Release 13 for Windows

# AutoCAD
## and its applications
## Basics

by

D1198569

**Terence M. Shumaker**
Manager
Autodesk Premier Training Center
Clackamas Community College, Oregon City, OR


**David A. Madsen**
Chairperson
Drafting Technology
Autodesk Premier Training Center
Clackamas Community College, Oregon City, OR
Former Board of Director
American Design Drafting Association

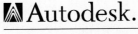

**Autodesk.**

Registered Author/Publisher

Publisher
**THE GOODHEART-WILLCOX COMPANY, INC.**
Tinley Park, Illinois

Library of Congress Catalog Card Number 95-9502
International Standard Book Number 1-56637-182-1

4 5 6 7 8 9 10    96    00 99 98 97

**Library of Congress Cataloging-in-Publication Data**
Shumaker, Terence M.
   AutoCAD and its applications–basics: release 13 for Windows / by Terence M. Shumaker, David A. Madsen.
      p. cm.
   Includes index.
   ISBN 1-56637-182-1
   1. Computer graphics. 2. AutoCAD for Windows
I. Madsen, David A. II. Title.
T385.S4616 1996
620'.0042'02855369--dc20                    95-9502
                                            CIP

Materials used for the cover art courtesy of Arthur Baker, CalComp, Moraine Valley Community College, David Ward, and FLIR Systems Inc.

# INTRODUCTION

*AutoCAD and its Applications—Basics, Release 13 for Windows* is a write-in text that provides complete instruction in mastering the AutoCAD Release 13 for Windows commands and drawing techniques. Typical applications of AutoCAD are presented with basic drafting and design concepts. The topics are covered in an easy-to-understand sequence, and progress in a way that allows you to become comfortable with the commands as your knowledge builds from one chapter to the next. In addition, *AutoCAD and its Applications—Basics, Release 13 for Windows* offers the following features:

- Step-by-step use of AutoCAD commands.
- In-depth explanations of how and why commands function as they do.
- Extensive use of font changes to specify certain meanings. These are fully explained in the next section, *Fonts Used in the Text*.
- Examples and discussions of industrial practices and standards.
- Actual screen captures of AutoCAD and Windows features and functions.
- Professional tips explaining how to use AutoCAD effectively and efficiently.
- Over 200 exercises involving several tasks to reinforce the chapter topics. These exercises also build on previously learned material.
- Chapter tests for review of commands and key AutoCAD concepts.
- A large selection of drafting problems supplement each chapter. Problems are presented as 3D illustrations, actual plotted industrial drawings, and engineering sketches.

With *AutoCAD and its Applications—Basics, Release 13 for Windows*, you not only learn AutoCAD commands, but you also become acquainted with:

- Office practices for firms using AutoCAD systems.
- Preliminary planning, sketches, and drawing plan sheets.
- Linetypes and their uses.
- Drawing geometric shapes and constructions.
- Special editing operations that increase productivity over manual drafting.
- Making multiview drawings.
- Dimensioning techniques and practices, as interpreted through accepted standards.
- Drawing section views and designing graphic patterns.
- Creating shapes and symbols for different uses.
- Creating and managing symbol libraries.
- Sketching with AutoCAD.
- Basic 3D drawing and display
- Plotting and printing drawings.
- Using Windows **File Manager** for organizing and managing files and directories.

The most important factor in learning AutoCAD is to find a reference that:

- Answers all your questions.
- Presents the commands in an easy-to-understand, logical sequence.
- Applies AutoCAD for Windows to typical drafting and design tasks.
- Provides proper drafting standards.
- Reduces the fear of using AutoCAD for Windows.

*AutoCAD and its Applications—Basics, Release 13 for Windows* does this... and even more!

## Fonts used in this text

Different type faces are used throughout each chapter to define terms and identify AutoCAD commands. Important terms always appear in ***bold-italic face, serif*** type. AutoCAD menus, commands, variables, dialog box names, and tool buttons are printed in **bold-face, sans serif** type. Filenames, directory names, paths, and keyboard-entry items appear in the body of the text in Roman, sans serif type. Keyboard keys are shown inside of square brackets [ ] and appear in Roman, sans serif type. For example, [Enter] means to press the enter (return) key.

Prompt sequences are set apart from the body text with space above and below, and appear in Roman, sans serif type. Keyboard entry items in prompts appear in **bold-face, sans serif** type. In prompts, the [Enter] key is represented by the ↵ symbol.

In addition, commands, menus, and dialog boxes related to Microsoft Windows appear in Roman, sans serif type. Two exceptions are Chapter 32 and Chapter 33. In these chapters, Windows-related terms appear in **bold-face, sans serif** type.

### Checking the AutoCAD reference manuals

No other reference should be needed when using this text. However, the authors have referenced relevant topic areas to the AutoCAD User's Guide and the AutoCAD Customization Guide. To the right of many heads in this text you will find an abbreviation and a chapter reference number. References are shown in a box similar to the following examples:

> AUG 4

> ACG 5

The AUG in the first example refers to the *AutoCAD User's Guide*. The 4 indicates Chapter 4 of that guide. The reference ACG 5 indicates that the topic is referenced to Chapter 5 of the *AutoCAD Customization Guide*. The AutoCAD software is also delivered with the *AutoCAD Command Reference*. Commands and variables are presented in alphabetical order in this manual.

### Other text references

For additional information, standards from organizations such as ANSI (American National Standards Institute) and ASME (American Society of Mechanical Engineers) are referenced throughout the text. These standards are used to help you create drawings that follow industrial, national, and international standards.

Also for your convenience, other Goodheart-Willcox textbooks are referenced. Textbooks that are referenced include *AutoCAD and its Applications* (Releases 10, 11, and 12), *AutoLISP Programming—Principles and Techniques*, and *AutoCAD AME—Solid Modeling for Mechanical Design*. All of these textbooks can be ordered directly from Goodheart-Willcox.

### Introducing the AutoCAD commands

There are several ways to select AutoCAD for Windows drawing and editing commands. Selecting commands from the toolbars, pull-down menus, or the digitizer tablet template menu is slightly different than entering them from the keyboard. All AutoCAD commands and related options in this text are presented using a variety of command entry methods.

Unless otherwise specified, command entries are shown as if they were typed at the keyboard. This allows the text to present the full command name and the prompts that appear on screen. Commands, options, and values you must enter are given in bold text, as shown in the following example. Pressing the [Enter] (return) key is indicated with the ↵ symbol. (Also, refer to the earlier section *Fonts used in this text*.)

```
Command: LINE ↵
From point: 2,2 ↵
To point: 4,2 ↵
To point: ↵
```

General input such as picking a point or selecting an object is presented in italic, serif font, as shown below.

    Command: **LINE** ↵
    From point: *(pick a point)*
    To point: *(pick another point)*
    To point: ↵

Other command entry methods presented throughout the text are toolbars and pull-down menus. When a toolbar button can be used to execute a command, it is illustrated in the margin next to the text reference. The text will indicate where the button is located. A grayscale button is an AutoCAD-related button. A green button is a Windows-related button. The AutoCAD digitizer tablet template is presented in Chapter 31. This gives you the opportunity to become familiar with other input formats before using the template menu. Experiment with all command entry methods to find the most convenient way for *you* to enter commands.

## Flexibility in design

Flexibility is the key word when using *AutoCAD and its Applications—Basics, Release 13 for Windows*. This text is an excellent training aid for individual, as well as classroom instruction. *AutoCAD and its Applications—Basics, Release 13 for Windows* teaches you AutoCAD in the Windows environment and how to apply AutoCAD to common drafting tasks. It is also an invaluable resource for any professional using AutoCAD.

When working through the text, you will see a variety of notices throughout. These notices include Professional Tips, Notes, and Cautions that help you develop your AutoCAD skills.

**PROFESSIONAL TIP**

These ideas and suggestions are aimed at increasing your productivity and enhancing your use of AutoCAD commands and techniques.

**NOTE**

A note alerts you to important aspects of a command function, menu, or activity that is being discussed. These aspects should be kept in mind while you are working through the text.

**CAUTION**

A caution alerts you to potential problems if instructions or commands are used incorrectly, or if an action can corrupt or alter files, directories, or disks. If you are in doubt after reading a caution, always consult your instructor or supervisor.

*AutoCAD and its Applications—Basics, Release 13 for Windows* provides several ways for you to evaluate your performance. Included are:
- **Exercises.** Each chapter contains in-text Exercises. These Exercises instruct you to perform tasks that reinforce the material just presented. You can work through the Exercises at your own pace.
- **Chapter Tests.** Each chapter includes a written test at the end of the chapter. Questions require you to give the proper definition, command, option, or response to perform a certain task.

- **Drawing Problems.** There are a variety of drafting and design problems at the end of each chapter. These are presented as real-world CAD drawings, 3D illustrations, and engineering sketches. The problems are designed to make you think, solve problems, use design techniques, research and use proper drawing standards, and correct errors in the drawings or engineering sketches.

  Each drawing problem deals with one of seven technical disciplines. Although doing all of the problems will enhance your AutoCAD skills, you may be focusing on a particular discipline. The discipline that a problem addresses is indicated by a text graphic in the margin next to the problem number. Each graphic and its description is as follows:

| | |
|---|---|
| **Mechanical Drafting** | These problems address mechanical drafting and designing applications, such as manufactured part designs. |
| **Architecture** | These problems address architectural and structural drafting and design applications, such as floor plans and presentation drawings. |
| **Electronics Drafting** | These problems address electronics drafting and designing applications, such as electronic schematics, logic diagrams, and electrical part design. |
| **Civil Drafting** | These problems address civil drafting and design application, such as plot plans, plats, and landscape drawings. |
| **Graphic Design** | These problems address graphic design applications, such as text creation, title blocks, and page layout. |
| **Piping** | These problems address piping drafting and design applications, such as piping flow diagrams, pump design, and pipe layout. |
| **General** | These problems address a variety of general drafting and design applications, and should be attempted by everyone learning AutoCAD for the first time. |

---

**NOTE**   Some problems presented in this text are given as engineering sketches. These sketches are intended to represent the kind of materials a drafter is expected to work from in a real-world situation. As such, engineering sketches often contain errors or slight inaccuracies, and are most often not drawn according to proper drafting conventions and applicable standards. Errors in these problems are *intentional* to encourage the user to apply appropriate techniques and standards in order to solve the problem. As in real-world applications, sketches should be considered to be preliminary layouts. Always question inaccuracies in sketches and designs, and consult the applicable standards or other resources.

---

## DISK SUPPLEMENTS

To help you develop your AutoCAD skills, Goodheart-Willcox offers a disk supplement package to use with *AutoCAD and its Applications—Basics, Release 13 for Windows*. The Autodesk software AutoCAD Release 13 for Windows is required for Goodheart-Willcox software to operate properly.

The *Student Work Disk* contains additional AutoCAD pull-down menus with a variety of activities. These activities are intended to be used as a supplement to the exercises and activities found in the text. The *Work Disk* activities correspond to Chapter 6 - Chapter 25 of the text. These activities allow you to progress at your own pace.

## ABOUT THE AUTHORS

Terence M. Shumaker is Manager of the Autodesk Premier Training Center, and a Drafting Technology Instructor at Clackamas Community College. Terence has been teaching at the community college level since 1977. He has commercial experience in surveying, civil drafting, industrial piping, and technical illustration. He is the author of Goodheart-Willcox's *Process Pipe Drafting*, and is co-author of the *AutoCAD and its Applications Release 13* series, *AutoCAD and its Applications* (Release 10, 11, and 12 editions), and *AutoCAD Essentials*.

David A. Madsen is the Chairperson of Drafting Technology and the Autodesk Premier Training Center at Clackamas Community College. David has been an instructor/department chair at Clackamas Community College since 1972. In addition to community college experience, David was a Drafting Technology instructor at Centennial High School in Gresham, Oregon. David also has extensive experience in mechanical drafting, architectural design and drafting, and construction practices. He is the author of several Goodheart-Willcox drafting and design textbooks, including *Geometric Dimensioning and Tolerancing*, and is co-author of the *AutoCAD and its Applications Release 13* series, *AutoCAD and its Applications* (Release 10, 11, and 12 editions), and *AutoCAD Essentials*.

## NOTICE TO THE USER

*AutoCAD and its Applications—Basics, Release 13 for Windows*, covers the basic AutoCAD for Windows applications that are mentioned in this introduction. For a text that covers the advanced AutoCAD for Windows applications, please refer to *AutoCAD and its Applications—Advanced, Release 13 for Windows*. The *Basics* and the *Advanced* texts are also available for the AutoCAD Release 13 for DOS format. Copies of any of these texts can be ordered directly from Goodheart-Willcox.

## ACKNOWLEDGMENTS

The authors and publisher would like to thank the following individuals and companies for their assistance and contributions:

### Special recognition

The authors are indebted to Rod Rawls for his professional expertise in providing in-depth research and testing, technical assistance, reviews, and development of new materials for use throughout the text. Rod is an AutoCAD consultant and principal instructor at the AutoCAD Premier Training Center, Clackamas Community College. He is also the co-author of *AutoLISP Programming: Principles and Techniques* published by Goodheart-Willcox.

### Technical assistance and contribution of materials

Margo Bilson of Willamette Industries, Inc.
Fitzgerald, Hagan, & Hackathorn
Dr. Stuart Soman of Briarcliffe College
Gil Hoellerich of Springdale, AR

### Contribution of materials

Cynthia B. Clark of the American Society of Mechanical Engineers
Marty McConnell of Houston Instrument, A Summagraphics Company
Grace Avila, Neele Johnston, and Wayne Hodgins of Autodesk, Inc.
Dave Hall of the Harris Group, Inc.

### Contribution of photographs or other technical information

Amdek Corporation
Applications Development, Inc.
Arthur Baker
Autodesk, Inc.
*CADalyst* magazine
*CADENCE* magazine
CalComp
Chris Lindner
Computer-Aided Design, Inc.
Digital Equipment Corp.
EPCM Services Ltd.
Far Mountain Corporation
FLIR Systems Inc.
Gateway 2000
GTCO Corporation
Harris Group, Inc.
Hewlett-Packard
Houston Instrument, A Summagraphics Company
International Source for Ergonomics

IOLINE Corporation
JDL, Inc.
Jerome Hart
Jim Armstrong
Jim Webster
Kunz Associates
Matt Slay
Mark Stennfeld
Mitsubishi Electronics America, Inc.
Microsoft Corporation
Mouse Systems Corporation
Myonetics Inc.
NEC Technologies, Inc.
Norwest Engineering
Schuchart & Associates, Inc.
Summagraphics Corporation
The American Society of Mechanical Engineers
The Xerox Engineering Systems Company
Weiser, Inc.
Willamette Industries, Inc.

### Technical assistance and reviews

Michael Jones, Autodesk Premier Training Center, Clackamas Community College
J.C. Malitzke, Autodesk Premier Training Center, Moraine Valley Community College
Kevin DeVoll, Margaret Burke, Earl Larson, Paul Masterson

### Hardware contributions

CalComp for use of the Inkjet plotter.
Moraine Valley Community College for use of laboratory, computer, monitor, and digitizer.

## TRADEMARKS

Autodesk, AutoCAD, and AutoLISP are registered in the U.S. Patent Trademark Office by Autodesk, Inc.
Autodesk Animator Pro, Autodesk 3D Studio, and DXF are trademarks of Autodesk, Inc.
dBase is a registered trademark of Ashton Tate
IBM is a registered trademark of International Business Machines
Windows and Windows 95 are trademarks of Microsoft Corporation
Pizazz Plus is a registered trademark of Applications Software Corporation
RenderMan is a registered trademark of Pixar used by Autodesk, Inc. by license
Microsoft Word is a trademark of Microsoft Corporation
MS-DOS is a registered trademark of Microsoft Corporation

# CONTENTS

## APPENDICES

# Chapter 1

# Introduction to Computer-Aided Drafting

## Learning objectives
After completing this chapter, you will be able to:
- ❍ Identify the tools (equipment) used in computer-aided drafting.
- ❍ Describe the methods and procedures used in computer-aided drafting.
- ❍ Explain the value of planning and system management.
- ❍ Follow the basic rules of hygiene for a computer lab.

## THE TOOLS OF CAD

The computer is the principal tool of the drafter's workstation. It is quickly replacing manual drafting tools such as drafting tables, pencils, scales, and templates. The drafter, designer, or engineer can create layouts and designs on a computer screen using the commands of a computer program. Points are chosen with an electronic pointing device such as a digitizer or mouse. Original drawings do not have to be copied with a blueprint machine. Instead, the drawing data is sent to a plotter for an inked original, or to a printer for a quick check print. The final drawing is saved on magnetic media such as floppy disks, hard disks, or magnetic tape. The optical CD is becoming a preferred method of data archival. It is much more durable and has greater storage capacity than magnetic media.

The AutoCAD software enables you to create your own drawing commands. This aspect of CAD is often overlooked, and is addressed in this book. You will be learning to use a new set of tools—the computer and AutoCAD. However, you will also be introduced to the methods of customization. Customization is modifying the basic program to meet your specific needs. For example, you may want to create a command to insert a specific symbol at an exact location. It is easy with AutoCAD. This skill allows you to become more productive, and prepares you to move into fields of expertise such as design, engineering, software development, animation and video production, or computer programming.

The nature of AutoCAD allows you to alter the basic program into something that is highly specialized and efficient. Along the way, however, you must pick up many new skills and ways of thinking about the drawing process.

## THE NEW METHODS OF CAD

As you begin to use AutoCAD, you will encounter many new drawing methods. These require that you organize your thoughts and plan the project in order to complete the drawing productively. For example, suppose you wish to draw a symmetrical object (an object that is the same on both sides of a centerline). You should not just begin drawing shapes on one side, and then redraw them on the other side. Rather, you should select drawing commands and pick positions on the computer screen using an input device to draw one-half of the object. A special command is then used to reflect or "mirror" the shapes just drawn to complete the object. With CAD, you should never draw the same shape twice.

As you begin your CAD training, plan your drawing sessions thoroughly to organize your thoughts. Sketch the problem or design, noting size and locations of features. List the drawing commands needed in the order they are to be used. Schedule a regular time to use the computer and adhere to that time. Follow the standards set by your school or firm. These might include: specific drawing names, project planning sheets, project logs, drawing layout procedures, special title blocks, and the location where drawings are to be stored. Standards and procedures must be followed by everyone using the computers in your school or company. Confusion may result if your drawings do not have the proper name, are stored in the wrong place, or have the wrong title block.

When using AutoCAD, you will be dealing with a machine that asks questions, follows instructions promptly, and executes every command you give it. Since the computer can destroy your drawing in a fraction of a second, you should develop the habit of saving your work regularly—at least every 10 to 15 minutes. (In Release 13, the **SAVETIME** system variable can be set to automatically save your drawings at predetermined intervals. **SAVETIME** is covered in detail in Chapter 5.) Drawings may be lost due to a software error, hardware malfunction, power failure, or your own mistakes. This is not common, but you should still be prepared for such an event.

You should develop methods of managing your work. This is critical to computer drafting and is discussed throughout the text. Keep the following points in mind as you begin your AutoCAD training.
- Plan your work and organize your thoughts.
- Learn and use your classroom or office standards.
- Save your work often.

If you remember to follow these three points, your grasp of the tools and methods of CAD will be easier. In addition, your experiences with the computer will be more enjoyable.

## THE APPLICATIONS OF AUTOCAD

You are embarking on a learning process that will take you through a broad range of commands, functions, and applications of the AutoCAD software. Along the way you will learn how to construct, layout, dimension, and annotate two-dimensional drawings. Should you wish to continue your study into 3D rendering and customization, *AutoCAD and its Applications—Advanced, R13 for Windows,* provides you with detailed instruction. Your studies will enable you to create a wide variety of drawings, designs, and models in any of the drafting, design, and engineering disciplines.

The AutoCAD software enables you to create designs and drawings that are more than just two-dimensional constructions. The drawings can have hundreds of colors, and *layers* that contain different kinds of information. See Figure 1-1A and Figure 1-1B. In addition, objects in the drawing can be given "intelligence" in the form of *attributes*. These attributes are various kinds of data that turn a drawing into a graphical database. You can then ask questions of your drawing and receive a variety of information.

Using AutoCAD you have the ability to construct 3D models that appear as wireframes, or have surface colors and textures. The creation of solid models that have mass properties, and can be analyzed is also possible with AutoCAD. The display on the monitor in Figure 1-2 is an example of a solid model created in AutoCAD. 3D drawings and models can be viewed in several ways. These models can also be colored and shaded, or *rendered*, to appear in a realistic format.

Figure 1-1. A—Colors and layers are used to emphasize components in this exploded isometric assembly. (Hewlett-Packard) B—Many different colors and layers were used to create this realistic architectural rendering. (SRG Partnership PC)

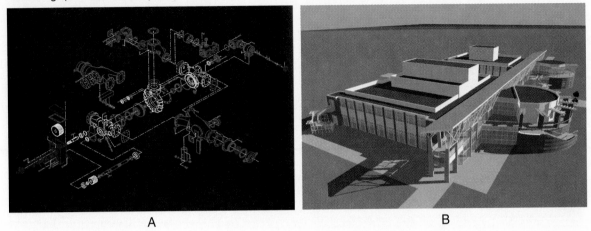

A

B

Figure 1-2. Solid models like this can be created with AutoCAD. (Digital Equipment Corporation)

A powerful application of CAD software and 3D models is animation. The simplest form of animation is to dynamically rotate the model in order to view it from any direction. Drawings and models can also be animated so that the model appears to move, rotate, and even explode into its individual components. An extremely useful form of animation is called a *walkthrough*. Using specialized software, you can plot a path through or around a model and replay it just like a movie. The logical next step in viewing the model is to actually be inside it and have the ability to manipulate and change the objects in it. This is called *virtual reality*, and is achieved through the use of 3D models, and highly specialized software and hardware. Figure 1-3A, Figure 1-3B, and Figure 1-3C illustrate several kinds of drawings and models that have been created with CAD software.

Figure 1-3.    A—The components of this rendered 3D piping model retain information in the form of attributes that makes the drawing a graphical database. (Applications Development, Inc.) B—The solid model on this monitor was created with AutoCAD. (Mitsubishi Electronics America, Inc.) C—This model of a F18 jet was created with AutoCAD. (Autodesk, Inc.)

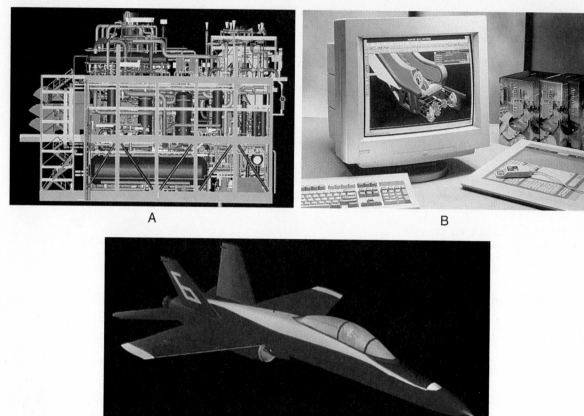

A        B

C

# HARDWARE

The physical pieces of equipment used in computer-aided drafting and design are referred to as *hardware*. The microcomputer is the main component. It is accompanied by several other devices called *peripherals*, Figure 1-4. The specific components included in a CAD workstation are presented in the following discussion.

Figure 1-4.    Components of an AutoCAD workstation.

## Computer

The most commonly used microcomputers for CAD in the education and industrial fields is the IBM, and other microcomputers called "IBM compatibles" or "clones." These clones must be 100% compatible with IBM models for AutoCAD to work properly. The important consideration, regardless of the brand of machine used, is that the computer has the proper components and memory. See Appendix B for the specific hardware requirements of AutoCAD.

A typical microcomputer is a rectangular-shaped metal box containing the central processing unit (CPU), memory, floppy disk drives, and hard disk drive(s).

The heart of the computer—the CPU—is a chip that handles all of the system's calculations. Several printed circuit boards, called *cards*, are found in the computer. These cards have a variety of integrated circuit chips and electronic components attached. Specific cards or "boards" are required for a video graphics display, the connection for a digitizer or mouse (called *serial ports*), and additional items such as extra memory for the computer.

The computer has a group of blank chips (like empty storage boxes), called *memory*. Memory is also referred to as *random access memory (RAM)*. Random access memory refers to the ability of the computer to randomly store and search for data in this area of the memory. When the computer is turned on, the operating system (such as DOS) is loaded into a small portion of the computer's memory. The operating system remains there because it can be accessed faster than if it was used directly from the hard disk drive.

When AutoCAD is loaded, it is placed into the computer's RAM. If your computer has a large amount of RAM, most of the AutoCAD program can be placed in the computer's memory. Then, when you work on a drawing, some (or all) of the drawing may also initially be placed in the computer's memory. If your drawing gets too big, some of it is removed from RAM, and copied, or *paged* to the hard disk. If the "page" of your drawing or AutoCAD is needed again, it is copied back into memory. If you are quick, you may notice when this happens by looking at the floppy and hard disk lights located on the front of your computer. Watch these lights and you will begin to get a good idea of when AutoCAD accesses the floppy disk and hard disk drives.

IBM compatible computers have 640K (640,000 bytes) of base memory. One byte is roughly equal to one character, such as a letter or number. Memory added to a computer above the basic 640K is called *extended memory*. In order to run AutoCAD Release 13, your computer must have a total of at least 8MB (8 million bytes) of memory, and 16MB is recommended. The more memory a computer has, the faster it can work. More memory allows the computer to load programs into memory and not have to work from the hard disk drive. Accessing the hard drive is much slower than accessing RAM.

## Monitor

The *monitor* is the output or display device that resembles a small TV, Figure 1-5. Common monitor sizes are 15", 17", and 21" (measured diagonally). Monitors are available in color and monochrome display. *Monochrome* refers to a single text and graphics color, most often white, amber, or green on a black background.

Display *resolution* determines how smooth or jagged text and objects appear on-screen. Resolution is measured in *pixels*. The word "pixel" means "picture element." A pixel appears as a dot on the screen, but it is actually a tiny rectangle. The display of a monitor is composed of horizontal rows and vertical columns of pixels. A typical display resolution is 640 × 480, meaning there are 640 dots horizontally and 480 dots vertically. High-resolution monitors may display 1024 × 768 pixels, or more.

The resolution of your monitor is directly related to a component in the computer called a *graphics card*. The graphics card is a "board" that contains a variety of computer chips. This board is inserted in a slot inside the computer that allows the CPU to communicate with the graphics card and monitor.

Figure 1-5.   The monitor lets
the drafter view the CAD
drawings. (NEC Technologies)

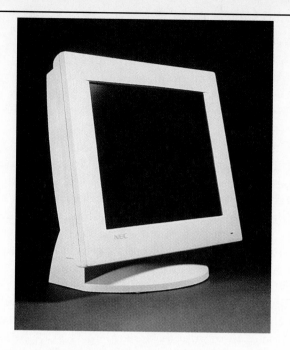

Graphics cards called *accelerator boards* may allow resolution of up to 1600 × 1200, and up to 16.7 million colors. Older computers may have VGA (Video Graphics Array) resolution that supports only 16 colors. However, the most common resolution is Super VGA that supports up to 16.7 million colors. Also, many industrial applications now need high-end graphics accelerator boards because of the complexity of the models, renderings, and animations.

## Keyboard

If you type well, you will soon discover that the keyboard is the most used input device at your workstation. It resembles a standard typewriter keyboard but has additional keys to the left, right, and top, Figure 1-6. The exact location and number of these keys varies from one model to another. In addition to typing commands, the keyboard can be used for entering precise coordinate values (see Chapter 6), text, and dimensions.

The keys labeled [F1] - [F10] (or [F1] - [F12]) are called *function keys*. These immediately perform commands that would otherwise have to be typed. AutoCAD uses function keys to control specific operations, many of which are discussed in Chapter 3.

Figure 1-6.   A computer keyboard has many types of keys.

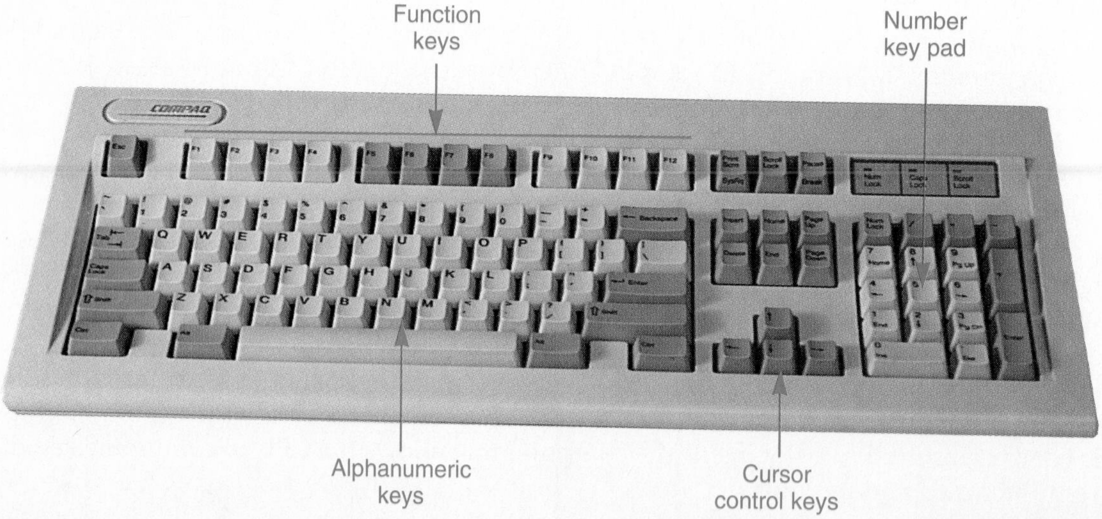

Function
keys

Number
key pad

Alphanumeric
keys

Cursor
control keys

## Pointing devices

Another important input device is the pointer, or pointing device. A ***pointing device*** moves the cursor or crosshairs on the screen. With it, you can select point locations and commands from a screen or digitizer tablet menu. The most commonly used pointing devices are a multibutton ***puck*** or a pen-shaped ***stylus***. See Figure 1-7. Pointing devices are connected to a ***digitizer tablet***. Digitizer tablet layout and use is discussed in Chapter 31 of this text.

Figure 1-7.   Digitizer pucks are available with different button arrangements. The stylus resembles a pen. (Kurta)

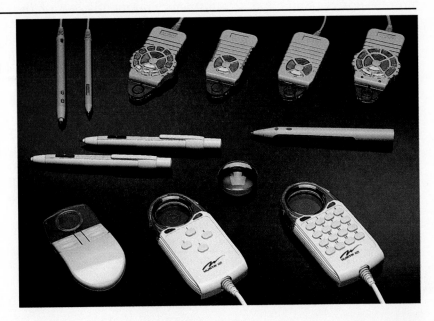

Other commonly used pointing devices include the ***mouse*** and ***trackball***. The mouse or trackball is often the best choice when cost and table space are concerns (since they do not require a digitizer). Each pointer functions differently, but all put information into the computer.

The digitizer tablet is the drawing board of the CAD workstation. Several examples are shown in Figure 1-8. A plastic or paper ***menu overlay*** containing AutoCAD commands and/or drawing symbols can also be placed on the digitizer. Items can be selected directly from the menu without looking at the screen. Movement of the puck or stylus is recorded

Figure 1-8.   Digitizers are available in many different sizes. (CalComp)

and displayed on the screen as the cursor position. Commands or menus can be picked on the screen by moving the pointing device to the desired item. Then press the pick button on the puck, or press down on the stylus.

The multibutton puck, used with a digitizer tablet may have from 1 to 16 buttons. The bottom surface of the puck slides on the digitizer surface. A set of fine crosshairs mounted in the puck serve as the pick point for this device. When the display screen crosshairs move, they are showing the position of the puck's crosshairs on the tablet. One button—the pick button—enters points and selects menu commands. All of the other buttons can be programmed to suit the user. See *AutoCAD and its Applications—Advanced, Release 13 for Windows,* for information on digitizer tablet and button customization.

The stylus, a pen-shaped pointer, attached to the digitizer with a cable, works in a different manner. The point of the stylus is pressed down on the surface of the digitizer. A slight click can be felt and heard. This indicates that a point or menu item at the cursor's position on the screen has been selected.

The mouse is the most inexpensive pointing device because it does not require a digitizer tablet. A mouse needs only a small flat surface to operate. The mouse is available in two forms: mechanical and optical. See Figure 1-9. An optical mouse uses a special reflective pad with grid lines. A light shines from the mouse to the pad. The location of the mouse is shown as the crosshairs location on the screen. The optical mouse must remain on the special pad in order to work.

Figure 1-9.   A—An optical mouse. Note the reflective pad and grid lines in the pad. (Summagraphics) B—A mechanical mouse can be used on almost any surface.

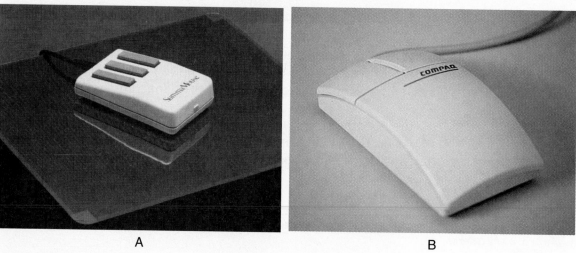

A                                                                                                    B

The mechanical mouse has a roller ball on the bottom. The movement of the roller on any flat surface is sent to the computer and displayed as the screen crosshairs movement. Unlike the stylus and puck, the mouse can be lifted and moved to another position without affecting the location of the screen crosshairs.

If you turn a mouse over, the roller ball is exposed. If this ball was increased in size and enlarged another inch, you would have a trackball. A trackball enables you to move the cursor on the screen by rolling a ball. A trackball requires only the amount of table space needed for it to sit on. The only part you move is the ball. There are a variety of trackballs available, but most have two or three buttons, much like a mouse. See Figure 1-10.

Figure 1-10.   A trackball is a pointing device, which is used by rolling the ball to move the screen cursor or crosshairs.

## Storage devices and media

Your computer will have at least one floppy and one hard disk drive. Small lights on the fronts of the disk drives indicate when they are being accessed. These are the storage areas for AutoCAD and its drawings. A standard 5.25″ floppy disk holds 360,000 (360K) characters of information. A character is referred to as a **byte**. A **high-density** 5.25″ disk holds 1.2 million bytes of information. Million is called **mega**. Therefore, a high-density disk's capacity is called 1.2 megabytes, or 1.2MB.

Many computer users prefer the 3.5″ flexible disk. It is smaller in size and enclosed in a hard plastic shell that protects it from damage. Originally designed to fit a shirt pocket, it is convenient to carry around. The 3.5″ disk can be formatted for either IBM/DOS compatible systems, or Apple Macintosh systems. The 3.5″ disk high-density drive is the standard for new computers, Figure 1-11. These disks hold up to 1.44MB of information.

For those who need to use both sizes of diskette, the dual disk drive is available. This drive allows either size diskette to be placed in the same drive slot and used. If you are using an older computer with a low-density disk drive, you will not be able to use high-density disks.

Figure 1-11.   A—Floppy disk drives with a hard disk drive to the left. Note the extra compartment that has a CD-ROM drive. B—An external CD-ROM drive. (NEC Technologies)

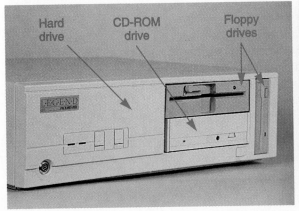

A                                                    B

Most new computers now come with a high-density compact optical digital disk drive (CD-ROM). The discs for CD-ROM drives are much like compact audio discs. The CD-ROM drive is found on most CAD workstations now. In fact, AutoCAD Release 13 is shipped on CD-ROM. An example of a CD-ROM drive is shown in Figure 1-11B.

In addition to floppy disk drives, your computer also has a hard disk drive. The hard drive is a sealed unit that contains one or more metal disks, or "platters." These disks have a much greater storage capacity than floppy disks, and are measured in megabytes. Common hard disk sizes are 540MB to over a gigabyte (1000MB). A small light on the front of the computer indicates when the hard disk drive is being accessed. Before AutoCAD can be used, it must be installed onto the hard disk drive. (See Appendix A for installation information.)

The need for greater storage capacity, and more reliable media has seen the increase in popularity of the readable/writable optical drive. The most popular of these drives uses optical disks that are about the same size as standard magnetic 3.5" floppy disks, except the optical disks are a little thicker. They typically store up to 256MB per disk (512MB compressed), however, optical drives that store over 4GB (gigabyte) of data are on the market. Optical drives provide the reliability of optical media without the cost or vulnerability of magnetic media. Optical disks can be rewritten with new data as required, just like magnetic floppies. They are also faster and more reliable for backups than magnetic tape drives.

## Selecting floppy disks

Avoid buying bulk quantities of unpackaged floppy disks that are sold without dust jackets. Often these are sitting out on a store counter exposed to dust, cigarette smoke, and handling. Be safe. Purchase packaged unformatted disks, keep them boxed, and store the box in a clean area. Keep disks away from extreme heat or cold and magnetic fields found around stereo speakers, telephones, and computer monitors.

A variety of disk drive configurations are now available for most new microcomputers. In some cases, you are able to specify the drive configuration you want when purchasing a computer. Since there is such a variety of drive configurations, be careful when purchasing floppy disks to make sure that you have the correct disks for your computer. Check the following:
- 5.25" vs. 3.5"
- High density vs. double density

Even if you store most drawings on the hard disk drive, you will probably use floppy disks for temporary storage of your drawing files, and to share drawings with clients or other computers.

Before files can be stored on a disk, it must be properly prepared. This process is called *formatting*. Formatting is discussed in detail in Chapter 32. Many disks can also be purchased preformatted from the store.

**CAUTION**

Before formatting a floppy disk, check with your instructor or supervisor for information about formatting disks. Some schools and companies have special menu selections that allow you to safely format disks in the floppy disk drives.

Floppy diskettes are available for purchase both formatted and unformatted. Most companies prefer to buy the diskettes that are already formatted. The formatting procedure takes over your computer system while in progress, so no other work can be done while waiting for the process to complete. Since high-density floppies may take several minutes each to format, formatting a quantity of diskettes can take up a significant amount of time. In a professional environment, it is actually less expensive to buy the preformatted diskettes at a slightly higher price, rather than using up valuable work time by formatting them yourself.

## Plotter

Paper and film drawings are most often output by a plotter. A plotter uses felt tip, ball-point, or wet ink pens, or pencils to put lines on paper. These devices can plot any size drawing, and are available in a variety of sizes. See Figure 1-12. Plotting is normally done for final documents. Drafters and designers can work for a long time before they ever need to plot their work. For that, and other reasons, most schools and companies have one plotter that is shared by several workstations. The plotting routine is covered in Chapter 12.

Figure 1-12.   Plotters are available in a variety of sizes and styles. (CalComp)

A                                    B

The *electrophotographic plotter* is increasing in popularity because of its speed and efficiency. A laser printer uses a single beam of light, however, an electrophotographic plotter uses an array of light-emitting diodes (LED) to draw the image. These tiny LEDs are packed 400 to the inch in the plotter shown in Figure 1-13. This produces a plot resolution of 400 dpi (dots per inch). Electrophotographic plotters produce more accurate images than laser printers for large-format drawings.

Figure 1-13. The electrophotographic plotter uses an array of LEDs to plot an image at 400 dpi. (CalComp)

A less expensive alternative to electrophotographic plotters is inkjet plotters. See Figure 1-14. Inkjet plotters use a cartridge that shoots tiny drops of ink at the paper. The cartridge requires no maintenance, and may provide from 200 to 400 prints. Resolutions of 300 to 600 dpi are common. A typical inkjet plotter may be three to eight times faster than a pen plotter, depending on the drawing complexity and printing mode.

Figure 1-14.    Inkjet plotters shoot tiny drops of ink at the paper and provide from 300 to 600 dpi resolution. (Hewlett-Packard Printers/CalComp)

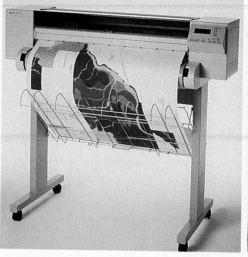 

Plotters fall into two basic groups—vector and raster. Pen plotters are vector plotters because they draw lines using the XY coordinates of the drawing geometry. Although they are accurate and produce fine quality drawings, they are the slowest of the various plotter technologies. Raster plotters, on the other hand, convert CAD vectors into rows and columns of dots, often called a *bitmap*. Raster plotters, such as the inkjet, print an entire row at a time as the paper advances, whereas the pen plotter must constantly move around the paper, drawing each vector.

## Printer

The raspy sounds of a dot matrix printer are familiar to people who have been to a store or bank. These same printers can render a quick check print of your AutoCAD drawing. Large-format dot matrix printers can produce prints up to C-size (17″ × 22″). However, other more quiet printing devices—inkjet, laser, and electrophotographic devices—also create high-quality prints. Laser printers can plot up to 1200 dpi. Some inkjet printers can plot up to 720 dpi. An example of a laser printer is shown in Figure 1-15.

Figure 1-15.   The laser printer "paints" an image on a sensitized drum and prints up to 600 dpi resolution. (Hewlett-Packard Printers)

## Network systems

There is an increasing need for drawing symbol consistency, accurate project time accounting, instant communication between coworkers, and data security. This has led to the popularity of "network systems." A *network* is nothing more than several computers, connected by a cable, that communicate with each other. Complex networks have hundreds of computers or terminals working from a central computer called a *server*. Each workstation on the network still requires a CPU, input device, and display device. A diagram of a typical network system is shown in Figure 1-16.

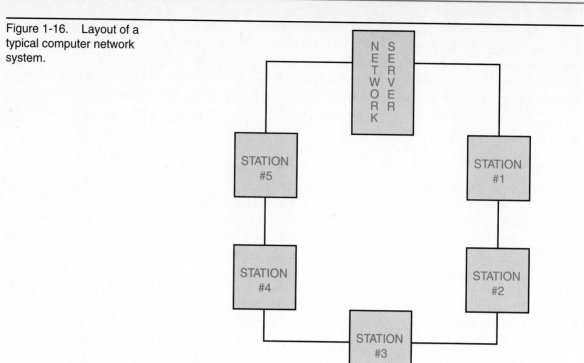

Figure 1-16.    Layout of a typical computer network system.

The hard disk drives in the server are normally large-capacity drives. They need to store a variety of software, and still have plenty of space for numerous files created by the computer users attached to the network. The network server can also store drawing files that may be needed by computer users in order to complete new drawings. For example, a base drawing of the walls of a structure can be stored on the server. When a student or employee needs to work on a new drawing of the plumbing or electrical layout of the structure, they simply load the base drawing from the server into their computer and begin working. In most cases, the base drawing is preserved in its original form and a different name is given to the new drawing. AutoCAD provides a facility that automatically locks a drawing when a person "checks it out" of the network. This means that only one person can work on a drawing at any given time, thus preventing several people from making different changes to the drawing.

## THE ERGONOMIC WORKSTATION

*Ergonomics* is the science of adapting the working environment to suit the needs of the worker. Since the advent of computers in the workplace in the early 1980s, an increasing number of work-related injuries and afflictions have been reported. By far, the most common of these are repetitive motion disorders. Carpal tunnel syndrome is probably the most well-known of these. Most injuries and disorders related to computer work are the result of the sedentary nature of the work, and the fast, repetitive motions of the hands and fingers on the keyboard and pointing devices.

Most disorders of this nature can be prevented to some extent by proper workstation configuration, good posture, and frequent exercises. Figure 1-17 illustrates an example of ergonomic equipment for the computer workstation. Review the following checklist, and try to adhere to as many of the items as possible. As is often the case, a small adjustment of equipment, or the investment of a few extra dollars, can prevent unnecessary future injuries and lost productivity.

Figure 1-17.   The forearm supports provide relief from muscle tension for computer operators, and assist in the prevention of repetitive motion disorders. This design was created with AutoCAD. (MyoNetics Inc.)

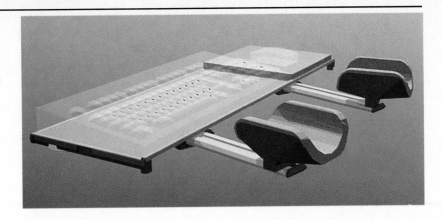

✓ Obtain a good chair with proper back support, height, and tilt adjustment.

✓ Use adaptive devices such as forearm supports, wrist and palm rests, and keyboard drawers to help maintain a level wrist position in relation to the keyboard and pointing device.

✓ Avoid resting your wrists on a table while typing, and use a light stroke on the keys.

✓ Investigate the variety of ergonomic keyboards on the market and test for comfort and efficiency.

✓ Position the equipment and supplies of your workstation for ease of use and access.

✓ The screen should be placed from 18 to 30 inches from the eyes and the top of the display screen should be at eye level.

✓ Lighting should not produce a glare on the screen.

✓ Provide under-desk space so that feet can be placed on a tilted footrest, or at minimum, flat on the floor.

✓ Take short breaks throughout the day.

✓ Practice refocusing your eyes, and engaging in stretching exercises for hands, arms, shoulders, and neck on a regular basis.

✓ Be aware of how your body feels, especially any changes you feel in your shoulders, arms, wrists, and hands.

✓ Consult your doctor if you notice any numbness, aching, or tingling in your hands, wrists, or arms.

## COMPUTER DRAFTING PROCEDURES

The finished product of a CAD drafter is similar to that of a manual drafter. However, some of the thought processes and procedures used to produce the final product are different. A drawing plan must be developed where all the aspects of the project are considered. This requires careful management of the CAD system and the creation and use of detailed standards for the planning and drawing process.

### Drawing planning

Drawing planning involves looking at the entire process or project that you as a drafter, designer, or engineer, are involved in. A plan determines how a project is going to be approached. It includes the drawings to be created, how they will be titled and numbered, the information to be presented, and the types of symbols needed to show the information.

More specifically, drawing planning applies to how you create and manage a drawing or set of drawings. Drafters who begin constructing a drawing from the seat of their pants—creating symbols and naming objects, shapes, and views as they go—do not possess a good drawing plan. Those who plan, use consistent techniques, and adhere to school or company standards are developing good drawing habits.

Throughout this text you will find aids to help you develop good drawing habits. One of the first steps in developing your skills is to learn how to plan your work. The importance of planning cannot be emphasized enough. There is no substitute.

## Creating and using drawing standards

*Standards* are guidelines for operating procedures, drawing techniques, and record keeping. Most schools and companies have established standards. It is important that standards exist and are used by all CAD personnel. Drawing standards may include:

- Methods of file storage: location and name.
- Dimensioning techniques.
- File naming conventions.
- Text styles.
- Drawing sheet sizes and title blocks to be used.
- Linetypes.
- Drawing symbols.
- Color schemes for plotting.
- File backup methods and times.

Your standards may vary in content, but the most important aspect of standards is that they are used. The more your standards are used, the more efficiently the classroom or office will run. In addition, it will be easier to manage the system and plan projects. As they are used, standards will change to reflect new methods, techniques, and symbols. All students and employees using the CAD system must be informed of changes immediately. This increases communication and maintains a high level of consistency and productivity.

## Planning your work

Study the planning pyramids in Figure 1-18. The horizontal axes of the pyramids represent the amount of time spent on the project. The vertical axes represent the life of the project. The top level is the planning stage and the bottom level is the final execution of the project. The pyramid on the right is pointed at the top and indicates a small amount of planning. As the project progresses, more and more time is devoted to planning and less time is available for other tasks. This is *not* an ideal situation. The inverted pyramid on the left shows a lot of time devoted to initial planning. As the project advances, less planning time is needed, thus freeing more time for other tasks.

Figure 1-18. Planning pyramids illustrate time required for well-planned and poorly-planned projects.

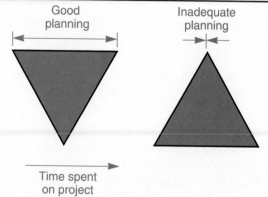

Remember the message of the planning pyramids as you begin your study of AutoCAD. When you feel the need to dive blindly into a drawing or project, restrain yourself. Take the time needed for development of the project goals. Then proceed with the confidence of knowing where you are heading.

During your early stages of AutoCAD training, write down all of the instructions needed to construct your drawing. Do this especially for your first few assignments. This means documenting every command and every coordinate point (dimension) needed. Develop a planning sheet for your drawings or use an example shown in Chapter 6. Your time spent at the computer with AutoCAD will be more productive and enjoyable.

## System management

The concepts of drawing planning and project planning are parts of system management. (See Appendix C.) *System management* means that the entire CAD system and related functions are governed by set guidelines. However, simply having guidelines does not mean that the system is being managed. A person or persons must see that procedures and standards are followed throughout the life of a project. If a system is not managed, it soon falls apart. A well-managed system functions smoothly.

Right now, you are probably anxious to begin learning AutoCAD and are wondering why planning, standards, and management are being discussed. It is because you are about to encounter many details, possibilities, methods, and options that you may have never dealt with before. Even if you have never drafted, a basic understanding of AutoCAD will provide you with a solid footing on which to build your experience and knowledge.

You personally may not be the ultimate manager of the CAD system. However, you still need to possess a knowledge of what is meant by system management. Therefore, it is important that you develop an early knowledge of:
- When to store drawings on floppy disks and when to store them on hard disks or other magnetic media.
- How names are assigned to drawings so other employees or your instructor understand their meaning.
- When and how to make backup copies of drawings and store them in a safe place.
- Where to physically store backup floppy disks and magnetic tapes.
- Who should have access to drawings you create.
- Who creates drawing standards and symbols.
- How symbols and standards are distributed to all CAD users.
- Who maintains the hardware and handles software upgrades.

These are just a few aspects of system management affecting your use of AutoCAD in the educational and industrial environments. Before you ever begin a drawing, you should be aware of the items listed above. Know how they relate to your standards and planning procedures because they are a part of system management.

## Interactive process

A CAD drafter "interacts" with the drawing much more than a manual drafter. The CAD program asks questions, provides hints, and prompts for information that is needed to complete certain steps. The drawing taped to a drafting board just lies there. It doesn't glow, ask questions, or make demands of the drafter. CAD drafters find themselves involved in an exciting, interactive process. They communicate with the computer to create a drawing.

As you begin learning AutoCAD, you will realize that several skills are required to become a proficient CAD user. The following list provides you with some hints to help you become comfortable with AutoCAD. They will also allow you to work quickly and efficiently. The following items are discussed in detail in later chapters.
- Plan all work with pencil and paper before using the computer.
- Check the screen menu bar to see if you are in the correct menu and are picking the right command. A command is an instruction that you give to the computer so it can perform a specific task. For example, the **LINE** command instructs the computer to draw a line between two points you pick.

- Check the **Properties** toolbar at the top of the display screen and the status bar at the bottom to see which layer(s) and drawing aid(s) are in effect.
- Read the command line at the bottom of the display screen. Constantly check for the correct command, instructions, or proper keyboard entry of data.
- Read the command line after keyboard entry of data before pressing the [Enter] or [Return] key. Backspacing to erase incorrect typing is quicker than redoing the command.
- If using a multibutton puck, develop a good hand position that allows easy movement. Your button-pressing finger should move without readjusting your grip of the puck.
- Learn the meanings of all the buttons on your puck or mouse and use them regularly.
- Watch the floppy disk and hard disk drive lights to see when the disks are being accessed. Some disk access may take a few seconds. Knowing what is happening will lessen frustration and impatience.
- Think ahead. Know your next move.
- Learn new commands every day. Don't rely on just a few that seem to work. Find commands that can speed your work and do it more efficiently.
- Save your work every 10 to 15 minutes in case a power failure or system crash deletes the drawing held in computer memory.
- If you're stumped, ask the computer for help. Use the **HELP** command to display valuable information about each command on the screen.

## Computer lab hygiene

Computer equipment is not only costly and complex, it is sensitive. Special cautions should be taken when working with computer equipment and magnetic media.

- It is better to leave computers on all day than to turn them on and off.
- Static electricity can damage computer memory chips. Always ground yourself by stepping on antistatic mats or touching static discharge plates or a metal chair before touching computer hardware.
- Touching the display screen often can build up a static charge in your body. If you must touch the screen, ground yourself often by touching some piece of metal not connected to the computer equipment.
- Keep computers out of dusty areas and away from chalkboards.
- Keep food and drinks away from computer hardware. Coffee and soft drinks spilled in keyboards can ruin your whole day.
- Use a gentle, but firm press on keyboard keys. Avoid sharp strikes.
- Keep magnetic media (floppy disks, magnetic tape) away from magnetic fields such as radio speakers, phones, digitizer tablets, and other computer equipment.
- Store magnetic media in rooms with a moderate, even temperature. Avoid extreme temperature changes.
- Write on disk labels before attaching them to disks.
- Avoid touching the exposed portions of floppy disks and magnetic tapes.

## CHAPTER TEST

*Write your answers in the spaces provided.*

1. How are points chosen on a screen in computer-aided drafting? _____

    _____

2. What type of machine produces an inked original drawing? _____

3. What is customization? _____

    _____

4. Why is drawing planning important? _____

    _____

5. Why should you save your work every 10 to 15 minutes? _____

    _____

6. List the seven components of a CAD workstation. _____

    _____

    _____

    _____

7. What is "drawing planning?" _____

    _____

    _____

    _____

8. What are standards? _____

    _____

9. Describe system management. _____

    _____

    _____

    _____

10. How do the CAD drafter and the computer "interact?" _____

    _____

    _____

11. Why should you read the command line at the bottom of the screen? _____

    _____

12. What type of storage device can be used for backup storage, hold up to 256MB of data, and be rewritten with new data as required? _____

    _____

13. Name three different types of plotter technologies. _____

    _____

14. What is the difference between vector and raster plotters? _____
_____

15. Why is static electricity an important concern in computer rooms? _____
_____

## PROBLEMS

General

1. Read through several computer magazines or AutoCAD journals and list three brand names of each piece of hardware required for a computer drafting workstation. Call or visit a local computer equipment dealer and get prices for each piece of equipment.

General

2. Write a comparative report on using dot matrix printers or pen plotters to satisfy your school or company requirements. Take into account the type of drawings you create and their uses. Determine the minimum quality print you need. Compare this to the final products produced by printers and pen plotters. Based on your needs, recommend a product and include in your recommendation the following:

   A. Price.

   B. Size.

   C. Location (where the equipment will be installed).

   D. Maintenance costs (maintenance contract, if available).

   E. Who will operate the equipment.

   F. Cost of supplies and frequency of purchase.

   G. Savings to school or company over a given period of time.

General

3. Compare the following types of input devices. List the advantages and disadvantages of each. Provide general price comparisons, ease of use, space, and maintenance requirements.

   A. Mouse.

   B. Digitizer with stylus.

   C. Digitizer with multibutton puck.

   D. Keyboard.

General

4. Visit an AutoCAD dealer, hardware vendor, or local engineering or manufacturing firm and request a plotter demonstration. Ask questions about paper sizes, speed, pen types, price, and maintenance. Call or visit a local plotting service. Get information on their services and rates. Write a report on the uses and benefits of owning a plotter. Compare this to the benefits of using a plotting service to create final plots.

General

5. Write a report on the benefits of using a dot matrix printer for generating all check prints. Visit hardware vendors and research the types and sizes of printers available.

General

6. Interview your drafting instructors or supervisors and try to determine what type of drawing standards exist at your school or company. Write this down and keep it with you as you learn AutoCAD. Make notes as you progress through this text on how you use these standards. Also note how the standards could be changed to match the capabilities of AutoCAD.

7. Research your drafting department standards. If you do not have a copy of the standards, acquire one. If AutoCAD standards have been created, make notes as to how you can use these in your projects.

   If no standards exist in your department or company, make notes as to how you can help develop standards. Write a report on why your school or company should create CAD standards and how they would be used. Discuss who should be responsible for specific tasks. Recommend procedures, techniques, and forms, if necessary. Develop this report as you progress through your AutoCAD instruction, and as you read through this book.

*General*

8. Work up an equipment proposal for the purchase of three different CAD workstation configurations that can run AutoCAD. Visit or call an Authorized AutoCAD Dealer to determine exactly what you need for each item listed below. Record prices for each piece of equipment. Write an introductory statement for each workstation proposal listing the benefits of each. The three proposals should include the following: (You may revise these lists to suit your needs or to reflect changing technologies.)

*General*

| EQUIPMENT | PROPOSAL #1 | PROPOSAL #2 | PROPOSAL #3 |
|---|---|---|---|
| Computer | CPU: 486/33 ISA<br>8MB RAM<br>2 serial ports<br>1 parallel port<br>MS-DOS | CPU: 486/66 VLB<br>16MB RAM<br>2 serial ports<br>1 parallel port<br>MS-DOS<br>Windows (optional) | CPU: Pentium 90MHz<br>32MB RAM<br>2 serial ports<br>1 parallel port<br>MS-DOS<br>Windows |
| Monitor and Graphics Array Card | 14" Multi-scan monitor<br>SVGA graphics card<br>w/512K VRAM | SVGA card with 2MB RAM<br>17" color monitor | SVGA card with 4MB RAM<br>21" color monitor |
| Storage Device | Single 3.5" HD floppy disk drive<br>340MB Hard disk drive | Dual floppy disk drive<br>540MB hard disk drive<br>256MB tape drive<br>Double speed CD-ROM | Dual floppy disk drive<br>1 gigabyte hard disk drive<br>256MB re-writable CD drive<br>4X speed CD-ROM |
| Input Devices | Keyboard and mouse | Keyboard & mouse<br>11 × 11 digitizer tablet with 4-button cursor<br>Scanner (optional) | Keyboard & mouse<br>11 × 11 digitizer tablet with 4-button cursor<br>Color scanner (optional) |
| Surge Protector | Power center with surge protection | Light duty UPS (Uninterruptible Power Supply) | Heavy duty UPS |
| Hardcopy Device | A-size and B-size inkjet printer,<br>or laser printer (2MB memory) | A-size through E-size pen plotter<br>8 1/2 × 11 inkjet printer | A-size through E-size color inkjet plotter<br>A-size and B-size color inkjet printer |
| Communications | 9600 bps modem | 14,400 bps FAX/Modem | 28,800 bps FAX/Modem |

9. Develop a drawing planning sheet for use in your school or company. List items that you think are important for planning a CAD drawing. Make changes to this sheet as you learn more about AutoCAD.

*General*

General

10. Interview your instructors or supervisors to determine how CAD system management is applied in your school or company. Ask questions about the following items:

   A. Drawing storage methods.

   B. Drawing naming standards.

   C. Drawing backup procedures.

   D. Symbol creation and storage.

   E. Hardware and software maintenance and upgrades.

General

11. List ways in which your computer room can be made cleaner and more secure. Look for problems such as chalkboards, traffic patterns, radios, telephones, garbage cans, heating vents and elements, and locations where people drink and eat.

AutoCAD R13

# Chapter 2

# Starting AutoCAD

## Learning objectives

After completing this chapter, you will be able to:

○ Identify the meaning of DOS disk drive prompts.
○ Define the meaning of directories and path names.
○ Start Microsoft Windows and load AutoCAD from the Program Manager.
○ Describe the AutoCAD screen layout and user interface.
○ Describe the function of dialog boxes.
○ Use the keyboard and an input device to select commands, enter text, and pick locations on the screen.
○ Use the **HELP** command for on-line assistance.

AutoCAD for Windows must be installed on the hard disk drive of your computer. The software is distributed on a CD-ROM with a single floppy disk, but all-disk sets are available. The floppy disk labeled Disk 1 is the installation disk, and contains an installation program called SETUP.EXE. On some systems, a program called WIN32S must first be installed before you can run AutoCAD Release 13. Installing this program is explained in your *Installation Guide for Windows™*. The SETUP.EXE program transfers files from the release disks to subdirectories on the computer's hard disk, and creates a program group in the Program Manager window. A *program group* contains program items graphically displayed as icons. *Icons* are small pictures that represent applications, accessories, files, or commands. An icon that starts an application like AutoCAD is called a *program-item icon*. The AutoCAD program group window is a separate window within the Program Manager and contains the AutoCAD for Windows program-item icon, as well as a variety of "README" documentation files, Figure 2-1. The Quick Tour icon starts a program that provides a brief overview of the AutoCAD program. The What's New icon is designed to highlight only the differences between AutoCAD Release 13 and Release 12 for users who have upgraded their old software. If you are using the CD-ROM version, you will also see an "AutoCAD Documentation" icon. This provides an electronic version of the AutoCAD documentation that can be viewed directly on your

Figure 2-1. The AutoCAD Release 13 installation procedure creates a new program group in the Program Manager window. This group (shown here) contains several icons. Double-clicking the AutoCAD R13 program-item icon starts AutoCAD Release 13.

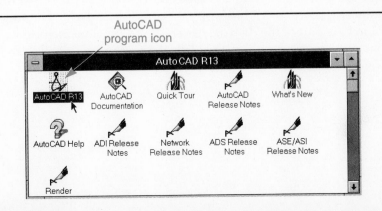

computer screen. Instructions are given on-screen during the installation process to assist you in proper installation. Refer to Appendix A for installation procedures.

After the AutoCAD files have been installed on the hard disk, AutoCAD must be configured. Configuring tells AutoCAD what equipment you are using. You can select from a variety of graphics devices, printers, plotters, and pointing devices. You are also able to choose the appearance of the screen display during configuration. Installing and configuring AutoCAD are discussed in detail in Appendix A.

This chapter discusses how to get started once you have configured AutoCAD. It shows how the screen display will look when you begin a drawing. You can choose either of two different screen formats, or switch between them if you wish. You will also learn how to select commonly used commands and special functions given to keyboard keys and digitizer puck buttons.

**PROFESSIONAL TIP**

The README files in the AutoCAD program group window are in Windows Write format, and include useful information about AutoCAD device drivers and special functions that may not be covered in the AutoCAD manuals. Be sure to read these files after installing AutoCAD for Windows on your hard disk.

## GETTING STARTED

When you turn on your computer, the DOS software is automatically loaded. As you may recall, DOS stands for Disk Operating System, and is the "traffic cop" of your computer system. DOS enables the computer to work with files (including drawings), peripheral equipment, and software such as Windows and AutoCAD. Some schools or companies have a menu displayed on the screen where you can make selections. The DOS prompt might be located below this menu. Many computers also start Windows automatically when the computer is turned on. In that case, you will not see a DOS prompt.

### DOS prompts

A *prompt* is a statement or response issued by the computer to show that it awaits your command. The first prompt you see is a letter followed by the greater-than symbol, or *closed chevron* (⟩). These prompts are part of your DOS software and not part of AutoCAD. The prompt on your screen may be A⟩, B⟩, C⟩, or D⟩. The prompt may also display other information.

The letter indicates the DOS name of the current disk drive. If your computer has both a 5.25″ and 3.5″ floppy drives, most newer configurations specify the 3.5″ drive as the A: drive, regardless of its location. If you have an older computer, the top or left floppy drive is named A: and the lower or right floppy drive is the B: drive. The first hard disk is the C: drive. The colon (:) is part of the disk drive name, and must be included when you type DOS commands that require the name of the disk drive. Figure 2-2 illustrates the names of the different drives.

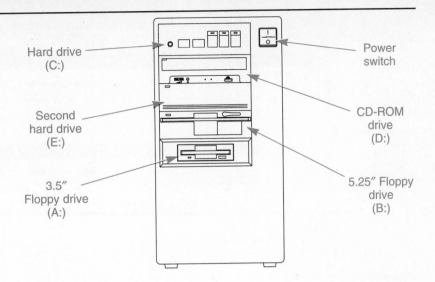

Figure 2-2.   This shows a typical configuration of drives on a computer and their DOS names. Note: The computer shown here is a "tower" computer.

## Starting Windows and AutoCAD

The prompt that is displayed on the computer screen always indicates the current disk drive (the drive being looked at by the computer). To run Windows, the prompt must display the letter of the hard disk drive. You need to change drives if the display is anything other than C⟩ or C:\⟩. To change drives, type:

> **C:** ↵

Now the display should read:

> C⟩ *or* C:\⟩

If the display on the screen was already C⟩ or C:\⟩, you are ready to start Windows and run AutoCAD. To load Windows, type the following at the DOS prompt:

> C:\⟩ **WIN** ↵

Remember, if your computer automatically loads Windows when it starts, you will not need to do this. As Windows loads, the Microsoft Windows logo will appear briefly. The display screen will then show the Program Manager window. The Program Manager is an application that is the center of the Windows operating environment, and continues to run as long as you are working with a Windows application such as AutoCAD.

### Starting AutoCAD from the Program Manager

The Program Manager window can appear several different ways, depending on how Windows has been configured on your computer. In Figure 2-3, the Program Manager is shown with the Main group window open inside the Program Manager window. The other group windows have been *minimized* and are represented by group icons located at the lower edge of the Program Manager. The group icons are clearly labeled so that each is easily identified.

Before AutoCAD can be run, you must first open the group window that contains the AutoCAD for Windows program-item icon. To open the AutoCAD group window, do one of the following:

- Double-click the AutoCAD group icon with the left mouse button.
- Press [Ctrl]+[F6] or [Ctrl]+[Tab] until the AutoCAD group icon is selected, and then press [Enter].
- Select AutoCAD from the list at the bottom of the Window pull-down menu.

Once the AutoCAD group window is open, you may start AutoCAD by double-clicking the program-item icon labeled AutoCAD R13.

Figure 2-3.   The Main group window is shown here open in the Program Manager window. Each of the other group windows have been minimized and are located along the bottom.

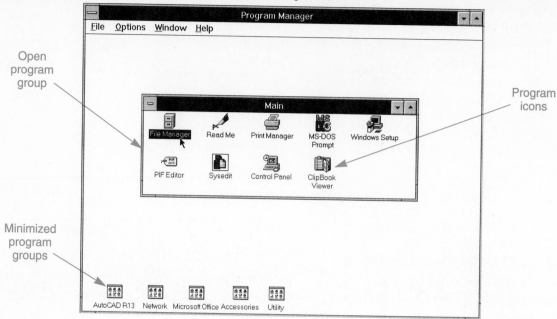

Open program group

Program icons

Minimized program groups

Another way the Program Manager window may appear on-screen is in a *tiled* display, Figure 2-4. In a tiled display, all group windows are already open and arranged side-by-side in the Program Manager workspace. Program-item icons are clearly visible in each of the open group windows, although there may not be enough room to display all of the program-item icons in the allotted space for each group. To rearrange all the open group windows in a tiled display, select Tile from the Window pull-down menu.

Figure 2-4.   These program groups are displayed using the Tile command in Program Manager.

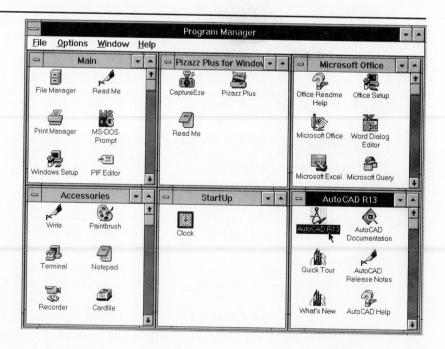

The Program Manager may also be displayed with each open group window arranged in a layered, or *cascading*, fashion. This option orients and resizes each group window to overlap one another with the title bar of each group window clearly visible, Figure 2-5. To rearrange all the open group windows in a cascading display, select Cascade from the Window pull-down menu. If the AutoCAD group window is not in front, simply pick the AutoCAD group window title bar.

Once you double-click the AutoCAD R13 program-item icon, AutoCAD begins loading into memory and a small hourglass icon appears on-screen. The AutoCAD® Release 13 logo is then displayed in the middle of your screen while the program loads. Finally, the AutoCAD graphics window appears as the program completes its loading process. The graphics window is where all drawing and editing operations are performed.

Figure 2-5. These program groups are displayed using the Cascade command in Program Manager.

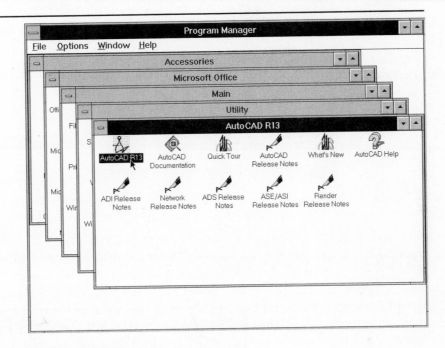

## THE AUTOCAD GRAPHICS WINDOW

The AutoCAD graphics window is similar to any other window within the Windows operating system. Picking the small square area in the upper-left corner displays a standard window control menu, and the arrows in the upper-right are used for minimizing and maximizing the AutoCAD graphics window. Window sizing operations are done as with any other window. AutoCAD for Windows uses the familiar Windows style interface, with buttons, pull-down menus and dialog boxes. Each of these items are discussed in detail in this chapter. Learning the layout, appearance, and proper use of these features allows you to master AutoCAD for Windows quickly.

### Standard screen layout

The standard screen layout provides a large graphics or drawing area. The drawing area is bordered by the toolbar at the top and the command line at the bottom. The graphics area is white, and the text appearing in the command line area is black on a white background (in its uncustomized format). Look at your screen now and study the illustration in Figure 2-6.

Figure 2-6.   This is the standard (uncustomized) AutoCAD graphics window.

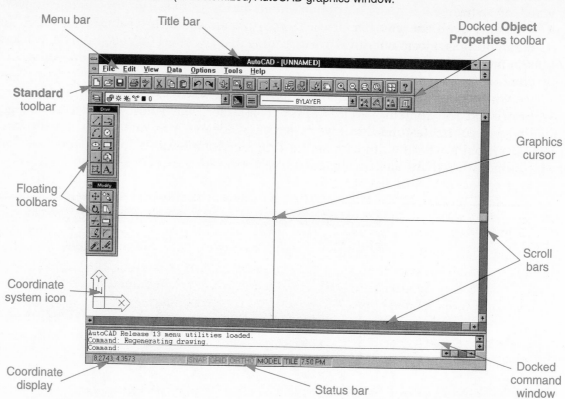

Note that the proportional size of the AutoCAD graphics window features may vary depending on the display resolution of your computer system. Many of the elements of the AutoCAD graphics window are referred to as *floating*. This means that the item can be freely moved about the screen into new positions as desired. When an item is floating, it has a standard Windows border and title bar. Floating windows are moved and adjusted for size in the same manner as any other window within the Windows program. Items that are floating can also be *docked* around the edges of the graphics window. To dock an item, drag it to the edge of the graphics window (top, bottom, left or right). When an item is docked, it loses its border and title bar and becomes a part of the graphics window. Moving a docked item away from the edge of the graphics window restores its title bar and border. Objects may be moved or docked at any time as needed.

Become familiar with these unique areas of the graphics window and the information provided by each. The following list describes the function of each area. Each of these features will be discussed in detail later in this text.

- **Floating command window.** In its default position, this window is docked at the bottom of the graphics window. It displays the **Command:** prompt and reflects any command entries you make. It also displays prompts that supply information to you or request values and/or text. This is where your primary communications with AutoCAD are displayed, so watch for any information shown on this line.
- **Menu bar.** The menu bar appears just below the title bar and displays a number of menu names. As with standard Windows menus, use the cursor to point at a menu name and press the pick button. This causes a *pull-down* menu to be displayed. Any time you pick an item followed by an *ellipsis* (…), a dialog box is displayed. A *dialog box* is a rectangular area that appears on the screen after you type or select certain commands. It contains a variety of options related to a specific command or function, and provides a convenient means of supplying information to AutoCAD.
- **Scroll bars.** The scroll bars allow you to adjust your view of the drawing area.

- **Graphics cursor.** This is your primary means of pointing to objects or locations within a drawing.
- **Coordinate system icon.** This indicates the current coordinate system and helps to determine point locations.
- **Floating toolbar.** Floating toolbars contain various buttons that activate AutoCAD commands. Two of these are displayed in the default screen configuration. The toolbars can be moved, resized, modified, hidden or docked as needed.
- **Status bar.** This contains several display fields that reflect the current state of specific drawing control features, plus the current time. When a menu item is highlighted or you are pointing at a button, a brief explanation of the item is shown here.
- **Coordinate display.** This display field, found on the status bar, shows the cursor location according to the current settings.
- **Standard Toolbar.** In the default AutoCAD screen configuration, the **Standard Toolbar** appears just above the graphics area. When you move your pointing device to the toolbar, the crosshairs change to the familiar Windows arrow pointer. Holding the cursor over a button for a moment displays **Tooltips**. This shows the function of the button. Some buttons show a small black triangle in the lower right corner. These buttons are called *flyouts*. Press and hold the pick button while pointing at a flyout to display a set of related buttons. The **Standard Toolbar** contains a series of buttons that provide access to several of AutoCAD's drawing setup and control commands. Each of these features is identified and briefly described in Figure 2-7. These features are discussed in detail later in this text.

Figure 2-7.  The **Standard Toolbar** and its components.

A— **New.** Begins a new drawing session.

B— **Open.** Allows existing drawings to be opened for editing and revision.

C— **Save.** Writes the drawing information currently in memory to a file.

D— **Print.** Sends drawing information to a hardcopy device, such as a printer or plotter.

E— **Spelling.** Performs a spell check of the text in your drawing.

F— **Cut.** "Cuts" a specified portion of your drawing geometry, storing it on the Windows Clipboard.

G— **Copy.** Copies a specified portion of your drawing geometry, storing it on the Windows Clipboard.

H— **Paste.** "Pastes" the contents of the Clipboard to a specified location in your drawing.

I— **Undo.** Cancels the effect of the last command or operation.

J— **Redo.** Can be used after **Undo,** to redo the previously canceled operation.

K— **Tool Bars Flyout.** Displays several buttons to activate various tool bars.

L— **Object Selection Flyout.** Displays a group of buttons to activate various object selection options.

M— **Object Group.** Groups objects together for easy editing.

N— **Object Snap Flyout.** Presents a series of buttons that activate tools for accessing specific geometric points within a drawing.

O— **Point Filter Flyout.** Displays buttons that provide several point specification options.

P— **Coordinate System Flyout.** Presents a series of buttons that activate various coordinate system options.

Q— **View Flyout.** Various options for changing the current view of your drawing are presented by this flyout.

R— **Redraw Flyout.** This flyout provides options for refreshing the drawing display.

S— **Pan.** Allows you to change the current drawing display location.

T— **Zoom In.** Doubles the magnification of the current drawing display.

U— **Zoom Out.** Decreases the magnification of the current view by 1/2.

V— **Zoom Window.** Allows the user to draw a window to define the desired display area.

W— **Zoom Flyout.** Presents the rest of the available zooming operations.

X— **Space Flyout.** Provides buttons to enable **Paper/Model** space options.

Y— **Help.** Activates AutoCAD's **On-line Help** facility.

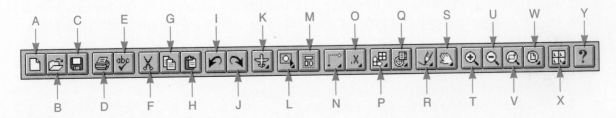

Figure 2-8.   The **Object Properties** toolbar and its components.

A— **Layers**. Accesses the **Layer Control** dialog box, where you can create and manage drawing layers.

B— **Layer Control**. Shows the current layer and its properties. Clicking on the down arrow on the right side of the **Layer Control** field shows information on all drawing layers and provides a handy shortcut to common layer control options.

C— **Color Control**. Displays the current object creation color and when picked, accesses the **Select Color** dialog box for selection of a new color option.

D— **Linetypes**. Accesses the **Select Linetype** dialog box for selecting and loading object linetypes.

E— **Linetype Control**. Displays the current object linetype. Clicking on the down arrow to the right allows you to select a new linetype from the currently loaded linetypes.

F— **Object Creation**. Accesses the **Object Creation** dialog box where detailed settings can be made regarding object layers, linetypes, colors, and other object creation modes.

G— **Multiline Style**. Accesses the **Multiline Styles** dialog box.

H— **Properties**. Allows modification to the properties of existing objects in a drawing.

I— **List**. Displays various information on a selected object.

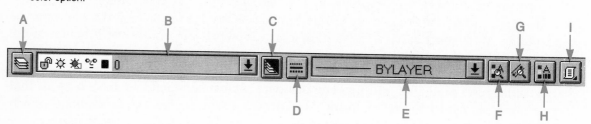

- **Object Properties Toolbar.** In the default AutoCAD screen configuration, the **Object Properties** toolbar appears just above the graphics area with the **Standard Toolbar**. This toolbar contains buttons and display fields for commonly used AutoCAD commands. Each of these features is identified and briefly explained in Figure 2-8.

## Pull-down menus

The AutoCAD for Windows pull-down menus are located on the menu bar at the top of the screen. As with a toolbar, when you move your pointing device to the menu bar, the crosshairs change to the arrow pointer. From Figure 2-9, you can see that the default menu bar has seven pull-down menu items. They are **File**, **Edit**, **View**, **Data**, **Options**, **Tools**, and **Help**.

Figure 2-9.   The standard pull-down menus for AutoCAD for Windows. These are located along the top of the screen, just as with any other Windows program.

| ☐ | **File**    **Edit**    **View**    **Data**    **Options**    **Tools**    **Help** |

By default, AutoCAD for Windows divides the command set between menus and toolbars, with some commands occurring in both. To see how a pull-down menu works, move your cursor to the **View** menu and press the pick button. A pull-down menu appears below **View**, Figure 2-10A. Commands are easily selected by picking a menu item with your pointing device.

Notice that several of the commands in the **View** pull-down menu have a small arrow to the right. When one of these items is selected, a *cascading menu* appears. A cascading menu has additional options for the previous selection, Figure 2-10B.

Some of the menu selections are followed by an ellipsis (...). If you pick one of these items, a dialog box is displayed. Dialog boxes are discussed later in this chapter.

Figure 2-10. Using the pull-down menus. A—When you pick **View**, this pull-down menu is displayed. B—A pull-down menu item followed by an arrow indicates a cascading menu. Selecting the item displays the cascading menu (shown here highlighted).

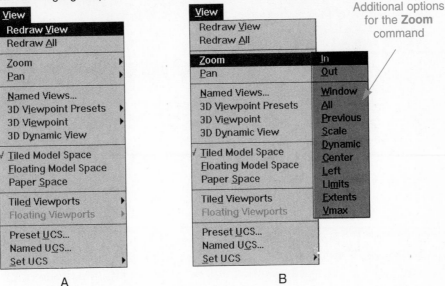

A                                                    B

If you pick the wrong pull-down menu, simply move the cursor to the one you want and pick it. The first menu is removed and the one you pick is displayed. The pull-down menu disappears after you pick an item in the menu, pick a point in the drawing area, or type on the keyboard.

**Accessing pull-down menus from the keyboard.** As you move through the pull-down menus, note that one character of each pull-down menu title is underlined. This allows access to any pull-down menu selection using an [Alt]+[*key*] combination on the keyboard. For instance, the **File** menu can be accessed by pressing [Alt]+[F]. Pressing [Alt]+[A] accesses the **Assist** menu, and so on.

Once a pull-down menu is displayed, a menu item can be selected using a single character key. For example, suppose you want to zoom in closer to your work. Referring once again to Figure 2-10B, first press [Alt]+[V] to access the **View** menu. Then, press Z to select the **Zoom** command. Finally, press I to select the **In** option. These shortcut keystrokes for accessing pull-down menu items are called *menu accelerator keys*.

---

**NOTE**      There are many individual character key and key combination shortcuts available for Windows and Windows-based applications. Refer to the Microsoft Windows *User's Guide* for a complete list of keyboard shortcuts.

---

## Dialog boxes

One of the most important aspects of AutoCAD Release 13 for Windows is the Graphical User Interface (GUI) offered by the Microsoft Windows operating environment. A *graphical user interface* is how information, options, and choices are displayed for you by the software. The most common aspect of the GUI is the dialog box. A *dialog box* is a box that may contain a variety of information. You can also select an item in a dialog box by simply moving your cursor to it and picking. This process eliminates a lot of typing, thus potentially saving time and increasing productivity.

Commands and selections in pull-down menus that are followed by an ellipsis (...) display a dialog box when they are picked. An example of a simple dialog box is shown in Figure 2-11. This dialog box is displayed when you pick **New...** from the **File** pull-down menu. This dialog box is discussed in detail in Chapter 5.

Figure 2-11.  A dialog box appears when you pick an item that is followed by an ellipsis. The dialog box shown here appears after you select **New...** from the **File** pull-down menu.

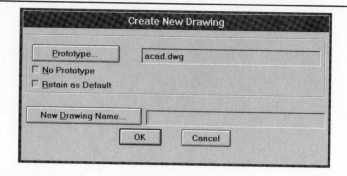

Buttons in a dialog box that are followed by an ellipses display a subdialog box when they are picked. The subdialog box will be displayed on top of the original dialog box, much like laying a sheet of paper on top of another. You must make a selection from the subdialog box before returning to the original dialog box.

There are standard parts to all dialog boxes. If you take a few minutes to review the brief descriptions here, you will find it much easier to work with the dialog boxes. Detailed discussions are provided in later chapters. You can become efficient in your use of dialog boxes by remembering two things—pick a button and enter text in a text box.

- **Buttons.** When you pick a button, something happens immediately. The most common buttons are **OK** and **Cancel**. Another very common button is **Help**. See Figure 2-12. If a button has a dark border (such as **OK** in Figure 2-12A), it is the default. Pressing the [Enter] key accepts the default. If a button is "grayed-out," then that button cannot be selected. Buttons can also lead to other things. A button with an ellipsis (...) leads to a subdialog box. A button with the symbol ⟩ requires that you make a selection in the graphics window, then returns you to the dialog box.
- **Radio buttons.** When you press a selector button on your car radio, the station changes. Only one station can play at a time. Likewise, only one item in a group of radio buttons can be highlighted or active at one time. See Figure 2-13.
- **Toggles.** A toggle, or check box, displays an "X" when it is on (active). If the box is empty, the option is off. See Figure 2-14.
- **List box.** A list box contains a list of items or options. You can scan through the list using the scroll bar (if present) or the keyboard arrow keys. Either highlight the desired item with the arrow keys and press [Enter], or simply select it using your pointing device. See Figure 2-15.

Figure 2-12.  When you select a button, something immediately happens. Three common buttons found in dialog boxes are the **OK**, **Cancel**, and **Help...** buttons. Note the dark border around the **OK** button. This means that this is the default button.

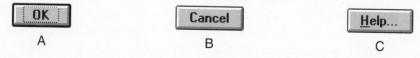

Figure 2-13. Only one radio button in a group can be highlighted at any one given time.

Radio buttons

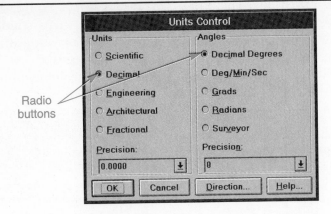

Figure 2-14. An "X" in a check box indicates that the item is active (on). Any number of check boxes can be active in a given group.

Active toggle (on)

Inactive toggle (off)

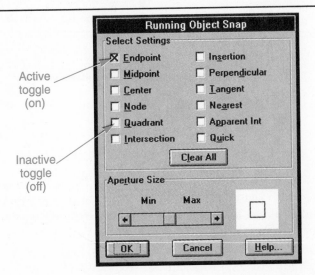

Figure 2-15. A list box contains a list of items related to the dialog box. Here, the list box (shown highlighted) shows the views defined for the current drawing.

List of items

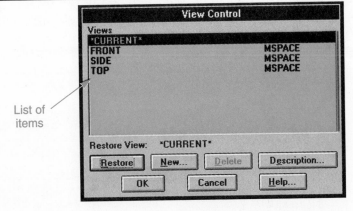

- **Pop-up list box.** The pop-up list box is similar to the standard list box, except only one item is initially shown. The remaining items are hidden until you pick the down arrow. When you pick the down arrow, the pop-up list is displayed below the initial item. As with a standard Windows "drop-down" list, you can then pick from the expanded list, or use the scroll bar to find the item you need. See Figure 2-16.

Figure 2-16.   A pop-up list box is displayed when you pick the down arrow. Many Windows applications call pop-up lists "drop-down" lists.

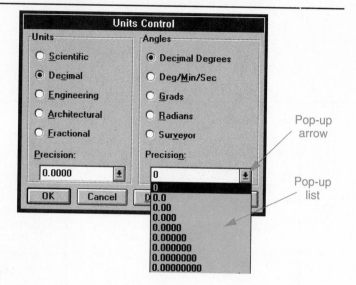

- **Edit box.** You can enter a name or single line of information using the edit box. See Figure 2-17. When a edit box is empty, the cursor appears as a flashing vertical bar positioned at the far-left side of the box. If there is existing text in the edit box, that text appears highlighted. Any characters you then type will replace the highlighted text. Pressing either the [Backspace] key, space bar, or the [Delete] key will delete all of the highlighted text. You can edit existing text using the cursor keys [Home], [End], right arrow, and left arrow. The [Home] key moves the cursor to the beginning of the line of text and the [End] key moves to the end of the line. The right arrow and left arrow keys move the cursor one character to the right or to the left, respectively. By using the [Ctrl] key in conjunction with the right arrow or left arrow key, you can move the cursor to the next word or the previous word, respectively.

Figure 2-17.   You can enter a name or single line of information in an edit box. Several edit boxes are shown here highlighted.

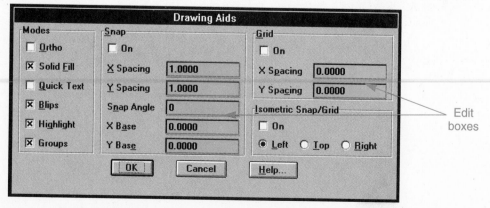

- **File dialog.** The file dialog provides a simple means of locating and specifying file-names using the familiar Windows Browse style dialog. The example in Figure 2-18 shows a file dialog for drawing filenames. By *double-clicking* a directory name in the directory window, you can "open" a directory. Its contents are then displayed in the file list box where items can be selected. The drive list box allows alternate drive names to be specified. The file type list box is used to specify the type of file being searched for. Once a filename is selected, it appears in the filename edit box. If needed, it can be edited. If the path and filename are already known, they can simply be typed into the edit box, regardless of the current values in the drive list box and directory window.

Figure 2-18.   The file dialog provides a simple means of locating filenames. The file dialog area of this dialog box is shown here highlighted.

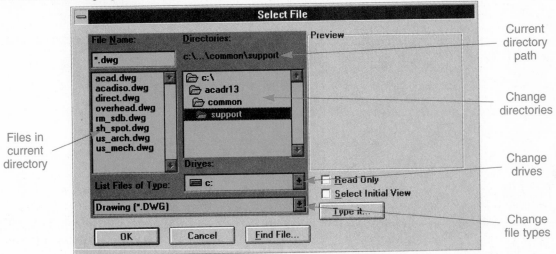

- **Scroll bar.** The scroll bar can be compared to an elevator sitting next to a list of files or directories. The top arrow points to the top floor, and the bottom arrow points to the basement. The box in the middle is the elevator. If you pick the elevator and hold down the pick button, you can move the box up or down. This displays additional files in the upper or lower floors of your directory. Pick the blank area above the elevator box to scroll up one page. Pick below the elevator box to scroll down one page. If you want to scroll up or down one file at a time, simply pick the up or down arrows. See Figure 2-19. The scroll bars on the side of the graphics window work in this same manner, and provide a quick and easy way to adjust the current view of a drawing.

Figure 2-19.   Use the scroll bar to scroll through a listing.

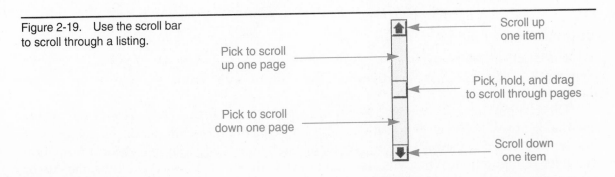

- **Image tile.** An image tile is an area of a dialog box that displays a "picture" of the item you selected, such as a hatching style, linetype, or text font. See Figure 2-20. For many image tiles, you can actually pick the image, or part of it, to adjust the selection.
- **Alerts.** Alerts can be displayed in two forms. A note may appear in the lower-left corner of the original dialog box. Or, a separate dialog box may appear with the alert. See Figure 2-21.

Figure 2-20. An image tile displays the selected setting. Many image tiles, such as the ones shown here, can be picked to change the setting.

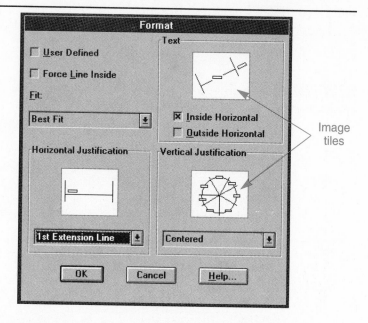

Figure 2-21. A—An alert may appear as a note in the corner of a dialog box. B—An alert may appear in a separate dialog box.

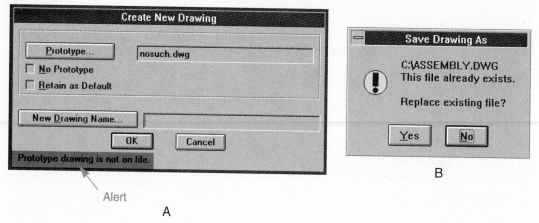

A

B

## AutoCAD tablet menu

The digitizer tablet can accept an overlay or menu that contains most of AutoCAD's commands. Other specialized programs that operate with AutoCAD may have similar menus.

This text presents commands as if they are typed at the keyboard or selected from menus and dialog boxes. If you wish to use your digitizer tablet to pick commands, the tablet must first be configured (arranged) before the menu can be used. See Chapter 31 for information on tablet configuration. When you use a digitizer with AutoCAD for Windows, the cursor can only be moved within the active drawing area on-screen. Therefore, menu selections can only be made from the tablet menu overlay. Since all of the AutoCAD commands do not fit on the tablet, you will still need to select toolbar buttons, or to make selections from the pull-down menus on the menu bar. In addition, using the tablet requires that you take your eyes off the screen and look down at the overlay. After picking a tablet command, look at the command line to be sure you picked what you desired.

The AutoCAD tablet menu is shown in Figure 2-22. If you plan on using a digitizer with a tablet menu, take some time and study its arrangement. Become familiar with the command groups and try to remember where each command is located. The quicker you learn the layout of the menu, the more efficient your drawing sessions will be.

Figure 2-22. The AutoCAD tablet menu. (Autodesk, Inc.)

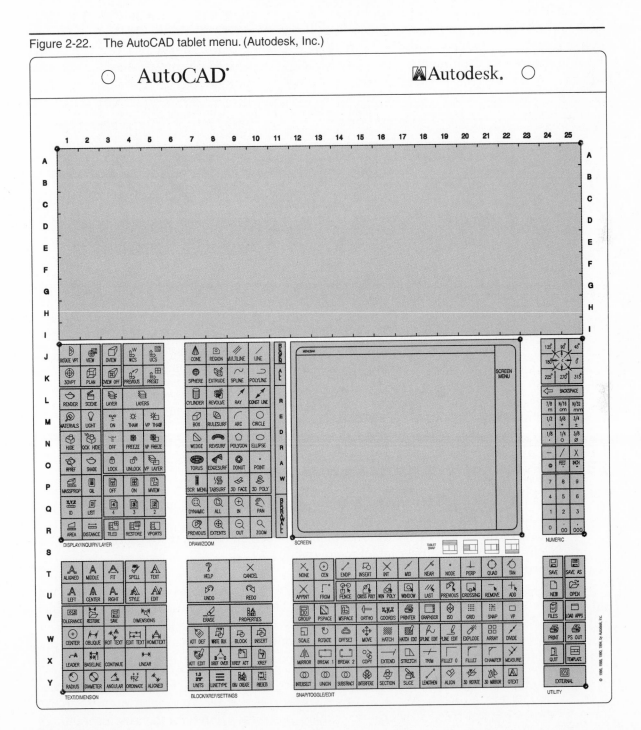

**NOTE**
Certain types of digitizer tablets can be configured to work both as a Windows system pointer (a mouse) and a digitizer. This type of configuration is called *absolute mode.* In order to operate in absolute mode, you must have a **Wintab Compatable Digitizer.** See the AutoCAD Release 13 for Windows *Installation Guide* for information on digitizer configuration.

## ICON MENUS

An icon is a symbol used to graphically represent an item, such as a pattern. AutoCAD uses several menus composed of icons or patterns. Figure 2-23 shows the icon menu for spline fit variables. To choose the spline fit style you want to use, simply pick the icon or text label in the list box. Icon menus allow for easy selection, since you can see the shape or item represented by the icon. To select an icon, move your pointing device to it and pick.

Figure 2-23.   Icon menus graphically display options or selections.

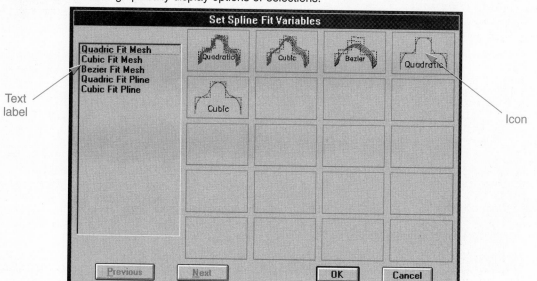

## SELECTING AUTOCAD COMMANDS

Commands may be selected in AutoCAD for Windows in four different ways. They can be:
- Executed by picking a toolbar button or icon.
- Selected from one of the pull-down menus (or screen menus, if so configured).
- Selected from the digitizer tablet menu overlay.
- Typed at the keyboard.

The advantage in using the toolbar and toolbar buttons, as well as the menus, is that you do not have to remove your eyes from the screen. However, when using a digitizer tablet, you must look down to pick tablet menu commands. On the other hand, a tablet menu overlay can show almost every command. Also, when configured as both a windows pointer and a digitizer (absolute mode), a tablet is a powerful and efficient input device.

Typed commands do not require that you turn your eyes from the screen. You can also learn commands quicker by typing them. Try typing commands before other selection methods are used. In some cases, work will progress faster and you will be able to concentrate on the screen for longer periods. The examples shown in this text illustrate each of the AutoCAD commands as they appear when typed at the **Command:** prompt.

## GETTING HELP                                        AUG 4

If you need help with a specific command, option, or program feature, AutoCAD for Windows provides a powerful and convenient on-line **Help** system. There are several ways to access this feature. The fastest method is to simply press the [F1] function key. This displays the **Table of Contents** for the **Help** system in the **AutoCAD Help** window, Figure 2-24. You can also display the **Table of Contents** by selecting **Contents** from the **Help** pull-down menu, or by typing ? or HELP at the **Command:** prompt.

Figure 2-24.   The **Table of Contents** for **Help** is displayed when you select **Contents...** from the **Help** pull-down menu or press [F1].

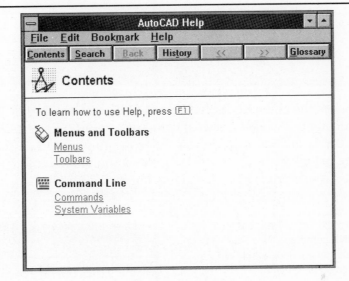

There are two major categories listed within the **Table of Contents**. These categories are:
- **Menus and Toolbars**
- **Command Line**

When you move the arrow pointer to one of the green underlined words within a category, the arrow changes to a hand with a pointer finger. If you click on an underlined word, you can get more information on that topic.

Suppose for example that you needed help with the **LINE** command. Pick the green underlined word **Commands** in the **Command Line** category. A display appears that shows a list of the AutoCAD commands and variable names that begin with the letters A, B, or C, Figure 2-25. Click the green underlined letters **E-L** and all command and variable names starting with the letters E through L are displayed.

Figure 2-25. AutoCAD Commands are displayed alphabetically in the **Help** window.

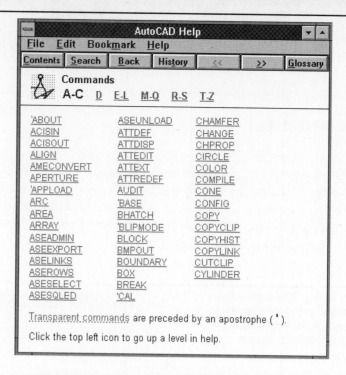

Click the green underlined word **LINE**, and another display appears that contains information about the **LINE** command and its options, Figure 2-26. On the upper-right side of this window is the **See Also** button. Selecting this button displays a pop-up box that tells you where to look in the AutoCAD documentation to find more information. A list of related topics and/or commands is also given, Figure 2-27.

Figure 2-26. The **Help** entry for the **LINE** command. The **See Also** button provides additional information on related commands and topics.

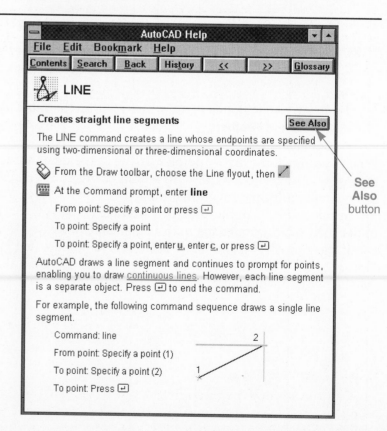

Figure 2-27.   Clicking the **See Also** button displays more information and related topics. The dialog box shown here is displayed after selecting the **See Also** button in the **Help** entry for the **LINE** command.

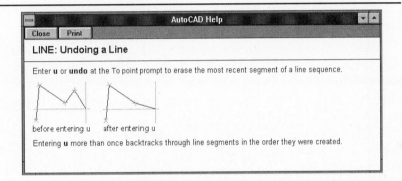

For more information on drawing lines, see "Drawing Line Objects" in chapter 2, "Creating Objects," in the *AutoCAD User's Guide*.

**Commands:** PLINE creates two-dimensional polylines. XLINE creates an infinite line. RAY creates a semi-infinite line.

Selecting a green word with a solid underline displays a subsequent window of information on the selected topic, Figure 2-28. Selecting a green word with a dotted underline displays a pop-up box with a definition for that word, Figure 2-29. You can exit the **Help** system and return to the AutoCAD graphics window by selecting **Exit** from the **File** menu of the AutoCAD **Help** window.

Figure 2-28.   Clicking a word underlined with a solid green line displays an additional window with more information.

**AutoCAD Help**

Close   Print

**LINE: Undoing a Line**

Enter **u** or **undo** at the To point prompt to erase the most recent segment of a line sequence.

before entering u     after entering u

Entering **u** more than once backtracks through line segments in the order they were created.

Figure 2-29.   Clicking a word underlined with a green dotted line displays a definition pop-up box (shown here highlighted).

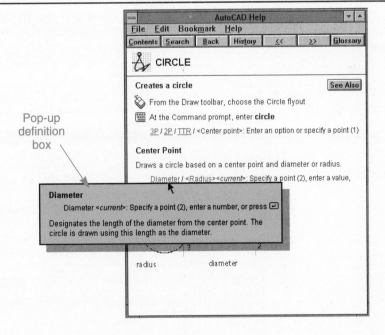

Pop-up definition box

**AutoCAD Help**

**File   Edit   Bookmark   Help**

Contents | Search | Back | History | << | >> | Glossary

**CIRCLE**

**Creates a circle**                              See Also

From the Draw toolbar, choose the Circle flyout

At the Command prompt, enter **circle**

3P / 2P / TTR / <Center point>: Enter an option or specify a point (1)

**Center Point**

Draws a circle based on a center point and diameter or radius.

Diameter / <Radius> <*current*>: Specify a point (2), enter a value,

**Diameter**

Diameter <*current*>: Specify a point (2), enter a number, or press

Designates the length of the diameter from the center point. The circle is drawn using this length as the diameter.

radius          diameter

## Help window buttons

Controls for moving through the **Help** system are provided by the seven buttons located near the top of the **Help** window. Any button that appears "grayed-out" is not currently available for selection. The seven buttons and the functions which they perform are:

- **Contents.** Returns you to the **Table of Contents**.

- **Search.** Enables you to research topics associated with particular words or phrases. (This is described in the next section.)
- **Back.** Returns you to the previously displayed **Help** window.
- **History.** Displays a list of every **Help** topic researched during a current **Help** session. You can return to a topic by double-clicking on it.
- 《. Displays the next topic in a sequence of related topics. To view the next topic, pick the button or press the period (.) key. When you reach the last topic in the sequence, or if there is no sequence, the 》 button is grayed-out.
- 》. Displays the previous topic in a sequence of related topics. To view the previous topic pick the button or press the comma (,) key. When you reach the first topic in the sequence, or if there is no sequence, the 《 button is grayed-out.
- **Glossary.** Displays the AutoCAD **Glossary** window. This feature provides quick definitions of AutoCAD terminology. Selecting one of the green underlined letters at the top of the window takes you directly to the section containing words beginning with that letter. Select the **Close** button to return to the AutoCAD Help window.

## Using Search

Just as you might look up a topic in a textbook by finding a certain word in the index, you can also research AutoCAD topics using a single word or phrase. The **Help** system **Search** function can be started from the AutoCAD graphics window by selecting **Search for Help on...** in the **Help** pull-down menu. If you are already in the **Help** system, click the **Search** button near the top of the **Help** window.

After selecting the command, the **Search** dialog box appears. There are several components to the **Search** dialog box. Near the top is located the *keyword text box*. Just below the keyword text box is the *keyword list box*. The *topics list box* is located at the very bottom of the dialog box.

In Figure 2-30, you can see that instructions for using the **Search** function are provided in the upper-left corner of the **Search** dialog box. You can use the scroll bar to find the word or phrase you want in the keyword list box and then highlight it with your cursor. You can also enter the word by typing it in the keyword text box.

Figure 2-30.   The **Search** dialog box can be used to find **Help** topics if you only know part of the command or term.

Once the word or phrase you want to research is shown in the text box, click the **Show Topics** button. All related topics are then displayed in the topics list box. (Double-clicking on a word or phrase from the keyword list box will also display all related topics in the topics list box.)

Click the topic you want from the topics list box, and then click the **Go To** button. (You may also double-click on a topic from the topics list box to obtain the same results.) The **Search** dialog box is closed, and the topic information appears in the **Help** window.

### New Features in Release 13

If you are curious about the changes that were made for the Release 13 version of AutoCAD, pick **What's New in Release 13...** from the **Help** pull-down menu. There are three selections available in the **What's New in Release 13** dialog box. The **Using What's New** selection helps you navigate this portion of AutoCAD's help files. **New Features** gives you a quick tour—with color image tiles—of some of the new features in Release 13. The **Command Summary** selection provides lists of new, changed, and deleted commands in Release 13.

---

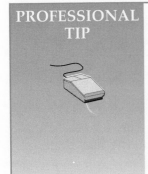

PROFESSIONAL TIP

AutoCAD's **Help** function can also be used while you are in the process of using a command. For example, suppose you are using the **ARC** command and forget what type of information is required by AutoCAD for the specific prompts that are on-screen. Simply press the [F1] function key and the help information for the currently active command is displayed. This *context oriented help* saves valuable time since you don't need to scan through the **Help** contents or perform any searches to find the information.

---

## KEYS, BUTTONS, FUNCTIONS, AND TERMINOLOGY

AutoCAD provides several ways of performing a given task. There are a variety of keys on the keyboard. Some of them you may find handy, but only if you know their meanings. Keyboard keys allow you to perform many functions. In addition, multibutton pointing devices also utilize the extra buttons for AutoCAD commands. Become familiar with the meaning of these keys and buttons.

### The Escape key

Any time it is necessary to cancel a command and return to the **Command:** prompt, press the *escape* key on your keyboard. This key is found on the upper-left corner of most keyboards and is typically labeled Esc. Some command sequences may require that the [Esc] key be pressed twice to completely cancel the operation.

### Control keys

Most computer programs use *control key* functions to perform common tasks. Control key functions are activated by pressing and holding the [Ctrl] key while pressing a second key. Keep the following list close at hand and try them occasionally. (If a command or key is noted as a "toggle," it is either on or off–nothing else.)

| | |
|---|---|
| [Ctrl]+[B] | *Snap mode (toggle).* |
| [Ctrl]+[D] | *Coordinate display on status line (toggle).* |
| [Ctrl]+[E] | *Crosshairs in isoplane positions left/top/right (toggle).* |
| [Ctrl]+[G] | *Grid (toggle).* |
| [Ctrl]+[H] | *Same as backspace.* |
| [Ctrl]+[L] | *Ortho mode (toggle).* |
| [Ctrl]+[O] | *Open.* |
| [Ctrl]+[T] | *Tablet mode (toggle).* |
| [Ctrl]+[V] | *Paste clip.* |
| [Ctrl]+[X] | *Cut clip.* |
| [Ctrl]+[Z] | *Undo.* |

**NOTE**

Computer users who are experienced in working with DOS, or those who have used previous versions of AutoCAD may be familiar with using the [Ctrl]+[C] key combination as a **Cancel** command. However, in AutoCAD Release 13, the [Ctrl]+[C] key combination by default activates the **COPYCLIP** command. By changing the settings in the **Preferences** dialog box, the [Ctrl]+[C] key combination can be changed so that it activates the **Cancel** command. See *AutoCAD and its Applications—Advanced, Release 13 for Windows,* for information on customizing preferences.

## Function keys

Function keys provide instant access to commands. They can also be programmed to perform a series of commands. The function keys are either to the left or along the top of the keyboard, Figure 2-31. Depending on the brand of keyboard, there will be either 10 or 12 function keys. These are numbered from [F1] to [F10] (or [F12]). AutoCAD uses only nine function keys. These are listed below. As you become proficient with AutoCAD, you might program the function keys to do specific tasks using other computer programs.

| | |
|---|---|
| [F1] | *Help.* |
| [F2] | *Flip screen from graphics to text (toggle).* |
| [F4] | *Tablet mode (toggle).* |
| [F5] | *Isoplane (toggle).* |
| [F6] | *Coordinate display (toggle).* |
| [F7] | **Grid** *(toggle).* |
| [F8] | **Ortho** *mode (toggle).* |
| [F9] | **Snap** *mode (toggle).* |
| [F10] | *Activates the menu bar.* |

Figure 2-31. Function keys are found along the top or side of a keyboard. In this photo, the function keys are along the top and labeled [F1] through [F12].

## Button functions

If you are using a multibutton pointing device, you can select control key functions by pressing a single button. The meaning of the pointing device buttons are:

| | |
|---|---|
| 0— Pick. | 5—Ortho mode (toggle). |
| 1— Return. | 6—Grid (toggle). |
| 2— Object snap cursor menu | 7—Coordinate display (toggle). |
| displayed on-screen. | 8—Crosshairs isoplane positions |
| 3— Cancel. | top/left/right (toggle). |
| 4— Snap mode (toggle). | 9—Tablet mode (toggle). |

## Understanding terminology

Become familiar with the following terms. These terms are used throughout the text and will help you select AutoCAD functions.

- **Default.** A value that is maintained by the computer until you change it.
- **Select.** Choose a command or option from the pull-down or tablet menu.
- **Pick or Click.** Use the pointing device to select an item on the screen or tablet.
- **Button.** One of the screen toolbar or pointing device (puck) buttons.
- **Key.** A key on the keyboard.
- **Function key.** One of the keys labeled [F1] - [F10] (or [F1] - [F12]) along the top or side of the keyboard.
- **[Enter] (⏎).** The [Enter] or [Return] key on the keyboard.
- **COMMAND.** An instruction issued to the computer.
- **Option.** An aspect of a command that can be selected. These are shown with the first letter capitalized and the rest lowercase.

## AVOIDING "DISK FULL" PROBLEMS

When you begin a new drawing, AutoCAD "looks" at the drawing filename to determine where the drawing will be stored (unless you have configured temporary file placement—see the Professional Tip on page 63). When you enter the drawing name, AutoCAD creates a space for it in the current directory of the active disk drive. AutoCAD does this automatically to the hard disk if you do not put a directory name in front of the filename. Suppose you give the name A:P15-5. AutoCAD creates a space on the floppy disk in the A: drive for drawing P15-5.

Creating a drawing on a floppy disk is not the best way to operate AutoCAD. This is because AutoCAD creates space for several temporary files that it uses during a drawing session. There must be room for these files, in addition to your drawing file, for AutoCAD to function properly. Floppy drives are slow to store and access data. In addition, limited space on the floppy disk can eventually lead to a "disk full" error, or worse, a system crash. The disk full error still allows you to save the current drawing. A system crash destroys the current drawing in memory. Avoid these problems by configuring temporary file placement.

---

**NOTE** Before a disk can be used by the computer, it must be formatted. This process divides the disk into pie-shaped sectors, checks it for defects, and creates a file directory on the disk. This is all accomplished with the Windows File Manager. See Chapter 32 for a complete discussion on this process.

## Creating a new drawing

It is best to begin new drawings and edit existing drawings on the hard disk during a drawing session. If you are starting a new drawing called P15-5, begin the drawing session with the new drawing name P15-5. AutoCAD then works on the hard disk, which should have plenty of room for the temporary open files. Save the drawing as A:P15-5 to store it on a floppy, then quit without saving. This places the drawing on the floppy disk, but does not put anything on the hard disk drive.

If you have configured temporary file placement, you will not need to worry about temporary files being stored on the floppy disk. In this case, you can name the new drawing A:P15-5. Then you can select **Save** from the **File** menu instead of the **Save As...** command.

## Editing an existing drawing

If you are in training with AutoCAD, you should save all of your drawings and exercises on floppy disks, not on the hard disk drive. Keep two copies of each floppy disk. One is the original and the other is a backup copy. Each time you save a drawing on a floppy disk, save it a second time on the backup disk. This is discussed again later in the text.

When you need to edit a drawing that is on a floppy disk, but preserve the original, select **New...** from the **File** pull-down menu. If the drawing is P15-5, enter the following in the **New Drawing Name...** text box and press [Enter], or click on the **OK** button:

> **P15-5=A:P15-5** ⏎

This technique instructs AutoCAD to retrieve a copy of drawing P15-5 from the floppy disk in the A: drive and begin a new drawing located on the hard disk named P15-5 using that copy. This is called the *prototype drawing method*, and preserves the original drawing.

Another way to use the prototype drawing method is by picking the **Prototype...** text box of the **Create New Drawing** dialog box. The drawing name ACAD should be the current name in the text box. Double-click on the word ACAD and type A:P15-5. Now pick the **New Drawing Name...** text box and type P15-5. When you pick the **OK** button, AutoCAD retrieves a copy of the prototype drawing and begins a new one with the same name. This process is explained in greater detail in Chapter 5.

When you are ready to save the drawing, type the **SAVE** command. Use A:P15-5 as the drawing name. You will then get an alert box that says:

> This file already exists.
> Replace existing file?

Pick the **YES** button. Saving the drawing as A:P15-5 means you want to place the drawing on the floppy drive. (Remember, you first loaded the drawing by this name from the floppy disk.) AutoCAD says that a drawing with the same name already exists on the floppy disk in that drive. By entering Y or YES, you replace the old copy with the edited (updated) version.

Use these techniques for working with drawings. You will avoid the problems associated with editing a drawing you want preserved as a prototype.

**PROFESSIONAL TIP**

You can instruct AutoCAD to store its temporary files in a specific directory by using the **CONFIG** command. First be sure that you have made a new directory on your hard disk with a name such as C:\ACADTEMP. Then type CONFIG at the **Command:** prompt, and press [Enter] three times until the **Configuration** menu is displayed. Then type 7 for **Configure operating parameters**. This displays the **Configure operating parameters** menu. Now type 5 for **Placement of temporary files**. You will be asked to enter a directory name for temporary files. Enter the following:

**C:\ACADTEMP**

Now AutoCAD will always place its temporary work files in the C:\ACADTEMP directory, and not in the current directory or the one that contains the drawing you are working on. This simplifies the process of purging old, unneeded temporary files from the hard disk. It also avoids "disk full" errors when working from a floppy disk.

## CHAPTER TEST

*Write your answers in the spaces provided.*

1. What is the difference between installing, configuring, and loading AutoCAD? _____

   _____

   _____

   _____

   _____

   _____

2. What do the following DOS prompts mean? _____

   A⟩ _____

   B⟩ _____

   C⟩ _____

3. What do you type at the DOS prompt to load Windows? _____

   _____

4. List four of the areas that comprise the AutoCAD for Windows (uncustomized) graphics window. _____

   _____

   _____

   _____

   _____

   _____

5. Which area displays the communication between AutoCAD and the user? _____

   _____

6.  What are the differences between a docked toolbar and a floating toolbar? _____

_____

_____

_____

7.  What are menu accelerator keys? How are they used? Give an example. _____

_____

_____

_____

8.  What is an option?_____

_____

_____

9.  List the seven AutoCAD for Windows pull-down menus._____

_____

_____

10. What is an icon?_____

_____

11. What must you do to the tablet before it can be used? _____

_____

12. What are the functions of the following control keys?

A.  [Ctrl]+[B] _____

B.  [Ctrl]+[C] _____

C.  [Ctrl]+[D] _____

D.  [Ctrl]+[G] _____

E.  [Ctrl]+[O] _____

13. Name the function keys that execute the same task as the following control keys.

     Control Key              Function Key

A.  [Ctrl]+[B] _____

B.  [Ctrl]+[D] _____

C.  [Ctrl]+[G] _____

D.  [Ctrl]+[O] _____

E.  [Ctrl]+[T] _____

14. What is the difference between a "button" and a "key"? _____

_____

15. What do you call a value that is maintained by the computer until you change it?_____

_____

16. What type of pull-down menu has an arrow to the right of the item? _____

_____

17. What type of menu contains a group of symbols or patterns?_____

18. The scroll bar is normally associated with what portion of the dialog box? _____

_____

19. What is an image tile? _____

_____

20. What is "content oriented help," and how is it accessed? _____

_____

_____

## PROBLEMS

1. Read the instructions in Appendix A for installing AutoCAD. Make a list of the steps required to perform the task. List the correct order that the disks should be copied in.

General

2. List the steps required to configure AutoCAD. (Do not list all the hardware options in the configuration routine.)

General

3. List the steps required to start Windows, run AutoCAD, and begin a new drawing named FIRST.

General

4. Begin AutoCAD and pick the **File** pull-down menu. Perform the following tasks using this menu:

General

   A. Open one of the drawings that is provided with AutoCAD. You may have to pick one or more of the directories to find them. (Hint: Try the SAMPLE subdirectory.)

   B. Open another drawing and do not save the previous one.

   C. Save the drawing you just opened as CH2TEST.

   D. Exit AutoCAD and do not save the changes.

5. Draw a freehand sketch of the screen display. Label each of the screen areas. To the side of the sketch, write a short description of each screen area's function.

General

6. Draw a freehand sketch of your keyboard by blocking each specific group of keys. Label the groups. Label the function keys, arrow keys, and control keys. To the side of your sketch write a short description of the function of each group of keys.

General

7. Draw a freehand sketch of the AutoCAD overlay menu. (Do not draw each individual box.) Block in the four menu areas and the screen area. Label each menu area that is shown in red on the template.

General

General

8. Identify the parts of the dialog boxes shown in the following screen displays.

A. _____

B. _____

C. _____

D. _____

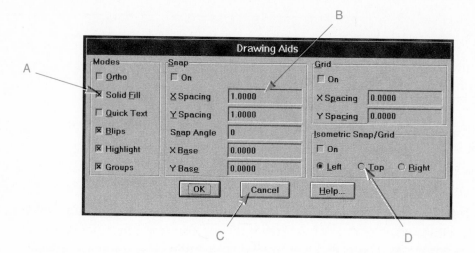

E. _____

F. _____

G. _____

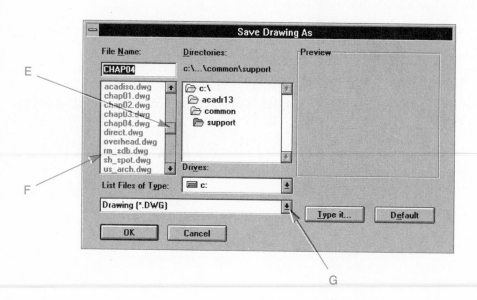

## Learning objectives

After completing this chapter, you will be able to:

○ Draw and erase lines.
○ Use the **UNITS** command to establish units of measure.
○ Set drawing limits.

Effective planning can greatly reduce the amount of time it takes to set up and complete a drawing. Drawing setup involves a number of factors that affect the quality and accuracy of your final drawing. Some basic planning decisions include:

• The sheet size needed to fit the drawing.
• The units of measure needed to create the drawing.
• The degree of accuracy required.
• The name of the drawing.

## STARTING A DRAWING

When you load AutoCAD, the standard AutoCAD graphics window (discussed in Chapter 2) is displayed. This is referred to as the *drawing editor*. See Figure 3-1.

Figure 3-1. The AutoCAD for Windows drawing editor.

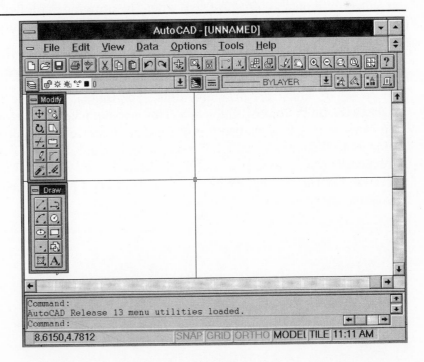

Now that you are in the drawing editor, you are ready to start drawing. Notice the screen crosshairs. Move your pointing device and the crosshairs also move. Now, try some drawing using the following command sequence.

Command: **LINE** ↵ *(Type LINE using the keyboard and press the [Enter] key)*
From point: *(move your pointer to any desired place on the screen and pick a point)*
To point: *(move your pointer and pick another point)*
To point: *(move your pointer and pick another point)*
To point: ↵
Command:

You should now have two lines drawn on-screen. Now erase the lines as follows:

Command: **ERASE** ↵
*(Notice that the crosshairs have changed to a small box called the pick box.)*
Select objects: *(move the pick box to one of the lines and pick it by pressing your
    pick button)*
Select objects: *(move pick box and pick the other line)*
Select objects: ↵

Now that the lines are erased, look at the screen and notice some points still remain. These points are called *blips*. They are located at points that you picked when drawing. If you want to get rid of the blips, enter the following command sequence. You can also pick **Redraw View** from the **View** pull-down menu or click on the **Redraw View** icon in the standard toolbar for the same results.

Command: **REDRAW** ↵

## SETTING UP DRAWING UNITS

AUG 1

When drawing with AutoCAD, you do not have to scale a drawing. All lines, circles, and other entities are drawn and measured full-size. For example, if a part is 36″ long, it is drawn 36 units (inches) long. Therefore, the size of the product determines the size of the drawing. Inches, millimeters, or feet can be used as the unit of measurement. The drawing may have to be scaled to fit on a given sheet size when the drawing is plotted. You can even position and plot different views of the drawing at different scales using AutoCAD's paper space capabilities. Paper space is explained in Chapter 10 and Chapter 26.

### Setting units with the Units Control dialog box

To set or adjust the drawing units, pick **Units...** from the **Data** pull-down menu. This accesses the **Units Control** dialog box. This is the quickest and easiest way to set units, though you can also use the **Command:** prompt. The **Units Control** dialog box in Figure 3-2A has the units set to three-place decimals, two-place decimal degrees. Pick **Direction...** to display the **Direction Control** dialog box. Refer to Figure 3-2 as you go through the next sections. The **Direction Control** dialog box in Figure 3-2B has settings of East angle direction and angles measured counterclockwise.

Figure 3-2. A—The **Units Control** dialog box. Select the appropriate unit and angle settings and the precision for each. B—The **Direction Control** subdialog box appears when you pick **Direction...** in the **Units Control** dialog box. Select the appropriate 0° angle setting and the direction for measuring angles.

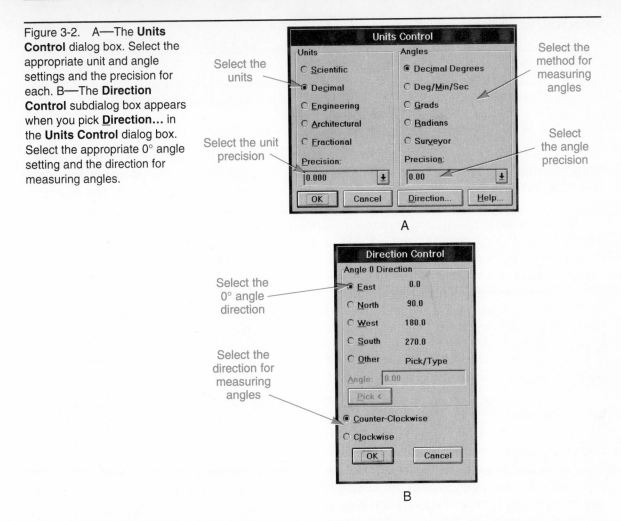

## Selecting decimal units

ASME Y14.5M-1994, *Dimensioning and Tolerancing*, specifies that decimal-inch, or metric units in millimeters, be used on engineering drawings. Decimal units are used widely in mechanical drafting. To set decimal units, select the **Decimal** radio button in the **Units** section of the **Units Control** dialog box.

## Selecting engineering units

Engineering units are used in civil drafting. *Civil drafting* deals with detailed construction drawings and topographic maps for the planning and construction of highways, harbors, drainage, and related projects. Engineering units are measured in feet, inches, and decimal parts of an inch. For example, 5'-6.75" would be used to denote 5 feet and 6 3/4 inches. Each engineering unit in AutoCAD is one inch. To set engineering units, select the **Engineering** radio button in the **Units** section of the **Units Control** dialog box.

## Selecting architectural units

Residential and commercial planning and construction drawings use architectural units. With these units, dimensions are given in feet, inches, and fractional parts of an inch. For example, 8'-10 3/4" would be used to denote 8 feet and 10 3/4 inches. To set architectural units, select the **Architectural** radio button in the **Units** area of the **Units Control** dialog box.

### Selecting fractional units

Units can also be fractional parts of a unit. The fractional units may take on any desired value such as inches, feet, or miles. Dimensions are shown giving whole units and parts of a unit as a fraction. For example, 24 3/4 indicates 24 units and 3/4 of a unit. To set fractional units, select the **Fractional** radio button in the **Units** area of the **Units Control** dialog box.

### Precision of units

The precision of units is based on either the number of decimal places or the smallest fraction. After you have selected the type of units, you need to set the precision for those units. At this point, you need to make some decisions about the accuracy of the drawing display.

For scientific, decimal, and engineering units, a two-place decimal unit is shown as 0.00, a three-place decimal is 0.000, and a four-place decimal is 0.0000. For mechanical drawings, three to four digits are normally adequate for inch drawings. For metric drawings, one or two place decimals are commonly used. Select the appropriate number of places behind the decimal from the **Precision:** pop-up list.

When architectural or fractional units are used, the accuracy is determined by the size of the fraction's denominator. The larger the denominator, the greater the precision. Select the appropriate fractional setting from the **Precision:** pop-up list.

### Setting angle measurements

The angular measurement format recommended by the American National Standards Institute is degrees (°), minutes ('), and seconds (") or decimal degrees. However, your drawing needs may be different. Select the appropriate setting in the **Angles** area of the **Units Control** dialog box.

The degree of accuracy is determined by the drawing requirements. Two-place decimal degrees or degrees and minutes are normally adequate for mechanical drawings. Select the appropriate setting from the **Precision** pop-up list.

Next, you need to specify the direction for a 0° angle. In other words, where the origin for making angular measurements is located. The AutoCAD default is an angle starting to the right (East) and heading in a counterclockwise direction, Figure 3-3.

---

Figure 3-3. The default AutoCAD settings for 0° angle and direction are East and counterclockwise.

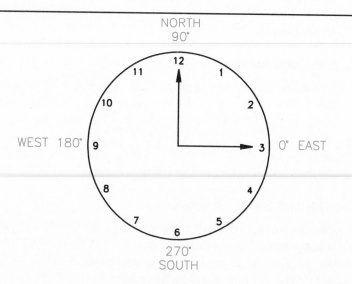

To set the direction for a 0° angle, first pick the **Direction...** button in the **Units Control** dialog box. This opens the **Direction Control** dialog box. Refer to Figure 3-2B. Select the appropriate direction for a 0° angle. Also, you need to select whether angles are measured counterclockwise or clockwise from a given point.

## Setting units using the Command: prompt

The units of measurement can also be set using the **Command:** prompt. However, this method is not as quick and easy as using the dialog box. To set the units of measurement, type UNITS at the **Command:** prompt as follows:

Command: **UNITS** ⏎

The display then changes to a text window. Here, you are given examples showing how the units are displayed. You must specify the type of units you want.

```
Report formats:          (Examples)
   1. Scientific         155E+01
   2. Decimal            15.50
   3. Engineering·       1'-3.50"
   4. Architectural      1'-3 1/2"
   5. Fractional         15 1/2
```
With the exception of Engineering and Architectural formats, these formats can be used with any basic unit of measurement. For example, Decimal mode is perfect for metric units as well as decimal English units.
Enter choice, 1 to 5 ⟨*default*⟩:

The examples given show how the value of 15.5 drawing units is displayed in each format. The default (in brackets) shows the units currently in effect. Decimal units are commonly used on mechanical drawings. To choose decimal units, enter 2 at the prompt and press [Enter]:

Enter choice, 1 to 5 ⟨*default*⟩: **2** ⏎

Next you need to select the precision of the units. For decimal-type units, you need to specify the number of digits to the right of the decimal point. For fraction-type units, you need to specify a number for the denominator.

## Setting angle measurements using the Command: prompt

After the accuracy of decimal or fractional units has been set, the next option determines the method of measuring angles. The screen displays the following:

```
Systems of angle measure:     (Examples)

   1. Decimal degrees          45.00002
   2. Degrees/minutes/seconds  45d0'0"3
   3. Grads                    50.0000g4
   4. Radians                   0.7854r5
   5. Surveyor's units         N 45d0'0" E

Enter choice, 1 to 5 ⟨default⟩:
```

The given examples show how a 45° angle is displayed in each format. Pressing the [Enter] key gives you the default value currently in effect. If the default is not appropriate, make the proper selection. The next prompt requests the accuracy of angular measurements:

Number of fractional places for display of angles (0 to 8) ⟨*default*⟩:

Select "2" for mechanical drawings. Select "2" or "5" for civil (mapping) drawings.

Next you are asked to specify the direction for a 0° angle. If the AutoCAD default of East is appropriate for your drawing, respond with "0" as follows:

Direction for angle 0:
East                                   3 o'clock = 0
North                                 12 o'clock = 90
West                                   9 o'clock = 180
South                                  6 o'clock = 270
Enter direction for angle 0 ⟨*default*⟩: **0** ⏎

The next prompt is:

Do you want angles measured clockwise? ⟨*default*⟩:

To maintain the default counterclockwise, enter N or NO. If you want angles to be measured clockwise, enter Y or YES. You are then returned to the drawing editor.

## SIZING OF THE DRAWING AREA                                             AUG 1

ASME/ANSI standard sheet sizes and format are specified in the documents ANSI Y14.1 *Drawing Sheet Size and Format*, and ASME Y14.1M *Metric Drawing Sheet Size and Format*. The proper presentation of engineering changes are given in ASME Y14.35M *Revision of Engineering Drawings and Associated Documents*. ANSI Y14.1 lists sheet size specifications in inches as follows:

| Size Designation | Size (in inches) Vertical X Horizontal |
|---|---|
| A | 8 1/2 X 11 (horizontal format) |
|   | 11 X 8 1/2 (vertical format) |
| B | 11 X 17 |
| C | 17 X 22 |
| D | 22 X 34 |
| E | 34 X 44 |
| F | 28 X 40 |

Sizes G, H, J, and K are roll sizes.

ASME Y14.1M provides sheet size specifications in metric (M). Standard metric drawing sheet sizes are designated as follows:

| Size Designation | Size in millimeters Vertical X Horizontal |
|---|---|
| A0 | 841 X 1189 |
| A1 | 594 X 841 |
| A2 | 420 X 594 |
| A3 | 297 X 420 |
| A4 | 210 X 297 |

Longer lengths are referred to as *elongated* and *extra-elongated* drawing sizes. These are available in multiples of the short side of the sheet size. Figure 3-4 shows standard ANSI/ASME sheet sizes.

Figure 3-4. A—Standard drawing sheet sizes. (ANSI Y14.1) B—Standard metric drawing sheet sizes. (ASME Y14.1M)

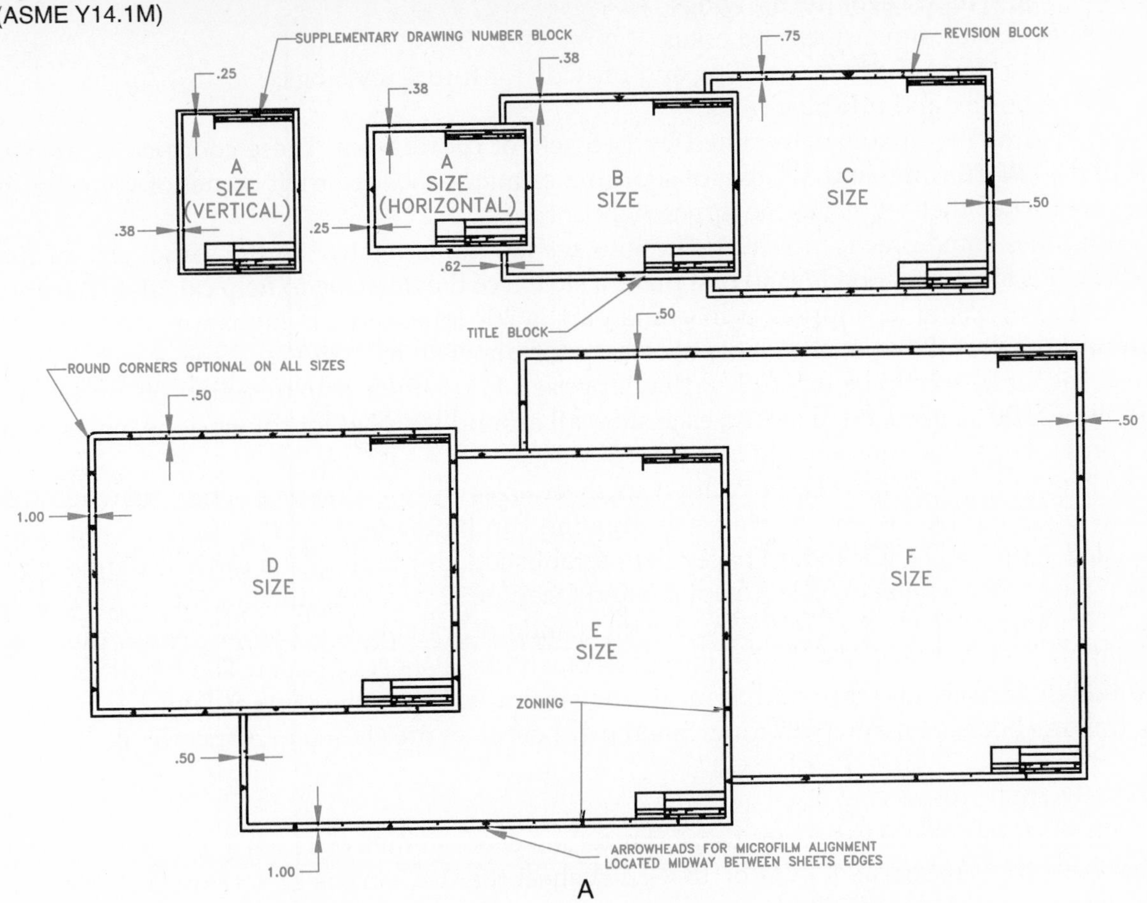

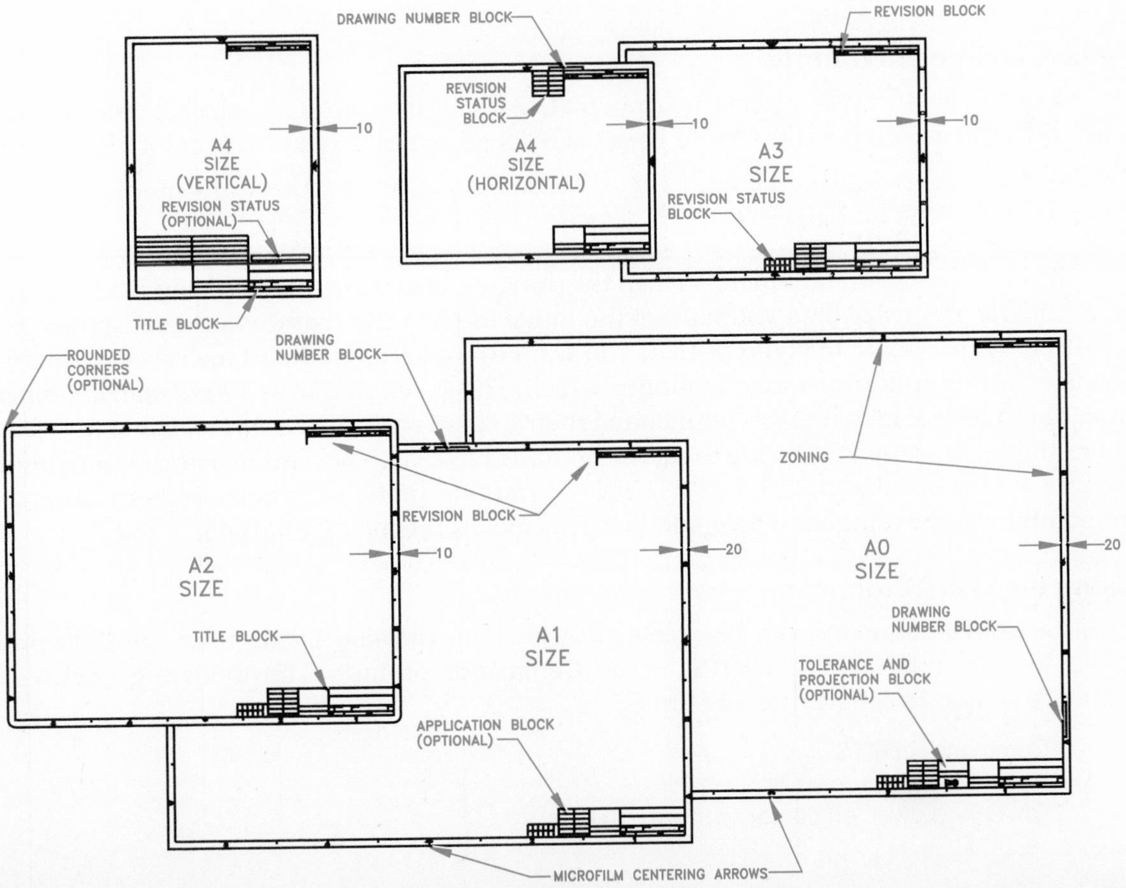

The size or limits of the AutoCAD drawing area is usually determined by:
- The actual size of the drawing.
- Space for dimensions and notes.
- Free space to avoid crowding and provide for future revisions.
- A border and title block area.

The drawing area is determined by two sets of coordinates. These coordinates are set with the **LIMITS** command. One set of coordinates marks the lower-left corner of your drawing area. The other set marks the upper-right corner.

It takes some practice to decide how to set the limits relative to the actual size of the object. It is always a good idea to first make a sketch of the drawing to help calculate the area needed. For example, suppose a machine part is 20″ long and 14″ high. An additional 4″ around the part (2″ on each side) is necessary for dimensions, notes, and free space. In this case, the limits should be set at 24″ × 18″. Suppose a house floor plan measures 68′ by 44′. An additional 20′ is needed (10 feet on each side) all around the plan for dimensions, notes, and a border. Then, the limits should be set at 88′ × 64′.

Plan your drawing area in relation to sheet sizes during drawing setup, or when the drawing is plotted. When plotting, the drawing can be made to fit the sheet or scaled as needed. AutoCAD has standard paper sizes established for plotting. You can also define your own paper size when you plot. Chapter 6 and Chapter 12 cover plotting an AutoCAD drawing. The preferred method is to consider the standard drawing sheet sizes when setting the required drawing area. The screen format is much like a sheet of paper. The length is measured horizontally and the width is measured vertically. This is the same as laying a sheet on a drawing board in manual drafting. Standard sheet sizes are shown in Appendix E.

## Setting inch limits

If the limits are based on an A-size sheet, then choose limits of 11 × 8.5 or 12 × 9. A sheet that is B-size is set up as 17 × 11 or 18 × 12. A sheet that is C-size is 22 × 17 or 24 × 18 and a D-size sheet is 34 × 22 or 36 × 24.

## Setting architectural limits

Most architectural floor plans are drawn at 1/4″ = 1′-0″ scale. If a C-size (22 × 17) sheet is used, then the drawing limits should be set at 88′ × 68′, since 4′ (4 units/inch) × 22 = 88′ and 4′ × 17 = 68′.

## Setting metric limits

The limits are set in millimeters when the drawing is in metric units. If you decide to use an A3 metric sheet size then you will set the limits to 420 × 297, based on the recommended ASME standard shown in Figure 3-4B. If you want to convert a standard inch sheet to metric, you use the multiplication factor 25.4mm = 1 inch. This is referred to as a *hard metric conversion*. This does not match the recommended metric standard, called a *soft metric conversion*. For example, suppose you decide to set the limits at 17″ × 11″. The hard metric drawing limits are 25.4 × 17 = 431.8 and 25.4 × 11 = 279.4. To provide limits with even units of measure, round off to the next higher whole number. This makes the metric limits 432 × 280.

## Using the LIMITS command

The **LIMITS** command can be accessed by picking **Drawing Limits** from the **Data** pull-down menu, or by typing **LIMITS** at the **Command:** prompt. The following command sequence is used to set the drawing limits:

```
Command: LIMITS ↵
Reset Model space limits:
ON/OFF/〈Lower left corner〉〈current 〉: 0,0 ↵
```

## CHAPTER TEST

*Write your answers in the spaces provided.*

1. When you type UNITS at the **Command:** prompt and press [Enter], what happens to the screen? _____

_____

_____

2. The display of a measurement will change when a different number of digits to the right of the decimal point is specified. If a 1.6250 dimension is to be displayed, and the number of digits to the right of the decimal points is as follows, what will actually be displayed?

   A. One digit _____

   B. Two digits _____

   C. Three digits _____

   D. Four digits _____

3. The AutoCAD default for an angle is in a(n) _____

   direction.

4. What are the limits of an architectural drawing using a C-size (22 × 17) sheet and a scale of 4 feet per inch when plotted?

   A. Lower-left corner _____

   B. Upper-right corner _____

5. Name the five systems of units options. _____

_____

_____

6. Name the pull-down menu that contains the **LIMITS** command._____

7. How do you access the **Units Control** dialog box? _____

_____

8. Give the entries or commands needed to set the drawing units to three-digit decimal, two-place decimal degrees, East direction for angle 0, and to measure angles counter-clockwise:

   Command:_____

   System of units:_____

   Enter choice 1 to 5 ⟨*default*⟩: _____

   Number of digits to right of decimal point (0 to 8) ⟨*default*⟩: _____

   System of angular measure: _____

   Enter choice, 1 to 5 ⟨*default*⟩: _____

   Number of fractional places for display of angles (0 to 8) ⟨*default*⟩: _____

   Enter direction for angle 0 ⟨*current*⟩:_____

   Do you want angles measured clockwise? ⟨*current*⟩: _____

9. Give the commands and coordinate entries to set the drawing limits to 22 × 17:

Command:_____

Reset Model space limits: _____

ON/OFF/⟨Lower left corner⟩⟨*current*⟩: _____

Upper right corner ⟨*current*⟩: _____

10. What should you do after setting the drawing limits? Identify the command and option
used to perform this task._____

_____

_____

## DRAWING PROBLEMS

*For the following problems, you should save the drawings for future use. Saving the draw-
ings as specified will save them to your floppy disk in the A: drive. If you prefer to save your
drawings on a floppy disk in the B: drive, insert your floppy disk in the appropriate drive,
and type B: before the filename. If in doubt, consult your instructor.*

*General*

1. A. Load AutoCAD for Windows.
   B. Enter the **UNITS** command. Select decimal units with four digits behind the
      decimal. Select decimal degrees with two digits behind the decimal point and
      90° (North) for direction of the 0° angle. Angles should be measured
      counterclockwise.
   C. Enter the **UNITS** command. Select architectural units with 32 as the
      denominator of the smallest fraction. Angles should be measured by
      degrees/minutes/seconds with 4 as the number of fractional places. The
      direction for angle 0° should be East. Angles are to be measured
      counterclockwise.
   D. Set the limits to correspond with a 12 × 9 (A-size) sheet. The scale to be used
      in calculating the limits is 1/4″ = 1′-0″. The lower-left corner of your drawing
      area should be at 0,0.
   E. Type SAVE at the **Command:** prompt and enter A:A12-9 to save your drawing.
   F. Type QUIT at the **Command:** prompt and press [Enter].

*General*

2. A. Load AutoCAD for Windows.
   B. Use the **Units Control** dialog box. Select decimal units with three digits behind
      the decimal point. Select decimal degrees with two digits behind the decimal
      point and 90° (North) for direction of the 0° angle. Angles should be
      measured counterclockwise.
   C. Set the limits to correspond with a 17 × 11 (B-size) sheet (0,0; 17,11).
   D. Save the problem as A:B17-11 and quit.

*General*

3. A. Load AutoCAD for Windows.
   B. Enter the **UNITS** command. Select decimal units with two digits behind the
      decimal point. Select decimal degrees with two digits behind the decimal and
      0° (East) for direction of the 0° angle. Angles should be measured
      counterclockwise.
   C. Set the limits to correspond with metric (millimeters) and an A3 size sheet.
   D. Save as A:A3 and quit.

## Chapter 4

**AutoCAD R13**

## Introduction to Drawing and Drawing Aids

### Learning objectives

After completing this chapter, you will be able to:
- ○ Set up the drawing aids in a prototype drawing, including limits, units, grid, and snap.
- ○ Use the **LINE** command to draw several different geometric shapes.
- ○ Experiment with snap grid turned on and off.

AutoCAD provides aids that help prepare the drawing layout, increase speed and efficiency, and ensure accuracy. These *drawing aids* include **GRID**, **SNAP**, and **ORTHO**. This chapter discusses each of these aids and how they are used to assist your drawing. Drawing aids may be accessed by picking **Drawing Aids...** from the **Options** pull-down menu or by typing the DDRMODES command at the **Command:** prompt.

### ESTABLISHING A GRID ON THE SCREEN

Some drafting paper used for manual drafting is printed with a grid to help the drafter lay out the drawing. A similar type of grid can be used in AutoCAD. The **GRID** command places a pattern of dots on the screen at any spacing, Figure 4-1. The grid pattern shows only

Figure 4-1. The **Grid** spacing is represented by dots.

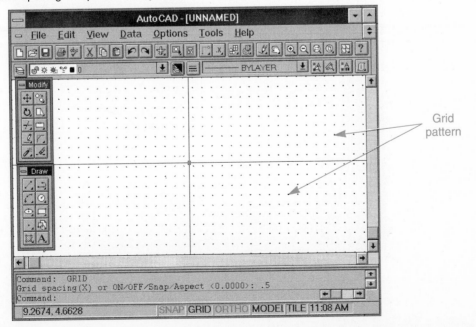

within the drawing limits to help clearly define the working area. Entering the **GRID** command provides a prompt showing the default grid spacing and several other options. You can press [Enter] to accept the default spacing value shown in brackets, or enter a new value as follows:

    Command: **GRID** ↵
    Grid spacing(X) or ON/OFF/Snap/Aspect ⟨0⟩: **.5** ↵

The dot spacing of the grid can be set by entering a specified unit of measure, such as the .5 grid shown in Figure 4-1. If the grid dot spacing you enter is too close to display on the screen, you will get the "Grid too dense to display" message. In this case, a larger grid spacing is required.

The grid spacing can be changed at any time. Also, the grid can be turned on (displayed) or off (not displayed) at any time by typing ON or OFF at the **GRID** prompt line. Other methods for turning the grid on and off include pressing [Ctrl]+[G], the [F7] function key, puck button 6, or selecting **Drawing Aids...** from the **Options** pull-down menu. When the grid is turned on, the previously set spacing is used.

## Setting a different horizontal and vertical grid

Type A (for the **Aspect** option) at the **GRID** prompt line to set different values for the horizontal and vertical grid dot spacing. For example, suppose you want a horizontal spacing of 1 and a vertical spacing of .5. Enter the following:

    Command: **GRID** ↵
    Grid spacing(X) or ON/OFF/Snap/Aspect ⟨*current*⟩: **A** ↵
    Horizontal spacing(X) ⟨0⟩: **1** ↵
    Vertical spacing(X) ⟨0⟩: **.5** ↵

This **Aspect** option provides the grid dot spacing shown in Figure 4-2.

---

Figure 4-2.   The X and Y **Grid** spacing can be set to different values using the **Aspect** option. Notice that the horizontal spacing is greater than the vertical spacing.

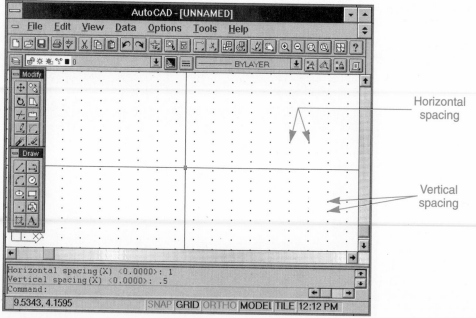

# INTRODUCTION TO DRAWING LINES

AUG 2

This section gives a brief introduction to drawing lines so you can get started with AutoCAD drawing commands. You will see how the different drawing setup options affect the speed and accuracy of drawing lines. There are several ways to use the **LINE** command, but for now only one method is discussed. (The **LINE** command is explained in detail in Chapter 6 of this text.)

Command: **LINE** ↵
From point: *(move the screen cursor to any position on the screen and pick that
   point)*
To point: *(move the screen cursor to another location and pick a point)*

Notice that a line has been drawn between the two points. A "rubber band" line is attached to the last point selected and the cursor. The "rubber band" shows where the line will be drawn if you picked the current cursor location. The next prompt is:

To point: *(pick the next point)*

You can continue to draw connected lines until you press the [Enter] key or space bar to exit the **LINE** command. The following command sequence is displayed in Figure 4-3.

Command: **LINE** ↵
From point: *(pick point number 1)*
To point: *(pick point number 2)*
To point: *(pick point number 3)*
To point: *(pick point number 4)*
To point: ↵
Command: *(meaning AutoCAD is ready for a new command)*

---

Figure 4-3.   Using the **LINE** command. Select the points in order from Point 1 to Point 4 to draw this three-segment line.

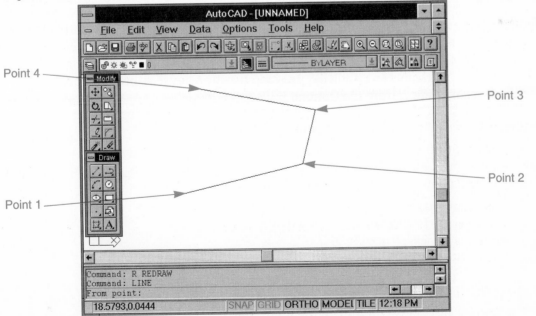

**EXERCISE 4-1**

❑ Turn on your computer, start Windows, and load AutoCAD.
❑ Set the grid spacing at .5.
❑ Use the **LINE** command to draw two sets of four connected line segments.
❑ Turn off the grid and draw two sets of three connected line segments. Notice how having the grid on provides some guidance for locating points.
❑ Type SAVE at the **Command:** prompt. When the **Save Drawing As** dialog box appears, type the filename EX4-1 to save this exercise on your hard disk, or type A:EX4-1 to save it on your floppy disk. Press [Enter] or pick the **OK** button.
❑ Type QUIT at the **Command:** prompt and press [Enter] if you want to exit AutoCAD.

## SETTING INCREMENTS FOR CURSOR MOVEMENT ┃ AUG 1,3

When you move your pointing device, the cursor crosshairs move freely on the screen. Sometimes it is hard to place a point accurately. You can set up an invisible grid that allows the cursor to move only in exact increments. This is called the *snap grid* or *snap resolution*. The snap grid is different than using the **GRID** command. The snap grid controls the crosshairs' movement. The grid discussed in the previous section is only a visual guide. However, the **SNAP** and **GRID** commands can be used together.

Properly setting the snap grid can greatly increase your drawing speed and accuracy. The **SNAP** command is used to set the invisible snap grid. Entering **SNAP** gives you the following prompt:

Command: **SNAP** ↵
Snap spacing or ON/OFF/Aspect/Rotate/Style ⟨*current*⟩:

Pressing [Enter] accepts the value shown in brackets. If a different snap spacing is required, such as .25, enter the new value as shown below:

Command: **SNAP** ↵
Snap spacing or ON/OFF/Aspect/Rotate/Style ⟨*current*⟩: **.25** ↵

This sets up the invisible snap spacing at .25 increments both horizontally and vertically.

The **OFF** selection turns snap off, but the same snap spacing is again in effect when you turn snap back on. The snap spacing can be turned on or off at any time by clicking the **SNAP** button on the toolbar, pressing [Ctrl]+[B], pressing function key [F9], pressing puck button 4, or selecting **Drawing Aids...** from the **Options** pull-down menu.

### Different horizontal and vertical Snap grid units

The **SNAP** command is usually set up with equal horizontal and vertical snap grid units. However, it is possible to set different horizontal and vertical snap grid units. This is done using the **SNAP** command's **Aspect** option as follows:

Command: **SNAP** ↵
Snap spacing or ON/OFF/Aspect/Rotate/Style ⟨*current*⟩: **A** ↵
Horizontal spacing ⟨*current*⟩: **.5** ↵
Vertical spacing ⟨*current*⟩: **.25** ↵

### Rotating the Snap grid

The normal snap grid pattern is horizontal rows and vertical columns. However, another option is to rotate the snap grid. This technique is helpful when drawing an auxiliary view that is at an angle to other views of the drawing. (Auxiliary views are discussed in Chapter 17.) When the snap grid is rotated, you are given the option of setting a new base point. The base point is the pivot that the snap grid is rotated around. The base point of a normal snap grid is the lower-left corner. It may be more convenient to set the base point at the location where you will begin the view. You will also be asked to set the rotation angle. The range is 0 to 90 or 0 to –90 degrees. The command sequence is as follows:

Command: **SNAP** ↵
Snap spacing or ON/OFF/Aspect/Rotate/Style ⟨*current*⟩: **R** ↵
Base point ⟨0,0⟩: (*press* [Enter] *or pick a new base point*)
Rotation angle ⟨0⟩: **25** ↵

The grid automatically rotates counterclockwise about the base point when a positive rotation angle is given, and clockwise when a negative rotation angle is given. Figure 4-4 shows the relationship between the regular and rotated snap grids. Remember, the snap grid is invisible.

Figure 4-4.   A—The **Snap** grid is usually horizontal rows and vertical columns. (The **Snap** grid is invisible, but represented here by dots.) B—You can rotate the **Snap** grid to help you draw.

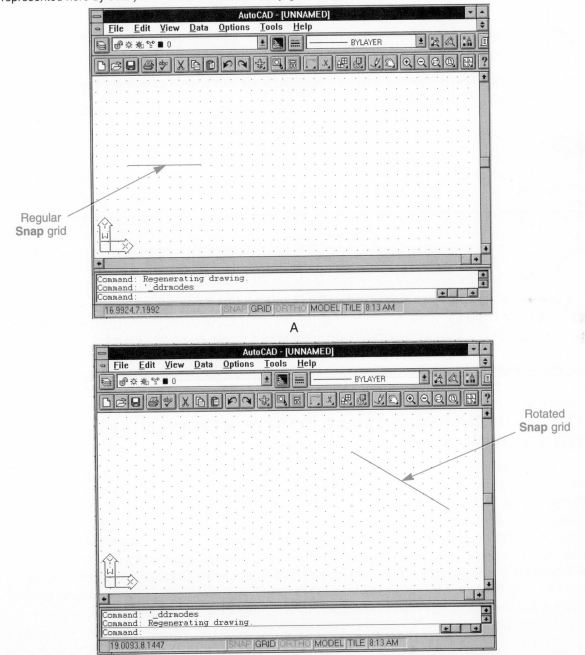

### Setting the Snap style

The **SNAP** command's **Style** option allows you to set the snap grid to either a standard (default) or isometric pattern. The isometric pattern is useful when doing isometric drawings (discussed in Chapter 23). If the snap grid is set to **Isometric**, use the **Style** option to return it to the **Standard** mode, as shown below:

Command: **SNAP** ↵
Snap spacing or ON/OFF/Aspect/Rotate/Style ⟨current⟩: **S** ↵
Standard/Isometric ⟨current⟩: **S** ↵

### Setting the Grid spacing relative to the Snap spacing

The visible grid can be set to coincide with the invisible snap grid by choosing the **Snap** option after entering the **GRID** command. You can also set the dot spacing as a multiple of the snap units by entering the number of snap units between grid points. For example, 2X places grid points at every other snap unit.

Command: **GRID** ↵
Grid spacing(X) or ON/OFF/Snap/Aspect ⟨current⟩: **2X** ↵

Therefore, if the snap units are .25 and you specify 2X at the **Grid spacing** prompt, the grid point spacing will be .5 units.

---

**EXERCISE 4-2**

❑ Start Windows and load AutoCAD.
❑ Set the units to decimal, and two digits to the right of the decimal point.
❑ Set the angular measure to decimal, one fractional place, 0 direction, and counterclock-wise.
❑ Set the limits to an A-size (12 x 9) sheet. (Lower-left corner: 0,0; upper-right corner: 12,9.)
❑ Set the **Grid** spacing to .5.
❑ Set the **Snap** spacing to .25.
❑ Use the **LINE** command to draw two sets of four connected line segments.
❑ Turn **Snap** off and draw two sets of three connected line segments. Notice how when **Snap** is on, you can "snap" exactly at .25 intervals.
❑ Type SAVE at the **Command:** prompt and save the drawing as A:EX4-2, and then quit the drawing editor.

---

## USING THE PULL-DOWN MENU TO SET OR CHANGE THE DRAWING AIDS

The AutoCAD drawing aids may be set or changed using the **Options** pull-down menu. Pick **Options** in the menu bar, and then select **Drawing Aids...** from the pull-down menu. The **Drawing Aids** dialog box then appears on the screen. Typing DDRMODES at the **Command:** prompt also displays the same dialog box.

Use the dialog box to set or change the **Grid** and **Snap** spacing values. Turn **Snap** and **Grid** on or off by picking the **On** check box. Enter your desired grid and snap spacing in the **X/Y Spacing** boxes as needed. Look at Figure 4-5 and notice that **Grid** and **Snap** are both on, as indicated by the "X" in the **On** check boxes. The **Grid** has an equal horizontal (X) spacing and vertical (Y) spacing of .500 units. The **Snap** has an equal X and Y spacing of .250.

Figure 4-5.  The **Drawing Aids** dialog box. Notice the Xs in the check boxes indicating options that are active. Also note the current **Snap** and **Grid** settings.

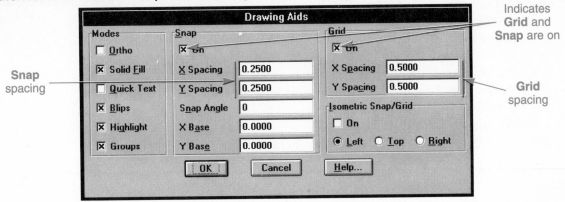

**PROFESSIONAL TIP**

    The most effective use of **Snap** quite often comes from setting an equal X and Y spacing to the lowest, or near lowest, increment of the majority of the feature dimensions. For example, in a mechanical drawing this might be .0625 units, or maybe 6" in an architectural application. If many horizontal features conform to one increment and vertical features to another, then a corresponding **Snap** grid can be set up using different X and Y values. The **Snap** and **Grid** drawing aids may be set at different values to complement each other. For example, the **Grid** may be set at .5 and the **Snap** at .25. With this type of format, each plays a separate role in assisting drawing layout. This may also keep the **Grid** from being too dense. You can quickly change these values at any time to have them best assist you.

## FACTORS TO CONSIDER WHEN SETTING DRAWING AIDS

Factors that influence drawing aid values include:
- The drawing units. If the units are decimal inches, set the **Grid** and **Snap** values to standard decimal increments such as .0625, .125, .25, .5, and 1 or .05, .1, .2, .5, 1. For architectural units, use 1, 6, and 12 inches, or 1, 2, 4, 5, and 10 feet increments.
- The drawing size. A very large drawing might have a 1.00 **Grid** spacing, while a small drawing may use a 0.5 spacing or less.
- Value of the smallest dimension. For example, if the smallest dimension is .125, then an appropriate **Snap** value would be .125 and a **Grid** spacing of .25.
- You can change the **Snap** and **Grid** values at any time without changing the location of points or lines already drawn. This should be done when larger or smaller values would assist you with a certain part of the drawing. For example, suppose a few of the dimensions are in .0625 multiples, but the rest of the dimensions are .250 multiples. Change the **Snap** spacing from .250 to .0625 when laying out smaller dimensions.
- Always prepare a sketch before starting a drawing. Use the visible grid to help you place views and lay out the entire drawing.
- Use whatever method works best and fastest for you when setting or changing the drawing aids.

## EXERCISE 4-3

❑ Start Windows and load AutoCAD.
❑ Set decimal units with three digits to the right of the decimal point.
❑ Set the angular measure to degrees/minutes/seconds, one fractional place, and default values for the rest of the options.
❑ Set the limits to 17,11. (Lower-left corner at 0,0 and upper-right corner at 17,11.)
❑ Zoom the screen using the **ZOOM All** option.
❑ Set the **Grid** spacing at .5 units.
❑ Set the **Snap** spacing at .25 units.
❑ Use the **LINE** command to draw two sets of eight connected line segments.
❑ Change the **Snap** value to .125 and the **Grid** spacing to .25. Draw several more lines and see what happens.
❑ Change the **Snap** value to .5 and the **Grid** spacing to 1. Draw several more lines and observe the results.
❑ Save the drawing as A:EX4-3 and quit.

## INTRODUCTION TO PROTOTYPE DRAWING           | AUG 1 |

When doing manual drafting you normally begin with a sheet of drafting paper. The paper may even have a preprinted border and title block. The title block might be labeled with the company name and address, and a place for the drawing title, part number, scale, material, and drafter's name. You tape down the sheet and add the views, dimensions, and fill in the title block information. It could be said that you began with a *prototype drawing*—the clean sheet of preprinted paper. The prototype, or drawing format, is then changed when adding the new information. The same type of process occurs when using AutoCAD for Windows. A simple prototype drawing is one set up with values for limits, grid, and snap. A complex prototype might have a border and title block, established text styles, layer names, and other drawing variables.

AutoCAD has a standard prototype drawing named ACAD that is available every time you start a new drawing. One big drawback with the ACAD prototype is that it is often too general to be used without some customization. In time, you will set up a prototype for each drawing size and type. For example, there may be a border and title block format for A-size, B-size, and C-size drawings. There may be a different prototype for mechanical, electrical, or architectural drawings. The values for limits, units, drawing aids, and other parameters are different for each.

When you design a prototype drawing in AutoCAD, set the units, limits, snap, and grid values to your own or to your company's or school's specifications. When you have all of the desired items set, save the prototype drawing with a name such as PROTODR1. A drawing name is limited to eight characters (with no spaces). To save the prototype drawing as PROTODR1, type SAVE at the **Command:** prompt or pick **Save...** from the **File** pull-down menu. Type the name PROTODR1 at the **File Name:** text box and then press [Enter] or click the **OK** button. The prototype is now saved as PROTODR1. The prototype is ready to use anytime you need it.

When you are ready to use the prototype, pick **Open...** from the **File** pull-down menu. When you get the **Open Drawing** dialog box, select PROTODR1 from the list of files. Now, use the prototype as the setup for your drawing. When finished with the drawing, pick **Save As...** from the **File** pull-down menu. Save your drawing with a new filename such as PROB4-1. By doing this, you now have the new drawing while the prototype remains as PROTODR1, to be used again. Additional prototype information is discussed in the following chapters. Saving a drawing is discussed in Chapter 5.

When you develop prototype drawings, it is a good idea to record the name of the prototype and the setup values. The following are some sample prototypes:

- A prototype for B-size mechanical drawings using inch values might be set up as:
  Name: M-IN-B (M = mechanical, IN = inches, B = B-size)
  Units: Three-place decimal, two-place decimal degrees
  Limits: 17,11
  Grid: .5
  Snap: .25
- A prototype for B-size mechanical drawings using metric values may be set up as:
  Name: M-MM-B (M = mechanical, MM = millimeters, B = B-size)
  Units: Two-place decimal, two-place decimal degrees
  Limits: 432,280
  Grid: 10
  Snap: 5
- A prototype for a C-size architectural floor plan may be set up as:
  Name: ARCHFL-C (ARCH = architectural, FL = floor plan, C = C-size)
  Units: Architectural, 16 fractional denominator, two-place degrees/minutes/seconds
  Limits: 88′,68′
  Grid: 6
  Snap: 2″

## EXERCISE 4-4

❏ Start Windows and load AutoCAD.
❏ Set the values for your prototype drawing as follows:
   **Units**: Three-place decimal, two-place angular decimals
   **Limits**: 12,9
   **Grid**: .5
   **Snap**: .25
❏ On a piece of notebook paper, record the prototype name and all of the specifications set in this exercise. Keep this record for future reference. This is part of preparing a drawing plan sheet, discussed in detail in Chapter 6.
❏ Save the drawing as PRODR1. This prototype is used in future exercises and problems. With a formatted disk in the A: drive, save it a second time as A:PRODR1 and quit.

## CHAPTER TEST

*Write your answers in the spaces provided.*

1. Give the command and value entered to set a **Grid** spacing of .25:
   Command:_____
   Grid spacing(X) or ON/OFF/Snap/Aspect ⟨*current*⟩:_____

2. Give the command and value entered to set the **Snap** spacing at .125:
   Command:_____
   Snap spacing or ON/OFF/Snap/Aspect/Rotate/Style ⟨*current*⟩: _____

3. Name the command used to place a pattern of dots on the screen. _____

4.  Identify the pull-down menu used to select drawing aids. _____
    _____

5.  How do you activate the **Snap** grid so the screen cursor will automatically move in pre-
    cise increments? _____
    _____
    _____

6.  How do you set different horizontal and vertical **Snap** units? _____
    _____
    _____

7.  Name three ways to access the drawing aids. _____
    _____
    _____

8.  Name two ways to access the **Drawing Aids** dialog box. _____
    _____
    _____

9.  Describe a prototype drawing. _____
    _____
    _____
    _____

10. A drawing name is limited to _____ characters.

## DRAWING PROBLEMS

**General**

1.  Load AutoCAD for Windows. Insert your floppy disk in the disk drive. Set up
    the following specifications for the new drawing.

    **Limits:** 12,9

    **Grid:** .5

    **Snap:** .25

    **Units:** Three-place decimals, two-place decimal angular, East direction for
    angle 0, angles measured counterclockwise.

    Save the *prototype* drawing as D12-9. (The D denotes decimal drawing units and
    the 12-9 specifies the limits.) Save the drawing as A:D12-9.

**General**

2.  Load AutoCAD for Windows. Insert your floppy disk in the disk drive. Pick
    **New...**from the **File** pull-down menu. Enter A:D12-9 in the **Prototype:** text box,
    and enter P4-2 in the **New Drawing Name:** text box. Then pick **OK**. Turn on the
    **Grid** and **Snap**. Draw the following objects using the **LINE** command so that they
    fit within the left half of the specified limits.

    A. Right triangle.

    B. Isosceles triangle.

    C. Rectangle.

    D. Square.

Type SAVE and save the drawing as A:P4-2. Do not quit this drawing session. Continue with Problem 3.

3. Draw the same object specified in Problem 2 on the right side of the screen. This time, make sure the **Snap** grid is turned off. Observe the difference between having snap on and off. Type SAVE at the **Command:** prompt, change the drawing name to A:P4-3, and pick **OK**. Then type QUIT at the **Command:** prompt and press [Enter] twice. This saves the drawing as A:P4-3 while the prototype remains as D12-9.

*General*

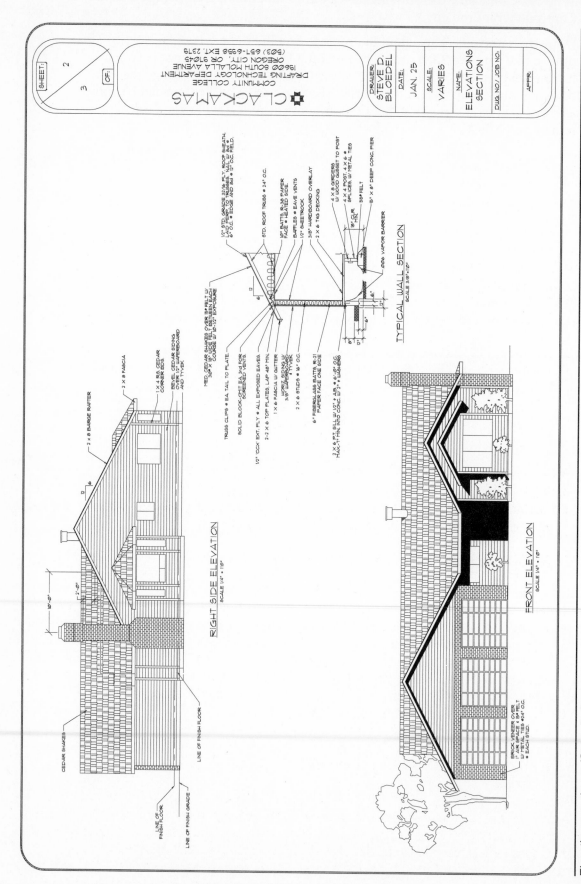

Elevations section.   (Steve D. Bloedel)

AutoCAD R13

## Learning objectives

After completing this chapter, you will be able to:
- ○ Open a saved drawing.
- ○ Identify the function of the **FILEDIA** system variable.
- ○ Change the **FILEDIA** system variable.
- ○ Save a drawing under a different name.
- ○ End a drawing session, saving all previous work with the current drawing name.
- ○ Quit a drawing.
- ○ Identify at least four ways to cancel a command.
- ○ Explain the difference between the **SAVE**, **SAVEAS**, and **QSAVE** commands.
- ○ Use the **SAVETIME** command to specify how often your work is automatically saved.
- ○ List two ways to move between the text window and the graphics window.
- ○ Explain the difference between the **END** and **QUIT** commands.
- ○ Determine the status of drawing parameters.

This chapter covers how to cancel command at any time. This chapter also covers the ways to save or end a drawing. The commands to save or end a drawing include **SAVE**, **SAVEAS**, **QSAVE**, **QUIT**, and **END**. Finally, this chapter covers the **STATUS** command. This command is used to display current default values and other drawing characteristics.

## CANCELING A COMMAND

AUG 1

If you press the wrong key or misspell a word when entering a command or answering a prompt, use the backspace key to correct the error. This only works if you notice your mistake *before* the [Enter] key is pressed. If you do enter an incorrect option or command, AutoCAD usually responds with an error message. You are then given another chance to enter the correct data or returned to the **Command:** prompt. If you are not sure what has happened, reading the error message should tell you what you need to know.

Occasionally, the entire message may not be visible in the **Floating Command Window**. Press the function key [F2] to display AutoCAD's text screen. This will allow you to read the entire message. Also, you will be able to review the commands and options you entered. This may help you better understand what happened. You can press the [F2] key again to return to the graphics screen, or use your cursor to pick any visible portion of the graphics screen to make it current again.

It is often necessary to stop the currently active command and return to AutoCAD's **Command:** prompt to either reenter a command or use an alternate command. This can occur if an incorrect entry is made and you need to restart the command using the correct method, or even if you simply decide to do something different. Some commands, such as the **LINE** command, can be discontinued by pressing the [Enter] key (or the spacebar). This exits the currently active command and returns to the **Command:** prompt, where AutoCAD awaits a new command entry. However, there are many situations where this does not work. One example of this is using the **Window** option of the **ZOOM** command. Pressing [Enter] does not discontinue the command. In this case, you must cancel the command. (The **ZOOM** command is discussed in detail in Chapter 10.)

You can cancel any active command, or abort any data entry, and return to the **Command:** prompt by pressing the [Esc] key. This is usually located in the upper-left corner of your keyboard. It may be necessary to press the [Esc] key twice to completely cancel certain commands. Many multibutton digitizer pucks use button number 3 to cancel a command. Additionally, most of the toolbar buttons and pull-down menu options automatically cancel any currently active command before entering the new command. So, in a case where you wish to abort the current command and start a new one, simply pick the appropriate menu option or toolbar button.

**PROFESSIONAL TIP**

Previous releases of AutoCAD, and the DOS version of Release 13, utilize the keystroke combination known as *control-C* to cancel an operation. This is accomplished by pressing and holding the [Ctrl] button on your keyboard, then pressing the [C] key and immediately releasing both. By default, [Ctrl]+[C] activates the **COPY** command. If you would like to use [Ctrl]+[C] to cancel a command, you can change the **Keystrokes** option in the **Preferences** dialog box to the **AutoCAD Classic** setting. The **Preferences** command is found on the **Options** pull-down menu, and is discussed in detail in *AutoCAD and Its Applications—Advanced, Release 13 for Windows.*

## INTRODUCTION TO SAVING AND QUITTING A DRAWING | AUG 1

In Chapter 3, you were shown how to begin drawing when you accessed the AutoCAD drawing editor. You also saved work or quit the drawing in the exercises and problems. The following discussion provides you with detailed information about saving and quitting a drawing.

When saving drawing files using either the **SAVE** or **SAVEAS** command, you can have a dialog box appear, or you can type everything at the **Command:** prompt. This is controlled by the **FILEDIA** system variable. A *system variable* is a command that lets you change the way AutoCAD works. These variables are remembered by AutoCAD and remain in effect until you change them again. There are two **FILEDIA** system variable options. The default is 1, which displays dialog boxes at the appropriate times. When **FILEDIA** is set to 0, dialog boxes do not appear. You must then type the desired information at the prompt line. You can quickly change the **FILEDIA** system variable as follows:

        Command: **FILEDIA** ↵
        New value for FILEDIA ⟨1⟩: **0** ↵

In the following discussion, the **FILEDIA** variable is set to 1, unless otherwise specified.

## NAMING DRAWINGS

Drawing names may be chosen to identify a product by name and number, for example, VICE-101, FLPLN-92, or 6DT1005. Your school or company probably has a drawing numbering system that you can use. These drawing names should be recorded in a part numbering or drawing name log for future reference.

It is important to set up a system where you can determine the content of a drawing by the drawing number. The following rules and restrictions apply to naming a drawing:
- Drawing names contain a maximum of 8 characters.
- Drawing names include only letters, numbers, dashes (–), dollar signs ($), or under-lines (_).
- Spaces, slashes (/ or \), periods, asterisks, or question marks cannot be used in a draw-ing name.

## STARTING A NEW DRAWING

AUG 1

Once you have entered the drawing editor, you can name a new drawing, or you can use a prototype drawing that was created earlier. To do this, type NEW at the **Command:** prompt and press [Enter], or pick **New...** from the **File** pull-down menu, Figure 5-1. You can also select the **New** button from the standard toolbar. The **Create New Drawing** dialog box appears. See Figure 5-2.

Figure 5-1. The **File** pull-down menu. To name a new drawing or use a prototype, select **New...** from the menu.

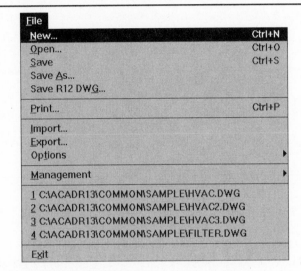

Figure 5-2. The **Create New Drawing** dialog box. Notice the prototype is the standard ACAD prototype and the new drawing name is TEST.

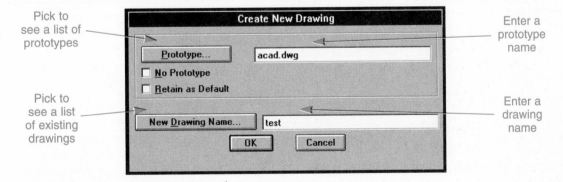

### The New **Drawing Name...** text box

This is where you enter the filename for the new drawing. For example, if you enter TEST and pick the **OK** button, AutoCAD creates a new drawing file called TEST.DWG. The drawing filename TEST is entered in Figure 5-2.

## The New Drawing Name... button

Pick the **New Drawing Name**... button to see a list of existing drawings. The **Create Drawing File** dialog box is then displayed. You can pick an existing drawing name from this dialog box. However, this will overwrite the existing file. See Figure 5-3A.

When you pick an existing drawing that was created in AutoCAD Release 13, a picture of the drawing is displayed in the **Preview** image tile. This is an easy way for you to get a quick look at the drawing without going into the AutoCAD drawing editor. You can view each drawing until you find the one you want. Hold the pick button down or use the keyboard arrow keys as you move the cursor arrow up or down the files list to view drawings very fast.

Figure 5-3.  A—The **Create Drawing File** subdialog box appears when  you select the **New Drawing Name...** button in the **Create New Drawing** dialog box. B—The **Prototype Drawing File** subdialog box appears when you select the **Prototype...** button in the **Create New Drawing** dialog box.

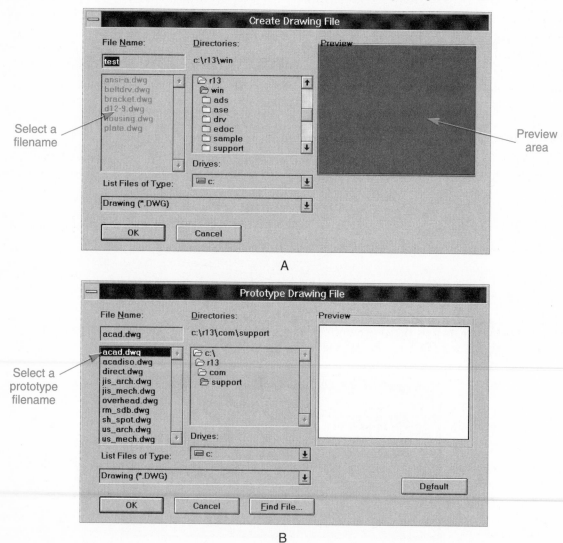

## The Prototype... text box

As you may recall, a prototype drawing contains all of the standard elements that you need in the drawing format. These elements might be a border, title block, text style, and AutoCAD system variables set for your application. The **Prototype...** text box is where you enter the name of the prototype drawing that you want to use as the basis for your new drawing. You can also create your own prototype drawing and enter its name in the **Prototype...** text box. The prototype drawing in Figure 5-2 is ACAD, which is the standard AutoCAD prototype. (All of the values of the ACAD prototype drawing are shown in Appendix E.)

In Chapter 4, you created a simple prototype drawing named D12-9 (A:D12-9 if the file is on your floppy disk). To use this prototype as the basis for a drawing named EX5-1, enter D12-9 in the **Prototype...** text box and EX5-1 in the **New Drawing Name...** text box. Now, any work you do is saved as EX5-1. The prototype remains unchanged and ready for use again.

## The Prototype... button

To see a list of the existing drawings, pick the **Prototype**... button to get the **Prototype Drawing File** dialog box shown in Figure 5-3B. Notice the D12-9 prototype in the file list (if you saved it to the hard disk drive). You can use D12-9 as your prototype by picking it and pressing [Enter] or picking the **OK** button. The **Prototype Drawing File** dialog box is closed and D12-9 is listed in the **Prototype...** text box of the **Create New Drawing** dialog box. Enter a drawing name in the **New Drawing Name...** text box and pick the **OK** button. You are then ready to start drawing.

In addition to the standard AutoCAD prototype, there are architectural and mechanical prototypes based on US and international standards. You will see these in the list of files when you pick the prototype button. These prototypes have preset values for units, limits, drawing aids, and dimensioning inches or millimeters depending on the application.

## The No Prototype check box

Pick this check box if you don't want to use a prototype drawing. An X in this box sets all variables to AutoCAD default values. This is essentially the same as using the ACAD prototype.

## The Retain as Default check box

If you pick this check box, the current prototype is kept for the next time you set up a new drawing.

**PROFESSIONAL TIP**   An entry in a dialog box can be accepted by moving the cursor arrow to the **OK** button and picking, or by simply pressing the [Enter] key.

### EXERCISE 5-1

❑ Load AutoCAD for Windows.
❑ Pick **New...** from the **File** pull-down menu and look at the **Create New Drawing** dialog box.
❑ Pick the **New Drawing Name...** button and see if there are any existing drawings identified in the **File** list. Pick the **Cancel** button.
❑ Enter a new drawing name called TEST at the **New Drawing Name...** text box and pick the **OK** button.
❑ The dialog box is closed and the AutoCAD title bar has [TEST.DWG] displayed. This means that the new drawing named TEST has set up a work space for temporary files. You are ready to begin drawing.
❑ Type QUIT at the **Command:** prompt and press [Enter].

## SAVING YOUR WORK

The **SAVE** command allows you to protect your work by writing the existing status of your drawing to disk while remaining in the drawing editor. While working in the drawing editor, you should save your drawing every 10 to 15 minutes. This is very important! If there is a power failure, a severe editing error, or other problems, all of the work saved prior to the problem will likely be usable. If you save only once an hour, a power failure results in an hour of lost work. Saving your drawing every 10 to 15 minutes will result in only 10 to 15 minutes of lost work if a problem occurs.

To use the **SAVE** command, type SAVE at the **Command:** prompt, click on the **Save** button in the toolbar, or pick **Save...** from the **File** pull-down menu. If the drawing you are saving is not yet named, the **Save Drawing As** dialog box is displayed. Refer to Figure 5-4 as you go through the following list.

- In this example, the current drive and directory is C:\R13\WIN. This is indicated by the "open folder" icons in the **Directories** box. The drawing will be saved to this directory unless another directory is selected. The list of directories in Figure 5-4 include ADS, SAMPLE, and SUPPORT.
- If the drawing is to be saved to another drive, click the down arrow in the **Drives** box to display a drop-down list of available drive options.
- Note that the file extension .DWG appears in the **List Files of Type** drop-down list. Since all AutoCAD drawing files have a .DWG file extension, .DWG is automatically added to the drawing filename.
- A list of existing drawing files appears in the **Files** list box at the left of the dialog box.

Figure 5-4. The **Save Drawing As** dialog box is used to specify the name and location of a file to be saved. In this example, the file type is a drawing (.DWG) file, the current directory is \R13\WIN on the C: drive, and the drawing to be saved is named FLRPLN in the **File Name:** text box.

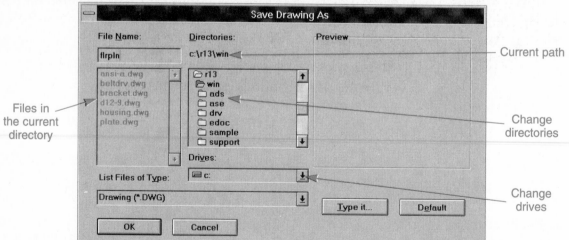

Enter the desired drawing name in the **File Name:** text box, pick a drawing name from the list, or click the **Type It** button to enter the drawing name at the command line. Remember to change to the drive and directory where you want the drawing saved. If you want to save your drawing to the floppy disk in the A: drive, enter A: before the filename. Or, click the down arrow in the **Drives** drop-down list and select the icon that represents the A: drive.

If you are working on a drawing and try to save it with a filename that already exists, AutoCAD displays the alert box shown in Figure 5-5. This box informs you of the existing drawing name and asks, "Replace existing file?". Click the **Yes** button if you want the existing file replaced with the current one. If you do not want it replaced, click **No**. Be sure to make the right choice. The existing drawing cannot be recovered after you pick the **Yes** button. Sometimes it may be appropriate to replace an existing drawing when you are changing it.

Figure 5-5. This AutoCAD alert box appears when a drawing with the same name already exists in the specified directory.

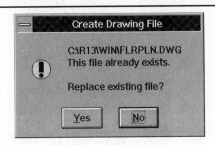

**PROFESSIONAL TIP**

Never begin a drawing on a floppy disk when in AutoCAD. All work during your drawing session should be done on the hard disk. Then, at the end of the drawing session, save your work to a floppy disk.

Save your work in two places. If anything happens to one disk, you have the other one to depend on. If you have two disk drives, backup disks may be placed in the A: and B: drives. When finished with your drawing, save it once with an A: prefix and a second time with the B: prefix. If you have only one floppy disk drive, then save your work on two separate disks in the A: drive.

While saving drawings on floppy disks may be practical at school, it is not recommended for industry applications. The most common practice in industry is storing drawings on a hard disk. Saving drawings on a hard disk is much more reliable and convenient than dealing with floppies, not to mention the noticeable speed difference when working on the hard drive. Large capacity hard drives are economical. Another growing practice is the use of rewritable optical disks as archival and drawing storage. Optical disks are safe because they are unaffected by magnetic fields, normal changes in temperature, and do not deteriorate over time. In industry, saving work on floppies is often the last choice, even when sending drawings between users. Sending work through a network or through modems are the safest and fastest methods of transmission.

## SAVING YOUR WORK AUTOMATICALLY

AutoCAD provides you with an automatic work-saving tool called the **SAVETIME** system variable. All you need to do is decide how often you want your work saved, and enter the amount of time (in minutes) between saves. The following example tells AutoCAD to save the drawing every 15 minutes:

    Command: **SAVETIME** ↵
    New value for SAVETIME ⟨*current*⟩: **15** ↵

The **SAVETIME** timer starts as soon as a change is made to the drawing. The timer is reset when the **SAVE**, **QSAVE**, or **SAVEAS** command is used.

The drawing is saved when the first command is given after the **SAVETIME** value has been reached. This is important to remember. For example, if you set **SAVETIME** to 15, work for 14 minutes, and then let the computer remain idle for 5 minutes, an automatic save is not executed until the 19 minute interval. Therefore, be sure to manually save your drawing if you plan to be away from your computer for an extended period of time.

The autosaved drawing is always saved with the name of AUTO.SV$. If you need to use the autosaved file, it can be renamed to a .DWG file using the Windows File Manager or the DOS RENAME command. Refer to Chapter 32 for more information on the Windows File Manager. Renaming files from within the AutoCAD drawing editor is covered in Chapter 17.

**PROFESSIONAL TIP**

While an automatic save is a safeguard, it's an inconvenience to rename the AUTO.SV$ file. Use the **SAVE** command to continually save work in progress. A quick shortcut to the **SAVE** command is the [Ctrl]+[S] key combination.

## WHERE TO SAVE THE DRAWING                          AUG 1

When you save a drawing, it is stored in the current directory. To save a drawing to the floppy drive, place the floppy disk in the A: drive, type SAVE, and enter the drawing name as A:NAME. The "A:" part of the name directs the drawing "NAME" to be saved on the A: drive where your floppy disk is located. Suppose you want the drawing saved on the disk in the B: drive. Place your disk in the B: drive and save the drawing as B:NAME.

Unless otherwise specified by your instructor or CAD manager, it is best to do your work on the hard drive and save to a floppy disk. In fact, save your work to two floppy disks so you have a backup in case something happens to one disk. After you save your work to a floppy disk and quit the drawing session, you will need to transfer the previous work from the floppy disk to the hard disk. Follow these steps for an example drawing saved as A:NAME.

- Load AutoCAD.
- Put your disk with the drawing NAME in the A: drive.
- Enter the **NEW** command to get the **Create New Drawing** dialog box.
- At the **New Drawing Name...** text box, type a drawing name, equal sign, and the name of the drawing on the A: drive as follows:

  WORK=A:NAME

  This method directs the A:NAME drawing to be copied to the hard drive with the name WORK.
- Now you are working on the hard drive. You can leave the disk in the A: drive or you can remove it.
- Save your work every 10 to 15 minutes.
- When finished for the day, save your work on the disk in the A: drive. Put the floppy disk in the A: drive (if removed) and enter the **SAVE** command.
- Change the directory to A: and type NAME in the **File Name:** text box, or type A:NAME in the **File Name:** text box.
- The alert box shown in Figure 5-5 is then displayed. Pick **Yes**. This saves the work you have done on the C: drive as A:NAME.

You can also use Windows File Manager to copy the file from the floppy disk to the hard drive. In many cases, this may be the easiest way. File Manager is covered in Chapter 32.

The **SAVEAS** command lets you save the current drawing under a new filename. For example, if you are working on an existing drawing and make changes that you want saved with a different name, then use the **SAVEAS** command. This leaves the current drawing intact with the old name (before changes were made), and saves the modified drawing with the new name. When you pick **Save As...** from the **File** pull-down menu, or type SAVEAS at the **Command:** prompt, the **Save Drawing As** dialog box appears. Refer to Figure 5-4. (The dialog box appears only if the **FILEDIA** system variable is set to 1.)

---

**CAUTION**

Do not use the **SAVEAS** command to save a drawing to a floppy disk. This causes AutoCAD to relocate its temporary work files to the floppy disk (if you have not reconfigured the temporary file location). Always use the **SAVE** command to save your drawing to a floppy disk. See Chapter 2 page 65 for instructions on configuring a temporary file location.

---

## SAVING YOUR DRAWING QUICKLY

AUG 1

The **QSAVE** (quick save) command works like the **SAVE** command, except that the **Save Drawing As** dialog box is not displayed. The drawing is automatically saved under the current name. If the drawing is not yet named, the **Save Drawing As** dialog box is displayed. Pick a filename from the **Files** list box, or type the drawing name in the **File Name:** text box.

To use the **QSAVE** command, click the **Save** button on the toolbar, or type QSAVE at the **Command:** prompt and press the [Enter] key. The drawing is then saved without allowing you to change the name, directory, or drive. Picking **Save** from the **File** pull-down menu or using the [Ctrl]+[S] key combination activates the **QSAVE** command if a drawing has been named and previously saved.

## SAVING A RELEASE 13 DRAWING FOR RELEASE 12

Your AutoCAD Release 13 drawings can be saved in a Release 12 format. This allows you to send Release 13 drawings to a business where Release 12 is being used, or if you use Release 13 at work or school and have Release 12 at home. To do this, type SAVEASR12 at the **Command:** prompt. The **Save release 12 drawing as** dialog box appears. Type the desired drawing name at the **File** edit box. It is best to save the drawing in Release 13 with one filename and again using the **SAVEASR12** command for a different filename. This protects you from accidentally writing over the Release 13 file.

Converting from Release 13 back to Release 12 adds handles to the drawing. *Handles* are an alphanumeric representation of the drawing in the AutoCAD database that can be accessed by other applications. Remove these handles by typing HANDLES at the **Command:** prompt after entering Release 12. The information that is unique to Release 13 is lost in the Release 12 conversion. However, during the process a log lists changes and lost information for your reference. You can look at the log by pressing the [F1] key to get the text screen.

---

**EXERCISE 5-2**

❑ Load AutoCAD for Windows.
❑ Insert your floppy disk in the A: drive, and type SAVE at the **Command:** prompt.
❑ Click the down arrow in the **Drives** drop-down list, and then click the A: drive icon.
❑ Type EX5-2 in the **File Name:** text box. Click the **OK** button or press [Enter].
❑ Type SAVE at the **Command:** prompt.
❑ Be sure C: is the current directory, then type A:EX5-2A in the **File Name:** text box and press [Enter]. You have now saved EX5-2 and EX5-2A to the floppy disk in the A: drive.
❑ Type QUIT at the **Command:** prompt and press [Enter].

## OPENING AN EXISTING DRAWING

An existing drawing is one that has been previously saved. You can easily access any existing drawing on the hard disk with the **OPEN** command. Click the **Open** button on the **Standard** toolbar, pick **Open...** from the **File** pull-down menu, or type OPEN at the **Command:** prompt. The **Select File** dialog box appears, Figure 5-6.

The **Select File** dialog box contains directory and file lists, just as in the **Save Drawing As** dialog box. Pick the desired directory or file from the lists for quick access, or type the file-name in the **File Name:** text box. If you specify a filename that does not exist, AutoCAD displays an alert box with the following messages:

> Cannot find this file.
> Please verify that the correct path and file name are given.

If this happens, be sure you have correctly entered the filename and that you are in the appropriate directory. You cannot open a drawing file that does not exist, or is not in the directory you have specified.

When you pick an existing drawing that was created in AutoCAD Release 13, a picture of the drawing is displayed in the **Preview** image tile. The **Preview** image tile is found just to the right of the **Files:** list. Refer to Figure 5-6. This is an easy way for you to get a quick look at the drawing without going into the AutoCAD drawing editor. You can view each drawing until you find the one you want. Hold the pick button down or use the keyboard arrow keys as you move the cursor arrow up or down the files list to view drawings very fast.

Figure 5-6. The **Select File** dialog box is used to select a drawing to open. Notice the drawing ASESMP.DWG has been selected from the files list box and appears in the **File Name:** text box.

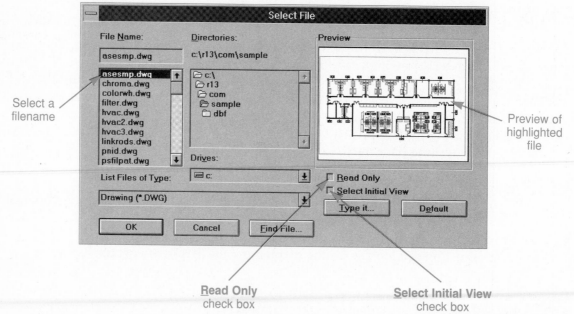

## EXERCISE 5-3

A quick way to become familiar with the **Preview** image tile feature is to look at the sample drawings that come with AutoCAD. To do this exercise, the sample drawings must have been loaded during the AutoCAD installation process.

❑ Load AutoCAD.

❑ Pick **Open...** from the **File** pull-down menu to access the **Open Drawing** dialog box.

❑ Double-click on the directory that contains AutoCAD Release 13, such as R13.

❑ Double-click on SAMPLE if it is displayed, or double-click on COM. This directory contains subdirectories that are common to both the DOS and Windows versions of AutoCAD. Then double-click on SAMPLE.

❑ The **Files:** list should display all of the sample AutoCAD files.

❑ Pick any sample drawing and look at the **Preview** image tile. Pick as many as you like to preview. Once a filename has been highlighted, you can use the cursor keys on your keyboard to quickly scroll up or down through the available files. Using the scroll bar to move up and down allows you to access additional drawings without having to view each one along the way.

❑ Pick the **Cancel** button.

❑ Type QUIT at the **Command:** prompt and press [Enter].

### Select initial view

Look at Figure 5-6 and notice the **Select Initial View** check box. When you pick this box, you are allowed to select a named view that is displayed when you open the drawing. This feature is discussed in detail in Chapter 10 when you learn to establish different views of your drawing.

Refer to Figure 5-6 again and note the **Read Only Mode** check box. When you pick this box, any changes or modifications made to the drawing cannot be saved. In other words, the drawing can only be used for viewing purposes. This is one way to protect your drawing file from any changes made by an unauthorized user. You can also use this mode if you want to practice on your drawing without the fear of altering it.

## OPENING RELEASE 11 AND 12 DRAWINGS

You can open AutoCAD Release 11 and Release 12 drawings in Release 13. When you open a drawing from a previous release and work on it, AutoCAD automatically updates the drawing to Release 13 standards when you save. After the previous release drawing is saved in Release 13, it can be viewed in the **Preview** image tile during future applications.

## MAKING A PREVIEW IMAGE OF OLDER RELEASE DRAWINGS

When working with older AutoCAD release drawings, the **MAKEPREVIEW** command can be used to allow previewing of files without saving in AutoCAD Release 13. To do this, enter AutoCAD Release 13, open a drawing file from a previous release, and enter the following:

Command: **MAKEPREVIEW** ↵
Command:

The **MAKEPREVIEW** command makes a compressed .BMP file of the drawing and places it in the same directory as the drawing file. You do not have to save the drawing to Release 13. When you open this drawing in the future, in Release 13, the **Select Drawing** dialog box displays the image in the preview image tile. See Figure 5-3A.

**NOTE:**    If you move a drawing file created in a previous release to another location after you have used the **MAKEPREVIEW** command, you must move the .BMP file as well to be able to preview the drawing in Release 13.

---

**EXERCISE 5-4**

❑ Load AutoCAD for Windows.
❑ Pick **Open...** from the **File** pull-down menu to access the **Open Drawing** dialog box.
❑ PRODR1 and D12-9 should be in the **Files** list if you did Exercise 4-4 and Drawing Problem 4-1.
❑ Pick D12-9 to insert it at the **File Name:** text box and press [Enter], or pick the **OK** button to open the prototype drawing D12-9.
❑ Type QUIT at the **Command:** prompt and press [Enter].

---

## Opening a drawing from the File pull-down menu list

AutoCAD for Windows stores the names and locations of the last four drawing files opened in the drawing editor. These filenames are listed at the bottom of the **File** pull-down menu. Refer back to Figure 5-1. Any one of these files can be quickly opened by clicking the filename with the arrow pointer. Notice that the drive and directory for each drawing is included with the filename. If you try to open one of these drawing files after it has been deleted or moved to a different drive or directory, AutoCAD will be unable to locate it. AutoCAD will display the message "Cannot find the specified drawing file." in the floating command window and open the **Select File** dialog box.

## Using File Find

There may be instances when you need to edit an existing drawing file, but you cannot remember the drawing name or where the drawing resides on disk. A drawing file (or any other AutoCAD file type) may be located by its name, type, date created, or time created. To locate a file:

1. Pick the **Find File...** button in the **Select File** dialog box to display the **Browse/Search** dialog box. There are two sections to this dialog, available by selecting the appropriate "tab." When you are looking for a specific file, and know either part or all of the name of the file, select the **Search** tab. This displays the **Search** dialog shown in Figure 5-7.
2. Set the **Search Pattern:** to look for the file you need. Either a complete filename can be specified or a partial name can be used with standard DOS "wildcard" characters. For example, the default specification of *.DWG finds all files that have a .DWG file extension (AutoCAD drawings). The asterisk can be used alone, or after other characters. The file specification of FLOOR*.DWG finds any drawing file that has the first five characters of FLOOR. It would find FLOOR_01.DWG, FLOOR.DWG and FLOORPLN.DWG. Question marks can also be used to position wildcards in single character positions. For example, the specification FL??R.DWG would find FLOOR.DWG and FLYER.DWG, but not FLOOR_01.DWG. Wildcard combinations can be used. For example, the specification FL??R*.DWG would find FLOOR.DWG, FLYER.DWG, FLOORPLN.DWG and FLOOR_01.DWG.
3. The **File Types:** pop-up displays the available options of file types for the current operation. Since you are opening a drawing, the only file type available is .DWG.
4. The **Date Filter** can be used to limit the search to files created within a specific date range. Selecting the pop-up allows you to specify whether the search should include only files

last edited before or after the date specified below. Note that the format for specifying time and date must be as follows:

>    Date: mm-dd-yy
>
>    Time: hh:mm  or  hh:mm:ss

5. The **Search Location** allows you to limit your search to specific drives or directory paths. First, select the appropriate radio button, then set the required specifications. For example, to limit your search to the contents of one disk drive you must first select the **Drives:** radio button, then use the pop-up list to select the disk drive to search. Selecting the **All Drives:** pop-up displays the options of searching only local fixed drives (hard disks) or searching all drives. Searching all drives will search all available hard and floppy disks, plus all available network drives. If you wish to limit your search to specific directory paths, select **Path:**. For a single path, type your entry directly into the edit box. For multiple path entries, select the **Edit...** button. This displays the **Edit Path** dialog. Additional paths can be added or deleted from the search path list. See Figure 5-8.

6. Finally, pick the **Search** button to begin the search. A dynamic display above the **Files:** window counts the number of files found matching the current search criteria, while the path names of the directories being searched are displayed below. The **Search** button changes to a **Stop Search** button, and can be pressed at anytime to halt the search. Once the search is complete, the found files and their locations are displayed in the **Files:** window. Only Release 13 drawing files will be displayed graphically, files from earlier releases are shown only as a rectangle with an "X" shape and the directory path location of the file. The scroll bars can be used to display the entire path or more files listings. To open a drawing in the **Files:** window, double-click on the desired file, or pick once and then pick the **Open** button.

Figure 5-7.   The **Browse/Search** dialog box. To search for a file, select the **Search** tab, as shown here. Search parameters can include drives and directories, file types, and can be limited by the date and/or time the files were created.

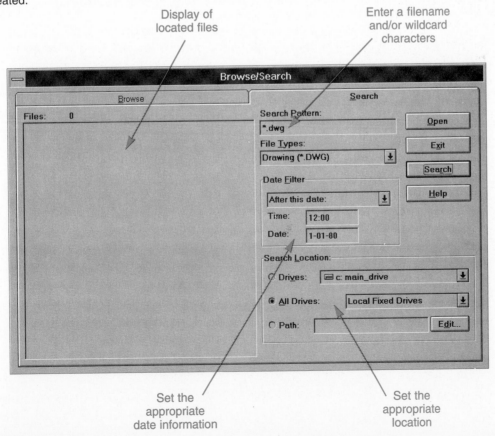

Figure 5-8.    The **Edit Path**
subdialog box. The
\R13\COM\SAMPLE directory
on the C: drive has been added
to the search path. Additional
paths can be entered in the
**Path:** text box and added to the
list by picking the **Add** button.

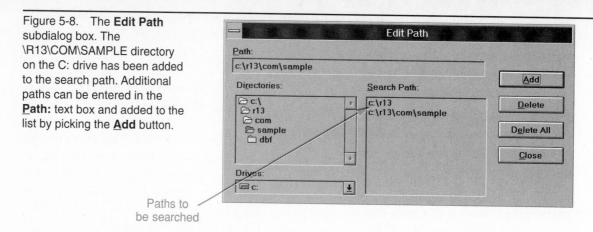

## Browsing through Drawing Files

When the filename is not known, and you would like to look through your drawing files to find a specific drawing, select the **Browse** tab to display the **Browse** dialog box. See Figure 5-9. This allows you to select directory path locations and look through the drawing files found there. To browse through a directory of drawings, use the following procedure:

1. Use the directory window to navigate to the desired directory location. Double-click on the directory you want to look through. If you need to change the current disk drive first, select the **Drives** pop-up and pick the appropriate disk drive. The **List Files of Type** pop-up shows only .DWG files, since the active command is **Open**.

2. The **File Name:** edit box can be used to indicate specific files to display. DOS wildcard characters can be used here as well. For example, A*.DWG displays only drawing files that have a filename beginning with an "A".

Figure 5-9.    When the filename is not known, select the **Browse** tab in the **Browse/Search** dialog box. Each individual drawing file can be viewed to find a specific drawing.

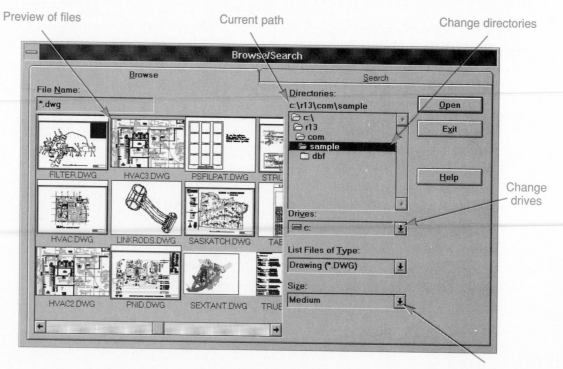

3. Use the scroll bar to view more files. To open a file from the **Browse** dialog, double-click on the drawing image, or pick the image and then pick the **Open** button. If you need to view another directory, simply double-click on the new directory, and the drawing files contained there will be displayed. The browser will display only the contents of a single directory.

4. To change the size of the drawing image displayed, pick the **Size** pop-up. Selecting **Small** allows up to 30 drawings to be displayed at one time. However, there will be very little detail since they are so small. The **Medium** setting completely displays 9 to 12 files a bit larger. The **Large** setting provides the best image, but only one drawing is completely displayed.

## ENDING A DRAWING

| AUG 1 |

When you have completed your drawing session, you can save your work, exit the drawing editor, and return to the Program Manager all at once using the **END** command. Simply type END at the **Command:** prompt as follows:

>   Command: **END** ↵

When you enter END, the revised drawing is saved with the drawing name and a .DWG file extension. The old version is saved as a backup, with a .BAK file extension. For example, if you work on the drawing named PROTO1 and enter END, it is saved as PROTO1.DWG. The previous version of PROTO1 is saved as PROTO1.BAK. Use the **OPEN** command when you want to work on PROTO1 again. AutoCAD looks for the .DWG file. If you need to open the previous version, you must rename the file from a .BAK extension to a .DWG extension.

Some caution should be considered before using the **END** command if you have done a lot of work on a drawing, because the **END** command writes the drawing to disk and exits AutoCAD, without purging deleted object data from the drawing file. Use the **SAVE, QSAVE,** or **SAVEAS** commands to have AutoCAD automatically reduce the file size.

## USING THE **QUIT** COMMAND

The **QUIT** command is another way to end a drawing session. You can pick **Exit** from the **File** pull-down menu, or type QUIT at the **Command:** prompt as follows:

>   Command: **QUIT** ↵

If you enter QUIT before saving your work, then AutoCAD gives you a chance to decide what you want to do with unsaved work. The AutoCAD alert box shown in Figure 5-10 appears. Press [Enter] to activate the highlighted **Yes** button. This saves the drawing. If the drawing is unnamed, the **Save Drawing As** dialog box appears. You can also pick the **No** button if you plan to discard any changes made to the drawing since the previous save. This is a good way to use AutoCAD for practice. Enter the **QUIT** command when you are done and pick the **No** button. All of the practice work is gone. Pick the **Cancel** button if you decide not to quit and want to return to the drawing editor.

Figure 5-10.   This AutoCAD alert box is shown if QUIT is entered before saving the work. This is an opportunity for deciding what will be done with unsaved work.

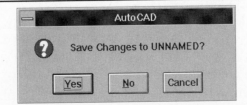

If you quit and pick the **Yes** button when the drawing is in **Read Only Mode**, then an alert box is displayed and the **QUIT** command is automatically canceled. Use the **SAVEAS** command and give the drawing a new name to save these changes.

**PROFESSIONAL TIP**

The **Save**, **Qsave**, and **Saveas** commands decrease the size of the drawing by varying amounts as compared to the **End** command. The actual amount of reduction can often be fairly insignificant. However, in larger drawings where much editing has occurred, the reduction in size can be considerable.

## DETERMINING THE DRAWING STATUS

AUG 3

While working on a drawing, you may want to refresh your memory about some of the drawing parameters, such as the limits, **Grid** spacing, or **Snap** values. All of the information about the drawing is displayed by typing STATUS at the **Command:** prompt. You can also select **Status** from the **Inquiry** menu item in the **Assist** pull-down menu. The graphics window automatically flips to the text window to display the information that you have requested. In Figure 5-11, the **STATUS** command has been issued for a B-size drawing called FILTER.

Figure 5-11. The **AutoCAD Text Window** displays a drawing's information when using the **STATUS** command.

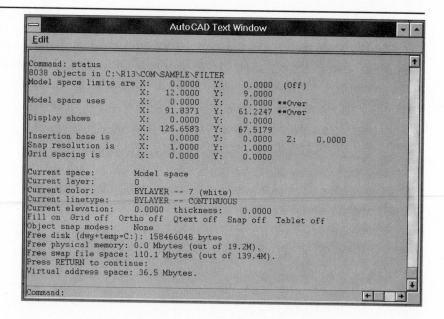

The number of objects in a drawing refers to the total number of entities—both erased and existing. The **(Off)** indication on the **Model space limits are** line refers to the limits check discussed in Chapter 3. If the message **Over appears to the right of **Model space uses**, this indicates that the drawing extends outside the drawing limits. Free disk represents the space left on the drive containing your drawing file.

When you have completed reading the status information in the text window, press the function [F2] key to flip back to the graphics window. This action automatically closes the active text window and restores the inactive graphics window. You can also switch to the graphics window without closing the text window by clicking anywhere inside the inactive graphics window.

**NOTE**

Another way to move between the graphics window and the text window is provided with the AutoCAD commands **GRAPHSCR** and **TEXTSCR**. Typing TEXTSCR at the **Command:** prompt flips to the text window. Typing GRAPHSCR flips to the graphics window. You can also flip to the text window from the drawing editor by selecting **Text Window** from the **Edit** pull-down menu.

**PROFESSIONAL TIP**

Refer to the drawing **STATUS** command periodically to see how much "free disk" space is available. If this free disk space becomes dangerously low, you may be unable to complete and save the drawing. This has been known to cause severe problems. AutoCAD automatically saves your work and ends the drawing editor if it runs out of disk space.

## EXERCISE 5-5

❑ Load AutoCAD for Windows.
❑ Pick **Open...** from the **File** pull-down to access the **Select File** dialog box. PRODR1 and D12-9 should be in the **Files** list if you did Exercise 4-4 and Drawing Problem 4-1.
❑ Pick D12-9 to insert it in the **File Name:** text box and press [Enter], or pick the **OK** button to open the prototype drawing D12-9.
❑ Enter the **STATUS** command and read all of the items displayed.
❑ Press the [F2] function key to get back to the graphics window.
❑ Type QUIT at the **Command:** prompt and press [Enter].

## CHAPTER TEST

*Write your answers in the spaces provided.*

1. Name the command used to start a new drawing. _____

2. What command saves your drawing and returns you to the Windows Program Manager?

   _____

3. Identify the command that you use to leave the drawing editor without saving. _____

   _____

4. What command would you use to save an existing drawing with a different name? _____

   _____

5. Identify at least four ways to cancel a command. _____

   _____

   _____

   _____

   _____

6. Explain the difference between the **SAVE**, **END**, and **QUIT** commands. _____

_____

_____

_____

_____

_____

_____

7. How do you change the name of a drawing while in the drawing editor? _____

_____

8. How often should work be saved? _____

_____

9. Name the command that allows you to quickly save your work without displaying the dialog box. _____

10. The status of an AutoCAD drawing is currently displayed on-screen. List one method to get back to the drawing editor. _____

11. Name the system variable that allows you to control the dialog box display._____

12. List the settings for the system variable described in the previous question that is used to achieve the following results:

Dialog box displayed _____

Dialog box not displayed _____

13. Why is it important to record drawing names in a log? _____

_____

14. List at least three rules and restrictions for drawing names. _____

_____

_____

_____

15. Name the pull-down menu where the **SAVE**, **SAVEAS**, and **OPEN** commands are located. _____

16. Identify two ways to exit AutoCAD without saving your work. _____

_____

17. Name the command that allows AutoCAD to automatically save your work at designated intervals. _____

18. Explain how you can get a list of existing drawing prototypes. _____

_____

_____

19. It is recommended that you resume work on the hard drive when you have saved the drawing file on a floppy disk. Name the file entry needed to transfer the drawing file named A:PROJECT to the hard disk in a file called WORK. _____

_____

_____

20. Why is it a good idea to save your work on two floppy disks? _____

_____

_____

21. What command do you use, and how do you use it, to save a drawing to a floppy disk?

_____

22. Why should you never use the **SAVEAS** and **OPEN** commands when saving or retrieving drawings from a floppy disk?_____

_____

23. How do you access the **Preview** image tile and what is its purpose? _____

_____

_____

_____

_____

24. Name the command used to change a drawing created in AutoCAD Release 13 back to Release 12. _____

_____

## DRAWING PROBLEMS

1. Start AutoCAD for Windows and open drawing D12-9. This is the prototype that you set up in Problem 4-1. (If you did not set up this prototype, refer back to Problem 4-1 and set up the drawing now.) Draw the same objects that you drew in Problem 4-2. Use the **SAVEAS** command and change the filename to P5-1. This keeps the prototype unchanged for future use and saves the drawing on the hard drive as P5-1 (P=Problem, 5=Chapter 5, 1=Problem 1). Now, type QUIT at the **Command:** prompt and press [Enter].

   *General*

2. Start AutoCAD for Windows and open drawing P5-1. Draw the objects in the same manner as required in Problem 4-3. Type QUIT, press the [Enter] key, and discard all changes. This procedure deletes all changes to the drawing and returns you to Windows Program Manager.

   *General*

3. Start AutoCAD for Windows and open drawing P5-1. Observe that the work done in Problem 2 does not exist. This is because you used the **QUIT** command. Now enter END. This saves P5-1 as is and returns you to Windows Program Manager.

   *General*

4. Start AutoCAD for Windows and access the **Create New Drawing** dialog box. Enter P5-4=P5-1 at the **New Drawing Name:** text box. This procedure does the following:

   • Creates a new drawing titled P5-4.

   • Copies the drawing P5-1 to P5-4.

   • When you save, there is a new drawing titled P5-4. The previous drawing, P5-1, remains unchanged.

   On the right side of the screen, draw a right triangle, a square, and a rectangle. Use the **SNAP** and **GRID** commands to your best advantage. Type END to save the drawing when finished.

5. Start AutoCAD for Windows and open drawing P5-4. Enter the **STATUS** command and observe the drawing status. Press the function [F2] key to return to the graphics window. Draw a box around the items previously drawn. Enter the **QSAVE** command and press [Enter]. Then, type QUIT and press [Enter] to go back to Windows Program Manager.

# Chapter 6

## Drawing Lines, Erasing Lines, and Making Prints

## Learning objectives

After completing this chapter, you will be able to:
- ○ Use the absolute, relative, and polar coordinate point entry systems.
- ○ Use the screen cursor for point entry.
- ○ Use the **Ortho** mode and coordinate display.
- ○ Select the **LINE** command to draw given objects.
- ○ Use a variety of linetypes to construct an object.
- ○ Make revisions to objects using the **ERASE** command and its options.
- ○ Make selection sets using the **Multiple**, **Window**, **Crossing**, **WPolygon**, **CPolygon**, and **Fence** options.
- ○ Use the **OOPS** command to bring back an erased object.
- ○ Draw objects in color.
- ○ Remove and add objects to the selection set.
- ○ Use the **MULTIPLE** command modifier.
- ○ Clean up the screen with the **REDRAW** command.
- ○ Draw objects with different linetypes.
- ○ Make a print of your drawing.
- ○ Use drawing plan sheets.

Drafting is a graphic language that uses lines, symbols, and words to describe products to be manufactured or constructed. Line conventions are standards based on line thickness and type, and are designed to enhance the readability of drawings. This chapter introduces line standards and shows you how to use the AutoCAD drawing editor to perform basic drafting tasks.

## LINE CONVENTIONS

The American National Standards Institute (ANSI) recommends two line widths to establish contrasting lines on a drawing. Lines are described as thick and thin. Thick lines are 0.6mm wide and thin lines are 0.3mm wide. Figure 6-1 shows recommended line width and type as taken from ANSI Y14.2M, *Line Conventions and Lettering*.

Figure 6-1.    Line conventions. (ANSI Y14.2M)

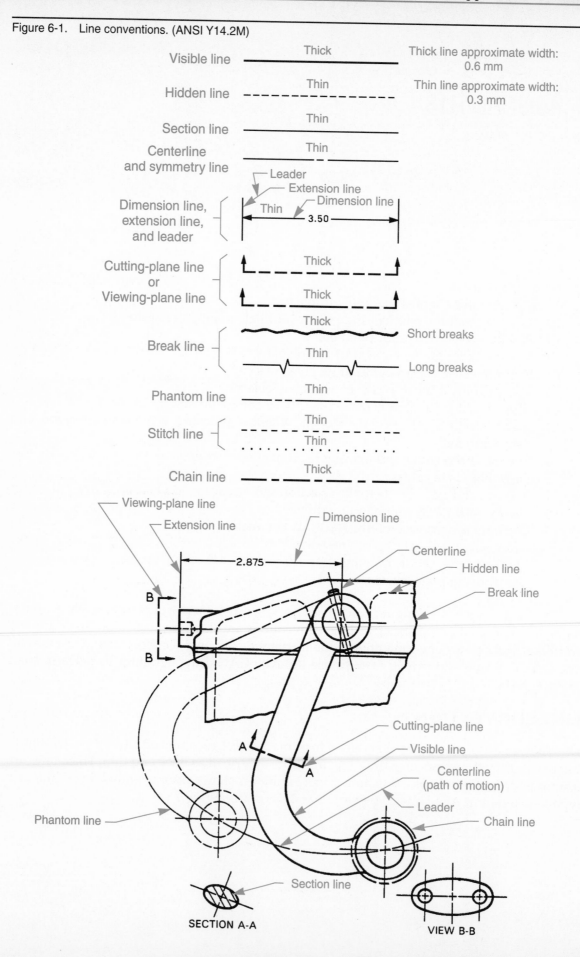

## Object lines

*Object lines*, also called *visible lines*, are thick lines used to show the outline or contour of an object, Figure 6-2. Object lines are the most common type of lines used on drawings. These lines should be twice as thick as thin lines.

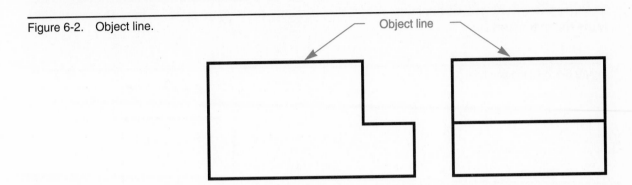

Figure 6-2.   Object line.

## Hidden lines

*Hidden lines*, often called *dashed lines*, are used to represent invisible features of an object, Figure 6-3. Hidden lines are drawn thin so they clearly contrast with object lines. When properly drawn at full size, the dashes are .125″ (3mm) long and spaced .06″ (1.5mm) apart. Be careful if the drawing is to be greatly reduced or scaled down during the plotting process. Reduced dashes may appear too small.

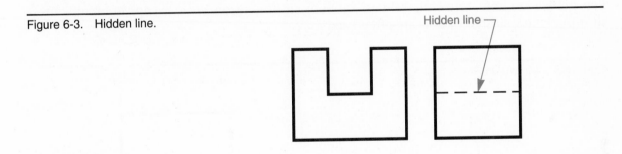

Figure 6-3.   Hidden line.

## Centerlines

*Centerlines* locate the centers of circles and arcs, and show the axis of a cylindrical or symmetrical shape, Figure 6-4. Centerlines are thin lines consisting of alternately spaced long and short dashes. The recommended dash lengths are .125″ (3mm) for the short dashes and .75″ to 1.5″ (19mm to 38mm) for the long dashes. These lengths can be altered depending on the size of the drawing. The dashes should be separated by spaces approximately .06″ (1.5mm). The small centerline dashes should cross only at the center of a circle.

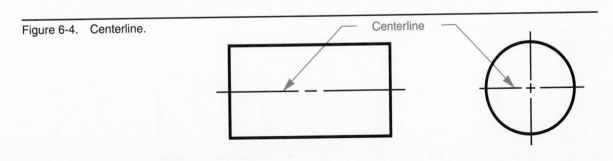

Figure 6-4.   Centerline.

## Extension lines

*Extension lines* are thin lines used to show the "extent" of a dimension, Figure 6-5. Extension lines begin a small distance from the object and extend .125" (3mm) beyond the last dimension line. Extension lines may cross object lines, hidden lines, and centerlines, but they may not cross dimension lines. Centerlines become extension lines when they are used to show the extent of a dimension. When this is done, there is no space where the centerline joins the extension line.

Figure 6-5.    Extension line.

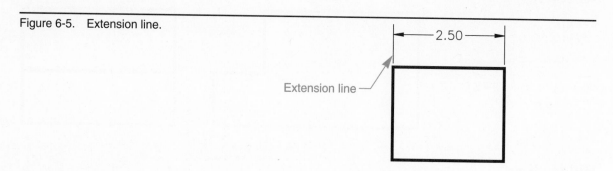

## Dimension lines

*Dimension lines* are thin lines placed between extension lines to indicate a measurement. In mechanical drafting, the dimension line is normally broken near the center for placement of the dimension numeral, Figure 6-6. The dimension line normally remains unbroken in architectural and structural drawings. The dimension numeral is placed on top of an unbroken dimension line. Arrows terminate the ends of dimension lines, except in architectural drafting where slashes or dots are often used.

Figure 6-6.    Dimension line.

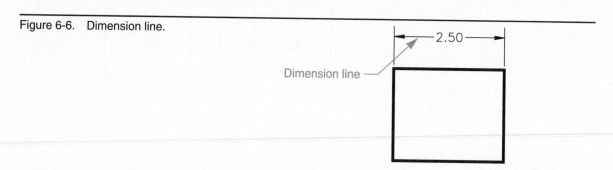

## Leader lines

*Leader lines* are thin lines used to connect a specific note to a feature on a drawing. A leader line terminates with an arrowhead at the feature and has a small shoulder at the note, Figure 6-7. Dimension and leader line usage is discussed in detail in Chapters 20 and 21.

Figure 6-7.    Leader line.

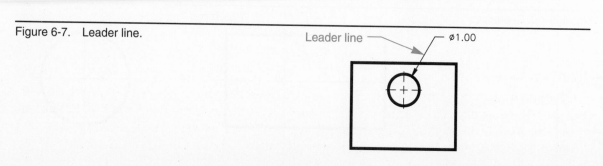

## Cutting-plane and viewing-plane lines

*Cutting-plane lines* are thick lines that identify the location of a section. *Viewing-plane lines* are drawn in the same style as cutting-plane lines, but identify the location of a view. Cutting-plane and viewing-plane lines may be drawn one of two ways, as shown in Figure 6-1. The use of viewing-plane and cutting-plane lines is discussed in detail in Chapter 19 and Chapter 24.

## Section lines

*Section lines* are thin lines drawn in a section view to show where material has been cut away, Figure 6-8. Types of section lines and applications are discussed in Chapter 24.

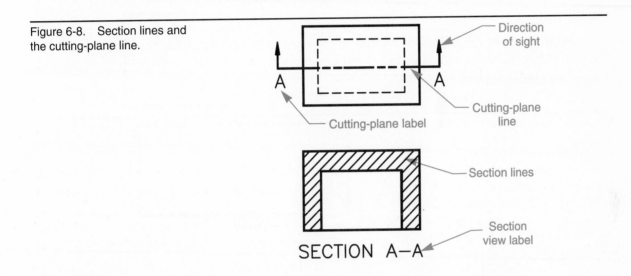

Figure 6-8.  Section lines and the cutting-plane line.

## Break lines

*Break lines* show where a portion of an object has been removed for clarity or convenience. For example, the center portion of a very long part may be broken out so the two ends can be moved closer together for more convenient representation. There are several types of break lines shown in Figure 6-9.

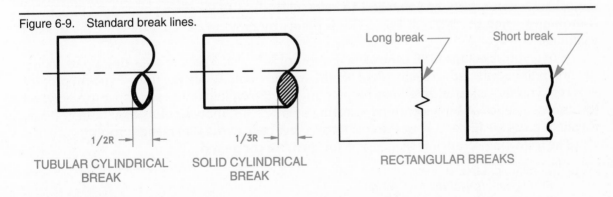

Figure 6-9.  Standard break lines.

## Phantom lines

*Phantom lines* are thin lines with two short dashes alternately spaced with long dashes. The short dashes are .125″ (3mm) and the long dashes range from .75″ to 1.5″ (19mm to 38mm) in length depending on the size of the drawing. Spaces between dashes are .06″ (1.5mm). Phantom lines identify repetitive details, show alternate positions of moving parts, or locate adjacent positions of related parts, Figure 6-10.

Figure 6-10.   Phantom lines.

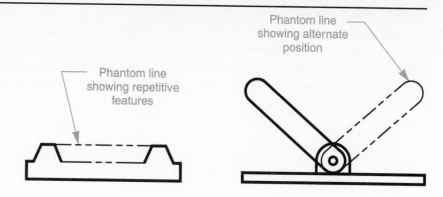

## Chain lines

*Chain lines* are thick lines of alternately spaced long and short dashes. They show that the portion of the surface next to the chain line has special features or receives unique treatment. See Figure 6-11.

Figure 6-11.   Chain lines.

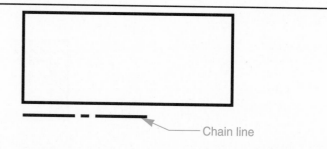

## DRAWING LINES WITH AUTOCAD

AUG 2

Individual line segments are drawn between two points on the screen. This is referred to as *point entry*. Point entry is the simplest form of drafting. After selecting the **LINE** command, enter the endpoints of a line.

To access the **Line** command, type LINE at the **Command:** prompt. It can also be selected by clicking the **LINE** button in the **Draw** toolbar. When you enter the **LINE** command, AutoCAD asks for the **From point:** and **To point:** of the line. Enter these points by typing point coordinates using the keyboard or picking points by moving the crosshairs to the desired locations.

When you select the **LINE** command, a prompt asks you to select a starting point. When the first point is selected, you are asked for the second point. When the third **To point:** prompt is given, you may stop adding lines by pressing the [Enter] key or the space bar. If you want to connect a series of lines, continue selecting as many additional points as you like. When finished, press the [Enter] key or the space bar to get back to the **Command:** prompt.

The following command sequence is for the **LINE** command:

Command: **LINE** ↵
From point: *(select the first point)*
To point: *(select the second point)*
To point: *(select the third point, or press* [Enter] *or the space bar to get a new*
    **Command:** *prompt)*
Command: *(this appears if you pressed* [Enter] *or the space bar at the previous*
    *prompt)*

## Responding to AutoCAD prompts with numbers

Many of the AutoCAD commands require specific types of numeric data. Some of AutoCAD's prompts require you to enter a whole number as the proper response. For example, later in this book you will learn how to draw a polygon using the **POLYGON** command. This command requires that you specify the number of sides as follows:

Command: **POLYGON** ↵
Number of sides ⟨*current*⟩: **6** ↵
Edge/⟨Center of polygon⟩: (*pick center of polygon*)
Inscribed in circle/Circumscribed about circle (I/C): (*respond with* I *or* C *and press* [Enter])
Radius of circle: (*type the radius, such as* 2 *and press* [Enter], *or pick a point on the
    screen at the desired distance from the center*)

The **Number of sides** ⟨*current*⟩: prompt illustrates the simplest form of numeric entry where any whole number may be used. Other entries require whole numbers that may be positive or negative. A number is understood to be positive without placing the plus (+) sign before the number. However, a negative number must be preceded by the minus (–) sign.

Much of your data entry may not be whole numbers. In these cases, any real number can be used, and can be expressed as decimals, fractions, or scientific notation. They may be positive or negative. Here are some examples of acceptable real numbers:

4.250
–6.375
1/2
1–3/4
2.5E+4 (25,000)
2.5E–4 (0.00025)

When entering fractions, the numerator and denominator must be whole numbers greater than zero. For example, 1/2, 3/4, and 2/3 are all acceptable fraction entries. Fractional numbers greater than one must have a dash between the whole number and the fraction. For example, 2-3/4 is entered for two and three quarters. The dash (–) separator is needed because a space acts just like pressing [Enter] and automatically ends the input. The numerator may be larger than the denominator as in 3/2 *only* if a whole number is not used with the fraction.

When you enter coordinates or measurements, the value used depends on the units of measure. Values on inch drawings are understood to be in inches without placing the inch marks (") after the numeral. For example, 2.500 is automatically understood to be 2.500 inches. When your drawing is set up for metric values, then any entry is automatically expressed as millimeters. If you are working in an engineering or architectural environment, any value greater than one foot is expressed in inches, feet, or feet and inches. The values can be whole numbers, decimals, or fractions. For measurements in feet, the foot symbol (') must follow the number, as in 24'. If the value is in feet and inches, there is no space between the feet and inch value. For example, 24'6 is the proper input for the value 24'-6". If the inch part of the value contains a fraction, the inch and fractional part of an inch are separated by a dash, such as 24'6-1/2. Never mix feet with inch values greater than one foot. For example, 24'18" is an invalid entry. In this case, you should enter 25'6.

**PROFESSIONAL TIP**

Placing the inch mark (") after an inch value at the prompt line is acceptable, but not necessary. It takes more time and reduces productivity.

## POINT ENTRY METHODS

There are several point entry techniques for drawing lines. Being familiar and skillful with these methods is very important. It is not necessary to use only one point entry system when drawing. A combination of techniques may be used to help reduce drawing time. Each of the point entry methods uses the Cartesian, or rectangular, coordinate system. The *Cartesian coordinate system* is based on selecting distances from two intersecting axes. Each distance is measured along a horizontal X axis and a vertical Y axis. The intersection of the axes, called the *origin*, divides the coordinate system into four quadrants. Points are located in relation to the origin where X = 0 and Y = 0, or (0,0). Figure 6-12 shows the X,Y values of points located in the Cartesian coordinate system.

Figure 6-12. The Cartesian coordinate system.

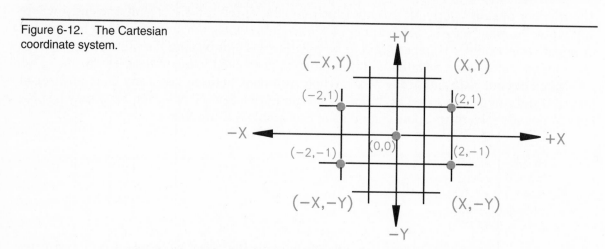

When using AutoCAD, the origin (0,0) is usually at the lower-left corner of the drawing. This point also coincides with the lower-left corner of the drawing limits. This setup places all points in the upper-right quadrant where both X and Y coordinate values are positive, Figure 6-13. Methods of establishing points in the Cartesian coordinate system include absolute coordinates, relative coordinates, and polar coordinates.

Figure 6-13. X,Y coordinate axes on the screen.

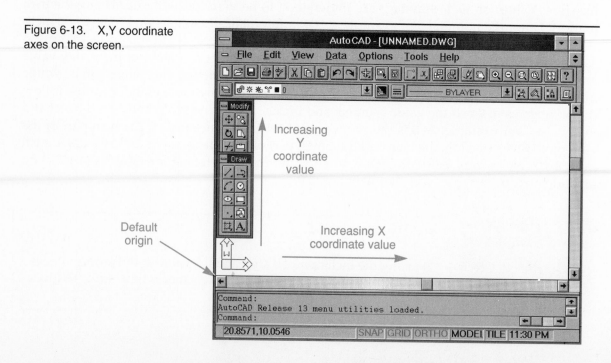

## Absolute coordinates

Points located using the absolute coordinate system are measured from the origin (0,0). For example, a point with X = 4 and Y = 2 (4,2) is measured 4 units horizontally and 2 units vertically from the origin, Figure 6-14. Notice that the coordinate display window on the toolbar registers the location of the selected point in X and Y coordinates. Also note that the coordinate display window reflects the current system of working units. The coordinate display can be turned on or off by clicking the coordinate display window with the arrow pointer, pressing function key [F6], using the [Ctrl]+[D] key combination, or pressing puck button 7.

Figure 6-14.  Locating points with absolute coordinates.

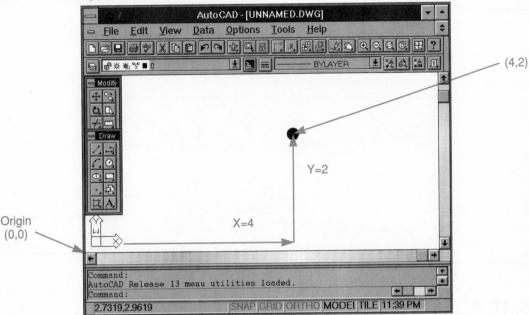

Remember, when the absolute coordinate system is used, each point is located from 0,0. Follow through these commands and point placements at your computer as you refer to Figure 6-15.

```
Command: LINE ↵
From point: 4,2 ↵
To point: 7,2 ↵
To point: 7,6 ↵
To point: 4,6 ↵
To point: 4,2 ↵
To point: ↵
Command: (press [Enter] or space bar to reinitiate the LINE command) LINE From point: 9,1.5 ↵
To point: 11,1.5 ↵
To point: 10,5.25 ↵
To point: 9,1.5 ↵
To point: ↵
Command:
```

Figure 6-15. Drawing simple shapes using the **LINE** command and absolute coordinates.

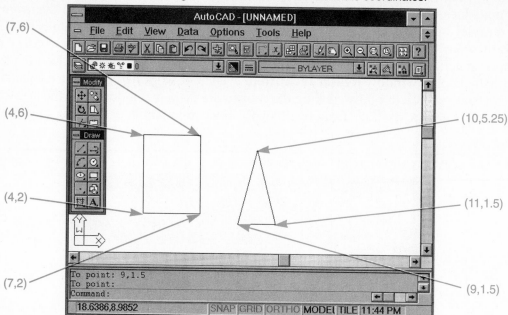

## EXERCISE 6-1

❏ Load AutoCAD for Windows and open **PRODR1** from Exercise 4-4, or start a new drawing and set up your own variables.
❏ Given the absolute coordinates in the chart below, use the **LINE** command to draw the object.
❏ Save the drawing as A:EX6-1 and exit AutoCAD.

| Point | Coordinates | Point | Coordinates |
|-------|-------------|-------|-------------|
| 1 | 0,0 | 5 | 0,2 |
| 2 | 9,0 | 6 | 0,1.5 |
| 3 | 9.5,.5 | 7 | .25,.5 |
| 4 | 9.5,2 | 8 | 0,0 |

## Relative coordinates

*Relative coordinates* are located from the previous position, rather than from the origin. The relationship of points in the Cartesian coordinate system shown in Figure 6-12 must be clearly understood before beginning with this method. For relative coordinates, the @ symbol must precede your entry. This symbol is selected by holding the [Shift] key and pressing the [2] key at the top of the keyboard. Follow through these commands and relative coordinate point placements as you refer to Figure 6-16.

Command: **LINE** ↵
From point: **2,2** ↵
To point: **@6,0** ↵
To point: **@2,2** ↵
To point: **@0,3** ↵
To point: **@–2,2** ↵
To point: **@–6,0** ↵
To point: **@0,–7** ↵
To point: ↵
Command:

Figure 6-16.   Drawing a simple shape using the **LINE** command and relative coordinates. Notice that the coordinates are entered clockwise from the first point (2,2).

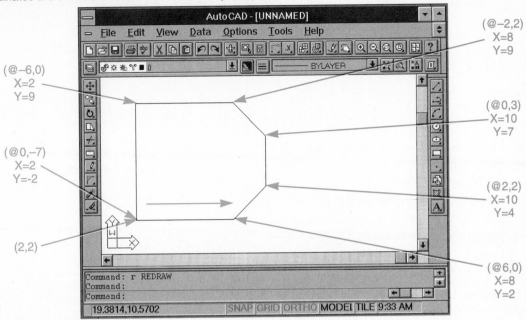

## EXERCISE 6-2

❑ Load AutoCAD for Windows and open PRODR1 from Exercise 4-4, or begin a new drawing using your own variables.
❑ Use the **LINE** command to draw the object with the relative coordinates given in the chart below.
❑ Save the drawing as A:EX6-2 and quit.

| Point | Coordinates | Point | Coordinates |
|-------|-------------|-------|-------------|
| 1 | 1,1 | 5 | @−9.5,0 |
| 2 | @9,0 | 6 | @0,−.5 |
| 3 | @.5,.5 | 7 | @.25,−1 |
| 4 | @0,1.5 | 8 | @−.25,−.5 |

## Polar coordinates

A point located using *polar coordinates* is based on the distance from a fixed point at a given angle. When using AutoCAD, a polar coordinate point is determined by distance and angle measured from the *previous point*, not the origin (0,0). The angular values used for the polar coordinate format are shown in Figure 6-17.

When establishing points using the polar coordinate system, AutoCAD needs a specific symbol entered. For example, if you want to locate a point 4 units from point 1,1 at a 45° angle, the following information must be typed:

    Command: **LINE** ↵
    From point: **1,1** ↵
    To point: **@4⟨45** ↵
    To point: ↵

Figure 6-17. Angles used in
the polar coordinate system.

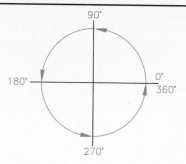

Figure 6-18 shows the result of this command. The entry @4⟨45 means the following:

@ Tells AutoCAD to measure from the previous point. This symbol must precede all polar coordinate input.

4 Gives the distance from the previous point.

⟨ Establishes a polar or angular increment to follow.

45 Determines the angle as 45° from 0°.

Figure 6-18. Using polar
coordinates for the **LINE**
command.

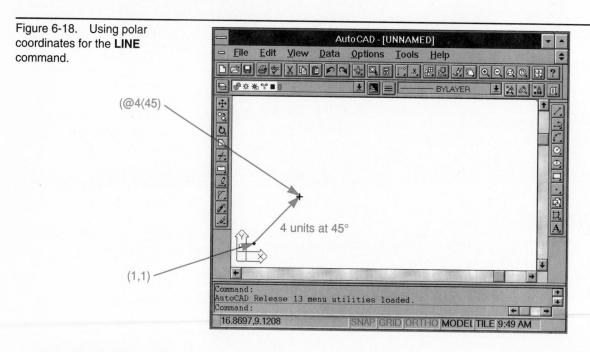

Now, follow through these commands and polar coordinate points on your computer as you refer to Figure 6-19.

```
Command: LINE ↵
From point: 1,1 ↵
To point: @4⟨0 ↵
To point: @2⟨90 ↵
To point: @4⟨180 ↵
To point: @2⟨270 ↵
To point: ↵
Command: ↵
LINE From point: 2,8 ↵
To point: @2.5⟨0 ↵
To point: @3⟨135 ↵
To point: 2,8 ↵
To point: ↵
Command:
```

Figure 6-19. Drawing simple shapes using polar coordinates.

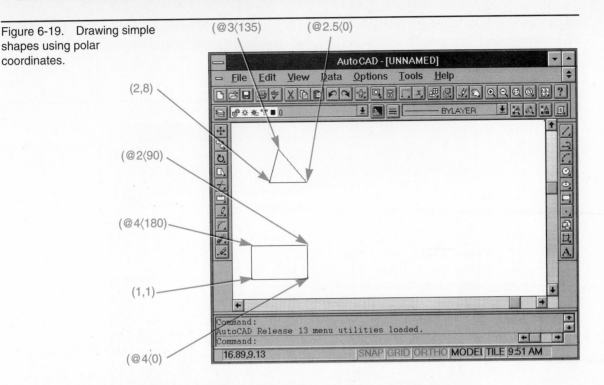

## EXERCISE 6-3

❑ Load AutoCAD for Windows and open PRODR1 from Exercise 4-4, or start a new drawing and set up your own variables.
❑ Use the **LINE** command to draw an object using the polar coordinates given in the chart below.
❑ Save the drawing as A:EX6-3 and quit.

| Point | Coordinates |
| --- | --- |
| 1 | 1,1 |
| 2 | @9⟨0 |
| 3 | @.7⟨45 |
| 4 | @1.5⟨90 |
| 5 | @9.5⟨180 |
| 6 | @2⟨270 |

## Picking points using the screen cursor

The cursor crosshairs may be moved to any location. Pick points at the cursor using the mouse, stylus, or puck. The **GRID** and **SNAP** modes normally should be turned on for precise point location. This assists in drafting presentation and maintains accuracy when using a pointing device. With the **SNAP** grid on, the crosshairs move in designated increments without any guesswork.

When using a pointing device, the command sequence is the same as using coordinates, except that points are picked when the crosshairs are at the desired location on the screen. After the first point is picked, the distance to the second point and the point's coordinates are displayed on the status line for reference. When picking points in this manner, there is a "rubberband" line connecting the "from point" and the crosshairs. The rubberband line moves as the crosshairs are moved. It provides a clue to where the new line will be placed. The rubberband line remains attached to the crosshairs until you complete the **LINE** command. See Figure 6-20.

Figure 6-20. The rubberband line is visible when using a pointing device to input points for lines.

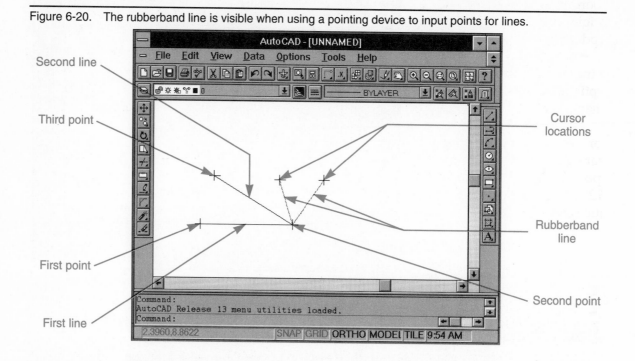

## DRAWING MULTIPLE LINES

The **MULTIPLE** command modifier is a method used to automatically repeat commands issued at the keyboard. This technique can be used to draw repetitive lines, polylines, circles, arcs, ellipses, or polygons. For example, if you plan to draw several sets of line segments, type the word **MULTIPLE** before **LINE** at the **Command:** prompt. AutoCAD automatically repeats the **LINE** command until you have finished drawing all of the desired lines. You must then cancel to get back to the **Command:** prompt. The **MULTIPLE** option is used as follows:

Command: **MULTIPLE LINE** ↵
From point: *(pick the first point)*
To point: *(pick the second point)*
To point: *(pick the third point or press* [Enter]*)*
To point: ↵
LINE From point: *(pick the first point of the next line)*
To point: *(pick the second point of the next line)*
To point: *(pick the third point or press* [Enter]*)*
To point: ↵
LINE From point: *(pick first point of third line)*
To point: *(pick the second point of third line)*
To point: ↵
LINE From point: *(press* [Esc] *to cancel)* *Cancel*
Command:

As you can see, AutoCAD automatically reissues the **LINE** command so you can draw another line (or lines). Press [Esc] to cancel the repeating command.

## The Coordinate Display

AUG 1

The area to the left side of the status bar shows the coordinate display window. The number of places to the right of the decimal point is determined by the units setting. The coordinate display changes to represent the location of the point or cursor in relation to the origin. Each time a new point is picked or the pointing device moved, the coordinates are updated.

The coordinate display is turned on and off by double-clicking the coordinate display window with the arrow pointer, pressing [Ctrl]+[D], [F6], picking **Coordinate Display** from the **Options** pull-down menu, or puck button 7. With coordinates on, the coordinates constantly change as the crosshairs move. With coordinates off, no coordinates are displayed.

There are three modes, controlled by the **COORDS** system variable. Set this variable to 0 for a static display. This displays coordinates only when points are selected. Set the **COORDS** variable to 1 for a dynamic absolute display. Set the variable to 2 for a dynamic length/angle (polar) display. A typical absolute coordinate display gives X and Y coordinates like 6.2000,5.9000. A polar coordinate display shows the distance and angle from the last point, such as 3.4000<180.

---

### EXERCISE 6-4

❑ Load AutoCAD for Windows and open PRODR1 from Exercise 4-4.
❑ Draw rectangles 3" (76.2mm) wide by 2" (50.8mm) high using each point entry method from the following list. Experiment with the coordinate display options as you draw the rectangles.
  ❑ Absolute coordinates.
  ❑ Relative coordinates.
  ❑ Polar coordinates.
  ❑ Using the screen cursor.
❑ Use the **MULTIPLE LINE** command to draw several different lines or shapes. Notice the advantage of remaining in the **LINE** command when several different line segments or shapes must be drawn.
❑ Save the drawing as A:EX6-4 and quit.

---

## DRAWING AT RIGHT ANGLES USING THE ORTHO COMMAND

AUG 3

The **ORTHO** command puts AutoCAD in the **Ortho** mode. Ortho allows lines drawn by the crosshairs movement to be only horizontal or vertical, in alignment with the current **Snap** grid. The term *ortho* comes from "orthogonal" which means "at right angles." The **Ortho** mode has a special advantage when drawing rectangular shapes because all corners are guaranteed to be square. It is impossible to draw a line at an angle using your pointing device while **Ortho** is on. See Figure 6-21. **Ortho** can be turned on or off by typing ORTHO at the **Command:** prompt, by double-clicking **ORTHO** on the status bar, or by using function key [F8], puck button 5, or [Ctrl]+[L].

Command: **ORTHO** ↵
ON/OFF ⟨*current*⟩: (ON *or* OFF *as desired*) ↵

Direct distance entry is a convenient way to enter point coordinate locations. Use this whenever you get a point prompt by moving the cursor in the direction of the desired point and type a distance value. This is easy and accurate for drawing horizontal and vertical lines with **ORTHO** on.

Figure 6-21.   A—Angled lines cannot be drawn with a pointing device while **ORTHO** mode is turned on.
B—With **ORTHO** mode turned off, angled lines can be drawn.

Screen
crosshairs

A

Screen
crosshairs

B

---

## EXERCISE 6-5

❑ Load AutoCAD for Windows and open PRODR1 from Exercise 4-4.
❑ Draw an equilateral triangle (three equal sides and angles). **Ortho** must be off to do this.
❑ Draw a 3″ (76.2mm) by 2″ (50.8mm) rectangle using the screen cursor for point entry with **Ortho** off. Draw a second rectangle with **Ortho** on. Compare the difference.
❑ Save the drawing as A:EX6-5 and quit.

---

### PROFESSIONAL TIP

Practice using the different point entry techniques and decide which method works best for certain situations. Keep in mind that you may mix methods to help enhance your drawing speed. For example, absolute coordinates may work best to locate an initial point or to draw a simple shape. These calculations are easy. Polar coordinates may work better to locate features in a circular pattern, or at an angular relationship. Practice with **ORTHO** and **SNAP** settings to see the advantages and disadvantages of each. Change the **SNAP** setting at any time to assist in drawing layout accuracy. Remember, **SNAP** is a drawing aid, so set the snap increment to assist in drawing accuracy.

---

## USING THE **CLOSE POLYGON** OPTION

A *polygon* is a closed plane figure with at least three sides. Triangles and rectangles are examples of polygons. Once you have drawn two or more line segments of a polygon, the endpoint of the last line segment can be connected automatically to the first line segment using the **Close** option. To use this option, select **Close** from the **Assist** pull-down menu, or type C or CLOSE at the prompt line. In Figure 6-22, the last line is drawn using the **Close** option as follows:

Command: **LINE** ↵
From point: *(pick point 1)*
To point: *(pick point 2)*
To point: *(pick point 3)*
To point: *(pick point 4)*
To point: **CLOSE** ↵
Command:

---

Figure 6-22.   Using the **Close** option to complete a box. **Close** may be selected from the **Assist** pull-down menu or entered at the prompt line.

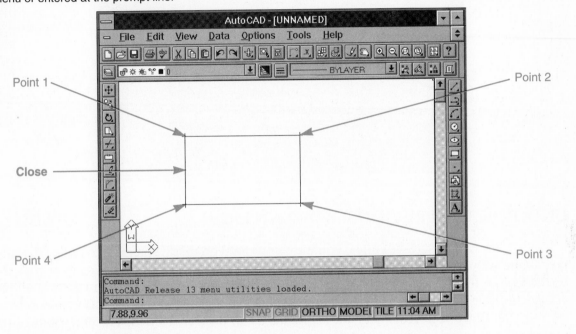

## USING THE **LINE CONTINUATION** OPTION

Suppose you draw a line, then exit the **LINE** command, but decide to go back and connect a new line to the end of the previous one. First, press the [Enter] key or the space bar to repeat the **LINE** command. This procedure, as shown in the following sequence, is an easy way to repeat any AutoCAD command. When the **From point:** prompt appears, simply press the [Enter] key or the space bar again. This action automatically connects the first endpoint of the new line segment to the endpoint of the previous one, as shown in Figure 6-23. The **Continuation** option can also be used for drawing arcs, as discussed in Chapter 8. The following command sequence is used for continuing a line:

**First line:**

Command: **LINE** ↵
From point: *(pick point 1)*
To point: *(pick point 2)*
To point: *(press [Enter] or the space bar to exit the command)*

**Next line:**

Command: *(press [Enter] or the space bar to repeat the command)*
From point: *(press [Enter] or the space bar and AutoCAD automatically picks the last endpoint of the previous line)*
To point: *(pick the next point)*
To point: *(press [Enter] or the space bar to exit the command)*
Command:

Figure 6-23.  Using the **Continue** option.

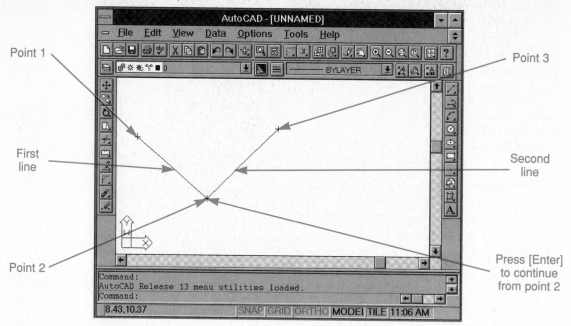

UNDOING THE PREVIOUSLY DRAWN LINE    AUG 1

When drawing a series of lines, you may find that you made an error. To delete the mistake while still in the **LINE** command, type U at the prompt line and press [Enter], or click the **UNDO** icon in the **Standard** toolbar. Doing this erases the previously drawn line and allows you to continue from the previous endpoint. A series of U's followed by [Enter]'s or successive clicks of the **UNDO** icon will erase line segments as far back as needed. The endpoints of the removed lines remain as blips (for reference) until you enter the **REDRAW** or **REGENERATE** command, or change the drawing display area. See Figure 6-24.

Command: **LINE** ↵
From point: *(pick point 1)*
To point: *(pick point 2)*
To point: *(pick point 3)*
To point: *(pick point 4)*
To point: *(pick point 5)*
To point: **U** ↵
To point: **U** ↵
To point: *(pick revised point 4)*
To point: *(press* [Enter] *or the space bar to exit the command)*
Command:

**NOTE**
When AutoCAD for Windows is configured to display screen menus in addition to the toolbar, the **Close**, **Continuation**, and **Undo** options appear in the **LINE** screen menu. Refer to Chapter 32 for information about enabling screen menus.

Figure 6-24.   Using the **Undo** option while in the **LINE** command. Notice that the original points 4 and 5 remain as blips until the screen is redrawn.

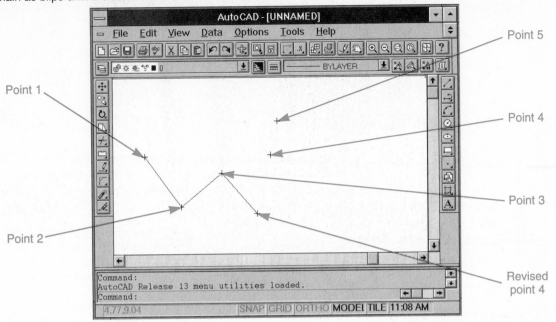

---

**EXERCISE 6-6**

❑ Load AutoCAD for Windows and open PRODR1, or begin a new drawing using your own variables.
❑ Experiment drawing lines using the following guidelines and options:
  ❑ Draw one triangle and one rectangle using the **Close** option.
  ❑ Draw two connected lines and end the **LINE** command. Then, repeat the **LINE** command and use the **Continuation** option to draw additional lines.
  ❑ Draw eight connected lines. Then use the **Undo** option to remove the last four lines while remaining in the **LINE** command. Finally, draw four new connected lines.
❑ Save the drawing as A:EX6-6 and quit.

---

## INTRODUCTION TO EDITING

AUG 5

*Editing* is the procedure used to correct mistakes or revise an existing drawing. There are many editing functions that help increase productivity. The basic editing operations **ERASE** and **OOPS** are introduced in the next sections.

To edit a drawing, you must select items to modify. The following prompt appears whenever you need to select items in the command sequence:

Select objects:

Whether you select only one entity, or hundreds of entities, you create a *selection set*. You can create a selection set using a variety of selection options, including **Window**, **Crossing**, **WPolygon**, **CPolygon**, and **Fence**. When you become familiar with the selection set options, you will find that they increase your flexibility and productivity.

In the discussion and examples that follow, several of the selection set methods are introduced using the **ERASE** command. Keep in mind, however, that these techniques can be used with most of the editing commands in AutoCAD whenever the **Select objects:** prompt appears. Any of the selection set methods can be enabled from the prompt line, or by picking the appropriate buttons in the **Select Objects** toolbar. See Figure 6-25.

Figure 6-25.   Pick the button for
the appropriate selection method
in the **Select Objects** toolbar.

## USING THE **ERASE** COMMAND

AUG 5

The **ERASE** command is similar to using an eraser in manual drafting to remove unwanted information. However, with the **ERASE** command you have a second chance. If you erase the wrong item, it can be brought back with the **OOPS** command. Access the **ERASE** command by typing **ERASE** at the **Command:** prompt, or by clicking the **ERASE** button in the **Modify** toolbar.

Whether you enter ERASE at the keyboard, or click the **ERASE** icon, you are prompted to select an object to be erased as follows:

      Command: **ERASE** ↵
      Select objects: *(select an object)*
      Select objects: ↵
      Command:

When the **Select objects:** prompt appears, a small box replaces the screen crosshairs. This box is referred to as the *pick box*. Move the pick box over the item to be erased and pick it. The object is highlighted. Then, press the [Enter] key again, or press the right mouse button, and the object is erased.

---

**NOTE**          The terms entity and object are interchangeable in AutoCAD. An entity or object is a predefined element that you place in a drawing by means of a single command. For example, a line, circle, arc, or single line of text is an entity or object.

---

After you pick the first object, the **Select objects:** prompt is redisplayed. You can then select another entity to erase, Figure 6-26. If you are finished selecting entities, press the [Enter] key at the **Select objects:** prompt to "close" the selection set. The **ERASE** operation is completed and you are returned to the **Command:** prompt.

Figure 6-26.   Using the **ERASE** command to erase a single entity.

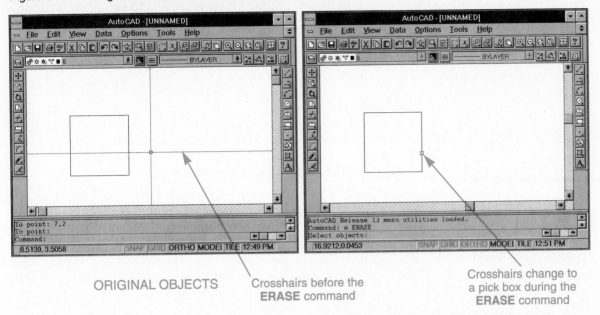

ORIGINAL OBJECTS          Crosshairs before the          Crosshairs change to
                          **ERASE** command              a pick box during the
                                                         **ERASE** command

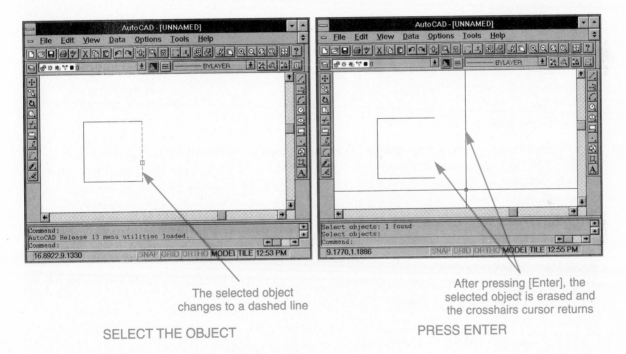

The selected object                    After pressing [Enter], the
changes to a dashed line               selected object is erased and
                                       the crosshairs cursor returns

SELECT THE OBJECT                      PRESS ENTER

## Making a single selection automatically

Normally, AutoCAD lets you pick as many items as you want for a selection set, and selected items are highlighted to let you know what has been picked. You also have the option of selecting a single item and having it automatically edited without first being highlighted. To do this, enter SI (for single) at the **Select objects:** prompt. To select several items with this method, use the **Window** or **Crossing** selection options (discussed later in this chapter). The command sequence is as follows:

Command: **ERASE** ↵
Select objects: **SI** ↵
Select objects: *(pick an individual item, or use the* **Window** *or* **Crossing** *option to pick several items)*
Command:

Note that the **Select objects:** prompt did not return after the items were picked. The entire group is automatically edited (erased in this example) when you press [Enter] or pick the second corner of a window or crossing box.

The **SI** (single) selection option is not commonly used as a command line option. This is because picking an object and pressing [Enter] requires less keystrokes than typing SI and pressing [Enter]. The **SI** option is most commonly utilized when developing menu macros that require single object selection.

### Using the Last selection option

The **ERASE** command's **Last** option saves time if you need to erase the last entity drawn. For example, suppose you draw a box using the **LINE** command. The **ERASE** command's **Last** option erases the last line drawn. The **Last** option can be selected by picking the **Select Last** button from the **Select Objects** toolbar, or by typing L at the **Select objects:** prompt as follows:

```
Command: ERASE ↵
Select objects: L ↵
1 found
Select objects: ↵
Command: (press space bar or [Enter])
Select objects: L ↵
1 found
Select objects: ↵
Command:
```

Keep in mind that using the **Last** option only highlights the last item drawn. You must press [Enter] for the object to be erased. If you need to erase more than just the last object, you can use the **ERASE** command and **Last** option repeatedly to erase items in reverse order. However, this is not as quick as using the **ERASE** command and selecting the objects.

### EXERCISE 6-7

❑ Load AutoCAD for Windows and open PRODR1, or begin a new drawing using your own variables.
❑ Use the **LINE** command to draw a square similar to the ORIGINAL OBJECT in Figure 6-26.
❑ Type ERASE at the **Command:** prompt and erase two of the lines.
❑ Draw another square, similar to the previous one.
❑ Type ERASE at the **Command:** prompt and enter L at the **Select objects:** prompt.
❑ Press [Enter] again and enter L to erase one more line.
❑ Type QUIT and exit AutoCAD without saving.

### The Window selection option                                                            AUG 5

The **W** or **Window** option can be used with several commands. This option allows you to draw a box or "window" around an object or group of objects to select for editing. Everything entirely within the window can be selected at the same time. If portions of entities project outside the window, they will not be selected. The command sequence looks like this:

```
Command: ERASE ↵
Select objects: (select a point to the left of the object or group of objects to be erased)
```

When the **Select objects:** prompt is shown, select a point clearly outside and to the left of the object to be erased. After you select the first point, the screen crosshairs change to a box-shaped cursor. It expands in size as you move the pointing device to the right. The box is a solid line. The next prompt is:

> Other corner: *(pick the other corner to the right of the object or group of objects)*
> Select objects: ⏎
> Command:

When the **Other corner:** prompt is shown, move the pointing device to the right so the box totally encloses the object(s) to be erased. Then pick to locate the second corner, Figure 6-27. All objects within the window become highlighted. When finished, press [Enter] to complete the **ERASE** command.

Figure 6-27.   Using the **ERASE Window** option.

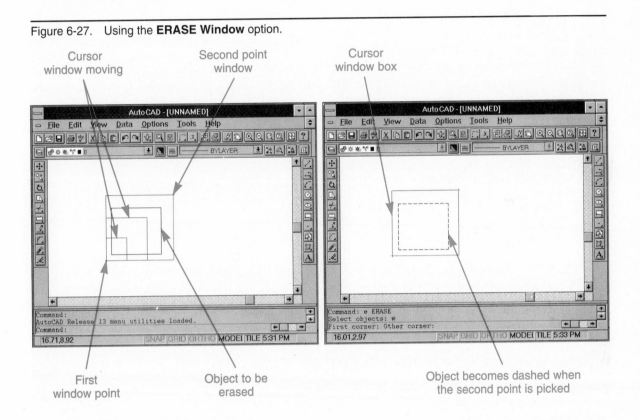

Cursor window moving

Second point window

Cursor window box

First window point

Object to be erased

Object becomes dashed when the second point is picked

You can also manually specify the **Window** option from the command line. You need to do this if the **PICKAUTO** variable (discussed later in this chapter) is set to 0. The command sequence is as follows:

> Command: **ERASE**
> Select objects: **W**
> First corner: *(select a point outside of the object)*

When you manually enter the **Window** option, you do not need to pick the first point to the left of the object(s) being erased. The "box" remains the **Window** box whether you move the cursor to the left or right.

## The Crossing selection option

The **Crossing** selection option is similar to the **Window** option. However, entities within and those *crossing* the box are selected. The **Crossing** box outline is dotted to distinguish it from the solid outline of the **Window** box. The command sequence for the **Crossing** option is as follows:

> Command: **ERASE** ↵
> Select objects: *(pick a point to the right of the object or group of objects to be erased)*

When the **Select objects:** prompt is shown, select a point to the right of the object to be erased. After you select the first point, the screen crosshairs change to a box-shaped cursor. It expands in size as you move the pointing device to the left. The next prompt is:

> Other corner: *(move the cursor to the left so that the box encloses or crosses the object or group of objects to be erased and pick)*
> Select objects: ↵
> Command:

Remember, the crossing box does not have to enclose the entire object to erase it; the window box does. The crossing box need only "cross" part of the object to be erased or edited. Figure 6-28 shows how to erase three of four lines of a rectangle using the **Crossing** option.

Figure 6-28.    Using the **Crossing** box to erase objects.

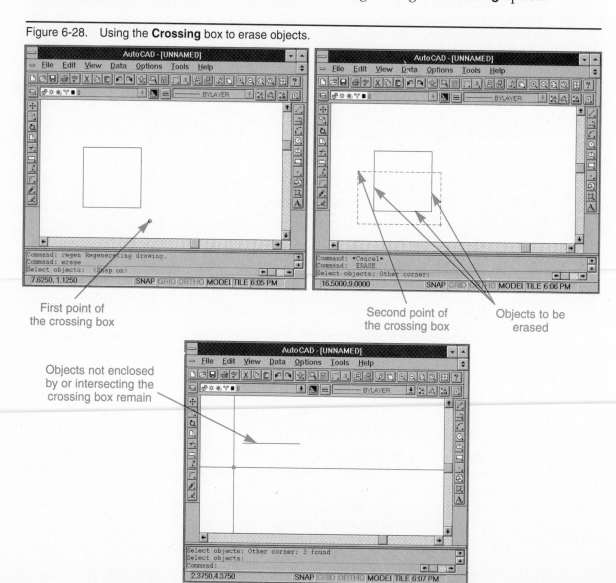

First point of
the crossing box

Second point of
the crossing box

Objects to be
erased

Objects not enclosed
by or intersecting the
crossing box remain

You can also manually specify the **Crossing** option from the command line. You need to do this if the **PICKAUTO** variable (discussed later in this chapter) is set to 0. The command sequence is as follows:

> Command: **ERASE**
> Select objects: **C**
> First corner: *(pick a point outside of the object)*

When you manually enter the **Crossing** option, you do not need to pick the first point to the right of the object(s) being erased. The "box" remains the **Crossing** box whether you move the cursor to the left or right.

## PICKAUTO variable

When the **PICKAUTO** system variable is on (1), you can automatically use the **Window** or **Crossing** selection process. By default, **PICKAUTO** is set to 1. The **PICKAUTO** system variable controls automatic windowing when the **Select objects:** prompt appears. The **PICKAUTO** settings are: ON = 1 (default) and OFF = 0. Change the **PICKAUTO** setting like this:

> Command: **PICKAUTO** ↵
> New value for PICKAUTO ⟨1⟩: **0** ↵

You can use the automatic **Window** or **Crossing** option even if **PICKAUTO** is 0 (off). To do this, enter AU (for auto) at the **Select objects:** prompt, and then proceed as previously discussed. The command sequence looks like this:

> Command: **ERASE** ↵
> Select objects: **AU** ↵
> Select objects: *(pick a point outside and to the left for a **Window** box, or pick a point*
>     *outside and to the right of the object for a **Crossing** box)*
> Other corner: *(move the cursor right so the **Window** box entirely encloses the object,*
>     *or move the cursor left so that the **Crossing** box encloses or crosses the object)*
> Select object: ↵
> Command:

**PROFESSIONAL TIP**

With **PICKAUTO** set to 1, pick any left point outside the object and then move the cursor to the right for a **Window** selection. The **Window** box outline is a solid line. Pick any right point outside the object and move the cursor to the left for a **Crossing** selection. The **Crossing** box is a dashed line.

## CLEANING UP THE SCREEN

AUG 1

After you draw or erase a number of objects on a drawing, the screen is cluttered with small crosses or markers called *blips*. In addition, many of the grid dots may be missing. This can be distracting. It is easy to clean up the screen, and restore the drawing, by choosing the **REDRAW** command. The **REDRAW** command cleans the screen in the current viewport. Viewports and the **REDRAWALL** command are discussed in detail in Chapter 10. The **REDRAW** command can be typed at the keyboard, selected from the **View** pull-down menu, or selected by clicking the **REDRAW** button in the toolbox.

> Command: **REDRAW** ↵

The screen will go blank for an instant, and the cleaned drawing and screen return.

**EXERCISE 6-8**

❏ Load AutoCAD for Windows and open PRODR1, or begin a new drawing using your own variables.

❏ Set the **PICKAUTO** system variable to 0 (off).

❏ Use the **LINE** command to draw a square similar to the ORIGINAL OBJECT shown in Figure 6-26.

❏ Type ERASE at the **Command:** prompt and use the **Window** selection option. Place the window around the entire square to erase it. Enter OOPS at the next **Command:** prompt to have the square reappear.

❏ Now, erase three of the four lines by typing C at the **Select objects:** prompt. Use the **Crossing** selection shown in Figure 6-28. Type OOPS and press [Enter] to bring the three lines back on the screen.

❏ Set the **PICKAUTO** system variable to 1 (on).

❏ Now, enter ERASE and automatically erase the square using a window. Type OOPS to get the square back again.

❏ Enter ERASE and erase three sides of the square (as shown in Figure 6-28) using the automatic **Crossing** selection.

❏ Use the **REDRAW** command to clean up the screen.

❏ Type QUIT and exit AutoCAD without saving.

## Using the WPolygon selection option

AUG 5

The **Window** selection option requires that you place a rectangle completely around the entities to be erased. Sometimes it is awkward to place a rectangle around the items to erase. When this situation occurs, you can place a polygon (closed figure with three or more sides) of your own design around the objects with the **WPolygon** option. To use the **WPolygon** option, type WP at the **Select objects:** prompt, or pick the **Window Polygon** button from the **Select Objects** toolbar. Then, draw a polygon that encloses the objects. As you pick corners, the polygon drags into place. The **WPolygon** line is a solid rubberband cursor. The command sequence for erasing the five squares in the middle of Figure 6-29A is as follows:

```
Command: ERASE ↵
Select objects: WP ↵
First polygon point: (pick point 1)
Undo/⟨Endpoint of line⟩: (pick point 2)
Undo/⟨Endpoint of line⟩: (pick point 3)
Undo/⟨Endpoint of line⟩: (pick point 4)
Undo/⟨Endpoint of line⟩: ↵
Select objects: ↵
Command:
```

If you do not like the last polygon point you picked, use the **Undo** option by entering U at the **Undo/⟨Endpoint of line⟩:** prompt.

Figure 6-29.   Using the **WPolygon** selection option to erase objects.

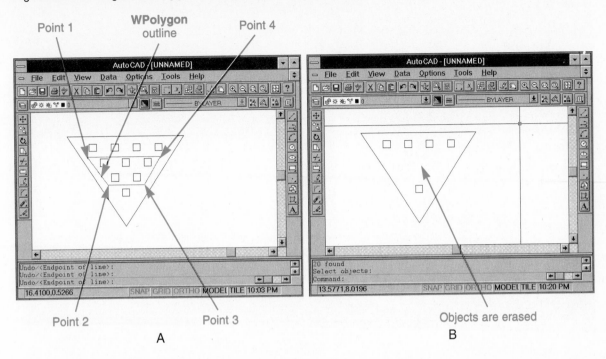

A

B

Point 1    WPolygon outline    Point 4

Point 2    Point 3

Objects are erased

---

❑ Load AutoCAD for Windows and open PRODR1, or begin a new drawing using your own variables.
❑ Draw an object similar to the one shown in Figure 6-29A.
❑ Use the **WPolygon** selection option to erase the same items as shown in the figure.
❑ Use the **REDRAW** command to clean up the screen.
❑ Save the drawing as A:EX6-9 and quit the drawing session.

## Using the **CPolygon** selection option

AUG 5

The **Crossing** selection option lets you place a rectangle around or through the objects to be erased. Sometimes it is difficult to place a rectangle around or through the items to be erased without coming into contact with other entities. When you want to use the features of the **Crossing** selection option, but prefer to use a polygon instead of a rectangle, enter CP at the **Select objects:** prompt, or pick the **Crossing Polygon** button from the **Select Objects** toolbar. Then, proceed to draw a polygon that encloses or crosses the objects to erase. As you pick the points, the polygon drags into place. The **CPolygon** line is a dashed rubberband cursor. Refer to Figure 6-30.

Suppose you want to erase everything inside the large triangle in Figure 6-30A except for the top and bottom horizontal lines. The command sequence to erase these lines is as follows:

```
Command: ERASE ↵
Select object: CP ↵
First polygon point: (pick point 1)
Undo/⟨Endpoint of line⟩: (pick point 2)
Undo/⟨Endpoint of line⟩: (pick point 3)
Undo/⟨Endpoint of line⟩: (pick point 4)
Undo/⟨Endpoint of line⟩: ↵
Select objects:
Command:
```

Figure 6-30.   Using the **CPolygon** selection option. Everything enclosed within or crossing the polygon is selected.

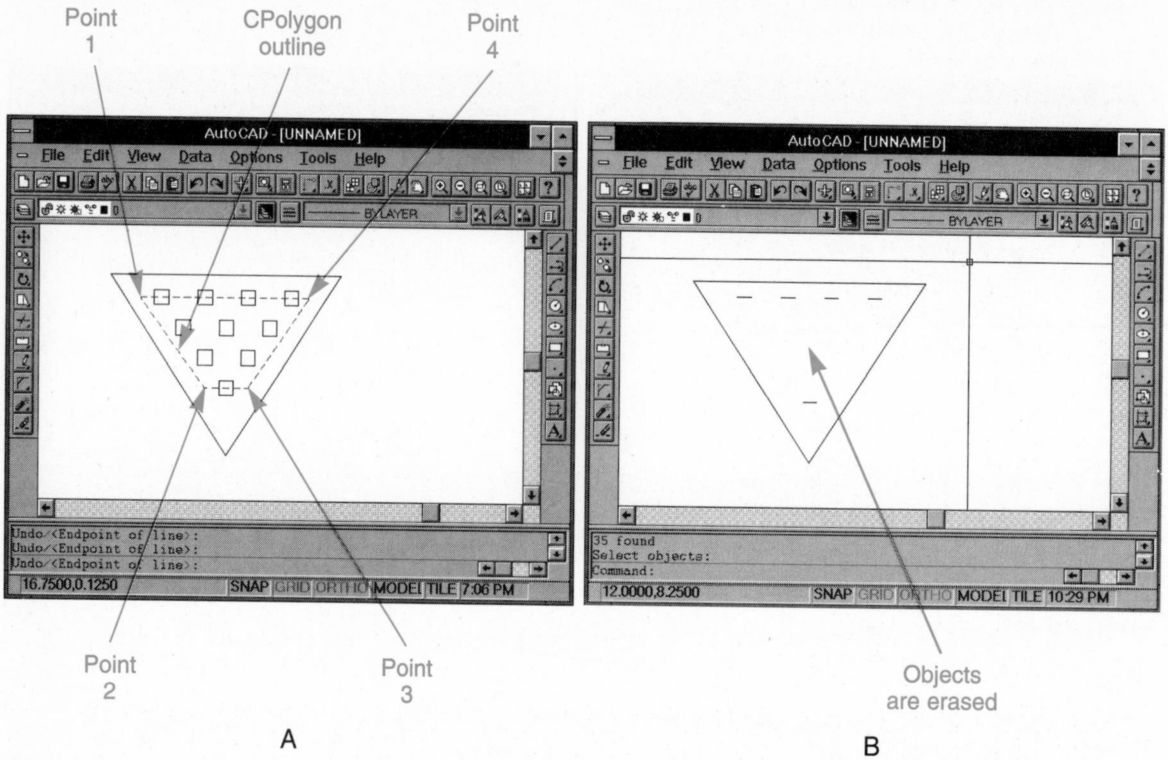

A

B

If you want to change the last **CPolygon** point you picked, enter U at the **Undo/⟨Endpoint of line⟩:** prompt.

## EXERCISE 6-10

❑ Load AutoCAD for Windows and open PRODR1, or begin a new drawing using your own variables.
❑ Draw an object similar to the one shown in Figure 6-30A.
❑ Use the **CPolygon** selection option to erase the same items as shown in the figure.
❑ Use the **REDRAW** command to clean up the screen.
❑ Save the drawing as A:EX6-10 and quit.

## Using the Fence selection option

AUG 5

    **Fence** is another selection option used to select several objects at the same time. When using the **Fence** option, you simply need to place a fence through the objects you want to select. Anything that the fence passes through is included in the selection set. The fence can be straight or staggered, as shown in Figure 6-31. Pick **Crossing Fence** button from the **Select Objects** toolbar or enter F at the **Select objects:** prompt as follows:

Command: **ERASE** ↵
Select objects: **F** ↵
First fence point: *(pick the starting point of the first fence)*
Undo/⟨Endpoint of line⟩: *(pick point 2)*
Undo/⟨Endpoint of line⟩: ↵
6 found
Select objects: **F** ↵
Undo/⟨Endpoint of line⟩: *(pick point 3)*
Undo/⟨Endpoint of line⟩: *(pick point 4)*
Undo/⟨Endpoint of line⟩: *(pick point 5)*
Undo/⟨Endpoint of line⟩: *(pick point 6)*
Undo/⟨Endpoint of line⟩: *(pick point 7)*
Undo/⟨Endpoint of line⟩: *(pick point 8)*
Undo/⟨Endpoint of line⟩: ↵
9 found
Select objects: ↵
Command:

Figure 6-31.    Using the **Fence** selection option to erase entities. Notice that the fence can be either straight or staggered.

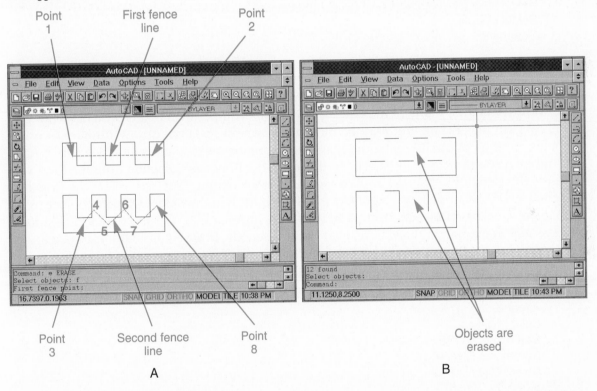

EXERCISE 6-11

❑ Load AutoCAD for Windows and open PRODR1, or start a new drawing using your own variables.
❑ Draw an object similar to the one shown in Figure 6-31A.
❑ Use the **Fence** selection option to erase the items shown in the figure.
❑ Use the **REDRAW** command to clean up the drawing.
❑ Save the drawing as A:EX6-11 and quit.

### Removing and adding entities to the selection set

When editing a drawing, a common mistake is to accidentally select an entity that you did not want, or not to select an entity that you want included. Do not worry; you can remove or add the entity to the selection set anytime you are at the **Select objects:** prompt. For example, suppose you are using the **ERASE** command and you selected several items to be erased. Then you decide that two of the items should not be erased. When this happens, pick the **Select Remove** button from the **Select Objects** toolbar, or enter R (for remove) at the **Select objects:** prompt like this:

> Command: **ERASE** ↵
> Select objects: *(pick several items using any of the selection techniques)*
> Select objects: **R** ↵
> Remove objects: *(pick the items you want removed from the selection set)*
> Remove objects: ↵
> Command:

Now if you decide that you want to add more items to the selection set, pick the **Select Add** button from the **Select Objects** toolbar, or enter A (for add), and pick the additional objects to be erased:

> Remove objects: **A** ↵
> Select objects: *(pick additional items to be erased)*
> Select objects: ↵
> Command:

### Using the Previous Selection

The object selection options given to this point in the chapter have used the example of the **ERASE** command. Many of the editing operations you perform in a typical drawing will not necessarily be erasing, but may be moving or rotating objects, or any number of other available editing options. Often, more than one sequential editing operation needs to be carried out on a specific group of objects. In this case, the **Previous Selection** option allows you to select the same object(s) you just edited for further editing. You can select the **Previous Selection** set by either picking the **Select Previous** button in the **Select Objects** toolbar or by typing P at the **Select Objects:** prompt. In the following example, a group of objects is erased and the **OOPS** command is used to recover them. Then, the **ERASE** command is issued again, this time using the **Previous Selection** option.

> Command: **ERASE** ↵
> Select objects: *(pick several items using any selection technique)*
> *n* found.
> Select objects: ↵
> Command: **OOPS** ↵
> Command: **ERASE** ↵
> Select objects: **P** ↵
> *n* found.
> Select objects: ↵
> Command:

### Selecting all entities on a drawing

Sometimes you may want to select every item on the drawing. To do this, pick the **Select All** button from the **Select Objects** toolbar, or enter ALL at the **Select objects:** prompt as follows:

> Command: **ERASE** ↵
> Select objects: **ALL** ↵
> Select objects: ↵
> Command:

This procedure erases everything on the drawing. You can use the **Remove** option at the second **Select objects:** prompt to remove certain objects from the set. You can also enter ALL after typing R to remove all objects from the set. If you leave the command, you can immediately get everything back with the **OOPS** or **UNDO** command.

---

**EXERCISE 6-12**

❑ Load AutoCAD for Windows and open PRODR1, or start a new drawing using your own variables.
❑ Draw an object similar to the one shown in Figure 6-31A.
❑ Use the **SI** selection option to erase one line.
❑ Use the **SI** selection option with a fence to erase any two lines.
❑ Experiment using the **Remove** and **Add** selection options by selecting six items to erase, remove two of the items from the selection set, and then add three different entities to the selection set.
❑ Use the **REDRAW** command to clean up the screen.
❑ Use the **ALL** selection option to erase everything from the drawing.
❑ Use the **UNDO** or **OOPS** command to get everything back that you erased.
❑ Save the drawing as A:EX6-12 and quit.

---

## Using the **Box** selection option

Another way to begin the window or crossing selection option is to type BOX at the **Select objects:** prompt. You are then prompted to pick the left corner of a **Window** box or the right corner of a **Crossing** box, depending on your needs. The command sequence is as follows:

```
Command: ERASE ↵
Select objects: BOX ↵
First corner: (pick the left corner of a Window box or the right corner of a Crossing box)
Select objects: ↵
Command:
```

## Using the **Multiple Selection** option

The **MULTIPLE** option provides easy access to stacked objects. *Stacked objects* occur when one feature, such as a line, overlays another in a 2D drawing. These lines have the same Z values, so one is no higher or lower than the other. However, the last object drawn will appear to be on top of all others. When a point on an object is picked in select mode, the data base is scanned and the first object found is the object selected. Additional picks will only duplicate the original results. This means, that unless **Window**, **Crossing**, **Fence**, or **Multiple** is used, the underlying objects are inaccessible. Using the **MULTIPLE** option allows multiple picks at the same point to find more than one entity. The first pick finds the first object. A second pick in the same place ignores the already selected object and finds the next object. This process continues for each pick made. The command sequence used to erase two stacked lines with the **Multiple** option is as follows:

```
Command: ERASE ↵
Select objects: M ↵
Select objects: (pick the stacked objects twice, then press the [Enter] key)
2 selected, 2 found
Select objects: ↵
Command:
```

Notice that the *n* **selected**, *n* **found** prompt does not appear until you press the [Enter] key. This may make it difficult to select all overlapping objects if you do not know how many are there.

PROFESSIONAL
TIP

When objects are selected using the **Multiple** option, the selected objects are not highlighted until the [Enter] key is pressed. This can speed up the selection process for text and other complex objects on workstations with slower display systems.

Often you may want to modify an object underlying another, without affecting the "top" object. To do this, enter the **Multiple** mode as previously discussed. For the previous example, pick a point on the object twice. Press [Enter] to end the multiple mode. AutoCAD tells you that both objects are selected. Now, use the **REMOVE** option and select the same point again. The "top" object is now removed from the selection set. The command sequence looks like this:

Command: **ERASE** ↵
Select objects: **M** ↵
Select objects: *(pick the object twice)*
2 selected, 2 found
Select objects: **R** ↵
Remove objects: *(pick the point again)*
1 found, 1 removed
Remove objects: ↵
Command:

NOTE

When selecting objects to be erased, AutoCAD only accepts qualifying objects. *Qualifying object* refers to an object that is not on a locked layer and that passes through the pickbox area at the point selected. Layers are discussed in Chapter 19 of this text.

### Cycling through stacked objects

Another way to deal with stacked objects is to let AutoCAD cycle through the objects. *Cycling* is repeatedly selecting one item from a series of stacked objects until the desired object is highlighted. This works best when several objects cross at the same place or are very close together. Look at Figure 6-32. To do this, hold down the [Ctrl] key and pick the object as you normally pick a single object. For the objects in Figure 6-32, pick where the four circles intersect. If there are two or more objects found crossing through the pick box area, the top object is highlighted. Now, you can release the [Ctrl] key. When you pick again, the top object returns and the next one is highlighted. Every time you pick, another object becomes highlighted. In this way, you cycle through all of the objects. When you have the desired object highlighted, press [Enter] to end the cycling process and return to the **Select objects:** prompt. Press [Enter] again to return to the **Command:** prompt. The following command sequence is used to erase one of the circles in Figure 6-32, but you can use this for any editing function:

Command: **ERASE** ↵
Select objects: *(hold down the [Ctrl] key and pick)* ⟨Cycle on⟩ *(pick until you high-
    light the desired object and press* [Enter])
⟨Cycle off⟩1 found
Select objects: *(select additional objects or press* [Enter])
Command:

Figure 6-32.   Cycling through a series of stacked circles until the desired object is highlighted.

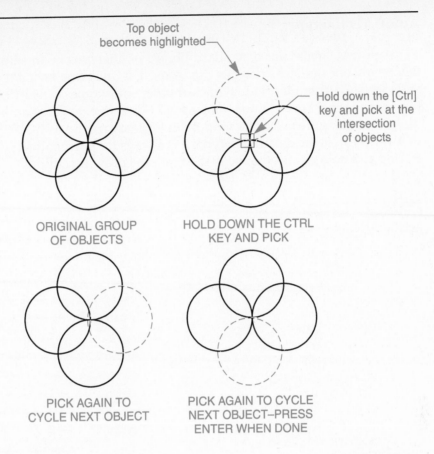

Top object becomes highlighted

Hold down the [Ctrl] key and pick at the intersection of objects

ORIGINAL GROUP OF OBJECTS

HOLD DOWN THE CTRL KEY AND PICK

PICK AGAIN TO CYCLE NEXT OBJECT

PICK AGAIN TO CYCLE NEXT OBJECT–PRESS ENTER WHEN DONE

## OOPS, I MADE A MISTAKE

AUG 5

The **OOPS** command is handy to bring back the last object you erased. If you erased several objects in the same command sequence, all are brought back to the screen. **OOPS** can only be used with the **ERASE** command. If you erased entities within a window, they can be brought back as follows:

Command: **ERASE** ↵
Select objects: **W** ↵
First corner: *(select a point)*
Other corner: *(select a point)*
Select objects: ↵
Command: **OOPS** ↵

## INTRODUCTION TO LINETYPE

AUG 6

Earlier in this chapter you were introduced to line standards. AutoCAD provides standard linetypes that can be used at any time. Standard AutoCAD linetypes are a single width. In order to achieve different line widths, it is necessary to use the **PLINE** or **TRACE** commands. These commands are introduced in Chapter 7 of this text.

Line width can also be varied using different plotter pen tip widths. To do this, draw different width lines on separate layers. Then, plot with the appropriate width of pen for each layer. This is further discussed in this chapter and in Chapter 12 of this text.

## AutoCAD linetypes

AutoCAD maintains a standard library of linetypes in an external file called ACAD.LIN. Before any one of these linetypes can be used, it must first be loaded into the drawing editor and then set current. Individual lines or other entity types can be drawn with a specified linetype at any time. You will note that a solid object line does not appear in the linetype library illustrated in Figure 6-33. The solid linetype is referred to as CONTINUOUS and is the default in AutoCAD. As the default linetype, it is always the current linetype when a new drawing is started and does not need to be loaded into the drawing editor.

Figure 6-33.    Standard AutoCAD linetype library.

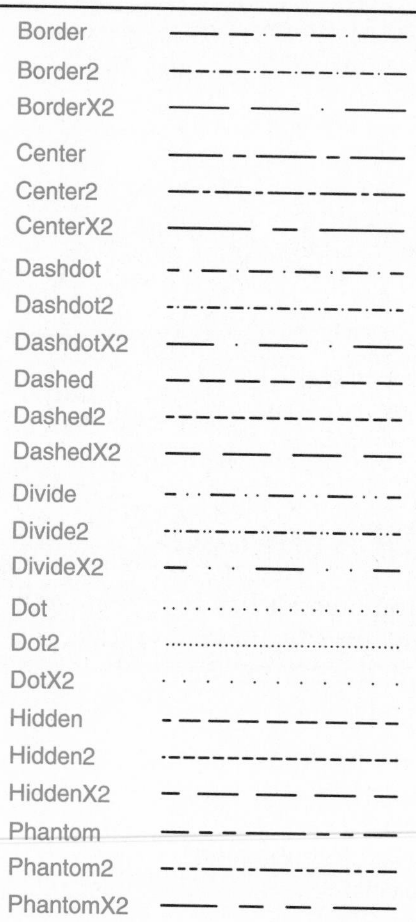

| Border | |
| Border2 | |
| BorderX2 | |
| Center | |
| Center2 | |
| CenterX2 | |
| Dashdot | |
| Dashdot2 | |
| DashdotX2 | |
| Dashed | |
| Dashed2 | |
| DashedX2 | |
| Divide | |
| Divide2 | |
| DivideX2 | |
| Dot | |
| Dot2 | |
| DotX2 | |
| Hidden | |
| Hidden2 | |
| HiddenX2 | |
| Phantom | |
| Phantom2 | |
| PhantomX2 | |

## Managing linetypes in AutoCAD

Selecting the **Linetype** button in the **Object Properties** toolbar activates the **Select Linetype** dialog box. This provides an easy means of loading linetypes and setting the current linetype. Figure 6-34A shows the default appearance of the dialog box. Each of the currently loaded linetypes is shown in the **Loaded Linetypes** section. To set a loaded linetype as current, click the image button that depicts the desired linetype. The name of the selected linetype appears in the **Linetype:** edit box. If necessary, another linetype can be selected or the name appearing in the edit box can be directly edited.

In a new drawing with no prototype, the three options initially available are CONTINUOUS, BYLAYER, and BYBLOCK. To add additional linetypes to the available options, select the **Load** button. The **Load or Reload Linetype** dialog box shown in Figure 6-34B displays the available linetypes contained within the file specified in the edit box to the right of the **File...** button.

Figure 6-34. Using the **Select Linetype** and **Load or Reload Linetype** dialog boxes.

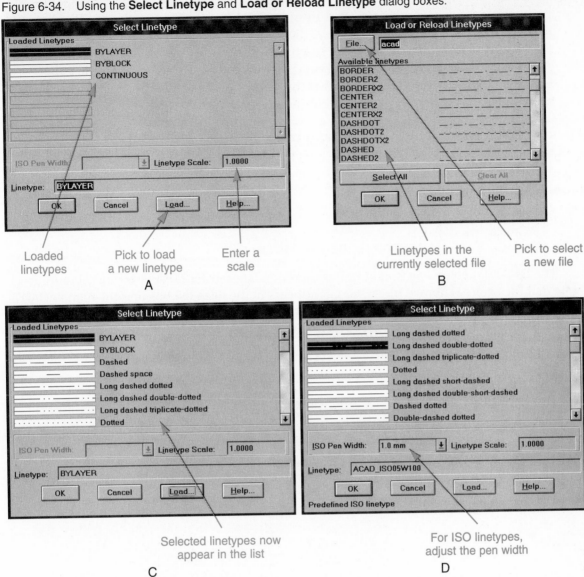

Pressing the **File...** button starts a file dialog to allow selection of a different linetype definition file (.LIN).

The **Available linetypes** list is used to specify which of the defined linetypes you wish to load into the current drawing session. Selected linetypes will appear highlighted, and any number can be selected. Picking a linetype has the effect of *toggling* the selection status, selecting or unselecting the option depending on its previous state. The **Select All** button selects all of the available linetypes. The **Clear All** button can be used to clear all of the selected linetypes. When all required linetypes have been selected, click the **OK** button and the specified linetypes are loaded. You are then returned to the **Select Linetype** dialog. See Figure 6-34C.

The appearance of a linetype can be adjusted by altering the linetype scale. A smaller scale means shorter dashes closer together and a larger scale causes linetypes to appear with longer dashes farther apart. The scale is changed by editing the value in the **Linetype Scale:** edit box. If the current linetype is an ISO linetype, the scale is changed using the **ISO Pen Width:** pop-up list. See Figure 6-34D.

The **LINETYPE** command also allows you to load different linetypes and change the current linetype. Linetypes can be assigned to individual layers. This method is discussed in Chapter 19. The **LINETYPE** command offers the following options:

- **?.** Lists the linetypes defined in a specified library file.
- **Create.** Allows creation of a new linetype and stores it in a specified library file.
- **Load.** Loads one or more linetypes from a specified library file.
- **Set.** Sets the current linetype used for newly drawn objects.

## Loading linetypes from the Command: prompt

To load one or more linetypes, enter LINETYPE at the **Command:** prompt. In the following example, three linetypes are loaded. When loading multiple linetypes, separate each linetype name with a comma.

    Command: **LINETYPE** ⏎
    ?/Create/Load/Set: **L** ⏎
    Linetype(s) to load: **CENTER,HIDDEN,PHANTOM** ⏎

The **Select Linetype File** dialog box is then displayed if **FILEDIA** is set to 1, Figure 6-35. Note that the external library file ACAD.LIN appears in the **Files** list box and the name ACAD is highlighted in the **File Name:** text box. Click the **OK** button or press [Enter]. The three linetypes are then loaded and the **LINETYPE** command options are redisplayed:

    ?/Create/Load/Set: *(select an option or press* [Enter] *to exit the command)*

Figure 6-35. The **Select Linetype File** dialog box.

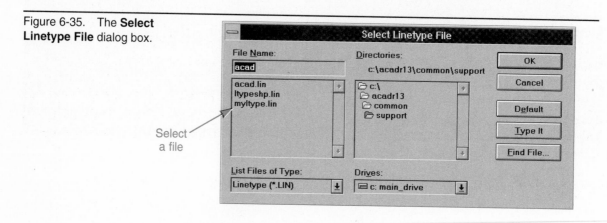

Select a file

## Setting a linetype current from the Command: prompt

You now have four linetypes loaded in the current drawing—the three which you just loaded plus the default CONTINUOUS linetype. Only one linetype can be current at a time. Once a linetype is loaded, it can be made current using the **Set** option of the **LINETYPE** command. In the sequence that follows, the current CONTINUOUS linetype is replaced with the HIDDEN linetype. The current linetype is shown in brackets. If you have just begun a new drawing and have not yet changed the linetype, the word BYLAYER appears in the brackets. If you want to see a sample of the current linetype, type ? at the **New entity linetype:** prompt.

    Command: **LINETYPE** ⏎
    ?/Create/Load/Set: **S** ⏎
    New entity linetype (or ?) ⟨BYLAYER⟩: **HIDDEN** ⏎

Once again the **LINETYPE** command options are redisplayed. Press [Enter] to exit the command. Any new entities created will now be drawn in the HIDDEN linetype until a different linetype is set current.

To save time and increase productivity, load the linetypes you use most often in your prototype drawing. Since a new drawing is based on the prototype, the linetypes you require will be preloaded. You need only set the desired linetype current before drawing.

### Listing linetypes

AutoCAD permits the creation of custom linetypes, or the modification of existing linetypes. This capability is covered in Chapter 19. The new or modified linetypes can be stored in the ACAD.LIN library file, or you can create an entirely new library file. The new file must have the .LIN extension. If you want to list the linetypes contained in an external library file, enter ? as follows:

        Command: **LINETYPE** ⌐
        ?/Create/Load/Set: **?** ⌐

If **FILEDIA** is set to 1, the **Select Linetype File** dialog box is then displayed. If additional linetype library files exist, they will appear in the **Files** list box along with the ACAD.LIN file. Enter the desired library file name in the **File Name:** text box, or accept the default ACAD.LIN file. Click the **OK** button or press [Enter]. The graphics window is then replaced with the text window which displays each of the available linetypes. To return to the graphics window, press the [F2] function key and exit the **LINETYPE** command by pressing [Enter].

**LINETYPE** can also be used as a *transparent command*. This means it can be used while you are working inside another command. When the transparent command is completed, the command you were using returns. Use the transparent command by entering an apostrophe (') before the command name, for example 'LINETYPE. Keep in mind, however, that you cannot begin a drawing command using one linetype, and then transparently use the **Set** to finish the command with another linetype. The newly set linetype will not become current until the drawing command in progress is terminated.

### EXERCISE 6-13

❑ Load AutoCAD for Windows and open PRODR1.
❑ Use the **LINETYPE** command to do the following:
  ❑ Look at the standard AutoCAD linetypes with the **?** option.
  ❑ Load the CENTER2 and HIDDEN2 linetypes.
❑ Save the PRODR1 drawing, but do not exit AutoCAD.
❑ Load four additional linetypes of your own choosing.
❑ Draw objects using each of the loaded linetypes. Remember that a linetype must be set current before it can be used.
❑ When you are done experimenting with the different linetypes, quit the drawing session without saving.

## ADDING COLOR TO THE DRAWING

You can change the color of any part of the drawing. Whether you are using a single layer or multiple layers, the color can be changed by typing COLOR at the **Command:** prompt. Then, enter the color name or number. The seven standard colors are:

- 1   Red
- 2   Yellow
- 3   Green
- 4   Cyan
- 5   Blue
- 6   Magenta

After entering the **COLOR** command, you are asked for the new color. Type the color name or number as follows:

Command: **COLOR**
New object color ⟨current⟩: *(type the color name or number,* BLUE *or 5 for example)*

**COLOR** is a transparent command. Enter 'COLOR to change the color while inside another command. Additional information on color is found in Chapter 19.

### EXERCISE 6-14

❑ Load AutoCAD and open PRODR1, or begin a new drawing using your own variables.
❑ Change the color to yellow. Use the **LINE** command to draw a 2 units by 4 unit rectangle.
❑ Change the color to blue. Use the **LINE** command to draw a 2 units by 4 unit rectangle.
❑ Save the drawing as A:EX6-14 and quit.

## INTRODUCTION TO PRINTING AND PLOTTING

A drawing created with CAD can exist in two distinct forms: hard copy and soft copy. The term *hard copy* refers to a physical drawing produced on paper by a printer or plotter. The term *soft copy* refers to the computer software version of the drawing, or the actual data file. The soft copy can only be displayed on the computer monitor, making it inconvenient to use for many manufacturing or construction purposes. If the power to the monitor is turned off, then the soft copy drawing is gone. A hard copy drawing, however, is extremely versatile in its uses. It can be rolled up or folded and taken down to the shop floor, or out to a construction site. A hard copy drawing can be checked and redlined without the need for a computer or CAD software. Although CAD is the new standard throughout the world for generating drawings, the hardcopy drawing is still a vital tool in industry.

AutoCAD supports two types of hard copy devices— printers and plotters. Printers and plotters take the soft copy images that you draw in AutoCAD and transfer them onto paper to make the hard copy. There are several types of printers including dot matrix, inkjet, laser, and thermal transfer. Dot matrix printers are normally used to make low-quality check prints, while inkjet, laser, and thermal printers may be used for quick check prints of formal drawings and the quality is generally much better. Print size for most of these printers is 8.5″ × 11″ or 8.5″ × 14″.

Large format hardcopy devices are commonly referred to as plotters. These include inkjet plotters, thermal plotters, electrostatic plotters, pen plotters, and pencil plotters. These plotters are capable of producing hardcopy with varying line widths and color output. The specific features of a plotter should be verified. Pen plotters have been the industry standard for preparing large format hardcopy. They are called pen plotters because they use liquid ink, fiber tip pens, or pens with pencil lead to reproduce computer drawings. Multi-pen plotters can provide different line thickness and colors. Even though pen plotters can plot very fast, it takes quite some time to plot a large complex drawing.

Since plotting with pen plotters can be time-consuming, they are rapidly being replaced in industry by inkjet, thermal transfer, and laser plotters. Laser printers and plotters draw lines on a revolving plate that is charged with high voltage. The laser light causes the plate to discharge while an ink toner adheres to the laser-drawn image. The ink is then bonded to the paper by pressure or heat. The quality of the laser printer or plotter depends mostly on the number of dots per inch (dpi). Laser printers are commonly 300 and 600 dpi. The thermal printer uses tiny heat elements to burn dots into treated paper. The electrostatic process uses a line of closely spaced, electrically charged wire nibs to produce dots on coated paper. Inkjet plotters spray droplets of ink onto the paper to produce dot-matrix images.

**PROFESSIONAL TIP**

The stereo lithography process involves using a movable table immersed in a bath of polymer. A laser beam is used to plot one very thin slice of a 3D CAD model on the tabletop. This has the effect of hardening the polymer wherever the beam passes. Then the table moves down slightly and the process continues until the entire object has been plotted into an accurate 3D model. Thus, an engineer can hold a prototype of the design in just minutes after completing the design. While AutoCAD does not yet "talk" directly to stereo lithography machines, it does output Stereo Lithography file formats (.STL). See chapter 17 for information on creating .STL files.

This chapter gives you an introduction to making prints and plots. Chapter 12 explores the detailed aspects of printing and plotting. Prints and plots are made using the **PLOT** command. This can be typed at the **Command:** prompt, by picking **Print...** in the **File** pull-down menu, or by picking the **Print** buttton in the **Standard** toolbar. Doing one of these things displays the **Plot Configuration** dialog box shown in Figure 6-36. Some of the features in the **Plot Configuration** dialog box are explained further in Chapter 12 of this text.

**PROFESSIONAL TIP**

Unlike other dialog boxes in AutoCAD for Windows that are controlled with the **FILEDIA** system variable, the **Plot Configuration** dialog box is controlled with the system variable **CMDDIA**. By default, **CMDDIA** is set to 1 (on) and will display the **Plot Configuration** dialog box regardless of the current value of **FILEDIA**. When **CMDDIA** is set to 0 (off), all printing and plotting parameters are specified in response to prompts on the command line.

## Device and default selection

As you look at the **Plot Configuration** dialog box, notice the **Device and Default Information** area in the upper-left corner. This is where AutoCAD for Windows displays information about the currently configured printer or plotter. For now, it is assumed that your instructor or CAD systems manager has taken care of the device and default selections.

## Pen parameters

The **Pen Parameters** area in the **Plot Configuration** dialog box allow you to set pen parameters based on your drawing standards or the type of printer/plotter you are using. You should be able to make a print at this time without changing any pen parameters. If not, these settings should be set by your instructor or your CAD systems manager. You will learn to make your own settings in Chapter 12 of this text.

## Additional parameters

Look at the **Additional Parameters** area of the **Plot Configuration** dialog box in Figure 6-36. You can see the options for the part of a drawing to be plottted, and how it is to be plotted. The options are **Display**, **Extents**, **Limits**, **View**, and **Window**. They are shown with radio buttons, and only one option can be selected at a time.

Figure 6-36.   The **Plot Configuration** dialog box.

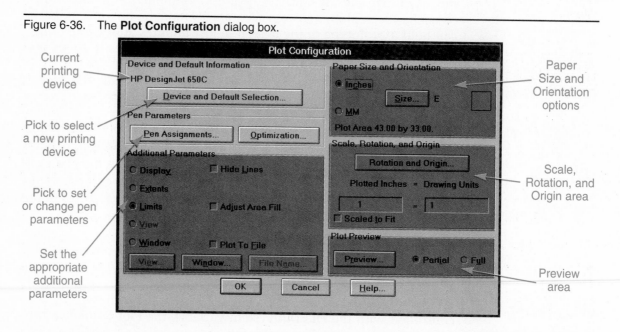

The following describes the function of each option:
- **Display.** This option prints or plots the current screen display.
- **Extents.** The **Extents** option prints or plots only the area of the drawing where objects (entities) are drawn. Before using this option, zoom the extents to verify exactly what will be plotted. Be aware that border lines around your drawing (like the title block) may be clipped off if they are at the extreme edges of the screen. This often happens because you are requesting the plotter to plot at the extreme edge of its active area.
- **Limits.** This option plots everything inside the defined drawing limits.
- **View.** Views saved with the **VIEW** command are plotted using this option. Until a view name has been provided, this option button is grayed-out. To specify a view name, pick the **View...** button to display the **View Name** subdialog box. Select the name of the view you want plotted and then click **OK**. The view name you select does not have to be currently displayed on the screen, but the **TILEMODE** variable must be off (0) to plot any saved view from paper space.

- **Window.** This option button appears grayed-out until you click the **Window...** button to display the **Window Selection** subdialog box shown in Figure 6-37. This option requires you to define two diagonally opposite corners of a window around the portion of the drawing to be plotted. The corners can be chosen with your pointing device or entered as absolute coordinates. Enter the **First Corner** and **Other Corner** coordinates of the desired window in the appropriate **X:** and **Y:** text boxes. If you want to define the window with your pointing device, click the **Pick** ⟨ button at the upper-left of the subdialog box. This clears the dialog boxes and redisplays the graphics window. You are then prompted at the command line to pick the window corners that surround the part of the drawing you want printed or plotted. After you have picked the corners, the **Window Selection** subdialog box is redisplayed. Click **OK** to return to the **Plot Configuration** dialog box.

Click the **Hide Lines** check box if you want to plot a 3D drawing with hidden lines removed. This function works the same as the **HIDE** command. Note that plotting takes a little longer when removing hidden lines since AutoCAD must calculate the lines to be removed. Do not check this box when plotting 2D drawings.

Activate the **Adjust Area Fill** check box if you want entities such as wide polylines, traces, doughnuts, and solids filled precisely. If you want to send the plot data to a file, pick the **Plot to File** check box. This activates the **File Name...** button. Pick this button to get the **Create Plot File** subdialog box.

Figure 6-37.   Specify a plot window using the **Window Selection** dialog box.

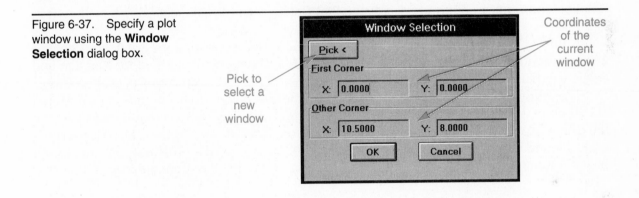

## Paper size and orientation

The upper-right area of the **Plot Configuration** dialog box shown in Figure 6-36 controls the paper size and orientation. Click either the **Inches** or **MM** option button to make inches or millimeters the units for all plot specifications.

Pick the **Size...** button to access the **Paper Size** subdialog box. This should already be set up by your instructor or CAD manager. You can make your own settings after studying Chapter 12. Also indicated is either landscape or portrait orientation. The orientation icon is a rectangle to the right of the **Size...** button. Figure 6-38A shows the icon in the landscape position and Figure 6-38B shows the portrait orientation. The term *landscape* comes from the idea that landscape artwork is normally displayed horizontally, while *portrait* artwork is usually prepared vertically.

Figure 6-38.   A—The landscape sheet size icon. B—The portrait sheet size icon.

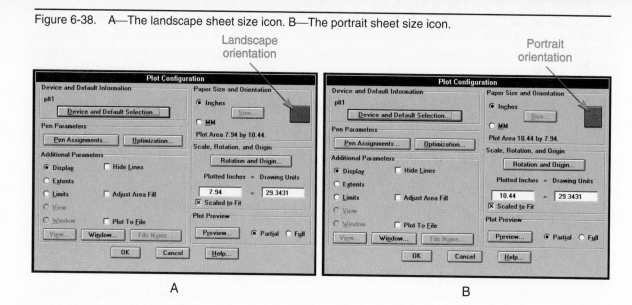

A                                                                 B

## Scale, Rotation, and Origin

Options to control the plot rotation and origin are located in the **Scale, Rotation, and Origin** area of the **Plot Configuration** dialog box. Refer back to Figure 6-36. Click the **Rotation and Origin...** button to access the **Plot Rotation and Origin** subdialog box shown in Figure 6-39.

AutoCAD can rotate plots in 90° clockwise increments. The options are **0**, **90**, **180**, and **270** for rotation settings. These are located in the **Plot Rotation** area of the **Plot Rotation and Origin** subdialog box. Figure 6-40 illustrates the result of the 90° increments of plot rotation.

The origin of a pen plotter is the lower-left of the plot media. To begin plotting a drawing at that point, leave the values shown in the **Plot Origin** text boxes at 0.00. If you want to move the drawing away from the default origin, set the required values in the text boxes accordingly. Remember that the units you enter should be consistent with the units specified with the option buttons in the **Paper Size and Orientation** area of the **Plot Configuration** dialog box.

Figure 6-39.   The **Plot Rotation and Origin** dialog box.

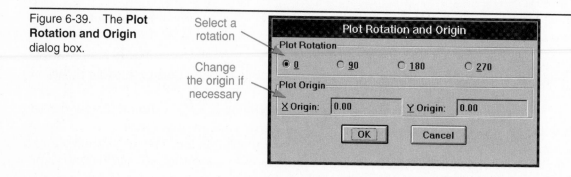

Figure 6-40.   An example of a drawing plotted at the different rotation angles.

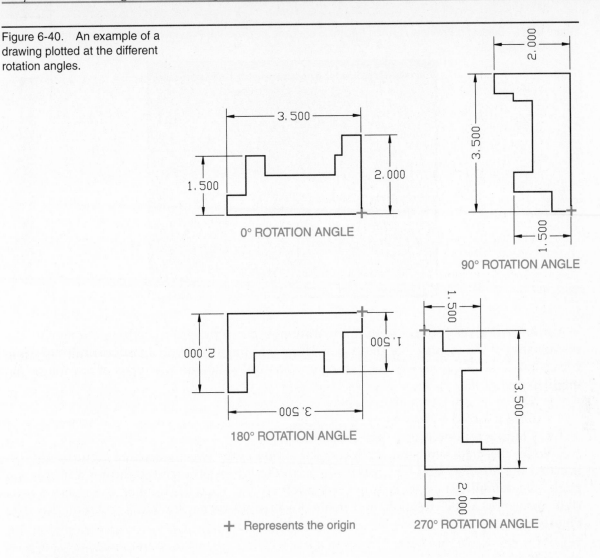

+ Represents the origin

## Scaling the plot

The **Plotted Inches = Drawing Units** text boxes (or **Plotted MM = Drawing Units** text boxes if using metric units) allow you to specify the plot scale as a ratio of plotted units to drawing units. Click the **Scale to Fit** check box if you want AutoCAD to automatically adjust your drawing to fit on the paper. For now, pick this box. You will study the other options in Chapter 12 of this text.

## Previewing the plot

The size and complexity of some drawings often makes the plotting time very long. By previewing a plot before it is sent to the output device, you can save material and valuable plot time. This feature is found in the **Plot Preview** area at the lower-right of the **Plot Configuration** dialog box. Refer back to Figure 6-36. The **Partial** and **Full** preview options are each controlled with a radio button.

When the **Partial** option is activated and you click the **Preview...** button, AutoCAD quickly displays the **Preview Effective Plotting Area** subdialog box shown in Figure 6-41. The red outline is the paper size. The paper dimensions are given at the bottom of the dialog box for reference. The area of the image is called the *effective area*. The blue outline is the effective area. The effective area dimensions are also given at the bottom with the paper dimensions. AutoCAD displays a red and blue dashed line when the effective area and the paper size are the same. While this shows you how the drawing compares to the paper size, the final plot depends on how the printer or plotter is set up.

Figure 6-41.   Selecting **Preview...** when **Partial** is checked displays the **Preview Effective Plotting Area** subdialog box.

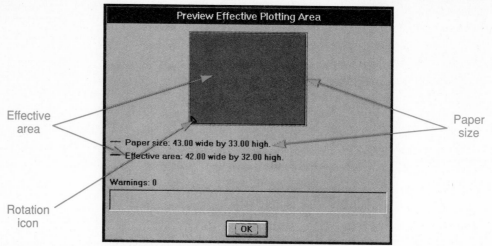

AutoCAD gives you messages in the **Warnings:** box if there is something wrong with the relationship of the display and the paper. These warnings give you an opportunity to make corrections and then preview the plot again. The following are the types of warnings you might expect.

- Effective area too small to display.
- Origin forced effective area off display.
- Plotting area exceeds paper maximum.

Notice the small symbol in the lower-left corner of the effective area in Figure 6-41. This is called the *rotation icon*. The rotation icon in the lower-left corner indicates a 0° rotation angle (the default). The icon is in the upper-left corner when the rotation is 90°, the upper-right corner for a 180° rotation, and in the lower-right corner for a 270° rotation. Refer to Figure 6-42.

Figure 6-42.   The rotation icon as it appears for each rotation angle setting.

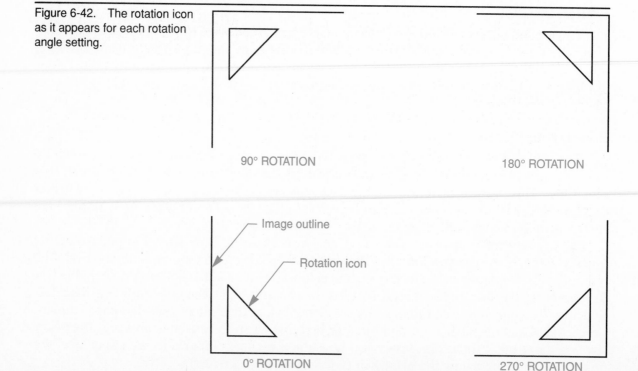

Pick the **Full** option button, then the **Preview...** button, if you want a full preview. The **Full** preview takes more time, but it displays the drawing in the graphics window as it will actually appear on the plotted hardcopy. This takes the same amount of time as a drawing regeneration so the drawing size determines how fast a full preview takes. AutoCAD displays a 0 – 100% meter in the lower-right corner of the **Plot Configuration** dialog box as the full plot preview is generated. The graphics window then returns with the drawing displayed inside the paper outline. At the same time, there is a **Plot Preview** dialog box positioned near the center of the screen. See Figure 6-45. If this dialog box obscures the drawing, you can move the box to a different location. To do so, move the cursor arrow to the title bar at the top of the dialog box, click and hold, then drag the dialog box to a more convenient location. Click the **End Preview** button to return to the **Plot Configuration** dialog box. The **Full** preview option also allows you to examine details on the drawing or evaluate how a multi-view arrangement fits together by clicking the **Pan and Zoom** button.

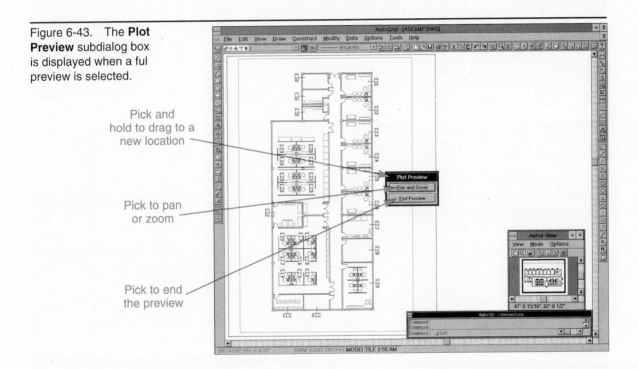

Figure 6-43.   The **Plot Preview** subdialog box is displayed when a ful preview is selected.

Pick and hold to drag to a new location

Pick to pan or zoom

Pick to end the preview

## Completing the print process

Setting up the **Plot Configuration** dialog box is easy. However, before you pick the **OK** button, there are several items you should check:
- Printer or plotter is plugged in.
- Cable from your computer to printer or plotter is secure.
- Printer has paper.
- Paper is properly loaded in the plotter and grips or clamps are in place.
- Plotter pens are inserted in the holder and the proper colors or thickness are in the correct places.
- Plotter area is clear for unblocked paper movement.

Pick the **OK** button when you are ready to send the print or plot to paper. You can also cancel or get help at any time by picking the **Cancel** or **Help** buttons. After you pick the **OK** button, you get one of the following messages:

Plot Complete, or
Position paper in plotter.
Press RETURN to continue or S to Stop for hardware setup.

If you get the second message, press the [Enter] key to send the drawing to the plotter.

**PROFESSIONAL TIP**

You can stop a plot in progress at any time by using the [Esc] key. Keep in mind that it may take awhile for some plotters or printers to terminate the plot, depending on the amount of the drawing file that has already been sent to the plotter or printer. You may also find it necessary to turn the plotter off and then turn it back on after pressing the [Esc] key. This action purges any remaining plot data from the plotter's internal buffer.

### EXERCISE 6-15

❑ Load AutoCAD and open any of your previous drawings.
❑ Access the **Plot Configuration** dialog box.
❑ There should be an X in the **Scale to Fit** check box, and the **Partial** and **Display** radio buttons should be highlighted.
❑ Pick the **Preview...** button and observe what happens. Pick **OK**.
❑ Pick the **Full** preview button and then pick the **Preview...** button to see the results. A full representation of your drawing should be displayed as it will appear when printed on the paper. Pick **End Preview**.
❑ Experiment by changing the rotation angle followed by doing a full preview each time.
❑ Pick the **Window...** button and then pick the **Pick⟩** button in the **Window Selection** dialog box. Window a small portion of your drawing and then pick OK.
❑ Do another full preview to see the results. End the preview.
❑ Pick the **Display** radio button, preview the drawing to see if it is what you want, and make a print if a printer is available for your use.
❑ Quit AutoCAD.

## USING DRAWING PLAN SHEETS

A good work plan generally saves drafting time in the long run. Planning should include sketches and drawing plan sheets. A rough preliminary sketch and completed drawing plan sheet help in the following ways:

- Determines the drawing layout.
- Sets the overall size or limits of the drawing by laying out the views and required free space.
- Confirms the drawing units based on the dimensions provided.
- Predetermines the point entry system and locates the points.
- Establishes the **Grid** and **Snap** settings.
- Presets some of the drawing variables, such as **LINETYPE**, **FILL**, and polyline width.
- Establishes how and when various activities are to be performed.

- Determines the best use of AutoCAD.
- Results in an even work load.
- Provides maximum use of equipment.

Drawing plan sheets may range in content depending on the nature of the drafting project. One basic drawing plan sheet is shown in Figure 6-44.

Figure 6-44.   A drawing plan sheet and project log combination. They are generally printed on the front and back of one piece of paper. (Courtesy of Harlton Terrie Gaines; Palmer, Alaska)

## DRAWING PLANNING SHEET      Page 1 of 2

The following information is to be furnished by the Assigned Project Engineer requesting design support:

PROJECT TITLE: _____

DISCIPLINE: _____

PROJECT NO. : _____      A.F.E. NO. : _____

PROJECT ENGINEER: _____      PHONE NO. : _____

CLIENT: _____

DRAWING SCOPE OF WORK: _____
_____
_____
_____

The following information will be furnished by the assigned Lead Designer:

LEAD DESIGNER: _____      PHONE NO. : _____

DISK NAME: _____

FILE NAME: _____      DRAWING NO.: _____

DWG. GHOST (SIZE & FORMAT): _____

DRAFTER: _____      PHONE NO. : _____

DATE ASSIGNED: _____      DATE REQUIRED: _____

DATE I.F.A. : _____      DATE I.F.C. : _____

ESTIMATED M.H. : _____      ACTUAL M.H. : _____

DRAWING STANDARD: _____      MAT'L SPEC.: _____

AFFECTED TAG NO'S:                    REFERENCE SHEETS

_____   _____   _____      _____   _____   _____
_____   _____   _____      _____   _____   _____

Freehand sketch by drafter:

Approved by: _____      Date: _____

Figure 6-44.   (Continued)

**DRAWING PLANNING SHEET**          Page 2 of 2

Drafters notes: _____

_____
_____
_____
_____
_____
_____
_____
_____
_____

Commands used by the drafter:

| Commands | Values | Commands | Values |
|---|---|---|---|
| 1. | | 34. | |
| 2. | | 35. | |
| 3. | | 36. | |
| 4. | | 37. | |
| 5. | | 38. | |
| 6. | | 39. | |
| 7. | | 40. | |
| 8. | | 41. | |
| 9. | | 42. | |
| 10. | | 43. | |
| 11. | | 44. | |
| 12. | | 45. | |
| 13. | | 46. | |
| 14. | | 47. | |
| 15. | | 48. | |
| 16. | | 49. | |
| 17. | | 50. | |
| 18. | | 51. | |
| 19. | | 52. | |
| 20. | | 53. | |
| 21. | | 54. | |
| 22. | | 55. | |
| 23. | | 56. | |
| 24. | | 57. | |
| 25. | | 58. | |
| 26. | | 59. | |
| 27. | | 60. | |
| 28. | | 61. | |
| 29. | | 62. | |
| 30. | | 63. | |
| 31. | | 64. | |
| 32. | | 65. | |
| 33. | | 66. | |

## CHAPTER TEST

*Write your answers in the spaces provided.*

1.  Give the commands and entries you must make to draw a line from point A to point B, to point C, back to point A. Then, return to the **Command:** prompt:

    Command:_____

    From point: _____

    To point:_____

    To point:_____

    To point:_____

    To point:_____

    Command:_____

2.  Give the commands needed to turn on the **Ortho** mode:

    Command:_____

    ON/OFF: _____

3.  Give the command and actions needed to quickly connect a line to an existing line, and then undo it because it was wrong:

    Command:_____

    From point: _____

    To point:_____

    To point:_____

    To point:_____

4.  Give the command sequence used to erase a group of objects at the same time and then bring them all back:

    Command:_____

    Select objects:_____

    First corner:_____

    Other corner: _____

    Select objects:_____

    Command:_____

5.  Give the command necessary to clean the screen:

    Command:_____

6.  Give the commands to change the linetype from a solid line to a centerline:

    Command:_____

    ?/Create/Load/Set: _____

    New entity linetype (or ?): ⟨continuous⟩: _____

7. Identify the following linetypes:

A. _____

B. _____

C. _____

D. _____

E. _____

F. _____

G. _____

H. _____

I. _____

J. _____

K. _____

A  ————————————————

B  - - - - - - - - - - - -

C  ————————— — · ————————

D, F, E (dimension line with arrows)

G  ————————————————

H  |- - - - - - - - - - -|

I  —————⌄————⌄—————

J  ——— - - ——— - - ———

K  ·····························

8. List two ways to discontinue drawing a line. _____

_____

_____

9. Name four point entry systems. _____

_____

_____

_____

10. Identify three ways to turn on the coordinate display. _____

_____

_____

11. What does a coordinate display of 2.750⟨90 mean? _____

_____

_____

12. What does the coordinate display of 5.250,7.875 mean? _____

_____

13. List four ways to turn on the **ORTHO** mode. _____

_____

_____

_____

_____

14. What do you enter at the **Command:** prompt if you want to have AutoCAD automatically repeat the **LINE** command? _____

_____

15. Identify two ways to continue drawing another line from a previously drawn line. _____

_____

_____

16. Name the screen menu where you can access several options that may be used for erasing applications. _____

_____

17. Define stacked objects. _____

_____

18. Name the command that you use if you want to draw new entities in red. _____

_____

19. How do you automatically use the **Window** selection method when you want to erase a group of objects? _____

_____

_____

_____

20. How do you automatically use the **Crossing** selection option when you want to erase three out of four lines of a square? _____

_____

_____

_____

21. How does the appearance of a window and crossing box differ? _____

_____

22. Name the command that is used to bring back the last object you erased before you issue another command. _____

23. What command and option do you use if you are drawing object lines and you want to change to draw hidden lines? _____

24. How do you get an alphanumeric screen showing the AutoCAD standard linetypes?

_____

25. List at least five ways to select an object to erase. _____

_____

_____

26. Define hard copy and soft copy. _____

_____

_____

_____

27. Identify three ways to access the **Plot Configuration** dialog box._____

_____

_____

_____

28. Describe the difference between the **Display** and the **Window** options for the **Plot Parameter** section. _____

_____

_____

_____

29. What is a major advantage of doing a plot preview? _____

_____

_____

30. Identify at least four reasons for using a drawing plan sheet. _____

_____

_____

_____

## DRAWING PROBLEMS

General

1. Draw an object by connecting the following point coordinates. Save your drawing as A:P6-1. Make a print of your drawing if a printer is available.

| Points | Coordinates | Points | Coordinates |
|--------|-------------|--------|-------------|
| 1 | 2,2 | 8 | @-1.5,0 |
| 2 | @1.5,0 | 9 | @0,1.25 |
| 3 | @.75⟨90 | 10 | @-1.25,1.25 |
| 4 | @1.5⟨0 | 11 | @2⟨180 |
| 5 | @0,-.75 | 12 | @-1.25,-1.25 |
| 6 | @3,0 | 13 | @2.25⟨270 |
| 7 | @1⟨90 | | |

General

2. With the absolute, relative, and polar coordinate entry methods, draw the following shapes. Be sure to use a drawing plan sheet. Set the limits to 22,17, units to decimal, grid to .5, and snap to .0625. Draw rectangle A three times using a different point entry system each time. Draw object B once using at least two methods of coordinate entry. Do not draw dimensions. Save your drawing as A:P6-2. Make a print of your drawing if a printer is available.

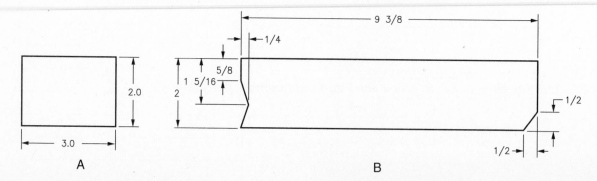

3. With the absolute, relative, and polar coordinate entry methods, draw the following object. Use a drawing plan sheet. Set the limits to 22,17, units to decimal, grid to .25, and snap to .0625. Use the **LINE** command. Do not draw dimensions. Save your drawing as A:P6-3. Make a print of your drawing if a printer is available.

*General*

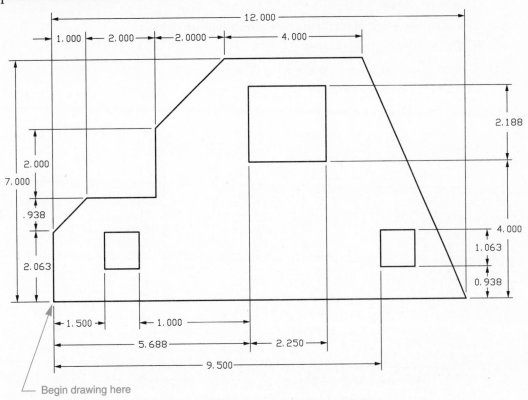

4. Edit problem **P6-3** so that it takes on the following changes. The dimensions shown are revisions and are not to be added. Save your drawing as A:P6-4. Make a print of your drawing if a printer is available.

*General*

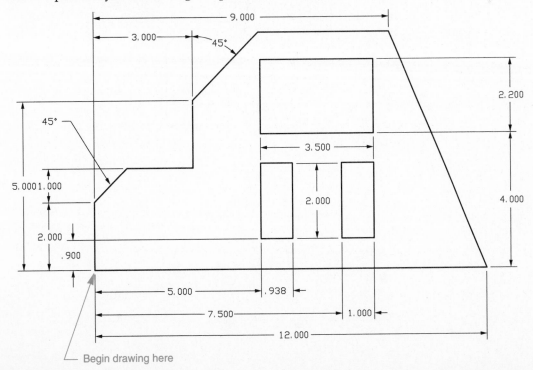

5. Draw the objects shown at A and B below using the following instructions:

   A. Use a drawing plan sheet.

   B. Draw each object using the **LINE** command.

   C. Start each object at the point shown and then discontinue the **LINE** command where shown.

   D. Complete each object using the **Continuation** option.

   E. Do not draw dimensions.

   F. Save the drawings as A:P6-5.

   G. Make a print of your drawing if a printer is available.

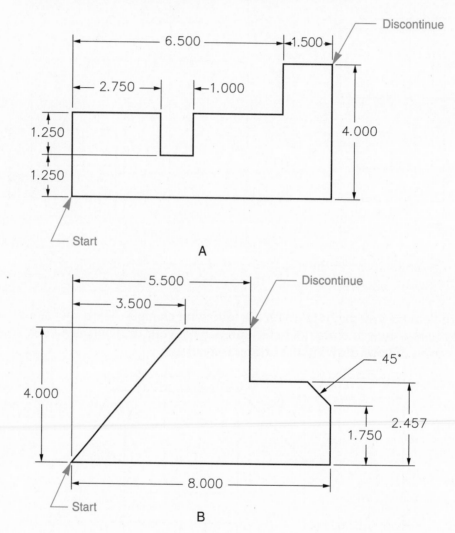

A

B

6.  Draw the plot plan shown below. Use the linetypes shown, which include:

   A. ACAD—CONTINUOUS, HIDDEN, PHANTOM, and CENTERLINE.

   B. LTYPESHP—FENCELINE1 and GAS-LINE.

   C. Make your drawing proportional to the given example.

   D. Save the drawing as A:P6-6.

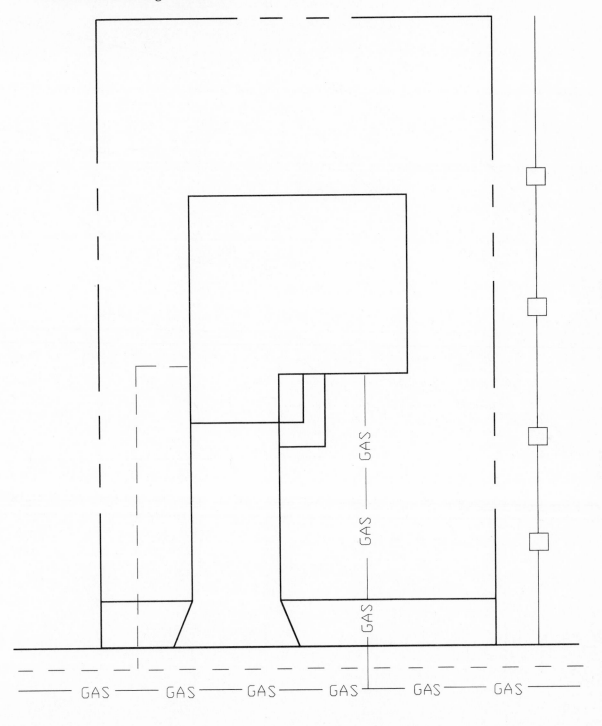

7. Draw the line chart shown below. Use the linetypes shown, which include:
   A. ACAD—CONTINUOUS, HIDDEN, PHANTOM, and CENTERLINE.
   B. LTYPESHP—FENCELINE1 and FENCELINE2.
   C. Make your drawing proportional to the given example.
   D. Save the drawing as A:P6-7.

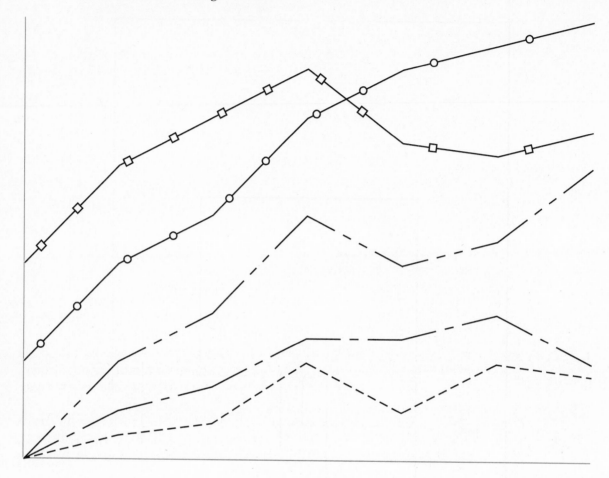

AutoCAD R13

# Chapter 7

# Introduction to Polylines and Multilines

## Learning objectives
After completing this chapter, you will be able to:
- ○ Use the **PLINE** command to draw objects.
- ○ Compare the results of using **FILL** on and off.
- ○ Explain the function of the **REDRAW** command.
- ○ Draw objects using the **TRACE** command.
- ○ Use the **MLINE** command to draw features.
- ○ Create your own multiline styles with the **MLSTYLE** command.
- ○ Sketch with AutoCAD.

AutoCAD has two features that provide you with endless possibilities for design and drafting applications. These are polylines and multilines. This chapter introduces you to the use of polylines and fully explains how to create drawing features with multilines. You will also see how to freehand sketch with AutoCAD. A complete discussion of polylines is given in Chapter 18 of this text.

The term *polyline* is composed of the words "poly" and "line." *Poly* means many, and a polyline is a single object that can be made up of one or more varied width line segments. Polylines are drawn with the **PLINE** command and its options. Another command that works similar to the **PLINE** command is the **TRACE** command.

Multilines are combinations of parallel lines consisting of between 1 and 16 individual lines called *elements.* You can offset the elements as needed to create any desired pattern for any field of drafting, including architectural, schematic, or mechanical. Multilines are drawn using the **MLINE** command and related options.

## INTRODUCTION TO DRAWING POLYLINES    AUG 2

The **PLINE** (polyline) command is used to draw polylines. Polylines have advantages over normal lines because there are an unlimited number of possibilities, including:
- • Making thick or tapered lines.
- • Much more flexibility than lines drawn with the **TRACE** command (discussed later in the chapter).
- • Can be used with any linetype.
- • Can be used to draw a filled circle or doughnut shape using the **DONUT** command found in Chapter 8.
- • Can be edited using advanced editing features.
- • Closed polygons can be drawn.
- • The area or perimeter of a polyline feature can be determined without extra effort.
- • Arcs and straight lines of varying thickness can be joined as a single entity.

The **PLINE** command basically functions like the **LINE** command. However, there are additional options and all segments of a polyline are a single entity. To draw a polyline, you can pick the **PLINE** button from the **Draw** toolbar, pick **Polyline** from the **Draw** pull-down menu, or PLINE can be typed at the **Command:** prompt:

Command: **PLINE** ⏎
From point: *(select a point)*
Current line-width is 0.0000

A line width of 0.0000 produces a line of minimum width. If this line width is acceptable, you may begin by selecting the endpoint of a line when the following prompt appears:

Arc/Close/Halfwidth/Length/Undo/Width/⟨Endpoint of line⟩: *(select a point)*

If additional line segments are added to the first line, the endpoint of the first line automatically becomes the starting point of the next line.

## Setting the polyline width

If it is necessary to change the line width, type W (for width) at the following prompt:

Arc/Close/Halfwidth/Length/Undo/Width/⟨Endpoint of line⟩: **W** ⏎

When the **Width** option is selected, you are asked for the starting and ending widths. If a tapered line is desired, enter different values for the starting and ending widths at the following prompts:

Starting width ⟨0.0000⟩: *(enter a width and press [Enter])*
Ending width ⟨starting width⟩: *(enter a different width and press [Enter])*

The starting width that you select becomes the default for the ending width. Therefore, to keep the line the same width, press [Enter] at the **Ending width:** prompt. The following command sequence draws the line shown in Figure 7-1. Notice that the start and endpoints of the line are located at the center of the line.

Command: **PLINE** ⏎
From point: **4,4** ⏎
Current line-width is 0.0000
Arc/Close/Halfwidth/Length/Undo/Width/⟨Endpoint of line⟩: **W** ⏎
Starting width is ⟨0.0000⟩: **.25** ⏎
Ending width ⟨.2500⟩: ⏎
Arc/Close/Halfwidth/Length/Undo/Width/⟨Endpoint of line⟩: **8,4** ⏎

Figure 7-1. A thick polyline drawn with the **PLINE Width** option.

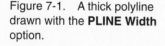

## Drawing a tapered polyline

Enter different starting and ending widths if you want to draw a tapered polyline, Figure 7-2. In the following example, the starting width is .25 units and the ending width is .5 units.

Command: **PLINE** ⏎
From point: **4,4** ⏎
Current line-width is 0.0000
Arc/Close/Halfwidth/Length/Undo/Width/⟨Endpoint of line⟩: **W** ⏎
Starting width is ⟨0.0000⟩: **.25** ⏎
Ending width ⟨.25⟩: **.5** ⏎
Arc/Close/Halfwidth/Length/Undo/Width/⟨Endpoint of line⟩: **8,4** ⏎

Figure 7-2.  Using **PLINE** to draw a wide tapered line.

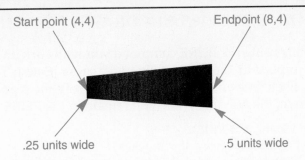

If you want to draw an arrowhead, give 0 as the starting width and then use any desired ending width.

## Using the **Halfwidth** option

The **Halfwidth** option allows you to specify the width from the center to one side. This is done by selecting the **Halfwidth** option of the **PLINE** command  and specifying the widths. Notice that the line in Figure 7-3 is twice as wide as the line in Figure 7-2.

Arc/Close/Halfwidth/Length/Undo/Width/⟨Endpoint of line⟩: **H** ↵
Starting half-width ⟨0.0000⟩: **.25** ↵
Ending half-width ⟨.2500⟩: **.5** ↵

Figure 7-3.  Using the **PLINE Halfwidth** option. Notice that a starting value of .25 produces a width of .5 units, and an ending value of .5 produces a width of 1 unit.

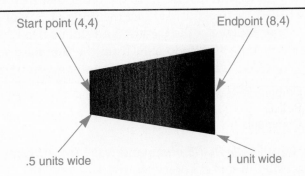

## Using the **Length** option

The **Length** option allows you to draw another polyline at the same angle as the previous polyline. To use this option, type L and give the desired length. For example:

Command: **PLINE** ↵
From point: (*pick a starting point for polyline number 1*)
Current line-width is 0.0000
Arc/Close/Halfwidth/Length/Undo/Width/⟨Endpoint of line⟩: (*pick the ending point for polyline number 1*)
Arc/Close/Halfwidth/Length/Undo/Width/⟨Endpoint of line⟩: ↵
Command: ↵
PLINE
From point: (*pick a starting point for polyline number 2*)
Current line-width is 0.0000
Arc/Close/Halfwidth/Length/Undo/Width/⟨Endpoint of line⟩: **L** ↵
Length of line: (*enter any desired length for polyline number 2*)
Arc/Close/Halfwidth/Length/Undo/Width/⟨Endpoint of line⟩: ↵
Command:

The second polyline is drawn at the same angle as the previous polyline, and at the length you specify.

## UNDOING PREVIOUSLY DRAWN POLYLINES

AUG 1

While using the **PLINE** command you may click on the **Undo** button in the **Standard** toolbar, or type U at the prompt line and press [Enter]. This erases the last polyline segment drawn. Each time you pick undo, another polyline segment is erased. A quick way to go back and correct the polyline while you remain in the **PLINE** command is as follows:

Command: **PLINE** ↵
From point: *(pick a starting point)*
Current line-width is 0.0000
Arc/Close/Halfwidth/Length/Undo/Width/⟨Endpoint of line⟩: *(pick the endpoint)*
Arc/Close/Halfwidth/Length/Undo/Width/⟨Endpoint of line⟩: *(pick another endpoint)*
Arc/Close/Halfwidth/Length/Undo/Width/⟨Endpoint of line⟩: *(pick another endpoint)*
Arc/Close/Halfwidth/Length/Undo/Width/⟨Endpoint of line⟩: **U** ↵
Arc/Close/Halfwidth/Length/Undo/Width/⟨Endpoint of line⟩: *(pick another endpoint or*
    enter U *again to remove an additional segment)*

After you type U followed by [Enter], the last polyline segment you drew is automatically removed. However, the rubber band cursor remains attached to the end of the polyline segment drawn previous to the last one. You can now continue drawing additional polyline segments, or type U again to undo more polyline segments. You can keep using the **Undo** option to remove all of the polyline segments up to the first point of the polyline. The polyline segments are removed in reverse from the order that they were drawn.

The **UNDO**, or **U**, command (*not* the **Undo** option of the **PLINE** command) works in much the same way. However, the **U** command can be used to undo any previous commands. This is done by picking the **Undo** icon from the **Standard** toolbar or typing U at the **Command:** prompt. AutoCAD gives you a message telling you which command was undone:

Command: **U** ↵
PLINE
Command:

In this example, the **PLINE** command was the last command undone. The **UNDO** command is discussed later in this chapter.

---

**EXERCISE 7-1**

❑ Load AutoCAD for Windows and open PRODR1, or begin a new drawing using your own variables.
❑ Use the **PLINE** command to draw several objects of your own design. Vary the width for each object.
❑ Draw three different types of arrows by specifying different starting and ending widths.
❑ Set the polyline width to .125. Draw a single polyline. Using the **Length** option, draw two more .125 wide polylines with a 4 unit length.
❑ Save the drawing as A:EX7-1 and quit.

---

## DRAWING THICK LINES USING THE **TRACE** COMMAND

When it is necessary to draw wide lines, the **TRACE** command can be used instead of the **PLINE** command. To use the **TRACE** command pick the **Trace** button from the **Pline** flyout in the **Draw** toolbox, or type **TRACE** at the **Command:** prompt. All of the **LINE** command procedures apply to **TRACE** except that the line width is set first, and it cannot be closed.

The current trace width is specified in brackets. Type .032 if you want to specify a trace width equal to the ANSI standard width for object lines. The following command and prompts produce a six-sided object. Try using the **TRACE** command while responding to the prompts as follows:

```
Command: TRACE ↵
Trace width ⟨current⟩: .032 ↵
From point: 2,2 ↵
To point: @6,0 ↵
To point: @2,2 ↵
To point: @0,3 ↵
To point: @–2,2 ↵
To point: @–6,0 ↵
To point: @0,–7 ↵
To point: 2,2 ↵
To point: ↵
Command:
```

When you use the **TRACE** command, the lines are made up of *trace segments*. The previous trace segment is not drawn until the next endpoint is specified. This is because trace segment ends are mitered to fit the next segment.

## EXERCISE 7-2

❑ Load AutoCAD for Windows and open PRODR1, or begin a new drawing using your own variables.
❑ Use the **TRACE** command to draw several objects of your own design. Vary the trace width for each object.
❑ Save the drawing as A:EX7-2 and quit.

## USING THE UNDO AND U COMMANDS 　　　　　　　AUG 1

Picking **Undo** from the **Edit** pull-down or typing UNDO at the **Command:** prompt works differently from using the **Undo** option of either the **PLINE** or **LINE** commands. The **UNDO** command can be used to undo any previous command. When you select the **UNDO** command, the following suboptions appear:

```
Command: UNDO ↵
Auto/Control/BEgin/End/Mark/Back/⟨Number⟩:
```

The default is Number. You designate the number of previous command sequences you want removed. For example, if you enter 1, the previous command sequence is removed. If you enter 2, the previous two command sequences are removed. When using this command, AutoCAD tells you which previous commands were undone with a message after you press [Enter]:

```
Command: UNDO ↵
Auto/Control/BEgin/End/Mark/Back/⟨Number⟩: 2 ↵
PLINE LINE
Command:
```

There are other options of the **UNDO** command. These are defined as follows:
- **Auto (A).** Entering A gives you the following prompt:

    ON/OFF ⟨current⟩: (*type* ON *or* OFF *and press* [Enter])

    With **UNDO Auto** turned on, any group of commands that are used to insert an item are removed together. For example, when a command contains other commands, all of the commands in that group are removed as one single command with **UNDO Auto** turned on. If **UNDO Auto** is off, each command in a group of commands is treated individually.

- **Control (C).** Allows you to decide how many of the **UNDO** suboptions you want active. You can even disable the **UNDO** command altogether. When you enter C, you get the following prompt:

  > All/None/One 〈All〉:

The control options do the following:
- **All (A)**—Keeps the full range of **UNDO** options active.
- **None (N)**—This suboption disables both the **U** and **UNDO** commands.

  > Auto/Control/BEgin/End/Mark/Back/〈Number〉: **C** ↵
  > All/None/One 〈All〉: **N** ↵

  You are now unable to use either the **U** or **UNDO** commands. If you try to use **UNDO**, all you get is the **Control** options:

  > Command: **UNDO** ↵
  > All/None/One 〈All〉:

  You must activate the **UNDO** options by pressing [Enter] for **All** or entering O for the **One** mode. If you have **U** and **UNDO** disabled and try to use the **U** command, AutoCAD gives you this message:

  > Command: **U** ↵
  > U command disabled: Use UNDO command to turn it on

- **One (O)**–This suboption limits **UNDO** to one operation only:

  > Auto/Control/BEgin/End/Mark/Back/〈Number〉: **C** ↵
  > All/None/One 〈All〉: **O** ↵

  Now, when you enter the **UNDO** command, you get the following prompt:

  > Command: **UNDO** ↵
  > Control/〈1〉:

  You can press [Enter] to undo only the previous command, or enter C to return to the **Control** options. With **One** active, you can remove only those items drawn with the previous command. AutoCAD acknowledges this with the message:

  > Command: **UNDO** ↵
  > Control/〈1〉: ↵
  > LINE
  > Everything has been undone
  > Command:

**PROFESSIONAL TIP**

When you use the **UNDO** command, AutoCAD maintains an "undo" file. This file saves previously used **UNDO** commands. All **UNDO** entries saved before disabling **UNDO** with the **Control None** option are discarded. This frees up some disk space, and may be valuable information for you to keep in mind if you ever get close to a full disk situation. If you want to continue using **U** or **UNDO** to some extent, then you might consider using the **UNDO Control One** suboption. This allows you to keep using **U** and **UNDO** to a limited extent while freeing disk space holding current **UNDO** information.

- **Begin (BE) and End (E).** These **UNDO** options work together to cause a group of commands to be treated as a single command. Entering the **U** command removes commands that follow the **Begin** suboption but precede the **End** suboption. These options can be used if you can anticipate the possible removal of a consecutive group of commands. For example, if you think you may want to undo the next three commands all together, then do the following:

> Command: **UNDO** ↵
> Auto/Control/BEgin/End/Mark/Back/⟨Number⟩: **BE** ↵
> Command: **LINE** ↵
> From point: *(pick a point)*
> To point: *(pick other endpoint)*
> To point: ↵
> Command: **PLINE** ↵
> From point: *(pick one endpoint)*
> Current line-width is 0.0000
> Arc/Close/Halfwidth/Length/Undo/Width/⟨Endpoint of line⟩: *(pick the other end point of the polyline)*
> Arc/Close/Halfwidth/Length/Undo/Width/⟨Endpoint of line⟩: ↵
> Command: **LINE** ↵
> From point: *(pick a point)*
> To point: *(pick other endpoint)*
> To point: ↵
> Command: **UNDO** ↵
> Auto/Control/BEgin/End/Mark/Back/⟨Number⟩: **E** ↵
> Command: **U** ↵

  This U undoes the three commands that you executed between entering **UNDO Group** and **UNDO End**.

- **Mark (M).** The **UNDO Mark** option inserts a marker in the undo file. The **Back** option allows you to delete commands "back" to the marker. For example, if you do not want any work to be undone by the **UNDO Back** option, then enter the **Mark** option following the work:

> Auto/Control/BEgin/End/Mark/Back/⟨Number⟩: **M** ↵
> Command:

  Then, use the **UNDO Back** option to undo everything back to the marker.

> Command: **UNDO** ↵
> Auto/Control/BEgin/End/Mark/Back/⟨Number⟩: **B** ↵

**PROFESSIONAL TIP**

The **UNDO Mark** option can be used to assist in the design process. For example, if you are working on a project and have completed the design on a portion of the structure you can mark the spot with the **Mark** option and then begin work on the next design phase. If anything goes wrong with this part of the design, you can simply use **UNDO Back** to remove everything back to the **Mark**.

- **Back (B).** This option undoes everything back to the last mark. If no marks have been entered, it will undo everything in the entire drawing. AutoCAD questions your choice with the following message:

> This will undo everything: OK? ⟨Y⟩:

If you want everything that you have drawn and edited to be undone, press [Enter]. If not, type N or NO followed by [Enter], or use [Esc].

## REDOING THE UNDONE

AUG 1

Type **REDO** or pick the **Redo** button from the **Standard** toolbar to bring back objects that were previously removed using the **UNDO** or **U** command:

Command: **REDO** ↵

**REDO** only works immediately after undoing something. **REDO** does *not* bring back polyline segments that were removed using the **Undo** option within the **PLINE** command.

---

### EXERCISE 7-3

❑ Load AutoCAD for Windows and open PRODR1, or begin a new drawing using your own variables.
❑ Use the **PLINE** command to draw the following:
  ❑ A rectangle 2 units by 4 units, 0 width.
  ❑ A rectangle 2 units by 4 units, .125 width.
  ❑ A line 6 units long with a .125 starting width and .250 ending width.
  ❑ A line 6 units long using the **Halfwidth** option. Starting width is .125 and ending width is .250.
❑ Use the **UNDO** command to remove the last three polylines.
❑ Use **REDO** to bring back the last removed polyline.
❑ Save the drawing as A:EX7-3 and quit.

---

## FILLING THE PLINE AND TRACE

AUG 2

In the discussion on the **PLINE** and **TRACE** commands, the results were shown as if they were solid, or filled in. You may decide to leave traces and polylines filled in, or show an outline. This is controlled by the **FILL** command, Figure 7-4. The **FILL** command only has **ON** and **OFF** options.

Command: **FILL** ↵
ON/OFF ⟨*current*⟩:

The value specified in brackets is the default, or previous setting. **FILL** may be turned on or off in the prototype drawing. When **FILL** is off, traces and polylines appear as outlines and the corners are mitered. After turning **FILL** off, type REGEN to have the fill removed.

---

Figure 7-4.   Examples of **FILL** when it is turned on and off.

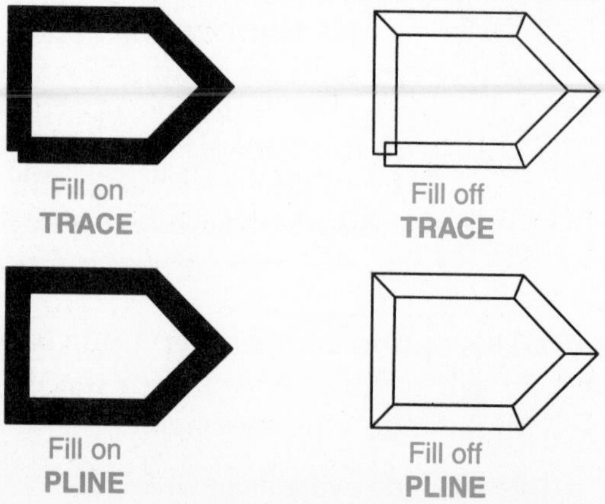

Fill on
**TRACE**

Fill off
**TRACE**

Fill on
**PLINE**

Fill off
**PLINE**

**PROFESSIONAL TIP**

When there are many wide polylines or traces on a drawing, it is best to have the **FILL** mode turned off. This saves time when redrawing, regenerating, or plotting a check copy. Turn the **FILL** mode on for the final drawing.

## EXERCISE 7-4

❑ Load AutoCAD for Windows and open PRODR1, or begin a new drawing using your own variables.

❑ Use the **TRACE** command to draw a 2 unit by 4 unit rectangle with a .125 line width. Draw another with .25 line width.

❑ Use the **PLINE** command to draw a rectangle 2 units by 4 units with .125 line width. Draw another with .25 line width.

❑ Turn **FILL** off and on and observe the difference.

❑ Use the **REGEN** command with **FILL** on and off, and notice the regeneration speed in each situation. There may not be much difference with a fast computer unless the file begins to get large.

❑ Save the drawing as A:EX7-4 and quit.

## DRAWING MULTILINES

AUG 2

The multiline function has two related commands: **MLINE** and **MLSTYLE**. The **MLINE** command actually draws the multiline. The **MLSTYLE** command allows configuration, or style, of the multiline to be set. A multiline consists of between 1 and 16 parallel lines. The lines in a set of multilines are called *elements*. The AutoCAD default style has two elements and is called STANDARD.

The **MLINE** command is accessed by picking **Multiline** button from the **Draw** toolbar, or by typing **MLINE** at the **Command:** prompt as follows:

```
Command: MLINE ↵
Justification = Top, Scale = 1.00, Style = STANDARD
Justification/Scale/STyle/⟨From point⟩: 2,2 ↵
To point: 6,2 ↵
Undo/To point: 6,6 ↵
Close/Undo/⟨To point⟩: 2,6 ↵
Close/Undo/⟨To point⟩: C ↵
Command:
```

Notice the familiar ⟨From point⟩: and ⟨To point⟩: prompts, plus some other options found in the **MLINE** command. These prompts work just as they did in the **LINE** command. The other options are **Close** and **Undo**. Use the **Close** option by typing C at the last prompt to close a polygon. Enter U during the command sequence to undo the previously drawn multiline segment. The object created in the previous command sequence is shown in Figure 7-5. Two lines are drawn because this is the STANDARD AutoCAD multiline style.

Figure 7-5. This multiline object was created with the command sequence given in the text.

## Multiline justification

Multiline justification determines how the resulting lines are offset, based on the definition points provided. The *definition points* are the points you enter when drawing the multilines. Justification can be specified only once during a single **MLINE** command sequence and is based on a counterclockwise rotation direction. The justification value is stored in the AutoCAD system variable **CMLJUST**. The justification options are **Top**, **Zero**, and **Bottom**. Top justification is the AutoCAD default, but the current value remains in effect until changed. To change the justification, enter J at the first prompt followed by the first letter of the desired justification format (T, Z, or B). Figure 7-6 shows the results of the three different justification options using the same point entries, as given in the following command sequence:

```
Command: MLINE ↵
Justification = Top, Scale = 1.00, Style = STANDARD
Justification/Scale/STyle/⟨From point⟩: J ↵
Top/Zero/Bottom ⟨top⟩:(type T, Z, or B, and press [Enter])
Justification = as specified, Scale = 1.00, Style = STANDARD
Justification/Scale/STyle/⟨From point⟩: 2,2 ↵
⟨To point⟩: 6,2 ↵
Undo/⟨To point⟩: 6,6 ↵
Close/Undo/⟨To point⟩: 2,6 ↵
Close/Undo/⟨To point⟩: C ↵
Command:
```

Figure 7-6.   Multiline justification options.

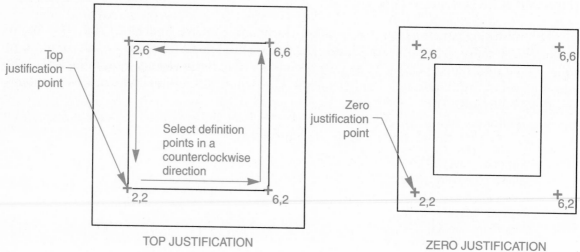

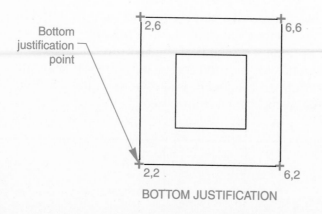

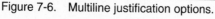

**PROFESSIONAL TIP**

As shown in Figure 7-6, the justification options control the direction of the offsets for multiline elements of the current style. These examples draw the multiline segments in a counterclockwise direction. Unexpected results can often happen, depending on the justification and drawing direction.

**EXERCISE 7-5**

❑ Load AutoCAD and open PRODR1, or begin a new drawing using your own variables.
❑ Use the **MLINE** command and justification options to draw three objects similar to the ones shown in Figure 7-6.
❑ Use your own point input that results in a layout that is similar to the illustration in Figure 7-6.
❑ Observe the difference between the justification options.
❑ Save the drawing as A:EX7-5 and quit.

## Adjusting the multiline scale

The **Scale** option controls the multiplier for the offset values specified in the **MLSTYLE** command. The multiplier is stored in the **CMLSCALE** system variable. For the command sequence given in the previous section, the **Scale** is 1.00. This means that the distance between multiline elements is 1 unit. In the case of **Zero** justification, the lines are offset 0.5 units on either side of the definition points picked. If the **Scale** value is 2, the result is 2 units offset for the **Top** and **Bottom** justification, and **Zero** offset of 1 and –1 each side of the definition points. Change the offset **Scale** to 2 by typing S and 2 at the appropriate prompts, as given below. Figure 7-7 shows a comparison between multilines drawn at several different offset **Scale** values.

```
Command: MLINE ↵
Justification = Top, Scale = 1.00, Style = STANDARD
Justification/Scale/STyle/⟨From point⟩: S ↵
Set Mline scale ⟨1.00⟩: 2 ↵
```

Figure 7-7.   Multiline scales.

SCALE = .25

SCALE = .5

SCALE = 2

SCALE = 1

**EXERCISE 7-6**

❑ Load AutoCAD and open PRODR1, or begin a new drawing using your own variables.
❑ Use the **MLINE** command and the scale option to draw three objects at scales similar to the ones shown in Figure 7-7.
❑ Use your own point input that results in a layout that is similar to the illustration in Figure 7-7.
❑ Observe the difference between the scales.
❑ Save the drawing as A:EX7-6 and quit.

### Setting your own multiline style

The **STyle** option in the **MLINE** command allows you to define multiline styles to be set as the current style. However, the multiline style has to be saved using the **MLSTYLE** command before it can be accessed. To use multiline styles that have been saved in the **MLSTYLE** command, type ST as follows:

> Command: **MLINE** ⏎
> Justification = Top, Scale = 1.00, Style = STANDARD
> Justification/Scale/STyle/⟨From point⟩: **ST** ⏎
> Mstyle name (or ?): **ROAD1** ⏎
> Justification = Zero, Scale = 1.00, Style = ROAD1

If you forget the name of the desired multiline style, you can type ? as follows to get the text screen shown in Figure 7-8:

> Justification/Scale/STyle/⟨From point⟩: **ST** ⏎
> Mstyle name (or ?): **?** ⏎

Figure 7-8. The AutoCAD text screen showing the loaded multiline styles.

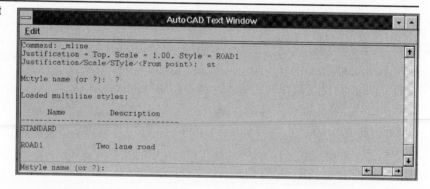

Styles are defined using the **MLSTYLE** command and stored in the **CMLSTYLE** system variable. The **MLSTYLE** command can be accessed by picking the **Multiline Style** button in the **Object Properties** toolbar, the **Multiline Style...** entry in the **Data** pull-down menu, or MLSTYLE can be typed at the **Command:** prompt. The **MLSTYLE** command displays the **Multiline Styles** dialog box. This is where multiline styles can be defined, edited, and saved. See Figure 7-9. Styles can be saved either to the drawing's symbol table, or externally in a file so they can be used in other drawings.

Figure 7-9. The **Multiline Styles** dialog box is used to define, edit, and save multiline styles.

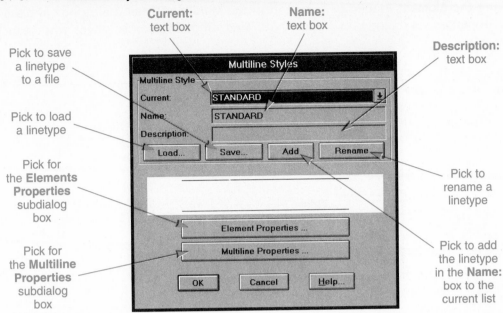

## Introduction to the Multiline Styles

Look at Figure 7-9. The options found in the **Multiline Style** part of the dialog box are described as follows:

- **Current: text box.** The **Current:** text box makes the identified multiline style current. This adjusts the value of the AutoCAD system variable **CMLSTYLE**. The use of this option provides a list box showing currently defined multiline styles. Use the down arrow to show the list and to pick the style that you want to make current. The only style listed is for the STANDARD AutoCAD multiline, until you create others.
- **Name: text box.** This is where you enter a new style name, but this is done after you have created a new style. This is discussed later in this chapter after you create a style.
- **Description: text box.** An optional description of your multiline style may be entered here. This is discussed later in this chapter after you create a style.
- **Load... button.** The **Load...** button allows you to load a multiline style contained in an external multiline definition file or from the symbol table of the current drawing. You can only load a style that has been created, so this is discussed again after you create a style.
- **Save... button.** The **Save...** button lets you save a style to an external file. The style is saved to an .MLN file. This is covered again later in this chapter after you have created a style.
- **Add button.** Pick the **Add** button after entering a multiline style name in the **Name:** text box. This adds the multiline style name to the **Current:** list.
- **Rename button.** Pick this button to rename a multiline style. The image tile in the center of the **Multiline Style** dialog box displays a representation of the current multiline elements.

## Using the Element Properties subdialog box

Picking the **Element Properties...** button in the **Multiline Styles** dialog box accesses the **Element Properties** subdialog box, Figure 7-10. This subdialog box is where you create new multiline styles.

Figure 7-10.   The **Element Properties** subdialog box is used to create multiline styles.

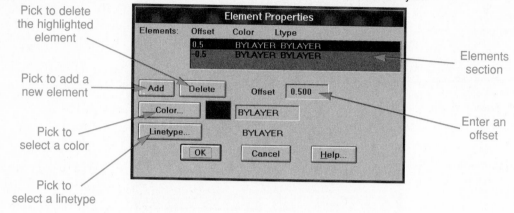

Pick to delete the highlighted element

Pick to add a new element

Pick to select a color

Pick to select a linetype

Elements section

Enter an offset

The following items describe how to use this subdialog box:

- **Elements: section.** This part of the dialog box displays the current **Offset** values, **Color**, and **Linetype**. Picking a set of elements highlights the items for further definition in this dialog box.
- **Add button.** Pick this button to add a new element to the multiline definition. Doing this adds an element with these settings: Offset = 0.0, Color = BYLAYER, and Ltype = BYLAYER. This allows you to draw a multiline element between the two existing elements shown in Figure 7-10.
- **Delete button.** Pick this button to delete the highlighted items in the **Elements:** list.
- **Offset text box.** Type either a positive or negative offset value for the highlighted offset in the **Elements:** list. Press [Enter] to accept what you type.
- **Color... button.** The **Color...** button accesses the **Select Color** subdialog box. Pick the desired color to change the color of the highlighted item in the **Elements:** list. Now the color is displayed in an image tile next to the **Color...** button.
- **Linetype... button.** Pick this button to get the **Select Linetype** subdialog box. Pick the desired linetype from the **Loaded Linetypes** list. Linetypes must be loaded before they can be used. Load needed linetype by picking **Load...** in the **Select Linetype** subdialog box followed by picking the linetypes from the **Load Linetypes** or **Reload Linetypes** subdialog box, and then pick **OK**. The selected linetype is now displayed at the highlighted items in the **Elements:** list.

If you add a new set of elements to the **Elements:** list, leave the color BYLAYER, and change the linetype to CENTER2, you get the display shown in Figure 7-10. Pick **OK** to leave the **Element Properties** subdialog box. The current status of the multiline is displayed in the **Multiline Style** image tile. You can continue in this manner to add up to 16 different color and linetype elements to the custom multiline style.

## Using the Multiline Properties subdialog box

You can continue to customize the multiline style by adding various end caps, segment joints, and background color by picking the **Multiline Properties...** button in the **Multiline Styles** dialog box. Doing this displays the **Multiline Properties** subdialog box shown in Figure 7-11. The following explains the options for you to use in the **Multiline Properties** subdialog box:

- **Display joints.** This is an on/off toggle for the display of joints. *Joints* are lines that connect the vertices between adjacent multiline elements. Joints are also referred to as *miters*. Figure 7-12 displays a multiline drawn with joints on and with joints off.

Figure 7-11.   The **Multiline Properties** subdialog box is used to customize a multiline style.

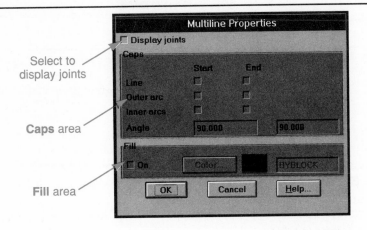

Figure 7-12.   How an object appears with multiline joints on and off.

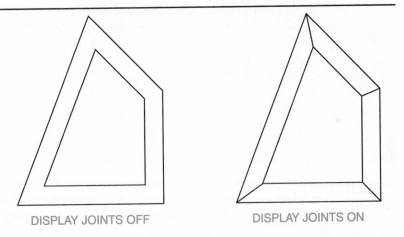

DISPLAY JOINTS OFF            DISPLAY JOINTS ON

- **Caps.** There are several selections in the category of caps that control the placement of end-caps on the multilines. End caps are lines drawn between the corresponding vertices of the beginning or ending points of the elements of the multiline. Caps can be set on either the start point, end point, or both points of the multiline. Arcs may also be specified. Arcs can be set to connect the ends of the outermost lines only, between pairs of interior elements, or both the outer and interior lines. These arcs are drawn tangent to the elements they connect. Drawing outermost arcs requires at least two multiline elements.

    You can also change the angle of the cap relative to the direction of the last drawn line segment. All you have to do to customize the end lines is to turn on or off the **Start** and **End** toggles in the **Caps** area as needed. An "X" in a box means that the end option is on. To change the ending angle, enter a new value in the **Angle** text boxes as desired. Figure 7-13 shows examples of several different end cap options.

Figure 7-13.   Several different
multiline end cap options.

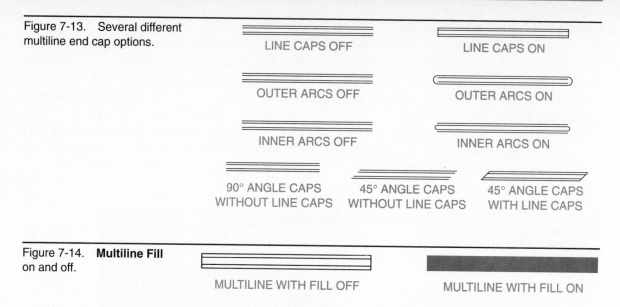

LINE CAPS OFF                    LINE CAPS ON

OUTER ARCS OFF                   OUTER ARCS ON

INNER ARCS OFF                   INNER ARCS ON

90° ANGLE CAPS        45° ANGLE CAPS        45° ANGLE CAPS
WITHOUT LINE CAPS    WITHOUT LINE CAPS    WITH LINE CAPS

Figure 7-14.   **Multiline Fill**
on and off.

MULTILINE WITH FILL OFF              MULTILINE WITH FILL ON

- **Fill.** If turned on, the multiline is filled with a solid fill pattern in the color specified using the fill color option. Pick the **On** switch to activate the **Color...** button. You can leave the color set BYLAYER or change it by picking the **Color...** button which displays the **Select Color** subdialog box. Figure 7-14 shows multilines drawn with **Fill** turned on and off.

## Steps in creating and drawing a multiline

Now that you have seen how the **MLINE** and **MLSTYLE** commands work, you can put it all together by creating and drawing your own multiline style. Suppose you need to draw a multiline for a two lane road to be used on a mapping project. The following procedure is used to draw the multiline:

1. Access the **Multiline Styles** dialog box, pick **Element Properties...** and set the following elements:

   | Elements: Offset | Color | Ltype |
   |---|---|---|
   | 0.25 | BYLAYER | BYLAYER |
   | 0.0 | BYLAYER | CENTER2 |
   | −0.25 | BYLAYER | BYLAYER |

2. Pick **OK**.
3. Pick the **Multiline Properties...** button in the **Multiline Styles** dialog box. Be sure the **Display joints**, **Caps**, and **Fill** toggles are turned off, and the **Caps Angle** is 90°.
4. Pick **OK**.
5. Type ROAD1 in the **Name:** text box in the **Multiline Style** area of the **Multiline Styles** dialog box.
6. In the **Description:** text box, type: TWO LANE ROAD WITH CENTERLINE.
7. Pick the **Save...** button in the **Multiline Styles** dialog box to get the **Save Multiline Style** subdialog box.
8. Double-click on the ACAD file, or pick ACAD and then **OK**.
9. Pick the **Load...** button in the **Multiline Styles** dialog box to access the **Load Multiline Styles** subdialog box.
10. Find the ROAD1 style and highlight it. Pick **OK**.
11. Pick **OK** to exit the **Multiline Style** dialog box.
12. Enter the **MLINE** command to draw the ROAD1 multiline. Set **Zero** justification like this:

```
Command: MLINE ↵
Justification = Top, Scale = 1.00, Style = ROAD1
Justification/Scale/STyle/⟨From point⟩: J ↵
Top/Zero/Bottom ⟨top⟩: Z ↵
Justification = Zero, Scale = 1.00, Style = ROAD1
```

If the **ROAD1** multiline style was not loaded in the **Multiline Style** dialog box but does exist, use the **STyle** option to access it. Then, draw the multiline shown in Figure 7-15 using the following command sequence:

```
Justification/Scale/STyle/⟨From point⟩: ST ↵
Mstyle name (or?): ROAD1 ↵
Justification = Zero, Scale = 1.00, Style = ROAD1
Justification/Scale/STyle/⟨From point⟩: 2,2 ↵
⟨To point⟩: 6,2 ↵
Undo/⟨To point⟩: ↵
Command:
```

Figure 7-15.   Drawing the ROAD1 multiline style.

---

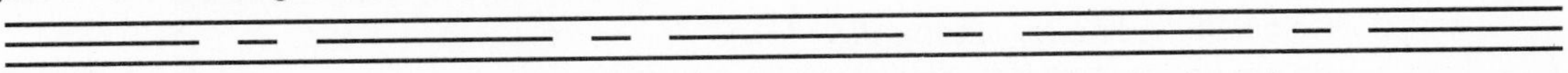

## EXERCISE 7-7

❑ Load AutoCAD and open PRODR1, or begin a new drawing using your own variables.
❑ Use the **MLSTYLE** and the **MLINE** commands to create and draw the following:
   ❑ A multiline with joints similar to Figure 7-12.
   ❑ Multilines with several end cap options similar to Figure 7-13.
   ❑ A multiline with **Fill** on.
   ❑ A multiline with a different linetype similar to Figure 7-15.
❑ Save the drawing as A:EX7-7 and quit.

## EDITING MULTILINES

| AUG 5 |
| :---: |

The **MLEDIT** command allows limited editing of multiline objects. The **MLEDIT** command can be accessed by picking the **Edit Multiline** button in the **Modify** toolbar or by typing **MLEDIT** at the **Command:** prompt. This displays the **Multiline Edit Tools** dialog box shown in Figure 7-16. The image buttons in this dialog box show you an example of what to expect when using each option.

Figure 7-16.   The **Multiline Edit Tools** dialog box has twelve different options. Refer to the text for an explanation of each option.

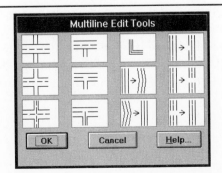

## Editing the crossing

The **Multiline Edit Tools** dialog box has four columns, each with three image buttons. The first (left) column displays three different types of intersections. Picking a button allows you to create the type of intersection shown. The name of the **MLEDIT** option is displayed in the lower-left corner of the dialog box when you pick an image button. The buttons in the first column are described below:

- **Closed Cross.** This option lets you create what is referred to as a *closed cross*. This is where the first multiline, called the foreground, remains unchanged while the second multiline is trimmed to intersect with the foreground multiline as shown in Figure 7-17. Note that the trimming is apparent, not actual. This means that the line visibility is changed, but it is still one multiline element. The command sequence is like this:

> Command: **MLEDIT** ↲ *(pick the* **Closed Cross** *image button and pick* **OK***)*
> Select first mline: *(pick the foreground multiline)*
> Select second mline: *(pick the intersecting multiline)*

The closed cross intersection is drawn. AutoCAD also issues a prompt to let you pick additional multilines for intersection, or type U to undo the intersection you just made. If you undo, AutoCAD gives the **Select first mline:** prompt again.

> Select first mline (or Undo): **U** ↲
> Select first mline: *(pick the foreground multiline)*
> Select second mline: *(pick the intersecting multiline)*
> Select first mline (or Undo): ↲
> Command:

Figure 7-17.    **MLEDIT Closed Cross** option.

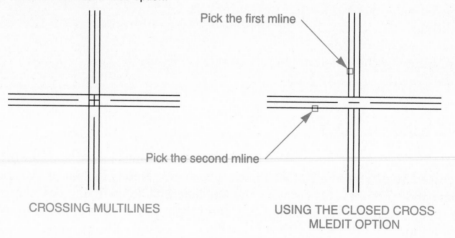

Pick the first mline

Pick the second mline

CROSSING MULTILINES

USING THE CLOSED CROSS
MLEDIT OPTION

- **Open Cross.** Select the **Open Cross** image button to trim all of the elements of the first picked multiline and only the outer elements of the second multiline are trimmed, as shown in Figure 7-18. The command sequence is the same as for the **Closed Cross**.
- **Merged Cross.** The **Merged Cross** image button allows you to trim all outer elements while all interior elements remain the same, as shown in Figure 7-19.

Figure 7-18. **MLEDIT Open Cross** option.

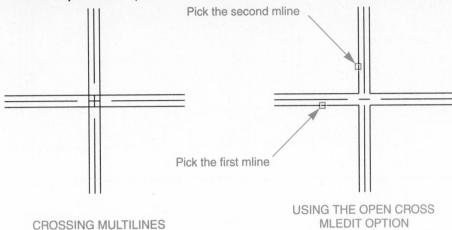

Pick the second mline

Pick the first mline

CROSSING MULTILINES

USING THE OPEN CROSS MLEDIT OPTION

Figure 7-19. **MLEDIT Merged Cross** option.

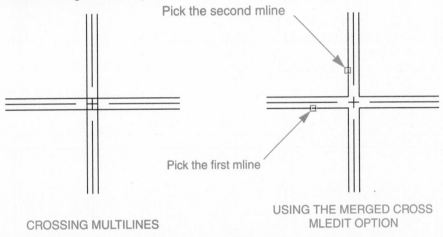

Pick the second mline

Pick the first mline

CROSSING MULTILINES

USING THE MERGED CROSS MLEDIT OPTION

## EXERCISE 7-8

❑ Load AutoCAD and open PRODR1, or begin a new drawing using your own variables.
❑ Use the **MLINE** and **MLEDIT** commands to do the following:
   ❑ Draw three sets of crossing multilines. Then, use the **Closed Cross** option to edit the first, **Open Cross** for the second, and **Merged Cross** to edit the third. Use Figure 7-17, Figure 7-18, and Figure 7-19 as examples.
❑ Save the drawing as A:EX7-8 and quit.

### Editing the tees

The second column of the **Multiline Edit Tools** dialog box is for editing tees. The **MLEDIT** tee options are illustrated in Figure 7-20. The options are described as follows:
- **Closed Tee.** Pick the **Closed Tee** option to have AutoCAD trim or extend the first selected multiline to its intersection with the second multiline.
- **Open Tee.** The first pick of the **Open Tee** option is the multiline to trim or extend and the second is the intersecting multiline. The intersecting multiline is trimmed and left open where the first multiline joins.
- **Merged Tee.** The **Merged Tee** option trims or extends the intersecting multiline by creating an open appearance with the outer elements and joining the interior elements.

Figure 7-20.  **MLEDIT Tee** options.

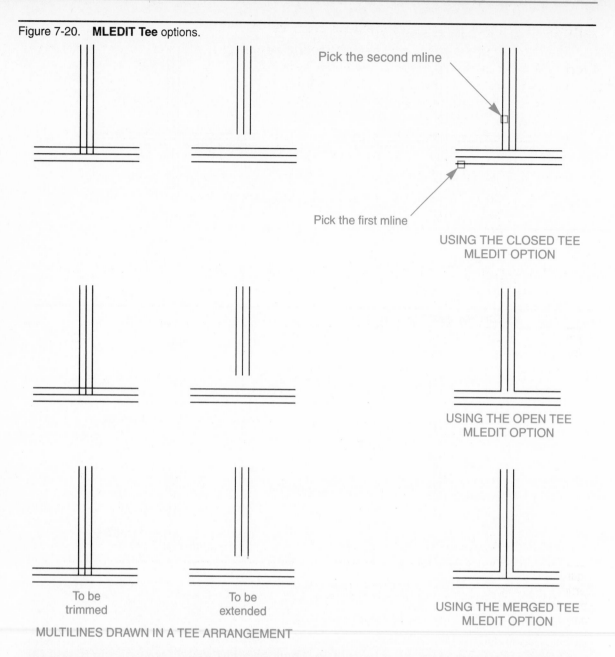

Pick the second mline

Pick the first mline

USING THE CLOSED TEE
MLEDIT OPTION

USING THE OPEN TEE
MLEDIT OPTION

To be
trimmed

To be
extended

USING THE MERGED TEE
MLEDIT OPTION

MULTILINES DRAWN IN A TEE ARRANGEMENT

### EXERCISE 7-9

❑ Load AutoCAD and open PRODR1, or begin a new drawing using your own variables.
❑ Use the **MLINE** and **MLEDIT** commands to do the following:
   ❑ Draw three sets of multilines that meet or nearly meet at a tee. Then, use the **Closed Tee** option to edit the first, **Open Tee** for the second, and **Merged Tee** to edit the third. Use Figure 7-20 as an example.
❑ Save the drawing as A:EX7-9 and quit.

## Editing the corner joint and multiline vertices

The third column of the **Multiline Edit Tools** dialog box has a corner joint option and vertex control options. These options are described below:

- **Corner Joint.** This **MLEDIT** option creates a corner joint between two multilines. The first multiline is trimmed or extended to its intersection with the second multiline, as shown in Figure 7-21.
- **Add Vertex.** This **MLEDIT** option adds a vertex to an existing multiline at the location where you pick, as shown in Figure 7-22. The command sequence is a little different than the previous options:

> Command: **MLEDIT** ↵ (*pick the* **Add Vertex** *image button and pick* **OK**)
> Select mline: (*pick the place on the mline for the new vertex*)
> Select mline (or Undo): ↵
> Command:

- **Delete Vertex.** The **Delete Vertex** option removes a vertex from an existing multiline nearest to the location where you pick, as shown in Figure 7-22.

Figure 7-21.  **MLEDIT Corner Joint** option.

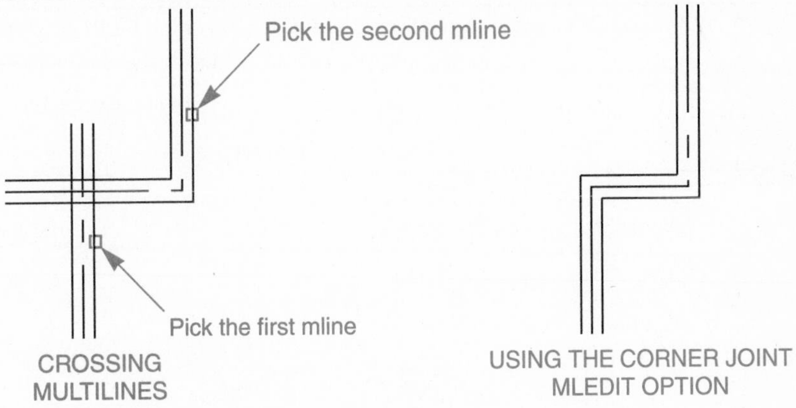

Pick the second mline

Pick the first mline

CROSSING
MULTILINES

USING THE CORNER JOINT
MLEDIT OPTION

Figure 7-22.  The **Add Vertices** and **Delete Vertices** options of the **MLEDIT** command.

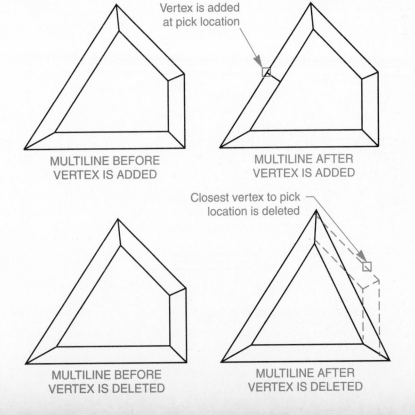

Vertex is added
at pick location

MULTILINE BEFORE
VERTEX IS ADDED

MULTILINE AFTER
VERTEX IS ADDED

Closest vertex to pick
location is deleted

MULTILINE BEFORE
VERTEX IS DELETED

MULTILINE AFTER
VERTEX IS DELETED

## EXERCISE 7-10

❏ Load AutoCAD and open PRODR1, or begin a new drawing using your own variables.
❏ Use the **MLINE** and **MLEDIT** commands to do the following:
  ❏ Draw multilines similar to the "before" example in Figure 7-21. Then, use the **Corner Joint** option to edit similar to Figure 7-21.
  ❏ Draw multilines similar to the "before" example in Figure 7-22. Then, use the **Add Vertex** and **Delete Vertex** options to edit similar to Figure 7-22.
❏ Save the drawing as A:EX7-10 and quit.

## Cutting and welding multilines

The fourth column of image buttons in the **Multiline Edit Tools** dialog box is for *cutting* a portion out of a single multiline element or the entire multiline, or connecting a space between multiline ends. AutoCAD refers to the connecting operation as *welding*. The options are illustrated in Figure 7-23.

Figure 7-23.   The **Cut Single**, **Cut All**, and **Weld** options of the **MLEDIT** command.

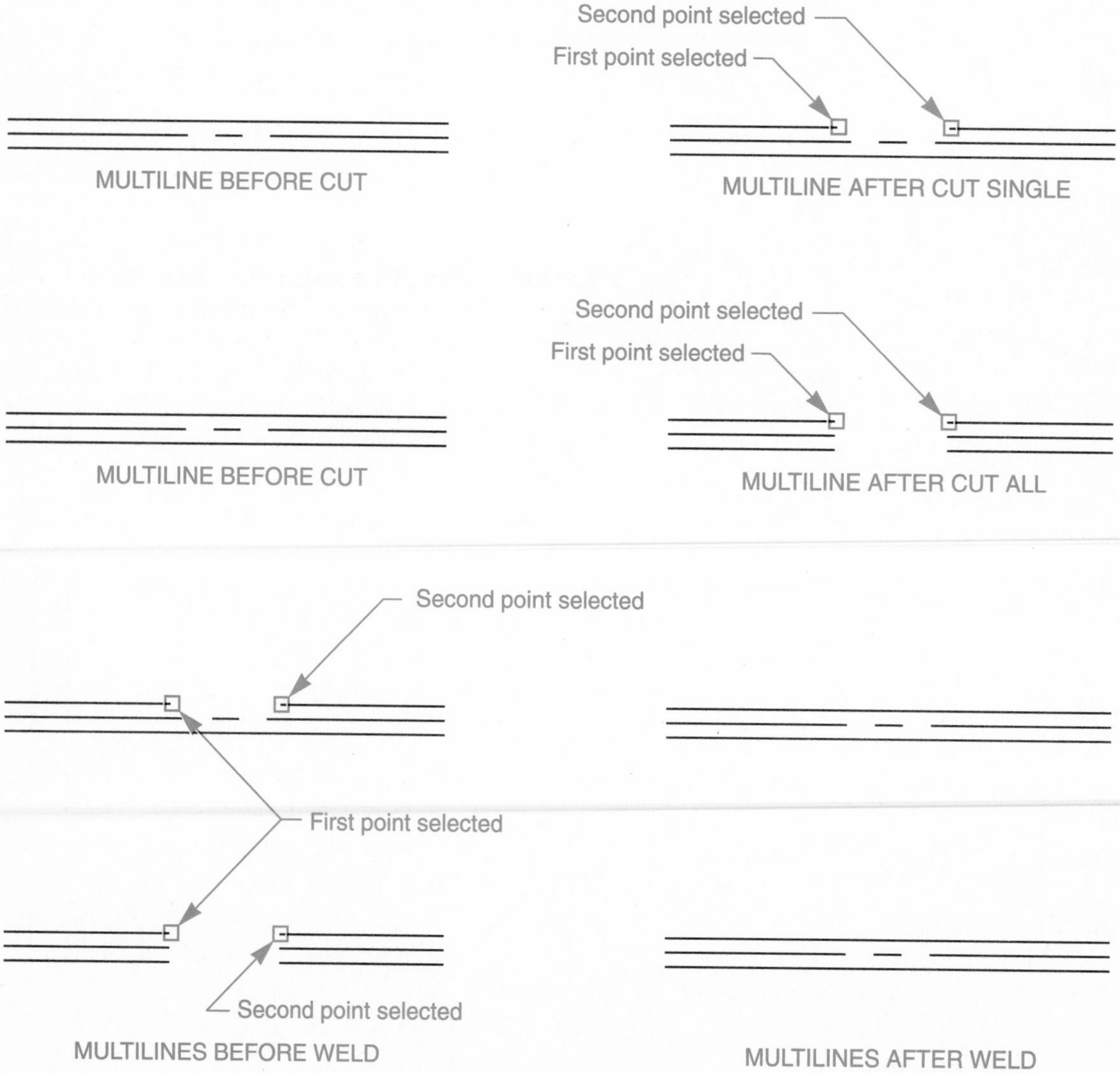

Second point selected
First point selected

MULTILINE BEFORE CUT

MULTILINE AFTER CUT SINGLE

Second point selected
First point selected

MULTILINE BEFORE CUT

MULTILINE AFTER CUT ALL

Second point selected

First point selected

Second point selected

MULTILINES BEFORE WELD

MULTILINES AFTER WELD

- **Cut Single.** This option allows you to cut a single element between two specified points. Cutting only affects visibility of elements, and does not separate a multiline object. The multiline is still a single object. AutoCAD uses the points you pick on the multiline as the cut points. Be sure you pick the points where you want the cut to occur, or enter U to undo the operation and try again. The command sequence is as follows:

> Command: **MLEDIT** ↵ *(pick the **Cut Single** image button and pick **OK**)*
> Select mline: *(pick the place for the first cut point on the mline)*
> Select second point: *(pick the place for the second cut point)*
> Select mline (or Undo): ↵
> Command:

- **Cut All.** This **MLEDIT** option cuts all of the elements of a multiline between specified points. The multiline is still a single object, even though it appears to be separated.
- **Weld All.** This option repairs all cuts in a multiline between two selected points.

**EXERCISE 7-11**

❑ Load AutoCAD and open PRODR1, or begin a new drawing using your own variables.
❑ Use the **MLINE** and **MLEDIT** commands to do the following:
  ❑ Draw multilines similar to those in Figure 7-23. Then, use the **Cut Single**, **Cut All**, and **Weld** options to edit the multilines similar to those shown in Figure 7-23.
❑ Save the drawing as A:EX7-11 and quit.

**PROFESSIONAL TIP**

Multiline objects are complex objects similar to blocks, and can be exploded. Multiline objects become individual line segments after being exploded. A block is a symbol that is created for future use. Blocks are discussed in detail in Chapter 25. The **EXPLODE** command is explained in Chapter 18, Chapter 22, and Chapter 25. The following is a brief look at the **EXPLODE** command sequence:

> Command: **EXPLODE** ↵
> Select objects: *(pick the object to explode)*
> Select objects: ↵
> Command:

## SKETCHING WITH AUTOCAD                     AUG 2

While the **SKETCH** command is not commonly used, it does have value for certain applications. Sketching with AutoCAD allows you to draw as if you are sketching with pencil and paper. The **SKETCH** command is sometimes used when it is necessary to draw a contour that is not defined by geometric shapes or straight lines. Examples of freehand sketching with AutoCAD include:

- Contour lines on topographic maps.
- Maps of countries and states.
- Architectural landscape symbols, such as trees, bushes, and plants.
- Graphs and charts.
- Graphic designs, such as those found on a greeting card.
- Short breaks, such as those used in mechanical drafting.

## USING THE **SKETCH** COMMAND                                    AUG 2

Before using the **SKETCH** command, it is best to turn **SNAP** and **ORTHO** modes off since they control the cursor's movement. Normally, you want total control over the cursor when sketching. The **SKETCH** command can be accessed from the keyboard or by selecting the **Sketch** button in the **Miscellaneous** toolbar. When you enter **SKETCH**, AutoCAD responds with the following:

> Command: **SKETCH** ⏎
> Record increment ⟨0.1000⟩:

The Record increment is the length of each sketch line element generated as you move the cursor. For example, if the record increment is 0.1 (default value), sketched images consist of 0.1 long lines. An increment setting of 1 creates sketched line segments 1 unit long. Reducing the record increment increases the accuracy of your sketched image. However, record increments less than .1 consume great amounts of computer storage. To view the chosen record increment, turn the **ORTHO** mode on and draw stair steps. Each horizontal and vertical element is the length of the record increment. If the **SNAP** mode is also on, the record increment automatically equals the snap increment. Figure 7-24 shows a comparison of .1 and 1 record increments.

Figure 7-24.    Sketching record increments.

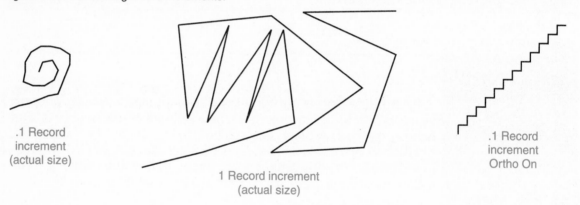

.1 Record
increment
(actual size)

1 Record increment
(actual size)

.1 Record
increment
Ortho On

To set a .1 record increment, type .1 and press [Enter], or press [Enter] to accept the default value.

> Record increment ⟨0.1000⟩: ⏎

AutoCAD then issues the following prompt:

> Sketch. Pen eXit Quit Record Erase Connect .

Once you see the **Sketch.** prompt, the buttons on your puck activate the **SKETCH** subcommands. If you do not use a puck, the subcommands may be entered at the keyboard by simply typing the capitalized letter in each option. The normal puck buttons for **SNAP** (4) and **ORTHO** (5) modes remain disabled as long as the **SKETCH** command is active. The following list shows the puck button and keyboard letters used to access each subcommand.

| Keyboard Entry | Puck Button | Subcommand Function |
|---|---|---|
| Pen (P) | 0 | Pen up, Pen down. |
| "." (period) | 1 | To draw a line from endpoint of sketched line. |
| Record (R) | 2 | Records sketched lines as permanent. |
| eXit (X, space, or Return) | 3 | Records sketched lines and exits **SKETCH** command. |
| Quit (Q, [Esc]) | 4 | Removes all entities created before R or X. |
| Erase (E) | 5 | Erases all entities created before R or X. |
| Connect (C) | 6 | Connects to endpoint of sketched line after a pen up has been issued. |

## Drawing sketched lines

Sketching is done with the **Pen** subcommand. It is similar to sketching with paper and pencil. When the pencil is "down," you are ready to draw. When the pencil is "up," you are thinking about what to draw next or moving to the next location. Type P to select "pen down," and sketch. You can also press your left mouse button to move the pen "up" and "down." Move your cursor around to create a line. Type P again to select pen up to stop sketching. When you type P or use puck button 0, the prompt line reads:

Sketch. Pen eXit Quit Record Erase Connect . ⟨Pen down⟩ ⟨Pen up⟩

**PROFESSIONAL TIP**

If you don't consider yourself an artist, trace an existing design. Tape it to a digitizer and move the cursor along the outline of the shape with the pen down. Don't forget to select "pen up" when moving to a new sketching location.

## Using the Period (.) subcommand

To draw a straight line from the endpoint of the last sketched line to a selected point, do the following:
1. Complete drawing the segment you are working on and make sure the "pen" is up.
2. Move the screen cursor to the desired point.
3. Type a period (.) or press puck button 1. A straight line is automatically drawn. If **ORTHO** is turned on, only vertical or horizontal lines are drawn.

## Using the Erase subcommand

You can erase while sketching. If you make a mistake, type E for the **Erase** command, or press puck button 5. The "pen" may be up or down. If the pen is down, it is automatically raised. AutoCAD responds with the message:

Erase: Select end of delete. ⟨Pen up⟩

Move the cursor to erase any portion of the sketch, beginning from the last point. When finished, type P or press pick button 0. If you decide not to erase, type E or press button 5. AutoCAD returns to the **SKETCH** command after issuing the message "Erase aborted."

### Recording sketched lines

As you sketch, the lines are displayed in color and are referred to as *temporary lines*. Temporary lines become *permanent lines*, and are displayed in their final color, after they are "recorded." You can record the lines and remain in the **SKETCH** command by typing R or pressing puck button 2. You can also record and exit the **SKETCH** command by typing X and pressing the right mouse button, the space bar, the [Enter] key, or puck button 3. AutoCAD responds with a message indicating the number of lines recorded. For example, suppose you created 32 lines, the message reads: "32 lines recorded."

### Quitting the SKETCH command

To quit the **SKETCH** command without recording temporary lines, type Q, press [Esc], or press puck button 4. This removes all temporary lines and returns the **Command:** prompt.

### Connecting the endpoint of the line

It is not uncommon to select "pen up" to pause or to make a menu selection. When the pen is up, return to the last sketched point and resume sketching by typing C or pressing puck button 6. AutoCAD responds with this message:

> Connect: Move to the endpoint of line.

Move the cursor to the end of the previously sketched temporary line. As soon as the crosshairs touch the previously drawn line, the pen automatically goes down and you can resume sketching.

### Consuming storage space with the SKETCH command

Sketching consumes computer storage rapidly. A drawing with fine detail will quickly fill your floppy disk. Therefore, the **SKETCH** command should be used only when necessary. The record increment should be set as large as possible, yet still appear pleasing. In commercial applications, such as topographical maps, the storage capacity is designed to accept the required input. Figure 7-25 shows a sketch of a rose. This drawing nearly filled one high-density 3.5" floppy disk (1,440,000 bytes).

---

Figure 7-25.   A rose drawn using the **SKETCH** command. (Courtesy of Susan Waterman)

## EXERCISE 7-12

❑ Load AutoCAD for Windows.
❑ Use the **SKETCH** command to sketch a bush, tree, or houseplant in plan (top) view.
❑ Save the drawing as A:EX7-12 and quit.

## CHAPTER TEST

*Write your answers in the spaces provided.*

1. Give the commands to draw a polyline from point A to point B with a beginning width
   of .500 and an ending width of 0. Then, undo the polyline as if you made a mistake.
   Finally, bring it back as if you realized you did not make a mistake:

   Command:_____

   From point: _____

   Current line-width is 0.0000 _____

   Arc/Close/Halfwidth/Length/Undo/Width/⟨End point of line⟩:_____

   Starting width ⟨0.0000⟩:_____

   Ending width ⟨.500⟩: _____

   Arc/Close/Halfwidth/Length/Undo/Width/⟨End point of line⟩:_____

   Arc/Close/Halfwidth/Length/Undo/Width/⟨End point of line⟩:_____

   Command:_____

   Auto/Back/Control/End/Group/Mark/⟨number⟩: _____

   Command:_____

2. Give the command and entries needed to draw two parallel lines, with a centerline
   between, with center justification, and end line caps, and the style is already saved
   as ROAD1:

   Command: _____

   Justification = Top, Scale = 1.00, Style = STANDARD _____

   Justification/Scale/STyle/⟨From point⟩: _____

   Mstyle name (or ?):  _____

   Justification = Top, Scale = 1.00, Style = ROAD1 _____

   Justification/Scale/STyle/⟨From point⟩: _____

   Top/Zero/Bottom ⟨top⟩: _____

   Justification = Zero, Scale = 1.00, Style = ROAD1 _____

   Justification/Scale/STyle/⟨From point⟩: _____

   ⟨To point⟩: _____

   Undo/⟨To point⟩:_____

3. How do you draw a filled arrow using the **PLINE** command?_____

   _____

   _____

4. Name two commands that can be used to draw wide lines. _____

_____

5. Which **PLINE** option allows you to specify the width from the center to one side? _____

_____

6. What is an advantage of leaving the **FILL** mode turned off? _____

_____

7. What is the difference between picking **Undo** from the **Pline:** screen menu and entering the **UNDO** command? _____

_____

_____

_____

8. Name the command that is used to bring back an object that was previously removed using **UNDO**. _____

9. Name the **MLINE** command option that establishes how the resulting lines are offset based on the definition points provided. _____

_____

10. Name the option that controls the multiplier for the offset values specified in the **MLINE** command. _____

11. How do you access the **Multiline Style** dialog box? _____

_____

12. Describe the function of the **Add** button in the **Element Properties** dialog box. _____

_____

_____

13. Describe the function of the **Linetype...** button in the **Element Properties** dialog box. ____

_____

_____

_____

_____

14. Define "end caps." _____

_____

_____

15. Name the **Multiline Properties Caps** options. _____

_____

16. Define "joints." _____

_____

17. What do you get when you enter the **MLEDIT** command? _____

_____

18. How do you access one of the **MLEDIT** options? _____

_____

19. List the three options that are used for editing crossings in the **MLEDIT** command. _____

20. Name the **MLEDIT** option where the intersecting multiline is trimmed or extended and left open where the first multiline joins. _____

21. Name the **MLEDIT** option that allows you to remove a vertex from a multiline. _____

22. Name the **MLEDIT** option that lets you remove a portion from an individual multiline element._____

23. Name the **MLEDIT** option that removes all of the elements of a multiline between two specified points._____

24. Name the **MLEDIT** option that repairs all cuts in a multiline._____

25. Explain why the **SNAP** and **ORTHO** modes should be turned off for most sketching applications. _____

---

## DRAWING PROBLEMS

1. Use the **PLINE** command to draw the following object with a .032 line width. Do not draw dimensions. Save the drawing as A:P7-1.

> Mechanical Drafting

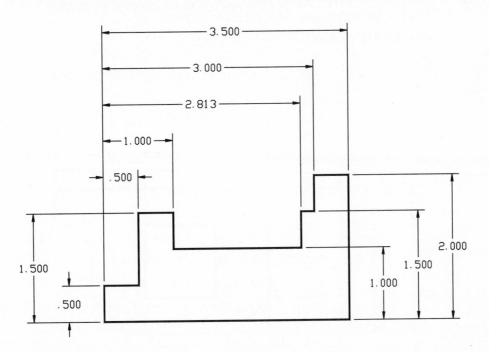

2. Use the **PLINE** command to draw the following object with a .032 line width. Do not draw dimensions. Save the drawing as A:P7-2.

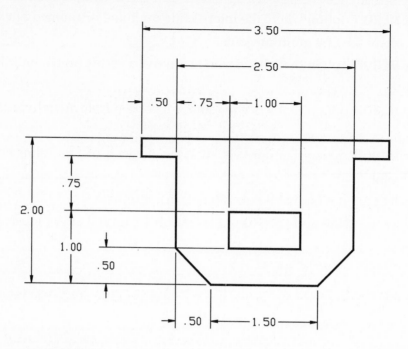

3. Use the **TRACE** command to draw the following object with a .032 line width. Do not draw dimensions.

A. Turn off the **FILL** mode and use the **REGEN** command. Then, turn on **FILL** and do **REGEN** again.

B. Observe the difference with **FILL** on and off.

C. Save the drawing as A:P7-3.

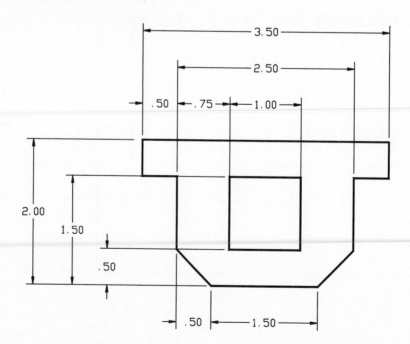

4. Use the **PLINE** command to draw the filled rectangle shown below. Do not draw dimensions. Save the drawing as A:P7-4.

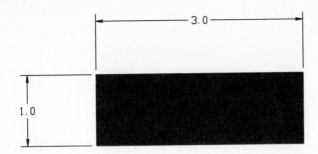

5. Draw the objects shown at A and B below. Then, use the **Undo** option to remove object B. Use the **REDO** command to get object B back. Save this drawing as A:P7-5.

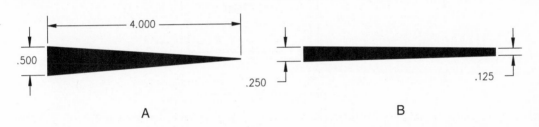

A                    B

6. Draw the object shown below. Set decimal units, .25 grid, .0625 snap, and limits at 11,8.5. Save your drawing as A:P7-6.

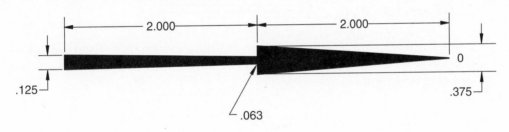

7. Draw the following objects using the **Multiline** command. Use the options indicated with each illustration. Set limits to 11,8.5, **Grid** at .50, and **Snap** at .25. Set the line offset to .125. Do not add text or dimensions to the drawings. Save the drawings as A:P7-7.

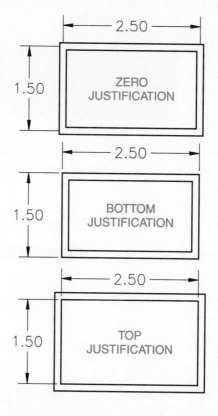

8. Draw the following objects using the multiline commands. Establish a line offset proportional to the given objects. Do not draw the dimensions or text. Save the drawing as A:P7-8.

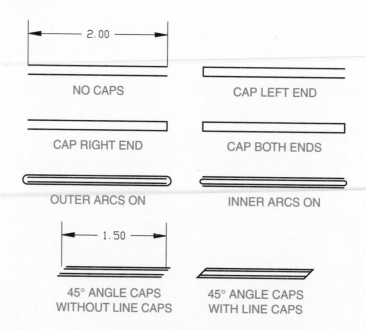

9. Draw the partial floor plan using the **MLINE** command. Carefully observe how the dimensions correlate with the double lines to determine your **Justification** settings. Also, use the **Cap** and **Break** options appropriately. Set limits to 88',68', **Grid** to 24, **Snap** to 12, and use architectural units. Make all walls 6" thick. Do not add text or dimensions to the drawing. Save the drawing as A:P7-9.

*Architecture*

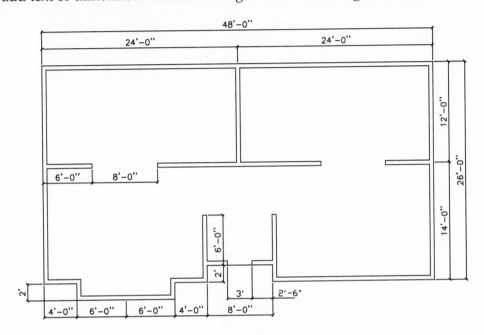

10. Draw the following proposed subdivision map using the multiline commands. Establish a line offset proportional to the given map. Use a centerline for the line-type at the center of the roads. The absolute coordinates are given at the road end and intersection centerlines. Do not draw the text. Save the drawing as A:P7-10.

*Civil Drafting*

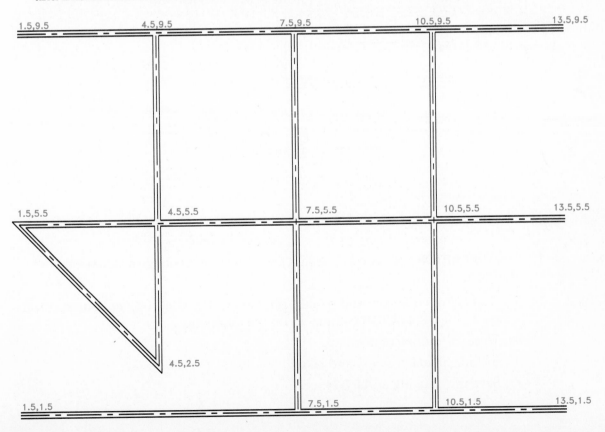

**Electronics Drafting**

11. Draw the following proposed electrical circuit using the multiline commands. Establish a line offset proportional to the given layout. Use a phantom line for the linetype at the center of the runs. The absolute coordinates are given at the connections. Do not draw the text. You establish any drawing features that are not defined by coordinates. Save the drawing as A:P7-11.

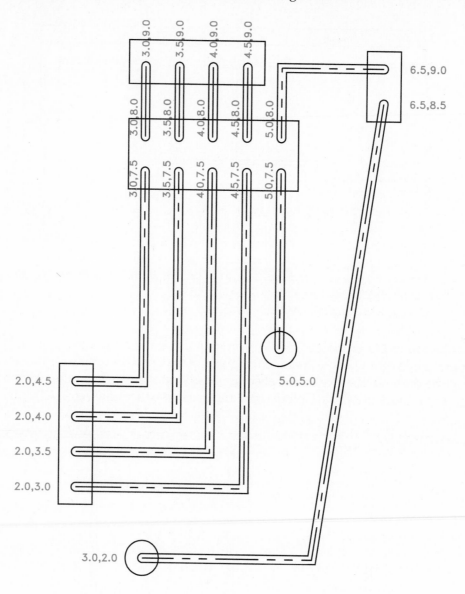

**General**

12. Use the **SKETCH** command to sign your name. Save the drawing as A:P7-12.

**General**

13. Use the **SKETCH** command to design the cover of a greeting card. Save the design as A:P7-13.

**Civil Drafting**

14. Find a map of your state and make a photocopy. Tape the copy to your digitizer tablet. Using the **SKETCH** command, do the following:

A. Trace the outline of the map.

B. Include all major rivers and lakes.

C. Save the drawing as A:P7-14.

**Chapter 8**

# Drawing Basic Shapes

## Learning objectives

After completing this chapter, you will be able to:

- ○ Use **DRAGMODE** to observe an object drag into place.
- ○ Draw circles using the **CIRCLE** command options.
- ○ Identify and use the **@** symbol function.
- ○ Draw arcs using the **ARC** command options.
- ○ Draw an arc extending from a previously drawn arc.
- ○ Draw an arc extending from a previously drawn line.
- ○ Use the **ELLIPSE** command to draw ellipses and elliptical arcs.
- ○ Draw polygons to given specifications.
- ○ Explain and use the **MULTIPLE** command modifier.
- ○ Draw doughnuts.
- ○ Preset polygon and doughnut specifications.

The decisions you make when drawing circles and arcs with AutoCAD are similar to those when drawing the items manually. AutoCAD provides many ways to create circles and arcs using the **CIRCLE** and **ARC** commands. These include the center location and radius or diameter, or where the outline of the circle or arc should be located. AutoCAD also provides the **ELLIPSE**, **POLYGON**, **RECTANG**, and **DONUT** commands. These commands can be used to draw a wide variety of shapes.

## WATCHING OBJECTS DRAG INTO PLACE

Chapter 6 showed how the **LINE** command displays an image that is "dragged" across the screen before the second endpoint is picked. This image is called a *rubberband.* The **CIRCLE, ARC, ELLIPSE, POLYGON**, and **RECTANG** commands also display a rubberband image to help you decide where to place the entity.

For example, when you draw a circle using the **Center Radius** option, a circle image appears on the screen after you pick the center point. This image gets larger or smaller as you move the pointer. When the desired circle size is picked, the dragged image is replaced by a solid-line circle, as shown in Figure 8-1.

Figure 8-1.   Dragging a circle to its desired size.

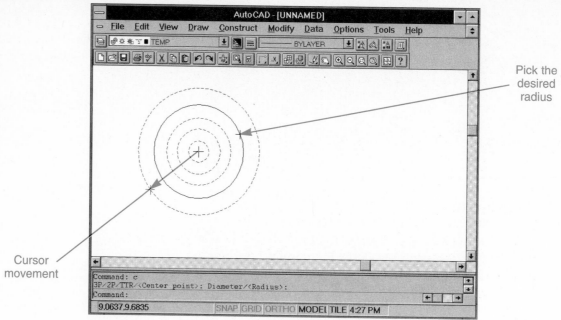

The **DRAGMODE** system variable affects the visibility of the rubberband. The **DRAGMODE** can be set to be on, off, or automatic by typing **DRAGMODE** at the **Command:** prompt and pressing [Enter] as follows:

Command: **DRAGMODE** ↵
ON/OFF/Auto ⟨*current*⟩: (*type* ON, OFF, *or* A *and press* [Enter])

The current (default) mode is shown in brackets. Pressing the [Enter] key keeps the existing status. Selecting **ON** turns **DRAGMODE** on. When **DRAGMODE** is on, you must enter DRAG during a command sequence to see the objects drag into place. Selecting **OFF** disables the **DRAGMODE.** This means that you will not see the objects drag into place. Even if you enter DRAG at the **Command:** prompt, AutoCAD will ignore the request. When you set **DRAGMODE** to **Auto**, you will automatically see objects dragged into place for all commands that support dragging. This is the default setting. Many users prefer to have the **DRAGMODE** set to **Auto**. However, some computer configurations slow down the drag process. When this occurs, you may prefer to turn **DRAGMODE** on or off. The following command sequence shows you how to activate the **DRAGMODE** while in the **CIRCLE** command.

Command: **CIRCLE** ↵
3P/2P/TTR/⟨Center point⟩: (*pick a center point*)
Diameter/⟨Radius⟩: **DRAG** ↵ (*the circle will drag into place as you pick the desired radius*)
Command:

---

**NOTE**

When AutoCAD is first installed, there are only seven pull-down menus displayed. These are **File**, **Edit**, **View**, **Data**, **Options**, **Tools**, and **Help**. This is the ACAD menu. This menu works well for users who are familiar with AutoCAD's command structure or who choose to use toolbars instead of menus. However, for this text you should load the full AutoCAD menu. This is called ACADFULL. To load this menu, simply type MENU at the **Command:** prompt. Then, select the ACADFULL.MNU file and pick the **OK** button. To change back to the default menu, type MENU and pick ACAD.MNU.

# DRAWING CIRCLES

AUG 2

The **CIRCLE** command may be issued by clicking the **Circle** icon in the **Draw** toolbar, selecting **Circle** from the **Draw** pull-down menu, or by typing CIRCLE or C at the **Command:** prompt. The **CIRCLE** command options can be seen in the **Circle** cascading submenu shown in Figure 8-2. The ACADFULL menu must be loaded to have the **Draw** pull-down menu.

Figure 8-2.   The **Circle** cascading submenu.

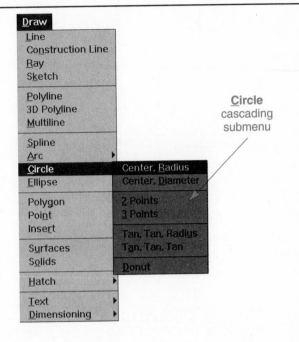

## Drawing a circle by radius

When you select the **Circle Center Radius** button in the **Draw** toolbar or the **Center, Radius** option in the **Circle** cascading submenu, AutoCAD asks you to first pick a center point. Then, either pick the radius on the screen or type the radius value, Figure 8-3. If the radius is picked on the screen, watch the coordinate display window to locate the exact radius. **Center, Radius** is the circle command's default option. The following is an example of using the **Center, Radius** option of the **CIRCLE** command:

> Command: **CIRCLE** ↵
> 3P/2P/TTR/〈Center point〉: *(select a center point)*
> Diameter/〈Radius〉: *(drag the circle to the desired radius and pick, or type the radius size and press* [Enter]*)*

Figure 8-3. Drawing a circle specifying the center and radius.

Pick a center point

Pick a point or type the radius

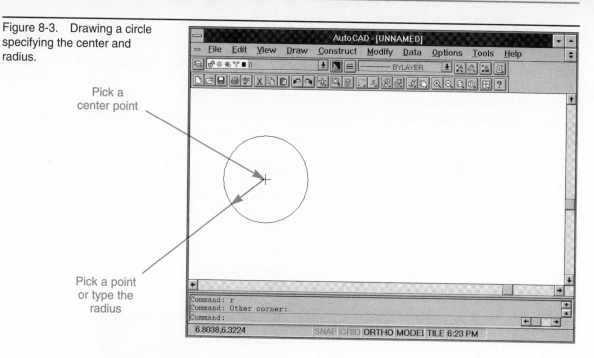

The radius value you enter becomes the default setting for the next time you use the **CIRCLE** command. Use the **CIRCLERAD** system variable if you want to set a radius default. This provides you with the same circle radius default value each time you use the **CIRCLE** command until you enter a different value for the variable. The **CIRCLERAD** system variable works like this:

> Command: **CIRCLERAD** ↵
> New value for CIRCLERAD ⟨*current*⟩: (*set the desired default, .50 for example*)

The **CIRCLE** command sequence then looks like this:

> Command: **CIRCLE** ↵
> 3P/2P/TTR/⟨Center point⟩: (*pick the center point*)
> Diameter/⟨Radius⟩ ⟨.50⟩: ↵
> Command:

When the **CIRCLERAD** system variable is set to a non-zero value, all you have to do is pick the center point of the circle and press [Enter] to accept the default value. You can always enter a different radius or pick a desired radius point if you want to ignore the default value. Set **CIRCLERAD** to 0 if you do not want a constant radius default.

## Drawing a circle by diameter

You can select the center point and the diameter of a circle by picking the **Circle Center Diameter** button from **Circle** flyout in the **Draw** toolbar. This option can also be selected by picking **Center, Diameter** in the **Circle** cascading submenu. If the **CIRCLE** command is entered at the **Command:** prompt, you must type a D for the **Diameter** option because **Radius** is the default:

> Command: **CIRCLE** ↵
> 3P/2P/TTR/⟨Center point⟩: (*select a center point*)
> Diameter/⟨Radius⟩: **D** ↵
> Diameter: (*drag the circle to the desired diameter and pick, or type the diameter size and press* [Enter])

Watch the screen carefully when using the **Center, Diameter** option. The pointer measures the diameter, but the circle passes midway between the center and the cursor, as shown in Figure 8-4. The **Center, Diameter** option is convenient because most circle dimensions are given as diameters.

Figure 8-4.   Drawing a circle using the **Center, Diameter** option. Notice that AutoCAD calculates the circle's position as you move the cursor.

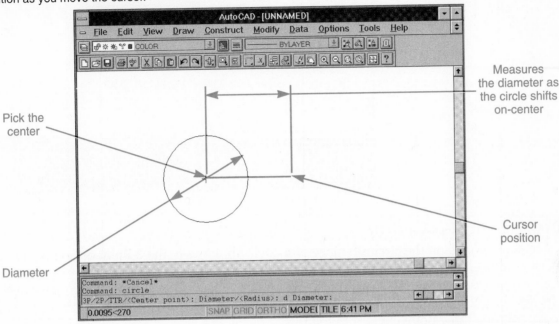

After you draw a circle, the radius you selected becomes the default for the next circle if **CIRCLERAD** is set to 0. If you use the **Diameter** option, the previous default setting is converted to a diameter. If you use the **Radius** option to draw a circle after using the **Diameter** option, AutoCAD changes the default to a radius measurement based on the previous diameter. If you set **CIRCLERAD** to a value such as .50, then the default for a circle drawn with the **Diameter** option is automatically 1.00 (twice the radius).

## Drawing a two-point circle

A two-point circle is drawn by picking two points on opposite sides of the circle, Figure 8-5. This option is useful if the diameter of the circle is known, but the center is difficult to find. One example of this is locating a circle between two lines. You can select the two points of the circle by picking the **Circle 2 Point** button from **Circle** flyout in the **Draw** toolbar. This option can also be selected by picking **2 Points** in the **Circle** cascading submenu. The command sequence for a two-point circle is as follows:

> Command: **CIRCLE** ↵
> 3P/2P/TTR/⟨Center point⟩: **2P** ↵
> First point on diameter: *(select a point)*
> Second point on diameter: *(select a point)*

AutoCAD uses the radius of the created circle as the default radius for the next time the **CIRCLE** command is used.

Figure 8-5. Drawing a circle by selecting two points on the circle.

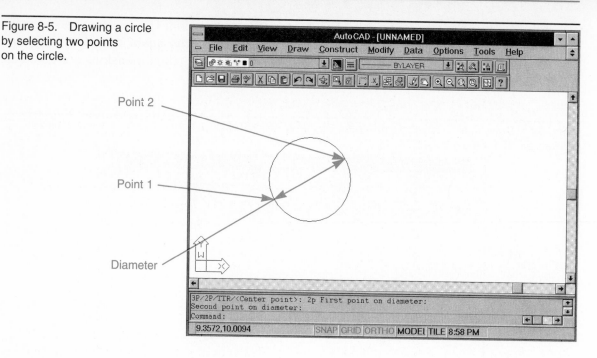

## Drawing a three-point circle

If three points on the circumference of a circle are known, the **3 Point** option is the best method to use. The three points can be selected in any order, Figure 8-6. You can select this option by picking the **Circle 3 Point** button from **Circle** flyout in the **Draw** toolbar. This option can also be selected by picking **3 Points** in the **Circle** cascading submenu. The command sequence for a three-point circle is as follows:

> Command: **CIRCLE** ⏎
> 3P/2P/TTR/⟨Center point⟩: **3P** ⏎
> First point: *(select a point)*
> Second point: *(select a point)*
> Third point: *(select a point)*

AutoCAD automatically calculates the radius of the circle and uses this value as the default for the next time the **CIRCLE** command is used.

Figure 8-6. Drawing a circle given three points on the circle.

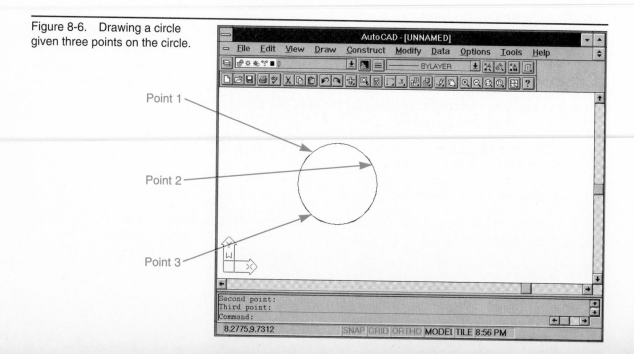

## Drawing a circle tangent to two objects

The term *tangent* refers to a line, circle, or arc that comes into contact with an arc or circle at only one point. That point is called the ***point of tangency***. A line drawn from the circle's or arc's center to the point of tangency is perpendicular to the tangent line. A line drawn between the centers of two tangent circles passes through the point of tangency. When you need to draw a circle tangent to given lines, circles, or arcs, pick the **Circle Tan Tan Radius** button in the **Circle** flyout. You can also select **Tan, Tan, Radius** from the **Circle** cascading submenu. Then, select the lines, or line and arc, that the new circle will be tangent to. The radius of the circle is also required. To assist you in picking the three objects, the screen cursor takes on the shape of a box and crosshairs. This is called an *aperture* and is discussed in detail in Chapter 9. When you see the aperture, move it to the objects that you want to pick. The command sequence for a circle tangent to two objects is as follows:

> Command: **CIRCLE** ↵
> 3P/2P/TTR/⟨Center point⟩: **TTR** ↵
> Enter Tangent spec: *(pick the first line, circle, or arc)*
> Enter second Tangent spec: *(pick the second line, circle, or arc)*
> Radius⟨current⟩: *(type a radius value and press* [Enter]*)*

If the radius entered is too small, AutoCAD gives you the message: Circle does not exist. If the **CIRCLERAD** system variable is set to 0, the radius you use for the **Tangent, Tangent, Radius** option becomes the default for the next circle. Two examples of this option are shown in Figure 8-7.

---

Figure 8-7. Two examples of drawing circles tangent to two given objects using the **Tangent, Tangent, Radius** option.

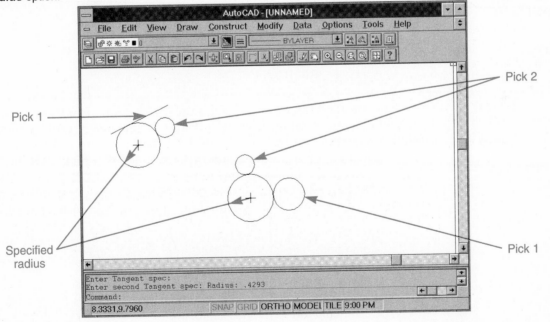

**PROFESSIONAL TIP**

Using the **CIRCLERAD** system variable to set a fixed default is helpful and saves drafting time when you plan to draw several circles with the same radius.

## Drawing a circle tangent to three objects

You can draw a circle tangent to three existing objects by using the **Tan,Tan,Tan** option in the **Circle** cascading submenu. This option creates a 3-point circle using the three points of tangency. The command sequence looks like the following, and is illustrated in Figure 8-8:

Command: _circle 3P/2P/TTR/⟨Center point⟩: _3p First point: _tan to (*pick an object*)
Second point: _tan to (*pick an object*)
Third point: _tan to (*pick an object*)
Command:

Figure 8-8. Two examples of drawing circles tangent to three given objects.

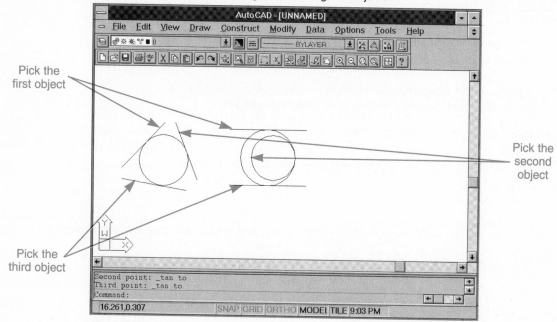

NOTE     The **Tan,Tan,Tan** option, unlike the **TTR** option, does not automatically recover when a point prompt is answered with a pick where no tangent exists. In such a case the **TAN** mode must be manually reactivated for subsequent attempts to make that pick. **TAN** (tangent) is one of the *object snap* modes discussed in Chapter 9. For now, if this happens type TAN and press [Enter] at the point selection prompt. This returns the aperture box so you can pick again as follows:

Command: _circle 3P/2P/TTR/⟨Center point⟩: _3p First point:
  _tan to (*pick an object*)
Second point: _tan to (*pick an object*)
Third point: _tan to (*you try, but fail to pick an object*)
No Tangent found for specified point.
Invalid 2D point.
Third point: **TAN** ↵
to (*pick an object*)
Command:

## The Copy Rad option

The AutoCAD screen menu for the **CIRCLE** command also contains the **Copy Rad** option. This menu is not visible by default and must be activated before it can be used. The process for activating the screen menu is covered in *AutoCAD and its Applications—Advanced, Release 13 for Windows*. Picking the **Copy Rad** option activates the AutoCAD geometry calculator (discussed in detail in Chapter 9). The **Copy Rad** option allows you to draw a circle with exactly the same radius as an existing circle or arc, or a polyline arc segment.

Figure 8-9 shows how to use the **Copy Rad** option with an existing circle. First, pick **Copy Rad** from the **Circle:** screen menu. Then, use the following command sequence:

> New value for CIRCLERAD 〈〉: '_cal Expression: rad
> 〉〉Select circle, arc or polyline segment for RAD function *(pick the existing circle)*
> Command: **CIRCLE** ↵
> 3P/2P/TTR/〈Center point〉: Diameter/〈Radius〉 〈*current*〉: ↵
> Command:

Figure 8-9.   Drawing a circle with the same radius as an existing arc or circle, or length of polyline, using the **Copy Rad** option. Pressing [Enter] at the **Radius:** prompt draws the new circle. Note the screen menu (shown highlighted). This must first be turned on to use the **Copy Rad** option.

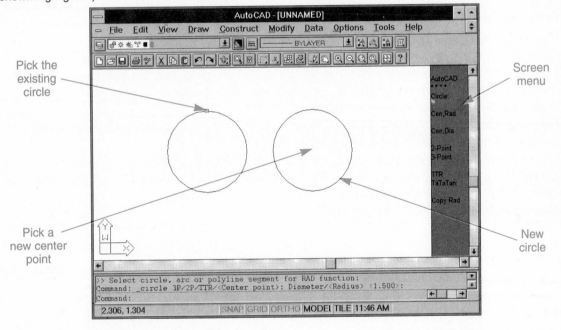

AUG 2

The @ symbol can be used to input the coordinates last entered. For example, suppose you want to draw a circle with a center at the end of the line you just drew. Enter the @ symbol at the 〈Center point〉: prompt as follows:

> Command: **LINE** ↵
> From point: **4,4** ↵
> To point: **8,4** ↵
> To point: ↵
> Command: **CIRCLE** ↵
> 3P/2P/TTR/〈Center point〉: **@** ↵

The @ symbol automatically issues the coordinate 8,4 (end of the last line) as the center of the circle. The 8,4 value is saved in the **LASTPOINT** system variable. The @ symbol retrieves the **LASTPOINT** value.

Another application of the @ symbol is drawing concentric circles (circles that have the same center). To do this, draw a circle using the **Center, Radius** or **Center, Diameter** options. Then, enter the **CIRCLE** command again and type @ at the ⟨Center point⟩: prompt. This automatically places the center of the new circle at the center of the previous circle.

---

### EXERCISE 8-1

❑ Load AutoCAD for Windows and open PRODR1, or start a new drawing using your own variables.
❑ Set the **CIRCLERAD** system variable to 0.
❑ Use the **Center, Radius** option of the **CIRCLE** command to draw a circle similar to the one shown in Figure 8-3.
❑ Use the **Center, Diameter** option of the **CIRCLE** command to draw the circle shown in Figure 8-4.
❑ Draw two vertical parallel lines two units apart. Then use the **2 Point** option of the **CIRCLE** command to draw the circle tangent to the two lines.
❑ Use the **3 Point** option of the **CIRCLE** command to draw the circle shown in Figure 8-6.
❑ Use the **Tangent, Tangent, Radius** option of the **CIRCLE** command to draw the circles shown in Figure 8-7.
❑ Draw objects similar to those in Figure 8-8 and then pick **Tan,Tan,Tan** from the **Circle** cascading menu to draw circles tangent to the existing objects as in Figure 8-8. (Note: The ACADFULL menu must be loaded.)
❑ Draw a line. Use the **Center, Radius** option of the **CIRCLE** command and the @ symbol to place the circle's center at the endpoint of the line.
❑ Draw three concentric circles using the @ and the **CIRCLE** command.
❑ Set **CIRCLERAD** to .5 and draw circles using each **CIRCLE** command option. Compare the prompts to those from the first circles drawn in this exercise.
❑ Save the drawing as A:EX8-1 and quit.

---

## DRAWING ARCS

AUG 2

An *arc* is defined as any part of a circle or curve. Arcs are commonly dimensioned with a radius, but can be drawn by a number of different methods. The **ARC** command can be accessed by clicking the **Arc** button in the toolbar, selecting **Arc** from the **Draw** pull-down menu, or by typing ARC at the **Command:** prompt. The ten **ARC** construction options can be seen in the **Arc** cascading submenu shown in Figure 8-10. (Note: The ACADFULL menu must be loaded.)

The **3 Point** option is the default when the **ARC** command is entered at the **Command:** prompt or when the **Arc** button is picked. The easiest way to select an arc option is by using the **Arc** cascading submenu or the **Arc** toolbar flyout. Figure 8-11 illustrates some of the commonly used options. Regardless of how the **ARC** command is executed, the last element of the arc is automatically dragged into place if **DRAGMODE** is set to **Auto**.

Figure 8-10. The **Arc** cascading submenu.

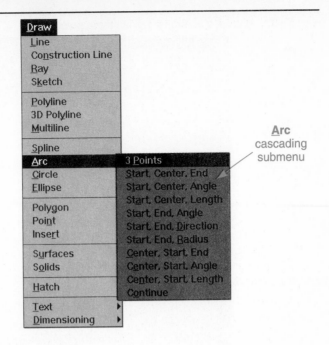

Arc cascading submenu

Figure 8-11. How several of the **ARC** command options work.

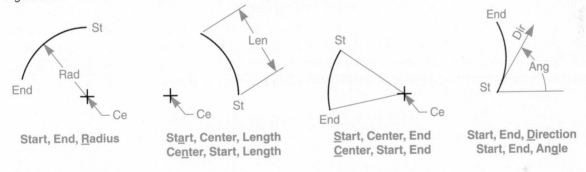

| Start, End, Radius | Start, Center, Length<br>Center, Start, Length | Start, Center, End<br>Center, Start, End | Start, End, Direction<br>Start, End, Angle |

**PROFESSIONAL TIP**

It is easiest to select the desired **ARC** option using the **Arc** button in the **Draw** toolbar or the **Arc** cascading submenu. When an **ARC** option is selected, AutoCAD automatically prompts you for the next required input (such as **End**, **Angle**, or **Start**).

## Drawing a three-point arc

The **3 Point** option asks for the start point, second point along the arc, and then the end-point, Figure 8-12. The arc can be drawn clockwise or counterclockwise, and is dragged into position as the endpoint is located. The following shows the command sequence for this option:

> Command: **ARC** ↵
> Center/⟨Start point⟩: *(select the first point on the arc)*
> Center/End/⟨Second point⟩: *(select the second point on the arc)*
> End point: *(select the arc's endpoint)*
> Command:

Figure 8-12.    Drawing an arc by picking three points.

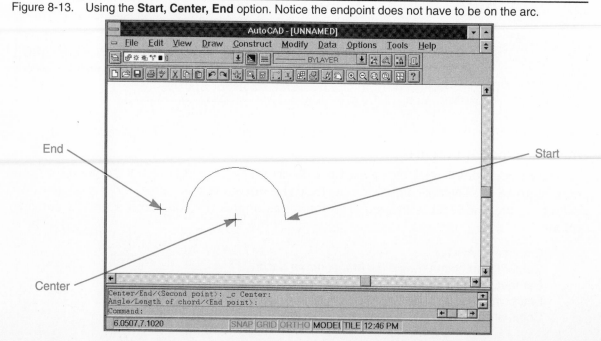

## Drawing an arc with the **Start, Center, End** option

Use **Start, Center, End** option when you know the start, center, and endpoints. Picking the start and center points establishes the arc's radius. The point selected for the endpoint determines the arc length. The selected endpoint does not have to be on the radius of the arc, Figure 8-13. The following shows the command sequence for this option:

Command: **ARC** ⏎
Center/⟨Start point⟩: *(select the first point on the arc)*
Center/End/⟨Second point⟩: **C** ⏎
Center: *(select the arc's center point)*
Angle/Length of chord/⟨End point⟩: *(select the arc endpoint)*

Figure 8-13.    Using the **Start, Center, End** option. Notice the endpoint does not have to be on the arc.

## Drawing an arc with the **Start, Center, Angle** option

When the arc's included angle is known, the **Start, Center, Angle** option may be the best choice. The *included angle* is an angle formed between the center, and start and endpoints of the arc. The arc is drawn counterclockwise, unless a negative angle is specified. See Figure 8-14. The following command sequence uses the **Angle** option and specifies a 45° included angle:

> Command: **ARC** ↵
> Center/⟨Start point⟩: *(select the first point on the arc)*
> Center/End/⟨Second point⟩: **C** ↵
> Center: *(select the arc center point)*
> Angle/Length of chord/⟨End point⟩: **A** ↵
> Included angle: **45** ↵

Figure 8-14.   How positive and negative angles work with the **Start, Center, Angle** option.

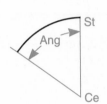
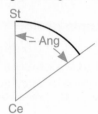
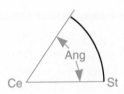
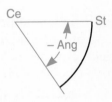

## Drawing arcs with the **Start, Center, Length of chord** option

The chord length can be determined using a chord length table. A one-unit radius arc with an included angle of 45° has a chord length of .765 units. Arcs are drawn counterclockwise. Therefore, a positive chord length gives the smallest possible arc with that length. A negative chord length results in the largest possible arc. See Figure 8-15. The command sequence for a chord length of .765 is as follows:

> Command: **ARC** ↵
> Center/⟨Start point⟩: *(select the first point on the arc)*
> Center/End/⟨Second point⟩: **C** ↵
> Center: *(select the arc center point)*
> Angle/Length of chord/⟨End point⟩: **L** ↵
> Length of chord: *(type .765 for the smallest arc, or –.765 for the largest arc, and press [Enter])*

Figure 8-15.   How positive and negative chord lengths work with the **Start, Center, Length** option.

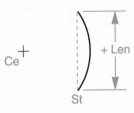
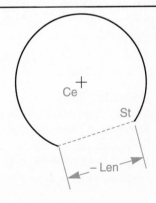

**EXERCISE 8-2**

❑ Load AutoCAD for Windows and open PRODR1, or begin a new drawing using your own variables.

❑ Use the **3 Point** option of the **ARC** command to draw arcs similar to those shown in Figure 8-12.

❑ Use the **Start, Center, End** option of the **ARC** command and draw the arc shown in Figure 8-13.

❑ Use the **Start, Center, Angle** of the **ARC** command option and draw the arcs shown in Figure 8-14.

❑ Use the **Start, Center, Length** option of the **ARC** command and draw the arcs shown in Figure 8-15.

❑ Save the drawing as A:EX8-2 and quit.

## Drawing arcs using the Start, End, Included Angle option

An arc can also be drawn by picking the start point, endpoint, and entering the included angle. A positive included angle draws the arc counterclockwise, while a negative angle produces a clockwise arc. See Figure 8-16. The command sequence is as follows:

Command: **ARC** ↵
Center/⟨Start point⟩: *(select the first point on the arc)*
Center/End/⟨Second point⟩: **E** ↵
End point: *(select the arc endpoint)*
Angle/Direction/Radius/⟨Center point⟩: **A** ↵
Included angle: *(type a positive or negative angle and press* [Enter]*)*

Figure 8-16.   How positive and negative angles work with the **Start, End, Angle** option.

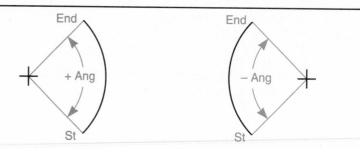

## Drawing arcs using the Start, End, Radius option

A positive radius value for the **Start, End, Radius** option results in the smallest possible arc between the start point and endpoint. A negative radius gives the largest arc possible, Figure 8-17. Arcs can only be drawn counterclockwise with this option. The command sequence is as follows:

Command: **ARC** ↵
Center/⟨Start point⟩: *(select the first point on the arc)*
Center/End/⟨Second point⟩: **E** ↵
End point: *(select the arc endpoint)*
Angle/Direction/Radius/⟨Center point⟩: **R** ↵
Radius: *(pick, or type a positive radius or negative radius and press* [Enter]*)*

Figure 8-17.   Using the **Start, End, Radius** option with a positive and/or a negative radius

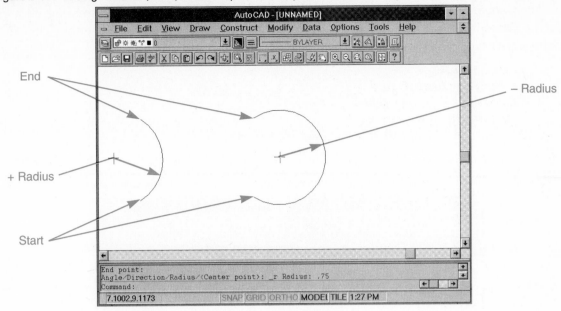

## Drawing arcs using the **Start, End, Direction** option

An arc can be drawn by picking the start point, endpoint, and entering the direction of rotation in degrees. The distance between the points and the number of degrees determines the arc's location and size. The arc is started tangent to the direction specified, as shown in Figure 8-18. The command sequence is as follows:

> Command: **ARC** ↵
> Center/⟨Start point⟩: *(select the first point on the arc)*
> Center/End/⟨Second point⟩: **E** ↵
> End point: *(select the arc endpoint)*
> Angle/Direction/Radius/⟨Center point⟩: **D** ↵
> Direction from start point: *(pick the direction from the start point, or type the direction in degrees and press* [Enter]*)*

Figure 8-18.   Using the **Start, End, Direction** option.

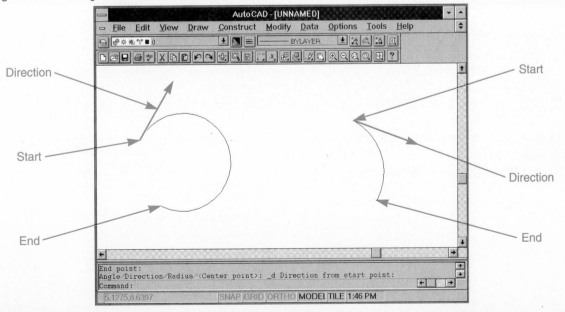

## Drawing arcs using the Center, Start, End option

The **Center, Start, End** option is a variation of the **Start, Center, End** option, Figure 8-19. Use the **Center, Start, End** option when it is easier to begin by locating the center. The command sequence is as follows:

Command: **ARC** ↵
Center/〈Start point〉: **C** ↵
Center: *(pick the center point)*
Start point: *(pick the start point)*
Angle/Length of chord/〈End point〉: *(pick the arc's endpoint)*

Figure 8-19. Using the **Center, Start, End** option. Note that the endpoint does not have to be on the arc.

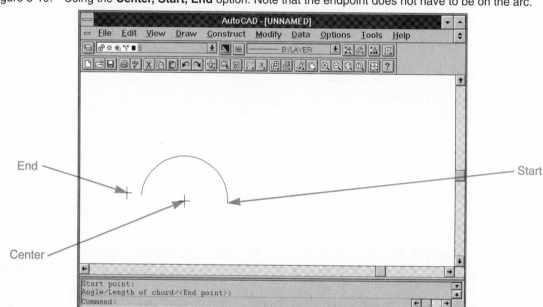

### EXERCISE 8-3

❏ Load AutoCAD and open PRODR1, or start a new drawing and set up your own variables.
❏ Use the **Start, End, Angle** option of the **ARC** command to draw arcs similar to those shown in Figure 8-16.
❏ Use the **Start, End, Radius** option of the **ARC** command to draw the arcs shown in Figure 8-17.
❏ Use the **Start, End, Direction** option of the **ARC** command to draw the arcs shown in Figure 8-18.
❏ Use the **Center, Start, End** option of the **ARC** command to draw the arc shown in Figure 8-19.
❏ Save the drawing as A:EX8-3 and quit.

## Drawing arcs using the Center, Start, Angle option

The **Center, Start, Angle** option is a variation of the **Start, Center, Angle** option. Use the **Center, Start, Angle** option when it is easier to begin by locating the center. Figure 8-20 shows how positive and negative angles work with this option. The command sequence is as follows:

> Command: **ARC** ↵
> Center/⟨Start point⟩: **C** ↵
> Center: *(pick the center point)*
> Start point: *(pick the start point)*
> Angle/Length of chord/⟨End point⟩: **A** ↵
> Included angle: *(pick the included angle or type a positive angle or negative angle and press* [Enter]*)*

Figure 8-20.   How positive and negative angles work with the **Center, Start, Angle** option.

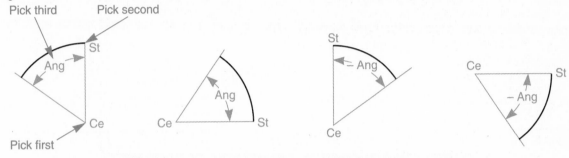

## Drawing arcs with the Center, Start, Length of chord option

The **Center, Start, Length of chord** option is a variation of the **Start, Center, Length** option. Use the **Center, Start, Length** option when it is easier to begin by locating the center. Figure 8-21 shows how positive and negative chord lengths work with this option. The command sequence is as follows:

> Command: **ARC** ↵
> Center/⟨Start point⟩: **C** ↵
> Center: *(pick the center point)*
> Start point: *(pick the start point)*
> Angle/Length of chord/⟨End point⟩: **L** ↵
> Length of chord: *(pick, or type the chord length and press* [Enter]*)*

Figure 8-21.   How positive and negative chord lengths work with the **Center, Start, Length** option.

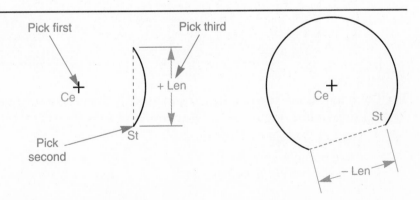

## Continuing an arc from a previously drawn arc or line

An arc can be continued from the previous arc or line. To do so, pick **Continue** from the **Arc** cascading submenu, pick the **Arc Continue** button in the **Arc** flyout, or press the [Enter] key or space bar at the 〈Start point〉: prompt.

When a series of arcs are drawn in this manner, each consecutive arc is tangent. The start points and direction are taken from the endpoint and direction of the previous arc. The arc continuation described below is shown in Figure 8-22.

> Command: **ARC** ⏎
> Center/〈Start point〉: *(select the first point on the arc)*
> Center/End/〈Second point〉: **E** ⏎
> End point: *(select the arc's endpoint)*
> Angle/Direction/Radius/〈Center point〉: **D** ⏎
> Direction from start point: *(pick, or specify the direction from the start point in degrees and press* [Enter]*)*
> Command: ⏎
> ARC Center/〈Start point〉: *(press the space bar or* [Enter]*)*
> End point: *(select the endpoint of the second arc)*
> Command: ⏎
> ARC Center/〈Start point〉: *(press the space bar or* [Enter]*)*
> End point: *(select the endpoint of the third arc)*

Figure 8-22.    Using the **Continue** option to draw three arcs.

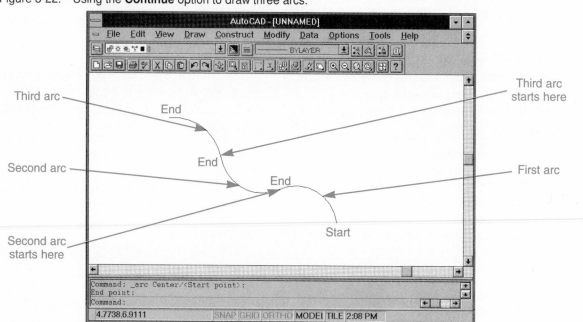

The **Continue** option can also be used to quickly draw an arc tangent to the endpoint of a previously drawn line, Figure 8-23. The command sequence is as follows:

> Command: **LINE** ⏎
> From point: *(select a point)*
> To point: *(select the second point)*
> To point: ⏎
> Command: **ARC** ⏎
> Center/〈Start point〉: *(press space bar or* [Enter] *to place start point of the arc at end of the previous line)*
> End point: *(select the endpoint of the arc)*

Figure 8-23. An arc continuing from the previous line. Point 2 is the start of the arc and Point 3 is the end of the arc.

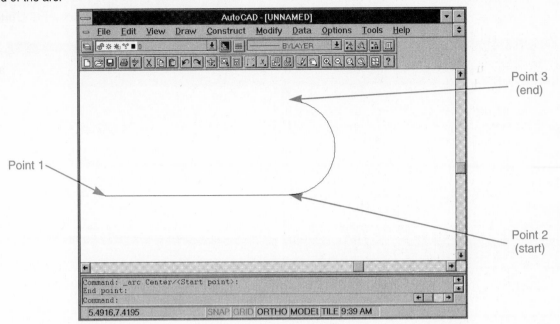

Look at the fully radiused slot in Figure 8-24A. This object can be drawn quite easily using the **Continue** methods just described. The command sequence is as follows:

Command: **LINE** ↵
From point: (*pick start point P1 in Figure 8-24B*)
To point: **@3⟨0** ↵
To point: (*press* [Enter] *or the space bar to exit the* **LINE** *command*)
Command: **ARC** ↵
Center/⟨Start point⟩: (*press* [Enter] *or the space bar to place the start point of arc, P2, at the end of the previous line*)
End point: **@1⟨90** ↵
Command: **LINE** ↵
From point: (*press* [Enter] *or the space bar to place the start point of line, P3, at the end of the previous arc*)
Length of line: **3** ↵
To point: (*press* [Enter] *or the space bar to exit the* **LINE** *command*)
Command: **ARC** ↵
Center/⟨Start point⟩: (*press* [Enter] *or the space bar to place the start point of arc, P4, at the end of the previous line*)
End point: **@1⟨270** ↵
Command:

Figure 8-24.   Fully radiused features, such as this slot, can be drawn quickly and easily using the **LINE** and **ARC** command **Continuation** options.

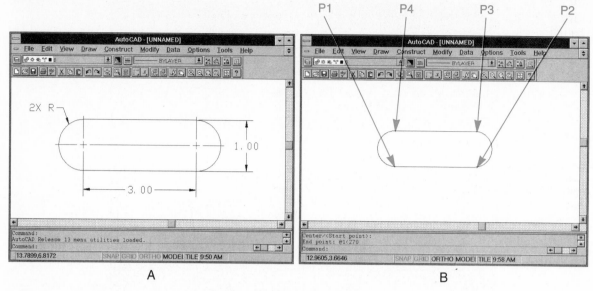

A                                            B

## DRAWING ELLIPSES

AUG 2

When a circle is viewed at an angle, an elliptical shape is seen. For example, a 30° ellipse is created if a circle is rotated 60° from the line of sight. The parts of an ellipse are shown in Figure 8-25.

Figure 8-25.   Parts of an ellipse.

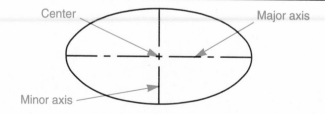

An ellipse can be drawn using different options of the **ELLIPSE** command. These options can be seen in the **Ellipse** cascading submenu shown in Figure 8-26. (The ACADFULL menu must be loaded.) The **ELLIPSE** command can be accessed by clicking the appropriate **Ellipse** button in the **Draw** toolbar, selecting **Ellipse** from the **Draw** pull-down menu, or typing ELLIPSE at the **Command:** prompt. Refer to Figure 8-27 as you go through the following command sequence:

> Command: **ELLIPSE** ↵
> Arc/Center/⟨Axis endpoint 1⟩: *(select an axis endpoint)*
> Axis endpoint 2: *(select the other endpoint of the axis)*
> ⟨Other axis distance⟩/Rotation: *(select a distance from the midpoint of the first axis to the end of the second axis and press* [Enter]*)*

Figure 8-26.   The **Ellipse**
cascading submenu.

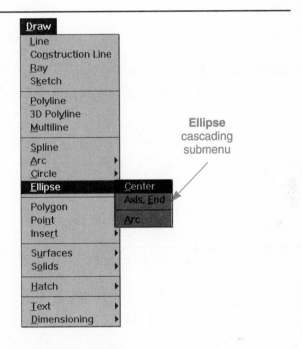

Figure 8-27.   Constructing the same ellipse by choosing different axis endpoints.

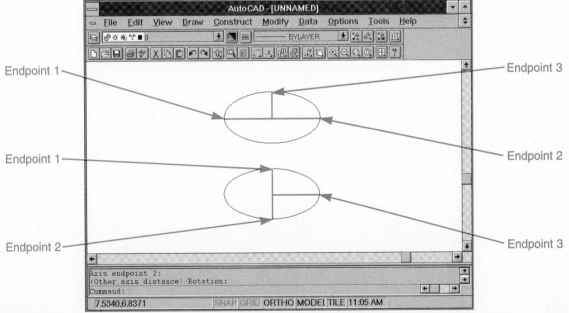

The **Axis, Endpoint 1** option establishes one endpoint of the first axis. This axis may be either the major or minor axis, depending on what is entered for the second axis. The longer of the two axes is always the major axis. After you pick the first axis, the ellipse is dragged by the cursor until the point is picked (if **DRAGMODE** is on).

If you respond to the ⟨Other axis distance⟩/Rotation: prompt with R for rotation, AutoCAD assumes you have selected the major axis with the first two points. The next prompt requests the angle that the ellipse is rotated from the line of sight at. The command sequence is as follows:

>   Command: **ELLIPSE** ↵
>   Arc/Center ⟨Axis endpoint 1⟩: *(select a major axis endpoint)*
>   Axis endpoint 2: *(select the other endpoint of the major axis)*
>   ⟨Other axis distance⟩/Rotation: **R** ↵
>   Rotation around major axis: *(type a rotation angle, such as* 30 *and press* [Enter])

The 30 response draws an ellipse that is 30° from the line of sight. A 0 response draws an ellipse with the minor axis equal to the major axis. This is a circle. Any angle greater than 89.4° is rejected by AutoCAD. Figure 8-28 shows the relationship between several ellipses having the same major axis length but different rotation angles.

Figure 8-28.   Ellipse rotation angles.

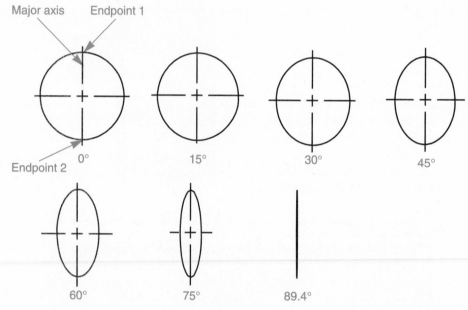

An ellipse can also be constructed by specifying the center point and one endpoint for each of the two axes, Figure 8-29. This can be done by picking the **Ellipse Center** button from the **Ellipse** flyout, picking the <u>**Center**</u> option from the <u>**Ellipse**</u> cascading submenu, or by using the following command sequence:

>   Command: **ELLIPSE** ↵
>   Arc/Center ⟨Axis endpoint 1⟩: **C** ↵
>   Center of ellipse: *(select the ellipse center point)*
>   Axis endpoint: *(select the endpoint of one axis)*
>   ⟨Other axis distance⟩/Rotation: *(select the endpoint of the other axis)*

Figure 8-29. Drawing an ellipse by picking the center and endpoint of two axes.

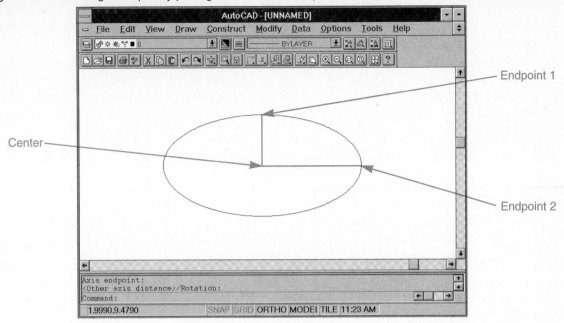

The rotation option can be used instead of selecting the second axis endpoint. See Figure 8-30. The command sequence is as follows:

Command: **ELLIPSE** ↵
Arc/Center ⟨Axis endpoint 1⟩: **C** ↵
Center of ellipse: *(select the ellipse center point)*
Axis endpoint: *(select the endpoint of one axis)*
⟨Other axis distance⟩/Rotation: **R** ↵
Rotation around major axis: **30** ↵

Figure 8-30. Drawing an ellipse using the **Center** option and the rotation angle. This ellipse was drawn using a 30° rotation angle.

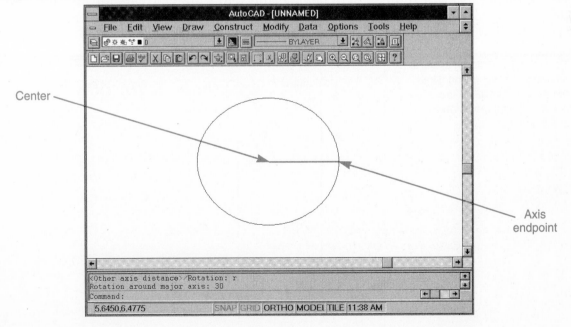

**EXERCISE 8-5**

❑ Load AutoCAD for Windows and open PRODR1, or begin a new drawing using your own variables.
❑ Use the **Axis, End** option of the **ELLIPSE** command to draw the ellipses shown in Figure 8-27.
❑ Use the **Center** option of the **ELLIPSE** command to draw the ellipse shown in Figure 8-29.
❑ Use the **Center** and **Rotation** options of the **ELLIPSE** command to draw the ellipse shown in Figure 8-30.
❑ Save the drawing as A:EX8-5 and quit.

## Drawing elliptical arcs

The **ELLIPSE** command can also be used to draw elliptical arcs with the **Arc** option. Pick **Arc** from the **Ellipse** pull-down menu, pick the **Ellipse Arc** button from the **Ellipse** flyout, or type ELLIPSE at the **Command:** prompt and enter the **Arc** option:

```
Command: ELLIPSE ↵
Arc/Center/〈Axis endpoint 1〉: A ↵
〈Axis endpoint 1〉/Center: (pick the first axis endpoint)
Axis endpoint 2: (pick the second axis endpoint)
〈Other Axis distance〉/Rotation: (pick the distance for the second axis)
Parameter/〈start angle〉: 0 ↵
Parameter/Included/〈end angle〉: 90 ↵
Command:
```

Once the second endpoint of the first axis is picked, you can drag the shape of a full ellipse (if **DRAGMODE** is on). This can be used to help you visually select the other axis distance. The distance for the second axis is from the ellipse center to the point picked. Next, enter a start angle. The start and end angles are the angular relation between the ellipse center and where arc begins. The angle of the elliptical arc is established from the angle of the first axis. A 0° start angle is the same as the first endpoint 1 of the first axis. A 45° start angle is 45° counterclockwise from the first endpoint of the first axis. End angles are also established counterclockwise from the start point. Figure 8-31 shows the elliptical arc drawn with the previous command sequence, and displays samples of different start and end angle arcs.

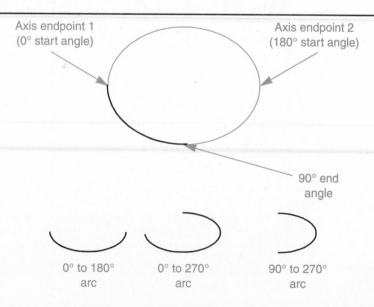

Figure 8-31. Drawing elliptical arcs with the **Arc** option. Note the three examples at the bottom using three different angle settings.

Axis endpoint 1
(0° start angle)

Axis endpoint 2
(180° start angle)

90° end angle

0° to 180° arc

0° to 270° arc

90° to 270° arc

### Using the **Parameter** option

The **Parameter** option requires the same input as the **Start, Angle** option. The difference is that AutoCAD creates the elliptical arc using a different means of vector calculation. The results are similar, but the command sequence looks like this:

> Parameter/⟨start angle⟩: **P** ↲
> Angle/⟨start parameter⟩: *(pick the start point)*
> Angle/Included/⟨end parameter⟩: *(pick the end point)*
> Command:

### Using the **Included** option

The **Included** option establishes an included angle beginning at the start angle. An included angle is an angle that is formed by two sides, or in this case, an angle that is formed as a number of degrees from the start angle. The command sequence looks like this:

> Command: **ELLIPSE** ↲
> Arc/Center/⟨Axis endpoint 1⟩: **A** ↲
> ⟨Axis endpoint 1⟩/Center: *(pick the first axis endpoint)*
> Axis endpoint 2: *(pick the second axis endpoint)*
> ⟨Other axis distance⟩/Rotation: *(pick the other axis distance)*
> Parameter/⟨start angle⟩: **0** ↲
> Parameter/Included/⟨end angle⟩: **I** ↲
> Included angle ⟨*current*⟩: **180** ↲
> Command:

### Rotating an ellipse arc around its axis

The **Rotation** option for drawing an elliptical arc is similar to the **Rotation** option when drawing a full ellipse discussed earlier. Refer back to Figure 8-28 for an example of various rotation angles. This option allows you to rotate the elliptical arc about the first axis by specifying a rotation angle as follows:

> Command: **ELLIPSE** ↲
> Arc/Center/⟨Axis end point 1⟩: **A** ↲
> ⟨Axis endpoint 1⟩/Center: *(pick the first axis endpoint)*
> Axis endpoint 2: *(pick the second axis endpoint)*
> ⟨Other axis distance⟩/Rotation: **R** ↲
> Rotation around major axis: **45** ↲
> Parameter/⟨start angle⟩: **90** ↲
> Parameter/Included/⟨end angle⟩: **180** ↲
> Command:

### Drawing an elliptical arc using the **Center** option

The **Center** option for drawing an elliptical arc lets you establish the center of the ellipse, as shown in Figure 8-32. The following is the command sequence:

> Command: **ELLIPSE** ↲
> Arc/Center/⟨Axis end point 1⟩: **A** ↲
> ⟨Axis endpoint 1⟩/Center: **C** ↲
> Axis endpoint: *(pick the first axis endpoint)*
> ⟨Other axis distance⟩/Rotation: *(pick the other axis distance)*
> Parameter/⟨start angle⟩: **0** ↲
> Parameter/Included/⟨end angle⟩: **180** ↲
> Command:

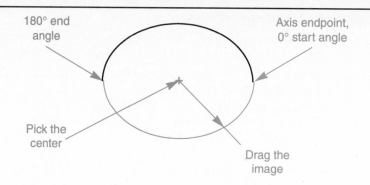

Figure 8-32. Drawing elliptical arcs with the **Center** option.

## The PELLIPSE system variable

**PELLIPSE** is an AutoCAD system variable having a value of either 0 or 1. When the value is 0, the object created using the **ELLIPSE** command is a true elliptical object. A true elliptical object can be grip edited while keeping the object elliptical. Grip editing is discussed in Chapter 14. If the **PELLIPSE** value is 1, the object created is a polyline ellipse. An elliptical polyline can be grip edited or "pedited" with each vertex able to move without maintaining the elliptical shape. The **Arc** option of the **ELLIPSE** command is not available when **PELLIPSE** is set to 1. The AutoCAD default is 0, but you can change it like this:

Command: **PELLIPSE** ↵
New value for PELLIPSE ⟨0⟩: **1** ↵
Command:

---

### EXERCISE 8-6

❑ Load AutoCAD and open PRODR1, or start a new drawing and set up your own variables.
❑ Use the **Arc** option of the **ELLIPSE** command to draw the following elliptical arcs:
❑ Use axis endpoints, axis distance, start angle = 0, and end angle = 90; similar to Figure 8-31.
❑ Use the same options as in the previous instructions to draw a 0° to 180° arc, 0° to 270° arc, and a 90° to 270° arc similar to the samples in Figure 8-31.
❑ Use the **Parameter** option to draw an elliptical arc of your own design.
❑ Use the **Rotation** option to rotate an elliptical arc 45° about its axis.
❑ Use the **Included** option to draw an elliptical arc with a 180° included angle and another with a 90° included angle.
❑ Use the **Center** option to draw an elliptical arc of your own design.
❑ Save the drawing as A:EX8-6 and quit.

---

## DRAWING REGULAR POLYGONS                                          AUG 2

A *regular polygon* is any closed-plane geometric figure with three or more equal sides and equal angles. A hexagon, for example, is a six-sided regular polygon. After drawing regular polygons using manual drafting techniques, you will be impressed with AutoCAD's **POLYGON** command. The command is used to draw any regular polygon with 3 to 1024 sides.

The **POLYGON** command can be accessed by clicking the **Polygon** button in the **Rectangle** flyout of the **Draw** toolbar, selecting **Polygon** from the **Draw** pull-down menu, or typing POLYGON at the **Command:** prompt. The options found in the **Polygon** cascading submenu are shown in Figure 8-33.

Figure 8-33.  The **Polygon** cascading submenu.

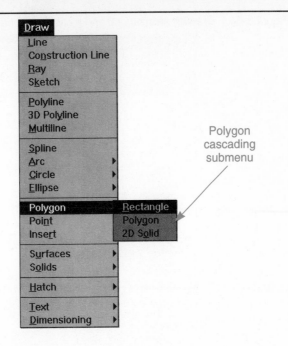

Polygon cascading submenu

PROFESSIONAL TIP

A large number of sides is usually impractical for a polygon. Too many sides make the polygon look like a circle.

Regardless of the method used to select the command, you are first prompted for the number of sides. If you want an octagon (polygon with eight sides), enter 8 as follows:

Command: **POLYGON** ⏎
Number of sides ⟨*current*⟩: **8** ⏎

The number of sides you enter becomes the default for the next time you use the **POLYGON** command. Next, AutoCAD prompts for the edge or center of the polygon. If you reply by picking a point on the screen, this point becomes the center of the polygon. You are then asked if you want to have the polygon inscribed within, or circumscribed outside, an imaginary circle, Figure 8-34. A polygon is *inscribed* when it is drawn inside a circle and its corners touch the circle. *Circumscribed* polygons are drawn outside of a circle where the sides of the polygon are tangent to the circle. You must then specify the radius of the circle. The command continues as follows:

Edge/⟨Center of polygon⟩: (*pick center of polygon*)
Inscribed in circle/Circumscribed about circle (I/C): (*respond with* I *or* C *and press* [Enter])
Radius of circle: (*type the radius, such as* 2 *and press* [Enter], *or pick a point on the screen at the desired distance from the center*)

The **I** or **C** option you select becomes the default for the next polygon.

Figure 8-34.   Drawing an inscribed and a circumscribed polygon.

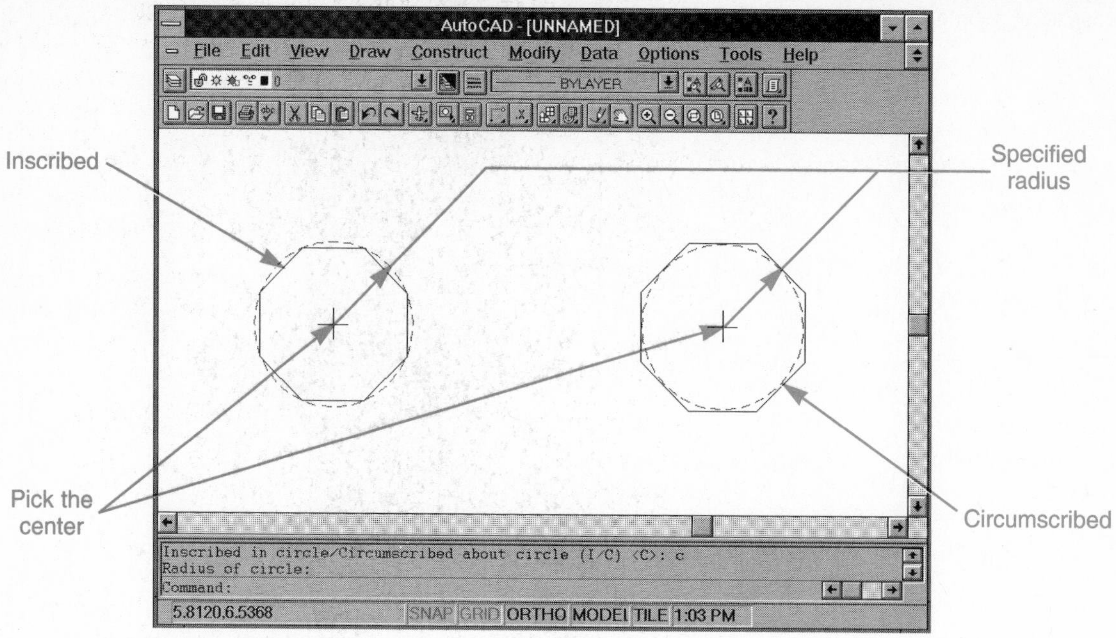

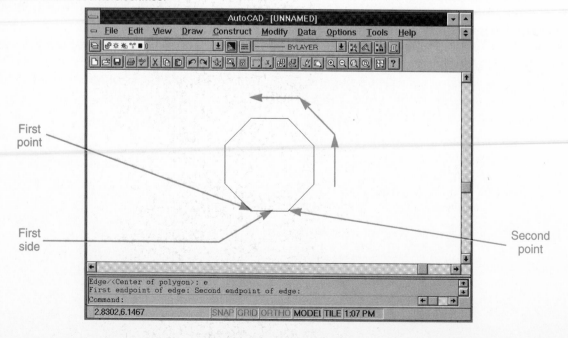

The Edge/⟨Center of polygon⟩: prompt allows you to pick the center or specify the edge. Notice that **Center of polygon** is the default. If you want to draw the polygon on an existing edge, specify the **Edge** option and pick edge endpoints as follows:

> Command: **POLYGON** ↵
> Number of sides: **8** ↵
> Edge/⟨Center of polygon⟩: **E** ↵
> First endpoint of edge: *(pick a point)*
> Second endpoint of edge: *(pick second point)*

After you pick the endpoints of one side, the rest of the polygon sides are drawn counter-clockwise, Figure 8-35.

Figure 8-35.   Drawing a polygon by giving the number of sides and the length of the first side. Note that the sides are drawn counterclockwise.

Polygons are polylines, and can be easily edited using the **PEDIT** (polyline edit) command. For example, a polygon can be given width using the **Width** option of the **PEDIT** command discussed in Chapter 18.

Hexagons (six-sided polygons) are commonly drawn as bolt heads and nuts on mechanical drawings. Keep in mind that these features are normally dimensioned across the flats. To draw a hexagon, or any polygon, dimensioned across the flats, circumscribe it. The radius you enter is equal to one-half the distance across the flats. The distance across the corners (inscribed polygon) is specified when the polygon must be confined within a circular area. One example is the boundary of a swimming pool in architectural drafting. Notice the distance across the flats and the distance across the corners in Figure 8-36.

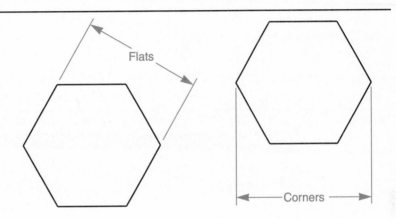

Figure 8-36. Specifying the distance across the flats and between corners of a polygon.

### Setting the Polygon SIDES default

AutoCAD allows you to set the default number of polygon sides with the **POLYSIDES** system variable. Set **POLYSIDES** like this:

> Command: **POLYSIDES** ⏎
> New value for POLYSIDES ⟨4⟩: **6** ⏎
> Command:

The value you specify for the default is used until you change the value again using the **POLYSIDES** system variable or the **POLYGON** command.

The **MULTIPLE** command modifier, introduced in Chapter 6, automatically repeats commands issued at the keyboard. It can be used to draw repetitive circles, arcs, ellipses, or polygons. For example, if you plan to draw multiple polygons, do the following:

> Command: **MULTIPLE POLYGON** ⏎
> Number of sides⟨6⟩: ⏎
> Edge/⟨Center of polygon⟩: *(pick the center of polygon)*
> Inscribed in circle/Circumscribed about circle (I/C) ⟨I⟩: ⏎
> Radius of circle: *(pick, or type the radius and press [Enter])*
> POLYGON Number of sides⟨6⟩: *(continue drawing additional polygons or cancel to get back to the* **Command:** *prompt)*

AutoCAD automatically re-issues the **POLYGON** command. Press [Esc] to cancel the repeating action.

## DRAWING RECTANGLES

AutoCAD's **RECTANGLE** command allows you to easily draw rectangles. When using this command, simply pick one corner and then the opposite corner. See Figure 8-37. The **RECTANGLE** command can be accessed from the **Polygon** cascading submenu in the **Draw** pull-down menu, by picking the **Rectangle** button in the **Draw** toolbar, or by typing RECTANG at the **Command:** prompt as follows:

> Command: **RECTANG** ↵
> First corner: (*pick first corner*)
> Other corner: (*pick the opposite corner*)
> Command:

As with ellipses and polygons, rectangles are polylines and may also be edited using the **PEDIT** command. Since a rectangle is a polyline, it is treated as one entity until exploded. After it is exploded, the individual sides can then be edited as desired. (The **EXPLODE** command is discussed in Chapter 18.)

Figure 8-37.    Using the **RECTANGLE** command. Simply pick opposite corners of the rectangle.

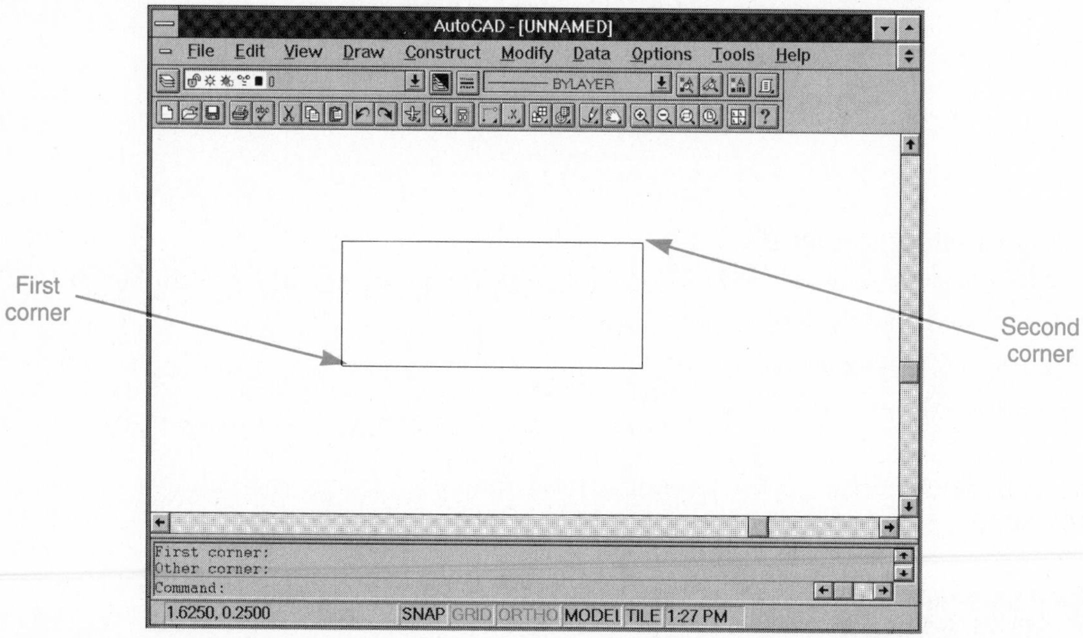

### EXERCISE 8-7

☐ Load AutoCAD for Windows and open PRODR1, or begin a new drawing using your own variables.
☐ Draw a hexagon with a distance of three units across the flats. Then draw another hexagon measuring three units across the corners.
☐ Draw an octagon with a horizontal edge that is 1.75 units long.
☐ Draw a pentagon circumscribed about a circle having a 2.25 inch diameter.
☐ Draw a rectangle measuring 3 × 5 units.
☐ Save the drawing as A:EX8-7 and quit.

# DRAWING DOUGHNUTS AND SOLID CIRCLES

Doughnuts drawn in AutoCAD are actually circular polylines. Drawing polylines was introduced in Chapter 6, and is covered in detail in Chapter 18. The **DONUT** command allows you to draw a thick circle. It can have any inside and outside diameter, or be completely filled in, Figure 8-38. The command can be selected from the **Draw** pull-down menu or issued as DOUGHNUT (or DONUT to save time), or the **Donut** button can be picked from the **Circle** flyout.

Command: **DONUT** ↵
Inside diameter ⟨current⟩: *(specify a new inside diameter and press* [Enter], *or press* [Enter] *to accept the current value)*
Outside diameter ⟨current⟩: *(specify a new outside diameter and press* [Enter], *or press* [Enter] *to accept the current value)*

Figure 8-38.  Examples of doughnuts. A—With **FILL** mode on. B—With **FILL** mode off.

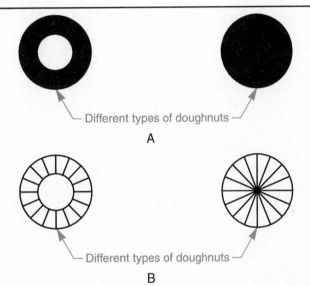

The previously set inside diameter is shown in brackets. A new inside diameter may be entered at this time, or press the [Enter] key to keep the existing value. A 0 response to the Inside diameter prompt gives you a solid circle, Figure 8-39. The next request is for a new outside diameter. Press [Enter] to keep the current value. AutoCAD then asks:

Center of doughnut: *(select the doughnut center point)*

When a center point is picked, the doughnut is drawn with its center at that point. Next, a new Center of doughnut: prompt is issued. You may pick another center point to draw the same size doughnut in a new location. Press [Enter] if you wish to get back to the **Command:** prompt. The **DONUT** command remains active until you press [Enter] or cancel the pressing [Esc] to end it.

Figure 8-39.  Doughnuts can be drawn with a 0 inside diameter to create solid circles.

Doughnut with ⌀0.00 inside

When the **FILL** mode is turned off, doughnuts appear as segmented circles or concentric circles as shown in Figure 8-38B. **FILL** can be used transparently by entering 'FILL while inside the **DONUT** command. Then, simply enter ON or OFF as needed. The fill in previously drawn doughnuts remains on until the drawing is regenerated.

If you want to draw a doughnut with a .5 inside diameter and a 1.25 outside diameter, use the following command sequence. This doughnut is shown in Figure 8-40.

> Command: **DONUT** ⏎
> Inside diameter ⟨*current*⟩: **.5** ⏎
> Outside diameter ⟨*current*⟩: **1.25** ⏎
> Center of doughnut: (*select the doughnut center point*)
> Center of doughnut: (*select the center point for another doughnut, or press* [Enter] *to discontinue the command*)

Figure 8-40. The doughnut that results from the command sequence given in the text.

Doughnut with ⌀.5 inside and ⌀1.25 outside

## Presetting the **DONUT** options

AutoCAD allows you to preset the **DONUT** options so the inside and outside diameters have defaults. This saves time when you plan to draw only doughnuts with a given inside and outside diameter. To set **DONUT** to automatically issue a default inside and outside diameter, use the **DONUTID** and **DONUTOD** system variables to set the inside and outside diameters, respectively. The **DONUTID** variable can be any value, including 0. The **DONUTOD** variable must be a nonzero value. If **DONUTID** is larger than **DONUTOD**, the two values are reversed by the next **DONUT** command. The command sequences for **DONUTID** and **DONUTOD** variables are as follows:

> Command: **DONUTID** ⏎
> New value for DONUTID ⟨*current*⟩: **.25** ⏎
> Command: **DONUTOD** ⏎
> New value for DONUTOD ⟨*current*⟩: **.75** ⏎
> Command:

---

### EXERCISE 8-8

❏ Load AutoCAD for Windows and open PRODR1, or begin a new drawing using your own variables.
❏ Draw a doughnut with a .5 inside diameter and a 1.5 outside diameter.
❏ Draw a doughnut with a 0 inside diameter and a 1.5 outside diameter.
❏ Turn the **FILL** mode off and type REGEN to see what happens to the doughnuts.
❏ Set **DONUTID** to .25 and **DONUTOD** to .75.
❏ Type DONUT at the **Command:** prompt and draw a doughnut using the defaults.
❏ Use a transparent **FILL** command ('FILL) to turn **FILL** on while in the **DONUT** command. Now, draw two more doughnuts.
❏ Select **Donut** from the **Draw** pull-down menu and draw three more doughnuts. Notice the inside and outside presets you set earlier are automatically used.
❏ Save the drawing as A:EX8-8 and quit.

## CHAPTER TEST

*Write your answers in the spaces provided.*

1. Give the command, entries, and actions required to draw a circle with a 2.5 unit diameter:

   Command:_____

   3P/2P/TTR/〈Center point〉: _____

   Diameter/〈Radius〉: _____

   Diameter:_____

2. Give the command, entries, and actions to draw a 1.75 unit radius circle tangent to an existing line and circle:

   Command:_____

   3P/2P/TTR/〈Center point〉: _____

   Enter Tangent spec: _____

   Enter second Tangent spec: _____

   Radius: _____

3. Give the command, entries, and actions needed to draw a three-point arc:

   Command:_____

   Center/〈Start point〉:_____

   Center/End/〈Second point〉:_____

   End point: _____

4. Give the command, entries, and actions needed to draw an arc, beginning with the center point and having a 60° included angle:

   Command:_____

   Center/〈Start point〉:_____

   Center: _____

   Start point:_____

   Angle/Length of chord/〈End point〉: _____

   Included angle: DRAG _____

5. Give the command, entries, and actions required to draw an arc tangent to the endpoint of a previously drawn line:

   Command:_____

   Center/〈Start point〉:_____

   End point: _____

6. Give the command, entries, and actions needed to draw an ellipse with the **Axis, End** option:

   Command:_____

   Axis/Center/〈Axis endpoint 1〉:_____

   Axis endpoint 2:_____

   〈Other axis distance〉/Rotation: _____

7. Give the command, entries, and actions necessary to draw a hexagon measuring 4 inches (101.6 mm) across the flats:

Command:_____

Number of sides: _____

Edge/⟨Center of polygon⟩: _____

Inscribed in circle/Circumscribed about circle (I/C): _____

Radius of circle:_____

8. Give the responses required to draw two doughnuts with a .25 inside diameter and a .75 outside diameter:

Command:_____

Inside diameter ⟨current⟩: _____

Outside diameter ⟨current⟩: _____

Center of doughnut: _____

Center of doughnut: _____

Center of doughnut: _____

9. Describe why the @ symbol can be used by itself for point selection. _____

_____

10. Define the term "included angle." _____

_____

11. List the two input options that can be used to draw an arc tangent to the endpoint of a previously drawn arc._____

_____

12. Given the distance across the flats of a hexagon, would you use the **Inscribed** or **Circumscribed** option to draw the hexagon?_____

_____

13. Describe how a solid circle can be drawn._____

_____

14. To use the **MULTIPLE** command modifier to draw a series of arcs, what command do you type? _____

_____

_____

15. Explain how you would turn the **FILL** mode off while inside the **DONUT** command. ____

_____

_____

16. Name the system variable used to set the default radius value when drawing circles.

_____

17. Name the system variables used to preset the inside and outside doughnut diameters.

_____

18. Identify one way to access the option that allows you to draw a circle tangent to three objects. _____

_____

19. Describe the purpose of the **Copy Rad** option. _____

_____

_____

_____

20. Identify three ways to access the **Arc** option for drawing elliptical arcs. _____

_____

_____

21. Name the AutoCAD system variable that lets you draw a true ellipse or a polyline ellipse with the **ELLIPSE** command. _____

22. Where is the **RECTANGLE** command found in a pull-down menu? _____

_____

23. What is the AutoCAD default if the **ARC** command is typed at the **Command:** prompt?

_____

24. Name the AutoCAD system variable that allows AutoCAD to automatically calculate the radius of the current circle and use this value as the default for the next circle. _____

_____

## DRAWING PROBLEMS

*Load AutoCAD for Windows for each of the following problems and use the prototype* PRODR1, *or start a new drawing with your own variables.*

1. You have just been given the sketch of a new sports car design (shown below). You are asked to create a drawing from the sketch. Use the **LINE** command and selected shape commands to draw the car. Do not be concerned with size and scale. Consider the commands and techniques used to draw the car, and try to minimize the number used. Save your drawing as A:P8-1 and quit.

*General*

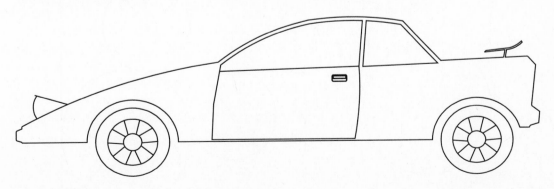

2. You have just been given the sketch of an innovative new truck design (shown below). You are asked to create a drawing from the sketch. Use the **LINE** and selected shape commands to draw the truck resembling the sketch. Do not be concerned with size and scale. Save your drawing as A:P8-2.

3. Use the **LINE** and **CIRCLE** command options to draw the objects below. Do not include dimensions. Save the drawing as A:P8-3.

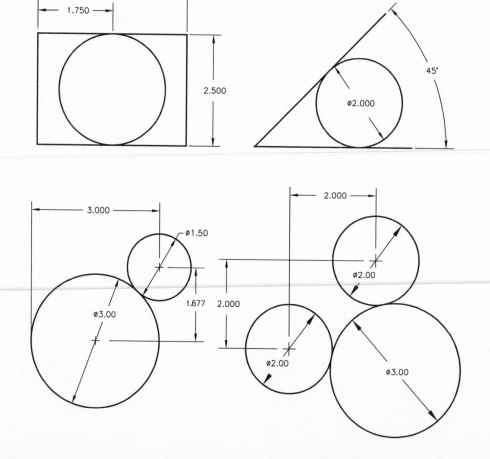

4. Use **CIRCLE** and **ARC** command options to draw the object below. Do not include dimensions. Save the drawing as A:P8-4.

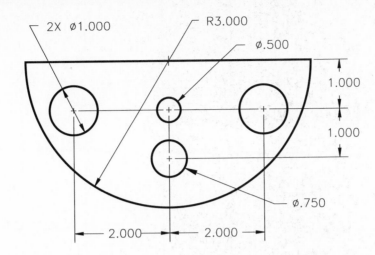

5. Select the **ELLIPSE** command to draw four ellipses using the following options. Then, save the drawing as A:P8-5.
   Ellipse 1: Axis endpoint 1/axis endpoint 2/other axis distance.
   Ellipse 2: Center/axis endpoint/other axis distance.
   Ellipse 3: Center/axis endpoint/rotation (use cursor and read coordinate angle display).
   Ellipse 4: Center/axis endpoint/rotation (type angle value).

6. Draw the pressure cylinder shown below. Use the **Arc** option of the **ELLIPSE** command to draw the cylinder ends. Do not draw the dimensions. Save the drawing as A:P8-6.

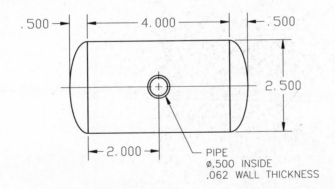

7. Use the **Arc** option of the **ELLIPSE** command to draw samples of elliptical arcs with different start and end angle arcs all with the same major axis length and a 45° rotation angle based on the following information: (see the samples at the bottom of Figure 8-31).
   Arc 1 = 0° to 90°
   Arc 2 = 0° to 180°
   Arc 3 = 0° to 270°
   Arc 4 = 90° to 180°
   Arc 5 = 90° to 270°
   Arc 6 = 180° to 0°

**Mechanical Drafting**

8.  Draw the hex head bolt pattern shown below. Do not draw dimensions. Save the drawing as A:P8-8.

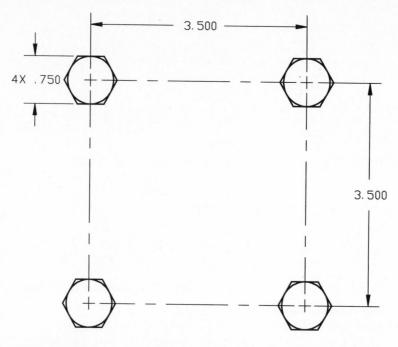

**General**

9.  Use the **POLYGON** command to draw the three polygons shown below. Save the drawing as A:P8-9.

A                B                C

**General**

10. Use the **DONUT** command to draw the objects shown below using the following values. Save the drawing as A:P8-10.

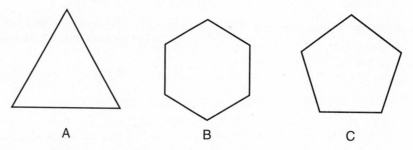

A          B          C

|   | Inner Diameter | Outer Diameter |
|---|---|---|
| A | .5 | 1.2 |
| B | 1.0 | 1.2 |
| C | 0 | .2 |

**General**

11. Use the **MULTIPLE** command modifier to draw four hexagons similar to the one shown in Problem 9, Example B. Save the drawing as A:P8-11.

**General**

12. Preset the doughnut inside diameter to .25 and the outside diameter to 1.25. Turn **FILL** on. Use the pull-down menu selection to draw four doughnuts with these settings. Place the doughnuts 1.5 units apart in a straight horizontal line. Save the drawing as A:P8-12.

## Learning objectives

After completing this chapter, you will be able to:

❍ Use the **OSNAP** command to set a running **Object Snap**.
❍ Use the **OSNAP** override.
❍ Identify three ways to discontinue a running **OSNAP**.
❍ List three ways to access the **Object Snap** modes.
❍ Describe the **QUICK** mode.
❍ Use the **Object Snap** interrupt and running modes to make several geometric constructions.
❍ Adjust aperture size.
❍ Use the **OFFSET** command to draw parallel lines and curves.
❍ Divide existing objects into equal parts using the **DIVIDE** command.
❍ Use the **MEASURE** command to set designated increments on an existing object.
❍ Set point sizes and options to draw points.
❍ Use the geometry calculator to draw and edit geometric constructions.
❍ Use X and Y filters to locate and project features and views.

This chapter explains how the powerful **OSNAP** command and its snap modes are used to perform geometric constructions. **OSNAP** is the command name for **Object Snap**. **Object Snap** allows you to precisely place points on existing objects. This chapter also explains how to draw parallel lines, divide objects, and place point symbols.

## SNAPPING TO SPECIFIC OBJECTS OR FEATURES

AUG 3

**Object Snap** is one of the most useful tools found in AutoCAD. It increases your drafting ability, performance, and productivity. The term *object snap* refers to the cursor's ability to "snap" exactly to a specific point or place on an object. The advantage of **Object Snap** is that you do not have to pick an exact point.

When using **Object Snap**, the screen cursor takes the shape of a box and crosshairs. This target box, called an *aperture*, is then used to pick the desired object. For example, suppose you want to connect a line to the end of another line. Move the aperture near the end of the line and pick. You do not have to place the aperture exactly at the endpoint. If you are drawing a line to the point of tangency on a circle, pick the **Tangent** option. Then, pick a point on the circle near the estimated point of tangency. See Figure 9-1.

Figure 9-1.   The **Object Snap** target box, or aperture. Simply move the cursor near the point to select and pick.

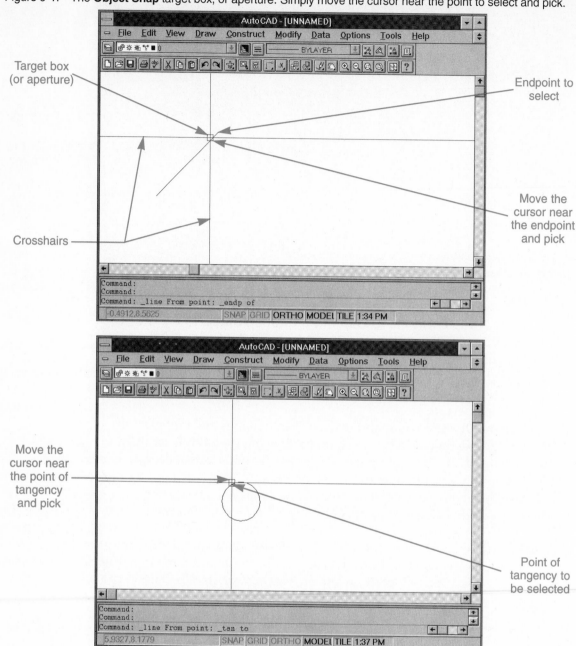

## THE **OBJECT SNAP** MODES

AUG 3

The **Object Snap** modes determine what the aperture snaps to. These modes can be activated using one of several different methods. An **Object Snap** can be typed at the prompt line or selected from the **Object Snap** cascading submenu in the **Edit** pull-down menu (if the ACADFULL menu is loaded), Figure 9-2. You can access a *cursor menu* with the same options by holding down the [Shift] key and clicking the [Enter] button on your mouse or puck. In addition, **Object Snap** modes are available as buttons in the **Object Snap** toolbar. To activate the **Object Snap** toolbar, select **Toolbars** from the **Tools** pull-down menu. Then, select **Object Snap** in the **Toolbar** cascading submenu.

Figure 9-2. The **Object Snap** cascading submenu (shown here highlighted) provides quick access to **Object Snap** modes.

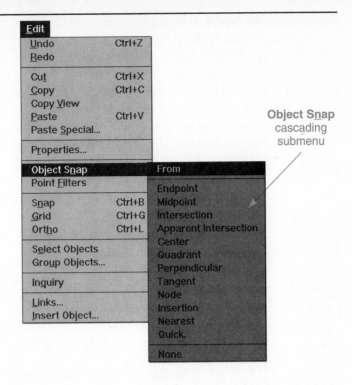

**NOTE**  When AutoCAD for Windows is configured to display screen menus, the **Object Snap** modes screen menu can be accessed by picking "* * * *" near the top of the current screen menu.

## Object Snap modes defined

Each **Object Snap** mode has a specific application. When typed at the prompt line, only the first three letters are required. The **Object Snap** modes are defined below. The letters in parentheses indicate what you need to type at the **Object snap modes:** prompt to activate the mode.

- **Snap to Apparent Intersection. (APP)** Finds the apparent intersection. In other words, the point where two objects would intersect if they were extended.
- **Snap to Center. (CEN)** Locates the center point of a radial object. This includes circles, arcs, ellipses, elliptical arcs, and radial solids.
- **Snap to Endpoint. (END)** Finds the nearest endpoint of a line, arc, elliptical arc, spline, ellipse, ray, solid, or mline.
- **Snap to Insertion. (INS)** Finds the insertion point of text objects and blocks.
- **Snap to Intersection. (INT)** Picks the closest intersection of two features.
- **Snap to Midpoint. (MID)** Finds the middle point of any object having two endpoints, such as a line, arc, elliptical arc, spline, ellipse, ray, solid, xline, or mline.
- **Snap to Nearest. (NEA)** Locates the point on an object closest to the crosshairs.
- **Snap to Node. (NOD)** Picks a point object drawn with the **POINT** command.
- **Snap to Perpendicular. (PER)** Finds a point that is perpendicular to an object from the previously picked point. Perpendicularity can be found with reference to an arc, elliptical arc, ellipse, spline, ray, xline, mline, solid, trace, or circle.
- **Snap to Quadrant. (QUA)** Picks the closest of the four quadrant points that can be found on circles, arcs, elliptical arcs, ellipses, and radial solids. (Not all of these objects may have all four quadrants.)

- **Snap to Quick. (QUI)** Finds the first selection in the database for the specified **Object Snap** mode that is selected immediately after **Snap to Quick**. For example, if you use the **Snap to Endpoint** option and two lines are found in the aperture area, then the entire drawing database is searched for all applicable points and the closest point is used. However, if **Snap to Quick** is specified, the database is searched and the first applicable point is used, with no further searching. Thus the term "quick," since it can be much faster in a large drawing file.
- **Snap to Tangent. (TAN)** Finds points of tangency between radial and linear objects.
- **Snap to None. (NON)** Turns running **Object Snap** off. This can also be used as an override that causes AutoCAD to ignore any currently running **Object Snap** modes.

### PROFESSIONAL TIP

Remember that **Object Snap** modes are not commands, but are used in conjunction with AutoCAD drawing and editing functions. If you type MID or PER at the **Command:** prompt for example, AutoCAD displays an "Unknown Command" error message.

If you choose to enter the **Endpoint** mode from the keyboard, be careful typing. If you type END at the **Command:** prompt, you will end the drawing session. For this reason, it is recommended that you type ENDP for the **Endpoint** mode until you become more familiar with the program, or select the **Object Snap** modes from the **Object Snap** toolbar.

## Using the **Object Snap** modes

Practice with the different **Object Snap** options to find which works best in various situations. **Object Snap** can be used during many commands, such as **LINE**, **CIRCLE**, **ARC**, **MOVE**, **COPY**, and **INSERT**. The most common **Object Snap** uses are discussed in the following sections.

## Finding the endpoint

In many cases, you need to connect a line, arc, or center point of a circle to the endpoint of an existing line or arc. Select the **Snap to Endpoint** option and move the aperture past the midpoint of the line or arc toward the end to be picked. To connect a line to the endpoint of the existing line A in Figure 9-3, the following command sequence is used:

Command: **LINE** ↵
From point: *(pick a point)*
To point: *(pick the* **Snap to Endpoint** *button from the* **Object Snap** *toolbar, type*
    END *and press* [Enter], *or pick* **Endpoint** *from the cursor or cascading submenus)*
of *(move the aperture near the end of line A and pick)*
To point: ↵
Command:

Figure 9-3.  Using **Object Snap** to find the endpoint of a line.

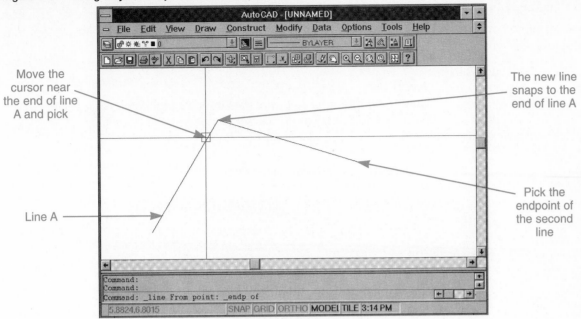

Another application is to snap an arc or line to the endpoint of an existing arc. To connect a new arc to the endpoint of the existing arc A in Figure 9-4, use the following command sequence:

Command: **ARC** ↵
Center/⟨Start point⟩: *(pick a point)*
Center/End/⟨Second point⟩: *(pick the second point)*
End point: *(pick the* **Snap to Endpoint** *button from the* **Object Snap** *toolbar, type* END
    *and press* [Enter], *or pick* **Endpoint** *from the cursor or cascading submenus)*
of *(move the aperture to somewhere near the end of arc A and pick)*

Figure 9-4.  Using **Object Snap** to find the endpoint of an arc.

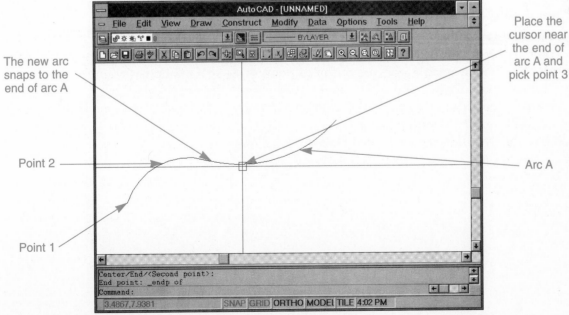

### Finding the midpoint

The **Snap to Midpoint** mode finds and picks the midpoint of a line, polyline, or arc. For example, to connect a line from any point to the midpoint of line A shown in Figure 9-5, use the following command sequence:

Command: **LINE** ↵
From point: *(pick a point)*
To point: *(pick the* **Snap to Midpoint** *button from the* **Object Snap** *toolbar, type* MID
    *and press* [Enter], *or pick* **Midpoint** *from the cursor or cascading submenus)*
of *(move aperture to anywhere on line A and pick)*

Figure 9-5.   Using **Object Snap** to find the midpoint of a line.

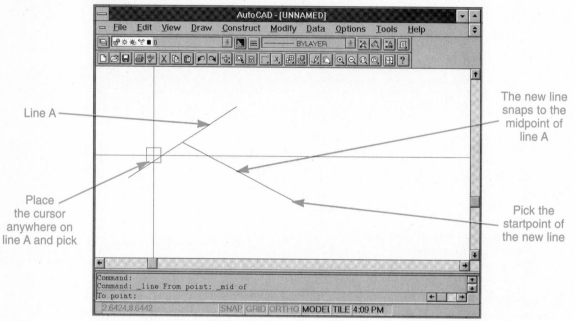

EXERCISE 9-1

❑ Load AutoCAD for Windows and open PRODR1, or begin a new drawing using your own variables.

❑ Use the **Object Snap** modes **Snap to Endpoint** or **Snap to Midpoint** to draw the object shown below. Draw line 1, then line 2 connecting to the endpoint of line 1. Draw line 3 from the endpoint of line 2 to the midpoint of line 1. Draw arc A with one end connected to the endpoint of line 1.

❑ Save the drawing as A:EX9-1 and quit AutoCAD.

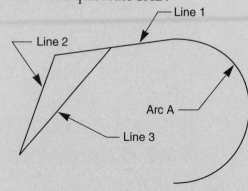

## Finding the center of a circle or arc

The **Snap to Center** option allows you to snap to the center point of a circle, doughnut, ellipse, elliptical arc, or arc. The following command sequence, as shown in Figure 9-6, draws a line from the center of circle A to the center of circle B.

> Command: **LINE** ↵
> From point: *(pick the* **Snap to Center** *button from the* **Object Snap** *toolbar, type*
>     CEN *and press* [Enter], *or pick* **Center** *from the cursor or cascading submenus)*
> of *(move aperture to anywhere on circle A and pick)*
> To point: *(pick the* **Snap to Endpoint** *button from the* **Object Snap** *toolbar, type*
>     CEN *and press* [Enter], *or pick* **Center** *from the cursor or cascading submenus)*
> of *(move aperture to anywhere on circle B and pick)*

Figure 9-6.   Using **Object Snap** to find the center of a circle.

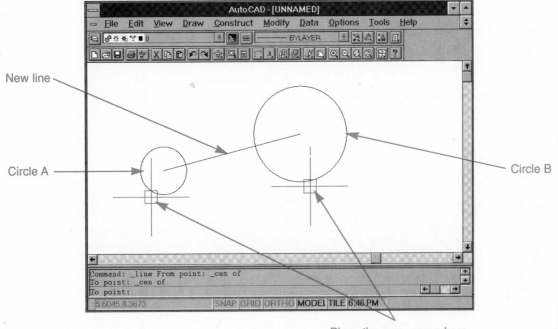

New line

Circle A

Circle B

Place the cursor anywhere
on the circles and pick

## Finding the quadrant of a circle or arc

A *quadrant* is a quarter section of a circle, doughnut, ellipse, elliptical arc, or arc. The **Object Snap** mode **Snap to Quadrant** finds the 0°, 90°, 180°, and 270° positions on a circle, doughnut, or arc, Figure 9-7.

Figure 9-7.   The quadrants
of a circle.

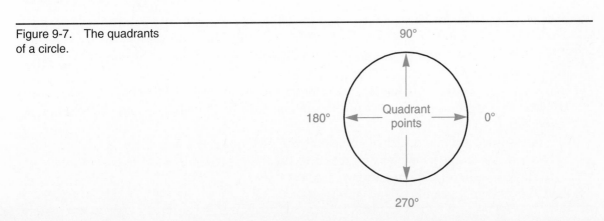

90°

180°

Quadrant
points

0°

270°

When picking quadrants, locate the aperture on the circle, doughnut, or arc closest to the intended quadrant. For example, circle B in Figure 9-8 may be drawn with its center located at one of the quadrants of circle A. The command sequence using the **Quadrant** option is as follows:

Command: **CIRCLE** ⏎
3P/2P/TTR/⟨Center point⟩: *(pick the* **Snap to Quadrant** *button from the* **Object Snap** *toolbar, type* QUA *and press* [Enter], *or pick* **Quadrant** *from the cursor or cascading submenus)*
of *(move the aperture to anywhere near the desired quadrant on circle A and pick)*
Diameter/⟨Radius⟩: *(pick a radius)*

Figure 9-8.   Using **Object Snap** to find the 0° quadrant of a circle.

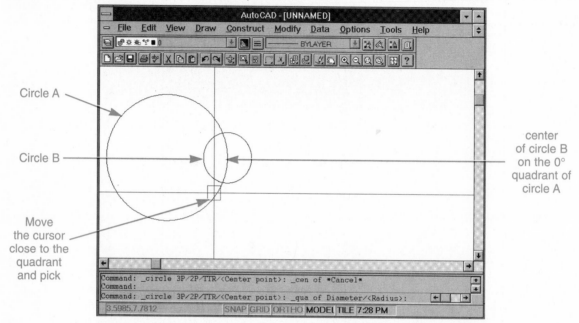

NOTE          Quadrant positions are unaffected by the current angle zero direction, but always coincide with the current **UCS** (User Coordinate System). The **UCS** is discussed in detail in Chapter 19 and Chapter 20 of this text. The quadrant points of a circle, doughnut, or arc are at the top, bottom, left, and right, regardless of the rotation of the object. However, the quadrant points of ellipses and elliptical arcs rotate with the object.

## EXERCISE 9-2

❏ Load AutoCAD for Windows and open PRODR1, or begin a new drawing using your own variables.
❏ Use the **Object Snap** mode **Center** or **Quadrant** for the following situations:
  ❏ Draw two separate circles and refer to the one on the left as circle A and the other as circle B.
  ❏ Draw a line from the center of circle A to the 180° quadrant of circle B.
  ❏ Draw a line from the center of circle B to the 270° quadrant of circle B to the 270° of circle A, and finally to the center of circle A.
❏ Save the drawing as A:EX9-2 and quit.

## Finding the intersection of lines

If it is necessary to snap to the intersection of two or more entities, use the **Snap to Intersection** option. Given line A intersecting arc A in Figure 9-9, the method to draw another line to the point of intersection is as follows:

> Command: **LINE** ↵
> From point: *(pick a point)*
> To point: *(pick the **Snap to Intersection** button from the **Object Snap** toolbar, type* INT *and press* [Enter], *or pick **Intersection** from the cursor or cascading submenus)*
> of *(move the cursor so the intersection is somewhere inside the aperture and pick)*
> To point: ↵

Figure 9-9.   Using the **Object Snap** mode **Intersection**.

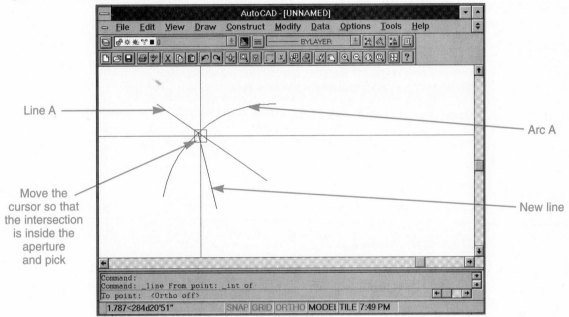

While picking with the aperture box over the intersection is the fastest way to select an intersection, the **Intersection** mode gives you an alternate means of finding the intersection. In an area of the drawing that is crowded, or if the current display doesn't show the actual intersection, pick one of the two intersecting objects. You are then prompted with "and" to allow you to pick the second object. The intersection point is found if these two objects intersect. The command sequence is as follows:

> Command: **LINE** ↵
> From point: *(pick a point)*
> To point: *(pick the **Snap to Intersection** button from the **Object Snap** toolbar, type* INT *and press* [Enter], *or pick **Intersection** from the cursor or cascading submenus)*
> of *(pick line A in Figure 9-9, not the intersection)*
> and *(pick arc A)*
> To point: ↵
> Command:

## Find the apparent intersection of lines

The **Object Snap** mode **Snap to Apparent Intersection** is used to find the point where two objects would intersect if they were extended far enough, as shown in Figure 9-10. For example, if you want to draw a line from the endpoint of an existing line to where it would intersect another line as if it is extended, use the following command sequence:

> Command: **LINE** ↵
> From point: **ENDP** ↵
> of *(pick the endpoint of line 1)*
> To point: *(pick the* **Snap to Apparent Intersection** *button from the* **Object Snap**
>     *toolbar, type* APP *and press* [Enter], *or pick* **Apparent Intersection** *from the cursor*
>     *or cascading submenus)*
> _appint of *(pick line 2)*
> and *(pick line 1 again)*
> To point: ↵
> Command:

Figure 9-10.   Using **Object Snap** to find the apparent intersection of two objects.

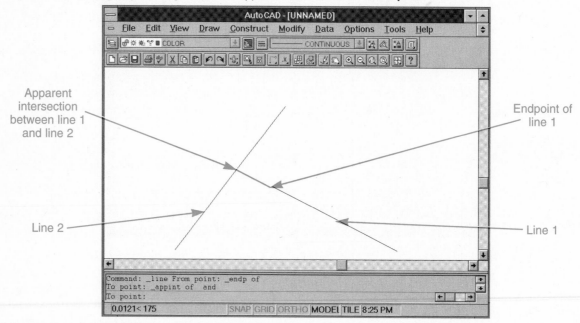

## Drawing a perpendicular line

A typical geometric construction is to draw one line or polyline perpendicular to another. This is easily done using the **Snap to Perpendicular** mode. For example, note line A and circle A in Figure 9-11. A line perpendicular to line A from the center point of circle A is drawn as follows:

> Command: **LINE** ↵
> From point: *(pick the* **Snap to Center** *button from the* **Object Snap** *toolbar, type*
>     CEN *and press* [Enter], *or pick* **Center** *from the cursor or cascading submenus)*
> of *(move the aperture to any location on the circumference of the circle and pick)*
> To point: *(pick the* **Snap to Perpendicular** *button from the* **Object Snap** *toolbar,*
>     *type* PER *and press* [Enter], *or pick* **Perpendicular** *from the cursor or cascading*
>     *submenus)*
> to *(move the aperture to any place on line A and pick)*
> To point: ↵

Figure 9-11.   Using the **Object Snap** modes **Perpendicular** and **Center**.

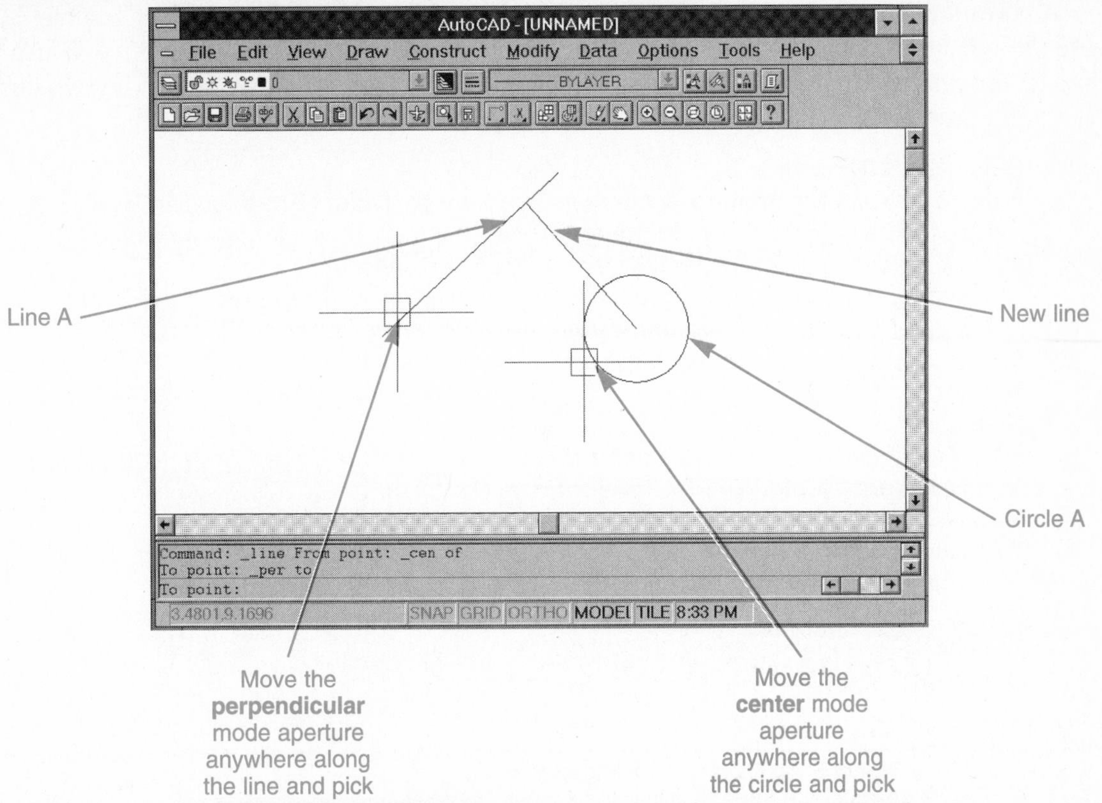

Line A

New line

Circle A

Move the
**perpendicular**
mode aperture
anywhere along
the line and pick

Move the
**center** mode
aperture
anywhere along
the circle and pick

**EXERCISE 9-3**

❑ Load AutoCAD for Windows and open PRODR1, or begin a new drawing using your own variables.

❑ Draw a horizontal line, then draw a circle above the line. Add a new line from the circle's center, perpendicular to the first line.

❑ Draw two intersecting lines and a separate circle. Add a line from the circle's center to the intersection of the lines.

❑ Draw two nonintersecting, nonparallel lines similar to Figure 9-10. Draw a line from the endpoint of one line to its apparent intersection with the other line.

❑ Save the drawing as A:EX9-3.

## Drawing a line tangent to a circle or arc

A common geometric construction is a line tangent to a circle or arc. In Chapter 7 you were shown how to draw circles tangent to lines, circles, and arcs. Now, you will use the **Snap to Tangent** mode to draw lines tangent to an existing circle or arc, given the two circles shown in Figure 9-12. The command sequence is:

Command: **LINE** ⏎
From point: *(pick the* **Snap to Tangent** *button from the* **Object Snap** *toolbar, type* TAN *and press* [Enter], *or pick* **Tangent** *from the cursor or cascading submenus)*
to *(pick a point on circle A near the intended point of tangency)*
To point: *(pick the* **Snap to Tangent** *button from the* **Object Snap** *toolbar, type* TAN *and press* [Enter], *or pick* **Tangent** *from the cursor or cascading submenus)*
to *(pick a point on circle B near the intended point of tangency)*
To point: ⏎
Command: ⏎
LINE From point: *(pick the* **Snap to Tangent** *button from the* **Object Snap** *toolbar, type* TAN *and press* [Enter], *or pick* **Tangent** *from the cursor or cascading submenus)*
to *(pick a point on circle A near the intended point of tangency)*
To point: *(pick the* **Snap to Tangent** *button from the* **Object Snap** *toolbar, type* TAN *and press* [Enter], *or pick* **Tangent** *from the cursor or cascading submenus)*
to *(pick a point on circle B near the intended point of tangency)*
To point: ⏎
Command:

Figure 9-12. Using **Object Snap** to draw lines tangent to circles.

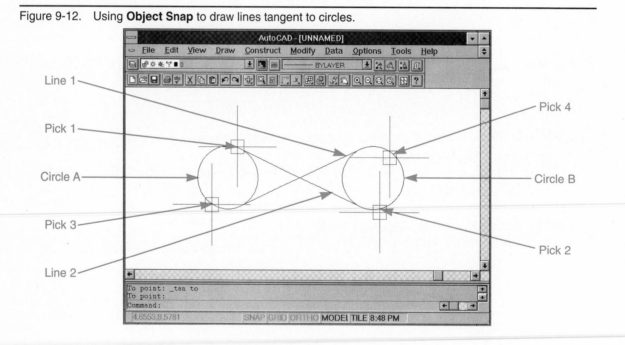

## EXERCISE 9-4

❑ Load AutoCAD for Windows and open PRODR1, or begin a new drawing using your own variables.
❑ Draw two circles with tangent lines similar to those shown in Figure 9-12 using the **Object Snap** mode **Tangent**.
❑ Use the **Object Snap** mode **Tangent** option to draw two lines that are tangent to the circles, but do not cross.
❑ Save the drawing as A:EX9-4 and quit.

### Using fast object snaps

When AutoCAD draws using **Object Snap** modes, it searches for the best solution to your request. In a simple drawing, this process happens very fast. However, as your drawing becomes complex, it may take some time for the snap object to be found. You can speed up the process by selecting the **Object Snap** mode **Quick**. To use this mode, select the **Snap to Quick** button from the **Object Snap** toolbar and then the desired **Object Snap** option. You can also type QUI, followed by a comma, and then the desired **Object Snap** option. (The **Quick** mode is not effective on the **Object Snap** mode **Intersection**.) The **Quick** mode directs AutoCAD to look only for the first solution to your request, and then end the search. The only problem you may find is that the first AutoCAD selection may not be the best choice. However, in most cases the **Quick** mode works to your advantage and helps increase productivity. The following command sequence shows the **Quick** mode used on the example illustrated in Figure 9-12.

```
Command: LINE ↵
From point: QUI,TAN ↵
to (pick a point on circle A near the intended point of tangency)
To point: QUI,TAN ↵
to (pick a point on circle B near the intended point of tangency)
To point: ↵
Command: ↵
LINE From point: QUI,TAN ↵
to (pick a point on circle A near the intended point of tangency)
To point: QUI,TAN ↵
to (pick a point on circle B near the intended point of tangency)
To point: ↵
Command:
```

### Using the cursor menu for **Object Snap**

Holding down the [Shift] key and clicking the [Enter] button on a mouse or puck activates the **Object Snap** options in a cursor menu. The cursor menu is displayed at the location of the screen crosshairs, Figure 9-13. This feature is very convenient and saves time. Simply move the arrow pointer to the desired **Object Snap** and click. The cursor menu disappears and the **Object Snap** is enabled for one pick.

Figure 9-13.   The **Object Snap** cursor menu.

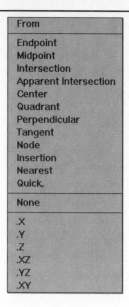

| From |
|---|
| Endpoint |
| Midpoint |
| Intersection |
| Apparent Intersection |
| Center |
| Quadrant |
| Perpendicular |
| Tangent |
| Node |
| Insertion |
| Nearest |
| Quick. |
| None |
| .X |
| .Y |
| .Z |
| .XZ |
| .YZ |
| .XY |

## Using the FROM point selection option

The **FROM** point selection mode allows you to establish a relative or polar coordinate entry from a specified reference base point. Access the **FROM** option by selecting the **Snap From** button in the **Object Snap** toolbar, select **From** in any of the **Object Snap** menus, or type FROM at a point selection prompt. The example in Figure 9-14 shows the center point for a circle being established as a polar distance from the midpoint of an existing line. The command sequence is shown here:

Command: **CIRCLE** ↵
3P/2P/TTR/⟨Center point⟩: **FROM** ↵
Base point: **MID** ↵
of *(pick the line)* ⟨offset⟩: **@2⟨45** ↵
Diameter/⟨Radius⟩: **.75** ↵
Command:

Figure 9-14.   Using the **FROM** point selection mode following the command sequence given in the text.

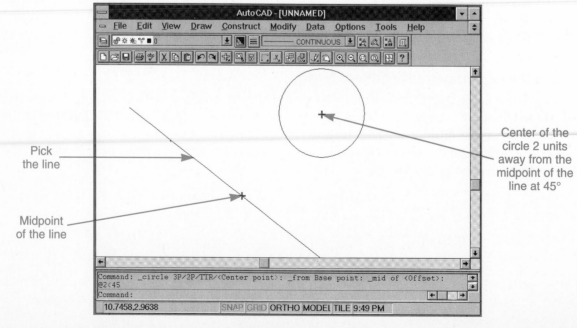

## SETTING A RUNNING OBJECT SNAP

AUG 3

The previous discussion explained how to use **Object Snap** options by typing the first three letters of the desired **Object Snap** at the prompt line, selecting the options from the pull-down or cursor menus, or clicking an **Object Snap** button in the **Object Snap** toolbar. These are called **OSNAP** *overrides*. The overrides work well in many situations. However, if you plan to use one **Object Snap** frequently, you can set *running object snaps*. AutoCAD automatically uses only the running **Object Snap** modes that you have selected.

### Using the dialog box to set running object snaps

You can set a running **Object Snap** using the **Running Object Snap** dialog box. Pick **Running Object Snap...** from the **Options** pull-down menu, or pick the **Running Object Snap** button from the **Object Snap** toolbar. You can also type DDOSNAP at the **Command:** prompt to access the dialog box. Notice in Figure 9-15 the **Endpoint**, **Perpendicular**, and **Tangent** are active. You can use this dialog box at any time to discontinue the running **Object Snap** or to set another **Object Snap**.

Figure 9-15.   Running **Object Snap** modes can be quickly set using the **Running Object Snap** dialog box. The aperture size can also be quickly set in this dialog box.

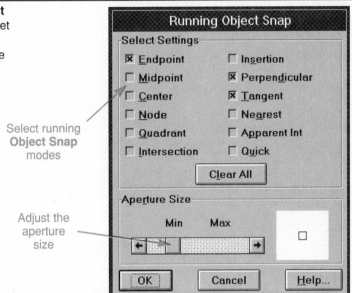

### Using the **Command:** prompt to set running object snaps

To set a running **Object Snap** at the **Command:** prompt, type OSNAP. The **Object snap modes:** prompt then appears. Enter the mode that you want to use as the running **Object Snap**. For example, if you want to set **Endpoint** as the running **Object Snap**, type END (or ENDP) as follows:

        Command: **OSNAP** ↵
        Object snap modes: **END** ↵

If you plan to use several **Object Snap** modes frequently, then set them by typing the first three letters of each, separated by commas. For example:

        Command: **OSNAP** ↵
        Object snap modes: **END,PER,TAN** ↵

Now the running **Object Snap** is set to perform endpoint, perpendicular, and tangency operations. All other **Object Snap** modes are ignored unless picked from the toolbar, the pull-down or cursor menus, or typed during a command in which case the override will be applied to a single pick.

### Overriding or getting out of the running OSNAP

You can temporarily override the running **OSNAP** by typing a different **Object Snap** request at the prompt. This is referred to as an **OSNAP** *override*. After the new **Object Snap** operation has been performed, the running snaps remain in effect.

The current running **OSNAP** can also be discontinued. Type NONE, OFF, or press the [Enter] key as follows:

        Command: **OSNAP** ↵
        Object snap mode: *(type* NONE *or* OFF *and press* [Enter], *or press* [Enter])

As needed, you can remove the active checks in the **Running Object Snap** dialog box to override running snaps. You can also pick the **Clear All** button to discontinue all modes.

---

### EXERCISE 9-5

❏ Load AutoCAD for Windows and open PRODR1, or begin a new drawing using your own variables.

❏ Set the **Endpoint**, **Midpoint**, and **Perpendicular** running **Object Snaps** and practice using them in at least two situations. Drawings similar to Figure 9-3, Figure 9-4, Figure 9-5, and Figure 9-11 can be used.

❏ Change the running **OSNAP** to **Center** and **Tangent**, and use each twice in creating a simple drawing. Drawings similar to Figure 9-6 and Figure 9-12 can be used.

❏ Discontinue the running **OSNAP**.

❏ Save the drawing as A:EX9-5 and quit.

---

**PROFESSIONAL TIP**

Use the **Object Snap** modes not only when drawing, but also when editing. With practice, using **Object Snap** becomes second nature, and greatly increases your productivity and accuracy.

---

## CHANGING THE APERTURE SIZE                                       AUG 3

Earlier in this chapter, you were introduced to the aperture. It appears on the screen when you enter **Object Snap** modes or use the **OSNAP** command. The size of the aperture may be enlarged to provide a bigger pick area. It may also be reduced in size to provide more accurate picking of a complex detail. The size of the aperture is measured in *pixels*. Pixels is short for "picture elements." Pixels are the dots that make up a display screen. The AutoCAD prototype drawing sets the aperture size at 10 pixels. If you want to change the size of the aperture, type APERTURE at the **Command:** prompt. You are then asked to enter the desired aperture box size in pixels. This is limited to a number between 1 and 50 pixels. To change the aperture size to 5 pixels, do the following:

        Command: **APERTURE** ↵
        Object snap target height (1-50 pixels) ⟨*current*⟩: **5** ↵
        Command:

Examples of different aperture box sizes are shown in Figure 9-16.

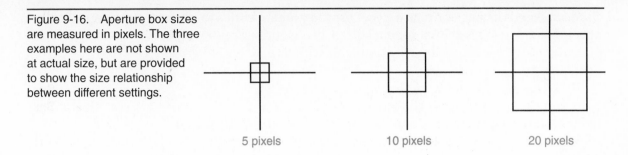

Figure 9-16.   Aperture box sizes are measured in pixels. The three examples here are not shown at actual size, but are provided to show the size relationship between different settings.

5 pixels                    10 pixels                    20 pixels

Keep in mind that the "aperture" and the "pick box" are different. The aperture is displayed on the screen when **Object Snap** modes are used. The pick box appears on the screen for any command that activates the **Select objects:** prompt. For example, the **ERASE** command issues the **Select objects:** prompt, thus displaying the pick box.

Another easy way to change the aperture size is found in the **Running Object Snap** dialog box. Look at Figure 9-15 and notice the **Aperture Size** area. Move the scroll bar between **Min** (minimum) and **Max** (maximum) and watch the sample aperture in the image tile change size accordingly. Pick **OK** when the aperture is the size you want.

---

### EXERCISE 9-6

❑ Load AutoCAD for Windows, insert your exercise floppy disk, and pick **New**... from the **File** pull-down menu. Enter A:EX9-5 in the **Prototype...** text box followed by entering EX9-6 in the **New Drawing Name...** text box. Pick the **OK** button to use EX9-5 as the prototype for EX9-6.
  ❑ Change the aperture size to 5 pixels. Draw lines to existing objects using the **Object Snap** modes of your choice.
  ❑ Change the aperture size to 20 pixels. Again, draw lines to the existing objects using the **Object Snap** modes of your choice.
  ❑ Observe the difference in aperture size. Determine your personal preference between the 5 and 20 pixel sizes as compared to the AutoCAD prototype set at 10 pixels.
❑ Save the drawing as A:EX9-6 and quit.

---

## DRAWING PARALLEL LINES AND CURVES                                    ⬚ **ARM 5**

The **OFFSET** command can be used to draw concentric circles, arcs, curves, polylines, or parallel lines. If the ACADFULL.MNU file is loaded, **Offset** is located in the **Construct** pull-down menu. Offset is also located as the **Copy Object** flyout in the **Modify** toolbar. OFFSET can also be typed at the **Command:** prompt as follows:

Command: **OFFSET** ↵
Offset distance or Through ⟨*current*⟩:

Type a desired distance or pick a point for the parallel entity to be drawn through. The last offset distance used is shown in brackets. If you want to draw two parallel circles a distance of .1 unit apart, use the following command sequence. Refer to Figure 9-17.

> Command: **OFFSET** ↵
> Offset distance or Through ⟨*current*⟩: **.1** ↵
> Select object to offset: *(pick the object)*
> Side to offset? *(pick the side of the object for the offset to be drawn)*
> Select object to offset: *(select another object or press* [Enter]*)*

Figure 9-17.  Drawing an offset using a designated distance.

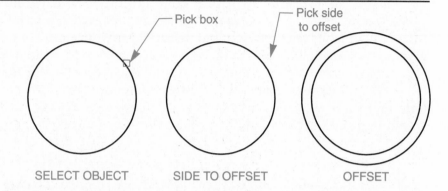

SELECT OBJECT        SIDE TO OFFSET        OFFSET

When the **Select object to offset:** prompt first appears, the screen cursor turns into a pick box. After the object is picked, the screen cursor turns back into crosshairs. None of the selection options work with the **OFFSET** command, with the exception of picking the object.

The other option is to pick a point that the offset is drawn through. Type T as follows to produce the results shown in Figure 9-18:

> Command: **OFFSET** ↵
> Offset distance or Through ⟨*current*⟩: **T** ↵
> Select object to offset: *(pick the object)*
> Through point: *(pick the point that the offset will be drawn through)*
> Select object to offset: ↵

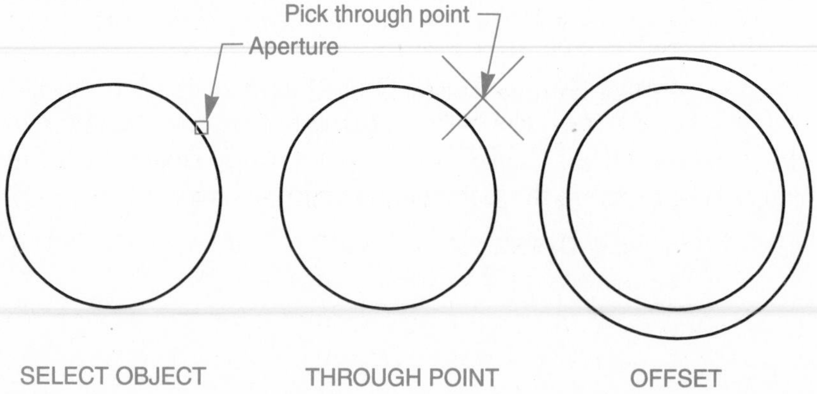

Figure 9-18.  Drawing an offset through a given point.

SELECT OBJECT        THROUGH POINT        OFFSET

PROFESSIONAL
TIP

**Object Snap** modes can be used to assist in drawing an offset. For example, suppose you have a circle apart from a line, as shown at A below. You want to draw another concentric circle tangent to the line, as shown at B below. Enter the following:

Command: **OFFSET** ↵

Offset distance or Through ⟨*current*⟩: *(pick the* **Snap to Quadrant** *button from the* **Object Snap** *toolbar, type* QUA *and press* [Enter], *or pick* **Quadrant** *from the cursor or cascading submenus)*

of *(pick the existing circle)*

Second point: *(pick the* **Snap to Perpendicular** *button from the* **Object Snap** *toolbar, type* PER *and press* [Enter], *or pick* **Perpendicular** *from the cursor or cascading submenus)*

to *(pick the existing line)*

Select object to offset: *(pick the existing circle)*

Side to offset? *(pick between the circle and line)*

Select object to offset: ↵

Command:

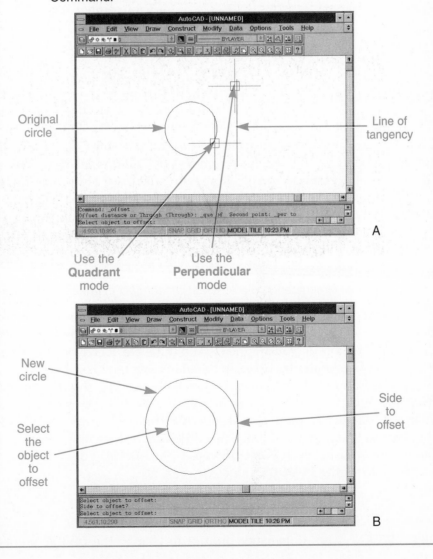

## Setting the offset distance default

The **OFFSETDIST** system variable creates an offset distance default. After setting the variable, the next time you offset an entity, the preset default will appear. To enter a .2 unit offset for the default value, use the following command sequence:

    Command: OFFSETDIST ↵
    New value for OFFSETDIST ⟨−1⟩: .2 ↵
    Command:

A setting of −1 makes the **Through** option the default.

---

### EXERCISE 9-7

❑ Load AutoCAD for Windows and open PRODR1, or begin a new drawing using your own variables.
❑ Draw two circles and two polylines made up of line and arc segments.
❑ Use the **OFFSET** command to draw parallels a distance of .2 unit on the inside of one circle and one polyline.
❑ Use the **OFFSET** command again, this time specifying **Through** point on the outside of the other circle and polyline.
❑ Use the command sequence shown in the Professional Tip on page 259 to draw a similar object.
❑ Save the drawing as A:EX9-7 and quit.

---

## DIVIDING AN OBJECT INTO AN EQUAL NUMBER OF PARTS     AUG 3

A line, circle, arc, or polyline can be divided into an equal number of segments using the **DIVIDE** command. The **Divide** button is found in **Point** flyout in the **Draw** toolbar, or DIVIDE can be typed at the **Command:** prompt. If the ACADFULL.MNU file is loaded, you can select **Divide** from the **Point** cascading submenu of the **Draw** pull-down menu.

Suppose you have drawn a line and want to divide it into eight equal parts. Enter the **DIVIDE** command and select the object to divide. Then, enter the number of divisions or segments. Refer to Figure 9-19. The procedure is as follows:

    Command: DIVIDE ↵
    Select object to divide: (pick the object)
    ⟨Number of segments⟩/Block: (enter the number of divisions and press [Enter])

The **Block** option of the **DIVIDE** command allows you to place a block at each division point. A *block* is a previously drawn symbol or shape. To initiate the **Block** option, type B or BLOCK at the prompt. You are then asked if the block is to be aligned with the object. Answer YES or NO. Blocks are discussed in detail in Chapter 25 of this text.

After the number of segments is given, the object is divided with dots. However, the dots may not show very well. Notice in Figure 9-19 that the appearance of the marks has been changed. The marks placed by the **DIVIDE** command are controlled by the **PDMODE** (point display mode) system variable. Basic **PDMODE** values range from 0 to 4. Figure 9-20 shows points drawn using each **PDMODE** value. The **PDMODE** default value is 0. Use the following sequence to set the **PDMODE** value:

    Command: PDMODE ↵
    New value for PDMODE ⟨0⟩: 3 ↵

Type REGEN at the **Command:** prompt to change the **DIVIDE** points to the new **PDMODE** setting.

Figure 9-19.  Using the **DIVIDE** command. Note that the default marks (points) have been changed to X's

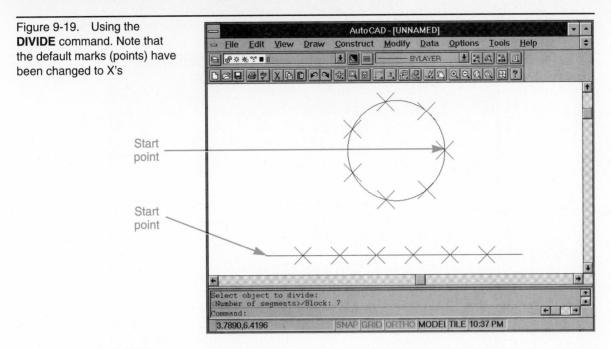

Figure 9-20.  The five basic **PDMODE** values and the corresponding symbols.

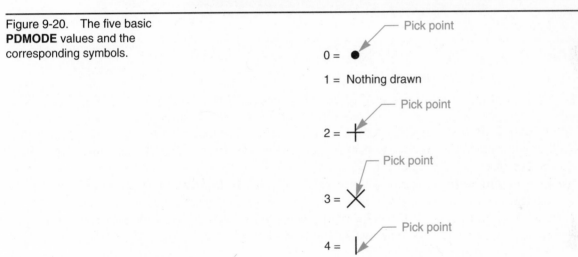

## MEASURE AN OBJECT INTO SPECIFIED DISTANCES

AUG 3

Unlike the **DIVIDE** command where an entity is divided into a specified number of parts, the **MEASURE** command places marks at a specified distance apart. The **Measure** button is found in the **Point** flyout in the **Draw** toolbar, or MEASURE can be typed at the **Command:** prompt. If the ACADFULL.MNU file is loaded, the **Measure** command is located in the **Point** cascading submenu of the **Draw** pull-down menu. The line shown in Figure 9-21 is measured with .75 unit segments as follows:

> Command: **MEASURE** ↵
> Select object to measure: *(pick an object)*
> ⟨Segment length⟩/Block: **.75** ↵

Measuring begins at the end closest to where the object is picked. All increments are equal to the entered segment length except the last segment. It may be shorter depending on the length of the entity. Refer to Figure 9-21. The **PDMODE** setting affects the marks placed on the object, just as it does with the **DIVIDE** command. Blocks can be inserted at the given distances using the **Block** option of the **MEASURE** command.

Figure 9-21.  Using the **MEASURE** command. Notice that the last segment may be shorter than the others, depending on the total length of the object.

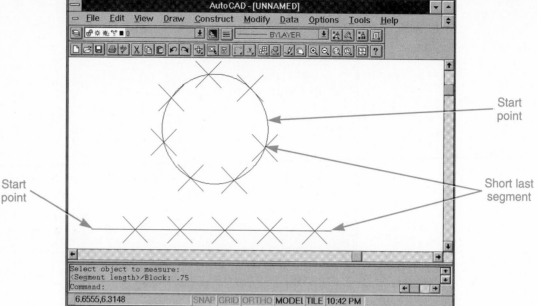

## EXERCISE 9-8

❏ Load AutoCAD for Windows and open PRODR1, or begin a new drawing using your own variables.
❏ Set the **PDMODE** to 3 before marks are drawn in this exercise.
❏ Draw two circles of any diameter, and two lines of any length.
❏ Use the **DIVIDE** command to divide one circle into 10 equal parts and one line into 5 equal parts.
❏ Use the **MEASURE** command to divide the other circle into .5 unit parts and the other line into .75 unit parts.
❏ Draw two parallel vertical lines. Make each line 3″ (76.2mm) long and space them 4″ (101.6mm) apart. Use the **DIVIDE** command to divide the line on the left into 10 equal increments. Draw horizontal parallel lines from each division on the left line over to the right line. Use the **OSNAP Node** and **Perpendicular** options to assist you.
❏ Save the drawing as A:EX9-8 and quit.

## DRAWING POINTS

AUG 2

You can draw points anywhere on the screen using the **POINT** command. The **Point** button can be picked from the **Draw** toolbar, or POINT can be typed at the **Command:** prompt. If the ACADFULL.MNU file is loaded, the **Point** command can be selected from the **Point** cascading submenu in the **Draw** pull-down menu. The specific type of point drawn is controlled by **PDMODE** discussed earlier. If you want to draw a dot (.), set the **PDMODE** to the default value of 0. Then proceed as follows:

    Command: **POINT** ↵
    Point: (type point coordinates or pick with pointing device)

Notice when you pick the point, it shows on the screen as a blip. The blip changes to a dot after using the **REDRAW** command, as shown in Figure 9-22. If you want to change the point style to a +, X, or |, set the **PDMODE** value as discussed earlier.

Figure 9-22.   Using the **POINT** command to change how a point appears on-screen.

Selected point shows as a blip

Selected point shows as a point after redraw

## Adding additional symbols to the point

So far you have changed the **PDMODE** to draw four different point types. You can also draw other symbols by adding another value to the original value, Figure 9-23. Draw a circle by adding 32 to the original **PDMODE** value. Add 64 to draw a square. Add 96 to draw a circle and square. For example, a point display of an X inside a circle has a **PDMODE** value of 35. That is the sum of the X value of 3 and the circle value of 32. If you want to draw a point with an X inside of a circle and square, enter the **PDMODE** value 99. Then use the **POINT** command as follows:

> Command: **PDMODE** ↵
> New value for PDMODE ⟨*current*⟩: **99** ↵
> Command: **POINT** ↵
> Point: (*pick the point*)
> Command:

When the **PDMODE** value is changed, all previously drawn points stay the same until the drawing is regenerated.

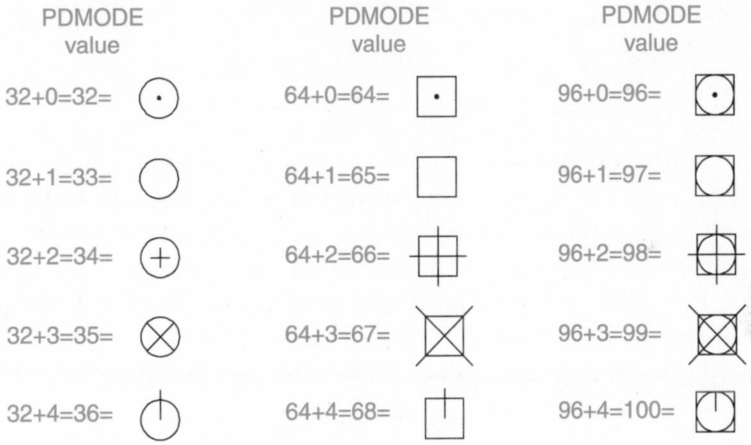

Figure 9-23.   By adding 32, 64, or 96 to the base **PDMODE** value, different symbols can be drawn.

| PDMODE value | | PDMODE value | | PDMODE value | |
|---|---|---|---|---|---|
| 32+0=32= | ⊙ | 64+0=64= | ▪ | 96+0=96= | ⊡ |
| 32+1=33= | ○ | 64+1=65= | □ | 96+1=97= | ⊡ |
| 32+2=34= | ⊕ | 64+2=66= | ⊞ | 96+2=98= | ⊕ |
| 32+3=35= | ⊗ | 64+3=67= | ⊠ | 96+3=99= | ⊠ |
| 32+4=36= | ⊖ | 64+4=68= | ⊥ | 96+4=100= | ⊡ |

## Changing the point size

The point size can be modified using the **PDSIZE** (point display size) system variable. The default **PDSIZE** value of 0 displays points at the size shown in Figure 9-20 and Figure 9-23. If you want to draw a point with a **PDSIZE** of 1, use the following command sequence:

> Command: **PDSIZE** ↵
> New value for PDSIZE ⟨0.0000⟩: **1** ↵
> Command: **POINT** ↵
> Point: (*pick the point*)
> Command:

The point retains the set **PDMODE** value, but the size changes. Figure 9-24 shows the point sizes of different **PDSIZE** values. Positive **PDSIZE** values change points in relation to different display options. For example, if the view is enlarged with the **ZOOM** command, the point size also increases. (Zoom is discussed in Chapter 10.) A negative **PDSIZE** value makes the points

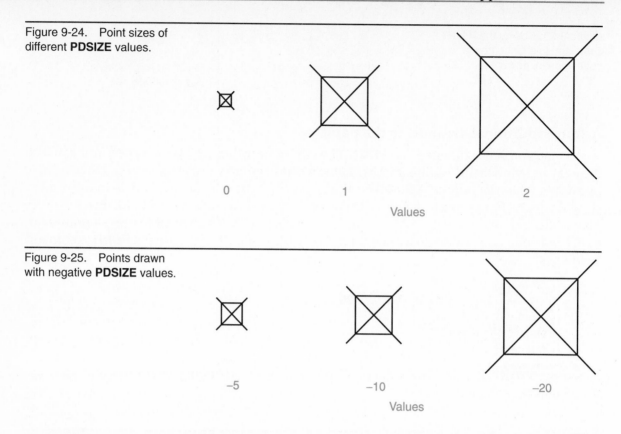

Figure 9-24.   Point sizes of
different **PDSIZE** values.

appear the same size no matter how much you **ZOOM** the drawing. Points drawn with negative **PDSIZE** values are shown in Figure 9-25.

### Using the Point Style icon menu

The **Point Style** icon menu is shown in Figure 9-26. It is accessed by selecting **Point Style...** from the **Display** cascading submenu in the **Options** pull-down menu. This is convenient since it lets you see and pick the point symbols displayed as graphic images. Pick the desired style from those displayed. Set the point size by entering a value in the **Point Size:** text box. Pick the **Set Size Relative to Screen** option button if you want the point size to change in relation to different display options (a positive value). Picking the **Set Size in Absolute Units** option button makes the points appear the same size no matter what display option is used (a negative value).

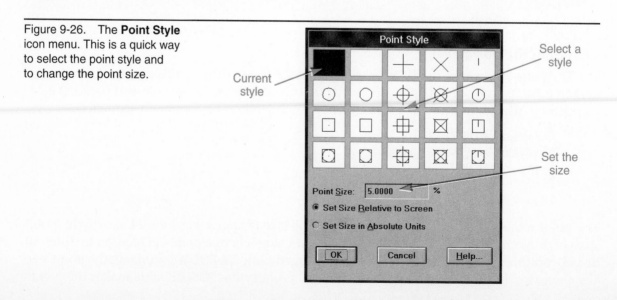

Figure 9-26.   The **Point Style**
icon menu. This is a quick way
to select the point style and
to change the point size.

## EXERCISE 9-9

❏ Load AutoCAD for Windows and open PRODR1, or begin a new drawing using your own variables.
❏ Draw a point with **PDMODE** set to the following values: 0, 1, 2, 3, 4, 32, 33, 66, 67, 98, 99, and 100.
❏ Type REGEN and observe the results.
❏ Set **PDMODE** to a value of 35. Then draw a point using each of the following **PDSIZE** values: 0, 1, 2, –5, –10, and –20.
❏ Save the drawing as A:EX9-9 and quit.

## USING THE CALCULATOR FOR GEOMETRIC CONSTRUCTION

AUG 3

AutoCAD's geometry calculator is a convenient tool to use when drawing and editing geometric constructions, and performing basic mathematical calculations. The geometry calculator is accessed by picking **Calculator** from the **Tools** pull-down menu, picking the **Calculator** button from the **Object Snap** toolbar, or by typing CAL at the **Command:** prompt. 'CAL can also be entered transparently when needed during any AutoCAD command. The calculator is especially helpful when entering points that are not easily located by other means, and for editing objects using mathematical calculations. You can also enter a math equation when you see the ⟩⟩ **Expression:** prompt, such as shown in the following command sequence:

```
Command: CAL ↵
⟩⟩ Expression: 2+2 ↵
4
Command:
```

The following discussion introduces the techniques and applications for using the geometry calculator.

### Making entries

Numbers are entered in the calculator in the same manner they are entered when locating coordinates on-screen. (Refer to Chapter 6 for details about entering numbers.) The standard format is inches. You can use decimal inches or scientific notation. Two formats are used for entering feet and inches: 0'–0" or 0'0". In the following example, 5'–6" is converted to 66". The value 5'6" could also be used.

```
Command: CAL ↵
⟩⟩ Expression: 5'–6" ↵
66.0
Command:
```

Angles are entered in decimal degrees. For example, 30d is 30 degrees. Minutes (') and seconds (") can be omitted if their values are 0. When minutes and seconds are included, they can be entered as 30d45'15". When *only* minutes and seconds are used, degrees are entered as 0d. You can also enter angles in radians by adding an "r" (3.5r), or in grads with a "g" (12.25g).

When entering coordinate values in the calculator, enclose them in square brackets ([ ]). Use standard absolute, relative, and polar coordinate notation (discussed in Chapter 6). Absolute values are entered as [X,Y,Z], such as [4,6,0]. Relative values are entered as [@X,Y,Z], such as [@2,4,0]. Polar values require a distance and angle value [distance⟨angle,Z], such as [6⟨45d,0]. The Z value is used for 3D applications. It can be entered as 0 or omitted for 2D applications. Coordinate values can be added in the calculator like this:

```
Command: CAL ⤶
⟩⟩ Expression: [4,2,0]+[2,6,0] ⤶
(6.0 8.0 0.0)
Command:
```

Other mathematical functions can also be performed using the calculator. The following symbols are used in mathematical expressions:

+ Add
− Subtract
* Multiply
/ Divide
∧ Exponents
( ) Grouped expressions

Parentheses are used to group the symbols and values into sets. Complex mathematical expressions where more than one set is involved are calculated beginning with the innermost grouped set. In any given set, exponents are calculated first, followed by multiplication and division, and then addition and subtraction. Calculations are then made from left to right.

## EXERCISE 9-10

❑ Load AutoCAD for Windows.
❑ Use the **CAL** command to make the following calculations:
  A. 28.125 + 37.625
  B. 16.875 − 7.375
  C. 6.25 + 3.5
  D. (25.75 ÷ 4) + (5.625 × 3)
❑ Do not save this exercise.

### Additional geometric calculations

In addition to the basic math functions previously discussed, AutoCAD's **CAL** command also allows you to obtain information about entities or make the following calculations:

| | |
|---|---|
| **RXOF**(*point*) | Provides the X coordinate of a point. |
| **RYOF**(*point*) | Provides the Y coordinate of a point. |
| **SIN**(*angle*) | Sine of angle. |
| **COS**(*angle*) | Cosine of angle. |
| **TANG**(*angle*) | Tangent of angle. |
| **ASIN**(*number*) | Arcsine of number between −1 and 1. |
| **ACOS**(*number*) | Arccosine of number between −1 and 1. |
| **ATAN**(*number*) | Arctangent of number. |
| **IN**(*number*) | Natural log of number. |
| **LOG**(*number*) | Base 10 logarithm of number. |
| **EXP**(*number*) | Natural exponent of number. |
| **EXP10**(*number*) | Base 10 exponent of number. |
| **SQR**(*number*) | Square of number. |
| **SQRT**(*number*) | Square root of positive number. |
| **ABS**(*number*) | Absolute value of number. |
| **ROUND**(*number*) | Rounds number to nearest integer. |

| **TRUNC**(*number*) | Provides integer part of number (portion preceding the decimal point). |
| **R2D**(*angle*) | Converts angle in radians to degrees. |
| **D2R**(*angle*) | Converts angle in degrees to radians. |
| **CVUNIT**(*value,from,to*) | Converts a value from one unit of measurement to another, such as inches to millimeters. For example, CVUNIT(6,IN,MM) converts 6″ to the equivalent in millimeters (152.4mm). |
| **PI** | Constant value π (3.1415926). |

An example of calculating the square root of 25 is as follows:

> Command: **CAL** ↵
> ⟩⟩ Expression: **SQRT(25)** ↵
> 5.0
> Command:

---

### EXERCISE 9-11

❑ Load AutoCAD for Windows.
❑ Use the **CAL** command to perform the following calculations:
  A. Sine of 30°
  B. Cosine of 18°
  C. Circumference of a 4 in. diameter circle. Use the formula: $C = \pi \times D$
  D. Round off 9.875 to nearest integer
  E. Convert 18 inches to millimeters
  F. $23^2$
  G. Square root of 79
❑ Do not save this exercise.

---

### 2D entity calculations

Some functions of the geometry calculator can be used to help create or edit a drawing. The following functions involve calculations in a 2D, or XY plane, environment. Some functions have shortcut versions that combine some functions and the **Endpoint Object Snap** mode. Additional functions are used for 3D (XYZ plane) vector calculations for descriptive geometry. 3D functions are detailed in the *AutoCAD Command Reference* under the **'CAL** listing. You can also use certain **Object Snap** modes in place of the variables. See the following section for more detail.

| **CUR** | Allows you to pick a point using the cursor. |
| **DEE** | Distance between endpoints of two entities. This command spelled out is DIST(END,END). |
| **DIST**(*P1,P2*) | Distance between points P1 and P2. |
| **DPL**(*P,P1,P2*) | Distance between point P and line P1-P2. |
| **ILL**(*P1,P2,P3,P4*) | Gives the intersection between lines P1-P2 and P3-P4. |
| **ILLE** | This is a shortcut version of **ILL**(*P1,P2,P3,P4*). |
| **MEE** | Gives the midpoint between two endpoints. This command is spelled out (END + END)/2. |
| **PLD**(*P1,P2,DIST*) | Point on line P1-P2, that is the specified distance (DIST) from P1. |
| **PLT**(*P1,P2,T*) | Point on line P1-P2 defined by parameter T. |
| **RAD** | Gives the radius of the circle or arc selected. |
| **ROT**(*P,ORIGIN,ANGLE*) | Rotates point P through an angle about the origin. |
| **ROT**(*P,P1AX,P2AX*) | Rotates point P through an angle using line P1-P2 as the rotation axis. |

To determine the length of a line, use the following command sequence:

> Command: **CAL** ⏎
> 》 Expression: **DEE** ⏎
> 》 Select one endpoint for DEE: *(pick one end of the line)*
> 》 Select another endpoint for DEE: *(pick the other end)*
> 6.30064

The radius of a circle, arc, or polyline is determined using the following procedure:

> Command: **CAL** ⏎
> 》 Expression: **RAD** ⏎
> Select circle, arc or polyline segment for RAD function: *(pick one of specified entities)*
> 1.06682
> Command:

### Using the Object Snap modes

The **Object Snap** modes can be used in place of point coordinates in 2D entity calculations. This instructs AutoCAD to automatically issue the **OSNAP** mode you need to easily pick an exact point, thus eliminating the need for you to enter the point coordinates at the keyboard. All you need to enter are the first three letters of the **Object Snap** mode, as with any **OSNAP** operation. The **CAL** command supports the following **OSNAP** modes:

- **Endpoint**
- **Insert**
- **Intersection**
- **Midpoint**
- **Center**
- **Nearest**
- **Node**
- **Quadrant**
- **Perpendicular**
- **Tangent**

### Calculating the angle between lines

Some calculator functions allow you to find the angle from the X axis or between given lines. The angle is measured counterclockwise. The formulas for these functions are:

**ANG(*P1,P2*)**  Provides the angle between the X axis and line P1-P2. Use the **Endpoint Object Snap** mode to pick the endpoints.

**ANG(*APEX,P1,P2*)**  Returns the angle between lines in an XY plane. For example, if you want to find the angle between the two lines in Figure 9-27, use the following command sequence:

> Command: **CAL** ⏎
> 》 Expression: **ANG(END,END,END)** ⏎
> 》 Select entity for END snap: *(pick the vertex)*
> 》 Select entity for END snap: *(pick P1)*
> 》 Select entity for END snap: *(pick P2)*
> 60.5
> Command:

The (END,END,END) notation instructs AutoCAD to use the **Endpoint Object Snap** mode to assist you in picking the desired points.

---

**EXERCISE 9-12**

❑ Load AutoCAD for Windows and open PRODR1.
❑ Use the **LINE** command to draw an angle similar to Figure 9-27.
❑ Determine the angle formed using the **CAL** command.
❑ Save the drawing as A:EX9-12 and quit.

Figure 9-27.  Using the geometry calculator to determine the angle between lines in an XY plane.

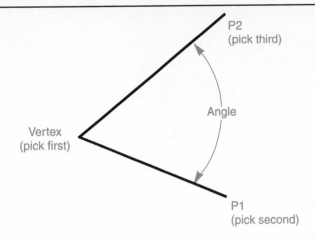

## Making point calculations

You can easily calculate the distance between two points using the following command sequence:

> Command: **CAL** ↵
> ⟩⟩ Expression: **DIST(NOD,NOD)** ↵
> ⟩⟩ Select entity for NOD snap: *(pick the first point)*
> ⟩⟩ Select entity for NOD snap: *(pick the second point)*

If you want to calculate one-half the distance between any two entities, such as the endpoints of a line, follow this procedure:

> Command: **CAL** ↵
> ⟩⟩ Expression: **DIST(END,END)/2** ↵
> ⟩⟩ Select entity for END snap: *(pick the first point)*
> ⟩⟩ Select entity for END snap: *(pick the second point)*

## Determining the radius of an arc or circle

You can use the **RAD** function to determine the radius of a circle, arc, or 2D polyline. The command sequence is as follows:

> Command: **CAL** ↵
> ⟩⟩ Expression: **RAD** ↵
> ⟩⟩ Select circle, arc or polyline segment for RAD function: *(pick the circle or arc to automatically obtain the radius value)*

### EXERCISE 9-13

❑ Load AutoCAD for Windows.
❑ Without the assistance of either **Snap** or **Grid**, use the **LINE** command to draw a single line anywhere on the screen.
❑ Use the **CAL** command to determine the distance between the endpoints.
❑ Use the **CAL** command to determine one-half the distance between the endpoints.
❑ Draw a circle without a specified radius or diameter.
❑ Use the **CAL** command's **RAD** function to determine the radius of the circle.
❑ Save the drawing as A:EX9-13 and quit.

# CALCULATOR APPLICATIONS

Using the geometry calculator to perform simple tasks that can be performed on a hand-held calculator may seem to be a poor use of time. However, the real power of AutoCAD's geometry calculator is apparent when using the calculator as part of your drawing and editing process. The following applications provide you with a few of the many tasks that can be performed using the geometry calculator.

## Circular applications

You can place a circle or other entity centered inside an object such as a rectangle using the following calculation. Refer to Figure 9-28. The following examples are only a few of the possibilities for using the **CAL** command. Although the examples shown here involve the **CIRCLE** command, similar tasks involving other commands can also be performed. More examples, related to editing drawings, are given in Chapter 14.

> Command: **CIRCLE** ↵
> 3P/2P/TTR/⟨Center point⟩: **'CAL** ↵
> ⟩⟩ Expression: **MEE** ↵

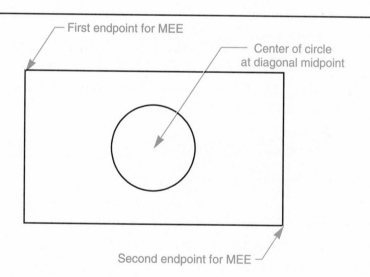

Figure 9-28. Centering a circle within a rectangle using the **CAL** command.

First endpoint for MEE

Center of circle at diagonal midpoint

Second endpoint for MEE

**MEE** is the midpoint between two endpoints. This expression allows you to pick the opposite corners of the rectangle to get the midpoint of the diagonal, which is the center of the rectangle.

> ⟩⟩ Select one endpoint for MEE: (*pick one corner of the rectangle*)
> ⟩⟩ Select another endpoint for MEE: (*pick the opposite corner*)
> Diameter/⟨Radius⟩ ⟨current⟩: (*enter a radius and press* [Enter], *or pick a radius*)

If you have an existing circle on a drawing, you can create another circle of equal radius using the **RAD** expression. The command sequence is as follows, and is shown in Figure 9-29:

> Command: **CIRCLE** ↵
> 3P/2P/TTR/⟨Center point⟩: (*pick a center point for the new circle*)
> Diameter/⟨Radius⟩⟨current⟩X: **'CAL** ↵
> ⟩⟩ Expression: **RAD** ↵
> ⟩⟩ Select circle, arc or polyline segment for RAD function: (*pick the original circle*)

After you pick the original circle, a circle equal in radius to the original, is automatically drawn at the new center point. This technique is helpful if you do not know the size of the original circle.

Figure 9-29.   Using the **RAD** function to create a circle equal in size to an existing circle.

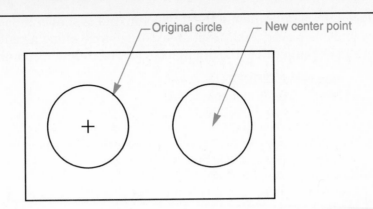

Original circle  —  New center point

---

**EXERCISE 9-14**

❑ Load AutoCAD for Windows and open PRODR1.
❑ Use the **CAL** command **MEE** function to assist you in making a drawing similar to Figure 9-28.
❑ Use the **CAL** command to assist you in making a drawing similar to Figure 9-29.
❑ Save the drawing as A:EX9-14 and quit.

Calculator functions can also be combined. For example, suppose you want to draw a new circle that is 25 percent the size of the original circle, and placed in a new position that also needs to be calculated. Refer to Figure 9-30 as you follow this command sequence:

> Command: **CIRCLE** ↵
> 3P/2P/TTR/〈Center point〉: **'CAL** ↵
> 〉〉 Expression: **(MID+MID)/2** ↵
> 〉〉 Select entity for MID snap: *(pick line 1)*
> 〉〉 Select entity for MID snap: *(pick line 2)*

Now, instruct AutoCAD to calculate a new radius that is 25 percent (.25) of the size of the original circle:

> Diameter/〈Radius〉〈*current*〉: **'CAL** ↵
> 〉〉 Expression:.**25\*RAD** ↵
> 〉〉 Select circle, arc or polyline segment for RAD function: *(pick one of the original circles)*

The new circle is automatically placed at the point specified, and at 25 percent of the size of the original circle.

---

Figure 9-30.   Combining calculator functions to resize a circle and place it in a new position.

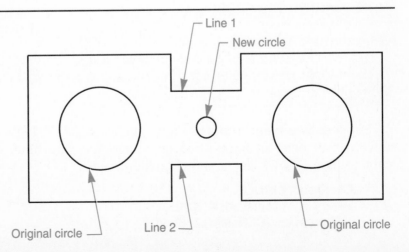

Line 1
New circle
Original circle  —  Line 2  —  Original circle

Another application of the **CAL** command is shown in Figure 9-31. In that illustration, a new circle is placed 3.00″ from an existing circle along a centerline. The new circle is 1 1/2 times (1.5X) larger than the original circle. The following command sequence can be used:

Command: **CIRCLE** ⏎
3P/2P/TTR/⟨Center point⟩: **'CAL** ⏎
⟩⟩ Expression: **PLD(CEN,END,3.00)** ⏎
⟩⟩ Select entity for CEN snap: *(pick the original circle)*
⟩⟩ Select entity for END snap: *(pick near the right end of the centerline)*
Diameter/⟨Radius⟩ ⟨current⟩: **'CAL** ⏎
⟩⟩ Expression: **1.5*RAD** ⏎
⟩⟩ Select circle, arc or polyline segment for RAD function: *(pick the original circle)*

Figure 9-31.   Copying a circle along a centerline and resizing it.

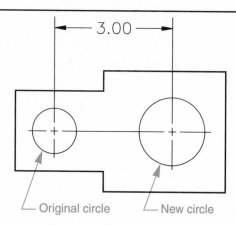

Original circle          New circle

If enabled, the **Circle:** screen menu, provides the **Copy Rad** option. Picking **Copy Rad** also activates the geometry calculator. You can use the **Copy Rad** option to draw a circle with exactly the same radius as an existing arc, circle, or polyline arc segment. To do this, draw the original circle shown in Figure 9-29. Next, pick **Copy Rad** from the **Circle:** screen menu to get the following prompt:

New value for CIRCLERAD⟨⟩: '_cal Expression: rad
⟩⟩Select circle, arc or polyline segment for RAD function: *(pick the existing circle)*
Command: **CIRCLE** ⏎
3P/2P/TTR/⟨Center point⟩: *(pick a point)*
Diameter/⟨Radius⟩ ⟨1.500⟩: ⏎
Command:

### EXERCISE 9-15

❑ Load AutoCAD for Windows and open PRODR1.
❑ Use the **CAL** command to assist you in creating a drawing similar to Figure 9-30.
❑ Use the **CAL** command to assist you in making a drawing similar to Figure 9-31.
❑ Save the drawing as A:EX9-15 and quit.

Suppose you want to draw a new circle that is .5″ higher than one-half the distance between the center of an existing circle and the side (line) of an object. The command sequence is as follows, and is shown in Figure 9-32:

Command: **CIRCLE** ⏎
3P/2P/TTR/⟨Center point⟩: **'CAL** ⏎
⟩⟩ Expression: **(CEN+MID)/2+[0,.5]** ⏎

The (CEN+MID)/2 expression finds a point one-half the distance between the center of the original circle and the midpoint of the line. Adding the [0,.5] locates the center point 0 units in the X direction and .5 units in the Y direction (higher) than the point located with the (CEN+MID)/2 expression.

〉〉 Select entity for CEN snap: *(pick the original circle)*
〉〉 Select entity for MID snap: *(pick the right line)*
Diameter/〈Radius〉 〈*current*〉: **'CAL** ↵
〉〉 Expression: **RAD** ↵
〉〉 Select circle, arc or polyline segment for RAD function: *(pick the original circle)*

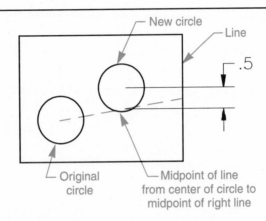

Figure 9-32.   Combining calculator functions to create a new circle not on the same centerline as the original.

New circle
Line
.5
Original circle
Midpoint of line from center of circle to midpoint of right line

**EXERCISE 9-16**

❑ Load AutoCAD for Windows and open PRODR1.
❑ Use the **CAL** command to assist you in making a drawing similar to Figure 9-32.
❑ Save the drawing as A:EX9-16 and quit.

## DRAWING WITH X AND Y FILTERS                            AUG 5

Filters allow you to select any aspect of an entity on the screen while "filtering out" other items or features. There are many uses for filters. A variety of applications for filters are presented throughout this text. However, this discussion centers on using the **LINE** command with X and Y filters. These are the filters that control X and Y coordinates. There is also a Z filter for the Z coordinate, but it is used in 3D applications. Refer to *AutoCAD and its Applications—Advanced, Release 13 for Windows* for more detail on the Z filter. If prompted for a Z value in the following examples, simply enter 0.

Suppose you want to construct an isosceles triangle with a given height of 4" on a baseline that already exists. Refer to Figure 9-33. First, use this command sequence to establish the base of the triangle:

Command: **LINE** ↵
From point: **2,2** ↵
To point: **@3〈90** ↵

Now, place the vertex (Y) 4" from the midpoint of the baseline:

To point: **.Y** ↵
of **MID** ↵
of *(pick the baseline)*
of (need XZ): **4,0** ↵

Finally, complete the triangle:

> To point: **END** ⏎
> of *(pick the endpoint of the baseline)*
> To point: ⏎
> Command:

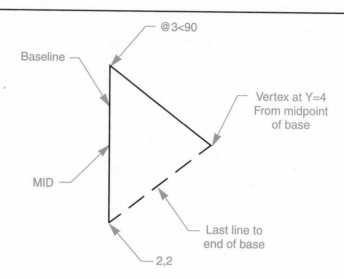

Figure 9-33.  Constructing an isosceles triangle using the **.Y** filter.

@3<90

Baseline

Vertex at Y=4
From midpoint
of base

MID

Last line to
end of base

2,2

---

## EXERCISE 9-17

❑ Load AutoCAD for Windows and open **PRODR1**.
❑ Use the X and Y filters as previously discussed to assist you in making a drawing similar to Figure 9-33.
❑ Save the drawing as A:EX9-17 and quit.

---

Earlier in this chapter you learned to construct a circle at the center of a rectangle using the geometry calculator **MEE** function (shown in Figure 9-28). The same operation can be performed using X and Y filters. As an example, suppose you want to place the center of a circle (or a polygon) at the center of a rectangle or square, Figure 9-34. In this example, the X value is filtered before the YZ value. However, the same operation can be performed by filtering the Y value first, and then the XZ value. The command sequence is as follows:

> Command: **CIRCLE** ⏎
> 3P/3P/TTR/⟨Center point⟩: **.X** ⏎
> of **MID** ⏎
> of *(pick the top horizontal line near point P1)*
> of (need YZ): **MID** ⏎
> of *(pick right vertical line near point P2)*
> Diameter/⟨Radius⟩ ⟨current⟩: *(enter the desired radius at P3)*
> Command:

Figure 9-34. Centering a circle inside of a box using X and Y filters.

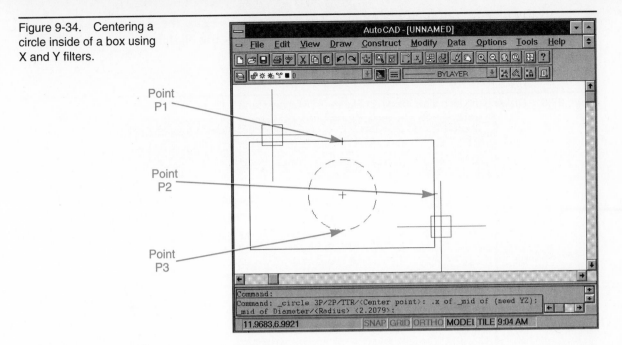

## Using X and Y filters to project views and view features

If you draw the object shown in Figure 9-35 on a drafting board, you would probably draw the front view first. Then, using drafting instruments, you might orthographically project construction lines and points in the front view to complete the right side view. This is usually the best way to draw the required views for a CAD drawing as well. Construction lines and other multiview drawing tools are discussed in Chapter 19 of this text.

Figure 9-35. A simple orthographic drawing.

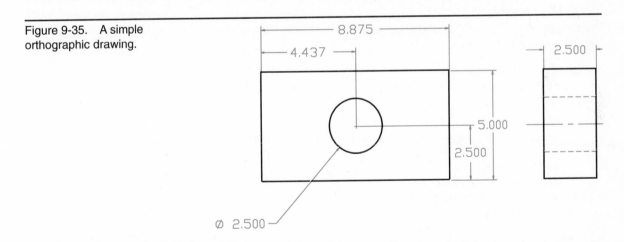

However, filters can be used to perform similar projection operations. The front view of a rectangular object can be drawn very efficiently using the **RECTANG** command, and the circle constructed using X and Y filters as previously described. The command sequence to draw the side view, shown in Figure 9-36, is as follows:

Command: **RECTANG** ↵
First corner: **.Y** ↵
of **END** ↵
of (*pick line near the endpoint of one of the horizontal lines*)
of (need XZ): (*pick point P2 to set distance between the views*)
Other corner: **@2.5,5** ↵
Command:

The rectangle that represents the side view is now complete. Since the side view's lower-left corner is located by filtering the Y value of the front view's lower-right corner, it is aligned orthographically with that view.

Figure 9-36.  Drawing the side view shown in Figure 9-35 using X and Y filters.

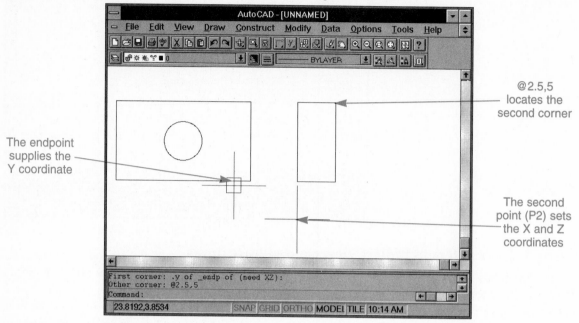

It is also a simple matter to draw the hidden lines that represent the circle seen in the side view. This operation is performed using the **Object Snap** modes **Quadrant**, **Nearest**, and **Perpendicular**. First, change the linetype to HIDDEN. Then, the command sequence is as follows. Refer to Figure 9-37.

Command: **LINE** ↵
From point: **.Y** ↵
of **QUA** ↵
of (*pick near the 90° or 270° quadrant on the circle*)
of (need XZ): **NEA** ↵
of (*pick near one of the vertical lines of the side view*)
To point: **PER** ↵
of (*pick on the opposite vertical line in the side view*)
To point: (*press* [Enter] *or the space bar to exit the command*)
Command:

Now that one of the hidden lines is drawn, you can repeat the procedure to draw the second hidden line. However, an easier way is to use the **OFFSET** command to offset the first hidden line at the required distance.

Figure 9-37. "Projecting" lines using X and Y filters to complete the side view shown in Figure 9-35.

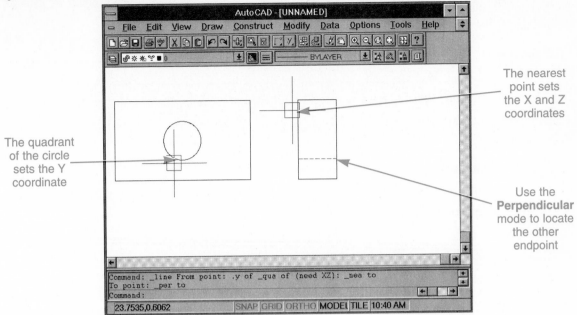

The nearest point sets the X and Z coordinates

The quadrant of the circle sets the Y coordinate

Use the **Perpendicular** mode to locate the other endpoint

```
Command: _line From point: .y of _qua of (need XZ): _nea to
To point: _per to
Command:
23.7535,0.6062        SNAP GRID ORTHO MODEL TILE 10:40 AM
```

### PROFESSIONAL TIP

You can greatly increase your productivity when you use **Object Snap** modes in conjunction with X and Y filters by setting running **Object Snaps**.

### EXERCISE 9-18

❑ Load AutoCAD for Windows and open PRODR1.
❑ Turn off **Grid** and **Snap**.
❑ Draw the front view of the object shown in Figure 9-36 and locate the circle's center using the X and Y filter technique discussed in this chapter.
❑ Construct the top view of the object using the appropriate running **Object Snap** modes and X and Y filters. For the top view, which coordinate values are filtered—X or Y?
❑ Save the drawing as A:EX9-18 and quit.

## CHAPTER TEST

*Write your answers in the spaces provided.*

1. Give the command and entries needed to draw a line to the midpoint of an existing line:

   Command:_____

   From point: _____

   To point: _____ of _____

2. Give the command and entries necessary to draw a line tangent to an existing circle and perpendicular to an existing line:

   Command:_____

   From point: _____ to _____

   To point: _____ to _____

3. Give the command and entries needed to set **Endpoint**, **Center**, and **Midpoint** as the running **Object Snap** modes:

   Command:_____

   Object snap modes: _____

4. Give the command sequence required to draw a concentric circle inside an existing circle at a distance of .25:

   Command:_____

   Offset distance or Through ⟨*current*⟩: _____

   Select object to offset:_____

   Side of offset?: _____

   Select object to offset:_____

5. Give the command and entries needed to divide a line into 24 equal parts:

   Command:_____

   Select the object to divide: _____

   ⟨Number of segments⟩/Block: _____

6. Give the command and entries used to draw a point symbol that is made up of a circle over "X":

   Command:_____

   New value for _____ ⟨0⟩:_____

   Command:_____

   Point:_____

7. After drawing the point in question 6, you find that it is too small. Give the command and prompts needed to draw the point larger:

   Command:_____

   New value for _____ ⟨0.000⟩: _____

8. Define **Object Snap**._____

   _____

9. What do you call the cursor box that appears on the screen when an **Object Snap** mode is selected? _____

10. List three methods to access the **Object Snap** modes. _____

    _____

    _____

    _____

11. When typed at the prompt line, which three letters are required to activate any desired
    **Object Snap**? _____

    _____

12. Define quadrant. _____

13. Describe the **Quick** mode. _____

    _____

    _____

14. Define running **Object Snap**. _____

    _____

    _____

15. Identify two ways to set a running **Object Snap**. _____

    _____

16. How do you access the **Running Object Snap** dialog box? _____

    _____

17. Describe the **OSNAP** override. _____

    _____

    _____

18. What command is used to change the aperture size? _____

19. In addition to the command identified in question 18, what is another way to change
    the aperture size? _____

    _____

20. What value would you specify to make the aperture half the default value? _____

21. How is the running **OSNAP** discontinued? _____

    _____

22. List two ways to establish an offset distance using the **OFFSET** command: _____

    _____

23. Name the system variable used to set the offset distance default. _____

24. The **DIVIDE** command is located in which pull-down menu? _____

25. What is the difference between the **DIVIDE** and **MEASURE** commands? _____

    _____

26. The **Object Snap Quick** mode is not effective on which **Object Snap** option? _____

    _____

27. If you use the **DIVIDE** command and nothing appears to happen, what should you do?

    _____

    _____

28. Name the system variable used to set a point style. _____

29. Name the system variable used to set a point size. _____

30. How do you access the **Point Style** icon menu? _____

    _____

31. How do you change the point size in the **Point Style** icon menu? _____

32. List the command that is used to make geometric calculations with AutoCAD. _____

33. Identify three ways the value "four feet and eight inches" can be entered in the calculator.

    _____

34. How is "45 degrees, 15 minutes, 30 seconds" entered in the calculator? _____

35. How are point coordinates entered in the AutoCAD calculator? _____

36. Cite the proper input for the following calculations:

    A. Sine of a 35° angle: _____

    B. Tangent of a 50° angle: _____

    C. Square root of 49: _____

    D. Convert 86 millimeters to inches: _____

    E. Area of a 6" diameter circle, where A=πXØ: _____

37. Give the calculator functions used to achieve the following results:

    A. Distance between two points: _____

    B. Intersection of two lines: _____

    C. Midpoint between two endpoints: _____

    D. Radius of a circle or arc: _____

38. Define "filters." _____

    _____

39. What value do you enter for Z when working with X and Y filters in a 2D drawing?

    _____

## DRAWING PROBLEMS

*Load AutoCAD for each of the following problems and use the* PRODR1 *prototype drawing, or start a new drawing using your own variables.*

General

1. Draw the object below using the **Object Snap** modes. Save the drawing as A:P9-1 (omit dimensions).

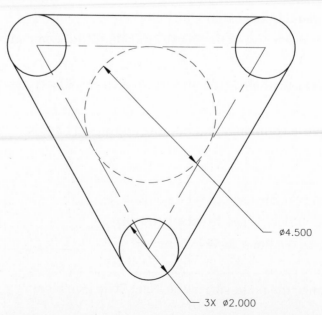

ø4.500

3X ø2.000

2. Draw the object below using the **Object Snap** modes indicated. Save the drawing as A:P9-2.

*General*

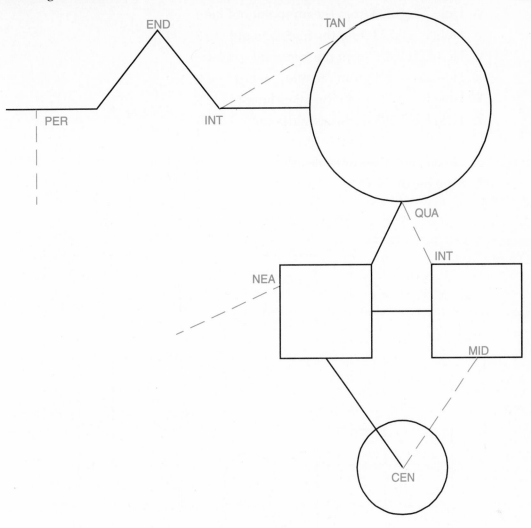

3. Draw the object below using **Endpoint**, **Tangent**, **Center**, **Perpendicular**, and **Quadrant Object Snap** modes. Save the drawing as A:P9-3.

*General*

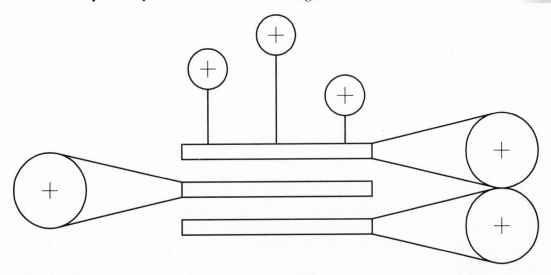

4. Draw the following object using the **FROM** option and these instructions:
   (Dimensions are in inches, do not draw dimensions.)

   A. Hole A is 0.523 from the midpoint of Line 1.

   B. Hole B is 0.523 from the midpoint of Line 2.

   C. Hole C is 0.833 from the midpoint of Line 3.

   D. Hole D is 0.399 from the midpoint of Line 4.

   E. Hole E is 0.738 from the midpoint of Line 5.

   F. Hole F is 1.295 from the midpoint of Line 6.

   G. Hole G is 0.574 from Corner 1.

   H. Hole H is 0.574 from Corner 2.

   I. Save the drawing as A:P9-4.

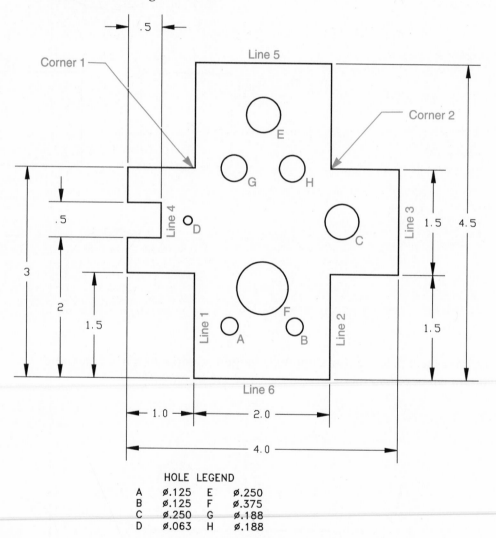

HOLE LEGEND

| A | Ø.125 | E | Ø.250 |
|---|-------|---|-------|
| B | Ø.125 | F | Ø.375 |
| C | Ø.250 | G | Ø.188 |
| D | Ø.063 | H | Ø.188 |

5. Draw the floor plan layout about three times the size of that shown. Use the following AutoCAD functions:

   A. Set architectural units; 48',36' limits; 2' grid; and 6" snap.

   B. Use the **PLINE** command to draw plan A. (The **LINE** command may be used, but it will take longer to complete the problem.)

   C. Use the **OFFSET** command to draw a parallel line 6" on the inside of plan A. Your final drawing should look like that shown in plan B.

   D. Save the drawing as A:P9-5.

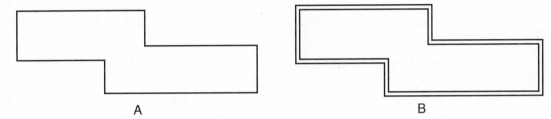

   A                                    B

6. Create a drawing proportional, but about three times the size of the object shown below. Proceed as follows:

   A. Draw the outer circle first.

   B. Use the **OFFSET** command to create other concentric circles. (Try to draw the object without leaving the **OFFSET** command.) Select the **Through** option and point to the spot where you want the offset circles to be placed.

   C. Save the drawing as A:P9-6.

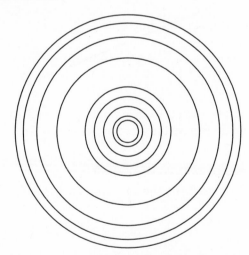

7. Draw two horizontal lines, each 8" (203.2mm) long. Use the **DIVIDE** command to divide one of the lines into 10 equal parts. Use the **MEASURE** command to set off .8" (20.3mm) increments on the second line. Save the drawing as A:P9-7.

8. Draw two circles, each having a 4" (101.6mm) diameter. Then use the **DIVIDE** command to divide one of the circles into 12 equal parts. Use the **MEASURE** command to set off .75" (19.1mm) increments on the second circle. Save the drawing as A:P9-8.

9. Draw two closed polylines each made up of line and arc segments. Then, use the **DIVIDE** command to divide one of the polylines into 24 equal parts. Use the **MEASURE** command to set off 1.5 increments on the second polyline. Save the drawing as A:P9-9.

*Note for Problems 10 through 13: If several **PDMODE** symbols are displayed on the screen, they will all be updated to the current **PDMODE** value when a regeneration occurs.*

General
10. Set the **PDSIZE** to 1 and draw points with each of the following **PDMODE** values: 0, 2, 3, and 4. Save the drawing as A:P9-10.

General
11. Set the **PDSIZE** to 2 and draw a point with each of the following **PDMODE** values: 32, 34, 35, 64, 65, 66, 96, 97, 98, 99, and 100. Save the drawing as A:P9-11.

General
12. Use the **Point Style** icon menu to draw five different point symbols. Save the drawing as A:P9-12.

General
13. Use the **Point Style** icon menu to change the size of each of five different point symbols. Save the drawing as A:P9-13.

General
14. Use the **LINE** command to draw the angle shown in the following illustration using the given coordinates. Use the **CAL** command to determine the angle, in degrees, between the lines. Save the drawing as A:P9-14.

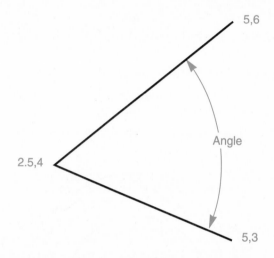

General
15. Draw a rectangle measuring 3.125 × 5.625. Use the **CAL** command to center a .75 diameter circle inside the rectangle. Save the drawing as A:P9-15.

Mechanical Drafting
16. Draw the following object. Then use the **CAL** command to place another circle to the left of the existing circle so the completed object is symmetrical. Do not include the dimensions. Save the drawing as A:P9-16.

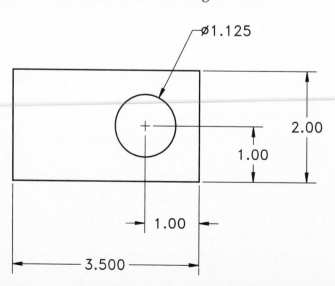

17. Draw the following object. Then use the **CAL** command to add another circle with a diameter which is 30 percent of the size of the existing circle. Center the new circle between the midpoints of line 1 and 2. Do not include dimensions. Save the drawing as A:P9-17.

*Mechanical Drafting*

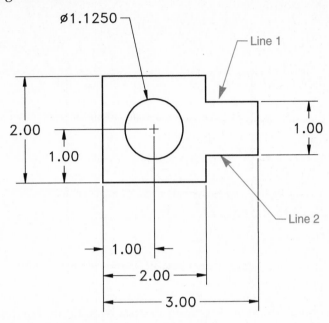

18. Draw the object shown below. Then use the **CAL** command to create another circle with a diameter which is 150 percent (1.5X) of the existing circle. Center the new circle 3″ horizontally to the right of the existing circle. Do not dimension the drawing. Save the drawing as A:P9-18.

*Mechanical Drafting*

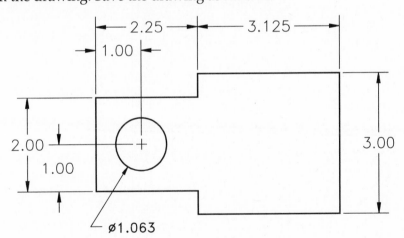

19. Draw the following object. Then use the **CAL** command to create another circle with the same diameter as the existing circle. Place the center of the new circle .5" above a point that is midway between the center of the existing circle and the midpoint of the right line of the object. Do not include dimensions. Save the drawing as A:P9-19.

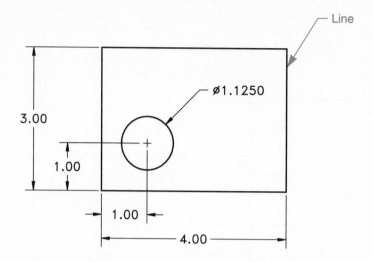

20. Use the X and Y filters to draw an isosceles triangle with a vertical baseline measuring 4.5" long and 5.75" high. Save the drawing as A:P9-20.

### Learning objectives

After completing this chapter, you will be able to:
○ Magnify a small part of the drawing to work on details.
○ Move the display window to reveal portions of the drawing outside the boundaries of the monitor.
○ Create named views that can be recalled instantly.
○ Use the **Aerial View** window.
○ Define the terms model space and paper space.
○ Create multiple viewports in the graphics window.
○ Explain the differences between **REDRAW** and **REGEN**.

You can view an exact portion of the drawing using the AutoCAD display commands. The **ZOOM** command allows you to enlarge or reduce the amount of the drawing displayed. The portion displayed can also be moved back and forth, or up and down, using the **PAN** command. Panning is like looking through a camera and moving the camera across the drawing. The **DSVIEWER** command enables the **Aerial View** window. This window displays the entire drawing. Using this window you can locate a particular area of the drawing to view, and move to it using **ZOOM** or **PAN** functions. The **VIEW** command allows you to create and name specific views of the drawing. When further drawing or editing operations are required in a saved view, the view can be quickly and easily recalled.

Specialized display functions allow you to work in "space." These functions are called model space and paper space. *Model space* is used for drawing and designing. *Paper space* is used for plotting. Both functions are found in the **View** pull-down menu. The **MVIEW** command provides options that allow you to switch between model space and paper space. Detailed information on the use of model space and paper space, as related to plotting multi-view drawings, is provided in Chapter 26.

This chapter also discusses the differences between the **REDRAW** and **REGEN** commands. Additionally, using the **REGENAUTO** and **VIEWRES** commands to achieve optimum display speeds and quality is discussed.

## REDRAWING THE SCREEN

AUG 1

The **REDRAW** command is used to clean the blips from the screen and refresh objects after editing operations. A *blip* is a small cross displayed when a point is picked on the screen, Figure 10-1. These blips are indicators of selected points and are not part of your drawing. They simply stay on the screen until it is redrawn.

Redraw the screen by clicking the **Redraw View** button in the **Standard** toolbar, selecting **Redraw View** from the **View** pull-down menu, or by typing REDRAW or R at the **Command:** prompt. The **REDRAW** command can be used to redraw the screen while working inside another command.

Figure 10-1.  Tiny crosshairs, or blips, show on the screen when a point is selected.

Blips

---

**PROFESSIONAL TIP**

Using **REDRAW** every time blips appear may begin to slow your drawing sessions. Only redraw the screen when the blips interfere with the drawing process.

## Working inside another command

To enter a new command, you usually need to complete or cancel the current command. Most menu picks automatically cancel the command in progress before issuing a new one. Some commands, however, can be used as transparent commands. A *transparent* command can be used while another command is active. This means that it is not necessary to first complete or cancel the current command. Many display options can be used transparently. Commands that can be used transparently include **REDRAW**, **PAN**, **VIEW**, **HELP**, **AV**, and several **ZOOM** options. Using a transparent command temporarily interrupts the active command, performs its function and then resumes the previous command.

Entering a command transparently from the command line requires that the command name be preceded with an apostrophe. For example, the following command sequence shows the **REDRAW** command entered transparently during the **LINE** command.

Command: **LINE** From point: *(select the first point)*
To point: **'REDRAW** *(this clears all blips so you can see the drawing better)*
Resuming LINE command.
To point: *(select the second point)*
To point: *(press* [Enter] *to end the command)*
Command:

All of the commands discussed in this chapter, with the exception of **DSVIEWER**, **REGEN**, **VIEWRES**, and **VPORTS** can be used transparently. A detailed discussion of transparent commands and how they are used is given later in the chapter.

## Using blips

Blips remind you where points were selected. However, they can be turned off to eliminate the need to redraw often. To turn blips off, use the **Drawing Aids** dialog box. To open this dialog box, select **Drawing Aids...** from the **Options** pull-down menu. To turn off blips, click the X in the **Blips** check box (or type B), Figure 10-2. The blips will not show on the screen for the current drawing until turned back on. Blips can also be turned off by entering the **BLIPMODE** command at the **Command:** prompt as follows:

> Command: **BLIPMODE** ↵
> ON/OFF ⟨*current*⟩: **OFF** ↵
> Command:

Figure 10-2.   **BLIPMODE** can be turned on or off from the **Drawing Aids** dialog box.

Deselect to turn blips off

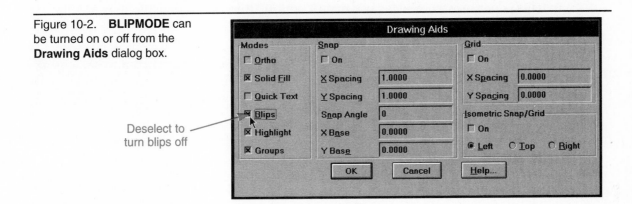

**PROFESSIONAL TIP**

Turning **BLIPMODE** off affects the current drawing only. If you want blips to be off in any new drawing, turn off **BLIPMODE** in the ACAD.DWG prototype and any other prototype drawings that you use.

# GETTING CLOSE TO YOUR WORK                          AUG 4

It is doubtful whether many drafters would create drawings on a computer screen if they could not move in close to their work. This ability to "zoom in" (magnify) a drawing allows designers to create extremely small items, such as the electronic circuits found in a computer. The **ZOOM** command is a tool that you will use often because it is so helpful. It also can be used as a transparent command while inside other commands. The twelve different options of the **ZOOM** command are discussed in the next sections.

## The ZOOM options

Each of the **ZOOM** options can be accessed by its corresponding button in the **Standard** toolbar and **Zoom** flyout, or by selecting **Zoom** from the **View** pull-down menu. Also, entering **ZOOM** at the **Command:** prompt lists the options as follows:

> Command: **ZOOM** ↵
> All/Center/Dynamic/Extents/Left/Previous/Vmax/Window/⟨Scale(X/XP)⟩:

Brief explanations of the **ZOOM** options are provided below.

- **In.** This option is available only on the toolbar and the pull-down menu. It automatically executes a 2X zoom scale factor.

- **Out.** This option is available only on the toolbar and the pull-down menu. It automatically executes a .5X zoom scale factor.

- **Limits.** This option is available only on the toolbar and the pull-down menu. This zooms to the limits of your drawing, but unlike **Zoom All** this option zooms to the limits without regard to the location or size of any objects in your drawing.

- **All.** Zooms to display drawing limits. If objects are drawn beyond limits, a **Zoom Extents** is performed. Always use the **All** option after you change the drawing limits.

- **Center.** Pick the center and height of the next screen display. A magnification factor instead of a height can be entered by typing a number followed by an X, such as 4X. The current value represents the height of the screen in drawing units. Entering a smaller number enlarges the image size, while a larger number reduces it. The command sequence is as follows:

      All/Center/Dynamic/Extents/Left/Previous/Vmax/Window/⟨Scale(X/XP)⟩: **C** ↵
      Center point: *(pick a center point)*
      Magnification or Height ⟨*current*⟩: **4X** ↵
      Command:

- **Dynamic.** Allows for a graphic pan and zoom with the use of a view box that represents the screen. This option is discussed in detail later in the chapter.

- **Extents.** Zooms to extents of the drawing. This is the portion of the drawing area that has entities drawn in it.

- **Left.** Pick the lower-left corner and height of next screen display. A magnification factor instead of a height can be entered as follows:

      All/Center/Dynamic/Extents/Left/Previous/Vmax/Window/⟨Scale(X/XP)⟩: **L** ↵
      Lower left corner point: *(pick a point)*
      Magnification or Height ⟨*current*⟩: **3X** ↵
      Command:

- **Previous.** Returns to the previous display. You can go back ten displays, one at a time, in Release 13.

- **Vmax.** AutoCAD maintains a "virtual screen" composed of 4 billion pixels in each axis (X and Y). This means that each time a regeneration is required, the virtual screen is recalculated. Then, you can view any detail of your drawing that you want within the virtual screen, and AutoCAD displays it at redraw speed. The image is redrawn (not regenerated) if the next display you request is inside the limits of the virtual screen. However, if the requested display (a small zoom window, for example) will not provide an accurate representation of the drawing entities, AutoCAD performs a regeneration. You can test **Vmax** by zooming in on a small detail on your drawing. You may want to do this a couple of times until AutoCAD regenerates. Then use **ZOOM Vmax**. The resulting display is the virtual screen.

- **Window.** Pick opposite corners of a box. Objects in the box enlarge to fill the display. The **Window** option is the default if you pick a point on the screen.

- **Scale(X).** A positive number is required here to indicate the magnification factor of the original display. You can enlarge or reduce relative to the current display by typing an X after the scale. Type 2X if you want the image enlarged two times. Type .5X if you want the image reduced by half. Typing just a number without the X zooms the *original* drawing. On the other hand, typing a number followed by an X zooms the *current* view by that scale value.
- **Scale(XP).** This option is used in conjunction with model space and paper space, both discussed later in this chapter. Its purpose is to scale a drawing in model space relative to paper space, and is used primarily in the layout of scaled multiview drawings for plotting purposes. A detailed discussion of this option is given in Chapter 26 *External References and Multiview Layouts.*

### Performing real-time zoom

The **RTZOOM** command allows you to see the model move on the screen as you zoom. This is a new feature in the R13c4 maintenance version of AutoCAD and is the dynamic version of the **ZOOM** command. It is the quickest and easiest methods for adjusting the magnification of drawings on the screen. After executing the **RTZOOM** command, press and hold the pick button and move the pointing device up to zoom in and down to zoom out. The command sequence is as follows:

Command: **RTZOOM** ↵
Press pick button and move cursor to pan [Enter or ESC to exit]:↵

The magnifying glass icon with a plus and minus is displayed when **RTZOOM** is executed.

---

**NOTE**  The **RTZOOM** and **RTPAN**, which is discussed later in this chapter, are not available before the R13c4 maintenance release of AutoCAD. If you are not sure which version you have, Pick **About AutoCAD...** in the **Help** pull-down menu. The version number is displayed in the copyright notice at the top of the screen.

---

### Enlarging with a window

The most-used **ZOOM** option is **Window.** Opposite corners of a rectangular window enclosing the feature to be zoomed are picked. The command sequence is as follows:

Command: **ZOOM** ↵
All/Center/Dynamic/Extents/Left/Previous/Vmax/Window/⟨Scale(X/XP)⟩: *(pick a corner)*
Other corner: *(pick the opposite corner)*
Command:

The first point you pick is automatically accepted as the first corner of the zoom window. After this corner is picked, a box appears attached to the crosshairs. It grows and shrinks as you move the pointing device. When the second corner is picked, the center of the window becomes the center of the new screen display. If you wish to return to the previous display, select **ZOOM** and use the **Previous** option. If you want to see the entire drawing, use the **All** option. Figure 10-3 shows **ZOOM Window** and **ZOOM Previous** used on a drawing.

The **Window** option can also be selected by entering a W at the options prompt. This method is useful for customized applications that are designed to operate on earlier releases of AutoCAD. See *AutoCAD and its Applications—Advanced, Release 13 for Windows* for information on customizing AutoCAD menus.

Figure 10-3.   A—When using the **ZOOM Window** command, select the corners of a window (shown here highlighted). B—The selected window will fill the drawing screen. C—To return to the last view of the drawing, use the **ZOOM Previous** command.

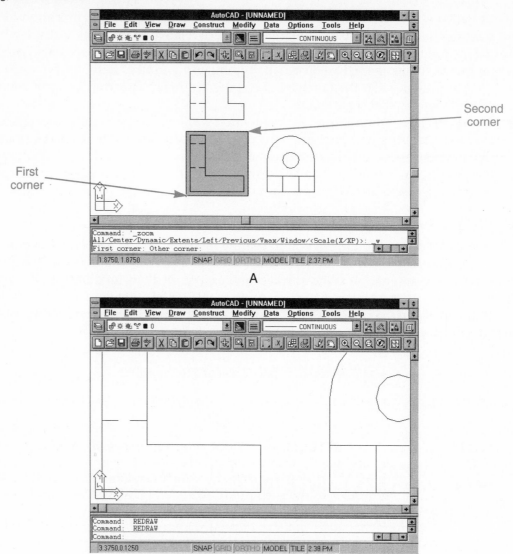

A

B

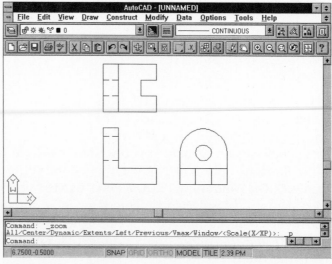

C

## Accurate displays with a dynamic zoom

The **ZOOM Dynamic** option allows you to accurately specify the portion of the drawing you want displayed. This is done by constructing a *view box*. This view box is proportional to the size of the display area. If you are looking at a zoomed view when **ZOOM Dynamic** is selected, the entire drawing is displayed on the screen. To practice with this command, load any drawing into AutoCAD. Then, select the **Zoom Dynamic** button from the **Standard** toolbar, or use the following command sequence:

Command: **ZOOM** ↵
All/Center/Dynamic/Extents/Left/Previous/Vmax/Window/⟨Scale(X/XP)⟩: **D** ↵

The screen is now occupied by four boxes, Figure 10-4. A fifth box is displayed later. Each one has a specific function. The boxes and their functions are:

- **Drawing extents.** (white line) This box shows the area of the drawing that is occupied by drawing features (entities). It is the same area that is displayed with **ZOOM Extents**.
- **Current view.** (green dotted line) This is the view that was displayed before you selected **ZOOM Dynamic**. It may be considerably smaller than the red corners of the generated area.
- **Generated area.** (red corners) This box represents the generated area of the drawing. AutoCAD keeps a *virtual screen* of over 4 billion pixels in both the X and Y coordinate directions. (Pixels are discussed in Chapter 9 of this text.) The virtual screen is the area AutoCAD calculates with the **REGEN** command. Many users have screens with 640 × 480 pixels. Thus, the virtual screen is much larger than the display area. Even the highest resolution monitors do not have more than two thousand pixels in the X and Y directions. This is why the generated area extends beyond the actual drawing.

Figure 10-4.   Features of the **ZOOM Dynamic** command. A—Drawing extents. B—Current view. C—Generated area. D—Panning view box/Zooming view box. E—Hourglass.

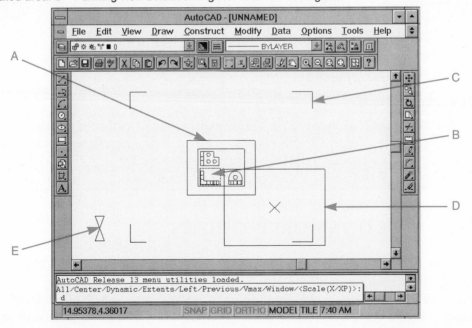

The generated area is important because it displays the portion of the drawing that can be zoomed without causing a regeneration. This means the next display is calculated at a faster redraw speed. If you select a zoom box that lies outside the generated area, a **REGEN** is performed, thus slowing the next display. Try to size your view and pan boxes inside the generated area.

- **Panning view box.** (X in the center) Move the pointing device to find the center point of the desired zoomed display. When you press the pick button, the zooming view box appears.
- **Zooming view box.** (arrow on right side) This box allows you to decrease or increase the area that you wish to zoom. Move the pointer to the right and the box increases in size. Move the pointer to the left and the box shrinks. You can also pan up or down with the zooming view box. The only restriction is that you cannot move the box to the left.

The **ZOOM Dynamic** command is not complete until you press [Enter]. If you press the pick button to select the zooming view box, the panning view box reappears. Then, you can reposition it if necessary. Press the pick button again and the zooming view box is displayed. In this manner, you can fine-tune the exact display needed. This is also helpful in defining permanent views, which is discussed later in this chapter.

One final aspect of **ZOOM Dynamic** is the "hourglass" displayed in the lower-left corner of the screen. Refer back to Figure 10-4. The hourglass informs you that the zooming view box is outside the generated area (red corners). AutoCAD is then forced to regenerate the drawing. The hourglass is a reminder to help you save time by avoiding unnecessary regeneration. As you adjust the view box, the hourglass may disappear. When it does, notice where the view box is located. All lines of the view box are inside the generated area. Move the view box so that one side is touching the generated area. The hourglass then reappears. If you pick that view box location, a regeneration takes place.

---

**EXERCISE 10-1**

❑ Load a drawing from a previous exercise or drawing problem.
❑ Select **ZOOM Window** and enlarge a portion of the drawing.
❑ Select **ZOOM Window** again to move in closer to a detail.
❑ Select **ZOOM Vmax** to show the virtual screen.
❑ Use **ZOOM Previous** to return to the last display.
❑ Select **ZOOM Extents** to show only the drawing entities.
❑ Select **ZOOM All** to display the entire drawing limits.
❑ Select **ZOOM Dynamic**. Maneuver the view box to select a portion of the drawing.
❑ Use **ZOOM Dynamic** to enlarge the display. Force a regeneration of the drawing by placing the view box partially outside the generated area.
❑ Save the drawing as A:EX10-1, then quit the drawing session.

---

## CREATING YOUR OWN WORKING VIEWS                              AUG 4

On a large drawing that involves a number of separate details, using the **ZOOM** command can be time-consuming. Being able to quickly specify a certain part of the drawing would be much easier. This is possible with the **VIEW** command. It allows you to create named views. A view can be a portion of the drawing, such as the upper-left quadrant, or it can denote an enlarged portion. After the view is created, you can instruct AutoCAD to display it at any time.

## Creating views with the View dialog box

AUG 4

The **VIEW** command can be accessed by picking the **Named Views** button in the **View** toolbar or selecting **Named Views...** from the **View** pull-down menu. This activates the **View Control** dialog box. See Figure 10-5.

**Defining views.** A list of currently defined views is shown in the **View Control** dialog box. If you wish to window a new view, pick the **New...** button. The **Define New View** dialog box is displayed. See Figure 10-6. Now, type the desired view name in the **New Name:** edit box. Click the **Define Window** radio button, and then click the **Window** 〈 button. You are prompted for the first corner. Select the window. After you pick the second corner, the **Define New View** dialog box reappears. Click the **Save View** button and the **View Control** dialog box is updated to reflect the new view.

Figure 10-5. Select a different view in the **View Control** dialog box. Create a new view by selecting the **New...** button.

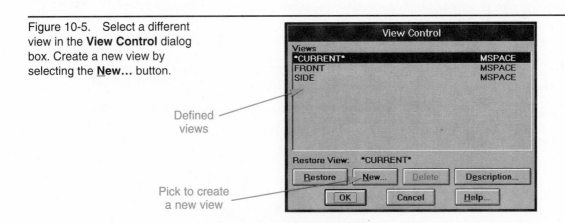

Figure 10-6. In the **Define New View** dialog box, name the new view and define the window.

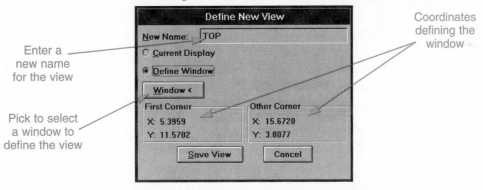

**NOTE** The crosshairs in a 3D view remain on the 3D axis until you pick the first window point, then the window is displayed. After entering a name in the **New Name:** text box, you must pick the **Save View** button, rather than pressing [Enter].

**Restoring a saved view.** If you wish to display any of the listed views, simply pick its name from the file list and click the **Restore** button. The name of the view to be restored appears in the **Restore View:** label. Now, pick the **OK** button and the screen displays the selected view.

**Saving the current display.** If you want to save the current display as a view, pick the **New...** button in the **View Control** dialog box, then type the new name. The **Current Display** option button is the default, so just click **Save View**, and the view name is added to the list.

**Deleting a view.** If you wish to delete a view displayed in the dialog box, first pick the view name in the list, then click **Delete**. Notice that the view name is immediately removed from the list. If no view name is highlighted, the **Delete** button is grayed out, and thus not a valid option.

**View description.** You can get a detailed description of the selected view by picking the **Description...** button. This opens the **View Description** dialog box that provides a variety of information about the view. See Figure 10-7. A discussion of these values related to 3D drawings is given in *AutoCAD and its Applications—Advanced, Release 13 for Windows.*

Figure 10-7. Picking the **Description...** button in the **View Control** dialog box accesses the **View Description** subdialog box. This subdialog box provides information about a view.

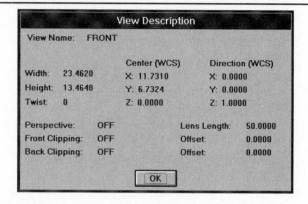

**Creating views at the Command: prompt**

When VIEW is typed at the **Command:** prompt, you are presented with five options. The **Save** and **Window** options allow you to create views. The **Save** option saves the current screen display under a name you enter. To name the view FRONT, use this procedure:

```
Command: VIEW ↵
?/Delete/Restore/Save/Window: S ↵
View name to save: FRONT ↵
Command:
```

The second method of choosing a view to save is by windowing. This is much like zooming in on an area with the **ZOOM Window** option.

```
Command: VIEW ↵
?/Delete/Restore/Save/Window: W ↵
View name to save: (enter the view name and press [Enter])
First corner: (pick one window corner)
Other corner: (pick the second corner)
Command:
```

**Getting information on existing views.** To obtain a listing of the currently defined view names, use the **?** option. You are prompted for which views to list, responding by pressing ↵ accepts the default and displays all currently defined view names.

```
Command: VIEW ↵
?/Delete/Restore/Save/Window: ? ↵
View(s) to list ⟨*⟩: ↵
Saved views:
View name       Space
FRONT           M
SIDE            M
Command:
```

**Recalling a saved view.** A saved view can be restored to the screen at any time by selecting the Restore option of the **VIEW** command. Then enter the name of the view you want to display. The view you enter is immediately displayed.

```
Command: VIEW ↵
?/Delete/Restore/Save/Window: R ↵
View name to restore: (type the view name and press [Enter])
Command:
```

**PROFESSIONAL TIP**

Part of your project planning should be view names. A consistent naming system makes sure that all users will know the view names without having to list them. The views can be set as part of the prototype drawings. Then, view names can be placed in a custom screen menu as discussed in *AutoCAD and its Applications—Advanced, R13 for Windows*.

## MOVING AROUND THE DISPLAY SCREEN

AUG 4

Imagine that you can put a hook in one side of the drawing, then drag the drawing across the screen. This is what the **PAN** command does. **PAN** allows you to move around the drawing without changing the magnification factor. You can then view objects that lie just outside the edges of the display screen.

### Picking the pan displacement

Type PAN at the **Command:** prompt, select **Point** from the **Pan** cascading submenu in the **View** pull-down menu, or pick the **Pan Point** button on the **Standard** toolbar. AutoCAD then prompts for a displacement. This is the point you want to drag. Pick that point. Next, you must pick where you want the first point to appear in the next display. The display window is moved the distance between the two points, Figure 10-8.

```
Command: PAN ↵
Displacement: (pick the point to drag)
Second point: (pick the final location of the first point)
Command:
```

### Performing real-time pan

The **RTPAN** command allows you to see the model move on the screen as you pan. This is a new feature in the R13c4 maintenance version of AutoCAD and is the dynamic version of the **PAN** command. It is the quickest and easiest methods for adjusting the location of drawings on the screen. After executing the **RTPAN** command, press and hold the pick button and move the pointing device in the direction you wish to pan. The command sequence is as follows:

Command: **RTPAN** ↵
Press pick button and move cursor to pan [Enter or ESC to exit]: ↵

The pan icon of the hand is displayed when **RTPAN** is executed.

Figure 10-8. **PAN** moves the drawing around the screen. A—Panning to the left. B—Panning up. C—Completed pan.

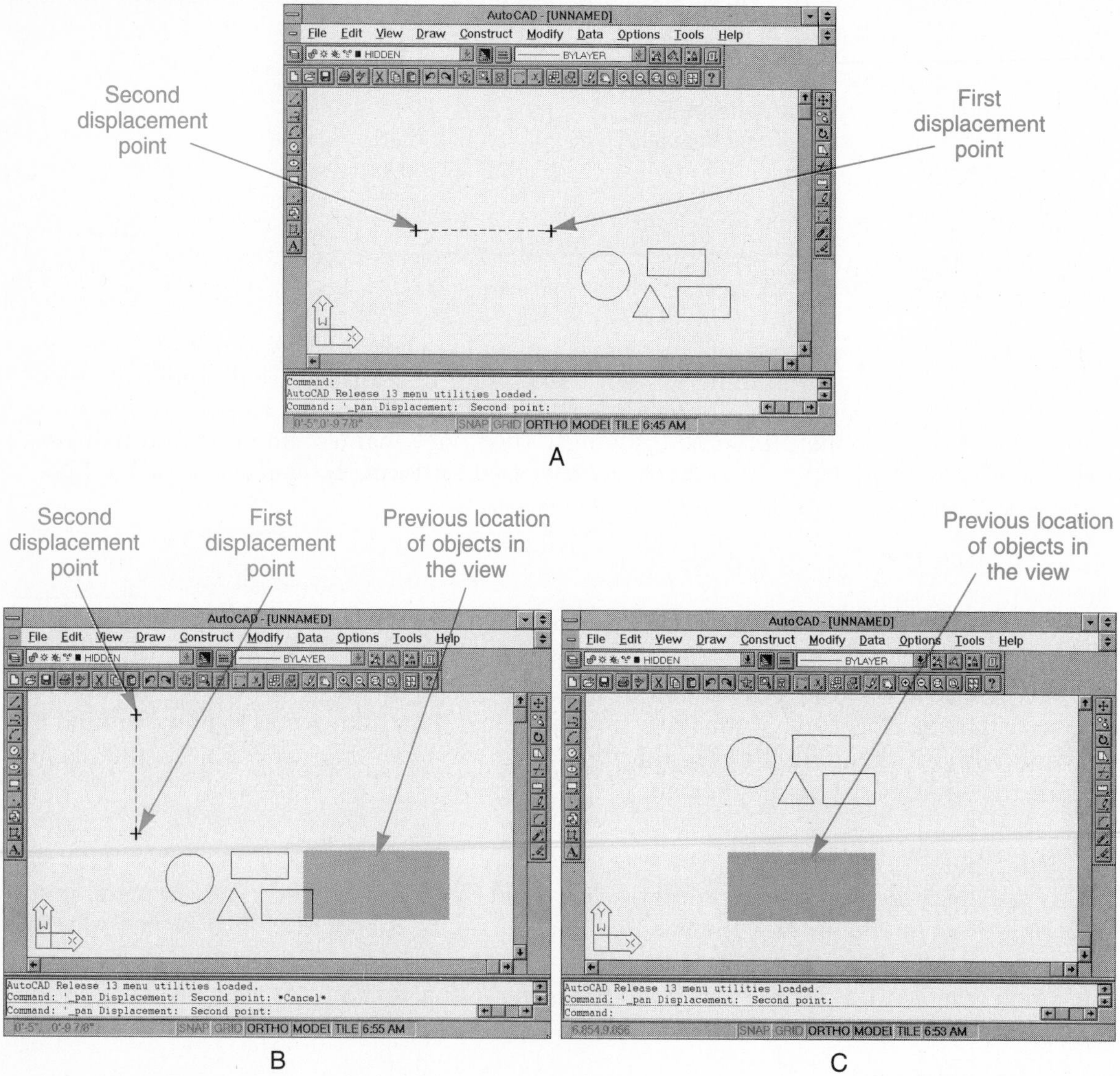

You can also enter the displacement, or the distance the display window is to be moved, by giving coordinates. See Figure 10-9. The coordinates can be either relative or absolute. A relative displacement to move the drawing 8 units to the right and 3 units up is:

Command: **PAN** ↵
Displacement: **8,3** ↵
Second point: ↵
Command:

Figure 10-9.  Relative coordinates can be used to pan across a drawing.

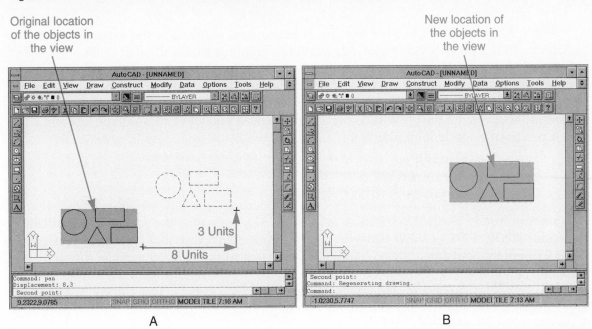

A                                                                B

Suppose the coordinate location of the point you referenced was 4,5. Then, the relative displacement for the above movement is calculated as 8,3 + 4,5 = 12,8 for the second point. Enter this as follows:

Command: **PAN** ↵
Displacement: **4,5** ↵
Second point: **12,8** ↵
Command:

### Using **PAN** presets

You can automatically pan from the center of your current drawing display to one of the four edges or corners by using one of the pan presets provided in the toolbar flyout and pull-down menu. The eight available options are shown in Figure 10-10 as they appear both in the **Pan Point** flyout in the **Standard** toolbar and in the **View** pull-down menu. Preset pan options can only be picked from one of these locations.

Figure 10-10.  The different **Pan** option can be found as buttons in the **Pan** flyout, or in the **Pan** cascading submenu of the **View** pull-down menu.

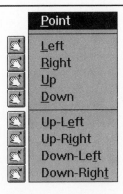

## SETTING VIEW RESOLUTION FOR QUICK DISPLAYS

AUG 4

AutoCAD allows you to save time on zooming and panning at the expense of display accuracy. On the other hand, AutoCAD provides highly accurate display at the expense of zoom and pan speed. The main factor is the view resolution. The *view resolution* refers to the number of lines used to draw circles and arcs. High resolution values display smooth circles and arcs. Low values display segmented circles and arcs. You can control the view resolution of circles and arcs with the **VIEWRES** command. It asks if you want zooms to be fast and what zoom percentage you want for circles:

> Command: **VIEWRES** ↵
> Do you want fast zooms? ⟨Y⟩ ↵
> Enter circle zoom percent (1-20000) ⟨100⟩:

If your response to the first prompt is Yes, AutoCAD "repaints" the screen using **REDRAW** speed for **ZOOM**, **PAN**, or **VIEW Restore**. The **REDRAW** speed can only be used if you do not reduce or enlarge outside of the generated areas. After zooming in on a circle, the circle will appear less smooth.

If speed is not a concern, then answer No to the first prompt. This causes AutoCAD to use **REGEN** when any display command is issued. Circles and arcs will always appear to have the same smoothness.

The actual smoothness of circles and arcs is controlled by the circle zoom percent. It can vary between 1 and 20000. The default is 100. This produces a relatively smooth circle. A number smaller than 100 causes circles and arcs to be drawn with fewer vectors (straight lines). A number larger than 100 places more vectors in the circles, as shown in Figure 10-11. The circle zoom percent is only used when AutoCAD is forced to do a regeneration. That is why a circle may appear to be composed of several straight sides after you zoom in on it. If you want a smooth circle, just use the **REGEN** command.

The **VIEWRES** command is a display function only and has no effect on the plotted or printed drawing. A drawing is printed or plotted using an optimum number of vectors for the size of circles and arcs. See Chapter 12 of this text for detailed information on plotting.

Figure 10-11. The higher the **VIEWRES** value, the smoother a circle will appear.

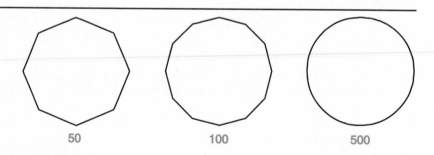

50          100          500

**PROFESSIONAL TIP**

If you are concerned with speed, set **VIEWRES** for fast zooms and set the circle zoom percent to 100 or less. Circles may look like they have straight line sides, but drawing regeneration takes less time.

**EXERCISE 10-2**

❑ Load AutoCAD for Windows and begin a new drawing named A:EX10-2.

❑ Draw three circles and three arcs of different sizes.

❑ Zoom in on the smallest circle using the **Dynamic** option. Notice the straight line segments that make up the circle.

❑ Keep zooming in on the circle edge (with **ZOOM Window**) until you force a regeneration. At that time, you have gone beyond the virtual screen.

❑ Set the **VIEWRES** command for fast zooms and a 10 percent circle zoom. **ZOOM All** and notice the shape of the circles and arcs after a regeneration.

❑ Select the **VIEWRES** command and answer No for fast zooms. Set circle zoom to 20 percent. Zoom in on a circle three times. Notice when any regeneration is performed.

❑ Save the drawing as A:EX10-2 and quit the drawing session.

## THE VIEW PULL-DOWN MENU

Often-used display commands can be accessed by selecting **View** from the menu bar. The **View** pull-down menu and one of its cascading submenus are shown in Figure 10-12.

The **View** pull-down menu provides access to most of AutoCAD's display and viewing commands. Four of the selections are followed by arrows. These selections lead to cascading submenus that provide additional options or other commands.

Figure 10-12.   The **View** pull-down menu with the **Zoom** cascading menu.

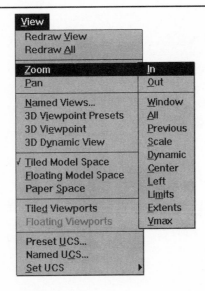

- **Redraw View.** Redraws the current viewport.
- **Redraw All.** Redraws all viewports in model space or paper space.
- **Zoom.** Provides access to all **ZOOM** command options.
- **Pan.** Provides access to all **PAN** command options.
- **Named Views....** Displays the **View Control** dialog box, enabling you to work with named views.
- **3D Viewpoint Presets.** Provides access to eleven different preset 3D views.
- **3D Viewpoint.** Provides access to three different methods of selecting a 3D viewpoint.
- **3D Dynamic View.** Activates the **DVIEW** command, providing total control over the creation of a 3D viewpoint and display.
- **Tiled Model Space.** This is the default display setting, and when a check mark is displayed it indicates that the current setting of the **TILEMODE** system variable is 1. A

**TILEMODE** setting of 1 means that model space is current and only *tiled* viewports can be created.

- **Floating Model Space.** Picking this option sets **TILEMODE** to 0, activating paper space. If no *floating* viewports currently exist in paper space, the **MVIEW** command is entered so the necessary viewports can be created.
- **Paper Space.** Switches **TILEMODE** to 0 and activates paper space. If floating viewports have been created, the crosshairs appear to be laying over the top of them. Paper space is a 2D environment. Therefore, when this item has a check mark by it, the 3D selections are grayed out and unselectable.
- **Tiled Viewports.** Enables you to create tiled viewports with the **VPORTS** command. This selection is available only when there is a check mark by **Tiled Model Space**, because the **VPORTS** command is only available when **TILEMODE** is set to 1.
- **Floating Viewports.** Enables you to create floating viewports with the **MVIEW** command. This selection is available only when there is a check mark by **Floating Model Space** or **Paper Space**, because the **MVIEW** command is only available when **TILEMODE** is set to 0.
- **Preset UCS....** Activates the **UCS Orientation** dialog box, in which you can graphically change the orientation of the User Coordinate System to a specific face of a cube. User coordinate systems are discussed in greater detail in Chapter 19.
- **Named UCS....** Activates the **UCS Control** dialog box in which you can display, delete, list or rename user coordinate systems that have been previously named and saved with the **UCS** command.
- **Set UCS.** Provides access to all of the options of the **UCS** command in a cascading submenu.

## USING TRANSPARENT DISPLAY COMMANDS

AUG 4

Certain commands can be used while you are inside another command. These commands are said to be *transparent* to the current command. The display commands **ZOOM**, **PAN**, and **VIEW** can be used transparently. Suppose that while drawing a line, you need to place a point somewhere off the screen. One option is to cancel the **LINE** command. Then zoom out to see more of the drawing and select **LINE** again. A more efficient method is to use **PAN** or **ZOOM** while still in the **LINE** command. An example of drawing a line to a point off the screen is as follows:

```
Command: LINE ↵
From point: (pick a point)
To point: 'PAN ↵
》Displacement: (pick a point to drag at edge of screen)
》Second point: (pick a second point of displacement)
Resuming LINE command.
To point: (pick a point)
To point: ↵
Command:
```

The double prompt (》) indicates that a command has been put on "hold" while you use a transparent command. The transparent command must be completed before the original command is returned. At that time, the double prompt disappears.

The above procedure is similar when using the **ZOOM** and **VIEW** commands. An apostrophe (') is entered before the command. To connect a line to a small feature, enter 'ZOOM at the **To point:** prompt. To perform a drawing or editing function across views, enter 'VIEW. If the current display you see is not a saved view, create a view. Then, you can do a transparent **PAN** or **ZOOM** to continue drawing. Finally, do a transparent **VIEW Restore**.

When trying to perform a transparent display, you may receive the following message:

**Requires a regen, cannot be transparent.
Resuming *current* command.

In this situation, you might try a less dramatic **ZOOM**, **PAN**, or **VIEW** that does not require AutoCAD to regenerate the display, or you can try **ZOOM Vmax**.

AutoCAD system variables can also be used in the transparent mode. Remember, when typing any transparent command, first type an apostrophe before the command name.

---

### EXERCISE 10-3

❏ Load AutoCAD for Windows and begin a new drawing named A:EX10-3.
❏ Set the drawing limits at 12,9, grid spacing at .5, and snap spacing at .25.
❏ Construct the two arcs shown below.
❏ Window a view of the left arc and name it 1. Restore view 1.
❏ Select the **LINE** command and snap to the top of the arc.
❏ Select **ZOOM Dynamic** transparently. Increase the zooming view box to include both arcs, but do not cause a regeneration.
❏ Extend the line to the top of the other arc. Begin a second line at the bottom of the right arc.
❏ Select **VIEW** transparently and restore view 1. Attach the line to the bottom of the left arc.
❏ **ZOOM Dynamic** to show the completed object.
❏ Save the drawing as A:EX10-3 and quit the drawing session.

VIEW 1

2 × R 1.0

---

## USING THE AERIAL VIEW

When you work on a large drawing, you can spend a lot of time zooming and panning the graphics window trying to locate a particular detail or feature. One of the most powerful display change features in AutoCAD for Windows is the **Aerial View** window. **Aerial View** is a navigation tool that lets you see the entire drawing in a separate window, locate the detail or feature you want, and move to it quickly. You can zoom in on an area, change the magnification, and match the view in the graphics window to the one in the **Aerial View** window (or vice versa). To open the **Aerial View** window, click the **Aerial View** button on the toolbar or enter DSVIEWER at the **Command:** prompt. The entire drawing is then displayed in the **Aerial View** window, Figure 10-13. The **Aerial View** window initially appears at the lower right of the graphics window, but can be moved to any convenient location on the screen. To do so, pick the title bar of the **Aerial View** window, hold down the left mouse button, and drag the **Aerial View** window to a new location.

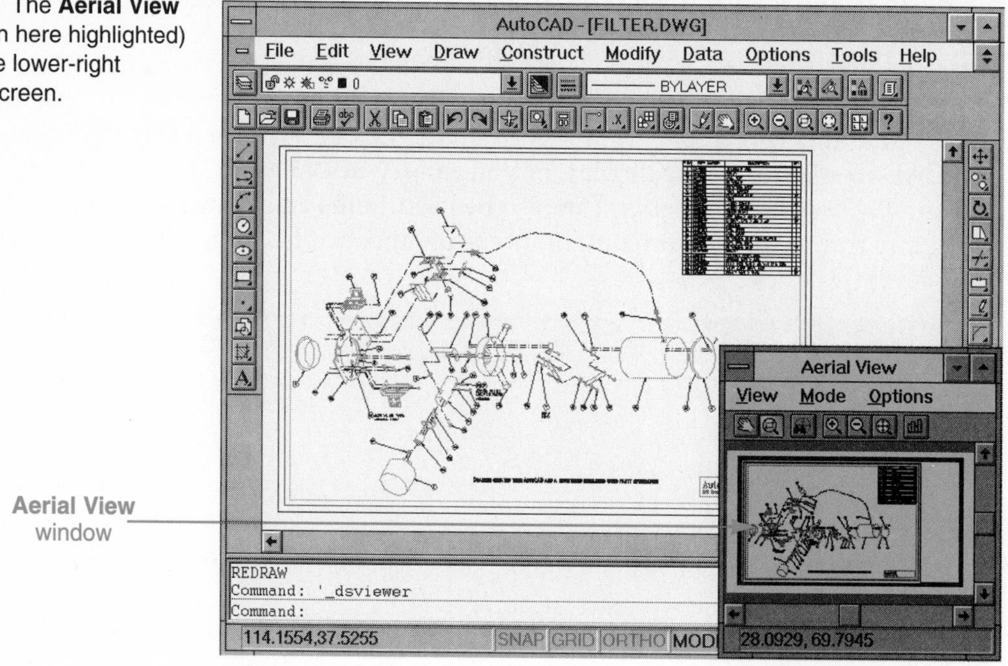

Figure 10-13. The **Aerial View** window (shown here highlighted) is initially in the lower-right corner of the screen.

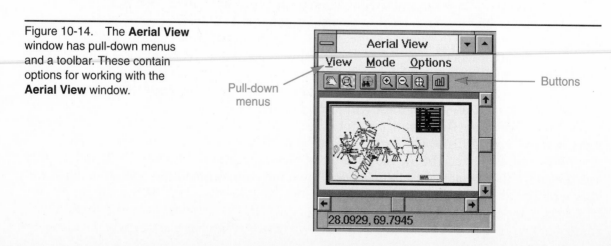

Aerial View
window

**NOTE**

AutoCAD must be configured for the Windows accelerated display driver to use **Aerial View**. This is the default AutoCAD for Windows configuration. If needed, change the display with the display-list option. Also, **Aerial View** cannot be used in paper space mode or if a perspective view is displayed using the **Distance** option to the **DVIEW** command. The **DVIEW** command and its options are covered in *AutoCAD and its Applications—Advanced, R13 for Windows*.

## Aerial View window description

The menu bar in the **Aerial View** window contains three pull-down menus and seven buttons. See Figure 10-14. The menus and buttons are described as follows:

- **Zoom In.** This is found as a button and in the **View** pull-down menu. Increases the magnification of the image in the **Aerial View** window.
- **Zoom Out.** This is found as a button and in the **View** pull-down menu. Decreases the magnification of the image in the **Aerial View** window.

Figure 10-14. The **Aerial View** window has pull-down menus and a toolbar. These contain options for working with the **Aerial View** window.

Pull-down
menus

Buttons

- **Global.** This is found as a button and in the **View** pull-down menu. Displays the entire generated area of the drawing in the **Aerial View** window.
- **Pan.** This is found as a button and in the **Mode** pull-down menu. Switches the aerial viewer into **Pan** mode, maintaining the current zoom display size and allowing you to reposition it in a new location.
- **Zoom.** This is found as a button and in the **Mode** pull-down menu. Switches the aerial viewer into **Zoom** mode, where you can draw a window anywhere in the generated area of the drawing.
- **Auto Viewport.** This is found only in the **Options** pull-down menu of the **Aerial View** window. When on, switching to a different tiled viewport will automatically cause the new viewport to be displayed in the aerial view window.
- **Dynamic Update.** This is found only in the **Options** pull-down menu of the **Aerial View** window. This causes the **Aerial View** window to update its display after each change in the drawing. Enable this only if your display system is very fast.
- **Locate Tool.** This is found only as a button. Press and hold this button down and drag the target image to the main AutoCAD display window. As you drag it around the drawing, the geometry appearing in the locator window is displayed in the **Aerial View** window. Release the pick button to make the shown display area current in the **Aerial View** window.
- **Locator Magnification....** This is found only in the **Options** pull-down menu of the **Aerial View** window. This controls the magnification factor used with the locator tool. The locator tool magnifies the view by a specified factor. To change the magnification, select **Locator Magnification....** The **Magnification** dialog box appears as shown in Figure 10-15. Click on the − or + button to decrease or increase the magnification value by one.
- **Display Statistics....** This is found as a button and in the **Options** pull-down menu. Displays a dialog box with statistics for the current driver. See Figure 10-16.

Note that you can also use the horizontal and vertical scroll bars in the **Aerial View** window to change the view. Best of all, you can use the **Aerial View** zoom and pan functions transparently while a drawing or editing command is in progress.

Figure 10-15.  The **Magnification** dialog box can be used to increase or decrease the magnification factor.

Figure 10-16.  Selecting **Display Statistics** from the **Aerial View Option** pull-down menu opens the **Display Driver Statistics** dialog box. This lists information about the current driver.

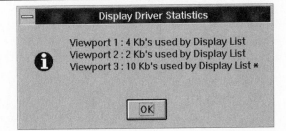

## Using the AutoCAD graphics window scroll bars

The scroll bars allow a quick and easy way to pan the drawing display. Picking the arrow buttons at the end of the scroll bar moves the display a small amount. Picking the scroll bar itself pans the drawing by its current height or width, depending on the direction of the pan. The "elevator" button can be picked and dragged as needed to move a desired amount. The scroll bars can be used to move the display anywhere within the generated area of the drawing.

PROFESSIONAL
TIP

Although regeneration has been virtually eliminated with Release 13, it is still possible. You should try to avoid regeneration because it slows your work and thought processes. Try the following tips for all your new drawings:

- Set your drawing limits to include a little extra for a border.
- **ZOOM All**.
- Create a view named **ALL** (or a name of your choice) of the entire drawing area.
- Avoid using **ZOOM All**, **ZOOM Extents**, or **REGEN** again.
- Create additional views as you need them.
- Use **Aerial View** whenever possible in place of all other display commands. To redisplay the entire drawing without causing a regeneration, double-click **Zoom** on the menu bar, or restore the view named ALL.
- If you have not configured AutoCAD for Windows to use the display-list driver, then use **ZOOM Dynamic** in place of the other display commands. The hourglass in the display will appear if AutoCAD will regenerate the drawing.
- Use **ZOOM Vmax** to check the contents of the virtual screen.

## EXERCISE 10-4

❑ Load AutoCAD for Windows and open the ASESMP drawing in the R13\COM\SAMPLE directory.

❑ Activate the **Aerial View** and zoom to office #109 in the upper-right corner of the drawing. Use the **Zoom** button in the **Aerial View** window.

❑ Using the **Aerial View Options** pull-down menu, set the **Locator Magnification** to 4. Pick the **Locate** button in the **Aerial View** window and hold the pick button down. Slowly move your pointer around the drawing to see the contents of room #109. Move the pointer back inside the **Aerial View** window then release the pick button

❑ Pick the **Pan** button in the **Aerial View** window. Move the zoom box in the **Aerial View** to the upper-left corner of the building and click so that office #101 is displayed in the drawing window.

❑ Set the **Locator Magnification** to 4. Pick the **Locate** button in the **Aerial View** window and hold the pick button down. Move the locator icon around the drawing until you can clearly see the green phone on the desk. Release the pick button.

❑ Zoom out to view the entire building using the **Zoom Out** button in the **Aerial View**.

❑ Resize your **Aerial View** window so it occupies at least one quarter of your display screen. Set **Locator Magnification** to 5. Pick the **Locate** button and take another tour of the building by moving the locator icon around the drawing. Do not release the pick button.

❑ Pick the **Zoom** button in the **Aerial View** window and create a zoom box just large enough to view one office.

❑ Pick the **Pan** button and move the zoom box around the **Aerial View**, picking different locations to look at as you go.

❑ When you are finished experimenting with the **Aerial View**, quit the session without saving.

## MODEL SPACE AND PAPER SPACE

**AUG 10**

*Model space* can be thought of as the method and "space" where you draw and design in AutoCAD. The term "model" has more meaning when working in 3D, but you can consider any drawing or design a model, even if it is two-dimensional. The best way to tell if you are in model space is to look at the **UCS** (User Coordinate System) icon. It is the symbol located in the lower-left corner of the screen, and represents the current directions of the X and Y coordinates. See Figure 10-17. A detailed discussion of User Coordinate Systems and the **UCS** icon is given in *AutoCAD and its Applications—Advanced, Release 13 for Windows*.

Figure 10-17.  The **UCS** icons for model space and paper space.

MODEL SPACE          PAPER SPACE

*Paper space*, on the other hand, is a "space" you create when you are ready to lay out a drawing or model to be plotted. Basically, it is as if you place a sheet of paper on the screen, then insert, or "reference," one or more drawings to the paper. In order to create this plotting layout, you must first enter paper space by typing PSPACE or PS at the **Command:** prompt.

    Command: **PS** ↵
    \*\*Command not allowed unless TILEMODE is set to 0\*\*

As you can see, AutoCAD does not allow you to enter paper space until you have changed how the viewports are handled. This system variable is called **TILEMODE**. The function of tiled viewports is discussed later in this chapter. For now, in order to enter paper space you must reset the **TILEMODE** value.

    Command: **TILEMODE** ↵
    New value for TILEMODE ⟨1⟩: **0** ↵
    Entering Paper space. Use Mview to insert Model space viewports.
    Regenerating drawing.
    Command:

After entering the **TILEMODE** variable of 0 you are automatically placed in paper space. Notice that the **P** button is highlighted on the toolbar and the paper space icon displayed in the lower-left corner of the screen.

    Remember that you should create all your drawings and designs in model space, not in paper space. Only paper layouts for plotting purposes should be created in paper space. Therefore, you should return to model space by entering either MSPACE or MS at the **Command:** prompt.

    Command: **MS** ↵
    MSPACE
    There are no active Model space viewports.
    Command:

Notice that you are *not* returned to model space. You must first reset the **TILEMODE** system variable to 1 to return to model space.

    Command: **TILEMODE** ↵
    New value for TILEMODE ⟨0⟩: **1** ↵
    Regenerating drawing.
    Command:

There are two quick ways to switch back and forth between model space and paper space. In the **View** pull-down menu, pick **Paper Space** to toggle your current space. Another method is to double-click on the space indicator tile found on the status bar. This toggles the space and updates the tile to display the name of the current space.

Do not be confused by **TILEMODE**, model space, and paper space. The detailed discussion in Chapter 26 will give you a better understanding. Right now, think of these terms in the following manner:

| ACTIVITY | SPACE | TILEMODE |
|---|---|---|
| Drawing and design | Model | 1 |
| Plotting and printing layout | Paper | 0 |

## CREATING MULTIPLE VIEWPORTS

AUG 4

Viewports are created with the **VPORTS** command. The AutoCAD graphics window can be divided into sixteen or more "tiled" viewports. The edges of tiled viewports butt against one another like floor tile. The **TILEMODE** variable must be set to 1 or ON to display tiled viewports. The arrangement of the viewports can vary, as indicated by the options of the **VPORTS** command. The default arrangement of viewports is 3, Figure 10-18.

```
Command: VPORTS ↵
Save/Restore/Delete/Join/SIngle/?/2/⟨3⟩/4: ↵
Horizontal/Vertical/Above/Below/Left/⟨Right⟩: ↵
Regenerating drawing.
Command:
```

Figure 10-18. The default arrangement of viewports.

By default, the large viewports is on the right

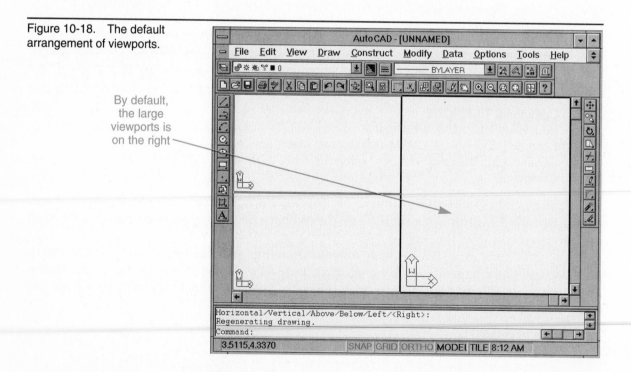

When you accept the defaults, AutoCAD displays an arrangement of two viewports on the left side of the screen, and a large viewport on the right. The possible combinations of three viewports are shown in Figure 10-19.

Move the pointing device around and notice that only one viewport contains crosshairs. This is called the *active viewport*. The pointer is represented by an arrow in the others. To make a different viewport active, move the pointer into it and press the pick button. As you draw in one viewport, the image is displayed in all of them. Try drawing lines and other

Figure 10-19.   A variety of viewport arrangements is possible with the **VPORTS** command and the 3 option.

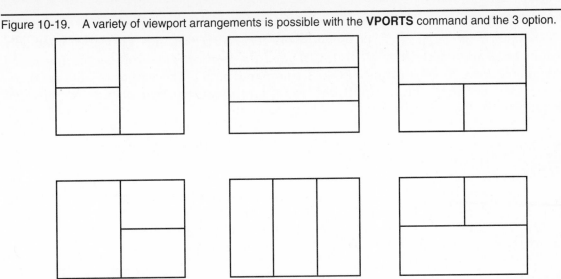

shapes and notice how the viewports are affected. Then use a display command, such as **ZOOM**, in the current viewport and notice the results. Only the current viewport reflects the use of the **ZOOM** command.

Preset tiled viewport layouts can be selected from an image tile menu. Pick the **View** pull-down menu, then select **Tiled Viewports**, **Layout**, and then **Tiled Viewports** to display the **Tiled Viewport Layout** icon menu. You can select a pre-arranged layout by either picking the image tile on the right, or by picking the written description from the list on the left. See Figure 10-20. After you pick a layout, the image tile and description are highlighted. If this is the desired layout, pick **OK** and the screen changes to the new configuration.

Notice in Figure 10-20 that there are several additional spaces in the image tile menu. You can create custom viewport layouts and add them to this image tile menu. See *AutoCAD and its Applications—Advanced, Release 13 for Windows* for menu customization techniques.

Figure 10-20.   The **Tiled Viewport Layout** icon menu.

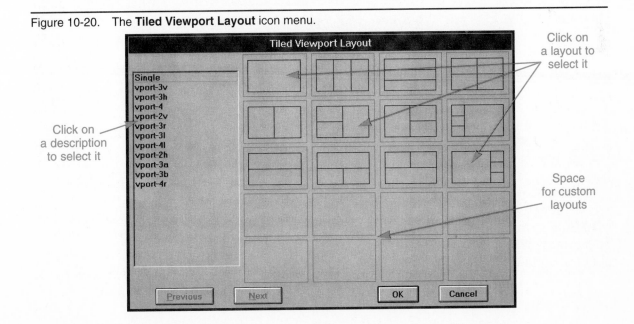

## Uses of viewports

Viewports in model space can be used for both 2D and 3D drawings. They are limited only by your imagination and need. See *AutoCAD and its Applications—Advanced, Release 13 for Windows* for examples of the **VPORTS** command in 3D. The nature of 2D drawings, whether they are mechanical multiview, architectural construction details, or unscaled schematic drawings, lend themselves well to viewports.

**PROFESSIONAL TIP**

When dialog boxes appear on-screen, many times they obstruct your view of the drawing. Click the title bar of the dialog box and hold down the pick button. You can then move the dialog box to a new location on-screen.

**PROFESSIONAL TIP**

Several sample drawings are included with the AutoCAD software. If AutoCAD was installed entirely, using default settings, the sample drawings should be located in the R13\COM\SAMPLE subdirectory. Check with your instructor or supervisor to locate these drawings, or browse through the directories and subdirectories to determine their locations. The sample drawings include a variety of drawing and design disciplines and are excellent for testing and practice. You should use these drawings, especially when learning the display commands.

### EXERCISE 10-5

❑ Load AutoCAD for Windows and open the SASKATCH drawing from the \R13\COM\SAMPLE subdirectory. (SASKATCH will reside here if AutoCAD was installed according to suggestions in the *Installation and Performance Guide*.)
❑ When the drawing is displayed on the screen, you should see a map of the Canadian province of Saskatchewan. Zoom into various locations to get familiar with the drawing.
❑ Use the **VPORTS** command to create the default arrangement of three viewports. (Make sure **TILEMODE** is set to 1.) The large viewport should be on the right.
❑ Use **PAN** to move the drawing up in the large viewport.
❑ In the upper-left viewport, use **ZOOM Window** to find the lower-left corner of the legend.
❑ Pick the lower-left viewport and zoom in on the center of the map. Locate the towns of McMahon and Neville.
❑ While in this same viewport, use **ZOOM Vmax**. This displays the virtual screen for the current viewport.
❑ Quit without saving the drawing.

## INTRODUCTION TO 3D DISPLAY COMMANDS

AUG 11

The commands **DVIEW** (dynamic view), and **VPOINT** (viewpoint) are used in 3D drawing. An introduction to the basics of 3D drawing is provided in Chapter 29. However, these two commands are discussed in the next sections.

### Establishing a dynamic view

When using the **DVIEW** command to view a 3D drawing, you can see the object move as you perform viewing commands such as **ROTATE**, **TURN**, **TWIST**, and **PAN**. Follow the given example for a brief overview of the **DVIEW** command. First, open the LINKRODS drawing. This drawing should be in the subdirectory R13\COM\SAMPLE. The drawing that appears is a 3D model of a link rod, and is displayed at an angle appropriate for 3D viewing.

Now use the **PLAN** command to see the plan, or top, view of the model. After the following command sequence, your display should look like Figure 10-21.

    Command: **PLAN** ⏎
    ⟨Current UCS⟩/Ucs/World: ⏎
    Regenerating drawing.
    Command:

Now, use the following commands to create viewports, and a dynamic view in the large viewport:

    Command: **VPORTS** ⏎
    Save/Restore/Delete/Join/SIngle/?/2/⟨3⟩/4: ⏎
    Horizontal/Vertical/Above/Below/Left/⟨Right⟩: ⏎
    Command:

Your screen should now look like Figure 10-22.

---

Figure 10-21.   The LINKRODS drawing displayed in a single viewport.

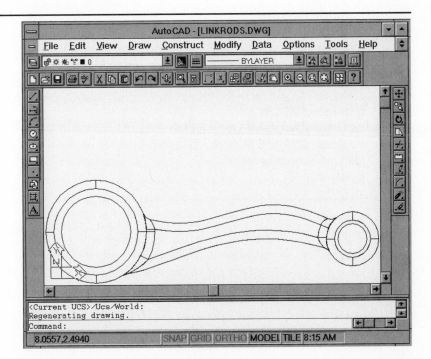

Figure 10-22.  The **VPORTS** command is used to display three viewports.

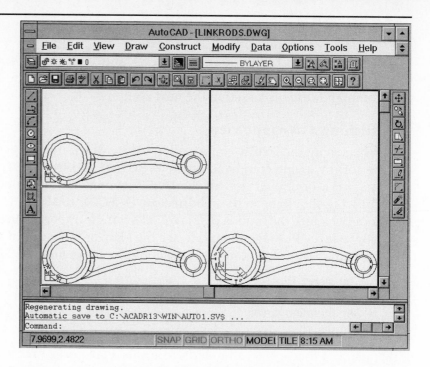

Next, use the **DVIEW** command to create a 3D view of the linkrod in the large viewport. First, make the large viewport active by clicking anywhere inside it. In order to speed up the **DVIEW** process, press [Enter] at the **Select objects:** prompt. This displays a small house that requires less regeneration time. Your drawing returns to the screen at the completion of the **DVIEW** command, and is displayed in the same viewpoint as the house. If you want to work with objects in your drawing on the screen using the **DVIEW** options, use any of the selection methods to select them.

Command: **DVIEW** ↵
Select objects: ↵
CAmera/TArget/Distance/POints/PAn/Zoom/TWist/CLip/Hide/Off/Undo/⟨eXit⟩: **TA** ↵
Toggle angle in/Enter angle from XY plane ⟨–90.00⟩: **–15** ↵
Toggle angle from/Enter angle in XY plane from X axis ⟨90.00⟩: **–40** ↵
CAmera/TArget/Distance/POints/PAn/Zoom/TWist/CLip/Hide/Off/Undo/⟨eXit⟩: ↵
Command: **ZOOM** ↵
All/Center/Dynamic/Extents/Left/Previous/Vmax/Window/
    ⟨Scale(X/XP)⟩: **E** ↵
Regenerating drawing.
Command

---

**NOTE**

When working in large drawings, it is best to use the house for **DVIEW**. If your drawing is complex, the computer slows down because it is constantly regenerating the highlighted display as the drawing is dynamically moved on the screen.

Try to determine the direction that you are viewing the linkrod from. Notice in the small viewports that the large end of the linkrod is toward the left of the screen, and the linkrod is oriented along the X axis. Now look at the **UCS** icon in the large viewport. If it appears that the large end is toward you, that is correct. Now look at the **UCS** icon in the top small viewport. If it appears that you are looking at the top of the linkrod, you are correct, Figure 10-23. If you have trouble visualizing this, make the large viewport active, and then type HIDE at the **Command:** prompt. The hide operation may take from 45 seconds to two minutes depending on the model and speed of your computer. This is because this drawing is a 3D solid model, and AutoCAD must first construct a "skin" to wrap around the model, and then calculate which parts of the model are hidden from view.

Figure 10-23. The **DVIEW** command is used in the large viewport.

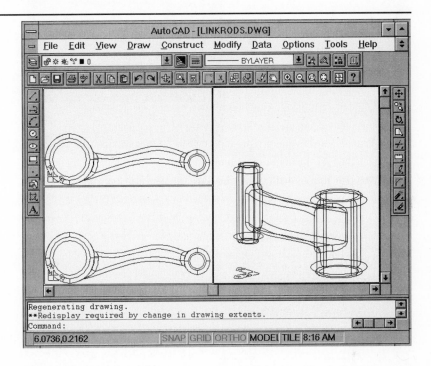

There are several other options and possibilities with the **DVIEW** command. You can create a true perspective view by specifying the distance from camera to target. In addition, you can zoom in or away from the object, or "clip" the front or rear of the screen image. Additional information regarding these options is found in *AutoCAD and its Applications—Advanced, Release 13 for Windows*.

### Creating a 3D viewpoint

The **VPOINT** command allows you to specify the direction that you will view the object from. You can enter XYZ coordinates, or you can visually determine your viewpoint using an XYZ "tripod." This example uses coordinate entry to determine both viewpoints. See Chapter 29 for a discussion of the tripod method. Make the upper-left viewport active and enter the following commands:

> Command: **VPOINT** ↵
> Rotate/⟨View point⟩ ⟨*current*⟩:**–1,–1,1** ↵
> Regenerating drawing.
> Command:

Figure 10-24.   The **VPOINT** command is used to create two different views in the small viewports.

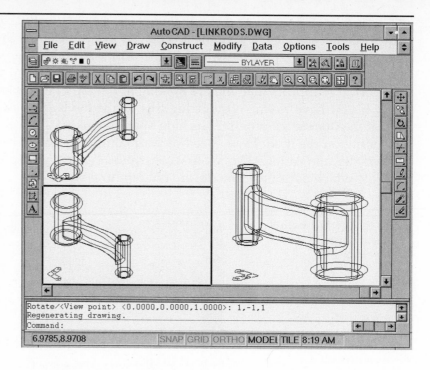

Activate the lower-left viewport and enter the following:

> Command: **VPOINT** ↵
> Rotate/〈View point〉 〈*current*〉: **1,–1,1** ↵
> Regenerating drawing.
> Command:

The screen should now resemble Figure 10-24.

One advantage of multiple viewports is that each viewport is a separate screen. Therefore, you can display any view of the drawing you wish in each screen. In addition, 3D drawings can appear as either wireframe or solid. A *wireframe* is an object that shows all lines, including those at the "back" of the object. The views currently on your screen show wireframes. To make an object look more realistic, use the **HIDE** command to represent a solid object.

First, make the lower-left viewport active and zoom in on the small end of the linkrod. Next, make the upper-left viewport active and zoom in on the large end of the linkrod. Now, use the **HIDE** command in all viewports to remove hidden lines. This process may take a few minutes depending on the speed of your computer.

> Command: **HIDE** ↵
> Regenerating drawing.
> Hiding lines 100% done
> Command:

The screen still shows three separate 3D views. However, the object in each view no longer appears as a wireframe. The hidden lines have been removed to represent a solid object. See Figure 10-25.

Figure 10-25. Three separate views of the LINKRODS drawing with hidden lines removed.

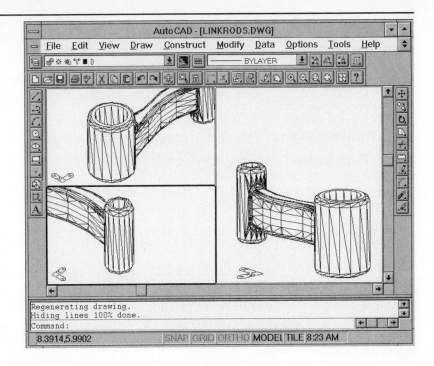

## REDRAWING AND REGENERATING VIEWPORTS

AUG 4

Since each viewport is a separate screen, you can redraw or regenerate a single viewport at a time without affecting the others. The **REGEN** (regenerate) command instructs AutoCAD to recalculate all of the entities in the drawing. This takes considerably longer than a **REDRAW**, especially if the drawing is large. However, **REGEN** can clarify a drawing by smoothing out circles, arcs, ellipses, and splines. In order to redraw all of the viewports, use the **REDRAWALL** command. If you need to regenerate all of the viewports, use the **REGENALL** command.

### EXERCISE 10-6

❑ Use the display of the LINKRODS drawing that is currently on your screen. If the display is not on your screen, refer to the previous section of this text entitled *Establishing a dynamic view* and follow the example to this point.
❑ Make the upper-left viewport active and draw some lines near the top of the linkrod. The lines should be displayed in all viewports.
❑ Make the lower-left viewport active and draw some lines.
❑ Use the **REDRAW** command while the lower-left viewport is active. Notice that only the lower-left viewport is redrawn.
❑ Use the **REDRAWALL** command.
❑ Pick the large viewport and use the **REGEN** command.
❑ Use the **REGENALL** command. Notice how much longer it takes to perform this command than the **REDRAWALL** command.
❑ Save your drawing as A:EX10-6, then quit the drawing session.

### Controlling automatic regeneration

When developing a drawing, you may use a command that changes certain aspects of the entities in it. When this occurs, AutoCAD does an automatic regeneration to update the entities. This may not be of concern to you when working on small drawings, but this regeneration may take a considerable amount of time on large and complex drawings. In addition, it may not be necessary to have a regeneration of the drawing at all times. If this is the case, set the **REGENAUTO** command to off.

> Command: **REGENAUTO** ↵
> ON/OFF ⟨*current*⟩: **OFF** ↵
> Command:

When **REGENAUTO** is off, you are given a warning if a regeneration is required:

> About to regen – proceed? ⟨Y⟩

If you answer No to this prompt, the command you issued is not executed. The commands that may automatically cause a regeneration are **ZOOM**, **PAN**, and **VIEW Restore**.

## MULTIPLE VIEWPORTS IN PAPER SPACE

The viewports created with the **VPORTS** command in model space are called *tiled viewports* because they butt against one another. However, the viewports created in paper space are constructed with the **MVIEW** command, and are separate entities. You can create as many paper space viewport entities as needed. They can also overlap.

AutoCAD can only display a certain number of active viewports. A model space drawing is displayed in an active viewport. The type of operating system used by your computer and the display device determine the number of active viewports. You can check this number by entering the **MAXACTVP** (maximum active viewports) system variable:

> Command: **MAXACTVP** ↵
> New value for MAXACTVP ⟨16⟩:

The viewports created by the **MVIEW** command are used when laying out a multiview drawing for plotting or printing. Since these viewports are created in paper space, and they can overlap, the **TILEMODE** system variable must be set to 0. This places you in paper space. Think of the relationship of **TILEMODE** and viewports as follows:

| ACTIVITY | SPACE | TILEMODE | COMMAND |
|---|---|---|---|
| Drawing and design | Model | 1 | VPORTS (tiled) |
| Plotting and printing layout | Paper | 0 | MVIEW (entities) |

This procedure, and all of the options of the **MVIEW** command, are discussed in detail in Chapter 26.

## CHAPTER TEST

*Write your answers in the spaces provided.*

1. What is the difference between the **REDRAW** and '**REDRAW** commands? _____

_____

_____

2. What are "blips" and how does **REDRAW** deal with them? _____

_____

_____

3. Which command allows you to change the display of blips? _____

4. Give the proper command option and value to zoom in on the center of a drawing with a magnification factor of 3. _____

5. What is the difference between **ZOOM Extents** and **ZOOM All**? _____

_____

6. During the drawing process, when should you use **ZOOM**? _____

_____

7. How many different boxes are displayed during the **ZOOM Dynamic** command? _____

8. What is a "virtual screen?" _____

_____

9. When using the **ZOOM Dynamic** option, what symbol informs you that a regeneration is about to take place? _____

10. Which command and option allows you to create a view, named FULL, of the current screen display? _____

11. What option would you choose to display an existing view? _____

12. How would you obtain a listing of existing views? _____

13. What is the purpose of the **PAN** command? _____

_____

14. How does **PAN** work? _____

_____

15. How do you access the **PAN** command presets? _____

_____

16. What is "view resolution?" _____

_____

17. What is the purpose of the **VIEWRES** command? _____

_____

18. If you answer No to the prompt Do you want fast zooms, what does AutoCAD do when you issue any display command? _____

19. What does the **VIEWRES** zoom percentage refer to? _____

_____

20. What is the difference between **Tiled Model Space** and **Floating Model Space**? _____

_____

_____

21. How is the **Locate** button in the **Aerial View** window used? _____

_____

_____

22. What is the affect of picking **Global** from the <u>View</u> pull-down menu, or the toolbar, found in the **Aerial View** window? _____

_____

23. How is a transparent display command entered at the keyboard? _____

_____

24. When will AutoCAD not execute a transparent display command? _____

_____

25. How must AutoCAD for Windows be configured before **Aerial View** can be used? _____

_____

_____

26. List two ways to enable the **Aerial View** window. _____

_____

_____

27. Cite several advantages of **Aerial View** over other display commands. _____

_____

_____

28. Explain the difference between model space and paper space. _____

_____

_____

29. What is the purpose of the **TILEMODE** system variable? _____

_____

_____

30. Describe the default viewport layout for the **VPORTS** command. _____

_____

31. What type of object does the **DVIEW** command use to initially establish a 3D view?

_____

32. How do the **DVIEW** and **VPOINT** commands differ? _____

_____

_____

33. Which command regenerates all of the viewports? _____
34. What is the function of **REGENAUTO**? _____

_____

## DRAWING PROBLEMS

General

1. Load a drawing from an earlier chapter. Use the following display commands and options on the drawing:

   A. **ZOOM All**

   B. **ZOOM Window** on one detail three times

   C. **ZOOM Previous**

   D. **ZOOM Extents**

    E. **ZOOM Center**

    F. **ZOOM Vmax**

    G. **PAN** in four directions

    H. **PAN** diagonally

2. Load a previous drawing that contains a large amount of detail. Use the **VIEW** command to create views of two areas to show detail. Also create a view that shows the entire drawing. Use the **VIEW** command to restore each of the views.

*General*

3. The purpose of this problem is to create and save seven individual views in a C-size drawing. Begin a new drawing and set the drawing limits to 22,17. Draw the six objects shown below so that they are proportional to the drawing limits. Use the following display aspects in your drawing:

*General*

    A. Create and save one view of the entire drawing limits and name it ALL.

    B. Use **Aerial View** or **ZOOM Dynamic** to window each object. Save each view with the name shown in the illustration.

    C. Set **VIEWRES** for fast zooms and a circle zoom percent of 50.

    D. Save the drawing as A:P10-3.

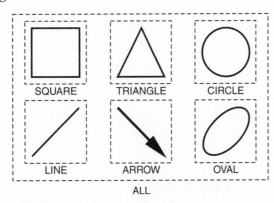

4. Open the drawing named TROL1. This drawing should be in the \R13\COM\SAMPLE subdirectory. Then, perform the following:

*General*

    A. Make sure you are in paper space. Thaw the VPORTS layer. Use the **VIEW** command to create views of the following parts of the drawing. Name the views using the names provided in parentheses.

        • Title block (TITLE).        • Section view (SECTION).

        • General notes (NOTES).     • Top view (TOP).

        • Entire drawing (ALL).       • Isometric (ISO).

    B. Use the **Restore** option of the **VIEW** command to check all the views you just made.

    C. Restore the entire drawing with the proper view.

    D. Set the **TILEMODE** system variable to 1. Try to restore one of your views. What happens?

    E. Set **TILEMODE** to 0. Switch to model space by typing MS.

    F. Restore the TITLE view. Note that views created in paper space are displayed on the entire screen. Restore the view named ALL. Now switch to model space.

    G. Create a new view named SECTION. Pick the isometric viewport, zoom in on the hub of the wheel, and create a view named ISO.

    H. Stay in model space and restore the SECTION view. Notice the difference between restoring a model space view and a paper space view.

I. Switch to paper space and restore the ISO view. Pick the outline of the isometric viewport when prompted to Select Viewport for view. Notice that AutoCAD automatically switches to model space because that is where the view was created.

J. Save the drawing as A:P10-4 only if required to by your instructor.

*Mechanical Drafting*

5. Open the drawing named sextant. It should be located in the R13\COM\SAMPLE subdirectory. The object is a 3D drawing that is displayed in a perspective view. In order to use the display commands such as **ZOOM**, you must first remove the perspective view.

   A. Set the **TILEMODE** system variable to 1.

   B. Type DVIEW, then press [Enter] at the Select objects: prompts. Now type OFF and press [Enter] twice to remove the perspective view and return to your drawing.

   C. Then perform the following display functions on the SEXTANT drawing:
   - Use **ZOOM Dynamic** to display the entire sextant on the screen.
   - Create an arrangement of three viewports using the **VPORTS** command. Place the large viewport on the right.
   - Use the **PAN** command to center the sextant in the large viewport.
   - Pick the upper-left viewport and type PLAN. This creates a top view. The **PLAN** command is discussed in Chapter 29.
   - Pick the lower-left viewport and use **Aerial View** to zoom in on the angled green box at the top of the sextant.
   - Pick the large viewport and type HIDE. This removes the hidden lines. Now type SHADE. This colors-in the solid faces of the object using the colors of the object. Your display should look similar to the one shown below. The **HIDE** command is discussed in Chapter 29.
   - Use the **VPORTS** command to save the present configuration as THREE.
   - Return the **TILEMODE** variable to 0.

   D. Save your drawing as A:P10-5 and quit the drawing session.

   E. Load AutoCAD for Windows and open P10-5 from your floppy disk using the prototype method.

   F. Set **TILEMODE** to 1. Notice the configuration that is displayed.

   G. Continue experimenting with naming views and creating other viewport configurations.

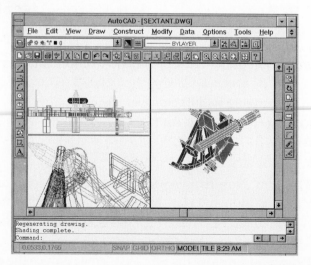

## Learning objectives

After completing this chapter, you will be able to:

❍ Use the **TEXT** command to add words to a drawing.
❍ Make multiple lines of text with the **MTEXT** command.
❍ Change text styles using the **STYLE** command.
❍ Use the **DTEXT** command to display text on the screen while typing.
❍ Draw special symbols using control characters.
❍ Underscore and overscore text.
❍ Explain the purpose of the **Quick Text** mode and use the **QTEXT** command.
❍ Identify and use the pull-down menus for creating and drawing text.
❍ Design prototype drawings with title blocks for A-size, B-size, and C-size drawings.
❍ Draw objects with associated text.
❍ Edit existing text.
❍ Check your spelling.

Words and notes on drawings have traditionally been added by hand lettering. This is a slow, time-consuming task. Computer-aided drafting programs have reduced the tedious nature of adding notes to a drawing. In computer-aided drafting, lettering is referred to as *text*. There are advantages of computer-generated text over hand-lettering techniques. Some of these advantages are that lettering is fast, easier to read, and follows the same consistent style. This chapter shows how text can be added using methods. Also explained is the proper text presentation stated in ASME Y14.2M-1992, *Line Conventions and Lettering*.

## TEXT STANDARDS

Company standards often dictate how text should appear on a drawing. The minimum recommended text height on engineering drawings is .125" (3mm). All dimension numbers, notes, and other text information should be the same height. Titles, subtitles, captions, revision information, and drawing numbers can be .188 to .25" (5 to 6.5mm) high. Many companies specify a .188, or 5/32" (5mm), lettering height for standard text. This text size is easy to read even after the drawing is reduced.

Vertical or inclined text may be used on a drawing, depending on company preference, Figure 11-1. One or the other is recommended, but do not use both. The recommended slant for inclined text is 68° from horizontal. Computer-generated text offers a variety of styles for specific purposes, such as titles or captions. Text on a drawing may be uppercase or lowercase letters. Most companies use uppercase letters.

---

Figure 11-1. Vertical and inclined text.

ABC.. abc.. 123..
*ABC.. abc.. 123..*

Numbers in dimensions or notes are the same height as standard text, excluding titles. Most number dimensions on an engineering drawing are in decimal inches or millimeters. On architectural drawings, enter dimensions as feet and inches. Fractional dimensions are not commonly used in mechanical drafting because they express a tolerance larger than the decimal equivalent. When fractions *are* used, each number should be the same height as the other drawing numbers. The ANSI standard recommends that the fraction bar be placed horizontally between the numerator and denominator using full-size numbers. However, this is difficult with computer-generated text. Therefore, the fraction bar is placed diagonally (/). A dash or space is placed between the whole number and the fraction, Figure 11-2. Dimensioning is discussed in detail from Chapter 20 through Chapter 23 of this text.

Figure 11-2.  Examples of numbers for different units of measure.

| UNITS | EXAMPLE |
|---|---|
| Decimal-Inches | 2.750 |
| Millimeters | 3                0.5 |
| Fractional Inches | 2 3/4 <br> 2-3/4 |

## DETERMINING DRAWING SCALE FACTORS FOR TEXT HEIGHT

AUG 1

Before plotting a drawing, you should determine the scale factor. You can do this at the time of plotting, but if you do, more work is required to update text heights. Scale factors are important because this value is used to make sure that the text is plotted at the proper height. The scale factor is multiplied by the desired plotted text height to get the AutoCAD text height. Scale factors and text heights should be determined before beginning a drawing, and are best incorporated as values within your prototype drawing files.

The scale factor is always a reciprocal of the drawing scale. For example, if you wish to plot a drawing at a scale of 1/2" = 1", calculate the scale factor as follows:

    1/2" = 1"
    .5" = 1"
    1/.5 = 2  The scale factor is 2.

An architectural drawing that is to be plotted at a scale of 1/4" = 1'-0" has a scale factor calculated as follows:

    1/4" = 1'-0"
    .25 = 12"
    12/.25 = 48  The scale factor is 48.

The scale factor of a civil engineering drawing that has a scale of 1" = 60' is calculated as follows:

    1" = 60'
    1" = (60 × 12)
    720/1 = 720  The scale factor is 720.

If your drawing is in millimeters where the scale is 1:1, the drawing scale factor can be converted to inches with the formula 1" = 25.4mm. Therefore, the scale factor is 25.4. When the metric drawing scale is 1:2, then the scale factor is 1" = 25.4 × 2, or 1" = 50.8. The scale factor is 50.8.

After the scale factor has been determined, you should then calculate the height of the AutoCAD text. If the text is to be plotted at 1/8" (.125") high, it should be drawn at that height. If the drawing scale is FULL (1″ = 1″), then the text height is 1/8″ (.125″). However, if you are working on a civil engineering drawing with a scale of 1″ = 60′, text drawn at 1/8″ high appears as a dot. Remember that the drawing you are working on is 720 times larger than it is when plotted at the proper scale. Therefore, you must multiply the text height by the 720 scale factor to get text that appears in correct proportion on the screen. If you want 1/8″ (.125″) high text to appear correctly on a drawing with a 1″ = 60′ scale, calculate the AutoCAD height as follows:

> 1″ = 60′
> 1″ = (60 × 12)
> 720/1 = 720 The scale factor is 720.
> text height × scale factor = scaled text height
> .125″ × 720 = 90 The proper text height is 90″.

An architectural drawing with a scale of 1/4″ = 1′-0″ has a scale factor of 48. Text that is to be 1/8″ high should be drawn 6″ high.

> 1/4″ = 1′-0″
> .25″ = 12″
> 12/.25 = 48 The scale factor is 48.
> .125 × 48 = 6 The proper text height is 6″.

## TEXT COMPOSITION

*Composition* refers to the spacing, layout, and appearance of the text. With manual lettering, it is necessary to space letters freehand. Spacing is performed automatically with computer-generated text.

Notes should be placed horizontally on the drawing. AutoCAD automatically sets lines of text apart a distance equal to one-half the text height. This helps maintain the identity of individual notes.

Most lines of text are left-justified. The term *justify* means to align the text to fit a given location. For example, left-justified text is aligned along an imaginary left border. Figure 11-3 shows the AutoCAD spacing between lines of left-justified text.

Figure 11-3.   Default spacing between lines of left-justified text.

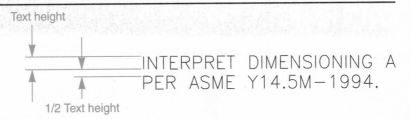

## USING AUTOCAD TO DRAW TEXT

AUG 8

The **TEXT** command places notes and other written information on a drawing. It can be accessed by picking the **Single-Line Text** button from the **Text** flyout in the **Draw** toolbar or **Single-Line Text** from the **Text** cascading submenu in the **Draw** pull-down menu. The command can also be entered by typing TEXT at the **Command:** prompt, as follows:

> Command: **TEXT** ↵
> Justify/Style/⟨Start point⟩:

The default option is **Start point**. If you want another option, type the option's first letter, such as J for **Justify** or S for **Style**, or select the option from the screen menu. The **TEXT** command allows you to compose in a variety of formats.

## Selecting the **Start point** option

The default mode is **Start point**. This option allows you to select a point on the screen where you want the text to begin. This point becomes the lower-left corner of the text. After you pick the point, the prompt reads:

Height ⟨0.2000⟩:

This prompt allows you to select the text height. The default value is 0.2000. The previously selected letter height may be displayed as the current value. If you want letters that are .5 unit high, then enter .5. The next prompt is:

Rotation angle ⟨0⟩:

The default value for the rotation angle is 0. This places the text horizontally at the specified start point. The values rotate text in a counterclockwise direction. The text pivots about the starting point, Figure 11-4. The starting point is the point you select to locate the text. Press [Enter] for 0° rotation to place horizontal text.
The last prompt is:

Text:

Type the desired text and press [Enter]. Text added with the **Start point** option is left-justified. Enter the following example:

Text: **AUTOCAD LEFT–JUSTIFIED TEXT** ↵
Command:

After you type the note, press [Enter] to insert the text. The information typed using the **Start point** option generates text as shown in Figure 11-5.

---

Figure 11-4. Different rotation angles for text. The starting point is indicated here with a plus sign.

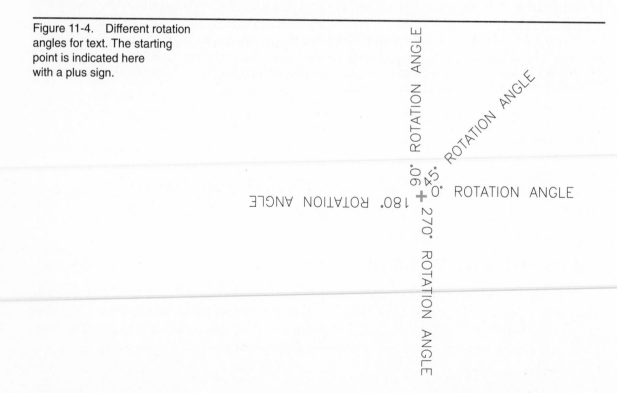

Figure 11-5. Left-justified text using the **Start point** option.

AUTOCAD LEFT–JUSTIFIED TEXT

## Justifying your text

When you select the **Justify** option, you can use one of several text alignment options. These options can be seen in the prompt line below, and are explained in the next sections.

```
Command: TEXT ↵
Justify/Style/⟨Start point⟩: J ↵
Align/Fit/Center/Middle/Right/TL/TC/TR/ML/MC/MR/BL/BC/BR:
```

## Using the **Align text** option

The **Align text** option allows you to pick two points that the text string is confined between. The beginning and endpoints can be placed horizontally or at an angle. AutoCAD automatically adjusts the text width to fit between the points selected. One caution with this option is that the text height is also changed. The height varies according to the distance between points and the number of characters. To use this option, enter J for **Justify**, and then A for **Align** as follows:

```
Command: TEXT ↵
Justify/Style/⟨Start point⟩: J ↵
Align/Fit/Center/Middle/Right/TL/TC/TR/ML/MC/MR/BL/BC/BR: A ↵
First text line point: (pick a point)
Second text line point: (pick a point)
Text: AUTOCAD ALIGNED TEXT ↵
Command:
```

Figure 11-6 shows how the text is aligned between the first and second points. Notice that the text is confined. The letter height and width changes in relation to the distance between points.

Figure 11-6. Examples of aligned text. Notice how AutoCAD adjusts the text height.

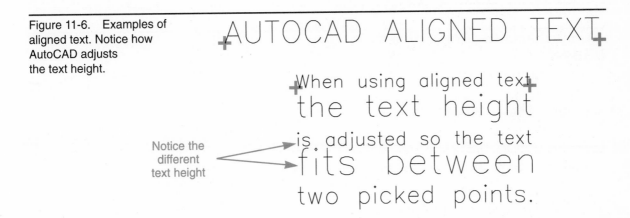

Notice the different text height

## Using the **Fit text** option

The **Fit text** option is similar to the **Align text** option, except that you can select the text height. AutoCAD adjusts the letter width to fit between two given points. The height default value is .20, but you can change this.

```
Command: TEXT ↵
Justify/Style/⟨Start point⟩: J ↵
Align/Fit/Center/Middle/Right/TL/TC/TR/ML/MC/MR/BL/BC/BR: F ↵
First text line point: (pick a point)
Second text line point: (pick a point)
Height ⟨current⟩: .5 ↵
Text: AUTOCAD FIT TEXT ↵
Command:
```

Figure 11-7 shows the note above as it appears on the screen in two different locations. Notice that the letter height remains the same, but the letter width is adjusted. In both cases, the line of text fits between the chosen points.

Figure 11-7. Using the **Fit** text option. Notice how AutoCAD adjusts the letter width.

Notice the different letter width

### The **Center text option**

The **Center text** option allows you to select the center point for the baseline of the text. Enter the letter height and rotation angle after picking the center point. This example uses a .5 unit height and a 0° rotation angle. The prompts appear as follows:

> Command: **TEXT** ↵
> Justify/Style/⟨Start point⟩: **J** ↵
> Align/Fit/Center/Middle/Right/TL/TC/TR/ML/MC/MR/BL/BC/BR: **C** ↵
> Center point: *(pick a point)*
> Height ⟨*current*⟩: **.5** ↵
> Rotation angle ⟨0⟩: ↵
> Text: **AUTOCAD CENTERED TEXT** ↵
> Command:

Figure 11-8 shows how the AUTOCAD CENTERED TEXT note appears. Notice that the text is centered horizontally, but placed above the pick point.

Figure 11-8. Using the **Center** text option.

AUTOCAD CENTERED TEXT

### Using the **Middle text** option

The **Middle text** option allows you to center text both horizontally and vertically at a given point. The letter height and rotation can also be changed. The command sequence is as follows and the result is shown in Figure 11-9:

> Command: **TEXT** ↵
> Justify/Style/⟨Start point⟩: **J** ↵
> Align/Fit/Center/Middle/Right/TL/TC/TR/ML/MC/MR/BL/BC/BR: **M** ↵
> Middle point: *(pick a point)*
> Height ⟨*current*⟩: **.5** ↵
> Rotation angle ⟨0⟩: ↵
> Text: **AUTOCAD MIDDLE TEXT** ↵
> Command:

Figure 11-9. Using the **Middle** text option.

AUTOCAD MIDDLE TEXT

## The **Right text** option

The **Right text** option is similar to **Start point**, except text is aligned with the lower-right corner. The text is right-justified. The letter height and rotation can also be entered. Figure 11-10 shows right-justified text. The command sequence is as follows:

Command: **TEXT** ↵
Justify/Style/⟨Start point⟩: **J** ↵
Align/Fit/Center/Middle/Right/TL/TC/TR/ML/MC/MR/BL/BC/BR: **R** ↵
End point: *(pick a point)*
Height ⟨*current*⟩: **.5** ↵
Rotation angle ⟨0⟩: ↵
Text: **AUTOCAD RIGHT–JUSTIFIED TEXT** ↵
Command:

---

Figure 11-10.    Using the **Right** text option.

AUTOCAD RIGHT—JUSTIFIED TEXT

---

## EXERCISE 11-1

❑ Load AutoCAD for Windows.
❑ Use the **TEXT** command to type the following information. Each time, change the text option to obtain the format given. Use .5 letter height and 0° rotation angle.
    AUTOCAD TEXT LEFT-JUSTIFIED USING THE START POINT OPTION.
    AUTOCAD TEXT RIGHT-JUSTIFIED USING THE RIGHT OPTION.
    AUTOCAD TEXT ALIGNED USING THE ALIGN OPTION.
    AUTOCAD TEXT CENTERED USING THE CENTER OPTION.
    AUTOCAD FIT TEXT USING THE FIT OPTION.
    AUTOCAD TEXT USING THE MIDDLE OPTION.
❑ Save the drawing as A:EX11-1 and quit.

---

**PROFESSIONAL TIP**

If you already know which text alignment option you want to use in your drawing, you can enter it at the Justify/Style/⟨Start point⟩: prompt without entering J for **Justify**.

---

## Using the other text alignment options

There are a number of text alignment options that allow you to place text on a drawing in relation to the top, bottom, middle, left, or right side of the text. These alignment options are shown in Figure 11-11. These options are shown as abbreviations that correlate to the **TEXT** prompt line, as shown below:

Command: **TEXT** ↵
Justify/Style/⟨Start point⟩: **J** ↵
Align/Fit/Center/Middle/Right/TL/TC/TR/ML/MC/MR/BL/BC/BR:

Figure 11-11.  Using the **TL**, **TC**, **TR**, **ML**, **MC**, **MR**, **BL**, **BC**, and **BR** text alignment options. Notice what the abbreviations stand for.

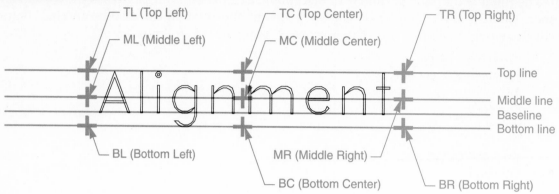

## Left-justified text

The **TL** option allows you to justify the text at the top left. An example of this type of justification is shown in Figure 11-12. The command line sequence is as follows:

Command: **TEXT** ↵
Justify/Style/⟨Start point⟩: **J** ↵
Align/Fit/Center/Middle/Right/TL/TC/TR/ML/MC/MR/BL/BC/BR: **TL** ↵
Top/left point: (*pick a point*)
Height ⟨*current*⟩: **.5** ↵
Rotation angle ⟨0⟩: ↵
Text: **AUTOCAD TOP/LEFT TEXT** ↵
Command:

Figure 11-12.  Using the **TL**
text alignment option.
⁺AUTOCAD TOP/LEFT TEXT

## Center-justified text

The **TC** option allows you to justify the text at the top center. An example of this type of justification is shown in Figure 11-13. The command line sequence is as follows:

Command: **TEXT** ↵
Justify/Style/⟨Start point⟩: **J** ↵
Align/Fit/Center/Middle/Right/TL/TC/TR/ML/MC/MR/BL/BC/BR: **TC** ↵
Top/center point: (*pick a point*)
Height ⟨*current*⟩: **.5** ↵
Rotation angle ⟨0⟩: ↵
Text: **AUTOCAD TOP/CENTER TEXT** ↵
Command:

Figure 11-13.  Using the **TC**
text alignment option.
AUTOCAD TOP⁺CENTER TEXT

## Right-justified text

The **TR** option allows you to justify the text at the top right. An example of this type of justification is shown in Figure 11-14. The command line sequence is as follows:

Figure 11-14.   Using the **TR**
text alignment option.

AUTOCAD TOP/RIGHT TEXT⁺

> Command: **TEXT** ↵
> Justify/Style/⟨Start point⟩: **J** ↵
> Align/Fit/Center/Middle/Right/TL/TC/TR/ML/MC/MR/BL/BC/BR: **TR** ↵
> Top/right point: *(pick a point)*
> Height ⟨*current*⟩: **.5** ↵
> Rotation angle ⟨0⟩: ↵
> Text: **AUTOCAD TOP/RIGHT TEXT** ↵
> Command:

## Other options

In the previous discussion you saw how the **TL**, **TC**, and **TR** options work. The remaining text alignment options function in the same manner, except are justified either middle or bottom. If you forget what the different abbreviations refer to, look back at Figure 11-11 for reference.

### EXERCISE 11-2

❑ Load AutoCAD for Windows.
❑ Use the **TEXT** command to type the following information. Each time, change the text option to obtain the format given in each statement. Use .5 letter height and 0° rotation angle.

> AUTOCAD TOP/LEFT OPTION.
> AUTOCAD TOP/CENTER OPTION.
> AUTOCAD TOP/RIGHT OPTION.
> AUTOCAD MIDDLE/LEFT OPTION.
> AUTOCAD MIDDLE/CENTER OPTION.
> AUTOCAD MIDDLE/RIGHT OPTION.
> AUTOCAD BOTTOM/LEFT OPTION.
> AUTOCAD BOTTOM/CENTER OPTION.
> AUTOCAD BOTTOM/RIGHT OPTION.

❑ Save the drawing as A:EX11-2 and quit.

## MAKING SEVERAL LINES OF TEXT                              AUG 8

Lines of text can be automatically spaced, each string having the same angle, height, and alignment. To do so, press [Enter] after the first line has been entered. This brings back the **Command:** prompt. A second [Enter] repeats the previous **TEXT** command. The **Start point:** prompt appears again and the previous line of text is highlighted. Press the [Enter] key to automatically justify the next line of text below the previous. The same procedure is used to continue drawing additional lines of text, Figure 11-15. The command sequence is as follows:

> Command: **TEXT** ↵
> Justify/Style/⟨Start point⟩: *(pick the start point)*
> Height ⟨*current*⟩: **.5** ↵
> Rotation angle ⟨0⟩: ↵
> Text: **THIS IS THE FIRST LINE OF TEXT** ↵
> Command: ↵
> TEXT Justify/Style/⟨Start point⟩: ↵
> Text: **THIS IS THE SECOND LINE OF TEXT** ↵
> Command:

Note that each line of text is an individual object in AutoCAD. In order to move or erase a paragraph of text created by this method, you need to select each and every line of text. The **MTEXT** command discussed in the next section creates multiline text objects where one or more paragraphs can be created as a single AutoCAD object.

---

Figure 11-15.   Drawing multiple lines of text with the **TEXT** command.

Words on a drawing have traditionally been referred to as lettering. Lettering has typically been a slow, time—consuming, task. Computer—aided drafting has reduced the tedious nature of preparing lettering on a drawing.

---

### EXERCISE 11-3

❏ Load AutoCAD for Windows.
❏ Use the **TEXT** command to type the following multiple lines of text exactly as shown. Use .25 letter height and 0° rotation angle.

LETTERING HAS TYPICALLY BEEN A SLOW, TIME-CONSUMING TASK.
COMPUTER-AIDED DRAFTING HAS REDUCED THE TEDIOUS NATURE OF
PREPARING LETTERING ON A DRAWING. IN CAD, LETTERING IS
REFERRED TO AS TEXT. COMPUTER-GENERATED TEXT IS FAST,
CONSISTENT, AND EASIER TO READ.

❏ Save the drawing as A:EX11-3 and quit.

---

### PROFESSIONAL TIP

Multiple lines of text can be placed in a box format with the **Fit** option. This justifies the text on both the left and right. The letter height is the same for each line of text. However, the letter width is adjusted to fit the boundary. Refer to the example below.

When using FIT text text height remains the same. The text width is adjusted to fit between the picked points.

Notice the different letter width

---

## MAKING MULTIPLE LINES OF TEXT WITH THE **MTEXT** COMMAND

AUG 8

The **MTEXT** command allows the creating of multiline text objects. Instead of each line being an individual object, all of the lines are part of the same object. Multiple text objects have a different set of rules from single-line text objects. The **MTEXT** command is accessed by picking the **Text** button in the **Draw** toolbar, or picking **Text** in the **Draw** pull-down then **Text** in the cascading submenu. You can also type MTEXT at the **Command:** prompt as follows:

> Command: **MTEXT** ↵
> Attach/Rotation/Style/Height/Direction/⟨Insertion point⟩:

The following gives a brief description of each **MTEXT** option:

- **Attach.** This sets the text justification method. The same text justification options discussed with single text lines apply. However, the alignment of the entire text boundary is set relative to the justification point. For example, all left justification options align the paragraph with the left margin, center justification centers each line of the paragraph, and all right justification options align the paragraph with the right margin, as shown in Figure 11-16.
- **Rotation.** This controls the rotation angle of the paragraph.
- **Style.**   Sets the text style to be used.
- **Height.** Sets the text height.
- **Direction.** This sets the reading direction. For example, English is read horizontally but Japanese is read vertically.
- **Width.** Numerically sets the paragraph width.
- **2Points.** Allows you to select 2 points to define the paragraph width, rather than a boundary box.
- **Insertion point.** This is the **MTEXT** default and lets you pick the first corner of a boundary used to enclose the paragraph.
- **Other corner.** This prompt asks you to pick the other corner of a text boundary box after you have picked the insertion point.

Figure 11-16.    The effects of the different **MText** justification options.

TOP LEFT
LEFT JUSTIFIED

TOP CENTER
CENTER JUSTIFIED

TOP RIGHT
RIGHT JUSTIFIED

MIDDLE LEFT
LEFT JUSTIFIED

MIDDLE CENTER
CENTER JUSTIFIED

MIDDLE RIGHT
RIGHT JUSTIFIED

BOTTOM LEFT
LEFT JUSTIFIED

BOTTOM CENTER
CENTER JUSTIFIED

BOTTOM RIGHT
RIGHT JUSTIFIED

This symbol represents the insertion point

You can use the **MTEXT** options to create desired text by setting each before you begin typing text. Plan how you want the paragraph to look before starting. The following shows the prompts and inputs you might use to set up the **MTEXT** command:

```
Command: MTEXT ↵
Attach/Rotation/Style/Height/Direction/⟨Insertion point⟩: A ↵
TL/TC/TR/ML/MC/MR/BL/BC/BR: BL ↵
Attach/Rotation/Style/Height/Direction/⟨Insertion point⟩: R ↵
Rotation angle ⟨0⟩: ↵
Attach/Rotation/Style/Height/Direction/⟨Insertion point⟩: S ↵
Style name (or ?) ⟨STANDARD⟩: ROMANS ↵ (Note: Text styles are explained later
    in this chapter)
Attach/Rotation/Style/Height/Direction/⟨Insertion point⟩: H ↵
Height ⟨0.080⟩: .125 ↵
Attach/Rotation/Style/Height/Direction/⟨Insertion point⟩: D ↵
Horizontal/Vertical: H ↵
Attach/Rotation/Style/Height/Direction/⟨Insertion point⟩: (pick the insertion point)
```

## Inserting multiline text

After you have set up the text the way you want it, the **MTEXT** default asks for an *insertion point*. Pick an insertion point or type the coordinates to start a corner of the text boundary. Now, the screen cursor forms a box, and you get the ⟨Other corner⟩: prompt. Pick the other corner of the box to establish the boundary for your paragraph of text. These are the prompts as continued from above:

```
Attach/Rotation/Style/Height/Direction/⟨Insertion point⟩: (pick the insertion point)
Attach/Rotation/Style/Height/Direction/Width/2Points/⟨Other corner⟩: (pick the other
    corner of the text boundary)
```

The ⟨Other corner⟩ selection sets the second corner of the text boundary. The boundary width is important because AutoCAD automatically starts the next line when your text gets to the boundary edge. The length is not as important, because if the text supplied spills over the defined boundary, the boundary is automatically resized to fit as related to the current attach setting. If the text is not enough to fill the boundary, the boundary size is reduced; accordingly. Once all options have been set and you are ready to enter the actual text content for the paragraph, AutoCAD opens the **Edit MTEXT** dialog box shown in Figure 11-17. This is a basic Windows-style text editor that allows simple text editing functions.

Figure 11-17. The **Edit MText** dialog box. The editing window (shown here highlighted) is where text is entered.

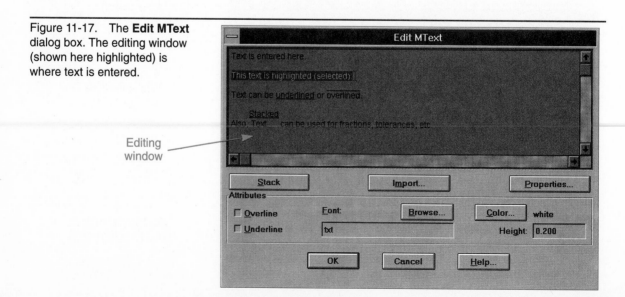

## Using the **Edit MTEXT** dialog box

The **Edit MTEXT** dialog box appears after you define the text boundaries, as shown above. The editing window is the primary feature of this dialog box, and is where text appears as you type. While typing text in the window, you can use many of the keystroke combinations that are available in Windows text editors. The following list shows the available keystroke functions:

| Keystroke | Function |
|---|---|
| [↑] [←] [→] [↓] | Arrow keys move the cursor through the text one position in the direction indicated by the arrow. |
| [Ctrl]+[→]<br>[Ctrl]+[←] | Moves the cursor one word in the direction indicated. |
| [Home] | Moves the cursor to the start of the current line. |
| [End] | Moves the cursor to the end of the current line. |
| [Delete] | Deletes the character immediately to the right of the cursor. |
| [Ctrl]+[Delete] | Deletes the word immediately to the right of the cursor. |
| [← Backspace] | The backspace key moves one character to the left, deleting the character as it moves. |
| [Ctrl]+[C] | Copy selection to the Clipboard. |
| [Ctrl]+[V] | Paste Clipboard contents to the selection or current cursor location. |
| [Ctrl]+[X] | Cut selection to the Clipboard. |
| [Ctrl]+[Shift]+[Space] | Insert non-breaking space (*the words on either side of a non-breaking space cannot be broken at the end of a line, instead both words are dropped to the next line*). |
| [Enter] | Ends the current paragraph, starting a new one on the next line. |

As you move the cursor into the editing window, it changes shape. If you have used other windows text editors, this will be a familiar cursor shape. Pointing to a character position within the text and pressing the pick button causes the cursor to be placed at the selected location. You can then begin typing or editing as needed.

Text is selected in the same way as with most standard Windows text editors. Place the cursor at one end of the desired selection, press and hold the pick button. Drag the cursor in the appropriate direction until the desired text is highlighted, then release the pick button. Now, any editing operations you perform will affect the highlighted text. For example, a **Copy** or **Cut** operation places the highlighted text on the Clipboard. To entirely replace the highlighted text with new text, either **Paste** the new text from the Clipboard or simply begin typing. The selection will be erased and the new text will appear in its place.

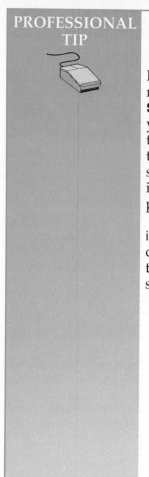

Normally, the specified font is displayed in the dialog box. However, certain font files are not recognized by Windows, and cannot be displayed in the **Edit MTEXT** dialog box. When this occurs, the **Select Font** dialog box is displayed. See the example below. Here, you can specify the substitute font to be used. Pick the pop-up list in the upper-right corner, and the available font files are shown. Select the desired font and set the **Bold** and **Italic** toggles. Then, this font is substituted for the actual font being used. Note that the substitution is shown only in the **Edit MTEXT** dialog, and the correct font is displayed in the drawing.

Your selected substitute font is displayed with the text Lorem ipsum dolor sit amet... in the **Sample** area. For those who might be curious, don't bother attempting a translation. This is nothing more than semi-Latin gibberish provided only to display a sample of the selected font.

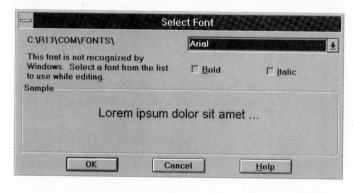

The following options are available in the **Edit MTEXT** dialog box. Refer to Figure 11-17.

- **Stack.** This option allows text parts to be stacked vertically. To use this feature, place a forward slash between the top and bottom items (for example, the fraction $1/2$ is written 1/2). Next, highlight the text to be stacked and pick the **Stack** button.
- **Import....** This displays the **Import Text File** dialog box allowing a text file to be selected and imported into the **Edit MTEXT** dialog box. This imported text can then be edited as needed.
- **Properties....** This displays the **MText Properties** dialog box. (See Figure 11-18.)
- **Overline.** Toggles the overline feature for the selected text.
- **Underline.** Toggles the underline feature for the selected text.
- **Font.** The desired font file can be typed in the edit box or you can use the **Browse...** button to find the desired file. If text is selected, the new font is applied only to the selection.
- **Color....** Displays the **Select Color** dialog box to set the color for the text. If text is selected, the new color is applied only to the selection.
- **Height:.** The current text height can be set in this edit box. If text is selected, the new height is applied only to the selection.

The formatting of the text within the **Edit MTEXT** dialog box may not always appear exactly as it will in the drawing. This is most commonly true when a substitute font is used for display in the editor. A substituted font may be wider or narrower than the font used in the drawing. AutoCAD automatically reformats the text to fit within the boundary defined in the drawing.

Figure 11-18.   The **MText Properties** subdialog box is used to change text parameters.

Set the text style, height, and direction

Set the attachment, width, and rotation options

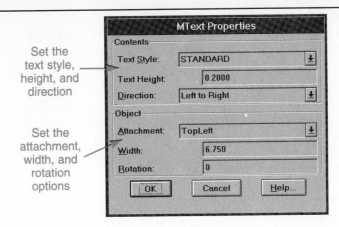

## Setting MTEXT properties

The **MText Properties** subdialog box is used to set the properties of the **MText**. The dialog box is shown in Figure 11-18. The available options are as follows:

- **Text Style:**. Displays a pop-up list of the defined text styles in the current drawing, selecting a style name makes it current.
- **Text Height:**. The value in the edit box specifies a new default text height.
- **Direction:**. Specifies the direction of the text.
- **Attachment:**. Specifies the attachment point and justification of the **MText**.
- **Width:**. Sets the width of the text boundary.
- **Rotation:**. Controls the rotation angle.

## Using an external text editor

If you are already familiar with another Windows text editing program, such as Notepad or Microsoft Word for Windows, you may prefer to use this external program. AutoCAD for Windows allows you to use any Windows-based text editor you wish. To set up your own editing program, select **Preferences...** from the **Options** pull-down menu. This displays the **Preferences** dialog box. Next, select the **Misc** tab to display the dialog page shown in Figure 11-19. Select the **Text Editor** edit box and type in the command line entry that starts the desired editor. Figure 11-19 shows the Notepad editor being specified, but any available editor can be specified. If you are not sure about the path you can select the **Browse...** button to display a file dialog that allows you to pick the path and file. To change back to the **Edit MTEXT** dialog, type INTERNAL in the **Text Editor** box. Also, when an external editor is running as a *child* process of AutoCAD, you must first exit the editor before you can return to AutoCAD.

Figure 11-19.   The **Misc** tab of the **Preferences** dialog box is where you can specify an external text editor.

Windows Notepad program is specified

Misc tab

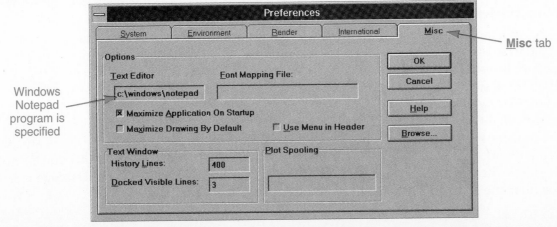

An external editor allows a greater amount of flexibility than the built-in editor. However, at first they can be a bit confusing. There are many codes used to format the text. Additionally, the text in the editor may appear much different than the text in your drawing. In the editor, you can simply type on the same line until your editor forces a word wrap, but it does not change the width of the text in your drawing. To force a new paragraph, type \P or press [Enter] and a new paragraph begins on the next line. When you return to AutoCAD, the text is automatically placed within the width of the boundary that you established. Note that if you type more text than can be displayed in the defined boundary, AutoCAD automatically adjusts the vertical size of the boundary to fit the text that you typed. See Figure 11-20.

Figure 11-20.  The multiline text boundary.

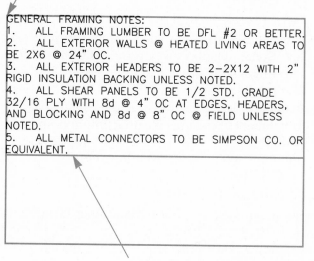

Insertion point–first corner of the text boundary

GENERAL FRAMING NOTES:
1.     ALL FRAMING LUMBER TO BE DFL #2 OR BETTER.
2.     ALL EXTERIOR WALLS @ HEATED LIVING AREAS TO BE 2X6 @ 24" OC.
3.     ALL EXTERIOR HEADERS TO BE 2–2X12 WITH 2" RIGID INSULATION BACKING UNLESS NOTED.
4.     ALL SHEAR PANELS TO BE 1/2 STD. GRADE 32/16 PLY WITH 8d @ 4" OC AT EDGES, HEADERS, AND BLOCKING AND 8d @ 8" OC @ FIELD UNLESS NOTED.
5.     ALL METAL CONNECTORS TO BE SIMPSON CO. OR EQUIVALENT.

The text boundary is automatically resized to fit the actual text that you type

**Note**

The boundary is adjusted vertically only if the text direction is horizontal. When the direction is vertical, the vertical boundary is held and the horizontal boundary is adjusted as necessary to fit the text.

## Saving the text

To save the text and return to the AutoCAD drawing editor, exit the editing program. If you have not yet saved the file, your editor should prompt you to save the changes. Make the appropriate selection to save the file. After the file is saved and the editor closed, the AutoCAD drawing editor returns. The text that you typed in the editor is displayed within the boundary you established earlier.

Note that the file you are editing has a name such as AC011551 without a file extension. The numbers may change from one drawing session to the next, but the filename will always begin with AC. In order for the text in the drawing to be updated, it is critical that you do not change this filename. The file is saved wherever your AutoCAD temporary file storage is set. If the filename is changed, any changes to the text will not be updated.

Most word processing programs allow you to change the format of the text. However, most formatting changes cannot be saved in an ASCII text format. For example, bold and italic text can easily be created in a word processor, but AutoCAD text uses different font files for italic and bold. These properties cannot be applied to other text fonts. When prompted by your word processor, be sure to specify *text only* (ASCII text) as the format for saving the file.

## Entering multiline text at the prompt line

If you prefer to enter multiple lines of text at the prompt line, use the **-MTEXT** command. You still get the **MTEXT** prompts that were previously described, but you enter the text at the prompt line after establishing the text boundary. If you have an external editor setup, this command overrides it. Everything else works the same as before, except these are the prompts:

> Command: **-MTEXT** ↵
> Attach/Rotation/Style/Height/Direction/⟨Insertion point⟩: *(pick the insertion point)*
> Attach/Rotation/Style/Height/Direction/Width/2Points/⟨Other corner⟩: *(pick the other*
>   *corner of the text boundary)*
> MText: **TYPE THE MULTIPLE LINES OF TEXT DIRECTLY AT THE PROMPT LINE.**
>   **AUTOCAD AUTOMATICALLY PLACES THE TEXT WITHIN THE BOUNDARY**
>   **THAT YOU HAVE ESTABLISHED.** ↵
> Command:

Setting a zero width causes lines of text to proceed in a continuous line until you press [Enter]. When you do this, AutoCAD only asks for the insertion point. You control the length of each line, so do not forget to press [Enter] when you want a new line to begin. This is the command sequence:

> Command: **-MTEXT**↵
> Attach/Rotation/Style/Height/Direction/⟨Insertion point⟩: *(pick the insertion point)*
> Attach/Rotation/Style/Height/Direction/Width/2Points/⟨Other corner⟩: **W** ↵
> Object width: **0** ↵
> MText: **ENTER THE DESIRED MULTIPLE LINES OF TEXT** ↵
> MText: **AT THE PROMPT LINE, BUT DO NOT FORGET TO** ↵
> MText: **PRESS ENTER TO HAVE YOUR TEXT GO TO THE** ↵
> MText: **NEXT LINE. PRESS ENTER TWICE TO GET BACK** ↵
> MText: **TO THE COMMAND: PROMPT.** ↵
> MText: ↵
> Command:

## EXERCISE 11-4

❑ Load AutoCAD and set your own variables as you feel are needed for this exercise.
❑ Type multiple lines of text based on the following requirements:
    Justification = TL, Rotation angle = 0, Style = STANDARD (AutoCAD's default),
    Text height = .125, Text direction = horizontal. Establish a text boundary beginning
    with the upper left corner that is 4″ wide by 5″ long.
❑ Type the following:
    The MTEXT command allows you to create multiline text objects. Instead of each line being
    an individual object, all of the lines are part of the same object. The command for multiple
    text objects is MTEXT. It is accessed in the pull-down menu by picking Text in the Draw pull-
    down and then Text in the flyout menu. After you have set up the text the way you want it, the
    MTEXT default asks for an insertion point. Pick an insertion point or type the coordinates to
    start a corner of the text boundary. Now, the screen cursor forms a box, and you get the
    〈Other corner〉: prompt. Pick the other corner of the box to establish the boundary for your
    paragraph of text. Once all options have been set and you are ready to enter the actual text
    content for the paragraph, AutoCAD opens the Edit MText dialog box or the external text editor.
❑ Save the drawing as A:EX11-4 and quit.

## AUTOCAD TEXT FONTS                                                    AUG 8,C

A *font* is all of the uppercase and lowercase letters and numbers of a particular letter
face design. The standard AutoCAD text fonts are shown in Figure 11-21.

Figure 11-21.    Standard AutoCAD text fonts. (Autodesk, Inc.)

**FAST FONTS**

| | |
|---|---|
| Txt | The quick brown fox jumps over the lazy dog. ABC123 |
| Monotxt | The quick brown fox jumps over the lazy dog. ABC123 |

**SIMPLEX FONTS**

| | |
|---|---|
| Romans | The quick brown fox jumps over the lazy dog. ABC123 |
| Scripts | *The quick brown fox jumps over the lazy dog. ABC123* |
| Greeks | Τηε ϑυιχκ βροων φοξ ϑυμπσ οεερ τηε λαζψ δογ. ABX123 |

**DUPLEX FONTS**

| | |
|---|---|
| Romand | The quick brown fox jumps over the lazy dog. ABC123 |

**COMPLEX FONTS**

| | |
|---|---|
| Romanc | The quick brown fox jumps over the lazy dog. ABC123 |
| Italicc | *The quick brown fox jumps over the lazy dog. ABC123* |
| Scriptc | *The quick brown fox jumps over the lazy dog. ABC123* |
| Greekc | Τηε ϑυιχκ βροων φοξ ϑυμπσ οεερ τηε λαζψ δογ. ABX123 |
| Cyrillic | Узд рфивк бсоцн еоч йфмпт охдс узд лащш гож. АББ123 |
| Cyriltc | Тхе цуичк брошн фож щумпс овер тхе лазй дог. АБЧ123 |

**Figure 11-21.** *Continued.*

### TRIPLEX FONTS

Romant    **The quick brown fox jumps over the lazy dog.   ABC123**

Italict    ***The quick brown fox jumps over the lazy dog.   ABC123***

### GOTHIC FONTS

Gothice    The quick brown fox jumps over the lazy dog.   ABC123

Gothicg    The quick brown fox jumps over the lazy dog.   ABC123

Gothici    The quick brown fox jumps over the lazy dog.   ABC123

The TXT font is the AutoCAD default when you begin a new drawing. The TXT font is rather rough in appearance and may not be the best choice for your application. On the other hand, TXT requires less time to regenerate than other fonts. The ROMANS (roman simplex) font is smoother than TXT. It closely duplicates the single-stroke Gothic lettering that has long been the standard for drafting. The COMPLEX and TRIPLEX fonts are multistroke fonts for drawing titles and subtitles. The GOTHIC and ITALIC fonts are ornamental styles. In addition, AutoCAD provides several standard symbol fonts, as shown in Figure 11-22.

Several additional AutoCAD fonts provide special alphabets or symbols that you must access by typing specific keys. This is called *character mapping*. Character mapping for non-Roman and symbol fonts is displayed in Figure 11-23.

**Figure 11-22.**  Standard AutoCAD symbol fonts. (Autodesk, Inc.)

### SYMBOL FONTS

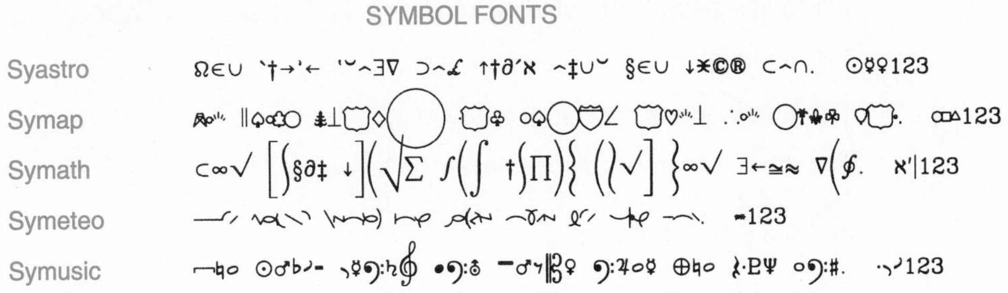

**Figure 11-23.**  Character mapping for non-Roman and symbol fonts. (Autodesk, Inc.)

AutoCAD Release 13 also provides PostScript™ fonts. See Figure 11-24. PostScript fonts are available by using the **STYLE** command and techniques previously discussed for the standard AutoCAD fonts. You can *set* a width factor or obliquing angle, but you cannot *apply* these options to PostScript fonts. Two of the PostScript fonts that might work well for architectural applications are the CIBT (city blueprint) and COBT (country blueprint). Additional information regarding PostScript fonts is included in *AutoCAD and its Applications—Advanced, Release 13 for Windows*. AutoCAD Release 13 also provides TrueType® fonts with a .TTF file extension. Refer to the *AutoCAD User's Guide* for a listing and description of these on pages 588 - 589, or open the TRUETYPE.DWG drawing.

Figure 11-24.   AutoCAD Release 13 PostScript fonts. (Autodesk, Inc.)

POSTSCRIPT FONTS

| Cibt | The quick brown fox jumped over the lazy dog. | ABC12 |
| Cobt | The quick brown fox jumped over the lazy dog. | ABC12 |
| Rom | The quick brown fox jumped over the lazy dog. | ABC12 |
| Romb | The quick brown fox jumped over the lazy dog. | ABC12 |
| Sas | The quick brown fox jumped over the lazy dog. | ABC12 |
| Sasb | The quick brown fox jumped over the lazy dog. | ABC12 |
| Saso | The quick brown fox jumped over the lazy dog. | ABC12 |
| Sasbo | The quick brown fox jumped over the lazy dog. | ABC12 |
| Te | THE QUICK BROWN FOX JUMPED OVER THE LAZY DOG. | ABC12 |
| Tel | THE QUICK BROWN FOX JUMPED OVER THE LAZY DOG. | ABC12 |
| Teb | THE QUICK BROWN FOX JUMPED OVER THE LAZY DOG. | ABC12 |
| Eur | The quick brown fox jumped over the lazy dog. àáâãäåæçèéêëìíîïðñòóÛŸßØµ¶©™®¢£¤¥¦§±‡†‡¿¡ | ABC12 |
| Euro | The quick brown fox jumped over the lazy dog. àáâãäåæçèéêëìíîïðñòóÜÝÞßØµ¶©™®¢£¤¥¦§±‡†‡¿¡ | ABC12 |
| Pan | The quick brown fox jumped over the lazy dog. ə√ÆæŊɲʔʰᵃđθßÐS¶áäâãāa̅ʻaa' ÂÄÃÄ | ABC12 |
| Suf | The quick brown fox jumped over the lazy dog. £đø±ß«»¶()∈Ł+ħſˊªáäâãʻaa'aÂÄ | ABC12 |

## SELECTING AUTOCAD TEXT STYLES                    AUG 8

Text styles are variations of fonts. A *text style* gives height, width, obliquing angle (slant), and other features to a text font. You may have several text styles that use the same font. Text styles may be created using the **STYLE** command, to be discussed later. The default style name used with the **TEXT** command is STANDARD. If the **Style** option is selected, you can select another text style. The **Style** option is entered at the **TEXT** prompt line by typing S. When AutoCAD for Windows is configured for screen menus, you can also select **Style** from the **TEXT** screen menu. Refer to Chapter 32. The following sequence shows the prompts for **Style** option of the **TEXT** command:

> Command: **TEXT** ⏎
> Justify/Style/⟨Start point⟩: **S** ⏎
> Style name (or ?) ⟨*current*⟩:

You can respond in one of the following ways:
- Press the [Enter] key to activate the current style.
- Type the name of a style that was previously created using the **STYLE** command. If you enter a text style that was not previously created using the **STYLE** command, AutoCAD gives this message:

  > Unknown or invalid text style name.
  > Style name (or ?) ⟨*current*⟩:

- Type ? to get a list of the available text styles. Entering ? gives you this prompt:

  > Style name (or ?)⟨*current*⟩: **?** ⏎
  > Text style(s) to list ⟨*⟩:

After entering ?, you can type the specific text style(s) to list, or press [Enter] to display all of the available text styles.

When you press [Enter] or type *, the available text styles are shown in the text window. The style name, font file, height, width factor, obliquing angle, and generation of each are listed. Press the [F2] key to return to the graphics window. AutoCAD displays the **Start point:** prompt for you to continue the **TEXT** command.

---

**PROFESSIONAL TIP**

The **Style** *option* of the **TEXT** command allows you to select text styles that have already been created. The **STYLE** *command* allows you to custom design one of the standard fonts to make a new style. The **Style** option then allows you to select that new style to use for text added to the drawing.

---

## MAKING FONT STYLES                                              AUG 8

The **STYLE** command is used to create and modify existing text styles or list existing styles. Access the **STYLE** command by picking **Text Style** from the **Data** pull-down menu or by typing STYLE at the **Command:** prompt. The prompts associated with the **STYLE** command are as follows:

> Command: **STYLE** ⏎
> Text style name (or ?) ⟨*current*⟩: *(enter text style name and press* [Enter]*)*

After entering the desired text style name, AutoCAD displays the **Select Font File** dialog box shown in Figure 11-25. If the style name you enter already exists, you get an Existing style message on the command line, and the current font is highlighted in the **File Name:** text box. If the entered style name is new, AutoCAD gives you a New style message and the default font for that style is shown highlighted in the **File Name:** text box.

Figure 11-25. The **Select
Font File** dialog box displays
the names of available fonts.

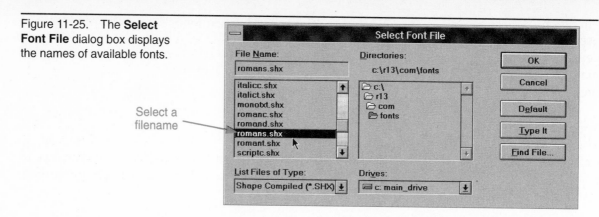

Select a
filename

In order to create or change a style, enter a style name at the **Text style name:** prompt.
Then, select a font in one of the following three ways:

1. Use the scroll bar to page through the list of available text fonts, move the arrow pointer
   to the desired font and click. This method is handy for both regular AutoCAD fonts with
   the .SHX extension, and for PostScript fonts with the .PFB extension. In Figure 11-25, the
   ROMANS.SHX font is selected and is shown in the **File Name:** text box.
2. Type the desired font filename in the **File Name:** text box. Be sure to add the extension
   .SHX to the font name you enter. Do not use this method for PostScript font names.
3. Move the arrow pointer to the **Type It** button and click. This removes the **Select Font File**
   dialog box and allows you to type the desired font name, without a file extension, at the
   **Command:** prompt as follows:

> Font file ⟨*current*⟩: **ROMANS** ↵

The rest of the prompts let you establish the style characteristics. These prompts are the same
no matter which of the three methods you choose. The next section explains each of the following prompts.

> Height ⟨*default*⟩: *(enter the height value,* .25 *for example, and press* [Enter])
> Width factor ⟨*default*⟩: *(enter the width factor,* 1 *for example, and press* [Enter])
> Obliquing angle ⟨*default*⟩: *(enter the obliquing angle,* 0 *for example, and press*
>   [Enter])
> Backwards? ⟨N⟩ *(type* Y *and press* [Enter], *or press* [Enter] *to accept the default)*
> Upside-down? ⟨N⟩ *(type* Y *and press* [Enter], *or press* [Enter] *to accept the default)*
> Vertical? ⟨N⟩ *(type* Y *and press* [Enter], *or press* [Enter] *to accept the default)*
> ROMANS is now the current text style.
> Command:

## STYLE command prompts

The following discussion explains each of the **STYLE** command prompts. The first
prompt in the **STYLE** command allows you to create a new style or modify an existing style.
The prompt is:

> Text style name (or ?) ⟨*current*⟩:

A ? response produces a list of existing styles. Pressing the space bar or [Enter] key selects the
current style shown in brackets. You can enter a name to create a new style, or modify an
existing one, as previously discussed. For example, suppose you want to create a ROMANS
style with a height of .125. Enter the style name as ROMANS-125. The style name can contain
up to 31 characters.

> Font file ⟨*default*⟩:

This prompt appears if the **FILEDIA** system variable is set to 0. Type the name of the font to be used. In this example, the font being used is **ROMANS**. If you respond by pressing the [Enter] key, the default font shown in brackets is made current. If **FILEDIA** is 1, the **Select Font File** dialog box appears. Select the desired font from the list, or enter the font filename using the procedure discussed earlier.

Height ⟨*default*⟩:

The **Height:** prompt allows you to enter a fixed character height. For example, typing .125 draws text .125" high for the text style. A 0 response gives you the opportunity to specify the text height each time you use this style. You can also press [Enter] to choose the default height shown in brackets.

Width factor ⟨*default*⟩:

The *width factor* is a numerical value that defines the character width relative to the height. A width factor of 1 is the default. A width factor greater than 1 expands the letters. A factor less than 1 compresses the letters, Figure 11-26.

Obliquing angle ⟨*default*⟩:

The obliquing angle allows you to slant the letters to the right or left. A 0 response draws vertical text. A value greater than 0 slants the letters to the right. A negative angle slants the characters to the left. See Figure 11-27.

Backwards ⟨N⟩

If you want the text to appear backwards, respond Y to this prompt. For text that appears normal, respond with N. Backwards characters may be used when the text is to be printed on the back of polyester film. When the film is turned around, the image will be legible. An example of backwards text is shown in Figure 11-28.

Figure 11-26. AutoCAD text width factors.

| Width factor | Text |
|---|---|
| 1 | ABCDEFGHIJKLM |
| .5 | ABCDEFGHIJKLMNOPQRSTUVWXY |
| 1.5 | ABCDEFGHI |
| 2 | ABCDEFG |

Figure 11-27. AutoCAD obliquing angles.

| Obliquing angle | Text |
|---|---|
| 0 | ABCDEFGHIJKLM |
| 15 | *ABCDEFGHIJKLM* |
| −15 | ABCDEFGHIJKLM |

Figure 11-28. Backward text.

ABCDEFG

Upside-down? ⟨N⟩

If you want the text to appear upside-down, respond with Y to this prompt. See Figure 11-29. For text that appears normal, respond with N.

Vertical? ⟨N⟩

Text is normally placed horizontally on a drawing. However, it is possible to add text in a vertical format. This application may be used for graphic designs or custom layouts. Vertical text is shown in Figure 11-30.

Figure 11-29.   Upside-down text.

Figure 11-30.   Vertical text.

Vertical text works best when the rotation angle is set at 270. For prompts that require two points, the second point should be directly below the first. Obliquing, underscoring, or overscoring are not intended for use with the vertical format. If vertical text is desired, then a Y response is required. Enter an N for standard horizontal text.

## CREATING A NEW TEXT STYLE                                          AUG 8

Assume that you have entered the drawing editor to begin a new drawing. Remember, the only text style available is STANDARD. The following command and prompts sets a new style called ROMANS-125:

    Command: **STYLE** ↵
    Text style name (or ?) ⟨STANDARD⟩: **ROMANS–125** ↵

The **Select Font File** dialog box then appears (if **FILEDIA** is 1). Type ROMANS.SHX in the **File Name:** text box, or select ROMANS.SHX from the list of fonts. Click **OK** to close the dialog box, and then enter the following values:

    Height ⟨*current*⟩: **.125** ↵
    Width factor ⟨*current*⟩: **1** ↵
    Obliquing angle ⟨*current*⟩: **0** ↵
    Backwards? ⟨N⟩ ↵
    Upside-down? ⟨N⟩ ↵
    Vertical? ⟨N⟩ ↵
    ROMANS-125 is now the current text style.

Keep reference notes stating the name and features of text styles that you design. However, if you forget, enter ? at the **Text style name:** prompt. A listing of created styles appears in the text window.

## Using the new text style

The new text style may now be used by entering the **TEXT** command. Select the **Start point** option or any of the other options. In this example, the ROMANS-125 style is now the default until you change it using the **Style** option. Remember, you can use the **Style** option of the **TEXT** command to select text styles already created with the **STYLE** command.

**PROFESSIONAL TIP**

TrueType, PostScript, and other complex text styles can be very taxing on system resources. This can slow down display changes and bring drawing regeneration time up significantly. Use these styles only when necessary. When you must use complex text styles, set your system variables to speed optimized settings.

System variables that control how text affects drawing display speeds include:

- TEXTQLTY. Lower values reduce display quality and speed up display changes. Significant speed increases result from a setting of 0.
- TEXTFILL. Set this to 0 to display PostScript and TrueType fonts as outlines only. Filled text fonts are very slow to display.

---

### EXERCISE 11-5

❑ Load AutoCAD for Windows, and set up your own variables.
❑ Use the **TEXT** command to type the following information. Change the text style to represent each of the four standard AutoCAD fonts named. Use .5 unit letter height and 0° rotation angle.

TXT–AUTOCAD'S DEFAULT TEXT FONT.
SIMPLEX–A SMOOTH FONT OF CONVENTIONAL LETTERING STYLE.
COMPLEX–A MULTISTROKE FONT THAT IS GOOD FOR TITLES.
ITALIC–AN ORNAMENTAL FONT SLANTED TO THE RIGHT.

❑ Save the drawing as A:EX11-5 and quit.

---

## Changing the format of existing styles

You can change text style without affecting existing text entities. The changes are applied only to newly added text using that style. However, you may not alter the text font or the orientation from horizontal or vertical. You can change the name of an existing text style using the **RENAME** command.

The **RENAME** command can be used to rename existing files such as blocks, dimension styles, layers, linetypes, and text styles. The options are discussed throughout this text where appropriate. The option relating to text styles is **Style**. Type the RENAME command and the **Style** option as follows:

```
Command: RENAME ↵
Block/Dimstyle/LAyer/LType/Style/Ucs/VIew/VPort: S ↵
Old text style name: ROMANS-125 ↵
New text style name: 125-ROMANS ↵
Command:
```

The **RENAME** command can also be accessed by picking **Rename...** in the **Data** pull-down menu. This selection opens the **Rename** dialog box. Using this dialog box, pick **Style** from the **Named Objects** list. This gives you an Items list where all of the current text styles are listed. A text style must have been loaded using the **STYLE** command for it to be listed here. Pick the current style that you want to rename from the Items list, or type the name of the current text style in the **Old Name:** file edit box. Next, type the new name in the **Rename To:** file edit box and finally pick the **Rename To:** button. The old name is changed and you can see the new name listed in the Items list.

Suppose you change the values of an existing text style, including the font and orientation. *All* text items with that style are redrawn with the new values. They are displayed when the drawing is regenerated. This type of a change causes automatic regeneration if the **REGENAUTO** mode is on.

**PROFESSIONAL TIP**

In AutoCAD 13 C4 maintenance release or later versions, a dialog box interface has been provided working with text styles. To access this dialog box, pick **Text Style...** from the **Data** pull-down menu or type **DDSTYLE** at the **Command:** prompt. The options in this dialog box work the same as at the command line, but the dialog interface allows greater flexibility and you can preview the font before you define it.

## SPECIAL CHARACTERS FOR SINGLE-LINE TEXT                    AUG 8

Many drafting applications require special symbols for text and dimensions. There are different methods for entering special characters, depending on if you are creating single-line text objects using the **TEXT** or **DTEXT** commands, or multiline text using the **MTEXT** command. In order to draw symbols, AutoCAD requires a sequence of *control characters*. The *control sequence* for a symbol begins with a double percent sign (%%). The next character you enter represents the symbol. These control characters are used for single-line text objects that are generated with the **TEXT** or **DTEXT** commands. **DTEXT** is discussed at the end of this chapter. The following list gives the most used control sequences:

    %%D = Draw degrees symbol (°).
    %%P = Draw plus/minus tolerance symbol (±).
    %%C = Draw diameter symbol (∅).
    %%% = Draw a single percent symbol (%).

In order to draw the note ∅2.75, the control sequence %%C2.75 is used. See Figure 11-31.

---

Figure 11-31.  The control sequence %%C creates the ∅ (diameter) symbol.

$\emptyset 2.75$

---

A single percent sign can be also drawn without using the %%% control sequence. Simply use the percent (%) key. However, when a percent sign must precede another control sequence, the %%% characters force a single percent sign. For example, suppose you want the note 25% ±2%. You must type the following sequence: 25 %%%%%P2%.

### Drawing underscored or overscored text

Text can be underscored (underlined) or overscored by typing a control sequence in front of the line of text. The control sequences are:

    %%O = overscore
    %%U = underscore

For example, the note <u>UNDERSCORING TEXT</u> must be typed as %%UUNDERSCORING TEXT. The resulting text is shown in Figure 11-32. A line of text may require both underscoring and overscoring. For example, the control sequence %%O%%ULINE OF TEXT produces the note with both underscore and overscore.

Figure 11-32. The control sequence %%U underscores text.

UNDERSCORING TEXT

The %%O and %%U control codes are toggles that turn overscoring and underscoring on and off. Type %%U preceding a word or phrase to turn underscoring on. Type %%U after the desired word or phrase to turn underscoring off. Any text following the second %%U will then appear without underscoring.

**PROFESSIONAL TIP**

Many drafters prefer to underline view labels such as <u>SECTION A-A</u> or <u>DETAIL B</u>. Rather than draw line or pline entities under the text, use **Middle** or **Center** justification modes and underscoring. The view labels are automatically underlined and centered under the views or details they identify.

## SPECIAL CHARACTERS AND FORMATTING FOR MULTILINE TEXT

**AUG 8**

The previous discussion explained the use of special characters in single-line text objects that are created with the **TEXT** and **DTEXT** commands. Special characters and formatting codes are also available in multiline text objects that are created with the **MTEXT** command (the **LEADER** command is discussed in Chapter 21). These multiline special characters are created in the text editor by using format codes for paragraphs and Unicode characters. Available format codes for multiline text and their results are as follows:

| PARAGRAPH FORMAT CODES | |
|---|---|
| **Format Code** | **Result** |
| \O | Overscore toggle on. |
| \o | Overscore toggle off. |
| \L | Underscore toggle on. |
| \l | Underscore toggle off. |
| \~ | Non-breaking space. |
| \\ | Backslash (\). |
| \{ *and* \} | Inserts opening and closing braces ({}). |
| \C*value*; | Changes to *value* color. For example, \Cred changes the color to red. |
| \H*value*; | Changes to *value* text height. For example, \H.250 changes the text height from its current value to .250. |
| \F*filnam*; | Changes font to *filnam*. For example, if the current font is ROMANS and you want a bolder ROMAND, then enter \Fromand. |

| PARAGRAPH FORMAT CODES *Continued* | |
|---|---|
| **Format Code** | **Result** |
| \S .../...;<br>or<br>\S...^...; | Stacks text at the / or ^ symbol. This is used for stacking fraction numerals, for example. |
| \T*value*; | Changes character spacing between .75X and 4X normal. Normal text spacing is 1X. Enter \T2; if you want double character spacing. |
| \Q*angle*; | Changes the obliquing angle of the text to *angle*. Standard obliquing angle is 0 . Change to a 15  slant on the characters with \Q15;. |
| \A0; | Changes the alignment for dimensions: \A0; = Baseline. |
| \A1; | Changes the alignment for dimensions: \A1; = Centerline. |
| \A2; | Changes the alignment for dimensions: \A2; = Topline. |
| \W*value*; | Changes the character width factor to *value*. For example, if you want to double the character width, enter \W2;. |
| \P | This entry begins a new paragraph on the next line. |

Using curly braces { } with the formatting code as the first entry applies the formatting changes only to the code and text within the braces. The braces are not needed for underscoring or overscoring. Type \L before the text to start the underscoring and \l after the text to end the underscoring. Overscoring uses \O and \o. The following are some special character entries and their results:

## Underscoring

If you enter the following:

INTERPRET DIMENSIONS AND TOLERANCES PER \LASME Y14.5M-1994\l FOR ALL
    DRAWING FEATURES.

The text result is:

INTERPRET DIMENSIONS AND TOLERANCES PER <u>ASME Y14.5M-1994</u> FOR ALL
    DRAWING FEATURES.

## Changing the font filename

If you enter the following:

INTERPRET DIMENSIONS AND TOLERANCES PER {\Fromand; ASME Y14.5M-1994}
    FOR ALL DRAWING FEATURES.

The text result is:

INTERPRET DIMENSIONS AND TOLERANCES PER **ASME Y14.5M-1994** FOR ALL
    DRAWING FEATURES.

## Changing the character spacing

If you enter the following:

All drawing titles are required to be entered with {\T2;DOUBLE SPACE TEXT} unless
    otherwise specified.

The text result is:

All drawing titles are required to be entered with D O U B L E  S P A C E  T E X T
    unless otherwise specified.

## Entering special characters using the Unicode system

AutoCAD Release 13 supports what is known as the *Unicode* character encoding standard. This standard replaces the old SHP and SHX file formats that will not be supported in releases after Release 13. This new font standard is no longer limited to 256 characters, as the SHP and SHX font files are. A Unicode font can have up to 65,535 separate characters in a font file, with figures for many different languages. This standard provides support for these languages by allowing the use of characters not on the keyboard. The Unicode standard is used for multiline text objects created with the **MTEXT** command (or the **LEADER** command discussed in Chapter 19). The prefix for a Unicode special character is \U+, and is followed by a four digit hexadecimal number indicating the value of the character in the font file. A *hexadecimal* number is a base 16 number, as opposed to a base 10 number previously used. The Unicode special characters are accessed by typing what is called an *escape sequence*. It is referred to as an escape sequence, probably because it allows you to escape the confines of the limited keyboard, or it "escapes" from the standard text processing. For example, \U+2205 is the escape sequence for entering a diameter symbol. The Unicode entry for special characters is in the format \U+*nnnn* where *nnnn* is the hexadecimal value of the character. The following are some examples that may commonly be used in drafting technology:

\U+2205    Enters the diameter symbol. For example: \U+2205.750 = Ø.750
\U+00B0    Places the degree symbol. For example: 45\U+00B0 = 45°
\U+00B1    Inserts the Plus/Minus symbol. For example: 2.625\U+00B1.005 = 2.626±.005

**PROFESSIONAL TIP**

In AutoCAD 13 C4 maintenance release or later versions, the %% codes used for single line text are also recongnized by text objects created using **MTEXT.**

**EXERCISE 11-6**

❑ Load AutoCAD and set up your own variables.
❑ Use the **TEXT** command and control characters to type the following:
  45°
  1.375±.005
  Ø3.875
  79%
  UNDERSCORING TEXT
❑ Use the **MTEXT** command and appropriate control characters to type the following:
  NOTE 1:
  EACH BEDROOM TO HAVE A <u>MINIMUM</u> WINDOW OPENING OF 5.7 SQ. FT. WITH A <u>MINIMUM</u> WIDTH OF 20" AND A SILL LESS THAN 44" OFF THE FLOOR.
  NOTE 2:
  BATHROOMS AND UTILITY ROOMS ARE TO BE VENTED TO THE OUTSIDE WITH A <u>MINIMUM</u> OF A 90CFM FAN WITH A <u>MINIMUM</u> Ø4" SCREENED DUCT.
❑ Save the drawing as A:EX11-6 and quit.

## DYNAMIC TEXT—SEE THE TEXT AS YOU TYPE      AUG 8

The **DTEXT** (dynamic text) command allows you to see the text on the screen as you type. All of the options are the same as the **TEXT** command. **DTEXT** also allows you to use the backspace key to edit what has been typed on the screen. The **TEXT** command only lets you backspace to edit at the prompt line. Enter multiple lines of text simply by pressing [Enter] at the end of each line. Press [Enter] twice to exit the **DTEXT** command. The sequence of prompts is the same as the **TEXT** command, except that the **Text:** prompt is repeated. When the **Text:** prompt appears, a cursor box equal in size to the text height also appears on the screen at the text start point.

The **DTEXT** command can be issued by entering **DTEXT** at the **Command:** prompt or clicking the **Dtext** button on the **Text** flyout in the **Draw** toolbar. If the ACADFULL.MNU file is loaded, the **Draw** pull-down menu also offers the **Dynamic Text** option. Select **Text** from the **Draw** pull-down menu, and then select **Dynamic Text** from the cascading submenu. Use the method that works best and fastest for you.

You can cancel the **DTEXT** command at any time by pressing the [Esc] key. This action erases all of the text entered during the command.

A great advantage of **DTEXT** over **TEXT** is that additional lines of text can be entered. Simply press [Enter] at the end of each line. The cursor box automatically moves to the start point one line below the preceding line. While in the **DTEXT** command, the screen crosshairs can be moved independently of the text cursor box. Selecting a new start point completes the line of text being entered and begins a new line at the selected point. Using **DTEXT**, multiple lines of text may be entered anywhere on the drawing without exiting the command. This saves a lot of drafting time.

A few aspects of the **DTEXT** command may cause you some concern at first. They are:
- When you end the **DTEXT** command, the entered text is erased from the screen, then regenerated.
- If you select **C, M, R, TL, TC, TR, ML, MC, MR, BL, BC,** or **BR** justification, the cursor box appears as if the text is left-justified. However, when you end the **DTEXT** command, the text disappears and is then regenerated with the alignment you requested.
- When you use a control code sequence for a symbol, the control code, not the symbol, is displayed. When you end the command, the text disappears and is then regenerated showing the proper symbol. For example, if the desired text is 98.6°F it first appears as typed, 98.6%%DF. However, when you end the **DTEXT** command, the note is redisplayed as 98.6°F.
- If you cancel the **DTEXT** command, all text entered while in the command is discarded. All **DTEXT** entries must be from the keyboard. Tablet menu and/or mouse button picks are ignored.

---

**PROFESSIONAL TIP**

**DTEXT** is not recommended for aligned text because the text height for each line is adjusted according to the width. Other justification options work well with the **DTEXT** command.

---

**EXERCISE 11-7**

❏ Load AutoCAD for Windows.
❏ Use the **STYLE** command to create the text styles described below. Change the options as specified. Then use the **DTEXT** command to type the text, changing the style for each of the four standard AutoCAD fonts. Enter a .5 letter height.
     TXT—EXPAND THE WIDTH.
     ROMANS—SLANT TO THE LEFT.
     ROMANC—SLANT TO THE RIGHT.
     ITALICC—BACKWARDS.
❏ Select any four fonts from the **Select Text Font** icon menu. Customize the text fonts to your own specifications such as height, width, or slant. Type the alphabet and numbers 1-10 for each of the four styles you developed.
❏ Save the drawing as A:EX11-7 and quit.

## PRESETTING TEXT HEIGHT

If you set a text height in the **STYLE** command, then this value is automatically used when you use the **TEXT** or **DTEXT** commands. If the text height in the **STYLE** command is set to 0, a default value for text height can be preset. When the text height is set to 0 in the **STYLE** command, then the **TEXTSIZE** system variable can be used to establish the text height default. The command sequence is as follows:

> Command: **TEXTSIZE** ⏎
> New value for TEXTSIZE ⟨*current*⟩: **.125** ⏎
> Command:

## QUICKLY REDRAWING TEXT

AUG 4

Text requires a great deal of time to regenerate, redraw, and plot. This is because each character is drawn with many individual vectors (line segments). The **Quick Text** mode makes text appear as rectangles equal to the height of each text string. This speeds regeneration and plotting time. The **Quick Text** mode is turned on and off with the **QTEXT** (quick text) command. Figure 11-33 shows a comparison between displays when **QTEXT** is on and off.

Figure 11-33.   Comparison of **QTEXT** turned on and off.

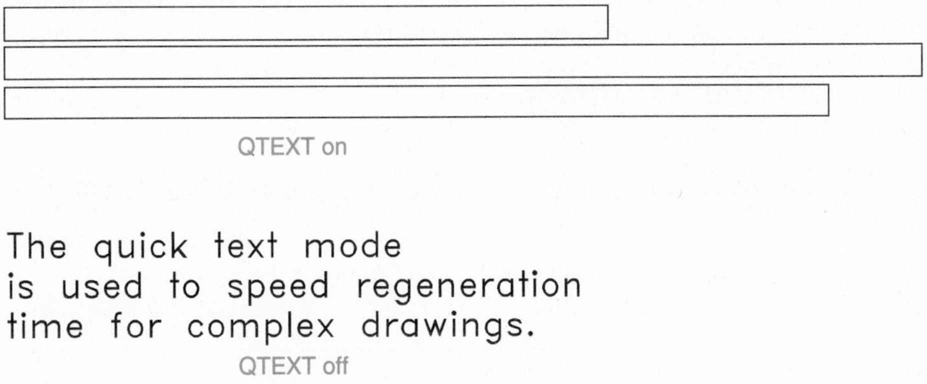

QTEXT on

```
The quick text mode
is used to speed regeneration
time for complex drawings.
```
QTEXT off

The **QTEXT** command is entered at the **Command:** prompt or picked from the **SETTINGS** screen menu when screen menus are enabled. The options **ON/OFF** are shown along with the current **QTEXT** setting. If the last setting was off, the command line appears as follows:

> Command: **QTEXT** ⏎
> ON/OFF ⟨Off⟩:

Type ON to quicken the redraw time. When quick text is on, new text entities first appear as text so you can check them. The text converts to the **QTEXT** appearance when the drawing is regenerated. If you want to review the text after **QTEXT** has been turned on, you need to turn **QTEXT** off. Follow this by the **REGEN** command to display the text in the normal format.

**PROFESSIONAL TIP**

To save valuable drafting time, consider setting up the following parameters in your prototype drawing:
- Create various text styles so that they are always available when needed.
- Set the **TEXTSIZE** variable if you consistently use the same text height.
- You might also set up **QTEXT**; ready to be used when a large amount of text or complex text begins to slow down screen redraw and regeneration.

## CHANGING THE LOCATION OF EXISTING TEXT

Existing text can be modified or moved to a new location using the **CHANGE** command. Enter the **CHANGE** command, and follow this command sequence:

```
Command: CHANGE ↵
Select objects: (pick text to be changed)
Select objects: ↵
Properties/⟨Change point⟩: ↵
Enter text insertion point: (pick a new text location)
Text style: ROMANS
New style or RETURN for no change: ↵
New height ⟨0.2000⟩: ↵
New rotation angle ⟨0⟩: ↵
New text ⟨selected text string⟩: (type new text or press [Enter] to keep the same text)
Command:
```

Figure 11-34 shows how text can be moved.

---

Figure 11-34.   Using the **CHANGE** command to move text.

THIS TEXT IS IN THE WRONG LOCATION

⎺ Pick the text to be changed

THIS TEXT IS NOW IN THE RIGHT LOCATION

⎺ Pick the new text location       ⎺ Type revised text at changed location

If the text location is acceptable, but you want to change other characteristics of your text, simply press [Enter] at the **Enter text insertion point:** prompt. If you want to change the text style and already have defined an ITALICC text style, do the following:

```
Properties/⟨Change point⟩: ↵
Enter text insertion point: (pick a new text location)
Text style: ROMANS
New style or RETURN for no change: ITALICC ↵
New height ⟨0.2000⟩: .25 ↵
New rotation angle ⟨0⟩: ↵
New text ⟨selected text string⟩: (type new text or press [Enter] to keep the same text)
Command:
```

Figure 11-35 shows the new text location and style.

Figure 11-35. Using the **CHANGE** command to relocate and change text style.

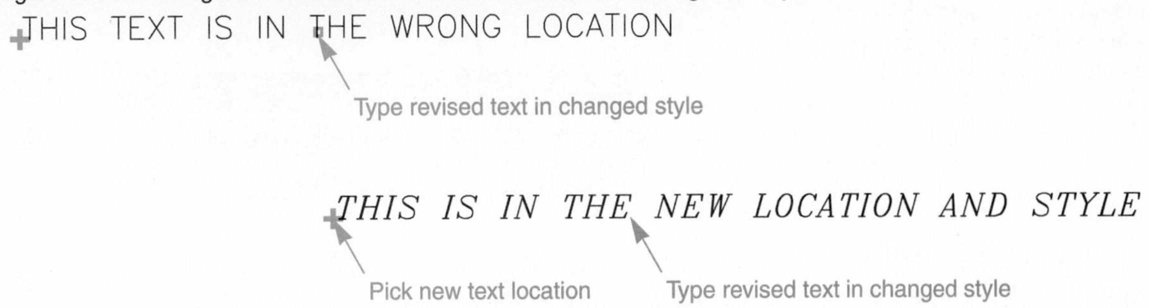

THIS TEXT IS IN THE WRONG LOCATION

Type revised text in changed style

*THIS IS IN THE NEW LOCATION AND STYLE*

Pick new text location          Type revised text in changed style

---

**EXERCISE 11-8**

❑ Load AutoCAD For Windows, and set your own variables.
❑ Place the following text on your drawing using .25 high letters: THIS IS THE ORIGINAL TEXT.
❑ Use the **CHANGE** command to move and change the above text to read: THIS IS THE REVISED TEXT IN A NEW LOCATION.
❑ Use the **CHANGE** command to move the previous text, change its style, and reword it as follows: THIS IS THE NEW TEXT WITH CHANGED STYLE AND LOCATION.
❑ Turn **QTEXT** on, then off. Observe the results. Do not forget to use **REGEN** to change the display.
❑ Save the drawing as A:EX11-8 and quit.

---

## ADDITIONAL TEXT TIPS

Text presentation is important on any drawing. It is a good idea to plan your drawing using rough sketches to allow room for text and notes. Some things to consider when designing the drawing layout include:

- Placement of the views.
- Arrange text to avoid crowding.
- Place related notes in groups to make the drawing easy to read.
- Place all general notes in a common location. Locate notes in the lower-left corner or above the title block when using ANSI standards. Place notes in the upper-left corner when using military standards.

## REVISING TEXT ON THE DRAWING

AUG 8

AutoCAD provides the means to revise existing text. This is referred to as *text editing*. Text editing is accomplished in a dialog box that is accessed using the **DDEDIT** command. **DDEDIT** is accessed by selecting the **Edit Text** button on the **Edit Polyline** flyout on **Modify** toolbar. **DDEDIT** is typed at the **Command:** prompt as follows:

    Command: **DDEDIT** ↵
    ⟨Select a TEXT or ATTDEF object⟩/Undo: *(pick the line of text to edit)*

The default prompt asks you to Select a TEXT and the screen cursor takes the shape of a pick box. Move the pick box to the desired text and pick. The **Edit Text** dialog box is then displayed with the line of text that you picked ready for editing. Figure 11-36 shows several lines of text and the **Edit Text** dialog box with the first line of text displayed.

Figure 11-36.   The first line of
the note has misspelled words.
After selecting the first text line,
it appears in the **Edit Text**
dialog box.

```
1. inTERPRET DEMENSIONS AND TOLERANCES PER ASME Y14.5M-1994
2. REMOVE ALL BURRS AND SHARP EDGES
3. ALL FILLETS AND ROUNDS R.125
```

First line of
text appears in
the edit box

If you press [Delete] or [Backspace], the highlighted text disappears and you can enter
new text. Pressing the key combination [Ctrl]+[V] to paste the contents of the Clipboard will
replace the highlighted text with the new text. If you make a mistake, use the editing keys or
press **Cancel** and pick the desired text again. Move the cursor arrow inside the **Text:** text box
and pick to remove the highlight around the text. Use the left and right arrow keys to move
through the entire line of text, and access the portion of the text that is hidden beyond the
limits of the text box. When you are ready to edit the text, move the cursor arrow just to the
right of the letters to be changed and pick. This places the text cursor in that location. Edit the
line of text shown in Figure 11-37 following this procedure:

- Notice the word inTERPRET should read INTERPRET. To see the beginning of the text,
  press [Home]. Use the cursor to highlight the "in" by picking and dragging the cursor
  through the text.
- Type IN.
- Notice the word DEMENSIONING is misspelled. Press [Ctrl]+[→] to move to the start of
  DEMENSIONING. Press [→] once and press [Delete] to delete the E. Now, type in an I, as
  shown in Figure 11-38.
- Pick **OK** or press [Enter] to accept the text changes. The revised text is then displayed
  on your drawing as shown in Figure 11-39.
- Press [Enter] or **Cancel** to exit the **DDEDIT** command, or enter U to undo the editing if
  you made a mistake.

Figure 11-37.   Highlight the
text you want to replace. Then,
type the revised text.

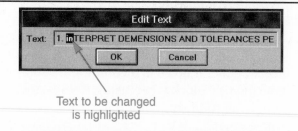

Text to be changed
is highlighted

Figure 11-38.   The two misspelled
words have been corrected. Select
**OK** to update the drawing.

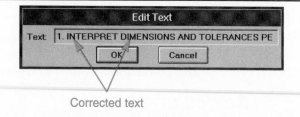

Corrected text

Figure 11-39.   After picking **OK**, the revised text is displayed on your screen.

```
1. INTERPRET DIMENSIONS AND TOLERANCES PER ASME Y14.5M-1994
2. REMOVE ALL BURRS AND SHARP EDGES
3. ALL FILLETS AND ROUNDS R.125
```

## Editing techniques

Although it is recommended that you enter text as carefully as possible initially, there will likely be times when you must revise text using the **DDEDIT** command. The following techniques can be used to help edit text:

- **Highlighting text in the Text: text box.** Text can be highlighted by moving the cursor arrow to the desired text and picking. Hold the pick button down while you move the cursor across the text to be highlighted. Release the pick button when you have highlighted all of the intended text.
- **Removing highlighted text in the Text: text box.** When the **Text:** text box, or a portion of the text in the **Text:** text box is highlighted, pressing [Space], [Delete], or [Backspace] removes the highlighted text.
- **Moving around inside the Text: text box.** Move the cursor arrow inside the **Text:** text box and click. Then use [←] to move the cursor to the left or [→] to move the cursor to the right.
- **Inserting text.** Type any desired text at the text cursor location. This inserts new text and shifts all existing text to the right.
- **[Backspace].** Pressing [Backspace] when text is not highlighted removes text to the left of the text cursor and moves the text at the right along with the text cursor.
- **[Space] (space bar).** Pressing [Space] when text is not highlighted moves all of the text to the right of the text cursor.
- **[←] (left arrow).** Moves the text cursor to the left.
- **[→] (right arrow).** Moves the text cursor to the right.
- **[Ctrl]+[X].** Deletes the entire string of highlighted text in the **Text:** text box.

The previous discussion explained how to edit single-line text objects by using the **DDEDIT** command to access the **Edit Text** dialog box. The **DDEDIT** command is also used when you want to edit multiline text, except the default text editor is opened with the selected text:

> Command: **DDEDIT** ↵
> ⟨Select a TEXT or ATTDEF object⟩/Undo: *(pick the multiline text)*

Use the text editor to edit the text as you wish and then pick the **OK** button return to the drawing editor as discussed previously with the **MTEXT** command.

You can also edit multiline text using the **DDMODIFY** command. **DDMODIFY** can be accessed by picking the **Properties** button on the **Object Properties** toolbar. It can also be accessed by selecting **Properties...** from the **Edit** pull-down menu. **DDMODIFY** is entered at the **Command:** prompt as follows:

> Command: **DDMODIFY** ↵
> Select object to modify: *(pick the line of text you want to edit)*

After you pick the specific line of text that you want to edit, the **Modify MText** dialog box shown in Figure 11-40 is displayed. The elements of the **Modify MText** dialog box are described below.

- The **Properties** area of the **Modify MText** dialog box lets you change color by picking the **Color...** button. This opens the **Select Color** dialog box where you can select a desired color. The **Layer...** button accesses the **Select Layer** dialog box which is explained in detail in Chapter 19.
- The **Insertion Point** area of the **Modify MText** dialog box lets you change the X, Y, and Z coordinates of the text insertion point by changing the values in the **X:**, **Y:**, or **Z:** edit boxes. You can also choose the **Pick Point** ⟨ button to change the pick point with the screen cursor.
- Pick the **Edit Contents...** button to edit the text found in the **Contents** edit box.
- The **Edit Properties...** button accesses the **MText Properties** dialog box. This dialog box is used to change the text style, text height, direction, attachment justification, width, or rotation.

Figure 11-40.   The **Modify MText** dialog box.

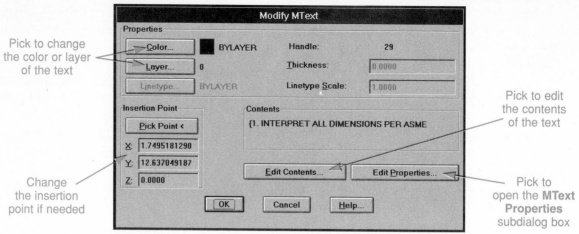

You can also use the **DDMODIFY** command to access the **Modify MText** dialog box for editing single-line text objects in a similar manner. This allows you to change the insertion point origin, justification, height, rotation, width factor, obliquing angle, style, properties, and edit the text.

### EXERCISE 11-9

❑ Load AutoCAD for Windows and set up your own variables.
❑ Use the **DTEXT** command to place the following text on your drawing (incorrectly as shown) using ROMANS style and .125 text height.
   1.  iNTERPRET DEMINSIONIN AND TOLERENCING PER ANSI Y14.5M.
   2.  MOVE ALL BURRS AND EDGES.
   3.  ALL FILLETS AND ROUNDS ARE .125 R.
   4.  FINISH ALL OVER.
❑ Use the **DDEDIT** command to revise the above text as follows:
   1.  INTERPRET DIMENSIONING AND TOLERANCING PER ASME Y14.5M.
   2.  REMOVE ALL BURRS AND SHARP EDGES.
   3.  ALL FILLETS AND ROUNDS R .125.
   4.  FINISH ALL OVER 62 MICROINCHES.
❑ Repeat this exercise, but create the text using **MTEXT**.
❑ Save the drawing as A:EX11-9 and quit.

## USING THE AUTOCAD SPELL CHECKER

You have been introduced to editing text on the drawing with the **DDEDIT** and **DDMODIFY** commands. You can use these commands to change lines of text and even correct spelling errors. However, AutoCAD has a powerful and convenient tool for checking the spelling on your drawing. To check spelling type SPELL at the **Command:** prompt, pick **Spelling...** from the **Tools** pull-down menu, or pick the **Spelling** button on the **Standard** toolbar. After entering the command, you are asked to select the text to be checked. You need to pick each line of single-line text or one pick on multiline text selects the entire paragraph. Enter the command and pick the text like this:

    Command: **SPELL** ↵
    Select objects: *(pick the text)*
    Select objects: ↵

The **Check Spelling** dialog box is displayed after picking the text that needs spell checking, Figure 11-41. The following describes the features found in the **Check Spelling** dialog box:

Figure 11-41. The **Check Spelling** dialog box.

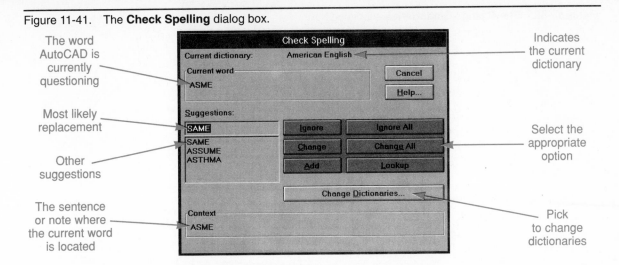

- **Current dictionary:** *American English.* The current dictionary that is being used to check the spelling of the text you picked is identified at the top of the dialog box. You can change to a different dictionary by picking the **Change Dictionaries...** button discussed later.
- **Current word.** The **Current word** box displays a word that AutoCAD thinks may be spelled incorrectly.
- **Context.** At the bottom of the dialog box, AutoCAD displays the line of text where the current word was found.
- **Suggestions:.** This gives you a list of possible correct spellings for the current word. The first box is called the Suggestion box and is AutoCAD's best guess. The word in the Suggestion box is highlighted. Following the highlighted word is a list of other possible choices. If there are many choices, the scroll bar is available for you to use. If you do not like the word that AutoCAD has highlighted, move the cursor arrow to another word and pick it. The word you pick then becomes highlighted in the list and is shown in the Suggestion box. When you think the highlighted word is correct, you have these options:
  - **Ignore.** Pick the **Ignore** button to skip the current word. For example, AutoCAD considers ASME in the Figure 11-39 note to be a misspelling, but ASME stands for American Society of Mechanical Engineers. So, you may chose to ignore this entry.
  - **Ignore All.** Pick this button if you want AutoCAD to ignore all of the words that match the current word.
  - **Change.** Pick the **Change** button to replace the **Current word** with the word in the Suggestion box.
  - **Change All.** Pick this button if you want to replace the **Current word** with the word in the **Suggestion** box throughout the entire text object.
  - **Add.** Pick this button to add the current word to the custom dictionary. You can add a word with up to 63 characters in length.
  - **Lookup.** The **Lookup** button asks AutoCAD to check the spelling of the word in the suggestion box. For example, if you want to verify the spelling of a word that you type in the **Suggestion** box and pick **Lookup**, a new suggestion and list of possible words follows.

## Changing Dictionaries

AutoCAD provides you with spelling dictionaries for 24 different languages. A full list of the available language dictionaries is in *Appendix A* of the *AutoCAD Command Reference*. Pick the **Change Dictionaries...** button in the **Check Spelling** dialog box to access the **Change Dictionary** dialog box shown in Figure 11-42.

Figure 11-42.   The **Change Dictionaries** subdialog box.

Name
of a custom
dictionary

Select a
main dictionary

```
┌─────────────────────────────────────────┐
│            Change Dictionaries           │
│  ┌─Main dictionary──────────────┐ ┌────┐ │
│  │ American English          ↓  │ │ OK │ │
│  └──────────────────────────────┘ └────┘ │
│                                  ┌──────┐ │
│                                  │Cancel│ │
│                                  └──────┘ │
│  ┌─Custom dictionary───────────┐ ┌──────┐ │
│  │                             │ │Help..│ │
│  │                             │ └──────┘ │
│  │        ┌─────────┐          │          │
│  │        │ Browse..│          │          │
│  │        └─────────┘          │          │
│  ┌─Custom dictionary words─────┐          │
│  │                      │ ┌─────┐          │
│  │                      │ │ Add │          │
│  │                      │ └─────┘          │
│  │                      │ ┌──────┐         │
│  │                      │ │Delete│         │
│  │                      │ └──────┘         │
│  └─────────────────────┘                   │
└─────────────────────────────────────────┘
```

The areas of the **Change Dictionary** dialog box are as follows:

- **Main dictionary.** This is where you can select one of the many language dictionaries to use as the current **Main dictionary**. To change the main dictionary, pick the down arrow to access the pop-up list. Next, pick the desired language dictionary from the pop-up list. The main dictionary is protected and cannot be added to.
- **Custom dictionary.** This displays the name of the current custom dictionary, or you can type the name of another custom dictionary in the text box. The name can take two forms:
  1. The name can be a textual description using up to 63 characters in sentence form. You can use spaces and characters such as #, or &. When named in this manner, it is referred to as volatile. This means that if an alternate custom dictionary is specified, the previous one is lost forever.
  2. If you wish to save a custom dictionary file for later access, name it in a standard DOS fashion using up to 8 characters and place a .CUS file extension after the name, like this: ARCH.CUS.

**PROFESSIONAL TIP**

Creating a .CUS file allows that name to be specified later for loading as the custom dictionary. A reason for this might be for a drafter who practices multiple disciplines. For example, when in a mechanical drawing, certain nonwords such as abbreviations or brand names that are commonly encountered might be added to a MECH.CUS file. In the same manner, a separate file named ARCH.CUS might contain common architectural abbreviations and frequently used brand names. These .CUS files are standard American National Standard Code for Information Interchange (ASCII) text files and can be edited in any standard text editor. This is where words can be added, deleted, or dictionaries can be combined. These should not be edited using a word processor such as MS Word or WordPerfect unless the output is saved as "text only" with no special text formatting or printer codes.

- **Browse....** Pick the **Browse...** button to get the **Select Custom Dictionary** dialog box.
- **Custom dictionary words.** Type a word in the text box that you either want to add or delete from the custom dictionary. For example, look at Figure 11-36 and see ASME Y14.5M entered in the text box. This is an example of custom text used in engineering drafting. Pick the **Add** button to accept the custom word in the text box, or pick the **Delete** button to remove the word from the custom dictionary. Custom dictionary entries may be up to 32 characters in length. Pick **OK** when you are done, or pick **Cancel**. Use the **Help...** button as needed.

When the spelling check is complete, you get the AutoCAD Alert shown in Figure 11-43. Pick the **OK** button or press [Enter] to return the drawing editor.

Figure 11-43.   When AutoCAD is finished spell-checking the selected text, this message box is displayed.

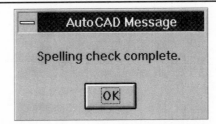

The current custom dictionary may be displayed at the prompt line by using the **DCTCUST** system variable like this:

    Command: **DCTCUST** ↵
    New value for DCTCUST, or . for none ⟨"MECHANICAL STANDARDS"⟩:

Typing the **DCTMAIN** system variable at the **Command:** prompt displays the current main dictionary:

    Command: **DCTMAIN** ↵
    New value for DCTMAIN, or . for none ⟨"enu"⟩:

The "enu" is the abbreviation for the American English main dictionary. The abbreviations for all available AutoCAD language dictionaries is found in *Appendix A* of the *AutoCAD Command Reference*.

---

**EXERCISE 11-10**

- ❑ Load AutoCAD and set up your own variables.
- ❑ Use the **MTEXT** command to type a short paragraph of your own choice with purposely made spelling errors.
- ❑ Check the spelling and correct the misspelled words.
- ❑ Save as A:EX11-10 and quit.

## CHAPTER TEST

*Write your answers in the spaces provided.*

1. Give the command and entities required to display IT IS FAST AND EASY TO DRAW TEXT USING AUTOCAD. The text must be .375 units high, have the default TXT font, and fit between two points:

   Command:_____

   Justify/Style/⟨Start point⟩: _____

   Align/Fit/Center/Middle/Right/TL/TC/TR/ML/MC/MR/BL/BC/BR: _____

   First text line point: _____

   Second text line point:_____

   Height ⟨.200⟩: _____

   Text:_____

2. Give the command and entries required to create a new text style. The style should have the following specifications. Assume **FILEDIA** equals 0.

   - Style name: 25-TITLES.
   - Double width.
   - Used for titles .25″ height.
   - ROMANC font.

   Command:_____

   Text style name (or ?) ⟨TXT⟩: _____

   Font file ⟨default⟩: _____

   Height ⟨*current*⟩: _____

   Width factor ⟨1⟩:_____

   Obliquing angle ⟨0⟩:_____

   Backwards? ⟨N⟩: _____

   Upside-down? ⟨N⟩: _____

   Vertical? ⟨N⟩: _____

   _____ is now the current text style.

3. Give the command and entries to underscore the following text and place it at a selected start point: VERIFY ALL DIMENSIONS DURING CONSTRUCTION.

   Command:_____

   Justify/Style/⟨Start point⟩: _____

   Height ⟨*current*⟩: _____

   Rotation angle ⟨0⟩:_____

   Text:_____

4. How do you turn on the **Quick Text** mode if it is currently off using the **Command:** prompt?

   Command:_____

   ON/OFF ⟨Off⟩: _____

5. Give the letter you must enter at the **TEXT** prompt to place text as follows:

    A. Left-justified text: _____

    B. Right-justified text: _____

    C. Text between two points without regard for text height:_____

    D. Center the text horizontally and vertically: _____

    E. Text between two points with a fixed height: _____

    F. Center text along a baseline:_____

    G. Top and Left horizontal: _____

    H. Middle and Right horizontal:_____

    I. Bottom and Center horizontal: _____

6. List the **Justify** options._____

7. How would you specify a text style with a double width factor? _____

   _____

8. How would you specify a text style with a 15° angle? _____

   _____

9. How would you specify vertical text? _____

   _____

10. How is the **Select Font File** dialog box accessed? _____

11. Give the control sequence required to draw the following symbols and associated text:

    | | **Single-Line Text** | **Paragraph or Unicode for multiline text** |
    |---|---|---|
    | A. 30° | _____ | _____ |
    | B. 1.375 ±.005 | _____ | _____ |
    | C. ⌀24 | _____ | _____ |
    | D. <u>NOT FOR CONSTRUCTION</u> | _____ | _____ |

12. What command is used so you can see the text on the screen as it is typed? _____

13. Why use the **Quick Text** mode rather than have the actual text displayed on the screen?

    _____

    _____

    _____

14. Name three ways to access the **DTEXT** command. _____

    _____

15. When setting text height in the **STYLE** command, what value do you enter at the **Height:** prompt so text height can be altered each time the **TEXT** or **DTEXT** commands are used? _____

    _____

16. Give the command that lets you alter the location, style, height, and wording of existing text. _____

    _____

17. Identify the command used to revise existing text on the drawing by using the **Edit Text** dialog box. _____

18. List the sequence of activities required to access the **Edit Text** dialog box. _____

    _____

19. When editing single-line text, how do you remove the character located in front of the text cursor? _____

    _____

20. When using the **Edit Text** dialog box, how do you move the text cursor to the left without removing text characters? _____

    _____

21. How do you remove all of the text to the right of the text cursor when editing text in the **Edit Text** dialog box? _____

    _____

    _____

22. When editing text in the **Text:** text box, the flashing vertical bar is called the _____.

23. Determine the AutoCAD text height for text to be plotted .188″ high using a half (1″ = 2″) scale. (Show your calculations.) _____

    _____

24. Determine the AutoCAD text height for text to be plotted .188″ high using a scale of 1/4″ = 1′-0″. (Show your calculations.) _____

    _____

25. What would you do if you just completed editing a line of text and discovered you made a mistake? Assume you are still in the **Edit Text** dialog box. _____

    _____

26. Identify two ways to move around inside the **Text:** text box of the **Edit Text** dialog box.

    _____

    _____

    _____

27. What happens when you press the space bar or the [Backspace] key when the text inside the **Text:** text box is highlighted? _____

28. What happens when you press [Ctrl]+[X] when the text within the **Text:** text box is highlighted? _____

    _____

    _____

29. Name the command that lets you make multiple line text objects. _____

30. What do you get when you pick **Text** from the **Draw** pull-down menu followed by selecting **Text** from the cascading submenu? _____

31. Describe the purpose of the **Attach** option when setting up multiline text. _____

    _____

    _____

    _____

32. How does the width of the multiline text boundary affect what you type? _____
_____
_____
_____

33. What happens if the multiline text that you are entering exceeds or is not as long as the boundary length that you initially establish? _____
_____
_____

34. What happens when you pick the insertion point followed by the other corner of the multiline text boundary? _____
_____
_____

35. Explain how an external text editor can be set up for creation of multiline text instead of the **Edit MTEXT** dialog box. _____
_____
_____

36. To return to using the **Edit MTEXT** dialog box, what must be specified as the name of the text editor in the **Preferences** dialog? _____

37. Describe how you save multiline text that you have created in an external text editor and return to AutoCAD. _____
_____
_____

38. Name the command that you enter if you want to enter multiple lines of text at the prompt line rather than in a text editor. _____

39. What command do you use if you want to change the name of a text style? _____
_____

40. Name two commands that allow you to edit multiline text. _____

41. Identify three ways to access the AutoCAD spell checker. _____
_____
_____
_____

42. What is the purpose of the word found in the **Current word** box of the **Check Spelling** dialog box? _____
_____

43. How do you change the **Current word** if you do not think the word that is displayed in the **Suggestion** box of the **Check Spelling** dialog box is the correct word, but one of the words in the list of suggestions is the correct word? _____
_____
_____
_____

44. What is the purpose of the **Add** button in the **Check Spelling** dialog box?_____

_____

_____

45. How do you change the main dictionary for use in the **Check Spelling** dialog box? _____

_____

_____

## DRAWING PROBLEMS

*General*

1. Make three prototype drawings with borders and title blocks for your future drawings. Use the following guidelines:

   A. Prototype 1 for A-size, 8 1/2 × 11 drawings, named TITLEA.

   B. Prototype 2 for B-size, 11 × 17 drawings, named TITLEB.

   C. Prototype 3 for C-size, 17 × 22 drawings, named TITLEC.

   D. Set the following values for the drawing aids:

      Units = three-place decimal.

      **Grid** = .500.

      **Snap** = .250.

   E. Draw a polyline border, .032 wide and 1/2″ from the drawing limits.

   F. Design a title block using created text styles. Place it in the lower-right corner of each drawing. The title block should contain the following information: company or school name, address, date, drawn by, approved by, scale, title, drawing number, material, revision number. See the following example.

   G. Set a standard text style titled ROMANS-125. This style was discussed in this chapter.

| SPECIFICATIONS | | | R - | CHANGE | | DATE | ECN |
|---|---|---|---|---|---|---|---|
| | | | HYSTER COMPANY | | | | |
| | | | THIS PRINT CONTAINS CONFIDENTIAL INFORMATION WHICH IS THE PROPERTY OF HYSTER COMPANY. BY ACCEPTING THIS INFORMATION THE BORROWER AGREES THAT IT WILL NOT BE USED FOR ANY PURPOSE OTHER THAN THAT FOR WHICH IT IS LOANED. | | | | |
| UNLESS OTHERWISE SPECIFIED DIMENSIONS ARE IN ~~INCHES~~ MILLIMETERS AND TOLERANCES FOR: | | | DR. | | SCALE | | DATE |
| ____ PLACE DIMS± _____ : ____ PLACE DIMS± _____ | | | CK. MAT'L. | | CK. DESIGN | | REL. ON ECN |
| ANGLES ± _____ ; WHOLE DIMS± _____ | | | NAME | | | | |
| MODEL | DWG. FIRST USED | SIMILAR TO | | | | | |
| DEPT. | PROJECT | LIST DIVISION | H | PART NO. | | | R |

2. Recall your TITLEA prototype drawing. Use the **TEXT** or **DTEXT** command to type the following information. Change the text style to represent each of the four standard AutoCAD fonts named. Use a .5 unit text height and 0° rotation angle. Save the drawing as A:P11-2 and quit.

*General*

TXT–AUTOCAD'S DEFAULT TEXT FONT WHICH IS AVAILABLE FOR USE WHEN YOU BEGIN A DRAWING.

ROMANS–SMOOTHER THAN TXT FONT AND CLOSELY DUPLICATES THE SINGLE-STROKE LETTERING THAT HAS BEEN THE STANDARD FOR DRAFTING.

ROMANC–A MULTISTROKE DECORATIVE FONT THAT IS GOOD FOR USE IN DRAWING TITLES

ITALICC–AN ORNAMENTAL FONT SLANTED TO THE RIGHT AND HAS THE SAME LETTER DESIGN AS THE COMPLEX FONT.

3. Recall your TITLEA prototype drawing. Use the **STYLE** command to create the following text styles. Change the options as noted in each line of text. Then use the **DTEXT** command to type the text, changing the text style to represent each of the four standard AutoCAD fonts named. Use a .25 unit text height. Save the drawing as A:P11-3 and quit.

*General*

TXT–EXPAND THE WIDTH BY THREE.

MONOTXT–SLANT TO THE LEFT –30°.

ROMANS–SLANT TO THE RIGHT 30°.

ROMAND–BACKWARDS.

ROMANC–VERTICAL.

ITALICC–UNDERSCORED AND OVERSCORED.

ROMANS–USE 16d NAILS @ 10" OC.

ROMANT–⌀32 (812.8).

4. Open drawing P11-3. Select the following fonts from the text font icon menu: SCRIPTC, ROMANT, GOTHICE, SYMAP, and SYMUSIC.

*General*

A. Type a complete alphabet and numbers 1-10 for the text fonts, and all available symbols for the symbol fonts.

B. Use .375 unit height with all other variables at default values.

C. Save the drawing as A:P11-4 and quit.

**General**

5. Draw a Parts List (similar to the one shown below) connected to your A-size prototype title block.

   A. Enter PARTS LIST with a COMPLEX style.

   B. Enter the other information using ROMANS text and the **DTEXT** command. Do not exit the **DTEXT** command to start a new line of text.

   C. Save the drawing as A:P11-5 and quit.

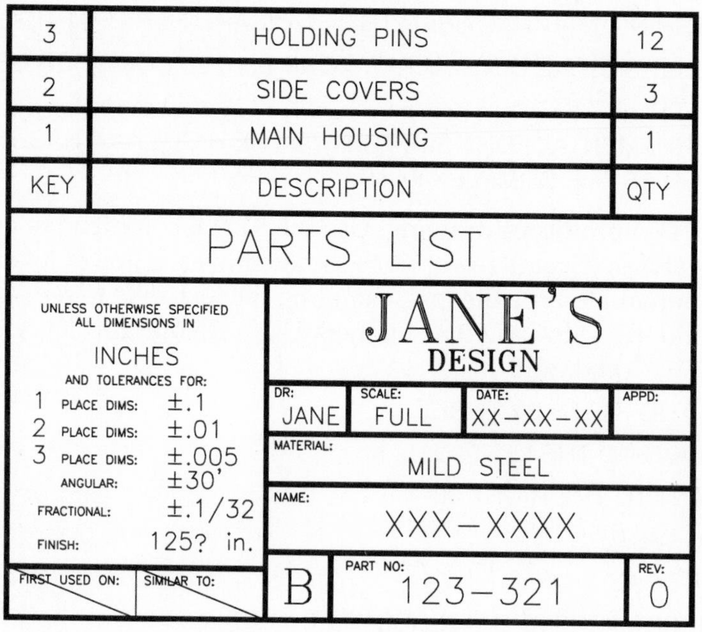

| 3 | HOLDING PINS | 12 |
|---|---|---|
| 2 | SIDE COVERS | 3 |
| 1 | MAIN HOUSING | 1 |
| KEY | DESCRIPTION | QTY |

PARTS LIST

UNLESS OTHERWISE SPECIFIED
ALL DIMENSIONS IN

INCHES

AND TOLERANCES FOR:

1 PLACE DIMS: ±.1
2 PLACE DIMS: ±.01
3 PLACE DIMS: ±.005
ANGULAR: ±30'

FRACTIONAL: ±.1/32

FINISH: 125? in.

JANE'S
DESIGN

| DR: JANE | SCALE: FULL | DATE: XX–XX–XX | APPD: |
|---|---|---|---|

MATERIAL:

MILD STEEL

NAME:

XXX–XXXX

FIRST USED ON: | SIMILAR TO: | B | PART NO: 123–321 | REV: 0

6. Draw an architectural prototype for a 17″ × 22″ or 22″ × 34″ sheet size with a title block along the right side similar to the one shown below. Save the drawing as A:P11-6 and quit.

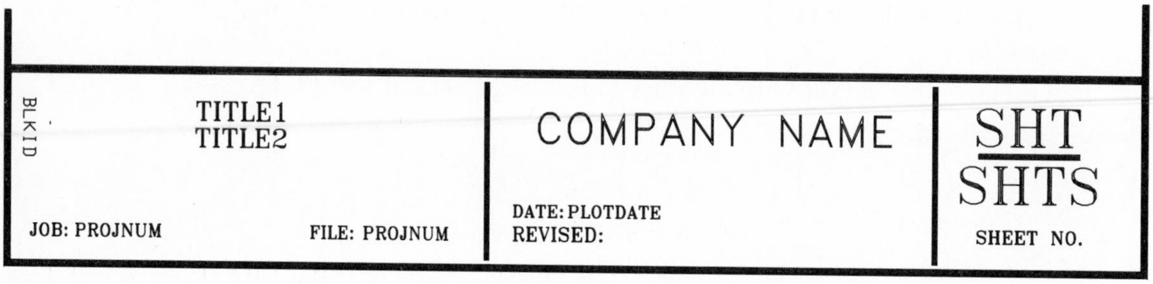

**General**

BLKID

TITLE1
TITLE2

COMPANY NAME

SHT
SHTS

JOB: PROJNUM          FILE: PROJNUM

DATE: PLOTDATE
REVISED:

SHEET NO.

7. Complete the following drawing.

    A. Make the symbols proportional to the ones shown. They will not necessarily be the same size.

    B. Use the **DTEXT** command and the variables studied in this chapter.

    C. Save the drawing as A:P11-7 and quit.

*Piping*

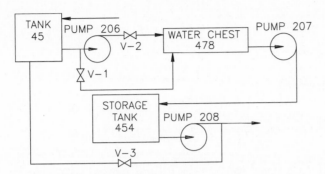

    4. ALL PUMPS ON 6" THICK CONCRETE PADS.
    3. ALL TANKS AND CHESTS BUILT TO CUSTOMERS SPECIFICATIONS.
    2. ALL VALVES FABRIVALVE FIG. 71.
    1. TEST ALL TANKS TO 175 PSI.

    NOTES:

8. Complete the drawing shown below.

    A. Make the symbols proportional to the ones shown, but not necessarily the same size.

    B. Use the **DTEXT** command and the variables studied in this chapter.

    C. Save the drawing as A:P11-8 and quit.

*Graphic Design*

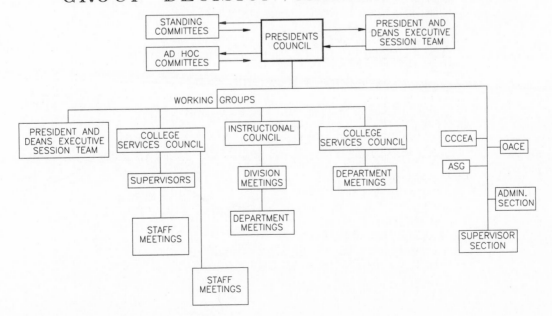

9. Use the **MTEXT** command to type the following text using the font settings of ROMANS and .125 text height with .25 heading text height.

## NOTES:

1. INTERPRET DIMENSIONS AND TOLERANCES PER ASME Y14.5M−1994.
2. REMOVE ALL BURRS AND SHARP EDGES.

CASTING NOTES UNLESS OTHERWISE SPECIFIED:
1. .31 WALL THICKNESS.
2. R.12 FILLETS.
3. R.06 ROUNDS.
4. 1.5°−3.0° DRAFT.
5. TOLERANCES:
   ± 1° ANGULAR
   ±.03 TWO PLACE DIMENSIONS.
6. PROVIDE .12 THK MACHINING STOCK ON ALL MACHINE SURFACES.

10. Use the **MTEXT** command to type the following text using the font settings of City Blueprint (CIBT) and .125 text height with .188 heading text height. After typing the text exactly as shown, edit the text with the following changes:

A. Change the \ in item 7 to 1/2.

B. Change the [ in item 8 to 1.

C. Change the 1/2 in item 8 to 3/4.

D. Change the ^ in item 10 to a degree symbol.

F. Save as drawing A:P11-10.

## COMMON FRAMING NOTES:

1. ALL FRAMING LUMBER TO BE DFL #2 OR BETTER.
2. ALL HEATED WALLS @ HEATED LIVING AREAS TO BE 2 X 6 @ 24" OC.
3. ALL EXTERIOR HEADERS TO BE 2−2 X 12 UNLESS NOTED, W/ 2" RIGID INSULATION BACKING UNLESS NOTED.
4. ALL SHEAR PANELS TO BE 1/2" CDX PLY W/ 8d @ 4" OC @ EDGE, HDRS, & BLOCKING AND 8d @ 8" OC @ FIELD UNLESS NOTED.
5. ALL METAL CONNECTORS TO BE SIMPSON CO. OR EQUAL.
6. ALL TRUSSES TO BE 24" OC. SUBMIT TRUSS CALCS TO BUILDING DEPT. PRIOR TO ERECTION.
7. PLYWOOD ROOF SHEATHING TO BE \ STD GRADE 32/16 PLY LAID PERP TO RAFTERS. NAIL W/ 8d @ 6"OC @ EDGES AND 12" OC @ FIELD.
8. PROVIDE [ 1/2" STD GRADE T&G PLY FLOOR SHEATHING LAID PERP TO FLOOR JOISTS. NAIL W/ 10d @ 6" OC @ EDGES & BLOCKING AND 12" OC @ FIELD.
9. BLOCK ALL WALLS OVER 10'−0" HIGH AT MID.
10. LET−IN BRACES TO BE 1 X 4 DIAG BRACES @ 45^ FOR ALL INTERIOR LOAD BEARING WALLS.

# Chapter *12*

## Plotting and Printing

### Learning objectives

After completing this chapter, you will be able to:
- ○ Identify options and variables found in the **PLOT** command.
- ○ Use the **Plot Configuration** dialog box to prepare a drawing for plotting.
- ○ Determine the scale factor of a drawing.
- ○ Print and plot a drawing.
- ○ Configure a new plotting device.

The *Introduction to Printing and Plotting* section in Chapter 6 provided a brief overview of the steps involved in generating a printed copy of your drawing. This chapter discusses the **Plot Configuration** dialog box in detail. In addition, suggestions for improving the quality and efficiency of your plots are given.

## USING THE PLOT COMMAND                    AUG 10

Before printing or plotting, make sure that your output device is configured properly, as described in the *AutoCAD Installation Guide.* With the output device properly configured, the **PLOT** command can be entered in several ways. Select **Print...** from the **File** pull-down menu, click the **Print** button in the **Standard** toolbar, or enter PLOT from the keyboard. The **Plot Configuration** dialog box appears, Figure 12-1. This dialog box allows you to define and preview each one of the parameters you specify for the final printing or plotting of your drawing.

Figure 12-1.  Plot parameters can be specified in the **Plot Configuration** dialog box.

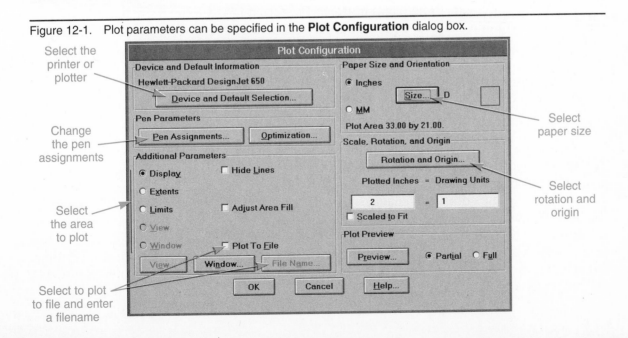

Dialog boxes are usually controlled with the **FILEDIA** system variable. However, this dialog box is controlled with the **CMDDIA** system variable. By default, **CMDDIA** is set to 1 (on). This displays the **Plot Configuration** dialog. When **CMDDIA** is set to 0 (off), all printing and plotting parameters must be entered on the command line.

### Device and default selection

As you look at the **Plot Configuration** dialog box, notice the **Device and Default Information** area in the upper-left corner. This is where AutoCAD displays information about the currently configured printer or plotter. Pick the **Device and Default Selection...** button to access the **Device and Default Selection** subdialog box shown in Figure 12-2. You can use this dialog box to change any of the printer or plotter specifications. The current device is highlighted in the **Select Device** area. When additional devices are shown, you can make a different one current by picking it from the list. In Figure 12-2, a Hewlett-Packard LaserJet IV laser printer is being set current. Add printers and plotters to the list with the **Configure plotter** option of the **CONFIG** command and choose the **Add a plotter configuration** selection.

Figure 12-2.    Available printers and plotters are listed in the **Device and Default Selection** subdialog box.

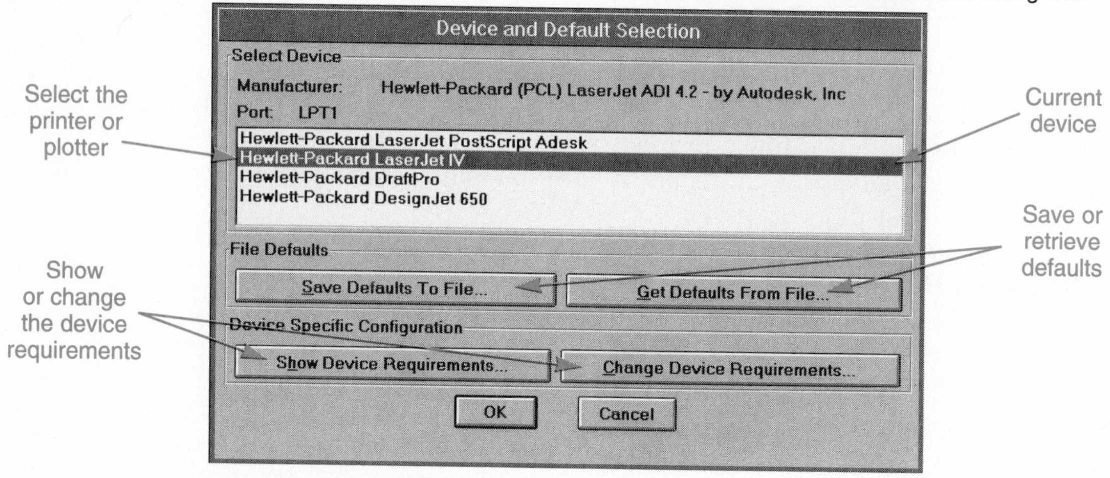

The **File Defaults** area of the **Device and Default Selection** subdialog box has **Save Defaults To File...** and **Get Defaults From File...** buttons. The files referred to by these buttons are plot configuration parameters (.PCP) files. You may create a PCP file for a number of reasons, including:

- Making changes to plot specifications before plotting.
- Making plot files for different drawing types.
- Making a plot file for each configured plotter or printer.
- Setting up a drawing to be plotted in a variety of formats.
- Giving a plot file to another person or company.

Each of the values you set in the **Plot Configuration** dialog box is saved in the PCP file. This means that you can set values for individual prototype drawings. Then, when a prototype is used to construct a new drawing, you only have to retrieve a PCP file and plot the drawing without making any additional changes to the plotting parameters. To save a PCP file, click the **Save Defaults To File...** button. Select the directory or drive where you want to save the file and enter the filename, as shown in Figure 12-3. Normally, the PCP file is saved to the \R13 directory and defaults to the current drawing name, but you may want to provide a name that is more descriptive of the saved parameters. In Figure 12-3, the filename of ARCH-D is being entered. When done, click the **OK** button to exit the **Save to File** subdialog box.

Figure 12-3.   The PCP (plot configuration parameters) **Save to File** subdialog box. Use this dialog box to save a PCP file.

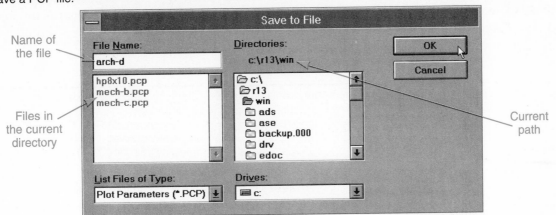

To retrieve a saved PCP file, click the **Get Defaults From File...** button. The **Obtain from File** subdialog box appears, Figure 12-4. Select the desired PCP file from the file list and click **OK**. If everything is fine with the PCP file you select, AutoCAD prints the message Plot configuration updated without error in the lower-left corner of the **Device and Default Selection** subdialog box. If there is an error, AutoCAD issues an Error Information on File Defaults dialog box. Click the **Create Error File** button to make an error file (.ERR extension) that can be used to correct the PCP file.

Figure 12-4.   Load a saved PCP file using the **Obtain from File** subdialog box.

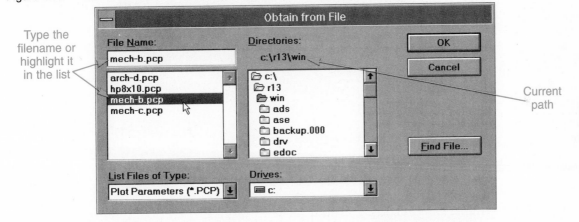

**PROFESSIONAL TIP**

Keep backup copies of your saved PCP files on a floppy disk. Should you need to reinstall AutoCAD for Windows, or upgrade to a new version, simply restore your saved PCP files onto your hard disk drive to avoid recreating the plotting parameters again.

Use the buttons in the **Device Specific Configuration** area to review or change your printer or plotter settings. The **Show Device Requirements...** button opens the **Show Device Requirements** subdialog box. Check the current device settings and click **OK** when you are satisfied. In Figure 12-5A, the device requirements for the currently configured system printer are shown (in the Windows environment, the system printer is the output device specified in the Print Manager). Click the **Change Device Requirements...** button to make any changes. If your currently configured device is the Windows system printer, several dialog boxes similar to those shown in Figures 12-5B through 12-5D are displayed. Change the settings as desired and click **OK** to continue. Remember that the type and number of dialog boxes presented are a function of your currently configured printer or plotter.

Figure 12-5.    A—The **Show Device Requirements** subdialog box. B—Changing the paper tray.
C—Changing the printer resolution. D—Setting the number of copies to be plotted.

Current device settings

> **Show Device Requirements**
>
> Number of copies = 1
> Resolution in dots per inch = 300
> Paper tray selected is Letter
>
> [ OK ]    [ Cancel ]

A

Available paper trays

Select the number of the paper tray installed

> **Change Device Requirements**
>
> Paper trays:
>
> 1. Manual Feed
> 2. Letter
> 3. A4 Sheet
> 4. Legal
>
> Select paper tray currently installed, 1 to 4                [2]
>
> [ OK ]    [ Cancel ]

B

Possible resolutions for the device

Select the number of the resolution you want to use

> **Change Device Requirements**
>
> Possible resolutions (dots/inch):
>
> 1.  75
> 2.  100
> 3.  150
> 4.  300
>
> Select desired resolution, 1 to 4                [4]
>
> [ OK ]    [ Cancel ]

C

Enter the number of copies you want

> **Change Device Requirements**
>
> How many copies of the plot would you like, 1 to 99       [1]
>
> [ OK ]    [ Cancel ]

D

**NOTE**            The changes that you make to the system printer only affect printed AutoCAD drawings. If you want the changes to be in effect for all printed Windows applications, make the changes using the Printers icon found in the Control Panel. Refer to the *Microsoft Windows User's Guide* for a complete description of the Control Panel.

## Pen parameters

The **Pen Parameters** area in the **Plot Configuration** dialog box allows you to set pen parameters based on your drawing standards or the type of printer/plotter you are using. To do this, click the **Pen Assignments...** button to get the **Pen Assignments** subdialog box, Figure 12-6. When you highlight a pen assignment by selecting it, the values for the selected pen are displayed in the **Modify Values** text boxes. The values that can be changed include the pen number, linetype, speed, and width.

Figure 12-6. The **Pen Assignments** subdialog box enables you to fine-tune the plotter pen specification.

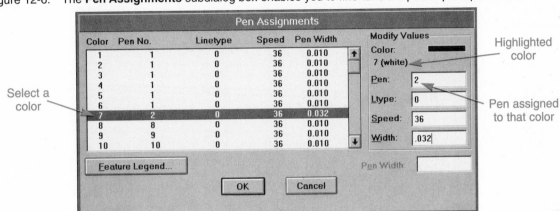

When you plot a drawing on a pen plotter, you must assign the color numbers used for your objects on-screen to the correct pen numbers in the plotter. For example, suppose you create a drawing using the first seven colors available in AutoCAD. Those colors—red, yellow, green, cyan, blue, magenta, and white (or black)—are mapped to color numbers 1 through 7. By default, these color numbers are automatically assigned to matching pen numbers. In other words, all red entities on-screen are plotted with pen number 1, all yellow entities with pen number 2, all green entities with pen number 3, and so on. If you did nothing to change this convention, you would need a separate pen for every color used in your drawing!

It is more efficient and cost-effective to map the various colors used in your drawing to only a few pens. Look at the **Pen Assignments** subdialog box shown in Figure 12-6. In this example, colors 1 through 6 are assigned to pen number 1. The entities drawn with these colors are to be plotted with a thin pen. These entities include dimensions, text, hatching, and centerlines. The object lines in the drawing were drawn with color number 7. Since object lines should be drawn thick, color number 7 is assigned to pen number 2. The line weight, or thickness, of pen number 2 is also set to .032 inches to conform to the ANSI standard for object lines. Therefore, only two pens are required to accurately plot all the drawing entities.

Fortunately, most pen plotters are capable of using various pen sizes. These types of pens are similar to the ink pens used for inking mylar. Therefore, they are available in a range of tip sizes. If your pen plotter is compatible with these types of pens, you need not set the pen width in the **Pen Assignments** subdialog box. Simply insert the correct pen size in the appropriate pen position on your plotter.

Other types of output devices, such as laser printers or electrophotographic plotters, do not use pens. However, you can still produce finished plots with the proper line weights by assigning the desired pen widths to the color numbers used in your drawing. This is particularly useful if you do not have a pen plotter.

You will also note that **Linetype** and **Speed** values can be changed in the **Pen Assignments** subdialog box. For most pen plotters, the linetype, pen speed, and pen force values are controlled by the plotter itself or the installed plotter driver. It is very unlikely that you will need to change these values. Also, notice the **Feature Legend...** button at the lower-left of the **Pen Assignments** subdialog box. Click this button to display the **Feature Legend** subdialog box shown in Figure 12-7. The linetypes shown in this subdialog box reflect the linetypes that are generated by your plotter. These linetypes are different than the linetypes created in your drawing. Therefore, entities drawn in linetypes other than CONTINUOUS will plot correctly as a function of the plotter itself. Thus, it is usually unnecessary to adjust the linetypes in the **Pen Assignments** subdialog box.

Figure 12-7.   The **Feature Legend** subdialog box displays the linetypes generated by the plotter, not AutoCAD.

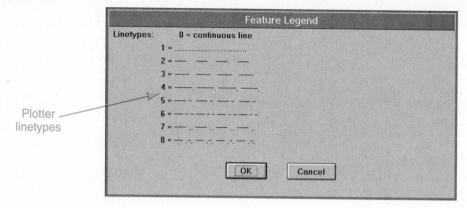

PROFESSIONAL TIP

In the unlikely event that you do need to adjust pen speeds, they should be set according to the type of paper or film you are using. In addition, you should consider the type of pen, such as liquid ink, fiber tip, or roller ball, and the lines or text to be plotted. A fast pen speed may not draw quality lines or text. Set a slower pen speed to improve the plot quality.

Also, since most pen plotters generate the required linetypes for AutoCAD drawings, leave the linetypes set to continuous (0) in the **Pen Assignments** subdialog box. Doing so makes sure that the lines in your drawing are properly plotted.

The **Optimization...** button in the **Plot Configuration** dialog box displays the **Optimizing Pen Motion** subdialog box. This subdialog box contains check boxes that let you control the efficiency of pen movement. By default, AutoCAD for Windows minimizes wasted pen motion with the settings shown in Figure 12-8. With the exception of the **No** optimization check box, each consecutive check box increases optimization. Picking a higher level option automatically checks all previous options. The options available in this subdialog box will vary depending on the type of printer or plotter that you are using. For nonpen plotters, like dot matrix printers, these options may not be available at all since they have no effect on these output devices.

Figure 12-8. The **Optimizing Pen Motion** subdialog box. Each box checked will increase the optimization. Check the **No Optimization** box if you don't want AutoCAD to optimize the plot.

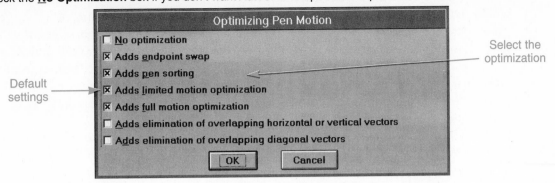

Default settings

Select the optimization

## Additional parameters—choosing what to plot

After selecting the desired output device and making the necessary pen assignments, you must decide what part of the drawing you want to plot. Look at the **Additional Parameters** area of the **Plot Configuration** dialog box, Figure 12-9.

Figure 12-9. The **Additional Parameters** area of the **Plot Configuration** dialog box is shown here highlighted.

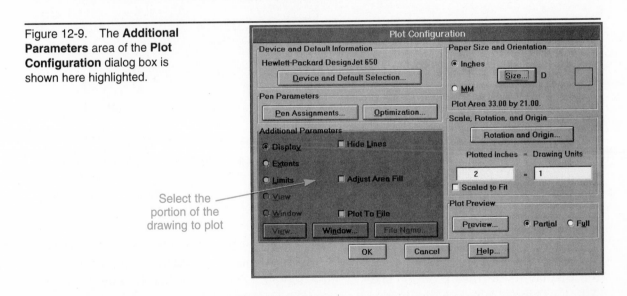

Select the portion of the drawing to plot

This section allows you to choose the portion of the drawing to be plotted, and how it is to be plotted. The functions performed by the five radio buttons labeled **Display**, **Extents**, **Limits**, **View**, and **Window** are described below:

- **Display.** This option prints or plots the current screen display.
- **Extents.** The **Extents** option prints or plots only that area of the drawing where objects (entities) are drawn. Before using this option, zoom the extents to include all drawn entities to verify exactly what will be plotted. Be aware that border lines around your drawing (like the title block) may be clipped off if they are at the extreme

edges of the screen. This often happens because you are requesting the plotter to plot at the extreme edge of its active area.

- **Limits.** This option plots everything inside the defined drawing limits.
- **View.** Views saved with the **VIEW** command are plotted using this option. Until a view name has been given, this option button is grayed-out. To specify a view name, pick the **View...** button to display the **View Name** subdialog box. Select the name of the view you want plotted and click **OK**. The view name you select does not have to be currently displayed on the screen, but the **TILEMODE** system variable must be off (0) to plot any saved view from either model space or paper space.
- **Window.** This button appears grayed-out until you click the **Window...** button to display the **Window Selection** subdialog box shown in Figure 12-10. This option requires that you define two diagonally opposite corners of a window around the portion of the drawing to be plotted. Enter the **First Corner** and **Other Corner** coordinates of the desired window in the appropriate **X:** and **Y:** text boxes. If you want to define the window with your pointing device, click the **Pick** ⟨ button at the upper-left of the subdialog box. This clears the dialog boxes and redisplays the graphics window. You are then prompted at the command line to pick the window corners that surround the part of the drawing you want printed or plotted. After you have picked the corners, the **Window Selection** subdialog box is redisplayed. Pick **OK** to return to the **Plot Configuration** dialog box.

Figure 12-10. Specify a plot window using the **Window Selection** subdialog box. Enter coordinates or pick a new window.

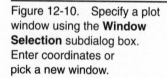
Select a new window

Coordinates of the current window

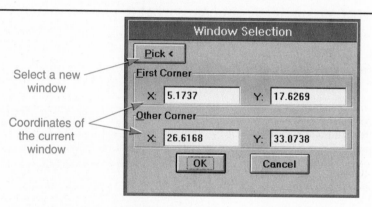

**Window Selection**

Pick ⟨

First Corner

X: 5.1737    Y: 17.6269

Other Corner

X: 26.6168    Y: 33.0738

OK      Cancel

**NOTE**      If the window you define is too close to an entity, some portion of that entity may be clipped off in your plot. Should this happen, simply adjust the window size the next time you plot.

Click the **Hide Lines** check box shown in Figure 12-9 if you want to plot a 3D drawing with hidden lines removed. This function works the same as the **HIDE** command does with the display. Note that plotting takes a little longer when removing hidden lines since AutoCAD must calculate the lines to be removed. Do not check this box when plotting 2D drawings.

Activate the **Adjust Area Fill** check box if you want entities such as wide polylines, traces, doughnuts, and solids filled completely. These precise plots are a result of the pen being adjusted inside the boundary of the entity by one-half the pen width. When this check box is turned off, the pen plots at the center of the boundary, which is fine for most applications, but may be poor for printed circuit board artwork.

**PROFESSIONAL TIP**

You may eventually work with paper space to create drawing layouts containing multiple views of varying scales. These layouts may contain 3D views inside paper space viewports in which the hidden lines must be removed for ease of visualization. The **Hide Lines** check box in the **Plot Configuration** dialog box will not automatically remove the hidden lines from a 3D object in a paper space viewport. You must first set the **Hideplot** option of the **MVIEW** command to on before plotting.

The **MVIEW** command and the use of paper space multiview layouts are discussed in detail in Chapter 27.

## Creating a plot file

Some computer operating systems allow you to continue working on a drawing, while other instructions are being handled by the computer. This capability is called *multitasking* and is a standard feature of the Windows 95, Windows NT, and Unix operating systems. For those operating systems capable of true multitasking, it can be extremely handy to redirect plot output to an external file. This plot file can then be sent directly to a configured plotter while you continue working on a drawing.

Unfortunately, DOS is not a multitasking operating system and can only run one program at a time. Many people confuse the Windows 3.1 and Windows for Workgroups 3.11 graphical user environments with multitasking operating systems. Since Windows has the ability to display multiple open windows on the display screen at one time, it gives the impression that several applications are running simultaneously. This is not the case, however. Only the application in the active window is running—another application is "dormant" until its window is reactivated.

Even though DOS and Windows are not multitasking operating environments, redirecting plot output to a .PLT file is good practice if you have only one office or class computer connected to a printer or plotter. This is also the case if your office or school uses a plot spooler. A plot spooler is connected to a plotter and is basically a "smart" disk drive with memory. It reads the .PLT file from disk and sends the drawing data to the plotter. A plot spooler removes the need of having a computer connected to the plotter. Additionally, plot files can be stored in a plot queue on the file server in a networked computer environment. A *plot queue* is a lineup, or list of files, waiting to be plotted. The .PLT files can be loaded in the queue and started while users on the network continue doing other work.

If you want to redirect plot output to a file, pick the **Plot To File** check box. This activates the **File Name...** button that is normally grayed-out. Clicking this button displays the **Create Plot File** subdialog box shown in Figure 12-11. Observe that saved plot files are automatically given the extension .PLT, and that the plot filename defaults to the current drawing name. If you have not yet provided a name for the current drawing, the plot file is saved with a filename of UNNAMED.PLT. To provide a different name for the plot file, enter the name in the **File Name:** edit box and pick **OK**. The **Plot Configuration** dialog box reappears. Click **OK** once more to close the dialog box and create the plot file. When the plot file is complete, you are so notified on the command line.

Figure 12-11.   The **Create Plot File** subdialog box. Select the destination and the name of the file.

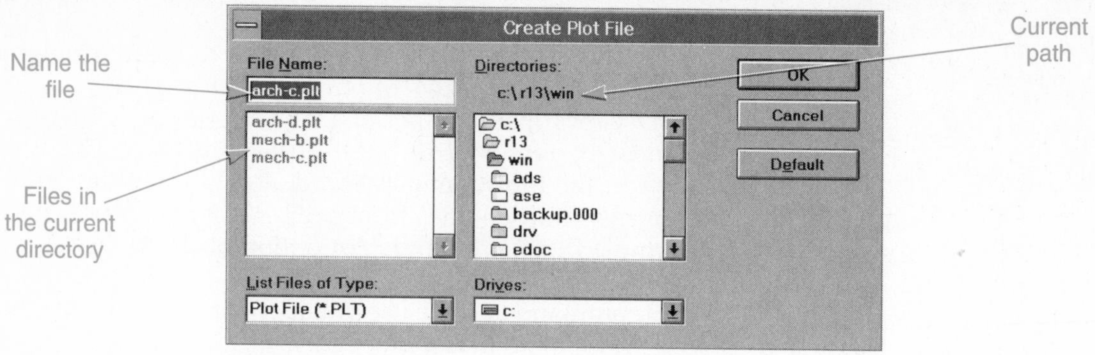

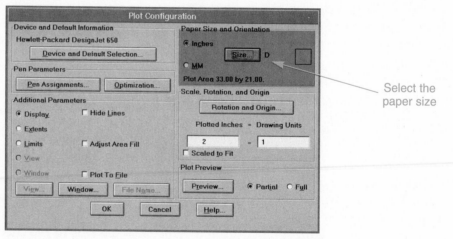

Name the file

Files in the current directory

Current path

## Paper size and orientation

The upper-right area of the **Plot Configuration** dialog box shown in Figure 12-12 controls the paper size and orientation. Click either the **Inches** or **MM** option buttons to make inches or millimeters the units for all plot specifications.

Click the **Size...** button to access the **Paper Size** subdialog box. Select the desired standard paper (or mylar) size, such as the D-size entry shown in Figure 12-13. You can also enter your own size specifications in one of the **USER Width** and **Height** text boxes. If you enter your own size specifications, make sure the values you enter do not exceed the maximum

Figure 12-12.   The **Paper Size and Orientation** area of the **Plot Configuration** dialog box is shown here highlighted.

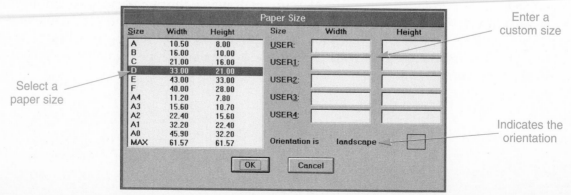

Select the paper size

Figure 12-13.   All available sheet sizes are listed in the **Paper Size** subdialog box. Select the size you want to use.

Select a paper size

Enter a custom size

Indicates the orientation

(**MAX**) size indicated in the list. This is because the **MAX** size is the largest size plot media your plotter can handle. Therefore, the sizes listed in the **Paper Size** subdialog box will vary according to the manufacturer and size of printer or plotter you have.

Remember that all pen plotters require margins around the edges of the plot media. This space allows for the plotter's grip wheels, clamps, or other holding devices. As a result, the available size may be smaller than the ANSI standard sizes. Figure 12-14 shows the standard paper sizes and the available plotting areas for each. Whether you select a standard size from the list in the **Paper Size** subdialog box, or enter your own size specifications, the available plotting area is reported in the **Paper Size and Orientation** area of the **Plot Configuration** dialog box.

Figure 12-14. Standard paper sizes and approximate plotting areas.

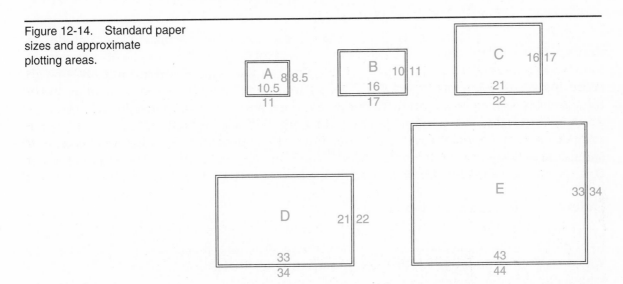

## Plot rotation and origin

Options to control the plot rotation and origin are located in the **Scale, Rotation, and Origin** area of the **Plot Configuration** dialog box. Click the **Rotation and Origin...** button to access the **Plot Rotation and Origin** subdialog box shown in Figure 12-15.

In AutoCAD, the horizontal screen measurement relates to the long side of the paper. This orientation is known as *landscape* format. However, you might create a drawing, form, or chart that must be placed in *portrait* format. This format orients the long side of the plot vertically. AutoCAD rotates plots in 90° clockwise increments, and **0**, **90**, **180**, and **270** options for degree rotation settings appear in the **Plot Rotation** area of the **Plot Rotation and Origin** subdialog box. Figure 12-16 illustrates the result of a 90° plot rotation.

Figure 12-15. The **Plot Rotation and Origin** subdialog box can be used to change the origin or rotation of the plot.

Select a plot rotation

Select a plot origin

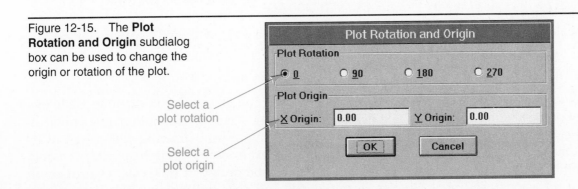

Figure 12-16.  A—Standard plot
with no rotation. B—Results of
a 90° clockwise rotation.

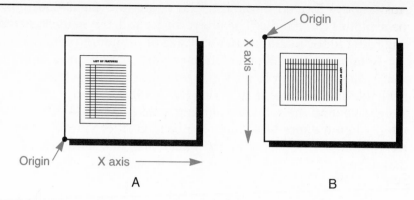

A                                              B

The origin of a pen plotter is the lower-left corner of the plot media. To begin plotting a drawing at that point, leave the values shown in the **Plot Origin** text boxes at 0.00. If you want to move the drawing away from the default origin, set the required values in the text boxes accordingly. For example, to move the drawing four units to the right and three units above the plotter origin, enter a 4 in the **X Origin:** edit box, and a 3 in the **Y Origin:** edit box. For printers, the origin is the upper-left corner of the paper. The coordinates of 4,3 will move the print origin four units to the right and three units down. Remember that the units you enter should be consistent with the units specified with the option buttons in the **Paper Size and Orientation** area of the **Plot Configuration** dialog box. Refer back to Figure 12-12.

### Determining drawing scale factors

The scale factor of the drawing should already be established by the time you are ready to plot. However, the plot scale can also be set now. Be aware, though, that you will have to spend some time updating dimensions and revising text heights and/or styles. The proper scale factor is vitally important because it makes sure that text, dimension values, and dimensioning entities (such as arrowheads and tick marks) are printed or plotted at the proper size. To obtain the correct AutoCAD text height, the desired plotted text height is multiplied by the scale factor. The scale factor is also used in the **DIMSCALE** dimension variable.

The scale factor is always the reciprocal of the drawing scale. For example, if you wish to plot a mechanical drawing at a scale of 1/2″ = 1″, calculate the scale factor as follows:

$$1/2″ = 1″$$
$$.5″ = 1″$$
$$1 \div .5 = 2 \ \textit{(The scale factor is 2 and } \textbf{DIMSCALE} = 2)$$

An architectural drawing to be plotted at a scale of 1/4″ = 1′-0″ has a scale factor calculated as follows:

$$1/4″ = 1′-0″$$
$$.25″ = 12″$$
$$12 \div .25 = 48 \ \textit{(The scale factor is 48 and } \textbf{DIMSCALE} = 48)$$

The scale factor of a civil engineering drawing that has a scale of 1″ = 60′ is calculated as:

$$1″ = 60′$$
$$1″ = 60 \times 12 = 720 \ \textit{(The scale factor is 720 and } \textbf{DIMSCALE} = 720)$$

Once the scale factor of the drawing has been determined, you should then calculate the height of the text in AutoCAD. If text height is to be plotted at 1/8″, it should not be drawn at that height. For example, if you are working on a civil engineering drawing with a scale of 1″ = 60′, the scale factor and **DIMSCALE** both equal 720. Text drawn 1/8″ high appears as a dot. Remember, all geometry created in AutoCAD should be drawn at full scale, regardless of your professional discipline. In this example, the full size civil engineering drawing in AutoCAD is 720 times larger than it will be when plotted at the proper scale. Therefore, you must multiply the text height by 720 in order to get text that appears in correct proportion on the screen. For 1/8″ high text to appear correctly on-screen, calculate the AutoCAD text height as follows:

$$1/8″ \times 720$$
$$.125 \times 720 = 90 \text{ (The proper height of the text is 90)}$$

Remember, scale factors, text heights, and **DIMSCALE** values should be determined before beginning a drawing. The best method is to incorporate these as values within your prototype drawing files.

## Scaling the plot

Since AutoCAD drawing geometry is created at full scale, the drawing is scaled at the plotter to fit on the sheet size. The **Plotted Inches = Drawing Units** section in the **Scale, Rotation, and Origin** area of the **Plot Configuration** dialog box is used to specify the plot scale. The **Plotted Inches = Drawing Units** text boxes (or **Plotted MM = Drawing Units** text boxes) allow you to specify the plot scale as a ratio of plotted units to drawing units. An architectural drawing to be plotted at 1/4″ = 1′-0″ can be entered in the text boxes as:

$$1/4″ = 1′ \text{ or } .25 = 12 \text{ or } 1 = 48$$

A mechanical drawing to be plotted at a scale of 1/2″ = 1″ can be entered in the text boxes as:

$$1/2″ = 1″ \text{ or } .5 = 1 \text{ or } 1 = 2$$

Click the **Scaled to Fit** check box if you want AutoCAD to automatically adjust your drawing to fit on the paper. This is useful if you have a C-size pen plotter, but need to plot a D-size or E-size drawing. However, keep in mind that you may have considerable blank space left on the paper depending on the size and proportions of your drawing. The **Scaled to Fit** feature is also useful if you are printing a large drawing on a dot matrix or laser printer that can only use A-size sheets. The drawing is automatically scaled down to fit the size of printer paper.

## Calculating the drawing area and limits

To calculate the available area on a sheet of paper or polyester film at a specific scale, use this formula:

$$\text{Unit} \div \text{Scale} \times \text{Media size} = \text{Limits}$$

For example, to find the limits of a B-size (17″ × 11″) sheet of paper at 1/2″ = 1″ scale:

$$1 \div .50 \times 17 = 17 \div .5 = 34 \text{ (X distance)}$$
$$1 \div .50 \times 11 = 11 \div .5 = 22 \text{ (Y distance)}$$

Thus, the limits of a B-size sheet at the scale of 1/2″ = 1″ are 34,22. The same formula applies to architectural scales. The limits of a C-size architectural sheet (24″ × 18″) at a scale of 1/4″ = 1″-0″ can be determined like this:

$$1′-0″ \div 1/4″ \times 24 = 12″ \div .25″ \times 24 = 48 \times 24 = 1152 \div 12 = 96 \text{ feet (X distance)}$$

Use the same formula to calculate the Y distance for the 18″ side of the paper. The chart in Figure 12-17 provides limits for common scales on various plot media sizes for each drafting field. It also lists text height, scale factors, and linetype scales for the best linetype quality.

Figure 12-17. Common scales and their drawing limits, text height, scale factors, and linetype scales.

| | Paper size | Approx. drawing area | Scale | Limits | Plotted text height (inches) 1/8 | 1/4 | Scale factor | Ltscale |
|---|---|---|---|---|---|---|---|---|
| **Mechanical** | 11 × 8.5 | 9 × 7 | 2″ = 1″<br>3/4″ = 1″<br>1/2″ = 1″<br>1/4″ = 1″ | 4.5″× 3.5″<br>12″ × 9.33″<br>18″ × 14″<br>36″ × 28″ | .0625<br>.167<br>.25<br>.5 | .125<br>.33<br>.5<br>1.0 | .5<br>1.33<br>2<br>4 | .25<br>.67<br>1<br>2 |
| | 17 × 11 | 15 × 10 | 2″ = 1″<br>3/4″ = 1″<br>1/2″ = 1″<br>1/4″ = 1″ | 7.5″ × 5″<br>20″ × 13.33″<br>30″ × 20″<br>60″ × 40″ | | | | |
| | 22 × 17 | 20 × 15 | 2″ = 1″<br>3/4″ = 1″<br>1/2″ = 1″<br>1/4″ = 1″ | 10″ × 7.5″<br>26.67″ × 20″<br>40″ × 30″<br>80″ × 60″ | | | | |
| | 34 × 22 | 32 × 20 | 2″ = 1″<br>3/4″ = 1″<br>1/2″ = 1″<br>1/4″ = 1″ | 16″ × 10″<br>42.67″ × 26.67″<br>64″ × 40″<br>128″ × 80″ | | | | |
| | 44 × 34 | 42 × 32 | 2″ = 1″<br>3/4″ = 1″<br>1/2″ = 1″<br>1/4″ = 1″ | 21″ × 16″<br>56″ × 42.67″<br>84″ × 64″<br>168″ × 128″ | | | | |

| | Paper size | Approx. drawing area | Scale | Limits | Plotted text height (inches) 1/8 | 1/4 | Scale factor | Ltscale |
|---|---|---|---|---|---|---|---|---|
| **Architectural** | 11 × 8.5 | 9 × 7 | 1″ = 1′–0″<br>1/2″ = 1′–0″<br>1/4″ = 1′–0″<br>1/8″ = 1′–0″ | 9′ × 7′<br>18′ × 14′<br>36′ × 28′<br>72′ × 56′ | 1.5<br>3.0<br>6.0<br>12.0 | 3.0<br>6.0<br>12.0<br>24.0 | 12<br>24<br>48<br>96 | 6<br>12<br>24<br>48 |
| | 17 × 11 | 15 × 10 | 1″ = 1′–0″<br>1/2″ = 1′–0″<br>1/4″ = 1′–0″<br>1/8″ = 1′–0″ | 15′ × 10′<br>30′ × 20′<br>60′ × 40′<br>120′ × 80′ | | | | |
| | 22 × 17 | 20 × 15 | 1″ = 1′–0″<br>1/2″ = 1′–0″<br>1/4″ = 1′–0″<br>1/8″ = 1′–0″ | 20′ × 15′<br>40′ × 30′<br>80′ × 60′<br>160′ × 120′ | | | | |
| | 34 × 22 | 32 × 20 | 1″ = 1′–0″<br>1/2″ = 1′–0″<br>1/4″ = 1′–0″<br>1/8″ = 1′–0″ | 32′ × 20′<br>64′ × 40′<br>128′ × 80′<br>256′ × 160′ | | | | |
| | 44 × 34 | 42 × 32 | 1″ = 1′–0″<br>1/2″ = 1′–0″<br>1/4″ = 1′–0″<br>1/8″ = 1′–0″ | 42′ × 32′<br>84′ × 64′<br>168′ × 128′<br>336′ × 256′ | | | | |

Figure 12-17.   Continued.

|  | Paper size | Approx. drawing area | Scale | Limits | Plotted text height (inches) | | Scale factor | Ltscale |
|---|---|---|---|---|---|---|---|---|
|  |  |  |  |  | 1/8 | 1/4 |  |  |
| **Civil Engineering** | 11 × 8.5 | 9 × 7 | 1″ = 10′<br>1″ = 20′<br>1″ = 30′<br>1″ = 50′ | 90′ × 70′<br>180′ × 140′<br>270′ × 210′<br>450′ × 350′ | 15<br>30<br>45<br>75 | 30<br>60<br>90<br>150 | 120<br>240<br>360<br>600 | 60<br>120<br>180<br>300 |
|  | 17 × 11 | 15 × 10 | 1″ = 10′<br>1″ = 20′<br>1″ = 30′<br>1″ = 50′ | 150′ × 100′<br>300′ × 200′<br>450′ × 300′<br>750′ × 500′ |  |  |  |  |
|  | 22 × 17 | 20 × 15 | 1″ = 10′<br>1″ = 20′<br>1″ = 30′<br>1″ = 50′ | 200′ × 150′<br>400′ × 300′<br>600′ × 450′<br>1000′ × 750′ |  |  |  |  |
|  | 34 × 22 | 32 × 20 | 1″ = 10′<br>1″ = 20′<br>1″ = 30′<br>1″ = 50′ | 320′ × 200′<br>640′ × 400′<br>960′ × 600′<br>1600′ × 1000′ |  |  |  |  |
|  | 44 × 34 | 42 × 32 | 1″ = 10′<br>1″ = 20′<br>1″ = 30′<br>1″ = 50′ | 420′ × 320′<br>840′ × 640′<br>1260′ × 960′<br>2100′ × 1600′ |  |  |  |  |

## Previewing the plot

The size and complexity of some drawings often requires a long time to finish a plot. By previewing a plot before it is sent to the output device, you can save material and valuable plot time. This feature is found in the **Plot Preview** area at the lower-right of the **Plot Configuration** dialog box, Figure 12-18. The **Partial** and **Full** preview options are each controlled with an option button.

Figure 12-18.   The **Plot Preview** area of the **Plot Configuration** subdialog box is shown here highlighted. Select **Partial** or **Full** and the **Preview...** button to preview the plot.

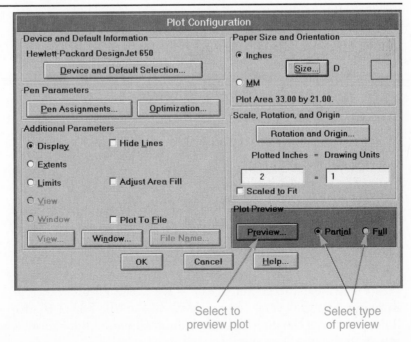

Select to preview plot

Select type of preview

When the **Partial** option is activated and you click the **Preview...** button, AutoCAD quickly displays the **Preview Effective Plotting Area** subdialog box shown in Figure 12-19. The red outline is the paper size, and the paper dimensions are given below for reference. The area the image occupies is called the *effective area*. The effective area dimensions are noted and the blue outline of this area is provided within the paper size. AutoCAD displays a red and blue dashed line when the effective area and the paper size are the same. While this shows you how the drawing compares to the paper size, the final plot depends on how the printer or plotter is set up. In Figure 12-19, the reported values indicate that a C-size drawing is being plotted on a D-size sheet of plot media.

Figure 12-19.   Selecting the **Preview...** button when **Partial** is checked displays the **Preview Effective Plotting Area** subdialog box. The red line indicates the paper size. The blue line indicates the plotting area.

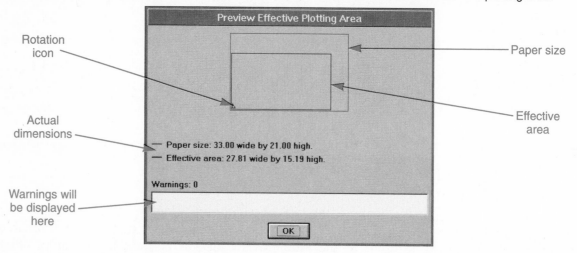

AutoCAD gives you messages in the **Warnings:** box if there is something wrong with the relationship of the display and the paper. These warnings give you an opportunity to make corrections and then preview the plot again. You may encounter the following warnings:
- Effective area too small to display.
- Origin forced effective area off display.
- Plotting area exceeds paper maximum.

Notice the small symbol in the lower-left corner of the effective area in Figure 12-19. This is called the *rotation icon*. When the rotation icon appears in the lower-left corner, it indicates the 0° default rotation angle. The icon is in the upper-left corner when the rotation is 90°, the upper-right corner for a 180° rotation, and in the lower-right corner for a 270° rotation, Figure 12-20.

Pick the **Full** option button followed by picking the **Preview...** button if you want a full preview. The **Full** preview takes more time, but it displays the drawing in the graphics window as it will actually appear on the plotted hard copy. This takes the same amount of time as a drawing regeneration. Therefore, the drawing size determines how fast this happens. AutoCAD displays a **0 – 100%** meter in the lower-right corner of the **Plot Configuration** dialog box as the full plot preview is generated. The graphics window then returns with the drawing displayed inside the paper outline. At the same time, there is a **Plot Preview** dialog box positioned near the center of the screen. See Figure 12-21. If this dialog box obscures the drawing, just move the cursor arrow to the title bar at the top of the dialog box. Click and hold, then drag the dialog box to a more convenient location. Click the **End Preview** button to return to the **Plot Configuration** dialog box.

Figure 12-20.   The rotation icon as it appears in each rotation angle selection.

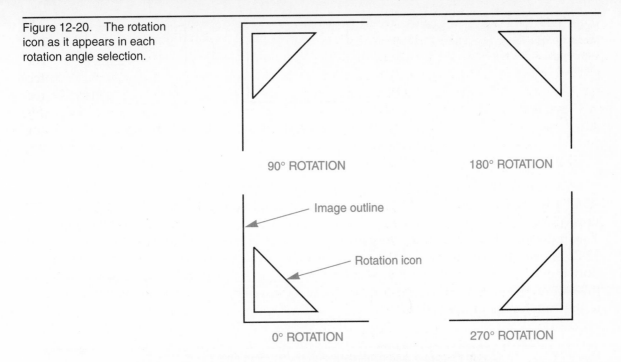

90° ROTATION

180° ROTATION

Image outline

Rotation icon

0° ROTATION

270° ROTATION

Figure 12-21.   The **Plot Preview** subdialog box is displayed when a full preview is selected.

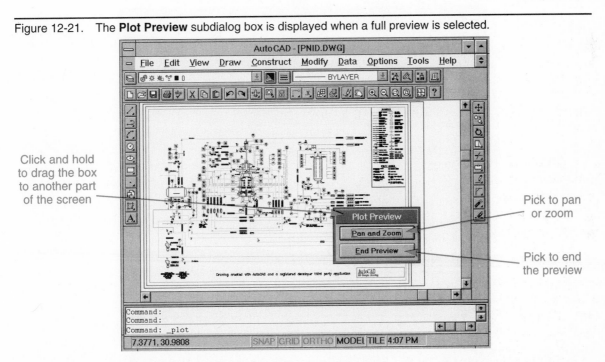

Click and hold to drag the box to another part of the screen

Pick to pan or zoom

Pick to end the preview

The **Full** preview option also allows you to examine details on the drawing or evaluate how a multiview arrangement fits together by clicking the **Pan and Zoom** button. When you first click the **Pan and Zoom** button, you get a small view box with an X inside for panning, as shown in Figure 12-22A. This is similar to the **Dynamic** option of the **ZOOM** command discussed in Chapter 10. Move the pan view box anywhere on the drawing. Clicking the pick button changes the image to a zoom view box. The zoom box image has an arrow on the right side, as shown in Figure 12-22B.

Figure 12-22.   The pan and zoom
boxes enable you to accurately
view areas of the drawing
during full preview.

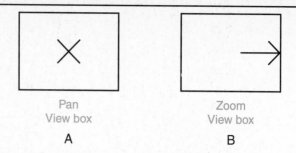

You can make the zoom box bigger by moving your pointing device to the right, or smaller by moving it to the left. The box can be moved vertically without changing its size. Press [Enter] when you have the size and position of the pan/zoom box where you want it. This redisplays the drawing at the pan location and zoom scale that you selected. Figure 12-23 shows the result of a selective pan and zoom to review some specific detail on the drawing. Also notice the **Plot Preview** subdialog box now has a **Zoom Previous** button. Click this button to return to the original full preview representation, or click **End Preview** to return to the **Plot Configuration** dialog box.

Figure 12-23.   The **Zoom Previous** button appears after picking **Pan and Zoom**.

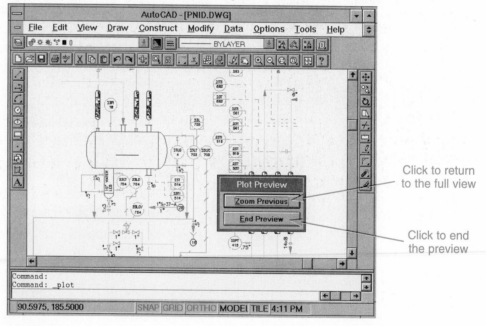

Before you pick **OK** in the **Plot Configuration** dialog box, there are several items you should check. Go through the following list before continuing.
- The printer or plotter is plugged in and turned on.
- The parallel or serial cable to the computer is secure.
- The pen carousel is loaded and secure or pen is in plotter arm.
- Pens of proper color and thickness are in correct locations in pen carousel or rack.
- The plot media is properly loaded in plotter and paper grips or clamps are in place.
- The printer or plotter area is clear for unblocked paper movement.

Further tips and suggestions for improving plot quality and productivity are given in the final section of this chapter.

Once you are satisfied with all printer or plotter parameters and are ready to plot, pick the **OK** button to exit the **Plot Configuration** dialog box. AutoCAD then displays the following message on the command line:

Effective plotting area: (*xx*) wide by (*yy*) high

These are the actual dimensions of the current plotting area. A dialog box is also displayed that indicates the name of the drawing being printed, and a meter shows the percentage of the file that has been regenerated and sent to the printer. See Figure 12-24.

Figure 12-24.   When you send a drawing to a printer or plotter, a progress meter appears allowing you to gage how long the plot will take.

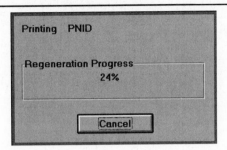

Printing   PNID

Regeneration Progress
24%

Cancel

**PROFESSIONAL TIP**

You can stop a plot in progress at any time by canceling with [Esc], or by clicking the **Cancel** button in the dialog box shown in Figure 12-24. Keep in mind that it may take a while for some plotters to terminate the plot, depending on the amount of the drawing file that has already been sent to the plotter. You may also find it necessary to turn the plotter off and then turn it back on after canceling. This action removes any remaining plot data from the plotter's internal buffer.

## PLOTTING HINTS

Plotting can slow down productivity in an office or a classroom if not done efficiently. Establish and follow a procedure for using the plotter. For a company, this might involve adding a special night shift to plot drawings when computer operators are not working. In a school, a student may be assigned to plot drawings, or specific times can be set aside for the task. In any situation, instruct all drafters, engineers, and other plotter users of the proper operating procedures. Post these in strategic locations.

### Planning your plots

Planning is again the key word when dealing with plots. In the same way you planned the drawing, you must plan the plot. A few items to consider when planning are:
- ✓ Size and type of plotting media, such as bond paper, vellum, or polyester film.
- ✓ Type of title block.
- ✓ Location and scale of multiple views.
- ✓ Origin location.
- ✓ Scale of the drawing.
- ✓ Color, thickness, and types of pens to be used.
- ✓ Speed of pens.
- ✓ Orientation of 3D views.
- ✓ Portion to be plotted: view, window, display, limits, or extents.

This is only a sample of decisions that should be made before you even walk up to the plotter. Remember, the plotter is the funnel that all the drawings must go through before they are evaluated, approved, and sent to production or the client. When a bottleneck develops at the plotter, the time savings of a CAD system can be drastically reduced.

Whether a school or business, it may help your organization to create a plotting request form. The example shown in Figure 12-25 is actually used in a school's CAD lab. Its purpose is to require AutoCAD users to prepare as much as possible before thinking about a plot. Use this form or develop one of your own to increase your plotting efficiency.

Figure 12-25.    An example of a plotting request form.

| PLOT REQUEST | |
|---|---|
| REQUESTED BY: | DATE: |
| DATE REQUIRED: | |

| CAD STATION NUMBER: | 1.   3.   5.   7   9.<br>2.   4.   6.   8.   10. |

SCALE:  ☐1=1  ☐1=12  ☐1=24  ☐1=32  ☐1=48
☐1=96  ☐FIT  ☐OTHER (      )

AREA OF DWG. TO PLOT:
☐DISPLAY      ☐EXTENTS      ☐LIMITS
☐VIEW        ☐WINDOW

TYPE OF PLOT & PAPER SIZE:

| CALCOMP: | ☐D−SIZE      ☐OTHER (      ) |
| JDL: | ☐D REDUCED TO C−SIZE<br>☐B−SIZE      ☐OTHER (      ) |
| H−P: | ☐D REDUCED TO B−SIZE<br>☐B−SIZE      ☐OTHER (      ) |
| LASER: | ☐LANDSCAPE   ☐PORTRAIT |
| PLOT WRITTEN TO FILE: | ☐NO      ☐YES |
| PLOTTED BY: | DATE: |

## PROFESSIONAL TIP

Use preprinted borders and title blocks whenever possible. Use attributes in a block for the information in the title block that will change with each drawing. This block can be inserted into any drawing, or plotted separately before or after the drawing. This eliminates drawing borders and title blocks each time. Refer to Chapter 27 for a review of title block attributes. If you develop title blocks using text entities now, you can always update them later to take advantage of the more efficient use of blocks and attributes.

## Establish a plotting center

Many companies and schools have discovered the problems associated with the plotting process. One solution is creating a plotting center. A person or department is responsible for plotting drawings and supervising plotter use. The type of center or procedure established depends on the number of plotters available. Other factors include the number of computers serving the plotters, the numbers of computer users, network usage, office space available, and the nature of the business.

The plotting center may be a special room with a dedicated computer, a terminal attached to the plotter, or a plot spooler cabled to a plotter. Disks are sent here at prearranged times or left in a "plot request" box with a plot form attached. Large companies that produce many drawings usually have a reproduction department. One or more people are responsible for making prints, copies, or photos. It is unproductive in a large office or classroom to allow all computer users to run their own plots.

Network users can operate a plotting center even more efficiently. Plot files are created and used by a plot spooler. A plot spooler is a program that creates a plot queue (list). Plots are made as fast as paper can be loaded in the plotter. The network or spooler may also have a method for leaving instructions for the person doing the actual plotting. These instructions might replace the items that would normally be listed on a plot request form.

### Establish plotting times in a classroom

In an educational environment, set a schedule for plot times. Have an instructor or lab assistant available to answer questions and solve problems. Options include:

✓ Plot at the end of the class or day.
✓ Plot once a week.
✓ Have a lab assistant make plots during the evening.

Plot only those drawings absolutely necessary during work or class hours. This might occur during final evaluation at the end of the term. Instructors should evaluate drawings on disk whenever possible.

### Eliminate unnecessary plots

A potential element in using computers for design and manufacturing is the elimination of paper drawings. This is a difficult concept for many people to grasp because there is nothing to hold in their hands. When design data proceeds directly to manufacturing, there is no paper drawing to approve, touch, mark on, or keep lying around. Therefore, people tend to make plots when they really don't need to do so.

When you create plots, a bottleneck is introduced into the classroom or production environment, decreasing productivity. The easiest way to eliminate the problems associated with plotting is to eliminate plotting. Simply don't plot. Make plots *only* when absolutely necessary. This results in time and money savings. A few additional suggestions include:

✓ Obtain approvals of designs while the drawings are on the screen. This procedure is good in theory, but for most people it is still easier to check a paper print of a drawing for errors.

✓ Transfer files or disks for the checker's comments or supervisor's input on layout or designs.

✓ Create a special layer with a unique color for mark-ups. Freeze or erase this layer when finally making a plot.

✓ Use a "redlining" software package, such as Autodesk View, that enables the checker to review the drawing and apply markups to it without using AutoCAD.

✓ Classroom instructors should check drawings on disk. Use a special layer for instructor comments.

✓ Make quick prints with a printer whenever check prints are sufficient.

✓ Avoid making plots for backups. Rather, save your drawing files in three different locations such as: hard disk, flexible disk at workstation, and flexible disk at another location. These may also be supplemented with a backup on tape cartridges or optical disks.

## If you must plot...

Industry still exists on a paper-based system. Therefore, it is important that plotters are used efficiently. That means using the plotter only for what is required. Here are a few hints for doing just that.

✓ Ask yourself, "Do I *really* need a plot?" If the answer is an unqualified *yes*, then proceed.

✓ Plan your plot!

✓ Pick the least busy time to make the plot.

✓ If more than one plotter is available, use the smallest, least complex model.

✓ Select the smallest piece of paper possible.

✓ Use the lowest quality paper possible. Select bond for check plots or vellum or polyester film for final plots.

✓ Decide on only one color and thickness of pen to make the plot.

✓ Use the most inexpensive pen possible. Obtain a fiber tip or disposable pen for check plots. Choose a wet ink, steel, jewel, or ceramic tip pen only for final plots on vellum or polyester film.

✓ Enter the fastest pen speed that will still achieve quality without the pen skipping.

✓ Use a continuous linetype when possible. Hidden and center linetypes increase plot time significantly, and cause pen wear. This is not as much of a factor with penless plotters such as laser and inkjet.

## Producing quality plots

The time comes when you must plot the highest quality drawing for reproduction, evaluation, or client use. Then, use your plotter in a manner that does the job right the first time. Keep in mind these points before making that final plot.

✓ If you have several plotters, choose the one that will produce the quality of print you need. Select the right tool for the job.

✓ Choose the paper size appropriate for the drawing.

✓ Set pen speeds slow enough to produce good lines without skipping.

✓ Use the proper ink for your climate.

## Plotter hygiene

Computer lab hygiene, discussed in Chapter 1, extends to plotters as well. It is true that when properly maintained and cleaned, mechanical equipment works longer, more efficiently, and develops fewer problems. Here are a few suggestions for dealing with plotters and plotter supplies.

✓ Keep the plotter clean. Purchase a plastic or cloth dust cover if possible. Dust or vacuum it regularly. Clean the grip wheels with a stiff bristle brush (usually provided by manufacturer). Use pressurized air to clean internal parts.

✓ Service as soon as problems develop.

✓ Lock wheels on plotters that roll.

✓ Locate plotters out of high traffic areas. A separate room is best.

✓ Properly instruct all plotter users on machine operation.

✓ Have regular plotter operation update sessions.

✓ Assign people on a rotating basis to regularly clean the plotter and plotting center, if a specific person is not in charge of plotting duties.

✓ Keep plotter supplies, paper, pens, attachments, in a storage area near the plotter.

✓ Adjust the humidity of the plotter room to suit the media used, or purchase plotter media that works best in the temperature and humidity of the plotter room.

✓ Avoid using wrinkled or creased paper or film in the plotter.

## CHAPTER TEST

*Write your answers in the spaces provided.*

1. What command is used to generate paper copies of your drawings? _____

2. What **CMDDIA** value is needed to issue plot prompts at the **Command:** line? _____

3. List the different displays of a drawing you can select to plot using the **Plot Configuration** dialog box. _____

4. Define a "plot file" and explain how it is used. _____

5. Define a "plot queue." _____

6. Explain when you would rotate a plot 90° clockwise. _____

7. What do you enter in the dialog box to make the plotted drawing twice the size of the soft copy drawing? _____

8. What do you enter to specify a scale of 1/4″ = 1′-0″? _____

9. Name the system variable that controls the display of the **Plot Configuration** dialog box. _____

10. How do you stop a plot in progress? _____

11. Name the pull-down menu where the **Print...** command is found. _____

12. How do you add several printers or plotters to the **Select Device** area of the **Device and Default Selection** dialog box? _____

13. What is a PCP file? _____

14. How do you save a plot file named PLOT1 to your floppy disk? _____

15. How do you set pen assignments in a dialog box? _____

16. Identify the two types of paper orientation. _____

17. Specify the option button that is picked to make millimeters the units for all plot specifications. _____

_____

18. List an advantage of the **Partial plot preview** format. _____

19. Enter the rotation indicated when each of the following rotation icons appears in the partial plot preview.

Image outline

Rotation icon

A. _____     B. _____     C. _____     D. _____

20. Cite at least two advantages of the **Full plot preview** format. _____

_____

_____

21. Identify at least one disadvantage of the **Full plot preview** format. _____

_____

22. Enter the name of symbols below that are used in the **Pan and Zoom** application of the **Full plot preview** format.

A. _____          B. _____

23. Explain the function of the **Pan** and **Zoom** boxes in the **Full plot preview** format. _____

_____

_____

_____

_____

24. Explain why you should plan your plots. _____

_____

_____

25. Provide the best method to speed up the plotting process in a classroom or company.

_____

_____

26. Quick, check prints are best generated on a(n) _____.

27. What type of paper and pens should be used for a check plot?_____

_____

28. What type of paper and pens should be used for a final plot?_____

_____


_____

## DRAWING PROBLEMS

1. Open one of your drawings from an earlier chapter. Print it on your printer.

   *General*

2. Use the same drawing from Problem 1 and generate two plots on your printer. The first should be rotated 90° and the second plot should not be rotated.

   *General*

3. Open one of your dimensioned drawings from a previous chapter. Use the **PLOT** command to generate a B-size half-scale drawing of the limits. Use **MVIEW** to create viewports. Set zoom magnification appropriately.

   *Mechanical Drafting*

4. Plot the drawing used in Problem 3 on appropriate size paper to give you a full-scale plot.

   *Mechanical Drafting*

5. Plot the same drawing used in Problem 3 on B-size paper, but with a scale that will fit the entire drawing on the paper. Add a title block and border to the drawing before making the plots.

   *Mechanical Drafting*

6. Open one of your drawings from Chapter 11. Plot the drawing on B-size paper using the **Limits** option. Use different color pens for each color in the drawing.

   *General*

7. Zoom in on a portion of the drawing in Problem 6 and select the **Display** option. Rotate the plot 90° and fit it on the paper.

   *General*

8. Using the same drawing from Problem 6, first be sure the entire drawing is displayed on the screen. Select **PLOT** and use the **Window** option. Then, window a detailed area of the drawing. Plot the drawing to fit the paper size chosen.

   *General*

9. Plot a title block and border on a C-size sheet of paper. Put the name PLOT TEST next to Drawing Name: in the title block. Next, plot six different views of a drawing from any previous chapter on a separate area of the paper. Use the following guidelines.

   *Mechanical Drafting*

   A. Determine the overall dimensions of the object before you plot.

   B. Determine the amount of paper space available for each object.

   C. Set the appropriate scale for each object so that it does not extend beyond the amount of space allotted to it.

   D. Use the appropriate plot format, such as **Display**, **View**, or **Window**.

   E. Be sure to change the plot origin before plotting each object.

General

10. Open your most detailed, dimensioned drawing. Generate a final plot with wet ink pens.

A. Display the entire drawing on the screen.

B. Load vellum or polyester film into the plotter.

C. Insert wet ink pens into the pen holder or carousel. Use different pen widths if available.

D. If you constructed the drawing on different layers, choose different color pens for each layer.

E. Set pen speeds to achieve good quality lines. See the manufacturer's specifications for your particular brand of pen.

F. Plot the drawing using the **Limits** or **Extents** option.

AutoCAD R13

## Chapter 13

# Basic Editing Commands

## Learning objectives

After completing this chapter, you will be able to:

○ Draw chamfers and angled corners with the **CHAMFER** command.
○ Use the **FILLET** command to draw fillets, rounds, and other rounded corners.
○ Preset chamfer and fillet specifications.
○ Remove a portion of a line, circle, or arc using the **BREAK** command.
○ Relocate an object using the **MOVE** command.
○ Use the **TRIM**, **EXTEND**, and **LENGTHEN** commands to edit an object.
○ Use the **CHANGE** command to revise an existing object.
○ Make single and multiple copies of existing objects using the **COPY** command.
○ Draw a mirror image of an object.
○ Change the angular position of an object using the **ROTATE** command.
○ Use the **ALIGN** command to move and rotate an object simultaneously.
○ Enlarge or reduce the size of an object using the **SCALE** command.
○ Change the length and height of an object using the **STRETCH** command.
○ Set the **PICKAUTO**, **PICKFIRST**, and **GRIPS** system variables to vary selection techniques.
○ Use the geometry calculator to edit drawings.
○ Create selection sets and object groups.

This chapter explains commands and methods for changing a drawing. With manual drafting techniques, editing and modifying a drawing can take hours or even days. AutoCAD, however, makes the same editing tasks simpler and quicker. In Chapter 6 you learned how to draw and erase lines. The **ERASE** command is one of the most commonly used editing commands. You also learned how to select objects by picking with the cursor or using a window box, crossing box, or fence. The items selected are referred to as a *selection set*.

Many of the same selection methods and techniques can be used for the editing commands given in this chapter. You will learn how to draw angled and rounded corners. You will also learn how to move, copy, rotate, scale, or create a mirror image of an existing object. These features are found in the **Construct** and **Modify** toolbars or pull-down menus. The editing commands discussed in this chapter are basically divided into two general groups—editing individual features of a drawing and editing major portions of a drawing. Commands typically used to edit individual features of a drawing are:

- **CHAMFER**
- **FILLET**
- **BREAK**

- **TRIM**
- **EXTEND**
- **LENGTHEN**

The following commands are used to edit entire drawings or major portions of a drawing, though they can be used to edit individual features:

- **MOVE**
- **COPY**
- **ROTATE**
- **MIRROR**
- **SCALE**
- **STRETCH**
- **CHANGE**
- **GROUP**

## DRAWING CHAMFERS

AUG 5

A *chamfer* in mechanical drafting is a small angled surface used to relieve a sharp corner. AutoCAD defines a chamfer as "any angled corner on the drawing." The size of a chamfer is determined by its distance from the corner. A 45° chamfer is the same distance from the corner in each direction, Figure 13-1.

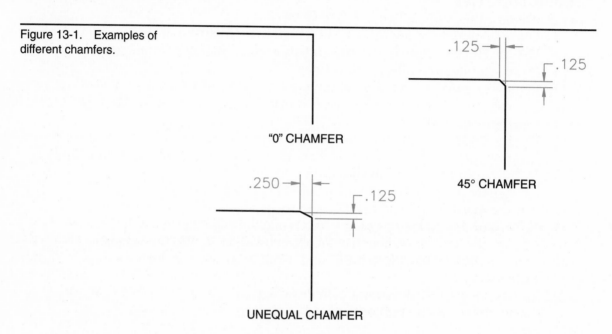

Figure 13-1. Examples of different chamfers.

"0" CHAMFER

.125 .125

45° CHAMFER

.250 .125

UNEQUAL CHAMFER

Chamfers are drawn between two lines that may, or may not, intersect. They are also used on polylines, xlines, and rays. The **CHAMFER** command can be accessed by selecting the **Chamfer** button in the **Chamfer** flyout on the **Modify** toolbar or by typing CHAMFER at the **Command:** prompt. If the ACADFULL menu file is loaded, the **CHAMFER** command can also be accessed by picking **Chamfer** from the **Construct** pull-down menu. The following shows the default values and the options that are available when you enter the **CHAMFER** command:

Command: **CHAMFER** ↵
(TRIM mode) Current chamfer Dist1 = 0.0, Dist2 = 0.0
Polyline/Distance/Angle/Trim/Method/⟨Select first line⟩:

The current settings are displayed for your reference. Chamfers are established with two distances, or a distance and angle. The default value is 0 for both distances. This produces a square corner. The following is a brief description of each **CHAMFER** option:

- **Polyline.** Use this option if you want to chamfer all of the eligible corners on a polyline. The term "eligible" means that the chamfer distance is small enough to work on the corner.
- **Distances.** This option lets you set the chamfer distance for each line from the corner.
- **Angle.** This option uses a chamfer distance on the first selected line and applies a chamfer angle to determine the second line chamfer.

- **Trim.** Enter this to set the **Trim** mode. If **Trim** is on, the selected lines are trimmed or extended as required from the corner before creating the chamfer line. If **No trim** is active, the **Trim** mode is off. In this case, the selected lines are not trimmed or extended and only the chamfer line is added.
- **Method.** This is a toggle that sets the chamfer method to either **Distances** or **Angle**. **Distance** and **Angle** values can be set without affecting each other.

### Setting the chamfer distance

The chamfer distance must be set before you can draw chamfers. The distances that you set remain in effect until changed. Most drafters set the chamfer distance as exact values, but you can also pick two points to set the distance. The chamfer distance is set like this:

Command: **CHAMFER** ↵
(TRIM mode) Current chamfer Dist1 = 0.0, Dist2 = 0.0
Polyline/Distance/Angle/Trim/Method/⟨Select first line⟩: **D** ↵
Enter first chamfer distance ⟨0⟩: *(specify a distance, such as .25)*
Enter second chamfer distance ⟨0.25⟩: *(press [Enter] for the current distance, or type a new value)*
Command:

Now you are ready to draw chamfers. Enter the **CHAMFER** command and select the first and second lines:

Command: **CHAMFER** ↵
(TRIM mode) Current chamfer Dist1 = 0.25, Dist2 = 0.25
Polyline/Distance/Angle/Trim/Method/⟨Select first line⟩: *(pick the first line)*
Select second line: *(pick the second line)*

After the lines are picked, AutoCAD automatically chamfers the corner. Objects can be chamfered even when the corners do not meet. AutoCAD will extend the lines as required to generate the specified chamfer unless **TRIMMODE** is off. This is discussed later. If the specified chamfer distance for an object is great enough to make the chamfered object disappear, AutoCAD will not perform the chamfer. Instead, a message such as **2 lines were too short** is given. If you want to chamfer additional corners, press [Enter] to repeat the **CHAMFER** command. The results of several chamfering operations are shown in Figure 13-2.

Figure 13-2.   Using the **CHAMFER** command.

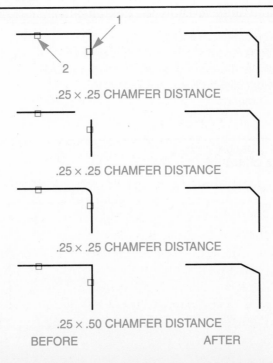

.25 × .25 CHAMFER DISTANCE

.25 × .25 CHAMFER DISTANCE

.25 × .25 CHAMFER DISTANCE

.25 × .50 CHAMFER DISTANCE

BEFORE                AFTER

## Chamfering the corners of a polyline

All corners of a closed polyline can be chamfered at one time. Enter the **CHAMFER** command, select the **Polyline** option, and then select the polyline. The corners of the polyline are chamfered to the distance values set. If the polyline was drawn without using the **Close** option, the beginning corner is not chamfered, Figure 13-3.

```
Command: CHAMFER ↵
Polyline/Distance/Angle/Trim/Method/⟨Select first line⟩: P ↵
Select 2D polyline: (pick the polyline)
Command:
```

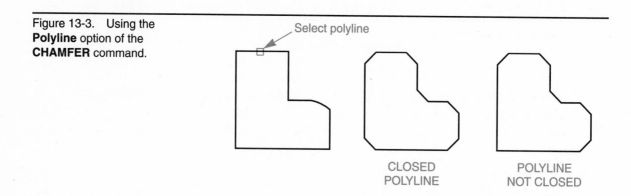

Figure 13-3.   Using the **Polyline** option of the **CHAMFER** command.

Select polyline

CLOSED POLYLINE

POLYLINE NOT CLOSED

## Setting the chamfer angle

Instead of setting two chamfer distances, you can set the chamfer distance for one line and an angle to determine the chamfer to the second line. To do this, use the **Angle** option:

```
Command: CHAMFER ↵
Polyline/Distance/Angle/Trim/Method/⟨Select first line⟩: A ↵
Enter chamfer length on the first line ⟨0⟩: (enter a chamfer distance, .5 for example)
Enter chamfer angle from the first line ⟨0⟩: (enter an angle, 45 for example)
Command:
```

Now, you are ready to enter the **CHAMFER** command again and draw a chamfer with the **Angle** option, as shown in Figure 13-4. You can see in the following command sequence that distance and angle are now the defaults:

```
Command: CHAMFER↵
(TRIM mode) Current chamfer Length = 0.5, Angle = 45.0
Polyline/Distance/Angle/Trim/Method/⟨Select first line⟩: (pick line 1)
Select second line: (pick line 2)
Command:
```

Figure 13-4.   Using the **Angle** option of the **CHAMFER** command.

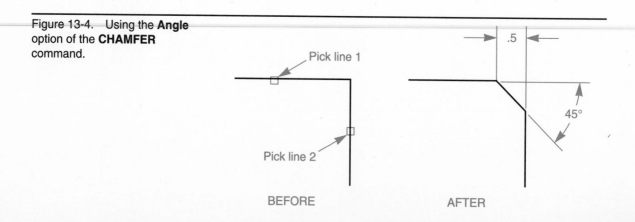

Pick line 1

Pick line 2

BEFORE

.5

45°

AFTER

## Setting the chamfer method

When you set the chamfer distances using the **Distance** option or set the distance and angle using the **Angle** option, AutoCAD keeps the setting until you change it. You can set the values for each method without affecting each other. Use the **Method** option if you want to toggle between drawing chamfers by **Distance** or by **Angle**. The default option contains the values that you previously set:

> Command: **CHAMFER** ↵
> (TRIM mode) Current chamfer Length = 0.5, Angle = 45.0
> Polyline/Distance/Angle/Trim/Method/⟨Select first line⟩: **M** ↵
> Distance/Angle ⟨Angle⟩: **D** ↵
> Polyline/Distance/Angle/Trim/Method/⟨Select first line⟩: *(pick line 1)*
> Select second line: *(pick line 2)*
> Command:

## Setting the chamfer Trim mode

You can have the selected lines automatically trimmed with the chamfer, or you can have the selected lines remain in the drawing after the chamfer, as shown in Figure 13-5. To use this, enter the **Trim** option and then select either T for **Trim** or N for **No trim**:

> Command: **CHAMFER** ↵
> Polyline/Distance/Angle/Trim/Method/⟨Select first line⟩: **T** ↵
> Trim/No trim ⟨Trim⟩: **N** ↵
> Polyline/Distance/Angle/Trim/Method/⟨Select first line⟩: *(pick line 1)*
> Select second line: *(pick line 2)*
> Command:

Figure 13-5. Using the **Trim** option of the **CHAMFER** command. A—With trim. B—With no trim. C—The result when the lines do not extend to the corners.

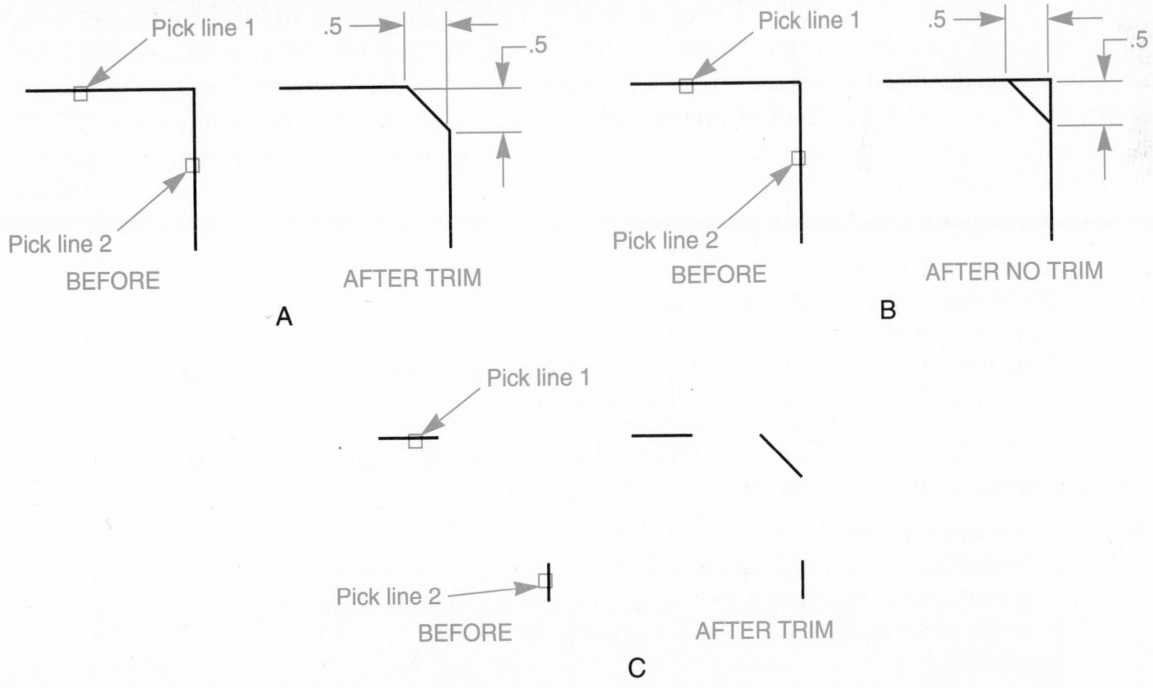

You can also use the **TRIMMODE** system variable to set **Trim** or **No trim**. A 1 setting trims the lines before chamfering, while a 0 setting does not trim the lines:

Command: **TRIMMODE** ↵
New value for TRIMMODE ⟨1⟩: **0** ↵
Command:

---

NOTE The **TRIMMODE** system variable affects the **FILLET** command in the same way as the **CHAMFER** command. The **FILLET** command is discussed next. If the **Polyline** option is used with the **No trim** mode active, any chamfer lines created are not part of the polyline.

---

PROFESSIONAL TIP

When the **CHAMFER** or **FILLET** command is set to **Trim**, lines that do not connect at a corner are automatically extended and the chamfer or fillet is applied. However, when the **No trim** option is used, these lines are not extended, but the chamfer or fillet is drawn anyway. If you have lines that are drawn short of a corner and want them to connect to the chamfer or fillet, you need to extend them before or after you draw in the **No trim** mode.

---

# DRAWING ROUNDED CORNERS                    AUG 5

In mechanical drafting, an inside rounded corner is called a *fillet*. An outside rounded corner is called a *round*. AutoCAD refers to all rounded corners as fillets. The **FILLET** command draws a rounded corner between intersecting and nonintersecting lines, circles, and arcs. To access the **FILLET** command, pick the **Fillet** button in the **Chamfer** flyout on the **Modify** toolbar or enter FILLET at the **Command:** prompt. If the ACADFULL menu file is loaded, the command can also be accessed by selecting **Fillet** from the **Construct** pull-down menu. Fillets are sized by radius. The radius is specified first by typing R on the prompt line for the **Radius** option of the **FILLET** command as follows:

Command: **FILLET** ↵
(TRIM mode) Current fillet radius = 0
Polyline/Radius/Trim/⟨Select first object⟩: **R** ↵
Enter fillet radius ⟨current⟩: *(type the fillet radius, .25 for example, and press* [Enter],
    *or press* [Enter] *to accept the current value)*

Once the fillet radius has been given, repeat the **FILLET** command to fillet the objects. The command sequence shown in Figure 13-6 is as follows:

Command: **FILLET** ↵
(TRIM mode) Current fillet radius = 0.25
Polyline/Radius/Trim/⟨Select first object⟩: *(pick the first object to be filleted)*
Select second object: *(pick the other object to be filleted)*
Command:

Figure 13-6. Using the
**FILLET** command.

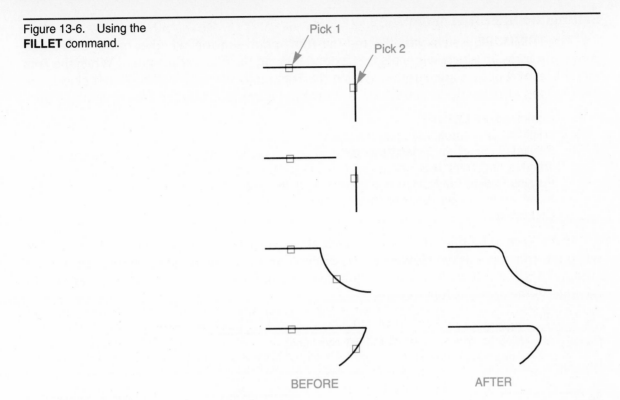

## Rounding the corners of a polyline

Fillets can be drawn at all corners of a closed polyline by selecting the **Polyline** option. The current fillet radius is used with this option. The command sequence shown in Figure 13-7 is as follows:

    Command: **FILLET** ↵
    (TRIM mode) Current fillet radius = 0.25
    Polyline/Radius/Trim/⟨Select first object⟩: **P** ↵
    Select 2D polyline: *(pick the polyline)*
    *n* lines were filleted
    Command:

AutoCAD tells you how many lines were filleted. Then the **Command:** prompt returns. If the polyline was drawn without using the **Close** option, the beginning corner is not filleted.

Figure 13-7. Using the
**Polyline** option of the **FILLET**
command.

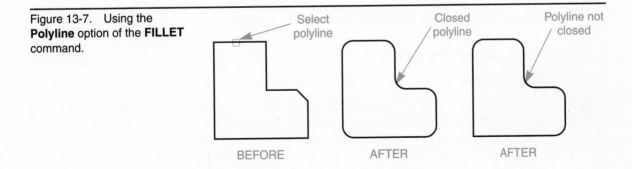

## Setting the fillet Trim mode

The **TRIMMODE** system variable and the **Trim** option controls whether or not the **FILLET** command trims off object segments that extend beyond the fillet radius point. When the **Trim** mode is active, objects are trimmed. When the **Trim** mode is inactive, the filleted objects are not changed after the fillet is inserted, as shown in Figure 13-8. Use the **Trim** option like this:

Command: **FILLET** ↵
(TRIM mode) Current fillet radius = 0.25
Polyline/Radius/Trim/⟨Select first object⟩: **T** ↵
Trim/No trim ⟨Trim⟩: **N** ↵
Polyline/Radius/Trim/⟨Select first object⟩: *(pick the first object)*
Select second object: *(pick the second object)*
Command:

If the lines to be filleted do not connect at the corner, they are automatically extended when the **Trim** mode is on. However, they are not extended when using **No trim**. The results are similar to the bottom example in Figure 13-5. If you do not want these results, then extend the lines to the corner before filleting.

Figure 13-8. Using the **Trim** option of the **FILLET** command.

Pick line 1
Pick line 2
Before                After
TRIM ACTIVE

Pick line 1
Pick line 2
Before                After
TRIM INACTIVE

## Filleting parallel lines

You can also draw a fillet between parallel lines. When parallel lines are selected, a radius is placed between the two lines. If one of the parallel lines is longer than the other, the longer line is trimmed to match the length of the shorter line with **Trim** mode on. The radius of a fillet between parallel lines is always half of the distance between the two lines, regardless of the **FILLETRAD** setting. The **FILLETRAD** setting does not change to this radius.

**PROFESSIONAL TIP**

Press [Enter] or the space bar to automatically return the **FILLET** or **CHAMFER** command after the settings are made. This saves you the time of retyping or repicking the command.

## Chamfering and filleting line and polyline objects together

In Figure 13-2 and Figure 13-6 you saw that line objects, such as lines and arcs, are chamfered or filleted at the corner where they meet. These line objects are automatically extended and chamfered if they do not meet. This also happens when a combination of line objects and polyline objects are chamfered or filleted. For example, if you have a line and a polyline that either meet or do not meet, you can draw a chamfer or fillet between them with the **CHAMFER** or **FILLET** command. When you do this, the line is automatically joined with the polyline. The result is a single polyline. This is only true when **TRIMMODE** is 1. When **TRIMMODE** is 0, neither object is affected.

## Presetting the chamfer distance and the fillet radius

AutoCAD lets you set the chamfer distance and fillet radius to a designated value. This saves time when the chamfer distance and fillet radius remains constant on your drawing. To do this, use the **CHAMFERA**, **CHAMFERB**, and **FILLETRAD** system variables. You can preset the chamfer distances to different or equal values. For example, if you want .125 for both chamfer distances, type the following:

> Command: **CHAMFERA** ⏎
> New value for CHAMFERA ⟨*current*⟩: **.125** ⏎
> Command: **CHAMFERB** ⏎
> New value for CHAMFERB ⟨*current*⟩: **.125** ⏎
> Command:

Now, enter **CHAMFER** at the **Command:** prompt and the preset values are automatically issued. The command sequence looks like this:

> Command: **CHAMFER** ⏎
> (TRIM mode) Current chamfer Dist1 = 0.125,Dist2 = 0.125
> Polyline/Distance/⟨Select first line⟩: *(pick the first line)*
> Select second line: *(pick the second line)*
> Command:

When presetting the fillet radius, first enter **FILLETRAD** at the **Command:** prompt. You are then asked to enter a new value. For example, if you want .25 radius, type the following:

> Command: **FILLETRAD** ⏎
> New value for FILLETRAD ⟨*current*⟩: **.25** ⏎
> Command:

To use the preset value, enter the **FILLET** command. The preset radius for the fillet is automatically issued. The command sequence looks like this:

> Command: **FILLET** ⏎
> (TRIM mode) Current fillet radius = 0.25
> Polyline/Radius/⟨Select first object⟩: *(pick the first object)*
> Select second object: *(pick the second object)*
> Command:

**PROFESSIONAL TIP**

Using the **FILLET** or **CHAMFER** command with a 0 fillet radius or 0 chamfer distances is a quick and convenient way to create square corners.

**EXERCISE 13-1**

❑ Load AutoCAD for Windows and open TITLEB.
❑ Draw two 4 × 2 rectangles using the **LINE** command. Use the **CHAMFER** command on the first rectangle to chamfer two corners a distance of .125 with the **Trim** mode on. Chamfer the other corners a distance of .25 with no trim. Use the **FILLET** command on the second rectangle to round two corners at a .125 radius with the **Trim** mode on. Round the other corners at a .25 radius with no trim.
❑ Draw two more 4 × 2 rectangles using the **PLINE** command. Use the **Close** option on one but *not* on the other. Use the **CHAMFER** command on the first rectangle to chamfer all corners a distance of .25. Use the **FILLET** command on the second rectangle to round all corners at .25 radius. Set **Trim** mode on for both drawings. Observe what happens on the polyline rectangle that was drawn without using the **Close** option.
❑ Save the drawing as A:EX13-1 and quit.

**PROFESSIONAL TIP**

While the previous chamfer and fillet examples were for mechanical applications, the **CHAMFER** and **FILLET** commands can be used in any drafting field. For example, angled or rounded corners are frequently used in architectural drafting. If you are working in architectural drafting at a scale of 1/4" = 1'-0", be sure to set the chamfer or fillet distances in feet and/or inches accordingly.

## REMOVING A SECTION FROM AN OBJECT                    AUG 5

The **BREAK** command is used to remove a portion of a line, circle, arc, trace, or polyline. If the ACADFULL menu file is loaded, the **BREAK** command can be accessed from the **Modify** pull-down menu. When you pick **Break**, a cascading submenu appears, displaying four options. These four options are also toolbar buttons in the **1 Point** flyout on the **Modify** toolbar. The options **1 Point**, **1 Point Select**, **2 Points**, and **2 Points Select** are explained as follows:

* **1 Point.** This is used to split an object in two without removing a portion. For example, if you pick a line with this option, the line becomes two lines. Both lines have one endpoint at the break point. The prompt line looks like this:

    Command: _break Select object: *(pick the desired point on the object)*
    Enter second point (or F for first point): @
    Command:

    Notice the @ symbol is automatically entered at the end of the second prompt. This means that the second break point is exactly where you picked the first break point. You can also do this manually by entering an @ symbol at the second prompt when typing the command.

* **1 Point Select.** This option asks you for a new first point after you select the object to break, then automatically picks the second point at the same location as your first point:

    Command: _break Select object: *(pick the object)*
    Enter second point (or F for first point): _f
    Enter first point: *(pick the first break point)*
    Enter second point: @
    Command:

- **2 Points.** This option gives you prompts as if you entered the command from the **Command:** prompt. Refer to the next section for a detailed discussion on manually entering the **BREAK** command.
- **2 Point Select.** This option automatically asks you for a first point after you select the object. You are then asked for a second point after you pick the first point:

> Command: _break Select object: *(pick the object)*
> Enter second point (or F for first point): _f
> Enter first point: *(pick the first break point)*
> Enter second point: *(pick the second break point)*
> Command:

## Using the BREAK command from the Command: prompt

When you issue the **BREAK** command by entering BREAK at the **Command:** prompt, AutoCAD asks you to first select the object, then pick break points as follows:

> Command: **BREAK** ↵
> Select object: *(pick the line, circle, or arc to be broken. If a pick point is used rather than a window, that point becomes the first break point.)*

If the object you pick is a line, the pick point is your first break point. You are then asked for the second break point:

> Enter second point (or F for first point): *(pick the second point, or type **F** and press [Enter] for another first point option)*

If you pick a second break point, the line is broken between the two points, Figure 13-9. You can also type F to specify a new first point:

> Enter second point (or F for first point): **F** ↵
> Enter first point: *(pick a new first point)*
> Enter second point: *(pick the second point)*
> Command:

---

Figure 13-9.  Using the **BREAK** command.

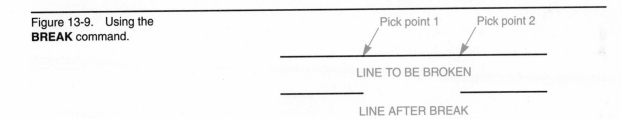

When breaking arcs or circles, always work in a counterclockwise direction. Otherwise, you may break the portion of the arc or circle that you want to keep. If you want to break off the end of a line or arc, pick the first point on the object. Then pick the second point slightly beyond the end to be cut off, Figure 13-10. When you pick a second point that is not on the object, AutoCAD selects the nearest point on the object to the point you picked.

If you want to break a line from the point of intersection with another line, use the object snap **Intersect** mode as follows:

> Command: **BREAK** ↵
> Select object: *(pick the line)*
> Enter second point (or F for first point): **INT** ↵
> of *(move the aperture to the intersection and pick)*
> Command:

The line is now broken between the first point and the point of intersection.

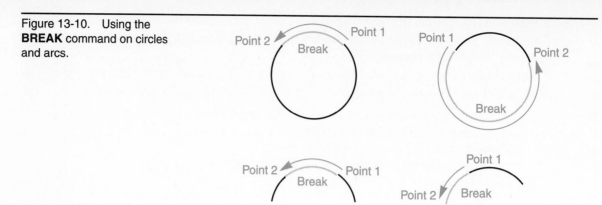

Figure 13-10. Using the **BREAK** command on circles and arcs.

## TRIMMING SECTIONS OF A LINE, CIRCLE, OR ARC | AUG 5

The **TRIM** command cuts off lines, polylines, circles, arcs, ellipses, splines, xlines, or rays that extend beyond a desired point of intersection. To access the **TRIM** command, pick the **Trim** button in the **Modify** toolbar or enter TRIM at the **Command:** prompt. If the ACADFULL menu file is loaded, it can also be accessed by selecting **Trim** from the **Modify** pull-down menu.

The command requires that you pick a "cutting edge" and the object(s) to trim. The *cutting edge* can be an object that defines the point where the object you are trimming will be cut. A cutting edge can be an object such as a line, arc, or text. If two corners of an object overrun, select two cutting edges and two objects. Refer to Figure 13-11 as you go through the following sequence:

Command: **TRIM** ↵
Select cutting edges: (Projmode = UCS, Edgemode = No extend)
Select objects: *(pick first cutting edge)*
Select objects: *(pick second cutting edge)*
Select objects: ↵
⟨Select object to trim⟩/Project/Edge/Undo: *(pick the first object to trim)*
⟨Select object to trim⟩/Project/Edge/Undo: *(pick the second object to trim)*
⟨Select object to trim⟩/Project/Edge/Undo: ↵
Command:

Figure 13-11. Using the **TRIM** command. Note the cutting edges.

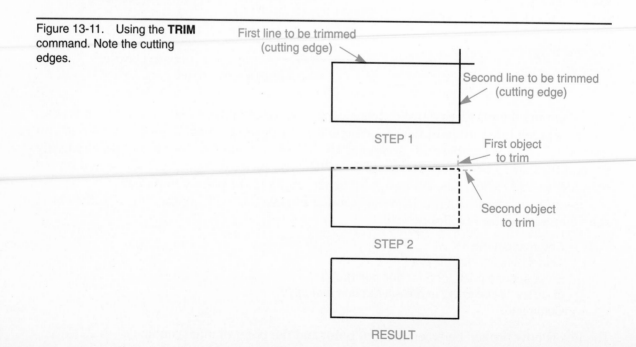

## Trimming to an implied intersection

An *implied intersection* is where two or more objects will meet if extended. Trimming to an implied intersection is possible using the **Edge** option of the **TRIM** command. When you enter the **Edge** option, the choices are **Extend** and **No extend**. When **Extend** is active, AutoCAD checks to see if the cutting edge object will extend to intersect the object to be trimmed. If so, the implied intersection point can be used to trim the object. This does not change the cutting edge object at all. The command sequence for the **TRIM** operation shown in Figure 13-12 is as follows:

```
Command: TRIM ↵
Select cutting edges: (Projmode = UCS, Edgemode = No extend)
Select objects: (pick the first cutting edge)
Select objects: (pick the second cutting edge)
Select objects: ↵
⟨Select object to trim⟩/Project/Edge/Undo: E ↵
Extend/No extend ⟨No extend⟩: E ↵
⟨Select object to trim⟩/Project/Edge/Undo: (pick the object to trim)
⟨Select object to trim⟩/Project/Edge/Undo: ↵
Command:
```

The **Edge** option can also be set using the **EDGEMODE** system variable. **Extend** is active when the **EDGEMODE** is 1. With this setting, the cutting edge object is checked to see if it will extend to intersect the object to be trimmed.

```
Command: EDGEMODE ↵
New value for EDGEMODE ⟨0⟩: 1 ↵
```

Figure 13-12. Trimming to an implied intersection.

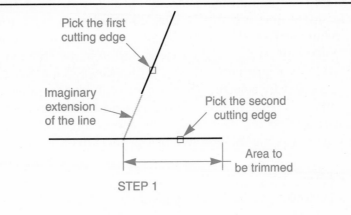

Pick the first cutting edge

Imaginary extension of the line

Pick the second cutting edge

Area to be trimmed

STEP 1

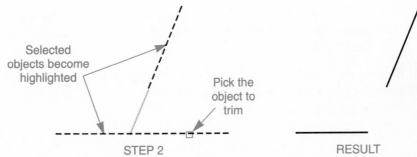

Selected objects become highlighted

Pick the object to trim

STEP 2

RESULT

## Using the Undo option

The **TRIM** command has an **Undo** option that allows you to reverse the previous **TRIM** without leaving the command. This is useful when the result of a trim is not what you expected. To undo the previous trim and try another trim, use the following procedure:

Command: **TRIM** ↵
Select cutting edges: (Projmode = UCS, Edgemode = No extend)
Select objects: *(pick the first cutting edge)*
Select objects: *(pick the second cutting edge)*
Select objects: ↵
⟨Select object to trim⟩/Project/Edge/Undo: *(pick the object to trim)*
⟨Select object to trim⟩/Project/Edge/Undo: **U** ↵
Command has been completely undone.
⟨Select object to trim⟩/Project/Edge/Undo: *(pick the object to trim)*
⟨Select object to trim⟩/Project/Edge/Undo: ↵
Command:

## An introduction to the Project mode

In a 3D drawing environment, some lines may appear to intersect in a given view, but may not actually intersect. In such a case, using the **Project** option of the **TRIM** command can allow trimming operations. This option is also controlled by the **PROJMODE** system variable. Using AutoCAD for 3D drawing is explained in *AutoCAD and its Applications—Advanced, Release 13 for Windows*.

## EXTENDING LINES

$\boxed{\text{AUG 5}}$

The **EXTEND** command can be considered the opposite of **TRIM**. The **EXTEND** command is used to lengthen lines, open polylines, elliptical arcs, rays, or arcs to meet other objects. **EXTEND** will not work on closed polylines since an unconnected endpoint does not exist. To use the **EXTEND** command, pick the **Extend** button in the **Trim** flyout on the **Modify** toolbar or enter EXTEND at the **Command:** prompt. If the ACADFULL menu file is loaded, the command can also be accessed by selecting **Extend** from the **Modify** pull-down menu. The command format is similar to **TRIM**. You are asked to select boundary edges, as opposed to cutting edges. *Boundary edges* are objects that the chosen objects extend to, such as lines, arcs, or text. The command sequence is shown below and illustrated in Figure 13-13:

Command: **EXTEND** ↵
Select cutting edges: (Projmode = UCS, Edgemode = No extend)
Select objects: *(pick the boundary edge)*
Select objects: ↵
⟨Select object to extend⟩/Project/Edge/Undo: *(pick the object to extend)*
⟨Select object to trim⟩/Project/Edge/Undo: ↵
Command:

If there is nothing for the selected line to meet, AutoCAD gives the message No edge in that direction or Entity does not intersect an edge.

Figure 13-13. Using the **EXTEND** command. Note the boundary edges.

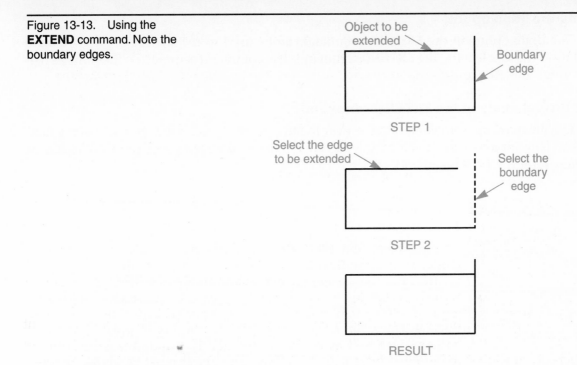

Object to be extended

Boundary edge

STEP 1

Select the edge to be extended

Select the boundary edge

STEP 2

RESULT

## Extending to an implied intersection

You can extend an object to an implied intersection using the **Edge** option in the **EXTEND** command. When you enter the **Edge** option, the choices are **Extend** and **No extend**, just as with the **TRIM** command. When **Extend** is active, the boundary edge object is checked to see if it intersects when extended. If so, the implied intersection point can be used as the boundary for the object to be extended, as shown in Figure 13-14. This does not change the boundary edge object at all.

    Command: **EXTEND** ↵
    Select boundary edges: (Projmode = UCS, Edgemode = No extend)
    Select objects: *(pick the boundary edge)*
    Select objects: ↵
    〈Select object to extend〉/Project/Edge/Undo: **E** ↵
    Extend/No extend 〈No extend〉: **E** ↵
    〈Select object to extend〉/Project/Edge/Undo: *(pick the object to extend)*
    〈Select object to extend〉/Project/Edge/Undo: ↵
    Command:

The **Edge** option can also be set using the **EDGEMODE** as previously discussed with the **TRIM** command.

Figure 13-14. Extending to an implied intersection.

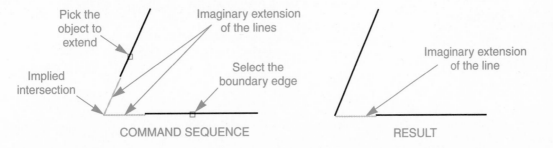

Pick the object to extend

Imaginary extension of the lines

Implied intersection

Select the boundary edge

Imaginary extension of the line

COMMAND SEQUENCE

RESULT

### Using the Undo option

The **Undo** option in the **EXTEND** command can be used to reverse the previous **Extend** operation without leaving the **EXTEND** command. The command sequence is the same as discussed for the **TRIM** command.

### The Project mode of the EXTEND command

In a 3D drawing, some lines may appear to intersect in a given view, but may not actually be able to intersect. In such a case, you can use the **Project** option or the **PROJMODE** as explained for the **TRIM** command.

**PROFESSIONAL TIP**

The **TRIM** and **EXTEND** commands have a convenient **Smart** mode. To use the **Smart** mode, press [Enter] rather than selecting a cutting or boundary edge. Then, when an object to trim or extend is picked, AutoCAD searches for the nearest intersecting object or implied intersection in the direction of your pick, depending on the **EDGEMODE** setting. AutoCAD then uses this object as the cutting or boundary edge. If an actual intersection is found, it is used even if the implied intersection is closer. The object must be visible on the screen, and cannot be a block or xref object. Also, trimming can be done between two actual or implied intersections, but not between a combination of one actual and one implied intersection.

## CHANGING LINES AND CIRCLES

The endpoint location of a line or the radius of a circle can be altered using the **CHANGE** command. The endpoint of one or more lines can be moved by picking a new point. This new point is called the *change point*. For example, suppose a corner where two lines meet is not correct. To access the **CHANGE** command, pick the **Point** button in the **Stretch** flyout on the **Modify** toolbar or type CHANGE at the **Command:** prompt. If the ACADFULL menu file is loaded, the command can also be accessed by picking **Point** from the **Modify** pull-down menu. You are then prompted to select the objects to change. Pick the two lines and press [Enter]. At the Properties/⟨Change point⟩: prompt, pick the new point or enter a coordinate. AutoCAD automatically relocates the endpoints of the selected lines, as shown in Figure 13-15. The command sequence is as follows:

```
Command: CHANGE ⏎
Select objects: (pick the lines individually or with a crossing box)
Select objects: ⏎
Properties/⟨Change point⟩: (pick the new point)
Command:
```

Figure 13-15.  Using the **CHANGE** command to relocate a corner.

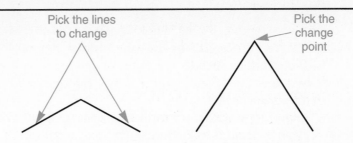

Pick the lines to change

Pick the change point

**NOTE:** If **ORTHO** is on for the **Change point** operation shown in Figure 13-15, the lines will be disconnected and extended parallel to each other up to the new point.

The **CHANGE** command can also be used to revise the radius of a circle. You can pick a change point that the new circle is to be drawn through, or a new circle radius can be specified, Figure 13-16. The command sequence is as follows:

Command: **CHANGE** ↵
Select objects: *(pick the circle to change)*
Select objects: ↵
Properties/⟨Change point⟩: *(pick a change point through which the new circle is to be drawn or press* [Enter] *to specify a new radius)*
Enter circle radius: *(enter a radius value and press* [Enter])
Command:

Using the **CHANGE** command to move text is discussed in Chapter 11. Changing common properties such as layer, linetype, and color is explained in Chapter 19. The 3D applications are discussed in *AutoCAD and its Applications—Advanced, Release 13 for Windows.*

Figure 13-16.  Using the **CHANGE** command to revise the radius of a circle.

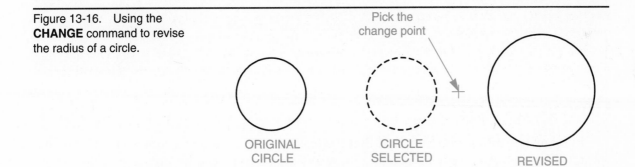

Pick the change point

ORIGINAL CIRCLE

CIRCLE SELECTED

REVISED CIRCLE

## EXERCISE 13-2

❏ Make a drawing similar to the one shown below. Perform the **BREAK**, **TRIM**, and **EXTEND** operations noted.
❏ Draw two new lines meeting at a corner that is not 90°. Use the **CHANGE** command to revise the corner to 90°.
❏ Draw a new circle with a .75 radius. Use the **CHANGE** command to revise the radius to 1.00. Revise the radius again to .25.
❏ Save the drawing as A:EX13-2 and quit.

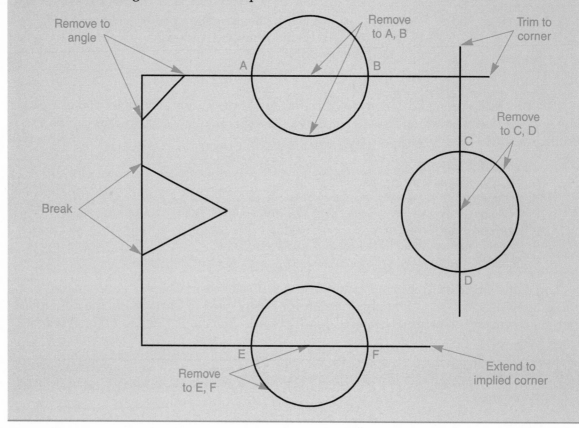

# MOVING AN OBJECT

AUG 5

   In many situations, you may find that the location of a view or feature is not where you want it. This problem is easy to fix using the **MOVE** command. You can access the **MOVE** command by clicking the **Move** button in the **Modify** toolbar or entering MOVE at the **Command:** prompt. If the ACADFULL menu file is loaded, you can also select **Move** from the **Modify** pull-down menu. After the **MOVE** command is accessed, AutoCAD asks you to select the objects to be moved. Use any of the selection set options to select the objects. Once all of the items are selected, press the [Enter] key or click the **Enter** button on your pointing device.

   The next prompt requests the base point. The *base point* is any point on or adjacent to the feature. It provides a reference point. Most drafters select a point on an object, corner of a view, or center of a circle. The next prompt asks for the second point of displacement. This is the new position. All selected entities are moved the distance from the base point to the displacement point. The following **MOVE** command relates to the object shown in Figure 13-17. As the base point is picked, the object is automatically dragged into position if the **DRAGMODE** variable is set to **Auto**.

Figure 13-17. Using the **MOVE** command. When you select the object to be moved, it becomes highlighted.

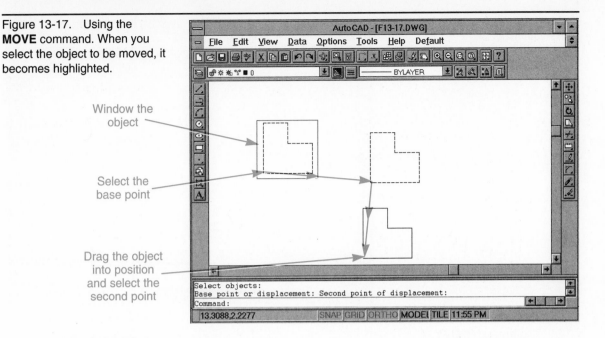

Window the object

Select the base point

Drag the object into position and select the second point

Command: **MOVE** ↵
Select objects: *(pick individual entities or window the object to be moved)*
Select objects: ↵
Base point or displacement: *(enter coordinates or pick a point on-screen)*
Second point of displacement: *(establish the new position by typing coordinates or picking a second point on-screen)*
Command:

**PROFESSIONAL TIP**

Always use object snap to your best advantage with editing commands. For example, suppose you want to move an object to the center point of a circle. Initiate the **OSNAP Center** option as follows:

Command: **MOVE** ↵
Select objects: *(select the object to be moved)*
Base point or displacement: *(pick the base point on the object)*
Second point of displacement: **CEN** ↵
of *(select an existing circle and snap to its center)*

## COPYING OBJECTS

AUG 5

The **COPY** command is used to make a copy of an existing view or object. To access the **COPY** command, enter **COPY** on the command line. It can be accessed by clicking the **Copy** button in the **Modify** toolbar, or by selecting **Copy** from the **Construct** pull-down menu if the ACADFULL menu file is loaded. The command prompts are the same as the **MOVE** command. However, when a second point of displacement is picked, the original object remains and a copy is drawn. The following command sequence is shown in Figure 13-18.

Figure 13-18.   Using the **COPY** command.

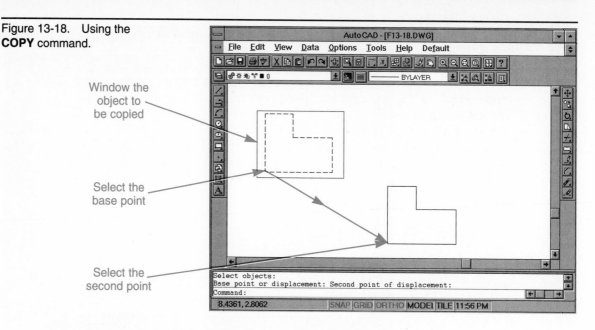

Command: **COPY** ↵
Select objects: *(pick individual entities or window the object to be copied)*
Select objects: ↵
〈Base point or displacement〉/Multiple: *(enter coordinates and press [Enter], or pick with the pointing device)*
Second point of displacement: *(establish the new position by typing coordinates and pressing [Enter], or pick a point on the screen)*
Command:

## Making multiple copies

To make several copies of the same object, select the **Multiple** option of the **COPY** command by typing M at the 〈Base point or displacement〉/Multiple: prompt. The prompt for a second point repeats. When you have made all the copies needed, press [Enter]. The command sequence is as follows. The results are shown in Figure 13-19.

Figure 13-19.   Using the **Multiple** option of the **COPY** command.

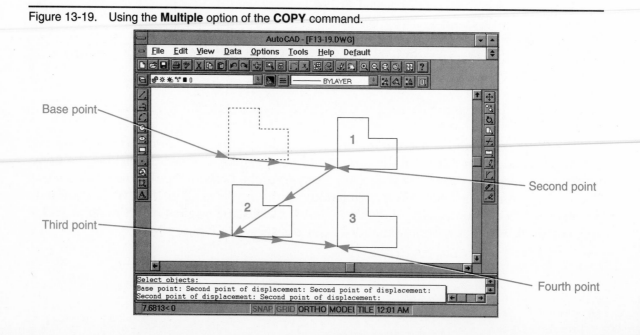

Command: **COPY** ↵
Select objects: *(pick individual entities or window the object to be copied)*
Select objects: ↵
⟨Base point or displacement⟩/Multiple: **M** ↵
Base point: *(enter coordinates and press* [Enter], *or pick a location with the pointing device)*
Second point of displacement: *(establish the new position by typing coordinates and pressing* [Enter], *or pick a location on screen)*
Second point of displacement: *(pick the second position)*
Second point of displacement: *(pick the third position)*
Second point of displacement: ↵
Command:

---

### EXERCISE 13-3

❑ Load AutoCAD for Windows and open TITLEA.
❑ Draw a square and an equilateral triangle (equal sides and angles). Use the **POLYGON** command.
❑ Move the square to a new location.
❑ Copy the triangle next to the new square position. Leave a small space between the two objects.
❑ Move all features to a new position in the upper-left corner of the screen.
❑ Make four copies of the square anywhere on the screen. The new copies should not touch other objects.
❑ Save the drawing as A:EX13-3 and quit.

## DRAWING A MIRROR IMAGE OF AN EXISTING OBJECT      AUG 5

It is often necessary to draw an object, symbol, or view in a reflected, or mirrored position. The **MIRROR** command performs this task. Mirroring an entire drawing is common in architectural drafting when a client wants a plan drawn in reverse.

The normal mirroring operation reverses everything, including words and dimensions. However, by using the system variable **MIRRTEXT**, text retains its normal position. **MIRRTEXT** is discussed later in the chapter.

### Selecting the mirror line

The *mirror line* is the hinge that objects are reflected about. Once you select objects to mirror, you must pick two points on the mirror line. The objects, plus any space between the objects and the mirror line are reflected, Figure 13-20.

---

Figure 13-20.   When an object is reflected about a mirror line, the space between the object and the mirror line is also mirrored.

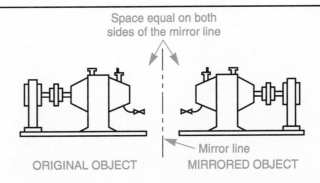

Space equal on both sides of the mirror line

ORIGINAL OBJECT

Mirror line
MIRRORED OBJECT

The mirror line can be placed at any angle. Once you pick the first endpoint, a mirrored image appears and moves with the cursor. Once you select the second mirror line endpoint, you have the option to erase the original objects. To access the **MIRROR** command, pick the **Mirror** button in the **Copy** flyout on the **Modify** toolbar or enter MIRROR on the command line. If the ACADFULL menu file is loaded, the **MIRROR** command can be accessed by selecting **Mirror** from the **Construct** pull-down menu. The command sequence shown in Figure 13-21 is as follows:

> Command: **MIRROR** ↵
> Select objects: *(use any selection method—a window is common)*
> Select objects: ↵
> First point of mirror line: *(pick the first point on the mirror line on or away from the object)*
> Second point: *(pick the second point on the mirror)*
> Delete old objects? ⟨N⟩ *(type Y and press* [Enter] *to delete the old objects, or press*
>     [Enter] *to accept the default)*
> Command:

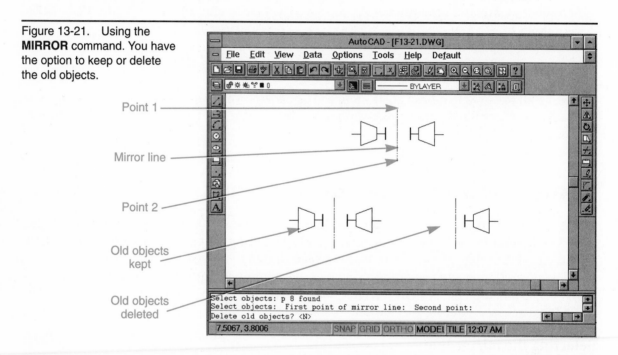

Figure 13-21.  Using the **MIRROR** command. You have the option to keep or delete the old objects.

---

**EXERCISE 13-4**

❑ Load AutoCAD for Windows and open TITLEA.
❑ Draw the half object shown below. Then, complete the entire object using the **MIRROR** command. Do not dimension.
❑ Save the drawing as A:EX13-4 and quit.

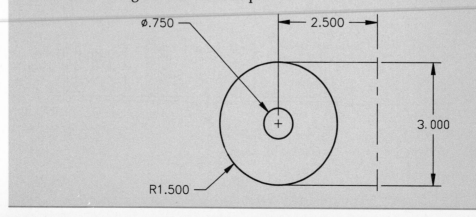

# MIRRORING TEXT

Normally, the **MIRROR** command reverses any text associated with the selected object. Backwards text is generally not acceptable. To keep the text readable, the **MIRRTEXT** system variable must be zero. There are two values for **MIRRTEXT**, Figure 13-22.

- 1 = Default value. Text is mirrored in relation to the original object.
- 0 = Prevents text from being reversed.

To draw a mirror image of an existing object, but leave the text readable, set the **MIRRTEXT** variable to 0. Then, proceed to the **MIRROR** command. The entire command sequence is as follows:

Command: **MIRRTEXT** ⏎
New value for MIRRTEXT ⟨1⟩: **0** ⏎
Command: **MIRROR** ⏎
Select objects: *(select objects to mirror)*
Select objects: ⏎
First point of mirror line: *(pick the first mirror line point)*
Second point: *(pick the second mirror line point)*
Delete old objects? ⟨N⟩ *(type Y and press [Enter], or press [Enter])*
Command:

Figure 13-22.  The **MIRRTEXT** system variable options.

Mirror line

MIRRTEXT(1)          (ꓸ)TXƎTЯЯIM

MIRRTEXT(0)          MIRRTEXT(0)

## EXERCISE 13-5

❑ Load AutoCAD for Windows and open TITLEA.
❑ Make a drawing similar to the "original" object shown below. With the **MIRRTEXT** variable set to 0, mirror the object as shown in the center example.
❑ Mirror the object as required to give the result on the right example.
❑ Save the drawing as A:EX13-5 and quit.

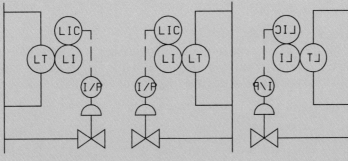

ORIGINAL

## ROTATING EXISTING OBJECTS

AUG 5

Design changes often require that an object, feature, or view be rotated. For example, the office furniture layout may have to be moved, copied, or rotated for an interior design. AutoCAD allows you to easily revise the layout to obtain the final design.

To rotate selected objects, pick the **Rotate** button on the **Modify** toolbar or enter ROTATE on the command line. If the ACADFULL menu file is loaded, the command can be accessed by selecting **Rotate** from the **Modify** pull-down menu. Objects can be selected using any of the selection set options, and are rotated about a base point. You must pick a base point and enter a rotation angle. A negative rotation angle revolves the object clockwise, Figure 13-23. A positive rotation angle revolves the object counterclockwise. The **ROTATE** command sequence appears as follows:

> Command: **ROTATE** ↵
> Select objects: *(pick the objects using any of the selection methods)*
> Select objects: ↵
> Base point: *(pick the base point on or near the object, or enter coordinates and press* [Enter]*)*
> ⟨Rotation angle⟩/Reference: *(type a positive or negative rotation angle and press* [Enter]*, or pick a point on-screen)*
> Command:

Figure 13-23. Different rotation angles.

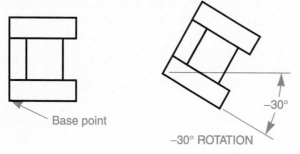
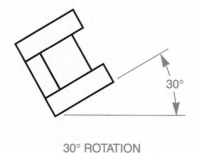

If an object is already rotated and you want a different angle, you can do this in two ways. Both ways involve using the **Reference** option after selecting the object for rotation. The first way is to specify the existing angle and then the new angle, Figure 13-24A:

> ⟨Rotation angle⟩/Reference: **R** ↵
> Reference angle ⟨0⟩: **135** ↵
> New angle: **180** ↵

The other method is to pick a reference line on the object and rotate the object in relationship to the reference line, Figure 13-24B:

> ⟨Rotation angle⟩/Reference: **R** ↵
> Reference angle ⟨0⟩: *(pick an endpoint of a reference line that forms the existing angle)*
> Second point: *(pick the other point of the reference line that forms the existing angle)*
> New angle: *(specify a new angle, such as 180, and press* [Enter]*)*

Figure 13-24.   Using the **Reference** option of the **ROTATE** command.

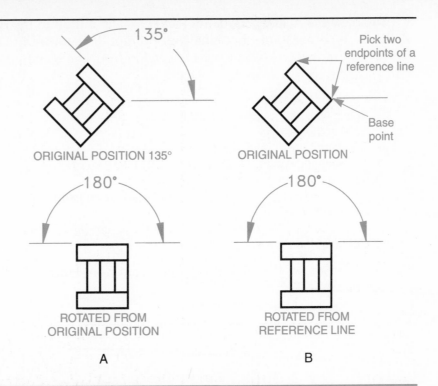

A

B

❑ Load AutoCAD for Windows and open TITLEA.
❑ Draw a 2.25 unit square with one horizontal side.
❑ Rotate the square to 75°. Then, using the **Reference** option, rotate the square another 45°. Finally rotate the square back to 0°.
❑ Save the drawing as A:EX13-6 and quit.

## PROFESSIONAL TIP

Always use the **OSNAP** modes to your best advantage when editing. For example, suppose you want to rotate an object. It may be difficult to find an exact corner without using **OSNAP** modes. To select the base point, use the **Endpoint** or **Intersect** option.

## MOVING AND ROTATING AN OBJECT AT THE SAME TIME   AUG 5

The **ALIGN** command is primarily used for 3D applications, but it has 2D applications when you want to both move and rotate an object at the same time. The command sequence asks you to select objects, and then asks for three source points and three destination points. For 2D applications, you only need two source and two destination points. The *source points* are points on the object in its original position. The *destination points* correspond to the location where the object is to be placed. Refer to Figure 13-25A. Press [Enter] when the prompt requests the third source and destination points.

To access the **ALIGN** command, pick the **Align** button in the **Rotate** flyout on the **Modify** toolbar or type ALIGN at the **Command:** prompt. If the ACADFULL menu file is loaded, the command can be accessed by selecting **Align** from the **Modify** pull-down menu. The command sequence is as follows:

Command: **ALIGN** ⏎
Select objects: *(select the objects)*
Select objects: ⏎
1st source point: *(pick the first source point)*
1st destination point: *(pick the first destination point)*
2nd source point: *(pick the second source point)*
2nd destination point: *(pick the second destination point)*
3rd source point: ⏎
⟨2d⟩ or 3d transformation: *(press [Enter] to accept the 2D default)*
Command:

Figure 13-25B shows the kitchen cabinet layout from Figure 13-25A moved and rotated into position on the wall.

Figure 13-25.   The **ALIGN** command rotates and moves an object at the same time.

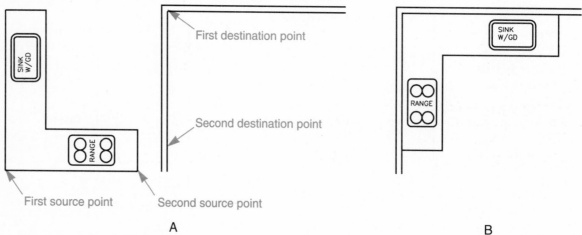

A                                                                                                B

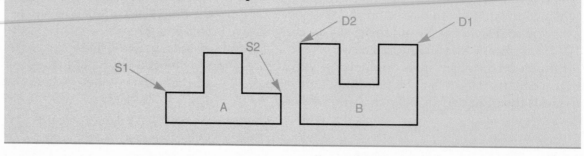

# CHANGING THE SIZE OF AN EXISTING OBJECT

AUG 5

A convenient editing command that saves hours of drafting time is the **SCALE** command. This command lets you change the size of an object or the complete drawing. The **SCALE** command enlarges or reduces the entire object proportionately. With AutoCAD, if an object is dimensioned and then scaled, the dimensions also change to reflect the new size. To scale objects, pick the **Scale** button on the **Stretch** flyout in the **Modify** toolbar or enter SCALE at the **Command:** prompt. If the ACADFULL menu file is loaded, the command can also be accessed by selecting **Scale** from the **Modify** pull-down menu. The command sequence is as follows:

> Command: **SCALE** ↵
> Select objects: *(use any selection technique to select objects)*
> Select objects: ↵
> Base point: *(select the base point)*
> ⟨Scale factor⟩/Reference:

## Scale factors

Specifying the scale factor is the default option. Enter a number to indicate the amount of enlargement or reduction. For example, if you want to double the scale, type 2 at the ⟨Scale factor⟩/Reference: prompt, Figure 13-26. The chart in Figure 13-27 shows sample scale factors.

An object can also be scaled by specifying a new size in relation to an existing dimension. For example, suppose you have a shaft that is 2.50" long and you want to make it 3.00" long. To do so, use the **Reference** option as follows, Figure 13-28:

> ⟨Scale factor⟩/Reference: **R** ↵
> Reference length ⟨1⟩: **2.5** ↵
> New length: **3** ↵
> Command:

Figure 13-26.    Using the **SCALE** command. A—The original object. B—The object after being scaled.

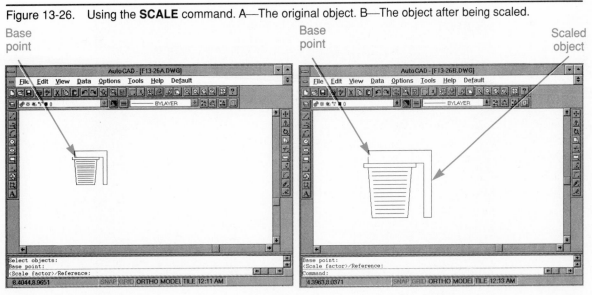

A

B

Figure 13-27.    Different scale factors and the resulting sizes.

| Scale Factor | Resulting Size |
|---|---|
| 10 | 10 × bigger |
| 5 | 5 × bigger |
| 2 | 2 × bigger |
| 1 | Equal to existing size |
| .75 | 3/4 of original size |
| .50 | 1/2 of original size |
| .25 | 1/4 of original size |

Figure 13-28.    Using the **Reference** option of the **SCALE** command.

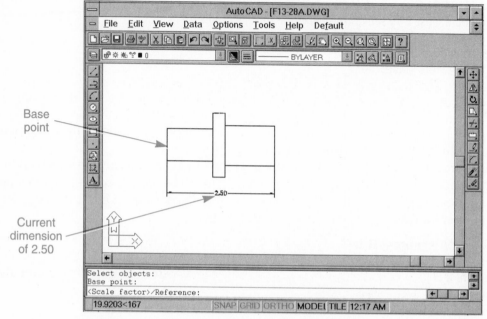

A

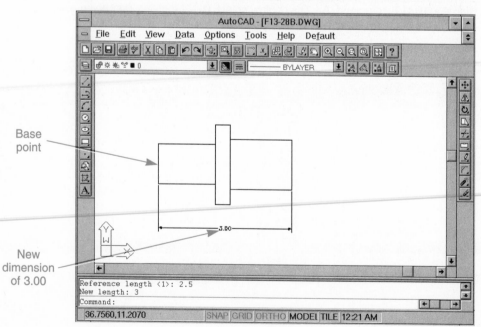

B

> **NOTE**  The **SCALE** command changes all dimensions of an object proportionately. If you want to change only the width or length of an object, use the **STRETCH** or **LENGTHEN** commands.

## EXERCISE 13-8

❑ Load AutoCAD for Windows and open TITLEA.
❑ Draw two 2.25″ squares so that two sides are horizontal.
❑ Double the size of one square.
❑ Use the **Reference** option to make the other square 3.25″ long on one side.
❑ Save the drawing as A:EX13-8 and quit.

## STRETCHING AN OBJECT                                    | AUG 5 |

The **SCALE** command changes the length and width of an object proportionately. The **STRETCH** command, on the other hand, changes only one dimension of an object or view. In mechanical drafting, it is common to increase the length of a part while leaving the diameter or width the same. In architectural design, room sizes may be stretched to increase the square footage.

When using the **STRETCH** command, you can select objects individually, or with the crossing window or crossing polygon options. For example, type C at the Select objects: prompt, and pick the opposite two corners of a crossing window around the objects you want to stretch.

To access the **STRETCH** command, pick the **Stretch** button in the **Modify** toolbar or type STRETCH at the **Command:** prompt. If the ACADFULL menu file is loaded, the command can also be accessed by selecting **Stretch** from the **Modify** pull-down menu. The command sequence is as follows:

    Command: **STRETCH** ↵
    Select objects to stretch by crossing-window or -polygon...
    Select objects: *(use a crossing window or one of the polygon options to select the*
        *first corner of a crossing box)*
    Other corner: *(pick the second corner)*
    Select objects: *(pick additional objects or press* [Enter]*)*

Select only the portion of the object to be stretched, Figure 13-29. If you select the entire object, the **STRETCH** command works like the **MOVE** command.

Next, you are asked to pick the base point. This is the point that the object will be stretched from. Then, pick a new position for the base point. As you move the screen cursor, the object is stretched or compressed. When the displayed object is stretched to the desired position, pick the new point. The command sequence after selecting objects is as follows:

    Base point or displacement: *(pick the base point for the stretch to begin)*
    Second point of displacement: *(pick the final location of the base point)*
    Command:

Figure 13-29.   Using the
**STRETCH** command.

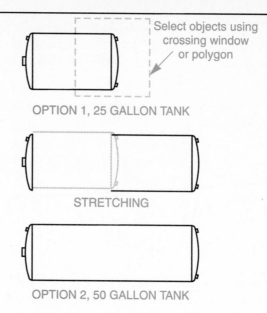

Select objects using
crossing window
or polygon

OPTION 1, 25 GALLON TANK

STRETCHING

OPTION 2, 50 GALLON TANK

The example in Figure 13-29 shows the object being stretched. This is a common use of the **STRETCH** command. You can also use the **STRETCH** command to reduce the size of an object.

## Using the Displacement option

The **Displacement** option works the same with the **STRETCH** command as with the **MOVE** and **COPY** commands.

> Command: **STRETCH** ↵
> Select objects to stretch by crossing-window or -polygon...
> Select objects: *(pick the first corner of a crossing-window, or one of the polygon options)*
> Other corner: *(pick the second corner)*
> Select objects: ↵
> Base point or displacement: *(enter an X and Y displacement value such as* 2,3*)*
> Second point of displacement: ↵
> Command:

When you press [Enter] at the Second point of displacement: prompt, the object is automatically stretched as you specified with the X and Y coordinates at the Base point or displacement: prompt. In this case, the object is stretched 2 units in the X direction and 3 units in the Y direction.

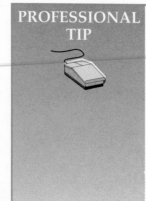

**PROFESSIONAL TIP**

It may not be common to have objects lined up in a convenient manner for using the **Crossing** selection method with the **STRETCH** command. You should consider using the **Window-polygon** or **Crossing-polygon** selection options to make selecting the objects easier. Also, make sure the **DRAGMODE** variable is turned on when stretching an object so you can watch the object stretch to its new size. If the stretched object is not what you expected, cancel the command with the [Esc] key. The **STRETCH** command and other editing commands discussed in this chapter work well with **ORTHO** on. This restricts the object movement to only horizontal and vertical directions.

---

**EXERCISE 13-9**

❑ Load AutoCAD for Windows and open TITLEB.
❑ Design and draw a cylindrical-shaped object similar to the tank in Figure 13-29.
❑ Stretch the object to approximately twice its original length.
❑ Stretch the object to about twice its original height.
❑ Save the drawing as A:EX13-9 and quit.

---

## LENGTHENING OR SHORTENING AN OBJECT          AUG 5

The **LENGTHEN** command can be used to change the length of objects and the included angle of an arc. Objects can only be lengthened one at a time. The **LENGTHEN** command does not affect closed objects. For example, you can lengthen a line, polyline, arc, elliptical arc, or spline but you cannot lengthen a closed polygon. Pick the **Lengthen** button in the **Modify** toolbar, pick **Lengthen** from the **Modify** pull-down menu, or type MODIFY at the **Command:** prompt. When you select an object, AutoCAD gives you the current length if the object is linear, or the included angle if the object is an arc:

> Command: **LENGTHEN** ↵
> DElta/Percent/Total/DYnamic/⟨Select object⟩: *(pick an object)*
> Current length: 1.500, included angle: 75.000
> DElta/Percent/Total/DYnamic/⟨Select object⟩:

Each option is described below:

- **Delta.** The **Delta** option allows you to specify a positive or negative change in length measured from the endpoint of the selected object. The lengthening or shortening happens closest to the selection point and changes the length by the amount entered. See Figure 13-30.

> Command: **LENGTHEN** ↵
> DElta/Percent/Total/DYnamic/⟨Select object⟩: *(pick an object)*
> Current length: 3.000
> DElta/Percent/Total/DYnamic/⟨Select object⟩: **DE** ↵
> Angle/⟨Enter delta length (0.000)⟩: *(enter the desired length, .75 for example)*
> ⟨Select object to change⟩/Undo: *(pick the object again)*
> ⟨Select object to change⟩/Undo: (press [Enter] *to make the change or type* U
>     *to undo the change)*
> Command:

---

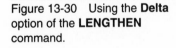

Figure 13-30   Using the **Delta**
option of the **LENGTHEN**
command.

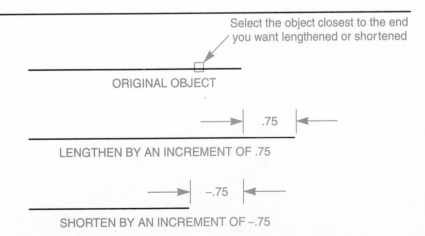

You can change the length of an arc as just demonstrated on a line. You can also change the included angle of an arc. The **Delta** option has an **Angle** suboption that lets you change the included angle of an arc by a specified angle. The command sequence is as follows, Figure 13-31:

> Command: **LENGTHEN** ↵
> DElta/Percent/Total/DYnamic/⟨Select object⟩: **DE** ↵
> Angle/⟨Enter delta length (0.000)⟩: **A** ↵
> Enter delta angle ⟨0.000⟩: *(enter an angle such as 45)*
> ⟨Select object to change⟩/Undo: *(pick the arc)*
> ⟨Select object to change⟩/Undo: ↵
> Command:

- **Percent.** The **Percent** option allows you to change the length of an object or the angle of an arc by a specified percentage. If you consider the original length 100%, then you can make the object shorter by specifying less than 100% or longer by specifying more than 100%. Look at Figure 13-32 and follow this command sequence:

> Command: **LENGTHEN** ↵
> DElta/Percent/Total/DYnamic/⟨Select object⟩: **P** ↵
> Enter percent length ⟨100.0⟩: **125** ↵
> ⟨Select object to change⟩/Undo: *(pick the object)*
> ⟨Select object to change⟩/Undo: ↵
> Command:

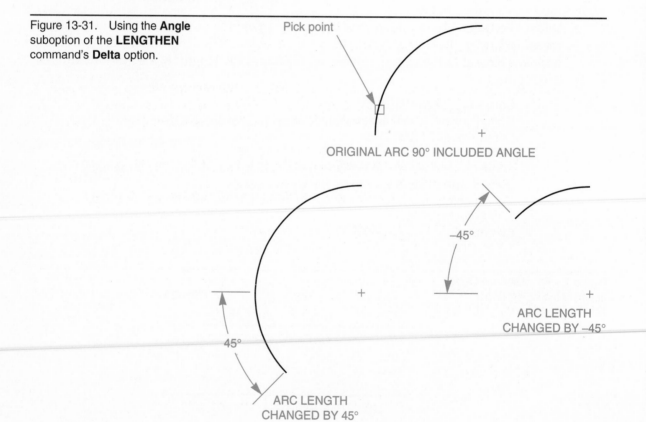

Figure 13-31. Using the **Angle** suboption of the **LENGTHEN** command's **Delta** option.

Pick point

ORIGINAL ARC 90° INCLUDED ANGLE

−45°

ARC LENGTH CHANGED BY −45°

45°

ARC LENGTH CHANGED BY 45°

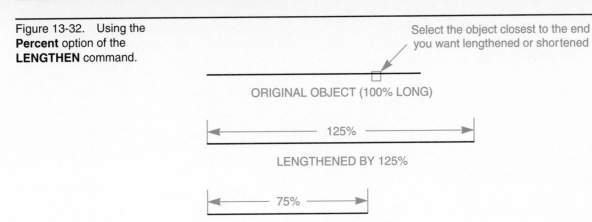

Figure 13-32. Using the **Percent** option of the **LENGTHEN** command.

- **Total.** The **Total** option allows you to set the total length or angle by the value that you specify. See Figure 13-33. You do not have to select the object before entering one of the options, but doing so lets you know the current length and, if an arc, angle of the object:

> Command: **LENGTHEN** ↵
> DElta/Percent/Total/DYnamic/⟨Select object⟩: *(pick an object)*
> Current length: 3.000
> DElta/Percent/Total/DYnamic/⟨Select object⟩: **T** ↵
> Angle/⟨Enter delta length (1.000)⟩: *(enter a new length such as* **3.75** *or* **A** *if it is an angle)*
> ⟨Select object to change⟩/Undo: *(pick the object)*
> ⟨Select object to change⟩/Undo: ↵
> Command:

- **Dynamic.** This option lets you drag the endpoint of the object to the desired length or angle with the screen cursor. See Figure 13-34. It is helpful to have the grid and snap set to usable increments when using this option. This is the command sequence:

> Command: **LENGTHEN** ↵
> DElta/Percent/Total/DYnamic/⟨Select object⟩: **DY** ↵
> Specify new end point.
> ⟨Select object to change⟩/Undo: *(pick the object and move the cursor to the desired length)*
> ⟨Select object to change⟩/Undo: ↵
> Command:

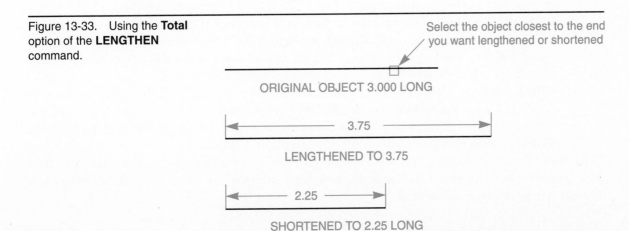

Figure 13-33. Using the **Total** option of the **LENGTHEN** command.

Figure 13-34.  Using the
**Dynamic** option of the
**LENGTHEN** command.

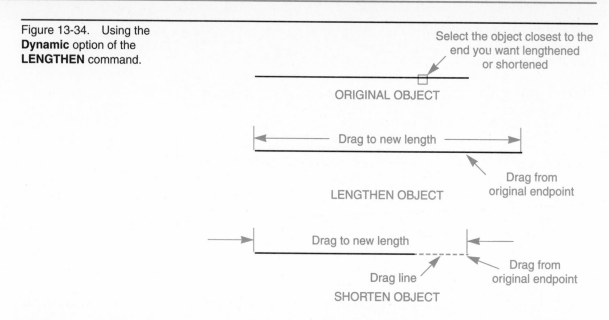

Select the object closest to the
end you want lengthened
or shortened

ORIGINAL OBJECT

Drag to new length

LENGTHEN OBJECT

Drag from
original endpoint

Drag to new length

Drag line
SHORTEN OBJECT

Drag from
original endpoint

## EXERCISE 13-10

❑ Load AutoCAD and set up your own variables or use a prototype.
❑ Use the **LENGTHEN** command and the following options to draw objects similar to the
ones specified in the given figure numbers: (Note: Use the **COPY** command to make two
copies of each original object for the lengthening or shortening.)
  **Delta** —Figure 13-30 and Figure 13-31.
  **Percent**—Figure 13-32.
  **Total**—Figure 13-33.
  **Dynamic**—Figure 13-34.
❑ Save the drawing as A:EX13-10 and quit.

## SELECTING OBJECTS BEFORE EDITING

Throughout this chapter, you have worked with the basic editing commands by entering
the command and then selecting the object to be edited. You can also set up AutoCAD to let
you select the object first and then enter the desired editing command. The system variables
that affect this procedure are **PICKAUTO**, **PICKFIRST**, and **GRIPS**. They should be set as follows:
  • **PICKAUTO = 1 (on).** This allows you to automatically pick objects by the method used
    to pick and move the cursor.
  • **PICKFIRST = 1 (on).** This system variable lets you pick the object before entering the
    editing command. When **PICKFIRST** is set to 0 (off), you must enter the command
    name before selecting the object. Notice the difference in the appearance of the
    crosshairs when **PICKFIRST** is on and off, and when **GRIPS** is off.
  • **GRIPS = 0 (off).** Grips are used for automatic editing, and are discussed in detail in
    Chapter 14. For **PICKFIRST** to have its best performance, turn **GRIPS** off. If you are fol-
    lowing along with this text while working at your computer, be sure to turn the
    **GRIPS** system variable back on when working in Chapter 14.
With these variable settings, you now have the flexibility of entering the command and then
selecting the object, or selecting the object and then entering the command. The editing commands work the same either way.

### EXERCISE 13-11

❑ Load AutoCAD for Windows and open EX13-3, or start a new drawing and draw a square and triangle of any size.
❑ Set the following system variables to the settings given:
   **PICKAUTO** = 1
   **PICKFIRST** = 1
   **GRIPS** = 0
❑ Select the square. Then, enter the **MOVE** command to move it to a new position.
❑ Select the triangle. Then, enter the **COPY** command to make a copy of it.
❑ Experiment by selecting objects followed by using some of the other editing commands such as **ROTATE** and **SCALE**.
❑ Erase an object by selecting the object before entering the **ERASE** command.
❑ Save the drawing as A:EX13-11 and quit.

## EDITING WITH THE GEOMETRY CALCULATOR          AUG3

Sometimes it is difficult to determine the exact position of an object you are trying to edit since the geometry does not fit into your grid and snap setup. When this occurs, it may be helpful to use the **CAL** command. There are an endless number of possibilities; this discussion provides you with a few of the many options.

You were introduced to the geometry calculator using the **CAL** command in Chapter 9. Review that chapter before proceeding, paying special attention to the symbols, equations, and format detailed there.

Assume you have a drawing similar to the one shown in Figure 13-35. You can easily locate points 1 and 2 using object snap modes. However, you cannot easily find the exact center between the points for the final destination of the circular object. Use the **MOVE** and **CAL** commands as follows:

> Command: **MOVE** ↵
> Select objects: *(select the circular object on the right)*
> Select objects: ↵
> Base point or displacement: **CEN** ↵
> of *(pick circular object)*

Now use the **CAL** command to locate the center point exactly halfway between points 1 and 2:

> Second point of displacement: **'CAL** ↵
> ⟩⟩ Expression: **(END+END)/2** ↵
> ⟩⟩ Select entity for END snap: *(pick point 1)*
> ⟩⟩ Select entity for END snap: *(pick point 2)*
> Command:

The circular object automatically moves to the exact center point between points 1 and 2.

Figure 13-35.   Centering an object between two endpoints using the **CAL** command.

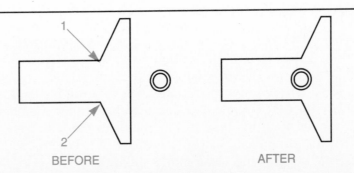

## EXERCISE 13-12

❑ Load AutoCAD for Windows and open **TITLEA**.
❑ Create a drawing similar to the "before" example in Figure 13-35.
❑ Use the **MOVE** and **CAL** commands to move the circular object exactly halfway between points 1 and 2. Your results should be similar to the "after" example.
❑ Save the drawing as **A:EX13-12** and quit.

The object at the left in Figure 13-36 is rotated at an unknown angle. This makes it difficult to rotate the object on the right to the same angle. To rotate the object on the right so that its base is parallel with the base of the object on the left, use the following command sequence:

> Command: **ROTATE** ↵
> Select objects: *(select the object on the right)*
> Select objects: ↵
> Base point: *(pick point 1)*
> ⟨Rotation angle⟩/Reference: **'CAL** ↵
> ⟩⟩ Expression: **ANG(END,END)** ↵
> ⟩⟩ Select entity for END snap: *(pick point 2)*
> ⟩⟩ Select entity for END snap: *(pick point 3)*
> Command:

Figure 13-36. Rotating an object so its base is parallel with an existing object.

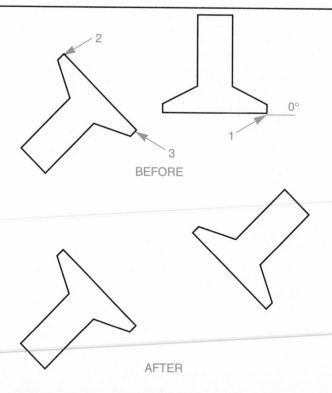

BEFORE

AFTER

## EXERCISE 13-13

❑ Load AutoCAD for Windows and open **TITLEA**.
❑ Make a drawing similar to the "before" example in Figure 13-36.
❑ Use the **ROTATE** and **CAL** commands to rotate the object on the right so that its base is parallel with the base of the object on the left. Your results should be similar to the "after" example.
❑ Save the drawing as **A:EX13-13** and quit.

## SELECTING OBJECTS FOR FUTURE EDITING

AUG 5

The **SELECT** command is used to preselect an object or group of objects for future editing. It is designed to increase your productivity. Often you are working with the same set of objects, moving, copying, or scaling them. Set these aside as a selection set with the **SELECT** command. Then continue to perform another drawing task. To return to those objects set aside, enter P for **Previous** at the Select objects: prompt. The command sequences for creating a selection set and then moving it are as follows:

> Command: **SELECT** ↵
> Select objects: *(use any method to select an individual object or group of objects)*
> Select objects: *(select additional objects or press* [Enter]*)*
> Command:

This creates a selection set. Later, when you want to move these objects, use the **Previous** option as follows:

> Command: **MOVE** ↵
> Select objects: **P** ↵ *(this selects the object or group of objects previously selected using the* **SELECT** *command)*
> Select objects: ↵
> Base point or displacement: *(pick the base point)*
> Second point of displacement: *(pick the new location of the base point)*
> Command:

---

### EXERCISE 13-14

❑ Load AutoCAD for Windows and open TITLEA.
❑ Draw two circles with 1.5″ (38.1mm) radii spaced .25″ (6.35mm) apart.
❑ Use the **SELECT** command to select both circles for future editing.
❑ Draw at least three other small objects.
❑ Use the **COPY** command and the **Previous** option to copy the original two circles to a new location.
❑ Save the drawing as A:EX13-14 and quit.

---

## CREATING OBJECT GROUPS

AUG 5

A group is a named selection set of objects. These selection sets are saved with the drawing and therefore exist between multiple drawing sessions. Objects can be members of more than one group and groups can be nested. *Nesting* means placing one group inside of another group. An object existing in multiple groups creates an interesting situation. For example, if a line and an arc are grouped and then the arc is grouped with a circle, moving the first group moves the line and arc, and moving the second group moves the arc and circle. Nesting can be used to place smaller groups into larger groups for easier editing.

The **PICKSTYLE** system variable is used to determine whether selecting a grouped object selects the individual object or the entire group. **PICKSTYLE** has the following settings:

0   No group selection or associative hatch selection. Hatch is used in sectioning and is discussed in Chapter 24. Associative hatch means that the hatch pattern is associated with the object. So, when the object is changed, the hatch pattern changes with it.
1   Group selection is the default.
2   Associative hatch selection.
3   Group selection and associative hatch selection.

Change the **PICKSTYLE** setting like this:

> Command: **PICKSTYLE** ↵
> New value for PICKSTYLE ⟨1⟩:

The **GROUP** command can be accessed by picking **Object Group** button in the **Standard** toolbar, typing GROUP at the **Command:** prompt, or accessed by picking **Group objects...** from the **Edit** pull-down menu. Any of these entry methods will display the **Object Grouping** dialog box shown in Figure 13-37.

Figure 13-37.  The **Object Grouping** dialog box. The different elements are shown here highlighted.

| | Object Grouping | |
|---|---|---|
| **Group Name** | | **Selectable** |
| FRONT | | Yes |
| NOTES | | Yes |
| SIDE | | Yes |
| TITLEBLOCK | | No |
| TOP | | Yes |

**Group Identification**
- Group Name: TITLEBLOCK
- Description: MECHANICAL TITLE BLOCK
- [Find Name <] [Highlight <] □ Include Unnamed

**Create Group**
- [New <] ☒ Selectable □ Unnamed

**Change Group**
- [Remove <] [Add <] [Rename] [Re-order...]
- [Description] [Explode] [Selectable]

[OK] [Cancel] [Help...]

*Currently defined groups* — *Group identification elements* — *Options for creating a new group* — *Options for changing a group*

The elements found in the **Object Grouping** dialog box are described below:
- **Group Name.** This shows currently defined groups.
- **Selectable.** If a group is selectable, picking any object in it selects the entire group. Making a group non-selectable allows individual objects to be edited while still in the group.
- **Group Identification.** This section of the **Object Grouping** dialog box shows the name of the selected group and its description. The elements found in this section are:
  - **Group Name:**—Displays the name of the currently selected group. Also, this is where a name for a new group is entered. Group names can be a maximum of 31 characters long and can include letters, numbers, and the special characters $, _, and -. The group name cannot have a space between words, but if you want to use two words, separate them with an underline or dash, such as CHART-EARNINGS.
  - **Description:**—Enter a text description for the group highlighted in the **Group Name:** section. A maximum of 64 characters can be used, including spaces.
  - **Find Name** ⟨—This button allows you to select an object, then displays a dialog list of all groups the object is associated with. When you pick this button, you get the following prompt:

    > Pick a member of a group:

    The drawing editor returns and you can pick an object. Once you pick an object, the **Group Member List** dialog box is displayed listing any groups the object is associated with.

- **Highlight** ⟨—This button allows a group name to be specified, then highlights all the members of the specified group in the drawing editor. This allows you to see the parts of the drawing that are identified as the members of that group. There is a **Continue** button that you can pick or press [Enter] to get back to the **Object Grouping** dialog box.
- **Include Unnamed**—This is a toggle that causes unnamed groups to be listed with named groups. Unnamed groups are given a default name by AutoCAD in the format: *A$x$, where $x$ is an integer value that increases with each new group, *A6 for example. Unnamed groups can be named later using the **Rename** option.
- **Create Group.** This section contains the options for creating a new group. The elements found in this section are:
  - **New** ⟨—This button creates a new group from the selected objects using the name entered in the **Group Name:** text box. AutoCAD issues these prompts after you enter a new name in the **Group Name:** text box:

    > Select objects for grouping:
    > Select objects: *(select the objects to group)*
    > Select objects: ↵

    The **Object Grouping** dialog box returns and the newly named group is shown in the **Group Name** list.
  - **Selectable**—A check in this box sets the initial status of the **Selectable** value as Yes for the new group. This is indicated in the **Selectable** list described earlier. No check here specifies No in the **Selectable** list. This can be changed later.
  - **Unnamed**—This indicates whether the new group will be named. If this box is checked, AutoCAD assigns its own default name as detailed previously.
- **Change Group.** This section of the **Object Grouping** dialog box shows the options for changing a group. The elements found in this section are:
  - **Remove** ⟨—Pick this button to remove objects from a group definition.
  - **Add** ⟨—This button allows objects to be added to a group definition.
  - **Rename**—Pick this button to change the name of an existing group. Unnamed groups having AutoCAD's default name can be renamed.
  - **Re-order...**—Objects are numbered in the order that they are selected when defining the group. The first object is numbered 0, not 1. This button allows objects to be re-ordered within the group. For example, if a group contains a set of instructions, you can re-order the instructions to suit the typical steps that are used to follow the instructions. The **Order Group** dialog box is displayed when you pick this button. The elements of this dialog box are briefly described as follows:
    - **Group Name.** Displays the name of the selected group.
    - **Description.** Displays the description that you entered for the selected group.
    - **Remove from position (0-$n$):.** Position number of the object to re-order, where $n$ is the total number of objects found in the group. You place the desired order in the text box to the right of this and the next two features.
    - **Replace at position (0-$n$):.** Position number to place the object at.
    - **Number of objects (1-$n$):.** Displays the number of objects or the range to re-order.
    - **Reverse Order.** Pick this button to have the order of all members in the group reversed.
  - **Description**—Updates the group with the new description entered in the **Description:** text box described earlier.
  - **Explode**—Pick this button to delete the selected group definition, but not the group's objects. The group name is removed and the original group is exploded, but copies of the group are not affected. The reason this happens is because copies of a group become unnamed groups. By toggling on the **Include Unnamed** switch, these unnamed groups are displayed and can then be exploded, if needed.

- **Selectable**—Toggles the selectable value of a group. This is where you can change the value in the **Selectable** list from Yes to No or back again.

---

**EXERCISE 13-15**

❑ Load AutoCAD and open one of your previous more complex drawings.
❑ Use the **GROUP** command to name and describe several different elements of the draw-ing as groups. For example, for views use FRONT, TOP, SIDE, TITLEBLOCK, or NOTES.
❑ Use each element of the **Object Grouping** dialog box to see the effect on the groups that you have named.
❑ Save as A:EX13-15.

---

## CHAPTER TEST

*Write your answers in the spaces provided.*

1. Give the command and entries used to draw a 45° × .125 chamfer:

    Command:_____

    Polyline/Distances/Angle/Trim/Method/⟨Select first line⟩: _____

    Enter first chamfer distance ⟨*current*⟩: _____

    Enter second chamfer distance ⟨*previous*⟩: _____

    Command:_____

    Polyline/Distances/Angle/Trim/Method/⟨Select first line⟩: _____

    Select second line: _____

2. Give the command and entries required to produce .50 radius fillets on all corners of a closed polyline:

    Command:_____

    Polyline/Radius/⟨Select first object⟩: _____

    Enter fillet radius ⟨*current*⟩: _____

    Command:_____

    Polyline/Radius/Trim/⟨Select first object⟩: _____

    Select 2D polyline: _____

3. Give the command, entries, and actions required to move an object from position A to position B:

    Command:_____

    Select objects:_____

    Select objects:_____

    Base point or displacement: _____

    Second point of displacement: _____

4. Give the command and entries needed to make two copies of the same object:

Command:_____

Select objects:_____

Select objects:_____

⟨Base point or displacement⟩/Multiple: _____

Base point: _____

Second point of displacement: _____

Second point of displacement: _____

Second point of displacement: _____

5. Give the command and entries necessary to draw a reverse image of an existing object and remove the existing object:

Command:_____

Select objects:_____

Select objects:_____

First point of mirror line: _____

Second point of mirror line: _____

Delete old objects? ⟨N⟩:_____

6. Give the command and entries needed to rotate an object 45° clockwise:

Command:_____

Select objects:_____

Select objects:_____

Base point: _____

⟨Rotation angle⟩/Reference: _____

7. Give the command and entries required to reduce the size of an entire drawing by one-half:

Command:_____

Select objects:_____

Select objects:_____

Base point: _____

⟨Scale factor⟩/Reference: _____

8. Give the command and entries needed to change the first break point picked to the intersection of two other lines:

Command:_____

Select object:_____

Enter second point (or F for first point):_____

Enter first point: _____

Enter second point: _____

of _____

9. Give the command sequence that revises the radius of a circle:

Command:_____

Select objects:_____

Select objects:_____

Properties/⟨Change point⟩: _____

10. Define the term "displacement" as it relates to the **MOVE** and **COPY** commands. _____

_____

_____

11. Explain the difference between the **MOVE** and **COPY** commands. _____

_____

_____

12. List two locations you normally choose as the base point when using the **MOVE** or **COPY** commands. _____

_____

13. Describe the purpose of the **SELECT** command. _____

_____

14. What is a selection set? _____

_____

15. How do you select objects for editing that have previously been picked using the **SELECT** command? _____

_____

16. How is the size of a fillet specified? _____

17. Identify the default selection method issued by AutoCAD when the **STRETCH** command is selected from the pull-down menu. _____

_____

18. List two ways to cancel the **STRETCH** command. _____

_____

19. The **EXTEND** command can be considered the opposite of the _____ command.

20. Name the system variable used to preset the fillet radius. _____

21. In what direction should you pick points to break a portion out of a circle or arc? _____

_____

22. Name the command which trims an object to a cutting edge. _____

23. Name the command associated with boundary edges._____

24. The **MOVE**, **COPY**, **TRIM**, **EXTEND**, and **STRETCH** commands are located in the _____ and _____ pull-down menus.

25. Name the command that can be used to move and rotate an object simultaneously. ____

_____

26. Describe the purpose of the **PICKFIRST** system variable. _____

_____

27. Describe the difference between **Trim** and **No trim** when using the **CHAMFER** and **FILLET** commands. _____

_____

_____

_____

28. What is the purpose of the **Method** option in the **CHAMFER** command? _____

_____

29. How can you split an object in two without removing a portion? _____

_____

_____

30. Name the option in the **TRIM** and **EXTEND** commands that allows you to trim or extend to an implied intersection. _____

31. How do you use the **Smart** mode? _____

_____

32. Identify the **LENGTHEN** command option with its descriptions by placing the letter of the command option in the blank in front of its description.

_____ Change a length or arc angle by a percentage of the total.          A. **Delta**

_____ Drag the end point of the object to the desired length or angle.     B. **Percent**

_____ Allows a positive or negative change in length from the end point.   C. **Total**

_____ Set the total length or angle to the value specified.                D. **Dynamic**

33. Define a group. _____

_____

34. How do you access the **Object Grouping** dialog box? _____

_____

_____

35. Describe how you create a new group. _____

_____

_____

_____

## DRAWING PROBLEMS

*Use the **TITLEA** or **TITLEB** prototypes as appropriate for each of the following problems. Start a new drawing for each problem, unless indicated otherwise.*

**General**

1.  Draw the object shown as view A. Change the angle of the object to 45° as shown in view B. Then rotate it to a 90° rotation angle as shown in view C. Save the drawing as A:P13-1.

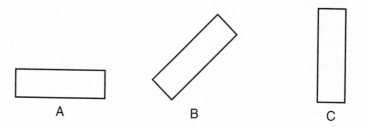

**General**

2.  Draw the object shown as view A. Scale it down to 1/4 size as shown in view B. Then scale the object 10 times as shown in view C. Save the drawing as A:P13-2.

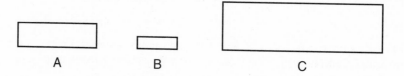

**General**

3.  Draw object A using the **LINE** command, making sure that the corners overrun. Then trim the lines all at the same time. Select all four lines when asked to select cutting edges. Pick all overruns when asked to select object to trim. The object should appear as shown in view B. Save the drawing as A:P13-3.

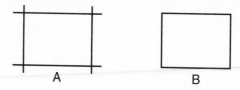

**General**

4.  Draw object A using the **LINE** and **ARC** commands. Make sure that the corners overrun and the arc is centered, but does not touch the lines. Then use the **TRIM**, **EXTEND**, and **MOVE** commands to make the object look like the example shown in view B. Save the drawing as A:P13-4.

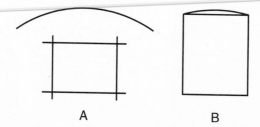

5. Open drawing P13-4 for further editing. Using the **STRETCH** command, change the shape to that shown in view B. Make a copy of the new revision. Change the copy to represent the example shown in view C. Save the drawing as A:P13-5.

General

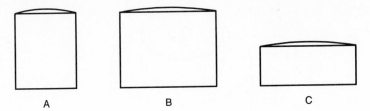

A                          B                          C

6. Refer to Figure 13-24 in this chapter for this problem. Draw and make three copies of the object shown in Option 1. Stretch the first copy to twice its length as shown as Option 2. Stretch the second copy to twice its height. Double the size of the third copy using the **SCALE** command. Save the drawing as A:P13-6.

Piping

7. Draw objects A, B, and C shown below without dimensions. Then, move objects A, B, and C to new positions. Select a corner of object A and the center of objects B and C as the base points. Save the drawing as A:P13-7.

Mechanical Drafting

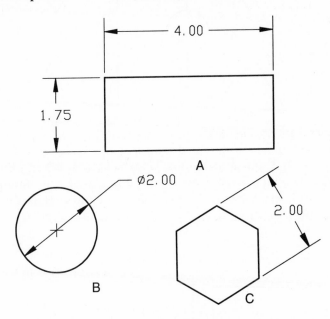

8. Draw objects A, B, and C shown in Problem 13-7 at the left side of the screen. Make a copy of object A two units to the right. Make four copies of object B three units, center-to-center, to the right using the **Multiple** option. Make three copies of object C three units, center-to-center, to the right. Save the drawing as A:P13-8.

Mechanical Drafting

9. Draw the object shown using the **ELLIPSE**, **COPY**, and **LINE** commands. The rotation angle of the ellipses is 60°. Use the **BREAK** or **TRIM** commands when drawing and editing the lower ellipse. Save the drawing as A:P13-9 and quit.

General

*General*

10. Call up drawing P13-9 for further editing. Shorten the height of the object using the **STRETCH** command as shown below. Next, add to the object as indicated. Save the drawing as A:P13-10 and quit.

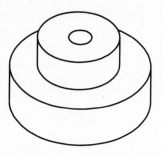

*General*

11. Draw the object shown as view A. Use the **TRIM** command to help change the object to the example shown as view B. Save the drawing as A:P13-11.

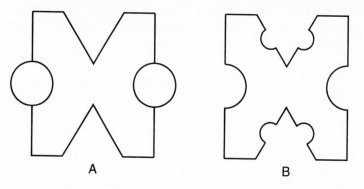

A                                                          B

*Mechanical Drafting*

12. Draw view A, without dimensions. Use the **CHAMFER** and **FILLET** commands to your best advantage. Then draw a mirror image of it as shown in view B. Now, remove the original view and move the new view so that point 2 is at the original point 1 location. Save the drawing as A:P13-12.

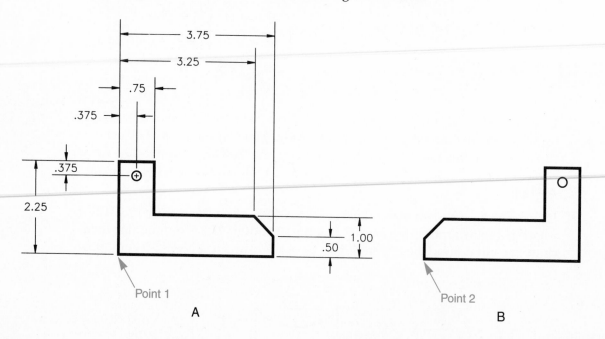

A                                                          B

Mechanical
Drafting

13. Draw the object shown below, without dimensions. The object is symmetrical; therefore, draw only the right half. Then mirror the left half into place. Use the **CHAMFER** and **FILLET** commands to your best advantage. Save the drawing as A:P13-13.

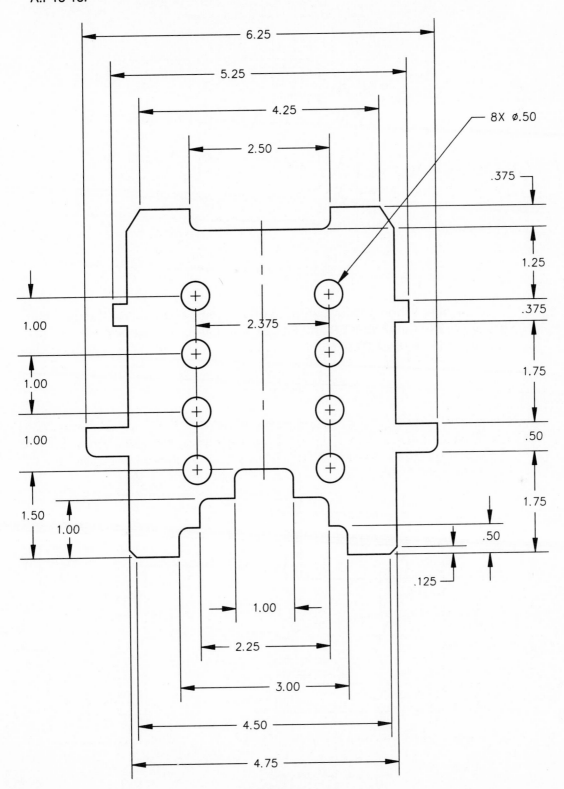

NOTE:   ALL FILLETS AND ROUNDS R.125.

14. Refer to the view shown below for this problem. Plan to use the **TRIM, OSNAP,** and **OFFSET** commands to assist you in drawing the view. Do not draw centerlines or dimensions. Save the completed drawing as A:P13-14.

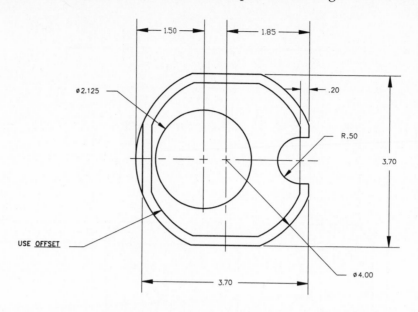

15. Draw the object shown below, without dimensions. Then mirror the right half into place. Use the **CHAMFER** and **FILLET** commands to your best advantage. Save the drawing as A:P13-15.

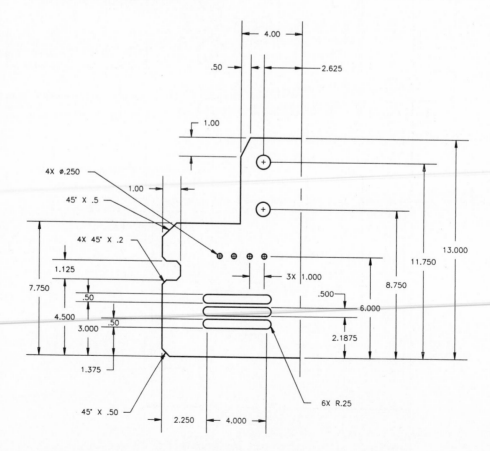

16. Redraw the objects shown below. Then mirror the drawing, but have the text remain readable. Delete the original image during the mirroring process. Save the drawing as A:P13-16.

*Piping*

2b1

TRANSFER

5a2  4a1  8a1

LTS. HTRS. FANS

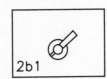

2b1

1b1

RESET

11b1

BYPASS

17. Draw the kitchen cabinet layout shown in view A and the partial floor plan shown at B. Make the cabinet 24″ (600mm) deep and the walls 6″ (150mm) wide. Make the sink and range proportional in size to the given illustration. Use the **ALIGN** command to move and rotate the cabinet layout into the wall location as shown in view C. Save the drawing as A:P13-17.

*Architectural*

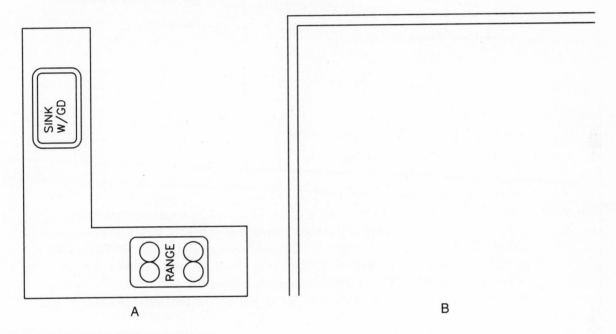

A                                                                                    B

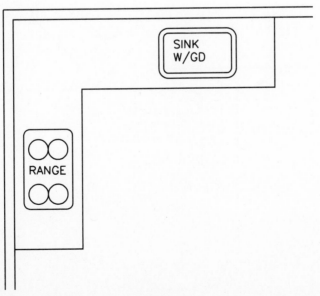

C

*General*

18. Draw the following objects. All rounds on the drawing are .250 unit radius. Use the **CAL** command to assist you in moving the circular object at the right to be centered exactly between points 1 and 2 on the object on the left. Do not dimension the drawing. Save the drawing as A:P13-18.

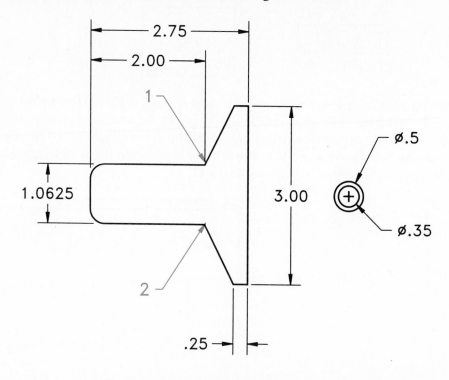

*General*

19. Open drawing P13-18. Make a copy of the object and rotate the copy to a horizontal position similar to the object shown at A below. Exact position is not critical. Rotate the original object to 225° as shown at B. Use the **ROTATE, MOVE,** or **ALIGN** commands as needed. Your objects should now look like A and B below. Use the **ROTATE** and **CAL** commands to rotate the object on the right so that the base is parallel to the base of the object on the left. Save the drawing as A:P13-19.

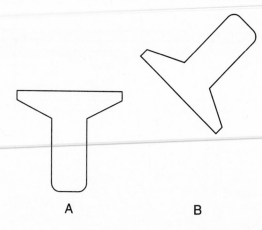

A                          B

20. Draw the objects shown at the left using the dimensions given, but do not draw the dimensions. Copy all of the objects to a position to the right and perform the specified **TRIM** and **EXTENT** operations to demonstrate a before and after representation. Save the drawing as A:P13-20.

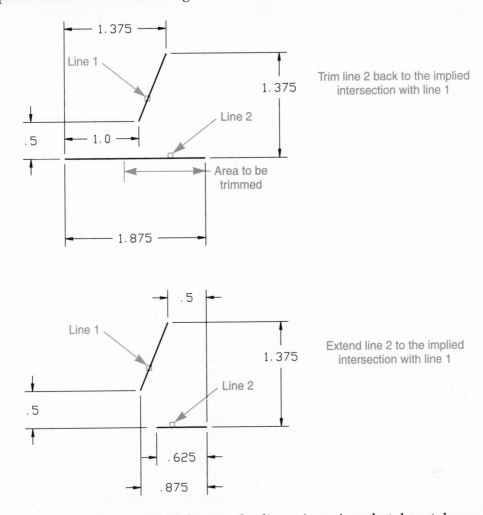

21. Draw the objects shown at the left using the dimensions given, but do not draw the dimensions. Copy all of the objects to a position to the right and perform the specified **LENGTHEN** operations to demonstrate a before and after representation. Perform all operations from the right end of the copied lines. Save the drawing as A:P13-21.

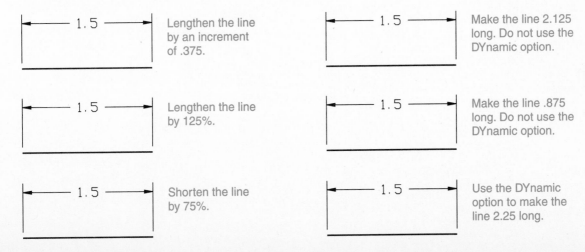

General

22. Draw the objects shown at the left using the dimensions given, but do not draw the dimensions. Copy all of the objects to a position to the right and perform the specified **LENGTHEN** operations to demonstrate a before and after representation. Perform all operations from the bottom-left end of the copied arcs. Save the drawing as A:P13-22.

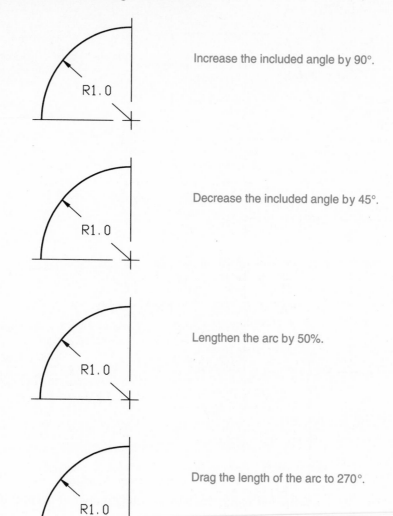

Increase the included angle by 90°.

R1.0

Decrease the included angle by 45°.

R1.0

Lengthen the arc by 50%.

R1.0

Drag the length of the arc to 270°.

R1.0

23. Draw the following object without dimensions. Note: Use the **TRIMMODE** to your advantage. Save the drawing as A:P13-23.

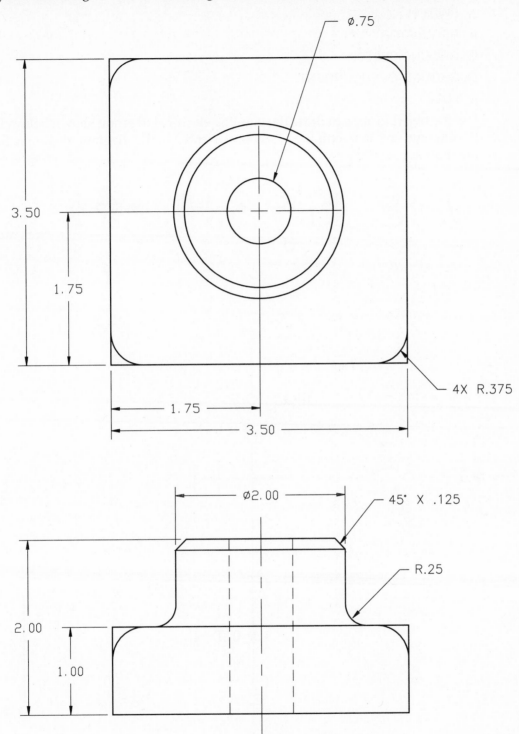

Piping

24. Draw the objects shown at A, B, C, D, and E below. Use the **GROUP** command to name each of the drawings as follows:

A. SWITCH

B. REGULATOR

C. GROUND-SWITCH

D. GROUND-OVERCURRENT

E. FUSE

Use the object groups to draw the one-line electrical diagram shown below. Use the **Explode** option to edit the symbols at 1 and 2 in the diagram as shown. Save the drawing as A:P13-24.

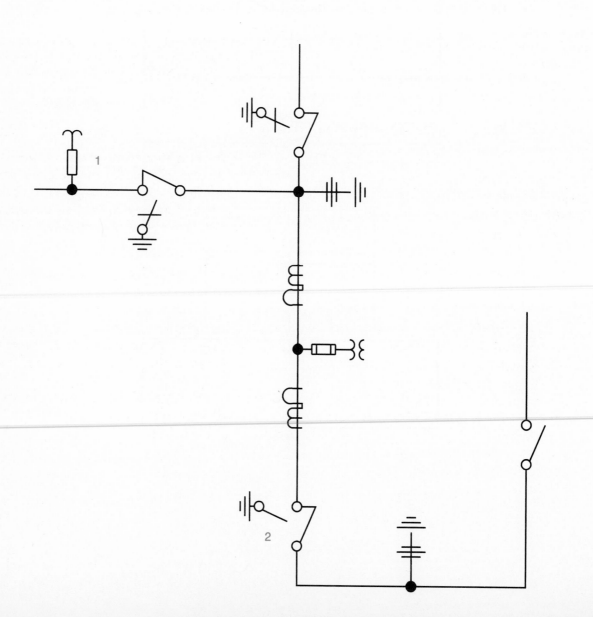

## Learning objectives

After completing this chapter, you will be able to:

○ Use grips to do automatic editing with the **STRETCH**, **COPY**, **MOVE**, **ROTATE**, **SCALE**, and **MIRROR** commands.

○ Identify the system variables used for automatic editing.

○ Perform automatic editing through the **Modify** dialog box.

○ Change the properties of an object.

○ Use the **FILTER** command to create a selection set.

In Chapter 13, you learned how to use commands that let you do a variety of drawing and editing activities with AutoCAD. These editing commands give you maximum flexibility and increase productivity. However, this chapter takes editing a step further by allowing you to select an object and automatically perform editing operations.

## AUTOMATIC EDITING WITH GRIPS

AUG 5

"Hold," "grab," and "grasp" are all words that are synonymous with grip. In AutoCAD, *grips* are features on an entity that are highlighted with a small box. For example, the grips on a straight line are the ends and midpoint. When grips are used for editing, you can select an object to automatically activate the grips. Then, pick any of the small boxes to perform stretch, copy, move, rotate, scale, or mirror operations. In order for grips to work the **GRIPS** system variable must be on.

```
Command: GRIPS ↵
New value for GRIPS ⟨0⟩: 1 ↵
Command:
```

When **GRIPS** is on and there is no command active, there is a pickbox located at the intersection of the screen crosshairs. You can pick any object with the pickbox to activate the grips. Figure 14-1 shows what grips look like on several different entities. For text, the grip box is located at the insertion point.

You can control grips settings by picking **Grips...** in the **Options** pull-down menu or by typing DDGRIPS at the **Command:** prompt. The **Grips** dialog box shown in Figure 14-2 is then displayed.

Figure 14-1.   Grips are placed at strategic locations on objects.

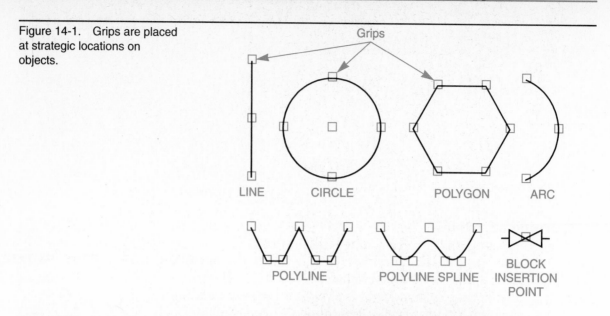

Figure 14-2.   The **Grips** dialog box.

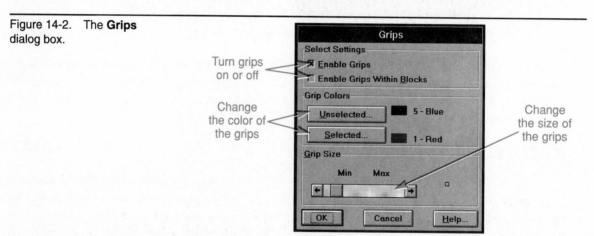

Notice the **Select Settings** check boxes in the **Grips** dialog box. Pick the **Enable Grips** check box to turn grips on or off. Pick the **Enable Grips Within Blocks** check box to have grips displayed on every sub-entity of a block. A *block* is a special symbol designed for multiple use. Blocks are discussed in detail in Chapter 25. When this check box is off, the grip location for a block is at the insertion point, as shown in Figure 14-1. Grips in blocks can also be controlled with the **GRIPBLOCK** system variable. The default for **GRIPBLOCK** is 0. Enter 1 and press [Enter] to turn on grips within blocks.

The **Grip Colors** buttons allow you to change the color of grips. The grips displayed when you first pick an entity are referred to as *unselected grips* because you have not yet picked a grip to perform an operation. An unselected grip is a square with a color outline. Unselected grips are blue by default and are called "warm." After you pick a grip it is called a *selected grip*. A selected grip appears as a filled-in square, as shown in Figure 14-3. Selected grips are red by default and are called "hot." If more than one entity is selected and they have warm grips, then they are all affected by what you do with the hot grips. Entities that have warm and hot grips are highlighted and are part of the selection set. You can remove highlighted entities from the selection set by holding down the [Shift] key and picking the entity to be removed. The highlighting goes away, but the grips remain. These are called "cold" grips. Entities with cold grips are not affected by what you do to entities with warm grips. Return the entity with cold grips to the selection set by picking it again.

Figure 14-3. Selected (hot) grips are filled-in squares. Unselected (warm) grips are colored outlines.

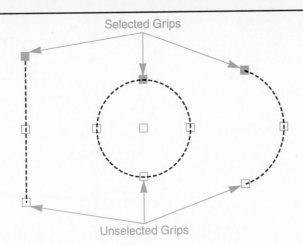

Selected Grips

Unselected Grips

You can also control grip color with the **GRIPCOLOR** and **GRIPHOT** system variables. **GRIPCOLOR** controls the color of unselected (warm) grips, while **GRIPHOT** regulates the color of selected (hot) grips. When you enter one of these variables, simply set the color number as desired.

The **Grip Size** scroll bar in the **Grips** dialog box lets you graphically change the size of the grip box. Change the grip size to whatever works best for your drawing. Very small grip boxes may be difficult to pick. However, the grips may overlap if they are too large.

The grip size can be given a numerical value at the command line using the **GRIPSIZE** system variable. To change the default of 3, enter GRIPSIZE at the **Command:** prompt and then type a desired size in pixels.

## Using grips

To activate grips, move the pick box to the desired entity and pick. The object is highlighted and the unselected grips are displayed. To select a grip, move the pick box to the desired grip and pick it. Notice that the crosshairs snap to a grip. When you pick a grip the command line changes to:

```
** STRETCH **
⟨Stretch to point⟩/Base point/Copy/Undo/eXit:
```

This activates the **STRETCH** command. All you have to do is move the cursor to make the selected object stretch, as shown in Figure 14-4. If you pick the middle grip of a line or arc, or the center grip of a circle, the object moves. These are the other options:

- **Base point.** Enter B and press [Enter] to select an new base point.
- **Copy.** Enter C and press [Enter] if you want to make one or more copies of the selected object.
- **Undo.** Enter U and press [Enter] to undo the previous operation.
- **eXit.** Enter X and press [Enter] to exit the command. The selected grip is gone, but the unselected grips remain. You can also use [Esc] key to cancel the command. Canceling twice removes the selected and the unselected grips and returns the **Command:** prompt.

Figure 14-4. Using the automatic **STRETCH** command. Note the selected grip. A—Stretching a line. B—Stretching a circle. C—Stretching an arc.

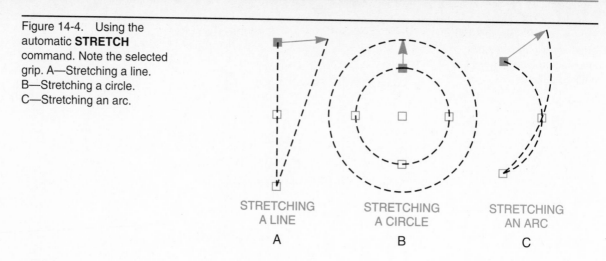

STRETCHING A LINE
A

STRETCHING A CIRCLE
B

STRETCHING AN ARC
C

Figure 14-5. Stretching an object. A—Select corners to stretch individually. B—Select several hot grips by holding down the [Shift] key.

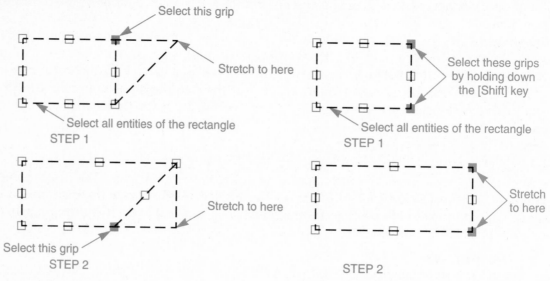

You can pick entities individually, or use a window or crossing box. Figure 14-5 shows how you can stretch features of an object after selecting all of the entities. Step 1 in Figure 14-5A illustrates stretching the first corner and Step 2 stretches the second corner. You can also make more than one grip hot at the same time by holding down the [Shift] key as you pick the grips, as shown in Figure 14-5B. Here are some general rules and guidelines that can help make grips work for you:

✓ Be sure the **GRIPS** system variable is on.
✓ Pick an entity or group of entities to activate grips.
✓ Entities in the selection set are highlighted.
✓ Pick a warm grip to make it hot.
✓ Make more than one grip hot by holding down the [Shift] key while picking warm grips.
✓ If more than one entity is selected and they have hot grips, then they are all affected by the editing commands.
✓ Remove entities from the selection set by holding down the [Shift] key and picking them, thus making the grips cold.
✓ Return entities to the selection set by picking them again.

✓ Remove hot grips from the selection set by pressing [Esc] key to cancel. Cancel again to remove all grips from the selection set. If you have not yet picked a hot grip, cancel twice at the keyboard.

---

**PROFESSIONAL TIP**

When editing with grips, you can enter coordinates to help improve your accuracy. Remember that any of the coordinate entry methods discussed in Chapter 6 will work.

---

## EXERCISE 14-1

❑ Load AutoCAD for Windows and open TITLEA.
❑ Draw a line with coordinates X = 2, Y = 4 and X = 2, Y = 7. Draw a circle with the center at X = 5.5, Y = 5.5, with a radius of 1.5. Finally, draw an arc with its center at X = 8.5, Y = 5.5, a start point of X = 9.5, Y = 4, and an endpoint of X = 9.5, Y = 7.
❑ In the space at the bottom of the screen, draw a polyline on the left similar to the one in Figure 14-1.
❑ Make sure **GRIPS** are on.
❑ Experiment with the **STRETCH** command using grips by picking the points as follows:
  ❑ Line—Pick the ends first and then the middle to see what happens.
  ❑ Circle—Pick one of the quadrants, and the center.
  ❑ Arc—Pick the ends and the middle.
  ❑ Polyline—Pick various grips.
❑ Save the drawing as A:EX14-1 and quit.

You can also use the **MOVE**, **ROTATE**, **SCALE**, and **MIRROR** commands to automatically edit entities. All you have to do is pick the object and then select one of the grips. When you see the ** STRETCH ** command, press [Enter] to cycle through the command options:

    ** STRETCH **
    ⟨Stretch to point⟩/Base point/Copy/Undo/eXit: ↵
    ** MOVE **
    ⟨Move to point⟩/Base point/Copy/Undo/eXit: ↵
    ** ROTATE **
    ⟨Rotation angle⟩/Base point/Copy/Undo/Reference/eXit: ↵
    ** SCALE **
    ⟨Scale factor⟩/Base point/Copy/Undo/Reference/eXit: ↵
    ** MIRROR **
    ⟨Second point⟩/Base point/Copy/Undo/eXit:

As an alternative to pressing [Enter], you can enter the first two characters of the desired command from the keyboard as follows. Type MO for move, MI for mirror, RO for rotate, SC for scale, and ST for stretch.

---

**NOTE**

When AutoCAD for Windows is configured to display a screen menu, the **Move**, **Mirror**, **Rotate**, **Scale**, and **Stretch** automatic editing commands appear in a separate screen menu whenever a grip is selected. See *AutoCAD and its Applications—Advanced, Release 13 for Windows*.

**PROFESSIONAL TIP**

Many of the conventional AutoCAD editing operations can be performed when warm grips are displayed on-screen and the **PICK-FIRST** variable is set to 1 (its default value). The editing commands can be selected from the pull-down menus, the toolbox, or entered at the **Command:** prompt. For example, the **ERASE** command can be used to clear the screen of all entities displayed with warm grips by first picking the entities and then selecting the **ERASE** command.

## Moving an object automatically

If you want to move an object with grips, select the object, pick a grip to use as the base point, and then cycle through the commands until you get to this prompt:

> \*\* MOVE \*\*
> 〈Move to point〉/Base point/Copy/Undo/eXit:

The selected grip becomes the base point. Then, move the object to a new point and pick. The **MOVE** operation is complete as shown in Figure 14-6. If you accidentally pick the wrong grip or decide to change the grip base point, enter B and press [Enter] for the **Base point** option and pick a new one.

Figure 14-6.   The automatic **MOVE** command. The selected grip becomes the base point for the move.

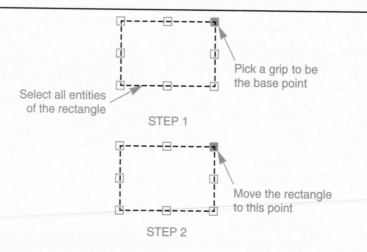

Pick a grip to be the base point

Select all entities of the rectangle

STEP 1

Move the rectangle to this point

STEP 2

**EXERCISE 14-2**

❏ Load AutoCAD for Windows and open TITLEA.
❏ Draw a 1.5″ (38.1mm) diameter circle with its center at X = 2, Y = 3.
❏ Use grips to move the circle 2″ (50.8mm) to the right.
❏ Save the drawing as A:EX14-2 and quit.

## Copying an object automatically

The **Copy** option is found in each of the editing commands. When using the **STRETCH** command, the **Copy** option allows you to make multiple copies of the entity you are stretching. Holding down the [Shift] key while performing the first **STRETCH** operation accesses the **Multiple** mode. The prompt looks like this:

> \*\* STRETCH (multiple) \*\*
> 〈Stretch to point〉/Base point/Copy/Undo/eXit: ↵

The **Copy** option in the **MOVE** command is the true form of the **COPY** command. You can activate the **Copy** option by entering C as follows:

    ** MOVE **
    ⟨Move to point⟩/Base point/Copy/Undo/eXit: **C** ↵
    ** MOVE (multiple) **
    ⟨Move to point⟩/Base point/Copy/Undo/eXit: *(make as many copies as desired and*
        *enter X to exit, or press* [Esc])

Holding down the [Shift] key while performing the first **MOVE** operation also puts you in the **Copy** mode. The **Copy** option works similarly in each of the editing commands. Try it with each to see what happens.

**PROFESSIONAL TIP**

When in the **Copy** option of the **MOVE** command, if you make the first copy followed by holding the [Shift] key, the distance of the first copy automatically becomes the snap spacing for additional copies.

## EXERCISE 14-3

❑ Load AutoCAD for Windows and open TITLEA.
❑ Use the **RECTANG** command to draw the objects shown at A, B, C, and D below. Do not draw dimensions.
❑ Use the **Copy** option of the **STRETCH** command to make object A look similar to the example at the right.
❑ Use the **Copy** option of the **STRETCH** command to make object B look similar to the example at the right. Make two grips hot for this to work.
❑ Use the **Copy** option of the **MOVE** command to make multiple copies to the right of object C.
❑ Use the **MOVE** command to make multiple copies to the right of object D while holding down the [Shift] key.
❑ Save the drawing as A:EX14-3 and quit.

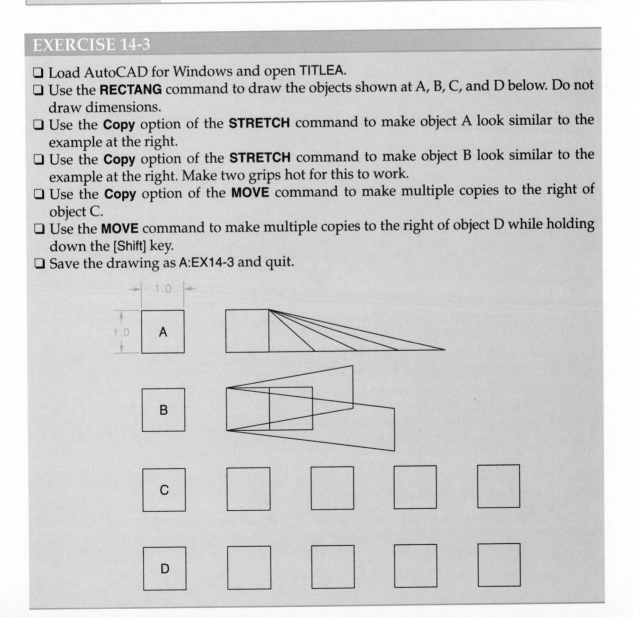

## Rotating an object automatically

To automatically rotate an object, select the object, pick a grip to use as the base point, and press [Enter] until you see this prompt:

```
** ROTATE **
⟨Rotation angle⟩/Base point/Copy/Undo/Reference/eXit:
```

Now, move your pointing device to rotate the object. Pick the desired rotation point, or enter a rotation angle like this:

```
⟨Rotation angle⟩/Base point/Copy/Undo/Reference/eXit: 45 ↵
```

Enter R and press [Enter] if you want to use the **Reference** option:

```
⟨Rotation angle⟩/Base point/Copy/Undo/Reference/eXit: R ↵
```

The **Reference** option may be used when the object is already rotated at a known angle and you want to rotate it to a new angle. The reference angle is the current angle and the new angle is the desired angle. Figure 14-7 shows the **Rotation** options.

```
Reference angle ⟨0⟩: 45 ↵
** ROTATE **
⟨New angle⟩/Base point/Copy/Undo/Reference/eXit: 10 ↵
```

Figure 14-7.   The **Rotation angle** option and **Reference** option of the **ROTATE** command.

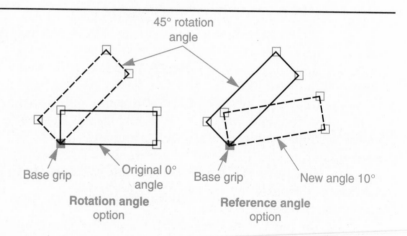

**EXERCISE 14-4**

❑ Load AutoCAD for Windows and open TITLEA.
❑ Use the **RECTANG** command to draw a rectangle similar to the one shown at the left of Figure 14-7. Orient the long sides so they are at 0°.
❑ Use grips to rotate the object 45°.
❑ Rotate the object again to 20° using the **Reference** option.
❑ Save the drawing as A:EX14-4 and quit.

## Scaling an object automatically

If you want to scale an object with grips, cycle through the editing options until you get this prompt:

```
** SCALE **
⟨Scale factor⟩/Base point/Copy/Undo/Reference/eXit:
```

Move the screen cursor and pick when the object is dragged to the desired size. You can also enter a scale factor to automatically increase or decrease the scale of the original object. Scale factors are given in Chapter 13 of this text. You can use the **Reference** option if you know a current length and a desired length. Enter R for the **Reference** option:

> ⟨Scale factor⟩/Base point/Copy/Undo/Reference/eXit: **R** ↵
> Reference length ⟨*current*⟩: **3.0** ↵
> ** SCALE **
> ⟨New length⟩/Base point/Copy/Undo/Reference/eXit: **5.25** ↵

The selected base point remains in the same place when the object is scaled. Figure 14-8 shows the two **Scale** options.

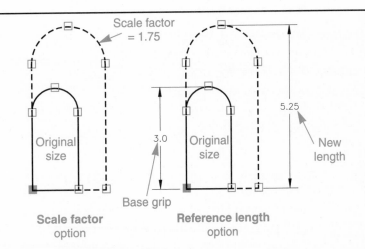

Figure 14-8. The options for the automatic **SCALE** command include the **Scale factor** option and the **Reference length** option.

---

## EXERCISE 14-5

❑ Load AutoCAD for Windows and open TITLEA.
❑ Draw an object similar to the original object on the left in Figure 14-8.
❑ Activate grips to make a copy of the object to the right of the original.
❑ Scale the first object using a scale factor of 1.5.
❑ Use the **Reference** option to scale the second object to any height.
❑ Save the drawing as A:EX14-5 and quit.

---

### Mirroring an object automatically

If you want to mirror an object using grips, the selected grip becomes the first point of the mirror line. Use the **Base point** option to reselect the first point of the mirror line. Then press [Enter] to cycle through the editing commands until you get this prompt:

> ** MIRROR **
> ⟨Second point⟩/Base point/Copy/Undo/eXit:

Pick another grip or any point on the screen as the second point of the mirror line, Figure 14-9. Unlike the **MIRROR** command accessed through the pull-down menu, toolbox, and keyboard, the automatic **MIRROR** command does not give you the option to delete the old objects. The old objects are deleted automatically. If you want to keep the original object while mirroring, use the **Copy** option in the **MIRROR** command.

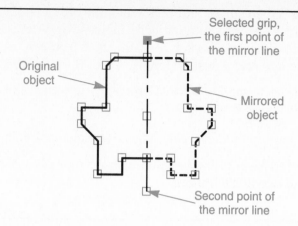

Figure 14-9. When using the automatic **MIRROR** command, the selected grip becomes the first point of the mirror line.

**EXERCISE 14-6**

❑ Load AutoCAD for Windows and open TITLEA.
❑ Draw a shape similar to the original object in Figure 14-9.
❑ Use grips to mirror the object along the centerline.
❑ Save the drawing as A:EX14-6 and quit.

## BASIC EDITING VS. AUTOMATIC EDITING

In Chapter 13 you were introduced to basic editing. Basic editing allows you to first enter a command and then select the desired object to be edited. You can also set system variables to first select the desired objects and then enter the desired command. The automatic editing features discussed in this chapter use grips and related editing commands to edit an object automatically by picking the object first.

The **Object Selection Settings** dialog box allows you to control the way that you use editing commands. This dialog box is displayed by typing DDSELECT at the **Command:** prompt, or by picking **Selection...** from the **Options** pull-down menu. See Figure 14-10. These are the items found in the **Object Selection Settings** dialog box:

- **Noun/Verb Selection.** When you first select objects and then enter a command, it is referred to as the *noun/verb* format. This technique is used throughout most of this book. The pick box is displayed at the screen crosshairs. An "X" in the **Noun/Verb Selection** check box means that the noun/verb method is active. The **PICKFIRST** system variable can also be used to set the noun/verb selection. The *verb/noun* format is when you enter the command before selecting the object. In this text, the verb/noun method is used primarily in Chapter 13. Remove the "X" from the **Noun/Verb Selection** check box to enter the command before making a selection. Some editing commands such as **FILLET, CHAMFER, DIVIDE, MEASURE, OFFSET, EXTEND, TRIM,** and **BREAK** require that you enter the command before you select the object.

- **Use Shift to Add.** When this check box is off, every entity or group of entities you select is highlighted and added to the selection set. If you pick this check box, it changes the way AutoCAD accepts entities you pick. For example, if you pick an entity, it is highlighted and added to the selection set. However, if you pick another entity, it is highlighted and the first one is removed from the selection set. This means that you can only include one entity by picking, or one group of entities with a selection window. If you want to add more items to the selection set, you must hold down the [Shift] key as you pick them. Turning on the **PICKADD** system variable does the same thing as turning on this feature.

- **Press and Drag.** This is the same as turning on the **PICKDRAG** system variable. With **Press and Drag** on, you create a selection window by picking the first corner, then moving the puck while holding down the pick button. Release the pick button when you have the desired selection window. By default, **Press and Drag** is off. This means that you have to pick both the first and second corner of the desired selection window.
- **Implied Windowing.** By default, this option is on. This means that you can automatically create a window by picking the first point, and moving the cursor to the right to pick the second point, or make a crossing box by picking the first point and moving the cursor to the left to pick the second point. This is the same as turning on the **PICKAUTO** system variable. This does not work if **PICKDRAG** is on.
- **Object Grouping.** This option controls whether or not AutoCAD recognizes grouped objects as singular entities. When off, the individual elements of a group can be selected for separate editing without having to first explode the group.
- **Default.** Picking this button sets the selection methods to the AutoCAD defaults, as shown in Figure 14-10.

Figure 14-10. The **Object Selection Settings** dialog box.

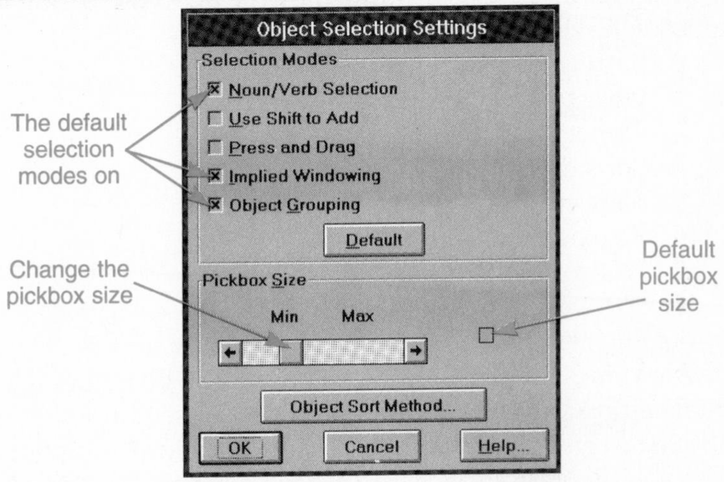

- **Pickbox Size.** This scroll bar lets you adjust the size of the pick box. The sample in the image tile will get smaller or larger as you move the scroll bar. Stop when you have the desired size. The pick box size is also controlled by the **PICKBOX** system variable.
- **Object Sort Method....** The **Object Sort Method** subdialog box shown in Figure 14-11 appears when you pick this button. The check boxes in the **Object Sort Method** subdialog box allows you to control the order that entities are displayed or plotted in. The check boxes are explained as follows:
  - **Object Selection**—Makes sure that objects selected using a windowing method are placed in the selection set in the order they occur in the drawing database.
  - **Object Snap**—Makes sure that object snap modes find objects in the order they occur in the drawing database.
  - **Redraws**—Makes sure that objects are displayed by a **REDRAW** command in the order they occur in the drawing database.
  - **Slide Creation**—Writes the slide file so that when viewing the slide, objects are displayed in the order they occur in the drawing database.
  - **Regens**—Makes sure that objects are displayed by a drawing regeneration in the order they occur in the drawing database.
  - **Plotting**—Makes sure that objects are plotted in the order they occur in the drawing database.

Figure 14-11. This subdialog box can be accessed by picking **Object Sort Method...** from the **Object Selection Settings** dialog box.

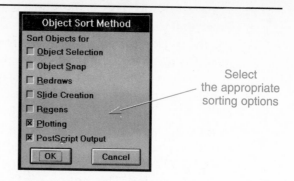

Select the appropriate sorting options

- **PostScript Output**—Makes sure that **PSOUT** processes objects in the order they occur in the drawing database. PostScript is a copyrighted page description language that is used in the desktop publishing industry. This is discussed further in *AutoCAD and its Applications—Advanced, Release 13 for Windows*. The **PSOUT** command converts any AutoCAD drawing to a PostScript file.

Entity sorting is also controlled by the **SORTENTS** system variable. The following values duplicate the check boxes in the dialog box:

  0  Sorting is turned off.
  1  Object selection sorting.
  2  Object snap sorting.
  4  Sorts entities in a redraw.
  8  Slide creation sorting.
 16  Regeneration sorting.
 32  Plot sorting.
 64  Sort for PostScript output.

The default, 96, specifies sorting for plotting and PostScript output. This is because the numeric values for each setting are *bit* values. Bit values allow you to add together the individual setting values to indicate each of the set values. Since the values $64 + 32 = 96$, this **SORTENTS** setting sorts both for **Plotting** and for **PostScript** output. If you wanted to set the object sort method to include **Object Selection** (1), **Object Snap** (2) and **Redraws** (4), the **SORTENTS** value should be 7 because $1 + 2 + 4 = 7$.

**PROFESSIONAL TIP**

Notice in Figure 14-11 that only two of the check boxes are checked. Entity sorting takes time and should only be used if the drawing or application software you are using requires entity sorting. Turn the **Object Selection** sorting on if you want AutoCAD to find the last object drawn when selecting overlapping entities.

**EXERCISE 14-7**

❑ Load AutoCAD for Windows.
❑ Enter the DDSELECT command to open the **Object Selection Settings** dialog box.
❑ Adjust the pick box size and observe the image tile.
❑ Pick **Object Sort Method...** to open the **Object Sort Method** subdialog box.
❑ Cancel both dialog boxes.
❑ Quit the drawing session.

# AUTOMATIC EDITING IN A DIALOG BOX

To edit an entity using the **Modify** dialog box, type DDMODIFY at the **Command:** prompt, click the **Properties** button from the **Object Properties** toolbar, or pick **Properties…** from the **Edit** pull-down menu. You are first asked to select an object to modify:

> Command: **DDMODIFY** ↵
> Select object to modify: *(pick a single object to modify)*

If you pick a line, you get the **Modify Line** dialog box. If you pick a circle you get the **Modify Circle** dialog box shown in Figure 14-12. Each of the **Modify** dialog boxes is slightly different. For example, the **Modify Line** dialog box contains information about the line from the two endpoints, and text boxes to change the endpoint coordinates. If you pick an entity such as a polygon, you get the **Modify Polyline** dialog box. This dialog box contains items that allow you to automatically edit various aspects of a polyline. Remember from Chapter 8 that polygons and rectangles are polylines.

Figure 14-12.   **Modify** dialog boxes, such as the **Modify Circle** dialog box, can be used to edit entities.

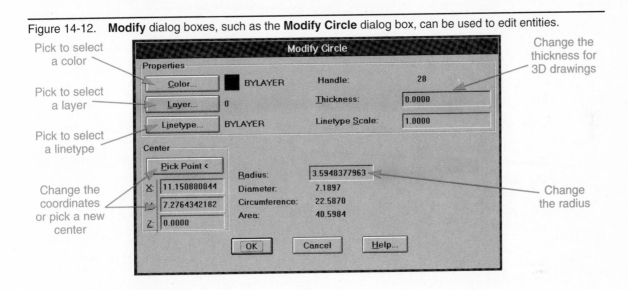

The **Modify Text** dialog box is an excellent way to quickly and easily edit text. To get the **Modify Text** dialog box shown in Figure 14-13, enter the **DDMODIFY** command and pick the single-line text to be modified. The **Properties** options allow you to change the color, linetype, layer, linetype scale, and thickness. You can edit the text wording by moving the cursor to the **Text:** edit box and remove, add, or change the text as needed. Change the text origin by selecting the **Pick Point** ⟨ button and picking a new point on the screen, or enter new X, Y coordinates. Automatically change the text height in the **Height:** text box, or change the rotation angle, width factor, or obliquing angle by altering the values in these text boxes. Pick the arrow at the right of the **Justify** box to get the justification pop-up list. Pick the desired justification from this list. Select a text style that has been previously created by picking the desired style from the **Style** pop-up list. Check either the **Upside Down** or the **Backward** boxes if you want these conditions to be in effect.

The next sections discuss features found in **Modify** dialog boxes. These features are common to all of the **Modify** dialog boxes.

Figure 14-13.  A simple means to edit text is through the use of the **Modify Text** dialog box.

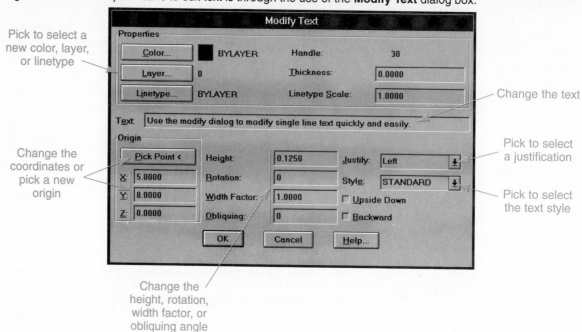

Pick to select a
new color, layer,
or linetype

Change the
coordinates or
pick a new
origin

Change the text

Pick to select
a justification

Pick to select
the text style

Change the
height, rotation,
width factor, or
obliquing angle

## Properties

The **Properties** section of all **Modify** dialog boxes contains several common elements. These are:

- **Color....** Pick this button to get the **Select Color** subdialog box. This subdialog box displays the available colors. Simply pick a desired color for this entity, or enter a color name or number in the **Color:** text box.
- **Linetype....** Pick this button to see the **Select Linetype** subdialog box. Here you can change the entity linetype by selecting one of the linetypes that has already been loaded.
- **Layer....** Picking this button displays the **Select Layer** dialog box where you can set the selected entity to a desired layer. Layers are discussed in Chapter 19.
- **Thickness:.** This text box lets you change the thickness of a 3D entity. This is discussed in Chapter 29.
- **Linetype Scale:.** This text box allows you to change the individual object linetype scale as a multiplier of the **LTSCALE** system variable.

## Changing the center point

When an object such as a circle or an arc is selected using **DDMODIFY**, the following information is provided:

- **Pick Point ⟨.** Pick this button to establish a new center point. The dialog box disappears, the graphics window returns, and you see this prompt:

  Center point: (*pick a new center point, or enter the coordinates for a new center location and press* [Enter])

- **X:, Y:, Z:.** Use these text boxes to change the values of the X, Y, or Z coordinates. The Z coordinate is for 3D drawings. The center location automatically changes when you enter new values and pick the **OK** button.

When modifying a circle, related information for the diameter, circumference, and area appear near the center of the **Modify** dialog box. The radius is also given in a text box. If you want to change the radius, double click on the **Radius:** text box and enter a new value. The circle automatically changes to the new radius.

> **NOTE**
>
> Changing an object's properties by picking the **Properties** button on the **Object Properties** toolbar or **Properties...** from the **Edit** pull-down menu will display different dialog boxes, depending on how many objects are selected. Only single objects can be modified using a **Modify** dialog box, so when more than one object is selected then the **Change Properties** dialog is displayed just as if you had used the **DDCHPROP** command. DDCHPROP and the **Change Properties** dialog are discussed in the next section of this chapter. If you type the **DDMODIFY** command, then AutoCAD doesn't allow you to select more than one object.

## EXERCISE 14-8

❑ Load AutoCAD for Windows and open TITLEA.
❑ Draw a line with endpoint coordinates X = 2, Y = 3, and X = 2, Y = 6.
❑ Draw a circle with a radius of 1.250 and a center location of X = 6, Y = 4.5.
❑ Use the **DTEXT** command with .25″ text height to position the word LINE below the line and CIRCLE below the circle.
❑ Use the **Modify Line** dialog box to edit the line as follows:
   ❑ Change the "from point" to X = 6.750, Y = 3.770.
   ❑ Change the "to point" to X = 6.750, Y = 6.750.
❑ Use the **Modify Circle** dialog box to edit the circle as follows:
   ❑ Change the center location to X = 7.125, Y = 5.25.
   ❑ Change the radius to .375.
❑ Change the LINE label to .125″ height and place it above the line.
❑ Change the CIRCLE label to read Circle and justify the middle of it with the center of the circle. Modify the text height to be .375″.
❑ Save the drawing as A:EX14-8 and quit.

> **PROFESSIONAL TIP**
>
> If you are trying to pick an entity that is on top of another, AutoCAD may not pick the one you want. However, AutoCAD picks the last thing you drew if **Object Selection** is on in the **Object Sort Method** dialog box.

## CHANGING THE PROPERTIES OF AN OBJECT

In Chapter 13 you learned how to make changes to an object using the **CHANGE** command. This is a popular command because it is easy to use and allows you to change either the location of an object or properties related to the object. In Chapter 13 you used the default, **Change point**, to change the location of an object. You can also change properties of the feature by entering P:

    Command: **CHANGE** ⏎
    Select objects: *(pick the object)*
    Select objects: ⏎
    Properties/⟨Change point⟩: **P** ⏎
    Change what property (Color/Elev/LAyer/LType/ltScale/Thickness) ?

The following properties can be changed with the **CHANGE** command:
- **Color.** Changes the color of the selected object.
- **Elev.** Used to change the elevation in 3D drawing.
- **Layer.** Changes the layer designation. Layers are discussed in Chapter 19.
- **LType.** Changes the current linetype of a selected object to a linetype that has been loaded using the **LINETYPE** command.
- **ItScale.** Changes the individual object linetype scale. The linetype scale representation can be changed using the **Linetype Scale:** edit box.
- **Thickness.** Used to change the thickness in 3D drawing.

The **CHPROP** (change property) command lets you change only properties of an object. It does not allow for a point changes as in the **CHANGE** command. This is the command sequence for **CHPROP**:

> Command: **CHPROP** ↵
> Select objects: *(pick the object)*
> Select objects: ↵
> Change what property (Color/LAyer/LType/ItScale/Thickness) ?

Except for **Elevation**, the **CHPROP** options are the same as those discussed for the **CHANGE** command.

If you prefer to use a dialog box, you can change properties by picking the **Properties** button on the **Object Properties** toolbar, entering **DDCHPROP** at the **Command:** prompt, or picking **Properties...** in the **Edit** pull-down menu. The command sequence for **DDCHPROP** is as follows:

> Command: **DDCHPROP** ↵
> Select objects: *(pick the object)*
> Select objects: ↵

The **Change Properties** dialog box shown in Figure 14-14 is displayed.

As you look at this dialog box you can see some of the items discussed earlier. You can pick **Color...** to change the entity color, pick **Layer...** to change the layer, or pick **Linetype...** to change the linetype. The thickness or linetype scale of an object can be changed using edit boxes.

Figure 14-14.   The **Change Properties** dialog box is accessed with the **DDCHPROP** command.

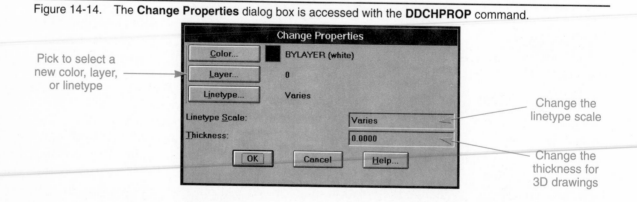

Pick to select a new color, layer, or linetype

Change the linetype scale

Change the thickness for 3D drawings

❑ Load AutoCAD for Windows and open TITLEA.
❑ Draw a vertical line on the left side of the screen, a circle in the middle, and a hexagon on the right side.
❑ Load the CENTER, HIDDEN, and PHANTOM linetypes.
❑ Use the **CHANGE** command to change the line's linetype to CENTER.
❑ Use the **CHPROP** command to change the circle's linetype to HIDDEN and the color to red.
❑ Enter the **Change Properties** dialog box and change the linetype of the hexagon to PHANTOM and the color to yellow.
❑ Save the drawing as A:EX14-9 and quit.

## USING FILTERS TO CREATE A SELECTION SET ┃ AUG 5 ┃

Even though the edit commands and selection methods that you have been using provide you with maximum flexibility, there are situations, especially on complex drawings, that limit your productivity. It would be nice, in these situations, if you could develop a selection set based on only specific characteristics of the drawing, such as all circles less than ∅1.00 or all text of a designated style. This is possible using filters. *Filters* allow you to create a selection set of only those items on the drawing that you designate.

### Creating entity filters

You can create a filter list of items based on specific properties that restrict a selection set. These filter list selection sets can be used in the current drawing or in a future drawing, if needed. This is done using the **FILTER** command. To access this command, select the **Selection Filters** button in the **Select Window** flyout on the **Standard** toolbar or type FILTER at the **Command:** prompt. It can also be accessed by picking **Selection Filters...** from the **Select Objects** ⟩ cascading submenu in the **Edit** pull-down menu. This command can be accessed transparently while inside another command at a **Select objects:** prompt by typing 'FILTER. These options access the **Object Selection Filters** dialog box shown in Figure 14-15. You can use this dialog box to identify filters for a variety of properties, including type of entity such as line or circle, linetype, color, text style, or layer.

Figure 14-15. The **Object Selection Filters** dialog box. The list box, **Selected Filters** area, and **Named Filters** area are highlighted here.

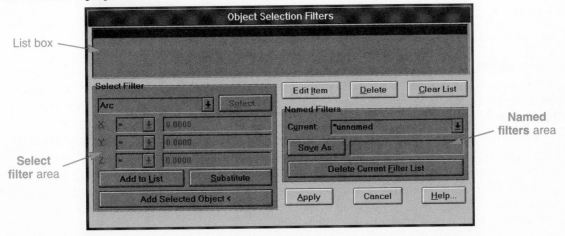

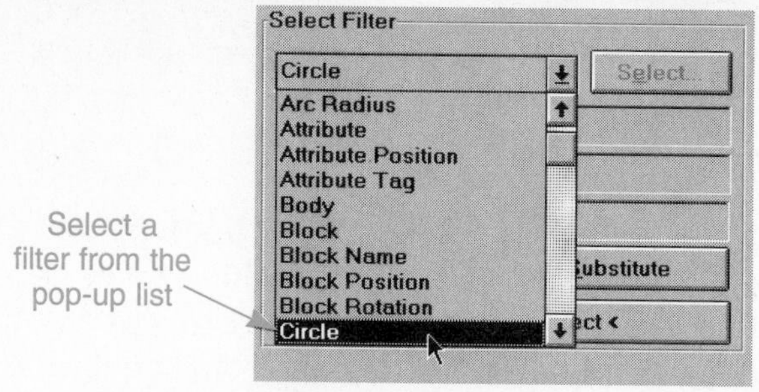

Figure 14-16.   Items picked
from the pop-up list appear
in the list box.

Select a
filter from the
pop-up list

There are three major areas of the **Object Selection Filters** dialog box, including the list box at the top of the dialog box, the **Select Filter** area, and the **Named Filters** area. You must first add items to the list box. This is done by picking an item from the pop-up list just below **Select Filter**. Use the scroll bar to access the desired item. For example, pick Circle as shown in Figure 14-16. Then, pick the **Add to List** button.

Now, Circle is placed in the list box. If you pick an item from the **Select Filter** list that has X, Y, and Z values such as **Circle Center** or **Line Start**, then the **X:**, **Y:**, and **Z:** coordinate pop-up lists and text boxes are no longer grayed-out. Picking a coordinate pop-up arrow accesses the expanded pop-up list shown in Figure 14-17. You can change the X, Y, and Z values in the text boxes, and you can establish relationships between the filtered items and designated units of measure. This is done by picking one of the symbols in the pop-up list. AutoCAD refers to these symbols as *relational operators*. A description of these symbols follow:

   =  Equals
   !=  Not equal to
   ⟨  Less than
   ⟨=  Less than or equal to
   ⟩  Greater than
   ⟩=  Greater than or equal to
   *  Multiply

Figure 14-17.   Relational
operators can be picked
from the pop-up list.

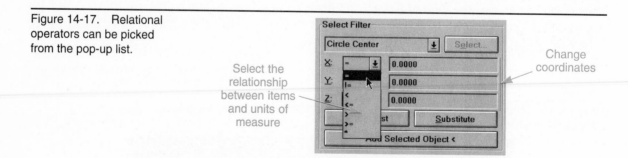

Select the
relationship
between items
and units of
measure

Change
coordinates

The **Select...** button is grayed-out unless you pick an item from the **Select Filter** pop-up list that accesses a dialog box. For example, picking **Text Style Name** and then the **Select...** button accesses the **Select Text Style Name(s)** subdialog box. This subdialog box shows you all of the currently defined text styles.

You can also add an entity from a drawing by picking the **Add Selected Object** ⟨ button. This button returns you to the drawing editor and prompts with **Select object:**. If you pick an item such as text, the properties of this entity are displayed in the list box. Figure 14-18 shows part of the list now present in the list box. Move the scroll bar to see all of the items listed. You can have as many items in the filter list box as you wish.

Figure 14-18.   The filters list is displayed in the list box. You can edit, apply, delete, and substitute these items.

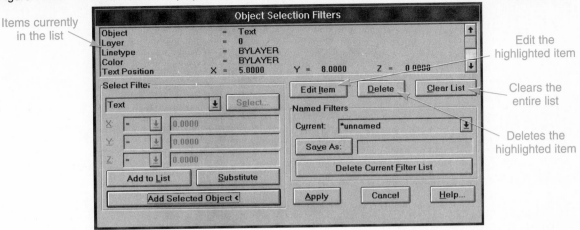

Now that you have a filters list you can use some of the other items in the dialog box. For example, pick the **Clear List** button to get rid of everything you just put in the list. You can highlight any item in the list by moving the pointer to the item and picking it. When an item is highlighted, you can remove it from the list by selecting the **Delete** button. You can substitute an item in the **Select Filter** list with a highlighted item in the filters list by picking the **Substitute** button. For example, if the filter list displays Text Style Name = ROMANS, you can change it to another existing text style, such as ROMANC. First, pick **Text Style Name** from the **Select Filter** pop-up list. Then, scroll down the list box and highlight the **Text Style Name** entry, followed by picking the **Select...** button. This accesses the **Select Text Style Name(s)** dialog box. Pick ROMANC followed by **OK** to close the dialog box. Finally, pick the **Substitute** button to execute the change.

If you want to edit an item in the list, first highlight it and then pick the **Edit Item** button. This places the current X, Y, and Z values of the item in the **Select Filter** text boxes for you to change as needed. Make the changes and pick the **Substitute** button for the alterations to take place.

The **Named Filters** area in Figure 14-15 shows the **Current:** filter as *unnamed. This appears when you start a drawing. Use the **Save As:** text box to save your current filter list. Enter the desired name in the text box followed by picking the **Save As:** button. This name becomes the current named filter. If there are several filter names, you can access these through the **Current:** pop-up list. You can delete the current named filter list by picking the **Delete Current Filter List** button.

Finally, pick the **Apply** button to exit the dialog box and have the selection set filters ready for use. If AutoCAD finds a problem with your filter list, you will get a message at the bottom of the dialog box. Pick the **Cancel** button if you decide not to continue with the filter list.

### Using filters on a drawing

Now, try using the filtering process on the drawing shown in Figure 14-19. Your supervisor likes the flowchart that you just finished, except you are asked to change all of the ROMANS text inside the flow chart and the note to a new layer and color for plotting or printing considerations. You could use the **CHPROP** command and individually select each word on the chart, but you decide to use the **FILTER** command to make the job easier. Access the **Object Selection Filters** dialog box and follow these steps:

1.  Pick the **Add Selected Object** ⟨ button. The drawing returns and you get this prompt:

        Command: FILTER
        Select object: *(pick one of the words in the chart such as* PRESIDENTS*)*

Figure 14-19.   Original flowchart requiring modification.

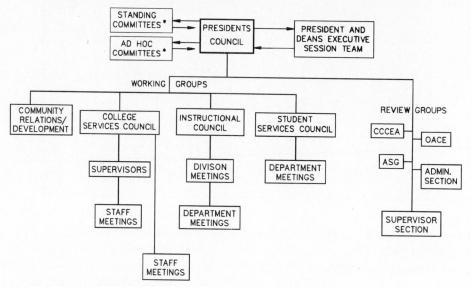

# GROUP DECISION MAKING PROCESS

*NOTE: STANDING OR AD HOC COMMITTEES MAY BE FORMED AT ANY LEVEL.

Figure 14-20.   Deleting selection filters.

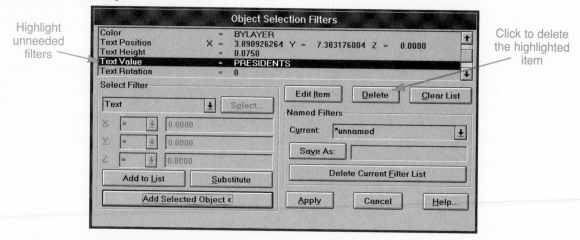

2.  The dialog box returns and displays the characteristics of the text you picked. Highlight items such as Text Position and Text Value, and pick the **Delete** button for each. These filters are not needed because they limit the filter list to specific aspects of the text. See Figure 14-20.

3.  Enter a filter name such as TEXT in the **Save As:** text box and then pick the **Save As:** button. The **Current:** filter name is TEXT, as shown in Figure 14-21.

4.  Pick the **Apply** button. The drawing returns and this prompt is given:

    Select object:
    Applying filter to selection.
    Select objects: *(window all of the drawing text to be included in the selection set)*
    Select objects: ↵

The text within the flowchart is now highlighted, and you see this prompt:

    Select objects: Other corner: 145 found
    107 were filtered out.

Figure 14-21.   Setting the filter name.

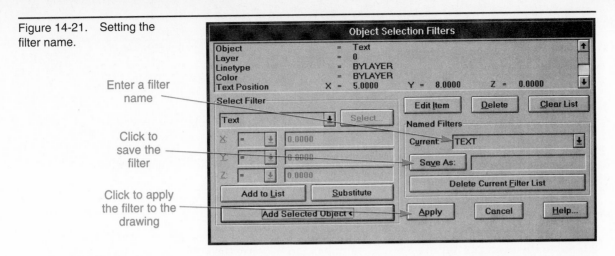

Enter a filter name

Click to save the filter

Click to apply the filter to the drawing

5. The highlighted text returns and the items that were previously highlighted become part of the selection set. Now that the desired items are part of a selection set, the next step is to access the set and change the layer.

6. At the **Command:** prompt, enter the **CHPROP** command. Enter P when you get the **Select objects:** prompt. This retrieves the selection set that was previously established with the **FILTER** command:

> Command: **CHPROP** ↵
> Select objects: **P** ↵
> 106 found
> Select objects: ↵
> Change what property (Color/LAyer/LType/ltScale/Thickness) ? **LA** ↵
> New layer ⟨0⟩: **COLOR** ↵
> Change what property (Color/LAyer/LType/ltScale/Thickness) ? ↵
> Command:

The **COLOR** layer was previously created with a color of red. You must create the layer before you can change to it. Now all of the text within the flow chart is on the **COLOR** layer in red color. The revised flowchart is shown in Figure 14-22.

Figure 14-22.   Revised flowchart. All text in the flow chart shown here in green should appear red on your screen.

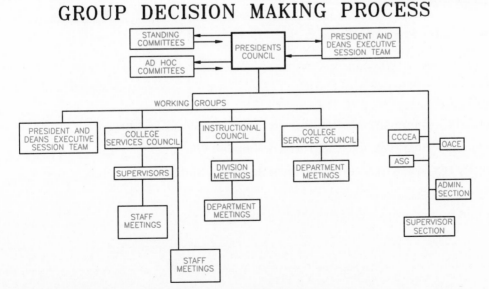

## CHAPTER TEST

*Write your answers in the spaces provided.*

1. Give the command and entries required to turn on grips:

   Command:_____

   New value for _____ ⟨⟩:_____

2. Give the prompts needed to rotate an object from an existing 60° angle to a new 25° angle:

   ⟨Rotation angle⟩/Base point/Copy/Undo/Reference/eXit: _____

   Reference angle ⟨⟩: _____

   ⟨New angle⟩/Base point/Copy/Undo/Reference/eXit: _____

3. Give the prompts required to scale an object to become three-quarters of its original size:

   ⟨Scale factor⟩/Base point/Copy/Undo/Reference/eXit: _____

4. Name the two system variables that control the color of grips._____

   _____

   _____

5. Name the six editing commands that can be accessed automatically. _____

   _____

   _____

   _____

6. Explain the difference between "noun/verb selection" and "verb/noun selection." ____

   _____

   _____

   _____

7. Name the system variable that allows you to set the "noun/verb selection." _____

8. What does **Use Shift to Add** mean?_____

   _____

   _____

   _____

9. Describe how **Press and Drag** works._____

   _____

   _____

   _____

10. Name the system variable that is used to turn on **Press and Drag**._____

11. Name the system variable that turns on **Implied Windowing**._____

12. Identify two ways to access the **Object Selection Settings** dialog box._____

   _____

13. Explain two ways to change the pick box size._____

   _____

   _____

14. Give the command sequence and explain how you would change the radius of a circle from 1.375 to 1.875 using a dialog box. _____

_____

_____

_____

_____

15. Identify the pull-down menu and the item you pick from this menu to access the dialog box described in Question 14. _____

_____

16. How would you change the linetype of an entity using the dialog box described in Question 14?_____

_____

_____

_____

17. Name three commands that allow you to change the properties of an object. _____

_____

_____

18. Which of the commands in Question 17 accesses the **Change Properties** dialog box?

_____

19. How do you access the **Change Properties** dialog box through a pull-down menu?

_____

20. How do you change the color of an entity using the **Change Properties** dialog box?

_____

_____

_____

## DRAWING PROBLEMS

*Use prototypes* **TITLEA** *or* **TITLEB** *as appropriate for each of the following problems. Use grips and the associated editing commands or other editing techniques discussed in this chapter.*

1. Draw the objects shown at A below and then use the **STRETCH** command to make them look like the objects at B. Do not include dimensions. Save the drawing as A:P14-1.

*General*

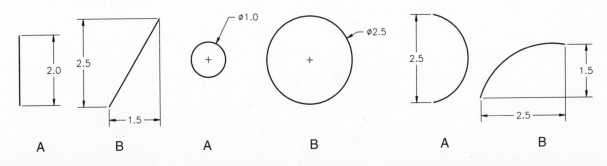

A        B        A        B        A        B

*General*

2. Draw the object shown at A below. Then using the **Copy** option of the **MOVE** command, copy the object to the position shown at B. Edit object A so that it resembles example C. Edit object B so that it looks like D. Do not include dimensions. Save the drawing as A:P14-2.

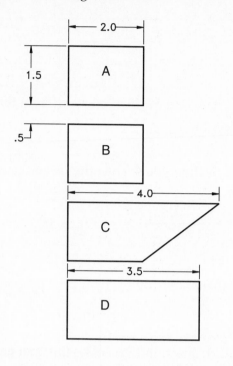

*General*

3. Draw the object shown at A below. Then copy the object, without rotating it, to a position below as indicated by the dashed lines. Then, rotate the object 45°. Copy the rotated object at B to a position below as indicated by the dashed lines. Use the **Reference** option to rotate the object at C to 25° as shown. Do not include dimensions. Save the drawing as A:P14-3.

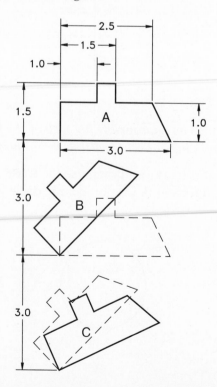

4. Draw the individual entities (vertical line, horizontal line, circle, arc, and "C" shape) at A below using the dimensions given. Then, use grips and the editing commands to create the object shown at B. Do not include dimensions. Save the drawing as A:P14-4.

*Piping*

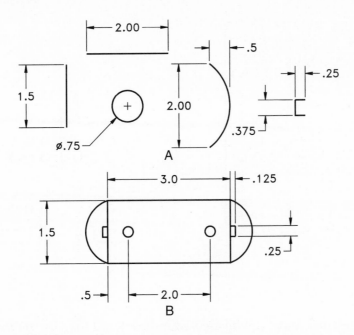

5. Use the completed drawing from Problem 14-4. Erase everything except the completed object and move it to a position similar to A below. Copy the object two times to positions B and C. Use the **SCALE** command to scale the object at B to fifty percent of its original size. Use the Reference option of the **SCALE** command to enlarge the object at C from the existing 3.0 length to a 4.5 length as shown in C. Do not include dimensions. Save as A:P14-5.

*Piping*

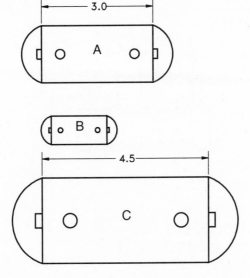

6. Draw the dimensioned partial object shown at A. Do not include dimensions. Mirror the drawing to complete the four quadrants as shown at B. Change the color of the horizontal and vertical parting lines to red and the linetype to CENTER. Save the drawing as A:P14-6.

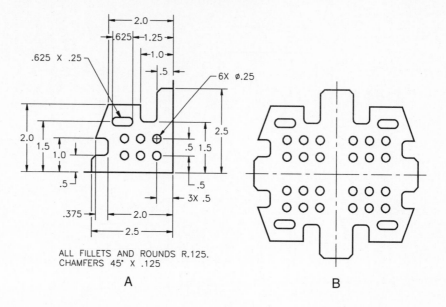

7. Load the final drawing you created in Problem 14-6. Use the **Modify Circle** dialog box to change the circles from ⌀.25 to ⌀.125. Use the **Change Properties** dialog box to change the linetype of the slots to PHANTOM. Be sure the linetype scale allows the linetypes to be displayed. Save the drawing as A:P14-7.

8. Use the editing commands discussed in this chapter to assist you in drawing the following object. Draw the object within the boundaries of the given dimensions. All other dimensions are flexible. Do not include dimensions in the drawing. Save the drawing as A:P14-8.

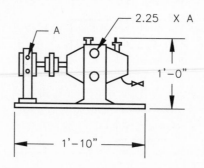

9. Draw the following object within the boundaries of the given dimensions. All other dimensions are flexible. Do not include dimensions. After drawing the object, create a page for a vendor catalog as follows:

- All labels should be ROMAND text centered directly below the view. Use a text height of .125.
- Keep the valve the same scale as the original drawing in each additional drawing.
- Label the existing drawing ONE-GALLON TANK WITH HORIZONTAL VALVE.
- Copy the original tank to a new location and scale it so that it is two times its original size. Rotate the valve 45°. Label this tank TWO-GALLON TANK WITH 45° VALVE.
- Copy the original tank to another location and scale it so that it is 2.5 times the size of the original. Rotate the valve 90°. Label this tank TWO- AND ONE-HALF GALLON TANK WITH 90° VALVE.
- Copy the two-gallon tank to a new position and scale it so that it is two times this size. Rotate the valve to 22°30'. Label this tank FOUR-GALLON TANK WITH 22°30' VALVE.
- Left-justify this note at the bottom of the page:
  - Combinations of tank size and valve orientation are available upon request.
- Use the **Modify Text** dialog box to make the following changes:
  - Change all tank labels to ROMANC, .25" high.
  - Change the note at the bottom of the sheet to ROMANS, centered on the sheet using uppercase letters.

Save the drawing as A:P14-9.

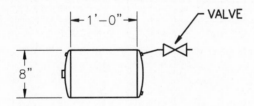

10. Open Problem 13-14 if you have already drawn it. If you have not yet drawn this object, refer to the problem on page 11-32 and draw it now. Do not include dimensions. Use the **DDMODIFY** command and other editing commands to change the drawing as follows:

- Change the ∅2.125 circle to ∅1.50.
- Change the R.50 dimension to R.375.
- Change the 3.70 length to 4.80.
- Save the drawing as A:P14-10.

11. Open Problem 11-8 and use the **FILTER** command as discussed in this chapter. Change all text to ROMAND. Save the drawing as A:P14-11.

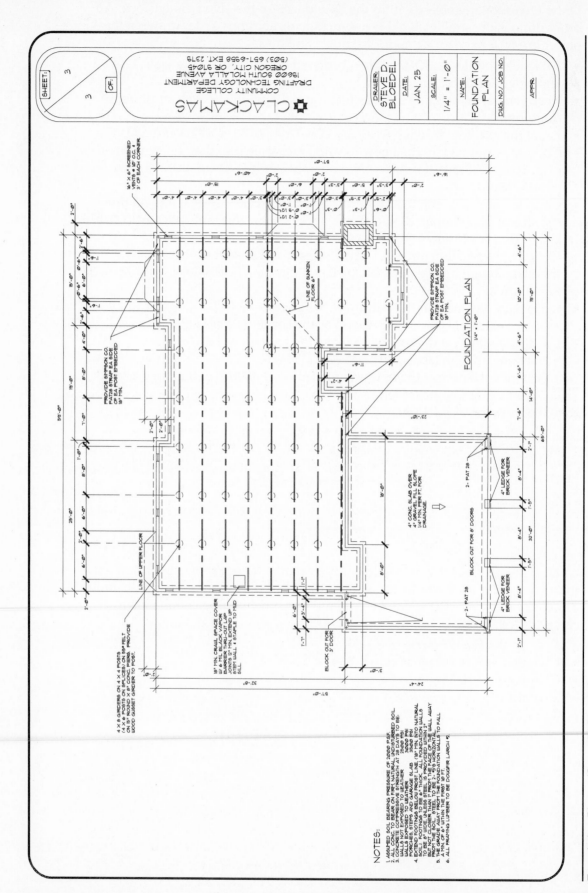

Foundation Plan. (Steve D. Bloedel)

AutoCAD R13

Chapter **15**

# Creating Multiple Objects with Array

## Learning objectives

After completing this chapter, you will be able to:
- ○ Create an arrangement of objects in a rectangular pattern.
- ○ Create an arrangement of any objects in a circular pattern.

Some designs require a rectangular or circular pattern of the same object. For example, office desks are often arranged in rows. Suppose your design calls for five rows, each having four desks. You can create this design by drawing one desk and copying it 19 times. You can also save the desk as a block and insert it 20 times. However, both of these options are time-consuming. A quicker method is to use AutoCAD's **ARRAY** command. Using **ARRAY**, you first select the object(s) to be copied. Then, enter the type of arrangement (rectangular or polar).

A *rectangular array* creates rows and columns of the selected items, and you must provide the spacing. A *polar array* constructs a circular arrangement. For a circular array, you must specify the number of items to array, the angle between items, and the center point of the array. Some examples are shown in Figure 15-1.

Figure 15-1.    Example arrays created with the **ARRAY** command.

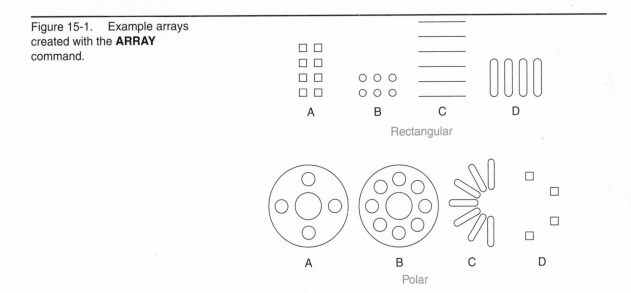

In this chapter, you will experiment with the **ARRAY** command on a .5 unit square. You may want to draw this object now to use as you study the chapter.

The **ARRAY** command is accessed by typing ARRAY at the **Command:** prompt. It can also be accessed by picking the **Rectangular Array** or the **Polar Array** button in the **Copy Object** flyout on the **Modify** toolbar. If the ACADFULL menu file is loaded, the **Array ⟩** cascading sub-menu can be selected from the **Construct** pull-down menu.

After you issue the **ARRAY** command, AutoCAD asks you to select objects. All of the selection set methods, such as window and crossing, are valid. After you select the desired objects, you must specify whether you want a rectangular or polar array. The command sequence is as follows:

Command: **ARRAY** ↵
Select objects: *(select the objects)*
1 found
Select objects: ↵
Rectangular or Polar array (R/P) ⟨*current*⟩: *(type R or P and press* [Enter]*)*

## RECTANGULAR PLACEMENT OF OBJECTS

| AUG 5 |

To create a rectangular array, type ARRAY at the **Command:** prompt and use the **Rectangular** option, or pick the **Rectangular Array** button in the **Copy Object** flyout in the **Modify** toolbar. If the ACADFULL menu file is loaded, select **Rectangular** in the **Array** ⟩ cascading submenu of the **Construct** pull-down menu.

A rectangular array places objects in line along the X and Y axes. You can specify a single row, a single column, or multiple rows and columns. *Rows* are horizontal and *columns* are vertical. AutoCAD reminds you of this by indicating the direction in parentheses: (---) for rows and (⫶) for columns. The following sequence creates a pattern having 3 rows, 3 columns, and .5 spacing between objects.

Rectangular or Polar array (R/P) ⟨*current*⟩: **R** ↵
Number of rows (---) ⟨1⟩: **3** ↵
Number of columns (⫶) ⟨1⟩: **3** ↵
Unit cell or distance between rows (---):**1** ↵
Distance between columns (⫶):**1** ↵
Command:

The original object and resulting array are shown in Figure 15-2. When giving the distance between rows and columns, be sure to include the width and height of the object. Figure 15-2 shows how to calculate the distance between objects in a rectangular array.

AutoCAD allows you to point to the distance separating objects. This is called the *unit cell*. The unit cell distance is the same as the distance between rows and columns. However, it is entered with the pointing device, just like selecting a window. See Figure 15-3. The second point's distance and direction from the first point determines the X and Y spacing for the array.

Unit cell or distance between rows (---): *(pick corner)*
Other corner: *(pick second corner)*

Figure 15-2.   The original object (dashed) and the created rectangular array. Note how the distance between rows and columns is determined.

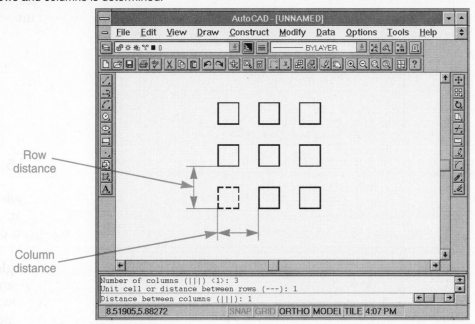

Figure 15-3.   The unit cell spacing box is the same as the distance between rows and columns.

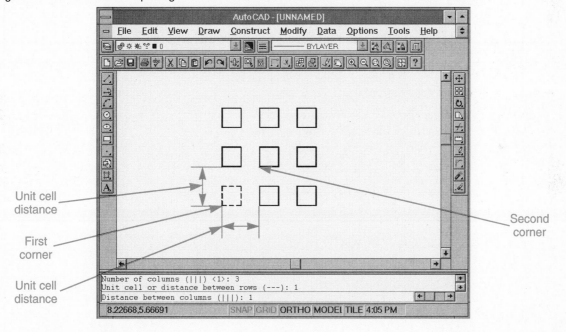

Figure 15-4 shows how you can place arrays in four directions by entering either positive or negative row and column distance values. The dashed box is the original object. The row and column distance is one unit and the box is .5 units square.

Specifying the unit cell distance can create a quick row and column arrangement in any direction. For example, in Figure 15-5 the second unit cell corner is picked to the left and below the first corner.

Figure 15-4.    Placing arrays in one of four directions by giving positive or negative row and column distance values. The original object is shown highlighted.

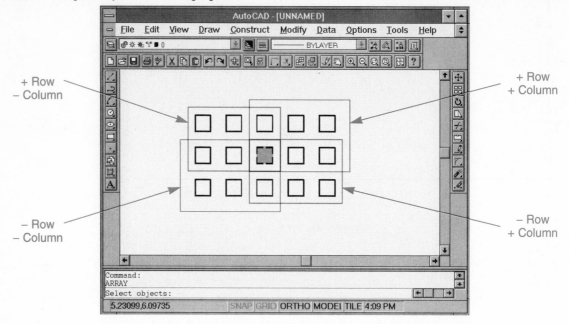

Figure 15-5.    Creating a rectangular array by picking a negative unit cell distance.

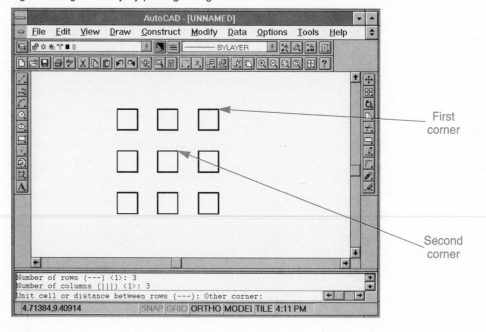

## PROFESSIONAL TIP

Plan your drawing so you can array blocks. Blocks are symbols and shapes that are treated as a single entity. They are discussed in Chapter 25. Blocks save time when selecting the object. They also save drawing storage space.

By setting the snap rotation to a specified angle before performing an array, a rotated rectangular array can be created. The **SNAP** command **Rotate** option is covered in Chapter 4 of this text.

## EXERCISE 15-1

❑ Load AutoCAD for Windows and open TITLEA, or start a new drawing and set up your own variables.

❑ Construct the Bill of Materials form shown below using the **LINE** and **ARRAY** commands. Line A is arrayed in nine rows and one column. The distance between rows is given. Line B is arrayed in one row and three columns. The distance between the columns is provided.

❑ Complete the headings using the **DTEXT** command with middle justification.

❑ Save the drawing as A:EX15-1 and quit.

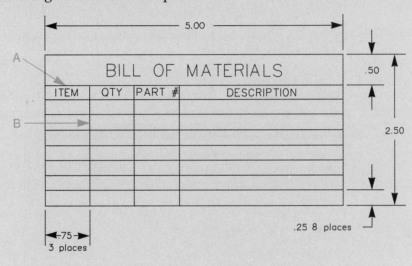

## ARRANGING OBJECTS AROUND A CENTER POINT

AUG 5

To create a polar array, type ARRAY at the **Command:** prompt and use the **Polar** option, or pick the **Polar Array** button in the **Copy Object** flyout on the **Modify** toolbar. If the ACADFULL menu file is loaded, select **Polar** in the **Array** ⟩ cascading submenu of the **Construct** pull-down menu.

First, erase everything on your screen except for one .5 unit square. Enter the following command sequence:

> Command: **ARRAY** ↵
> Select objects: *(select the object)*
> 1 found
> Select objects: ↵
> Rectangular or Polar array (R/P) ⟨*current*⟩: **P** ↵
> Center point of array: *(pick the center point)*

Next, AutoCAD requests the number of objects you want in the array. If you know the exact number needed, enter that value. If you would rather specify an angle between items, just press [Enter]. In the example below, [Enter] is pressed.

> Number of items: ↵
> Angle to fill (+ =ccw, – =cw) ⟨360⟩:

Notice the letters +=ccw and –=cw in parentheses. You can array the object in a counterclockwise direction by entering a positive angle value. Numbers entered without the plus sign are positive. Objects can be arrayed clockwise by entering the minus sign before the angle value. Pressing [Enter] at this prompt without entering a value copies the object through 360°. This is the default value.

The final value needed is the angular spacing between the arrayed objects.

Angle between items: **45** ⏎

A number entered at this prompt is assumed to be the angle. This prompt is only displayed if you pressed [Enter] at the Number of items: prompt. If you specify the number of items, AutoCAD calculates the angle for you. The last prompt is:

Rotate objects as they are copied? ⟨Y⟩ **N** ⏎
Command:

You can have the objects rotated as they are copied around the pivot point. This keeps the same face of the object always pointing toward the pivot point, as on the left in Figure 15-6. If objects are not rotated as they are copied, they remain in the same orientation as the original object, as on the right in Figure 15-6.

Figure 15-6.    Using polar **ARRAY** to rotate a box. A—The box is rotated as it is arrayed. B—The box is not rotated as it is arrayed.

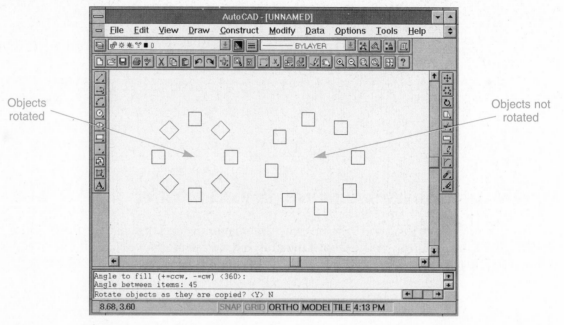

Objects rotated

Objects not rotated

---

**EXERCISE 15-2**

❏ Load AutoCAD for Windows and open the TITLEA drawing, or start a new drawing and set up your own variables.
❏ Draw a .5 radius circle near the top of the screen.
❏ Create a 360° polar array of five circles.
❏ Copy one of the circles to the side of the polar array.
❏ Create an array with the copied circle. Each circle should be 30° apart through 270°.
❏ Save the drawing as A:EX15-2 and quit.

## CHAPTER TEST

*Write your answers in the spaces provided.*

1.  What is the difference between polar and rectangular arrays? _____

    _____

    _____

2.  What four values should you know before you create a rectangular array? _____

    _____

    _____

3.  Define "unit cell." _____

    _____

4.  Suppose an object is 1.5" (38.1mm) wide and you want a rectangular array with .75" (19.05mm) spacing between objects. What should you specify for the distance between columns? _____

5.  How do you create a rectangular array that is rotated? _____

6.  What values should you know before you execute a polar array? _____

    _____

7.  Suppose you enter a value for the Number of items: prompt in a polar array. Which of the following values are you not required to give? Circle one.

    A.  Angle to fill.

    B.  Angle between items.

    C.  Center point.

    D.  Rotate objects as they are copied.

8.  What happens to an object when it is not rotated as it is arrayed? _____

    _____

9.  How do you specify a clockwise array rotation? _____

    _____

## DRAWING PROBLEMS

1. Draw the following object views using the dimensions given. Use **ARRAY** to construct the bolt hole arrangement. Place the drawing on your prototype drawing TITLEB. Do not add dimensions. Save the drawing as A:P15-1.

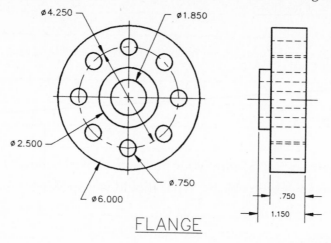

FLANGE

2. Draw the object views shown below using the dimensions given. Use **ARRAY** to construct the hole arrangement. Place the drawing on your prototype drawing TITLEB. Do not add dimensions. Save the drawing as A:P15-2.

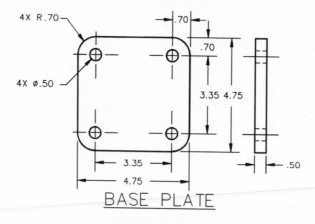

BASE PLATE

3. You have been given an engineer's sketches and notes, and asked to construct a drawing of a sprocket. Create a front and side view of the sprocket using the **ARRAY** command. Place the drawing on your prototype drawing TITLEB. Do not add dimensions. Save the drawing as A:P15-3 and quit.

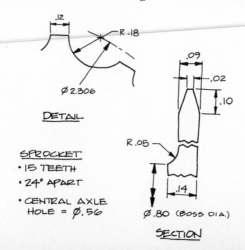

4. The following engineering sketch shows a steel column arrangement on a concrete floor slab for a new building. The steel columns are represented by I-shaped symbols. The columns are arranged in "bay lines" and "column lines." The column lines are numbered 1, 2, and 3. The bay lines are labeled A through G. The width of a bay is 20'-0". Line balloons, or tags, identify bay and column lines. Draw the arrangement using **ARRAY** for the steel column symbols and for the tags. The following guidelines will help you.

A. Begin a new drawing named P15-4.

B. Select architectural units and 36 × 24 sheet size. Determine the scale required for this floor plan to fit on this sheet size, and determine your limits accordingly.

C. Set the grid spacing at 2'-0" (24").

D. Set the snap spacing at 12".

E. Use the **PLINE** command to draw the steel column symbol.

F. Do not dimension the drawing.

G. Draw all objects to dimensions given.

H. Place text inside the tag balloons. Set **OSNAP** to **Center**, use **DTEXT Middle**, text height 6".

I. Place a title block on the drawing.

J. Save the drawing as A:P15-4.

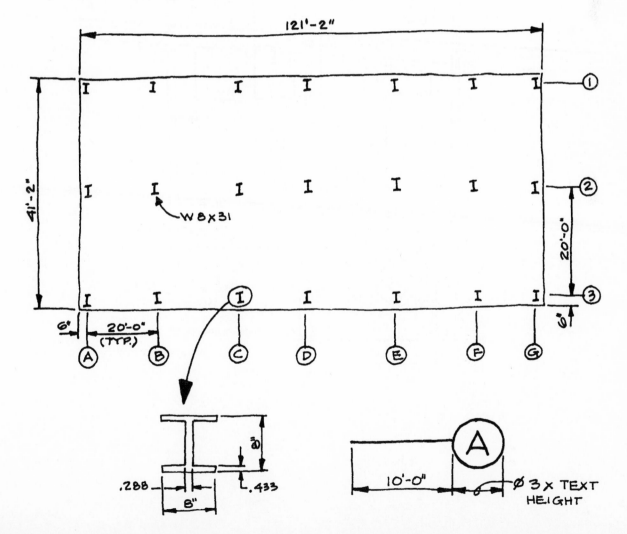

5. The engineering sketch given is a proposed office layout of desks and chairs. One desk has been shown with the layout of chair, keyboard, monitor, and tower-mounted computer (dotted lines). All of the desk workstations should have the same configuration. Exact size and locations of doors and windows is not important for this problem. Set the **SAVETIME** variable to save your drawing every ten minutes. Use the following guidelines to complete this problem.

A. Begin a new drawing called P15-5.

B. Choose architectural units.

C. Select an appropriate paper size. If you want to use the paper space prototype drawing for the final layout, be sure to create this drawing in model space without a border and title block.

D. Use the appropriate drawing and editing commands to complete this problem quickly and efficiently.

E. Draw the desk and computer hardware to the dimensions given.

F. Do not dimension the drawing.

G. Save the drawing as A:P15-5.

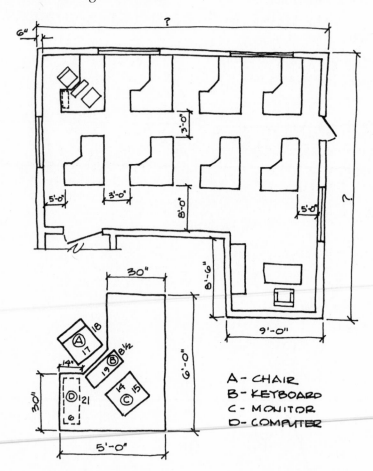

A - CHAIR
B - KEYBOARD
C - MONITOR
D - COMPUTER

## Learning objectives

After completing this chapter, you will be able to:
- ○ Use AutoCAD to calculate the area of an object by adding and subtracting entities.
- ○ List data related to a single point, entity, group of entities, or an entire drawing.
- ○ Determine the amount of time spent in a drawing session.

When working on a drawing, you may need to ask AutoCAD for information about the drawing, such as distances and areas. You can also ask AutoCAD how much time you have spent on a drawing. The commands that allow you to do this include **AREA**, **DBLIST** (database list), **DIST** (distance), **ID** (identification), **LIST**, **STATUS**, and **TIME**. The **STATUS** command was discussed in Chapter 5 of this text. The **STATUS** and **TIME** commands are found in the **Data** pull-down menu. The **LIST**, **ID**, **DIST**, and **AREA** command buttons are found in the **List** flyout on the **Object Properties** toolbar or in the **Inquiry** 〉 submenu of the **Edit** pull-down menu. These commands can also be typed at the **Command:** prompt.

The **Mass Properties** command is also located in the **Inquiry** 〉 submenu of the **Edit** pull-down menu. This command provides data related to the properties of a region or 3D object created with solids. These topics are discussed in *AutoCAD and its Applications— Advanced, Release 13 for Windows.*

## FINDING THE AREA OF SHAPES AND OBJECTS ⎧ AUG 3 ⎫

The most basic function of the **AREA** command is to find the area of any object, circle, polyline, or spline. To select an entity, use the **Object** option as follows:

> Command: **AREA** ⏎
> 〈First point〉/Object/Add/Subtract: **O** ⏎
> Select objects: *(pick objects)*
> Area = *(n.nn)*, Circumference = *(n.nn)*
> Command:

The *n* given above represents the numeric values of the area and circumference of the object. The second value that is returned by the **AREA** command varies depending on the type of object selected.

| Object | Value returned |
|--------|----------------|
| Line   | Perimeter |
| Pline  | Perimeter |
| Circle | Circumference |
| Spline | Length |

**PROFESSIONAL TIP**

AutoCAD gives you the area between three or more points picked on the screen, even if the three points are not connected by lines. The perimeter of the selected points is also given.

Shapes drawn with lines or polylines do not have to be closed for AutoCAD to calculate their area. AutoCAD calculates the area as if a line connects the first and last points.

To find the area of a shape created with the **LINE** command, pick all the vertices of that shape. See Figure 16-1. This is the default mode of the **AREA** command. Set a running object snap such as **Endpoint** or **Intersection** to help you pick the vertices.

Command: **AREA** ↵
⟨First point⟩/Object/Add/Subtract: *(pick point 1)*
Next point: *(pick point 2)*
Next point: *(continue picking points until all corners of the object have been selected;*
   *then press* [Enter])
Next point: ↵
Area = *(n.nn)*, Perimeter = *(n.nn)*
Command:

Figure 16-1.   Pick all corners to find the area of an object drawn with the **LINE** command.

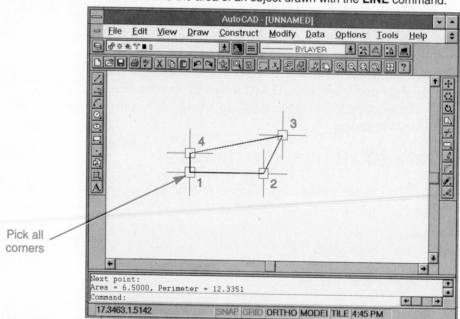

Pick all corners

## Adding and subtracting areas

If you select the **Add** option, you can pick objects drawn with the **PLINE** command. They are then automatically added to calculate the total area. After entities have been added, the **Subtract** option allows you to remove selected areas. Once either of these options is entered, the **AREA** command remains in effect until you cancel the command. You can continue to add or subtract entities and shapes using the **Add** and **Subtract** options.

The next example uses both the **Add** and **Subtract** options. It also shows how entities drawn with the **PLINE** command are easier to pick. Refer to Figure 16-2 as you go through the following sequence:

```
Command: AREA ↵
⟨First point⟩/Object/Add/Subtract: A ↵
⟨First point⟩/Object/Subtract: O ↵
(ADD mode) Select object: (pick the polyline)
Area = 5.51, Perimeter = 13.61
Total area = 5.51
(ADD mode) Select object: ↵
⟨First point⟩/Object/Subtract: S ↵
⟨First point⟩/Object/Add: O ↵
(SUBTRACT mode) Select object: (pick the first circle)
Area = 0.11, Circumference = 1.18
Total area = 5.40
(SUBTRACT mode) Select object: (pick the second circle)
Area = 0.11, Circumference = 1.18
Total area = 5.29
(SUBTRACT mode) Select object: ↵
⟨First point⟩/Object/Add: ↵
```

The total area of the object in Figure 16-2, subtracting the area of the two holes, is 5.29. Circumferences and perimeters are given for each object as it is selected. These are not affected by the adding or subtracting functions.

Notice in the previous command sequence that if you are finished adding and wish to subtract, you must press [Enter] at the (ADD mode) Select objects: prompt. The same is true if you have completed subtracting and wish to add.

Figure 16-2.   First select the outer boundary of the object using the **AREA** command **Add** option. Then, select the inner boundaries (the circles) using the **AREA** command **Subtract** option. This  will calculate the area of the object.

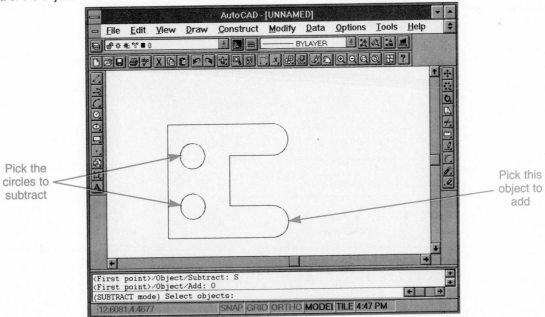

**PROFESSIONAL TIP**

Calculating area, circumference, and perimeter of shapes made with the **LINE** command can be time-consuming. You must pick each vertex on the object. If you know you have to calculate areas, it is best to create lines and arcs with the **PLINE** or **SPLINE** command. Then choose the **Object** option when adding or subtracting entities.

## EXERCISE 16-1

❑ Load AutoCAD for Windows, and begin a new drawing using the default AutoCAD prototype drawing. Set up your own variables.
❑ Draw the objects shown below. Use the size dimensions given. The exact locations of the cutout and holes are not important.
❑ Use the **AREA** command to calculate the area of the entire object.
❑ Use the **AREA** command to subtract the areas of the rectangle and two circles.
❑ List the following information:
  A. Area of large rectangle _____
  B. Perimeter of large rectangle _____
  C. Perimeter of small rectangle _____
  D. Circumference of one circle _____
  E. Area of large rectangle minus the areas of the three shapes _____
❑ Save the drawing as A:EX16-1. This drawing is used for the next exercise.

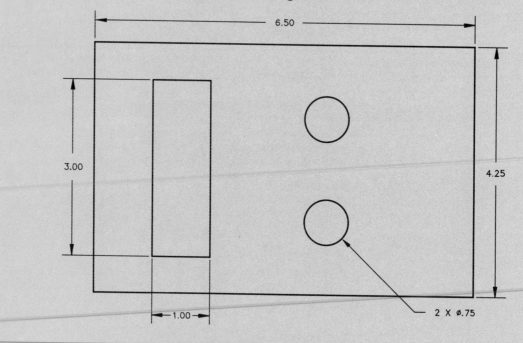

## LISTING DRAWING DATA

AUG 3

The **LIST** command displays data about any AutoCAD entity. Line length, circle or arc locations and radii, polyline widths, and object layers are just a few of the items AutoCAD gives you with the **LIST** command. You can select several objects to list.

> Command: **LIST** ↵
> Select objects: *(pick objects using any selection option)*
> Select objects: ↵

When you press [Enter], the data for each of the objects picked is displayed in the text window. The data given for a line are:

```
       LINE          Layer:  (layer name)
                      Space:  Model space
                      Handle = (nn)
     from point, X = (nn.nn)    Y = (nn.nn)    Z = (nn.nn)
       to point, X = (nn.nn)    Y = (nn.nn)    Z = (nn.nn)
   Length = (nn.nn)    Angle in XY Plane = (nn.nn)
          Delta X = (nn.nn)    Delta Y = (nn.nn)    Delta Z = (nn.nnn)
```

The Delta X and Y numbers show the horizontal and vertical distance between the *from point* and *to point* of the line. These two numbers, the length, and angle provide you with four measurements for a single line. An example of the data provided for two-dimensional lines is shown in Figure 16-3. If a line is three-dimensional, the **LIST** command displays an additional line of information as follows:

> 3D Length = *(nn.nn)* Angle from XY Plane = *(nn.nn)*

The data given by the **LIST** command for text, multiline text, circles, and splines are as follows:

```
       TEXT          Layer:  (layer name)
                      Space:  Model space
       Handle  = (nn)
        Style  = (name) Font file = (name)
        start  point, X = (n.nn) Y = (n.nn) Z = (n.nn)
       height  (n.nn)
         text  (text label)
     rotation  angle (nn)
        width  scale factor (n.nn)
     obliquing  angle (nn)
   generation  normal

       MTEXT         Layer:  (layer name)
                     Space:  Model space
        Handle  = (nn)
      Location:  X = (n.nn) Y = (n.nn) Z = (n.nn)
         Width:  (n.nn)
        Normal:  X = (n.nn) Y = (n.nn) Z = (n.nn)
      Rotation:  (n.nn)
    Text style:  (style name)
   Text height:  (n.nn)
    Attachment:  (corner of multiline text insertion point)
 Flow direction:  (direction text is read based on language)
      Contents:  (multiline text contents)
```

```
       CIRCLE          Layer: (layer name)
                       Space: Model space
          Handle = (nn)
    center point, X = (n.nn)  Y = (n.nn)  Z = (n.nn)
          radius (n.nn)
   circumference (n.nn)
            area (n.nn)

       SPLINE          Layer: (layer name)
                       Space: Model space
          Handle = (nn)
         Length: (n.nn)
          Order: (n.nn)
      Properties: Planar, Non-Rational, Non-Periodic
 Parametric Range: Start (n.nn)
                   End (n.nn)
   Control Points: X = (n.nn) , Y = (n.nn) , Z = (n.nn)
                   (All XYZ control points listed)
       User Data: Fit Points
                   X = (n.nn) , Y = (n.nn) , Z = (n.nn)
                   (All XYZ fit points listed)
```

Figure 16-3.  Measurements of a line provided by the **LIST** command.

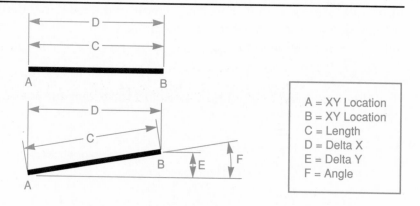

A = XY Location
B = XY Location
C = Length
D = Delta X
E = Delta Y
F = Angle

**PROFESSIONAL TIP**

The **LIST** command is probably the most powerful inquiry command in AutoCAD. It provides all of the information you need to know about a selected object. Practice by listing as many different objects as possible in your drawings. This exercise will help you to gain a greater understanding of the different kinds of data stored with each AutoCAD object.

## LISTING ALL THE DRAWING DATA                                     AUG 3

The **DBLIST** (database list) command lists all of the data about every entity in the current drawing. The information provided is in the same format as the with **LIST** command. As soon as you enter **DBLIST**, the data begins to quickly scroll up the screen. The scrolling stops when a complete page (screen) is filled with database information. Press [Enter] to scroll to the end of the next page. If you find the data you need, press the [Esc] key to exit the **DBLIST** command.

# FINDING THE DISTANCE BETWEEN TWO POINTS

AUG 3

The **DIST** command finds the distance between two points. Use object snap modes to accurately pick locations. See Figure 16-4. The **DIST** command provides distance and angle of the line. It also gives delta X, Y, and Z dimensions.

> Command: **DIST** ↵
> First point: *(select point)* Second point: *(select point)*
> Distance = 2.85,  Angle in XY Plane = 353,  Angle from XY Plane = 0
> Delta X = 2.83,  Delta Y = –0.37  Delta Z = 0.0000
> Command:

If you pick the **Edit** pull-down menu, then **Inquiry** and **Distance**, notice the syntax that is displayed at the **Command:** prompt.

> Command: '__dist First point:

The apostrophe that appears before "dist" indicates that this is a transparent command. Transparent commands can be used while you are working inside of another command. The **ID** command, discussed in the next section, is transparent if selected from the pull-down menu.

---

Figure 16-4.   Use the running object snap **Endpoint** and the **DIST** command to find the distance between two endpoints of a line.

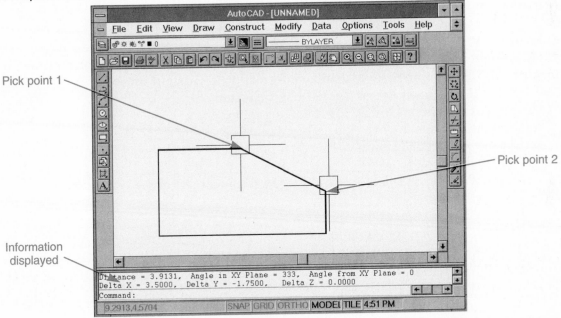

# IDENTIFYING A POINT LOCATION

AUG 3

The **ID** command gives the coordinate location of a single point on the screen. This can be used to find the endpoint of a line or the center of a circle. Simply pick the point to be identified. Use the object snap modes for accuracy. The **ID** command is listed as **Locate Point** in the **Inquiry** cascading submenu of the **Edit** pull-down menu.

> Command: **ID** ↵
> Point: *(select the point)*
> X = *(nn.nn)*  Y = *(nn.nn)*  Z = *(nn.nn)*
> Command:

The **ID** command can also help you identify a coordinate location on the screen. Enter the exact coordinate values you wish to find. Suppose you want to see where the point X = 8.75, Y = 6.44 is located. Enter these numbers at the Point: prompt. AutoCAD responds by placing a blip (marker) at that exact location if the **BLIPMODE** variable is on.

Command: **ID** ↵
Point: **8.75,6.44** ↵
X = 8.75 Y = 6.44 Z = 0.00
Command:

**PROFESSIONAL TIP**

The **ID** command can also be used to specify a point as the origin for relative coordinates. For example, if you wish to begin drawing a line 10'-6" on the X axis from the corner of a building, select **ID** and pick the corner. Next, select **LINE** and enter the following for the From point: prompt:

From point: **@10'6",0** ↵

When you use the **ID** command, it automatically resets the system variable called **LASTPOINT** to the value of the **ID** point. When you include the @ sign, AutoCAD works from the **LASTPOINT** value.

**EXERCISE 16-2**

❑ Load AutoCAD for Windows and open EX16-1 if it is not currently on the screen.
❑ Use the **LIST** command to display information about one circle and one line on the drawing.
❑ Select the **DBLIST** command to display information about your drawing.
❑ Select **DBLIST** again and press [Esc] to end the listing.
❑ Use object snap options to find the following information:
  A. Distance between the two circle center points. _____
  B. Distance between the lower circle center point and the left edge of the large rectangle.
    _____
  C. Distance between the lower-left and upper-right corners of the large rectangle. ____
    _____
  D. **ID** of the center point of the upper circle._____
  E. **ID** of the lower-left corner of the small rectangle._____
  F. **ID** of the midpoint of the large rectangle's right side. _____
  G. **ID** of point (6,4) on your screen._____
❑ Save the drawing as A:EX16-2 and quit.

## CHECKING THE TIME                                                       | AUG 3 |

The **TIME** command displays the current time, the time related to your drawing, and the time related to the current drawing session. The display for the **TIME** command is as follows:

Command: **TIME** ↵
Current time: Wednesday, February 14, 19XX at 13:39:22.210PM
Times for this drawing:
  Created: Monday, February 12, 19XX at 10:24:48.130AM
  Last updated: Monday, February 12, 19XX at 14:36:23.46PM
  Total editing time: 0 days 01:23:57.930
  Elapsed timer (on): 0 days 00:35:28.650
  Next automatic save in: 0 days 01:35:26.680
Display/ON/OFF/Reset:

There are a few things to keep in mind when checking the **TIME** display. First, the drawing creation time starts when you "OK" a new drawing with the **NEW** command, or by using the **BLOCK** command discussed in Chapter 25. Second, the **END** and **SAVE** commands affect the Last updated: time. However, when **QUIT** is used to end a drawing session and you do not save the drawing, all time in that session is discarded. Finally, you can time a specific drawing task by using the **Reset** option to reset the elapsed timer.

While the **TIME** display is on the screen, it is static. That means that none of the times are being updated. You can request an update by choosing the **Display** option as follows:

Display/ON/OFF/Reset: **D** ↵

When you enter the drawing editor, the timer is on by default. If you want to stop the timer, just enter OFF at the prompt. If the timer is off, enter ON to start it again.

If the date and time are incorrect, they can be reset from the Windows Control Panel. Control Panel is located in the Main group window of Program Manager, Figure 16-5. The Control Panel allows you to modify certain aspects of your system, such as screen colors and system time. Using the Date/Time option, you can change your system's date and time, Figure 16-6. It is important that your system date and time are always accurate. Date and time changes are recognized by other Windows applications that use the system clock like File Manager, Clock, and Calendar. File Manager functions are covered in Chapter 32 of this text.

To change the system date and time, do the following:

1. Load Windows.
2. Activate the Main group window of Program Manager.
3. Double-click the Control Panel icon to activate the Control Panel window.
4. In the Control Panel window, double-click on the Date/Time icon.
5. Select the part of the date or time you want to change, and then type a new value or click the up or down arrow to increase or decrease the number by one, Figure 16-7.
6. Click the OK button and select Exit from the pull-down Settings menu in the Control Panel window.

Figure 16-5.  The Control Panel is located in the Main group window of Program Manager.

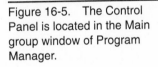
Control Panel icon

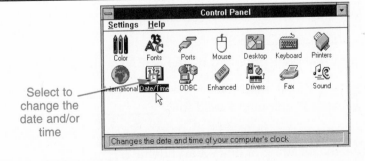

Figure 16-6.  Select the Date/Time icon to change the system clock settings.

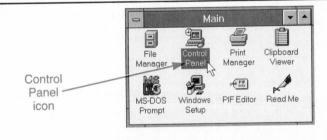

Select to change the date and/or time

Figure 16-7.   Highlight the item to change and enter the new setting. You can also click on the up or down arrows to change the setting of the highlighted item.

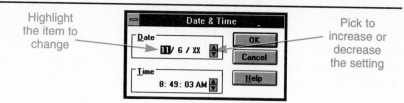

Highlight the item to change

Pick to increase or decrease the setting

## PROFESSIONAL TIP

You do not need to exit AutoCAD for Windows to return to the Program Manager. You can cycle quickly through open Windows applications by simultaneously holding down the [Alt] key, then pressing the [Tab] key. Continue to hold down the [Alt] key. With each press of the [Tab] key, a small dialog box displays the icon and name of an open application. When the one you wish to use is displayed, release the [Alt] key and that application becomes active. Since Program Manager is always open, you can [Alt]+[Tab] to it from AutoCAD. Then, set the system date and time as described in the text.

## EXERCISE 16-3

❑ Open any one of your previous drawings.
❑ Select the **TIME** command and study the information that is displayed.
❑ If the current date and time are incorrect, inform your instructor or supervisor. Then, use the Windows Control Panel to set the correct date and time.
❑ Update the **TIME** display.
❑ Reset the elapsed timer.
❑ Exit AutoCAD for Windows without saving.

## CHAPTER TEST

*Write your answers in the spaces provided.*

1. To add entity areas, when do you select the **Add** option? _____

   _____

2. When using the **AREA** command, explain how picking a polyline is different than picking an object drawn with the **LINE** command. _____

   _____

3. What information is provided by the **AREA** command? _____

   _____

4. What is the **LIST** command used for? _____

   _____

5. Describe the meaning of delta X and delta Y. _____

   _____

   _____

6.  What is the function of the **DBLIST** command? _____

_____

7.  How do you cancel the **DBLIST** command? _____

8.  What are the two purposes of the **ID** command? _____

_____

_____

9.  What information is provided by the **TIME** command? _____

_____

10.  When does the drawing time start? _____

_____

11.  It is necessary to exit AutoCAD for Windows to reset the date and time. (True/False)

_____

## DRAWING PROBLEMS

*Load AutoCAD for windows and start a new drawing for each of the following problems.*
*Insert your floppy disk and name the drawing as* **P16-(problem number)**.

1.  Draw the object shown below using the dimensions given. Draw all of the features
    using **PLINE** and **CIRCLE** commands. Follow these instructions as you proceed:

    A.  Check the time when you enter the drawing editor.

    B.  Use the default units and limits.

    C.  Set the grid spacing to .5 and snap spacing to .25.

    D.  Measure the area of object A and subtract the areas of the other three features.

    E.  Write your answers for the areas and perimeters in the chart provided.

    F.  Use the **Add, Subtract**, and **Object** options of **AREA** to find the measurements.
        Do not exit the **AREA** command. Complete all of the following calculations in
        one selection of **AREA**.

    G.  Select **TIME** and note your time in the drawing editor.

    H.  Save the drawing as A:P16-1.

| | OBJECT A | OBJECT B | OBJECT C | OBJECT A–OBJECT B | OBJECT A–CUTOUTS AND HOLES |
|---|---|---|---|---|---|
| AREA | | | | | |
| PERIMETER | | | | | |

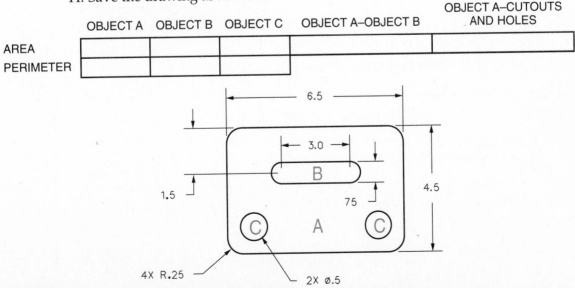

2. Draw the object shown below using the **LINE** command. Draw the hexagon using the **POLYGON** command. Use the following settings and provide all measurements listed.

    A. Set architectural units. Use 1/2″ fractions and decimal degrees. Leave remaining units settings at default values.

    B. Set the limits to 100′,80′ and **ZOOM All**.

    C. Set the grid spacing to 2′ and snap spacing to 1′.

    D. Calculate the measurements requested in the charts below.

    E. Select the **DBLIST** command.

    F. Select **TIME** and note the time in the drawing editor.

    G. Save the drawing as A:P16-2.

|  | OBJECT A | OBJECT B | OBJECT A – OBJECT B |
|---|---|---|---|
| AREA |  |  |  |
| PERIMETER |  |  |  |

|  | LINE CD | DISTANCE EC |
|---|---|---|
| DISTANCE |  |  |

|  | POINT C | POINT D | POINT F |
|---|---|---|---|
| ID |  |  |  |

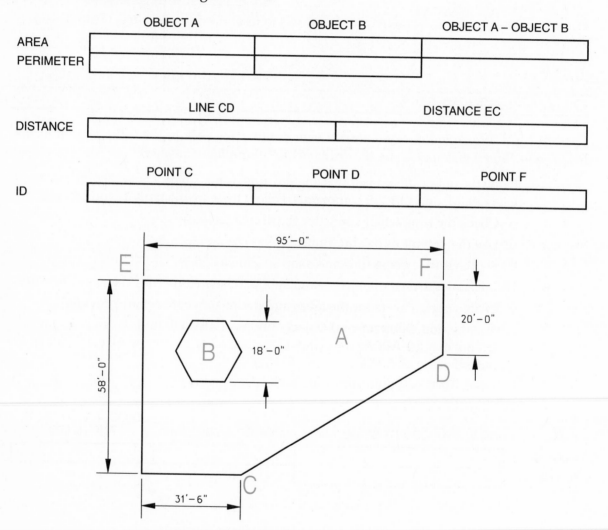

3. In this problem you will draw a piece of property in the form of a plat. A *plat* is a map of a piece of land. The lengths of the sides are measured, as well as the bearing. A *bearing* is a direction measured from the north or south to the east or west. A bearing is never greater than 90°. Refer to the drawing as you do this problem.

A. Set units to engineering. Select four digits to right of decimal.

B. Select surveyor's units, and four fractional places for angle display.

C. Select **East** (E) for angle direction.

D. Set the limits at 440',340' and **ZOOM All**.

E. Draw the property lines using the **LINE** command. Enter the distance and bearing at the To point: prompt as follows:

> From point: (*pick a point*)
> To point: **@130'〈N45dE** ↵
> To point: **@245'〈S76d30"E** ↵

F. Continue in this manner for the next two sides. When entering tenths of a foot, they must be entered as feet and inches; for example, 264.5' should be entered as 264'6". Convert tenths of a foot to inches by multiplying by 12. Use the **Close** option to draw the fifth line.

G. Select **LIST** and get the bearing of the last line.

H. Use the **PLINE**, **SPLINE**, or **LINE** command to draw the road. It can be straight or curved. See Chapter 18 for more information on the **PLINE** and **SPLINE** command. The road should be 12' wide.

I. Use **TRIM** and **EXTEND** to clean up the ends of the road. You will have to use **PLINE** and **PEDIT** to establish the road as a closed polyline.

J. Fill-in the information in the chart below.

K. Label the drawing as shown.

L. Select **TIME** and note the time in drawing editor.

M. Save the drawing as A:P16-3.

| | Areas | Perimeters |
|---|---|---|
| Property | | |
| Lake | | |
| Road | | |
| Property – Lake | | |
| Lake + Road | | |
| Property – Lake + Road | | |

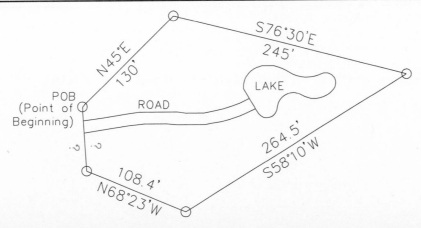

4. This problem requires that you create a drawing of the proposed parking lot shown below. Do not dimension the drawing.

A. Set units to architectural.

B. Set the limits to 400′,300′ and **ZOOM All**.

C. Use the **PLINE** command to draw the parking lot outline.

D. Calculate the following and record your answers:

Area of asphalt (without landscape dividers). _____

Area of landscape dividers (all trees and flowers)._____

Area of landscape dividers (trees only). _____

E. Select **TIME** and note the time in the drawing editor. _____

F. Save the drawing as A:P16-4.

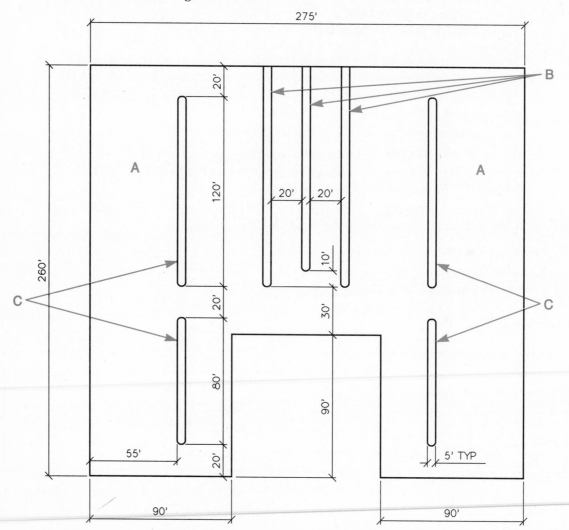

A—Parking Lot (asphalt)    B—Landscape Dividers (flowers)    C—Landscape Dividers (trees)

# Chapter 17

# Working with AutoCAD Files

## Learning objectives

After completing this chapter, you will be able to:
- ○ Explain the meaning and use of DOS file extensions.
- ○ List any type of file using the **File Utilities** dialog box.
- ○ Copy, rename, and delete files using the **File Utilities** dialog box.
- ○ Explain the use of file locking and unlocking.
- ○ Import and export a variety of file types in AutoCAD.
- ○ Define DOS file extensions.

AutoCAD for Windows works with several types of computer files. These can be identified by a three-letter file type extension on the end of the filename. The **File Utilities** dialog box in AutoCAD allows the user to list, copy, rename, delete, and unlock files.

The AutoCAD drawing file format is potentially compatible with a variety of other software applications. You can export the industry standard DXF file for use with other CAD packages, or specific applications. Files can also be exported for use in the design and animation software 3D Studio, or for use in the stereolithography process. In addition, you can import several different file types into AutoCAD. Working with files in this fashion is easier than using the Windows File Manager, discussed in Chapter 32.

## FILENAME TYPES

AUG 14

Drawing filenames can be up to eight characters long. They can contain letters, numbers, the dollar sign ($), hyphens (-), and underscores (_). When you begin a new drawing, AutoCAD adds a file extension to the end of the filename. This extension is .DWG. If you began a drawing called BLDG-34, AutoCAD creates the file as BLDG-34.DWG. When you open the drawing to edit, you only have to type BLDG-34. AutoCAD knows to look for that file, plus the .DWG extension.

After you edit the BLDG-34.DWG file and save it again, the original is converted to a backup file. Its file extension is automatically changed to .BAK (backup). AutoCAD maintains a current .DWG file and one .BAK file. If you revise the BLDG-34 drawing again, the .BAK file is erased and the previous .DWG copy becomes the backup. Only a newly revised drawing is given the .DWG file extension.

There are other extensions given to files by AutoCAD, MS-DOS, and Windows. Some common file extensions are listed on the following page.

### AutoCAD

- .BAK   Backup copy of a drawing file.
- .DCL   Dialog control language description file.
- .DWG   Drawing file.
- .DWK   Locked drawing file.
- .LIN    File containing the linetypes used by AutoCAD.
- .MNU   Menu source file.
- .PAT   Hatch patterns file.
- .PLT    Plot file.

### MS-DOS

- .BAT   Batch file.
- .COM   Command file.
- .EXE   Executable file.

### Windows

- .BMP   Bitmap file.
- .DLL   Dynamic-link library file.
- .INI    Initialization file.
- .WMF   Windows metafile.

## FILE UTILITIES DIALOG BOX                                            AUG 14

The **File Utilities** dialog box contains options that allow you to perform file management functions other than creating and editing drawings. See Figure 17-1. This dialog box can be accessed by selecting the **Utilities...** option in the **Management** ⟩ cascading submenu in the **File** pull-down menu or entering FILES at the **Command:** prompt.

Figure 17-1.   The **File Utilities** dialog box can be used to manipulate files in a number of ways.

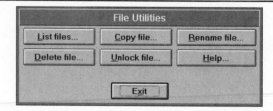

### List your drawings

It is easy to find out which drawings are stored on a particular disk. The **File Utilities** dialog box allows you to list the drawings on any disk or directory. AutoCAD only needs to know which disk drive or directory you wish to list. Remember, if you have two floppy disk drives, the top drive is usually designated as the A: drive and the bottom is usually designated B: drive. The first hard disk is usually the C: drive. If there is more than one hard disk on your computer, the second hard disk is usually the D: drive, and the third hard disk is usually E: drive. To list the drawing files on a floppy disk in the A: drive, first insert the diskette. Then pick the **List files...** button in the **File Utilities** dialog box.

This displays the **File List** dialog box that is similar to the **Open Drawing** dialog box. Notice in Figure 17-2 that two list boxes are displayed. The box on the right contains a list of directories on the current drive. The box on the left contains a list of files of the current type. The current type of file is shown in the lower-left section of the dialog box in the **List Files of Type:** pop-up list. Additionally, the current type of file is always given in the **File Name:** text box in the upper-left section of the dialog box.

Pick the arrow in the **Drives:** pop-up list to see the other available drives on your computer. Now, pick the A: drive icon and a list of files on the floppy disk is displayed in the **File Name:** list. See Figure 17-3. If necessary, use the vertical scroll bar to move up and down through the list. When you are done, click the **Cancel** button, or press the [Esc] key to exit.

Figure 17-2.  The **File List** dialog box shows directories and files.

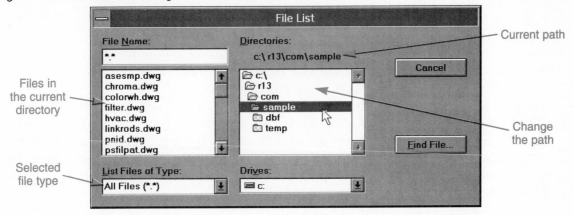

Figure 17-3.  You can use the **File List** dialog box to show the files on a disk drive or in a different directory.

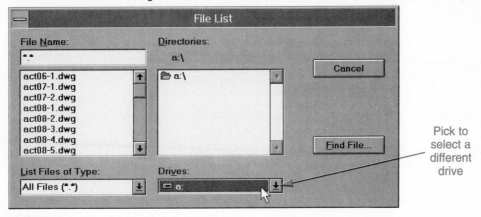

**PROFESSIONAL TIP**

Since all functions in the **File Utilities** dialog box use the same basic dialog box, use the following basic steps for all file management operations.
1. Pick the button for the operation you want to do.
2. If necessary, use the **Drives** pop-up list and the vertical scroll bar in the **Directories:** list box to find the drive or directory you wish to work in.
3. Use the **List Files of Type:** pop-up to specify the type of file(s) you wish to work with.
4. Select the required file(s).
5. Provide any necessary final information, such as a new name or location.

## List any file type

You are not limited to listing just .DWG file types (drawing files). A variety of file types is available in the **List Files of Type:** pop-up list. Simply click on the desired file type in the pop-up list, and the files will display in the Files list box. Not all file types appear in the pop-up list, however. Suppose you need a list of all backup (.BAK) files in the \R13\PROJ-01 subdirectory. Although backup files are not included in the **List Files of Type:** pop-up list, they can still be listed using the following method:

1. Click the **List files...** button in the **File Utilities** dialog box.
2. Pick anywhere inside the **File Name:** edit box. You can use the cursor keys, [Backspace], and [Delete] keys to edit the line of existing text. However, if you double-click in the box, the item is highlighted. Now when you type the first character, the new text replaces everything in the box. Enter *.BAK in the **File Name:** edit box.
3. Double-click the folder icon that represents the \R13\PROJ-01 subdirectory.
   All of the files that have a .BAK file extension are listed in the **Files** list box. The asterisk (*) used in the above entry is a DOS wild-card character. It represents any number of characters. Used in this manner, it instructs AutoCAD to list all files with a .BAK extension.

If you are searching for one particular file, enter that filename and extension. If the file is not on the specified drive or directory, it will not be listed.

---

### EXERCISE 17-1

❏ Load AutoCAD for Windows and insert a floppy disk that contains drawing files.
❏ Use the **File Utilities** dialog box to do the following:
   A. List all .DWG files on the hard disk drive in the \R13\COM\SAMPLE subdirectory.
   B. List all .DWG files on the floppy disk.
   C. List all files with a .EXE extension on the hard disk drive in the \R13\WIN directory.
   D. List all file types beginning with acad.
   E. List all files with a .LSP extension on the hard disk drive in the \R13\COM\SAMPLE subdirectory.
❏ Exit the **File Utilities** dialog box.

---

## Deleting files

Deleting files is a drastic measure to take with any type of file. *Before deleting a file, be sure that the filename you enter is the one you want to delete.* Select **Delete file...** in the **File Utilities** dialog box. The **File(s) to Delete** dialog box then appears.

Suppose you want to delete the JUNK.DWG drawing on the disk in the A: drive. First, be sure the A: drive is current. Scroll to find the file and highlight it. The selected name is displayed in the **File Name:** edit box. See Figure 17-4. If the filename displayed is correct, pick **OK**. Before AutoCAD deletes the file, it prompts you with an alert box, as shown in Figure 17-5.

Figure 17-4.   The selected file to be deleted is placed in the **File Name:** edit box.

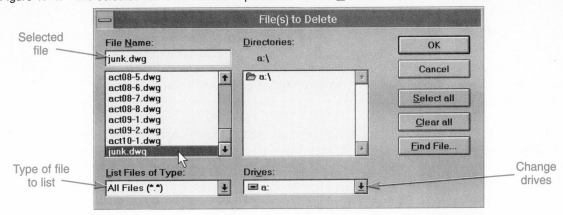

Selected file

Type of file to list

Change drives

Figure 17-5.   AutoCAD alerts you before deleting a file.

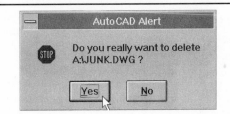

**PROFESSIONAL TIP**

You may have noticed that many of the buttons and dialog boxes contain underlined characters. These buttons can be activated by simply pressing the keyboard key of the underlined character key. Menus with underlined characters can be activated by pressing the [Alt] key and the keyboard key of the character. Such keys are called *accelerator keys*. It is not necessary to press the [Enter] key after using an accelerator key. You can move from button to button within a dialog box from left to right and top to bottom by pressing the [Tab] key. Pressing [Shift]+[Tab] moves in reverse order. To cancel or exit a dialog box, press the [Esc] key. Refer to the *Microsoft Windows User's Guide* for a complete description of shortcut keys.

You can select more than one file at a time to delete. After you pick the second file, no name is displayed in the **File Name:** text box. If you wish to "clean house" and delete all files on a disk or directory, simply pick the **Select all** button and all files are highlighted. If you do this by mistake, pick the **Clear all** button and all files are unselected.

If you want to delete a specific group of files, such as all drawing files that begin with PIPE and end with any three characters, you can first list them by typing the following in the **File Name:** edit box:

**PIPE???.DWG**

This displays only the specific files you requested. The question mark (?) is a DOS wild-card character that represents any single character. To delete the listed files, pick the **Select all** button, then pick **OK**. AutoCAD displays an alert before deleting each file.

Remember, a question mark represents any single character. The files PIPE123.DWG and PIPEABC.DWG are selected for deletion by the previous entry. However, the file PIPE1234.DWG is not selected because four characters follow PIPE.

**PROFESSIONAL TIP**

Users who keep their drawing files on one or more backup disks or tapes occasionally erase all .BAK files on working disks in order to make room for additional files. Do not do this unless you are sure that you have backup copies of your files elsewhere.

In order to manage your files properly, a working knowledge of directories and subdirectories is important. AutoCAD for Windows displays the current directory under the **Directories:** label in many dialog boxes. A label such as D:\R13\COM\SAMPLE indicates that the \SAMPLE subdirectory located under the \R13\COM directory on the D: drive is the current directory. This is referred to as a *path*.

As mentioned at the beginning of this chapter, managing files and directories can also be done using Windows File Manager. The File Manager is discussed in Chapter 32.

**PROFESSIONAL TIP**

Deleting files can be dangerous. Even with some of the undelete file software utilities commercially available, a deleted file sometimes cannot be recovered. Always be very careful when entering a filename, and verify the filename you typed in the **File Name:** edit box or selected from the **Files** list box before clicking the **OK** button.

## Changing filenames

You can rename files by selecting **Rename file...** from the **File Utilities** dialog box. The **Old File Name** dialog box used for all file utility commands is displayed. Use the same method discussed previously to first select the disk drive or directory you wish to work in. Remember, you can specify the type of file so that only specific filenames are displayed. Then select the filename you wish to change from the **File Name:** list box and pick **OK**, or double click on the filename.

The **New File Name** dialog box appears. You can type the new name in the **File Name:** edit box and pick **OK**. Be sure to include the three letter extension. A message indicates if the renaming operation was successful. If you want to put the file in another directory on the current disk drive, first pick the directory, then type the new name.

## Copying files

Copying files is similar to the functions previously discussed. When you pick **Copy file...** from the **File Utilities** dialog box, the **Source File** dialog box is displayed. First, select the disk drive and directory you wish to copy from, then select the file you wish to copy, such as P16-8.DWG. Then, pick **OK**. You can also double click on the filename. The **Destination File** dialog box is displayed. Now, select the disk drive and directory where you want the copy placed. Finally, type the full name of the file, in this case P16-8.DWG, and pick **OK**. If you wish to change the name of the file in addition to copying it, simply type the new name in the **Destination File** dialog box. A message Copied *xxxx* bytes is displayed indicating the file was successfully copied. See Figure 17-6.

Figure 17-6. The size of the copied file is indicated with a message in the **File Utilities** dialog box.

Indicates the file was copied and gives the size of the file

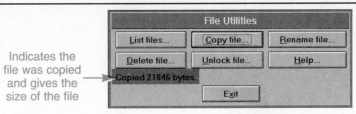

---

**PROFESSIONAL TIP**

AutoCAD can use a .BAK file if it is renamed to a .DWG file. This may be necessary when a drawing file is accidentally erased or is unreadable due to a disk failure. It is best to copy the backup file to another disk. Then, rename the backup with a .DWG extension. If you use the **Copy file...** button to do this, you will still have the backup copy as well as the .DWG file.

## Unlocking a file

File locking can be set when AutoCAD for Windows is initially installed, or by using the **CONFIG** command. If you choose to enable file locking using the **CONFIG** command, be sure to save your current drawing *before* doing so! This type of configuration change requires AutoCAD to exit, and you are not given the option to save your work. Use the **CONFIG** command as follows:

1. First, save your current drawing.
2. Type CONFIG at the **Command:** prompt, or select **Configure** from the **Options** pull-down menu.
3. The graphics window now flips to the text window and the current configuration is displayed. Press [Enter].
4. Select 7 Configure operating parameters.
5. Select 12 File locking.
6. Answer yes (Y) to the Do you wish to enable file-locking? prompt.
7. Select 0 Exit to configuration menu.
8. Select 0 Exit to drawing editor.
9. Answer yes (Y) to the Keep configuration changes? prompt. The following message and prompt is now displayed:

    This configuration change requires AutoCAD to exit.
    Press [Enter] to continue:

10. Press [Enter] at the prompt, and the program is terminated. The next time AutoCAD for Windows is loaded, file locking is enabled.

**NOTE**

File locking should not be changed and files should not be unlocked unless you have proper authorization. File locking is enabled for a reason, and should you unlock and revise a file at the wrong time, it may cause problems in your classroom or company. Be sure you have permission before enabling or disabling file locking.

When AutoCAD is run on a single-user workstation, file locking is not needed. However, should you wish to safeguard a file and protect it from being overwritten during an editing session, you can open it and assign *read-only* status to it. Select **Open...** from the **File** pull-down menu. Pick the **Read Only** check box in the **Select file** dialog box. See Figure 17-7. You can edit the drawing as you wish, but when you try to save it, an AutoCAD Message is displayed. See Figure 17-8.

A file (or group of files) can be unlocked by using the **Unlock file...** button in the **File Utilities** dialog box. The **File(s) to Unlock** dialog box is displayed. You can list only the locked files by entering *.DWK in the **File Name:** edit box. Pick the file you need to unlock, then pick **OK**. The AutoCAD Alert shown in Figure 17-9 is displayed. Click the **Yes** button to proceed with the unlocking.

Figure 17-7.  Pick the **Read Only** check box to safeguard a file from being overwritten.

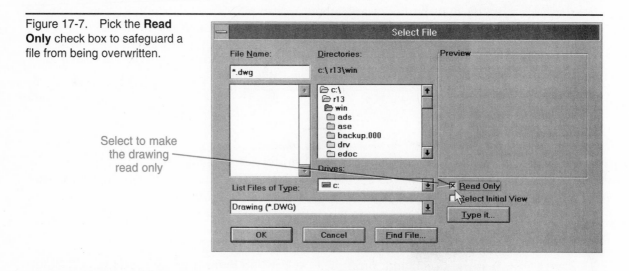

Select to make the drawing read only

Figure 17-8.  AutoCAD alerts you if you attempt to save a file that has read-only status.

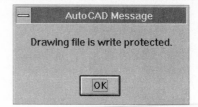

Figure 17-9.  Information about the locked file and who locked it is provided in an **AutoCAD Alert** box.

Filename

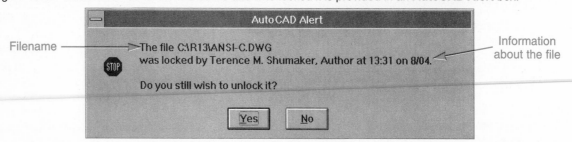

Information about the file

**NOTE**     One common function that creates a locked file is by an "ungraceful" exit from AutoCAD as a result of a power failure or system crash. These drawings may require unlocking before they can be edited again.

**PROFESSIONAL TIP**

If your class or company works with drawings that must be accessed by more than one student or employee, it is good practice to enable file locking. Drawings such as basic site plans, floor plans, templates, or outlines that must have additional information added to them are examples of drawings that must be accessed by more than one person.

When file locking is enabled, AutoCAD automatically creates a small lock file with a .DWK extension. Therefore, when the ANSI-C.DWG file is loaded, a file named ANSI-C.DWK is also created. When the drawing file is unlocked, the ANSI-C.DWK file is deleted.

If file locking is enabled, AutoCAD creates locked versions of several file types. Keep this in mind when working with files other than drawings. The following list shows the activities that create locked versions of the associated file. It is not important that you understand the meaning of all of the file types right now. As you work through this text and gain experience with AutoCAD, you will become more familiar with these activities, and the file types that are used in each.

| Activity | File type | Lock file |
|---|---|---|
| Auditing a drawing for errors. | .ADT | .ADK |
| Working with a drawing file. | .DWG | .DWK |
| Working with drawing interchange files. | .DXF, .DXB | .DFK, .DBK |
| Working with attribute extraction. | .DXX, .TXT | .DXK, .TXK |
| Altering line types. | .LIN | .LIK |
| Creating multiline styles. | .MLN | .MNK |
| Compiling an AutoCAD menu file. | .MNX | .MNK |
| Writing mass properties to a text file. | .MPR | .MPK |
| Converting an older AutoCAD drawing. | .OLD | .OLK |
| Working with a plot configuration parameters file. | .PCP | .PCK |
| Creating plot files. | .PLT | .PLK |
| Working with an ASCIS (3D solids) file. | .SAT | .SAK |
| Altering shape or font files. | .SHX | .SXK |
| Creating and displaying slides. | .SLD | .SDK |
| Creating a stereolithography file. | .STL | .STK |
| Using reference drawings. | .XLG | .XLK |

## RECOVERING A DAMAGED DRAWING                     AUG 14

A damaged drawing file is one that has been corrupted and cannot be loaded into the AutoCAD drawing editor. Drawing files can be damaged in a number of ways. When they are damaged, it can be a frustrating experience, especially if you do not have a backup. Drawings are most often corrupted by:

- Removing a floppy disk before properly exiting AutoCAD.
- Changing floppy disks during a drawing session.
- Running out of disk space during a drawing session.
- Power failures.
- Hardware or software problems.

**NOTE**    Never start a new drawing on the floppy disk using the following naming convention:

> A:FILENAME

This can lead to disk full errors and damaged drawings. Always start a new drawing on the hard disk. Create subdirectories in the \R13 directory for your drawing and data files using Windows File Manager. In the following example, a subdirectory called \DWGS is created under the \R13 directory on the C: drive.

First, open File Manager. Then, select the R13 "folder" in the directory tree. Select Create Directory... from the File menu. Enter DWGS in the Name: text box of the Create Directory dialog box. Pick OK and the new directory is created.

Now, you can load Windows and AutoCAD for Windows and start a new drawing called FRAMUS as follows:

1. Select **New** from the **File** pull-down menu.
2. When the **Create New Drawing** dialog box displays, type the following in the **New Drawing Name...** text box:

> **C:\R13\DWGS\FRAMUS**

This tells AutoCAD where to create and store a new drawing file. You should not run out of disk space as long as there are five or more megabytes of open storage space on the hard disk that contains your directory.

You can add a measure of security by specifying the name of a directory that AutoCAD can use for storage of temporary drawing files. This is an operating parameter option in the **Configuration** menu, which is accessed with the **CONFIG** command. This is discussed in the section titled *Understanding Disk Drives and Directories* in Chapter 2. Always get permission from your instructor or supervisor before altering any of the settings in the **Configuration** menu.

AutoCAD provides a method for recovering most damaged files. You can type RECOVER at the **Command:** prompt, or select **Recover...** in the **Management** ⟩ cascading submenu from the **File** pull-down menu. Select the proper path and file and AutoCAD attempts to recover the damaged drawing.

For example, if the bad file is named \R13\STRUCT\SLAB.DWG, pick the \STRUCT subdirectory. Then, pick the SLAB drawing name. AutoCAD then tries to recover the damaged file. If it is successful, the file is loaded into the drawing editor, and it can be worked on normally. If you do not save the file before exiting AutoCAD, the recovered drawing is lost.

## USING THE AUDIT COMMAND                                          AUG 14

You can perform a diagnostic check on your drawing files with the **AUDIT** command. This checks for, and corrects, errors. You have the option of fixing errors or leaving them.

Command: **AUDIT** ↵
Fix any errors detected? ⟨N⟩ ↵
1                                        Blocks audited
Pass 1      145                          objects audited
Pass 2      145                          objects audited
Total errors found 0                          fixed 0
Command:

If you answer no, as in the above example, any errors are listed for your reference, but they are not fixed. To fix errors in the transferred drawing, answer yes as follows:

> Command: **AUDIT** ↵
> Fix any errors detected? ⟨N⟩: **Y** ↵

AutoCAD displays the errors and notifies you that they are fixed like this:

> 3 Blocks audited
> Pass 29                              objects audited
> Pass 14                              objects audited
> total errors found 2 fixed 2

If the system variable **AUDITCTL** is set to 1 (on), AutoCAD automatically creates an audit report that lists the corrections made. This report is given the same name as the drawing, but has an .ADT file extension. The file is placed in the same directory as the drawing. This is a ASCII text file (American Standard Code for Information Interchange). You can open this file and read the information using any ASCII text editor, such as Windows Notepad.

## Listing the audit report

It is not necessary to leave AutoCAD and exit Windows to display the audit report. Use the [Alt]+[Tab] key combination and switch to Program Manager. Double-click on the Notepad icon located in the Accessories group window, Figure 17-10.

To list the audit report, first select Open... from the File menu. Then, change to the directory where the audit report is, select All Files (*.*) for the type of file, and select the audit file. Pick OK and the contents of the FRAMUS.ADT file are then displayed on the screen. After reviewing the file, you can exit Notepad or [Alt]+[Tab] back to AutoCAD.

Figure 17-10.   The Notepad icon is located in the Accessories group window of Program Manager.

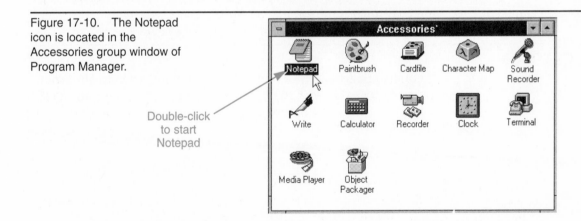

Double-click to start Notepad

---

### EXERCISE 17-2

❑ Insert one of your floppy disks with drawings into the A: drive.
❑ Use the **File Utilities** dialog box for this exercise.
❑ Copy one of your files and rename it using an .OLD file extension.
❑ Change the name of the file in the previous step to TEST.OLD.
❑ Copy and rename TEST.OLD to TEST-2.OLD.
❑ List all files with the .OLD extension.
❑ Delete all files with the .OLD extension.
❑ List the files on the floppy disk in the A: drive. Check to see whether there are any files with the .OLD extension.
❑ Exit the **File Utilities** dialog box.

## UNDERSTANDING AUTOCAD'S TEMPORARY FILES

AutoCAD maintains several temporary files while you are working on a drawing. You might consider these as "worksheets" that AutoCAD opens, much like the notes, references, sketches, and calculations you may have scattered around your desk. These files are created automatically to store portions of the AutoCAD program not currently in use, and for information related to the current drawing file. These files are critical to AutoCAD's operation, and must be maintained and safeguarded properly.

### Program swap files

AutoCAD uses a virtual memory system. *Virtual memory* is a combination of RAM and hard disk space. The main program file for AutoCAD is named ACAD.EXE. It is a very large file—over 5.6MB. If there is not enough room in your computer's physical memory (RAM) to store the program, AutoCAD creates *pages* of the program in free space on your hard disk drive.

A virtual memory system keeps only the part of the program that is currently being used in physical memory. If additional portions of the program are needed, AutoCAD creates a *page* on the hard disk and writes the least-used portion of the program to that page. The new portion of the program that is requested is written to physical memory. Thus, AutoCAD creates a *paging* system using virtual memory. The least-used pages are written to a page called a *swap file*, and are held there until needed again.

The important point to note regarding AutoCAD's paging system is that when required, it creates a swap file in the root directory of the current disk drive, and gives it a .SWR extension. These files are critical to AutoCAD, and must never be deleted while you are in a drawing session. Should you experience an improper termination of AutoCAD, and the drawing file is not saved properly, these swap files may be left open. In that case the files are no longer of use and can be deleted, but only *after* you have exited AutoCAD.

> **CAUTION**
>
>
>
> If you feel that swap files have been left behind after an abnormal exit from AutoCAD, you may delete all files that have an .SWR extension, or that have names such as AOBCGFFE and have no extension. Never delete any of these temporary files while you are working in AutoCAD. Doing so may damage the current drawing and cause AutoCAD to terminate improperly.

### Temporary files

The second piece of AutoCAD's virtual memory system is called the *pager*. This works similar to the swap file system, but creates temporary storage space for drawing file information. The entire contents of a small drawing may fit into your computer's physical memory, but as the drawing grows larger, portions of it must be temporarily removed. AutoCAD creates a *page file* for the least-used portion of your drawing, and opens the physical memory for new drawing data. When the drawing data contained in the page file is needed, it is *paged* back into memory. These temporary files are given the file extension of .AC$. These are vital files and must never be deleted while working in AutoCAD.

If AutoCAD should terminate improperly, these page files are left open in the current drawing directory. The .AC$ files that are left behind are no longer of any use, and can be deleted. Always delete these files with File Manager, and never while you are working in AutoCAD.

You can specify a directory on the hard disk drive for the storage of page files. Use the **ACADPAGEDIR** environment variable in the batch file that runs AutoCAD. A normal installation of AutoCAD creates a batch file titled ACADR13.BAT. The line in that file that specifies a directory for page files may look like this:

    SET ACADPAGEDIR=C:\R13\TEMP

Never alter the contents of a batch file unless you have the permission of your instructor or supervisor.

### Create a workspace for temporary files

The default workspace for AutoCAD's temporary files is the current disk drive and directory, or the drive and directory specified by the **SAVE** or **SAVEAS** commands. You can create a directory on your hard drive and tell AutoCAD to always use that directory for storage of temporary files. Use the following procedure to allocate space for these files.

1. Use the **CONFIG** command and press [Enter] until the **Configuration** menu is displayed.
2. Select  7 Configure operating parameters.
3. Select  5 Placement of temporary files.
4. Enter a hard disk drive and directory where you want the temporary files located. The \WINDOWS\TEMP directory is created when Windows is installed. This is a convenient location.

The default setting is DRAWING, which causes temporary files to be stored in the same drive and directory as the drawing being edited. By setting this to a path that contains plenty of free space, you can be reasonably protected from "disk full" situations. AutoCAD places temporary files on the floppy disk if it is specified as the path with **SAVE** or **SAVEAS**. Therefore, never pick either of these commands from the pull-down menu to save to a floppy disk.

### Automatically saved drawing files

The **SAVETIME** system variable allows you to specify the time interval that AutoCAD uses to automatically save the current drawing file. This becomes your first line of backup, and is also considered a temporary file. Should you encounter a problem in AutoCAD and find your drawing file is corrupted as a result of an improper termination or system crash, this file may be a valuable backup. As a default setting, AutoCAD names the automatically saved file AUTO.SV$. If you ever need to use this drawing because the original is corrupt, you must rename it as a .DWG file.

For example, first start File Manager. Highlight the filename in the directory tree. Then, select Re<u>n</u>ame... from the <u>F</u>ile menu and enter a name with the .DWG extension, such as TEST.DWG. This renaming action allows AutoCAD to load the file as a drawing.

The default name of the autosave file is established by AutoCAD, but can be changed by using the **CONFIG** command. If you want to have this file saved under a name other than AUTO.SV$, use the **CONFIG** command as follows:

1. Execute the **CONFIG** command.
2. Select 7 in the **Configuration** menu.
3. Select 7 in the **Configure operating parameters** menu.
4. Type the time between saves and the new filename at the following prompts and press [Enter].

> Interval between automatic saves, in minutes
> (1 - 600, or 0 for no automatic saves) ⟨120⟩: **10** ↵
> Enter filename for automatic saves
> ⟨AUTO.SV$⟩: **AUTOSAVE** ↵

5. Select 0 Exit to configuration menu.
6. Select 0 Exit to drawing editor.
7. Answer yes (Y) to the Keep configuration changes? prompt.

Remember, any time you wish to change the interval between automatic saves, just use the **SAVETIME** system variable at the AutoCAD **Command:** prompt.

## AUTOCAD'S DXF FILE FORMAT                          ACG 16

AutoCAD users may need to exchange files with other programs, or import other software files into AutoCAD. For this purpose, Autodesk, Inc. created the DXF (drawing interchange file) file format. This format has become an accepted standard for microcomputer CAD programs.

Files prepared using the DXF format are standard ASCII code. *ASCII* stands for American National Standard Code for Information Interchange. This means that the information contained in the file can be read by any computer that "understands" the ASCII format.

Unfortunately computer translations, as with spoken languages, often lose something in the translation. The problem is not the ASCII code, but rather the way that CAD systems create entities, layers, and other drawing characteristics. For example, AutoCAD allows layer names. Some other programs use numbers. Even if layer numbers are used in AutoCAD, they may not translate to be the same number in another program. AutoCAD has polylines and some other programs do not. AutoCAD's blocks may become individual entities in other programs.

This may seem like a roadblock to drawing file translation. However, often it creates only minor problems, depending on the drawings and the systems involved. These problems may soon be eliminated. The field of microcomputer CAD (microCAD) is still young. Companies are beginning to realize the importance of standardization. The ability to translate files will become an even more valuable tool in the near future.

### Binary DXF file

The standard DXF file is in ASCII format, but you also have the option of creating a binary form of the DXF file. A *binary code* is one composed of data in the form of bits having a value of either 1 or 0. This type of file can be up to 25% smaller than an ASCII file, and it is just as accurate. The binary file is given the same extension of .DXF. It can be read quicker than an ASCII file, and AutoCAD can create it and load it using the **DXFOUT** and **DXFIN** commands. Since DXF files are so much smaller than drawing files, and binary files are even smaller, using the **Binary** option of the **DXFOUT** command may be a good practice if you must provide interchange files to a coworker or client who works with Release 10 or newer versions of AutoCAD.

### Contents of an ASCII DXF file

You do not need to understand the contents of a DXF file to successfully translate drawings. Yet, when customizing or programming AutoCAD and using AutoLISP, you will use information like that found in a DXF file. The contents of a DXF file is arranged into four sections.
- **Header.** Every drawing variable and its value is listed in this section.
- **Tables.** Named items, such as layers, linetypes, styles, and views, are found in this section.
- **Blocks.** All entities and their values that comprise blocks are listed in this section.
- **Entities.** Objects in the drawing are located here.

A quick method of displaying and examining a .DXF file is to open it using your favorite text editor or word processing program, or the Windows Notepad program. You can quickly [Alt]+[Tab] to Program Manager and open the word processor or Notepad.

Once in Notepad, open the .DXF file. The file is long, and contains a list of all the variables and settings used by AutoCAD. If you plan to study menu customization or programming, you should become familiar with the components of .DXF files and the syntax used. Refer to the *AutoCAD Customization Guide* for detailed information on this type of file.

## Exporting a DXF file

The **DXFOUT** command creates a .DXF file extension ASCII drawing file from an AutoCAD drawing. To test the use of the **DXFOUT** command, begin a new drawing and name it DXFTEST. Draw a single line on your screen using the **LINE** command. The DXF commands can be selected from a cascading submenu by picking **Export...** in the **File** pull-down menu. This displays the **Export Data** dialog box. This is a general files dialog box and is used for creating export files of a variety of types. It is described later in this chapter. Enter the **DXFOUT** command at the **Command:** prompt as follows:

> Command: **DXFOUT** ↵

The **Create DXF File** dialog box is displayed when the **FILEDIA** system variable is set to 1, Figure 17-11. The DXF filename default in the **File Name:** edit box is the same as the drawing name, but with the .DXF extension. Notice that the .DXF extension does not appear in the **File Name:** box, but it automatically appears in the **List Files of Type:** pop-up list at the lower-left of the dialog. Click the **OK** button to accept the filename.

Figure 17-11.   The **DXFOUT** command displays the **Create DXF File** dialog box. Enter a filename and select a directory for the file.

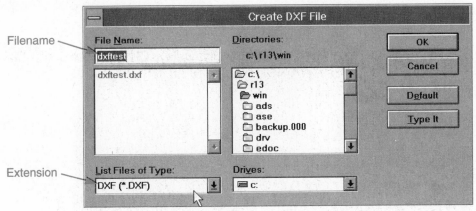

AutoCAD then asks you on the command line to indicate the degree of accuracy you want for numeric values. The choices range between 0 and 16 decimal places. In this example, the default accuracy of six decimal places is accepted by pressing [Enter]. The DXF file is created and stored on disk.

> Enter decimal places of accuracy (0 to 16)/Objects/Binary ⟨6⟩: ↵
> Command:

The **Objects** option allows you to select specific shapes or objects to include in the DXF file. If you use this option, only the objects that you pick are placed in the file. When you pick the specific objects, AutoCAD asks for the desired accuracy as before:

> Enter decimal places of accuracy (0 to 16)/Binary ⟨6⟩: ↵

Check to be sure the DXF file was created by using the **File Utilities** dialog box. To access the **File Utilities** dialog box, select **Utilities...** from the **Management** cascading submenu in the **File** pull-down menu. Next, click the **List files...** button to display the **File List** subdialog box, Figure 17-12. Use the **List Files of Type:** pop-up list to list only those files with a .DXF extension. The file DXFTEST.DXF should appear in the file list box.

When using the **DXFOUT** command, you can specify a filename other than the default. *Do not* enter a .DXF extension—AutoCAD automatically adds this to the filename that you specify. If the filename you provide already exists, AutoCAD informs you accordingly and displays the **Create DXF File** alert box shown in Figure 17-13. Click the **Yes** button to replace the file or click the **No** button to cancel.

After using the **DXFOUT** command to create the DXF file, use the **SAVEAS** command to save your drawing file. The **Save Drawing As** dialog box appears. Accept the filename DXFTEST by picking the **OK** button. Notice the file type is .DWG. Now exit AutoCAD for Windows.

Figure 17-12.   The **File List** subdialog box can be used to list .DXF files only.

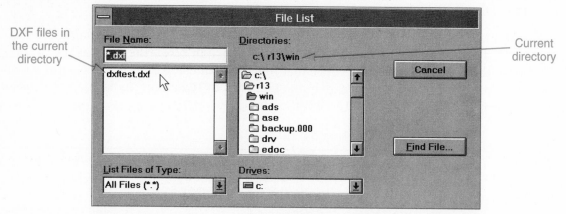

Figure 17-13.   The **Create DXF File** alert box warns you if a file with the same name already exists.

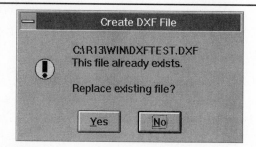

---

**CAUTION**

Remember that if **FILEDIA** is set to 0 (off), no dialog box is displayed when you create a DXF file. In these instances, you are prompted for the filename on the AutoCAD command line. If you give a filename that already exists, AutoCAD cannot display an alert box. The existing DXF file is automatically overwritten.

---

### Importing a DXF file

The **DXFIN** command allows you to create an AutoCAD drawing file (.DWG extension) from a .DXF file. It is important that you begin a new drawing in AutoCAD first. Do not add entities or make setup steps. If you use an old drawing, only the entities of the DXF file are inserted. The layers, blocks, and other drawing definitions of the old drawing will override those of the DXF file.

Begin a new drawing and name it DXFTEST1. Select **Import...** from the **File** pull-down menu or type DXFIN at the **Command:** prompt. When the **Select DXF File** dialog box appears, select DXFTEST.DXF from the file list box or enter the filename DXFTEST in the **File Name:** edit box, Figure 17-14. Then, click the **OK** button or press [Enter]. The dialog box disappears and the drawing is regenerated.

Figure 17-14. The **DXFIN** command displays the **Select DXF File** dialog box. Enter a filename or select it from the list.

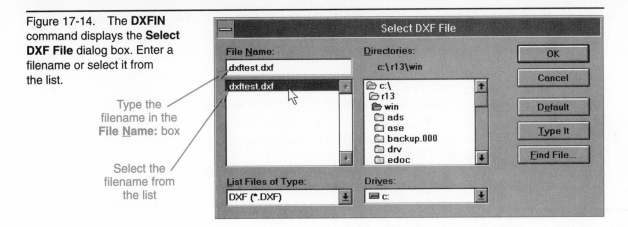

Type the filename in the **File Name:** box

Select the filename from the list

The line should appear on the screen as it was in the original DXFTEST drawing. The new drawing DXFTEST1 with the inserted DXF file, is not given the .DWG extension until you save it.

## DXF applications

There are several applications where you will want to convert an AutoCAD file to DXF format. The most common application is sharing drawings with CAM systems or other CAD systems. Numerical control (NC) programs such as SmartCAM™ and NCProgrammer™ use DXF files. The file is used to translate the shape and features of a machine part to code that can be used for lathes, milling machines, and drill presses. In addition, desktop publishing programs like Quark XPress®, Ventura Publisher®, and Pagemaker™ use DXF files to translate drawings into images that can be inserted into a page layout. Also, programs that perform stress analysis and calculations often rely on DXF drawings.

## Importing a scanned file

*Scanning* is the process of creating an electronic file from a hard copy. Scanners reflect light off the hard copy and translate this data into an electronic file. Many scanning programs create a DXB (drawing interchange binary) file after scanning an existing paper drawing with a camera or plotter-mounted scanner. A plotter-mounted scanner is shown in Figure 17-15.

Figure 17-15. This scanner is attached to a large format plotter and is capable of detecting lines as fine as 0.007 inch. (Houston Instrument, A Summagraphics Company)

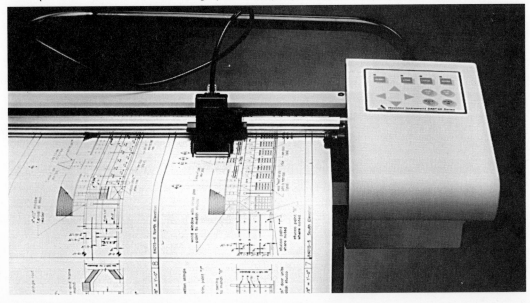

The file created is a binary code. The **DXBIN** command converts this code into drawing data. This drawing data becomes an AutoCAD drawing file with a .DWG extension. The command is used as follows:

Command: **DXBIN** ⏎

The **FILEDIA** system variable determines what you see on the screen. If **FILEDIA** is 1, the **Select DXB File** dialog box appears. Accept the default filename, or enter the filename of a specific scanned drawing, and pick the **OK** button. You can then edit the drawing using typical AutoCAD commands.

If **FILEDIA** is 0, the file dialog box is replaced with a filename prompt. The following prompt appears after you enter DXBIN at the **Command:** prompt:

DXB file: *(enter filename and press* [Enter]*)*

After you enter a filename, the drawing file created can then be edited.

## LOCATING ERRORS IN A TRANSFERRED FILE

AutoCAD generally does not check a DXF file for errors, but you can do this if you need to. To do so, instruct AutoCAD to automatically list errors in the file before you transfer a DXF file. Use the following steps:

Command: **CONFIG** ⏎

- Press [Enter] until the **Configuration** menu is displayed.
- Select 7 Configure operating parameters from the **Configuration** menu.
- Select 10 Automatic Audit after DXFIN, or DXBIN from the **Configure** operating parameters menu.
- Answer Y to this question:

Do you want an automatic audit after DXFIN or DXBIN? ⟨N⟩: **Y** ⏎

- The automatic audit is ready to be performed. Press [Enter] until you get back to the **Configuration** menu.
- Be sure to press [Enter] to update the configuration.

The automatic auditing process does not correct errors in the file. Errors must be corrected by editing the DXF file or by using the **AUDIT** command while working on the drawing. See the section earlier in this chapter titled *USING THE AUDIT COMMAND* for a discussion on the use of this command.

## EXPORTING AND IMPORTING FILES

AutoCAD provides you with the ability to work with files other than DXF. You can export the current drawing to files that can be used in other programs for rendering, animation, desktop publishing, presentations, stereolithography, and solids modeling. This section provides a brief overview of AutoCAD's capabilities in exporting and importing a variety of different files. All of these options can be selected from the **File** pull-down menu by picking either the **Import...** or **Export...** command.

Figure 17-16 illustrates the **Import Data** and **Export Data** dialog boxes. These dialog boxes are basically the standard dialog for selecting files. First, pick the type of file you wish to work with in the **List Files of Type:** pop-up list at the lower-left corner of the dialog box. Next, select the file. The **File Name:** edit box is located in the upper-left corner. Enter the filename here, or select it from the files displayed in the file list. Use the **Drives:** pop-up list to select the proper drive, and the **Directories:** list to choose a directory. The next sections cover the different importing and exporting commands.

Figure 17-16. A—A variety of files can be imported into AutoCAD using the **Import File** dialog box.
B—A variety of file types can be exported from AutoCAD for use in other software with the
**Export Data** dialog box.

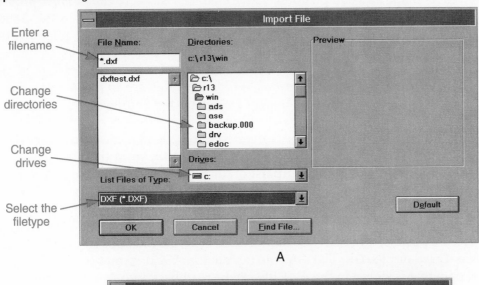

A

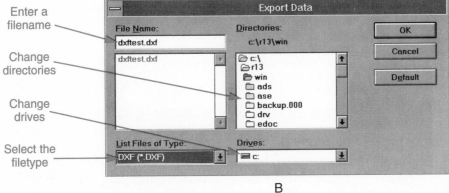

B

## AutoCAD Release 12 files

The **SAVEASR12** command allows you to export an AutoCAD Release 13 drawing file in
Release 12 format. This function can be selected from the **File** pull-down menu or entered at
the **Command:** prompt. If **FILEDIA** is set to 1 (on), the **Save Release 12 Drawing As** dialog box
is displayed. You can select any .DWG file from the files list, or enter a filename in the **File
Name:** edit box. Press [Enter] or pick **OK** when you are finished. If you select an existing filename, AutoCAD saves the Release 13 drawing with a .BAK extension.

## 3D Studio files

The program 3D Studio is an Autodesk product that allows you to design, render, and
animate 3D models. You can export or import 3D Studio files with AutoCAD Release 13.
When you type 3DSOUT at the **Command:** prompt to export a 3D Studio file, you are prompted to select objects. Select all of the 3D objects you wish to export and press [Enter]. The **3D
Studio Output File** dialog box is displayed. Enter the filename in the **File Name:** edit box. Press
[Enter] or pick **OK** when you are finished. Exporting a 3D Studio file can also be executed by
picking the 3D Studio (*.3DS) file type in the **Export Data** dialog box.

You can also import an existing 3D Studio file into AutoCAD by selecting **Import...** from
the **File** pull-down menu. The **Import File** dialog box is displayed. Select the appropriate .3DS
file from the list and press [Enter]. You can also import a 3D Studio file by typing 3DSIN at the
**Command:** prompt.

## Solid model files

A *solid* is a 3D object that is composed of a specific material, and possesses unique characteristics related to its shape and composition. These characteristics are called *mass properties*. Solids are created in AutoCAD with one of several commands found in the **Solids** cascading submenu of the **Draw** pull-down menu. The term *solid modeling* refers to the process of constructing a part from one or more 3D solid shapes called *primitives*, and performing any necessary editing functions to create the final product. This procedure is discussed in detail in *AutoCAD and its Applications—Advanced, Release 13 for Windows*, and in *AutoCAD AME—Solid Modeling for Mechanical Design* by Ted Saufley.

A solid model is frequently used with analyzing and testing software, or in the manufacturing of the part. AutoCAD drawings can be converted into a file that can be used for these purposes. To do so, use the **ACISOUT** command. Choose **Export...** from the **File** pull-down menu. Pick ACIS (*.SAT) in the file type pop-up list of the **Export Data** dialog box. When you pick **OK**, you are prompted to select objects. Use any of the standard selection methods to choose the solid objects, then press [Enter]. If ACISOUT is typed at the **Command:** prompt, the **Create ACIS File** dialog box is displayed instead of the **Export Data** dialog box. Notice that the .SAT extension is the default setting. Do not change this. Type the filename in the **File Name:** edit box and press [Enter] or pick **OK**. The .SAT file is stored in ASCII format.

Solid model data that is stored in the .SAT file can be read back into AutoCAD using the **ACISIN** command. When you enter this command, the **Select ACIS File** dialog box is displayed. Pick the file from the list, then pick **OK** or press [Enter].

**PROFESSIONAL TIP**

The ASCII file created by the **ACISOUT** command may be from three to four times smaller than the .DWG drawing file. For this reason, it may be efficient to store 3D solid models as .SAT files instead of drawings. When you need to work with the model for any purpose in AutoCAD, simply use the **ACISIN** command. This command creates solid objects from the model data stored in the ASCII file.

## Stereolithography files

*Stereolithography* is a technology where a plastic prototype 3D model is created using a computer-generated solid model, a laser, and a vat of liquid polymer. This technology is also referred to as *rapid prototyping* because a prototype 3D model can be designed and formed in a short amount of time, without using standard manufacturing processes. Most software used to create a stereolithograph can read a .STL file. AutoCAD can export a drawing file to the .STL format, but *cannot* import an .STL file.

After entering the **STLOUT** command, you are prompted to select a single object as follows:

```
Command: STLOUT ↵
Select a single solid for STL output:
Select objects:
```

If you select more than one object AutoCAD prompts you:

```
Only one solid per file permitted.
```

Select one object and press [Enter]. You are then asked if you want to create a binary .STL file. If you answer no to this prompt, an ASCII file is created. Keep in mind that a binary STL file may be at least five times smaller than the ASCII STL file. After you choose the type of file to create, the **Create STL File** dialog box is displayed. Type the filename in the **File Name:** edit box and pick **OK** or press [Enter].

### PostScript files

PostScript is a copyrighted page description language developed by Adobe Systems. This language is widely used in the desktop publishing industry. AutoCAD drawing files can be exported to the .EPS PostScript file format by typing PSOUT at the **Command:** prompt. The **Create PostScript File** dialog box is displayed. You can also pick **Export...** from the **File** pull-down menu to display the **Export Data** dialog box. Then, pick Encapsulated PS (*.EPS) in the files type pop-up list. Type the filename in the **File Name:** edit box and pick **OK** or press [Enter].

PostScript files can be imported into AutoCAD by picking **Import...** from the **File** pull-down menu. The **Import Data** dialog box is displayed. Then, pick Encapsulated PS (*.EPS). Type the filename in the **File Name:** edit box and pick **OK** or press [Enter].

## CHAPTER TEST

*Write your answers in the spaces provided.*

1. What is a file type extension? _____

   _____

2. What do the following file extension types mean:
   A. .BAK _____
   B. .LIN _____
   C. .MNU _____
   D. .PLT _____
   E. .BAT _____
   F. .EXE _____

3. Which pull-down selection leads to the **File Utilities** dialog box? _____

4. How do you list the drawing files on the floppy disk in the A: drive? _____

   _____

5. How do you list all .MNU files on the floppy disk in the B: drive? _____

   _____

6. How do you delete all .BAK files from the current C:\R13 directory? The files begin with PROJ2 and have three additional letters in their names. _____

   _____

   _____

7. What is the procedure for changing a filename? _____

   _____

   _____

8. What two functions can the **Rename files** option perform? _____

9. How is the **Copy files** option similar to the **Rename files** option? _____

   _____

10. Describe the function of dialog box accelerator keys. _____

   _____

11. Why are files locked? _____

_____

12. What type of file is created when file locking is enabled? _____

13. How can a file be unlocked? _____

_____

14. How can a damaged file be recovered? _____

_____

15. What command allows you to run a diagnostic check of a drawing file? ____

_____

16. What type of memory system does AutoCAD use to create pages of the program on the hard disk? _____

17. What file type is created by the system in question 16, and what is its three-letter file extension? _____

18. What is AutoCAD's pager system, and what is the three-letter file extension that it creates?

_____

_____

_____

_____

_____

19. What is the name of the backup drawing file that AutoCAD creates automatically based on the value of the **SAVETIME** variable? _____

20. Explain why drawing file translations are needed. _____

_____

21. Define the following abbreviations.
    DXF _____
    DXB _____

22. What is the purpose of the **DXFOUT** command? _____

_____

23. When would you use the **DXFIN** command? _____

_____

24. List the four sections contained in a DXF file. _____

_____

25. Suppose you plan to import a DXF file. What setup steps must you perform to the new drawing before importing the DXF file? _____

_____

26. List some of the programs that can use DXF files. _____

_____

_____

27. When would you use the **DXBIN** command? _____
    _____

28. Is the DWG, DXF, or DXB file type typically the largest? _____

29. What **FILEDIA** system variable value must be used to ensure that a file dialog box appears when needed? _____

30. Does AutoCAD automatically list errors in a transferred DXF file? _____

31. Does the automatic auditing process correct errors in a file? _____

32. Describe the function of the **AUDIT** command when used to correct errors in a transferred file. _____
    _____

33. Name five types of files, other than DXF, that can be imported into AutoCAD. _____
    _____
    _____
    _____

34. Why might it be more efficient to store solid models in the form of .SAT files rather than as drawing files? _____
    _____

35. What is an .STL file and what is it used for? _____
    _____
    _____

## DRAWING PROBLEMS

1. Write a short report on the importance of file maintenance. Present some uses of the **File Utilities** dialog box in file maintenance. Suggest a procedure to save drawing files and other types of files. Cover the following points in your report:

   *General*

   A. Where drawing files are to be stored now—hard disk or floppy disks?
   B. When files should be backed up?
   C. How many backups of each file should exist?
   D. Where should the original and backup disks be located?
   E. How often should .BAK files be deleted, or should they be deleted at all?
   F. What file naming system should be used?

2. Make backup copies of all your diskettes. Use the **Copy File** option in the **File Utilities** dialog box. Copy the files in two different ways.

   *General*

   A. Copy all files with the .DWG extension to the new disk. Then copy all .BAK files to the new disk.
   B. Copy a second disk, or recopy the first disk.
   C. List the files on your backup disk. Be sure that files with both .DWG and .BAK extensions have been copied. Then rename all files with the .BAK extension to have an .OLD extension.

General

3. Get a printed listing of the files contained on one disk. Ask your instructor or supervisor for assistance if you are not familiar with the printer. See Chapter 12 for instructions on making a printout of text printed on the screen.

General

4. Get a printed list of all drawing files contained on your floppy disk.

General

5. Load one of your simple drawings into the AutoCAD graphics window. Create a DXF file of the drawing. Generate a printed copy of the contents of the DXF file.

General

6. The purpose of this drawing is to create entities and generate a DXF file. Then, edit the DXF file with a text editor and use the **DXFIN** command to view the revised drawing. You must refer to Chapter 16 of the *AutoCAD Customization Guide* to complete this problem. Use the following steps:

A. Begin a new drawing and name it P17-2.

B. Draw circle A at 4,4 with a 1″ radius.

C. Draw circle B at a distance of 3,0 from circle A with radius of .5″.

D. Save the drawing.

E. Make a DXF file of the drawing using the name of the drawing.

F. Load the DXF file into your text editor and make the following changes to circles. They are listed in the **ENTITIES** section of the DXF file. Use a Search function of your text editor to find this section.
   • Change the radius of circle B to 2.
   • Change the location of circle A to 4,2.

G. Save the DXF file.

H. Begin a new drawing named P17-6A. Use the **DXFIN** command to load the P17-6.DWG file. Do you notice any changes? Save the drawing.

General

7. If you have access to a scanner, create a DXB file from an old, hand-drawn print. Import the DXB file using the **DXBIN** command. Compare the new AutoCAD drawing with the original.

General

8. Use one of the previous problems to fix errors that may exist in the transferred file using the **AUDIT** command.

*Problems 9 and 10 require that you have access to another microCAD program, or a program that is designed to work with AutoCAD output. Another school or company in your area may have one such program that you can use to exchange files.*

General

9. Load one of your drawings that contains layers, blocks, and a variety of entities into AutoCAD. Create a DXF file of the drawing. Import the file into another program that can accept DXF file translations. Compare the new drawings with the AutoCAD version. Look especially at layers, block definitions, and entities such as polylines.

General

10. Obtain a DXF file from another microCAD or CAD/CAM program. Use the **DXFIN** command to convert it to an AutoCAD drawing file. Compare the new AutoCAD drawing with the original version.

## Learning objectives

After completing this chapter, you will be able to:
- ○ Use the **PLINE** command to draw polylines and polyarcs.
- ○ Preset the polyline width.
- ○ Use the **PEDIT** command to make changes to existing polylines.
- ○ Identify the **PEDIT** options.
- ○ Use the **EXPLODE** command to remove all polyline width characteristics.
- ○ Make a polyline boundary.
- ○ Draw and edit spline curves.

The **PLINE** command was introduced in Chapter 6 as a way to draw thick lines. As you will find, the **PLINE** command also draws a variety of special shapes, limited only by your imagination. The section on **PLINE** in Chapter 6 focused on line-related options, such as **Width**, **Halfwidth**, and **Length**. The editing functions were limited to the **ERASE** and **UNDO** commands. This chapter covers using **PLINE** to make polyline arcs and advanced editing commands for polylines. You can access the **PLINE** command by clicking the **Polyline** button in the **Draw** toolbox or typing PLINE at the **Command:** prompt. If the ACADFULL menu is loaded, you can select **Polyline** from the **Draw** pull-down menu. If you do so, you have the option to create 2D or 3D polylines.

## DRAWING PLINE ARCS

AUG 2

The **Arc** option of the **PLINE** command functions like the **ARC** command, except that **PLINE** options include **Width** and **Halfwidth**. The arc width can range from 0 up to the radius of the arc. A polyline arc with different end widths is drawn by changing the **Width**. The arc shown in Figure 18-1 was drawn with the following command sequence:

Command: **PLINE** ↵
From point: *(pick the first point)*
Current line-width is (status specified)
Arc/Close/Halfwidth/Length/Undo/Width/⟨Endpoint of line⟩: **W** ↵
Starting width ⟨current⟩: *(specify a starting width, such as .1, and press [Enter])*
Ending width ⟨current⟩: *(specify an ending width, such as .4, and press [Enter])*
Arc/Close/Halfwidth/Length/Undo/Width/⟨Endpoint of line⟩: **A** ↵
Angle/CEnter/CLose/Direction/Halfwidth/Line/Radius/Second
    pt/Undo/Width/⟨Endpoint of arc⟩: *(pick the arc endpoint)*
Angle/CEnter/CLose/Direction/Halfwidth/Line/Radius/Second
    pt/Undo/Width/⟨Endpoint of arc⟩: ↵
Command:

Figure 18-1.  A polyline arc
with different starting and
ending widths.

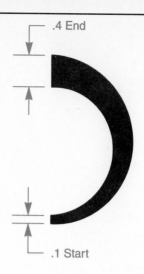

## Drawing a continuous polyline arc

A polyline arc continued from a previous line or polyline is tangent at the last point entered. The arc's center is determined automatically, but you can pick a new center. If a polyline arc is drawn before a straight polyline, the arc's direction is the same as the previous line, arc, or polyline. This may not be what you want. In this case, it may be necessary to set one of the **PLINE Arc** options. These include **Angle**, **CEnter**, **Direction**, **Radius**, or **Second pt** (second point). They work much like the **ARC** command options.

## Specifying the included angle

The following command sequence is used to enter the **Angle** option for a polyline arc, as shown in Figure 18-2:

    Command: **PLINE** ↵
    From point: *(pick the first point)*
    Current line-width is (status specified)
    Arc/Close/Halfwidth/Length/Undo/Width/⟨Endpoint of line⟩: **A** ↵
    Angle/CEnter/CLose/Direction/Halfwidth/Line/Radius/Second pt/Undo/Width/
        ⟨Endpoint of arc⟩: **A** ↵
    Included angle: *(specify the included angle, such as* 60, *and press* [Enter])
    Center/Radius/⟨Endpoint⟩: *(select the arc endpoint)*
    Angle/CEnter/CLose/Direction/Halfwidth/Line/Radius/Second pt/Undo/Width/
        ⟨Endpoint of arc⟩: ↵
    Command:

Figure 18-2.  Drawing a polyline
arc with a specified angle.

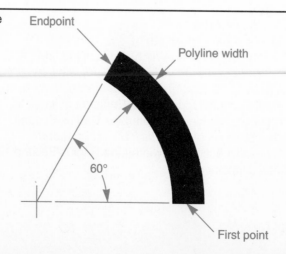

## Selecting the **CEnter** option

When a polyline arc continues from a drawn item, the center point is calculated automatically. You may want to pick a new center point when the polyline arc does not continue from another item or if the one calculated is not suitable. The **CEnter** option is used as follows:

```
Command: PLINE ↵
From point: (select the first point)
Current line-width is (status specified)
Arc/Close/Halfwidth/Length/Undo/Width/⟨Endpoint of line⟩: A ↵
Angle/CEnter/CLose/Direction/Halfwidth/Line/Radius/Second pt/Undo/Width/
    ⟨Endpoint of arc⟩: CE ↵ (notice that two letters, CE, are required for this option)
Center point: (select the arc center point)
Angle/Length/⟨Endpoint⟩: (select the arc endpoint, or type A or L and press [Enter])
```

If A is entered at this prompt, the next prompt is:

```
Included angle: (select an included angle and press [Enter])
```

If L is entered, the next prompt is:

```
Length of chord: (select a chord length and press [Enter])
```

The **Command:** prompt then returns.

## Using the **Direction** option

The **Direction** option alters the bearing of the arc. It changes the default option of placing the polyline arc tangent to the last polyline, arc, or line. This option can also be entered when you are drawing an unconnected polyline arc. The **Direction** option functions much like the **Direction** option of the **ARC** command. After D is typed, the following prompt appears:

```
Direction from start point: (enter a direction in positive or negative degrees, or specify
    a point on either side of the start point)
End point: (select the endpoint of the arc)
```

## Drawing a polyline arc by radius

Polyline arcs can be drawn by giving the arc's radius. This is done by typing R. Then, respond to these prompts:

```
Angle/CEnter/CLose/Direction/Halfwidth/Line/Radius/Second
    pt/Undo/Width/⟨Endpoint of arc⟩: R ↵
Radius: (type the arc radius and press [Enter])
Angle/⟨End point⟩: (pick the arc endpoint)
```

or

```
Angle/CEnter/CLose/Direction/Halfwidth/Line/Radius/Second
    pt/Undo/Width/⟨Endpoint of arc⟩: A ↵
Included angle: (type the included angle of the arc and press [Enter])
Direction of chord ⟨current⟩: (enter chord direction and press [Enter])
```

## Specifying a three-point polyline arc

A three-point arc can be drawn by typing S for **Second pt**. The prompts are as follows:

```
Angle/CEnter/CLose/Direction/Halfwidth/Line/Radius/Second pt/Undo/Width/
    ⟨Endpoint of arc⟩: S ↵
Second point: (pick the second point on the arc)
End point: (pick the endpoint to complete the arc)
```

## Using the CLose option

The **CLose** option saves drafting time by automatically adding the last segment to close a polygonal shape. The **PLINE Arc** option will close the shape with a polyline arc segments, rather than a straight polyline. Notice that CL is typed at the prompt line to distinguish this option from the **CEnter** option. You can also close a shape by selecting **Close** from the **Assist** pull-down menu. Figure 18-3 shows how the command sequence below encloses a shape.

Angle/CEnter/CLose/Direction/Halfwidth/Line/Radius/Second pt/Undo/Width/
⟨Endpoint of arc⟩: **CL** ↵

Figure 18-3.   Using the **CLose** option of the **PLINE** command.

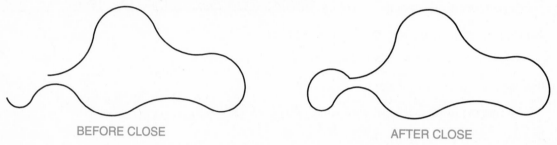

BEFORE CLOSE                                                                                    AFTER CLOSE

### EXERCISE 18-1

❑ Open TITLEA from Problem 11-1.
❑ Draw a continuous polyline arc with at least four segments. Select the **CLose** option to close the polyline.
❑ Draw a polyline arc using endpoints and a 90° included angle. Then continue from the first arc with another 90° polyline arc.
❑ Draw a polyline arc using end and center points.
❑ Choose the endpoint, center, and included angle to draw a polyline arc.
❑ Select endpoints and a positive direction to draw a polyline arc. Then see how using a negative direction affects the arc.
❑ Specify the endpoints of a 1.5 unit radius arc.
❑ Draw a polyline arc using three points.
❑ Save the drawing as A:EX18-1 and quit.

## Presetting polyline widths

You can preset the constant width of polylines and rectangles with the AutoCAD system variable **PLINEWID**. This can save you valuable drafting time. The **PLINEWID** system variable is entered at the **Command:** prompt as follows:

Command: **PLINEWID** ↵
New value for PLINEWID ⟨*current*⟩: *(enter a width and press* [Enter]*)*

Although polygon objects are constructed with polylines, they are not affected by the **PLINEWID** variable. When you are done drawing wide polylines or rectangles, be sure to set the value of **PLINEWID** to 0 (zero).

# REVISING POLYLINES USING THE PEDIT COMMAND

Polylines are drawn as single segments. A polyline joined to another polyline might then be joined to a polyline arc. Even though you draw connecting segments, AutoCAD puts them all together. The result is one polyline. When editing a polyline, you must edit it as one entity or divide it into its single segments. These changes are made with the **PEDIT** and **EXPLODE** commands.

## INTRODUCTION TO PEDIT

AUG 5

The **PEDIT** command is accessed by clicking the **Edit Polyline** button in the **Modify** toolbar or by entering PEDIT at the **Command:** prompt. If the ACADFULL menu file is loaded, the **PEDIT** command is also found in the **Modify** pull-down menu as **Edit Polyline**. The following prompt appears:

> Command: **PEDIT** ↵
> Select polyline: *(use one of the selection set options and press [Enter] when completed)*

Move the cursor and pick the polyline to be changed or use any selection option. If you are using a pickbox on a wide polyline, you must place the pickbox on an edge, rather than in the center.

If the polyline you want to change was the last object drawn, simply type L for **Last**. If the object you select is a line or arc entity, this message is displayed:

> Object selected is not a polyline.
> Do you want to turn it into one? ⟨Y⟩

A Y response, or [Enter], turns the selected object into a polyline. Type N to leave the object as is. Note that if the selection set contains more than one object, only the first object found in the drawing database will be converted to a polyline. The rest of the objects are ignored.

**PROFESSIONAL TIP**

A group of connected lines and arcs can be turned into a continuous polyline using the **Join** option. The **Join** option is discussed later in this chapter.

## REVISING A POLYLINE AS ONE UNIT

A polyline can be edited as a single entity, or it can be divided to revise each individual segment. This section shows you the options for changing the entire polyline. Notice the number of options given in the prompt:

> Command: **PEDIT** ↵
> Select polyline: *(pick a polyline)*
> Close/Join/Width/Edit vertex/Fit/Spline/Decurve/Ltype gen/Undo/eXit ⟨X⟩:

The default option in brackets is X for **eXit**. Pressing [Enter] returns you to the **Command:** prompt.

### Closing an open polyline or opening a closed polyline

You may decide that you need to close an open polyline, or you may need to reopen a closed polyline. Both of these functions are done with the **Close** option of the **PEDIT** command. Type C at the prompt line.

If you select **Close** for a polyline that is already closed, AutoCAD converts the request to **Open**. Also, typing O opens a closed polyline. Picking an open polyline and the **Close** option returns the **Close** prompt. The **Open** option will *not* work on a polyline that was closed by manually drawing the final segment. The polygon must have been closed with the **Close** option. Figure 18-4 shows open and closed polylines.

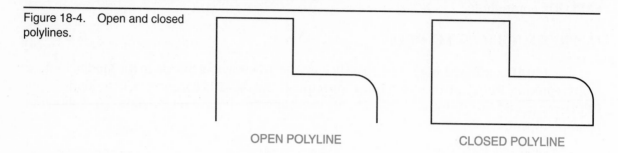

Figure 18-4. Open and closed polylines.

OPEN POLYLINE           CLOSED POLYLINE

## Joining polylines to other polylines, lines, and arcs

Polylines, lines, and arcs can be joined to create one polyline. The **Join** option works only if the polyline and other entities meet exactly. They cannot cross, nor can there be spaces or breaks within the entities. Refer to Figure 18-5. The command sequence to join objects is as follows:

Command: **PEDIT** ↵
Select polyline: *(select the original polyline)*
Close/Join/Width/Edit vertex/Fit/Spline/Decurve/Ltype gen/Undo/eXit ⟨X⟩: **J** ↵
Select objects: *(select all of the objects to be joined)*
Select objects: ↵
*nn* segments added to polyline
Close/Join/Width/Edit vertex/Fit/Spline/Decurve/Ltype gen/Undo/eXit ⟨X⟩: ↵
Command:

Select each object to be joined or group them with one of the selection options. The original polyline can be included in the selection set, but it does not have to be. See Figure 18-6.

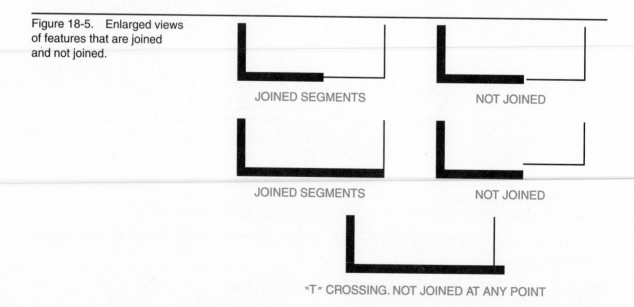

Figure 18-5. Enlarged views of features that are joined and not joined.

JOINED SEGMENTS          NOT JOINED

JOINED SEGMENTS          NOT JOINED

"T" CROSSING. NOT JOINED AT ANY POINT

Figure 18-6.   Joining a polyline
to other connected lines
and arcs.

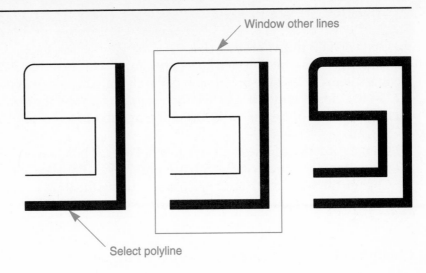

Window other lines

Select polyline

**PROFESSIONAL TIP**

Once items have been joined into a continuous polyline, the polyline can be closed using the **Close** option.

## Changing the width of a polyline

The **Width** option of the **PEDIT** command changes a polyline width to a new width. The width of the original polyline can be constant or it can vary. To change a polyline from a .06 width to a .1 width, follow these steps:

Command: **PEDIT** ↵
Select polyline: *(pick the polyline)*
Close/Join/Width/Edit vertex/Fit/Spline/Decurve/Ltype gen/Undo/eXit ⟨X⟩: **W** ↵
Enter new width for all segments: **.1** ↵
Close/Join/Width/Edit vertex/Fit/Spline/Decurve/Ltype gen/Undo/eXit ⟨X⟩: ↵
Command:

Circles drawn with the **CIRCLE** command cannot be changed to polylines. Polyline circles can be produced using the **PLINE Arc** option and drawing two 180° arcs, or by using the **DONUT** command. Change the width of doughnuts by individually picking each using the **PEDIT** command and **Width** option previously discussed. A **Window**, **Crossing**, or **Fence** selection will not change all doughnut widths at the same time. Figure 18-7 shows an existing polyline and a new polyline using the **PEDIT Width** option.

Figure 18-7.   Changing the
width of a polyline.

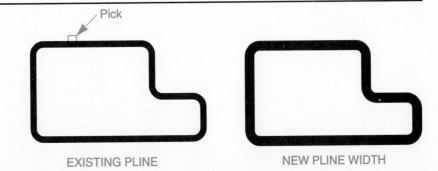

Pick

EXISTING PLINE          NEW PLINE WIDTH

---

### EXERCISE 18-2

❑ Open TITLEB from Problem 11-1.
❑ Draw a series of connected lines and arcs. Then, use the **PEDIT** command to change these items to a single polyline. Finally, change the width of the polyline.
❑ Draw a closed polyline. Use the **Close** option to draw the final segment.
❑ Use the **Open** option of the **PEDIT** command to open the polyline, and use **Close** to close it again.
❑ Connect a series of lines and arcs to a polyline. Then join all items as one polyline.
❑ Draw two doughnuts, each with a .5 unit inside diameter and 1.0 unit outside diameter. Change the width of the doughnuts to .1 using the **PEDIT** command.
❑ Save the drawing as A:EX18-2 and quit.

---

### Changing a polyline corner or point of tangency

Another **PEDIT** option is **Edit vertex**. When you enter E for this option, an X appears on screen at the first vertex or point of tangency. This **PEDIT** option has nine suboptions, as shown in the following prompts:

Close/Join/Width/Edit vertex/Fit/Spline/Decurve/Ltype gen/Undo/eXit ⟨X⟩: **E** ⏎
Next/Previous/Break/Insert/Move/Regen/Straighten/Tangent/Width/eXit ⟨N or P⟩:

The suboptions of the **Edit vertex** option are defined as follows:
- **Next (N).** Moves the screen X to the next vertex or point of tangency on the polyline.
- **Previous (P).** Moves the X to the previous vertex or tangency on the polyline.
- **Break (B).** Breaks a portion out of the polyline.
- **Insert (I).** Adds a new polyline vertex.
- **Move (M).** Moves a polyline vertex to a new location.
- **Regen (R).** Generates the revised version of the polyline.
- **Straighten (S).** Straightens polyline segments.
- **Tangent (T).** Specifies tangent direction for curve fitting.
- **Width (W).** Changes a polyline width.
- **eXit (X).** Returns to the **PEDIT** prompt.

Only the current point is affected by editing functions, Figure 18-8. If you edit the vertices of a polyline and nothing appears to happen, use the **Regen** option to regenerate the revised edition of the polyline.

---

Figure 18-8.   Using the **Next** and **Previous** suboptions of the **Edit vertex** option. Note the position of the X.

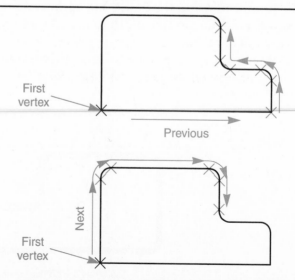

## Making breaks in a polyline

The **Break** suboption of the **Edit vertex** option breaks out a portion of a polyline. Select the **Next** or **Previous** suboptions to move the X to the correct vertex. Then, follow this command sequence:

Close/Join/Width/Edit vertex/Fit/Spline/Decurve/Ltype gen/Undo/eXit ⟨X⟩: **E** ↵
Next/Previous/Break/Insert/Move/Regen/Straighten/Tangent/Width/eXit ⟨N⟩: *(move the screen X to the position where you want the break to begin)*
Next/Previous/Break/Insert/Move/Regen/Straighten/Tangent/Width/eXit ⟨N⟩: **B** ↵

AutoCAD enters the point shown with an X as the first point to break.

Next/Previous/Go/eXit ⟨N⟩: *(move the screen X to the next or previous position)*

Move the screen X to the vertex you want as the second break point. Then, enter G for **Go**. This instructs AutoCAD to remove the portion of the polyline between the two selected points. The steps below are illustrated in Figure 18-9.

Next/Previous/Break/Insert/Move/Regen/Straighten/Tangent/Width/eXit ⟨N or P⟩: **B** ↵
Next/Previous/Go/eXit ⟨N⟩: **P** ↵ *(this is point 1)*
Next/Previous/Go/eXit ⟨P⟩: ↵ *(this is point 2)*
Next/Previous/Go/eXit ⟨P⟩: ↵ *(this is point 3)*
Next/Previous/Go/eXit ⟨P⟩: **G** ↵ *(this is point 4)*

Figure 18-9.   Using **Edit vertex** to break out a portion of a polyline.

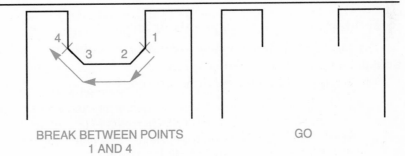

BREAK BETWEEN POINTS
1 AND 4

GO

## Insert a new vertex in a polyline

A new vertex can be added to a polyline using the **Insert** suboption. Use the Next or Previous suboptions to locate the vertex next to where you want the new vertex. Refer to the following command sequence and Figure 18-10:

Close/Join/Width/Edit vertex/Fit/Spline/Decurve/Ltype gen/Undo/eXit ⟨X⟩: **E** ↵
Next/Previous/Break/Insert/Move/Regen/Straighten/Tangent/Width/eXit ⟨N⟩: *(move the X cursor to the desired location using **Next** or **Previous**)*
Next/Previous/Break/Insert/Move/Regen/Straighten/Tangent/Width/eXit ⟨N⟩: **I** ↵
Enter location of new vertex: *(move the screen crosshairs to the new vertex location using your pointing device and pick or type the coordinates)*

Figure 18-10.   Using the **Insert** suboption of the **Edit vertex** option to a new vertex.

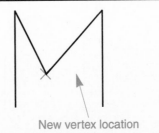

New vertex location

New vertex inserted

## Moving a polyline vertex

The **Move** suboption of **Edit vertex** moves a vertex. The screen X cursor must be placed on the point to move before you enter M. The following sequence is shown in Figure 18-11:

Close/Join/Width/Edit vertex/Fit/Spline/Decurve/Ltype gen/Undo/eXit ⟨X⟩: **E** ↵
Next/Previous/Break/Insert/Move/Regen/Straighten/Tangent/Width/eXit ⟨N⟩: *(move the X cursor to the vertex to be moved using **Next** or **Previous**)*
Next/Previous/Break/Insert/Move/Regen/Straighten/Tangent/Width/eXit ⟨N⟩: **M** ↵
Enter new location: *(pick the new point with your pointing device or type the coordinates)*

Figure 18-11.   Using the **Move** suboption **Edit vertex** option to place a vertex in a new location.

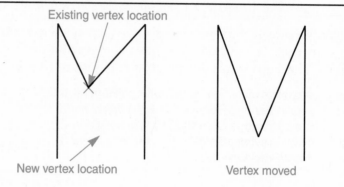

## Straightening polyline segments or arcs

You can straighten polyline segments or polyline arcs between two points. Use the **Straighten** option of **Edit vertex** as follows:

Close/Join/Width/Edit vertex/Fit/Spline/Decurve/Ltype gen/Undo/eXit ⟨X⟩: **E** ↵
Next/Previous/Break/Insert/Move/Regen/Straighten/Tangent/Width/eXit ⟨N⟩: *(move the X cursor to the first point of the segments to be straightened)*
Next/Previous/Break/Insert/Move/Regen/Straighten/Tangent/Width/eXit ⟨N⟩: **S** ↵
Next/Previous/Go/eXit ⟨N⟩: *(move the X to the last point)*
Next/Previous/Go/eXit ⟨N⟩: **G** ↵

If the X is not moved before G is entered, AutoCAD straightens the segment to the next vertex. This option provides a quick way to straighten an arc, Figure 18-12.

Figure 18-12.   Straightening polylines.

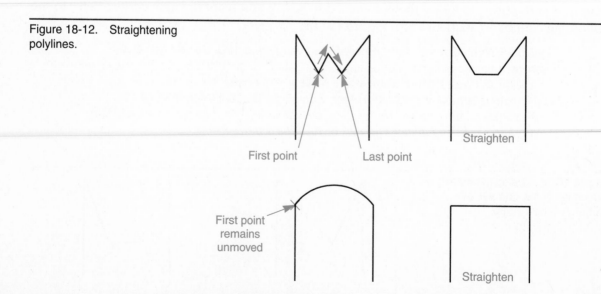

## Changing polyline segment widths

The **Width** option of **Edit vertex** is the only command that changes the starting and ending widths of an existing polyline segment. Move the screen X to the segment before the one to be altered. The command sequence is as follows:

> Close/Join/Width/Edit vertex/Fit/Spline/Decurve/Ltype gen/Undo/eXit ⟨X⟩: **E** ↵
> Next/Previous/Break/Insert/Move/Regen/Straighten/Tangent/Width/eXit ⟨N⟩: **N** ↵
> *(move the X cursor to the segment prior to the one to be changed)*
> Next/Previous/Break/Insert/Move/Regen/Straighten/Tangent/Width/eXit ⟨N⟩: **W** ↵
> Enter starting width ⟨*current*⟩: *(enter the revised starting width and press* [Enter]*)*
> Enter ending width ⟨*revised start width*⟩: *(enter the revised ending width and press*
> [Enter], *or press* [Enter] *to keep the width the same as the starting width)*
> Next/Previous/Break/Insert/Move/Regen/Straighten/Tangent/Width/eXit ⟨N⟩: **R** ↵

Notice that the starting width default is the current setting. The ending width default is the same as the revised starting width. When you press [Enter] to complete this command, nothing happens. You must select the **Regen** option to have AutoCAD draw the revised polyline. See Figure 18-13.

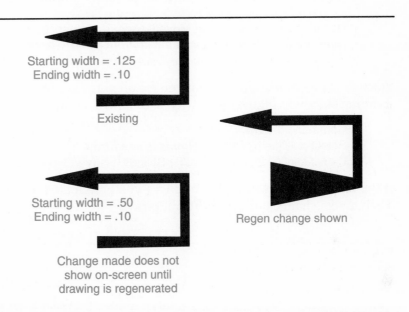

Figure 18-13. Changing the starting and ending widths of existing polylines. Use the **Regen** option to display the change.

Starting width = .125
Ending width = .10

Existing

Starting width = .50
Ending width = .10

Change made does not show on-screen until drawing is regenerated

Regen change shown

---

**EXERCISE 18-3**

❑ Open TITLEB from Problem 11-1.
❑ Draw a polyline with a series of segments. Have at least eight corners and three arcs.
❑ Enter the **Edit vertex** option and move the screen X cursor around using the **Next** and **Previous** suboptions.
❑ Break the polyline between any three points. Then, undo the breaks.
❑ Insert a new vertex in the polyline.
❑ Move one vertex of the polyline.
❑ Straighten one arc segment or at least three line segments.
❑ Change the starting and ending widths of one segment.
❑ Save the drawing as A:EX18-3 and quit.

## Making a smooth curve out of polyline corners

In some situations, you may need to convert a polyline into a series of smooth curves. One example is a graph. A graph may show a series of plotted points as a smooth curve rather than straight segments. This process is called *curve fitting* and is done using the **Fit** suboption of **Edit vertex**. The **Fit** suboption constructs pairs of arcs passing through control points. You can specify control points, or you can use the vertices of the polyline's corners. Closely spaced control points produce a smooth curve.

Prior to curve fitting, each vertex can be given a tangent direction. AutoCAD then fits the curve based on the tangent directions that you set. However, you do not have to enter tangent directions. Specifying a tangent direction is used to edit vertices when **Fit** did not produce the best results.

To edit tangent directions, enter the **Edit vertex** option of the **PEDIT** command. Move the screen X to each vertex to be changed. Enter the **Tangent** option and specify a tangent direction in degrees or pick a point in the expected direction. The direction you choose is indicated by an arrow placed at the vertex.

    Close/Join/Width/Edit vertex/Fit/Spline/Decurve/Ltype gen/Undo/eXit ⟨X⟩: **E** ↵
    Next/Previous/Break/Insert/Move/Regen/Straighten/Tangent/Width/eXit ⟨N⟩: *(move the
        screen X to the desired vertex)*
    Next/Previous/Break/Insert/Move/Regen/Straighten/Tangent/Width/eXit ⟨N⟩: **T** ↵
    Direction of tangent: *(specify a direction in positive or negative degrees and press
        [Enter], or pick a point in the desired direction)*

Once the tangent directions are given for all vertices to be changed, select the **Fit** option. The polyline shown in Figure 18-14 was made into a smooth curve with the following steps:

    Command: **PEDIT** ↵
    Select polyline: *(pick the polyline to be edited)*
    Close/Join/Width/Edit vertex/Fit/Spline/Decurve/Ltype gen/Undo/eXit ⟨X⟩: **F** ↵

If the result does not look like the curve you anticipated, return to the **Edit vertex** suboption. Then, make changes using **PEDIT** options.

---

Figure 18-14.   Using the **Fit** option of the **PEDIT** command.

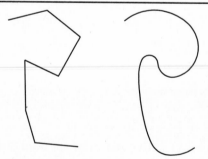

## Using the **Spline** option

With the **Fit** option, the curve passes through polyline vertices. The **Spline** option also smoothes the corners of a straight segment polyline. However, this option produces a different result. The curve passes through the first and last control points or vertices. However, the curve *pulls* toward the other vertices but does not pass through them. The **Spline** option is used as follows:

    Command: **PEDIT** ↵
    Select polyline: *(pick the polyline to be edited)*
    Close/Join/Width/Edit vertex/Fit/Spline/Decurve/Ltype gen/Undo/eXit ⟨X⟩: **S** ↵

A comparison of the **Fit** and **Spline** options is shown in Figure 18-15.

Figure 18-15.  A comparison between **Fit** and **Spline** options.

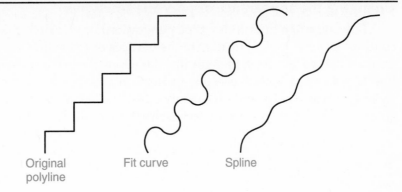

Original polyline         Fit curve         Spline

## Straightening all segments of a polyline

The **Decurve** option returns a polyline edited with **Fit** or **Spline** options to its original form. However, the information entered for tangent direction is kept for future reference. The **Decurve** option steps below are shown in Figure 18-16.

> Command: **PEDIT** ↵
> Select polyline: *(pick the polyline to be edited)*
> Close/Join/Width/Edit vertex/Fit/Spline/Decurve/Ltype gen/Undo/eXit ⟨X⟩: **D** ↵

Figure 18-16.  Using the **Decurve** option.

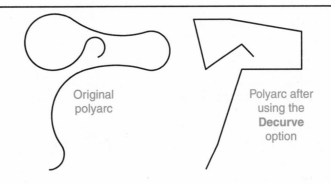

Original polyarc                    Polyarc after using the **Decurve** option

**PROFESSIONAL TIP**

If you make a mistake, remember that the **Undo** option is available within the **PEDIT** command. Using **Undo** more than once steps backwards through each option used. Use the **eXit** option to return to the **Command:** prompt. The **UNDO** command can be used at the **Command:** prompt to undo the effects of the last **PEDIT** command.

### EXERCISE 18-4

❑ Open TITLEB from Problem 11-1.
❑ Draw a polyline with at least five vertices. Smooth the polyline using the **Fit** option of the **PEDIT** command.
❑ Decurve the new polyline.
❑ Practice with **Undo** by first drawing a series of polyline segments. After using **PEDIT** to make some changes, select **Undo** to return to the original polyline. Finally, use the **REDO** command to work on the edited polyline again.
❑ Save the drawing as A:EX18-4 and quit.

## Changing the appearance of polyline linetypes

The **Ltype gen** option (linetype generation) option determines how linetypes, other than continuous lines, look in relation to the vertices of a polyline. For example, when a centerline is used and **Ltype gen** is off, then the line has a long dash at each vertex. When **Ltype gen** is on, the line is generated with a constant pattern in relation to the vertices. Look at the difference between **Ltype gen** on and off in Figure 18-17, and also notice the effect these settings have on spline curves. The **Ltype gen** option is either on or off. To turn this option on, follow these steps:

Command: **PEDIT** ⏎
Select polyline: *(pick the polyline)*
Close/Join/Width/Edit vertex/Fit/Spline/Decurve/Ltype gen/Undo/eXit ⟨X⟩: **L** ⏎
Full PLINE linetype ON/OFF ⟨Off⟩: **ON** ⏎

You can also change the **Ltype gen** value using the **PLINEGEN** system variable as follows:

Command: **PLINEGEN** ⏎
New value for PLINEGEN ⟨0⟩: **1** ⏎

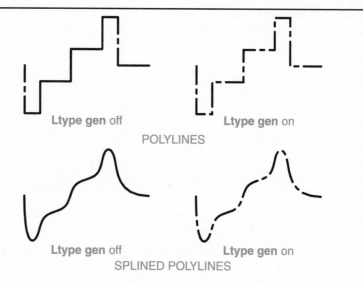

Figure 18-17. Comparison of
**Ltype gen** on and off.

Ltype gen off          Ltype gen on
POLYLINES

Ltype gen off          Ltype gen on
SPLINED POLYLINES

## CONVERTING A POLYLINE INTO INDIVIDUAL LINE AND ARC SEGMENTS

AUG 5

A polyline is a single entity composed of polyline and polyline arc segments. The **EXPLODE** command changes the polyline to a series of lines and arcs. To explode an object, pick the **Explode** button in the **Modify** toolbar or type EXPLODE at the **Command:** prompt. If the ACADFULL menu is loaded, the **Explode** command can also be accessed from the **Modify** pull-down menu.

When a wide polyline is exploded, the resulting line or arc is redrawn along the centerline of the original polyline, Figure 18-18. When the **EXPLODE** command is accessed, you are asked to select objects:

Command: **EXPLODE** ⏎
Select objects: *(pick the polyline to be exploded)*
Select objects: ⏎

The **EXPLODE** command removes all width characteristics and tangent information. However, AutoCAD gives you a chance to change your mind by offering this message:

Exploding this polyline has lost *(width/tangent)* information.
The UNDO command will restore it.

Figure 18-18.  Exploding a wide polyarc.

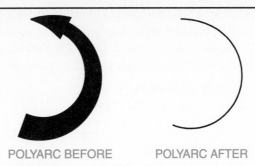

POLYARC BEFORE          POLYARC AFTER

## EXERCISE 18-5

❑ Load AutoCAD for Windows and open TITLEB.
❑ Draw a polyline of your own design. Include some width changes. Then, explode it and observe what happens.
❑ Restore the exploded polyline using the **UNDO** command.
❑ Save the drawing as A:EX18-5 and quit.

## ADDITIONAL METHODS FOR SMOOTHING POLYLINE CORNERS

AUG 5

Earlier in this chapter, the **Fit** and **Spline** options of the **PEDIT** command were discussed. With the **Fit** option, the resulting curve passes through the polyline vertices. The **Spline** option creates a curve that passes through the first and last control points, or vertices. The curve then *pulls* toward the other vertices but does not pass through them. There are also two spline curve options— **Cubic** and **Quadratic**. These options create B-spline curves. The *cubic curve* is extremely smooth because the elements of the curve pass through the first and last control points, and close to intermediate control points. The *quadratic curve* is not as smooth as the cubic curve. However, it is smoother than a curve made with the **Fit** option. Like a cubic curve, a quadratic curve passes through the first and last control points. The remainder of the curve is tangent to the polyline segments between intermediate control points, Figure 18-19.

Figure 18-19.  A comparison of the **Fit**, **Quadratic** spline curve, and **Cubic** spline curve options.

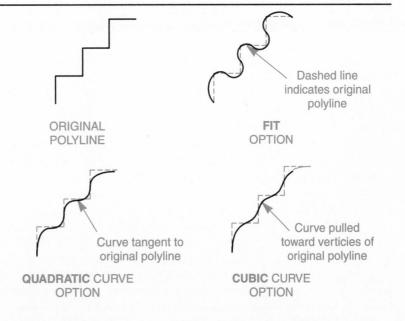

ORIGINAL
POLYLINE

FIT
OPTION

Dashed line indicates original polyline

Curve tangent to original polyline

**QUADRATIC** CURVE
OPTION

Curve pulled toward vertices of original polyline

**CUBIC** CURVE
OPTION

The system variable **SPLINETYPE** determines whether AutoCAD draws cubic or quadratic curves. The default setting is 6. This draws a cubic curve when using the **Spline** option of the **PEDIT** command. If you set **SPLINETYPE** to 5, a quadratic curve is generated. Set the **SPLINETYPE** variable to draw a quadratic curve as follows:

> Command: **SPLINETYPE** ↵
> New value for SPLINETYPE ⟨6⟩: **5** ↵

If you want to draw a cubic curve, reset **SPLINETYPE** to 6. The values 5 and 6 are the only valid values for **SPLINETYPE**.

---

**EXERCISE 18-6**

❏ Draw a polyline similar to the ORIGINAL POLYLINE shown in Figure 18-19.
❏ Use the **COPY** command to make three copies of the original polyline.
❏ Use the **Fit** option of the **PEDIT** command to smooth the first copy.
❏ Set **SPLINETYPE** to 5 for a quadratic curve.
❏ Use the **Spline** option of the **PEDIT** command to smooth the second copy.
❏ Set **SPLINETYPE** to 6 for a cubic curve.
❏ Use the **Spline** option again to smooth the third copy.
❏ Compare the original polyline with the three new curves.
❏ Save the drawing as A:EX18-6 and quit.

---

The **SPLINESEGS** system variable controls the number of line segments used to construct spline curves. The **SPLINESEGS** default value is 8. This setting creates a fairly smooth spline curve with moderate regeneration time. If you decrease the value, the spline curve is less smooth. If you increase the value, the spline curve is smoother. Although increasing the value above 8 creates a more precise spline curve, it also increases regeneration time and drawing file size. Change the **SPLINESEGS** variable as follows:

> Command: **SPLINESEGS** ↵
> New value for SPLINESEGS ⟨8⟩: **20** ↵

Figure 18-20 shows the relationship between several **SPLINESEGS** values.

---

Figure 18-20.   A comparison of **SPLINESEGS** values.

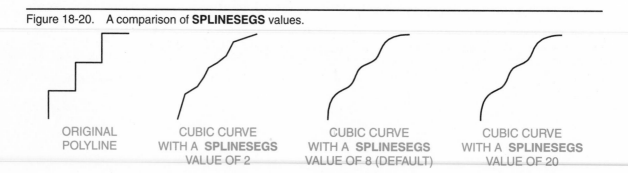

ORIGINAL
POLYLINE

CUBIC CURVE
WITH A **SPLINESEGS**
VALUE OF 2

CUBIC CURVE
WITH A **SPLINESEGS**
VALUE OF 8 (DEFAULT)

CUBIC CURVE
WITH A **SPLINESEGS**
VALUE OF 20

---

**NOTE**

When AutoCAD for Windows is configured to display screen menus and you select a polyline to edit, the first **PEDIT** screen menu changes to display some of the **PEDIT** options. Also displayed near the bottom of this screen menu is **PolyVars** (polyline variables). Selecting **PolyVars** accesses the **Set Spline Fit Variables** dialog box displaying five options, including **Quadratic**, **Cubic**, and **Bezier**.

## EXERCISE 18-7

❑ Draw a polyline similar to the ORIGINAL POLYLINE shown in Figure 18-20.
❑ Use the **COPY** command to make three copies of the original polyline.
❑ Set **SPLINETYPE** to 6 for a cubic curve.
❑ Set the **SPLINESEGS** system variable to 2.
❑ Use the **Spline** option of the **PEDIT** command to smooth the first copy.
❑ Set **SPLINESEGS** to 8.
❑ Use the **Spline** option to smooth the second copy.
❑ Set **SPLINESEGS** to 20.
❑ Use the **Spline** option to smooth the third copy.
❑ Compare the original polyline and the smoothness of the three new curves.
❑ Save the drawing as A:EX18-7 and quit.

## MAKING CURVES USING THE SPLINE COMMAND

You can use the **SPLINE** command to create NURBS curves. A NURBS curve (non-uniform rational B-spline) is considered to be a true spline. The spline created by fitting a spline curve to a polyline is merely a linear approximation of a true spline and is not as accurate. An additional advantage of spline objects over smoothed polylines is that splines use less memory and disk space. To access the **SPLINE** command pick the **Spline** button of the **Edit Polyline** flyout in the **Draw** toolbar, pick **Spline** in the **Draw** pull-down menu, or type SPLINE at the **Command:** prompt. A spline is created by specifying the control points along the curve using any standard coordinate entry method:

```
Command: SPLINE ↵
Object/⟨Enter first point⟩: 2,2 ↵
Enter point: 4,4 ↵
Close/Fit Tolerance/⟨Enter point⟩: 6,2 ↵
Close/Fit Tolerance/⟨Enter point⟩: ↵
Enter start tangent: ↵
Enter end tangent: ↵
Command:
```

When you have given all of the necessary points along the spline, pressing [Enter] ends the point specification process and allows start tangency and end tangency to be entered. Specifying the tangents allows the direction that the spline curve begins and ends with to be changed. Pressing [Enter] at these prompts accepts the default direction, as calculated by AutoCAD, for the specified curve. The results of the previous command sequence is shown in Figure 18-21.

Figure 18-21. Using the **SPLINE** command with the AutoCAD defaults for start and end tangents.

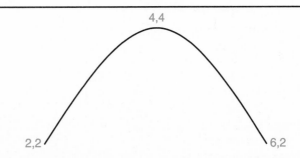

**NOTE**        If only two points are specified along the spline curve, an object that looks like a line is created, but the actual object is still a spline.

## Drawing closed splines

The **Close** option can be used to draw closed splines. The following command sequence is used. Refer to Figure 18-22.

        Command: **SPLINE** ↵
        Object/⟨Enter first point⟩: **2,2** ↵
        Enter point: **4,4** ↵
        Close/Fit Tolerance/⟨Enter point⟩: **6,2** ↵
        Close/Fit Tolerance/⟨Enter point⟩: **C** ↵
        Enter tangent: ↵
        Command:

After closing a spline, you are prompted to specify a tangent direction for the start/end point of the spline. Pressing [Enter] accepts the AutoCAD default.

---

Figure 18-22.   Using the **Close** option of the **SPLINE** command with AutoCAD default tangents. Compare this to object in Figure 18-21.

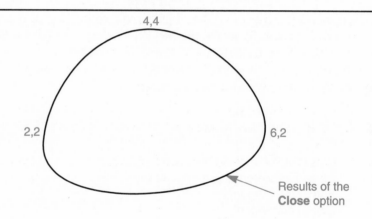

## Altering the Fit Tolerance specifications

Different results can be achieved by altering the **Fit Tolerance** specifications. The outcome of different settings varies, depending on the configuration of the individual spline object. The setting specifies a tolerance that the spline curve passes through the fit points within.

Figure 18-23 displays the **Fit Tolerance** for three test cases. The following is the command sequence for the example shown in color:

        Command: **SPLINE** ↵
        Object/⟨Enter first point⟩: **0,0** ↵
        Enter point: **2,2** ↵
        Close/Fit Tolerance/⟨Enter point⟩: **4,0** ↵
        Close/Fit Tolerance/⟨Enter point⟩: **5,5.5** ↵
        Close/Fit Tolerance/⟨Enter point⟩: **6,0** ↵
        Close/Fit Tolerance/⟨Enter point⟩: **F** ↵
        Enter Fit Tolerance ⟨0.00⟩: **3** ↵
        Enter start tangent: ↵
        Enter end tangent: ↵
        Command:

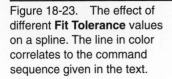

Figure 18-23.   The effect of different **Fit Tolerance** values on a spline. The line in color correlates to the command sequence given in the text.

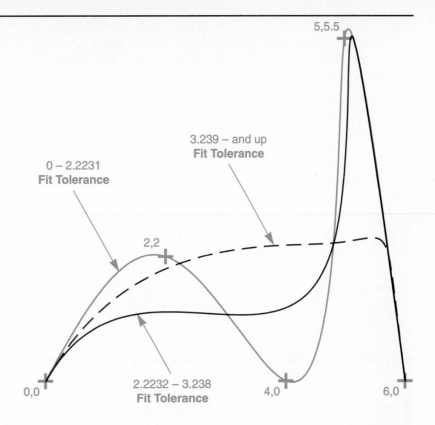

## Specifying the start and end tangents

The previous examples used AutoCAD's default start and end tangents. You can also specify a start and an end tangency using the **Tangent** or **Perpendicular** object snap modes. The tangency direction is in the direction of the selected point. An illustration showing the results of the **Tangent** and **Perpendicular** object snaps on two splines with the same point entries is given in Figure 18-24. This is the command sequence for the **Perpendicular** selection:

```
Command: SPLINE ↵
Object/⟨Enter first point⟩: 2,2 ↵
Enter point: 4,4 ↵
Close/Fit Tolerance/⟨Enter point⟩: 6,2 ↵
Close/Fit Tolerance/⟨Enter point⟩: ↵
Enter start tangent: _per to (pick the line)
Enter end tangent: _per to (pick the line)
Command:
```

Figure 18-24.   Examples of start and end tangents perpendicular to a line and tangent to a line.

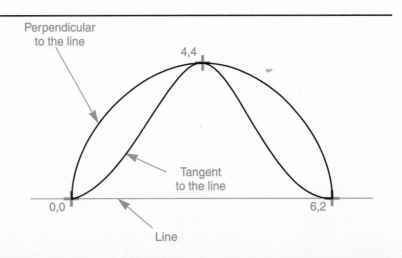

### Converting a spline-fitted polyline to a spline

A spline-fitted polyline object can be converted to a spline object using the **Object** option of the **SPLINE** command. This option works for either 2D or 3D objects. The command sequence is as follows:

> Command: **SPLINE** ↵
> Object/⟨Enter first point⟩: **O** ↵
> Select object to convert to splines.
> Select objects: *(pick the spline-fitted polyline)*
> Select objects: ↵
> Command:

---

### EXERCISE 18-8

❑ Load AutoCAD and open TITLEB.
❑ Draw a spline with control points similar to Figure 18-21. Use the AutoCAD default tangents.
❑ Draw a spline similar to the right of the first one using the **Close** option and default tangents.
❑ Draw three splines each with the same control points similar to Figure 18-23. Set the **Fit Tolerance** for the splines at 0, 3, and 4 respectively.
❑ Draw a line and two splines similar to Figure 18-24. Use the **Perpendicular** object snap mode for the start and end tangents on one spline. Use the **Tangent** object snap mode on the other.
❑ Save as A:EX18-8.

---

## EDITING SPLINES

The **SPLINEDIT** command allows you to edit spline objects. Fit points can be added or moved to alter the shape of a curve. The spline can be opened, closed, or joined. Start and endpoint tangents can also be changed. To access the **SPLINEDIT** command, pick the **Edit Spline** button in the **Edit Polyline** flyout on the **Modify** toolbar or type SPLINEDIT at the **Command:** prompt. If the ACADFULL menu file is loaded, **Edit Spline** can be picked from the **Modify** pull-down menu. The command sequence is as follows:

> Command: **SPLINEDIT** ↵
> Select spline: *(pick a spline)*

When you pick a spline, the control points and fit tolerance data are displayed in the grip color, as shown in Figure 18-25. The command continues with this prompt:

> Fit Data/Close/Move Vertex/Refine/rEverse/Undo/eXit ⟨X⟩:

The **SPLINEDIT** command options are described in the following sections.

---

Figure 18-25.   The control points on a spline when using the **SPLINEDIT** command.

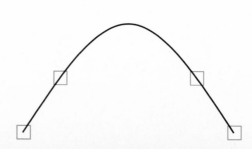

### Editing fit data

The **Fit Data** option of the **SPLINEDIT** command allows spline control points to be edited. These control points are called *fit points*. Entering the **Fit Data** option gives you the suboptions shown in the following command sequence:

> Command: **SPLINEDIT** ↵
> Select spline: (*pick a spline*)
> Fit Data/Close/Move Vertex/Refine/rEverse/Undo/eXit ⟨X⟩: **F**↵
> Add/Close/Delete/Move/Purge/Tangents/toLerance/eXit ⟨X⟩:

The purpose of these suboptions is described in the following section. Also, refer to Figure 18-26 for examples.

- **Add.** This allows new fit points to be added to the spline definition. When adding, a fit point must be located with the cursor, or you can type the X,Y location of the fit point. Fit points appear as unhighlighted grip boxes. When one is selected, it becomes highlighted along with the next fit point in the spline. The added fit point occurs between the two highlighted fit points. If the start or end of the spline is selected, a prompt is issued asking whether to insert the new fit point before or after the existing one. Respond with B or F accordingly. When a fit point is added, the spline curve is refit through the added point. See Figure 18-26.

Figure 18-26. Demonstrations of using the **SPLINEDIT** command **Fit Data** suboptions. Compare the original spline to edited objects.

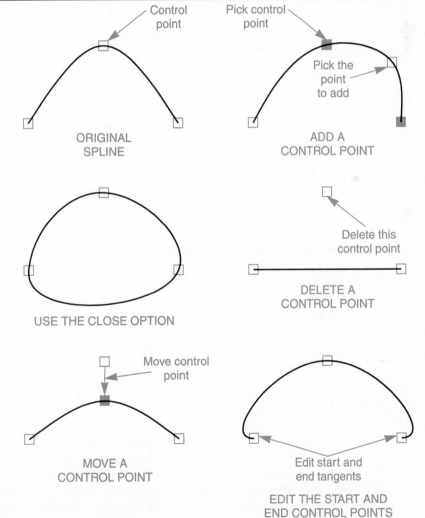

The **Add** option functions in a running mode. This means that you can continue to add points as needed. By pressing [Enter] at an Enter new point: prompt, you can continue to select existing fit points. Therefore, points can be added anywhere on the spline until finished. The command sequence looks like this:

> Command: **SPLINEDIT** ⏎
> Select spline: *(pick a spline)*
> Fit Data/Close/Move Vertex/Refine/rEverse/Undo/eXit ⟨X⟩: **F** ⏎
> Add/Close/Delete/Move/Purge/Tangents/toLerance/eXit ⟨X⟩: **A** ⏎
> Select point: *(pick a fit point)*
> Enter new point: *(pick a location to add a point)*
> Enter new point: *(pick a location to add a point)*
> Enter new point: ⏎
> Select point: ⏎
> Add/Close/Delete/Move/Purge/Tangents/toLerance/eXit ⟨X⟩: ⏎
> Fit Data/Close/Move Vertex/Refine/rEverse/Undo/eXit ⟨X⟩: ⏎
> Command:

- **Close/Open.** If the selected spline is open, the option is **Close**. If the spline is closed, the option is **Open**. Using this option lets you open a closed spline or close an open spline, as shown in Figure 18-26.
- **Delete.** The **Delete** option allows fit points to be deleted as needed. However, at least two fit points must remain. Even when only two points remain, the object is still listed as a spline and not a line. See Figure 18-26. This also operates in the running mode, allowing as many deletions as needed. The spline curve is refit through the remaining fit points when fit points are deleted. The prompts work like this:

> Command: **SPLINEDIT** ⏎
> Select spline: *(pick a spline)*
> Fit Data/Close/Move Vertex/Refine/rEverse/Undo/eXit ⟨X⟩: **F** ⏎
> Add/Close/Delete/Move/Purge/Tangents/toLerance/eXit ⟨X⟩: **D** ⏎
> Select point: *(pick a fit point)*
> Select point: *(pick a fit point)*
> Select point: ⏎
> Add/Close/Delete/Move/Purge/Tangents/toLerance/eXit ⟨X⟩: ⏎
> Fit Data/Close/Move Vertex/Refine/rEverse/Undo/eXit ⟨X⟩: ⏎
> Command:

- **Move.** This option allows fit points to be moved as necessary. See Figure 18-26. When **Move** is specified, the following options are available:
  - **Next**—Highlights the next fit point.
  - **Previous**—Highlights the previous fit point.
  - **Select Point**—Allows you to pick a different point to move rather than using the **Next** or **Previous** options.
  - **eXit**—Returns you to the **Fit Data** option prompt.
  - **⟨Enter new location⟩**— Moves the currently highlighted point to the specified location.

> Command: **SPLINEDIT** ⏎
> Select spline: *(pick a spline)*
> Fit Data/Close/Move Vertex/Refine/rEverse/Undo/eXit ⟨X⟩: **F** ⏎
> Add/Close/Delete/Move/Purge/Tangents/toLerance/eXit ⟨X⟩: **M** ⏎
> Next/Previous/Select Point/eXit/⟨Enter new location⟩ ⟨N⟩: **S** ⏎
> Next/Previous/Select Point/eXit/⟨Enter new location⟩ ⟨N⟩: ⏎
> Add/Close/Delete/Move/Purge/Tangents/toLerance/eXit ⟨X⟩: ⏎
> Fit Data/Close/Move Vertex/Refine/rEverse/Undo/eXit ⟨X⟩: ⏎
> Command:

- **Purge.** This option removes fit point data from a spline. After doing this, the spline is not as easy to edit. In very complex drawings, such as Geographical Information Systems (GIS), where many very complex splines are created, purging them reduces the file size by simplifying the definition. Once purged, the **Fit Data** option is no longer presented by the **SPLINE** command for the purged spline.
- **Tangents.** This option allows editing of the start and end tangents for an open spline and editing of the tangent for a closed spline. Selecting a point causes the tangency direction to be in the direction of the selected point. See Figure 18-26. The **System Default** option sets the tangency values to the AutoCAD defaults. This is how you use the **Tangents** option to set the **System Defaults**:

> Command: **SPLINEDIT** ⏎
> Select spline: *(pick a spline)*
> Fit Data/Close/Move Vertex/Refine/rEverse/Undo/eXit ⟨X⟩: **F** ⏎
> Add/Close/Delete/Move/Purge/Tangents/toLerance/eXit ⟨X⟩: **T** ⏎
> System Default/⟨Enter start tangent⟩: **S** ⏎
> System Default/⟨Enter end tangent⟩: **S** ⏎
> Add/Close/Delete/Move/Purge/Tangents/toLerance/eXit ⟨X⟩: ⏎
> Fit Data/Close/Move Vertex/Refine/rEverse/Undo/eXit ⟨X⟩: ⏎
> Command:

- **Tolerance.** The **Fit Tolerance** values can be adjusted using this option. The results are immediate, so the fit tolerance can be adjusted as necessary to produce different results.
- **eXit.** Returns you to the **SPLINEDIT** option line.

## Opening or closing a spline

This option depends on the status of the spline object currently being edited. Using this option lets you open a closed spline or close an open spline. If the spline is open, the option is **Close**:

> Fit Data/Close/Move Vertex/Refine/rEverse/Undo/eXit ⟨X⟩:

If the spline is closed, the option is **Open**:

> Fit Data/Open/Move Vertex/Refine/rEverse/Undo/eXit ⟨X⟩:

## Moving a vertex

This **SPLINEDIT** option allows the control points for the spline to be moved. When you access this option, you get a series of suboptions, as shown in the following prompts:

> Command: **SPLINEDIT** ⏎
> Select spline: *(pick a spline)*
> Fit Data/Close/Move Vertex/Refine/rEverse/Undo/eXit ⟨X⟩: **M** ⏎
> Next/Previous/Select Point/eXit/⟨Enter new location⟩ ⟨N⟩: ⏎

Each of the **Move Vertex** options are explained below:
- **Next.** Highlights the next fit point.
- **Previous.** Highlights the previous fit point.
- **Select Point.** Allows you to pick a different point to move, rather than using the **Next** or **Previous** options.
- **eXit.** Returns you to the **Fit Data** option prompt.
- ⟨**Enter new location**⟩. Moves the currently highlighted point to the specified location.

**EXERCISE 18-9**

❑ Load AutoCAD and open TITLEB.
❑ Draw a spline with control points similar to the ORIGINAL SPLINE in Figure 18-26. Use the AutoCAD default tangents.
❑ Copy the original spline to five locations similar to the layout of Figure 18-26.
❑ Use the **SPLINEDIT** command on the upper-right spline to add a control point similar to Figure 18-26.
❑ Use the **SPLINEDIT** command to close the middle-left spline similar to Figure 18-26.
❑ Use the **SPLINEDIT** command on the middle-right spline to delete the top control point similar to Figure 18-26.
❑ Use the **SPLINEDIT** command on the lower-left spline to move the top control point similar to Figure 18-26.
❑ Use the **SPLINEDIT** command on the lower-right spline to edit the start and end tangents with the **Tangent** object snap similar to Figure 18-26.
❑ Save as A:EX18-9.

### Smoothing or reshaping a section of the spline

The **Refine** option allows fine tuning of the spline shape. Control points can be added to help smooth or reshape a section of the spline. Using **Refine** removes the fit point data from the spline. Entering the **Refine** option gives you these suboptions:

```
Command: SPLINEDIT ⏎
Select spline: (pick a spline)
Fit Data/Close/Move Vertex/Refine/rEverse/Undo/eXit ⟨X⟩: R ⏎
Add control point/Elevate Order/Weight/eXit ⟨X⟩:
```

The following gives a description of each **Refine** suboption:
- **Add control point.** This allows new control points to be specified on a spline as needed. See Figure 18-26.
- **Elevate Order.** The order of a spline is the degree of the spline polynomial +1. For example, a cubic spline has order 4. Elevating the order of a spline causes more control points to appear on the spline for greater control. One of the spline examples in Figure 18-27 has the control point order elevated from 5 to 9. The setting can be between 4 and 26, but cannot be adjusted downward. For example, once set to 24, the only remaining settings are 25 and 26. Integers less than 24 are rejected.
- **Weight.** The default value is 1.0 and can be adjusted up or down from there. This controls the weight of individual control points. When all of the control points have the same weight factor, they all exert the same amount of pull on the resulting spline. When a weight value is lessened, that control point is not able to pull the spline as close to it as before. Likewise, when the weight is increased, the control point pulls harder and brings the spline closer to it, as shown in Figure 18-27. The only valid settings for this are positive real numbers. The control point selection options of this subcommand are the same as those discussed with **Move Vertex**, except the request to change weight is ⟨New weight data⟩:

```
Add control point/Elevate Order/Weight/eXit ⟨X⟩: W ⏎
Next/Previous/Select Point/eXit/⟨New weight data⟩ ⟨N⟩: (enter a positive
    number up to 26)
```

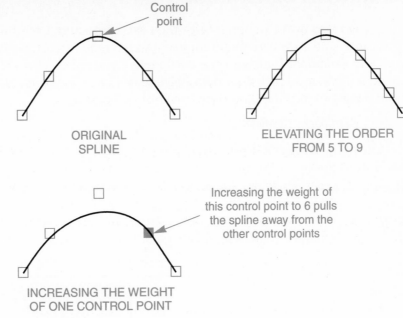

Figure 18-27.   The effects on a curve of elevating the order of control points and increasing the weight of a control point.

Control point

ORIGINAL SPLINE

ELEVATING THE ORDER FROM 5 TO 9

Increasing the weight of this control point to 6 pulls the spline away from the other control points

INCREASING THE WEIGHT OF ONE CONTROL POINT

## Reversing the order of spline control points

The **rEverse** option of the **SPLINEDIT** command reverses the listed order of the spline control points. This makes the previous start point the new end point, and the previous end point the new start point. This has an effect on various selection options of the **SPLINEDIT** subcommand. For example, the control points are reversed, and the **Tangent** option changes the start, first, and end order.

## Undoing SPLINEDIT changes

The **Undo** option undoes the previous change. You can also use this option to undo to the beginning of the current **SPLINEDIT** command.

## Exiting the SPLINEDIT command

Using the **eXit** option in the **SPLINEDIT** command returns you to the **Command:** prompt. You can press the [Enter] key, since X (for exit) is the default.

---

### EXERCISE 18-10

❏ Load AutoCAD and open TITLEB.
❏ Draw a spline with control points similar to the ORIGINAL SPLINE in Figure 18-27. Use the AutoCAD default tangents.
❏ Copy the original spline to two locations similar to the layout of Figure 18-27.
❏ Use the **SPLINEDIT** command on the upper-right spline to elevate the order of control points similar to Figure 18-27.
❏ Use the **SPLINEDIT** command on the lower spline to increase the weight of a control point similar to Figure 18-27.
❏ Save as A:EX18-10.

# MAKING A POLYLINE BOUNDARY

When you draw an object with the **LINE** command, each line segment is a single entity. You can create a polyline boundary of an area made up of closed line segments. To do this, pick the **Boundary** button in the **Rectangle** flyout of the **Draw** toolbar, or if the ACADFULL menu file is loaded pick **Bounding Polyline** from the **Construct** pull-down menu. You can also type BOUNDARY at the **Command:** prompt as follows:

Command: **BOUNDARY** ↵

Now, the **Boundary Creation** dialog box shown in Figure 18-28 is displayed. **Object Type:** is the first option in the **Boundary Creation** dialog box. This can be set to either **Polyline** or **Region**. If set to **Polyline**, AutoCAD creates a polyline around the area. If set to **Region**, AutoCAD creates a closed 2D area. A region may be used for area analysis, shading, or other purposes. The **Define Boundary Set** features are discussed in Chapter 24. The items in this dialog box related to hatching are also discussed in detail in Chapter 24.

Figure 18-28.   The **Boundary Creation** dialog box.

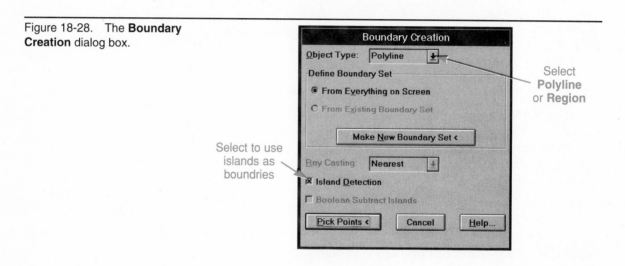

The **Island Detection** check box causes all objects within the outermost boundary to be used as boundary objects. Objects inside of a boundary are called *islands*, as shown in Figure 18-29. The **Ray Casting** options are disabled when **Island Detection** is checked. The **Boolean Subtract Islands** check box causes islands to be included in the outer boundary. Ray casting and Boolean subtraction are explained in Chapter 24.

Figure 18-29.   An example showing a boundary and islands.

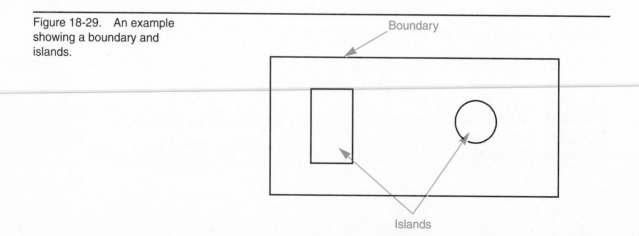

When you select the **Pick Points** button, the following prompts appear:

> Select internal point: *(pick a point inside a closed polygon)*
> Selecting everything…
> Selecting everything visible…
> Analyzing the selected data…
> Select internal point: *(pick a point inside another closed polygon)*
> Select internal point: ↵
> Command:

If the point you pick is inside a closed polygon, then the boundary is highlighted, as shown in Figure 18-30. If the area you want does not close, as in the lower-right example in Figure 18-30, then the **Boundary Definition Error** alert box appears. Pick **OK**, close the area, and try again.

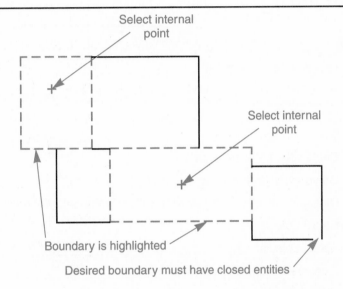

Figure 18-30. When you select an internal point, the boundary becomes highlighted. Boundaries must be closed objects.

Select internal point

Select internal point

Boundary is highlighted

Desired boundary must have closed entities

Unlike the **PEDIT Join** option, the polyline boundary created with the **BOUNDARY** command does not replace the original objects used to create it. The polyline simply *traces* over the defining entities with a polyline. Thus, the separate entities still exist and are *underneath* the newly created boundary. To avoid duplicate geometry, move the boundary to another screen location, erase the original defining entities, and then move the boundary back to its original position.

**PROFESSIONAL TIP**

Area calculations can be simplified by first using the **BOUNDARY** command, or by joining entities with the **PEDIT Join** option, before issuing the **AREA** command. Then, use the **AREA Entity** option to perform the area calculation. If you want to retain the original separate entities and **PEDIT Join** was used, explode the joined polyline. If **BOUNDARY** was used, simply erase the polyline boundary.

## CHAPTER TEST

*Write your answers in the spaces provided.*

1.  Give the command and entries required to make a polyline arc with a starting width of 0 and ending width of .25. Draw it from a known center to an endpoint.

    Command:_____

    From point: _____

    Current line width is (status) _____

    Arc/Close/Halfwidth/Length/Undo/Width/⟨Endpoint of line⟩: _____

    Starting width ⟨*current*⟩: _____

    Ending width:_____

    Arc/Close/Halfwidth/Length/Undo/Width/⟨Endpoint of line⟩: _____

    Angle/CEnter/CLose/Direction/Halfwidth/Line/Radius/Second pt/Undo/Width/⟨Endpoint of arc⟩:__

    Angle/Length/⟨Endpoint⟩ _____

2.  Give the command and entries required to turn three connected lines into a polyline:

    Command:_____

    Select polyline: _____

    Entity selected is not a polyline _____

    Do you want to turn it into one? ⟨Y⟩: _____

    Close/Join/Width/Edit vertex/Fit/Spline/Decurve/Ltype gen/Undo/eXit ⟨X⟩: _____

    Select objects:_____

    Select objects:_____

    2 segments added to polyline _____

    Close/Join/Width/Edit vertex/Fit/Spline/Decurve/Ltype gen/Undo/eXit ⟨X⟩: _____

3.  Give the command and entries needed to change the width of a polyline from .1 to .25:

    Command:_____

    Select polyline: _____

    Close/Join/Width/Edit vertex/Fit/Spline/Decurve/Ltype gen/Undo/eXit ⟨X⟩: _____

    Enter new width for all segments: _____

    Close/Join/Width/Edit vertex/Fit/Spline/Decurve/Ltype gen/Undo/eXit ⟨X⟩: _____

*For Questions 4 through 10, give the* **PEDIT Edit vertex** *option that relates to the definition given.*

4.  Moves the screen X to the next position. _____

5.  Moves a polyline vertex to a new location. _____

6.  Breaks a portion out of a polyline. _____

7.  Required for AutoCAD to redraw the revised edition of a polyline. _____

8.  Specifies tangent direction. _____

9.  Adds a new polyline vertex. _____

10. Returns you to the **PEDIT** options. _____

11. Which **PEDIT** option and suboption allows you to change the starting and ending widths of a polyline? _____

12. Why does it appear that nothing happens after you change the starting and ending widths of a polyline? _____
_____

13. How do you change the width of a doughnut? _____

14. Which command will remove all width characteristics and tangency information from a polyline? _____
_____

15. What happens to the screen cursor after you select the **PEDIT** command? _____
_____

16. What happens if you select **Close** for a polyline that is already closed? _____
_____

17. When you select the **Edit vertex** option of the **PEDIT** command, where is the screen cursor X placed by AutoCAD? _____

18. How do you move the screen X to edit a different vertex? _____
_____

19. Can you use the **Fit** option of the **PEDIT** command without using the **Tangent** option first? _____

20. Explain the difference between a fit curve and spline curve. _____
_____
_____

21. Explain the relationship between the **Quadratic curve**, **Cubic curve**, and **Fit** options. _____
_____
_____

22. Discuss the construction of a quadratic curve. _____
_____
_____
_____

23. What **SPLINETYPE** setting allows you to draw a quadratic curve? _____

24. What **SPLINETYPE** setting allows you to draw a cubic curve? _____

25. Name the system variable that adjusts the smoothness of a spline curve. _____

26. Name the pull-down menu where the **Polyline Edit** options are found. _____

27. Explain how you can adjust the way polyline linetypes are generated with the **PLINE** command. _____
_____
_____

28. Name the system variable that allows you to alter the way polyline linetypes are generated. _____
_____

29. Name the command used to create a polyline boundary. _____

30. Name the command that can be used to create a true spline. _____

31. How do you accept the AutoCAD defaults for the start and end tangents of a spline?
    _____

32. Name the option that allows you to turn a spline fitted polyline into a true spline. _____
    _____

33. Name the command that allows you to edit splines._____

34. What is the purpose of the **Add** suboption in the **Fit Data** option? _____
    _____
    _____

35. What happens to the spline if you use the **Delete** option and only two control points
    remain? _____
    _____

36. Name the options that let you move fit points in a spline._____

37. What is the purpose of the **Redefine** option in the **SPLINEDIT** command? _____
    _____
    _____
    _____

38. Identify the **SPLINEDIT** option that lets you increase the number of control points that
    appear on a spline for greater control. _____

39. This option in the **SPLINEDIT** command controls the pull that a control point exerts on
    the spline. _____

40. How many changes can you undo in a the **SPLINEDIT** command when using the **Undo**
    option? _____
    _____

## DRAWING PROBLEMS

*Start a new drawing for the following problems. Set up your own units, limits, and other variables to suit each problem.*

Graphic
Design

1. Draw the polyline shown below. Use the **Line**, **Arc**, **Width**, and **Close** options to complete the shape. The polyline width will be 0, except at those points indicated. Save the drawing as A:P18-1.

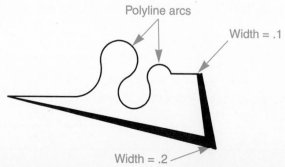

Polyline arcs

Width = .1

Width = .2

2. Draw the two curved arrows below using the **PLINE Arc** and **Width** options. The arrowhead should have a starting width of 1.4 and ending width of 0. The arrow body should have a beginning width of .8 and ending width of .4. To draw the clockwise arrow, select the **tanDir** option of the **PLINE Arc** menu. Save the drawing as A:P18-2.

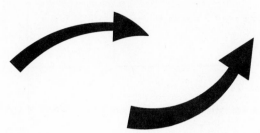

3. Change the object from Problem 18-1 into a rectangle. Use the **PEDIT** options **Decurve**, **Straighten**, **Width**, **Insert**, and **Move**. First, open P18-1, then make a second copy of the object to edit. Save the completed drawing as A:P18-3.

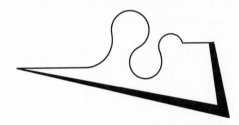 

4. Open P18-2 and make the following changes. Then, save the drawing as A:P18-4.

A. Combine the two polylines using the **Join** option.

B. Change the beginning width of the left arrow to 1.0 and the ending width to .2.

C. Draw a polyline .062 wide similar to the one labeled as B.

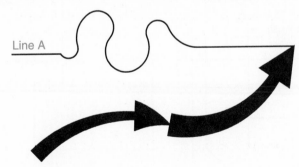

Line A

5. Draw the object shown below using the **LINE** command. Do not dimension the object. Then, change the object to a polyline, making the polyline .032 wide. Save the drawing as A:P18-5.

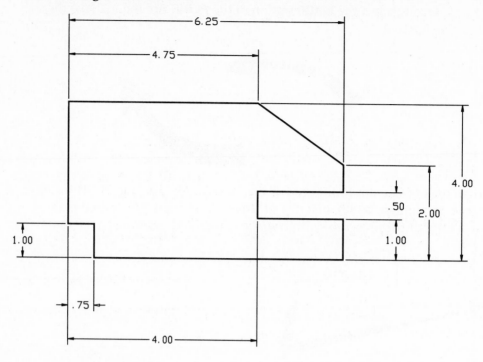

6. Use the **PLINE** command to draw object A below. Then, copy object A to a position directly below the original. Use the **PEDIT** command to edit object B as shown below. Save the drawing as A:P18-6.

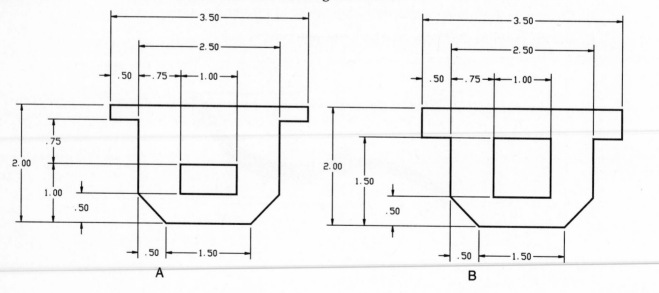

7. Load AutoCAD for Windows and open drawing P18-1. Explode the polyline and observe the results. Restore the original polyline using the **UNDO** command. Save the drawing as A:P18-7 and quit.

*General*

8. Draw a polyline .032 wide using the following absolute coordinates:

*Graphic Design*

| | | |
|---|---|---|
| Point 1  1,1 | Point 5  3,3 | Point 9   5,5 |
| Point 2  2,1 | Point 6  4,3 | Point 10  6,5 |
| Point 3  2,2 | Point 7  4,4 | Point 11  6,6 |
| Point 4  3,2 | Point 8  5,4 | Point 12  7,6 |

Copy the polyline three times. Use the **PEDIT Fit** option to smooth the first copy. Use the **PEDIT Spline** option to smooth the second copy. Use the **PEDIT Quadratic curve** option to smooth the third copy. Use the **PEDIT Decurve** option to return one polyline to its original form. Save the drawing as A:P18-8.

9. Open drawing P18-8 for further editing. Change all of the object lines to .032 wide polylines. Then, add centerlines. Save the revised version as A:P18-9.

*Graphic Design*

10. Draw a patio plan similar to the example shown at A below. Draw the house walls 6″ wide. Copy the A drawing to the positions shown at B, C, and D. Your client wants to see at least four different designs. Use the **Fit** option at B, a cubic spline at C, and a quadratic spline at D. Change the **SPLINETYPE** variable as required. Save the drawing as A:P18-10.

*Architecture*

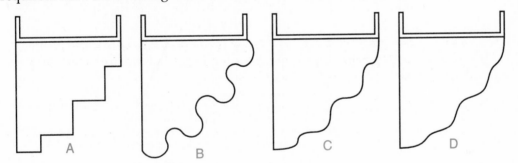

11. Open drawing P18-10 and make some new designs since your client is not satisfied with the first four proposals. This time, use the grips to edit the patio designs similar to the examples shown at A, B, C, and D below. Save the drawing as A:P18-11 and quit.

*Architecture*

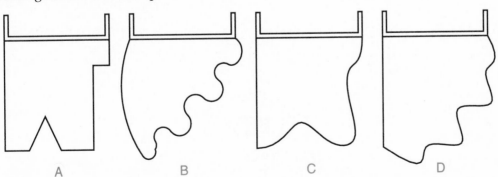

12. Use the **SPLINE** command to draw the curve for the cam displacement diagram below. Use the following instructions and the given drawing to complete this problem:

A. Total rise = 2.000

B. Total displacement can be any length.

C. Divide the total displacement into 30° increments.

D. Draw a half circle on one end divided into 6 equal parts.

E. Draw a horizontal line from each part of the half circle into the cam displacement diagram.

F. Draw the displacement curve with the **SPLINE** command by picking points where horizontal and vertical lines cross.

G. Label the degree increments along the horizontal scale.

Save as A:P18-12.

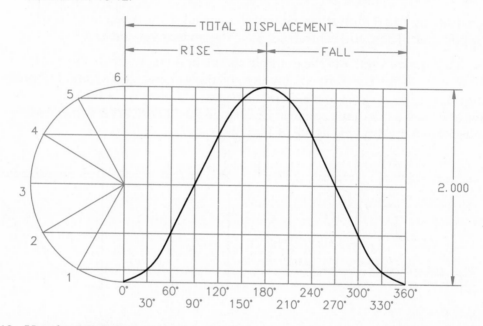

13. Use the **SPLINE** command and other commands such as **ELLIPSE, MIRROR, OFFSET,** and **PLINE** to design an architectural door knocker similar to the one shown below. Use GOTHICE text font to place your initials in the center. Save as A:P18-13.

14. Draw a spline similar to the ORIGINAL SPLINE shown below. Copy the original spline to seven locations similar to the layout shown below. Perform the **SPLINEDIT** operation identified under each of the seven splines. Save as A:P18-14.

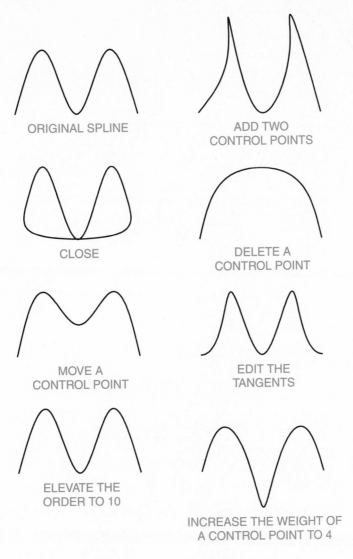

ORIGINAL SPLINE

ADD TWO
CONTROL POINTS

CLOSE

DELETE A
CONTROL POINT

MOVE A
CONTROL POINT

EDIT THE
TANGENTS

ELEVATE THE
ORDER TO 10

INCREASE THE WEIGHT OF
A CONTROL POINT TO 4

*Graphic Design*

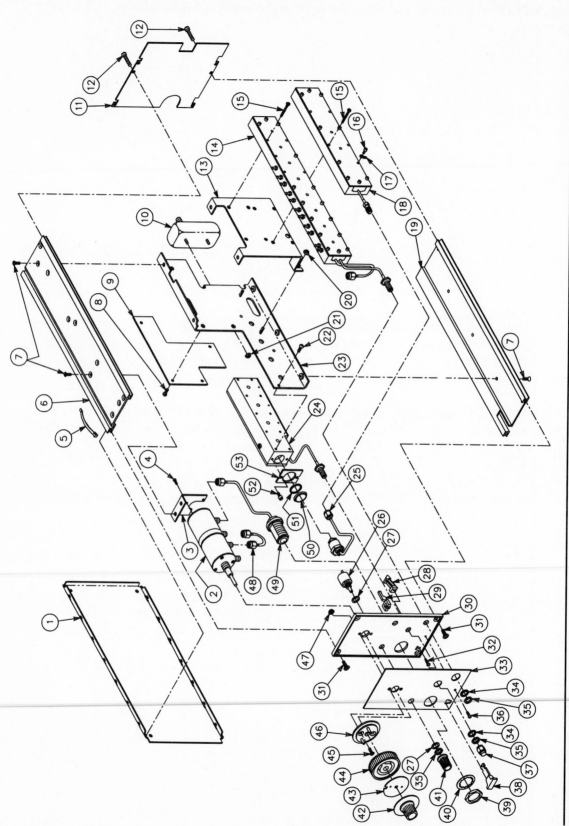

Assembly drawing. (Tektronix, Inc.)

# Multiview Drawings and Layers

## Learning objectives

After completing this chapter, you will be able to:

- ○ Draw multiviews and associated auxiliary views from a sketch.
- ○ Identify guidelines for selecting the front view.
- ○ Properly draw object lines, hidden lines, viewing-plane lines, and centerlines.
- ○ Use construction lines and rays to layout views.
- ○ Load, set, and create linetypes using the **LINETYPE** command.
- ○ Change the current color using the **COLOR** command.
- ○ Draw items on separate layers using the **LAYER** command.
- ○ Create and manage drawing layers using a dialog box.
- ○ Use standard borders and title block formats provided by AutoCAD.
- ○ Customize the standard title block for your company or school.

Each field of drafting has its own method to present views of a product. Architectural drafting uses floor plans and other plan views, exterior elevations, and sections. In electronics drafting, symbols are placed in a schematic diagram to show the circuit layout. In civil drafting, contour lines are used to show the topography of the land. Mechanical drafting uses *multiview drawings*.

This chapter discusses multiview drawings. Multiview drawings are based on the standard ANSI Y14.3.

## DRAWING MULTIVIEWS

Multiviews are made using orthographic projection. *Orthographic projection* is projecting object features onto an imaginary plane. This imaginary plane is called a *projection plane*. The imaginary projection plane is placed parallel to the object. Thus, the line of sight is perpendicular to the object. This results in views that appear two-dimensional, Figure 19-1.

Figure 19-1. How the front view is obtained by orthographic projection.

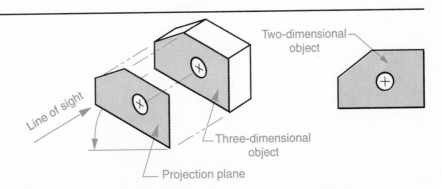

Six two-dimensional views completely show all sides of an object. The six views are the front, right side, left side, top, bottom, and rear. The views are placed in a standard arrangement so others can read the drawing. The front view is the central, or most important view. Other views are placed around the front view, Figure 19-2.

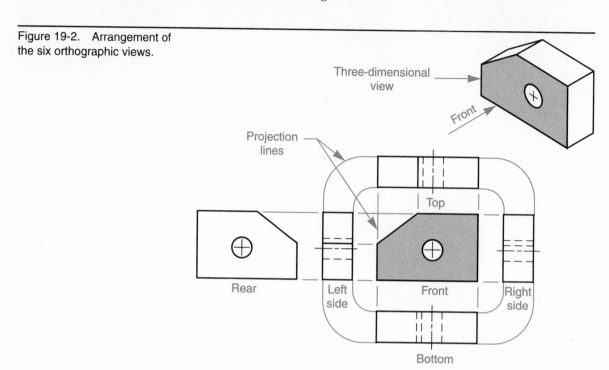

Figure 19-2.   Arrangement of the six orthographic views.

Views are aligned, rather than scattered about the drawing. It is easy to visualize the shape by looking from one view to the next. Chapter 20, Chapter 21, and Chapter 22 cover how this layout helps you read dimensions.

Six views are not always necessary. Actually, there are very few products that require all six views. The number of views needed depends on the complexity of the object. Use only enough views to completely describe the object. Drawing too many views is time-consuming and can clutter the drawing. In some cases, a single view may be enough to describe the object. The object shown in Figure 19-3 needs only two views. These two views completely describe the width, height, depth, and features of the object.

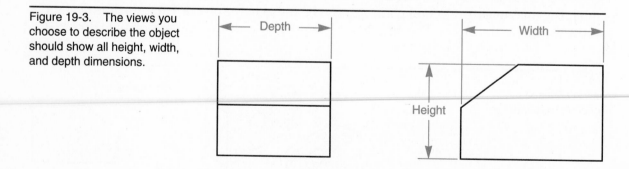

Figure 19-3.   The views you choose to describe the object should show all height, width, and depth dimensions.

## Selecting the front view

The front view is usually the most important view. The following guidelines should be considered when selecting the front view:

- Look for the best shape or most contours.
- Show the most natural position of use.
- Display the most stable position.
- Provide the longest dimension.
- Contain the least hidden features.

Look at Figure 19-4 and review the above guidelines. Do you agree with the front view chosen? Additional views are selected relative to the front view. Choose only the number of views needed to completely describe the object's features.

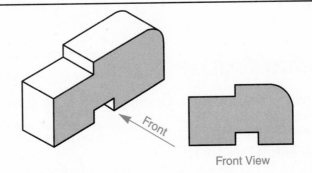

Figure 19-4.   The front view should contain the most details whenever possible.

Front View

## Showing hidden features in multiview drawings

Hidden features are parts of the object not visible in the view you are looking at. A visible edge appears as a solid line. A hidden edge is shown with a hidden line. Hidden lines were discussed in Chapter 6. Notice in Figure 19-5 how hidden features are shown as hidden lines.

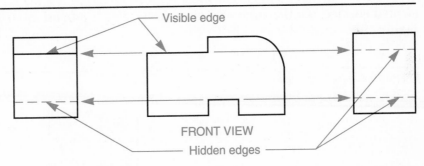

Figure 19-5.   Hidden features in a view are parts of the object not visible in that view.

Visible edge

FRONT VIEW

Hidden edges

## One-view drawings

In some instances, an object can be fully described using one view. A thin part, such as a gasket, is drawn with one view, Figure 19-6. The thickness is given as a note in the drawing or in the title block. A cylindrical object also can be drawn with one view. The diameter dimension is given to tell that the object is round.

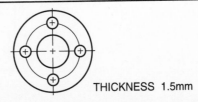

Figure 19-6.   A one-view drawing of a gasket. The thickness is given in a note.

THICKNESS  1.5mm

## Showing symmetry and circle centers

The centerlines of symmetrical objects and the centers of circles are shown using center-lines. For example, in one view of a cylinder, the axis is drawn as a centerline. In the other view, centerlines cross to show the center in the circular view. See Figure 19-7. The only place that the small centerline dashes should cross is at the center of a circle.

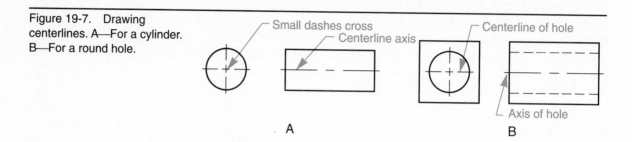

Figure 19-7. Drawing centerlines. A—For a cylinder. B—For a round hole.

# DRAWING AUXILIARY VIEWS

In most cases, an object is completely described using a combination of one or more of the six standard views. However, sometimes the multiview layout is not enough to properly identify some object surfaces. It may then be necessary to draw auxiliary views.

*Auxiliary views* are typically needed when a surface on the object is at an angle to the line of sight. These slanted surfaces are *foreshortened*, meaning they are shorter than the true size and shape of the surface. To show this surface in true size, an auxiliary view is needed. Auxiliary views are needed to show dimensions in views where a feature is true size and shape. Foreshortened dimensions are not recommended.

Auxiliary views are drawn by projecting perpendicular (90°) to a slanted surface. Usually, one projection line remains on the drawing. It connects the auxiliary view to the view where the slanted surface appears as a line. The resulting auxiliary view shows the sur-face in true size and shape. For most applications, the auxiliary view need only show the slanted surface, not the entire object. This is called a *partial auxiliary view* and is shown in Figure 19-8.

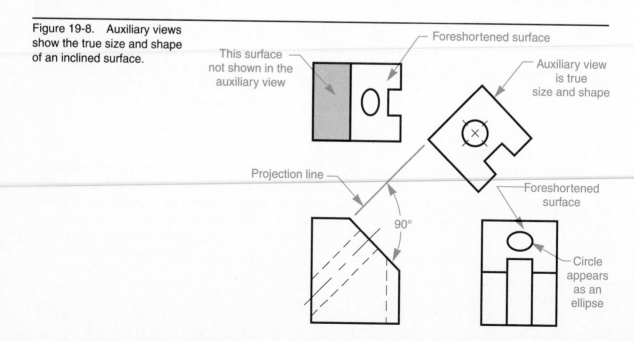

Figure 19-8. Auxiliary views show the true size and shape of an inclined surface.

In many situations, there may not be enough room on the drawing to project directly from the slanted surface. The auxiliary view is then placed elsewhere, Figure 19-9. A viewing-plane line is drawn next to the view where the slanted surface appears as a line. The *viewing-plane line* is drawn with a thick dashed or phantom line in accordance with ANSI Y14.2M. It is terminated with bold arrowheads that point toward the slanted surface. Each end of the viewing-plane line is labeled with a letter such as A. The letters relate the viewing-plane line with the proper auxiliary view. A title such as VIEW A-A is placed under the auxiliary view. When more than one auxiliary view is drawn, labels continue with B-B through Z-Z (if necessary). The letters I, O, and Q are not used because they may be confused with numbers. An auxiliary view drawn away from the multiview retains the same angle as if it is projected directly.

Figure 19-9.  Identifying an auxiliary view with a viewing-plane line. If there is not enough room, the view can be moved to a different location.

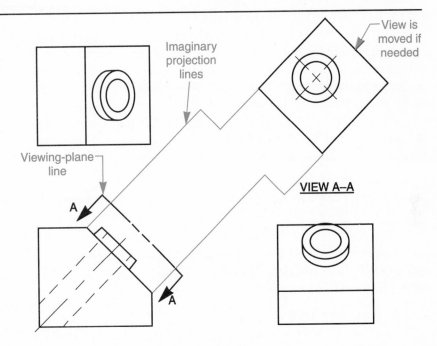

**Changing the snap grid rotation angle**

Changing the rotation angle of the snap grid is especially useful for drawing auxiliary views. This was discussed in Chapter 4. After the views have been drawn, access the **SNAP** command. Then, pick the base point for rotation on the line that represents the slanted surface. Enter the snap rotation angle equal to the angle of the slanted surface. If you do not know the angle, use object snap modes and pick points on the slanted surface to define the angle. The steps are as follows:

> Command: **SNAP** ↵
> Snap spacing or ON/OFF/Aspect/Rotate/Style ⟨*current*⟩: **R** ↵
> Base point ⟨0,0⟩: (*pick an endpoint on the line that represents the slanted surface*)
> Rotation angle ⟨0⟩: (*enter the angle of the slanted surface or pick two points on the surface*)
> Command:

PROFESSIONAL TIP

A viewing-plane line can be drawn with a polyline using an AutoCAD DASHED or PHANTOM linetype. Set the width of the polyline accordingly to draw the viewing-plane line wide, and to terminate with arrowheads. When labeling an auxiliary view, toggle underscoring mode on to produce an underlined view label, such as <u>VIEW A-A</u>.

Once you have placed and rotated the snap grid, you may want to place grid points on the snap grid. Select the **Snap** option of the **GRID** command. Then, complete the auxiliary view as shown in Figure 19-10A. When you finish drawing the auxiliary view, return the snap grid rotation value to 0°.

## Using the User Coordinate System for auxiliary views

All of the features on your drawing originate from the *World Coordinate System (WCS)*. This is the X, Y, and Z coordinate values measured from the origin 0,0,0. The WCS is fixed. The *User Coordinate System (UCS)*, on the other hand, can be moved to any orientation. The UCS is discussed in detail in *AutoCAD and its Applications—Advanced, Release 13 for Windows*. In general, UCS allows you to set your own coordinate origin. The UCS 0,0,0 origin has been in the lower-left corner of the screen for the drawings you have done so far. In many cases this is fine, but when drawing an auxiliary view it is best to have the measurements originate from a corner of the view. This in turn makes all auxiliary view features and the coordinate display true as measured from the corner of the view. This method makes it easier to locate and later dimension the auxiliary view features as compared with the rotated snap grid previously discussed.

First, draw the principal views such as the front, top, and right side. Then, move the UCS origin to a location that coincides with a corner of the auxiliary view using this command sequence:

> Command: **UCS** ↵
> Origin/ZAxis/3point/Object/View/X/Y/Z/Prev/Restore/Save/Del/?/⟨World⟩: **0** ↵
> Origin point ⟨0,0,0⟩: *(pick the origin point at the desired corner of the auxiliary view as shown in Figure 19-10B)*

Next, realign the UCS grid with the angle of the auxiliary view by adjusting the Z axis to the same angle. For example, if the auxiliary view is projected at 45° from the slanted surface in the front view, then rotate the Z axis as follows:

> Command: **UCS** ↵
> Origin/ZAxis/3point/Object/View/X/Y/Z/Prev/Restore/Save/Del/?/⟨World⟩: **Z** ↵
> Rotation angle about Z axis ⟨0⟩: **45** ↵

If you want the UCS icon displayed at the current UCS origin, use the **UCSICON** command as follows:

> Command: **UCSICON** ↵
> ON/OFF/ALL/Noorigin/ORigin/⟨ON⟩: **OR** ↵

This automatically moves the UCS icon to the revised UCS origin at the corner of the auxiliary view, as shown in Figure 19-10C. Although this is not required, it is convenient to see the location of the UCS origin. Before you begin drawing the auxiliary view, use the **Save** option of the **UCS** command to name the new UCS and save it:

> Command: **UCS** ↵
> Origin/ZAxis/3point/Object/View/X/Y/Z/Prev/Restore/Save/Del/?/⟨World⟩: **S** ↵
> ?/Desired UCS name: **AUX** ↵

Now, proceed by drawing the auxiliary view, as shown in Figure 19-10. When you have finished drawing the auxiliary view, use the **Previous** option of the **UCS** command to move the UCS icon to its previous position:

> Command: **UCS** ↵
> Origin/ZAxis/3point/Object/View/X/Y/Z/Prev/Restore/Save/Del/?/⟨World⟩: **P** ↵

Figure 19-10.  A—Using the rotated snap grid and grid points to help draw the auxiliary view. B—Relocating the origin and rotating the Z axis of the UCS system. Notice how the position of the UCS icon has been aligned with the auxiliary view angle. C—Moving the UCS icon display to the current UCS origin at the corner of the auxiliary view.

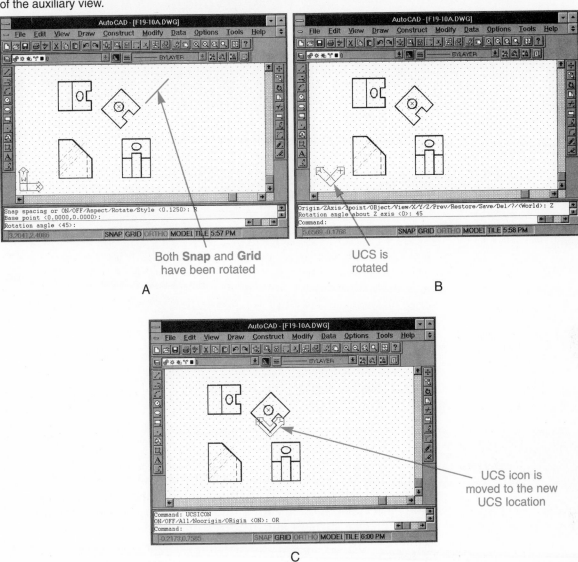

Both **Snap** and **Grid**
have been rotated

UCS is
rotated

A

B

UCS icon is
moved to the new
UCS location

C

You can also press [Enter] to accept the World default and send the UCS icon display back to the WCS origin:

> Command: **UCS** ↵
> Origin/ZAxis/3point/Object/View/X/Y/Z/Prev/Restore/Save/Del/?/⟨World⟩: ↵

The **UCS** command options can be used by selecting **UCS** from the **View** pull-down menu. As shown in Figure 19-11, the cascading submenu provides each of the available options. You can also use the **UCS** ⟩ selection in the **Options** pull-down menu to turn the UCS icon off or move the icon to the new origin of a UCS. Each of these options are covered thoroughly in *AutoCAD and its Applications—Advanced, Release 13 for Windows*.

Figure 19-11.   The **UCS**
command can be selected from
**View** pull-down menu.

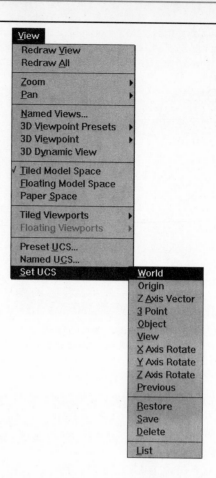

PROFESSIONAL
TIP

Use the orthogonal mode (**ORTHO** command) to help align the projected auxiliary view with the slanted surface. Also, consider using object snap modes with X and Y filters to assist you in projecting the precise corners and features on the slanted surface to the auxiliary view.

# DRAWING CONSTRUCTION LINES AND PROJECTING BETWEEN VIEWS

Construction lines in drafting terminology are lines used for layout purposes. They are not part of the drawing, and in manual drafting, they are either drawn very lightly or removed so they do not reproduce. AutoCAD has lines that can be used for such purposes. These are called *construction lines* and *rays*. For example, you can use construction lines and rays to project features between views for accurate placement, for geometric constructions, or to coordinate geometric locations for object snap selections. The AutoCAD command that lets you draw construction lines is **XLINE**, while rays are drawn with the **RAY** command. Both commands can be used for similar purposes, however, the **XLINE** command has more options and flexibility than the **RAY** command.

## Using the XLINE command

The **XLINE** command creates xline objects. An *xline object* is an infinite length line designed for use as a construction line. Although these lines are infinite, they do not change the drawing extents. This means that they have no effect on zooming operations such as **Extents** or **All**. The xlines can be modified by moving, copying, trimming and other editing operations. Editing commands such as **TRIM** or **FILLET** change the object type. For example, if one end of an xline is trimmed off, then it becomes a ray object. A *ray* is considered semi-infinite since it is infinite in one direction only, as you will see later. If the infinite end of a ray is trimmed off, then it becomes a line object.

Construction lines and rays print and plot the same as any other objects. Construction lines and rays are drawn on the current layer. This may cause conflict with the other lines on that layer. A good way to handle this problem is to set up a special layer just for construction lines. Perhaps call it CONST and use a color such as blue. This is discussed in detail later in this chapter with the **LAYER** command.

The **XLINE** command can be accessed by picking the **Construction Line** button in the **Line** flyout of the **Draw** toolbar or by typing XLINE at the **Command:** prompt. If the ACADFULL menu file is loaded, **XLINE** can be accessed by picking **Construction Line** in the **Draw** pulldown menu. The **XLINE** command sequence is:

> Command: **XLINE** ↵
> Hor/Ver/Ang/Bisect/Offset/⟨From point⟩:

The **XLINE** options are described as follows:

- ⟨**From point**⟩. This is the **XLINE** default option. This allows you to specify two points that the construction line passes through. After you pick the first point, you get a Through point: prompt. You can pick two points that the first construction line is drawn through, then draw another construction line by picking a third point. The first point of an xline is called the *root point*. Use the object snap modes to help you accurately pick points:

> Command: **XLINE** ↵
> Hor/Ver/Ang/Bisect/Offset/⟨From point⟩: *(pick a point)*
> Through point: *(pick a second point)*
> Through point: *(pick another second point)*
> Through point: *(draw more construction lines or press* [Enter]*)*
> Command:

Figure 19-12 shows how construction lines can be used to help project features between views.

- **Hor.** This option draws a horizontal construction line through a single specified point. It serves the same purpose as the default option, but the line is automatically drawn horizontally and you only have to pick one point:

> Command: **XLINE** ↵
> Hor/Ver/Ang/Bisect/Offset/⟨From point⟩: **H** ↵
> Through point: *(pick a point)*
> Through point: *(draw more construction lines or press* [Enter]*)*
> Command:

- **Ver.** This option draws a vertical construction line through the specified point:

> Command: **XLINE** ↵
> Hor/Ver/Ang/Bisect/Offset/⟨From point⟩: **V** ↵
> Through point: *(pick a point)*
> Through point: *(draw more construction lines or press* [Enter]*)*
> Command:

Figure 19-12.   Using the **XLINE** command default option. You can also use the **XLINE Hor** option in this example.

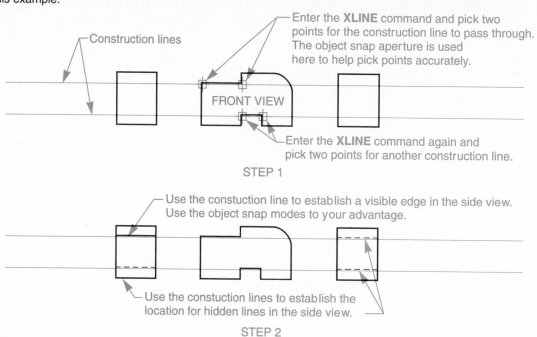

Construction lines

Enter the **XLINE** command and pick two points for the construction line to pass through. The object snap aperture is used here to help pick points accurately.

FRONT VIEW

Enter the **XLINE** command again and pick two points for another construction line.

STEP 1

Use the constuction line to establish a visible edge in the side view. Use the object snap modes to your advantage.

Use the constuction lines to establish the location for hidden lines in the side view.

STEP 2

## EXERCISE 19-1

❑ Load AutoCAD and open TITLEB from Problem 11-1.
❑ Draw four views of the object shown below. Do not draw dimensions.
❑ The top and side views are currently incomplete. Use construction lines to help you complete all views by adding in the missing lines. You were introduced to the **LINETYPE** command in Chapter 6. You may need to review before drawing the hidden lines.
❑ Save the drawing as EX19-1 and quit.

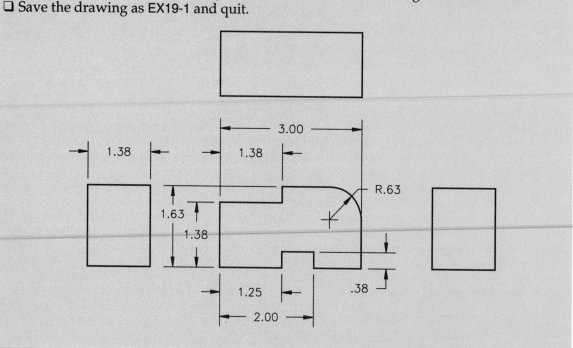

- **Ang.** This option draws a construction line at a specified angle through a specified point. The default lets you specify an angle and then pick a point for the construction line to be drawn through. This works well if you know the angle, or you can pick two points in the drawing to describe the angle:

> Command: **XLINE** ↵
> Hor/Ver/Ang/Bisect/Offset/⟨From point⟩: **A** ↵
> Reference/⟨Enter angle (0.0000)⟩: *(enter an angle, such as 45)*
> Through point: *(pick a point)*
> Through point: *(draw more construction lines or press* [Enter]*)*
> Command:

A reference angle from the angle of an existing line object can be specified by using the **Reference** suboption. This can be used when you do not know the angle of the construction line, but you know the angle between an existing object and the construction line:

> Command: **XLINE** ↵
> Hor/Ver/Ang/Bisect/Offset/⟨From point⟩: **A** ↵
> Reference/⟨Enter angle (45.0000)⟩: **R** ↵
> Select a line object: *(pick a line)*
> Enter angle ⟨45.0000⟩: **90** ↵
> Through point: *(pick a point)*
> Through point: *(draw more construction lines or press* [Enter]*)*
> Command:

Figure 19-13 shows the **Ang** option used to draw construction lines establishing the location of an auxiliary view.

Figure 19-13.   Using the
**XLINE** command **Ang** option.

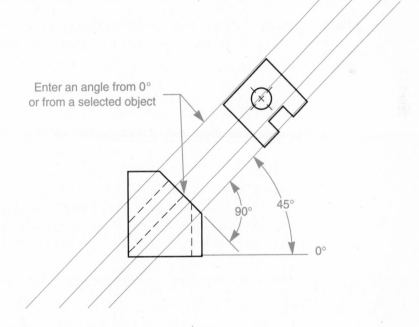

## EXERCISE 19-2

❏ Load AutoCAD and open TITLEB from Problem 11-1.
❏ Draw the front and auxiliary views of the object shown below. Do not draw dimensions or the top view. The top view is given to help you visualize the object.
❏ The front view is currently incomplete. Use construction lines to help you complete the views by adding the missing lines.
❏ Save the drawing as A:EX19-2 and quit.

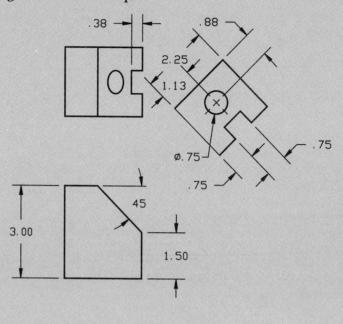

- **Bisect.** This option draws a construction line that bisects a specified angle. This is a convenient tool for use in some geometric constructions, as shown in Figure 19-14:

      Command: **XLINE** ↵
      Hor/Ver/Ang/Bisect/Offset/⟨From point⟩: **B** ↵
      Angle vertex point: *(pick the vertex)*
      Angle start point: *(pick a point on a side of the angle)*
      Angle end point: *(pick a point on the other side of the angle)*
      Angle end point: *(draw more construction lines or press* [Enter]*)*
      Command:

- **Offset.** This **XLINE** option draws a construction line a specified distance (offset) from a selected line object. It works just like the **OFFSET** command that you learned about in Chapter 9. You have the option of specifying an offset distance or using the **Through** suboption to pick a point for the construction line to be drawn through:

Figure 19-14.   Using the **XLINE** command **Bisect** option.

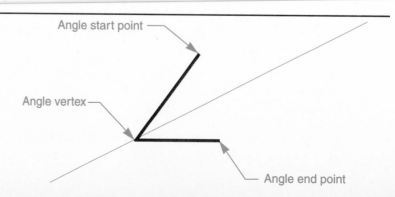

        Command: **XLINE** ↵
        Hor/Ver/Ang/Bisect/Offset/⟨From point⟩: **O** ↵
        Offset distance or Through ⟨0.0000⟩: **0.75** ↵
        Select a line object: *(pick a line)*
        Side to offset? *(pick any point on the side for the xline to be drawn)*
        Select a line object: *(draw more construction lines or press* [Enter]*)*
        Command:

The **Through** suboption works like this:

        Command: **XLINE** ↵
        Hor/Ver/Ang/Bisect/Offset/⟨From point⟩: **O** ↵
        Offset distance or Through ⟨0.7500⟩: **T** ↵
        Select a line object: *(pick a line)*
        Through point: *(pick a point for the xline to be drawn through)*
        Select a line object: *(draw more construction lines or press* [Enter]*)*
        Command:

---

**EXERCISE 19-3**

❏ Load AutoCAD and set the limits at 0,0 and 8.5,11.
❏ Draw the angle shown below using the given absolute coordinates.
❏ Use the **XLINE** command to bisect the angle and to draw a construction line parallel to the outer side of each leg of the angle offset at a distance of 0.525.
❏ Save the drawing as A:EX19-3 and quit.

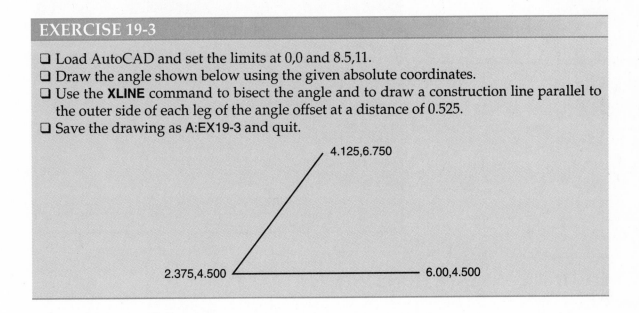

---

## Using the RAY command

The **RAY** command is limited when compared to the **XLINE** command. The **RAY** command allows you to specify the point of origin and a point the ray passes through. In this manner, the **RAY** command works much like the default option of the **XLINE** command. However, the ray extends out beyond the second pick point only. The **XLINE** command results in a construction line that extends both ways from the pick points.

The **RAY** command can be accessed by picking the **Ray** button in the **Line** flyout of the **Draw** toolbar or by typing RAY at the **Command:** prompt. If the ACADFULL menu file is loaded, **RAY** can be accessed by picking **Ray Line** in the **Draw** pull-down menu. The **RAY** command sequence is as follows:

        Command: **RAY** ↵
        From point: *(pick a point)*
        Through point: *(pick a second point)*
        Through point: *(pick another second point)*
        Through point: *(draw more construction lines or press* [Enter]*)*
        Command:

Both the **RAY** command and the **XLINE** command allow the creation of multiple objects, until you press [Enter] to end the command. They do *not* allow you to undo a construction line that you have already drawn.

## MODIFYING AN XLINE                              AUG 6

In earlier chapters, you used the **DDMODIFY** command to edit the properties of existing objects such as lines, circles, and text. You can also use this command to modify xlines and rays. When you pick the **Properties** button or enter the **DDMODIFY** command and select an xline, you get the **Modify Xline** dialog box shown in Figure 19-15. You can use this dialog box to edit the properties of color, layer, and linetype. You can change the root point, the second point, and direction vector. The *direction vector* represents a point on the xline that is one unit away from the root point. If you pick a ray while in the **DDMODIFY** command, you get the **Modify Ray** dialog box that has the same options as the **Modify XLINE** dialog box.

Figure 19-15. The **Modify Xline** dialog box.

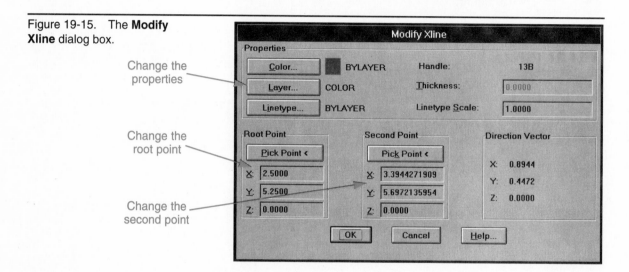

Change the properties → 

Change the root point →

Change the second point →

## EDITING CONSTRUCTION LINES AND RAYS           AUG 5

The construction lines that you create using the **XLINE** and **RAY** commands can be edited using standard editing commands. These lines will change into a new object type when infinite ends are trimmed off using **TRIM**, **FILLET**, **CHAMFER**, or **BREAK**. A trimmed xline becomes a ray. A ray that has its infinite end trimmed becomes a normal line object. Therefore, in many cases, your construction lines can be modified to become final geometry. This approach can save a significant amount of time in many drawings.

## USING DIFFERENT LINETYPES                       AUG 6

The objects that you have constructed so far have been drawn with solid lines. From Chapter 6, you learned that AutoCAD calls these linetypes *continuous*. You may also recall that AutoCAD maintains a standard library of linetypes in an external file called ACAD.LIN. Before a linetype in the ACAD.LIN file can be used, it must first be loaded into the drawing editor and set current. The continuous linetype is the default and does not need to be loaded into the drawing editor.

## Setting the linetype current

A loaded linetype can quickly be set current using the **Object Creation Modes** dialog box shown in Figure 19-16. To access this dialog box, click the **Object Creation** button on the **Object Properties** toolbar, select **Object Creation...** from the **Data** pull-down menu, or type DDEMODES at the **Command:** prompt.

Click the **Linetype...** button and the **Select Linetype** subdialog box shown in Figure 19-17 appears. Only the AutoCAD linetypes that have been loaded are displayed here. Use the scroll bar if needed to see more linetypes. If you want to set the DASHED linetype current, select the graphical representation of the DASHED linetype from the list (not the word DASHED) and pick the **OK** button.

When you pick an ACAD_ISO linetype that has been loaded in the **Select Linetype** dialog box, it also activates the **ISO Pen Width:** pop-up list shown in Figure 19-18. Pick the down arrow to display the pop-up list box. This list displays several line width options given in millimeters. You can also control the setting in the **Linetype Scale:** text box for the ISO pen width you selected. *ISO* stands for International Organization for Standardization.

Figure 19-16.   The **Object Creation Modes** dialog box.

Figure 19-17.   The **Select Linetype** dialog box displays linetypes that have been loaded.

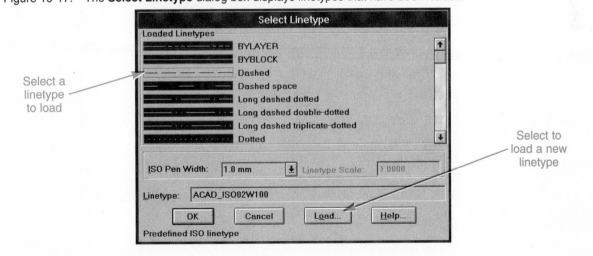

Figure 19-18.   Picking one of the AutoCAD ISO linetypes makes the ISO options available. Make any changes necessary and then pick **OK**.

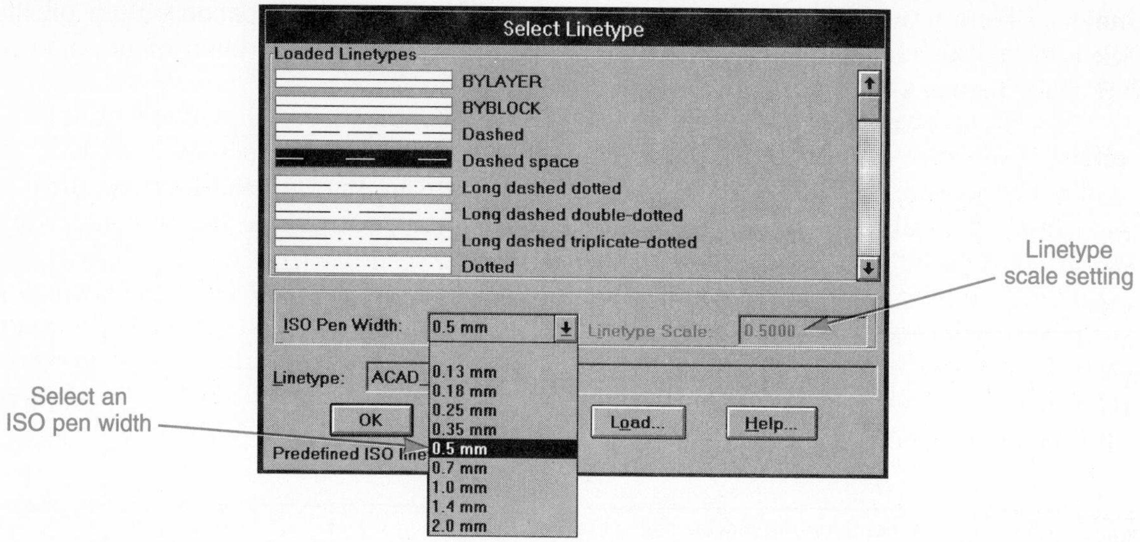

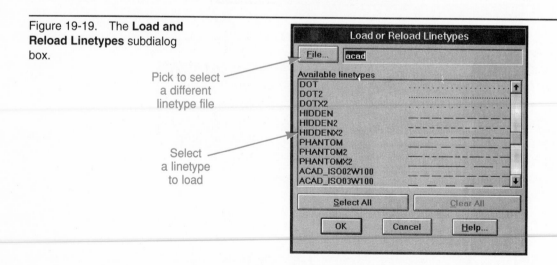

## Loading a linetype

The **Select Linetypes** subdialog box also offers an option to load linetypes. To load linetypes, pick the **Load...** button to get the **Load or Reload Linetypes** subdialog box shown in Figure 19-19. Scroll through the available linetypes and pick the linetype(s) you want to load. You can also pick the **Select All** button to automatically highlight all of the available linetypes. To clear a linetype, just pick it again and the highlight is removed. Pick the **Clear All** button to have all the selections cleared. The **Clear All** button is inactive until at least one linetype has been selected. Pick the **OK** button to have the selected linetypes loaded and listed in the **Select Linetype** subdialog box.

Figure 19-19.   The **Load and Reload Linetypes** subdialog box.

## Selecting a different linetype file

Pick the **File...** button in the **Load or Reload Linetypes** subdialog box to access the **Select Linetype File** subdialog box. Here, you can pick other linetype files that may be available. Pick a linetype file and then pick **OK** to have these linetypes listed and displayed in the **Load or Reload Linetypes** subdialog box. Then, load them as needed.

## Setting the linetype scale

Look at the **Select Linetype** subdialog box in Figure 19-18. Notice the **Linetype Scale:** text box. You can use this to quickly adjust the individual object linetype scale before returning to the drawing editor. If you forget to change the linetype scale in the **Select Linetype** subdialog box, you can also do it in the **Object Creation Modes** dialog box shown in Figure 19-16. You can also change the global linetype scale factor at the **Command:** prompt using the **LTSCALE** system variable that is discussed later in this chapter. Refer to the section *CHANGING THE LINETYPE SCALE* on page 582 for a detailed discussion. Figure 19-20 gives you an example of how changing the linetype scale affects the way a line is displayed.

Figure 19-20.   A comparison of linetype scale factors.

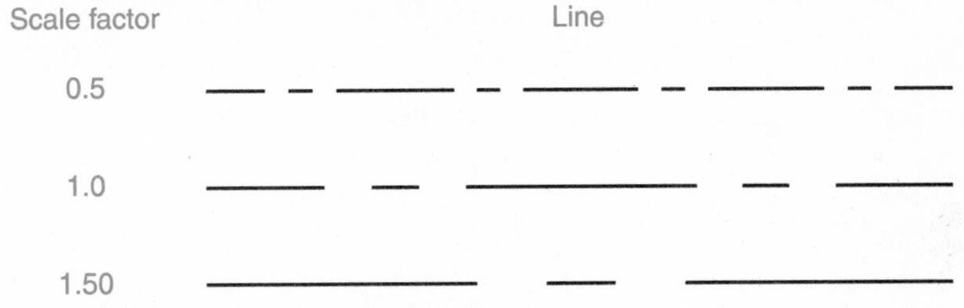

| Scale factor | Line |
| --- | --- |
| 0.5 | — – — – — – — – — – — – — – — – — |
| 1.0 | —— — — —— — —— |
| 1.50 | —— — —— |

## Working with linetypes using the Command: prompt

The **LINETYPE** command allows you to load different linetypes, change the current linetype, and create custom linetypes. The **LINETYPE** command options were introduced in Chapter 6, and are repeated here to refresh your memory:

- **?.** Lists the linetypes defined in a specified library file.
- **Create.** Allows creation of a new linetype and stores it in a specified library file.
- **Load.** Loads one or more linetypes from a specified library file.
- **Set.** Sets the current linetype used for newly drawn entities.

**Listing linetypes.** To get a listing of the available linetypes, type LINETYPE at the **Command:** prompt. Then, use the **?** option to open the **Select Linetype File** dialog box. The default linetype filename is ACAD.LIN. Pressing [Enter] lists the linetypes in that file. To display the standard linetype library, use the **LINETYPE** command as shown here:

```
Command: LINETYPE ↵
?/Create/Load/Set: ? ↵
```

The listing shown in Figure 19-21 is displayed on the text screen. Note that you may have to press enter a couple of times to see the entire listing.

Enter the **LINETYPE** command again and type ?. This time notice the LTYPESHP filename in the **Select Linetype File** dialog box. This file defines several complex linetypes. Pick LTYPESHP to highlight it and press [Enter] to see the text screen displaying the complex linetypes found in this file. See Figure 19-22.

Figure 19-21. AutoCAD's standard linetype library.

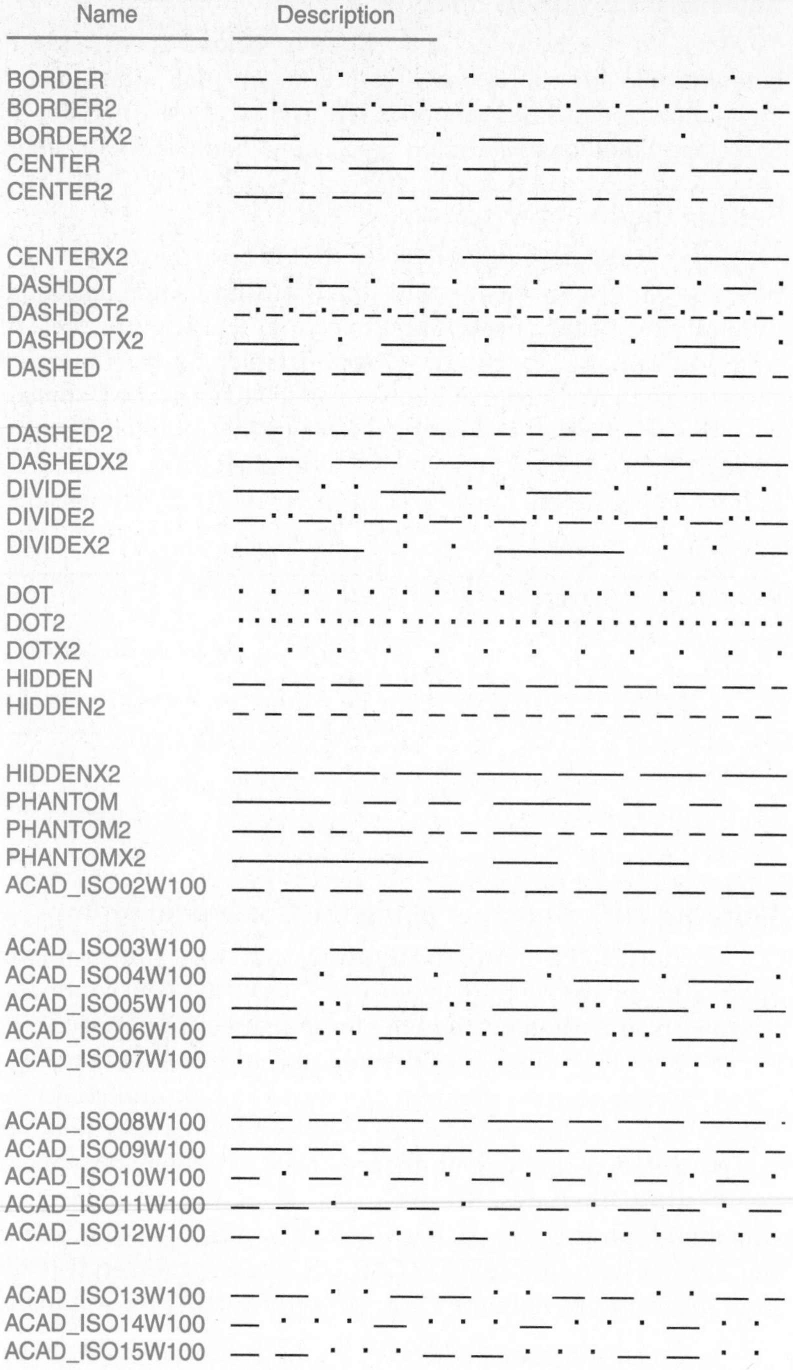

| Name | Description |
| --- | --- |
| BORDER | |
| BORDER2 | |
| BORDERX2 | |
| CENTER | |
| CENTER2 | |
| | |
| CENTERX2 | |
| DASHDOT | |
| DASHDOT2 | |
| DASHDOTX2 | |
| DASHED | |
| | |
| DASHED2 | |
| DASHEDX2 | |
| DIVIDE | |
| DIVIDE2 | |
| DIVIDEX2 | |
| | |
| DOT | |
| DOT2 | |
| DOTX2 | |
| HIDDEN | |
| HIDDEN2 | |
| | |
| HIDDENX2 | |
| PHANTOM | |
| PHANTOM2 | |
| PHANTOMX2 | |
| ACAD_ISO02W100 | |
| | |
| ACAD_ISO03W100 | |
| ACAD_ISO04W100 | |
| ACAD_ISO05W100 | |
| ACAD_ISO06W100 | |
| ACAD_ISO07W100 | |
| | |
| ACAD_ISO08W100 | |
| ACAD_ISO09W100 | |
| ACAD_ISO10W100 | |
| ACAD_ISO11W100 | |
| ACAD_ISO12W100 | |
| | |
| ACAD_ISO13W100 | |
| ACAD_ISO14W100 | |
| ACAD_ISO15W100 | |

Figure 19-22. LTYPESHP examples from \R13\COM\SUPPORT\LTYPESHP.LIN.

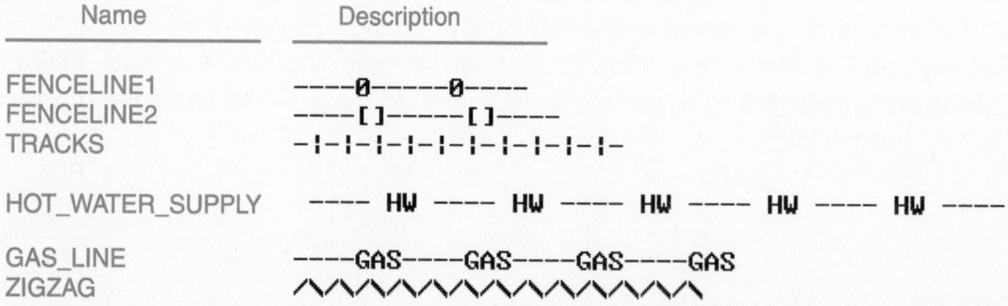

| Name | Description |
| --- | --- |
| FENCELINE1 | ----0-----0---- |
| FENCELINE2 | ----[]-----[]---- |
| TRACKS | -|-|-|-|-|-|-|-|-|-|-|- |
| HOT_WATER_SUPPLY | ---- HW ---- HW ---- HW ---- HW ---- HW ---- |
| GAS_LINE | ----GAS----GAS----GAS----GAS |
| ZIGZAG | /\/\/\/\/\/\/\/\/\/\ |

**Loading linetypes.** To load one or more linetypes, type LINETYPE at the **Command:** prompt and type L for the **Load** option. When loading multiple linetypes, separate each linetype name with a comma. In the following example, two linetypes are loaded:

>Command: **LINETYPE** ↵
>?/Create/Load/Set: **L** ↵
>Linetype(s) to load: **CENTER,HIDDEN** ↵

If the **FILEDIA** system variable is on (1), the **Select Linetype File** dialog box is displayed. If the **FILEDIA** system variable is off (0), the following prompt is displayed:

>File to search ⟨acad⟩: ↵

After selecting the desired linetype library, the **LINETYPE** command options reappear:

>?/Create/Load/Set: *(select an option or press* [Enter] *to exit the command)*

**Selecting a linetype.** When drawing views of an object, you may need to draw hidden lines and centerlines. Select the linetype using the **Set** option of the **LINETYPE** command. Type S at the prompt. You are then asked to name the linetype:

>Command: **LINETYPE** ↵
>?/Create/Load/Set: **S** ↵
>New object linetype (or ?) ⟨BYLAYER⟩: **HIDDEN** ↵
>?/Create/Load/Set:

Press [Enter] to get the **Command:** prompt. Now, any lines you add are drawn with the new linetype. You must again use the **Set** option to draw continuous lines or set another linetype.

**Loading custom linetypes.** Many companies have custom linetypes. For example, cartographers may need special styles of lines to draw maps. These linetypes are usually stored in library files other than the ACAD library. For example, if your company or school has installed a custom linetype library named MAPLINES, then this filename is listed. To list one of the available linetypes, type ? as previously shown. This will list and describe the linetypes contained in the file. The sequence for this is as follows:

>Command: **LINETYPE** ↵
>?/Create/Load/Set: **L** ↵
>Linetype(s) to load: *(enter linetype name)*

If **FILEDIA** is set to on (1), the **Select Linetype File** dialog box is displayed. Pick MAPLINES from the files list, or type it in the **File Name:** text box. If the **FILEDIA** variable is 0, the following prompt appears:

>Linetype(s) to load: *(enter linetype names)*
>File to search ⟨ACAD⟩: **MAPLINES** ↵

Now, suppose you want to use the PROPERTY linetype found in the MAPLINES linetype library. Enter PROPERTY as the name of the linetype to load and MAPLINES as the file to search.

If you try to load a linetype that is already loaded, such as the standard AutoCAD HIDDEN linetype, you get this message:

>Linetype(s) to load: **HIDDEN** ↵
>Linetype HIDDEN is already loaded. Reload it? ⟨Y⟩ ↵

Press [Enter] to reload the linetype, or type N and press [Enter] if you decide not to reload it.

## CREATING LINETYPES

To create custom linetypes, or modify AutoCAD standard linetypes, use the **Create** option of the **LINETYPE** command.

> Command: **LINETYPE** ↵
> ?/Create/Load/Set: **C** ↵

After typing C, AutoCAD requests the name of the linetype to create. It also must know the file for storing the linetype. Select a linetype name that represents the line's features. For example, suppose you are designing a line having long lines that alternate with three short dashes. This linetype might be for drawing property boundaries in mapping. Call the line D3D. You can store the linetype in the ACAD default file by pressing [Enter] as follows:

> Name of linetype to create: **D3D** ↵ *(the* **Select Linetype File** *dialog box appears.*
> *Pick and highlight* ACAD.LIN *and pick* **OK***)*
> Wait, checking if linetype already defined…

If the **FILEDIA** system variable is set to 0, the **Select Linetype File** dialog does not appear and you get this prompt:

> Name of linetype to create: **D3D** ↵
> File for storage of linetype ⟨C:\R13\COM\SUPPORT\ACAD.LIN⟩: ↵

AutoCAD first checks to see if the linetype already exists. Then, you are asked for descriptive text. As the name implies, *descriptive text* describes the new linetype. The text should be in the format *\*linetype-name ,description* and should be no more than 47 characters long. The D3D linetype being created here might be described as follows:

> Descriptive text: **\*D3D ,LONG AND 3 SHORT DASHES** ↵

The Enter pattern: prompt then appears. Describe the line based on the following code:

| CODE | | DEFINITION |
|------|---|-----------|
| A, | = | alignment. *This instructs AutoCAD to balance out the line ends with equal beginning length segments. The* **A***, always begins the set of pattern code.* |
| – numeral | = | length of a space. |
| + numeral | = | length of a dash. |
| 0 | = | dot. |

Suppose the D3D linetype is designed to be drawn as:

| LINE SEGMENT | LENGTH | CODE |
|--------------|--------|------|
| Long dash | = 1.5 units | = 1.5 |
| Space | = .062 units | = −.062 |
| Short dash | = .125 units | = .125 |
| Space | = .062 units | = −.062 |
| Short dash | = .125 units | = .125 |
| Space | = .062 units | = −.062 |
| Short dash | = .125 units | = .125 |
| Space | = .062 units | = −.062 |

The linetype pattern is given as follows:

> Enter pattern (on next line):
> **A,1.5,−.062,.125,−.062,.125,−.062,.125,−.062** ↵

AutoCAD then responds with:

> New definition written to file.
> ?/Create/Load/Set: **S** ↵

You must first set the new linetype current before you can use it. Respond with an S to the previous prompt. When asked for the name of the new linetype, enter D3D. The new linetype D3D is set to draw, as shown in Figure 19-23.

Figure 19-23. The new D3D linetype.

## Creating complex linetypes

You can create your own custom complex linetypes that use dashes, dots, and spaces like simple linetypes, but you can also add shapes or text. The complex linetypes are used and managed the same as simple linetypes in every aspect except creation. Even in creation, the dash/dot definition is the same. However, additional options are available for defining symbols and parameters to be used in the complex linetype. Creating a complex linetype can only be done using a text editor, unlike simple linetypes. Pen down and pen up lengths are done as usual, with positive and negative numeric values. The symbols can be drawn from either .SHX shape files or .SHX font files.

Shape files are similar to font files in the means of description, and they have the same .SHX file extension. The actual creation of .SHX files is beyond the scope of this discussion, but AutoCAD Release 13 comes with the following sample shape files:

*Common linetype symbol shapes*
File: C:\R13\COM\SUPPORT\LTYPESHP.SHX

| | |
|---|---|
| TRACK | ZIG |
| BOX | CIRC1 |
| BAT | |

*Electronics symbol shapes*
File: C:\R13\COM\SUPPORT\ES.SHX

| | | | |
|---|---|---|---|
| CON1 | ZENER | RES | OR |
| CAP | NOR | DIODE | XOR |
| PNP | AND | NPN | NAND |
| MARK | BUFFER | ARROW | INVERTER |
| JUMP | BOX | CON2 | NEG |

Other shape files include:

*Printed circuit symbol shapes*
File: C:\R13\COM\SUPPORT\PC.SHX
*Surface finish symbol shapes*
File: C:\R13\COM\SUPPORT\ST.SHX

To access shapes within a shape file, the shape file must first be loaded using AutoCAD's **LOAD** command. The **LOAD** command activates the **Select Shape File** dialog box if **FILEDIA** is set to 1. Otherwise, the following sequence is used when the file is located on the ACAD library path:

> Command: **LOAD** ↵
> Name of shape file to load (or ?): **LTYPESHP** ↵
> Command:

Do this in the **Select Shape File** dialog by accessing the directory C:\R13\COM\SUPPORT and then pick the LTYPESHP file, or enter the filename in the **File:** edit box and pick **OK**. Any valid shape file can be specified. However, a font file also has the .SHX file extension but cannot be loaded. An error message is issued if you try to load a font file.

Now, the **SHAPE** command can be used to list the available shapes or to insert a shape. The listings shown previously for LTYPESHP.SHX and ES.SHX are displayed when the **?** option of the **SHAPE** command is used after these files have been loaded.

After loading shape files, you are ready to proceed with creating a complex linetype definition. You do not have to load a shape file before it can be referenced in a linetype definition, but it may be necessary in order to obtain a listing of available shapes within a given file. Remember that only simple linetypes can be created at the command line, complex linetypes must be created by entering them directly into the .LIN file using a text editor.

## Syntax for a shape

The word *syntax* means the way words are put together. When used to describe a computer program requirement, syntax is the way commands or specifications are entered. The syntax for specifying a shape to use in a linetype definition is as follows:

> [*shapename,shxfilename*]

> or

> [*shapename,shxfilename,transform*]

The *shapename* should correspond to the name of a shape existing in the specified *shxfilename*. The *transform* field refers to a series of optional modifiers for the shape as follows, where $n$ = any number:

R=$n$     Relative rotation angle, defaults to degrees. Can be appended
          with *d* for degrees, *r* for radians or *g* for grads. Default=0.

A=$n$     Absolute rotation angle, defaults to degrees. Can be appended
          with *d* for degrees, *r* for radians or *g* for grads. Default=0.

S=$n$     Scale factor.

X=$n$     X offset value, used for proper alignment.

Y=$n$     Y offset value, used for proper alignment.

The X and Y offsets are adjustments from the default insertion points. Angle specifications are numerical as specified; however, the S, X and Y are in linetype scaled drawing units and are calculated with this formula: n(LTSCALE)=value.

These transform parameters can be used in any series with the $n$ above indicating a signed decimal number such as 1, 0.125, or –3. The values are based on any desired size, rotation and offset of shape or text. Some or all may be used in any order. An example of a shape and a transform specification is as follows:

> [CAP,es.shx,S=2,R=10,X=0.5]

The elements of the shape transformation mean this:

- **CAP.** Shape name
- **es.shx.** Shape filename
- **S=2.** Scale factor of 2
- **R=10.** Rotation angle of 10°
- **X=0.5.** X axis offset is 0.5

To use this in a linetype definition, place the specification as you would a dash or dot specification. For example:

> A,.25,–.125,[CAP,es.shx,S=2,R=10,X=0.5],–.125

A shape or text description may not be the first specification in the linetype definition, and square brackets must enclose the shape or text description. The complete sequence required to create, load, and set the complex linetype shown in Figure 19-24 is as follows:

> **\*CIR-SQ, Dashed line with alternating circles and squares**
> **A,1.25,–.5,[CIRC1,ltypeshp.shx,s=.1,x=–.125],–.5,1.25,–.5,[BOX,ltypeshp.shx,**
>     **s=.1,x=–.125],–.5**

Figure 19-24. A new linetype created with the command sequence in the text.

The following gives a brief description of each element in the above statement:
- **\*.** All linetype names must be preceded with an asterisk.
- **CIR-SQ.** Linetype name is followed by short descriptive text.
- **A.** Linetype is aligned, meaning start and end dashes are equalized.
- **–.5,.125,–.5.** Pen up and down are the same as a simple linetype.
- **CIRC1.** The name of the first shape.
- **BOX.** The name of the second shape.
- **ltypeshp.shx.** Shape filename for both shapes above.
- **S=.1.** Insert objects at a 0.1 scale factor of actual description.
- **X=–.125.** Offset value helps center the shape within the pen up area between dashes. X axis is considered to be the direction of the line and Y axis is the direction plus 90°.

Finally, save the file and exit the text editor, and return to AutoCAD. The linetype definition is now contained in the file named MYLTYPE.LIN. To load and set the new linetype, use the linetype command:

```
Command: LINETYPE ↵
?/Create/Load/Set: L ↵
Linetype(s) to load: CIRC-SQ ↵
?/Create/Load/Set: S ↵
New object linetype(or ?)⟨BYLAYER⟩: CIRC-SQ ↵
?/Create/Load/Set: ↵
Command:
```

Now, use any object creation command, such as **LINE**, **PLINE**, **CIRCLE** or **ARC** to draw objects with the new linetype. See Figure 19-24.

## Introduction to creating complex linetypes with text

Creating a linetype that uses text is much the same as creating a shape linetype. The primary difference is that the specification is for text and style names instead of shapes and shape files. The linetype is still complex, and must be entered directly into the .LIN file with a text editor. All other steps in the process are the same, except for the actual linetype specification entered into the .LIN file. The syntax for a text linetype is as follows:

["*string*",*stylename*]

or

["*string*",*stylename*,*transform*]

The "*string*" field refers to any text to appear in the linetype, and must be placed in quotation marks as shown. The *stylename* can be specified or left out. If left out, the default text style in the current drawing is used. The effects of the transform parameters are the same as for shapes. The linetype shown in Figure 19-25 is created with the linetype definition shown here:

**\*TEXT, Sample linetype with text**
**A,1.25,–.25,["TEXT",romans,S=.1,X=–.18],–.25**

Figure 19-25. A sample linetype with text.

The following gives a brief description of each element in the above statement:
- **\*.** All linetype names must be preceded with an asterisk.
- **TEXT.** Linetype name is followed by short descriptive text.
- **A.** Linetype is aligned, meaning start and end dashes are equalized.
- **.125,–.25.** Pen up and down are the same as a simple linetype.
- **"TEXT".** Text string to place along line.
- **romans.** Text style filename to reference. Note that this style must exist in the current drawing before the linetype can be loaded.
- **S=.1.** Scale factor for defined text height, or if current style has zero height, the absolute height in drawing units.
- **X=–.125.** Offset value helps center the text within the pen up area between dashes. X axis is considered to be the direction of the line and Y axis is the direction plus 90°.

Open the file MYLTYPE.LIN and enter this definition, then save and exit. You can then load the linetype during a drawing session using the **LINETYPE** command.

**PROFESSIONAL TIP**

When working within the Windows environment, a text editor and AutoCAD can be active simultaneously. While this is an efficient way to work when defining linetypes, some problems may be encountered. Once a linetype file is opened by AutoCAD to load a definition, the file can be opened by your editor but you may not be able to easily save your work. Your text editor may report that the file is in use by another application. An easy way to get around this is to either save the file under a different name or exit and restart AutoCAD.

## CHANGING THE LINETYPE SCALE                                   AUG 6

The linetype scale sets the length of dashes in linetypes having them. The default global linetype scale factor is one. Any line with dashes initially assumes this factor.

You can change the scale factor to 1.5 as follows:

Command: **LTSCALE** ↵
New scale factor ⟨*current*⟩: **1.5** ↵

A "regenerating drawing" message appears as the linetype scale is changed for all lines on the drawing.

### Changing the linetype scale of individual objects

The **LTSCALE** variable can be used to make a global change to the linetype scale. *Global* means that the change affects everything in the current drawing. Sometimes you may want to change the linetype scale of an individual object or a select group of objects. One way to do this is by using the **CHPROP** command. This command allows you to change many properties, each of which is identified by name in a list of options. The **CHPROP** command is a handy tool that works like this:

Command: **CHPROP** ↵
Select objects: *(select the objects to change)*
Select objects: ↵
Change what property (Color/LAyer/LType/ltScale/Thickness)? **S** ↵
New linetype scale ⟨1.0000⟩: **.5** ↵
Change what property (Color/LAyer/LType/ltScale/Thickness)? ↵
Command:

You can also change the linetype scale of specific objects by using the **DDMODIFY** command. Remember that the **Properties** button on the **Object Properties** toolbar will start the **DDMODIFY** command if one object is selected, or **DDCHPROP** if multiple objects are selected. Another option is to type the **DDMODIFY** command:

> Command: **DDMODIFY** ↵
> Select object to modify: *(select the object to modify)*

If a line object is selected, **Modify Line** dialog box is displayed. All primitive objects (including lines, arcs, circles, etc.) have a field available for changing the **Linetype Scale:** within the **Properties** area. Pick the **OK** button when you have changed the values as desired.

## Using the CELTSCALE system variable

The **CELTSCALE** system variable controls the "current entity linetype scale." The **LTSCALE** variable is a global setting that can be changed at any time and all objects in the drawing then use the new value. However, the **LTSCALE** variable is only a multiplier for the individual object linetype scale value. For example, if an object has an individual linetype scale of 0.5, and the **LTSCALE** is set at 0.5, then the apparent linetype scale displayed on screen is 0.25 for that object. The **CELTSCALE** variable assigns a property directly to newly created objects, similar to the **COLOR** or **LINETYPE** commands. Subsequent changes to the variable do not affect already created objects, just objects that are created after the change is made. **CELTSCALE** may be set at the **Linetype Scale:** edit box within the **Select Linetype** subdialog box. **CELTSCALE** can also be typed directly at the **Command:** prompt as follows. Refer to Figure 19-26.

> Command: **CELTSCALE** ↵
> New value for CELTSCALE ⟨1.0⟩: **.5** ↵
> Command:

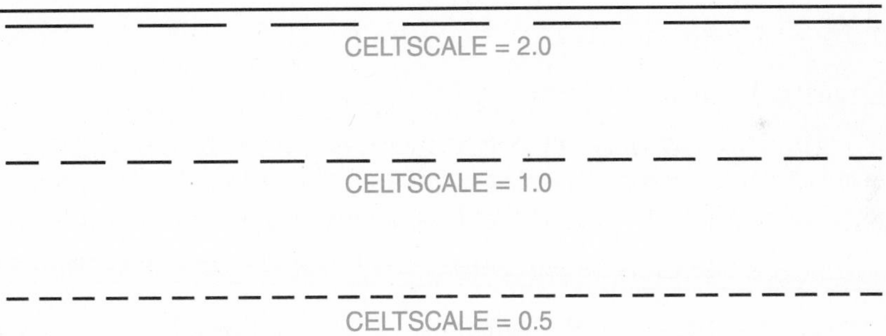

Figure 19-26. Drawing the same linetype at different **CELTSCALE** settings.

CELTSCALE = 2.0

CELTSCALE = 1.0

CELTSCALE = 0.5

## EXERCISE 19-4

❑ Open TITLEB from Problem 11-1.
❑ Draw the two objects shown below to approximate size.
❑ Change the linetype scale to .5, to 1.5, and then back to 1. Observe the effect each time it is changed.
❑ Save the drawing as A:EX19-4 and quit.

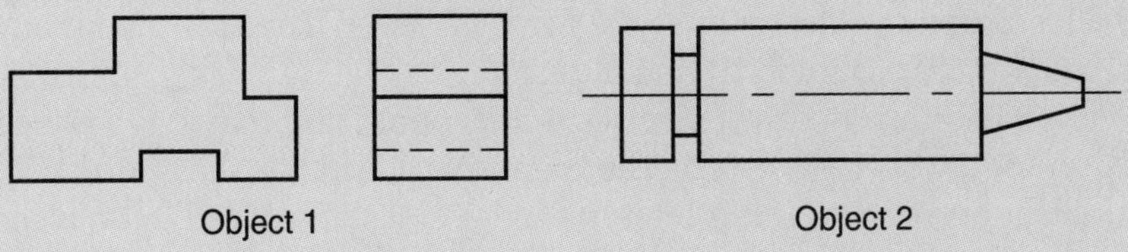

Object 1

Object 2

# LAYERS

In manual drafting, details of a design might be separated by placing them on different sheets of media. This is called *overlay* or *pin register* drafting. Each overlay is perfectly aligned with the others. All of the layers can be reproduced together to reflect the entire design. Individual layers might also be reproduced to show specific details. In AutoCAD, overlays are called *layers*. Using layers has certain benefits. These increase productivity.

- Specific information can be grouped on separate layers. For example, the floor plan can be drawn on one layer, the electrical plan on another, and the plumbing plan on a third layer.
- Drawings can be reproduced by individual layers or combined in any desired format. For example, the floor and electrical plan can be reproduced together and sent to an electrical contractor for a bid. The floor and plumbing plan can be reproduced together and sent to the plumbing contractor.
- Several drafters can work on a project at the same time to increase productivity.
- Each layer can be assigned a different color to help improve clarity.
- Each layer can be plotted in a different color or pen width.
- Selected layers can be turned off or frozen to decrease the clutter of information displayed on the screen, and to speed up drawing regeneration.
- Changes can be made to a layer promptly, often while the client watches.

## Layers used in different drafting fields

In mechanical drafting, views, hidden features, dimensions, sections, notes, and symbols might be placed on separate layers. In architectural drafting, there may be over a hundred layers. Layers may be created for floor plans, foundation plan, partition layout, plumbing, electrical, structural, roof drainage, reflected ceiling, and HVAC (heating, ventilating, and air conditioning) systems. Interior designers may use floor plan, interior partition, and furniture layers. In electronics drafting, each level of a multilevel circuit board is drawn on a separate layer.

## Layer colors

The number of layer colors available depends on your graphics card and monitor. A monochrome monitor displays only one color, usually white, amber, or green. Color systems usually support at least 256 colors. Many graphics cards support up to 16.7 million colors. Layer colors are coded by name and number. The first seven standard color numbers are given below. Assigning colors to layers is described later in the chapter.

| Number | Color |
|--------|---------|
| 1 | Red |
| 2 | Yellow |
| 3 | Green |
| 4 | Cyan |
| 5 | Blue |
| 6 | Magenta |
| 7 | White |

## Setting linetype by layer

AutoCAD allows you to select a linetype for each layer. Then, any item added to a layer is drawn with the linetype assigned to that layer.

As you have worked through the exercises in this book, you may have noticed that Layer 0 appears in the **Current Layer Name** box on the menu bar. Layer 0 is the AutoCAD default layer. It has a continuous linetype. Assigning linetype to layers is discussed later in this chapter.

## Naming layers

Layers should be given names to reflect what is drawn on them. Layer names can have up to 31 characters and can include letters, numbers, and special characters. Typical mechanical, architectural, and civil drafting layer names are as follows:

| <u>Mechanical</u> | | <u>Architectural</u> | <u>Civil</u> |
|---|---|---|---|
| OBJ | OBJECT | WALLS | PROPERTYLN |
| HID | HIDDEN | WINDOWS | STRUCTURES |
| CEN | CENTER | DOORS | ROADS |
| DIM | DIMENSION | ELECT | WATER |
| CONS | CONSTR | PLUMB | CONTOURS |
| HAT | HATCH | | |
| BOR | BORDER | | |

For simple drawings, layers can be named by linetype and color. For example, the layer name OBJECT-WHITE would have a continuous linetype drawn in white. The linetype and layer color number, such as OBJECT-7, can also be used. Another option is to assign the linetype a numerical value. For example, object lines can be 0, hidden lines 1, and centerlines 2. If you use this method, keep a written record of the numbering system for reference.

Lastly, layers can be given more complex names. The name might include the drawing number, color code, and layer content. The name DWG100-2-DIMEN refers to drawing DWG100, color 2, and DIMENSIONS layer.

## INTRODUCTION TO THE **LAYER** COMMAND

> AUG 6

When a layer is *current*, newly created objects are placed on that layer. The **LAYER** command has a variety of options dealing with layers. These options can be used in the **Layer Control** dialog box or at the **Command:** prompt.

### Using the **Layer Control** dialog box

> AUG 6

The **LAYER** command and all of its options can be used by accessing the **Layer Control** dialog box. To display this dialog box, pick the **Layers** button at the far left of the **Object Properties** toolbar, select **Layers...** from the **Data** pull-down menu, or type DDLMODES at the **Command:** prompt. Refer to Figure 19-27.

Many of the dialog box items are grayed-out until you move the arrow and click one of the listed layers. You can select as many layers as you want. When layers are selected, the

Figure 19-27. The **Layer Control** dialog box.

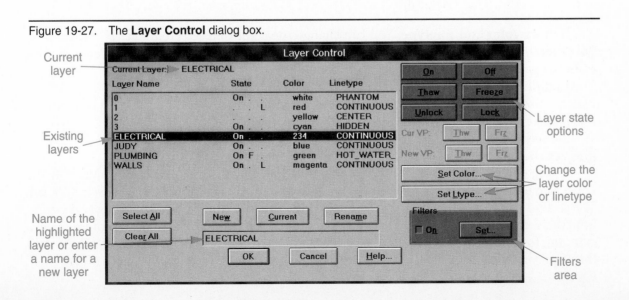

layer names are highlighted. When only one layer is selected, its name also appears in the text box at the bottom of the dialog box.

The **Layer Name list box.** The name of the current layer is displayed in the upper-left corner of the dialog box. Directly below the current layer name is the **Layer Name** list box. Here you see the names of the existing layers with their state, color, and linetype. The *state* is the layer status, such as on, frozen, or locked.

The **Select All** and **Clear All buttons.** Below the layer list are the **Select All** and **Clear All** buttons. Pick the **Select All** button if you want to select all of the layers in the list. Pick the **Clear All** button if you want to clear the list and remove the highlighting on all items picked. You can clear individual selections by repicking highlighted layers.

The **New, Current,** and **Rename buttons.** To add a new layer to the list, first pick in the edit box to activate the text cursor. Then, type the new layer name, such as PLUMBING, and pick the **New** button. The new layer name is added to the list, with the color white and linetype continuous. To make another layer current, pick a layer from the **Layer Name** list box to highlight, and then click the **Current** button.

When a layer is picked from the list, its name appears in the edit box. To change the layer name, make the changes in the edit box and click the **Rename** button. Notice in Figure 19-28 that the PLUMBING layer is being renamed as PLUMB.

Figure 19-28.   All layers can be selected or unselected using the **Select All** or **Clear All** buttons. To create a new layer, enter a name in the edit box and pick the **New** button.

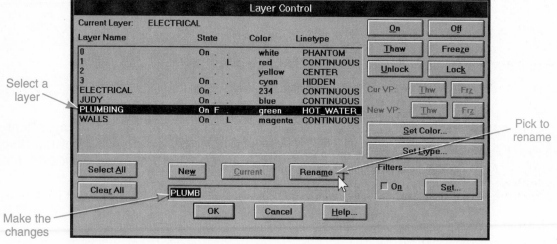

**Setting color and linetype.** You can change the color of a selected layer by picking the **Set Color...** button. Selecting this button displays the **Select Color** dialog box. Select the color from the palette, or enter the name or number of the color.

In order for a linetype to be changed, the linetype you want to use must first be loaded. Pick the **Set Ltype...** button to access the **Select Linetype** dialog box. Pick a linetype from the line list to change the highlighted layer to that linetype.

Notice in Figure 19-29 that the PLUMB layer is being changed to magenta and a dashed linetype. Be sure to click **OK** when you have completed making changes.

**Using the On, Off, Thaw, Freeze, Lock,** and **Unlock buttons.** The **State** column in the **Layer Name** list box provides the status of each layer. The first column in this list is for on/off. The second column indicates freeze/thaw, and the third column is for lock/unlock. A period (.) in these columns indicates off, thaw, or unlock. On, F, or L appearing in these columns indicates on, freeze, or lock. Highlight the desired layer in order to change the status. Then, click the appropriate button as needed. The current layer cannot be frozen, but can be turned off. Figure 19-30 shows several layers with different states.

Figure 19-29. A—Selecting **Set Color...** in the **Layer Control** dialog box opens the **Select Color** subdialog box. Choose a new color and then pick **OK**. B—Selecting **Set Ltype...** in the **Layer Control** dialog box opens the **Select Linetype** subdialog box. Choose a new linetype and then pick **OK**.

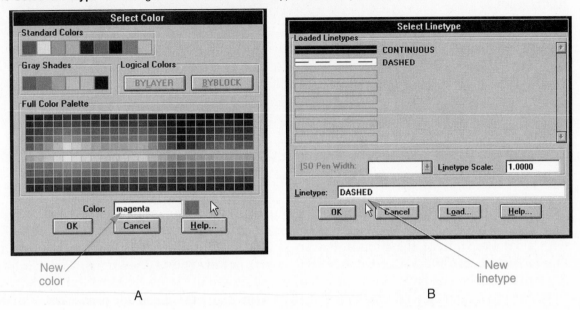

A

B

New color

New linetype

Figure 19-30. When you highlight layers in the **Layer Name** list box, the state of the layers can be changed. The state option buttons are shown here highlighted.

On/off column

Freeze/thaw column

Lock/unlock column

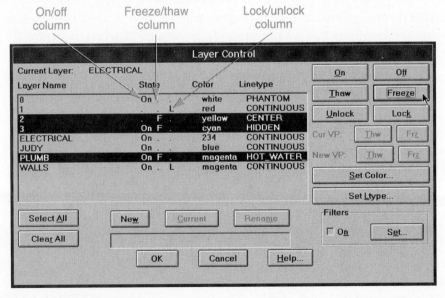

**Filtering layers.** *Layer filters* are used to screen, or filter, out any layers that have features that you do not want displayed in the **Layer Control** dialog box. These filters may include layer features such as name, color, or linetype. Filters can also involve the status of layers.

The **Filters** box has an **On** check box and a **Set...** button. The filters let you display only the layers you want in the **Layer Name** list box. For example, assume you are working on an electrical drawing, and want layers 0, 1, 3, and ELECTRICAL displayed. You can freeze the other layers and filter only the thawed layers. Layers can be filtered by any variable, such as name, state, color, or linetype. To do this, pick the **Set...** button to get the **Set Layer Filters** subdialog box. Filter the layer name, color, or linetype by entering the desired item in the related text box. If you want to display only the ELECTRICAL layer, then list its name as shown in Figure 19-31.

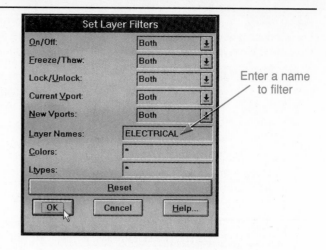

Figure 19-31.   Layers can be filtered by any variable using the **Set Layer Filters** subdialog box.

Enter a name to filter

You can use the wild card (*) to list a group of similar layers if desired. For example, if you want to filter all of the WALL layers, enter W*. This filters every layer name that starts with a W. Pick one of the drop-down arrows in the upper right to filter either **On/Off**, **Freeze/Thaw**, **Lock/Unlock**, **Current Vport** (viewport), or **New Vports** (viewports). For example, filter all of the thawed layers by setting **Thawed**, as shown in Figure 19-32A. Notice in Figure 19-32B that only the thawed layers are listed, and the filters **On** check box is checked. The **On** button is automatically checked when you pick the **OK** button in the **Set Layer Filters** dialog box. However, you can turn filters on or off at any time by clicking this check box.

## Using the LAYER command at the Command: prompt

The **LAYER** command and its options can also be entered at the **Command:** prompt. A list of **LAYER** command options and a brief description of each is given in Figure 19-33.

**Making new layers.** The **MAKE** option of the **LAYER** command is used to create a new layer, and at the same time, make the new layer current. For example, if you want to establish a new layer named JUDY and make it current, enter the following:

```
Command: LAYER ↵
?/Make/Set/New/ON/OFF/Color/Ltype/Freeze/Thaw/LOck/Unlock: M ↵
New current layer ⟨0⟩: JUDY ↵
?/Make/Set/New/ON/OFF/Color/Ltype/Freeze/Thaw/LOck/Unlock: ↵
```

Figure 19-32.   A—Layer filters being set. B—The result of filtering layers.

Select what to filter

Only layers that meet the filter setting are listed

Filters are turned on

A                                                            B

Figure 19-33. **LAYER** command options and their descriptions.

| | |
|---|---|
| **?** | Used to list layer names. Specific names can be entered, or an * can be entered to list all names. |
| **Make** | Used to create a new layer and make it current. |
| **Set** | Changes the current layer to the one specified. |
| **New** | Creates new layers without affecting the status of the current layer. |
| **ON** | Turns a layer on. Layers that are turned on are displayed, objects on them can be edited, and these layers are plotted. |
| **OFF** | Turns a layer off. Layers that are turned off are *not* displayed, objects on them *cannot* be edited, and these layers are *not* plotted. |
| **Color** | Changes the color of specific layers. You must supply the name or number of the color. |
| **Ltype** | Changes the linetype of specific layers. |
| **Freeze** | Freezes layers. Frozen layers are *not* displayed, objects on them *cannot* be edited, and these layers are *not* plotted. However, unlike layers that are off, frozen layers are not calculated by AutoCAD when a drawing is regenerated. |
| **Thaw** | Thaws layers. Thawed layers are displayed, objects on them can be edited, and these layers are plotted. |
| **LOck** | Locks layers. Layers that are locked are visible, but objects on them *cannot* be edited. |
| **Unlock** | Unlocks layers. Unlocked layers are visible and objects on them can be edited. |

However, new layers are usually created prior to beginning drawing, and then made current using the **Set** option. To create a new layer without making it current, use the **New** option as follows:

```
Command: LAYER ↵
?/Make/Set/New/ON/OFF/Color/Ltype/Freeze/Thaw/LOck/Unlock: N ↵
New layer name(s): ELECTRICAL ↵
?/Make/Set/New/ON/OFF/Color/Ltype/Freeze/Thaw/LOck/Unlock: ↵
```

The new layer named ELECTRICAL is created and ready to use when you need it. Notice the New layer name(s): prompt is either singular or plural. This means you can enter one or more layer names at the same time. Separate each name by a comma if you are specifying more than one layer. The following example creates three new layers:

```
New layer name(s): ELECTRICAL,PLUMBING,WALLS ↵
```

**Setting a current layer.** Layers must be created using the **Make** or **New** options before they can be set as current. However, once layers have been created, they can be set at any time. Layer 0 is the current layer set in the AutoCAD prototype drawing. If you want to make the ELECTRICAL layer (which you created earlier) current, follow this command sequence:

```
Command: LAYER ↵
?/Make/Set/New/ON/OFF/Color/Ltype/Freeze/Thaw/LOck/Unlock: S ↵
New current layer ⟨0⟩: ELECTRICAL ↵
?/Make/Set/New/ON/OFF/Color/Ltype/Freeze/Thaw/LOck/Unlock: ↵
```

**Layer color and linetype.** You can set a new layer's color and linetype, or change the color and linetype of an existing layer at any time. Use the **Color** and **Ltype** options as follows:

```
Command: LAYER ↵
?/Make/Set/New/ON/OFF/Color/Ltype/Freeze/Thaw/LOck/Unlock: C ↵
Color: (enter 5, B, or BLUE and press [Enter])
Layer name(s) for color 5 (blue) ⟨0⟩: ELECTRICAL ↵
?/Make/Set/New/ON/OFF/Color/Ltype/Freeze/Thaw/LOck/Unlock: L ↵
Linetype (or ?) ⟨CONTINUOUS⟩: PHANTOM ↵
Layer name(s) for linetype PHANTOM ⟨0⟩: ELECTRICAL ↵
?/Make/Set/New/ON/OFF/Color/Ltype/Freeze/Thaw/LOck/Unlock: ↵
```

**Putting it all together.** The following procedure is used to create three new layers named 1, 2, and 3 with colors red, yellow, and green, respectively. Assign these layers the linetypes hidden, center, and continuous, respectively. Remember, you can name layers individually or enter several layer names separated by commas.

```
Command: LAYER ↵
?/Make/Set/New/ON/OFF/Color/Ltype/Freeze/Thaw/LOck/Unlock: N ↵
New layers name(s): 1,2,3 ↵
?/Make/Set/New/ON/OFF/Color/Ltype/Freeze/Thaw/LOck/Unlock: C ↵
Color: 1 ↵
Layer name(s) for color 1 (red) ⟨0⟩: 1 ↵
?/Make/Set/New/ON/OFF/Color/Ltype/Freeze/Thaw/LOck/Unlock: C ↵
Color: 2 ↵
Layer name(s) for color 2 (yellow) ⟨0⟩: 2 ↵
?/Make/Set/New/ON/OFF/Color/Ltype/Freeze/Thaw/LOck/Unlock: C ↵
Color: 3 ↵
Layer name(s) for color 3 (green) ⟨0⟩: 3 ↵
?/Make/Set/New/ON/OFF/Color/Ltype/Freeze/Thaw/LOck/Unlock: L ↵
Linetype (or ?) ⟨CONTINUOUS⟩: HIDDEN ↵
Layer name(s) for linetype HIDDEN ⟨0⟩: 1 ↵
?/Make/Set/New/ON/OFF/Color/Ltype/Freeze/Thaw/LOck/Unlock: L ↵
Linetype (or ?) ⟨CONTINUOUS⟩: CENTER ↵
Layer name(s) for linetype CENTER ⟨0⟩: 2 ↵
```

Layer 3 contains dimensions. Dimension lines are continuous (solid) lines. Since CONTINUOUS is the default linetype, it is not necessary to assign it. After entering layer values, type ? to show a revised layer listing:

```
?/Make/Set/New/ON/OFF/Color/Ltype/Freeze/Thaw/LOck/Unlock:? ↵
Layer name(s) to list ⟨*⟩: ↵
```

| Layer name | State | Color | Linetype |
| --- | --- | --- | --- |
| 0 | On | 7 (white) | CONTINUOUS |
| 1 | On | 1 (red) | HIDDEN |
| 2 | On | 2 (yellow) | CENTER |
| 3 | On | 3 (green) | CONTINUOUS |
| ELECTRICAL | On | 5 (blue) | PHANTOM |
| JUDY | On | 7 (white) | CONTINUOUS |

```
Current layer: 0
?/Make/Set/New/ON/OFF/Color/Ltype/Freeze/Thaw/LOck/Unlock: ↵
Command:
```

Now, items added to layer 0 have white object lines. Items added to layer 1 have red hidden lines. Objects added to layer 2 have yellow centerlines. Dimensions added to layer 3 have solid green lines.

Once new layers and parameters are established, you can begin making the drawing. The steps below outline the sequence for completing a mechanical drawing. Keep records listing how you set up drawing prototypes. If your notes are not handy, list the layers, colors, and linetypes by typing ?.

- Make a sketch and prepare a plan sheet.
- Draw all object lines.
- Use the **Set** option of the **LAYER** command to select a new current layer to draw on. At this point, select layer 1 (that has hidden linetype).
- Draw all hidden lines.
- Set layer 2 as the current layer (that has centerlines).
- Draw all centerlines.
- Use the **Set** option of the **LAYER** command to select layer 3.
- Add dimensions. Dimensioning is discussed in Chapter 20 through Chapter 23.
- Set the current layer as necessary when editing the drawing.

## EXERCISE 19-5

❏ Load AutoCAD for Windows and open PRODR1.
❏ Set up six layers, each having a different color and linetype as follows:

| Layer name | Linetype | Color |
|---|---|---|
| Object | Continuous | White |
| Hidden | Hidden | Red |
| Center | Center | Yellow |
| Electric | Continuous | Green |
| Phantom | Phantom | Cyan |
| Dot | Dot | Blue |
| Dim | Continuous | Magenta |

❏ Save as A:PRODR2, thus establishing a new prototype with the specified layers.
❏ Draw the objects shown below. Place objects on the layer that has their linetype. The dimension layer will not be used at this time.
❏ Save the drawing as A:EX19-5 and quit.

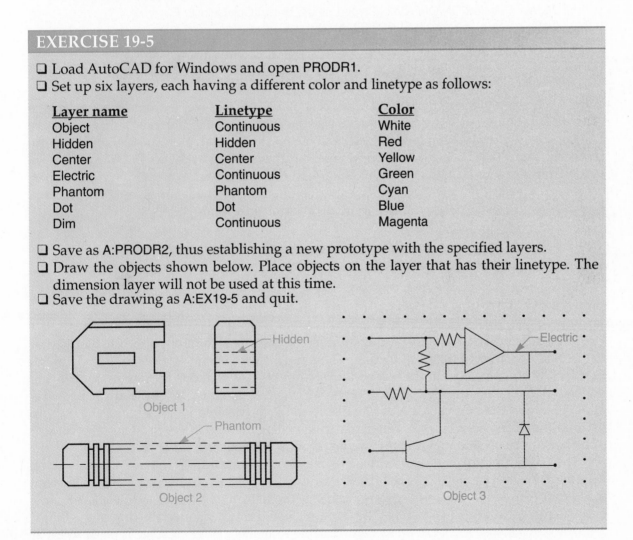

Object 1

Object 2

Object 3

**Turning layers on and off.** Layers that are turned on are displayed and plotted, but layers that are turned off are not displayed or plotted. Even though a layer is turned off, it is still regenerated with the rest of the drawing. To turn off a layer, follow this procedure:

>Command: **LAYER** ↵
>?/Make/Set/New/ON/OFF/Color/Ltype/Freeze/Thaw/LOck/Unlock: **OFF** ↵
>Layer name(s) to turn Off: **ELECTRICAL** ↵

If the layer you are turning off is the current layer, the following message appears:

>Really want layer ELECTRICAL (the CURRENT layer) off? ⟨N⟩ ↵

Press [Enter] if you do not want the current layer turned off, or enter Y and press [Enter] if you do want it turned off. Do not try to draw with the current layer off. You can draw with the current layer off, but you will not see the results until you turn it back on. Either turn it on or set another layer current. Simply use the **ON** option to turn layers back on.

**Freezing and thawing layers.** Frozen layers are not displayed and are not calculated by the computer when a regeneration occurs, thus saving time. Freeze layers like this:

>Command: **LAYER** ↵
>?/Make/Set/New/ON/OFF/Color/Ltype/Freeze/Thaw/LOck/Unlock: **F** ↵
>Layer name(s) to Freeze: **ELECTRICAL** ↵

If you try to freeze the current layer, AutoCAD responds with this message:

>Cannot freeze layer ELECTRICAL. It is the CURRENT layer.

If you really want to freeze the current layer, first make another layer current. Then, freeze the layer that was previously the current layer. Use the **Thaw** option to unfreeze a frozen layer.

**Locking and unlocking layers.** Unlocked layers can be drawn on, and objects on those layers can be edited. Locked layers are visible, but they cannot be drawn on. The objects on locked layers cannot be edited. Current layers can even be locked. For example, lock a layer (or several layers) if you want to be sure that no one tampers with the objects drawn on it. Lock a layer as follows. Note the use of the two-character response LO.

>Command: **LAYER** ↵
>?/Make/Set/New/ON/OFF/Color/Ltype/Freeze/Thaw/LOck/Unlock: **LO** ↵
>Layer name(s) to Lock: **ELECTRICAL** ↵

## QUICKLY SETTING A LAYER CURRENT

You can quickly change to another layer using the **Layer Control** pop-up list located at the left side of **Object Properties** toolbar. The name of the current layer is displayed in the box. Pick the down arrow in the box and a list appears that contains the names of all layers defined in the current drawing, Figure 19-34. When a command is active, the arrow button is grayed-out and the pop-up list is not available. Click the desired layer name in the pop-up list, and that layer is set current. When many layers are defined in the drawing, the vertical scroll bar can be used to move up and down through the list.

The **Layer Control** pop-up also has several icons indicating the status of each layer. Including the layer name, there are six fields for each layer. The meaning of each icon is given in Figure 19-35. By picking an icon, you can change the state of the layer. Selecting a layer name to set as current automatically closes the pop-up list and returns you to the drawing editor.

You can also use the **CLAYER** system variable to make a layer current. Type **CLAYER** at the **Command:** prompt as follows:

>Command: **CLAYER** ↵
>New value for CLAYER ⟨current layer⟩: (enter the name of an existing layer and
>    press [Enter])

Figure 19-34.  The **Layer Control** pop-up list is located at the left side of **Object Properties** toolbar. All layers are listed with icons representing their state and color.

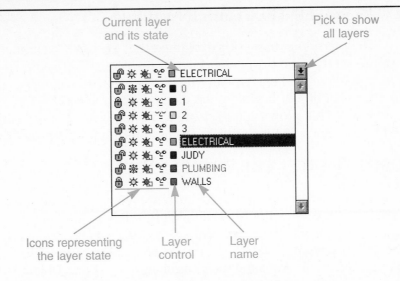

Current layer and its state

Pick to show all layers

Icons representing the layer state

Layer control

Layer name

Figure 19-35.  The icons that appear in the **Layer Control** pop-up and their meaning.

| Icon | Meaning |
|------|---------|
|  | Layer is currently unlocked. Picking this icon locks the layer. |
|  | Layer is currently locked. Picking this icon unlocks the layer. |
|  | Layer is currently frozen. Picking this icon thaws the layer. |
|  | Layer is currently thawed. Picking this icon freezes the layer. |
|  | Viewport layer status (disabled). This is covered in Chapter 26. |
|  | Layer is currently on. Picking this icon turns the layer off. |
|  | Layer is currently off. Picking this icon turns the layer on. |
|  | Current layer color assignment. Picking this icon does nothing. |
| ELECTRICAL | Current layer name. Pick a layer name to make it current. |

**PROFESSIONAL TIP**

Layers are meant to simplify the drafting process. They separate different details of the drawing and can reduce the complexity of what is displayed. If you set color and linetype by layer, do not reset and mix entity linetypes and color on the same layer. Doing so can mislead you and your colleagues when trying to find certain details. Maintain accurate records of your prototype setup for future reference.

# CONTROLLING LAYERS IN VIEWPORTS

The preceding discussion explained that the **LAYER** command's **Freeze/Thaw** and **On/Off** options set the visibility of layers in all viewports. This is known as *global control*. For example, if you freeze a layer globally, it is invisible in all viewports. If you want to set the visibility or invisibility of layers in one viewport or a specific set of viewports, use the **VPLAYER** command. This allows you to create a specific layer that is visible in a designated viewport. Refer to Chapter 26 for complete discussions of viewports and the **VPLAYER** command.

# USING ENTITY CREATION MODES

You can see the properties of current layers, or set the color, linetype, text style, or layer using the **Object Creation Modes** dialog box. It is accessed by clicking the **Object Creation** button in the **Object Properties** toolbar, picking **Object Creation...** from the **Data** pull-down menu, or by typing DDEMODES at the **Command:** prompt. The changes made may not be displayed until you enter the next command. A typical **Object Creation Modes** dialog box is shown in Figure 19-36. Notice that the color is currently set as BYLAYER, which is a common practice. Select a new color by picking the **Color...** button to access the **Select Color** subdialog box. Pick the **Layer...** button to make changes to the layer or add a new layer using the **Layer Control** subdialog box.

The **Text Style...** button accesses the **Select Text Style** subdialog box shown in Figure 19-37. This is a convenient way to change the text style. Simply pick one of the available styles in the list box, or type the name of a loaded text style in the **Style Name:** text box. When you pick a style, the image tile changes to display a sample of the selected style. You can enter your own text in the **Sample Text:** text box. The current font, height, width, obliquing angle, and generation format are also given at the lower-left of the subdialog box. Click the **Show All...** button to display the **Text Style Symbol Set** subdialog box. This dialog box shows all of the current text fonts. The elevation and thickness items in this dialog box refer to 3D values, which are discussed in Chapter 29.

Figure 19-36. The **Object Creation Modes** dialog box is used to view properties of the current layer. These properties can be changed, as well as a different layer made current or a new layer created (by accessing the **Layer Control** dialog box).

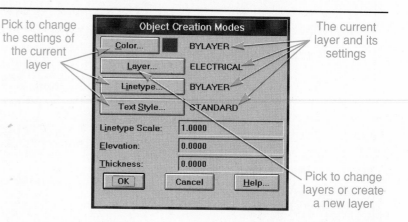

Pick to change the settings of the current layer

Object Creation Modes

The current layer and its settings

Pick to change layers or create a new layer

Figure 19-37.   The **Select Text Style** subdialog box is a convenient way to view and change the text style.

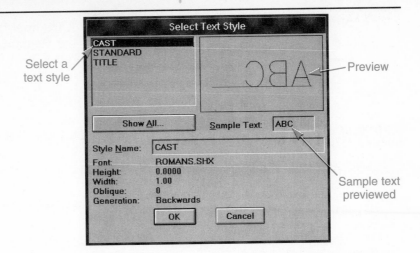

## CHANGING LAYERS

In Chapters 11, 13, and 14, you were introduced to the **CHANGE**, **CHPROP**, and **DDCHPROP** commands. These commands are convenient for editing a drawing. The **CHPROP** and **DDCHPROP** commands are the most convenient for changing layer, linetype, or color since they directly access the property options. For example, the **LA** option of the **CHPROP** command moves an object from one layer to another. This option only works if the intended layer has been created. When you enter LA and press [Enter], AutoCAD asks for the new layer. Suppose the current layer, shown in brackets, is FLPLAN. If the object should be on the ELECTRIC layer, proceed as follows:

> Command: **CHPROP** ↵
> Select objects: *(pick or window the object to be changed)*
> Select objects: ↵
> Change what property (Color/LAyer/LType/ltScale/Thickness)? **LA** ↵
> New layer ⟨FLPLAN⟩: **ELECTRIC** ↵
> Change what property (Color/LAyer/LType/ltScale/Thickness)? ↵

## RENAMING LAYERS

Using the **DDRENAME** command, you can rename many items, including layer, linetype, and text style. This command accesses the **Rename** dialog box shown in Figure 19-38. Pick any of the named objects, such as **Layer**, to get a list of items related to the object. To change the name of a layer, pick that layer from the **Items** list. Picking ELECTRICAL, for example, places it in the **Old Name:** text box. Next, type the new name in the **Rename To:** text box, followed by clicking the **Rename To:** button. Finally, click the **OK** button to exit the dialog box.

Figure 19-38.   The **Rename** dialog box is used to rename named objects such as layers, viewports, and views.

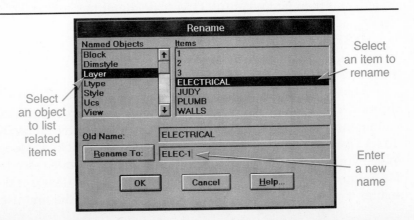

**NOTE**

Layer 0 and the CONTINUOUS linetype cannot be renamed and, therefore, do not appear in the **Rename** dialog box list of named objects. All other layers, linetypes, and text styles can be renamed using this dialog box.

---

## EXERCISE 19-6

❑ Load AutoCAD for Windows, open EX19-5, and erase the drawing shown on-screen.
❑ Change the layers as follows:

| Layer name | Linetype | Color |
|------------|----------|-------|
| VIEW | Continuous | White |
| HIDDEN | Hidden | Red |
| CENTER | Center | Blue |

❑ Omit layers 3-3, 4-4, and 5-5.
❑ Save the drawing as A:EX19-6.
❑ Given the pictorial drawing and three incomplete orthographic views of the object below, draw the three orthographic views without dimensions. Add any object, hidden, or centerlines needed to complete the views. Place object lines on the VIEW layer, hidden lines on the HIDDEN layer, and centerlines on the CENTER layer. Use X and Y filters to help project features from one view to another.
❑ Save the drawing again as A:EX19-6 and quit the drawing session.

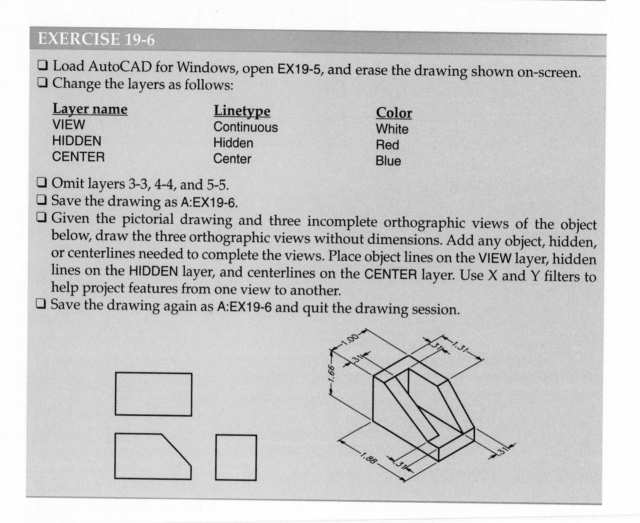

---

## SETTING UP YOUR SHEET FOR MULTIVIEW LAYOUT          `AUG 10`

AutoCAD has the **MVSETUP** command that allows you to insert one of several different predrawn standard border and title block formats based on ANSI, ISO, architectural, or generic layouts. The border and title block can be set up before plotting where they can be scaled, and then plotted at full (1:1) scale. Refer to Chapter 12 for information regarding the use of paper space viewports, and scaling a viewport.

**MVSETUP** is an AutoLISP routine that can be customized to insert any type of border and title block. AutoLISP is covered in *AutoCAD and its Applications—Advanced, Release 13 for Windows*.

To use **MVSETUP**, first open a drawing that you want to display. To access **MVSETUP** through the pull-down menus, you must first be in paper space. The **Floating Viewports** cascading menu in the **View** pull-down is disabled when the **TILEMODE** system variable is set to 1. To set **TILEMODE** to 0 and enable paper space, select **Floating Model Space** from the **View** menu. When you reselect the **View** menu, the **Floating Viewports** cascading menu is enabled. Pick the **MV Setup** option from this cascading menu. The current state of the **TILEMODE** variable doesn't matter if you type in the **MVSETUP** command. After the first use of **MVSETUP**, you can enter

MVS as the command name. The following is the command sequence for using **MVSETUP** the first time:

> Command: **MVSETUP** ↵
> Initializing…
> Enable paper space?(No/⟨Yes⟩): ↵

Pressing [Enter] to accept the default Yes automatically turns off the **TILEMODE** system variable. Notice the paper space UCS icon is displayed and your drawing has disappeared. If you turn **TILEMODE** off before entering **MVSETUP**, the Enable paper space? prompt does not appear. The **TILEMODE** system variable is discussed more later.

The **Title block** option of the **MVSETUP** command lets you establish a drawing border and title block. The title block is created on the current layer and with the current linetype and color. Therefore, it is a good idea to create a layer specifically for the drawing border and title block and set it as the current layer *before* using the **MVSETUP** command. If you forget to set the layer current before entering the command, use **Options** choice of the **MVSETUP** command. This option allows you to set a different layer current, change your drawing limits, or change drawing units before the drawing border and title block are drawn. **Options** is discussed later in the chapter.

> Align/Create/Scale viewports/Options/Title block/Undo: **T** ↵
> Delete objects/Origin/Undo/⟨Insert title block⟩: ↵

The default suboption of the **Title block** option allows you to insert a title block. The **Title block** suboptions are:
- **Delete objects.** Allows you to select objects to delete from paper space.
- **Origin.** Permits you to relocate the sheet origin.
- **Undo.** Undoes the previous operation.
- **Insert title block.** This is the default. When selected, the following is displayed in the text window:

> Available title block options:
>
> | | |
> |---|---|
> | 0: | None |
> | 1: | ISO A4 Size(mm) |
> | 2: | ISO A3 Size(mm) |
> | 3: | ISO A2 Size(mm) |
> | 4: | ISO A1 Size(mm) |
> | 5: | ISO A0 Size(mm) |
> | 6: | ANSI-V Size(in) *(this is the vertical A-size format)* |
> | 7: | ANSI-A Size(in) *(this is the horizontal A-size format)* |
> | 8: | ANSI-B Size(in) |
> | 9: | ANSI-C Size(in) |
> | 10: | ANSI-D Size(in) |
> | 11: | ANSI-E Size(in) |
> | 12: | Arch/Engineering (24 × 36 in) |
> | 13: | Generic D size Sheet (24 × 36 in) |
>
> Add/Delete/Redisplay/⟨Number of entry to load⟩: *(type the desired sheet size format, such as 7, and press [Enter])*

Next, you get a message that asks if you want to create a drawing with the sheet size specifications you selected. The following prompt appears if you select number 7 and a file named ANSI-A.DWG is not in your AutoCAD directory:

> Create a drawing named ansi-a.dwg? ⟨Y⟩: ↵

Pressing [Enter] at this prompt creates a drawing file with the name shown. ANSI-A.DWG is now available to be used as a prototype for the future. AutoCAD automatically draws the border and title block shown in Figure 19-39.

Figure 19-39. One of the border and title block arrangements available with the **MVSETUP** command.

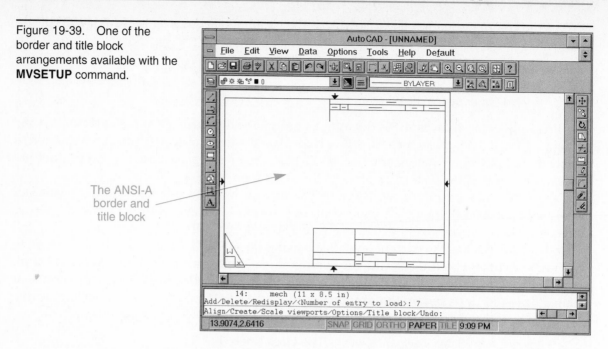

The ANSI-A border and title block

The **Create** option is used to establish the viewports once the border and title block are inserted. The command sequence is:

> Align/Create/Scale viewports/Options/Title block/Undo: **C** ⏎
> Delete objects/Undo/⟨Create viewports⟩: ⏎

Press [Enter] and a list of the viewport layout options is displayed:

> Available Mview viewport layout options:
> 0:      None
> 1:      Single
> 2:      Std. Engineering
> 3:      Array of Viewports
> Redisplay/⟨Number of entry to load⟩: **1** ⏎

A single viewpoint works best for this application. The next prompt asks you to identify the boundary for the viewport by picking the opposite corners. This is similar to forming a window.

> Bounding area for viewports. Default/⟨First point⟩: (*pick a point*)
> Other point: (*move the cursor and pick the second point*)

The model space drawing that you started with is now displayed inside the paper space viewport, Figure 19-40.

The **Scale** option of the **MVSETUP** command is used to scale the drawing. This option uses a ratio of paper space units to model space units. For example, 1:2 is one paper space unit for two model space units, or a one-half scale, as shown in Figure 19-41. The defaults are full scale, or 1:1, and are used in the following example. The drawing may not change much in size, depending on the size of the viewports. The command sequence is:

> Align/Create/Scale viewports/Options/Title block/Undo: **S** ⏎
> Select the viewports to scale:
> Select objects: (*pick the viewport outline, not the drawing*)
> Select objects: ⏎
> Enter the ratio of paper space units to model space units...
> Number of paper space units. ⟨1.0⟩: ⏎
> Number of model space units. ⟨1.0⟩: ⏎
> Align/Create/Scale viewports/Options/Title block/Undo: ⏎

Figure 19-40.   Opening a viewport.

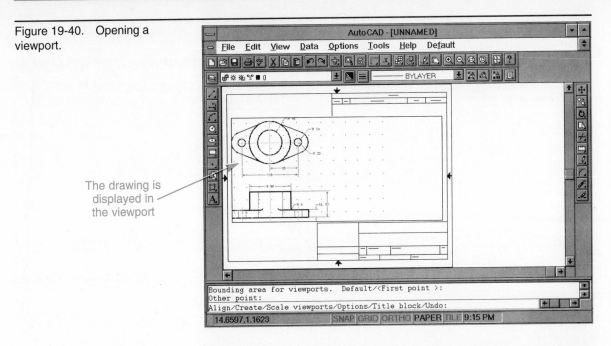

The drawing is displayed in the viewport

Figure 19-41.   Viewports are scaled with the **Scale viewport** option of the **MVSETUP** command.

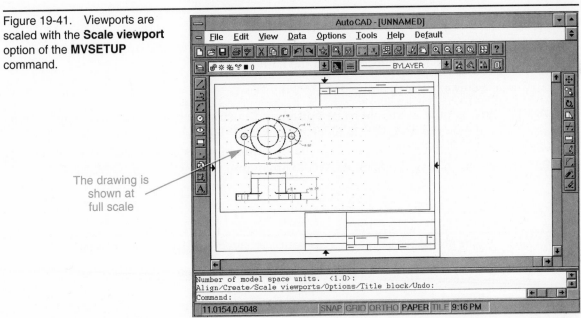

The drawing is shown at full scale

A viewport is an entity that can be altered in paper space using **MOVE**, **STRETCH**, or grips as needed. Part of your drawing may extend past the edge of the viewport after using the **Scale** option. Simply use the **STRETCH** command to compensate for the miscalculation. Figure 19-42A shows the results of using the **MOVE** command to position the drawing shown in Figure 19-40.

You can also use grips to scale the viewport so the viewport borders do not overlap the title block and sheet border. To do this, pick the viewport, activate a hot grip, and press [Enter] to access the **SCALE** command. Then, enter a new scale factor like this:

```
** SCALE **
⟨Scale factor⟩/Base point/Copy/Undo/Reference/eXit: .8 ↵
```

The results are shown in Figure 19-42B. Notice that this only affects the viewport, not the drawing.

Figure 19-42.   You can **Move**, **Stretch**, or **Scale** a viewport using grips, or by first entering the desired command.

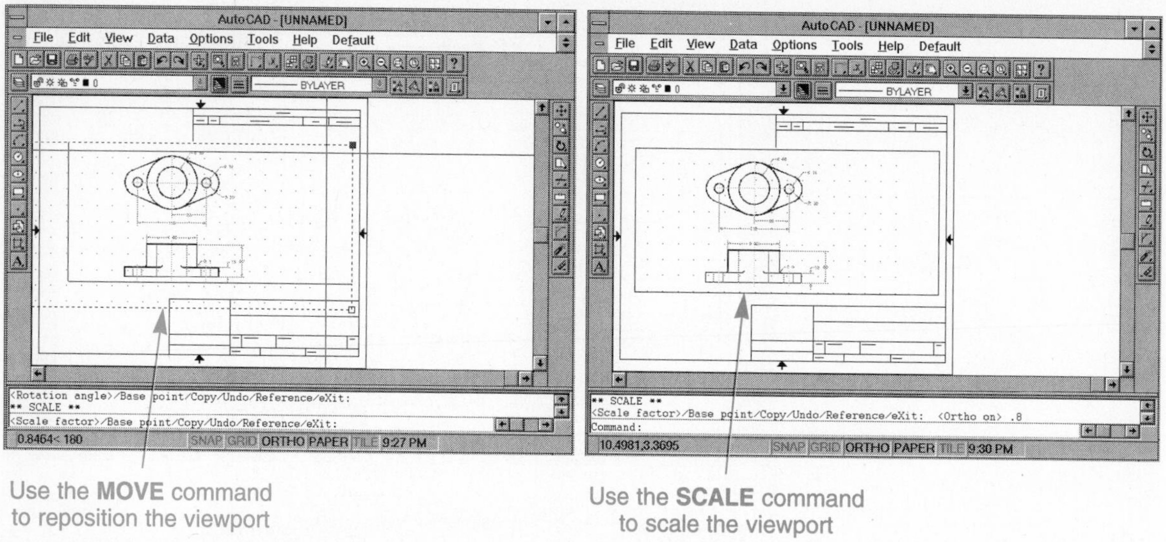

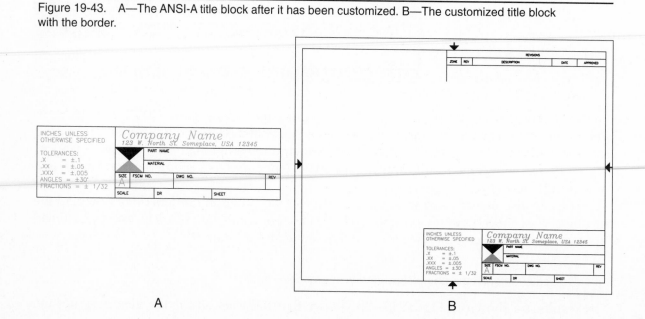

Use the **MOVE** command
to reposition the viewport

A

Use the **SCALE** command
to scale the viewport

B

## Creating your own title block format

Making a selection from the list of Available title block options: and answering Y to the following prompt creates a drawing file with the name shown:

Create a drawing named ansi-a.dwg? ⟨Y⟩: ↵

The ANSI-A.DWG is now available to be edited and customized for your own applications. Figure 19-43A shows the ANSI-A title block customized. Figure 19-43B shows the entire border with the customized title block. Now that the title block is customized, you can use the **SAVEAS** command to save the ANSI-A.DWG to any name you wish, such as MECH-A.

Figure 19-43.   A—The ANSI-A title block after it has been customized. B—The customized title block with the border.

A

B

When you begin a new drawing, use MECH-A as the prototype and provide a new drawing name, such as PART001, Figure 19-44. When you pick **OK**, the MECH-A format is loaded and ready for you to create the PART001 drawing.

You can also use the MECH-A format and insert a drawing that was previously created. This is useful to create several prototypes for different sheet sizes and title block formats. This is also often used to customize a list of drawings, as explained in the next section.

Figure 19-44.   Using the MECH-A prototype for a drawing called PART001.

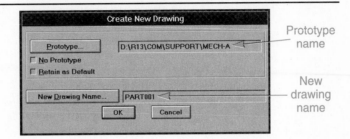

## Adding title blocks to the MVSETUP list

Following the list of available title block options is the Add/Delete/Redisplay/⟨Number of entry to load⟩: prompt. The **Add** option allows you to customize the list of prototype drawings by naming the drawing type and size, and inserting a specific drawing. The following sequence gives you an idea of how this works:

> ALign/Create/Scale viewports/Options/Title block/Undo: **T** ↵
> Add/Delete/Redisplay/⟨Number of entry to load⟩: **A** ↵
> Title block description: **MECH (11 X 8.5 IN)** ↵
> Drawing to insert (without extension): **SAMPLE** ↵
> Specify default usable area? ⟨Y⟩: **N** ↵

If you press [Enter] to accept the default yes to this prompt, AutoCAD asks you to pick two points that define the usable area. However, the N response shown above is more convenient and works well in most situations. If you do define the usable area, it is a good idea to locate the lower-left of the title block at 0,0. You are then prompted to locate the upper-right corner of the title block. You may enter coordinates or pick a diagonal corner at this second prompt.

The **File Utility** menu flashes briefly on the text screen and then a new Available title block options: list is displayed. The new border and title block design you specified appears in the revised list as one of the options:

> 14. MECH (11 X 8.5 IN)
> Add/Delete/Redisplay/⟨number of entry to load⟩: *(enter a desired sheet format, such as 14, and press* [Enter]*)*

If you press [Enter] at this prompt without typing a number, the **MVSETUP** command option line is redisplayed as follows:

> Align/Create/Scale viewports/Options/Title block/Undo: *(select another option or press* [Enter] *to exit* **MVSETUP***)*

## Additional MVSETUP options

The following descriptions outline the remaining **MVSETUP** options:

- **Align.** This option is used to align views in multiple viewports. You get this prompt when you use the **Align** option:

  Angled/Horizontal/Vertical alignment/Rotate view/Undo:

  - **Angled**—This suboption is used to pan a drawing in a viewport at a desired angle. The following prompts are displayed:

    Base point: (*pick a point as an origin*)
    Other point: (*pick a point in the viewport to be panned*)
    Distance from base point: (*enter a distance and press* [Enter], *or pick two points to establish a distance from the base point*)
    Angle from base point: (*enter an angular value and press* [Enter], *or pick two points representing an angle where the second point is to be positioned from the base point*)

  - **Horizontal**—This suboption allows you to align views in horizontal viewports:

    Base point: (*pick a point as an origin*)
    Other point: (*pick a point in the viewport to be aligned*)

  - **Vertical alignment**—This suboption allows you to align entities in vertical viewports in a manner similar to the **Horizontal** option.
  - **Rotate view**—This suboption allows you to rotate a drawing in a viewport around a selected base point:

    Specify in which viewport the view is to be rotated.
    Base point: (*pick a point as the pivot point for the rotation*)
    Angle from base point: (*enter an angle and press* [Enter], *or pick two points representing the angle*)

- **Options.** This option lets you establish several different functions that are associated with your layout. The prompt issued with **Options** is:

  Set Layer/LImits/Units/Xref:

- **Set Layer**—This suboption allows you to specify an existing layer or create a new layer for your border and title block. It is a good idea to put your border and title block on a separate layer, perhaps BORDER. This gives you the flexibility to freeze, thaw, or otherwise manipulate the layer as needed. Enter L for layer to get this prompt:

  Layer name for title block or . for current layer: **BORDER** ↵

- **Limits**—This suboption instructs AutoCAD to reset the drawing limits so it is equal to the extents when the border is inserted. The prompt has a No default:

  Set drawing limits? ⟨N⟩: ↵

- **Units**—This suboption allows you to specify the value that drawing information is presented in. Inch units are the default. You can also enter F for feet, ME or meters, or M for millimeters:

  Paper space units are in Feet/Inches/MEters/Millimeters? ⟨in⟩:

- **Xref**—This suboption determines if the border and title block is to be inserted in the drawing, or referenced to a master drawing. A referenced drawing is not added to the current drawing file, but is displayed. A referenced drawing is also referred to as *attached*. This helps to keep the file smaller. Referencing drawings is discussed in detail in Chapter 26. The default is **Insert**, or you can type A and press [Enter] for **Attach** as follows:

> Xref Attach or Insert title block? ⟨Insert⟩: ↵

## Working with the **TILEMODE** system variable

The **TILEMODE** system variable is on when it is set to 1. **TILEMODE** must be turned off to have AutoCAD provide you with the standard border and title block formats that were previously discussed. You can also answer yes to the Enable paper space? (No/⟨Yes⟩): prompt. The **TILEMODE** can be set to on (1) or off (0) like this:

> Command: **TILEMODE** ↵
> New value for TILEMODE ⟨0⟩: **1** ↵
> Regenerating drawing.
> Command:

You get the Enable paper space? (No/⟨Yes⟩): prompt with **TILEMODE** on when you enter the **MVSETUP** command:

> Command: **MVSETUP** ↵
> Enable paper space?(No/⟨Yes⟩): **N** ↵

Answering no to the above prompt gives you the opportunity to establish your own model space drawing units, scale, and paper size. The prompts continue like this:

> Units type (Scientific/Decimal/Engineering/Architectural/Metric): *(enter the desired units, D for example.)*

The text screen is displayed with several scale options to choose from. Each of the **Units type** options give you a different list. This is the **Decimal scales** list:

> Decimal Scales
> (4.0)    4 TIMES
> (2.0)    2 TIMES
> (1.0)    FULL
> (0.5)    HALF
> (0.25)   QUARTER
> Enter the scale factor: *(enter the desired scale, such as 1)*
> Enter the paper width: *(enter the paper width, such as 11)*
> Enter the paper height: *(enter the paper height, such as 8.5)*
> Command:

AutoCAD now uses the settings that you establish to draw a polyline border at the drawing limits.

## EXERCISE 19-7

❑ Use the **MVSETUP** command to insert the drawing from Exercise 19-6 (EX19-6) into a standard ANSI-A border and title block format.
❑ Adjust the scale and orientation as needed.
❑ Save the drawing as A:EX19-7 and quit the drawing session.

## CHAPTER TEST

*Write your answers in the spaces provided.*

1. Give the command and entries required to display AutoCAD's standard linetypes:

   Command:_____

   ?/Create/Load/Set: _____

   File to list ⟨ACAD⟩:_____

   ?/Create/Load/Set: _____

2. Supply the command and entries needed to make CENTER the new linetype:

   Command:_____

   ?/Create/Load/Set: _____

   New entity linetype (or ?) ⟨*current*⟩: _____

   ?/Create/Load/Set: _____

3. Provide the command and entries that change the linetype scale to .5:

   Command:_____

   New scale factor ⟨1⟩: _____

4. Give the command and entries to create three layers named HIDDEN, CENTER, and
   DIMENSION. The names and associated linetypes and colors are:

   | **Layer Name** | **Linetype** | **Color** |
   |---|---|---|
   | HIDDEN | HIDDEN | RED |
   | CENTER | CENTER | YELLOW |
   | DIMENSION | CONTINUOUS | GREEN |

   Command:_____

   ?/Make/Set/New/ON/OFF/Color/Ltype/Freeze/Thaw/LOck/Unlock: _____

   New layer name(s):_____

   ?/Make/Set/New/ON/OFF/Color/Ltype/Freeze/Thaw/LOck/Unlock: _____

   Color:_____

   Layer name(s) for color red ⟨0⟩: _____

   ?/Make/Set/New/ON/OFF/Color/Ltype/Freeze/Thaw/LOck/Unlock: _____

   Color:_____

   Layer name(s) for color yellow ⟨0⟩: _____

   ?/Make/Set/New/ON/OFF/Color/Ltype/Freeze/Thaw/LOck/Unlock: _____

   Color:_____

   Layer name(s) for color green ⟨0⟩: _____

   ?/Make/Set/New/ON/OFF/Color/Ltype/Freeze/Thaw/LOck/Unlock: _____

   Linetype (or ?) ⟨CONTINUOUS⟩: _____

   Layer name(s) for linetype HIDDEN ⟨0⟩: _____

   ?/Make/Set/New/ON/OFF/Color/Ltype/Freeze/Thaw/LOck/Unlock: _____

   Linetype (or ?) ⟨CONTINUOUS⟩: _____

   Layer name(s) for linetype CENTER ⟨0⟩: _____

   ?/Make/Set/New/ON/OFF/Color/Ltype/Freeze/Thaw/LOck/Unlock: _____

5. How do you change the color from yellow to magenta at the **Command:** prompt? Assume that you are working on a single layer.

   Command:_____

   New entity color ⟨yellow⟩: _____

6. Identify five guidelines to consider when selecting the front view.

   _____

   _____

   _____

   _____

   _____

7. Suppose the axis of a hole is perpendicular to a slanted surface. The auxiliary view shows the hole as _____.

8. The default linetype in AutoCAD _____.

9. Name at least ten of AutoCAD's standard linetypes.

   _____     _____

   _____     _____

   _____     _____

   _____     _____

   _____     _____

10. In the chart provided, list the seven standard color names and their number.

| Color Name | Color Name |
|------------|------------|
|            |            |
|            |            |
|            |            |
|            |            |
|            |            |
|            |            |
|            |            |

11. When you enter the **LAYER** command and select the **?** option, the prompt Layer name(s) for listing ⟨*⟩: appears. What does the asterisk ⟨*⟩ in default brackets mean? _____

    _____

12. Describe the **Make** option of the **LAYER** command. _____

    _____

    _____

13. Describe the **Set** option of the **LAYER** command. _____

    _____

14. Describe the **New** option of the **LAYER** command. _____

    _____

    _____

15. How are the new layer names entered when creating several layers at the same time? __

    _____

16. Which pull-down menu contains the **Layer Control...** option? _____

17. Identify two ways to access the **Layer Control** dialog box. _____

_____

_____

18. What condition must exist before a linetype can be chosen from the **Layer Control** dialog box?

_____

19. How do you make another layer current in the **Layer Control** dialog box? _____

_____

20. How do you change a layer's linetype in the **Layer Control** dialog box? _____

_____

21. When is the **Select Color** dialog box displayed? _____

_____

22. How do you load several linetypes at the same time? _____

_____

23. When is a linetype displayed in the **Select Linetype** dialog box? _____

_____

24. What is the state of a layer that is not displayed on the screen and is not calculated by the computer when the drawing is regenerated? _____

25. Describe the purpose of locking a layer. _____

_____

_____

26. Are locked layers visible? _____

27. If you get the message Cannot freeze layer PROD002. It is the CURRENT layer, what should you do if you want to freeze the layer? _____

_____

28. How do you select all of the layers in the **Layer Control** dialog box list at the same time?

_____

_____

29. When looking at the **State** column in the **Layer Control** dialog box, how do you know if a layer is either off, thawed, or unlocked? _____

30. Describe the purpose of layer filters. _____

_____

31. Identify two ways to access the **Object Creation Modes** dialog box. _____

_____

32. List at least four items that can be set using the **Object Creation Modes** dialog box. _____

_____

33. Name two commands that allow you to directly access property options for changing layer, linetype, or color. _____

34. Name the command that lets you rename layers, linetypes, and text styles. _____

35. The command that allows you to insert one of several different predrawn standard border and title block formats is _____

36. Name the system variable that must be off (0) in order to enter paper space. _____

37. Explain the **Insert title block** default obtained after entering the **Title block** option in the **MVS** command. _____

_____

38. What happens when you press [Enter] at this prompt?
Create a drawing named ansi-a.dwg?⟨Y⟩: _____

_____

39. Describe the purpose of the **Create** option of the **MVS** command. _____

_____

40. How is a drawing displayed when you set the **Scale** option of the **MVS** command to 1 paper space unit and 2 model space units? _____

41. What should you do if the drawing is initially displayed too far to the upper right of the sheet format when inserted in the viewport using the **MVS** command? _____

_____

_____

42. Describe how you can customize a standard title block available in the **MVS** command and save it as a prototype called MECH-A. _____

_____

_____

43. How do you begin a new drawing named WALLEYE using the prototype described in question 42? _____

_____

_____

44. How do you add the custom title block name ARCH-C to the **Available title block options** list?_____

_____

45. Describe the function and importance of the **Set Layer** suboption in the **Options** selection of the **MVS** command. _____

_____

46. Explain the difference between the results obtained from the **XLINE** command and the **RAY** command._____

_____

_____

47. Describe how the **XLINE** default option works. _____

_____

48. Name the **XLINE** option that lets you draw a construction line at a specified angle through a specified point. _____

49. Identify the pull-down menu and the selection used to access the **Object Creation** dialog box and then the pick needed to get the **Select Linetype** dialog box. _____

_____

_____

50. How is it possible to load all of the available linetypes when using the **Load or Reload Linetypes** subdialog box? _____

_____

_____

_____

## DRAWING PROBLEMS

*Mechanical Drafting*

1. Draw the views necessary to describe the object completely. Draw on one layer and use the **LINETYPE** command to change linetypes. Do not dimension. Save your drawing as A:P19-1.

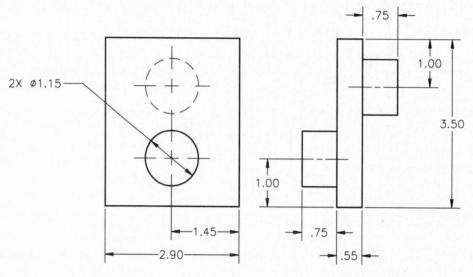

*Mechanical Drafting*

2. Draw the views necessary to describe the object completely. Draw on one layer and use the **LINETYPE** command to change linetypes and the **COLOR** command to change colors. Draw object lines white, hidden lines red, and centerlines yellow. Do not dimension. Save as A:P19-2.

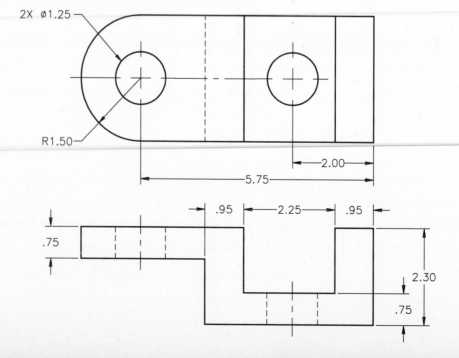

3 - 15. Draw the views necessary to describe each object completely. Set up the following layers, colors, and linetypes:

| LAYER | COLOR | LINETYPE |
|-------|-------|----------|
| OBJECT | WHITE | CONTINUOUS |
| HIDDEN | RED | HIDDEN |
| CENTER | YELLOW | CENTER |
| CONST | BLUE | CONTINUOUS |

Do not dimension. Save each drawing on your floppy disk.

3.

*Mechanical Drafting*

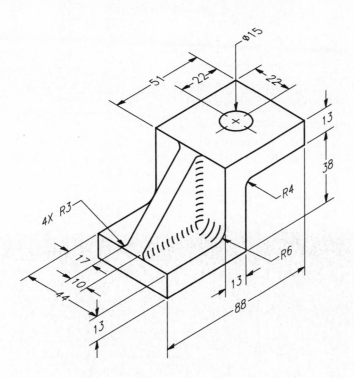

4.

*Mechanical Drafting*

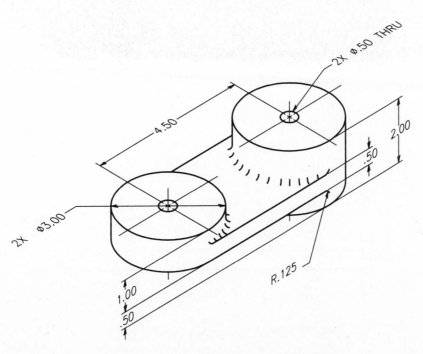

*Mechanical Drafting*

5.

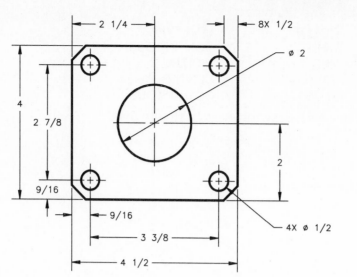

*Mechanical Drafting*

6.

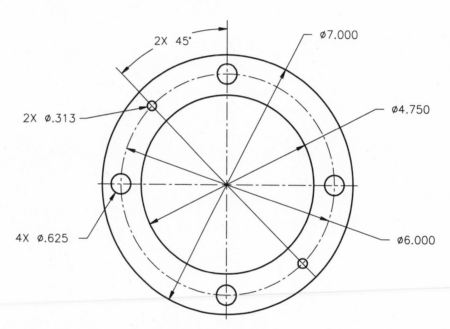

*Mechanical Drafting*

7.

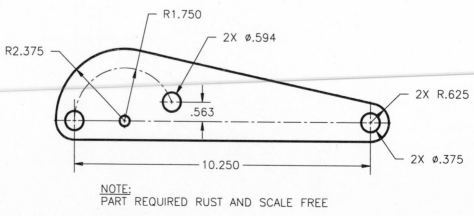

NOTE:
PART REQUIRED RUST AND SCALE FREE

8.

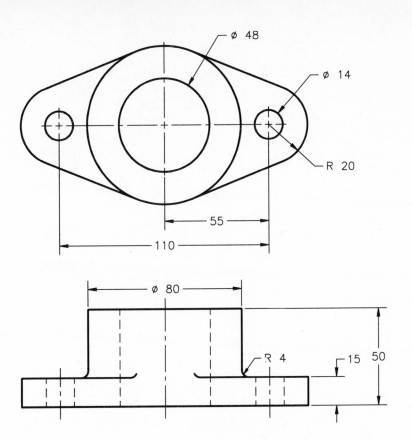

9.

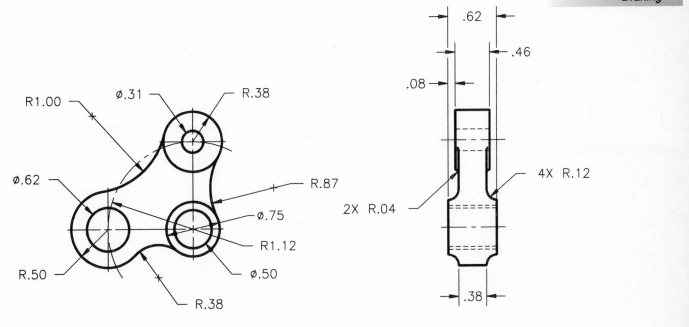

10.

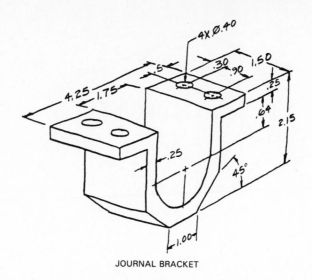

JOURNAL BRACKET

11.

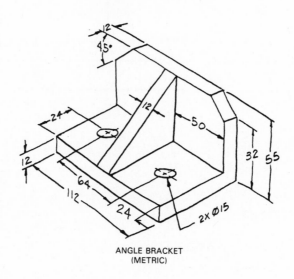

ANGLE BRACKET
(METRIC)

12.

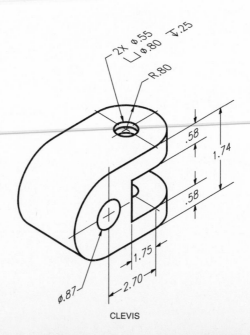

CLEVIS

13.

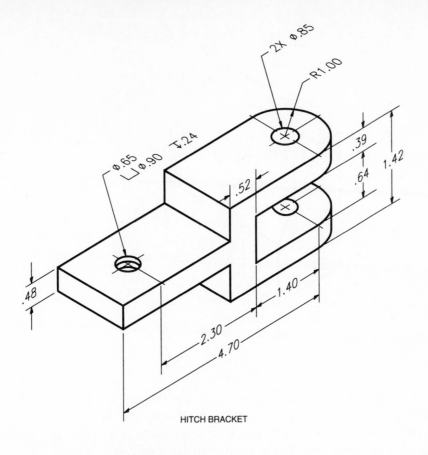

HITCH BRACKET

14.

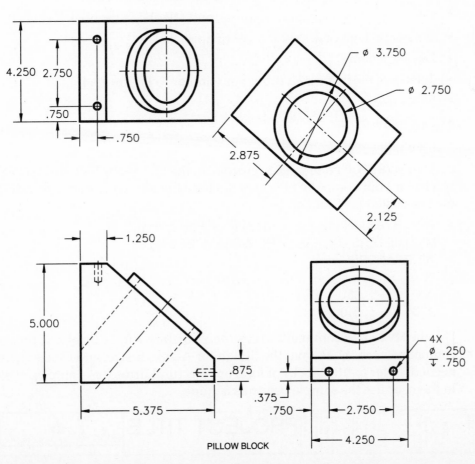

PILLOW BLOCK

**Mechanical Drafting**

15.

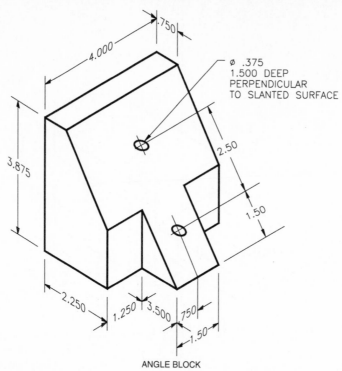

ANGLE BLOCK

**General**

16. Use the **MVSETUP** command to customize the ANSI-A, ANSI-B, and ANSI-C title blocks for your company or school. An example is provided in Figure 19-43, or refer to the border and title block arrangements of local industries. Be sure to include the following elements in your customized title block:

- Company or school name, address, and telephone number.
- Corporate logo or school mascot (if applicable).
- Drafter's name.
- Tolerance block for inch drawings (similar to Figure 19-43).
- Sheet size.
- Part name.
- Material.

**General**

17. Use the **MVSETUP** command to customize the ISO A4, ISO A3, and ISO A2 title blocks for your company or school. Include the following items in addition to the ones listed for Problem 16.

- Tolerance block for metric drawings. For example:
  MILLIMETERS UNLESS OTHERWISE SPECIFIED.
  TOLERANCES:
  .X          = ± .1
  .XX        = ± .05
  .XXX      = ± .010

**Architecrure**

18. Use the **MVSETUP** command to customize architectural title blocks for your company or school. Format the design for A-size, B-size, and C-size sheets as needed. Refer to title blocks of local architectural firms for examples of elements in them, or use the sample below as a guide.

PROJECT TITLE

SODERSTROM ARCHITECTS, P.C.

AutoCAD R13

# Chapter *20*

# Basic Dimensioning Practices

## Learning objectives

After completing this chapter, you will be able to:

○ Use the dimensioning commands to dimension given objects to ASME and other drafting standards.
○ Identify and set variables that affect the appearance of dimensions.
○ Add linear, angular, diameter, and radius dimensions to a drawing.
○ Set the appropriate units and decimal places for dimension numbers.
○ Use text size and style consistent with ASME and other professional standards.
○ Use the proper character codes to display symbols with dimension text.
○ Add dimensions to a separate layer.
○ Place general notes on drawings.

Dimensions are given on product designs for manufacturing and construction to describe the size, shape, and location of features on an object or structure. The dimension may consist of numerical values, lines, symbols, and/or notes, Figure 20-1. Each drafting field (mechanical, architectural, civil, electronics, etc.) uses a different type of dimensioning technique. Therefore, it is important for a drafter to place dimensions in accordance with company and industry standards. The standard emphasized in this text is ASME Y14.5M-1994 *Dimensioning and Tolerancing*. The M in Y14.5M means the standard is written with metric numeric values. ASME Y14.5M-1994 is published by The American Society of Mechanical Engineers (ASME). The standard can be ordered directly from ASME, 345 E. 47th Street, New York, NY 10017. It can also be obtained from The American National Standards Institute (ANSI), 1430 Broadway, New York, NY 10018. This text discusses the correct application of both inch and metric dimensioning.

AutoCAD's dimensioning functions provide you with unlimited flexibility. Available commands allow you to dimension linear distances (**DIMLINEAR** and **DIMALIGNED**), circles (**DIMDIAMETER**), and arcs (**DIMRADIUS**). The **LEADER** command allows you to place a note with an arrow and leader line pointing to the feature. In addition to these commands, AutoCAD includes a number of variables that allow you to modify the appearance of dimensions. These affect the height, width, style, and spacing of individual components of a dimension.

This text covers the comprehensive elements of AutoCAD dimensioning in four chapters: this chapter, *Basic Dimensioning Practices,* covers fundamental standards and practices; Chapter 21, *Intermediate Dimensioning,* covers special applications and coordinate dimensioning; Chapter 22, *Advanced Dimensioning,* covers dimension styles and editing dimensions; and Chapter 23, *Geometric Dimensioning and Tolerancing (GD&T),* covers geometric dimensioning and tolerancing practices.

Figure 20-1.   Dimensions describe size and location. Follow accepted conventions when dimensioning drawings.

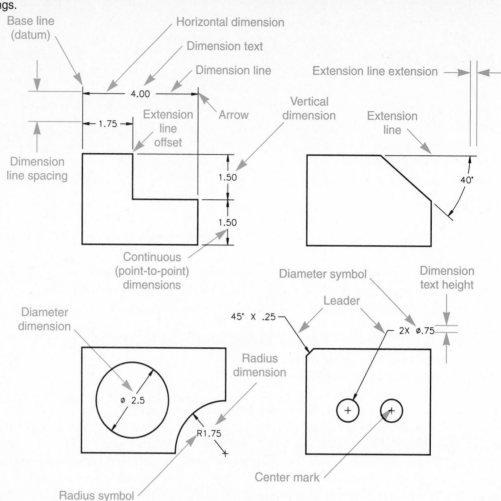

## THE AUTOCAD DIMENSIONING COMMANDS

AUG 9

AutoCAD's dimensioning commands can be picked from the **Dimensioning** toolbar or entered directly at the **Command:** prompt. If the ACADFULL menu file is loaded, the commands can also be picked from the **Dimensioning** cascading menu in the **Draw** pull-down menu. For those who prefer to use the keyboard for command entry, it is possible to enter a *dimensioning mode* where it is no longer necessary to precede the dimensioning commands with DIM. For example, a diameter dimension is created by typing DIMDIA at the **Command:** prompt. However, if you are in dimensioning mode, the command entry is simply DIA. To enter dimensioning mode, type the following at the **Command:** prompt:

Command: **DIM** ↵
Dim:

The **Dim:** prompt indicates that dimensioning mode is active and each of the dimensioning subcommands can now be issued. Once you enter dimensioning mode, it remains active until you return to normal command mode. To exit dimensioning mode and return to the **Command:** prompt, enter E for **Exit**, or press [Esc].

## Dimensioning mode subcommands

The various dimensioning mode subcommands are explained below. While in dimensioning mode, each of the subcommands can be abbreviated with the capital letters indicated.

**ALigned.** A linear dimension that is aligned with the extension line origins.

**ANgular.** An angular dimension.

**Baseline.** A dimension that continues from the first extension line of the previous dimension.

**CEnter.** Draws center mark or center lines through circles and arcs.

**COntinue.** A dimension that continues from the second extension line of the previous dimension.

**Diameter.** A diameter dimension.

**Exit.** Returns to normal command mode (the **Command:** prompt).

**HORizontal.** A linear dimension with a horizontal dimension line.

**Leader.** Draws a leader to the dimension text.

**ORdinate.** Ordinate point (arrowless) dimensioning.

**RAdius.** A radius dimension.

**Redraw.** Redraws the display.

**REStore.** Changes to a stored dimension style.

**ROtated.** A linear dimension at a specified angle.

**SAve.** Stores the current variable settings as a dimension style.

**STAtus.** Lists dimensioning variables and their current values.

**STYle.** Switches to a new text style.

**Undo.** Reverses the last dimensioning command.

**VErtical.** A linear dimension with a vertical dimension line.

The following dimension editing commands can be used to change a dimension. These commands can also be abbreviated while in dimensioning mode with the capital letters indicated.

**HOMetext.** Moves dimension text back to its home (default) position.

**Newtext.** Modifies the text of selected dimensions.

**OBlique.** Sets the oblique angle of dimension extension lines.

**OVerride.** Overrides a subset of the dimension variable settings.

**TEdit.** Changes the position of the dimension text.

**TRotate.** Rotates the dimension text.

**UPdate.** Redraws the dimensions in the current settings of all dimensioning variables.

**VAriables.** Lists variable settings.

**PROFESSIONAL TIP**

The **DIM** keyboard entry command is provided in AutoCAD Release 13 to help drafters make the transition from previous releases. However, this feature may not be available in future releases of the software. Therefore, you are encouraged to enter the dimensioning commands using toolbar options or menu selections, rather than typing the **DIM** command. This text presents both toolbar/menu and keyboard entry methods. You should experiment and do what works best for you.

## Accessing dimensioning commands from the pull-down menus and toolbars

The **Dimensioning** toolbar is an easy way of accessing the dimensioning commands. The **Dimensioning** toolbar is shown in Figure 20-2. It can be moved around the screen as needed or docked in a convenient location.

If the ACADFULL menu file is loaded, the dimensioning commands can also be accessed through the **Draw** pull-down menu. Pick **Dimensioning** ⟩ to display a cascading submenu with several options. As shown in Figure 20-3, three of the submenu options have additional cascading submenu selections.

The dimensioning pull-down menus and toolbar use the full dimensioning command. This means that you do not remain in dimensioning mode after performing a dimensioning operation, but are immediately returned to the **Command:** prompt.

Figure 20-2.   Many of the dimensioning commands can be accessed from the dimensioning buttons on the **Dimensioning** toolbar.

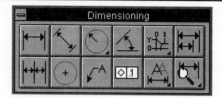

Figure 20-3.   Many of the dimensioning commands can be accessed from the **Dimensions** cascading submenus in the **Draw** pull-down menu.

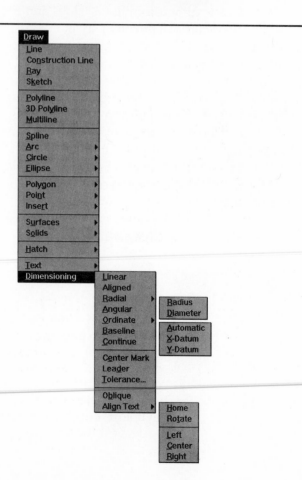

## Accessing dimensioning commands from the screen menus

When AutoCAD for Windows is configured to display screen menus, dimensioning commands can be entered by first selecting **DRAW DIM** from the AutoCAD root menu and then picking the desired option. When an option is selected, related dimensioning commands are displayed on the second submenu. To configure AutoCAD for screen menus, see *AutoCAD and its Applications—Advanced, Release 13 for Windows.*

## INTRODUCTION TO AUTOCAD'S DIMENSIONING VARIABLES

ACR A

AutoCAD provides options that control the appearance and format of dimensions. These are called *dimensioning system variables*, or *dim vars* for short. All default values for dimensioning variables are set in the AutoCAD prototype drawing ACAD.DWG. Many of the variables are on/off switches, where a value of 1 turns the variable on and a 0 value turns it off. Some of the variables hold numeric values or text. To change a variable, enter the name of the variable at the **Command:** prompt. The following appears when you change the extension line offset:

> Command: **DIMEXO** ↵
> New value for DIMEXO ⟨0.12⟩:

You can also change a dimension variable if you are already in the **DIM** command without preceding it with the DIM prefix, like this:

> Dim: **EXO** ↵
> Current value ⟨0.12⟩ New value:

The default, or current value is shown in brackets. Retain this value by pressing [Enter], or type a new value and press [Enter].

In this chapter, dimensioning variables are introduced following the sequence in which you might use them. Figure 20-4 displays the variables in a chart with a brief description of each. Notice that each of the variables begins with the prefix DIM. The remaining letters are a code giving the purpose of each variable. Page numbers are also included in the chart indicating the page number in this text to refer to for additional information. Variables may also be set in the **Dimension Styles** dialog box. This dialog box is covered thoroughly later in this chapter.

**PROFESSIONAL TIP**

Regardless of what prompt you are at, the **DIMCEN** variable cannot be changed without using the DIM prefix. Typing CEN at the **Dim:** prompt accesses the **CENTER** dimensioning subcommand rather than the **DIMCEN** variable. If you are at a point prompt, even within a dimensioning operation, typing CEN accesses the center object snap (**OSNAP**) mode. Be sure to type the entire name when changing this variable at the **Command:** prompt.

Figure 20-4.   This chart gives AutoCAD dimensioning variables and their abbreviated meanings. The page numbers given refer to where explanations of each variable are found in this text.

## Dimensioning Variables

| Variable | Meaning | Pg | Variable | Meaning | Pg | Variable | Meaning | Pg |
|----------|---------|----|----------|---------|----|----------|---------|----|
| DIMALI | Aligned dimensioning | 635 | DIMDEC | Dimensioning decimal places | 623 | DIMSOXD | Suppress outside extension-dimension lines | 681 |
| DIMALT | Alternate units | 739 | DIMDIA | Diameter dimensioning | 652 | DIMSTYLE | Gives current dimension style and accesses the dimension style edit options | 621 |
| DIMALTD | Alternate units decimal places | 739 | DIMDLE | Dimension line extension | 632 | DIMTAD | Text above dimension line | 631 |
| DIMALTF | Alternate units scale factor | 739 | DIMDLI | Dimension line increment | 651 | DIMTDEC | Tolerance decimal places | 732 |
| DIMALTTD | Alternate tolerance decimal places | 740 | DIMEXE | Extension line extension | 630 | DIMTFAC | Tolerance text scale factor | 735 |
| DIMALTTZ | Alternate tolerance zero suppression | 740 | DIMEXO | Extension line offset | 630 | DIMTIH | Text inside extension lines, horizontal | 631 |
| DIMALTU | Alternate units format | 739 | DIMGAP | Dimension line gap | 674 | DIMTIX | Text inside extension lines | 680 |
| DIMALTZ | Alternate units zero suppression | 739 | DIMLFAC | Length factor | 689 | DIMTM | Dimension with minus tolerance | 732 |
| DIMANG | Dimensioning angles | 638 | DIMFIT | Fit text | 655 | DIMTOFL | Text outside, force line inside | 654 |
| DIMAPOST | Alternate units text suffix | 739 | DIMJUST | Justification of text on dimension line | 682 | DIMTOH | Text outside extension line, horizontal | 631 |
| DIMASO | Associative dimensioning | 747 | DIMLIM | Limits tolerancing | 735 | DIMTOL | Dimension with tolerance | 730 |
| DIMASZ | Arrow size | 632 | DIMLIN | Linear dimensions | 628 | DIMTOLJ | Vertical tolerance justification | 733 |
| DIMAUNIT | Dimensioning angular units format | 641 | DIMPOST | Dimension text suffix | 737 | DIMTP | Dimension with plus tolerance | 732 |
| DIMBASE | Baseline dimensioning | 648 | DIMRAD | Radius dimension | 660 | DIMTSZ | Tick size | 632 |
| DIMBLK | Arrow block display | 633 | DIMRND | Round dimension units to specified value | 740 | DIMTVP | Text vertical placement | 682 |
| DIMBLK1 | Custom block 1st extension line | 684 | DIMSAH | Separate custom arrowheads | 684 | DIMTXSTY | Text style | 621 |
| DIMBLK2 | Custom block 2nd extension line | 684 | DIMSCALE | Overall dimension scale factor | 688 | DIMTXT | Dimension text size | 622 |
| DIMCEN | Center mark size | 652 | DIMSD1 | Suppress dimension line 1 | 631 | DIMTZIN | Toggles zero suppression in feet and inch values | 731 |
| DIMCLRD | Color of dimension line | 689 | DIMSD2 | Suppress dimension line 2 | 631 | DIMZIN | Zero supression in feet and inch values | 623 |
| DIMCLRE | Color of extension line | 689 | DIMSE1 | Suppress extension line 1 | 630 | DIMUNIT | Dimensioning units format | 623 |
| DIMCLRT | Color of text | 689 | DIMSE2 | Suppress extension line 2 | 630 | DIMUPT | User positioned text | 656 |
| DIMCONT | Continuing dimensioning | 649 | DIMSHO | Show dragged dimensions | 747 | | | |

# DIMENSIONING UNITS

The standard units of measurement on engineering drawings are decimal inches or millimeters. When all dimensions are given in inches or millimeters, this general note should appear on the drawing: UNLESS OTHERWISE SPECIFIED, ALL DIMENSIONS ARE IN INCHES (or MILLIMETERS). When using metric dimensions, a zero precedes the decimal point for measurements less than one millimeter. However, a zero does not precede the decimal point for dimensions less than one inch. An equivalent metric measurement requires one less digit behind the decimal to maintain the same degree of accuracy, Figure 20-5. In other words, when a three-place decimal-inch measurement is converted to millimeters, only two decimal places are required.

When dimensioning architectural or structural drawings, it is common to use feet and inches. For dimensions greater than one foot, the units are shown as feet(')-inches("), such as 12'-6". Distances less than one foot are noted in inches and fractions of an inch, Figure 20-6.

The recommended ASME height for dimension numbers and notes on a drawing is .125" (3mm). The larger text is recommended if the drawing is to be reduced. Titles and subtitles are usually .188" to .125" (5mm to 6mm) in height so they stand out from the rest of the drawing.

Figure 20-5.  Examples of decimal-inch and metric dimensions. Note the zero preceding the decimal point for metric dimensions less than 1.

| INCHES | MILLIMETERS |
|--------|-------------|
| 1.250 | 31.75 |
| .500 | 12.70 |
| .12 | 0.3 |
| 2.505 | 63.63 |

Figure 20-6.  Dimension formats for the construction trade.

DIMENSIONS GREATER THAN ONE FOOT

8'-10 1/2"      4'-0"      24'-6"

DIMENSIONS LESS THAN ONE FOOT

0'-8"      8"      6 1/4"

# DIMENSIONING TEXT OPTIONS

AutoCAD gives you the flexibility to control the way the dimension text looks on your drawing. The way you set the text-related dimensioning variables may depend on your school or company standards and on the type of drawing, such as mechanical or architectural.

## Text styles

When you begin a drawing, dimension text is drawn using the STANDARD text style. The text style on mechanical drawings is commonly ROMANS (roman simplex). AutoCAD also has the CIBT (city blueprint) PostScript font that works well for architectural applications. Use the **STYLE** command to create the drawing text style and the **DIMTXSTY** (text style) variable to use the new style for new dimensions. Note that a text style must have first been created before it can be used by dimension objects. Use the **DIMTXSTY** variable like this to change the dimension style to ROMANS:

```
Command: DIMTXSTY ↵
New value for DIMTXSTY ("STANDARD"):
```

This can also be entered at the **Dim:** prompt as TXSTY.

## Text size

If the text height is set to 0 in the **STYLE** command, then the dimension text height is controlled by the **DIMTXT** (dimension text) variable. The **DIMTXT** default is .1800. To change text to the standard .125 height used by many companies, use the following sequence:

    Command: **DIMTXT** ↵
    Current value ⟨0.1800⟩ New value for DIMTXT ⟨0.1800⟩: **.125** ↵
    Command:

If text height is set with the **STYLE** command, then the dimension text has that height. If you want to control the text height for each individual application, set the text height to 0 with the **STYLE** command. Dimensioning variables associated with text appearance can also be adjusted as needed. The prompts for the **STYLE** command are explained below.

    Command: **STYLE** ↵

Defining a new text style does not change the currently referenced dimension text style. Be sure to set the **DIMTXSTY** variable accordingly.

    Text style name (or ?) ⟨STANDARD⟩: **DIMENSION** ↵

If you want the text style being used for text on the drawing also used for dimensions, then you can redefine the STANDARD style. Otherwise, it is best to define a new style name. Select a font such as ROMANS for mechanical drawings or CIBT for architectural.

    Height ⟨0.2000⟩: **0** ↵

Defining a style with a height of 0 causes AutoCAD to prompt you for the height of each text object you create with that style. The **DIMTXT** variable setting is used for the text height. Doing this gives you the greatest flexibility. If you are defining a specific style intended only for dimension text, setting a constant height at this prompt makes sure all text created using this style is the same height.

    Width factor ⟨1.0⟩: ↵

The width factor can be adjusted as needed to meet requirements. If you are using a larger dimension text height, such as .188, a width factor slightly less than 1.0 helps to fit a bit more text within extension lines. Do not set the width factor so low that the text is difficult to read. A factor of .8 or above can be used with most fonts.

    Obliquing angle ⟨0⟩: ↵

For most standard dimensions, obliquing is not required or recommended. For isometric drawings, obliquing and rotation angles can be used to make text appear as if it is on the isometric plane being dimensioned.

    Backwards ⟨N⟩: ↵
    Upside-down ⟨N⟩: ↵
    Vertical ⟨N⟩: ↵
    Command:

These prompts are used to create backwards, upside-down, or vertical text. It is unlikely that you will ever dimension a drawing using any of these options.

## Determining drawing scale factors for dimension text height

Before plotting a drawing, you should determine the scale factor of the drawing. You can do this at the time of plotting. However, more work is required to update text heights.

After the scale factor has been determined, you should then calculate the height of the text in AutoCAD. To do this, multiply the desired text height by the scale factor to get text that appears in correct proportion on the screen.

Scale factors and dimension text heights should be determined before beginning a drawing. They are best incorporated as values within your prototype drawing files.

## Dimension units

The **DIMUNITS** (dimension units) variable is used to set the unit format for dimension text. The options are the same as you use in the **UNITS** command. Enter a value of 1 through 7 for the applications given in the chart below. The command sequence is:

Command: **DIMUNIT** ↵
New value for DIMUNIT ⟨2⟩: **4** ↵
Command:

| Value | Units | Example |
|---|---|---|
| 1 | Scientific | 1.55E+01 |
| 2 *(default)* | Decimal | 12.50 |
| 3 | Engineering | 1'-3.50" |
| 4 | Architectural Stacked | $1'\text{-}3\frac{1}{2}''$ |
| 5 | Fractional Stacked | $12\frac{1}{2}''$ |
| 6 | Architectural | 1'-3 1/2" |
| 7 | Fractional | 12 1/2 |

## Decimal places

The **DIMDEC** (dimension decimal places) variable is used to set the number of decimal places used to represent a dimensional value. The AutoCAD default is 4, but you can enter any number from 0 to 8 as follows:

Command: **DIMDEC** ↵
New value for DIMDEC ⟨4⟩: **3** ↵
Command:

**PROFESSIONAL TIP**

Any settings that you make with the **UNITS** command are not altered by changes made with the **DIMUNIT** or **DIMDEC** dimension variables. It is sometimes helpful to set the drawing units precision to 8 or more places. However, it is rarely a requirement to dimension a drawing with that precision. Use each of the related variables to your best advantage for each drawing application.

## Zero inch dimension

The **DIMZIN** (dimension zero inch) variable allows you to control the -0" part of feet-inch dimensions. When architectural or fractional units are used, the **DIMZIN** variable controls whether the dimension includes a "0" feet or "0" inches measurement. For architectural dimensioning, use settings of 0, 1, 2, or 3. The following chart shows the results of selecting one of the **DIMZIN** variables. These examples use fractional units for architectural drafting.

| Value | Results | Inches | | Feet and Inches | |
|---|---|---|---|---|---|
| 0 *(default)* | Removes 0' or 0" | 1/2" | 4" | 2' | 1'-0 1/2" |
| 1 | Includes 0' and 0" | 0'-0 1/2" | 0'-4" | 2'-0" | 1'-0 1/2" |
| 2 | Includes 0' omits 0" | 0'-0 1/2" | 0'-4" | 2' | 1'-0 1/2" |
| 3 | Includes 0" omits 0' | 1/2" | 4" | 2'-0" | 1'-0 1/2" |

Other settings are preferred for mechanical drafting. For example, AutoCAD places a zero in front of all decimal dimensions when **DIMZIN** is set to the default (0). According to ANSI standards, this is preferred for metric dimensions, but not for inch dimensions.

| **Metric** | **Inch** |
|---|---|
| 0.50 | .50 |

In order to have AutoCAD remove the leading zero for dimensions less than 1, set **DIMZIN** to 4 or 7. The following shows a comparison for **DIMZIN** set to 0 and 7:

| **DIMZIN** = 0 | **DIMZIN** = 7 |
|---|---|
| 0.50 | .50 |

You can have AutoCAD remove zeros to the right of the last nonzero number behind the decimal point by setting **DIMZIN** to 8. However, the **UNITS** command is used more often to control this. The following shows a comparison of **DIMZIN** set to 0 and 8:

| **DIMZIN** = 0 | **DIMZIN** = 8 |
|---|---|
| 0.50 | 0.5 |

You can remove the zeros before the decimal point and to the right of the last nonzero number behind the decimal with a **DIMZIN** setting of 15 (**DIMZIN** 7 + **DIMZIN** 8 = 15). The following shows a comparison of **DIMZIN** set to 0 and 15:

| **DIMZIN** = 0 | **DIMZIN** = 15 |
|---|---|
| 0.50 | .5 |

# DIMENSION ARRANGEMENT

Dimensions are meant to communicate information about the drawing. Different industries and companies apply similar techniques for presenting dimensions. The two most-accepted arrangements of text are unidirectional and aligned.

## Unidirectional dimensioning

Unidirectional dimensioning is typically used in the mechanical drafting field. The term *unidirectional* means one direction. This system has all dimension numbers and notes placed horizontally on the drawing. They are read from the bottom of the sheet.

Unidirectional dimensions normally have arrowheads on the ends of dimension lines. The dimension number is usually centered in a break near the center of the dimension line, Figure 20-7.

Figure 20-7.   When applying unidirectional dimensions, all dimension numbers and notes are placed horizontally on the drawing.

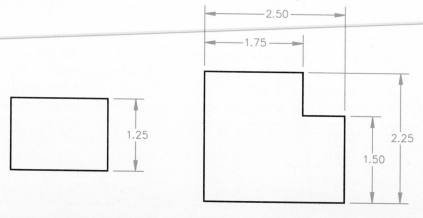

## Aligned dimensioning

Aligned dimensions are typically placed on architectural or structural drawings. The term *aligned* means the dimension numbers are lined up with the dimension lines. The dimension numbers for horizontal dimensions read horizontally. Dimension numbers for vertical dimensions are placed so they are right-reading from the right side of the sheet, Figure 20-8. Numbers for dimensions placed at an angle read at the same angle as the dimension line. Notes are usually placed so they read horizontally.

When using the aligned system, terminate dimension lines with tick marks, dots, or arrowheads. In architectural drafting, the dimension number is generally placed above the dimension line and tick marks are used, Figure 20-9.

Figure 20-8.   In the aligned dimensioning system, dimension numbers for horizontal dimensions read horizontally. Dimension numbers for vertical dimensions are placed so they read from the right side of the sheet.

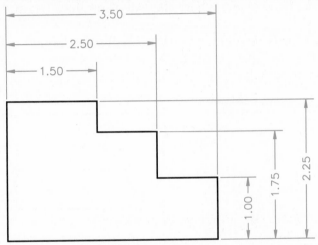

Figure 20-9.   An example of aligned dimensioning in architectural drafting. Notice the tick marks used in place of the arrowheads and the placement of the dimensions above the dimension line.

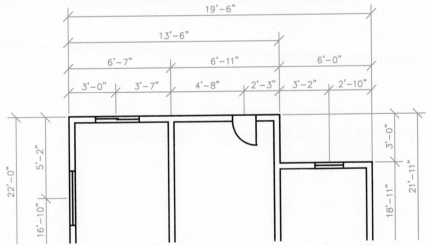

# DRAWING LINEAR DIMENSIONS

Linear means straight. In most cases, dimensions measure straight distances, such as horizontal, vertical, or slanted surfaces. The **DIMLINEAR** command allows you to measure the length of an object and place extension lines, dimension lines, dimension text, and arrowheads automatically. To do this, pick the **Linear Dimension** button from the **Dimensioning** toolbar or type DIMLINEAR or DIMLIN, at the **Command:** prompt. If the ACADFULL menu is loaded, you can also pick **Linear** from the **Dimensioning** cascading menu of the **Draw** pulldown menu. The prompts are as follows:

Command: *(type* DIMLIN *or* DIMLINEAR *and press* [Enter]*)*
First extension line origin or RETURN to select: *(pick the origin of the first extension line)*
Second extension line origin: *(pick the origin of the second extension line)*

The points you pick are the extension line origins, Figure 20-10. Place the crosshairs directly on the corners of the object where the extension lines begin. Use one of the object snap modes for accuracy.

Dimensioning standards recommend that a small space be left between the object and the start of the extension line. Use the **DIMEXO** variable to set the appropriate distance. Once you place a dimension, the small spaces may not show until you redraw the screen.

Figure 20-10.   Establishing extension line origins. The **Endpoint** or **Intersection** object snap modes are useful in accurately locating the origins.

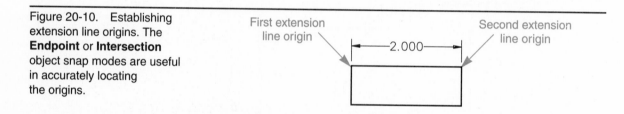

The **DIMLINEAR** command has many features, allowing you to generate horizontal, vertical, aligned, or rotated dimensions. After selecting the object or points of origin for dimensioning, the following prompt appears:

Dimension line location (Text/Angle/Horizontal/Vertical/Rotated):

These options are outlined as follows:

* **Dimension line location.** This is the default. Simply drag the dimension line to a desired location and pick, as shown in Figure 20-11. This is where preliminary plan sheets and sketches help you determine proper distances to avoid crowding. The extension lines, dimension line, dimension text, and arrowheads are automatically drawn, and the **Command:** prompt returns:

Dimension line location (Text/Angle/Horizontal/Vertical/Rotated): *(pick the dimension line location)*
Command:

Figure 20-11.   Establishing the dimension line's location.

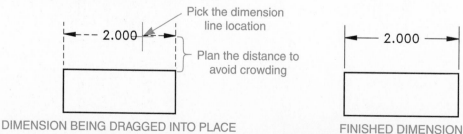

- **Text.** With this option, you can provide a specific measurement or text format for the dimension. For example, you can type a number with parenthesis to create a reference dimension. When you type T, the **Edit MText** dialog box is opened, Figure 20-12. The chevrons (⟨⟩) represent the current dimension number. Enter the new text and pick **OK**. If you want the dimension line drawn without text, delete the chevrons and pick **OK**.

Figure 20-12.   When you enter T for the **Text** option, the **Edit MText** dialog box appears. The chevrons (⟨⟩) represent the dimension number that AutoCAD has calculated. If you enter the dimensioning command at the **Dim:** prompt, this dialog box does not appear and you must enter the new or revised text on the command line.

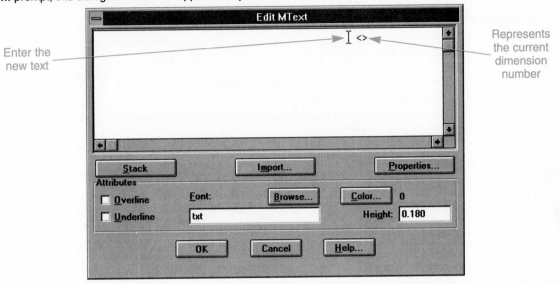

- **Angle.** This option allows you to change the dimension text angle. This option can be used when creating aligned dimensions and the sequence is as follows:

      Dimension line location (Text/Angle/Horizontal/Vertical/Rotated): **A** ↵
      Enter text angle: **90** ↵
      Dimension line location (Text/Angle/Horizontal/Vertical/Rotated): *(pick the dimension line location)*
      Command:

- **Horizontal.** This option sets the dimension being created to a horizontal dimension only. This may be helpful when dimensioning the horizontal distance of a slanted surface. The **Text** and **Angle** options are available again in case you want to change the dimension text number or angle. The command sequence looks like this:

      Dimension line location (Text/Angle/Horizontal/Vertical/Rotated): **H** ↵
      Dimension line location (Text/Angle): *(use the **Text** or **Angle** option, or pick the dimension line location)*
      Command:

- **Vertical.** This option sets the dimension being created to a vertical dimension only, Figure 20-13. This option may be helpful when dimensioning the vertical distance of a slanted surface. The command sequence is as follows:

      Dimension line location (Text/Angle/Horizontal/Vertical/Rotated): **V** ↵
      Dimension line location (Text/Angle): *(use the **Text** or **Angle** option, or pick the dimension line location)*
      Command:

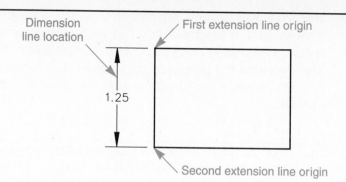

Figure 20-13. Drawing a vertical dimension.

- **Rotated.** This option allows an angle to be specified for the dimension line. A practical application is dimensioning to angled surfaces and auxiliary views, discussed later in this chapter. The command sequence looks like this:

    Dimension line location (Text/Angle/Horizontal/Vertical/Rotated): **R** ↵
    Dimension line angle ⟨0⟩: **45** ↵
    Dimension line location (Text/Angle/Horizontal/Vertical/Rotated): *(pick the dimension line location)*
    Command:

**NOTE:**          If you are in dimensioning mode and enter LIN at the **Dim:** prompt, using the **Text** option will not open the **Edit MText** dialog box. Instead, you are prompted on the command line for the new or revised text.

## PLACING HORIZONTAL AND VERTICAL DIMENSIONS IN DIMENSIONING MODE

AUG 9

While the **DIMLINEAR** command offers much flexibility, you can also draw horizontal and vertical dimensions with the **DIM** command. When you are inside the **DIM** command, the **Horizontal** and **Vertical** options work just like the **Horizontal** and **Vertical** options of the **DIMLINEAR** command.

After entering the dimensioning mode, use the following sequence to create a horizontal dimension:

    Dim: **HOR** *(type HOR or HORIZONTAL and press* [Enter]*)*
    First extension line origin or RETURN to select: *(pick one end of the feature to dimension)*
    Second extension line origin: *(pick the other point of the feature to dimension)*
    Dimension line location (Text/Angle): *(pick the dimension line location)*
    Dimension text ⟨2.0000⟩: ↵

When the dimension line location is picked, AutoCAD displays the measurement on the prompt line and allows you to change it. You can also alter dimension text by entering T for the **Text** option, or A for the **Angle** option at the Dimension line location (Text/Angle): prompt. If you enter T and press [Enter], AutoCAD gives you the opportunity to provide a specific text format that you want displayed with the dimension. The value shown in brackets is the current dimension number. Press [Enter] to accept this value, or enter a new value.

    Dimension line location (Text/Angle): **T** ↵
    Dimension text ⟨2.750⟩: **(2.750)** ↵
    Dimension line location (Text/Angle): ↵

You can have the dimension line drawn without text by pressing the space bar followed by pressing [Enter]:

> Dimension line location (Text/Angle): **T** ↵
> Dimension text ⟨2.750⟩: *(press the space bar once and then press* [Enter]*)*

The **Angle** option allows you to change the text angle as follows:

> Dimension line location (Text/Angle): **A** ↵
> Enter text angle: **90** ↵
> Dimension line location (Text/Angle): *(pick a point)*
> Dimension text ⟨2.750⟩: ↵

The **Dim:** prompt is issued after each dimension is complete. For drawing a vertical dimension, enter VE or VERTICAL at the **Dim:** prompt. The sequence is the same as for a horizontal dimension.

---

PROFESSIONAL TIP

Dimensioning in AutoCAD, like dimensioning on a conventional drafting board, should be performed as accurately and as neatly as possible. You can achieve consistently professional results by adhering to the following guidelines:

- Always construct drawing geometry as precisely as possible. Never truncate, or round-off, decimal values when entering coordinates. In other words, enter .4375 for 7/16 and not .44.
- For decimal dimensioning, set the system variable **DIMDEC** to the desired number of decimal places before creating any dimensions.
- Use running object snap modes like **Endpoint** and **Intersection** to place exact extension line origins.
- *Never* type in a different dimension value than what appears in the brackets. If a dimension needs to change, revise the drawing or dimensioning variables accordingly. The ability to change the dimension in the brackets is provided by AutoCAD so that a different text format can be specified for the dimension. Prefixes and/or suffixes can also be added to the dimension in the brackets. A typical example of a prefix might be to specify the number of times a dimension occurs, such as 4X 1.750. Other examples of this capability appear later in this chapter.

---

## USING DIMENSION VARIABLES TO CONTROL DIMENSION FORMAT

There are a number of dimension variables that control the basic dimension format. These variables control such things as extension line offset, alignment of extension lines, placement of text, and size of arrowheads. Dimension variables are discussed in the following sections.

## Setting the extension line offset

The *extension line offset* is the gap between the object and the start of the extension line. You can control the size of this space with **DIMEXO** (dimension extension offset) variable. The default gap of 0.0625 units is the ASME standard, based on a full-scale drawing. Suppose you needed to change the gap to .1 units. The following command sequence is used:

    Command: DIM ↵
    Dim: DIMEXO ↵
    Current value ⟨0.0625⟩ New value for DIMEXO ⟨0.0625⟩:.1 ↵

## Setting the extension line extension

Normally, extension lines extend beyond the last dimension line a short distance. In AutoCAD, this is called the *extension line extension* and is controlled by the **DIMEXE** (dimension extension extension) variable. The default distance of 0.18 units is an accepted standard, based on a full-scale drawing. Figure 20-14 shows the extension line offset and extension. To change the extension line extension, enter DIMEXE at the **Command:** prompt or EXE at the **Dim:** prompt, and enter a new value.

Figure 20-14. The **DIMEXE** and **DIMEXO** variables.

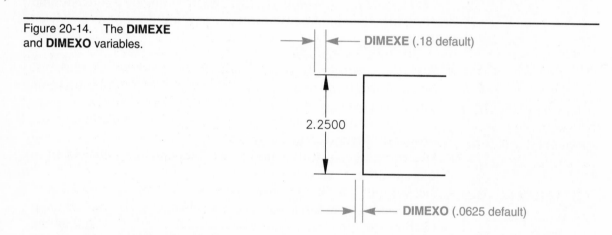

## Suppressing extension lines

Normally, extension lines are placed on both ends of the dimension line. The extension lines mark the edges of the feature being dimensioned. However, a situation may occur where you do not want the first extension line. For example, suppose the extension line coincides with an object line. In that case, it is then best to omit the extension line, Figure 20-15.

The **DIMSE1** dimensioning variable is used to suppress the first extension line. The **DIMSE2** variable allows you to suppress the second extension line. The variables are either on (1) or off (0). Off (default) places the extension line on the drawing.

Suppressing extension lines is not a typical application in mechanical drafting, and should be avoided unless absolutely necessary. Be sure to turn **DIMSE1** and **DIMSE2** back off before resuming normal dimensioning.

Figure 20-15. The **DIMSE1** and **DIMSE2** variables are used to suppress extension lines.

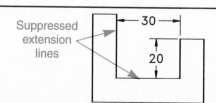

## Suppressing dimension lines

The **DIMSD1** variable is used to suppress the dimension line and arrowhead referencing the first extension line. The **DIMSD2** variable is used to suppress the dimension line and arrowhead referencing the second extension line. The options are on (1) and off (0), the default is off. Be sure to turn **DIMSD1** and **DIMSD2** off before resuming normal dimensioning. Figure 20-16 compares the **DIMSD1** and **DIMSD2** variables.

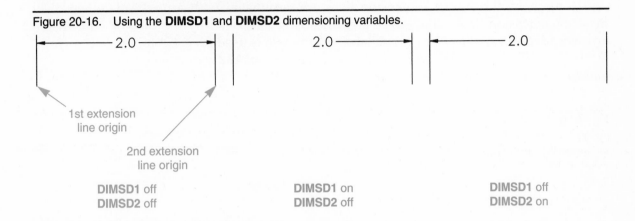

Figure 20-16.   Using the **DIMSD1** and **DIMSD2** dimensioning variables.

## Alignment of dimension text between extension lines

When there is room, the dimension line, arrowheads, and text is placed between the extension lines. The numbers are placed horizontally when the **DIMTIH** (dimension text inside horizontal) variable is on. The **DIMTIH** variable is on for unidirectional dimensioning, but off for aligned dimensioning. **DIMTIH** off allows the text inside extension lines to align with the dimension line angle, and the dimension numbers are placed as shown in Figure 20-8.

## Alignment of dimension text outside of extension lines

When there is not enough room between extension lines, AutoCAD automatically places the dimension lines, arrowheads, and numbers outside of the extension lines. In this instance, the **DIMTOH** (dimension text outside horizontal) variable works the same as **DIMTIH**. When this variable is on, text is drawn horizontally for unidirectional dimensioning. When it is off, text is drawn at the dimension line angle for aligned dimensioning, Figure 20-17.

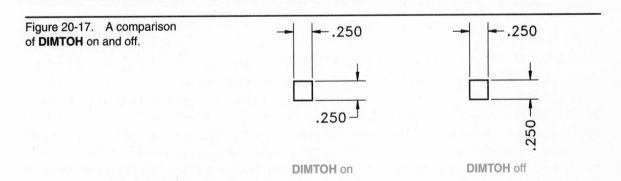

Figure 20-17.   A comparison of **DIMTOH** on and off.

## Placing the dimension text above the dimension line

In architectural drafting, the dimension number often appears above the dimension line. To do this, the **DIMTAD** (dimension text above dimension line) variable must be set to on. The default off places dimension numbers in a break in the dimension line. Figure 20-18 shows the effects of **DIMTAD** when turned on and off.

Figure 20-18.   Using the **DIMTAD** variable.

DIMTAD off                         DIMTAD on

## Controlling the size of arrowheads

In mechanical drafting, dimension lines are terminated with arrowheads where they meet the extension lines. The size of arrowheads is controlled by the **DIMASZ** (dimension arrowhead size) variable. The default size of 0.18 units is used for most full-scale drawings, Figure 20-19. To change the arrowhead size, enter the **DIMASZ** variable and the revised size value.

Figure 20-19.   The **DIMASZ** variable can be used to change the arrowhead size. The default value is .18.

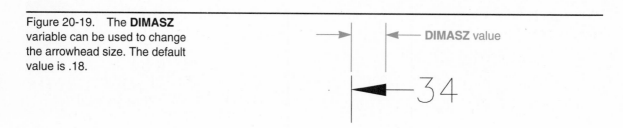

DIMASZ value

## Drawing dimension line tick marks and controlling their size

In architectural drafting, tick marks are often drawn at the ends of dimension lines. The **DIMTSZ** (dimension tick size) variable controls the size of the tick marks drawn and if they are drawn. When **DIMTSZ** is set to 0 (default), arrowheads are drawn. If you want tick marks, enter a value other than 0, Figure 20-20. The larger the value, the larger the size of the tick mark. Notice that the size is measured from the dimension line to the end of the tick, not from each end. If **DIMTSZ** is set to a value other than 0, the **DIMASZ** value is ignored.

Figure 20-20.   Effects of the **DIMTSZ** variable.

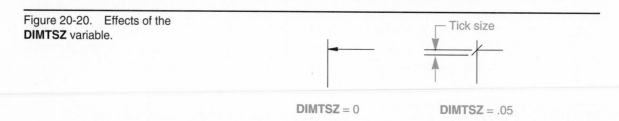

Tick size

DIMTSZ = 0                         DIMTSZ = .05

## Extending the dimension line past the extension line

Normally, dimension lines meet, but do not cross extension lines. When tick marks are used in architectural drafting, the dimension line may extend slightly beyond the extension line, depending on your school or company standard. This is controlled with the **DIMDLE** (dimension line extension) variable. When **DIMDLE** is set to 0 (default), there is no dimension line extension. To extend the dimension line, enter a value such as .0625. See Figure 20-21. Notice that the size is measured from the extension line to the end of the tick, not from each end.

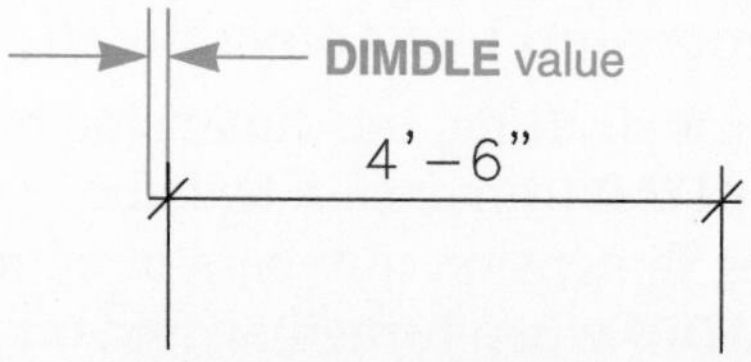

Figure 20-21.   Using the **DIMDLE** variable to allow the dimension line to extend past the extension line. With the default value of 0, the dimension line will not extend.

DIMDLE value

4'–6"

## Changing an arrowhead to a block

The **DIMBLK** (dimension block) dimensioning variable replaces arrowheads with a specific block. A *block* is an object, such as a symbol, that is called up for use on the drawing. Blocks are discussed in Chapter 25. A custom-designed arrow or symbol might be created as a block and used instead of an arrowhead. The **DIMBLK** default allows the standard arrowhead to be drawn.

AutoCAD has a standard block called DOT that you can use. Some architectural drafters prefer dots instead of tick marks to terminate dimensions. The command sequence to use dots as terminators is:

> Command: **DIM** ↵
> Dim: **DIMBLK** ↵
> Current value ⟨ ⟩ New value: **DOT** ↵

Figure 20-22A shows an example of the architectural dot. If the default dot is too big, make it smaller as follows:

> Command: **DIMASZ** ↵
> New value for DIMASZ ⟨0.18⟩: **.1** ↵

Another common architectural arrowhead block is a bold tick mark, Figure 20-22B. To define a customized tick mark as a block, first draw the block and give it a name, such as TICK1. The block should be one unit square, and you must also draw a tail to connect with the dimension line. Then, set the **DIMBLK** variable with the block name:

> Command: **DIM** ↵
> Dim: **DIMBLK** ↵
> Current value ⟨ ⟩ New value: **TICK1** ↵
> Dim:

Now place a horizontal dimension using this value. The **DIMASZ** and **DIMTSZ** variables should be set to their defaults. The **DIMASZ** variable affects the block size. Disable the established **DIMBLK** by entering a period as follows:

> Dim: **DIMBLK** ↵
> Current value ⟨ ⟩ New value: **.** ↵

Additional block dimensioning variables are discussed later in this chapter. Detailed information on creating and inserting blocks is found in Chapter 25.

Figure 20-22.   A block can be assigned to the **DIMBLK** variable. A—The **DIMBLK** variable is set to dot, supplied by AutoCAD. B— A custom block can also be assigned to the **DIMBLK** variable.

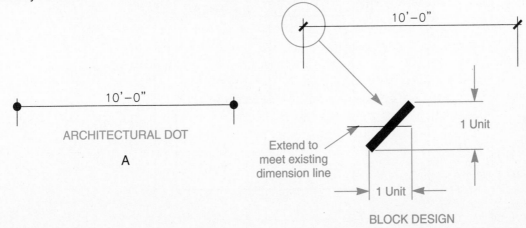

## EXERCISE 20-1

❏ Load AutoCAD for Windows and open PRODR2.
❏ Draw the object lines of the following views on layer Object. Place all dimensions on layer Dim.
❏ Use the proper dimensioning techniques and commands to dimension the objects exactly as shown.
❏ Save the drawing as A:EX20-1.

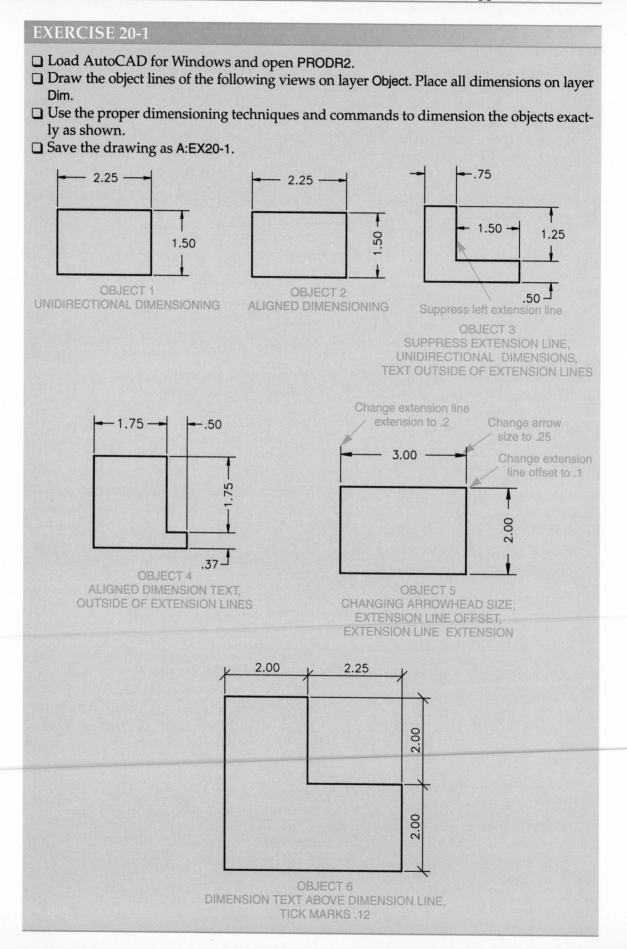

OBJECT 1
UNIDIRECTIONAL DIMENSIONING

OBJECT 2
ALIGNED DIMENSIONING

Suppress left extension line

OBJECT 3
SUPPRESS EXTENSION LINE,
UNIDIRECTIONAL DIMENSIONS,
TEXT OUTSIDE OF EXTENSION LINES

OBJECT 4
ALIGNED DIMENSION TEXT,
OUTSIDE OF EXTENSION LINES

Change extension line
extension to .2
Change arrow
size to .25
Change extension
line offset to .1

OBJECT 5
CHANGING ARROWHEAD SIZE,
EXTENSION LINE OFFSET,
EXTENSION LINE EXTENSION

OBJECT 6
DIMENSION TEXT ABOVE DIMENSION LINE,
TICK MARKS .12

# DIMENSIONING ANGLED SURFACES AND AUXILIARY VIEWS

When dimensioning a surface drawn at an angle, it may be necessary to align the dimension line with the surface. For example, auxiliary views are normally placed at an angle. In order to properly dimension these features, the **Rotated** option of the **DIMALIGNED** or **DIMLINEAR** can be used.

## Using the DIMALIGNED command

The **DIMALIGNED** command can be accessed by picking **Aligned Dimension** from the **Dimensioning** toolbar, or if the ACADFULL menu file is loaded by picking **Dimensioning** and then **Aligned** in the **Draw** pull-down menu. You can also type DIMALIGNED or DIMALI at the **Command:** prompt, or if you are inside of the **DIM** command, you can type ALIGNED or ALI at the **Dim:** prompt. The results of the **DIMALIGNED** command are displayed in Figure 20-23. The following shows the command sequence if you are using the **DIMALIGNED** or the **DIM** command:

> Command: *(type* DIMALIGNED *or* DIMALI *and press* [Enter]*)*

or

> Command: **DIM** ⏎
> Dim: **ALIGNED** ⏎
> First extension line origin or RETURN to select: *(pick first extension line origin)*
> Second extension line origin: *(pick second extension line origin)*
> Dimension line location (Text/Angle): *(pick the dimension line location)*
> Dimension text ⟨2.250⟩: ⏎

Figure 20-23. The **DIMALIGNED** dimensioning command allows you to place dimension lines parallel to angled features.

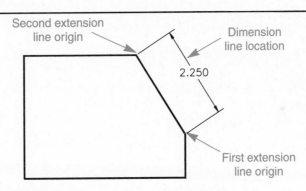

## Using the Rotate option of the DIMLINEAR command and Dim: ROTATE

Earlier, you were introduced to the **Rotate** option of the **DIMLINEAR** command. This discussion continues with an explanation and example of how this option and the **DIM** command can be used to provide rotated dimensions to angled surfaces. This technique is different from other dimensioning commands because you are asked to provide a dimension line angle, as shown in Figure 20-24. The command sequence is as follows when you use either the **DIMLINEAR** command or the **DIM** command:

> Command: *(type* DIMLIN *or* DIMLINEAR *and press* [Enter]*)*
> First extension line origin or RETURN to select: *(pick the first extension line origin)*
> Second extension line origin: *(pick the second extension line origin)*
> Dimension line location (Text/Angle/Horizontal/Vertical/Rotated): **R** ⏎
> Dimension line angle ⟨0⟩: *(type a dimension line angle such as* 45 *and press* [Enter], *or pick two points on the line to be dimensioned)*
> Dimension line location (Text/Angle/Horizontal/Vertical/Rotated): *(pick the dimension line location)*
> Command:

or

Command: **DIM** ↵
Dim: *(type* RO *or* ROTATED *and press* [Enter])
Dimension line angle ⟨0⟩: *(type the dimension line angle and press* [Enter], *or pick two points on the line to be dimensioned)*
First extension line origin or RETURN to select: *(pick the origin of the first extension line)*
Second extension line origin: *(pick the origin of the second extension line)*
Dimension line location (Text/Angle): *(pick the dimension line location)*
Dimension text ⟨2.000⟩: ↵

Figure 20-24. Using the
**DIMROTATED** command
allows you to dimension
an angled view.

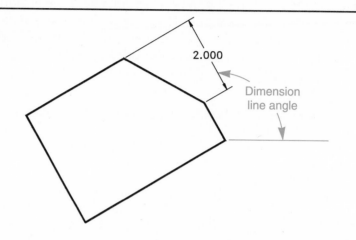

EXERCISE 20-2

❏ Open PRODR2.
❏ Draw the object lines of the following views on layer Object. Place all dimensions on layer Dim.
❏ Use the proper dimensioning techniques and commands to dimension the objects exactly as shown.
❏ Save the drawing as A:EX20-2.

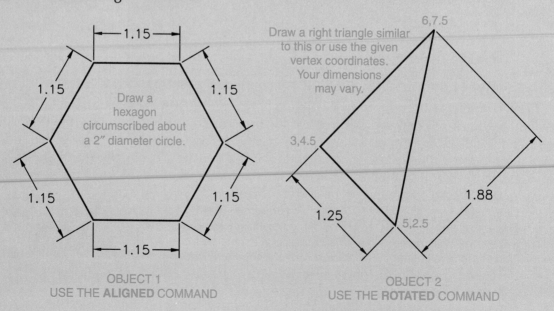

## SELECTING AN OBJECT TO DIMENSION

AUG 9

In the previous discussion, the extension line origins were picked in order to establish the extents of the dimension. Another powerful AutoCAD option allows you to pick a single line, circle, or arc to dimension. This works when you are using the **DIMLINEAR**, **DIMALIGNED** commands, and the **DIM** subcommands **HOR**, **VERT**, **ALI**, and **ROT**. You can use this AutoCAD feature any time you see the First extension line origin or RETURN to select: prompt. At this prompt, just press the [Enter] key or the space bar to be asked to Select an object to dimension:. When you select a line or arc, AutoCAD automatically selects the endpoints of the object to originate the extension lines. If you pick a circle, the extension lines are drawn from the closest quadrant and its opposite quadrant. If the **Rotate** option is used with a circle, the extension lines are drawn tangent to the circle from the dimension line location.

The **DIMLINEAR** command is used for this procedure as follows. Refer to Figure 20-25.

> Command: **DIMLIN** ↵
> First extension line origin or RETURN to select: ↵
> Select line, arc, or circle: *(pick any line, arc, or circle on the drawing)*
> Dimension line location (Text/Angle): *(pick the dimension line location)*
> Dimension text ⟨1.250⟩: ↵

Figure 20-25. Pressing [Enter] at the First extension line origin or RETURN to select: prompt allows you to pick the line, arc, or circle to be dimensioned. The cursor will change to the pick box.

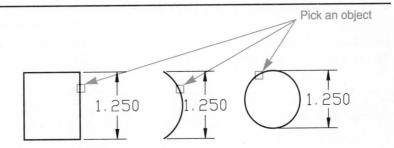

**PROFESSIONAL TIP**

AutoCAD does not place a diameter symbol in front of the dimension number when dimensioning a circle. You may want to add a diameter symbol to follow ASME standards. To do so, use the **Text** option to open the **Edit MText** dialog box. Then, enter %\U+2205 before the chevrons. Remember, the chevrons represent the current dimension value, such as 1.250. Pick **OK** to close the dialog box, and pick to place the dimension. The resulting dimension is displayed as Ø1.250. Note: If you enter the dimensioning command while in dimensioning mode (the **Dim:** prompt), the **Text** option will not open the **Edit MText** dialog box. Instead, you must enter \U+2205⟨⟩ on the command line.

Dimension text is multiline text. Therefore, you need to use Unicode entries to create special symbols. See Chapter 11.

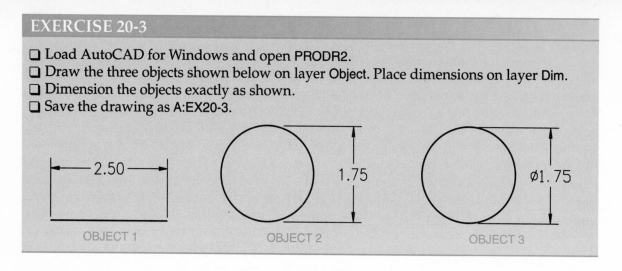

**EXERCISE 20-3**

❑ Load AutoCAD for Windows and open PRODR2.
❑ Draw the three objects shown below on layer Object. Place dimensions on layer Dim.
❑ Dimension the objects exactly as shown.
❑ Save the drawing as A:EX20-3.

OBJECT 1          OBJECT 2          OBJECT 3

# DIMENSIONING ANGLES IN DEGREES

Coordinate and angular dimensioning are both accepted for dimensioning angles. *Coordinate* dimensioning of angles can be accomplished with **DIMLINEAR** command. These dimensions locate the corner of the angle, Figure 20-26.

*Angular* dimensioning locates one corner with a dimension and provides the value of the angle in degrees, Figure 20-27. The type of angular unit depends on the **DIMAUNIT** setting. To use the angular method, type DIMANG at the **Command:** prompt or ANG at the **Dim:** prompt.

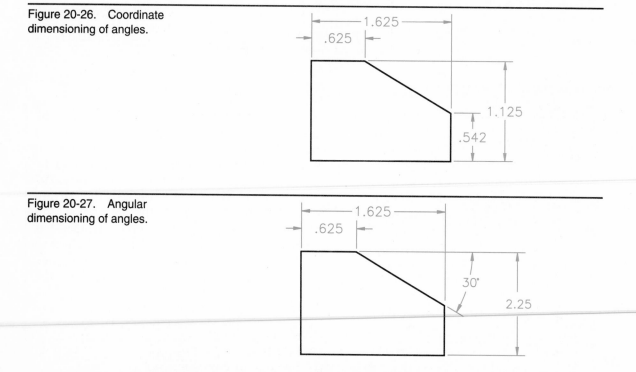

Figure 20-26.   Coordinate dimensioning of angles.

Figure 20-27.   Angular dimensioning of angles.

## Dimensioning the angle between two nonparallel lines

You can dimension the angle between two nonparallel lines. The intersection of the lines is the angle's vertex, Figure 20-28. AutoCAD automatically draws extension lines if they are needed. The command sequence is as follows:

Command: *(type* DIMANG *or* DIMANGULAR *and press* [Enter]) or

> Command: **DIM** ↵
> Dim: *(type* AN *or* ANGULAR *and press* [Enter]*)*
> Select arc, circle, line, or RETURN: *(pick the first leg of the angle to be dimensioned)*
> Second line: *(pick the second leg of the angle to be dimensioned)*
> Dimension arc line location (Text/Angle): *(pick the desired location of the dimension*
>    *line arc)*
> Dimension text ⟨45⟩: *(press* [Enter] *to accept the text, or type in a new value and press*
>    [Enter]*)*
> Enter text location (or RETURN): ↵

The last prompt asks you to enter the text location. Press [Enter] to have AutoCAD draw the dimension line and center the number in the dimension line, as shown in Figure 20-28. If there is not enough room between extension lines for the arrowheads and numbers, AutoCAD automatically places the arrowheads outside and the number inside the extension lines.

   You can manually place the text outside the extension lines, or locate the text other than in the center. To do so, pick the text location on the screen at the Enter text location (or RETURN): prompt. The position you pick is important. A leader is not connected to the number. Do not place the number where it may be confused with another part of the drawing. See Figure 20-29.

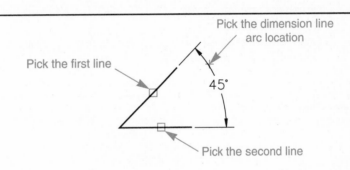

Figure 20-28.   Dimensioning angles with the text centered within the dimension line.

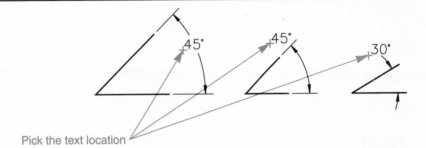

Figure 20-29.   Manually locating the dimension number for an angle.

## Placing angular dimensions on arcs

   The **DIMANGULAR** command can be used to dimension the included angle of an arc. The arc's center point becomes the angle vertex and the two arc endpoints are the origin points for the extension lines, Figure 20-30. The command sequence is as follows:

> Command: **DIMANG** ↵
> Select arc, circle, line, or RETURN: *(pick the arc)*
> Dimension arc line location (Text/Angle): *(pick the desired dimension line location)*
> Dimension text ⟨128⟩: ↵
> Enter text location (or RETURN): *(press* [Enter] *to accept the AutoCAD text location,*
>    *or pick a desired location for the text)*

Figure 20-30.   Placing angular
dimensions on arcs.

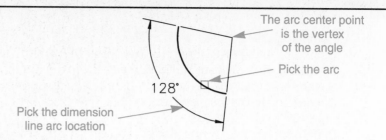

The arc center point
is the vertex
of the angle

Pick the arc

128°

Pick the dimension
line arc location

## Placing angular dimensions on circles

The **DIMANGULAR** command can also be used to dimension a portion of a circle. The circle's center point becomes the angle vertex and two picked points are the origin points for the extension lines, as shown in Figure 20-31. The command sequence is as follows:

> Command: **DIMANG** ↵
> Select arc, circle, line, or RETURN: *(pick the circle)*

The point you pick on the circle becomes the endpoint of the first extension line. You are then asked for the second angle endpoint. This becomes the endpoint of the second extension line. The command sequence is as follows:

> Second angle endpoint: *(pick the second point)*
> Dimension arc line location (Text/Angle): *(pick the desired dimension line location)*
> Dimension text ⟨85⟩: ↵
> Enter text location (or RETURN): *(press* [Enter] *to accept the AutoCAD text location, or pick a desired location for the text)*

Figure 20-31.   Placing angular
dimensions on circles.

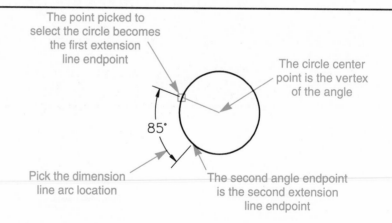

The point picked to
select the circle becomes
the first extension
line endpoint

The circle center
point is the vertex
of the angle

85°

Pick the dimension
line arc location

The second angle endpoint
is the second extension
line endpoint

**PROFESSIONAL
TIP**

Using angular dimensioning for circles increases the number of possible solutions for a given dimensioning requirement, but the actual uses are limited. The first angle point is where the circle is selected. If this point is to be accurately located, it must coincide with a known point on the circle, such as the intersection of a line and the circle. The **OSNAP Intersection** mode or the quadrant of a circle using the **OSNAP Quadrant** mode must be used to locate the point.

One professional application is dimensioning an angle from a quadrant point to a particular feature without having to first draw a line to dimension. Another benefit of this option is the ability to specify angles that exceed 180°.

## Angular dimensioning through three points

You can also establish an angular dimension through three points. The points are the angle vertex and the two angle line endpoints. See Figure 20-32. To do this, press [Enter] after the first prompt:

> Command: **DIMANG** ↵
> Select arc, circle, line, or RETURN: ↵
> Angle vertex: *(pick a vertex point and a "rubberband" connects between the vertex and the cursor to help locate the first point)*
> First angle endpoint: *(pick the first endpoint)*
> Second angle endpoint: *(pick the second endpoint)*
> Dimension arc line location (Text/Angle): *(pick the desired dimension line location)*
> Dimension text ⟨60⟩: ↵
> Enter text location (or RETURN): *(press [Enter] to accept the AutoCAD text location, or pick a desired location for the text)*

Figure 20-32.   Angular dimensioning using three points.

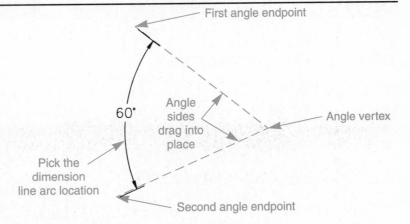

## Setting the angular units

The **DIMAUNIT** command allows you to set the dimension value format for angular units. The 0 setting for decimal degrees is the default value. The settings are as follows:

| Value | Format | Example |
|-------|--------|---------|
| 0 | Decimal degrees | 45.00 |
| 1 | Degrees/minutes/seconds | 45d30'15" |
| 2 | Gradients | 50.00g |
| 3 | Radians | 0.7549r |
| 4 | Surveyor's units | N45d30'15"E |

In the following example, the default setting of decimal degrees is being changed to the setting for surveyor's units:

> Command: **DIMAUNIT** ↵
> New value for DIMAUNIT ⟨0⟩: **4** ↵
> Command:

**PROFESSIONAL TIP**

The **DIMUNIT** and **DIMAUNIT** variables affect *dimensions only*. The **UNITS** command, and the **LUNITS** and **AUNITS** variables still apply to coordinate displays and inquiry commands.

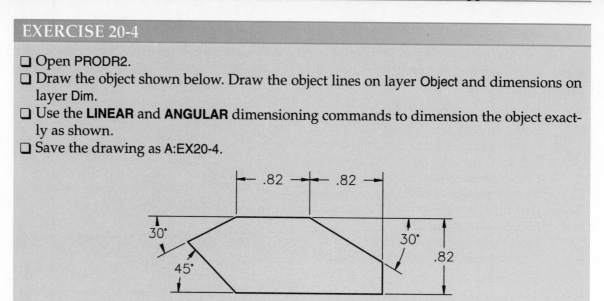

**EXERCISE 20-4**

❑ Open PRODR2.
❑ Draw the object shown below. Draw the object lines on layer **Object** and dimensions on layer Dim.
❑ Use the **LINEAR** and **ANGULAR** dimensioning commands to dimension the object exactly as shown.
❑ Save the drawing as A:EX20-4.

## DIMENSIONING PRACTICES

Dimensioning practices often depend on product requirements, manufacturing accuracy, standards, and tradition. Dimensional information includes size dimensions, location dimensions, and notes. Two techniques that identify size and location are chain and datum dimensioning. The method used depends on the accuracy of the product and the drafting field.

## SIZE DIMENSIONS AND NOTES

*Size dimensions* provide the size of physical features. They include lines, notes, or dimension lines and numbers. Size dimensioning practices depend on the techniques used to dimension different geometric features, Figure 20-33. A *feature* is considered any physical portion of a part or object, such as a surface, hole, window, or door. Dimensioning standards are used so an object designed in one place can be manufactured or built somewhere else.

There are two types of notes on a drawing: specific notes and general notes. *Specific notes* relate to individual or specific features on the drawing. They are attached to the feature being dimensioned using a leader line. *General notes* apply to the entire drawing and are placed in the lower-left corner, upper-left corner, or above or next to the title block. Where they are placed depends on company or school practice.

Figure 20-33.   Size
dimensions and specific notes.

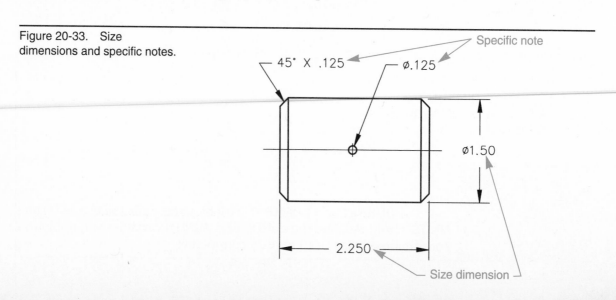

## Dimensioning flat surfaces and architectural features

In mechanical drafting, flat surfaces are dimensioned by giving measurements for each feature. If there is an overall dimension provided, you can omit one of the dimensions. The overall dimension controls the omitted dimension. In architectural drafting, it is common to place all dimensions without omitting any of them. The idea is that all dimensions should be shown to help make construction easier. See Figure 20-34.

## Dimensioning cylindrical shapes

Both the diameter and length of a cylindrical shape can be dimensioned in the view where the cylinder appears rectangular, Figure 20-35. This allows the view where the cylinder appears as a circle to be omitted.

---

Figure 20-34.  Dimensioning flat surfaces and architectural features.

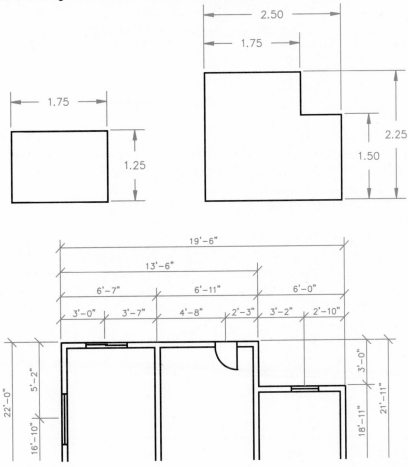

---

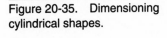

Figure 20-35.  Dimensioning cylindrical shapes.

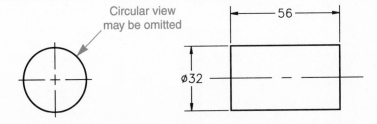

## Dimensioning square and rectangular features

Square and rectangular features are usually dimensioned in the views where the length and height are shown. The square symbol can be used preceding the dimension for the square feature, Figure 20-36. The square symbol must be created as a block and inserted. Blocks are discussed in Chapter 25.

## Dimensioning cones and hexagonal shapes

There are two ways to dimension a conical shape. One method is by giving the diameters at both ends and the length, as shown in Figure 20-37. Another method is to give the taper angle and length. Hexagonal shapes are dimensioned by giving the distance across the flats and the length. See Figure 20-38.

Figure 20-36.   Dimensioning square and rectangular features.

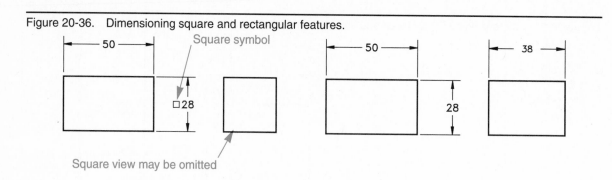

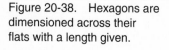

Figure 20-37.   Dimensioning conical shapes. These shapes can also be dimensioned with an angle and length.

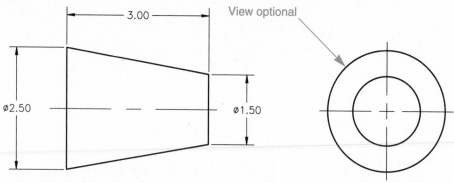

Figure 20-38.   Hexagons are dimensioned across their flats with a length given.

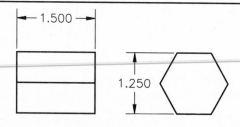

## EXERCISE 20-5

❑ Open PRODR2.
❑ Draw the objects shown below. Draw the object lines on layer Object, the centerlines on layer Center, and place all dimensions on layer Dim.
❑ Hint: To orient the hexagon as shown, use a six-sided circumscribed polygon. When prompted to enter the radius value, type @.625<0. Use X and Y filters with the appropriate object snap modes to assist you in drawing the side view of the hexagon.
❑ Dimension the objects exactly as shown using the proper dimensioning commands and techniques.
❑ Save the drawing as A:EX20-5.

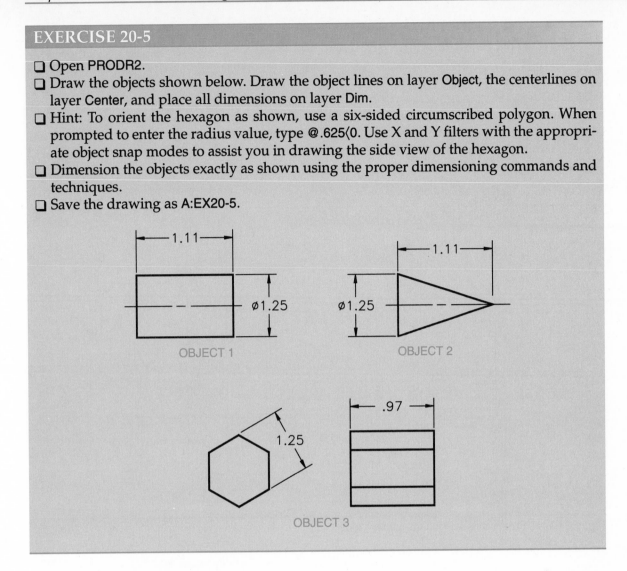

## LOCATION DIMENSIONS

*Location dimensions* are used to locate features on an object. They do not provide the size. Holes and arcs are dimensioned to their centers in the view where they appear circular. Rectangular features are dimensioned to their edges, Figure 20-39. In architectural drafting, windows and doors are dimensioned to their centers on the floor plan.

Figure 20-39.   Locating circular and rectangular features.

Rectangular coordinates and polar coordinates are the two basic location dimensioning systems. *Rectangular coordinates* are linear dimensions used to locate features from surfaces, centerlines, or center planes. AutoCAD performs this type of dimensioning using a variety of dimensioning subcommands. The most frequently used dimensioning command is **DIMLINEAR** and its options. See Figure 20-40.

The *polar coordinate system* uses angular dimensions to locate features from surfaces, centerlines, or center planes. The angular dimensions in the polar coordinate system are drawn using AutoCAD's **DIMANGULAR** command. Results of the **DIMANGULAR** command are shown in Figure 20-41.

Figure 20-40.   Rectangular coordinate location dimensions.

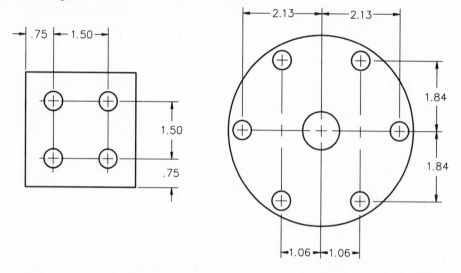

Figure 20-41.   Polar coordinate location dimensions.

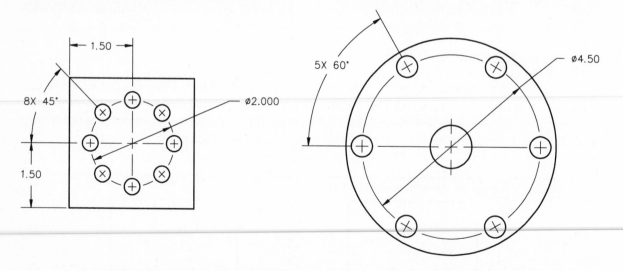

# DATUM DIMENSIONING

With *datum*, or *baseline dimensioning*, dimensions on an object originate from common surfaces, centerlines, or center planes. Datum dimensioning is commonly used in mechanical drafting because each dimension is independent of the others. This achieves more accuracy in manufacturing, Figure 20-42.

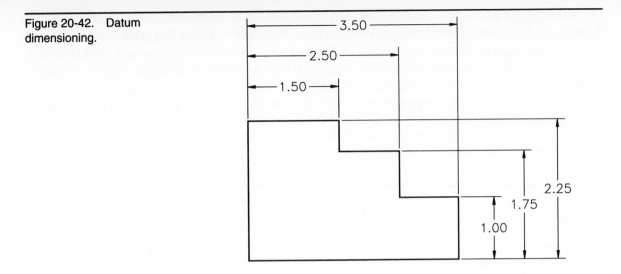

Figure 20-42.    Datum dimensioning.

# CHAIN DIMENSIONING

*Chain dimensioning*, also called *point-to-point dimensioning*, places dimensions in a line from one feature to the next. Chain dimensioning is sometimes used in mechanical drafting. However, there is less accuracy than with datum dimensioning since each dimension is dependent on other dimensions in the chain. Architectural drafting uses chain dimensioning in most applications. Figure 20-43 shows an example of chain dimensioning. In mechanical drafting, it is common to leave one dimension blank and provide an overall dimension. Architectural drafting practices usually show dimensions all the way across plus an overall dimension.

Figure 20-43.    Chain dimensioning.

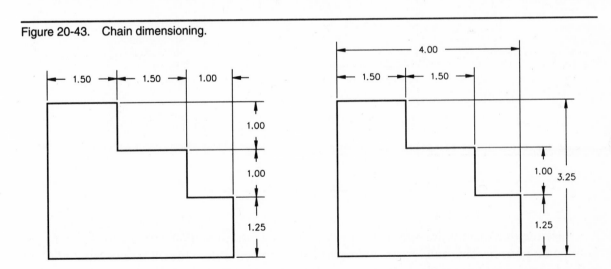

# MAKING DATUM AND CHAIN DIMENSIONING EASY        AUG 9

AutoCAD refers to datum dimensioning as *baseline* and chain dimensioning as *continue*. You can access these commands by picking the **Baseline Dimension** or **Continue Dimension** button in the **Dimensioning** toolbar, or typing either DIMBASE or DIMCONT at the **Command:** prompt. If the ACADFULL menu file is loaded, you can pick **Baseline** or **Continue** from the **Dimensioning** cascading menu of the **Draw** pull-down menu. If you are using the **DIM** command, you can type BA for baseline or CO for continue at the **Dim:** prompt. Baseline dimensions can be created with linear, ordinate, and angular dimensions. Ordinate dimensions are discussed in Chapter 21.

When you begin a new drawing and enter the **DIMBASE** command, AutoCAD asks you to Select base dimension:. Therefore, a dimension must exist before using **Baseline**. AutoCAD will use the most recently drawn dimension as the base dimension, unless you specify a different one. You can add additional datum dimensions to the previous dimension. AutoCAD automatically spaces and places the extension lines, dimension lines, arrowheads, and numbers. For example, to dimension the series of horizontal baseline dimensions shown in Figure 20-44, use the following procedure:

Command: *(type DIMLIN or DIMLINEAR and press [Enter])*
First extension line origin or RETURN to select: *(pick the origin of the first extension line)*
Second extension line origin: *(pick the origin of the second extension line)*
Dimension line location (Text/Angle): *(pick the dimension line location)*
Command: *(type DIMBASE or DIMBASELINE and press [Enter])*
Second extension line origin or RETURN to select: *(pick the second extension line origin for the next baseline dimension)*
Second extension line origin or RETURN to select: *(pick the second extension line origin for the next baseline dimension)*
Second extension line origin or RETURN to select: ↵
Select base dimension: ↵
Command:

Figure 20-44.    Using **DIMBASELINE** command. AutoCAD automatically spaces and places the extension lines, dimension lines, arrowheads, and numbers.

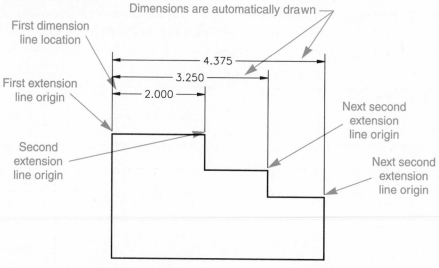

Baseline dimensions are automatically drawn until you press [Enter] twice to return to the **Command:** prompt. This only occurs when **DIMBASE** is used. When the **DIM** subcommand **Base** is used, only one dimension is drawn and the **Dim:** prompt returns. However, you can get immediately back to using the **Base** subcommand by pressing [Enter] at the next **Dim:** prompt:

Command: **DIM** ↵
Dim: *(type BASE or BA and press [Enter])*
Second extension line or RETURN to select: *(pick the second extension line origin for the next baseline dimension)*
Dimension text ⟨3.250⟩: ↵
Dim: ↵
BASE
Second extension line or RETURN to select: *(pick another second extension line origin for the next baseline dimension)*
Dimension text ⟨4.375⟩: ↵
Dim:

In some cases, you may want to draw datum dimensions to existing dimensions other than the most recently drawn dimension. To do so, use the following command sequence:

Command: *(type* DIMBASE *or* DIMBASELINE *and press* [Enter]*)*
Second extension line origin or RETURN to select: ↵
Select base dimension: *(pick the existing linear dimension)*
Second extension line origin or RETURN to select: *(pick the second extension line origin for the next baseline dimension)*
Second extension line origin or RETURN to select: ↵
Select base dimension: ↵
Command:

You can also draw baseline dimensions to angular features. First, draw an angular dimension and enter the **DIMBASE** command, or enter the command and pick an existing angular dimension. The result of the following command sequence is shown in Figure 20-45:

Command: *(type* DIMBASE *or* DIMBASELINE *and press* [Enter]*)*
Select next feature or RETURN to select: *(pick the next extension line origin for the next baseline dimension)*
Select next feature or RETURN to select: *(pick the next extension line origin for the next baseline dimension)*
Second extension line origin or RETURN to select: ↵
Select base dimension: ↵
Command:

The **DIMCONTINUE** command is used in the same manner as the **DIMBASELINE** command. The prompts and options are the same. The result is the chain dimensioning shown in Figure 20-46.

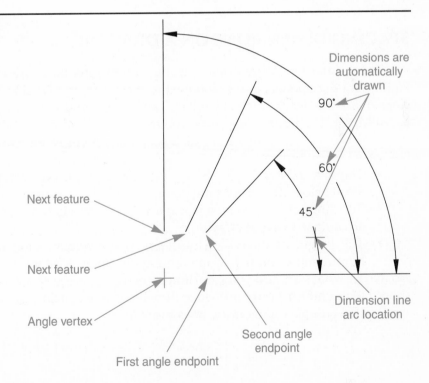

Figure 20-45. Using **DIMBASE** command to datum dimension angular features.

Figure 20-46.   Using the
**DIMCONTINUE** command.

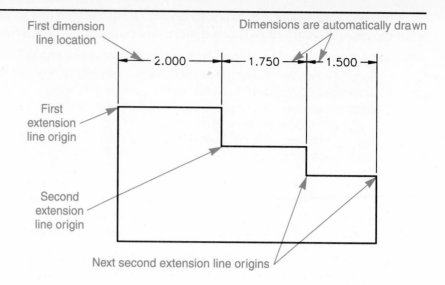

You do not have to use **DIMBASELINE** or **DIMCONTINUE** immediately after a dimension that is to be used as a base or chain with other dimensions. You can come back later and do it by pressing the [Enter] key at the Select extension line origin or RETURN to select: prompt. Then, select the dimension you want to use and draw the datum or chain dimensions that you need.

## SPACING DIMENSIONS ON A DRAWING                                         AUG 9

The primary concern when spacing dimensions on a drawing is to avoid crowding. Begin with the smallest dimension next to the object, followed by increasingly larger dimensions. Place the overall dimension last. The minimum dimension line spacing recommended by ASME is .4" (10mm) away from the object. Place additional dimension lines .25" (6mm) apart. However, these minimum distances are generally too close for most dimensioning. Use your own judgment. Dimension line spacing depends on:

- The size and complexity of the drawing. Complex drawings require careful consideration before dimensions are placed to avoid crowding.
- The amount of open area is important. If there is space available, use it to your best advantage to avoid crowding.
- The length of dimension numbers is important. Long numbers, such as 24.8750, require more space than small numbers, such as 24.88.

No matter what standard you use, dimension line spacing should be consistent. The drawing should look uniform. You can change dimension line spacing on different views, but keep the spacing for groups of dimension lines the same.

## Setting dimension line spacing

The **DIMDLI** (dimension line increment) variable controls the spacing between datum (baseline) dimension lines. The default spacing set in AutoCAD's prototype drawing is 0.38 units, Figure 20-47. However, this default is too close for many applications. Additional spacing, such as .50, can be specified as follows:

    Command: DIMDLI ↵
    New value for DIMDLI ⟨.3800⟩: .5 ↵
    Command:

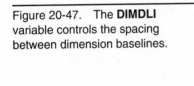

Figure 20-47.   The **DIMDLI** variable controls the spacing between dimension baselines.

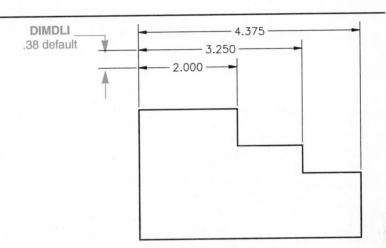

## INCLUDING SYMBOLS WITH DIMENSION TEXT

AUG 8

After you select a feature to dimension, AutoCAD responds with the measurement, or dimensioning number. In some cases such as dimensioning radii and diameters, AutoCAD automatically places the radius (R) or diameter (Ø) symbol before the dimension number. However, in other cases related to linear dimensioning this is not automatic. The recommended ASME standard for a diameter dimension is to place the diameter symbol (Ø) before the number. To add the diameter symbol, you must type the Unicode followed by ⟨ ⟩. The chevrons (⟨ ⟩) tell AutoCAD to use the measurement it calculated. See Chapter 11 for symbol codes. You can also type the symbol code and the number to achieve the same result. This can be done using the **Text** option of the **DIMLINEAR** command. Notice that when the **Edit MText** dialog box appears, the chevrons are already in place. Enter %\U+2205 before the chevrons and pick **OK**. If you enter the dimensioning command from the **Dim:** prompt, you need to enter the Unicode at the command line and include the chevrons or the dimension number, as shown below. Notice that the % sign is not needed. Either method places the dimension text Ø1.750 on your drawing.

    Dimension text ⟨1.750⟩: \U+2205 ⟨⟩ ↵

or

    Dimension text ⟨1.750⟩: \U+22051.750 ↵

Additional symbols are used in dimensions to point out certain features on the drawing. The diameter symbol (Ø) for circles and the radius symbol (R) for arcs are easily drawn. Additional symbols, such as □ for a square feature, can be drawn individually. However, this can be time-consuming. Instead, save the symbol as a block and insert it in the drawing before the dimension text. Storing and inserting blocks is discussed in Chapter 25. Symbols used often are shown in Figure 20-48.

Figure 20-48.  Common dimensioning symbols and how to draw them.

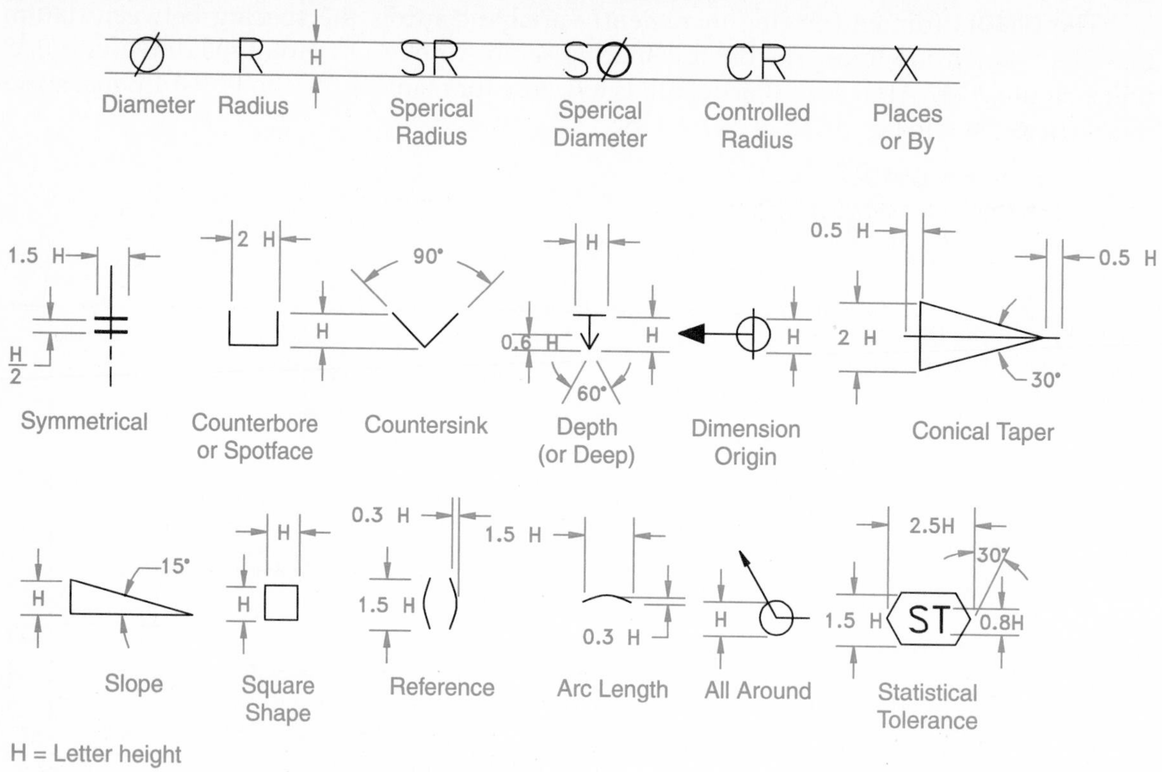

Ø        R      SR      SØ      CR      X

Diameter  Radius    Sperical    Sperical    Controlled    Places
                    Radius      Diameter    Radius        or By

Symmetrical   Counterbore   Countersink   Depth      Dimension        Conical Taper
              or Spotface                 (or Deep)  Origin

Slope     Square     Reference   Arc Length   All Around   Statistical
          Shape                                            Tolerance

H = Letter height

## DRAWING CENTER DASHES OR CENTERLINES IN A CIRCLE OR ARC

AUG 9

When small circles or arcs are dimensioned, the **DIMDIAMETER** and **DIMRADIUS** commands leave center dashes. If the dimension of a large circle crosses through the center, the dashes are left out. When you want to draw center dashes or centerlines, pick the **Center Mark** button in the **Dimensioning** toolbar or type DIMCENTER at the **Command:** prompt. If the ACADFULL menu file is loaded, you can also pick **Center Mark** in the **Dimensioning 〉** cascading menu of the **Draw** pull-down menu. The command sequence is as follows:

Command: **DIMCENTER** ↵
Select arc or circle: *(pick the arc or circle)*
Dim:

You can also enter CEN or CENTER at the **Dim:** prompt:

Command: **DIM** ↵
Dim: *(type CEN or CENTER and press [Enter])*
Select arc or circle: *(pick the arc or circle)*
Dim:

When the circle or arc is picked, center dashes are automatically drawn. The size of the center dashes, or the amount that the centerlines extend outside the circle or arc, is controlled by the **DIMCEN** (dimension centerline) variable. The default provides center dashes 0.09 units long. If **DIMCEN** is set to 0, center dashes or centerlines are not drawn. A positive value gives center dashes. For example, the value .125 displays center dashes that are .125 units long. When decimal-inch units are used, this is the recommended length. A negative **DIMCEN** value draws complete centerlines in addition to center dashes. With a negative value, centerlines extend beyond the circle or arc by the value entered. For example, a −.125 value extends centerlines .125 units beyond the circle or arc, Figure 20-49. A zero (0) **DIMCEN** setting will not draw any center marks. The command sequence is as follows:

>    Command: **DIMCEN** ⏎
>    New value for DIMCEN ⟨0.09⟩: −**.125** ⏎
>    Command:

Figure 20-49.   Using the **DIMCEN** variable. A positive value draws center dashes. A negative value draws complete centerlines. A value of 0 will not draw any center marks.

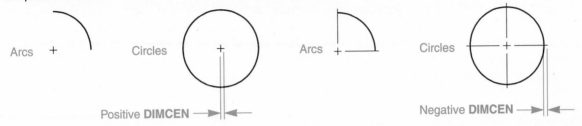

## PROFESSIONAL TIP

A negative **DIMCEN** value for small circles may result in placement of center dashes only. This is because AutoCAD needs room for the center dash and a space before the rest of the centerline is placed. Don't be alarmed if this happens. Either try a smaller negative **DIMCEN** value or accept the results with the value you have set.

## EXERCISE 20-6

☐ Load AutoCAD for Windows and open PRODR2.
☐ Draw circles and arcs similar to those shown in Figure 20-49.
☐ Set the **DIMCEN** value to add center dashes as shown. Use positive and negative values of .125.
☐ Place center dashes on layer 2-2.
☐ Save the drawing as A:EX20-6.

## DIMENSIONING CIRCLES                         AUG 9

Circles are normally dimensioned by giving the diameter. The ASME standard for dimensioning arcs is to give the radius. However, AutoCAD allows you to dimension either a circle or arc with a diameter dimension. To produce diameter dimensions, pick the **Diameter Dimension** button on the **Dimensioning** toolbar, type DIMDIA or DIMDIAMETER at the **Command:** prompt, or type either DIA or DIAMETER while in the **DIM** command at the **Dim:** prompt. If the ACADFULL menu file is loaded, you can also pick **Dimensioning** ⟩ from the **Draw** pull-down menu, followed by **Radial** ⟩ and then **Diameter**. You are then asked to select the arc or circle.

When the AutoCAD dimension variables are set to their default values, the **DIMDIA** command automatically places the dimension line, arrowheads, and diameter dimension inside of a circle, if the circle is large enough. For medium size circles, the dimension line and arrowheads may be placed inside or outside, depending on how you drag these items into place. The diameter dimension is placed with a short leader when the circle is small. Examples of these applications are shown in Figure 20-50.

The **DIMDIA** command is easy to use. All you have to do is pick a circle or arc to dimension and drag the dimension line or leader to the needed location. The dimension line automatically passes through the center, or the leader points to the center, as preferred by ASME Y14.5M-1994. This is the command sequence:

Command: *(type* DIMDIA *or* DIMDIAMETER *and press* [Enter]*)*
Dimension line location (Text/Angle): *(pick the dimension line location)*
Command:

You also have the **Text** and **Angle** options that were introduced earlier. Use the **Text** option if you want to change the text number or the **Angle** option if you want to change the angle of the text. The **Text** option might be used if you are dimensioning an arc, because an R should precede the dimension number rather than a diameter symbol. When you enter T for the **Text** option, the **Edit MText** dialog box appears. Delete the chevrons (⟨⟩) and the type R plus the dimension value. Then pick **OK** and the dimension text is placed.

Figure 20-50.    Using the **DIMDIA** command with the AutoCAD dimensioning variable defaults.

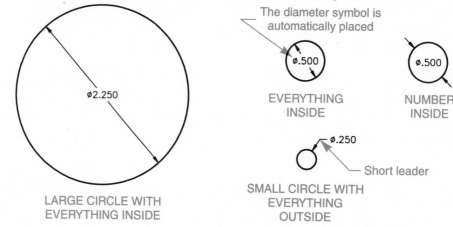

**NOTE:**    If you enter the diameter dimensioning command at the **Dim:** prompt, you will need to enter the R and the dimension text on the command line.

### Adjusting dimension variables to dimension circles with more flexibility

With the dimensioning method discussed in the previous section, there is little flexibility in placing the location of the dimension. This practice is generally not the best solution when trying to place dimensions on a real drawing. There are dimension variables that can be set to help gain more flexibility when dimensioning circles using the **DIMDIA** command. These dimension variables include **DIMTOFL**, **DIMFIT**, and **DIMUPT**.

### Using the DIMTOFL variable

The **DIMTOFL** (dimension text outside, force line inside) variable allows you to force a dimension line to be drawn between the arrowheads, even when the text and arrowheads are placed outside, Figure 20-51. The settings are off (0) (the default) and on (1):

Command: **DIMTOFL** ↵
New value for DIMTOFL ⟨Off⟩: **ON** ↵
Command:

Figure 20-51. Diameter dimensions placed with **DIMTOFL** off and on.

DIMTOFL off          DIMTOFL on

## Using the DIMFIT variable

The **DIMFIT** (fit text) variable controls the placement of arrowheads and text inside or outside of extension lines, based on the space available. There are five settings available, but all of the settings will fit text and arrows inside if there is room, or outside in some cases based on how you drag the dimension. The **DIMFIT** settings are as follows:

| | |
|---|---|
| 0 | If there is not enough room for both text and arrows, all are placed outside. |
| 1 | If there is room for text only, the text is placed inside and the arrowheads are placed outside. Otherwise, all are placed outside. |
| 2 | If there is room for arrows only, they are placed inside and the text is placed outside. Otherwise, all are placed outside. |
| 3 *(default)* | If there is room for arrows only, arrows are placed inside. If there is room for text only, text is placed inside. Otherwise all are placed outside. |
| 4 | If there is room for text only, text is placed inside. Otherwise, a leader line is created. |

Figure 20-52 shows how the **DIMFIT** variable can be used to alter the results of the **DIMDIA** command with **DIMTOFL** off. Figure 20-53 shows how the **DIMFIT** variable can be used to alter the results of the **DIMDIA** command with **DIMTOFL** on. Change the **DIMFIT** setting like this:

```
Command: DIMFIT ↵
New value for DIMFIT ⟨3⟩: 4 ↵
Command:
```

In AutoCAD 13 C4 maintenance release or later versions, a new **DIMFIT** setting is available. Setting **DIMFIT** at 5 works exactly like the setting of 4, except that no leader line is created.

Figure 20-52. Diameter dimensions placed with the different **DIMFIT** options. Drag the dimensions if there is room inside, otherwise everything is placed outside. All examples are with **DIMTOFL** off.

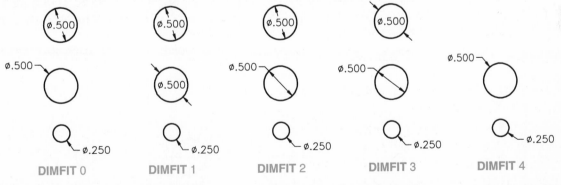

| DIMFIT 0 | DIMFIT 1 | DIMFIT 2 | DIMFIT 3 | DIMFIT 4 |

Figure 20-53. Diameter dimensions placed with **DIMTOFL** on and different **DIMFIT** options.

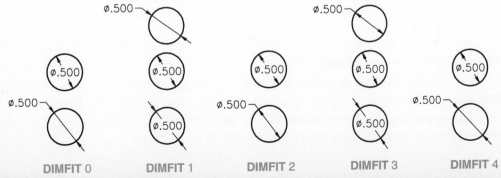

| DIMFIT 0 | DIMFIT 1 | DIMFIT 2 | DIMFIT 3 | DIMFIT 4 |

## Using the DIMUPT variable

The **DIMUPT** (user positioned text) variable gives you even more control of dimension text placement than the methods described to this point. Part of the problem with the **DIMTOFL** and **DIMFIT** applications is that the leader length cannot be adjusted. In practical use, this may not provide the clearance you need to place the dimension correctly on a drawing. Also, the dimension text is placed at the center of the circle when the dimension line and text are placed inside. This text placement is not normally a recommended practice. The text should be offset from the center of the circle to allow for center marks. The **DIMUPT** variable allows you to adjust the leader length and control the dimension text location, Figure 20-54. The **DIMUPT** variable is off (0) by default, but can be turned on (1):

> Command: **DIMUPT** ⏎
> New value for DIMUPT ⟨Off⟩: **ON** ⏎
> Command:

Figure 20-54.   Using the **DIMUPT** variable provides more flexibility in placing dimension text with the **DIMDIA** command.

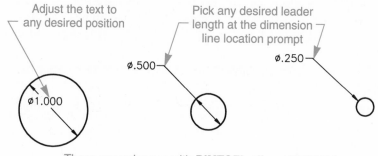

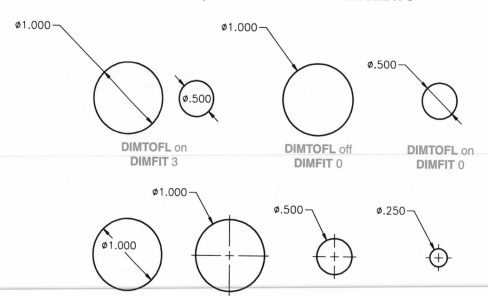

These circles are dimensioned
with the **DIMDIA** command and a **DIMCEN** setting of −.125

## Draw the center marks automatically

When you use the **DIMDIA** or **DIMRAD** command, center dashes are automatically drawn if the **DIMCEN** variable is set to a positive value. Centerlines are drawn if **DIMCEN** is a negative value. The automatic centers are drawn if the dimension is placed outside of the circle or arc. Otherwise no centers are drawn. See Figure 20-54.

**PROFESSIONAL TIP**

Dimensioning variables can be entered transparently while in another command. For example:

> Command: **DIMDIA** ↵
> Select arc or circle: **'DIMCEN** ↵

While dimensioning, if you are not at a point or object selection prompt, there is no need for the apostrophe. Transparent changes to variable settings can be very helpful for on-the-spot adjustments to dimension appearance. For example, in the following sequence, last minute changes are made to the **DIMCEN** and **DIMZIN** variables while in the process of creating a diameter dimension:

> Command: **DIMDIAMETER** ↵
> Select arc or circle: *(select a circle)*
> Dimension line location (Text/Angle): **DIMCEN** ↵
> Current value ⟨0.0900⟩ New value: **−.09** ↵
> Dimension line location (Text/Angle): **ZIN** ↵
> Current value ⟨0⟩ New value: **4** ↵
> Dimension line location (Text/Angle): *(complete your dimension)*

It is important to remember that when dimension variables are set transparently, the setting is temporary. This means the variable is only in effect during the dimensioning operation that it was set in. The variable is immediately reset to the previous value upon completion or cancellation of the current dimensioning command.

---

## EXERCISE 20-7

❏ Open PRODR2.
❏ For this exercise, draw the object lines on layer Object. Place all center marks and dimensions on layer Dim. Use the proper dimensioning techniques and commands to dimension the objects. Set the **DIMCEN** variable to −.125.
❏ With all dimension variables other than **DIMCEN** at their default settings, draw and dimension four circles similar to Figure 20-50.
❏ Draw and dimension a .500 diameter circle with **DIMTOFL** off and another .500 diameter circle with **DIMTOFL** on, like Figure 20-51. Label each dimensioned circle with its related **DIMTOFL** setting.
❏ With **DIMTOFL** off, experiment with the **DIMFIT** settings by drawing and dimensioning the circles shown in Figure 20-52. Label each group of dimensioned circles with their correlated **DIMFIT** application.
❏ With **DIMTOFL** on, experiment with the **DIMFIT** settings by drawing and dimensioning the circles shown in Figure 20-53. Label each group of dimensioned circles with their correlated **DIMFIT** application.
❏ Turn the **DIMUPT** variable on. Use Figure 20-54 as reference as you draw and dimension the following:
  ❏ Three circles with diameters of 1.000, .500, and .250 using **DIMTOFL** off and **DIMFIT** set to 3.
  ❏ Two circles with diameters of 1.000 and .500 using **DIMTOFL** on and **DIMFIT** (3).
  ❏ A 1.000 diameter circle with **DIMTOFL** off and **DIMFIT** (0).
  ❏ A .500 diameter circle with **DIMTOFL** on and **DIMFIT** (0).
❏ Save the drawing as A:EX20-7.

## Dimensioning holes

Holes are dimensioned in the view where they appear as circles. Give location dimensions to the center and a leader showing the diameter. Leader lines can be drawn as previously discussed. The **DIMUPT** (on) variable gives you the most flexibility. Set the **DIMCEN** variable to produce center marks. Multiple holes of the same size can be noted with one hole dimension, such as 2X ∅.50, Figure 20-55. However, this must be typed using the **Text** option at the Dimension line location (Text/Angle): prompt.

Figure 20-55.  Dimensioning holes.

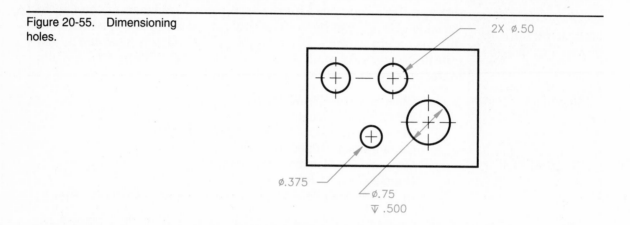

## Dimensioning for manufacturing processes

A *counterbore* is a larger diameter hole machined at one end of a smaller hole. It provides a place for the head of a bolt. A *spotface* is similar to a counterbore except that it is not as deep. The spotface provides a smooth recessed surface for a washer. A *countersink* is a cone-shaped recess at one end of a hole. It provides a mating surface for a screw head of the same shape. A note for these features is provided using symbols. First, locate the centers in the circular view. Then, place a leader providing machining information in a note, Figure 20-56. Symbols for this type of application must be customized and are discussed in Chapter 25. These symbols are displayed in Figure 20-48. Turn **DIMUPT** on to give you the maximum flexibility using the **DIMDIA** command. **DIMDIA** gives you one line of text to use during the creation of the dimension. Additional text can be added by editing the dimension text, since it is actually an **MTEXT** object.

Figure 20-56.  Dimension notes for machining processes.

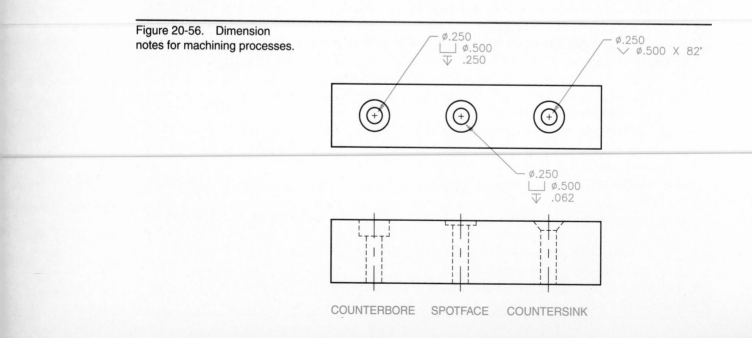

PROFESSIONAL
TIP

After creating any dimension, the dimension text can be directly edited using the **DDEDIT** command. This allows you to enter multi-line text and special notations.

## Dimensioning repetitive features

*Repetitive features* refer to many features having the same shape and size. When this occurs, the number of repetitions is followed by an X, a space, and the size dimension. The dimension is then connected to the feature with a leader, as shown in Figure 20-57.

Figure 20-57. Dimensioning repetitive features (shown in color).

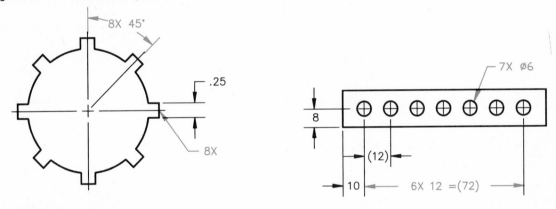

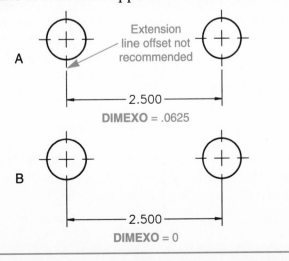

PROFESSIONAL
TIP

The ASME standard recommends a small space between the object and the extension line, as shown in Figure 20-1. This happens when the **DIMEXO** variable is set to its default or some other desired positive value. This is very useful *except* when providing dimensions to centerlines for the location of holes. A positive **DIMEXO** value leaves a space between the centerline and the beginning of the extension line when the endpoint of the centerline is picked, as shown at A below. This is not a preferred practice. It is recommended that you change **DIMEXO** to 0 for these applications. See B below.

**EXERCISE 20-8**

❑ Load AutoCAD for Windows and open PRODR2.
❑ Draw the object lines of the following objects on layer Object, centerlines on layer Center, and place all dimensions on layer Dim.
❑ Use the proper dimensioning techniques and commands to dimension the objects exactly as shown.
❑ Save the drawing as A:EX20-8.

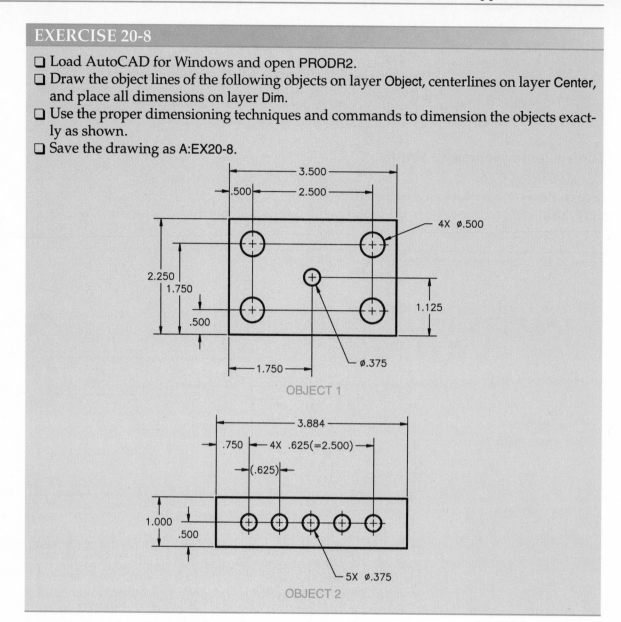

DIMENSIONING ARCS                                                           AUG 9

The standard for dimensioning arcs is a radius dimension. A radius dimension is placed with the **DIMRADIUS** command. You can pick the **Radius Dimension** button on the **Dimensioning** toolbar, type either DIMRAD or DIMRADIUS at the **Command:** prompt, or type either RAD or RADIUS while in the **DIM** command at the **Dim:** prompt. If the ACADFULL menu file is loaded, you can also pick **Dimensioning** ❭ from the **Draw** pull-down menu, followed by **Radial** ❭ and then **Radius**.

Using the **DIMRADIUS** command, AutoCAD places a leader line with an arrowhead pointing at the arc. The leader line either extends away from the arc or from the arc through the center point, depending on the size of the arc. When the dimension variables are set to their default values, the leader length is automatically determined by AutoCAD. This leader length is often too short for practical applications. Examples using the **DIMRAD** command with default variables are shown in Figure 20-58. The command sequence is as follows:

Command: *(type* DIMRAD *or* DIMRADIUS *and press* [Enter]*)*
Select arc or circle: *(pick an arc)*
Dimension line location (Text/Angle): *(drag the leader to a desired location and pick)*
Command:

As with the previous dimensioning commands, you can use the **Text** option to change the dimension text or use the **Angle** option to change the angle of the text numbers.

Figure 20-58.   Using the **DIMRAD** command to dimension arcs with AutoCAD dimensioning variable defaults.

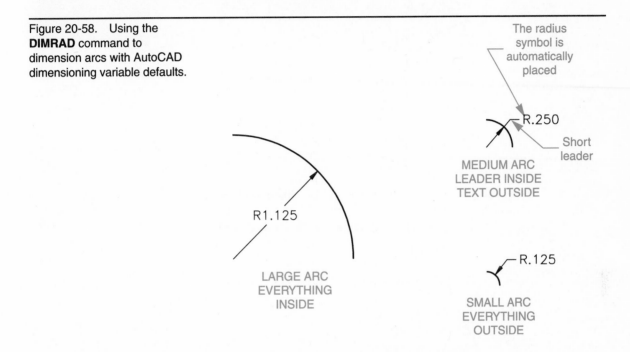

## Adjusting the dimension variables with the **DIMRAD** command

Changing the dimension variables when using the **DIMRAD** command alters the way dimensions are placed similar to the **DIMCIRCLE** command. While the effect of using the **DIMTOFL** variable is minor, it does force the leader inside when the arc is small, as shown in Figure 20-59.

The **DIMUPT** variable gives you the flexibility to place the radius dimension for a large arc either inside or outside of the arc. **DIMUPT** also lets you adjust the text location when the leader is inside, and allows you to control the leader length when the leader is outside. See Figure 20-60.

Figure 20-59.   Using the **DIMRAD** with **DIMTOFL** off and on.

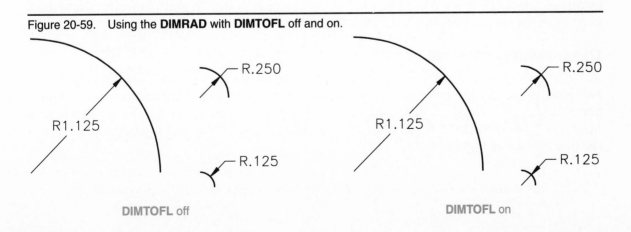

Figure 20-60.   Using the **DIMUPT** variable provides more flexibility in placing dimension text with the **DIMRAD** command.

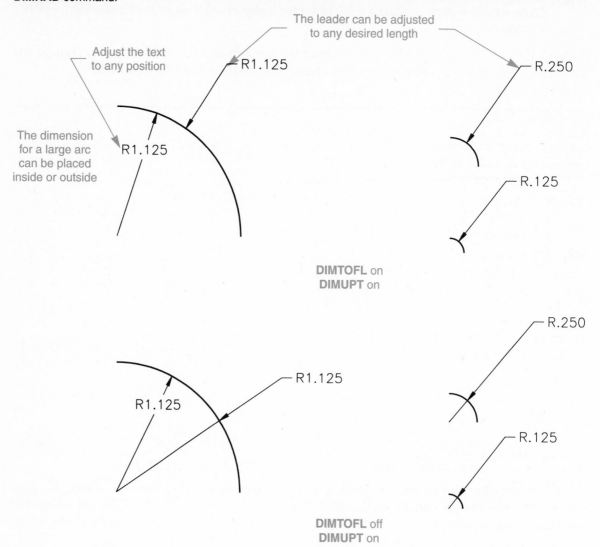

AutoCAD automatically adds the center dashes when the **DIMCEN** variable is nonzero, and when the leader is placed outside the arc. If decimal-inch units are used and the value is less than 1, AutoCAD places a 0 in front of the decimal. ASME Y14.5M-1994 recommends that a decimal-inch be shown without a 0 in front of the decimal point. Metric decimals, however, should have a 0 placed in front of the decimal point. To automatically delete the 0 in front of the decimal point, set the **DIMZIN** variable to 4.

### Dimensioning fillets and rounds

Small inside arcs are called *fillets*. Small arcs on outside corners are called *rounds*. Fillets are designed to strengthen inside corners. Rounds are used to relieve sharp corners. Fillets and rounds can be dimensioned individually as arcs or in a general note. The general note is ALL FILLETS AND ROUNDS R.125 UNLESS OTHERWISE SPECIFIED and is usually placed near the title block. See Figure 20-61.

Figure 20-61. Dimensioning fillets and rounds.

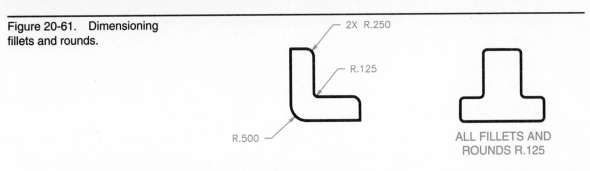

ALL FILLETS AND
ROUNDS R.125

---

## EXERCISE 20-9

❏ Open PRODR2.
❏ For this exercise, draw object lines on layer Object, and place all center dashes and dimensions on layer Dim. Use the proper dimensioning techniques, variables, and commands to dimension the objects. Set the **DIMCEN** variable to .125.
❏ With all dimension variables other than **DIMCEN** at their default settings, draw and dimension three arcs similar to Figure 20-58.
❏ Draw and dimension three arcs with **DIMTOFL** off and three arcs with **DIMTOFL** on similar to Figure 20-59.
❏ Turn **DIMUPT** on. Draw and dimension three arcs with **DIMTOFL** off and three arcs with **DIMTOFL** on similar to Figure 20-60.
❏ Save the drawing as A:EX20-9.

---

## CHAPTER TEST

*Write your answers in the spaces provided.*

1. Give the command and entries required to change the dimensioning text style from STANDARD to ROMANS:

   Command: _____

   New value for _____ ⟨"STANDARD"⟩: _____

2. If the dimension reads 2.875 and you want it to read ⌀2.875, what should you enter in the **Edit MText** dialog box or on the command line?_____

3. Give the command and entries needed to change the dimensioning text from the default size of 0.18 to .25:

   Command: _____

   New value for _____ ⟨0.1800⟩: _____

4. Give the command and entries required to dimension a 30° angle between two existing intersecting lines. Let AutoCAD center the text in the dimension line.

   Command: _____

   Select arc, circle, line, or RETURN: _____

   Second line: _____

   Dimension arc line location (Text/Angle): _____

   Dimension text ⟨30⟩: _____

   Enter text location (or RETURN): _____

5. Give the command and related responses used to dimension four holes, all having .250″ diameter:

Command: _____

Select arc or circle: _____

Dimension line location (Text/Angle): _____

Dimension text ⟨0.250⟩: _____

Dimension arc line location (Text/Angle): _____

6. Give the command and entries required to dimension an arc. The text should read R1.750.

Command: _____

Dim:_____

Select arc or circle: _____

Dimension line location (Text/Angle): _____

Dimension text ⟨1.750⟩: _____

Command: _____

7. Give the command and entries needed to set and draw centerlines that extend .25 units beyond a circle's circumference.

Command: _____

New value for _____ ⟨0⟩: _____

Command: _____

Select arc or circle: _____

8. Describe the function of dimension variables. _____

_____

_____

_____

9. Identify three ways to return to the **Command:** prompt when in the **DIM** command.

_____

_____

_____

10. What are the recommended standard units of measure on engineering drawings and related documents? _____

_____

11. Name the units of measure commonly used in architectural and structural drafting, and show an example. _____

12. What is the recommended height for dimension numbers and notes on drawings?

_____

13. Name the command option used to change the dimension text style. _____

14. Give the control code necessary to display the Ø symbol. _____

15. Name the pull-down menu where the **Linear**, **Aligned**, and **Radial** dimensioning commands are found. _____

16. Name the two dimensioning commands that provide linear dimensions for angled surfaces. _____

_____

17. Name the command used to dimension angles in degrees. _____

18. What are the two types of notes found on a drawing? _____

19. AutoCAD refers to chain dimensioning as _____.

20. AutoCAD refers to datum dimensioning as _____.

21. The command used to provide diameter dimensions for circles is _____.

22. The command used to provide radius dimensions for arcs is _____.

23. What does the M mean in the title of the standard ASME Y14.5M-1994? _____

_____

_____

24. Does a text style have to be loaded using the **STYLE** command before it can be accessed for use in dimension text? _____

_____

25. If the text height is set to 0 in the **STYLE** command, then the dimension text height is controlled by this dimension variable. _____

26. How do you access the **DIMRADIUS** and **DIMDIAMETER** in a pull-down menu? _____

_____

_____

27. How do you place a datum dimension from the origin of the previously drawn dimension? _____

_____

_____

_____

28. How do you place a datum dimension from the origin of a dimension that was drawn during a previous drawing session? _____

_____

_____

_____

_____

*For Questions 29 - 50, identify the dimensioning variable that does each of the following:*

29. Controls the dimension text height. _____

30. Controls the -0" part of a feet-inches dimension. _____

31. Controls the size of the gap between the object and extension line. _____

32. Controls the distance the extension line projects past the last dimension line. _____

33. Suppresses the second extension line. _____

34. Provides for aligned dimensioning of dimensions inside of extension lines. _____

35. Places dimension text above the dimension line for architectural drafting. _____

36. Changes the arrowhead size. _____

37. Controls the display and size of dimension line ticks for architectural drafting. _____

_____

38. Controls dimension line spacing. _____

39. Used to set the dimension text style. _____

40. Sets the units format for dimension numbers. _____

41. Establishes the number of decimal places for the value of the dimension numbers.

_____

42. Sets the dimension value format for angular dimensions. _____

43. Controls the placement of arrowheads and text inside or outside of extension lines
    based on the space available._____

44. Allows you to control the dimension text placement and leader length._____

45. Establishes center marks for circles and arcs. _____

_____

46. Name the dimensioning variable that, when turned on, forces dimension text inside the
    extension lines only when the dimension lines and arrowheads are placed outside.

_____

_____

47. Give an example of a proper inch and millimeter decimal number less than one.

_____

_____

48. Name the dimensioning variable and its value which is used to draw architectural dots
    at the end of the dimension lines. _____

_____

49. Name the dimensioning variable and its setting for suppressing the lead zero on
    decimal-inch dimensions. _____

50. It is recommended that no gap exist between an extension line and a centerline when
    providing location dimensions to holes. Give the dimension variable and its value to
    use to achieve this task. _____

## DRAWING PROBLEMS

***1 - 15.   Open each of the completed drawings in Chapter 19 (P19-1 through P19-15), or start a new drawing for those drawings not completed. Set limits, units, dimensioning variables, and other parameters as needed. Follow these guidelines:***

A. Draw the views to exact size.

B. Use grid, object snap modes, and the **OSNAP** command to your best advantage.

C. Apply dimensions accurately using ASME standards.

D. Set dimensioning variables to suit the drawing.

E. Use the **LAYER** command to set separate layers for views and dimensions.

F. Draw object lines using .032" wide polylines, or use the **LINE** command and plot object lines with a wide pen.

G. Place general notes 1/2" from lower-left corner.

    2.   REMOVE ALL BURRS AND SHARP EDGES.

    1.   INTERPRET PER ASME Y14.5M-1994.

    NOTES:

H. Save the drawings to your floppy disk with names A:P20-1 through P20-15.

***16 - 19. Draw and completely dimension the following manufacturing problems with the same general notes specified in Problems 1 - 15.***

16.

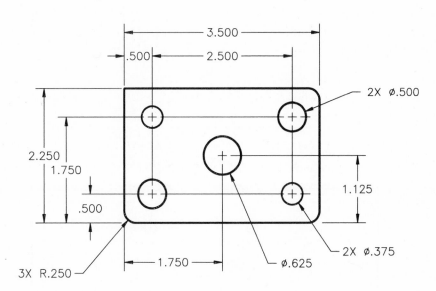

**Mechanical
Drafting**

17.

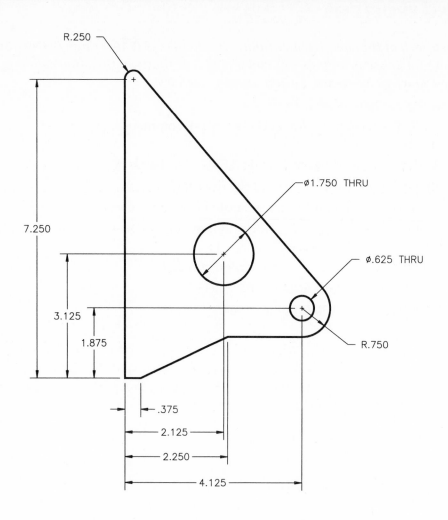

**Mechanical
Drafting**

18.

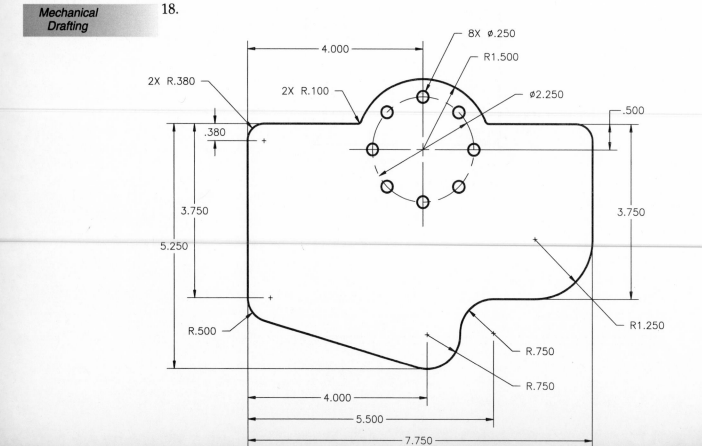

19.

*Mechanical Drafting*

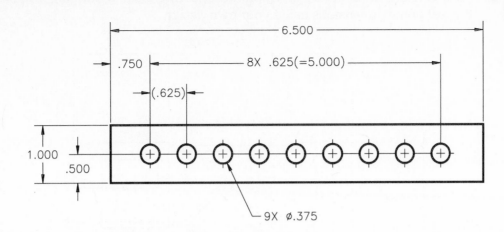

20 - 21. **Draw and completely dimension the following partial architectural floor plans.**

20.

*Architecture*

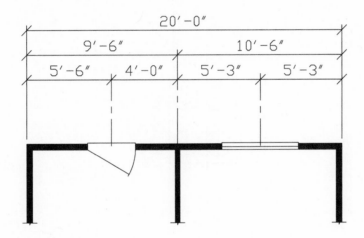

21.

*Architecture*

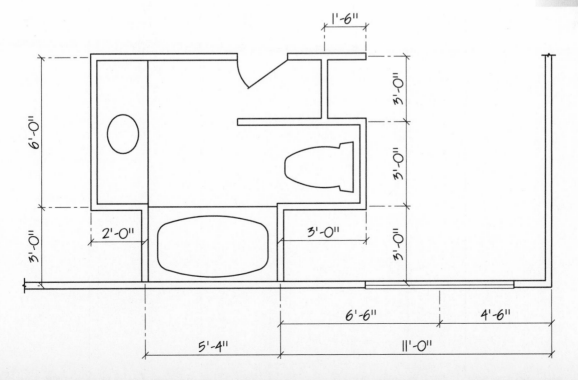

22. The overall dimensions are given on the following kitchen drawing. Establish the rest of the dimensions using your own design.

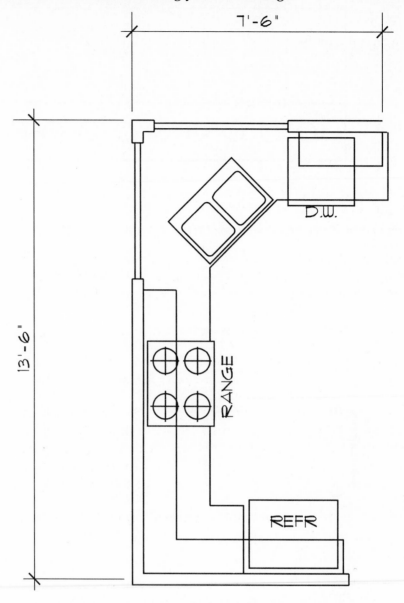

AutoCAD R13

## Chapter 21

# Intermediate Dimensioning

## Learning objectives

After completing this chapter, you will be able to:

- ○ Dimension curves that are not a specified radius.
- ○ Draw oblique dimensions.
- ○ Use the **LEADER** command to draw specific notes.
- ○ Use dimensioning variables to modify dimension text placement.
- ○ Alter dimension scales.
- ○ Change the color of dimension elements.
- ○ Edit dimensions.
- ○ Draw ordinate dimensions.
- ○ Place thread notes on a drawing.
- ○ Use dialog boxes to control dimensioning variables.

Chapter 20 introduced you to the basic dimensioning commands and how dimensioning variables can be used to provide flexibility in placing dimensions. This chapter presents additional dimensioning techniques used in a variety of situations where the applications require special consideration. The practices include dimensioning curves and drawing leaders to place specific notes. You will learn to use *ordinate dimensioning*. This is also called *arrowless dimensioning* because it replaces the traditional dimension lines and arrowheads. This chapter concludes with how to use the **Dimension Styles** dialog box.

## DIMENSIONING CURVES

When possible, curves are dimensioned as arcs. When they are not in the shape of a constant-radius arc, they should be dimensioned to points along the curve using the **DIMLINEAR** commands. See Figure 21-1.

Figure 21-1. Dimensioning curves that are not a constant radius.

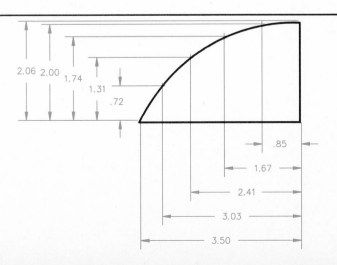

### Dimensioning curves with oblique extension lines

The curve shown in Figure 21-1 is dimensioned using the normal practice, but in some cases, spaces may be limited and oblique extension lines are used. First, dimension the object using the **DIMLINEAR** command as appropriate, even if dimensions are crowded or overlap, as shown in Figure 21-2A.

The .150 and .340 dimensions are to be placed at an oblique angle above the view. The **OBLIQUE** command can be accessed by picking the **Oblique Dimensions** button in the **Dimension Style** flyout in the **Dimensioning** toolbar. It can also be accessed by typing OBLIQUE at the **Dim:** prompt. If the ACADFULL menu file is loaded, the command can also be accessed by selecting **Oblique** in the **Dimensioning** 〉 cascading submenu in the **Draw** pulldown menu. Another way to produce oblique dimensions is to use the **Oblique** option of the **DIMEDIT** command.

After selecting the command, you are asked to select the objects. Pick the dimensions to be redrawn at an oblique angle. In this case, the .150 and .340 dimensions are selected.

> Command: **DIM** ↵
> Dim: *(type* OB *or* OBLIQUE *and press* [Enter]*)*
> Select objects: *(pick the .150 and .340 dimensions)*
> Select objects: ↵

Next, you are asked for the obliquing angle. Careful planning is needed to make sure the correct obliquing angle is selected. Obliquing angles originate from 0° East and revolve counterclockwise:

> Enter obliquing angle (RETURN for none): **135** ↵
> Dim:

The result is shown in Figure 21-2B.

Figure 21-2. Drawing dimensions with oblique extension lines.

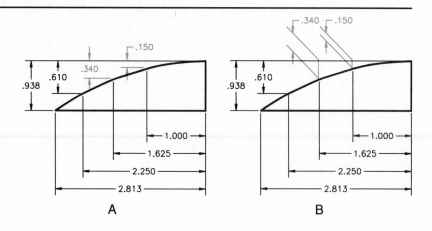

## DRAWING LEADER LINES

AUG 9

The **DIMDIAMETER** and **DIMRADIUS** options automatically place leaders on the drawing. The **LEADER** command allows you to begin and end a leader line where you desire. You can also place single or multiple lines of text with the leader. This command is ideal for the following situations:

- When you are working on a drawing and need more control of dimension placement than is available by adjusting dimensioning variables and using **DIMDIA** and **DIMRAD**.
- Adding specific notes to the drawing.
- When a leader line must be staggered to go around other drawing features. Keep in mind that staggering leader lines is not a recommended ASME standard.
- Where a double leader is required. Drawing two leaders from one note is not recommended.
- When making custom leader lines.

AutoCAD's **LEADER** command creates leader lines and related notes that are considered complex objects. This command provides you with the flexibility to place tolerances and multiple lines of text with the leader. The leader line characteristics, such as arrowhead size and text positioning, are controlled by the dimension variable settings. Other features, such as the leader format and annotation style, are controlled by options in the **LEADER** command. *Annotation* means the addition of notes or text and is commonly used in computer-aided drafting.

The **LEADER** command is accessed by typing **LEADER** at the **Command:** prompt, or by picking the **Leader** button in the **Dimensioning** toolbar. If the ACADFULL menu file is loaded, it can be accessed by selecting **Lea̲der** from the **Dimensioning** ⟩ cascading submenu in the **Draw** pull-down menu. The initial prompts look like the **LINE** command, with the From point: and To point: prompts. This allows you to pick where the leader starts and ends. In mechanical drafting, properly drawn leaders have one straight segment extending from the feature to a horizontal shoulder, which is 1/4″ (6mm) long. While most other fields also use straight leaders, AutoCAD provides the option of drawing curved leaders. Examples are shown in Figure 21-3. The command sequence begins like this:

```
Command: LEADER ↵
From point: (pick the leader start point)
To point: (pick the second leader point, which is the start of the leader shoulder)
To point (Format/Annotation/Undo) ⟨Annotation⟩:
```

Figure 21-3. Using the **LEADER** command to draw a curved leader and a straight leader, and identification of the leader elements.

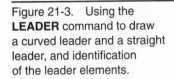
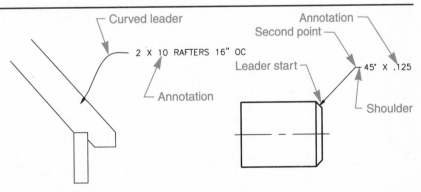

AutoCAD automatically draws a leader shoulder unless the leader line is 15° or less off of horizontal. While the ASME standard does not recommend a leader line that is less than 15° or greater than 75° from horizontal, it is sometimes necessary. If you need to create a shoulder, pick the endpoint of the leader shoulder like this:

Command: **LEADER** ↵
From point: *(pick the leader start point)*
To point: *(pick the second leader point, which is the start of the leader shoulder)*
To point (Format/Annotation/Undo) ⟨Annotation⟩: *(pick the end of the leader shoulder)*
To point (Format/Annotation/Undo) ⟨Annotation⟩:

Annotation is the default, which means that you can press [Enter] to access the **Annotation** option. Type the desired note at the next prompt and then press [Enter] to get the MText: prompt. Press [Enter] to get back to the **Command:** prompt, or type as many lines of text as you want and press the [Enter] key after each line of text. The prompts continue like this for placing one line of text:

Annotation (or RETURN for options): **2 X 6 STUDS 16″ OC** ↵
MText: ↵
Command:

If you wanted to place more than one line of text, the prompts would have continued like this:

Annotation (or RETURN for options): **2 X 6 STUDS 16″ OC** ↵
MText: **W/ 5 1/2″ BATTS R-19 MIN** ↵
MText: **FOIL FACE 1 SIDE** ↵
MText: ↵
Command:

The results of using the previous leader commands are shown in Figure 21-4. Text placed using the **LEADER** command is a multiline text object (all of the lines of text are one object). You may want to review the **MTEXT** command in Chapter 11. When there is more than one line of text, the lines are justified on the left side if the leader is on the left and justified on the right if the leader is on the right. The leader shoulder is centered on the multiple lines of text, as shown in Figure 21-4. The **DIMGAP** variable controls the distance from the end of the leader shoulder to the text.

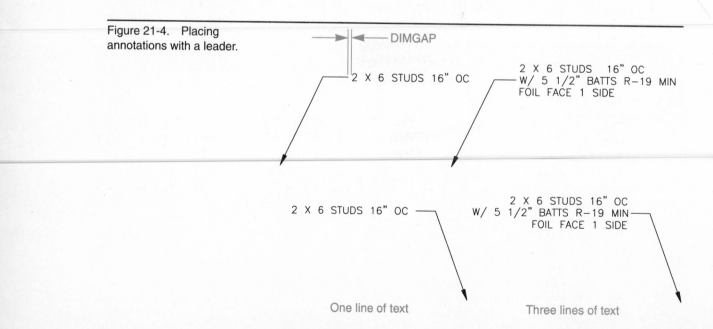

Figure 21-4.  Placing annotations with a leader.

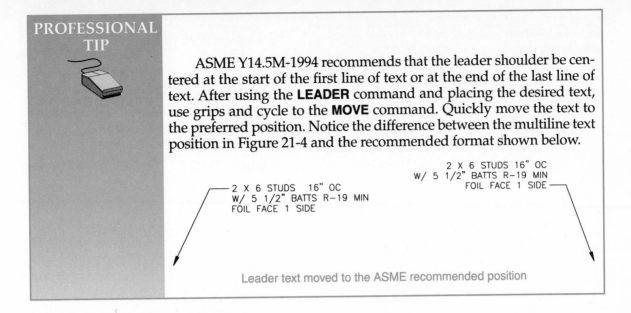

Leader text moved to the ASME recommended position

2 X 6 STUDS  16" OC
W/ 5 1/2" BATTS R—19 MIN
FOIL FACE 1 SIDE

2 X 6 STUDS 16" OC
W/ 5 1/2" BATTS R—19 MIN
FOIL FACE 1 SIDE

**PROFESSIONAL TIP**

ASME Y14.5M-1994 recommends that the leader shoulder be centered at the start of the first line of text or at the end of the last line of text. After using the **LEADER** command and placing the desired text, use grips and cycle to the **MOVE** command. Quickly move the text to the preferred position. Notice the difference between the multiline text position in Figure 21-4 and the recommended format shown below.

## Using the Annotation suboptions

The **Annotation** option can be accessed by pressing the [Enter] key as previously described. Typing A and pressing the [Enter] key will also access the option. If you press [Enter] again, you get the **Annotation** suboptions:

> To point (Format/Annotation/Undo) 〈Annotation〉:
> Annotation (or RETURN for options): **A** ↵
> Tolerance/Copy/Block/None/〈MText〉:

Now, you can press [Enter] to access the MS-DOS text editor. In the text editor, you can type paragraph text or use one of the other options:

- **Tolerance.** Type T to use the **Tolerance** option. This displays the **Geometric Tolerance** dialog boxes for creation of a feature control frame. An example is shown in Figure 21-5A. Geometric tolerancing is explained in detail in Chapter 23.
- **Copy.** This option copies text, mtext, feature control frame, or a block and connects the new object to the leader being created. The option begins with the Select object: prompt. All you have to do is pick a single object feature and it is automatically copied to a position at the leader shoulder, as shown in Figure 21-5B:

> Annotation (or RETURN for options): **A** ↵
> Tolerance/Copy/Block/None/〈MText〉: **C** ↵
> Select object: *(pick the object)*
> Command:

- **Block.** This option inserts a specified block at the end of the leader. A *block* is a symbol that was previously created and saved. Blocks can be then inserted into other drawings. These multiple-use symbols are explained in detail in Chapter 25. Blocks can be scaled during the insertion process. A special symbol block called TARGET is inserted in Figure 21-5C. The command to insert the block at the default scale of 1:1 and 0° rotation angle is:

> Annotation (or RETURN for options): **A** ↵
> Tolerance/Copy/Block/None/〈MText〉: **B** ↵
> Block name (or ?): **TARGET** ↵
> Insertion point: X scale factor 〈1〉 / Corner / XYZ: ↵
> Y scale factor (default=X): ↵
> Rotation angle 〈0〉: ↵
> Command:

Figure 21-5. Examples of using the **LEADER** command **Annotation** options.

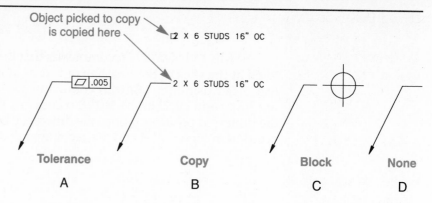

|  |  |  |  |
|---|---|---|---|
| Tolerance | Copy | Block | None |
| A | B | C | D |

- **None.** This option ends the leader with no annotation of any kind. See Figure 21-5.

    Annotation (or RETURN for options): **A** ↵
    Tolerance/Copy/Block/None/⟨MText⟩: **N** ↵
    Command:

## Using the LEADER command Format options

The **LEADER** command also allows you to modify the way a leader line is presented. This is done by accessing the **Format** option:

    Command: **LEADER** ↵
    From point: (*pick the leader start point*)
    To point: (*pick the second leader point, which is the start of the leader shoulder*)
    To point (Format/Annotation/Undo) ⟨Annotation⟩: **F** ↵
    Spline/STraight/Arrow/None/⟨Exit⟩:

The **Format** options are explained as follows:
- **Spline.** Enter S for the **Spline** option. This lets you draw leader lines using a spline object rather than straight segments. This practice is commonly used in architectural drafting. See Figure 21-6A.
- **STraight.** If you are inside the **LEADER** command and previously set **Format** to draw **Spline** leaders, then type ST to change back to straight segments. AutoCAD automatically defaults back to drawing straight segment leaders when you leave the **LEADER** command. See Figure 21-6B.
- **Arrow.** Use the **Arrow** option if you selected the **None** (no arrow) option and then decided to change back to using an arrow while in the **LEADER** command. AutoCAD automatically defaults back to using an arrow when you leave the **LEADER** command. See Figure 21-6C.
- **None.** This allows you to draw a leader without an arrow. See Figure 21-6D.
- **Exit.** Exit is the default here. Press the [Enter] key or type E to exit the **Format** options and return to the To point: prompt.

Figure 21-6. Examples of using the **LEADER** command **Format** options.

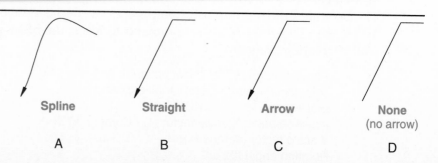

|  |  |  |  |
|---|---|---|---|
| Spline | Straight | Arrow | None (no arrow) |
| A | B | C | D |

## Using the Undo option

The **Undo** option removes the last leader segment that you drew. This is handy if you accidentally draw an extra leader shoulder and want to remove it. You can use the **Undo** option by typing U at the following prompt:

> To point (Format/Annotation/Undo) 〈Annotation〉: **U** ⏎

## Using multiple leaders

The **LEADER** command can be used to connect notes to various features on a drawing. While a single leader line is the preferred ASME standard, some companies allow multiple leaders, as shown in Figure 21-7. In order to draw multiple leader lines to the same note, use the **LEADER** command to place the first leader and the note. Then enter the **LEADER** command again and pick the beginning of the previous leader shoulder as the second point. Use the **None Annotation** option to terminate the command. The welding symbol shown in Figure 21-7B was created as a block and then inserted using the **Annotation Block** option.

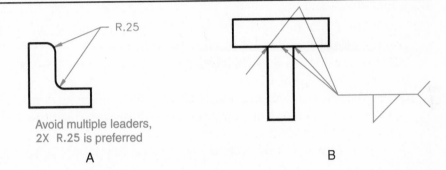

Figure 21-7. Alternate applications of the **LEADER** command.

Avoid multiple leaders, 2X R.25 is preferred

A

B

## Using the LEADER command inside the DIM command

You can also use the **LEADER** command inside of the **DIM** command by typing **LEADER** at the **Dim:** prompt. When you draw a leader in this manner, each element of the leader, including the arrow, straight segments, and text, are individual objects. Leaders must have straight segments and multiline text cannot be placed.

The **LEADER** subcommand acts like the **LINE** command. AutoCAD asks for the endpoints of the line segments. The second point determines the start of the leader shoulder. You must press enter to stop drawing other leader segments. The leader shoulder is automatically drawn unless the leader line is 15° or less from horizontal. You can then type the desired dimension text. You must cancel to get out of the **DIM** command:

> Command: **DIM** ⏎
> Dim: **LEADER** ⏎
> Leader start: *(pick a point on the feature to be dimensioned)*
> To point: *(pick the second leader point, which is usually the start of the shoulder)*
> To point: *(pick the end of the leader shoulder)*
> To point: ⏎
> Dimension text 〈1.500〉: *(type the desired text)*
> Dim: *(type EXIT and press [Enter], or press [Esc])*
> Command:

This is a version of the leader from previous AutoCAD releases. This type of leader generates a leader line that allows only one line of text to be entered, with no further options.

When using the **LEADER** subcommand of the **DIM** command, the text in brackets at the Dimension text: prompt is the default text for the last drawn dimension in the current drawing. This includes any special symbols. For example, if the last drawn dimension was a 2.500 diameter, the default leader text is ⟨Ø2.500⟩.

When the **DIMRADIUS** or **DIMDIAMETER** commands do not give you enough flexibility to meet special dimensioning requirements, you can use the **LEADER** subcommand to manually place the leader.

## EXERCISE 21-1

❑ Load AutoCAD and open PRODR2 or begin a new drawing with your own variables. Use the **LEADER** command to draw the following:
  ❑ Place one line of text with a straight leader and three lines of text with another leader as shown in Figure 21-4.
  ❑ Use the **Copy** and **None Annotation** options to place leaders similar to Figure 21-5. The **Tolerance** and **Block** options are not suggested at this time because these topics have not yet been explained.
  ❑ Use the **Spline**, **STraight**, **Arrow**, and **None Format** options to draw leaders similar to Figure 21-6. Annotation can be placed, if you wish.
❑ Use the **LEADER** subcommand of the **DIM** command to draw a leader with a 1/4" shoulder and place the note: R.250. Notice the difference between using the **LEADER** command at the **Command:** prompt and at the **Dim:** prompt.
❑ Save the drawing as A:EX21-1.

## Dimensioning chamfers

A *chamfer* is an angled surface used to relieve sharp corners. The ends of bolts are commonly chamfered to allow them to engage the threaded hole better. Chamfers of 45° are dimensioned with a leader giving the angle and linear dimension, or with two linear dimensions. This can be accomplished using the **LEADER** command, as shown in Figure 21-8.

Chamfers other than 45° must have either the angle and a linear dimension or two linear dimensions placed on the view. See Figure 21-9. The **DIMLINEAR** command is used for this purpose.

Figure 21-8.   Dimensioning
45° chamfers.

45° X .125

.125 X .125

Figure 21-9. Dimensioning chamfers that are not 45°.

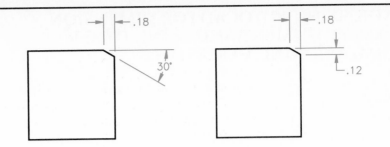

PROFESSIONAL TIP

Use the object snap modes to your best advantage when dimensioning. This saves time and increases accuracy.

**EXERCISE 21-2**

❏ Open PRODR2.
❏ Draw the object lines of the views on layer 0-7, centerlines on layer 2-2, and place dimensions on layer 3-3.
❏ Use the proper dimensioning techniques and commands to dimension the objects exactly as shown.
❏ Save the drawing as A:EX21-2.

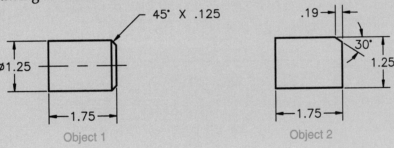

## DIMENSIONING IN LIMITED SPACES

When space between extension lines is limited, AutoCAD places the dimension line, arrowheads, and number outside the extension lines depending on the current **DIMFIT** setting. The number is placed outside of the last extension line selected, so you control its location by your selection order. See Figure 21-10. Remember, if you do not like where the dimension is placed, **UNDO** and try again.

Figure 21-10. When dimensioning in limited spaces, care must be used to properly select the dimension lines.

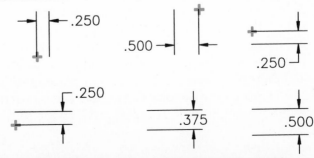

✛ This symbol is used to represent the first extension line origin point when the text does not fit between the extension lines

# ADJUSTING AUTOCAD FOR DIMENSION TEXT PLACEMENT AND USING OTHER DIMENSIONING VARIABLES

AUG 9

AutoCAD provides you with maximum flexibility to make your dimensioning reflect proper drafting standards. For example, if you are dimensioning a limited space and you want the number inside the extension lines with the arrowheads and extension lines outside the extension lines, dimensioning variables can be set to produce this.

## Placing dimension text inside the extension lines

The **DIMTIX** (dimension text inside extension lines) variable, when set on, forces the dimension text inside the extension lines. This occurs only when the dimension lines and arrowheads are placed outside. The **DIMTIX** default value is off. See Figure 21-11.

Figure 21-11. How the **DIMTIX** variable affects the placement of dimension text between extension lines.

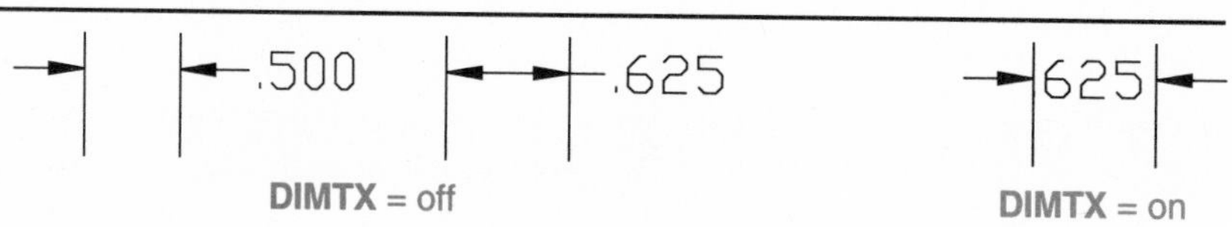

## Drawing the dimension line between the extension lines when the text and arrowheads are outside

Some drafters prefer to place a dimension line between extension lines when the dimension text is outside. To do so, set **DIMTOFL** to on and **DIMTIX** to off as shown in Figure 21-12. The default for **DIMTOFL** is off.

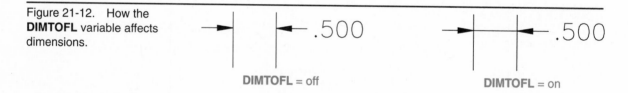

Figure 21-12. How the **DIMTOFL** variable affects dimensions.

## A review of the DIMFIT variable

The **DIMFIT** (fit text) variable was introduced in Chapter 20. This variable controls the placement of arrowheads and text inside or outside of extension lines. There are five settings available, all of which fit text and arrows inside if there is room. The different options are for times when the text and arrows do not fit between the extension lines. The **DIMFIT** settings are the options 0 through 4 and are used as follows:

- **0.** If there is not enough room for both text and arrows, all are placed outside.
- **1.** If there is room for text only, the text is placed inside and the arrowheads are placed outside. Otherwise, all are placed outside.
- **2.** If there is room for arrows only, they are placed inside and the text is placed outside. Otherwise, all are placed outside.
- **3.** This option is the default. If there is room for arrows only, arrows are placed inside. If there is room for text only, text is placed inside. Otherwise all are placed outside.
- **4.** If there is room for text only, text is placed inside. Otherwise, a leader line is created.

Figure 21-13 shows how the **DIMFIT** variable can be used to alter dimensions placed in limited spaces. Some options will, at times, produce the same result.

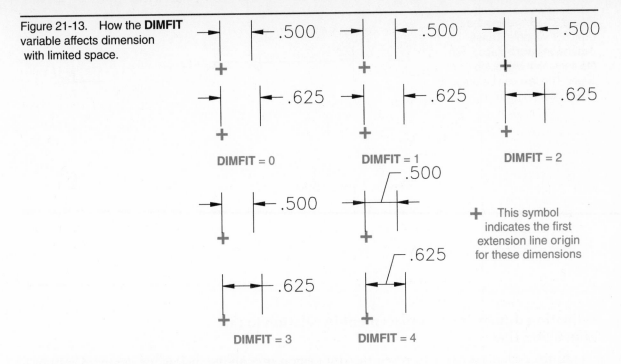

Figure 21-13.   How the **DIMFIT** variable affects dimension with limited space.

## Placing the dimension text inside the extension lines and suppressing the dimension line

When several dimensions are adjacent, you may want to place one number inside the extension lines and suppress the dimension lines and arrowheads. To do this, set **DIMTIX** to on and **DIMSOXD** (dimension suppress outside extension dimension lines) to on. The default value for each is off. The results are shown in Figure 21-14.

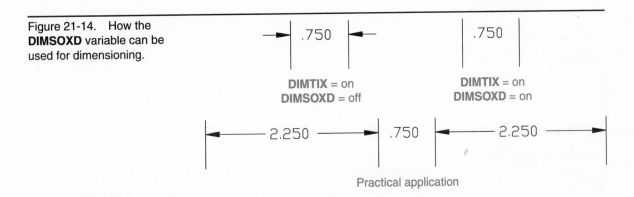

Figure 21-14.   How the **DIMSOXD** variable can be used for dimensioning.

## A review of the **DIMUPT** variable

The **DIMUPT** variable allows you to adjust the dimension line length and control the dimension text location by dragging the text, as shown in Figure 21-15. Turning the **DIMUPT** variable on enables this tool.

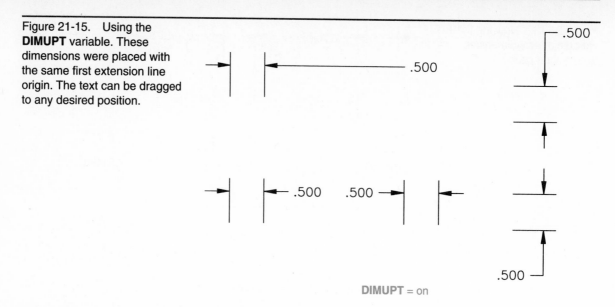

Figure 21-15.   Using the **DIMUPT** variable. These dimensions were placed with the same first extension line origin. The text can be dragged to any desired position.

DIMUPT = on

## Adjusting dimension text placement in relation to the dimension line

AutoCAD allows you to place the dimension text above, below, or centered within a break in the dimension line. This is called *text vertical position* and is controlled by the **DIMTVP** variable. As shown in Figure 21-16, **DIMTVP** has three settings:

- **DIMTVP = 0 (default).** Dimension text is centered within a break in dimension line. This is the normal practice for mechanical drafting.
- **DIMTVP = 1.** Dimension text is placed above the dimension line. This is common practice for architectural drafting and the construction trades.
- **DIMTVP = –1.** Dimension text is placed below the dimension line. This is an uncommon practice.

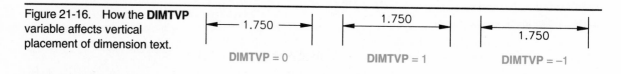

Figure 21-16.   How the **DIMTVP** variable affects vertical placement of dimension text.

DIMTVP = 0          DIMTVP = 1          DIMTVP = –1

**PROFESSIONAL TIP**

**DIMTVP** can be set to any value between 1 and –1 to achieve a text location that is off-center of the dimension line, but not completely above or below it.

## Using the DIMJUST variable

**DIMJUST** (justification) is used to justify text on the dimension line. There are five settings ranging from 0 to 4, with 0 being the default. Here are the results of these settings:

- **0.** This is the default. It center justifies the text on the dimension line.
- **1.** Places the text next to the first extension line.
- **2.** Places the text next to the second extension line.
- **3.** This option places the text aligned with and at the end of the first extension line.
- **4.** Places the text aligned with and at the end of the second extension line.

Results of the **DIMJUST** variable settings are displayed in Figure 21-17. Turn **DIMTAD** on if you want similar results with the text placed above the dimension line.

Figure 21-17.   How the **DIMJUST** variable affects dimension text.

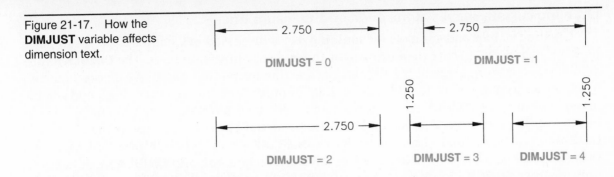

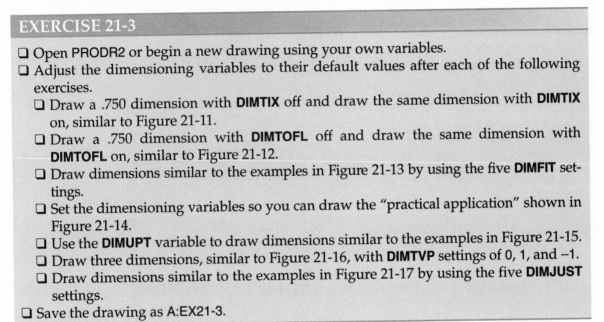

**EXERCISE 21-3**

❑ Open **PRODR2** or begin a new drawing using your own variables.
❑ Adjust the dimensioning variables to their default values after each of the following exercises.
  ❑ Draw a .750 dimension with **DIMTIX** off and draw the same dimension with **DIMTIX** on, similar to Figure 21-11.
  ❑ Draw a .750 dimension with **DIMTOFL** off and draw the same dimension with **DIMTOFL** on, similar to Figure 21-12.
  ❑ Draw dimensions similar to the examples in Figure 21-13 by using the five **DIMFIT** settings.
  ❑ Set the dimensioning variables so you can draw the "practical application" shown in Figure 21-14.
  ❑ Use the **DIMUPT** variable to draw dimensions similar to the examples in Figure 21-15.
  ❑ Draw three dimensions, similar to Figure 21-16, with **DIMTVP** settings of 0, 1, and –1.
  ❑ Draw dimensions similar to the examples in Figure 21-17 by using the five **DIMJUST** settings.
❑ Save the drawing as A:EX21-3.

## Controlling the gap between the dimension line and dimension text

When the dimension line is broken for placement of the dimension text, the space between the dimension line and text is controlled by the **DIMGAP** variable. The default distance for **DIMGAP** is .09. The default gap works well in most cases. However, in some instances the dimension text may be forced outside the extension line. Closing the dimension line gap allows more text to remain between the extension lines. Figure 21-18 shows the dimension line gap.

Figure 21-18.   The dimension line gap established with the **DIMGAP** dimensioning variable.

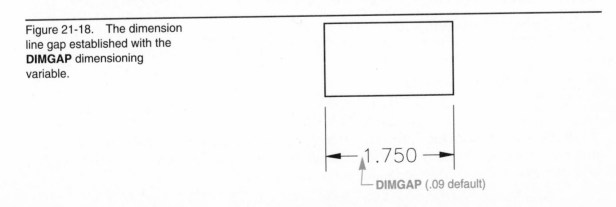

## Drawing custom shapes at the ends of dimension lines

Creating shapes and symbols for multiple use is discussed in Chapter 25. You can place user-defined blocks (rather than arrows) at the ends of dimension lines. The **DIMBLK1** variable places a custom block at the first end of the dimension line. **DIMBLK2** places a custom block at the second end of the dimension line. In order to place a block at both ends of the dimension line, set **DIMBLK** to the block name and have **DIMSAH** (separate custom arrow heads) off. To place a block at one end and use the default arrowhead type at the other end, **DIMSAH** must be on, and either **DIMBLK1** or **DIMBLK2** set to the appropriate block name. **DIMSAH** must be on for either **DIMBLK1** or **DIMBLK2** to be used, and **DIMBLK** must be set to none. Setting **DIMBLK1** to one value and **DIMBLK2** to another allows different blocks to be placed at each end of the dimension line. Figure 21-19 shows the dimension origin symbol used as a custom block at the first extension line. With **DIMSAH** set on, you can specify a custom block at both extension lines. Refer to Chapter 20 of this text for a discussion regarding the use of the **DIMBLK** variable.

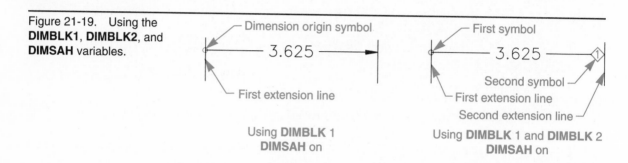

Figure 21-19. Using the **DIMBLK1**, **DIMBLK2**, and **DIMSAH** variables.

## USING **DIMEDIT** TO EDIT DIMENSION TEXT POSITION      AUG 9

In addition to the dimensioning variables that control the dimension text placement, the **DIMTEDIT** command lets you control the placement and orientation of an existing associative dimension. Remember, an associative dimension is a dimension drawn with **DIMASO** on, and all elements of the dimension act as one object. Good dimensioning practice requires that adjacent dimension numbers be staggered rather than stacked, as shown in Figure 21-20A. The **DIMJUST** can be used to stagger dimensions, if it is set before the dimension is placed. Use the **DIMTEDIT** command to stagger the text after a dimension has been placed. Access this command by typing **DIMTEDIT** at the **Command:** prompt, by typing TE or TEDIT at the **Dim:** prompt, or by picking one of the **DIMTEDIT** buttons on the **Dimensioning** toolbar. If the ACADFULL menu file is loaded, the **DIMTEDIT** options are also found by picking **Align Text** ⟩ in the **Dimensioning** ⟩ cascading menu of the **Draw** pull-down menu. You can also type TE at the **Command:** prompt:

> Command: **DIMTEDIT** ↵
> Select dimension: *(pick the dimension to be altered)*

or

> Command: **DIM** ↵
> Dim: *(type TE or TEDIT and press [Enter])*
> Select dimension: *(pick the dimension to be altered)*

If **DIMASO** was on when the dimension was created, the text of the selected dimension automatically drags with the screen cursor. This allows you to see where to place the text at the next prompt:

> Enter text location (Left/Right/Home/Angle): *(pick the desired text location)*

AutoCAD automatically moves the text and re-establishes the break in the dimension line, as shown in Figure 21-20B.

Figure 21-20.   Using the **DIMTEDIT** command to stagger dimensions.

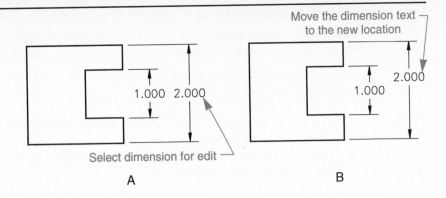

The **DIMTEDIT** command also allows you to automatically move the dimension text to the left or right, place it at an angle, or move it back to the original position. This is how the text location options work:

- **Left (L).** Moves horizontal text to the left or vertical text down.
- **Right (R).** Moves horizontal text to the right or vertical text up.
- **Home (H).** Moves text that had been changed previously back to its original position.
- **Angle.** Allows you to place dimension text at an angle. This works similar to the **TROTATE** command to be discussed later in this chapter. The text rotates around its middle point. The angle can be entered numerically or by selecting two points:

> Enter text location (Left/Right/Home/Angle): **A** ↵
> Text angle: **45** ↵

If you want to move text to the left, enter L as follows:

> Enter text location (Left/Right/Home/Angle): **L** ↵

Figure 21-21 shows the effects of the **DIMTEDIT** options.

Figure 21-21.   A comparison of the **DIMTEDIT** options.

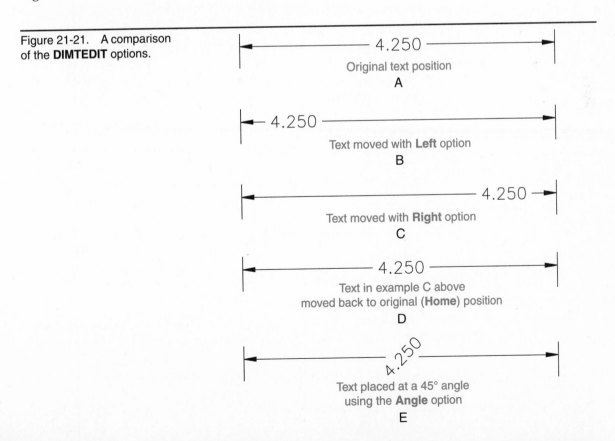

## Using the **DIMEDIT** command

The **DIMEDIT** command can be used to change the text or extension lines of existing text. Type DIMEDIT or DIMED at the **Command:** prompt to use this command:

Command: (type DIMEDIT or DIMED and press [Enter])
Dimension Edit (Home/New/Rotate/Oblique) ⟨Home⟩:

This command has four options that can be used to edit individual or multiple dimensions. The options are described as follows:

- **Home.** Home is the default option. You can press the [Enter] key or type H and then press [Enter]. This option restores the position and rotation of the dimension text to the original default position, as shown in Figure 21-22. Use the **Home** option like this:

    Command: **DIMED** ⌐
    Dimension Edit (Home/New/Rotate/Oblique) ⟨Home⟩: ⌐
    Select objects: (select the dimension or dimensions)
    Select objects: ⌐
    Command:

- **New.** Type N for the **New** option, which allows specification of new dimension text like this:

    Dimension Edit (Home/New/Rotate/Oblique) ⟨Home⟩: **N** ⌐
    Dimension text ⟨0⟩: **NEW TEXT** ⌐
    Select objects: (select the dimension or dimensions)

    See the example in Figure 21-22.

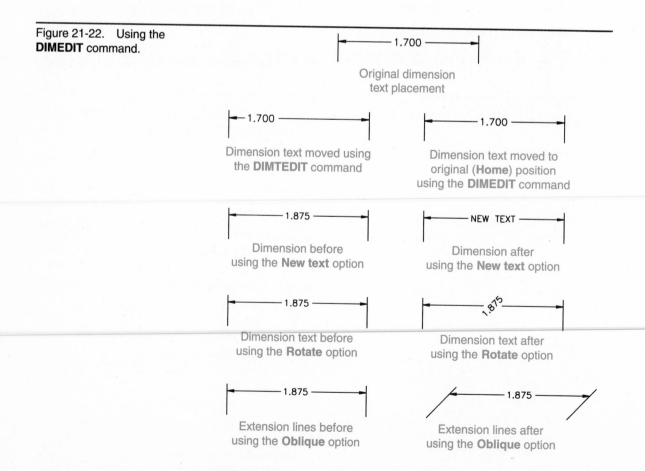

Figure 21-22.  Using the **DIMEDIT** command.

Original dimension text placement — 1.700

Dimension text moved using the **DIMTEDIT** command — 1.700

Dimension text moved to original (**Home**) position using the **DIMEDIT** command — 1.700

Dimension before using the **New text** option — 1.875

Dimension after using the **New text** option — NEW TEXT

Dimension text before using the **Rotate** option — 1.875

Dimension text after using the **Rotate** option — 1.875

Extension lines before using the **Oblique** option — 1.875

Extension lines after using the **Oblique** option — 1.875

- **Rotate.** This option rotates the dimension text to an angle that you specify (see Figure 21-22):

> Dimension Edit (Home/New/Rotate/Oblique) ⟨Home⟩: **R** ↵
> Enter text angle: **45** ↵
> Select objects: *(select the dimension or dimensions)*

- **Oblique.** Changes the extension line angle to your specifications. This has the same effect as using the **OBLIQUE** command inside of the **DIM** command, which was discussed previously in this chapter. See Figure 21-21 and Figure 21-22.

> Dimension Edit (Home/New/Rotate/Oblique) ⟨Home⟩: **O** ↵
> Select objects: *(select the dimension or dimensions)*
> Select objects: ↵
> Enter obliquing angle (RETURN for none): *(press* [Enter] *for no obliquing angle or type an angle such as 45)*

---

## EXERCISE 21-4

❑ Open PRODR2 or start a new drawing with your own variables.
❑ Using Figure 21-21 as an example, draw an original dimension similar to A. Copy the original dimension to four places represented by B, C, D, and E. Use the **DIMTEDIT** command to perform the following.
  ❑ Use the **Left** option to edit the dimension at B.
  ❑ Use the **Right** option to edit the dimension at C.
  ❑ Use the **Left** option to edit the dimension at D. Then use the **Home** option to move the text back to the original position.
  ❑ Use the **Angle** option to edit the dimension at E and place the text at a 45° angle.
❑ Using Figure 21-22 as an example, draw the original dimensions that are located on the left.
  ❑ Copy the original dimensions to the positions at the right.
  ❑ Perform the **DIMTEDIT** function on the middle top dimension.
  ❑ Use the **DIMEDIT** options on the rest of the dimensions as indicated in the caption for each example.
❑ Save the drawing as A:EX21-4.

---

## USING THE UPDATE SUBCOMMAND

AUG 9

The **UPDATE** subcommand changes existing dimensions to reflect the current settings for dimensioning variables. The only dimensions not affected by **UPDATE** are those drawn using the **BASELINE** or **CONTINUE** commands. For example, suppose you change the **DIMDLI** variable, which changes the dimension string spacing. All new dimensions drawn with the **BASELINE** or **CONTINUE** commands reflect the revised dimension line spacing. However, the **UPDATE** command would not alter the existing dimension line spacing. Although, if you use the **DIMASZ** variable to change the arrowhead size, then any dimensions picked with the **UPDATE** command are automatically changed to reflect the new arrowhead size. The **UPDATE** command works like this:

> Command: **DIM** ↵
> Dim: *(type* UP *or* UPDATE *and press* [Enter]*)*
> Select objects: *(select dimension entities to be updated)*
> Select objects: ↵
> Dim:

## USING THE DIMOVERRIDE COMMAND

AUG 9

The **DIMOVERRIDE** command overrides dimensioning variables associated with an individual dimension or a specific selected group of dimensions. You can use this command by typing either **DIMOVER** or **DIMOVERRIDE** at the **Command:** prompt. This variable does not affect the current dimension variable settings on the rest of the drawing. For example, you are dimensioning features with a **DIMEXO** setting of .0625 and find that several extension lines have an undesirable .0625 space where they meet centerlines, similar to Figure 21-23A. Use the **DIMOVERRIDE** command to change the **DIMEXO** setting and get the desired results, shown in Figure 21-23B:

Command: *(type* DIMOVER *or* DIMOVERRIDE *and press* [Enter])
Dimension variable to override (or Clear to remove overrides): **DIMEXO** ↵
Current value ⟨0.0625⟩ New value: **0** ↵
Dimension variable to override: *(enter another dim var to override or press* [Enter])
Select objects: *(select the dimension or dimensions to override)*
Select objects: ↵
Command:

Figure 21-23. Using the **DIMOVERRIDE** command. Notice that the offset is removed in B.

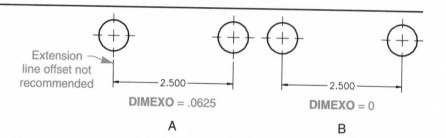

Extension line offset not recommended

DIMEXO = .0625     A

DIMEXO = 0     B

### EXERCISE 21-5

❑ With **DIMTIX** set to off, draw a .750″ dimension, as shown in Figure 21-11.
❑ Set **DIMTIX** on.
❑ Use the **UPDATE** command and pick the dimension again.
❑ With **DIMTOFL** set to off, draw a .750″ dimension as shown in Figure 21-12.
❑ Turn on the **DIMTOFL** variable.
❑ Use the **UPDATE** command and pick the dimension again.
❑ With **DIMEXO** set to .0625, draw and dimension the objects in Figure 21-23A.
❑ Use the **DIMOVERRIDE** command to change **DIMEXO** to 0 as in 21-23B.
❑ Save the drawing as A:EX21-5.

## DIM VARS THAT AFFECT DIMENSION SCALES

AUG 9

There are two dimensioning variables that alter the dimension scales. The **DIMSCALE** variable is an overall scale factor. It applies to all dimensioning variables that specify size, distance, or offset. When **DIMSCALE** is set to the default factor of 1, all dimensioning variables are displayed as set. If it is changed to 2, all variable values are doubled. See Figure 21-24. Changing the **DIMSCALE** affects only future dimensions.

If you are creating a drawing to be plotted at full (1:1) scale, then the **DIMSCALE** should equal 1. However, if the drawing is to be plotted at any other scale, the **DIMSCALE** should be set to the scale factor. The scale factor is the reciprocal of the drawing scale. For example, the scale factor for half scale (1:2) is 2, 1:2 is .5 = 1, and 1/.5 = 2. For the architect using a 1/4″ = 1′-0″

scale, the calculation is: .25″ = 12″, 12/.25 = 48 scale factor. Refer to the charts in Chapter 12 to assist you in determining scale factors.

Another dimensioning variable, **DIMLFAC** (dimension length factor), sets a scale factor for all linear dimensions, except angles. The default value of 1 represents a 1:1, or full scale factor. A factor of 2 multiplies dimension numbers by two, as shown in Figure 21-25.

The **DIMLFAC** variable is extremely convenient when dimensioning detail or section views that are scaled differently from the main views of the drawing. As an example, suppose you wanted to dimension a detail view that is at a scale of 4:1. Simply set **DIMLFAC** to a value of .25. When you dimension the view, AutoCAD automatically divides the values that appear in the brackets by a factor of 4 and displays the dimensions as if the view were drawn at 1:1.

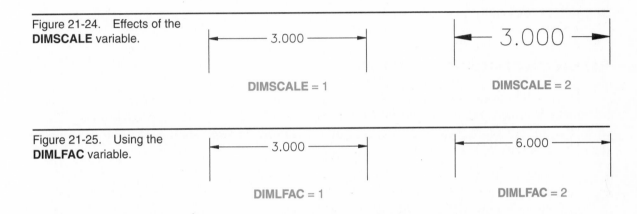

Figure 21-24.   Effects of the **DIMSCALE** variable.

DIMSCALE = 1

DIMSCALE = 2

Figure 21-25.   Using the **DIMLFAC** variable.

DIMLFAC = 1

DIMLFAC = 2

**EXERCISE 21-6**

❏ Draw the dimension shown on the left side of Figure 21-24 with a **DIMSCALE** value of 1. Copy it to a position at the right.
❏ Use the **UPDATE** command to change the **DIMSCALE** of the right dimension to 2.
❏ Draw the dimension shown on the left side of Figure 21-25 with a **DIMLFAC** value of 1. Copy it to a position at the right.
❏ Use the **DIMOVERRIDE** command to change the **DIMLFAC** of the right dimension to 2.
❏ Save as A:EX21-6.

## VARIABLES THAT ASSIGN COLOR TO DIMENSION COMPONENTS

There are three dimensioning variables that let you assign any valid color to dimension components. These variables are **DIMCLRD**, **DIMCLRE**, and **DIMCLRT**. You can set color values by number as follows:

1 = Red          5 = Blue
2 = Yellow       6 = Magenta
3 = Green        7 = White
4 = Cyan

The **DIMCLRD** variable is used to set the color of all dimension lines, arrowheads, and leaders. Use the **DIMCLRD** variable as follows:

Command: **DIMCLRD** ⏎
New value for DIMCLRD: *(enter desired color number, such as* **1** *for red, and press* [Enter]*)*

Now all new dimension lines, arrowheads, and leaders are drawn with red. Use the **UPDATE** command to change existing dimension colors.

The **DIMCLRE** variable changes the color of the extension lines. The **DIMCLRT** variable is used to alter the color of the dimension text. All three of these dimensioning variables are used in the same manner as previously described for the **DIMCLRD** variable.

**PROFESSIONAL TIP**

**DIMCLRD, DIMCLRE,** and **DIMCLRT** variables override any layer color settings. For example, even though a layer color may be yellow, the dimensions can still be different colors. It is usually the best practice to create objects using BYLAYER colors.

## ROTATING THE DIMENSION TEXT

The unidirectional and aligned dimensioning systems are the standard methods of placing dimension text. However, AutoCAD does allow you to rotate the dimension text. First, draw the dimension in the usual way, as shown in Figure 21-26A. Then, rotate the dimension text with the **TROTATE** subcommand as follows:

Command: **DIM** ⏎
Dim: *(type* TR *or* TROTATE *and press* [Enter]*)*
Enter text angle: *(set a text angle,* 45 *for example)* ⏎
Select objects: *(pick the dimension text to rotate)*

The selected dimension number is automatically rotated, as shown in Figure 21-26B.

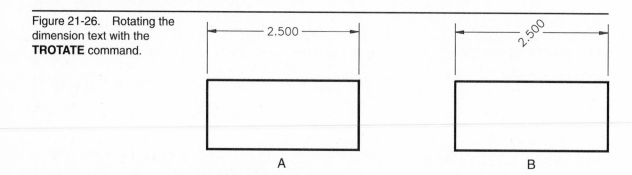

Figure 21-26. Rotating the dimension text with the **TROTATE** command.

A

B

# ERASING DIMENSIONS USING VARIOUS SELECTION OPTIONS

In Chapter 6 you were introduced to the **ERASE** command. There are different ways to select objects for erasure. These include **Last**, **Previous**, **Window**, **Crossing**, **WPolygon**, **CPolygon**, and **Fence**.

Erasing features, such as large groups of dimensions, often becomes difficult. They are very close to other parts of the drawing. It is time-consuming to erase them individually. When this situation occurs, the **Crossing**, **CPolygon**, and **Fence** selection options are useful. Figure 21-27 shows a comparison between using **ERASE Window** and **ERASE Crossing** on a group of dimensions. For a review of these techniques, refer to Chapter 6.

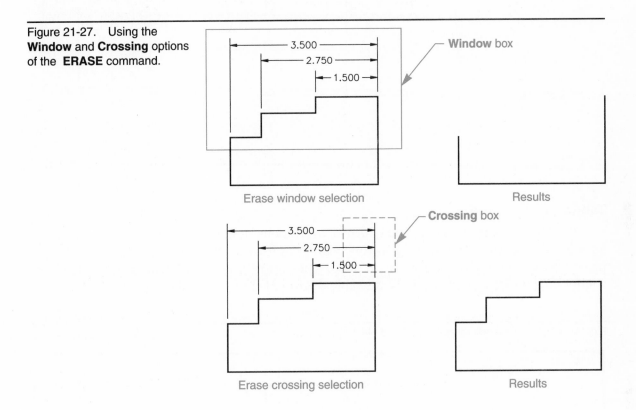

Figure 21-27. Using the **Window** and **Crossing** options of the **ERASE** command.

# ALTERNATE DIMENSIONING PRACTICES

In industries where computer-controlled machining processes are used, it is becoming common to omit dimension lines. This type of dimensioning is called arrowless, or tabular dimensioning. Where changing values of a product are involved, dimensions are shown in a chart. This is referred to as *chart dimensioning*.

## Arrowless dimensioning

*Arrowless dimensioning* is becoming popular in mechanical drafting. It is also used in electronics drafting, especially for chassis layout. This type of dimensioning has only extension lines and numbers. Dimension lines and arrowheads are omitted. Dimension numbers are aligned with the extension lines. Each dimension number represents a dimension originating from a common point. This starting, or 0 dimension is typically known as a *datum*, or *baseline*. Holes or other features are labeled with identification letters. Sizes are given in a table placed on the drawing, as shown in Figure 21-28.

Figure 21-28.   Arrowless dimensioning.

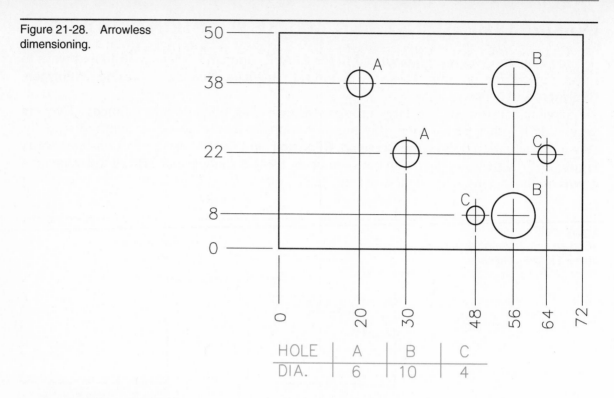

## Tabular dimensioning

*Tabular dimensioning* is a form of arrowless dimensioning where dimensions to features are shown in a table. The table gives the location of features from an X- and Y- axes. It also provides the depth of features from a Z-axis, when appropriate. Each feature is labeled with a letter or number that correlates to the table, Figure 21-29.

Figure 21-29.   Tabular dimensioning. (Doug Major)

| HOLE | QTY. | DESCRIP. | X | Y | Z |
|------|------|----------|----|----|------|
| A1 | 1 | ø7 | 64 | 38 | 18 |
| B1 | 1 | ø5 | 5 | 38 | THRU |
| B2 | 1 | ø5 | 72 | 38 | THRU |
| B3 | 1 | ø5 | 64 | 11 | THRU |
| B4 | 1 | ø5 | 79 | 11 | THRU |
| C1 | 1 | ø4 | 19 | 38 | THRU |
| C2 | 1 | ø4 | 48 | 38 | THRU |
| C3 | 1 | ø4 | 5 | 21 | THRU |
| C4 | 1 | ø4 | 30 | 21 | THRU |
| C5 | 1 | ø4 | 72 | 21 | THRU |
| C6 | 1 | ø4 | 19 | 11 | THRU |
| D1 | 1 | ø2.5 | 48 | 6 | THRU |

UNLESS OTHERWISE SPECIFIED
▬▬ — MILLIMETERS AND TOLERANCES FOR:
1 PLACE DIMS: ± .1
2 PLACE DIMS: ± .01
3 PLACE DIMS: ± .005
ANGULAR:       ± 30'
FRACTIONAL:    ± 1/32
FINISH:  3.2 ?m

✳ MAJOR  DESIGN ✳
DR:         | SCALE: | DATE:  | APPD:
D. MAJOR | 1.5:1   | 27FEB |
MTRL:
STAINLESS  STEEL
NAME:
MOUNTING  BASE
B | PART NO:     10099 | REV: 0

2. REMOVE ALL BURRS AND SHARP EDGES.
1. INTERPRET DIMENSIONS AND TOLERANCES PER ASME Y14.5M—1994.
NOTES:

## Chart dimensioning

*Chart dimensioning* may take the form of unidirectional, aligned, arrowless, or tabular dimensioning. It provides flexibility in situations where dimensions change as requirements of the product change. The views of the product are drawn and variable dimensions are shown with letters. The letters correlate to a chart where the different options are shown, Figure 21-30.

Figure 21-30. Chart dimensioning.

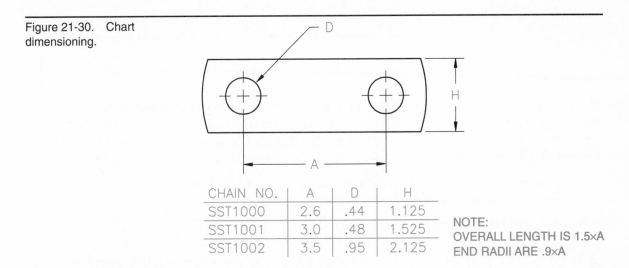

| CHAIN NO. | A | D | H |
|-----------|-----|-----|-------|
| SST1000 | 2.6 | .44 | 1.125 |
| SST1001 | 3.0 | .48 | 1.525 |
| SST1002 | 3.5 | .95 | 2.125 |

NOTE:
OVERALL LENGTH IS 1.5×A
END RADII ARE .9×A

## Ordinate dimensioning

AutoCAD refers to arrowless dimensioning as *ordinate dimensioning*. This type of dimensioning is done using the **DIMORDINATE** command. This command is accessed by typing DIMORDINATE or DIMORD at the **Command:** prompt, by typing ORDINATE or ORD at the **Dim:** prompt in the **DIM** command, or by picking the **Ordinate Dimension** button in the **Ordinate Dimension** flyout on the **Dimensioning** toolbar. If the ACADFULL menu file is loaded, you can pick **Dimensioning** ⟩ in the **Draw** pull-down menu, followed by **Ordinate** ⟩ and **Automatic**. When using this command, AutoCAD automatically places an extension line and number along X and Y coordinates. Since you are working in the X-Y axes, it is often best to have **ORTHO** on.

The World Coordinate System (WCS) 0, 0 coordinate has been in the lower-left corner of the screen for the drawings you have already completed. In most cases, this is fine. However, when doing ordinate dimensioning, it is best to have the dimensions originate from a primary datum, which is often a corner of the object. The WCS is fixed; the User Coordinate System (UCS), on the other hand, can be moved to any orientation desired.

All of the ordinate dimensions originate from the current UCS origin. The UCS is discussed in detail in Chapter 3 of *AutoCAD and its Applications—Advanced, Release 13 for Windows*. In general, UCS allows you to set your own coordinate system. If you do this, all of the Dimension text: prompts display the actual dimensions from the X-Y coordinates on the object. Move the UCS origin to the corner of the object using the following command sequence:

Command: **UCS** ↵
Origin/ZAxis/3point/Entity/View/X/Y/Z/Prev/Restore/Save/Del/?/⟨World⟩: **0** ↵
Origin point ⟨0,0,0⟩: *(pick the origin point at the corner of the object to be dimensioned as shown in Figure 21-31A)*

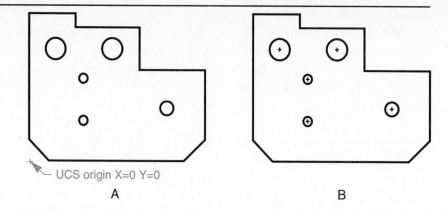

Figure 21-31.   A—Draw the object and move the UCS origin to the X-Y corner. B—Add the center marks to the circular features using the **CENTER** command.

A                                                                    B

Next, if there are circles on your drawing, use the **CENTER** command to place center marks in the circles, as shown in Figure 21-31B. This makes your drawing conform to ASME standards and provides something to pick when dimensioning the circle locations. Now, you are ready to start placing the ordinate dimensions. Enter the **DIMORDINATE** command as follows:

> Command: *(type* DIMORD *or* DIMORDINATE *and press* [Enter])
> Select Feature: *(pick the feature to be dimensioned)*

When the Select Feature: prompt appears, move the screen cursor to the point or feature to be dimensioned. If the feature is the corner of the object, pick the corner. If the feature is a circle, pick the end of the center mark. This leaves the required space between the center mark and the extension line. Zoom in if needed and use the object snaps to help. The next prompt asks for the leader endpoint, which actually refers to the extension line endpoint.

> Leader endpoint (Xdatum/Ydatum): *(pick the endpoint of the extension line)*
> Dimension text: ⟨X.XXX⟩: ↵

If the X-axis or Y-axis distance between the feature and the extension line endpoint is large, the default axis may not be the desired axis for the dimension. When this happens, use the **Xdatum** or **Ydatum** option to tell AutoCAD which axis originates the dimension:

> Leader endpoint (Xdatum/Ydatum): **X** ↵
> Leader endpoint: *(pick the endpoint of the extension line)*

Figure 21-32 shows the ordinate dimensions placed on the object. Notice the dimension text is aligned with the extension lines. Aligned dimensioning is standard with ordinate dimensioning, and is not altered by any change in the **DIMTIH** or **DIMTOH** variables. **DIMTAD** is off for the dimensions placed in Figure 21-32. You can have the dimension text placed above the extension line if you turn **DIMTAD** on.

Figure 21-32. Placing the
ordinate dimensions.

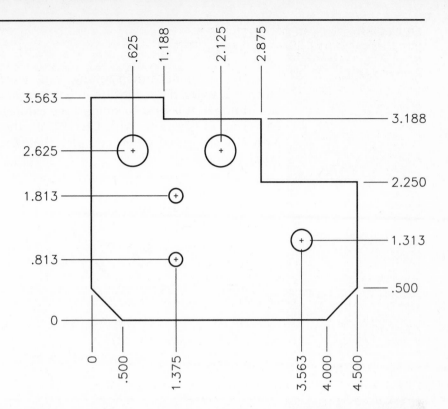

Finally, complete the drawing by adding any missing lines, such as centerlines or fold lines. Identify the holes with letters and correlate a dimensioning table, as shown in Figure 21-33.

You can leave the UCS origin at the corner of the object, or move it back to the corner of the screen (WCS) by pressing [Enter] for the World default:

Command: **UCS** ↵
Origin/ZAxis/3point/Entity/View/X/Y/Z/Prev/Restore/Save/Del/?/⟨World⟩: ↵

Figure 21-33. Completing
the drawing.

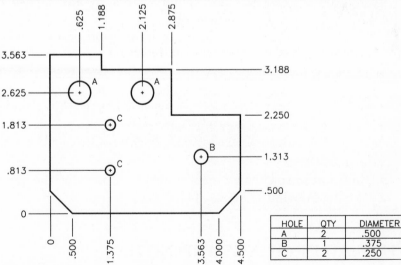

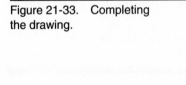

| HOLE | QTY | DIAMETER |
|------|-----|----------|
| A | 2 | .500 |
| B | 1 | .375 |
| C | 2 | .250 |

**PROFESSIONAL TIP**

Most ordinate dimensioning tasks work best with **ORTHO** on. However, when the extension line is too close to an adjacent dimension number, it is best to stagger the extension line as shown in the following illustration. With **ORTHO** off, the extension line is automatically staggered when you pick the offset second extension line point as demonstrated.

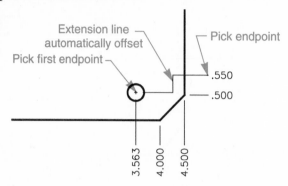

**PROFESSIONAL TIP**

AutoCAD's powerful **DIMORDINATE** dimensioning command allows you to quickly and accurately prepare arrowless dimensioning if you follow these steps:
- Draw the object carefully, making sure that all features are accurate.
- Set the UCS origin to the X = 0, Y = 0 coordinates of the object.
- Place center marks in any circles or arcs requiring location dimensions.
- Set the units to the appropriate number of decimal places.
- Dimension the object.

---

**EXERCISE 21-8**

❑ Open PRODR2.
❑ Draw and use ordinate dimensioning to dimension the object shown in Figure 21-28.
❑ Save the drawing as A:EX21-14.

---

## THREAD DRAWINGS AND NOTES

There are many different thread forms. The most common forms are the Unified and metric screw threads. The parts of a screw thread are shown in Figure 21-34.

Threads are commonly shown on a drawing with a simplified representation. Thread depth is shown with a hidden line. This method is used for both external and internal threads, Figure 21-35.

Figure 21-34.   Parts of a screw thread.

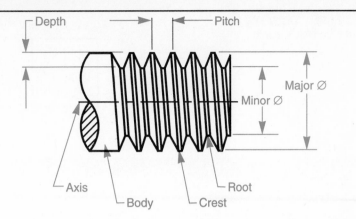

Figure 21-35.   Simplified thread representations.

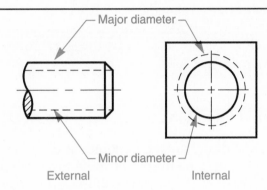

## Showing the thread note

The view shows the reader that a thread exists, but the thread note gives exact specifications. The thread note for Unified screw threads must be given in the following order:

**3/4 - 10UNC - 2A**
(1)    (2) (3)   (4) (5)
1.  Major diameter of thread, given as fraction or decimal inch.
2.  Number of threads per inch.
3.  Thread series. UNC = Unified National Course. UNF = Unified National Fine.
4.  Class of fit. 1 = large tolerance. 2 = general purpose tolerance. 3 = tight tolerance.
5.  A = external thread. B = internal thread.

The thread note for metric threads is displayed in the following order:

**M 14 X 2**
(1) (2)   (3)
1.  M = metric thread.
2.  Major diameter in millimeters.
3.  Pitch in millimeters.

There are too many Unified and metric screw threads to discuss here. Refer to the *Machinery's Handbook* or a comprehensive drafting text for more information.

The thread note is typically connected to the thread view with a leader, Figure 21-36. Notice in Figures 21-35 and 21-36 that a chamfer is often placed on the external thread. This makes it easier to engage the mating thread.

Figure 21-36.  Displaying the thread note with a leader.

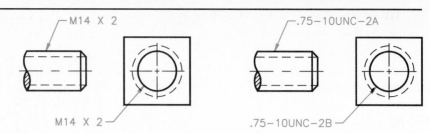

M14 X 2

M14 X 2

.75—10UNC—2A

.75—10UNC—2B

### EXERCISE 21-9

❑ Open drawing PRODR2.
❑ Draw a simplified representation of an external and internal Unified screw thread. Do the same for a metric screw thread.
❑ Use the **LEADER** command to label each view. Label the Unified screw thread as 7/8-14UNF-2 and the metric screw thread as M25 X 1.5.
❑ Your drawing should look similar to Figure 21-36.
❑ Save the drawing as A:EX21-9.

## USING DIALOG BOXES TO CONTROL DIMENSIONING VARIABLES

Entering the dimensioning variables at the **Command:** and **Dim:** prompts, as you have done so far, has given you the opportunity to see exactly how each variable controls the way a dimension is drawn. The same variables can be accessed through the **Dimension Styles** dialog box shown in Figure 21-37. You can access this dialog box by entering DDIM at the **Command:** or **Dim:** prompts, by picking the **Dimension Style** button on the **Dimensioning** toolbar, or by selecting **Dimension Style...** from the **Data** pull-down menu. It may be helpful to refer back to explanations and examples earlier in this chapter as you review each dimension variable in the following discussion.

When you become familiar with using the **Dimension Styles** dialog boxes, you will find that command-line adjustment of the dimensioning variables is slow by comparison. The dimensioning variables are changed in the dialog boxes by simply picking buttons or providing new settings in edit boxes. Some of the features are represented by image tiles. You can click on these image tiles with the cursor to cycle through the values while you see a display of the results. This can greatly speed up the dimension definition process.

Figure 21-37.  The **Dimension Styles** dialog box.

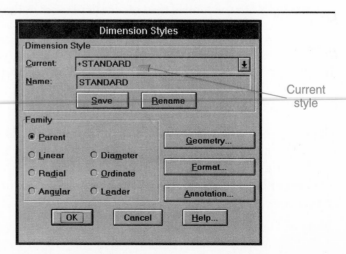

Current style

## An introduction to dimension styles

A *dimension style* in AutoCAD is a standard or customized set of dimensioning variables that conform to a particular drafting standard or practice. How to create and use dimension styles is explained in detail in Chapter 22 of this text, *Advanced Dimensioning*. The **Dimension Style** area of the dialog box displays dimension style names, makes existing styles current, and can be used to save and rename dimension styles. The dimension style with all of the AutoCAD defaults is called STANDARD. If you change any of the standard dimensioning variables, AutoCAD stores the changes in another style named +STANDARD. See Figure 21-37 and notice the +STANDARD style listed as current. This is a slightly modified version of the STANDARD dimension style.

Pick the down arrow in the **Current** box to access any available dimension styles. When you place dimensions on a drawing, they are displayed in the current style. The only dimension styles that are available in this example are STANDARD and +STANDARD. The **Name** edit box is where you display a dimension style name to save or rename. The STANDARD dimension style is AutoCAD's default and cannot be renamed.

## The dimension style family members

The **Family** area of the **Dimension Styles** dialog box contains AutoCAD's dimension style family members. A family member is turned on by picking the radio button next to the name. The family member that is turned on is displayed in the **Dimension Style** subdialog boxes that are discussed later. The **Parent** is default and contains all of the dimension style settings for the current style. The other family members contain only the specific dimensioning variables that are associated with their applications.

---

### EXERCISE 21-10

❑ Begin a new drawing using the standard AutoCAD prototype.
❑ Access the **Dimension Styles** dialog box and notice the selections in the **Current:** list. Pick **Cancel**.
❑ Change any dimension variable. For example, enter DIMTXT and change the text height to .125.
❑ Access the **Dimension Styles** dialog box and notice the selections in the **Current:** list. +STANDARD should be an additional option. Pick **Cancel**.
❑ Save as A:EX21-10 or quit without saving.

---

## Using the Geometry dialog box

If you pick the **Geometry** button in the **Dimension Styles** dialog box, you get the **Geometry** dialog box. This is shown in Figure 21-38 with the default values displayed. The dialog box controls the appearance of dimension lines, extension lines, arrowheads, center marks, and dimension scale. The dimension variable name and related figure number from Chapter 20 and Chapter 21 are placed in parenthesis with each part of the following discussion. The elements of the **Geometry** dialog box are described as follows:

- **Dimension Line.** This part of the dialog box controls dimensioning variables that relate to the dimension line. The specific controls are as follows:
  - **Suppress**—Pick the first check box if you want to suppress the first dimension line (**DIMSD1**, Figure 20-16). Pick the second check box if you want to suppress the second dimension line (**DIMSD2**, Figure 20-16).
  - **Extension**—This option is not available unless the dimension is set to draw tick marks (**DIMTSZ**, Figure 20-20). If **DIMTSZ** is set, this option allows you to enter a setting for dimension line extension beyond the extension line (**DIMDLE**, Figure 20-21).

Figure 21-38.   The **Geometry** dialog box is accessed by picking the **Geometry...** button in the **Dimension Styles** dialog box.

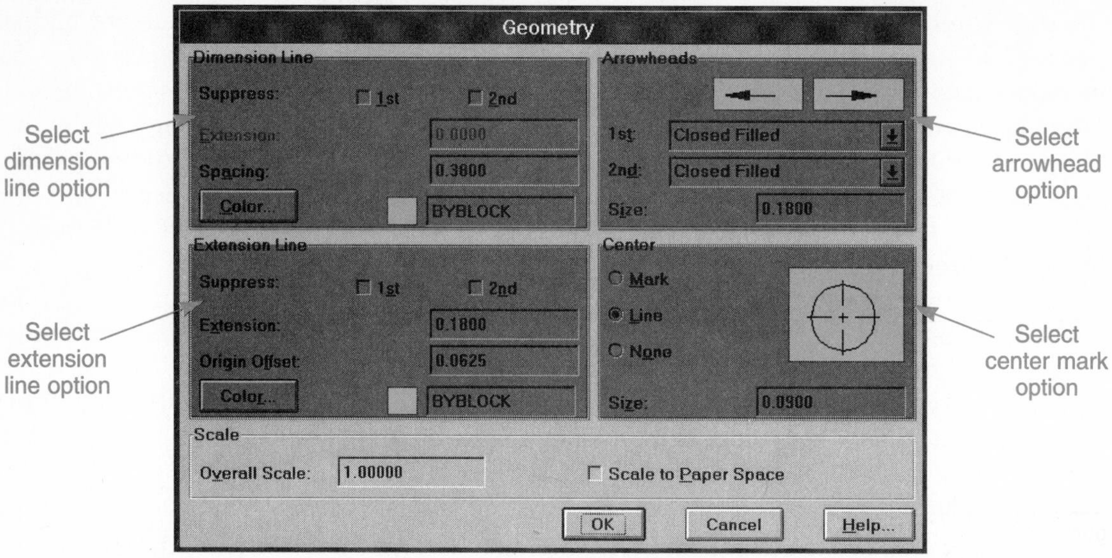

Select dimension line option

Select extension line option

Select arrowhead option

Select center mark option

- **Spacing**—This text box lets you change the spacing between dimension lines (**DIMDLI**, Figure 20-47) when the **DIMBASELINE** command is used.
- **Color...**—Pick the **Color** button to get the **Select Color** dialog box. Here you can pick a desired color for the dimension line (**DIMCLRD**). The currently selected color is displayed in the color swatch.
- **Extension Line.** This part of the dialog box controls dimensioning variables that relate to the extension line. The specific controls are as follows:
  - **Suppress**—Pick the 1st check box if you want to suppress the first extension line (**DIMSE1**, Figure 20-15). Pick the 2nd check box if you want to suppress the second extension line (**DIMSE2**, Figure 20-15).
  - **Extension**—Enter the amount that you want the extension line to extend beyond the last dimension line (**DIMEXE**, Figure 20-14).
  - **Origin Offset**—Enter the distance of the space that you want between the extension line origin and the object being dimensioned (**DIMEXO**, Fig 20-14). Enter a value of 0 if you do not want a space between the extension line and the object (Figure 21-23).
  - **Color...**—Pick the **Color...** button to get the **Select Color** dialog box. Here you can pick a desired color for the extension line (**DIMCLRE**). The color currently selected is displayed in the color swatch.
- **Arrowheads.** This part of the dialog box controls dimensioning variables that relate to arrowheads. You can change 1st, 2nd, or both arrowheads. To change arrowheads, pick the down arrow next to the **1st:** list. The list contains the arrowhead options shown in Figure 21-39. When you pick an arrowhead option from the **1st:** list, the 2nd arrowhead is automatically changed to match. You need to pick an arrowhead from the **2nd:** list if you want the arrowheads to be different. Notice that the arrowhead image tile changes to display a representation of your selection. Arrowhead options are shown in Figure 21-40. Picking the arrowhead image tile itself allows you to change the settings as well. You can continue to click on the image until the desired arrowhead is visible. The **None** option draws a dimension line or leader without an arrowhead. The **Origin Indication** option gives you the origin symbol that is used to display where a specific dimension is intended to originate on the drawing. Picking the **User Arrow...** option accesses the **User Arrow** dialog box, where you enter the name of a customized arrowhead block (Figure 20-22), and the text **USER...** appears in the image tile. The **Size** text box lets you change the arrowhead size as needed (**DIMASZ**, Figure 20-19).

Figure 21-39. Setting desired arrowheads using the **Geometry** dialog box.

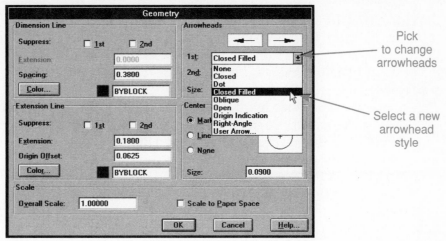

Figure 21-40. Examples of the arrowhead options available in the **Geometry** dialog box.

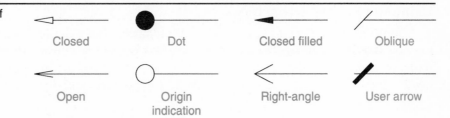

Closed   Dot   Closed filled   Oblique

Open   Origin indication   Right-angle   User arrow

- **Center.** The **Center** area includes radio buttons that allow you to quickly set desired center marks when using the **DIMCENTER**, **DIMDIAMETER**, and **DIMRADIUS** commands (**DIMCEN**, Figure 20-49). The circle image tile at the right automatically displays your selection. Picking the image tile also adjusts the setting. Figure 21-41 shows the image tile when the different options are selected. The options include:
  - **Mark**—Pick this button to get the center marks that would be drawn with a positive **DIMCEN** value.
  - **Line**—This option allows you to draw the center mark and centerlines that project beyond the circle as with a negative **DIMCEN** value.
  - **None**—Pick this if you want circles and arcs dimensioned without any center marks.
  - **Size**—Enter a value in the text box that you want used for the center mark length.
- **Scale.** The **Scale** options allow you to change the overall scale factor by entering a value in the text box (**DIMSCALE**, Figure 21-24). Pick the **Scale to Paper Space** check box if you want the dimension scaling to be a factor based on settings between model space and paper space. The **Overall Scale:** text box is disabled when the **Scale to Paper Space** check box is picked.

Figure 21-41. The **Center** image options found in the **Geometry** dialog box. Pick the desired **Center** button or pick on the image to cycle through the available options.

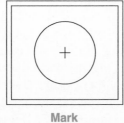
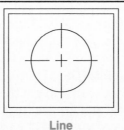
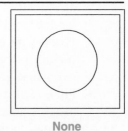

Mark   Line   None

## EXERCISE 21-11

❑ Begin a new drawing using the standard AutoCAD prototype.
❑ Access the **Dimension Styles** dialog box and pick the **Geometry** button.
❑ Experiment with the options in the **Geometry** dialog box by doing the following:
   ❑ Change the dimension line spacing to .5.
   ❑ Change the extension line extension to .125.
   ❑ Access the **Arrowhead** list and pick each of the options while you observe the results. Pick inside the left image tile as you watch the image and the option in the text box change. Pick the right image tile and see the results. Pick the left image tile until you get the **Closed Filled** arrowhead option.
   ❑ Pick each of the **Center** radio buttons and observe the changing image tile at the right. Now, pick inside the image tile and see the results.
   ❑ Pick either the **OK** or **Cancel** button.
❑ Save as A:EX21-11.

### Using the Format dialog box

If you pick the **Format** button in the **Dimension Styles** dialog box, you get the **Format** dialog box shown in Figure 21-42. This dialog box is used to control the dimensioning variables that are used to adjust the location of dimension lines, dimension text, arrowheads, and leader lines. The elements of the **Format** dialog box are described in the following:

Figure 21-42.   The **Format** dialog box is accessed by picking the **Format...** button in the **Dimension Styles** dialog box.

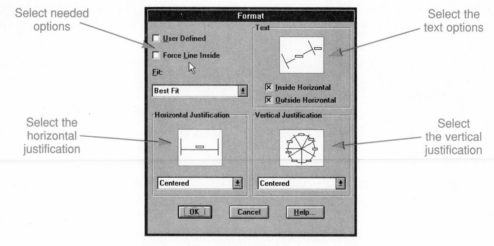

- **User Defined.** Picking the **User Defined** check box turns on the **DIMUPT** variable. In earlier applications, you learned that **DIMUPT** allows you to place dimension text at any desired position. This variable also allows you to drag the dimension line and leader length. (Figure 20-54, Figure 20-60, and Figure 21-15)
- **Force Line Inside.** Pick this check box if you want the dimension lines to be forced inside of the extension lines, even when the arrowheads are placed outside of the extension lines (**DIMTOFL**, Figure 20-51, Figure 20-53, Figure 20-59, and Figure 21-12).
- **Fit.** Pick the down arrow to get the list of **Fit** options. **Best Fit** is the default, but the list also includes **Text and Arrows**, **Text Only**, **Arrows Only**, and **Leader**. These options are the various settings of the **DIMFIT** variable (Figure 20-52, Figure 20-53, and Figure 21-13). The options are described as follows:

- **Best Fit**—If there is room for arrowheads only, arrowheads are placed inside of the extension lines. If there is room for text only, then text is placed inside of the extension lines. Otherwise all are placed outside. **DIMFIT** = 3
- **Text and Arrows**—If there is not enough room for both text and arrows, all are placed outside of the extension lines. **DIMFIT** = 0
- **Text Only**—If there is room for text only, it is placed inside of the extension lines and the arrowheads are placed outside. Otherwise all are placed outside. **DIMFIT** = 1
- **Arrows Only**—If there is room for arrowheads only, they are placed inside of the extension lines and the text is placed outside. Otherwise all are placed outside. **DIMFIT** = 2
- **Leader**—If there is room for text only, it is placed inside of the extension lines. Otherwise a leader line is created that connects the text to the dimension line. **DIMFIT** = 4

- **Horizontal Justification.** Pick the down arrow to access a list of horizontal justification options or click on the image to flip through the available options. These options are the settings of the **DIMJUST** variable (Figure 21-17). Notice the image tile just above the **Horizontal Justification** list in Figure 21-42. The rectangle in the image tile represents the dimension text position. You can also pick on the image tile to cycle through the options. The following describes the options and the representative images displayed in Figure 21-43:
  - **Centered**—This is the default and it center justifies the text on the dimension line. **DIMJUST** = 0
  - **1st Extension Line**—Places the text next to the first extension line. **DIMJUST** = 1
  - **2nd Extension Line**—Places the text next to the second extension line. **DIMJUST** = 2
  - **Over 1st Extension**—This option places the text aligned with and at the end of the first extension line. **DIMJUST** = 3
  - **Over 2nd Extension**—Places the text aligned with and at the end of the second extension line. **DIMJUST** = 4

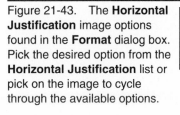
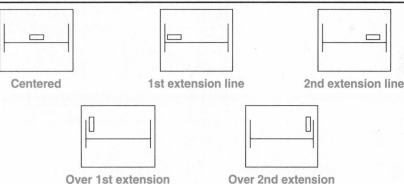

Figure 21-43. The **Horizontal Justification** image options found in the **Format** dialog box. Pick the desired option from the **Horizontal Justification** list or pick on the image to cycle through the available options.

Centered · 1st extension line · 2nd extension line · Over 1st extension · Over 2nd extension

- **Text.** The **Text** options in the **Format** dialog box allow you to control the alignment of dimension text inside (**DIMTIH**, Figure 20-7, Figure 20-8) and outside (**DIMTOH**, Figure 20-17) of the extension lines. The options are available by using two check boxes or clicking on the image tile. Note that your changes here may affect the image in the **Vertical Justification** image (described below). These boxes are checked by default. Any change to the settings is represented by a change in the image tile. The image tile represented when both boxes are checked is shown in Figure 21-42. Examples of the other image tile displays are shown in Figure 21-44. The options are explained in the following:

Figure 21-44.   The **Text** options found in the **Format** dialog box. Look at Figure 21-42 to see the defaults with the **Inside Horizontal** on and **Outside Horizontal** on. Notice how the image changes as the check boxes are adjusted. A—**Inside Horizontal** off and **Outside Horizontal** on. B—**Inside Horizontal** on and **Outside Horizontal** off. C—**Inside Horizontal** off and **Outside horizontal** off.

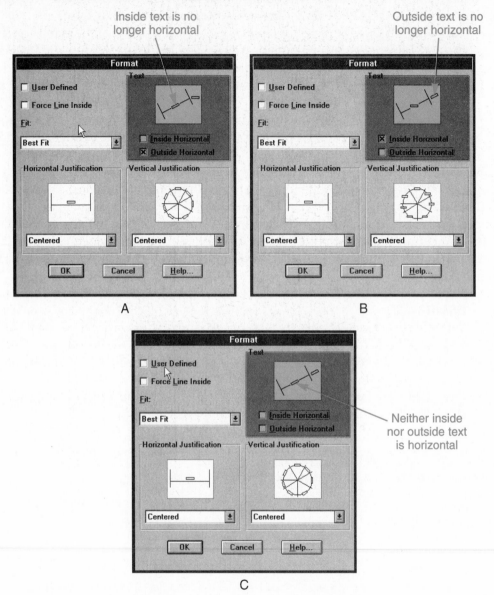

- **Inside Horizontal**—When there is room, the dimension line, arrowheads, and text is placed between the extension lines. The numbers are normally placed horizontally when this box is checked. If it is not checked, text is aligned with the dimension line.

- **Outside Horizontal**—When there is not enough room between extension lines, AutoCAD automatically places the dimension lines, arrowheads, and numbers outside, depending on the status of the **DIMFIT** variable. When this box is checked, text placed outside of the extension lines is drawn horizontally. When not checked, the dimension text placed outside is aligned with the dimension lines.

- **Vertical Justification.** Pick the down arrow to access a list of **Vertical Justification** options or pick the image tile to change the setting. These options affect the settings of the **DIMTAD** variable (Figure 20-18). Notice the image in the **Vertical Justification** area in Figure 21-42. The rectangle in the image represents the dimension text position. The following describes the options:

- **Centered**—This is the default and it center justifies the text on the dimension line. The image in Figure 21-42 represents the **Centered** option.
- **Above**—This option places the dimension text above the dimension line (**DIMTAD** on). This is a common practice in architectural drafting. The distance that the text is placed above the dimension line is equal to the **DIMGAP** (Figure 21-18) setting. The dialog box image is shown in Figure 21-45A.
- **Outside**—Using this option places the dimension text on the side of the dimension line that is farthest away from the first extension line origin. This is an uncommon practice. The dialog box image that displays this is shown in Figure 21-45B.
- **JIS**—This option allows you to place dimension text as related to the Japanese Industry Standard (JIS). See the image in Figure 21-45C.

Figure 21-45. The **Vertical Justification** image options found in the **Format** dialog box. Notice the **Centered** default shown in Figure 21-42. Pick the desired option from the **Vertical Justification** list or pick on the image to cycle through the available options. A—The **Above** option. B—The **Outside** option. C—The **JIS** option.

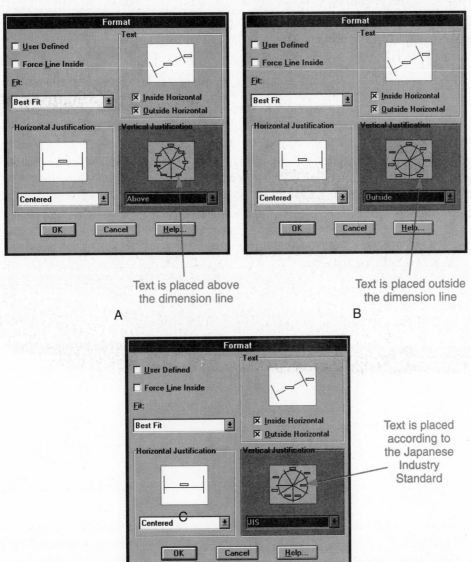

**EXERCISE 21-12**

❏ Begin a new drawing using the standard AutoCAD prototype.
❏ Access the **Dimension Styles** dialog box and pick the **Format** button.
❏ Experiment with the options in the **Format** dialog box by doing the following:
  ❏ Pick the **User Defined** check box.
  ❏ Access the **Fit:** list and see the options.
  ❏ Pick each of the options in the **Horizontal Justification** list and see what happens to the image tile. Now, pick the image tile several times and observe the results.
  ❏ Watch the results when you pick the **Text** check boxes.
  ❏ Pick each of the options in the **Vertical Justification** list and observe the image tile. Pick the image tile several times.
❏ Save as A:EX21-12.

## Using the Annotation dialog box

If you pick the **Annotation...** button in the **Dimension Styles** dialog box, you get the **Annotation** dialog box shown in Figure 21-46. This dialog box is used to control the dimensioning variables that display the dimension text. Some of the features found in this dialog box relate to topics that are discussed in Chapter 22, *Advanced Dimensioning and Tolerancing*. These elements are introduced here and explained in detail in Chapter 22:

- **Primary Units.** *Primary units* are the main part of the dimension text. When dual dimensioning is being used, the first dimension represents primary units. A dual dimension might appear as 1.00[25.4]. Where only one style of units is used, the primary units settings affect the main part of the dimension text. For example, if you have the dimension 2.875±.005, the primary units is 2.875. This is also referred to as the *specified dimension* in mechanical drafting. There may be items added to the primary units, such as prefixes, suffixes, tolerances, or symbols. The following items are found in the **Primary Units** compartment of the **Annotation** dialog box:

Figure 21-46. The **Annotation** dialog box is accessed by picking the **Annotation...** button in the **Dimension Styles** dialog box.

The **Primary Units** area

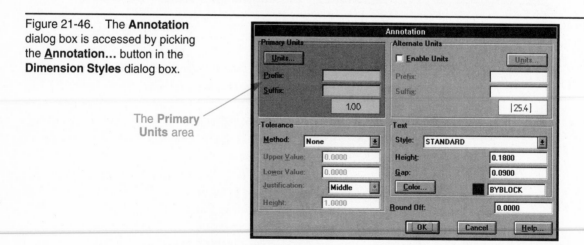

- **Units...**—Pick the **Units...** button to access the **Primary Units** dialog box shown in Figure 21-47. This is where you find items such as **Units**, **Dimension Precision**, and **Zero Suppression**. Each of the items in the **Primary Units** dialog box are described in the following:
  - **Units.** Pick the down arrow to access the traditional list of dimension unit options (**DIMUNIT**). These options include **Decimal** (default), **Scientific**, **Engineering**, **Architectural**, and **Fractional**. Pick the desired units format.

Figure 21-47.   The **Primary Units** dialog box is accessed by picking the **Units...** button in the **Primary Units** area of the **Annotation** dialog box.

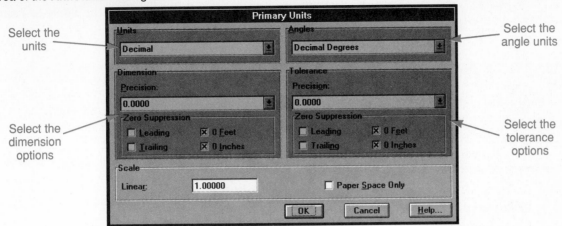

Select the units

Select the angle units

Select the dimension options

Select the tolerance options

- **Dimension**. The **Dimension** area has a pop-up list box with selections that are used to control the number of decimal places (**DIMDEC**) for the primary units. Pick the down arrow to access the choices, from 0 to 8 decimal places. Four decimal places (0.0000) is the default.
  - **Zero Suppression**—The **Zero Suppression** area gives you four check boxes. These options are used to suppress or keep leading and trailing zeros for the primary units (**DIMZIN**). Refer to Chapter 20 for a complete review of the **DIMZIN** variable and its options. The options are explained as follows:
    - **Leading**. Check this box to remove the zero that is placed before the decimal point in units less than one. Omit the check in this box to keep the zero. The ASME dimensioning standard recommends that inch values less than one have the zero removed, while metric values less than one keep the zero. **DIMZIN** = 4
    - **Trailing**. This box is not checked by default. This leaves the zeros after the decimal point up to the number of zeros specified in the **Dimension Precision** (**DIMDEC**) option. Put a check in this box to remove zeros after the decimal point. **DIMZIN** = 8
    - **0 Feet**. A check in this box is the default that removes the zero in foot-inch measurements ( 2', for example). Remove the check to keep the zero ( 2'-0"). **DIMZIN** = 0
    - **0 Inches**. A check in this box is the default which removes the zero in inch measurements (1/2", for example). Remove the check to keep the zero (0'-0 1/2"). **DIMZIN** = 3
- **Angles**. Pick the down arrow to access the traditional list of angular unit options (**DIMAUNIT**). These options include **Decimal Degrees** (default), **Deg/Min/Sec**, **Grads**, **Radians**, and **Surveyor**. Pick the selection that you want to make active.
- **Tolerance**. The **Tolerance** area has the same options as the **Dimension** area. They control the **Precision** (**DIMTDEC**) and **Zero Suppression** (**DIMTZIN**) for dimension tolerances. This is explained in Chapter 22.
- **Scale**. This area of the dialog box controls the scale factor of linear dimension numbers on the entire drawing (**DIMLFAC**, Figure 21-25). This does not affect angles, text height, or tolerance values. The options are:
  - **Linear**—The default is 1, which represents a 1:1 or FULL scale factor. A factor of 2 will multiply dimension numbers by 2. For example, if a dimension number reads 3.000 with a **Linear** setting of 1, it would read 6.000 with a setting of 2.

- **Paper <u>S</u>pace Only**—Pick the **Paper <u>S</u>pace Only** check box if you want the dimension scaling to be a factor based on settings between model space and paper space. The **Overall Scale:** text box is disabled when the **Scale to Paper Space** check box is picked.

## EXERCISE 21-13

- ❑ Begin a new drawing using the standard AutoCAD prototype.
- ❑ Access the **Dimension Styles** dialog box and pick the **<u>A</u>nnotation...** button.
- ❑ Experiment with the options in the **Annotation** dialog box by doing the following:
  - ❑ Pick the **Units...** button.
    - ❑ Look at the options in the **Units** list.
    - ❑ Set the **Dimension Precision** to three places (0.000).
    - ❑ Suppress the leading zeros for inch dimensioning.
    - ❑ Look at the options in the **Angles** list.
  - ❑ Pick **OK**.
  - ❑ Pick each of the options in the **Tolerance <u>M</u>ethod:** list and observe the **Primary Units** image tile. Pick the image tile several times.
  - ❑ Pick the **Text Style:** list and see the options.
  - ❑ Pick **OK**.
- ❑ Use the **STYLE** command to set the ROMANS and ROMAND text fonts.
- ❑ Access the **Dimension Styles** dialog box again and pick the **<u>A</u>nnotation...** button. Do the following:
  - ❑ Pick the **Text Style:** list and see the options.
  - ❑ Change the text height to .125.
  - ❑ Pick **OK**.
- ❑ Pick **OK**.
- ❑ Save as A:EX21-13.

## CHAPTER TEST

*Write your answers in the spaces provided.*

1. Oblique extension lines are drawn using the _____ command and by typing _____ or _____ at the **Dim:** prompt.

2. Define annotation. _____

3. Identify how to access the leader command using the following methods:
   Toolbar—_____
   Pull-down menu—_____
   Typing at the **Command:** prompt—_____

4. Text placed using the **LEADER** command is a _____ text object where all of the lines of text are _____ object.

5. Describe the purpose of the **Annotation Copy** option of the **LEADER** command. _____
   _____
   _____

6. Name and briefly describe the five **Format** options of the **LEADER** command. _____

_____

_____

_____

_____

_____

7. Which **LEADER** command option removes the last leader segment that you drew? _____

_____

8. Name the command that can be used to easily move the text in the dimension line after the dimension has been placed. _____

9. Identify the **DIMEDIT** command option from the following brief descriptions:

Restores the position and rotation of the dimension text to the original default values—

_____

Allows specification of new dimension text— _____

Rotates the dimension text to a specified angle— _____

Changes the extension line angle— _____

10. This command can be used to override dimensioning variables associated with an individual dimension or selected group of dimensions. _____

11. Define arrowless dimensioning. _____

_____

_____

12. AutoCAD refers to arrowless dimensioning as _____ dimensioning.

13. Name the pull-down menu selection that allows you to draw arrowless dimensions.

_____

14. What is the importance of the User Coordinate System (UCS) when doing arrowless dimensioning? _____

_____

_____

15. Identify the elements of this Unified screw thread note: 1/2-13 UNC-2B

1/2— _____

13— _____

UNC— _____

2— _____

B— _____

16. Identify the elements of this metric screw thread: M 14 X 2.

M— _____

14— _____

2— _____

17. Name the dialog box that is used to control dimensioning variables. _____

_____

18. Identify at least three ways to access the dialog box identified in question number 17.

_____

_____

_____

19. Define an AutoCAD dimension style. _____

_____

_____

20. If you change any of the standard dimensioning variables, AutoCAD stores the changes in another style named _____.

21. Provide a general description of dimension style family members. _____

_____

_____

_____

_____

22. Identify the parent family member. _____

_____

_____

23. Name the subdialog box that is used to control the appearance of dimension lines, extension lines, arrowheads, center marks, and dimension scale._____

_____

24. Name the subdialog box that is used to control dimensioning variables that adjust the location of dimension lines, dimension text, arrowheads, and leader lines. _____

_____

25. Name the subdialog box that is used to control the dimensioning variables that display the dimension text. _____

26. This subcommand of the **DIM** command is used to change existing dimensions to reflect the current settings for dimensioning variables. _____

27. This command can be used to change the text or extension lines of existing dimensions.

_____

28. This command is used to move dimension text within the dimension line of an existing dimension. _____

*For 29 through 40, identify the dimensioning variables associated with each of the following short definitions:*

29. Forces dimension text inside of extension lines._____

30. Places a dimension line between extension lines when the dimension text is outside.

_____

_____

31. Used to suppress the dimension lines and arrowheads._____

_____

32. Allows you to place the dimension text above, below, or centered in a break in the dimension line. _____

    _____

33. Controls the space between the dimension line and the dimension text. _____
34. Lets you insert a block in place of the first arrowhead. _____
35. Allows you to adjust the dimension line or leader length and control the dimension text location by dragging the text to the right or left side of the extension line. _____
36. This variable is an overall scale factor that applies to all dimensioning variables that specify size, distance, or offset. _____
37. Sets a scale factor for all linear dimensions, except angles. _____
38. Sets the color of all dimension lines, arrowheads, and leaders. _____
39. This variable controls the placement of arrowheads and text inside or outside of extension lines based on the space available. _____
40. Used to adjust the placement of the dimension text relative to the extension line. _____

    _____

## DRAWING PROBLEMS

*Set limits, units, dimensioning variables, and other parameters as needed. Use the following guidelines.*

A.  Draw the needed multiviews to exact size. Problems presented in 3D require you to select the proper multiviews.

B.  Use grids, object snap options, and the **OSNAP** command to your best advantage.

C.  Apply dimensions accurately using ASME standards. Dimensions are in inches unless otherwise specified.

D.  Set dimensioning variables to suit the drawing.

E.  Use the **LAYER** command to set separate layers for views and dimensions.

F.  Draw object lines using .032″ wide polylines, or use the **LINE** command and plot with a wide pen.

G.  Place general notes 1/2″ from lower-left corner:

    3.  UNLESS OTHERWISE SPECIFIED, ALL DIMENSIONS ARE IN INCHES *(or* MILLIMETERS *as applicable)*.

    2.  REMOVE ALL BURRS AND SHARP EDGES.

    1.  INTERPRET PER ASME Y14.5M-1994.

    NOTES:

H.  Save the drawing to a floppy disk as **P21-***(problem number)*.

## 1. Dimensioning Undefined Curve

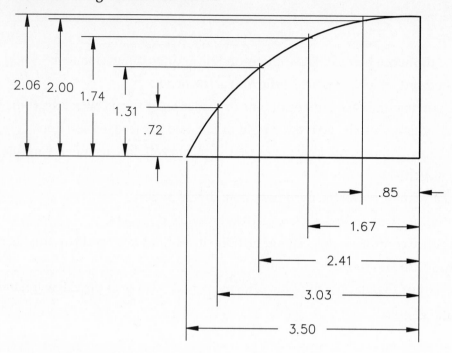

## 2. Placing Oblique Dimensions

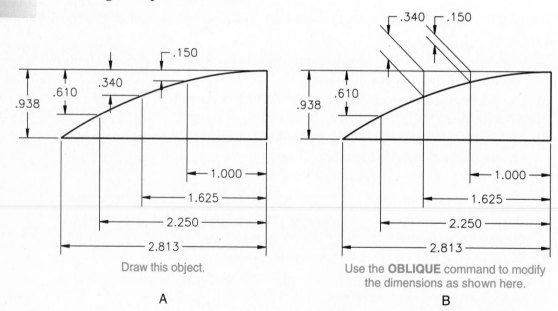

Draw this object.

A

Use the **OBLIQUE** command to modify
the dimensions as shown here.

B

3. **Shaft SAE 1030**

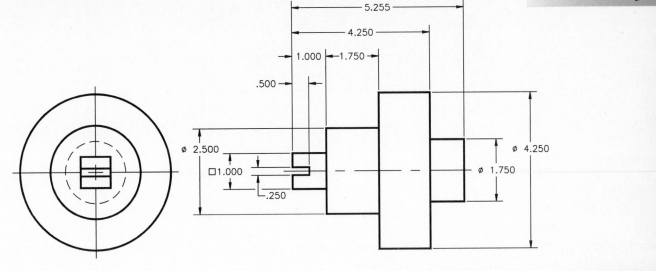

4. **Step Block**

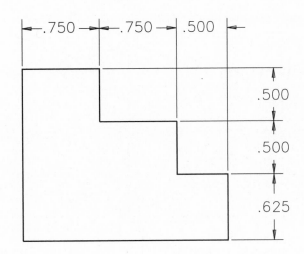

5. **Step Block 2**

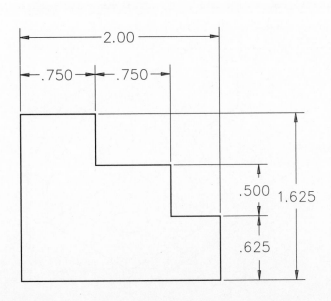

6. **Pin SAE 4320**

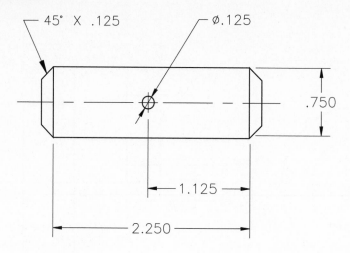

7. **Spline—MS .125 THK**

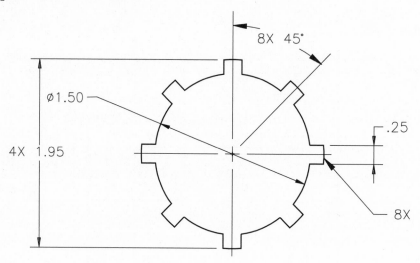

8. **Bracket—Aluminum**

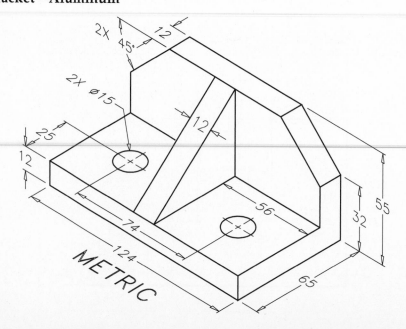

9. **Chain Link—Steel**

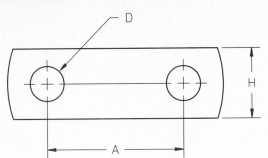

| CHAIN NO. | A | D | H |
|---|---|---|---|
| SST1000 | 2.6 | .44 | 1.125 |
| SST1001 | 3.0 | .48 | 1.525 |
| SST1002 | 3.5 | .95 | 2.125 |

NOTE:
OVERALL LENGTH IS 1.5×A
END RADII ARE .9×A

10. **Base—Bronze** Convert the given drawing to a drawing with the holes located using arrowless dimensioning based on the X and Y coordinates given in the table. Place a table above your title block with Hole (identification), Quantity, Description, and Depth (Z-axis).

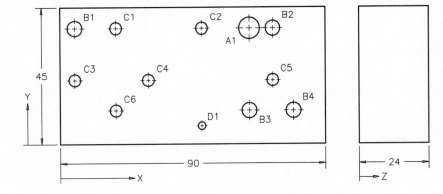

| HOLE | QTY. | DESCRIP. | X | Y | Z |
|---|---|---|---|---|---|
| A1 | 1 | ⌀7 | 64 | 38 | 18 |
| B1 | 1 | ⌀5 | 5 | 38 | THRU |
| B2 | 1 | ⌀5 | 72 | 38 | THRU |
| B3 | 1 | ⌀5 | 64 | 11 | THRU |
| B4 | 1 | ⌀5 | 79 | 11 | THRU |
| C1 | 1 | ⌀4 | 19 | 38 | THRU |
| C2 | 1 | ⌀4 | 48 | 38 | THRU |
| C3 | 1 | ⌀4 | 5 | 21 | THRU |
| C4 | 1 | ⌀4 | 30 | 21 | THRU |
| C5 | 1 | ⌀4 | 72 | 21 | THRU |
| C6 | 1 | ⌀4 | 19 | 11 | THRU |
| D1 | 1 | ⌀2.5 | 48 | 6 | THRU |

### 11. Chassis—Aluminum .100 THK

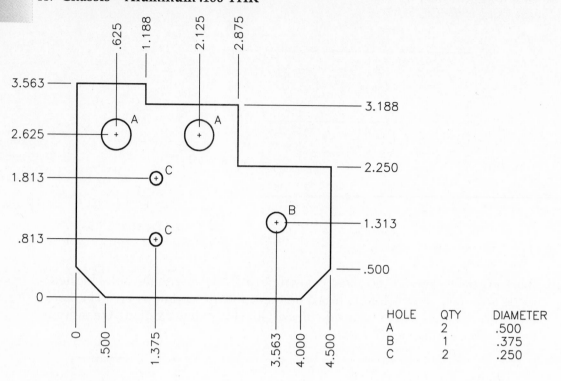

| HOLE | QTY | DIAMETER |
|------|-----|----------|
| A | 2 | .500 |
| B | 1 | .375 |
| C | 2 | .250 |

### 12. Shim MS

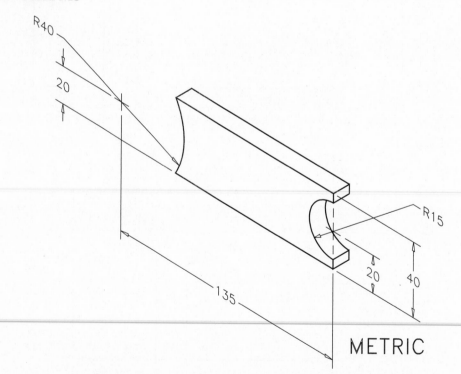

METRIC

13. **Shaft Support—Cast Iron (CI)** Half of the object is removed for clarity. The
entire object should be drawn.

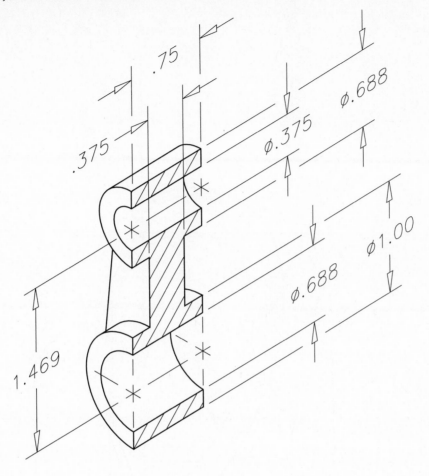

14. **Transmission Cover—Cast Iron (CI)** Half of the object is removed for clarity.
    The entire object should be drawn.

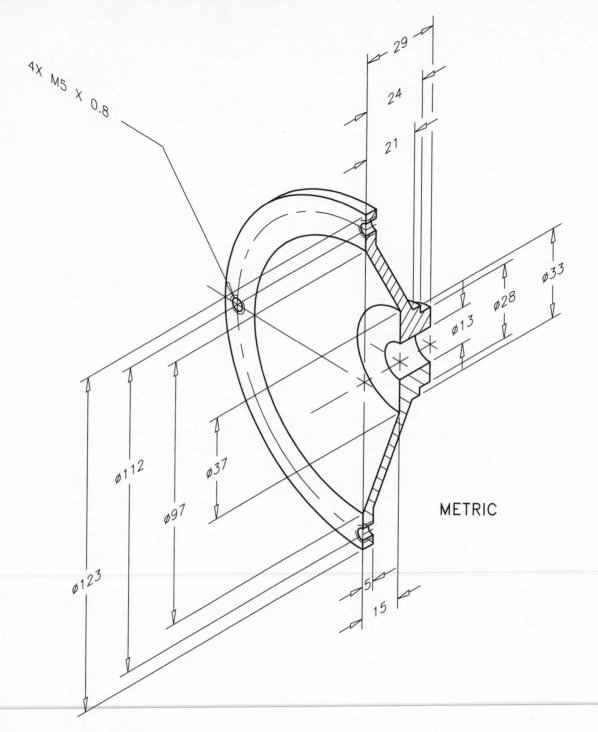

4X M5 X 0.8

29

24

21

ø33

ø28

ø13

ø112

ø37

ø97

ø123

METRIC

5

15

AutoCAD R13

# Chapter 22

# Advanced Dimensioning and Tolerancing

## Learning objectives

After completing this chapter, you will be able to:

○ Establish AutoCAD dimensioning styles to conform with drafting standards.
○ Override existing dimensioning variables.
○ Prepare drawings with dimensions and tolerances from engineering sketches.
○ Modify dimensioning variables to perform specific dimensioning and tolerancing operations.
○ Identify and use dual dimensioning techniques.
○ Apply associative dimensioning.
○ Use the **STRETCH**, **TRIM**, and **EXTEND** commands to revise existing dimensioned objects.
○ Make changes to existing dimension entities using the **UPDATE**, **HOMETEXT**, and **NEWTEXT** commands.

This chapter shows you how to establish AutoCAD dimensioning styles to conform with drafting standards. It explains tolerancing and dual dimensioning, along with the AutoCAD techniques used to edit dimensions. Also introduced is *associative dimensioning*. This is a technique that allows you to revise drawings using the **STRETCH**, **TRIM**, and **EXTEND** commands. Changes made to an object automatically affect associative dimensions.

The number of decimal places usually reflects the accuracy of a dimension. For example, a three-place decimal dimension is more precise than a two-place decimal. You can control the number of places behind the decimal point using dimension variables that control the dimensioning and tolerancing format. These are setups that you should enter on the drawing plan sheet.

## CREATING AND CONTROLLING DIMENSIONING STYLE $\boxed{\text{AUG 9}}$

AutoCAD refers to dimensioning standards as *style*. You can customize your dimensioning style to correspond to drafting standards such as ASME/ANSI, ISO (International Organization for Standardization), military (MIL), architectural, structural, civil, or your own corporate or school standards. Now that you have learned basic AutoCAD dimensioning techniques and how to control the dimensioning variables, you can decide how to establish your own dimensioning styles. You can set up AutoCAD to assist you in preparing the type of dimensioning needed. This will help if you do more than one type of drafting, such as mechanical and architectural. This can also help if you create drawings for clients who each requires different standards, such as ASME/ANSI, ISO, or MIL. The **DIMSTYLE** command allows you to identify and create dimensioning styles. Access the command by typing DIMSTYLE at the **Command:** prompt or STYLE at the **Dim:** prompt. The command sequence is as follows:

```
Command: DIMSTYLE ↵
dimension style: STANDARD
Dimension Style Edit (Save/Restore/STatus/Variables/Apply/?) ⟨Restore⟩:
```

After you enter the **DIMSTYLE** command, AutoCAD gives you a message identifying the current dimension style. The dimension style identified in the above command sequence is STANDARD. This is the AutoCAD default dimension style set up in the AutoCAD prototype.

## Creating dimension styles

Dimension styles can be created in a prototype drawing. This allows you to begin a new drawing and set the dimensioning style(s) that you need. For example, you may typically do drawings that are drawn to ARCHFL (architectural floor plans), ASME-IN (inch), or ASME-MM (metric) standards. If this is the case, make a complete list of the dimensioning variables that you commonly use for each type of drafting. Then, create dimensioning styles accordingly. Lists for architectural or mechanical styles may look like this:

| ARCHFL (1/4″=1′0″) | ASME–IN | ASME–MM |
|---|---|---|
| DIMTSZ = .05 | DIMASZ = .125 | DIMASZ = .125 |
| DIMCEN = .125 | DIMCEN = −.1 | DIMCEN = −.1 |
| DIMDLI = .75 | DIMDLI = .5 | DIMDLI = .5 |
| DIMDLE = .1 | | |
| DIMEXE = .125 | | |
| DIMEXO = .063 | | |
| DIMSCALE = 48 | DIMSCALE = 1 | DIMSCALE = 25.4 |
| DIMTAD = on | DIMTAD = off | DIMTAD = off |
| DIMTIX = on | | |
| DIMTXT = .125 | DIMTXT = .125 | DIMTXT = .125 |
| DIMZIN = 1 | DIMZIN = 4 or 7 | DIMZIN = 8 |
| DIMTIH = off | | |
| DIMTOH = off | | |
| DIMUNIT = 4 | | |
| DIMAUNIT = 1 | | |
| DIMTOFL = 1 | | |
| | DIMDEC = 3 | DIMDEC = 0 |

*(the following dimension variables are for tolerance control and are explained later in this chapter)*

| | | |
|---|---|---|
| DIMFIT = 4 | DIMTZIN = 1 | |
| | DIMTDEC = 3 | DIMTDEC = 0 |
| DIMUPT = 1 | DIMUPT = 1 | DIMUPT = 1 |
| STYLE = CIBT | STYLE = ROMANS | STYLE = ROMANS |
| DIMTXSTY = CIBT | DIMTXSTY = ROMANS | DIMTXSTY = ROMANS |

Any of the dimensioning variables that remain unchanged continue as AutoCAD default values. You can change a dimensioning variable and modify the dimensioning style at any time.

## Saving dimension styles

Now, you are ready to create each of the dimensioning styles listed. Start with the ARCHFL style. Change all of the dimensioning variables that you have listed for your ARCH standard, such as the settings shown above. Then, use the **Save** option of the **DIMSTYLE** command to enter the dimension style name. The command sequence is as follows:

```
Command: DIMSTYLE ↵
dimension style: STANDARD
Dimension Style Edit (Save/Restore/STatus/Variables/Apply/?) ⟨Restore⟩: S ↵
?/Name for new dimension style: ARCHFL ↵
Command:
```

When used at the **Dim:** prompt, the **SAVE** subcommand saves the current dimensioning variable settings to a dimension style and makes the new dimension style current. Type the desired dimension style:

> Command: **DIM** ↵
> Dim: *(type* SA *or* SAVE *and press* [Enter]*)*
> ?/Name for new dimension style: **ARCHFL** ↵

Now, proceed in the same manner to change the dimensioning variables reflecting your proposed ASME/ANSI style. Use the **Save** command for each of the created styles. Do this for any dimensioning style that you want created in your prototype drawing.

### Listing the dimension styles

Enter ? to list the dimension styles created for the current drawing. List the name or names of styles you want listed to help you remember if they have been created, or press [Enter] to accept the wild card ⟨*⟩ for all dimension styles:

> Command: **DIMSTYLE** ↵
> dimension style: STANDARD
> Dimension Style Edit (Save/Restore/STatus/Variables/Apply/?) ⟨Restore⟩: **?** ↵
> Dimension style(s) to list ⟨*⟩: ↵

The AutoCAD **Text Window** is displayed showing the list of available dimension styles:

> Named dimension styles:
>   ARCH
>   ASME-IN
>   ASME-MM
>   STANDARD
> Command:

Press the [F2] key to toggle between the **Text Window** and the drawing window. You can also double-click the **Text Window** control menu to close the **Text Window** and return to the drawing editor. The **Text Window** control menu is the box with a horizontal bar located above the word **Edit** located in the upper-left corner of the **Text Window**.

This is how you list the dimension styles in the **DIM** command:

> Command: **DIM** ↵
> Dim: *(type* SA *or* SAVE *and press* [Enter]*)*
> ?/Name for new dimension style:**?** ↵
> Dimension style(s) to list ⟨*⟩: ↵
> Named dimension styles:
>   ARCH
>   ASME-IN
>   ASME-MM
>   STANDARD
> ?/Name for new dimension style:

### Using the Restore option

The **Restore** option lets you change dimensioning variable settings by reading new settings from an existing dimension style. You can access **Restore** at the keyboard. The current style is listed when you enter the **DIMSTYLE** command. Change to a different dimension style by entering that dimension style name as follows:

> Command: **DIMSTYLE** ↵
> dimension style: STANDARD
> Dimension Style Edit (Save/Restore/STatus/Variables/Apply/?) ⟨Restore⟩: ↵
> ?/Enter dimension style name or RETURN to select dimension: **ARCHFL** ↵
> Command:

or in the **DIM** command:

>     Command: **DIM** ↵
>     Dim: **RES** ↵
>     ?/Enter dimension style name or RETURN to select dimension: **ARCHFL** ↵
>     Dim:

You can also press [Enter] and pick any existing dimension to determine the style. **Restore** is the default in the **DIMSTYLE** command, so you can type R and press [Enter] or just press the [Enter] key:

>     Command: **DIMSTYLE** ↵
>     dimension style: ARCHFL
>     Dimension Style Edit (Save/Restore/STatus/Variables/Apply/?) ⟨Restore⟩: ↵
>     ?/Enter dimension style name or RETURN to select dimension: ↵
>     Select dimension: *(pick a dimension on the drawing)*
>     dimension style: ARCHFL
>     Command:

or in the **DIM** command:

>     Command: **DIM** ↵
>     Dim: *(type RES or* RESTORE *and press* [Enter]*)*
>     Current dimension style: ARCHFL
>     ?/Enter dimension style name or RETURN to select dimension: ↵
>     Select dimension: *(pick a dimension on the drawing)*
>     Current dimension style: ARCHFL

Now you know that the dimension you picked was drawn using the ARCHFL style, which is the current style.

The **Restore** option lets you list the dimension styles in the current drawing. To do so, enter ? in the same manner as described with the **Save** option.

If you want to display the difference between one of your dimension styles and the current style, enter the tilde character (~) and the style to compare:

>     ?/Enter dimension style name or RETURN to select dimension: **~ASME–IN** ↵

When you press [Enter], AutoCAD shows you the difference between styles in the **Text Window**:

>     Difference between ASME–IN and current settings:
>
>     | ASME-IN | | Current Setting |
>     |---|---|---|
>     | DIMASZ | 0.125 | 0.180 |
>     | DIMCEN | −0.100 | 0.125 |
>     | DIMDEC | 3 | 4 |
>     | DIMDLI | 0.500 | 0.750 |
>     | DIMSCALE | 1 | 48 |
>     | DIMTAD | off | on |
>     | DIMTDEC | 3 | 4 |
>     | DIMTXSTY | ROMANS | CIBT |
>     | DIMTZIN | 1 | 0 |
>     | DIMZIN | 4 | 1 |

Keep in mind that the **Text Window** only displays the dimension variable settings that are *different* between the current style and the style name that you entered. You can do the same thing while in the **Dim: SAVE** command at the ?/Name for new dimension style: prompt.

## Using the STatus option

The **STatus** option of the **DIMSTYLE** command is used to display the settings of all dimension variables for the current dimension style. Pick the **Status** option in the **DimStyle:** screen menu or type ST as follows:

> Command: **DIMSTYLE** ↵
> dimension style: ARCHFL
> Dimension Style Edit (Save/Restore/STatus/Variables/Apply/?) ⟨Restore⟩: **ST** ↵

The **Text Window** displays all of the dimension variable names, the settings, and a descriptive statement about each variable. There are three pages, so press [Enter] to read each of the additional pages. Press [F2] or double-click the **Text Window** control menu to get back to the drawing window when done. This works the same as the **STATUS** subcommand:

> Command: **DIM** ↵
> Dim: **STATUS** ↵

## Using the Variables option

Another way to list the current dimension style and variable settings of a dimension style without changing the current settings is with the **Variable** option. You can name a dimension style to list the variables, or pick a dimension on the screen just as with the **Restore** option:

> Command: **DIMSTYLE** ↵
> dimension style: ARCHFL
> Dimension Style Edit (Save/Restore/STatus/Variables/Apply/?) ⟨Restore⟩: **V** ↵
> ?/Enter dimension style name or RETURN to select dimension: ↵
> Select dimension: *(pick a dimension on the drawing)*

or in the **DIM** command:

> Command: **DIM** ↵
> Dim: *(type* VA *or* VARIABLES *and press* [Enter]*)*
> Current dimension style: ARCH
> ?/Enter dimension style name or RETURN to select dimension: ↵
> Select dimension: *(pick a dimension on the screen)*

The screen changes to the **Text Window** listing of the current dimensioning variable settings for the dimension you picked. Press [Enter] to see more pages of the list, or press the [F2] key to return to the drawing window.

Use the **?** option if you want to look at the dimensioning variables used in the current drawing. You can compare the current dimension style with another style by entering ~ and the style name to compare as follows:

> Command: **DIMSTYLE** ↵
> dimension style: ARCHFL
> Dimension Style Edit (Save/Restore/STatus/Variables/Apply/?) ⟨Restore⟩: **V** ↵
> ?/Enter dimension style name or RETURN to select dimension: ~**ASME–IN** ↵
> Differences between ASME-IN and current settings:
> ASME-IN                    Current Setting
> DIMSCALE        1.0000      48.000

The text window then displays only the dimension variables that are different between the current style and the ASME–IN style.

## Using the Apply option

Use the **Apply** option in the **DIMSTYLE** command if you want to select a dimension and have it applied to the current dimension style settings. The command sequence is as follows:

> Command: **DIMSTYLE** ⏎
> Dimension Style Edit (Save/Restore/STatus/Variables/Apply/?) ⟨Restore⟩: **A** ⏎
> Select objects: *(select the dimension or dimensions that you want to have applied to the current dimension style)*
> Select objects: ⏎
> Command:

---

### EXERCISE 22-1

❑ Open one of your previous mechanical drawings or exercises containing dimensions.
❑ Design dimensioning variables that can be used for the two different dimension styles. Name one ARCHFL for drawing architectural floor plans at a scale of 1/4"=1'-0", and name the other ASME–IN for inch dimensioned ASME standard drawings. Use the following dimension variable settings:

| ARCHFL | ASME–IN |
|---|---|
| **DIMTSZ** = 4 | **DIMTSZ** = .125 |
| **DIMCEN** = 6 | **DIMCEN** = –.1 |
| **DIMDLE** = 2 | **DIMDLI** = .5 |
| **DIMEXO** = 2 | **DIMEXE** = .125 |
| **DIMEXE** = 3 | **DIMTXT** = .125 |
| **DIMTAD** = on | **DIMZIN** = 4 |
| **DIMTIX** = on | **DIMDEC** = 3 |
| **DIMTXT** = 6 | **DIMUPT** = 1 |
| **DIMZIN** = 1 | **STYLE** = ROMANS |
| **DIMTIH** = off | **DIMTXSTY** = ROMANS |
| **DIMTOH** = off | **DIMTDEC** = 3 |
| **DIMUNIT** = 4 | **DIMTZIN** = 4 |
| **DIMAUNIT** = 1 | |
| **DIMFIT** = 4 | |
| **DIMTOFL** = 1 | |
| **DIMUPT** = 1 | |
| **STYLE** = CIBT | |
| **DIMTXSTY** = CIBT | |

❑ Save these dimension styles under the name identified with each.
❑ Use the **Restore** option to restore the dimension style that is not currently set.
❑ Use the tilde (~) to have AutoCAD show you the difference between the styles.
❑ Use the **?** option to list the available dimension styles.
❑ Use the **STatus** option to display the dimension variable names of the current dimension style.
❑ Access the dimension variable status screen with the **Variable** option.
❑ Restore the ASME-IN dimension style if it is not current. Use the **Apply** option and select the dimensions on the drawing to convert to the current dimension style.
❑ Save as A:EX22-1.

## OVERRIDING EXISTING DIMENSIONING VARIABLES AUG 9

Generally, it is appropriate to have one or more dimensioning variables set to perform specific tasks that relate to your dimensioning practices. However, situations may arise where it is necessary to alter dimensioning variables to modify one or more specific dimensions on the final drawing. For example, assume you have the **DIMEXO** (dimension extension line offset) variable set at .062. This conforms to ASME standards. However, in your final drawing there are three specific dimensions that require a 0 extension line offset. You can pick these three dimensions and alter the **DIMEXO** variable exclusively using the **DIMOVERRIDE** command that was introduced in Chapter 21. As a review, the command works like this:

> Command: *(type* DIMOVER *or* DIMOVERRIDE *and press* [Enter]*)*
> Dimension variable to override (or Clear to remove overrides): **DIMEXO** ↵
> Current value ⟨.062⟩ New value: **0** ↵
> Dimension variable to override: *(type another variable name to override or press* [Enter]*)*
> Select objects: *(select the dimension or dimensions to override)*
> Select objects: ↵
> Command:

You can also override a dimension variable in the **DIM** command:

> Command: **DIM** ↵
> Dim: *(type* OVER *or* OVERRIDE *and press* [Enter]*)*
> Dimension variable to override: **DIMEXO** ↵
> Current value ⟨.0625⟩: New value: **0** ↵
> Dimension variable to override: ↵
> Select objects: *(pick the specific dimensions for change)*

The **DIMEXO** variable automatically changes from .062 to 0 on the three selected dimensions. You can also clear any previous overrides by using the **Clear** option like this:

> Command: **DIMOVER** ↵
> Dimension variable to override (or Clear to remove overrides): **C** ↵
> Select objects: *(select the dimension or dimensions to clear an override)*
> Select objects: ↵
> Command:

**PROFESSIONAL TIP**

It may be better to use the **DDIM** command rather than the **OVERRIDE** command, depending on the nature of the change. In the dialog box you can pick an existing style, change the variable, then make a new style.

It is also sometimes better to generate a new style, because certain situations require specific dimension styles in order to prevent conflicts with drawing geometry or dimension crowding. For example, if a number of the dimensions in the current drawing all require the same overrides, then generating a new dimension style is a good idea. If only one or two dimensions need the same overrides, then just using the **OVERRIDE** command may be more productive.

## EXERCISE 22-2

❑ Load AutoCAD for Windows and open PRODR2.
❑ Make a drawing similar to Figure 21-1 with dimensioning variables set as follows:

**DIMASZ** = .1
**DIMGAP** = .05
**DIMDLE** = .12
**DIMDLI** = .5
**DIMEXO** = .06

❑ Use datum (baseline) dimensioning to make your job easier.
❑ After completing the entire drawing, with the dimensioning variables set as required, use the **DIMOVERRIDE** command to change only the **DIMEXO** variable to 0 on all dimensions except the overall dimensions.
❑ Save the drawing as A:EX22-2.

## USING THE DIALOG BOX TO CONTROL DIMENSION STYLES

AUG 9

The **Dimension Styles** dialog box was introduced in Chapter 20 as an easy way to work with dimension variables. This box is also used to list, save, and restore dimension styles. The dialog box is accessed by selecting **Dimension Style...** from the **Data** pull-down menu, picking the **Dimension Styles** button on the **Dimensioning** toolbar, or by typing DDIM at the **Command:** or **Dim:** prompts.

The **Dimension Style** area of the dialog box is where you can access dimension styles that were previously created, or name and save additional dimension styles. See Figure 22-1. The currently active dimension style is identified in the **Current:** list box. Figure 22-1 shows STANDARD as the current dimension style. STANDARD is the AutoCAD default dimension style. Pick the down arrow to see additional dimension styles that are available, Figure 22-2. These are dimension styles that were saved earlier using the **DIMSTYLE** command. Each of the dimension styles that are saved using the **DIMSTYLE** command or in the **Dimension Styles** dialog box are referred to as a *dimension style family* by AutoCAD.

Figure 22-1. The **Dimensions Styles** dialog box can be used to list, save, and restore dimension styles.

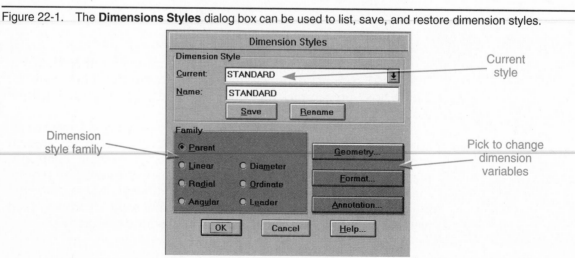

Figure 22-2.   Pick the down arrow next to the **Current:** edit box to see additional dimension styles
that are available.

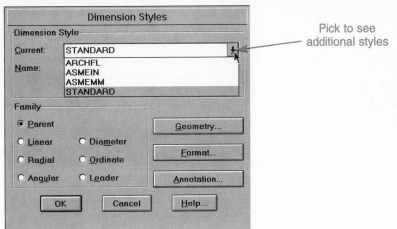

You can return to the drawing editor and make changes to the dimension variables or
change dimension variables using the **Geometry** subdialog box, **Format** subdialog box, and
**Annotation** subdialog box inside the **Dimension Styles** dialog box. When you have made the
dimension variable changes, use the **Dimension Styles** dialog to type the name of a new
dimension style in the **Name:** text box. A dimension style name can have up to 31 characters.
For example, you can modify the ARCHFL dimension style by changing the variables to use
on roof plan drawings at a 1/8"=1'-0" scale. Then, type ARCHRP (architectural roof plans) in
the **Name:** text box and pick the **Save** button, Figure 22-3. AutoCAD gives you the following
message at the bottom of the **Dimension Styles** dialog box: Created ARCHRP from ARCHFL.
Creating a new dimension style from an existing style is an easy way to establish new dimension styles.

The **Rename** button is used to rename a current dimension style. To rename a dimension
style, type the style name in the **Name:** text box and the pick the **Rename** button. However,
you cannot rename the AutoCAD STANDARD dimension style.

Figure 22-3.   To create a new dimension style, type the name in the **Name:** edit box and pick the **Save**
button. Note the message in the lower-left corner of the dialog box (shown here highlighted).

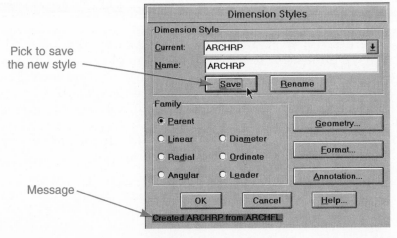

Although AutoCAD allows a dimension style name to be up to 31 characters, care should be taken in applying long names. You will learn in advanced topics that dimension style names and drawing names are linked together for certain applications. The combination of characters in these linked names cannot exceed 31 characters. If a drawing name has 8 characters, then the dimension style name should have no more than 23 characters.

## Using dimension style family members

Dimension style family members are very useful in AutoCAD. Just as with people, members of dimension families have different needs. This feature makes it possible to have various types of dimensions use alternate dimension variable settings. For example, in a drawing, you may want to show linear dimensions with the text placed above the dimension line, but maintain centered placement on radial dimensions. Rather than create and maintain an additional dimension style, you can specify that the parent of this style uses **DIMTAD** = 1 (text above dimension line), then select the radial member of this dimension family and specify centered text placement with **DIMTAD** = 0. Now the **DIMTAD** variable is on for linear dimensions and not for radial dimensions.

A second example of dimension family use might be if you want all diameter dimensions to place text outside the feature and force a dimension line (**DIMTOFL**) inside, without affecting any other types of dimensions. Again, using **DDIM**, select the parent of the current style and specify all settings that are used globally. Then select the diameter members of the family and turn **DIMTOFL** on.

A third example of dimension family use is for center marks placed by diameter dimensions (**DIMCEN** = .09 or −.09), but not by radius dimensions (**DIMCEN** = 0). This is a common practice in mechanical drafting, especially when the radii are small. To do this, use the **Geometry** dialog box and set the **Center** to **None** for the parent and then set the **Center** to either **Mark** or **Line** for the diameter family member.

There are many possible uses of the dimension style families. Using the dimension style families allows maximum flexibility with a minimal number of dimension styles.

**NOTE**

The descriptive nature of the term *family* may be used to explain the dimension style family. For example, in a family, many family members may share specific qualities or features, yet each member is unique having certain qualities or features all their own. My son and daughter share my name (**DIMSTYLE** name) and some of my general tendencies and features (parent setting), yet each of them look and act different than I do (individual family member settings).

**EXERCISE 22-3**

❑ Open EX22-1.
❑ Access the **Dimension Styles** dialog box.
❑ Look at the list of current dimension styles.
❑ Make the ASME–IN style current.
❑ Note that the **Parent Family** member radio button is active.
❑ Use the **Dimension Styles** dialog box to change the following dimension variables to the values indicated. Pick the **OK** button when done. Answer Yes when AutoCAD asks if you want to Save changes to current style?:
  ❑ Use the **Geometry** subdialog box:
  ❑ **Center = None (DIMCEN = 0)**
❑ Pick the **Diameter** family button to make it active and then set these dimension variables:
  ❑ In the **Geometry** subdialog box:
  ❑ **Center = Line, Size = .125 (DIMCEN = –.125)**
  ❑ In the **Format** dialog box:
  ❑ **Force Line Inside (DIMTOFL = on)**
❑ The changes are for a new dimension style that is slightly different from the ASME–IN style. This may be used for drawings standards that require the centerlines to be placed with diameter dimensions, but not with radius dimensions. This also forces the dimension line inside when using the **DIMDIAMETER** command. Name this dimension style ASME-IN2 and save it.
❑ You should keep a list of the dimension style names and their family member dimension variable settings for reference.
❑ Save as A:EX22-3.

## USING EXTERNALLY REFERENCED DIMENSION STYLES

In Chapter 19 you had a brief introduction to the **XREF** command. Remember, an external reference drawing is one that is not added to the current drawing, but rather *referenced* to it. This is explained in detail in Chapter 26 and Chapter 30. The **Dimension Style** list box may contain externally referenced styles. These referenced styles cannot be made current, changed, or renamed. You can easily identify these names since the xref name is given first, followed by a vertical bar, and then the dimension style name. For example, FOUNDATIONIARCH has the FOUNDATION style referenced to an external drawing.

If you want to use an externally referenced style, simply pick the style from the list box and then change the name and pick the **Save** button. Now, the new dimension style contains all the characteristics of the referenced style.

## TOLERANCING

A *tolerance* is the total amount that a specific dimension is allowed to vary. It is the difference between the maximum and minimum limits. A tolerance is not given to values that are identified as reference, maximum, minimum, or stock sizes. The tolerance may be applied to the dimension, indicated by a general note, or identified in the drawing title block.

The dimension in Figure 22-4 is 2.750±.005. This is referred to as *plus/minus tolerancing*. The maximum and minimum limits of the feature are then 2.755 (2.750 + .005) and 2.745 (2.750 – .005). By subtracting the lower limit from the upper limit, you find the tolerance is .010. The limits are calculated from the specified dimension 2.750.

However, the dimension on the drawing may show only the limits, without the specified dimension, as shown in Figure 22-5. This is referred to as *limits dimensioning*. Many companies prefer limits dimensioning over plus/minus tolerancing. Since the limits are shown, calculating them is not required.

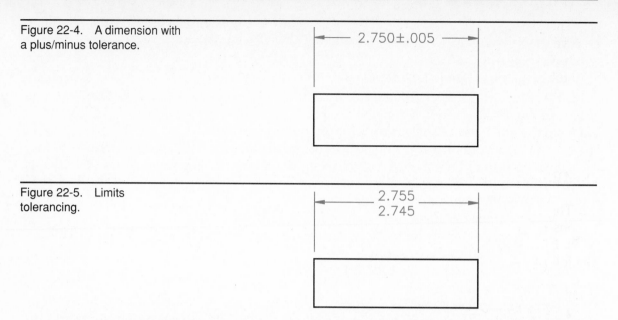

Figure 22-4.   A dimension with
a plus/minus tolerance.

$2.750 \pm .005$

Figure 22-5.   Limits
tolerancing.

$\dfrac{2.755}{2.745}$

A **bilateral tolerance** can vary in both directions from the specified dimension. The dimension 2.750± .005 is an equal bilateral tolerance. The variation from the specified dimension 2.750 is the same in both directions. An **unequal bilateral tolerance** occurs when the variation is not equal. The dimension $2.750^{+.005}_{-.003}$ is an unequal bilateral tolerance. A **unilateral tolerance** allows the dimension to vary in only one direction. The dimensions $2.750^{+.000}_{-.005}$ and $2.750^{+.005}_{-.000}$ are unilateral tolerances.

The tolerancing for inch and metric dimensions are shown differently on a drawing. The following shows several examples:

| INCH | METRIC |
|---|---|
| 1.500±.005 | $25 \pm 0.5$ |
| $1.500^{+.000}_{-.005}$ | $25 \, _{-\,0.5}^{\phantom{-}0}$ |
| $1.500^{+.005}_{-.000}$ | $25 \, _{\phantom{+}0}^{+\,0.5}$ |

Notice the 0 preceding the decimal point for metric values less than one, while the 0 is not shown for inch dimensions less than one. Also, compare the unique differences between inch and metric unilateral tolerances in the above examples.

### Drawing tolerance dimensions with AutoCAD

The **DIMTOL** (dimension tolerance) variable is used to draw dimension numbers with or without tolerances. The default value (off) draws dimensions without specified tolerances. Turn **DIMTOL** on to have tolerances drawn with the specified dimension:

```
Command: DIMTOL ↵
New value for DIMTOL ⟨Off⟩: ON ↵
Command:
```

### Setting AutoCAD to draw metric or inch dimension numbers

In Chapter 20 you learned that you can control whether or not a zero is placed in front of a decimal unit less than one. When the values are in millimeters, a zero should precede a value less than one millimeter, such as 0.5mm. However, when the dimensions are in inches, a zero is not drawn in front of a decimal inch, such as .5″. The **DIMZIN** variable controls this for the specified dimension. **DIMZIN** is set to its default value of 0 for metric dimensioning. **DIMZIN** is set to 4 or 7 for inch dimensioning.

The **DIMTZIN** (tolerance zero inch) variable allows you to suppress the zero for the tolerance values. The default (0) places the zero in front of tolerance values. A **DIMTZIN** setting of 4 removes the zeros in front of any decimal tolerance number. If your drawing is in inches with tolerance dimensions, set **DIMTZIN** like this:

Command: **DIMTZIN** ↵
New value for DIMTZIN ⟨0⟩: **4** ↵
Command:

# DIMENSION AND TOLERANCE DECIMAL PLACES

The ASME Y14.5M-1994 *Dimensioning and Tolerancing* standard has separate recommendations for the way the number of decimal places is displayed for inch and metric dimensions. Examples of inch and metric decimal dimension numbers are shown in Figure 22-6. The following are some general rules:

## Inch

- A specified inch dimension is expressed to the same number of decimal places as its tolerance. Zeros are added to the right of the decimal point if needed. For example, the inch dimension .250±.005 has an additional zero added to the .25 to match the three decimal tolerance. The dimensions 2.000±.005 and 2.500±.005 both have zeros added to match the tolerance.
- Both plus and minus values of an inch tolerance have the same number of decimal places. Zeros are added to fill in where needed. For example, +.005/−.010 *not* +.005/−.01.

## Metric

- The decimal point and zeros are omitted when the metric dimension is a whole number. For example, the metric dimension 12 has no decimal point followed by a zero. This rule is true unless tolerance values are displayed.
- When a metric dimension is greater than a whole number by a fraction of a millimeter, the last digit to the right of the decimal point is not followed by a zero. For example, the metric dimension 12.5 has no zero to the right of the five. This rule is true unless tolerance values are displayed.
- Both plus and minus values of a metric tolerance have the same number of decimal places. Zeros are added to fill in where needed.
- Zeros are not added after the specified dimension to match the tolerance. For example, both 24±0.25 and 24.5±0.25 are correct. However, some companies prefer to add zeros after the specified dimension to match the tolerance, as in 24.00±0.25 or 24.50±0.25.

---

Figure 22-6.  Examples of inch and metric decimal dimension numbers.

$$28 \quad 24.5$$
$$0.5$$
$$24^{+0.08}_{-0.20}$$
$$24 \pm 0.1$$
$$24^{\ \ 0}_{-0.2} \quad 24^{+0.2}_{\ \ 0}$$
$$24.25$$
$$24.30$$

METRIC

$$2.375 \quad .625$$
$$.750^{+.002}_{-.003}$$
$$.750 \pm .005$$
$$.625^{+.000}_{-.004}$$
$$.625^{+.004}_{-.000}$$

INCH

$$24.5° \quad 30°15'35" \quad 30°\pm0°5'$$

ANGLE

### Controlling the decimal places with AutoCAD

The **DIMDEC** (dimension decimal) variable was introduced in Chapter 20. This variable is used to set the number of decimal places for the value of the primary units. The default is 4, but you can set between 0 and 8. Inch dimensions for manufacturing drawings are often set to three place decimals:

        Command: **DIMDEC** ↵
        New value for DIMDEC ⟨4⟩: **3** ↵
        Command:

With metric dimensions, the last digit to the right of the decimal point is not followed by a zero. This is true unless the metric dimension needs to have places added after the decimal point to match tolerances given in a general note or in the title block.

When **DIMTOL** is on and dimensions are drawn with plus/minus tolerances displayed, it is important to match the number of decimal places in the tolerance with the number of decimal places in the specified dimension. This is done with the **DIMTDEC** (dimension tolerance decimal) variable. **DIMTDEC** also has a default of 4 and options between 0 and 8. If the specified dimension is set to three decimal places, then the tolerance decimal places should be three places:

        Command: **DIMTDEC** ↵
        New value for DIMTDEC ⟨4⟩: **3** ↵
        Command:

## DRAWING BILATERAL AND UNILATERAL TOLERANCES WITH AUTOCAD

AUG 9

Three dimension variables control how bilateral and unilateral tolerances are set up in AutoCAD. These are **DIMTOL**, **DIMTP** (tolerance plus), and **DIMTM** (tolerance minus). **DIMTOL** was introduced earlier and must be turned on before tolerance dimensions can be drawn. **DIMTP** sets the plus part of the tolerance, while **DIMTM** is used for the minus part of the tolerance.

### Setting an equal bilateral tolerance

Use the **DIMTP** and **DIMTM** variables and the following procedure to set an equal bilateral tolerance of .001:

        Command: **DIMTP** ↵
        New value for DIMTP ⟨0.000⟩: **.001** ↵
        Command: **DIMTM** ↵
        New value for DIMTM ⟨0.000⟩: **.001** ↵
        Command:

Before you set **DIMTP** and **DIMTM**, be sure that **DIMZIN**, **DIMTZIN**, **DIMDEC**, and **DIMTDEC** are in the desired settings and values. Any dimensions drawn from now on are given the plus and minus tolerance shown in Figure 22-7.

Figure 22-7.   Once an equal bilateral tolerance of .001 is set up, all dimensions drawn will have a tolerance that looks like this.

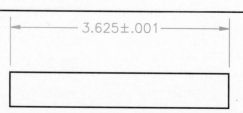

## Setting an unequal bilateral tolerance

Use the **DIMTP** and **DIMTM** variables and the following procedure to set an equal bilateral tolerance of .001:

Command: **DIMTP** ↵
New value for DIMTP ⟨0.000⟩: **.002** ↵
Command: **DIMTM** ↵
New value for DIMTM ⟨0.000⟩: **.005** ↵
Command:

Now you can use a dimensioning command, such as **DIMLIN**, to draw the dimension shown in Figure 22-8.

Figure 22-8.  A dimension with an unequal bilateral tolerance.

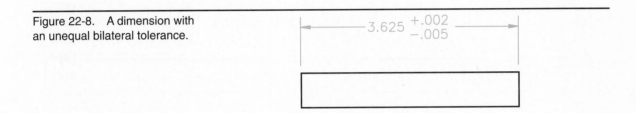

## Controlling the tolerance position of a bilateral tolerance

The **DIMTOLJ** (tolerance justification) variable can be used to control vertical justification of the bilateral tolerance in relation to the specified dimension. Using an option other than the default may not be practical because the default places the bilateral tolerance centered on the specified dimension, as shown in examples throughout this chapter. The options for the **DIMTOLJ** variable are as follows:

| Option | Results |
|--------|---------|
| 0 | The specified dimension text is aligned with the lower tolerance text. |
| 1 *(default)* | The specified dimension text is centered vertically between the tolerance text. |
| 2 | The specified dimension text is aligned with the upper tolerance text. |

### Setting a unilateral tolerance

To set a unilateral tolerance, enter 0 for either the **DIMTP** or **DIMTM** variables as needed. Remember, **DIMTP** is tolerance plus and **DIMTM** is tolerance minus. Setting the following dimension variables allows you to draw the dimension shown in Figure 22-9:

Command: **DIMTP** ↵
New value for DIMTP ⟨0.000⟩: **0** ↵
Command: **DIMTM** ↵
New value for DIMTM ⟨0.000⟩: **.005** ↵
Command:

Notice in Figure 22-9 that AutoCAD automatically omits the plus (+) symbol in front of the zero part of the unilateral tolerance. The plus (+) symbol is removed if the unilateral tolerance is +.000. The minus (–) symbol is removed if the unilateral tolerance is –.000. This is in violation of the ASME standard for inch dimensioning. However, for metric dimensions, the ASME and ISO standards say the plus and minus symbols should be removed for the zero part of a unilateral tolerance.

When **DIMTZIN** is 0 for metric dimensions, AutoCAD leaves the zero in front of the decimal point. This is a preferred practice. When **DIMTDEC** is 1, AutoCAD places a decimal point and a zero, as shown in Figure 22-10A. This is not a preferred way to display a metric unilateral tolerance. If you set **DIMTDEC** to 0, then you will only be able to place a tolerance equal to or

Figure 22-9.    Notice that AutoCAD automatically omits the plus (+) symbol in front of the zero part of a unilateral tolerance.

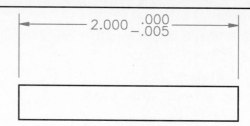

$$2.000 \, {}^{.000}_{-.005}$$

Figure 22-10.    A—For metric tolerances, a zero should not be followed by a decimal and another zero, as shown here. B—The proper way to show a metric tolerance of zero is with no decimal.

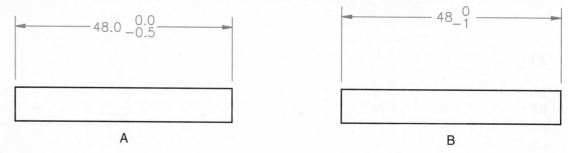

$$48.0 \, {}^{0.0}_{-0.5}$$

A

$$48 \, {}^{0}_{-1}$$

B

greater than 1, because the tolerance is rounded up to the nearest whole number. This makes the metric format correct, as shown in Figure 22-10B. However, this may not be an acceptable tolerance. See Figure 22-6 for examples of the recommended dimension text formats.

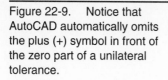

**PROFESSIONAL TIP**

As previously discussed, ASME Y14.5M-1994 recommends a plus and minus symbol be displayed for inch tolerances, even for a unilateral tolerance. AutoCAD does not do this automatically. There *is* a way to have the plus or minus symbol placed with the zero part of a unilateral tolerance, but use caution. If the specified dimension and the tolerance values are three place decimals, then set **DIMDEC** = 3 and **DIMTDEC** = 3. Now, turn **DIMTOL** on. If you want the plus tolerance to be .005, then set **DIMTP** to .005. If you want the minus tolerance to be .000 then set the **DIMTM** to .0001 for a four place decimal. The **DIMTDEC** value of 3 automatically sets the tolerance value to a three place decimal regardless of the **DIMTM** setting. Therefore, if you set **DIMTM** to .0001, the last digit (1) is automatically removed. This results in a display of −.000 for the minus tolerance. This is because AutoCAD thinks the tolerance has a value other than zero, but it is not displayed because **DIMTDEC** only allows a three place decimal.

Caution should be taken when using this method if the drawing is transmitted in electronic format or is run through a translator. In this application, the four place value that you set may be transferred to the destination drawing resulting in incorrect information. If this is the case, but you want to continue with this technique, set the tolerance out to 8 places (.00000001). Hopefully it will be recognized as a ridiculous value and questioned, rather than simply integrated into the manufacturing plan. If you are in doubt, stick with the normal AutoCAD application.

**PROFESSIONAL TIP**

The dimension text often becomes very long for dimensions having a plus/minus tolerance. Horizontal dimension text takes up more space between extension lines. Vertical dimension text requires more space between dimension lines. Allow for this space during the planning and sketching process. If you make an error when dimensioning, simply try again or move the dimension text. Remember to keep dimension lines equally spaced for a uniform appearance. The **DIMDLI** variable controls the dimension line spacing for baseline and continue dimensions.

## DRAWING DIMENSIONS USING LIMITS TOLERANCING    AUG 9

Limits tolerances can be drawn with AutoCAD by setting one extra variable in addition to **DIMTP**, and **DIMTM**. Enter the **DIMLIM** variable and respond with ON. This automatically turns **DIMTOL** off if it is on. Enter the **DIMTP** and **DIMTM** values if you have not already done so. AutoCAD calculates the upper and lower limits and places this as the dimension text. The following sequence was used before drawing the dimension shown in Figure 22-11.

    Command: **DIMLIM** ↵
    New value for DIMLIM ⟨Off⟩: **ON** ↵
    Command: **DIMTP** ↵
    New value for DIMTP ⟨Off⟩: **.005** ↵
    Command: **DIMTM** ↵
    New value for DIMTM ⟨Off⟩: **.005** ↵
    Command:

The specified dimension in Figure 22-11 is 3.625. AutoCAD automatically adds .005 and subtracts .005 (3.625 + .005 = 3.630 and 3.625 − .005 = 3.620).

Figure 22-11.   Limits tolerancing.

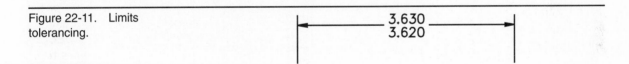

### Setting the tolerance text height

You can control the text height for tolerance dimensions when **DIMTOL** is on and **DIMTP** is different than **DIMTM**, or when **DIMLIM** is on and **DIMTP** and **DIMTM** are at any setting. Then, use the **DIMTFAC** (dimension tolerance scale factor) variable. With **DIMTFAC** set at the default of 1, the tolerance text height is equal to the specified dimension text height. This practice is consistent with the ASME standard. However, if you want to change the text height of the tolerance to, for example,  3/4 (.75) of the normal text height, then alter the **DIMTFAC** variable as follows:

    Command: **DIMTFAC** ↵
    New value for DIMTFAC ⟨1⟩: **.75** ↵
    Command:

Figure 22-12 shows how changing the **DIMTFAC** variable affects the dimension text.

Figure 22-12.   The affect of different **DIMTFAC** settings on plus/minus tolerances and limits tolerances.

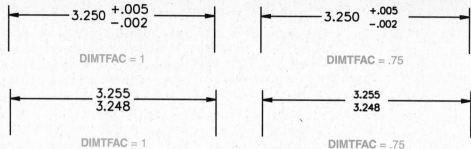

## EXERCISE 22-4

❑ Load AutoCAD for Windows and open PRODR2 or begin a new drawing with your own variable settings.

❑ Draw object lines of the views on layer 0-7, centerlines on layer 2-2, and place dimensions on layer 3-3.

❑ Create the circles for Object 3 and Object 4 at their nominal diameters of 1.120 and .750.

❑ Set the dimensioning variables as required to create the toleranced dimensions exactly as shown. Objects 1, 2, 3, and 4 are in inches. Objects 5, 6, and 7 are metric.

❑ Use **DIMTFAC** to change the tolerance text height in objects 2 and 3 to .75. Observe the difference and then change **DIMTFAC** back to 1.

❑ Save the drawing as A:EX22-4.

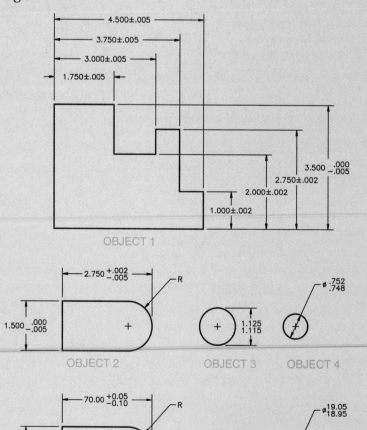

## DIMENSIONING UNITS AND DUAL DIMENSIONING     $\boxed{\text{AUG 9}}$

Dimensions in the standard ASME Y14.5M-1994, *Dimensioning and Tolerancing,* are given in SI (International System of Units) units. The accepted SI linear unit for engineering drawings and related documents is the millimeter. The accepted US linear unit for engineering drawings is the decimal-inch. The unit of measurement chosen should be in accordance with the policy of your company or school, or the product design. When all dimensions on a drawing are given in either millimeters or inches, place the following general note on the drawing:

UNLESS OTHERWISE SPECIFIED, ALL DIMENSIONS ARE IN MILLIMETERS *(or* INCHES*)*.

The abbreviation IN follows all inch dimensions on a drawing dimensioned in millimeters. The abbreviation mm follows all millimeter dimensions on a drawing dimensioned in inches.

### Placing a dimension suffix or prefix

AutoCAD allows you to place IN or mm after any or all dimension numbers using the **DIMPOST** variable (post meaning after). Common suffixes might be IN. for inch on mechanical drawings, mm for millimeters, MAX for maximum, or MIN for minimum in mechanical drafting. Architectural drafting may have suffixes such as " for inch, TYP for typical, or OC for on center. Use the suffix IN. like this:

> Command: **DIMPOST** ⏎
> New value for DIMPOST, or . for none ⟨""⟩: **IN.** ⏎
> Command:

Now, any new dimensions carry the IN. suffix. The **DIMPOST** default is no suffix. You can remove a suffix by typing a period (.) like this:

> Command: **DIMPOST** ⏎
> New value for DIMPOST, or . for none ⟨"IN."⟩: **.** ⏎
> Command:

It is not likely that a specific suffix will be used on all dimensions. One possible situation is having some inch dimensions on a metric drawing. Rather than using **DIMPOST**, it may be better to enter a desired suffix by using the **Text** option during the dimensioning process. This is done by placing the desired suffix after the closed brackets ⟨⟩. When you use this symbol ⟨⟩, it tells AutoCAD to automatically place the measured dimension text in the place of the symbol. The following command sequence is used to place IN. after the dimension text:

> Dimension line location (Text/Angle/Horizontal/Vertical/Rotated): **T** ⏎
> Dimension text ⟨2.750⟩: ⟨⟩ **IN.** ⏎
> Dimension line location (Text/Angle/Horizontal/Vertical/Rotated): *(pick the dimension line location)*
> Command:

**PROFESSIONAL TIP**

Using the brackets ⟨⟩ as previously discussed to keep the default text also maintains the associative dimension. An ***associative dimension*** allows the dimension to automatically change as the object is edited. Associative dimensions are explained in detail later in this chapter. If the text is typed without using the default text ⟨⟩, then the text is not changed when the dimension is edited. This is the normal application, but there may be some specific applications when you need to type a value that is different from the default text.

It is not a common practice to have a prefix or suffix on every dimension on the drawing. A general note usually takes care of these applications effectively. Additionally, you need to be careful when using the **DIMPOST** variable to set a prefix. This prefix takes the place of any standard AutoCAD prefixes, such as the R symbol for radius and the Ø symbol for diameter.

You can also use **DIMPOST** to place a prefix, or a prefix and a suffix, with dimension text. This is done by placing the desired prefix in front of open and closed brackets ⟨⟩. This keeps the default text as previously discussed. For example, enter the prefix SR (spherical radius) followed by ⟨⟩ if you need to dimension a group of spherical radii.

Command: **DIMPOST** ↵
New value for DIMPOST, or . for none ⟨""⟩: **SR⟨⟩** ↵
Command:

You can enter both a prefix and a suffix with the following command sequence:

Command: **DIMPOST** ↵
New value for DIMPOST, or . for none ⟨""⟩: **SR⟨⟩ IN.** ↵
Command:

### Dual dimensioning

*Dual dimensioning* means to place both inches and millimeters on each dimension. The current ASME standard *does not* recognize dual dimensioning. Yet, a few companies prefer to use it. One technique is to show inch dimensions followed by millimeter equivalents in brackets. This is referred to as the *bracket method*. The opposite is millimeters followed by inch equivalents in brackets. When this is done, the general note DIMENSIONS IN [ ] ARE MILLIMETERS or DIMENSIONS IN [ ] ARE INCHES should be placed on the drawing. Another method of dual dimensioning separates inch and millimeter dimensions with a slash. This is referred to as the *position method*. When this is done, the general note MILLIMETER/INCH or INCH/MILLIMETER should be placed on the drawing.

Military (MIL) standards recommend the bracket method when dual dimensioning is used, or by displaying a decimal equivalent table in the upper left corner of the drawing. This conversion table lists the inch and metric equivalent values of every dimension on the drawing. The table begins with the smallest dimension and continues to the largest. This eliminates the need for dual dimensioning at each dimension and cleans up the drawing. Examples of dual dimensioning are shown in Figure 22-13.

---

Figure 22-13. Two different ways of showing dual dimensions.

1.250 [31.75]

IN [MM]

31.75 [1.250]

MM [IN]

BRACKET METHOD

1.250
31.75

IN/MM

31.75
1.250

MM/IN

POSITION METHOD

To convert inches to millimeters, use the formula: $25.4 \times$ inch = millimeter. To convert millimeters to inches, use the formula: millimeter $\div 25.4$ = inch. Convert millimeters to decimal inch values with the ratio: .0394 inch = 1 millimeter.

The same degree of accuracy is achieved by giving one less digit to the right of the decimal point for millimeter dimensions. The following are considered equivalent conversions:

| INCH | MILLIMETER |
|------|------------|
| .1 | 2.5 |
| .01 | 0.3 |
| .001 | 0.03 |
| .0001 | 0.003 |

## USING AUTOCAD FOR DUAL DIMENSIONING

AutoCAD refers to dual dimensions as *alternate dimensions*. The **DIMALT**, **DIMALTF**, and **DIMALTD** variables set a dual dimensioning system for the specified dimension. The variables are as follows:

**DIMALTU** = alternate units.
**DIMALTZ** = alternate unit zero suppression.
**DIMALT** = alternate units.
**DIMALTF** = alternate units scale factor.
**DIMALTD** = alternate units decimal places.

The **DIMALTU** variable sets the units format for alternate units dimensions. The options are the normal unit formats:

| Options | Format |
|---------|--------|
| 1 | Scientific |
| 2 *(default)* | Decimal |
| 3 | Engineering |
| 4 | Architectural Stacked |
| 5 | Fractional Stacked |
| 6 | Architectural |
| 7 | Fractional |

**DIMALTZ** is the variable that controls alternate unit zero suppression. The options are the same as the **DIMZIN** variable where the default (0) places a zero before decimals less than one. Use this setting for metric dimensions. A value of 4 automatically removes the zero in front of decimals less than one. Review the **DIMZIN** variable in Chapter 20 for additional options and their applications.

**DIMALTF** allows you to set the multiplication factor. The **DIMALTF** default value for metric conversion is 25.4. Next, select the **DIMALTD** variable. This allows you to set the number of decimal places for the conversion value. If one-place millimeters are desired, set the **DIMALTD** value to 1. (The default is 2.) After setting the **DIMALTF** and **DIMALTD** variables, set the **DIMALT** variable on. This places the millimeter dual dimensions in brackets after each dimension number, such as 2.500 [63.50].

The **DIMAPOST** variable places information after the alternate dimension. The normal dual dimension appears as 2.50 [63.5]. With **DIMAPOST** set to mm, the same dimension reads 2.50 [63.5mm]. You can remove the suffix by typing a period (.) at the New value: prompt. The general note discussed earlier is better for dual dimensioning. Do not confuse **DIMAPOST** with **DIMPOST**. **DIMPOST** sets up a dimension prefix or suffix for the non-dual dimensioning system.

### Displaying alternate units with tolerance dimensions

When tolerance dimensions are placed on a dual dimensioning drawing, the alternate units need to be applied to the specified dimension and the tolerance. AutoCAD gives you these variables to help control the alternate unit tolerance values:

**DIMALTTD** = alternate tolerance decimal places.
**DIMALTTZ** = alternate tolerance zero suppression.

The **DIMALTTD** variable is used to set the number of decimal places for the tolerance values of an alternate dimension. The options are integers between 0 and 8, with 2 being the default. These options are the same as any variable controlling decimal places. **DIMALTTZ** controls zero suppression of alternate unit tolerances. The options are the same as the **DIMZIN** variable.

### Rounding dimensions

Dimension numbers can be rounded using the **DIMRND** variable. The **DIMRND** default value of 0 means no rounding takes place. Dimension numbers are given exactly as measured. If **DIMRND** is set at .5, then all numbers are rounded to the nearest .5 unit. For example, 2.875 is rounded to 3.000. Rounding is seldom needed.

---

### EXERCISE 22-5

❏ Open PRODR2 or begin a new drawing with your own variables.
❏ Draw the object lines on layer 0-7 and place dimensions on layer 3-3.
❏ Undimensioned features can be drawn to your own specifications.
❏ Set these dimension variables:
    **DIMTXSTY** = ROMANS
    **DIMTXT** = .125
    **DIMUPT** = on
    **DIMZIN** = 4
    **DIMCEN** = .1
❏ In addition to the previous settings, use the appropriate dimension variables to draw the dimensions shown below.
❏ Save the drawing as A:EX22-5.

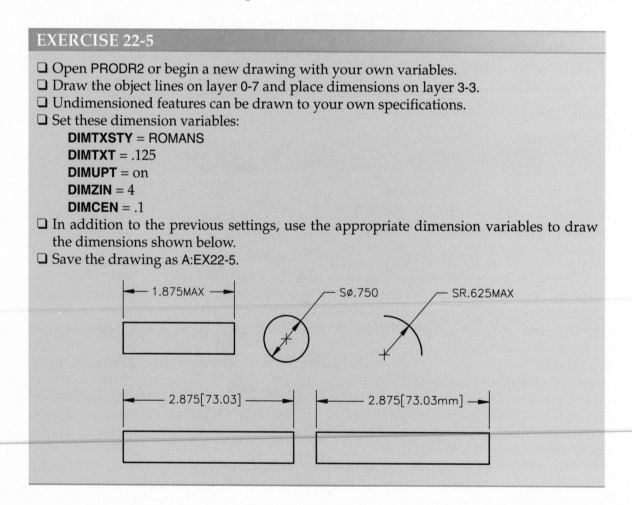

# USING THE DIALOG BOX TO CONTROL TOLERANCING AND DUAL DIMENSIONING

AUG 9

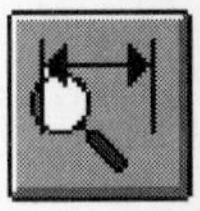

The **Dimension Styles** dialog box is a convenient way to work with dimension variables. The **Dimension Styles** dialog box was introduced in Chapter 21, but as a review, you can access this dialog box by picking the **Dimension Styles** button from the **Dimensioning** toolbar, pick **Dimension Style...** from the **Data** pull-down menu, or type DDIM at the **Command:** prompt. Pick the **Annotation...** button, as shown in Figure 22-14, to access the **Annotation** sub-dialog box shown in Figure 22-15.

Review Chapter 21 for an overview of the **Dimension Styles** dialog box and the **Annotation** subdialog box. The following sections explain the elements of the **Annotation** sub-dialog that control dimension tolerance, prefix, suffix, and alternate units:

Figure 22-14. Pick the **Annotation...** button in the **Dimension Styles** dialog box to open the **Annotation** subdialog box.

Figure 22-15. The different areas of the **Annotation** subdialog box (shown here highlighted).

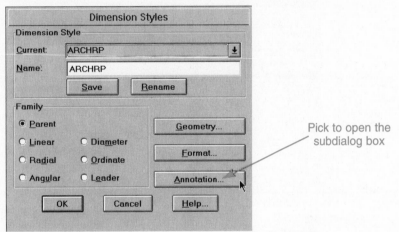

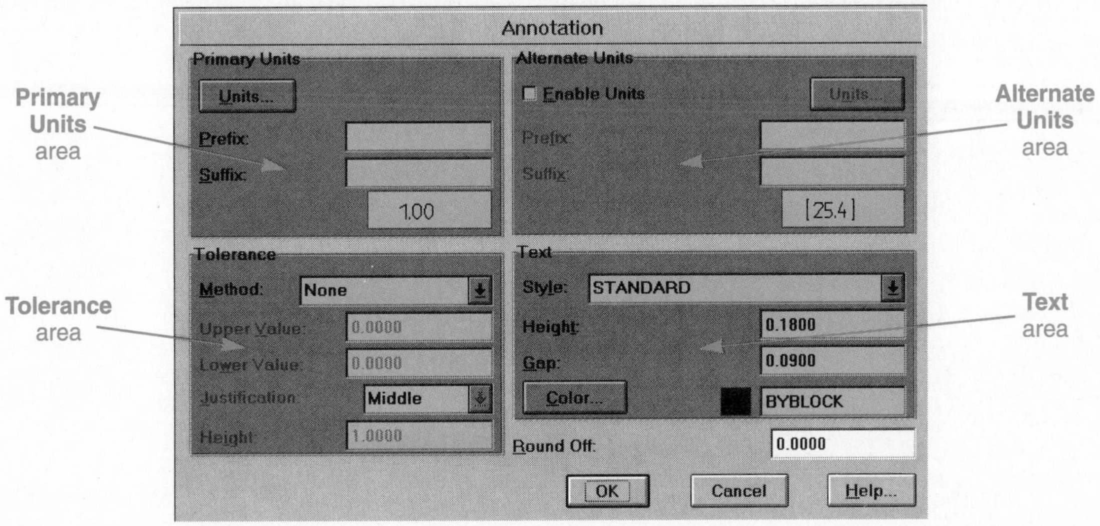

## Primary units

In the **Annotation** subdialog box, pick the **Units...** button to access the **Primary Units** sub-dialog box shown in Figure 22-16. The features that control the specified dimension were explained in Chapter 21. For this discussion, look at the **Tolerance** section. Adjust the **DIMDEC** variable by picking one of the options in the **Precision:** list box. Access this list box by picking the down arrow. The default is 0.0000 (four digits past the decimal place). If you want three place tolerance units, pick 0.000 as shown in Figure 22-17.

Figure 22-16.   Select the units, dimension precision, zero suppression, and tolerance precision in the **Primary Units** subdialog box. Note that the zero suppression has **0 Feet** and **0 Inches** checked by default (shown here highlighted).

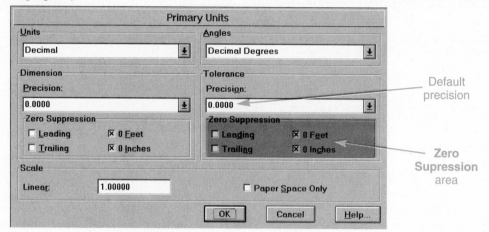

Figure 22-17.   Pick the drop-down arrow next to **Precision:** and select a new precision. Here, a three-place precision is being selected.

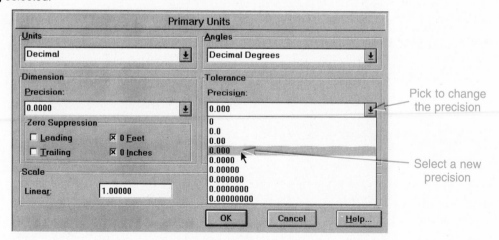

The **Zero Suppression (DIMZIN)** area has **0 F<u>ee</u>t** and **0 In<u>ch</u>es** suppressed by default. This is indicated by the checks in the check boxes. See Figure 22-16. The **Leading** and **Trailing** boxes are not checked by default. The **Lea<u>d</u>ing** box remains unchecked for metric dimensioning. Pick the **Lea<u>d</u>ing** check box if you want zeros omitted before decimal units less than one for inch dimensioning. The **Trailing** check box is normally left unchecked since **Precisio<u>n</u>:** sets the number of units past the decimal point, including zeros. In most cases, the number of decimal places is the same between the tolerance of a plus/minus or a limits tolerance. However, you can pick the **Trailing** check box if you want any zeros removed from the end of a tolerance value.

The **<u>P</u>refix:** and **<u>S</u>uffix: (DIMPOST)** text boxes, in the **Annotation** subdialog box, are where you can type a desired prefix, suffix, or both. Figure 22-18 shows SR entered in the **<u>P</u>refix:** box and IN. in the **<u>S</u>uffix:** box. When a suffix is used, it is added to the specified dimension and the tolerance. Keep in mind that a prefix entered here or with the **DIMPOST** variable takes the place of a diameter or radius symbol when using the **DIMDIA** and **DIMRAD** commands. You can have AutoCAD draw special symbols by typing the text control characters or the Unicode in the **<u>P</u>refix:** and **<u>S</u>uffix:** text boxes. For example, type %%C or \U+2205 to have a diameter symbol drawn, or %%D or \U+00B0 for a degrees symbol.

Figure 22-18.  In the **Annotation** subdialog box, you can enter a prefix and/or a suffix for all dimensions. Here, SR (spherical radius) is entered as a prefix and IN (inches) is entered as a suffix. The image box changes to reflect the settings you choose in this subdialog box.

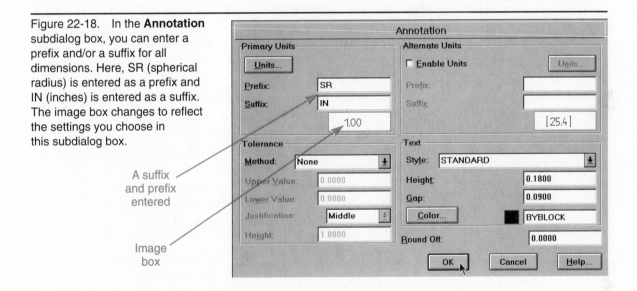

A suffix and prefix entered

Image box

## Tolerance

Look at Figure 22-18 and notice the box with 1.00 inside. This is an image box. Moving the cursor to here and picking changes the image and also changes display in the **Tolerance** area of the **Annotation** subdialog box. The images change to represent the various tolerance options that are available.

The **Tolerance** area of the **Annotation** subdialog box is where you set the dimension variables. These variables control tolerance dimensioning for the specified dimension (primary units) and the alternate units.

The **<u>M</u>ethod:** list box displays the tolerance options. **None** is the default. This displays no tolerance. Pick the down arrow to get the list of options shown in Figure 22-19. The options can be picked from the list or accessed automatically by picking the tolerance image in the **Primary Units** area or in the **Alternate Units** area, if alternate units are enabled. Alternate units tolerance is discussed later. Keep picking the image until it cycles to the option you want, or access the desired option in the **<u>M</u>ethod:** list.

Figure 22-19.   Pick the pop-up
button next to **Method:** in the
**Tolerance** area to select the
tolerancing option
that you want.

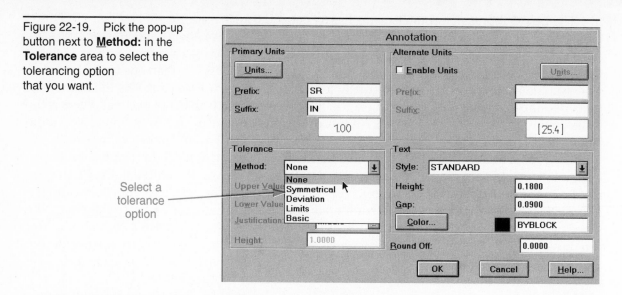

Select a
tolerance
option

The **Symmetrical** option (**DIMTOL** = on and **DIMLIM** = off) lets you draw equal bilateral tolerances. Picking the **Symmetrical** option changes the image in the primary **Units** area. The image is similar to what you can expect the tolerance dimension to look like, but keep in mind that it is only a representation. The image representing each of the **Tolerance Method:** options is shown in Figure 22-20. The **Upper Value:** text box is activated when you select the **Symmetrical** option. Type the desired tolerance such as .001 (**DIMTP** and **DIMTM** = .001). Then, when you draw a dimension such as 2.750, it reads 2.750±.001. The **Lower Value:** text box is deactivated because it is not needed for an equal bilateral tolerance.

The **Deviation** option (**DIMTOL** = on and **DIMLIM** = off) lets you draw unequal bilateral tolerances. The representative tolerance image is shown in Figure 22-20. The **Upper Value:** and **Lower Value:** text boxes are now both active, so you can enter the desired plus and minus tolerance values. If you type .001 (**DIMTP** = .001) in the **Upper Value:** box and .002 (**DIMTM** = .002) in the **Lower Value:** box, a 2.750 dimension looks like this: $2.750 \,^{+.001}_{-.002}$ . AutoCAD places a + symbol for positive values and a – symbol for negative values. The plus or minus symbol is omitted for zero tolerance values in a unilateral tolerance.

The **Limits** option (**DIMTOL** = off and **DIMLIM** = on) allows you to draw limit dimensions. The tolerance image shown in Figure 22-20 is kind of a strange representation of limits dimensioning. However, it does show one value above another. The image is meant to indicate that AutoCAD adds the tolerance you specify in the **Upper Value:** box, and subtracts the value you enter in the **Lower Value:** box. If you type .002 (**DIMTP** = .002) in the **Upper Value:** box and .002 (**DIMTM** = .002) in the **Lower Value:** box, a 2.750 dimension looks like this: $^{2.752}_{2.748}$ .

Figure 22-20.   Examples of
the different tolerancing options
available in the **Method:** drop-
down list of the **Annotation**
subdialog box.
(See Figure 22-19.)

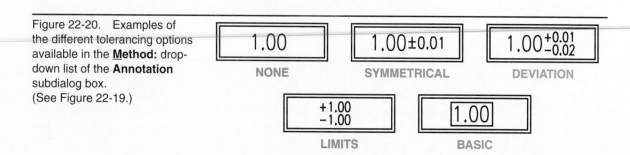

The **Basic** option allows you to draw a basic dimension. A basic dimension is one with a box drawn around it. This type of dimension is used in geometric dimensioning and tolerancing (GD&T) and is discussed in detail in Chapter 23. The representative tolerance image is shown in Figure 22-20. The **Upper Value:** and **Lower Value:** text boxes are both inactive, because a basic dimension has no tolerance values displayed with it.

The **Justification: (DIMTOLJ)** list box contains the tolerance justification options in name form. These can be used to control vertical justification of the bilateral tolerance in relation to the specified dimension. Using an option other than the **Middle** default may not be practical. The options provide the following results:

| Option | Results |
|--------|---------|
| **Top** | The specified dimension text is aligned with the upper tolerance text. |
| **Middle** | The specified dimension text is centered vertically between the tolerance text. This is the default and is the common practice. |
| **Bottom** | The specified dimension text is aligned with the lower tolerance text. |

The **Height: (DIMTFAC)** text box allows you to change the tolerance text height relative to the specified dimension text height. The default 1.0 draws the tolerances text equal to the specified dimension text height. The default setting is the preferred practice. Examples of different **DIMTFAC** settings are shown in Figure 22-12.

## Alternate units

This is the area of the **Annotation** subdialog box where you set dual dimensioning with inches followed by millimeters in brackets, or millimeters followed by inches in brackets. Look at the **Alternate Units** area of Figure 22-19. While this practice is not a recommended standard, it is recognized by the MIL standard. Other applications displaying equivalents in brackets might be used for specific purposes. The **Enable Units (DIMALT)** check box is used to activate the dual dimensioning feature. **DIMALT** is on when this box is checked. The **Prefix:** and **Suffix: (DIMAPOST)** text boxes allow you to enter a desired prefix or suffix to go along with the alternate units.

The **Units...** button is used to access the **Alternate Units** subdialog box shown in Figure 22-21. The features found in this dialog box work just like those found in the **Primary Units** subdialog box except that the controls are for alternate units. The following provides a brief overview of the items found in this dialog box:

- **Units—(DIMALTU)** Pick the down arrow to access the units options that include **Scientific**, **Decimal** (default), **Engineering**, **Architectural**, and **Fractional**. The selection you make establishes the units for the alternate dimension numbers.
- **Dimension**—The **Precision: (DIMALTD)** list allows you to select the number of digits past the decimal point for the alternate units associated with the primary dimension. **Zero Suppression (DIMALTZ)** provides check boxes for you to control the display of zeros before and after the alternate primary units decimal point.
- **Scale—(DIMALTF)** The **Linear:** text box allows you to set the multiplication factor for the conversion units. The default factor for inch to metric conversion is 25.4.
- **Angles**—You cannot access the **Angles** options for alternate units applications.
- **Tolerance**—The **Precision: (DIMALTTD)** lists allow you to select the number of digits past the decimal point for the alternate units associated with the tolerance dimension. **Zero Suppression (DIMALTTZ)** provides check boxes for you to control the display of zeros before and after the tolerance alternate units decimal point.

Figure 22-21.   Select the various options you need in the **Alternate Units** subdialog box. This subdialog box functions like the **Primary Units** subdialog box. Note that the **Angles** option is not available.

Type of units

Unit precision

Zero supression

Tolerance precision

Zero supression

**Alternate Units**

| Units | Angles |
| --- | --- |
| Decimal | Decimal Degrees |

**Dimension**
Precision:
0.00

**Tolerance**
Precision:
0.00

Zero Suppression
☐ Leading    ☒ 0 Feet
☐ Trailing   ☒ 0 Inches

Zero Suppression
☐ Leading    ☒ 0 Feet
☐ Trailing   ☒ 0 Inches

Scale
Linear:   25.40000

☐ Paper Space Only

[ OK ]    [ Cancel ]    [ Help... ]

The features found in the **Tolerance** area of the **Annotation** subdialog box were discussed earlier. Any changes made to the tolerance options for primary units also affect the alternate units if alternate units are enabled. As a review, the **Method:** list box displays the options **None**, **Symmetrical**, **Deviation**, **Limits**, and **Basic**. These options mean the same thing to alternate units as they do to primary units. You may change the tolerance method for primary and alternate units by picking one of the options from the **Method:** list or by picking the image box in the **Alternate Units** area if alternate units are enabled. Every time you pick the image box, a different tolerance method option is displayed and the items in the **Tolerance** area automatically change to match. The image representing each of the alternate tolerance **Method:** options is shown in Figure 22-22.

Figure 22-22.   Examples of the tolerancing options available in the **Alternate Units** subdialog box. (See Figure 22-21.)

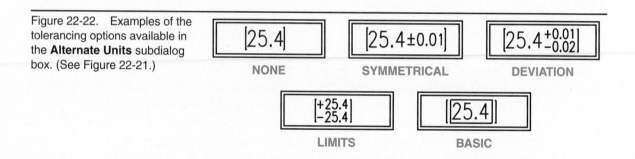

NONE          SYMMETRICAL          DEVIATION

LIMITS          BASIC

## EXERCISE 22-6

❑ Open PRODR2 or begin a new drawing with your own variables.
❑ Draw the object lines on layer 0-7 and place dimensions on layer 3-3.
❑ Undimensioned features can be drawn to your own specifications.
❑ Set these dimension variables:
   **DIMTXSTY** = ROMANS
   **DIMTXT** = .125
   **DIMUPT** = on
   **DIMZIN** = 4
   **DIMCEN** = .1
❑ In addition to the previous settings, use the appropriate dimension variables by using the **DDIM** command to draw the dimensions shown below.
❑ Save the drawing as A:EX22-6.

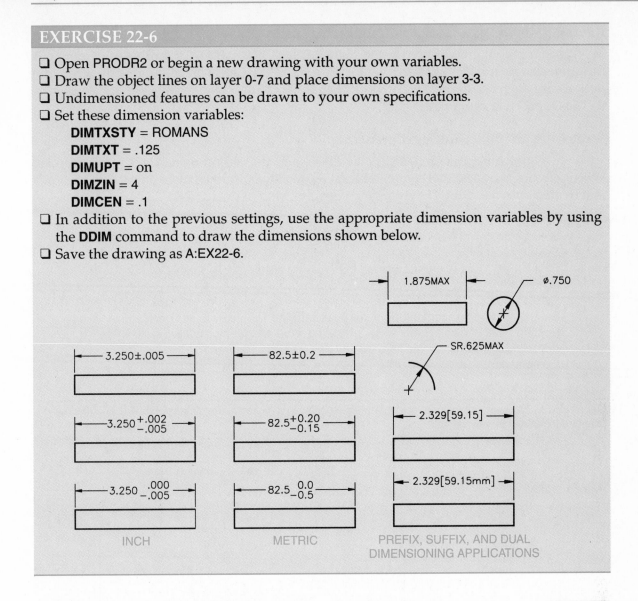

## USING AUTOCAD'S ASSOCIATIVE DIMENSIONING    AUG 9

*Associative dimensioning* permits dimensions to change as an object is edited. With the **DIMASO** variable turned on, stretching, trimming, or extending an object also changes the dimensions associated with that object. **DIMASO** is on by default. With the **DIMASO** variable turned off, elements of the dimension are considered separate. Thus, you can edit the dimension line, arrowheads, extension lines, and dimension numbers as individual items. With **DIMASO** turned on, these items act together as one entity. You can then erase the entire dimension by picking any part of the dimension. The **DIMALIGNED**, **DIMANGULAR**, **DIMDIAMETER**, **DIMLINEAR**, **DIMORDINATE**, and **DIMRADIUS** commands are influenced by associative dimensioning. The **DIMCENTER** and **DIMLEADER** commands remain as unique items and are not affected.

Another variable that works with associative dimensioning is **DIMSHO**. If **DIMASO** and **DIMSHO** are both on, the dimension for an object being stretched (for example) is visually recalculated as the object is dragged into position. Both **DIMASO** and **DIMSHO** are on by default.

## Revising drawings and associated dimensions

When a drawing is changed using the **GRIPS**, **MIRROR**, **ROTATE**, or **SCALE** commands, the dimensions are also changed when **DIMASO** is on. **Linear** and **Angular** dimensioning options are altered by the **STRETCH** command. Only linear dimensions are affected by the **EXTEND** and **TRIM** commands.

## Stretching an object and its dimensions

When stretching an object, select the object and dimension using the **Crossing** option. When selecting the **STRETCH** command from the **Modify** pull-down menu, the **Crossing** option is activated automatically. The command sequence shown in Figure 22-23 is as follows:

Command: **STRETCH** ↵
Select objects to be stretched by crossing-window or -polygon…
Select objects: **C** ↵
First corner: *(pick the first corner of the crossing box)*
Other corner: *(pick the second crossing box corner)*
Select objects: ↵
Base point or displacement: *(pick the base point on the object to be stretched)*
Second point of displacement: *(pick the new point to where the object is to be stretched and observe the object being dragged into position)*
Command:

---

Figure 22-23.   When you stretch an object and an associative dimension, the dimension text is automatically changed to reflect the new values.

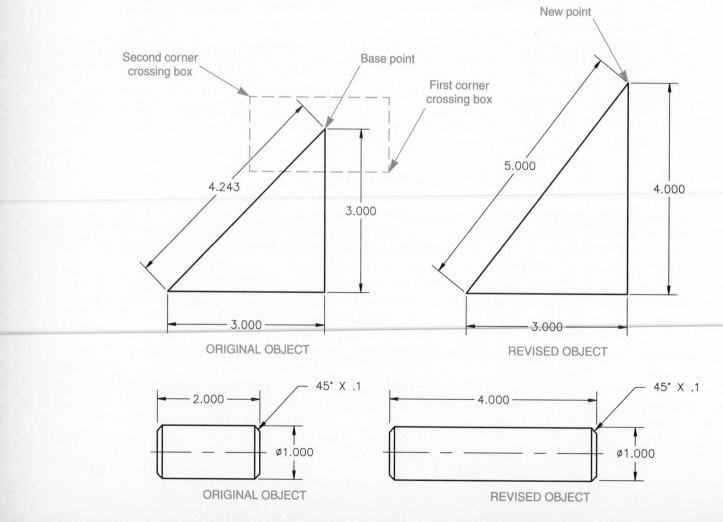

**PROFESSIONAL TIP**

The examples of editing associative dimensions that are discussed throughout this section demonstrate the power and efficiency that can be achieved when the **DIMASO** variable is on. When the two objects in Figure 22-23 were stretched, the dimensions automatically assumed the actual size of the object after the editing process was complete. You may not fully understand the power of this feature until you try to edit an object without associative dimensions. For example, if the original objects in Figure 22-23 had been drawn with **DIMASO** turned off, then the dimension values remain the same even when the objects are stretched, as shown below. In order to make the dimensions in the example below read to the correct size of the objects you would first need to calculate the correct values followed by using the **DIMEDIT** command to change the dimension text. If you compare this example with Figure 22-23 you quickly see the advantage of associative dimensions.

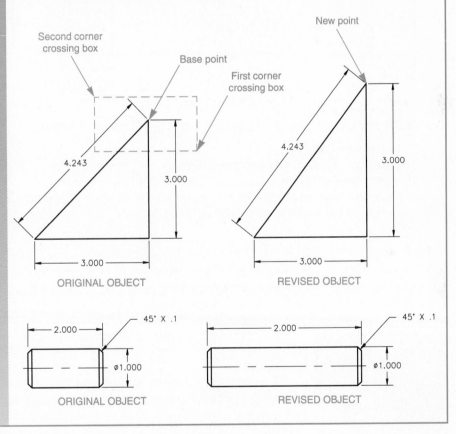

## Moving a dimension number

The ASME standards advise that adjacent dimensions be staggered. However, AutoCAD centers all dimension text unless **DIMUPT** is on. The **STRETCH** command can be used to move dimension text within the dimension line as follows, Figure 22-24:

Command: **STRETCH** ↵
Select objects to be stretched by crossing-window or -polygon...
Select objects: **C** ↵
First corner: Other corner: *(place the crossing box around the text to be moved)*
Select objects: ↵
Base point or displacement: *(pick the base point at the center of the existing text)*
Second point of displacement: *(pick the new point at the desired text location)*
Command:

Figure 22-24.    You can stretch text to a different location when needed.

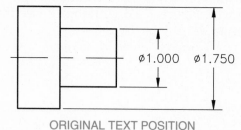

ORIGINAL TEXT POSITION

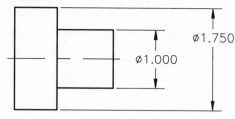

TEXT STRETCHED INTO NEW POSITION

The **TEDIT** command also works well for this application. Try this:

Command: **DIM** ↵
Dim: *(type* TE *or* TEDIT *and press* [Enter]*)*
Select dimension: *(pick the dimension number to be moved)*
Enter text location (Left/Right/Home/Angle): *(move the text to a new location and pick, or use one of the available options)*
Dim:

Refer to Chapter 21, Figure 21-21 for a detailed comparison of all **TEDIT** options.

You can also add or subtract size from an object to be stretched using relative coordinates. For example, at the Second point of displacement: prompt, typing @2,0 adds 2 units horizontally. Typing @–1.25,0 deletes 1.25 units horizontally. Typing @0,–.5 deletes .5 units vertically.

**PROFESSIONAL TIP**

The **DIMUPT** variable allows you to position the text as desired during the dimensioning process. The default for this variable is off, but you can turn it on if you want this flexibility. **DIMUPT** was explained in Chapter 20 as related to Figure 20-54 and reviewed again in Chapter 21 with Figure 21-15.

## Trimming and extending

It is possible to extend or trim an object and related dimensions to meet another object. The **TRIM** and **EXTEND** commands were introduced in Chapter 13. The **EXTEND** command format is as follows:

Command: **EXTEND** ↵
Select boundary edges (Projmode = UCS, Edgemode = No extend)
Select objects: *(pick the boundary edge)*
Select objects: ↵

The boundary edge is the line that the desired object will extend to, Figure 22-25A. Then pick the dimension and lines to extend.

⟨Select object to extend⟩/Project/Edge/Undo: *(pick the dimension to be extended)*
⟨Select object to extend⟩/Project/Edge/Undo: *(pick a line to extend)*
⟨Select object to extend⟩/Project/Edge/Undo: *(pick a line to extend)*
⟨Select object to extend⟩/Project/Edge/Undo: ↵
Command:

Notice in Figure 22-25C that one line of the original object remains. This line can be removed using the **ERASE** command.

---

Figure 22-25.   When you extend an associative dimension, the dimension text is automatically updated to reflect the new value.

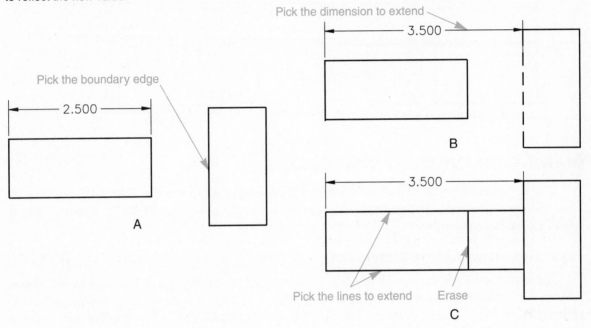

The **TRIM** command is the opposite of the **EXTEND** command. Look at Figure 22-26. First, draw a line on the original object to trim to. Then, follow this **TRIM** command sequence:

Command: **TRIM** ↵
Select cutting edges (Projmode = UCS, Edgemode = No extend)
Select objects: *(pick cutting edges that lines and dimensions will be shortened to)*
Select objects: ↵

The location where you pick the dimension establishes the trim position for the dimension.

⟨Select object to extend⟩/Project/Edge/Undo: *(pick the dimension to be trimmed)*
⟨Select object to extend⟩/Project/Edge/Undo: *(pick the line to be trimmed)*
⟨Select object to extend⟩/Project/Edge/Undo: *(pick the line to be trimmed)*
⟨Select object to extend⟩/Project/Edge/Undo: ↵
Command: **ERASE** ↵
Select objects: *(select the line on the right)*
Select objects: ↵
Command:

Figure 22-26.   When you trim an associative dimension, the dimension text is automatically updated
to reflect the new value.

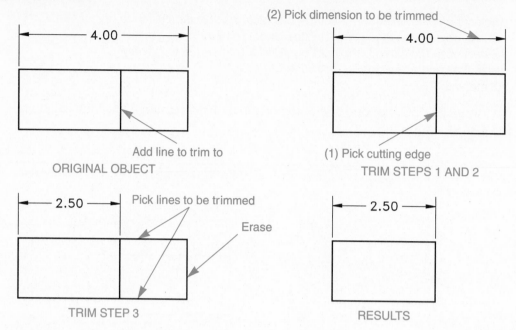

## MAKING CHANGES TO DIMENSIONS

AUG 9

The component parts of a dimension can be edited after using the **EXPLODE** command.
Dimensions also can be changed individually or in groups using the **UPDATE**, **HOMETEXT**, or
**NEWTEXT** subcommands.

### Exploding an associative dimension

AUG 5

An associative dimension is treated as one entity even though it consists of extension
lines, a dimension line, arrowheads, and numbers. At times, it is necessary to work with the
individual parts so you can select parts to edit. For example, you can erase the text without
erasing the dimension line, arrowheads, or extension lines. To do this, you must break the
dimension into its individual parts with the **EXPLODE** command. Be careful when exploding
dimensions because they may lose their layer assignment.

Command: **EXPLODE** ↵
Select objects: (*pick the dimension to be exploded*)
Select objects: ↵
Command:

---

**PROFESSIONAL TIP**

Caution should be exercised when using the **EXPLODE** command
on dimensions, they loose their layer and color definitions. Once
exploded, the dimension is placed on layer 0. This is not normally
acceptable. You may want to use the **CHPROP** command to put the
exploded dimension elements back to the dimensioning layer and
color, and set them to BYLAYER. An easier way to remove the associative dimension feature from a dimension is to use the **DIMOVERRIDE**
command or the **UPDATE** option discussed next. If you know in
advance that you need to work with the individual elements of the
dimensions, then turn the **DIMASO** variable off before starting the
drawing.

## Changing variables or text of existing dimensions

You can change the text or variables of individual dimensions or all dimensions on the drawing. The **UPDATE**, **HOMETEXT**, and **NEWTEXT** subcommands can be used to perform these tasks when you are inside the **DIM** command. The **HOMETEXT** and **NEWTEXT** subcommands work just like the **DIMEDIT** command discussed in Chapter 21 with Figure 21-22.

The **UPDATE** subcommand updates existing dimensions with the current dimensioning variables, units, or text style. For example, the **DIMASZ** (dimension arrowhead size) default value is .18. Suppose that after completing a drawing you learn the company standard requires .25 arrowheads. This is easy to fix. Select **DIMASZ** and enter the new value as .25. At the **Dim:** prompt, type UP or UPDATE and press [Enter]. Then select the items to be changed by picking them individually or windowing. It is common to change the entire drawing using the window selection process. The steps are as follows:

Command: **DIM** ↵
Dim: *(type* UP *or* UPDATE *and press* [Enter]*)*
Select objects: *(pick individual dimensions, a group of dimensions, or window the entire drawing)*

The selected objects are now automatically updated with the new current variables, Figure 22-27.

The **HOMETEXT** subcommand changes the position of dimension text to its original location. For example, suppose the **STRETCH** or **TEDIT** command is used to move a dimension number to a new location. The **HOMETEXT** subcommand moves the number back to the center, Figure 22-28.

Command: **DIM** ↵
Dim: *(type* HOM *or* HOMETEXT *and press* [Enter]*)*
Select objects: *(pick the dimension to be changed)*
Select objects: ↵
Dim:

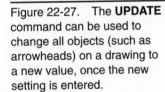

Figure 22-27.   The **UPDATE** command can be used to change all objects (such as arrowheads) on a drawing to a new value, once the new setting is entered.

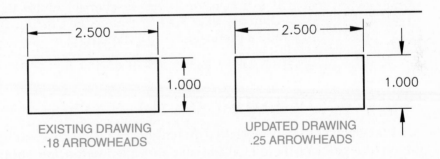

EXISTING DRAWING
.18 ARROWHEADS

UPDATED DRAWING
.25 ARROWHEADS

Figure 22-28.   The **HOMETEXT** command can be used to return a dimension to the center.

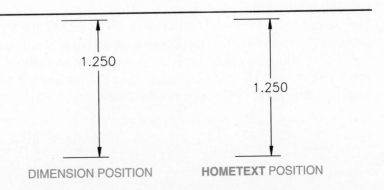

DIMENSION POSITION

**HOMETEXT** POSITION

The **NEWTEXT** subcommand can be used to add a prefix or suffix, or edit the text format of existing dimensions. Suppose you find that a diameter symbol was left off a linear dimension. Issue the **NEWTEXT** subcommand to select and change the dimension text format as follows, Figure 22-29:

Command: **DIM** ↵
Dim: *(type* N *or* NEWTEXT *and press* [Enter]*)*
Dimension text ⟨0.0000⟩: **%%C** ⟨ ⟩
Select objects: *(pick the dimension to be edited)*
Select objects: *(press* [Enter] *to close the selection set)*
Dim:

Figure 22-29.   The **NEWTEXT** command can be used to change the value, add a prefix, or add a suffix to an existing dimension.

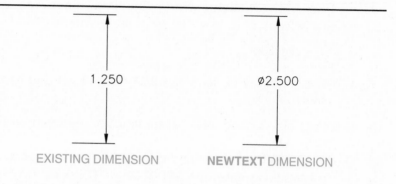

1.250                    ⌀2.500

EXISTING DIMENSION          **NEWTEXT** DIMENSION

**PROFESSIONAL TIP**

Never use the **NEWTEXT** command to type in a different dimensional value than appears in the brackets. Doing so destroys the associativity between the dimension and the associated feature. Should the dimensioned object then be stretched, trimmed, or extended as described in this chapter, the dimension *will not* update. If a dimension needs to change, revise the drawing accordingly. Only use **NEWTEXT** to change the existing dimension text format or add a prefix/suffix to a dimension.

# DIMENSION DEFINITION POINTS                                    AUG 9

When you draw an associative dimension, the points used to specify the dimension and the middle point of the dimension text are called *definition points*, or *defpoints*. When a dimension is redefined, the revised position is based on the definition points. The definition points are located on the DEFPOINTS layer. This layer is automatically created by AutoCAD. The definition points are displayed with the dimension. The **DEFPOINTS** layer does not plot. The definition points are plotted only if the **DEFPOINTS** layer is renamed. The definition points are displayed when the dimensioning layer is on, even if the **DEFPOINTS** layer is off.

If you select an object for editing and wish to include the dimensions in the edit, then you must include the definition points of the dimension in the selection set. If you need to snap to a definition point only, use the **Node** object snap.

# PAPER SPACE DIMENSIONING

Be cautious when placing associative dimensions on a drawing created in model space when you are currently in the paper space mode. These dimensions remain unchanged when you use editing commands like **STRETCH**, **TRIM**, or **EXTEND**, or display commands such as **ZOOM** or **PAN** in a model space viewport. To make sure that AutoCAD calculates a scale factor that is compatible between model and paper space, check the **Paper Space Scaling** check box in the subdialog boxes accessed through the **Dimension Styles** dialog box.

When you draw dimensions in paper space that describe something from your model space drawing, first set the **Viewport** option in the **DIMLFAC** variable while in paper space like this:

> Command: **DIM** ↵
> Dim: **LFAC** ↵
> Current value ⟨1.000⟩ New value (Viewport): **V** ↵
> Select viewport to set scale: *(pick the desired viewport)*

AutoCAD automatically makes the **DIMLFAC** variable adjust to the zoom scale factor of the model space viewport. This does not work when dimensioning with the **ORDINATE** command.

---

**PROFESSIONAL TIP**

Dimensions should normally be created in model space. Use caution when dimensioning in paper space. Linear dimensions of model space objects can be created in paper space, but radius and diameter dimensions of model space objects cannot be created in paper space. This means that some of your dimensions are in model space and others in paper space. This situation would require a lot of dimension variable juggling and space swapping. However, there are valid reasons to place notes in paper space when they are part of the drawing format.

---

## EXERCISE 22-7

❑ Open EX22-6.
❑ Set the following dimensioning variable values:
    **DIMEXE** = .125
    **DIMEXO** = .08
    **DIMCEN** = –.25
    **DIMASZ** = .25
    **DIMDLI** = .75
    **DIMTXT** = .140
❑ Use the **STRETCH** or **TEDIT** command to stagger the last vertical dimension.
❑ For Object 2, use the **STRETCH** subcommand to make it .25″ longer and .5″ higher.
❑ Enter the **UPDATE** subcommand to change the entire drawing to the current variables.
❑ Use the **HOMETEXT** subcommand to move the staggered vertical dimension in Object 1 back to its original position.
❑ Use the **NEWTEXT** subcommand to remove the plus/minus tolerances from the horizontal dimensions on Object 1.
❑ Save the drawing as A:EX22-6.

## CHAPTER TEST

*Write your answers in the spaces provided.*

1. The _____ option of the _____ command saves dimensioning variable settings to a dimension style and makes the new dimension style current.

2. The _____ option of the _____ command lets you change dimensioning variable settings by reading new settings from an existing dimension style.

3. Give the command and responses needed to list all of the available dimension styles through the **DIMSTYLE** command:

    Command: _____

    dimension style: _____

    Dimension Style Edit (Save/Restore/STatus/Variables/Apply/?) ⟨Restore⟩: _____

    Dimension style(s) to list ⟨*⟩: _____

4. Give the command and responses used to have AutoCAD display the difference between an existing MIL dimension style and the current dimension style:

    Command: _____

    dimension style: _____

    Dimension Style Edit (Save/Restore/STatus/Variables/Apply/?) ⟨Restore⟩: _____

    Dimension style(s) to list ⟨*⟩: _____

5. Give the command and responses used to override the **DIMEXO** variable on an existing dimension from the existing setting of .06 to 0, without changing the current dimension style:

    Command: _____

    Dimension variable to override (or clear to remove overrides): _____

    Current value ⟨.062⟩:New value: _____

    Dimension variable to override:_____

    Select objects:_____

    Select objects:_____

    Command:_____

6. Give the command and entries required to create all dimensions with a tolerance of ±.005:

    Command: _____

    New value for ⟨⟩ ⟨Off⟩: _____

    Command: _____

    New value for ⟨⟩ ⟨0.000⟩: _____

    Command:_____

    New value for ⟨⟩ ⟨0.000⟩: _____

    Command:_____

7. Give the command and entries needed to create all dimensions with limits tolerancing of ±.002:

   Command: _____

   New value for ⟨⟩ ⟨Off⟩: _____

   Command:_____

   New value for ⟨⟩ ⟨0.0000⟩: _____

   Command:_____

   New value for ⟨⟩ ⟨0.0000⟩: _____

   Command:_____

8. Define "tolerance." _____

   _____

9. Give an example of a bilateral tolerance._____

10. Give an example of a unilateral tolerance. _____

11. What are the limits of the dimension 1.875±.002? _____

12. Give the general note that should accompany a drawing dimensioned in millimeters.

    _____

    _____

13. Give the general note used when millimeter dimensions are provided in brackets next to inch dimensions. _____

14. Name the dialog box that allows you to work with dimension styles._____

    _____

15. Identify at least two ways to access the dialog box discussed in question number 14.

    _____

    _____

16. How do you save a new dimension style using the dialog box that was accessed in question number 14?_____

    _____

17. Describe the procedure to display dimensions with plus/minus equal bilateral tolerances of ±.002 using the dialog box. _____

    _____

    _____

    _____

18. Describe the procedure to display dimensions with limits dimensioning ±.005 from the specified dimension using the dialog box. _____

    _____

    _____

    _____

19. Define "definition points."_____

    _____

    _____

20. What is the importance of selecting definition points when editing an object and its dimensions? _____

_____

_____

_____

21. Name the object snap mode used to snap to a definition point. _____

**22 - 35. Identify the dimensioning variable associated with each of the definitions.**

22. The dimension variable used when in paper space to make the dimension scale factor adjust to the zoom scale factor of the model space viewport. _____

23. Identifies the current dimension style. _____

24. Used to change the text height for tolerance dimensions without affecting the primary dimension text height. _____

25. When on, shows a dimension number with tolerance. _____

26. Controls the plus part of a tolerance. _____

27. Controls the minus part of a tolerance. _____

28. When on, automatically calculates and displays tolerance limits. _____

29. Allows you to place a specified suffix after dimension numbers. _____

30. Automatically places millimeter dual dimensions in brackets. _____

31. Allows you to set a multiplication factor for alternate units. _____

32. Sets the number of decimal places for alternate units. _____

33. Used to turn on or off associative dimensioning. _____

34. Allows dimensions to be shown as they are edited. _____

35. Allows dimension numbers to be rounded as specified. _____

**36 - 40. Name the commands that do the following:**

36. Moves dimension text within a dimension line. _____

37. Breaks an existing associative dimension into its individual parts. _____

38. Changes existing dimensions to take on current dimensioning variable values. _____

39. Changes the position of dimension text to its original location. _____

40. Edits existing dimension text. _____

41. When would it be better to create a new dimension style rather than using the **DIMOVERRIDE** command? _____

_____

_____

_____

_____

42. Define "dimension style family" and "dimension style family members." _____

_____

_____

_____

_____

_____

_____

43. Give a practical example of how dimension style family members might have different settings for an application in AutoCAD. _____

_____

_____

_____

44. Give the following dimension variable settings needed before you can draw an equal bilateral tolerance of ±.001 in inches:

**DIMDEC** _____

**DIMTDEC** _____

**DIMZIN** _____

**DIMTZIN** _____

**DIMTOL** _____

**DIMTP** _____

**DIMTM** _____

45. Give the following dimension variable settings if you plan to draw this limits dimension: $\frac{2.752}{2.748}$

**DIMLIM** _____

**DIMTP** _____

**DIMTM** _____

46. What is the purpose of typing ⟨⟩IN. at the Dimension text: prompt as follows:

Dimension text ⟨2.750⟩: ⟨⟩IN.

_____

_____

_____

_____

## DRAWING PROBLEMS

Set limits, units, dimensioning variables, and other parameters as needed. Follow these guidelines.

- A. Draw the needed multiviews to exact size. You must select the proper multiview for the problems presented in 3D.
- B. Use grids, object snap options, and the **OSNAP** command to your best advantage.
- C. Apply dimensions accurately using ASME standards. Dimensions are in inches unless otherwise specified.
- D. Set dimensioning variables to suit the drawing.
- E. Use the **LAYER** command to set separate layers for views and dimensions.
- F. Draw object lines using .032" wide polylines, or use the **LINE** command and plot with a wide pen.
- G. Place the following general notes 1/2" from lower-left corner:
    - 3.  UNLESS OTHERWISE SPECIFIED, ALL DIMENSIONS ARE IN MILLIMETERS *(or* INCHES *as applicable)*.
    - 2.  REMOVE ALL BURRS AND SHARP EDGES.
    - 1.  INTERPRET PER ASME Y14.5M-1994.

    NOTES:
- H. Create dimension styles with family members that suit the specific needs of each drawing. For example, save dimension styles for metric, inch, or architecture drawings as appropriate.
- J. Save the drawings as **A:P22-***(problem number)*.

*Mechanical Drafting*

1.

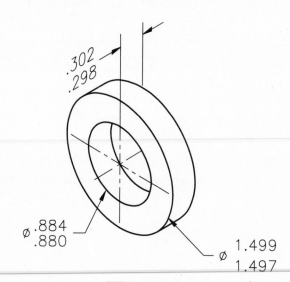

.302
.298

ø .884
.880

1.499
ø
1.497

TITLE: WASHER
MATERIAL: SAE 1020

2.

SØ.562  Ø.375 FLAT

$\emptyset.249 \begin{array}{l} +.000 \\ -.001 \end{array}$

↧.400

TITLE: HANDLE
MATERIAL: BRONZE

3.

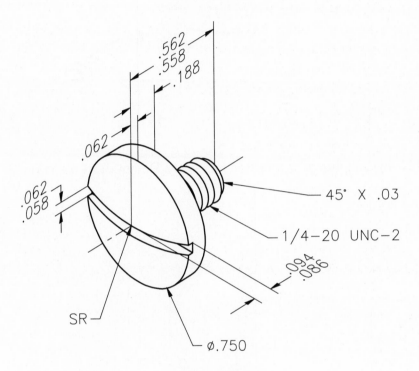

.562
.558
.188

.062

.062
.058

45° X .03

1/4−20 UNC−2

.094
.086

SR

Ø.750

TITLE: SCREW
MATERIAL: SAE 4320

4.

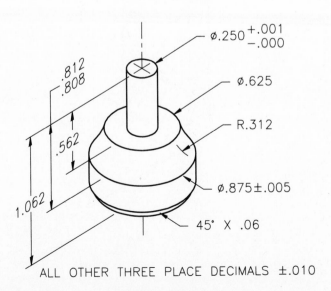

$\emptyset.250 \begin{array}{l} +.001 \\ -.000 \end{array}$

.812
.808

Ø.625

R.312

.562

Ø.875±.005

1.062

45° X .06

ALL OTHER THREE PLACE DECIMALS ±.010

TITLE: PIN
MATERIAL: MILD STEEL

Mechanical
Drafting

5.

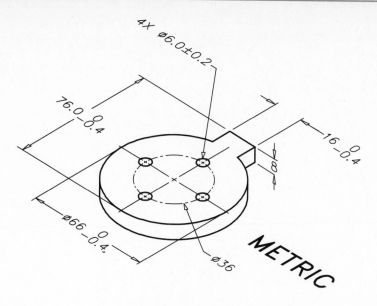

TITLE: SPACER
MATERIAL: COLD ROLLED STEEL

Mechanical
Drafting

6. This object is shown as a section for clarity. Do not draw a section.

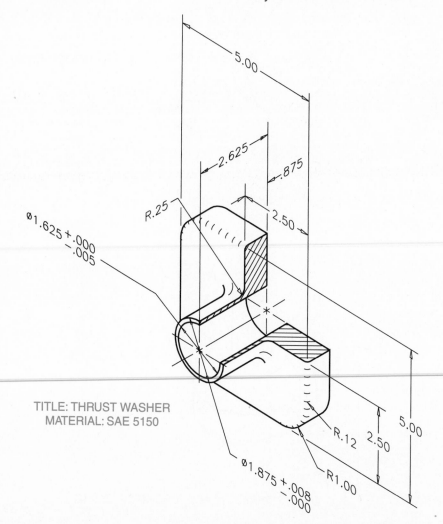

TITLE: THRUST WASHER
MATERIAL: SAE 5150

7.

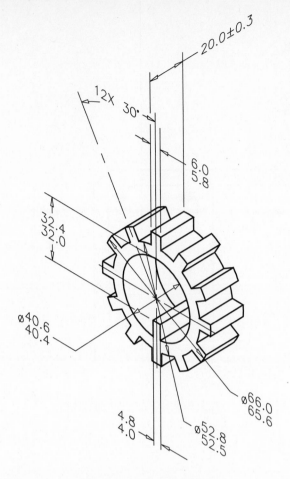

TITLE: LOCKING COLLAR
MATERIAL: SAE 1080

8.

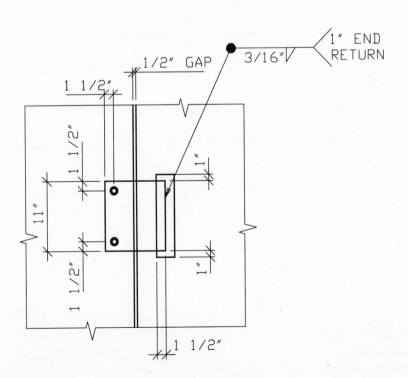

TITLE: COLUMN BASE

9.

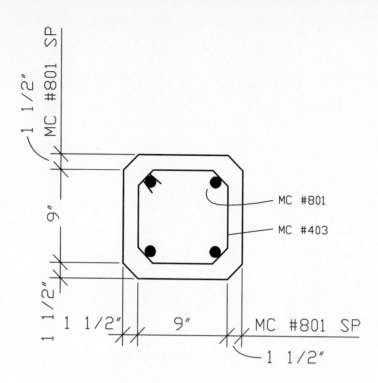

TITLE: COLUMN REINFORCING

10.

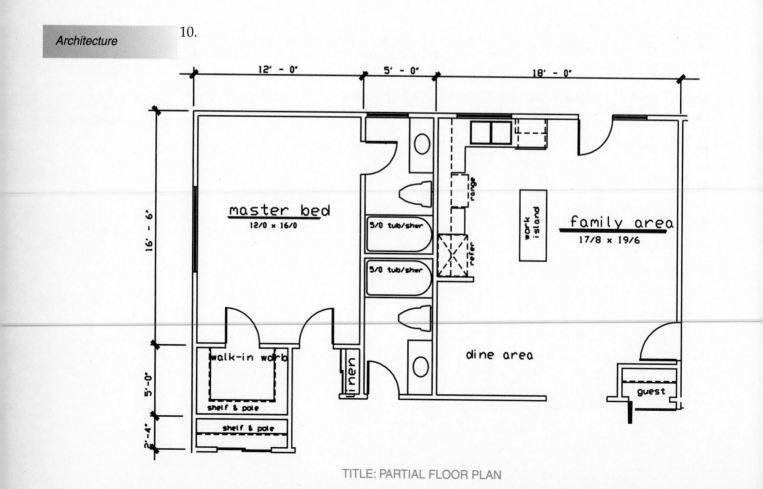

TITLE: PARTIAL FLOOR PLAN

**AutoCAD R13**

# Chapter 23

# Geometric Dimensioning and Tolerancing

## Learning objectives

After completing this chapter, you will be able to:
- ○ Identify geometric tolerancing symbols.
- ○ Use the **TOLERANCE** and **LEADER** commands.
- ○ Draw feature control frames.
- ○ Edit feature control frames.
- ○ Place basic dimensions on a drawing.
- ○ Draw datum feature symbols.
- ○ Identify how to draw projected tolerance zone symbols.

This chapter is an introduction to geometric dimensioning and tolerancing (GD&T) as adopted by the American National Standards Institute (ANSI) and published by the American Society of Mechanical Engineers (ASME) for engineering and related document practices. The standard is titled ASME Y14.5M-1994, *Dimensioning and Tolerancing*. **Geometric tolerancing** is a general term that refers to tolerances used to control form, profile, orientation, runout, and location of features on an object.

The drafting applications identified in this chapter use the AutoCAD geometric tolerancing capabilities and additional recommendations to comply with the ASME Y14.5M-1994 standard. This chapter is only an introduction to geometric dimensioning and tolerancing (GD&T). For complete coverage of GD&T refer to *Geometric Dimensioning and Tolerancing* published by The Goodheart-Willcox Company, Inc. Before beginning this chapter, it is recommended that you have a solid understanding of dimensioning and tolerancing standards and AutoCAD applications, which is covered in Chapter 20 through Chapter 22 of this text. The discussion in this chapter divides the dimensioning and geometric tolerancing symbols into the following five basic types:
- Dimensioning symbols.
- Geometric characteristic symbols.
- Material condition symbols.
- Feature control frame.
- Datum feature and datum target symbols.

When you draw GD&T symbols, it is recommended that you use a dimensioning layer so the symbols and text can be plotted as lines that are the same thickness as extension and dimension lines (.01″ or .3mm). The suggested text font is ROMANS. These practices correspond with ASME Y14.2M-1992 *Line Conventions and Lettering*.

## DIMENSIONING SYMBOLS

*Symbols* represent specific information that would otherwise be difficult and time-consuming to duplicate in note form. Symbols must be clearly drawn to the required size and shape so they communicate the desired information uniformly. Symbols are recommended by ASME Y14.5M because symbols are an international language, read the same way in any country. In an international economy, it is important to have effective communication on engineering drawings. Symbols make this communication process uniform. ASME Y14.5M also states that the adoption of dimensioning symbols does not prevent the use of equivalent terms or abbreviations in situations where symbols are considered inappropriate.

Symbols aid in clarity, ease of drawing presentation, and reducing drawing time. Creating and using AutoCAD symbols is covered later in this chapter and in Chapter 25 of this text. Figure 23-1 shows recommended dimensioning symbols.

Figure 23-1.   Dimensioning symbols recommended by ASME Y14.5M-1994.

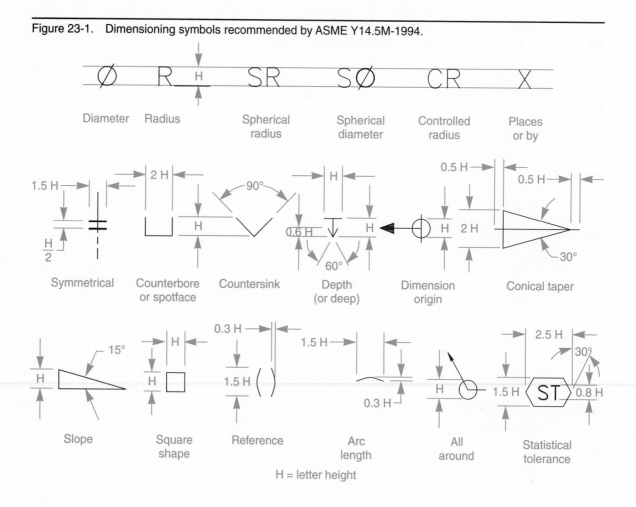

## GEOMETRIC CHARACTERISTIC SYMBOLS

In geometric dimensioning and tolerancing, symbols are used to provide specific controls related to the form of an object, the orientation of features, the outlines of features, the relationship of features to an axis, or the location of features. These are known as *geometric characteristic* symbols. Geometric characteristic symbols are separated into five types: form, profile, orientation, location, and runout, as shown in Figure 23-2. The symbols in Figure 23-2 are drawn to the actual size and shape recommended by ASME Y14.5M, based on .125″(3mm) high lettering.

Figure 23-2.   Geometric characteristic symbols recommended by ASME Y14.5M-1994.

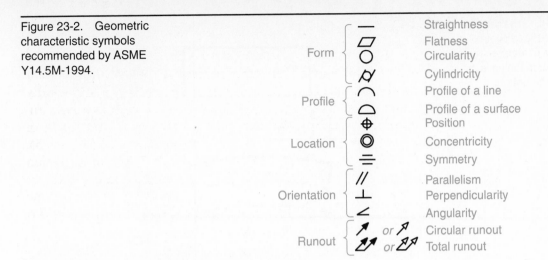

| | |
|---|---|
| | Straightness |
| | Flatness |
| Form | Circularity |
| | Cylindricity |
| Profile | Profile of a line |
| | Profile of a surface |
| | Position |
| Location | Concentricity |
| | Symmetry |
| | Parallelism |
| Orientation | Perpendicularity |
| | Angularity |
| Runout | Circular runout |
| | Total runout |

# MATERIAL CONDITION SYMBOLS

*Material condition symbols* are often referred to as "modifying symbols" because they modify or change the geometric tolerance in relation to the produced size or location of the feature. Material condition symbols are only used in geometric dimensioning applications. The symbols used in the feature control frame to indicate maximum material condition (MMC) or least material condition (LMC) are shown in Figure 23-3. Regardless of feature size (RFS) is also a material condition. However, there is no symbol for RFS because it is assumed for all geometric tolerances and datum references unless MMC or LMC is specified.

Figure 23-3.   Material condition symbols. In ASME Y14.5M-1994, there is no symbol for RFS, since it is assumed.

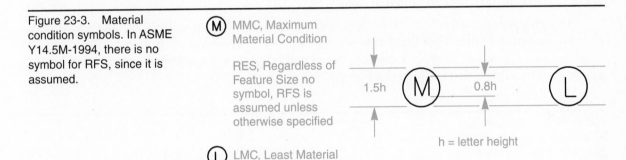

Ⓜ MMC, Maximum Material Condition

RES, Regardless of Feature Size no symbol, RFS is assumed unless otherwise specified

Ⓛ LMC, Least Material Condition

1.5h        Ⓜ        0.8h        Ⓛ

h = letter height

## Surface control regardless of feature size

Regardless of feature size is assumed when there is no material condition symbol following the geometric tolerance in the feature control frame. *Regardless of feature size* means that the geometric tolerances remain the same regardless of what the actual produced size happens to be. The term *produced size*, when used here, means the actual size of the feature when measured after manufacture. When the feature control frame is connected to a feature surface with a leader or an extension line, it is referred to as *surface control*, as shown in the drawing in Figure 23-4. Even though the geometric characteristic symbol is straightness, the applications are the same for any geometric characteristic.

Look at the chart in Figure 23-4 and notice the possible sizes range from 6.20 (MMC) to 5.80 (LMC). With surface control, perfect form is required at MMC. *Perfect form* means that the object cannot exceed a true geometric form boundary established at maximum material condition. This means that the geometric tolerance at MMC is zero, as shown in the chart in Figure 23-4. Then, as the produced size goes away from MMC, the geometric tolerance increases until it equals the amount specified in the feature control frame, at which time the geometric tolerance remains the same as shown in the chart in Figure 23-4.

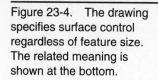

Figure 23-4. The drawing specifies surface control regardless of feature size. The related meaning is shown at the bottom.

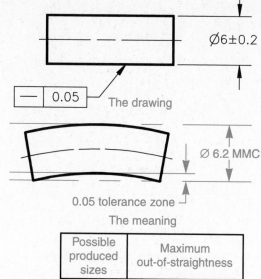

| | Possible produced sizes | Maximum out-of-straightness |
|---|---|---|
| MMC | 6.20 | * 0 |
| | 6.10 | 0.05 |
| | 6.00 | 0.05 |
| | 5.90 | 0.05 |
| LMC | 5.80 | 0.05 |

* Perfect form required

## Axis control regardless of feature size

*Axis control* is used when the feature control frame is shown with the diameter dimension, as shown in Figure 23-5. Regardless of feature size is assumed. With axis control, perfect form is not required at MMC. Therefore, the specified geometric tolerance stays the same at every produced size. See the chart in Figure 23-5.

Figure 23-5. The drawing specifies axis control regardless of feature size. The related meaning is shown at the bottom.

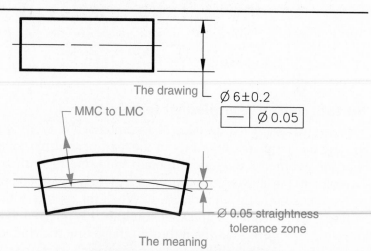

| | Possible produced sizes | Maximum out-of-straightness |
|---|---|---|
| MMC | 6.20 | 0.05 |
| | 6.10 | 0.05 |
| | 6.00 | 0.05 |
| | 5.90 | 0.05 |
| LMC | 5.80 | 0.05 |

## Maximum material condition control

If the material condition control is maximum material condition, then the symbol for MMC must be placed in the feature control frame, as shown in Figure 23-6. When this application is used, the specified geometric tolerance is held at the maximum material condition-produced size. See the chart in Figure 23-6. Then, as the produced size goes away from MMC, the geometric tolerance increases equal to the change. The maximum geometric tolerance is at the LMC-produced size.

Figure 23-6.   The drawing specifies maximum material condition applied to a feature (highlighted here). The related meaning is shown at the bottom.

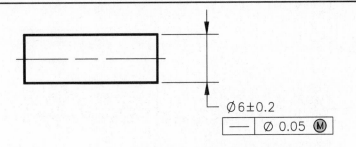

Ø6±0.2

— | Ø 0.05 Ⓜ

The meaning

|  | Possible produced sizes | Maximum out-of-straightness |
|---|---|---|
| MMC | 6.20 | 0.05 |
|  | 6.10 | 0.15 |
|  | 6.00 | 0.25 |
|  | 5.90 | 0.35 |
| LMC | 5.80 | 0.45 |

## Least material condition control

If the material condition control is least material condition, then the symbol for LMC must be placed in the feature control frame. When this application is used, the specified geometric tolerance is held at the least material condition-produced size. Then, as the produced size goes away from LMC, the geometric tolerance increases equal to the change. The maximum geometric tolerance is at the MMC produced size.

## FEATURE CONTROL FRAME

A geometric characteristic, geometric tolerance, material condition, and datum reference (if any) for an individual feature are specified by means of a feature control frame. The *feature control frame* is divided into compartments containing the geometric characteristic symbol in the first compartment followed by the geometric tolerance. Where applicable, the geometric tolerance is preceded by the diameter symbol, which describes the shape of the tolerance zone, and followed by a material condition symbol, if other than RFS. See Figure 23-7.

Figure 23-7. Feature control frames with geometric characteristic symbol, geometric tolerance, diameter symbol (when used), and material conditions symbol (when used). The material condition symbol is left off for RFS, since it is assumed. Note that the geometric tolerance is total, not plus/minus.

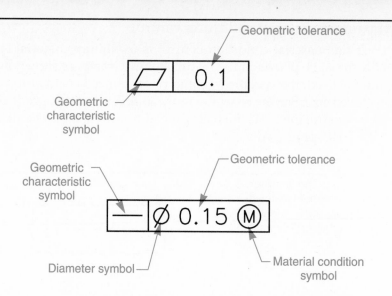

Where a geometric tolerance is related to one or more datums, the datum reference letters are placed in compartments following the geometric tolerance. Where a datum reference is multiple, both datum reference letters, separated by a dash, are placed in a single compartment after the geometric tolerance. A *multiple datum reference* is established by two datum features, such as an axis established by two datum diameters. Figure 23-8 shows several feature control frames with datum references.

The order of elements in a feature control frame is shown in Figure 23-9. Notice that the datum reference letters can be followed by a material condition symbol where applicable.

Figure 23-8. Feature control frames with datum references.

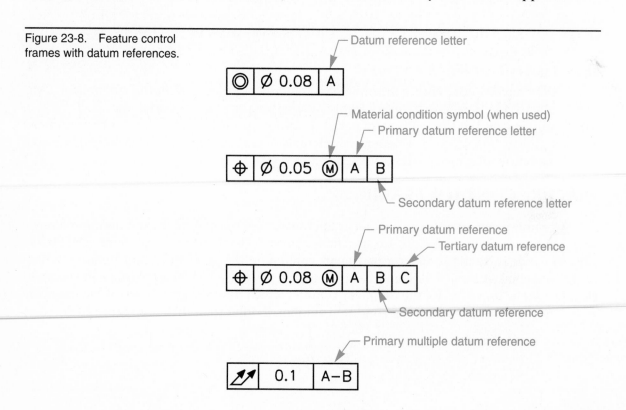

Figure 23-9.  Order of
elements in a feature
control frame.

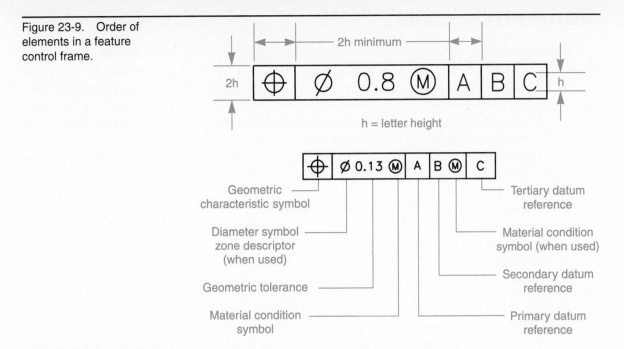

## BASIC DIMENSIONS

A basic dimension is considered a theoretically perfect dimension. Basic dimensions are used to describe the theoretically exact size, profile, orientation, and location of a feature. These dimensions provide the basis from which permissible variations are established by tolerances on other dimensions, in notes, or in feature control frames. In simple terms, a basic dimension tells you where the geometric tolerance zone or datum target is located.

Basic dimensions are shown on a drawing by placing a rectangle around the dimension, as shown in Figure 23-10. A general note can also be used to identify basic dimensions in some applications. For example, the note UNTOLERANCED DIMENSIONS LOCATING TRUE POSITION ARE BASIC indicates the dimensions that are basic. The basic dimension symbol around a dimension is a signal to the reader to look for a geometric tolerance in a feature control frame related to the features being dimensioned.

Figure 23-10.  Basic
dimensions.

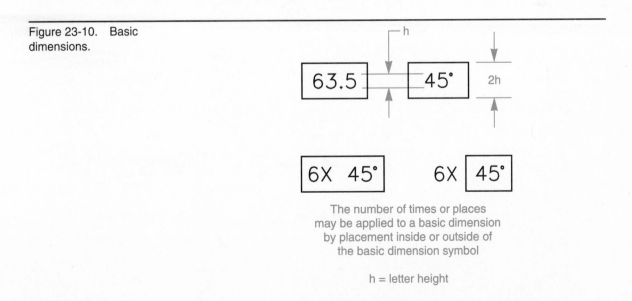

## ADDITIONAL SYMBOLS

Other symbols used in geometric dimensioning and tolerancing are shown in Figure 23-11. These symbols are used for specific applications, and are identified as follows:

- **Free state.** Free state describes distortion of a part after the removal of forces applied during manufacture. The free state symbol is placed in the feature control frame after the geometric tolerance and the material condition (if any), if the feature must meet the tolerance specified while in free state.
- **Tangent plane.** A tangent plane symbol is placed after the geometric tolerance in the feature control frame when it is necessary to control a feature surface by contacting points of tangency.
- **Projected tolerance zone.** A projected tolerance zone symbol is placed in the feature control frame to inform the reader that the geometric tolerance zone is projected away from the primary datum.
- **Between.** The between symbol is used with profile geometric tolerances to identify where the profile tolerance is applied.
- **Statistical tolerance.** The statistical tolerance symbol is used to indicate that a tolerance is based on statistical tolerancing. *Statistical tolerancing* is the assigning of tolerances to related dimensions based on the requirements of statistical process control (SPC). Statistical process control is a method of monitoring and adjusting a manufacturing process by using statistical signals. The statistical tolerancing symbol is placed after the dimension or geometric tolerance that requires SPC. See Figure 23-12. When the feature can be manufactured either by using SPC or by using conventional means, both the statistical tolerance with the statistical tolerance symbol and the conventional tolerance must be shown. An appropriate general note should accompany the drawing. Either of the two notes shown below are acceptable:
- FEATURES IDENTIFIED AS STATISTICAL TOLERANCED SHALL BE PRODUCED WITH STATISTICAL PROCESS CONTROL.
- FEATURES IDENTIFIED AS STATISTICAL TOLERANCED SHALL BE PRODUCED WITH STATISTICAL PROCESS CONTROL, OR THE MORE RESTRICTIVE ARITHMETIC LIMITS.

Figure 23-11.   Additional
dimensioning symbols.

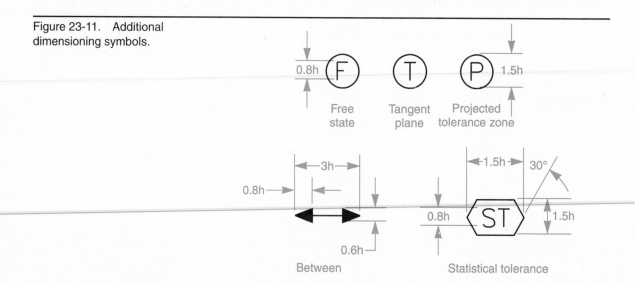

Figure 23-12. Different ways to apply a statistical tolerance. The statistical tolerance symbol is shown here highlighted.

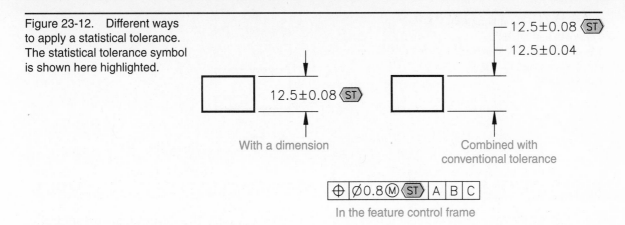

With a dimension

Combined with conventional tolerance

In the feature control frame

## DATUM FEATURE SYMBOL

*Datums* are considered theoretically perfect surfaces, planes, points, or axes. In this introduction to datum-related symbols, the datum is assumed. In geometric dimensioning and tolerancing, the datums are identified with a *datum feature symbol*.

Each datum feature requiring identification must have its own identification letter. Any letter of the alphabet can be used to identify a datum except for I, O, or Q. These letters can be confused with the numbers 1 or 0. On drawings where the number of datums exceed the letters in the alphabet, double letters are used, starting with AA through AZ, and then BA through BZ. Datum feature symbols can be repeated only as necessary for clarity. Figure 23-13 shows the datum feature symbol recommended by ASME Y14.5M-1994.

The datum feature used in drawings prior to the release of ASME Y14.5M-1994 is distinctively different. Figure 23-14 shows the old datum feature.

Figure 23-13. Datum feature symbol based on ASME Y14.5M-1994.

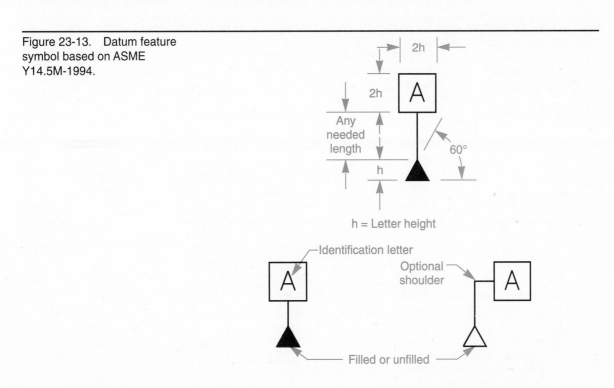

h = Letter height

Identification letter

Optional shoulder

Filled or unfilled

Figure 23-14.   Datum feature symbol based on ANSI Y14.5M-1982. This standard has been revised to ASME Y14.5M-1994.

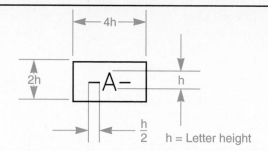

# APPLICATIONS OF THE ASME Y14.5M-1994 DATUM FEATURE SYMBOL

When a surface is used to establish a datum plane on a part, the datum feature symbol is placed on the edge view of the surface or on an extension line in the view where the surface appears as a line. Refer to Figure 23-15. A leader line can also be used to connect the datum feature symbol to the view.

When the datum is an axis, the datum feature symbol can be placed on the drawing using one of the following methods, Figure 23-16:

- The symbol can be placed on the outside surface of a cylindrical feature.
- The symbol can be centered on the opposite side of the dimension line arrowhead.
- The symbol can replace the dimension line and arrowhead when the dimension line is placed outside of the extension lines.
- The symbol can be placed on a leader line shoulder.
- The symbol can be placed below, and attached to, the center of a feature control frame.

Elements on a rectangular symmetrical part or feature can be located and dimensioned in relationship to a datum center plane. Datum center plane symbols are shown in Figure 23-17.

Figure 23-15.   The datum feature symbol is placed on the edge view or on an extension line in the view where the surface appears as a line.

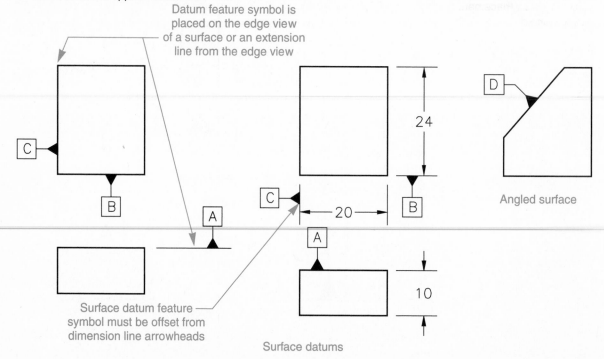

**Figure 23-16.** Methods of representing the datum axis.

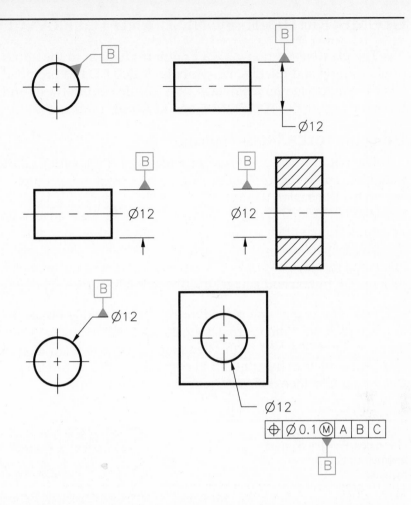

**Figure 23-17.** Placement of center plane datum feature symbols. Axis and center plane datum feature symbols must align with, or replace, the dimension line arrowhead. Or, the datum must be placed on the feature, leader shoulder, or feature control frame.

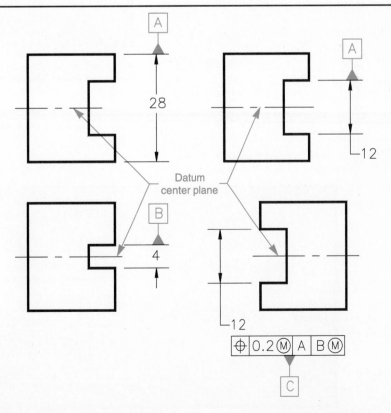

# GEOMETRIC DIMENSIONING AND TOLERANCING WITH AUTOCAD

The previous section gave a brief introduction to the appearance and use of geometric dimensioning and tolerancing symbols. AutoCAD has provided you with the ability to add GD&T symbols to your drawings. The feature control frame and related GD&T symbols can be created using the **TOLERANCE** and **LEADER** commands.

## Using the TOLERANCE command

The **TOLERANCE** command provides tools for creating GD&T symbols. Access this command by typing TOL or TOLERANCE at the **Command:** prompt, or picking the **Tolerance** button on the **Dimension** toolbar. If the ACADFULL menu file is loaded, the command can also be accessed by picking **Dimensioning** ⟩ followed by **Tolerance... Draw** pull-down menu. When you enter this command, you get the **Symbol** dialog box, shown in Figure 23-18.

The **Symbol** dialog box contains the geometric characteristic symbols. The last option is blank and displays no symbol. When you pick a desired symbol, it becomes highlighted. Next, pick the **OK** button and you get the **Geometric Tolerance** subdialog box shown in Figure 23-19.

The symbol that you picked in the **Symbol** dialog box is displayed in the **Sym** text box. You can pick the **Sym** box to get the **Symbol** dialog box back again if you want to pick a different symbol. The rest of the **Geometric Tolerance** subdialog box is divided into compartments that relate to the compartments found in the feature control frame. The elements of the **Geometric Tolerance** dialog box are described as follows:

Figure 23-18.   The **Symbol** dialog box. Pick the desired geometric characterisic symbol.

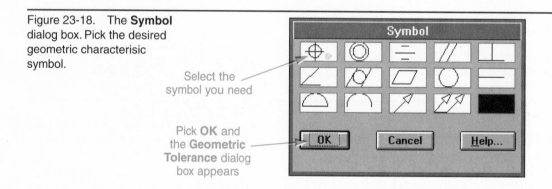

Figure 23-19.   The **Geometric Tolerance** subdialog box is used to build a feature control frame to desired specifications.

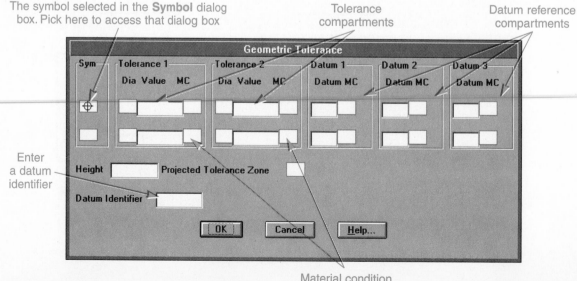

- **Tolerance 1.** This compartment allows you to enter the first geometric tolerance value found in the feature control frame. You can also add a diameter symbol by picking below the **Dia** and a material condition symbol by picking below **MC**. When you pick below **MC**, the **Material Condition** dialog box shown in Figure 23-20 appears. Highlight the desired material condition symbol by picking it, and then pick the **OK** button. The material condition symbol is now displayed under **MC**. Notice the ⓢ symbol in Figure 23-20. This is the regardless of feature size (RFS) symbol used in ANSI Y14.5M-1982. In ASME Y14.5M-1994, RFS is assumed unless otherwise specified.
    - There are two text edit boxes in each compartment. The text edit boxes are located below **Value**. The top text edit box is for the information found in a single feature control frame, while the bottom text edit box is for information needed for a double-feature control frame. Double-feature control frames are used for applications such as unit straightness, unit flatness, composite profile tolerance, composite positional tolerance, and coaxial positional tolerance. Refer to *Geometric Dimensioning and Tolerancing* published by The Goodheart-Willcox Company, Inc., or ASME Y14.5M-1994 for a complete discussion and examples. Figure 23-21 shows 0.5 entered in the **Tolerance 1** first text box, preceded by a diameter symbol and followed by an MMC symbol.
- **Tolerance 2.** This compartment is used for the addition of a second geometric tolerance to the feature control frame. This is not a common application, but it may be used in some cases where there are restrictions placed on the geometric tolerance specified in the first compartment. For example, ⌀0.8 MAX, which means that the specification given in the first compartment is maintained but cannot exceed 0.8 maximum.

Figure 23-20.   The **Material Condition** dialog box. Pick the desired material condition symbol for the geometric tolerance and datum reference as needed. Notice the symbol for RFS appears here. This symbol is not used in ASME Y14.5M-1994, but may be needed when editing older drawings.

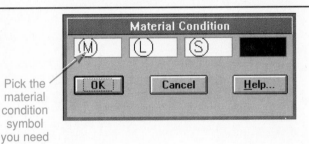

Figure 23-21.   The **Geometric Tolerance** subdialog box with a diameter symbol, geometric tolerance, and MMC material condition symbol added to the **Tolerance 1** area (shown here highlighted).

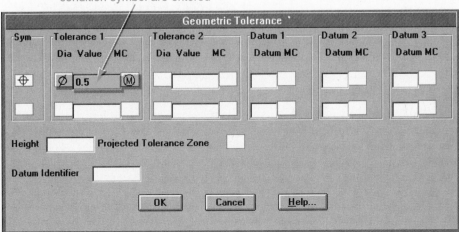

- **Datum 1.** This is used to establish the information needed in the primary datum reference compartment. You can also enter a material condition symbol by picking **MC**.
- **Datum 2** and **Datum 3.** These work the same as **Datum 1**, but are for setting the secondary and tertiary datum reference information. Look back at Figure 23-9 to see how the datum reference and related material condition symbols are placed in the feature control frame.
- **Height.** Enter the height of a projected tolerance zone and pick to the right of **Projected Tolerance Zone** to access the symbol. This topic is discussed later in this chapter.
- **Datum Identifier.** If working in accordance with the ANSI Y14.5M-1982 standard, you can specify a datum feature symbol here. If you want to comply with ASME Y14.5M-1994, you need to design a datum feature symbol and save it as a block. Creating your own dimensioning symbols is discussed later in this chapter and in Chapter 25.

When you have entered all of the desired information in the **Geometric Tolerance** subdialog box shown in Figure 23-22, pick the **OK** button. Now the following prompt is issued:

Enter tolerance location: *(pick the place for the feature control frame to be drawn)*
Command:

The feature control frame from the previous command sequence is shown in Figure 23-23.

Figure 23-22.   The **Geometric Tolerance** dialog box with a diameter symbol, geometric tolerance, and MMC material condition symbol added to the **Tolerance 1** area. Identifiers A at **Datum 1**, B and the MMC symbol at **Datum 2**, and C at **Datum 3** are also added. (These items are shown here highlighted.)

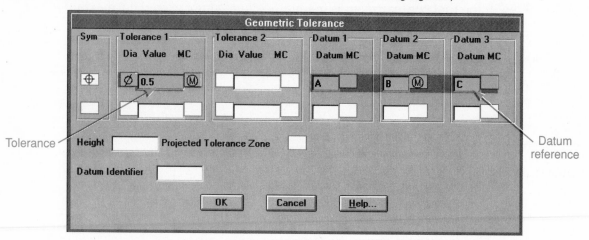

Figure 23-23.   The feature
control frame created by the
sequence displayed in
Figure 23-22.

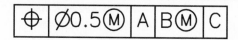

## EXERCISE 23-1

❏ Load AutoCAD and open one of your prototypes, or begin a new drawing with these settings:
**Limits**: 8.5,11.
**GRID**: .25
ROMANS text font for dimensioning.
**SNAP**: .125
❏ Draw the same feature control frames that are displayed in Figure 23-7 and Figure 23-8.
❏ Save the drawing as A:EX23-1.

## Using the LEADER command to place GD&T symbols

You can also use the **LEADER** command to access the same dialog boxes and draw a feature control frame connected to a leader line. This can be accomplished by using the following command sequence:

Command: **LEADER** ⏎
From point: *(pick the leader starting point)*
To point (Format/Annotation/Undo) ⟨Annotation⟩: *(pick the end of the shoulder)*
To point (Format/Annotation/Undo) ⟨Annotation⟩: *(press* [Enter] *for the default)*

*Annotation* means notes. The **Annotation** option allows you to enter a single line of text to go with the leader, or you can press the [Enter] key to get a list of **Annotation** options:

Annotation (or RETURN for options): ⏎
Tolerance/Copy/Block/None/⟨MText⟩: **T** ⏎

Enter T to access the **Tolerance** option. This activates the **Symbol** dialog box and the **Geometric Tolerance** dialog box, previously discussed. Establish the feature control frame information and pick **OK**. The feature control frame is connected to the leader shoulder, as shown in Figure 23-24.

Figure 23-24.   Using the **LEADER** command to draw a feature control frame.

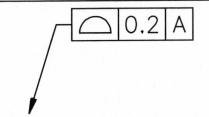

---

## PROJECTED TOLERANCE ZONE INTRODUCTION

In some situations where positional tolerance is used entirely in out-of-squareness, it may be necessary to control perpendicularity and position next to the part. The use of a *projected tolerance zone* is recommended when variations in perpendicularity of threaded or press-fit holes could cause the fastener to interfere with the mating part. A projected tolerance zone is usually specified for a fixed fastener, such as the threaded hole for a bolt or the press-fit hole for a pin. The length of a projected tolerance zone can be specified as the distance the fastener extends into the mating part, the thickness of the part, or the height of a press-fit stud. The normal positional tolerance extends through the thickness of the part.

However, this application can cause an interference between the location of a thread or press-fit object and its mating part. This is because the attitude of a fixed fastener is controlled by the actual angle of the threaded hole. There is no clearance available to provide flexibility. For this reason, the projected tolerance zone is established at true position and extends away from the primary datum at the threaded feature. The projected tolerance zone provides a bigger tolerance because it is projected away from the primary datum, rather than within the thread.

The projected tolerance is also easier to inspect than the tolerance applied to the pitch diameter of the thread, because a thread gage with a post projecting above the threaded hole can be used to easily verify the projected tolerance zone with a coordinate measuring machine (CMM).

One method for displaying the projected tolerance zone is by placing the projected tolerance zone symbol and height in the feature control frame after the geometric tolerance and related material condition symbol. The related thread specification is then connected to the sectional view of the thread symbol. With this method, the projected tolerance zone is assumed to extend away from the threaded hole at the primary datum. Refer to Figure 23-25.

To provide additional clarification, the projected tolerance zone can be shown using a chain line in the view where the related datum appears as an edge and the minimum height of the projection is dimensioned. Refer to Figure 23-26. The projected tolerance zone symbol is shown alone in the feature control frame after the geometric tolerance and material condition symbol (if any). The meaning is the same as previously discussed.

Figure 23-25. Projected tolerance zone representation with the length of the projected tolerance zone given in the feature control frame. The projected tolerance zone symbol is shown here highlighted.

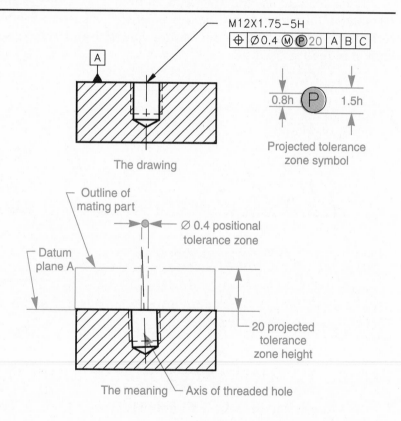

Figure 23-26. Projected tolerance zone representation with the length of the projected tolerance zone shown with a chain line and a minimum dimension in the adjacent view. The projected tolerance zone symbol is shown here highlighted.

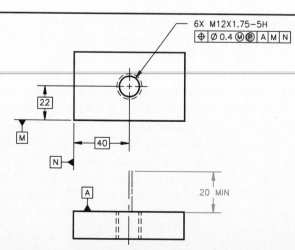

## Drawing the projected tolerance zone with AutoCAD   **AUG 9**

You can add projected tolerance zone specifications to the feature control frame by using the **Geometric Tolerance** subdialog box. To do this, use either the **TOLERANCE** or **LEADER** command to access the **Symbol** dialog box. Select the desired geometric characteristic symbol and press the **OK** button to access the **Geometric Tolerance** subdialog box. Type the desired geometric tolerance, diameter symbol, material condition symbol, and datum reference as previously discussed. Type the projected tolerance zone height in the **Height** text box. Notice that 24 is entered in the **Height** text box in Figure 23-27. Pick to the right of **Projected Tolerance Zone** to insert the projected tolerance zone symbol. Pick the **OK** button when ready.

Figure 23-27.   Entering the projected tolerance zone height and symbol in the **Geometric Tolerance** subdialog box.

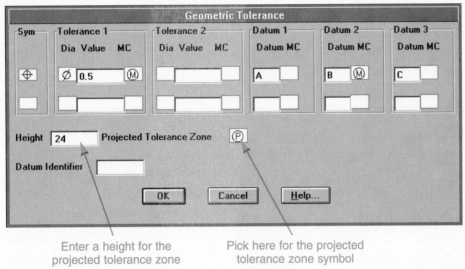

Enter a height for the projected tolerance zone

Pick here for the projected tolerance zone symbol

Now follow the screen prompts and place the feature control frame in the desired location. Notice in Figure 23-28 that AutoCAD displays the projected tolerance zone height in a separate compartment below the feature control frame. This representation is in accordance with ANSI Y14.5M-1982, but does not match the ASME Y14.5M-1994 examples that are displayed in Figure 23-25. If you want to dimension the projected tolerance zone height with a chain line, as in Figure 23-26, then omit the **Height** in the **Geometric Tolerance** subdialog box and only pick the projected tolerance zone symbol. This adds a compartment below the feature control frame with only the projected tolerance zone symbol.

Figure 23-28.   The AutoCAD feature control frame and projected tolerance zone compartment conforms to ANSI Y14.5M-1982 standards.

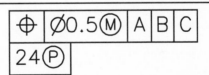

### EXERCISE 23-3

❏ Load AutoCAD and open EX23-1.
❏ Draw the feature control frame and projected tolerance zone compartment shown in Figure 23-28.
❏ Save the drawing as A:EX23-3.

## DRAWING A DOUBLE FEATURE
## CONTROL FRAME WITH AUTOCAD

AUG 9

Several GD&T applications require that the feature control frame be doubled in height, with two sets of geometric tolerancing information provided. These applications include unit straightness and flatness, composite positional tolerance, and coaxial positional tolerance. Use the **TOLERANCE** or **LEADER** command (as previously discussed) and pick the desired geometric characteristic symbol from the **Symbol** dialog box. When the **Geometric Tolerance** subdialog box is displayed, pick below current geometric characteristic symbol in the **Sym** box. The **Symbol** dialog box is displayed again. Pick another geometric characteristic symbol. This results in two symbols displayed in the **Sym** box, as in Figure 23-29. Continue picking and typing the needed information in both sets of tolerance and datum compartments.

If the two symbols in the **Sym** box are the same, then the double-feature control frame is drawn with one geometric characteristic symbol displayed in the first compartment, as shown in Figure 23-30A. If you are drawing a double-feature control frame with different geometric characteristic symbols for a combination control, then the feature control frame is drawn, as shown in Figure 23-30B.

Figure 23-29.   Double-feature control frame information displayed in the **Geometric Tolerance** subdialog box.

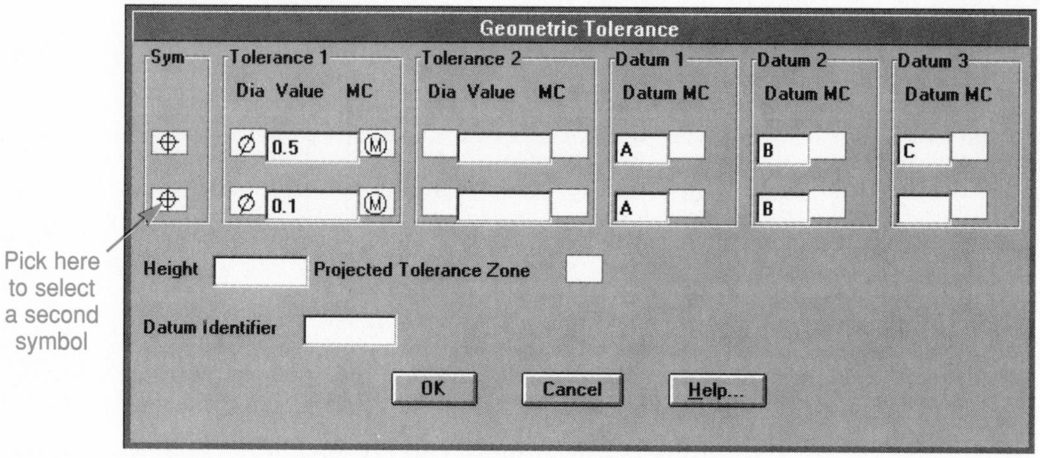

Figure 23-30.   A—If the same symbol is entered in the **Sym** box of the **Geometric Tolerance** subdialog box, it will be displayed once in the first compartment of the feature control frame.
B—Enter two different symbols in the **Sym** box of the **Geometric Tolerance** subdialog box to have them displayed in two separate compartments of the feature control frame.

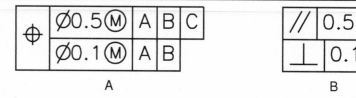

A

B

## DRAWING THE DATUM FEATURE SYMBOL WITH AUTOCAD

AUG 9

To draw the datum feature symbol with AutoCAD, use the **TOLERANCE** or **LEADER** command. When you get the **Symbol** dialog box, pick the blank option and then pick **OK**. This accesses the **Geometric Tolerance** subdialog box without any geometric characteristic symbol displayed. Type the desired datum identification (–A–) in the **Datum Identifier** text box as shown in Figure 23-31.

Pick the **OK** button and then place the datum feature symbol in the desired position on the drawing. The resulting datum feature symbol correlating with ANSI Y14.5M-1982 is shown in Figure 23-32A. You can also draw an ANSI Y14.5M-1982 datum feature symbol connected to a feature control frame, as shown in Figure 23-32B, by selecting the desired geometric characteristic symbol and entering the needed information in the **Geometric Tolerance** subdialog box.

Figure 23-31. Enter a datum identifier in the text box found in the **Geometric Tolerance** subdialog box.

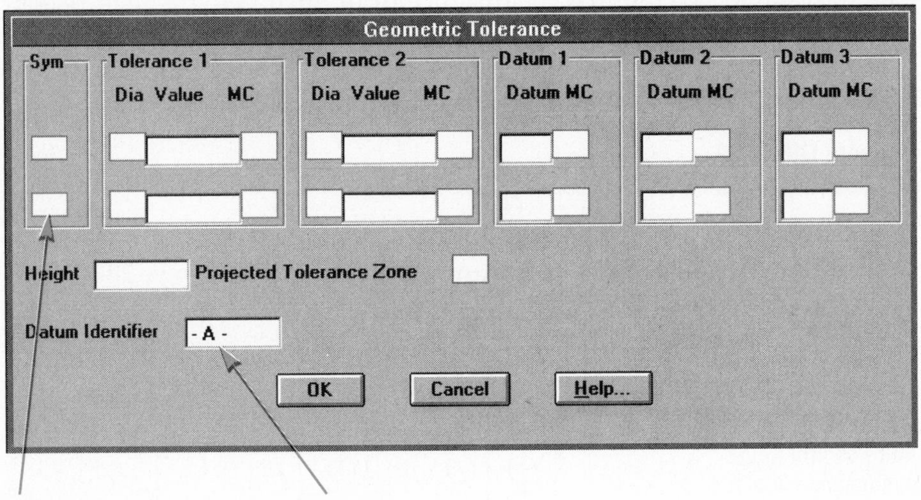

Picking the blank area in the **Symbol** dialog box leaves this area blank

Enter a datum identifier

Figure 23-32. A—A datum feature symbol drawn without a feature control frame. B—A datum feature symbol drawn with a feature control frame. Note that these datum feature symbols are drawn to the ANSI Y14.5M-1982 standards.

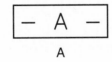

A

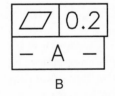

B

### EXERCISE 23-5

❑ Load AutoCAD and open EX23-1.
❑ Draw the datum feature symbol shown in Figure 23-32A.
❑ Draw the feature control frame and datum feature symbol shown in Figure 23-28.
❑ Save the drawing as A:EX23-5.

**PROFESSIONAL TIP**

Chapter 25 of this text gives you a detailed discussion on how to create your own custom symbol libraries. It is recommended that you design dimensioning symbols that are not available in AutoCAD. Dimensioning symbols might include the counterbore, countersink, depth, and other symbols displayed in Figure 23-1. Geometric tolerancing symbols can include the datum feature symbol that is currently recognized by ASME Y14.5M-1994, as shown in Figure 23-13.

## CONTROLLING THE HEIGHT OF THE FEATURE CONTROL FRAME

Figure 23-8 showed the height of the feature control frame as being twice the height of the text. Text on engineering drawings is generally .125″ (3mm). This makes the feature control frame height equal to .25″ (6mm). The distance from the text to the feature control frame is controlled by the **DIMGAP** dimension variable. The **DIMGAP** default is .09″. If the drawing text is .125″, then the space between the text and the feature control frame should be .0625″ to get a .25″ high frame. Change the **DIMGAP** like this:

    Command: **DIMGAP** ↵
    New value for DIMGAP ⟨0.09⟩: .0625
    Command:

The results of this setting is shown in the feature control frame in Figure 23-33.

Figure 23-33. The **DIMGAP** dimension variable controls the distance from the text to the box in the feature control frame and the basic dimension. Note: This value applies to both sides of the text.

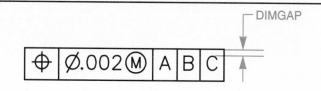

## DRAWING BASIC DIMENSIONS WITH AUTOCAD      AUG 9

You can have AutoCAD automatically draw basic dimensions by using the **Dimension Styles** dialog box. Remember, access this dialog box by picking the **Dimension Styles** button on the **Dimensioning** toolbar, by picking **Dimension Style...** in the **Data** pull-down menu, or by typing DDIM at the **Command:** prompt.

When inside the **Dimension Styles** dialog box, pick the **Annotation** button to get the **Annotation** subdialog box. To access the basic dimension feature, go to the **Tolerance Method:** list and pick BASIC, as shown in Figure 23-34. Notice that the image tile in the **Primary** and **Alternate Units** areas display basic dimension examples.

You can also activate the basic dimension feature by picking the image tile and cycling through the options until you get the basic dimension example. Pick the **OK** button in the **Annotation** subdialog box and the **Dimension Styles** dialog boxes to return to the drawing editor and begin drawing basic dimensions, as shown in Figure 23-35. The **DIMGAP** variable also controls the space between the basic dimension text and the box around the dimension.

Figure 23-34. Use the **DDIM** command to access the **Dimension Styles** dialog box. Then, pick Basic in the **Annotation** subdialog box to draw basic dimensions. You can also click on the image tile to cycle through the options.

The image tile adjusts to basic dimensions

Select Basic from the list

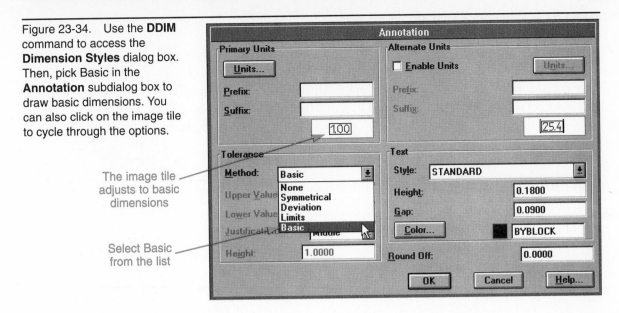

Figure 23-35. An AutoCAD basic dimension.

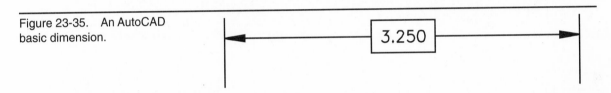

## EXERCISE 23-6

❏ Load AutoCAD and open EX23-1.
❏ The dimension text height was set to .125″ in EX23-1. Set the **DIMGAP** dimension variable so the feature control frame height is two times the text height.
❏ Draw the feature control frame shown in Figure 23-33.
❏ Draw the basic dimension shown in Figure 23-35.
❏ Save the drawing as A:EX23-6.

## EDITING THE FEATURE CONTROL FRAME

AUG 9

A feature control frame acts as one object. When you pick any place on the frame, the entire object is selected. You can edit feature control frames using **ERASE**, **COPY**, **MOVE**, **ROTATE**, and **SCALE**. The **STRETCH** command and **GRIPS** only move the feature control frame, similar to when they are used with text objects.

You can edit the information inside of a feature control frame by using the **DDEDIT** command. When you enter **DDEDIT** and select the desired feature control frame, the **Geometric Tolerance** subdialog box is displayed with all of the current feature control frame values displayed. Make any desired changes and pick the **OK** button. The feature control frame is now revised as needed. You can also use the **DDEDIT** command to edit basic dimensions. This displays the **Edit MText** dialog box where you can edit the basic dimension as any other dimension.

## SAMPLE GD&T APPLICATIONS

This chapter is intended to give you a general overview of GD&T applications and how to draw GD&T symbols using AutoCAD. If you are in the manufacturing industry, you may have considerable use for geometric dimensioning and tolerancing. The support information may be a review or it may inspire you to learn more about this topic. The drawings in Figure 23-36 are intended to show you some common GD&T applications using the available geometric characteristics.

Figure 23-36.   Examples of typical geometric dimensioning and tolerancing applications using the various geometric characteristics.

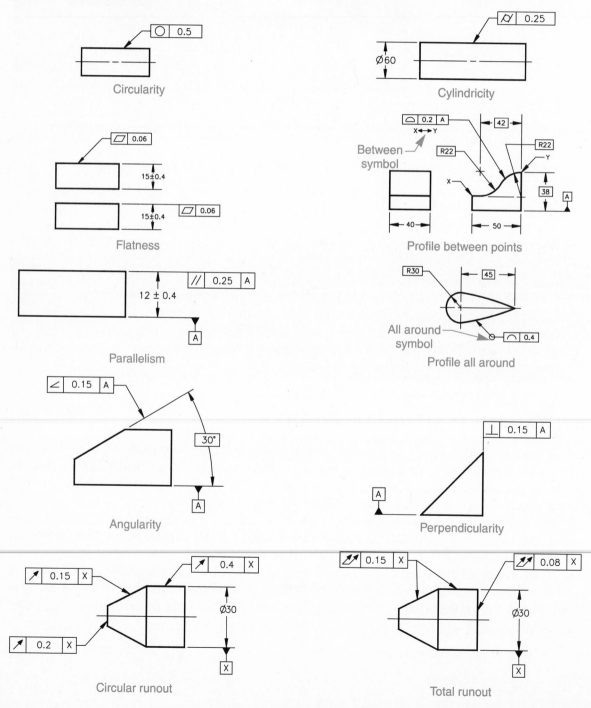

## CHAPTER TEST

*Write your answers in the spaces provided:*

1. Name each of the following geometric characteristic symbols:

   —  A. _____         ◎  H. _____

   ▱  B. _____         ≡  I. _____

   ○  C. _____         //  J. _____

   ⌀  D. _____         ⊥  K. _____

   ⌒  E. _____         ∠  L. _____

   ⌓  F. _____         ↗  M. _____

   ⊕  G. _____        ↗↗  N. _____

2. Label the parts of the following feature control frame:

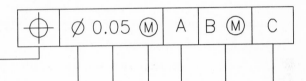

   A. _____

   B. _____

   C. _____

   D. _____

   E. _____

   F. _____

   G. _____

3. Name two commands that can be used to draw a feature control frame. _____

   _____

4. Identify the dialog box that contains the geometric characteristic symbols. _____

   _____

5. What appears after you pick a geometric characteristic symbol followed by picking **OK**
   in the dialog box identified in Question 4? _____

   _____

6. Identify the procedure used to draw a feature control frame connected to a leader.

_____

_____

_____

_____

7. Describe how to place a projected tolerance zone height and symbol compartment with the feature control frame. _____

_____

_____

_____

8. How do you get one symbol in the first compartment of a double-feature control frame?

_____

_____

_____

9. How do you get two different geometric characteristic symbols in the first compartments of a double-feature control frame? _____

_____

_____

_____

_____

10. Describe how to draw a basic dimension with AutoCAD. _____

_____

_____

_____

11. Identify the dimension variable that controls the space between the text in a feature control frame and basic dimension and the box surrounding these items. _____

_____

12. Describe how to draw a datum feature symbol with AutoCAD, without drawing an attached feature control frame. _____

_____

_____

_____

13. Name the command that can be used to change the information in an existing feature control frame. _____

_____

14. How do you get a **Geometric Tolerance** subdialog box without any symbol shown in the **Sym** box? _____

_____

15. Name the current standard for dimensioning and tolerancing that is adopted by the American National Standards Institute. _____

_____

## DRAWING PROBLEMS

*Create dimension styles that will assist you in the solution of these problems. Draw fully dimensioned multiview drawings. The required number of views depends upon the problem and is to be determined by you. Apply geometric tolerancing as discussed in this chapter. Use ANSI Y14.5M-1982 standards as applied by AutoCAD, or modify the available applications to use ASME Y14.5M-1994 standards. The problems are presented with ASME Y14.5M-1994 standards.*

1. Open P22-5 and edit by adding the geometric tolerancing shown below. If you did not draw P22-5, then open a new drawing or a prototype and draw the problem. Untoleranced dimensions are ±0.5. Save as A:P23-1.

   *Mechanical Drafting*

   METRIC
   Name:   SPRING CLIP
   Material:   SAE 1085

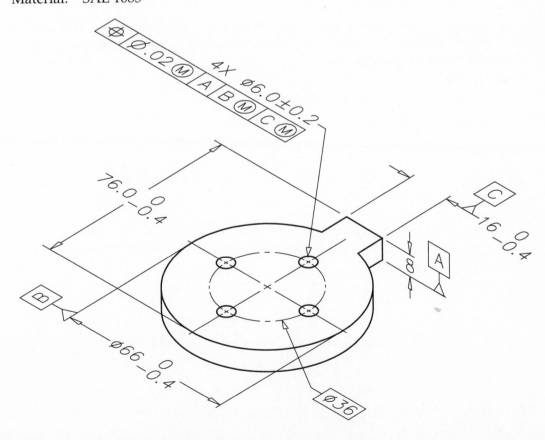

*Mechanical
Drafting*

2. Open P22-6 and edit by adding the geometric tolerancing shown below. If you did not draw P22-6, then open a new drawing or a prototype and draw the problem. Note: The problem is shown with a cutaway for clarity. You do not need to draw a section. Untoleranced dimensions XX = ±.02 and XXX = ±.005. Save as A:P23-2.

INCH

Name:   THRUST WASHER

Material:   SAE 5150

*Mechanical
Drafting*

3. Open P22-7 and edit by adding the geometric tolerancing shown below. If you did not draw P22-7, then open a new drawing or a prototype and draw the problem. Save as A:P23-3.

METRIC

Name:   LOCKING COLLAR

Material:   SAE 1080

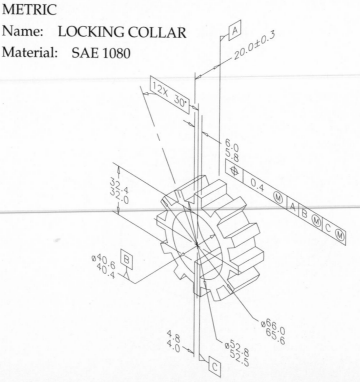

4. Draw the following object as previously instructed. Untoleranced dimensions are ±0.3. Save as A:P23-4.

METRIC

Name:   SHAFT GUIDE

Material:   CAST IRON

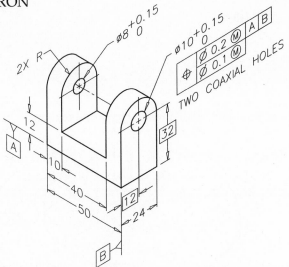

5. Draw the following object as previously instructed. Note: The problem is shown with a cutaway for clarity. You do not need to draw a section. Untoleranced dimensions are ±.010. Save as A:P23-5.

INCH

Name:   VALVE PIN

Material:   PHOSPHOR BRONZE

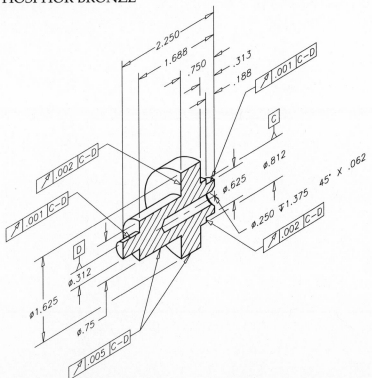

6. Draw the following object as previously instructed. Note: The problem is shown with a cutaway for clarity. You do not need to draw a section. Untoleranced dimensions are ±.010. Save as A:P23-6.

INCH

Name:   HUB

Material:   CAST IRON

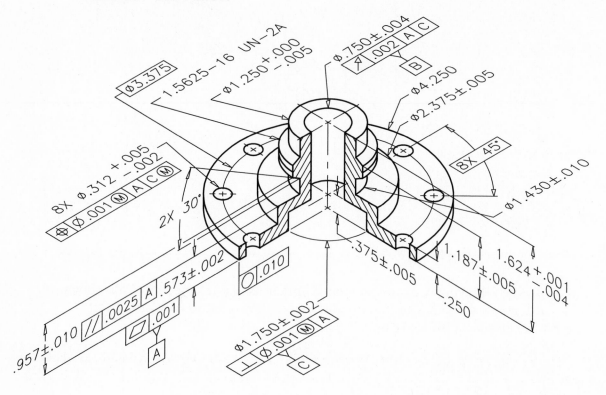

# Chapter 24

# Drawing Section Views and Graphic Patterns

## Learning objectives

After completing this chapter, you will be able to:

❍ Identify sectioning techniques.

❍ Use sections and dimensioning practices to draw objects given in engineering sketches.

❍ Draw section material using the **HATCH**, **BHATCH**, and **SOLID** commands.

❍ Prepare graphic displays, such as graphs and logos, using the **HATCH** and **SOLID** commands.

❍ Interpret a hatch pattern definition and create your own custom hatch pattern using the Windows Notepad.

❍ Edit existing associative hatch patterns using **HATCHEDIT**.

In mechanical drafting, internal features in multiviews appear as hidden lines. These features must be dimensioned. However, it is poor practice to dimension to hidden lines. Therefore, section views are used to clarify the hidden features.

Section views show internal features as if a portion of the object is cut away. They are used in conjunction with multiviews to completely describe the exterior and interior features of an object.

When sections are drawn, a *cutting-plane line* is placed in one of the views to show where the cut was made. The cutting-plane line is the "saw" that cuts through the object to expose internal features. It is drawn with a thick dashed or phantom line, in accordance with ANSI Y14.2M. The arrows on the cutting-plane line indicate the line of sight when looking at the section view.

The cutting-plane lines are often labeled with letters that relate to the proper section view. A title, such as SECTION A-A, is placed under the view. When more than one section view is drawn, labels continue with B-B through Z-Z. The letters I, O, and Q are not used because they may be confused with numbers.

Labeling multiple section views is necessary for drawings with multiple sections. When only one section view is present and its location is obvious, a label is not needed. Section lines are used in the section view to show where the material has been cut away. See Figure 24-1.

Sectioning is also used in other drafting fields, such as architectural and structural drafting. Cross sections through buildings show the construction methods and materials. See Figure 24-2. The cutting-plane lines used in these fields are often composed of letter and number symbols. This helps coordinate the large number of sections found in a set of architectural drawings.

**Figure 24-1.** A three-view multiview drawing with a section view.

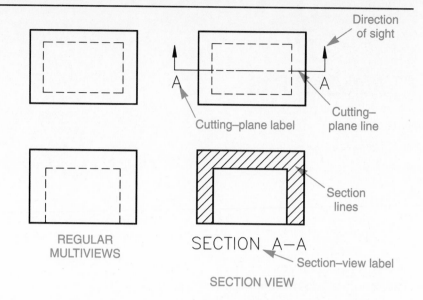

**Figure 24-2.** An architectural section view. (Alan Mascord, Design Associates)

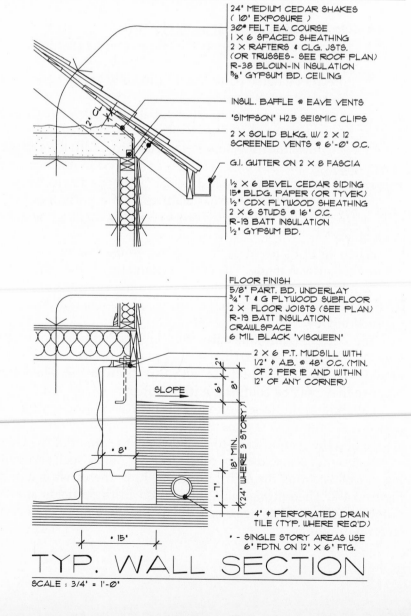

## TYPES OF SECTIONS

There are many types of sections available for the drafter to use. The section used depends on the detail to be sectioned. For example, one object may require the section be taken completely through the object. Another may only need to remove a small portion to expose the interior features.

### Full sections

*Full sections* "remove" half of the object, as in Figure 24-1. In this type of section, the cutting-plane line passes completely through the object along a center plane.

### Offset sections

*Offset sections* are the same as full sections, except that the cutting-plane line is staggered. This allows you to cut through features that are not in a straight line, Figure 24-3.

Figure 24-3.   An offset section.

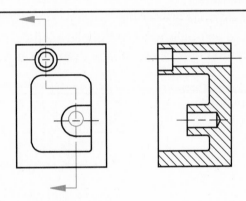

### Half sections

*Half sections* show one-quarter of the object removed. The term half is used because half of the view appears in section and the other half is shown as an exterior view. Half sections are commonly used on symmetrical objects. A centerline is used to separate the sectioned part of the view from the unsectioned portion. Hidden lines are normally omitted from the unsectioned side, Figure 24-4.

Figure 24-4.   A half section.

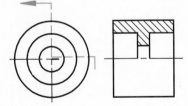

### Aligned sections

*Aligned sections* are used when a feature is out of alignment with the center plane. In this case, an offset section will distort the image. The cutting-plane line cuts through the feature to be sectioned. It is then rotated to align with the center plane before projecting into the section view. See Figure 24-5.

Figure 24-5. An aligned
section.

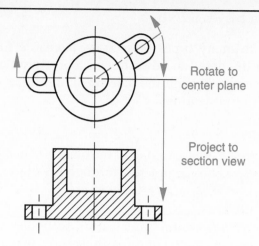

Rotate to
center plane

Project to
section view

## Revolved sections

*Revolved sections* clarify the contour of objects that have the same shape throughout their length. The section is revolved in place within the object, or part of the view may be broken away. Refer to Figure 24-6. This section makes dimensioning easier.

Figure 24-6. A revolved
section.

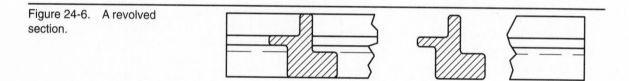

## Removed sections

*Removed sections* serve much the same function as revolved sections. The section view is removed from the regular view. A cutting-plane line shows where the section was taken. When multiple removed sections are taken, the cutting planes and related views are labeled. The section views are placed in alphabetical order. The letters I, O, and Q are not used because they may be mistaken for numbers. Drawing only the ends of the cutting-plane lines simplifies the views. See Figure 24-7.

Figure 24-7. Removed
sections.

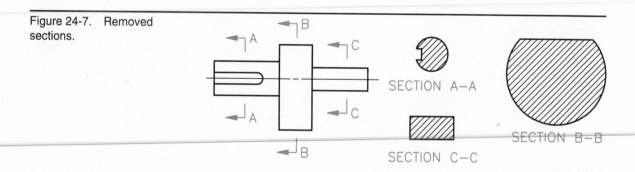

SECTION A–A

SECTION B–B

SECTION C–C

## Broken-out sections

*Broken-out sections* show only a small portion of the view removed to clarify a hidden feature. See Figure 24-8.

Figure 24-8.   A broken-out section.

## SECTION LINE SYMBOLS

AUG C

Section lines are placed in the section view to show where material has been cut away. Some rules that govern section line usage are:

- Section lines are placed at 45° unless another angle is required to satisfy the next two rules.
- Section lines should not be drawn parallel or perpendicular to any other adjacent lines on the drawing.
- Section lines should not cross object lines.

Section lines may be drawn using different patterns to represent the specific type of material. The equally-spaced section lines shown in the preceding examples represent a general application. This is adequate in most situations. Additional patterns are not necessary if the type of material is clearly indicated in the title block. Different section line material symbols are needed when connected parts of different materials are sectioned.

AutoCAD has standard section line symbols available. These are referred to as *hatch patterns*. These symbols are located in the ACAD.PAT file. The AutoCAD pattern labeled ANSI31 is the general section line symbol and is the default pattern in a new drawing. It is also used for cast iron. The ANSI32 symbol is used for sectioning steel. Other standard AutoCAD hatch patterns are shown in Figure 24-9. When very thin objects are sectioned, the material may be completely blackened or filled in. AutoCAD refers to this as *solid*. When you change to a different hatch pattern, the new pattern becomes the default in the current drawing until it is changed.

Figure 24-9.   Standard AutoCAD hatch patterns. (Autodesk, Inc.)

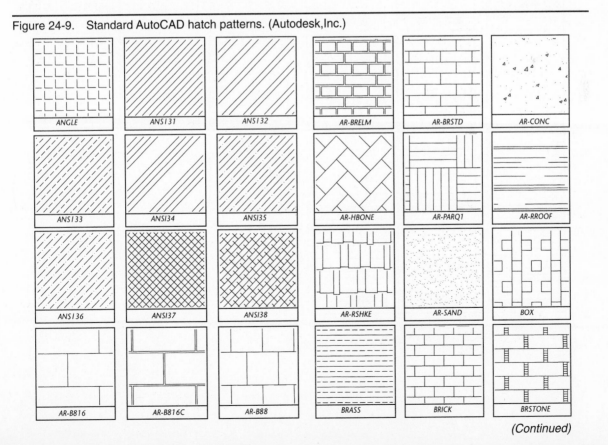

*(Continued)*

Figure 24-9.  (Continued)

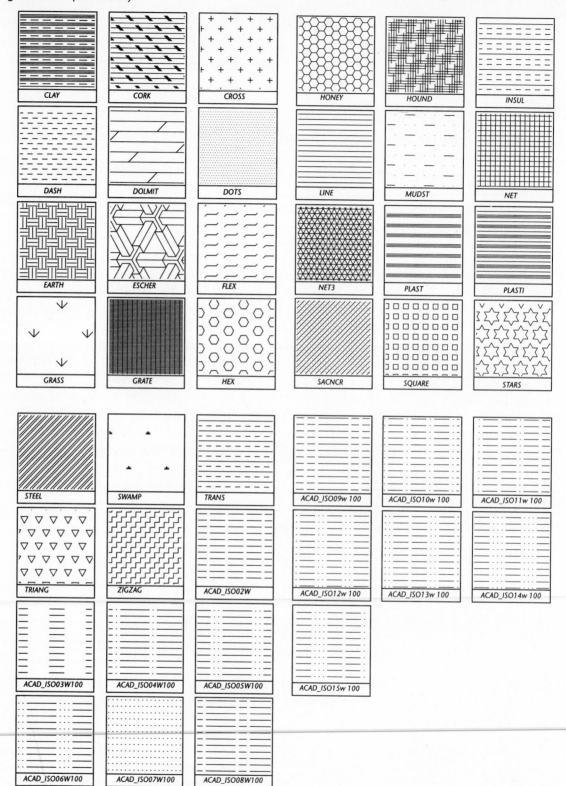

## DRAWING SECTION LINES AND HATCH PATTERNS　　AUG 2

AutoCAD hatch patterns are not limited to sectioning. They can be used as artistic patterns in a graphic layout for an advertisement or promotion. They might also be added as shading on an architectural elevation or technical illustration.

### Introduction to the HATCH command

AutoCAD allows you to draw section lines or other patterns using the **HATCH** command. Typing HATCH at the **Command:** prompt displays the following syntax and options:

```
Command: HATCH ↵
Pattern (? or name/U,style) ⟨ANSI31⟩:
```

Typing ? gives you this prompt:

```
Pattern(s) to list ⟨*⟩:
```

You can type the name or names of specific hatch patterns, or press [Enter] to accept the wildcard (*) and list all the hatch patterns in the text window. AutoCAD displays the names of all the standard hatch patterns in alphabetical order with a brief description of each following the pattern name. The list of pattern names is several pages long, so press [Enter] or the space bar after each page. Press function key [F2] to flip back to the graphics window when you are finished.

To draw a hatch pattern, press [Enter] to accept the default pattern ANSI31, or type a different pattern name and press [Enter]. You are then asked to define the pattern scale and angle.

```
Pattern (? or name/U,style) ⟨ANSI31⟩: ↵
Scale for pattern ⟨1.0000⟩: ↵
Angle for pattern ⟨0⟩: ↵
```

Press [Enter] after each prompt to use the default value shown in brackets. The pattern scale default is 1 (full scale). If the drawn pattern is too tight or too wide, type a new scale. Figure 24-10 shows different scale factors.

Figure 24-10.　Hatch pattern scale factors.

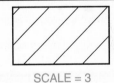

SCALE = 1　　　SCALE = 2　　　SCALE = 3

The default scale factor of 1 specifies one drawing unit. The relationship between the hatch scale in model space and paper space is controlled by the scale factor. Respond to the scale prompt with the desired size of the pattern in model space or paper space.

The hatch scale can be specified referencing model space, if desired. However, it is much simpler to reference the scale to paper space. This allows the scale factor to be based on the plotted scale of the drawing. To do this, enter XP after the scale. The XP indicates relative to paper space units. Therefore, entering 1XP as the scale factor causes AutoCAD to automatically calculate the actual scale required within model space to match the specified value of 1 in paper space:

```
Scale for pattern ⟨1.0000⟩: 1XP ↵
```

When you do this, notice that the next use of the **HATCH** command offers the actual pattern scale that was calculated by AutoCAD as a default. It is not necessary to re-enter 1XP since the default value shown is the model space equivalent of this already. Model space and paper space are discussed in detail in Chapter 26.

An alternate method of entering values for this prompt is by picking two points in the drawing. AutoCAD then measures the distance and uses it as the scale factor. This method does not allow the **XP** option to be used.

The pattern default angle is 0. This gives you the same pattern angle shown in Figure 24-9. To alter the pattern angle, type a new value.

**PROFESSIONAL TIP**

Enter a larger scale factor when hatching large areas. This makes your section lines look neater and saves regeneration and plot time. For metric drawings, set the hatch scale to 25.4.

## Selecting objects to be hatched

It is important to consider the boundary of the area you plan to hatch. It is easy to hatch within a circle or square. When you see the Select objects: prompt, pick the circle, or window the square. If the square was drawn as one closed polyline, then pick it as one entity. The circumference of the circle and the perimeter of the square automatically become the hatch boundary. See Figure 24-11.

```
Command: HATCH ↵
Pattern (? or name/U,style) ⟨ANSI31⟩: ↵
Scale for pattern ⟨1.0000⟩: ↵
Angle for pattern ⟨0⟩: ↵
Select hatch boundaries or RETURN for direct hatch option,
Select objects: (pick the circle)
1 found
```

Now select a square that was drawn as four lines.

```
Select objects: W ↵
First corner: (pick the first window corner)
Other corner: (pick the second window corner)
```

Now select a square that was drawn as one closed polyline.

```
Select objects: (pick the closed polyline)
1 found
Select objects: ↵
Command:
```

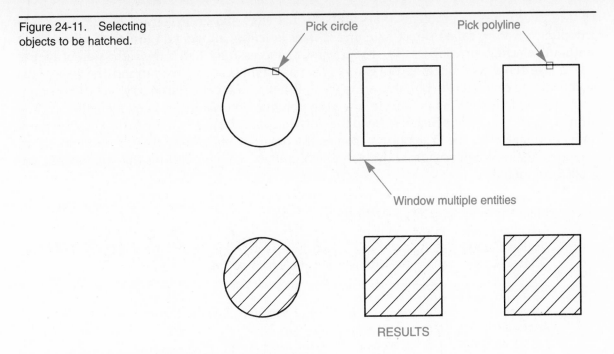

Figure 24-11.   Selecting objects to be hatched.

## Drawing a hatch without selecting objects

A problem may arise when you try to hatch an object that is composed of more than one enclosed area. If adjacent areas are drawn with interconnecting lines, the hatching may not be what you expect. Only the right side of each pair of blocks in Figure 24-12 is to be hatched. Notice the possible results using **Window** selection and picking the lines of the right side.

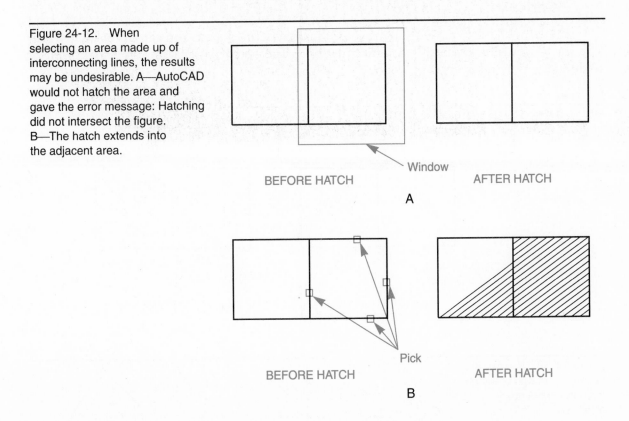

Figure 24-12.   When selecting an area made up of interconnecting lines, the results may be undesirable. A—AutoCAD would not hatch the area and gave the error message: Hatching did not intersect the figure. B—The hatch extends into the adjacent area.

To overcome the problems that can occur (as were shown in Figure 24-12), AutoCAD provides a feature called direct hatching. ***Direct hatching*** allows you to define a boundary without selecting any objects. So, if you want to successfully hatch the right side of Figure 24-12, use the direct hatching option to place a polyline boundary around the area to be hatched. You can keep the polyline or delete it. When you see the Retain polyline? ⟨N⟩: prompt, press [Enter] to accept the default to have the polyline boundary removed after the hatch is drawn. Type Y and press [Enter] to keep the polyline boundary. If you type Y to keep the polyline boundary, then the ⟨Y⟩ option becomes the default for the next **HATCH** operation until changed again. When you draw the polyline boundary, you get options that are just like the **PLINE** command:

> Command: **HATCH** ⏎
> Pattern (? or name/U,style) ⟨ANSI31⟩: ⏎
> Scale for pattern ⟨1.0000⟩: ⏎
> Angle for pattern ⟨0⟩: ⏎
> Select hatch boundaries or RETURN for direct hatch option,
> Select objects: ⏎
> Retain polyline? ⟨N⟩ ⏎
> From point: (pick the first point at a corner of the right square in Figure 24-13)
> Arc/Close/Length/Undo/⟨Next point⟩: (pick point 2)
> Arc/Close/Length/Undo/⟨Next point⟩: (pick point 3)
> Arc/Close/Length/Undo/⟨Next point⟩: (pick point 4)
> Arc/Close/Length/Undo/⟨Next point⟩: **C** ⏎

You can draw another polyline boundary or you can press [Enter] to have the hatch drawn in the boundary that you just finished:

> From point or RETURN to apply hatch: ⏎
> Command:

You do not have to draw a hatch pattern in a predefined area. You can draw a hatch pattern anyplace using the direct hatching method. The hatch pattern can be drawn with or without the polyline boundary, as shown in Figure 24-14.

---

Figure 24-13.   Using direct hatching.

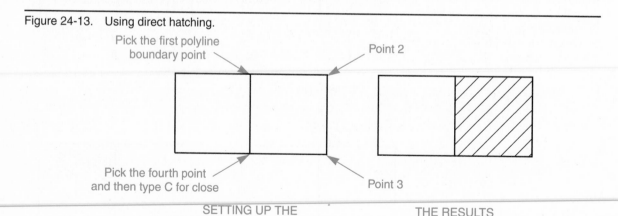

SETTING UP THE
DIRECT HATCHING BOUNDARY                    THE RESULTS

---

Figure 24-14.   You can draw a
hatch pattern with or without
the polyline boundary
displayed.

HATCH PATTERN                    HATCH PATTERN
WITHOUT THE BOUNDARY             WITH THE BOUNDARY

## The hatch pattern is nonassociative

An associative dimension is a dimension that is automatically updated when an object is edited. Patterns drawn with the **HATCH** command are nonassociative. This means that if you pick only the hatch boundary to edit, the hatch pattern does not change with it. For example, if you pick a hatch boundary to scale, only the boundary is scaled while the pattern remains the same. You need to select both the boundary and the pattern before editing.

## Making individual line hatch patterns

When you use the **HATCH** command and draw a hatch pattern using any of the designated hatch names, the pattern is drawn as a block. This means that the entire hatch pattern acts as one object. For example, if you pick one line of the pattern to erase, the entire hatch pattern is erased. You can make each line of the hatch pattern act as an individual object by typing an asterisk (*) before the hatch pattern name:

> Command: **HATCH** ↵
> Pattern (? or name/U,style) ⟨ANSI31⟩: **\*ANSI31** ↵

The rest of the command sequence works as previously discussed. Now, each line in the hatch pattern is a single object. This allows you to edit the lines individually. Include all of the lines in a selection set if you want to edit them together. The individual line hatch pattern remains as default until changed. Be sure to change it if you want to draw the next hatch pattern as a block. A hatch pattern can also be exploded to create individual lines.

---

**EXERCISE 24-1**

❑ Load AutoCAD and open PRODR2.
❑ Draw all object lines on layer 0-7.
❑ Create a new layer for hatch lines and set the color as magenta. Name the layer HATCH.
❑ Practice using the **HATCH** command by drawing the objects from the following figures with the specified patterns:
  ❑ Figure 24-10. Set the scale as shown. Use ANSI31 and angle 0.
  ❑ Figure 24-11. The first object is a circle. The second object is a square drawn using the **LINE** command and the last line closed. The third object is a square drawn using the **PLINE** command and the last polyline segment closed. Use ANSI31, scale 1, and angle 0.
  ❑ Figure 24-13. Draw the figure shown on the left using any combination of interconnecting lines. Hatch only the right side using the direct hatching option. Use ANSI31, scale 1, and angle 0.
  ❑ Figure 24-14. Use the direct hatching option to draw shapes that are similar to the examples. Draw one with the polyline boundary deleted and the other with the polyline boundary kept. Use ANSI31, scale_1, and angle 0.
❑ Save the drawing as A:EX24-1 and quit.

---

## Hatching around text

AutoCAD automatically places an imaginary box around the text in a hatch boundary. Hatch patterns are not placed inside of these imaginary boxes. The text must also be selected as an element of the hatch boundary for this to work properly. An example is the bar graph shown in Figure 24-15. Always place the text before hatching the area. Be sure you pick the object and the text:

```
Command: HATCH ↵
Pattern (? or name/U,style) ⟨current⟩: ↵
Scale for pattern ⟨1.0000⟩: ↵
Angle for pattern ⟨0⟩: ↵
Select hatch boundaries or RETURN for direct hatch option,
Select objects: (pick the object to be hatched)
n found
Select objects: (pick the text to be hatched around)
Select objects: ↵
Command:
```

In the previous example, the object and the text were picked individually. You can also window both for this to work.

Figure 24-15.    Hatching
around text.

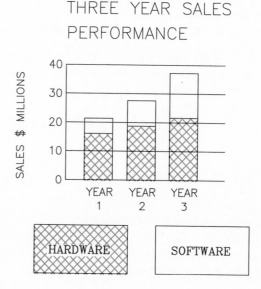

### Drawing your own simple hatch patterns

When you type HATCH at the **Command:** prompt, one of the options is **U**. This allows you to provide angle, spacing, and single or double specifications for a very simple hatch pattern, Figure 24-16. The commands are as follows:

```
Command: HATCH ↵
Pattern (? or name/U,style) ⟨current⟩: U ↵
Angle for crosshatch lines ⟨0⟩: (specify an angle, or pick two points on the screen and
    press [Enter] to accept the default angle)
Spacing between lines ⟨1.0000⟩: (type in the spacing desired, or pick two points on
    the screen to define the spacing and press [Enter] to accept the default spacing)
Double hatch area? ⟨N⟩ (type Y and press [Enter] for double hatch lines, or press
    [Enter] for the single hatch default)
Select hatch boundaries or RETURN for direct hatch option,
Select objects: (pick the object to be hatched)
n found
Select objects: ↵
Command:
```

Figure 24-16. Using the **U** option of the **HATCH** command.

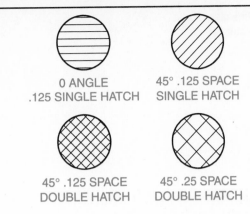

0 ANGLE
.125 SINGLE HATCH

45° .125 SPACE
SINGLE HATCH

45° .125 SPACE
DOUBLE HATCH

45° .25 SPACE
DOUBLE HATCH

The relationship between the hatch line spacing in model space and paper space is controlled by the scale factor. If you are planning to plot a drawing at a 1/2″ = 1″ (half scale) then the scale factor is 2. This means that one model space unit is equal to 2 paper space units. AutoCAD automatically controls this line spacing when you enter a line spacing of 2XP:

Spacing between lines ⟨1.00⟩: **2XP** ↵

This was discussed earlier in this chapter. Model space and paper space are explained in Chapter 26.

**PROFESSIONAL TIP**

Sometimes the hatch spacing is too wide or too close. Select **ERASE Last** or **Undo** to remove the pattern. Try a smaller or larger value.

### Using the HATCH Style option

An object may have several areas enclosed within each other. See Figure 24-17. The **Style** option of the **HATCH** command allows you to choose the features to be hatched. The three style options are:

- **N.** Normal style. This hatches every other feature.
- **O.** Hatches outermost feature area only.
- **I.** Ignores all interior features and hatches the entire object.

Any one of the options can be used. Type the desired pattern followed by a comma and the option. For example:

Command: **HATCH** ↵
Pattern (? or name/U,style) ⟨*current*⟩: **NET3,N** ↵
Scale for pattern ⟨1.0000⟩: *(for example, type* 2 *and press* [Enter]*)*
Angle for pattern ⟨0⟩: ↵
Select hatch boundaries or RETURN for direct hatch option,
Select objects: **W** ↵
First corner: *(pick first corner)*
Other corner: *(pick second corner)*
*n* found
Select objects: ↵
Command:

Figure 24-18 shows the results of using each **HATCH** style option on the object in Figure 24-17.

Figure 24-17.   This object has
three enclosed features.

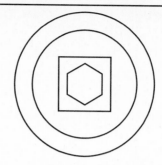

Figure 24-18.   The **Style** option of the **HATCH** command allows you to hatch enclosed features differently.
Shown here is the object in Figure 24-17.

  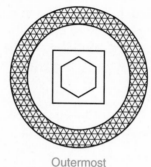  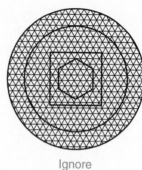

Normal                              Outermost                              Ignore

**PROFESSIONAL
TIP**

You can fill an area solid by specifying a dense pattern scale or
close line spacing. Set the scale or line spacing equal to the width of
the plotter pen. This creates a solid fill without excessive use of plot
or regeneration time. However, keep this type of application to a
minimum because it *does* slow down regeneration and plot time.

**EXERCISE 24-2**

❑ Load AutoCAD for Windows and open PRODR2.
❑ Create a new layer for hatch lines. Set the color as magenta. Name the layer HATCH-
MAGENTA.
❑ Practice using the **HATCH** command by drawing the objects from the following figures
with the patterns as shown. Draw all object lines on layer 0-7.
  ❑ Figure 24-15. Draw the HARDWARE and SOFTWARE legend boxes to practice hatch-
  ing around text.
  ❑ Figure 24-16. Set the pattern, space, and angle the same as examples.
  ❑ Figure 24-18. Set the pattern, scale, and angle the same as examples.
❑ Save the drawing as A:EX24-2 and quit.

## AUTOMATIC BOUNDARY HATCHING

AUG 2

So far you have seen how the **HATCH** command is used to place hatch patterns inside
defined areas. In addition, you were cautioned about hatching adjacent areas, as demonstrated in Figure 24-12. It is important that the hatch boundary be clearly defined, otherwise
strange things could happen.

The **BHATCH** command simplifies the hatching process by automatically hatching any enclosed area. Simply pick inside an enclosed area, rather than picking the entities or drawing a polyline to be hatched as with the **HATCH** command. The **BHATCH** command creates associative hatch patterns by default, but can be set to create nonassociative patterns.

*Associative hatch patterns* update automatically when the boundary is edited. If the boundary is stretched, scaled, or otherwise edited, the hatch pattern automatically fills the new area with the original hatch pattern scale, angle, and other settings. Associative hatch patterns can be edited using the **HATCHEDIT** command, discussed later in this chapter.

The **BHATCH** command is accessed by picking the **Hatch** button on the **Draw** toolbar or typing BHATCH at the **Command:** prompt. If the ACADFULL menu file is loaded, the command can also be accessed by picking **Hatch ⟩** and **Hatch...** in the **Draw** pull-down. Entering the **BHATCH** command displays the **Boundary Hatch** dialog box, shown in Figure 24-19.

Figure 24-19. The **Boundary Hatch** dialog box.

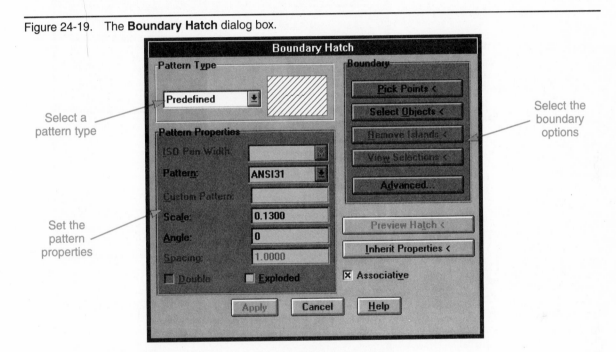

The **Boundary Hatch** dialog box contains the following elements:
- **Pattern Type.** This area has the **Pattern Type** pop-up list and an image tile at the right. The **Pattern Type** pop-up list has three options described as follows:
  - **Predefined**—This is AutoCAD's standard hatch patterns, which are stored in the ACAD.PAT file. A predefined pattern is displayed in the image tile.
    When the predefined patterns are active, picking on the image tile at the right allows you to scroll through the available AutoCAD hatch patterns until you find the one you want. This is a convenient way to see and select a hatch pattern. These patterns are shown in Figure 24-9.
  - **User-defined**—When you pick this option, the image tile is removed. This selection allows you to draw a user-style pattern using the current linetype, just as described earlier and shown in Figure 24-16.
  - **Custom**—This allows you to access a custom pattern defined in a pattern file other than the ACAD.PAT file.

- **Pattern Properties.** This is the area of the **Boundary Hatch** dialog box where you set the properties related to the selected hatch pattern. The features are:
    - **ISO Pen Width:**—This is a pop-up list available when a predefined ISO pattern is selected. The pop-up list shown in Figure 24-20 allows you to pick a pen width for ISO pattern scaling.
    - **Pattern:**—This list provides an easy way to access predefined patterns. When you pick a pattern name from this list, the image tile automatically displays a representation of the pattern, as shown in Figure 24-21.

Figure 24-20.   Pick the desired pen width for ISO pattern scaling list (shown here highlighted).

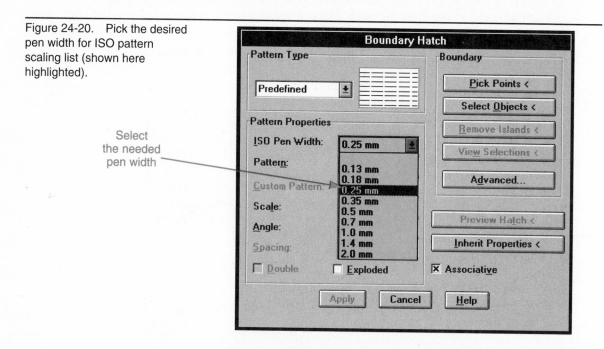

Figure 24-21.   The **Pattern Type** image tile automatically displays a representation of the pattern selected from the list. (The list and the image tile are shown here highlighted.)

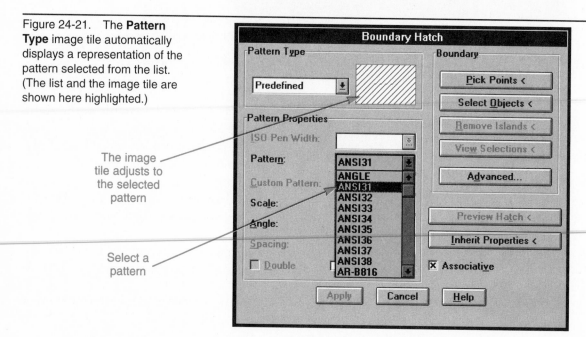

- **Custom Pattern:**— This allows you to enter a custom pattern name in the text box. This is available only if **Custom** is selected.
- **Scale:**—This text box allows you to set the pattern scale, as discussed earlier and shown in Figure 24-10. AutoCAD stores the hatch pattern scale in the **HPSCALE** system variable.
- **Angle:**—This text box allows you to set the pattern angle, as discussed earlier in this chapter. AutoCAD stores the hatch pattern angle in the **HPANG** system variable.
- **Spacing:**—This text box is available if **User-defined** is selected in the **Pattern Type** area. It allows you to set user-defined hatch spacing, as explained earlier and shown in Figure 24-16. AutoCAD stores the hatch pattern spacing in the **HSPACE** system variable.
- **Double**—Pick this check box to activate double hatch lines for a user-defined hatch pattern, as shown in Figure 24-16. AutoCAD stores this setting in the **HPDOUBLE** system variable.
- **Explode**—Pick this check box if you want the hatch pattern to be drawn with individual line objects rather than as a block pattern. When this box is checked, an asterisk is placed in front of the pattern name in the **HPNAME** system variable.
- **Boundary.** This area of the **Boundary Hatch** dialog box controls the way you hatch objects. The features are described as follows:
  - **Pick Points** ⟨— You can hatch the feature in Figure 24-13 using **BHATCH** and picking inside the area to be hatched. The **Pick Points** ⟨ button is highlighted as default. Press [Enter] or use the cursor and pick this button. The drawing now returns and the following prompts are displayed:

    > Select internal point: *(pick a point inside the area to be hatched)*
    > Analyzing the selected data…
    > Analyzing internal islands…
    > Select internal point: *(pick an internal point of another object or* [Enter] *if
    >     you are done selecting objects)*
    > Command:

    When you press [Enter], the **Boundary Hatch** dialog box returns. You can make adjustments to the hatch pattern, such as changing the pattern, scale, or angle. You can also preview the pattern. **Preview Hatch** is explained later. Pick the **Apply** button. **Apply** is now highlighted as the default, so you can also press the [Enter] key. The feature is automatically hatched, as shown in Figure 24-22. When you are at the Select internal point: prompt, you can type U or UNDO to undo the last selection, in case you picked the wrong area. You can also undo the hatch pattern by typing U at the **Command:** prompt after the pattern is drawn. However, you can preview the hatch before applying it to save time.

Figure 24-22.   Applying a hatch to a feature.

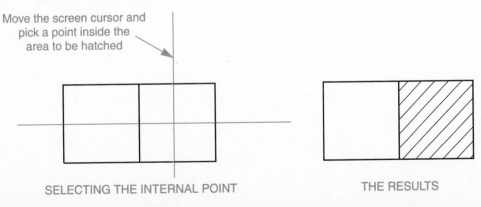

SELECTING THE INTERNAL POINT                                      THE RESULTS

- **Select <u>O</u>bjects** 〈—This button is used if you have items that you want to hatch by picking the object, rather than picking inside the object. These items can be circles, polygons, or closed polylines. This method works especially well if the object to be hatched is crossed by other objects, such as the graph lines that cross the bars in Figure 24-23. Picking a point inside the bar results in the hatch displayed in Figure 24-23A. You can pick inside each individual area of each bar, but this can be time-consuming. If the bars were drawn using a closed polyline, all you have to do is use the **Select <u>O</u>bjects** 〈 button to pick each bar, as shown in Figure 24-23B.

Figure 24-23.   A—Applying a hatch pattern to objects that cross each other using the **<u>P</u>ick Points** 〈 button. B—Applying a hatch pattern to a closed polygon using the **Select <u>O</u>bjects** 〈 button.

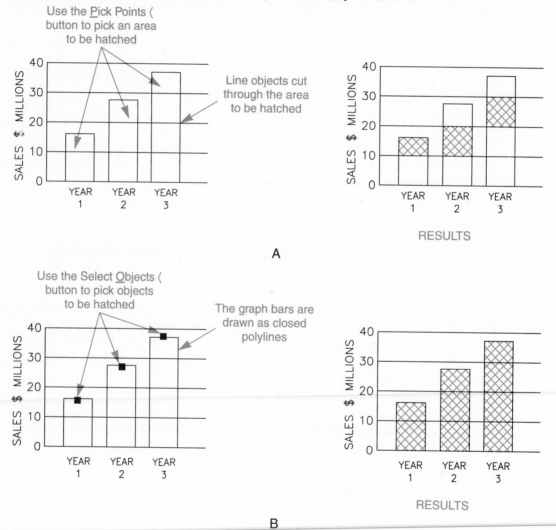

The **Select Objects** ⟨ button can also be used to pick an object inside an area to be hatched to exclude it from the hatch pattern. An example of this is the text shown inside the hatch area of Figure 24-24. When you pick the **Select Objects** ⟨ button, the following prompts appear:

    Select objects: *(pick or select an object or objects)*
    Select objects: *(pick the object or objects to be removed from the hatch)*
    Select objects: ↵

The **Boundary Hatch** dialog box returns. Preview the hatch, make any desired changes, and press [Enter] to apply the hatch.

Figure 24-24.   Using the **Select Objects** ⟨ button to exclude an object from the hatch pattern.

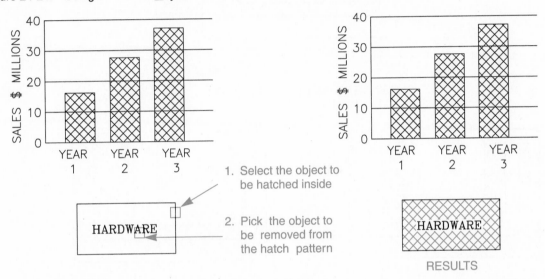

- **Remove Islands** ⟨ —An *island* is a closed area inside of a hatch area. When you use the **Pick Points** ⟨ button to hatch an internal area, islands are automatically left unhatched, as shown in Figure 24-25A. However, if you want islands to be hatched, follow these steps:
  1. Use the **Pick Points** ⟨ button and select an internal point, as shown in Figure 24-25B.
  2. When the **Boundary Hatch** dialog box returns, pick the **Remove Islands** ⟨ button. The following prompts now appear:

         Select island to remove: *(pick the islands to remove)*
         ⟨Select island to remove⟩/Undo: ↵

  The **Boundary Hatch** dialog box returns. Preview the hatch pattern, make any needed changes, and pick the **Apply** button. The results of removing an island is shown in Figure 24-25B.
- **View Selection** ⟨ —You can instruct AutoCAD to let you see the boundaries of selected objects. The **View Selections** ⟨ button is available after picking objects to be hatched. Pick this button to have the drawing displayed with the hatch boundaries highlighted. Look at the highlighted boundary and then pick the **Continue** button to return to the **Boundary Hatch** dialog box.
- **Advanced...**—Picking the **Advanced...** button accesses the **Advanced Options** dialog box, explained later in this chapter.

Figure 24-25.   A—Using the **Pick Points** ⟨ button to hatch an internal area leaves islands unhatched.
B—After picking an internal point, use the **Remove Islands** ⟨ button to pick an island. This allows the
island to be hatched.

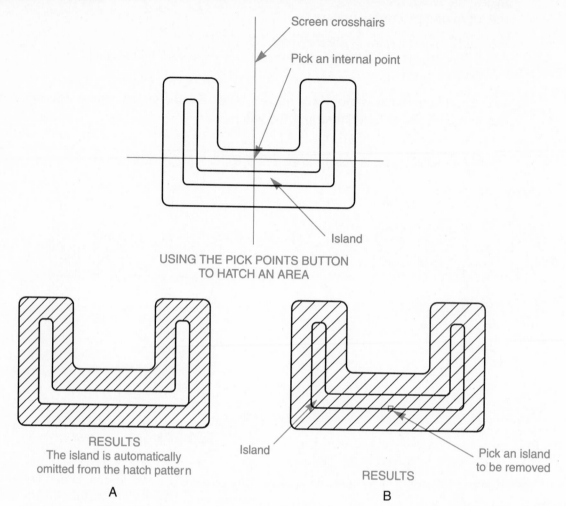

USING THE PICK POINTS BUTTON
TO HATCH AN AREA

RESULTS
The island is automatically
omitted from the hatch pattern

A

RESULTS

B

- **Preview Hatch** ⟨—Pick the **Preview Hatch** ⟨ button if you want to look at the hatch pattern before you apply it to the drawing. This allows you to see if any changes need to be made before the hatch is drawn. When using this option, AutoCAD temporarily places the hatch pattern on your drawing and displays the **Boundary Hatch Continue** dialog box. When finished with the preview, press [Enter] or pick **Continue**. The **Boundary Hatch** dialog box is displayed again. Change the hatch pattern as needed, preview the hatch again, and pick the **Apply** button to have the hatch pattern drawn.
- **Inherit Properties** ⟨—This button allows you to select a previously drawn hatch pattern and use it as the current hatch pattern settings. The prompt looks like this:

    Select hatch object: *(pick the desired hatch pattern)*

- The **Boundary Hatch** dialog box is displayed with the hatch pattern settings of the selected pattern.
- **Associative**—This check box is on by default (with an X). As discussed earlier, an associative hatch pattern is automatically updated to match any changes to the boundary area. When this box is empty, the hatch drawn is not associative.

## EXERCISE 24-3

❑ Open PRODR2.

❑ Use the **LINE** command to draw an object similar to the one shown below. The exact dimensions are up to you. Be sure each area of the object is closed.

❑ Use the **BHATCH** command to make a full section of the object, as shown on the right. Use the ANSI31 hatch pattern.

❑ Draw the bar graph shown in Figure 24-24 without text, except for HARDWARE inside the legend box. Use a closed polyline to draw the graph bars and the box around the HARDWARE legend. Use the **BHATCH Select Objects** option to select the bars for hatching. Use the same option to hatch the area inside the HARDWARE legend box without hatching through the text.

❑ Use closed polylines to draw the object at the left in Figure 24-25. Copy the object to a position directly below the original. Use the **Pick Points** option to hatch the top object, as shown in Figure 24-25A. Use the **Pick Points** button and the **Remove Islands** button to hatch the bottom object, as shown in Figure 24-25B.

❑ Preview each hatch pattern before you apply it, to be sure the results are what you expect.

❑ Enter the **BHATCH** command and pick the **Inherit Properties** ⟨ button. Pick a hatch pattern on your drawing that is different from the current hatch pattern settings. Notice that the name and settings of the selected pattern becomes current.

❑ Save the drawing as A:EX24-3.

OBJECT TO BE HATCHED          APPLIED HATCH

## Correcting errors in the boundary

The **BHATCH** command works well unless you have an error in the hatch boundary. The most common error is a gap in the boundary. This can be very small and difficult to detect. However, AutoCAD is quick to let you know by displaying the **Boundary Definition Error** alert box shown in Figure 24-26. Pick the **OK** button and then return to the drawing to find and correct the problem. Figure 24-27 shows an object where the corner does not close. The error is too small to see on the screen, but using the **ZOOM** command reveals the problem.

Another error message occurs when you pick a point outside the boundary area. When this happens, you also get the **Boundary Definition Error** alert. All you have to do is pick **OK** and select a new point that is inside the boundary you want hatched.

Figure 24-26.   A **Boundary Definition Error** alert box is displayed if problems occur in your hatching operation.

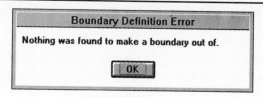

Figure 24-27.   Using the **ZOOM** command to find the source of the hatching error.

LOOK AT THE BOUNDARY ERROR    HATCH AFTER THE ERROR IS FIXED

**PROFESSIONAL TIP**

When creating an associative hatch, it is usually best to specify only one internal point per hatch block placement. Specifying more than one internal point for the same hatch pattern can produce unexpected results when you edit the hatch boundary.

## Improving boundary hatching speed using the Advanced option

In most situations, boundary hatching works with satisfactory speed. Normally the **BHATCH** command evaluates the entire drawing that is visible on the screen when establishing a boundary around the internal point that you pick. This process can take some time on a large drawing. You can improve the hatching speed, or resolve other problems by picking the **Advanced...** button in the **Boundary Hatch** dialog box. This displays the **Advanced Options** subdialog box, shown in Figure 24-28. Notice in the **Define Boundary Set** area that the **From Everything on Screen** option button is active. This evaluates everything on screen for hatching.

Figure 24-28.   The **Advanced Options** subdialog box.

Pick to define a Boundary area

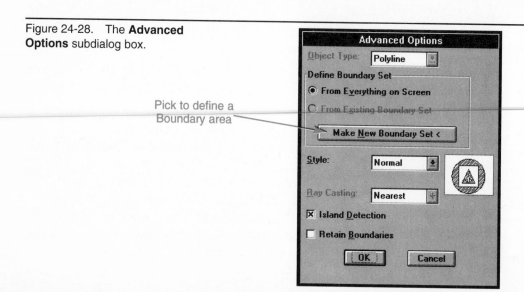

If you want to limit what AutoCAD evaluates when hatching, you can define the boundary area so the **BHATCH** command only considers a specified portion of the drawing. To do this, click the **Make New Boundary Set** ⟨ button in the **Advanced Options** subdialog box. Then, use a window to select the features of the object to be hatched. This is demonstrated in Figure 24-29 by using the following command sequence:

> (*click the* **Make New Boundary Set** ⟨ *button in the* **Advanced Options** *subdialog box*)
> Command: _bhatch Select objects
> Select objects: (*pick the first window corner*)

Notice that the window is automatic if you move the box to the right of the first pick point.

> Other corner: (*pick the second corner of the window*)
> Select objects: ↵
> Analyzing the selected data...

Figure 24-29.   The boundary set limits the area that AutoCAD evaluates during a boundary hatching operation.

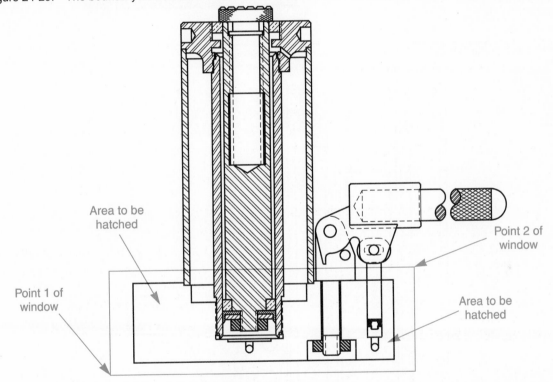

Now the **Advanced Options** subdialog box returns and the **From Existing Boundary Set** option button is active, as shown in Figure 24-30. Click the **OK** button and the **Boundary Hatch** dialog box appears. Use the **Pick Points** ⟨ button to pick the areas to be hatched. The results are shown in Figure 24-31.

You can make as many boundary sets as you wish. However, the last one made remains current until another is created. The **Retain Boundaries** check box can be selected as soon as a boundary set is made. Checking this box allows you to keep the boundary of a hatched area as a polyline, and continues to save these as polylines every time you create a boundary area. The default is no check in this box, so the hatched boundaries are not saved as polylines.

Figure 24-30.   When the **From Existing Boundary Set** option is selected, AutoCAD only evaluates objets in the boundary for the hatch.

Now the
current selection

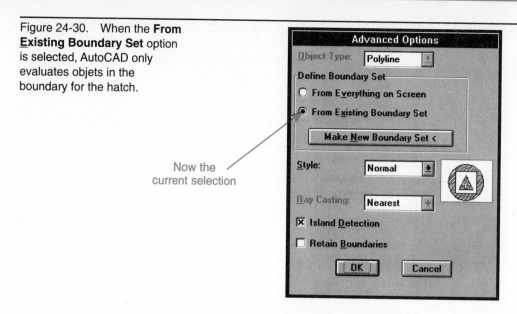

Figure 24-31.   Results of hatching the drawing in Figure 24-29 after selecting a boundary set.

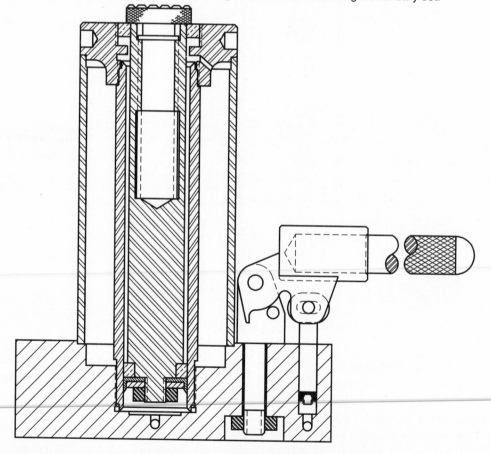

## Directing the way AutoCAD selects a boundary for hatching

When you pick an internal point for hatching an area, AutoCAD projects an imaginary line, by default, to the nearest object and then turns left in an effort to make a boundary around the object. This is known as *ray casting*. If the first ray hits an internal area or internal text, a boundary definition error is given. For example, look at the internal area in Figure 24-32.

Figure 24-32. Ray casting affects the objects selected for boundary hatching. If the first ray hits an internal area or internal text, a boundary definition error is given.

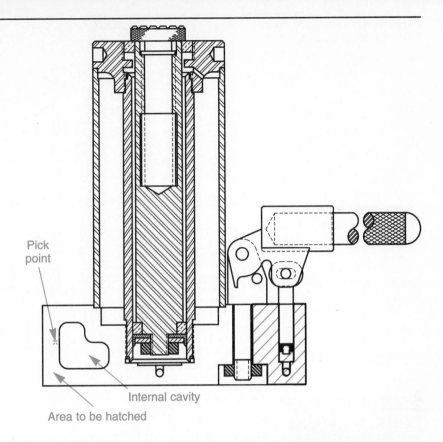

A **Boundary Definition Error** occurred because AutoCAD made a boundary around the cavity and could not continue with the desired hatch. You can control the way AutoCAD does ray casting if the **Island Detection** box is not checked. Notice in Figure 24-28 the **Ray Casting:** text box specifies **Nearest**. This is the default, but you can change it by picking the arrow to access the ray casting drop-down list. Figure 24-33 shows the ray casting options: **+X, −X, +Y,** and **−Y.** Selecting one of these determines which way the first ray is cast. For example, selecting a −X value for ray casting causes the same pick point in Figure 24-32 to make the correct boundary definition. Picking this point followed by picking inside the cavity area results in the hatching shown in Figure 24-34.

Figure 24-33. A—The **Ray Casting:** list box (shown highlighted). B—Ray casting directions as defined from the pick point.

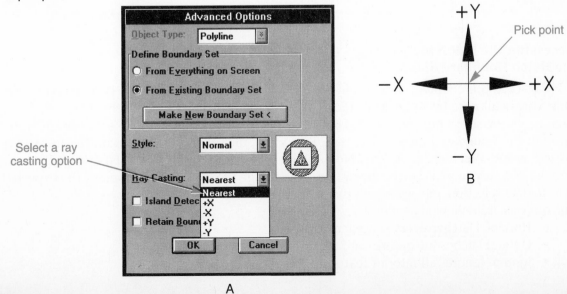

Figure 24-34.   The results of
using the appropriate ray
casting selection on the
drawing in Figure 24-29.

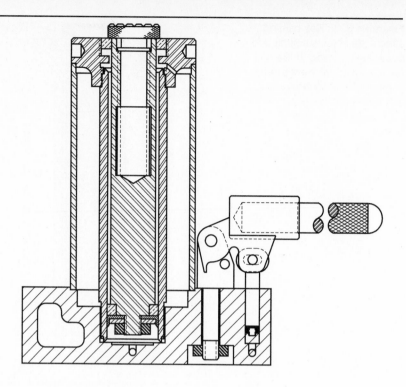

## PROFESSIONAL TIP

There are a number of techniques that can help save you time when hatching, especially with large and complex drawings. These include the following:

✓ Zoom in on the area to be hatched to make it easier for you to define the boundary. When you zoom into an area to be hatched, the hatch process is much faster because AutoCAD doesn't have to search the entire drawing to find the hatch boundaries.

✓ Preview the hatch before you apply it. This allows you to easily make last minute adjustments.

✓ Turn off layers where there are lines or text that might interfere with your ability to accurately define hatch boundaries.

✓ Create boundary sets of small areas within a complex drawing to help save time.

## Accessing the Hatch Style options through the Hatch Boundary dialog box

Earlier in this chapter, you learned about using the **Style** option in the **HATCH** command. This feature allows you to decide which features are to be hatched and which are not. Refer back to Figure 24-17 and Figure 24-18 for examples. You can create the same hatch styles through the **Boundary Hatch** dialog box. To do this, pick the **Advanced...** button to display the **Advanced Options** dialog box. Now, pick the down arrow in the **Style:** list to get the options. When you pick one of the options, the image tile to the right displays the expected results. The selection and representative image tile for each option is shown in Figure 24-35. The options are reviewed as follows:

- **Normal.** Hatches every other feature.
- **Outer.** Hatches the outermost feature only.
- **Ignore.** Ignores all interior features and hatches the entire object.

Figure 24-35.   Shown are the three options for hatch style. Notice how the image tile (shown here highlighted) changes to reflect how the hatch will appear on the drawing.

Select Normal

Image tile

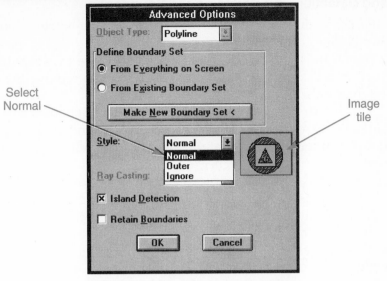

A

Select Outer

Image tile

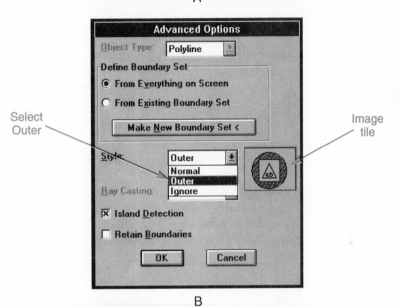

B

Select Ignore

Image tile

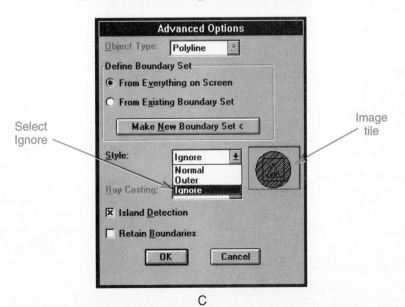

C

## Island Detection and Retaining the Boundaries

Earlier in this chapter, you were introduced to hatching around or through islands, as shown in Figure 24-25. Look at Figure 24-30, which displays the **Advance Options** dialog box. Notice that the **Island Detection** check box is active by default. This setting leaves internal objects (islands) unhatched. Pick the check box to remove the check if you want to hatch through islands.

Notice also in Figure 24-30 that the **Retain Boundaries** check box is not checked by default. When you use the **BHATCH** command and pick an internal area to be hatched, AutoCAD automatically creates a temporary boundary around the area. If the **Retain Boundaries** check box is unchecked, the temporary boundaries are automatically removed when the hatch is complete. However, if you check the **Retain Boundaries** check box, the hatch boundaries are kept when the hatch is completed.

Additionally, when the **Retain Boundaries** check box is checked, the **Object Type** list at the top of the **Advanced Options** dialog box is activated, as shown in Figure 24-36. Notice in Figure 24-36 that the **Object Type:** list has two options: **Polyline** and **Region**. **Polyline** is the default. This means that the boundary is a polyline object around the hatch area. If you select the **Region** option, then the hatch boundary is the hatched region. A *region* is a closed two-dimensional area.

Figure 24-36.   There are two object type options for the boundary. These options are only available if **Retain Boundaries** is checked.

The **Object Type:** list is available when **Retain Boundaries** is checked

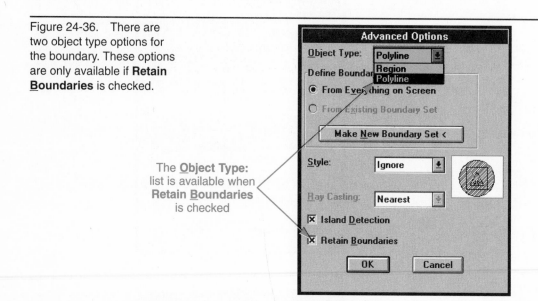

## EDITING HATCH PATTERNS

| AUG 5 |

You can edit hatch boundaries and hatch patterns with **GRIPS** and editing commands such as **ERASE, COPY, MOVE, ROTATE,** and **SCALE.** If a hatch pattern is associative, then whatever you do to the hatch boundary is automatically done to the associated hatch pattern. As explained earlier, a hatch pattern is associative if the **Associative** check box in the **Boundary Hatch** dialog box is active.

A convenient way to edit a hatch pattern is by using the **HATCHEDIT** command. You can access this command by typing HATCHEDIT at the **Command:** prompt, or by picking the **Edit Hatch** button in **Edit Polyline** flyout on the **Modify** toolbar. If the ACADFULL menu file is loaded, it can be accessed by picking **Edit Hatch...** in the **Modify** pull-down menu. The command sequence is as follows:

Command: **HATCHEDIT** ↵
Select hatch object: *(pick the hatch pattern to edit)*

When you select a hatch pattern or patterns to edit, the **Hatchedit** dialog box is displayed, Figure 24-37. The **Hatchedit** dialog box has the same features as the **Boundary Hatch** dialog box, except that only the items that control hatch pattern characteristics are available. The available features work just like they do in the **Boundary Hatch** dialog box. You can change the **Pattern Type**, **Scale**, **Angle**, **Explode** the pattern, remove the **Associative** qualities, **Inherit Properties** of an existing hatch pattern, or use the **Advanced Options** dialog box to edit the hatch pattern.

Figure 24-37. The **Hatchedit** dialog box is used to edit hatch patterns. Notice that only the options related to the hatch are available.

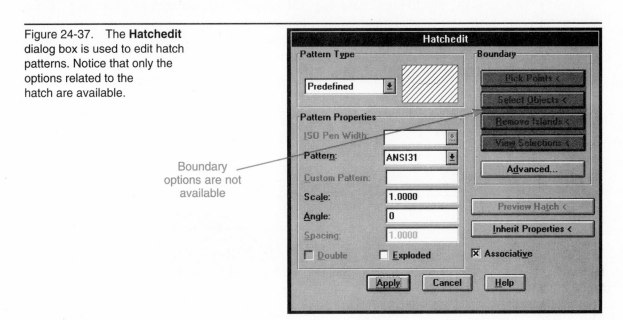

Boundary options are not available

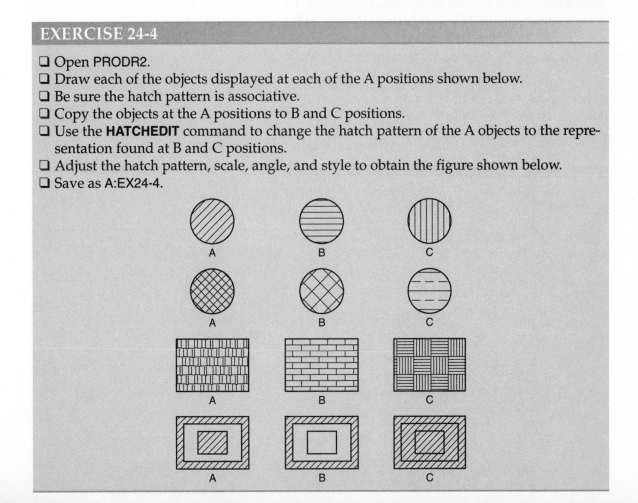

EXERCISE 24-4

❑ Open PRODR2.
❑ Draw each of the objects displayed at each of the A positions shown below.
❑ Be sure the hatch pattern is associative.
❑ Copy the objects at the A positions to B and C positions.
❑ Use the **HATCHEDIT** command to change the hatch pattern of the A objects to the representation found at B and C positions.
❑ Adjust the hatch pattern, scale, angle, and style to obtain the figure shown below.
❑ Save as A:EX24-4.

## DRAWING OBJECTS WITH SOLID FILLS

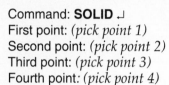

In previous chapters you have learned that polylines, polyarcs, trace segments, and doughnuts may be filled in solid when **FILL** mode is on. When **FILL** is off, these objects are drawn as outlines only. The **SOLID** command works in much the same manner except that it fills objects or shapes that are already drawn and fills areas that are simply defined by picking points. To access the **SOLID** command, type SOLID at the **Command:** prompt, or pick the **2D Solid** button from the **Rectangle** flyout on the **Draw** toolbar. You are then prompted to select points. If the object to fill solid is rectangular, pick the corners in the numbered sequence shown in Figure 24-38. The command procedure is as follows:

    Command: **SOLID** ↵
    First point: *(pick point 1)*
    Second point: *(pick point 2)*
    Third point: *(pick point 3)*
    Fourth point: *(pick point 4)*
    Third point:

Figure 24-38.   Using the **SOLID** command. **Select** the points in the order shown.

Notice that AutoCAD prompts you for another third point after the first four. This prompt allows you to fill in additional parts of the same object, if needed. The subsequent points you select fill in the object in a triangular fashion. Press [Enter] when you want to stop, or continue picking points. The following sequence draws the object shown in Figure 24-39.

    Command: **SOLID** ↵
    First point: *(pick point 1)*
    Second point: *(pick point 2)*
    Third point: *(pick point 3)*
    Fourth point: *(pick point 4 and the rectangular portion is drawn)*
    Third point: *(pick point 5)*
    Fourth point: *(press [Enter] and the triangular portion is drawn)*
    Third point: *(press [Enter] to end the command)*

Figure 24-39.   The **SOLID** command allows you to enter a second "third" point (point 5 here) after entering the fourth point.

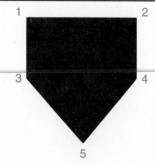

Different types of **SOLID** arrangements can be drawn by altering the numbering sequence. See Figure 24-40. Also, the **SOLID** command can be used to draw filled shapes without prior use of the **LINE**, **PLINE**, or **RECTANG** commands; simply pick the points. Consider using various object snap modes when picking the points.

Figure 24-40.    Using a different numbering sequence for the **SOLID** command will give you different results.

---

PROFESSIONAL
TIP

- It is very difficult and time-consuming to fill a circle using the **SOLID** command. Instead, use the **DONUT** command and set a 0 (zero) inside diameter. You can also use the **HATCH** command with a dense pattern, but this is not recommended.
- An irregular shape, such as a lake on a map, may be filled in solid to denote water. First, draw the lake outline—preferably with polylines and polyarcs. The lake must be a full enclosure. Then, set a dense hatch pattern and select the polyline lake outline with a single pick. If lines and arcs are used to draw the lake, a Window selection is best.
- Keep in mind that many solids and dense hatches require extensive regeneration. Therefore, create filled solids and hatching on a separate layer and keep the layer frozen until you are ready to plot the drawing. Many solids and dense hatch patterns also adversely affect plot time. Make check plots with **FILL** mode off.

---

EXERCISE 24-5

❑ Open PRODR2.
❑ Draw all object lines on layer 0-7.
❑ Create a new layer named SOLID-MAGENTA and draw all solids on this layer.
❑ Practice using the **SOLID** command by drawing the objects shown in Figure 24-38, Figure 24-39, and Figure 24-40.
❑ Save the drawing as A:EX24-5.

## CHAPTER TEST

*Write your answers in the spaces provided.*

1. Give the command and entries required to use the ANSI37 hatch pattern with double scale to hatch the inside of a given circle:

   Command:_____

   Pattern (? or name/U,style) ⟨*current*⟩:_____

   Scale for pattern ⟨1.0000⟩: _____

   Angle for pattern ⟨0⟩: _____

   Select hatch boundaries or RETURN for direct hatch options,

   Select objects:_____

   Select objects:_____

   Command:_____

2. Give the command and entries needed to draw your own hatch pattern. Set a 30° hatch angle, 1.5 spacing, and single hatch lines pattern to hatch the inside of a rectangle drawn with polylines:

   Command:_____

   Pattern (? or name/U,style) ⟨*current*⟩:_____

   Angle of crosshatch lines ⟨0⟩: _____

   Spacing between lines ⟨1.0000⟩:_____

   Double hatch area? ⟨N⟩: _____

   Select hatch boundaries or RETURN for direct hatch options,

   Select objects:_____

   Select objects:_____

   Command:_____

3. Given a square within a square, provide the command and entries used to hatch between the two squares (the outermost area). Use the default values of the ANSI31 hatch pattern:

   Command:_____

   Pattern (? or name/U,style) ⟨*current*⟩:_____

   Scale for pattern ⟨1.0000⟩: _____

   Angle for pattern ⟨0⟩: _____

   Select hatch boundaries or RETURN for direct hatch options,

   Select objects:_____

   First corner: _____

   Other corner: _____

   Select objects:_____

   Command:_____

4. Give the command and entries needed to fill in a rectangular area. Identify specific corners on the rectangle as you give the prompts. For example, specify the upper-right corner.

   Command:_____

   First point: _____

   Second point: _____

   Third point: _____

   Fourth point: _____

   Third point: _____

5. Give the command and responses to show a list and description of all the hatch patterns:

   Command:_____

   Pattern (? or name/U,style): _____

   Pattern(s) to list ⟨*⟩:_____

6. Give the command and responses used to hatch an object while providing an imaginary box around text located inside the hatch area.

   Command:_____

   Pattern (? or name/U,style) ⟨*current*⟩:_____

   Scale for pattern ⟨1.0000⟩: _____

   Angle for pattern ⟨0⟩: _____

   Select objects:_____

   Select objects:_____

   Select objects:_____

*For Questions 7 - 12, name the type of section identified in each of the following statements:*

7. Half of the object is removed; the cutting-plane line generally cuts completely through along the center plane. _____

8. Used primarily on symmetrical objects; the cutting-plane line cuts through one-quarter of the object. _____

9. The cutting-plane line is staggered through features that do not lie in a straight line. ___

   _____

10. The section is rotated in place to clarify the contour of the object. _____

11. This section is rotated and removed from the object. The location of the section is normally identified with a cutting-plane line. _____

12. Remove a small portion of the view to clarify an internal feature. _____

13. AutoCAD's standard section line symbols are called_____.

14. To use the same hatch pattern again, you must_____.

15. Give the code and results of using the three **HATCH Style** options:_____

    _____

    _____

    _____

16. In which pull-down menu is **Hatch** located?_____

17. Name the command that lets you automatically hatch an enclosed area just by picking a point inside the area. _____

18. Identify at least two ways to select a predefined hatch pattern in the **Boundary Hatch** dialog box. _____

_____

19. Explain how you set a hatch scale in the **Boundary Hatch** subdialog box. _____

_____

20. Identify two ways to change a hatch pattern (where all elements of the hatch are one unit) so that each element is an individual entity. _____

_____

21. Explain how to use an existing hatch pattern on a drawing as the current pattern for your next hatch. _____

_____

_____

22. Describe the purpose of the **Preview Hatch ⟨** button found in the **Boundary Hatch** dialog box. _____

_____

_____

23. What happens if you try to hatch an area where there is a gap in the boundary? _____

_____

_____

24. How do you limit AutoCAD hatch evaluation to a specific area of the drawing?

_____

_____

_____

25. Define ray casting. _____

_____

_____

26. Define associative hatch pattern. _____

_____

_____

_____

27. How do you change the hatch scale and angle in the **Boundary Hatch** dialog box?

_____

_____

28. Describe the fundamental difference between using the **Pick Points ⟨** and the **Select Objects ⟨** buttons in the **Boundary Hatch** dialog box. _____

_____

_____

_____

29. If you use the **Pick Points** ⟨ button inside the **Boundary Hatch** dialog box to hatch an area, how do you remove an island inside the area from the hatch pattern?_____

_____

_____

_____

_____

30. How do you use the **BHATCH** command to hatch an object with text inside without hatching the text? _____

_____

_____

_____

_____

31. How do you access the hatch style options through the **Boundary Hatch** dialog box? ___

_____

_____

_____

_____

32. Name the command that may be used to edit existing associative hatch patterns. _____

_____

_____

_____

_____

33. What do you get when you enter the command identified in Question 32? _____

_____

34. How does the item identified in Question 33 compare to what you get when you enter the **BHATCH** command? _____

_____

_____

_____

_____

35. What would you do if you want an existing hatch pattern on a drawing to take on the same characteristics as another hatch pattern on the same drawing?_____

_____

_____

_____

_____

_____

## DRAWING PROBLEMS

*Name each of the drawings* **P24-***(problem number). Follow these guidelines for all of the problems.*

1 - 8. Draw the full sections as indicated.

A. Draw the views to full size.

B. Set grid, snap, limits, and units values as needed. Use object snaps.

C. Apply dimensions accurately following ASME standards.

D. Set dimensioning variables to suit the drawing.

E. Use the **LAYER** command to set separate layers for views, dimensions, and section lines.

F. Place the following general notes 1/2" from the lower-left corner.

2. REMOVE ALL BURRS AND SHARP EDGES

1. INTERPRET PER ASME Y14.5M-1994

NOTES:

*Mechanical Drafting*    1.

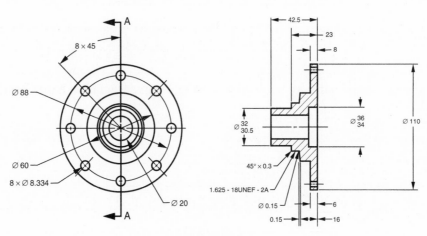

NAME: HUB
MATERIAL: CAST IRON

*Mechanical Drafting*    2.

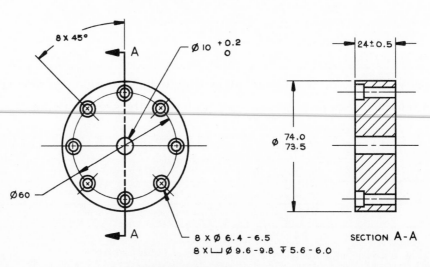

NAME: COLLAR
MATERIAL: SAE 1020

3. Draw the half section. Add the additional notes: OIL QUENCH 40-45C, CASE HARDEN .020 DEEP, and 59-60 ROCKWELL C SCALE.

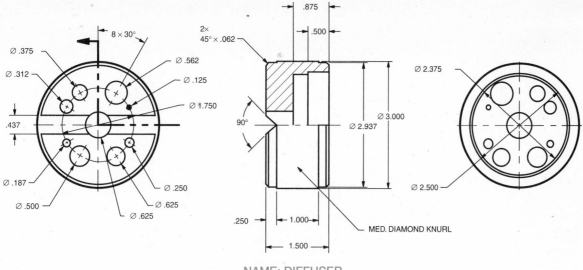

NAME: DIFFUSER
MATERIAL: AISI 1018

4 - 5. Draw the aligned sections as indicated. Add the additional notes: FINISH ALL OVER 1.63mm UNLESS OTHERWISE SPECIFIED and ALL DIMENSIONS ARE IN MILLIMETERS.

4.

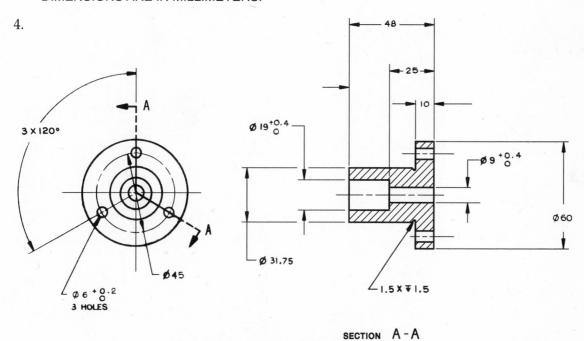

SECTION  A - A

NAME: BUSHING
MATERIAL: SAE 1030

**Mechanical Drafting**

5.

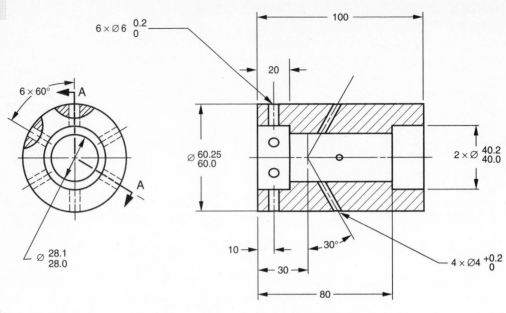

SECTION A-A

NAME: NOZZLE
MATERIAL: PHOSPHOR BRONZE

**Mechanical Drafting**

6. Draw the offset sections.

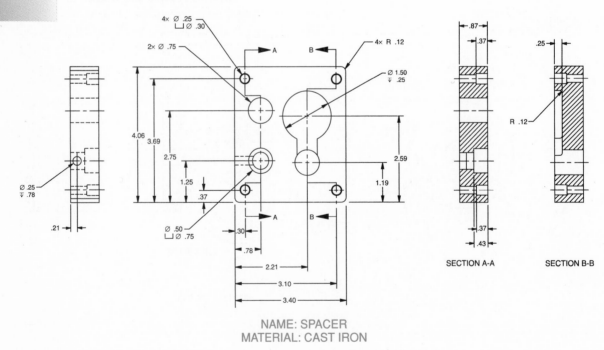

NAME: SPACER
MATERIAL: CAST IRON

7. Draw the removed section and enlarged view.

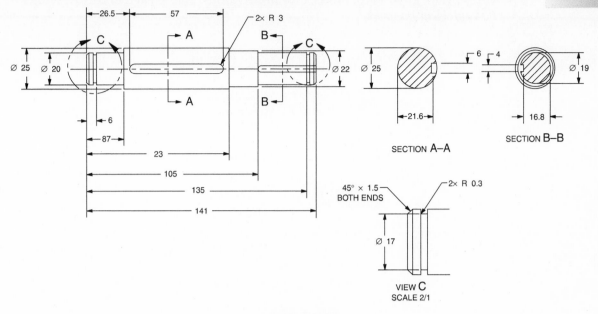

NAME: SHAFT
MATERIAL: SAE4320

8. Draw the revolved section. Use the **SOLID** command to fill in the thin section.

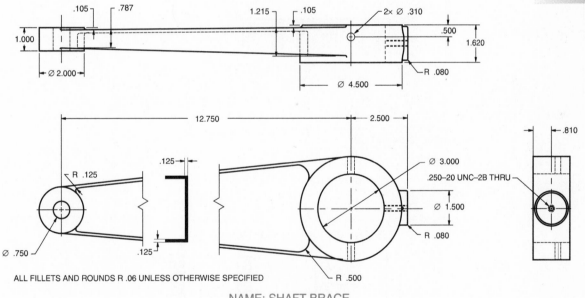

ALL FILLETS AND ROUNDS R .06 UNLESS OTHERWISE SPECIFIED

NAME: SHAFT BRACE
MATERIAL: MILD STEEL

*Graphic
Design*

9 - 16.  Use the **HATCH**, **BHATCH**, and **SOLID** commands as necessary. Establish
appropriate grid, snap, limits, and units values. Name each of the drawings
P24-*(problem number)*.

9.

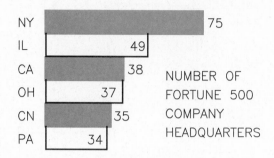

STATES WITH TOP COMPANIES

*Graphic
Design*

10.

COMPONENT LAYOUT

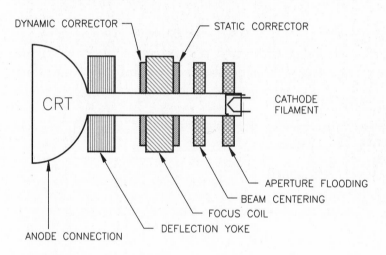

*Graphic
Design*

11.

SOLOMAN SHOE COMPANY

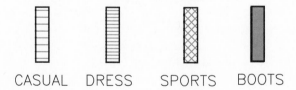

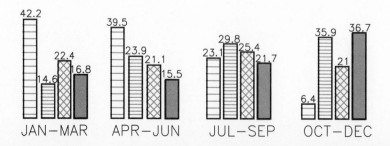

12.

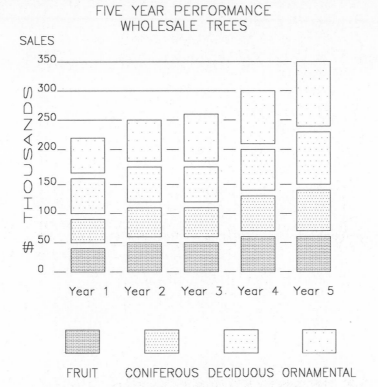

FIVE YEAR PERFORMANCE
WHOLESALE TREES

13.

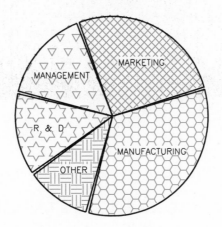

DIAL TECHNOLOGIES
EXPENSE BUDGET
**FISCAL YEAR**

*Graphic Design*    14.

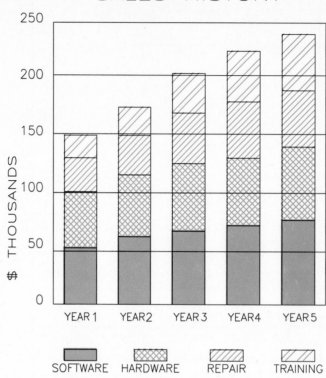

*Graphic Design*    15.

*Graphic Design*    16.

## Learning objectives

After completing this chapter, you will be able to:
- ○ Create and save blocks.
- ○ Insert blocks into a drawing.
- ○ Edit a block and update it in a drawing.
- ○ Create, or write blocks that are saved independent of the drawing.
- ○ Construct and use a symbol library of blocks.

One of the greatest benefits of AutoCAD is its ability to store symbols for future use. These symbols, or *blocks*, can be inserted into a drawing scaled and rotated. If a block is edited, drawings having the block can be updated to include the new version. The term *wblock* refers to the command **WBLOCK**, which is used to write a block description as a separate drawing file. Since any AutoCAD drawing can be inserted into another drawing, this provides *global* access (any drawing), as opposed to *local* access (current drawing). Therefore, a block can be used only in the drawing in which it was created. Both types can be used to create a symbol library, which is a related group of symbols.

When a drawing is referenced, it becomes part of the drawing on the screen, but its content is not added to the current drawing file. Any named entities, such as blocks and layers, are referred to as *dependent symbols*. When a dependent symbol is revised, a drawing that references it is automatically updated the next time it is loaded into AutoCAD.

## CREATING SYMBOLS AS BLOCKS

AUG 7

The ability to draw and store a symbol is the greatest time-saving feature of CAD. AutoCAD provides the **BLOCK** command to create a symbol and keep it with a specific drawing file. The predrawn block can be inserted as many times as needed into any drawing. Upon insertion, the block can be scaled and rotated to meet the drawing requirements.

### Constructing blocks

A block can be any shape, symbol, view, or drawing that you use more than once. Before constructing a block, review the drawing you are working on. (This is where a sketch of your drawing is convenient.) Look for shapes, components, notes, and assemblies that are used more than once. These can be drawn once and then saved as blocks.

Existing drawings can also be used as blocks. This can be done two different ways:
- Use the **BASE** command on the drawing to assign an insertion point.
- Insert the existing drawing into the drawing you are working on.

These two methods are discussed later in this chapter.

**PROFESSIONAL TIP**

Blocks that vary in size from one drawing to the next should be drawn to fit inside a one unit square. It does not matter if the object is measured in feet, inches, or millimeters. This makes it easy to scale the symbol when you later insert it in a drawing.

### Drawing the block components

Draw a block as you would any other drawing geometry. Use any AutoCAD commands you need. If you want the block to have the color and linetype of the layer it will be inserted on, be sure that you set layer 0 as current before you begin drawing the block. If you forget to do this, and draw the objects on another layer, simply use the **CHPROP** or **DDCHPROP** command to place all the objects on layer 0 before using the **BLOCK** command.

When you finish drawing the object, decide what is the best place on the symbol to use as an insertion point. When you insert the block into a drawing, the symbol is placed with its insertion point on the screen cursor. Figure 25-1 illustrates some common blocks and their insertion points (shown as dots).

Figure 25-1. Common symbols and their insertion points for placement on drawings. The insertion points are shown here as colored dots.

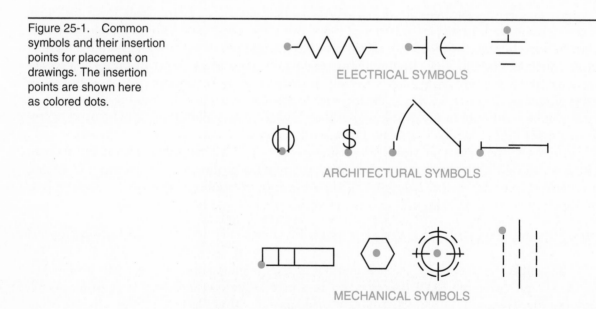

If it is important that the block maintains a specific color and linetype, regardless of the layer it is to be used on, be sure to set the color and linetype before drawing the objects. On the other hand, if it is okay for the block to assume the current color and linetype when the block is inserted into the drawing, use the **BYBLOCK** options of the **COLOR** and **LINETYPE** commands. This is achieved by picking the **Object Creation** button on the **Object Properties** toolbar, or pick **Object Creation...** in the **Data** pull-down menu. The **Object Creation Modes** dialog box displays the current settings of color, layer, linetype, text style, linetype scale, elevation, and thickness. See Figure 25-2.

Figure 25-2. The **Object Creation Modes** dialog box displays the current settings of object characteristics. You can change these settings by clicking on one of the four buttons or entering new values in the text boxes.

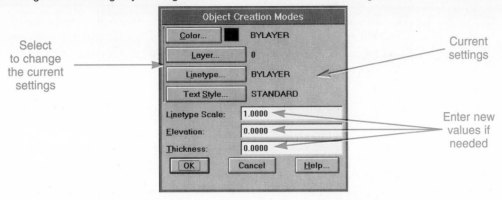

Select the **Color...** button and then pick the **BYBLOCK** button in the **Select Color** subdialog box, as shown in Figure 25-3. Pick the **OK** button and you are returned to the **Object Creation Modes** dialog box.

Next pick the **Linetype...** button in the **Object Creation Modes** dialog box to display the **Select Linetype** subdialog box. See Figure 25-4. Scroll to the top of the linetype list, pick the BYBLOCK entry, and then pick the **OK** button. This returns you to the **Object Creation Modes** dialog box.

The settings of BYBLOCK for color and linetype should now be displayed in the **Object Creation Modes** dialog box. See Figure 25-5. Now you can use any AutoCAD commands to create your block shapes. Whenever a block created with these BYBLOCK settings is inserted into a drawing, it will assume the current color and linetype, regardless of the current layer values.

Figure 25-3. The **Select Color** subdialog box is used to change the color of an object. Select a new color or enter a logical color.

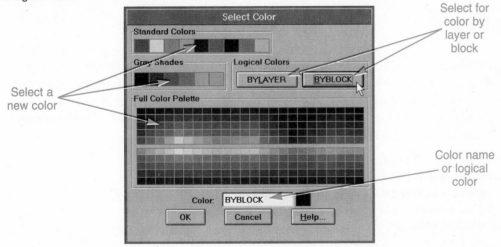

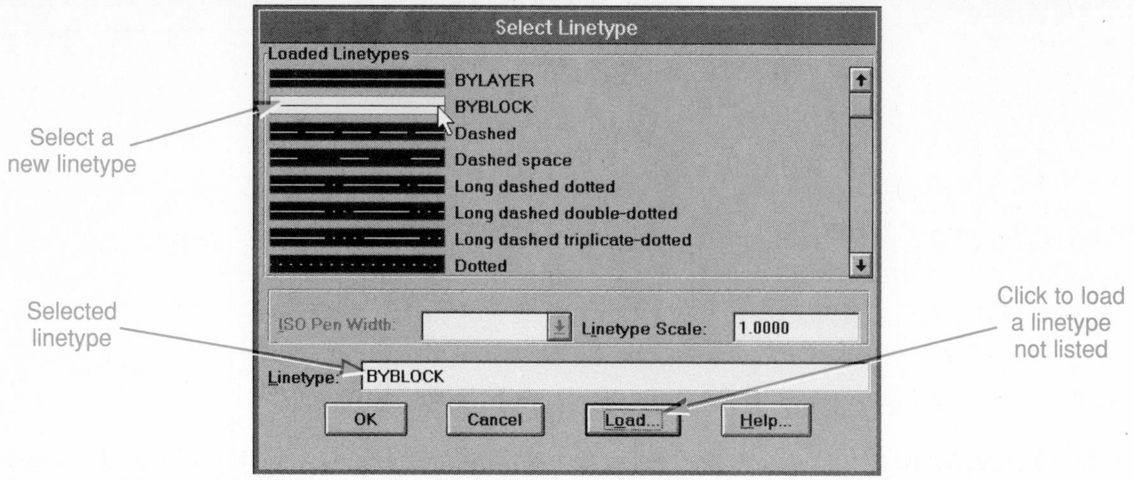

Figure 25-4.   The **Select Linetype** subdialog box is used to change an object's linetype.

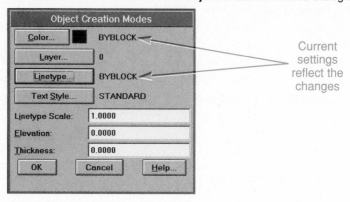

Select a
new linetype

Selected
linetype

Click to load
a linetype
not listed

Figure 25-5.   The color and linetype have been set to BYBLOCK in the **Object Creation Modes** dialog box.

Current
settings
reflect the
changes

## Creating blocks

Although you may have drawn a shape, you have not yet created a block. To save your object as a block, enter BLOCK at the **Command:** prompt, or pick the **Block** button in the **Insert Block** flyout on the **Draw** toolbar. If the ACADFULL menu file is loaded, the command can be accessed by selecting **Block** from the **Construct** pull-down menu. You are then prompted to specify a name and insertion point. Finally, you must select those objects on the screen that will compose the block. In the following example, a block symbol is created with the name PUMP.

> Command: **BLOCK** ⏎
> Block name (or ?): **PUMP** ⏎
> Insertion base point: *(pick the insertion point)*
> Select objects: *(select the entities that compose the symbol)*
> Select objects: *(press* [Enter] *to end the BLOCK command)*

The block name you provide cannot exceed 31 characters. In addition, be accurate when selecting the insertion point. Use the appropriate **OSNAP** option, or enter coordinate values. Select the entities that make up the block using any of the selection set options, such as **Window**, **Crossing**, and **Fence**.

AutoCAD informs you that the block was created by erasing the original, defining object from the screen. The block is now part of the current drawing file. Remember, a block can only be used in the drawing in which it was created. If you want the block geometry to return to screen, type OOPS at the **Command:** prompt. If the ACADFULL menu file is loaded, **Oops!** can be selected from the **Modify** pull-down menu. The defining objects reappear on screen in their original position.

To verify that the block was saved properly, select the **BLOCK** command again. At the prompt, type a question mark:

> Command: **BLOCK** ↵
> Block name (or ?): **?** ↵
> Block(s) to list ⟨*⟩:

Press [Enter] to list all of the blocks in the current drawing. The following information is then displayed in the text window:

> Defined blocks.
> PUMP

| User Blocks | External Reference | Dependent Blocks | Unnamed Blocks |
|---|---|---|---|
| 1 | 0 | 0 | 0 |

This text window display reports the name and number of blocks. When you create a block, you have actually created a *block definition*. Therefore, the first entry in the block listing is that of *defined* blocks. *User blocks* are those created by you. *External references* are drawings referenced with the **XREF** command, discussed in Chapter 26. Blocks that reside in a referenced drawing are called *dependent blocks*. *Unnamed blocks* are entities such as associative dimensions, and hatch patterns.

Step through the process of drawing a block again. Draw a one unit square and name it PLATE. See Figure 25-6. Draw the object using the **LINE** command. Select the **BLOCK** command. Name the block PLATE. Pick the insertion point at the lower-left corner. Select the object using the **Window** option. Select **BLOCK** again and use the **?** option to see that it was saved.

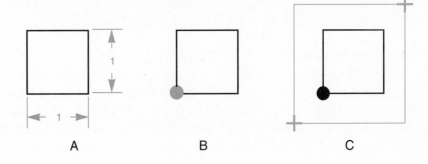

Figure 25-6.   The procedure for drawing a one unit square block. A—Draw the block. B—Pick the insertion point. C—Select the box using a window or other select option.

**EXERCISE 25-1**

❑ Load AutoCAD for Windows and open one of your prototype drawings with decimal units.
❑ Draw a circle with a one unit diameter and add centerlines on layer 0.
❑ Make a block of the circle and centerlines and name it CIRCLE.
❑ Pick the center of the circle as the insertion point.
❑ Save the drawing as A:EX25-1 and quit.

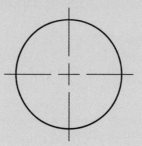

**PROFESSIONAL TIP**

Blocks can be used when creating other blocks. Suppose you design a complex part or view that will be used repeatedly. You can insert existing blocks into the view and then save the entire object as a block. This is called *nesting*; larger blocks contain smaller blocks. The larger block must be given a different name. Proper planning and knowledge of all existing blocks can speed the drawing process and creation of complex parts.

## USING BLOCKS IN A DRAWING                                    AUG 7

Once a block has been created, it is easy to insert it into a drawing. Before inserting a block, give some thought to the size the block should be and the rotation angle needed. Blocks are normally inserted on specific layers. Set the proper layer *before* inserting the block. Once a block has been inserted into a drawing it is referred to as a *block reference*.

### Inserting blocks

Blocks are placed on your drawing with the **INSERT** command. To access the **INSERT** command and its options, pick the **Insert Block** button in the **Draw** toolbar or type INSERT at the **Command:** prompt. If the ACADFULL menu file is loaded, pick **Insert 〉** in the **Draw** pull-down menu. Know beforehand where the insertion point of the block will be located in the drawing. Insert the PLATE block into your drawing as follows:

Command: **INSERT** ↵
Block name (or ?): **PLATE** ↵
Insertion point: *(pick the point)*
X scale factor ⟨1⟩ / Corner / XYZ: *(pick a point, type a number and press* [Enter], *or press* [Enter] *to accept the default)*
Y scale factor (default=X): *(type a number and press* [Enter], *or press* [Enter] *to accept the default)*
Rotation angle ⟨0⟩: *(pick a point, or type a number and press* [Enter])

The X and Y scale factors allow you to stretch or compress the block to suit your needs. This is why it is a good idea to draw blocks to fit inside a one unit square. It makes the block easy to scale because you can type the exact number of units for the X and Y dimensions. If you want the block to be three units long and two units high, respond:

> X scale factor ⟨1⟩ / Corner / XYZ: **3** ↵
> Y scale factor (default=X): **2** ↵

Notice that the Y prompt allows you to accept the X value for Y by just pressing [Enter]. The object shown in Figure 25-7 was given several different X and Y scale factors during the **INSERT** command.

Figure 25-7.   Shown is a comparison of the PLATE block inserted using different X and Y scale factors.

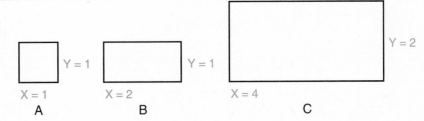

## Block insertion options

It is possible to obtain a mirror image of a block just by typing a negative value for the scale factor. For example, a –1,–1 scale factor mirrors the block to the opposite quadrant of the coordinate system and retains the original size. Figure 25-8 illustrates mirroring techniques. The insertion point is indicated with a dot.

An approximate dynamic scaling technique is achieved using the **Corner** option. You can see the block change size as you move the cursor if **DRAGMODE** is set to **Auto**. Select the **Corner** option at the X scale factor prompt as follows:

> X scale factor ⟨1⟩ / Corner / XYZ: **C** ↵
> Other corner: (*move cursor to change size and pick a point*)

A coordinate value can be typed or a point can be picked. Be sure to pick a point above and to the right of the insertion point to insert the block as drawn. Picking corner points to the left or below the insertion points will generate mirror images such as those in Figure 25-8.

Figure 25-8.   Negative and positive scale factors have different effects when inserting a block.

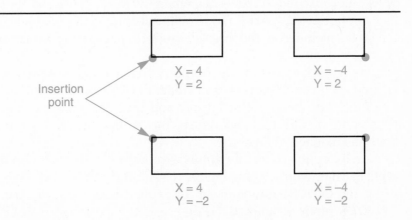

| **NOTE** | Before a block can be edited, it must be returned to its original objects with the **EXPLODE** command. Block editing and redefinition is covered later in this chapter. |

## EXERCISE 25-2

❏ Open EX25-1 if it is not currently on your screen.
❏ Draw a 1 × 1 square on layer 0 and make it a block named PLATE.
❏ Insert the PLATE block into the drawing. Enter an X scale factor of 6 and a Y scale factor of 4.
❏ Insert the CIRCLE block twice into the PLATE block as shown. The small circle is one unit in diameter and the large circle is 1.5 units in diameter.
❏ Make a block of the entire drawing and name it PLATE-1. Pick the lower-left corner as the insertion point.
❏ Insert the PLATE-1 block on your drawing and enter a scale of –1, –1. Also rotate the object 45°.
❏ Save the drawing as A:EX25-2.

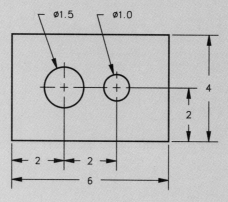

### The effects of layers on blocks

Blocks retain the property characteristics of the layer on which they were drawn. From Chapter 19, you learned that all entities in AutoCAD are created in **BYLAYER** mode by default. This means that the entity properties color and linetype are dictated by the layer on which they were created. For example, suppose the CIRCLE block was drawn on layer 1 having the color red and a dashed linetype. When inserted, the block appears red and dashed, no matter what layer it is inserted on. If different colors, linetypes, or even layers are used in a block, they also remain the same when the block is inserted on a different layer. Therefore, a block defined in **BYLAYER** mode retains its properties when inserted into another drawing. If the layers included in the inserted block do not exist in the drawing, AutoCAD automatically creates them.

For a block to assume the property characteristics of the layer it is inserted on, it must be created on layer 0. Suppose you create the CIRCLE block on layer 0 and insert it on layer 1. The block becomes part of layer 1 and thus assumes the color and linetype of that layer. Exploding the CIRCLE block returns the entities back to layer 0 and to the original color and linetype assigned to layer 0.

An exception occurs if entities within the block are drawn using an explicit color or linetype; in other words, not using the default **BYLAYER** mode. Whenever an explicit color is set using the **COLOR** command, or an explicit linetype is set using the **LINETYPE** command, **BYLAYER** mode is ignored. In this case, the exploded CIRCLE block entities would retain their original properties.

## Changing the layer, color, and linetype of a block

If you insert a block on the wrong layer, select **CHPROP** (change properties) to move it to the proper layer. Then enter the **LAyer** option of the **CHPROP** command:

```
Command: CHPROP ↵
Select objects: (pick the block to change)
Select objects: ↵
Change what property (Color/LAyer/LType/Thickness) ? LA ↵
New layer ⟨current layer⟩: (enter new layer name and press [Enter])
Change what property (Color/LAyer/LType/Thickness) ? ↵
```

The block is now changed to the proper layer. If the block was originally created on layer 0, it will assume the color and linetype of the new layer. If it was created on another layer, it will retain its original color and linetype.

To prevent a block from assuming a different color than the assigned layer color, set the **COLOR** command to BYLAYER before creating blocks:

```
Command: COLOR ↵
New object color ⟨current⟩: BYLAYER ↵
```

Now any entities or blocks that are drawn assume the color of the current layer.

The same is true of the linetype of an entity. In order to avoid problems, the linetype should be set as a function of the layer rather than using the **LINETYPE** command. Check to be sure the **LINETYPE** command is set to BYLAYER.

```
Command: LINETYPE ↵
?/Create/Load/Set: S ↵
New objects linetype (or ?) ⟨HIDDEN⟩: BYLAYER ↵
```

## INSERTING MULTIPLE COPIES OF A BLOCK

The **INSERT** and **ARRAY** features are combined in the **MINSERT** (multiple insert) command. This method of inserting and arraying not only saves time, but also disk space. To access the **MINSERT** command, type MINSERT at the **Command:** prompt, or pick the **Insert Multiple Blocks** button on the **Miscellaneous** toolbar. If the ACADFULL menu file is loaded, from the **Draw** pull-down menu select **Insert ⟩** and then **Multiple Blocks**.

An example of an application using **MINSERT** is to place an arrangement of desks on a drawing. Suppose you want to draw the layout shown in Figure 25-9. Change to architectural units and set the limits to 30',22'. Draw a rectangle 4' by 3' and save it as a block called DESK. The arrangement is to be three rows and four columns. Spacing between desks should be two feet horizontally and four feet vertically. Follow this sequence:

```
Command: MINSERT ↵
Block name (or ?): DESK ↵
   Insertion point: (pick a point)
   X scale factor ⟨1⟩/Corner/XYZ: ↵
   Y scale factor ⟨default=X⟩: ↵
   Rotation angle ⟨0⟩: ↵
Number of rows (—) ⟨1⟩: 3 ↵
Number of columns (III) ⟨1⟩: 4 ↵
Unit of cell or distance between rows (—): 7' ↵
Distance between columns (III): 6' ↵
```

The resulting arrangement is shown in Figure 25-9. The total pattern takes on the characteristics of a block, except that a **MINSERT** array cannot be exploded. If the initial block is rotated, all arrayed objects are also rotated about their insertion points.

Figure 25-9. To create an arrangement of desks using **MINSERT**, first create a block called DESK.

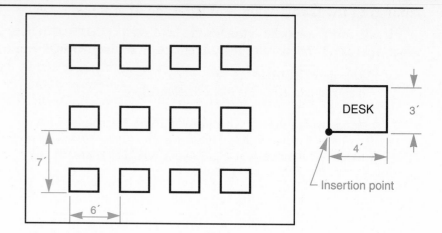

In the previous example, if you were working with different desk sizes, a one unit square may serve your purposes better than an exact size block. To create a 5′ × 3′-6″ (60″ × 42″) desk, insert a one unit square block using **INSERT** or **MINSERT**, and enter the following for the X and Y values:

X scale factor ⟨1⟩/Corner/XYZ: **60** ↵
Y scale factor ⟨default = X⟩: **42** ↵

A one unit square block can be used in this manner for a variety of objects.

## EXERCISE 25-3

❑ Load AutoCAD for Windows and start a new drawing named EX25-3. Set architectural units and 80′,60′ limits. Then, **ZOOM All**.
❑ Draw the chair shown below and save it as a block named CHAIR.
❑ Use the **MINSERT** command twice to create the theater arrangement. The sides of the chairs should touch. Each row on either side of the aisle should have 10 chairs. The spacing between rows is 4 feet. The width of the center aisle is 5 feet.
❑ Consider where you should insert the first chair to obtain the pattern.
❑ Save the drawing as A:EX25-3.

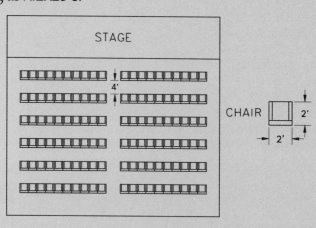

## Inserting entire drawings

The **INSERT** command can be used to insert an entire drawing into the current drawing. When one drawing is inserted into another, the inserted drawing becomes a block reference. As a block, it may be moved to a new location with a single pick. The drawing is inserted on the current layer, but does not inherit the color, linetype, or thickness properties of that layer. You can explode the inserted drawing back to its original objects if desired. Once exploded, the drawing objects revert back to their original layers.

By default, every inserted drawing has a base insertion point of 0,0,0. If necessary, you can change the insertion point using the **BASE** command. The nature of the drawing will determine the best location for the base point.

> Command: **BASE** ↵
> Base point ⟨0.0000,0.0000,0.0000⟩: *(pick a point or enter a new coordinate)*

The new base point now becomes the insertion point.

**PROFESSIONAL TIP**

It is common practice in industry to refer to other drawing prints to check features or dimensions while working on a drawing. Unfortunately, the prints that are referenced are occasionally out of date, resulting in erroneous information. In other instances, the prints are not available and must be produced. This is usually handled by a document control organization after a formal print request is issued. You can avoid such problems and delays by using the **INSERT** command. When you need to reference another drawing, simply insert it into your current drawing. When you are done checking the features or dimensions you need, simply **UNDO** the **INSERT** operation or erase the inserted drawing. Drawings may also be inserted into other drawings using the "drag and drop" capability of the Windows File Manager. See Chapter 32 of this text for a complete description of this powerful feature.

## EXERCISE 25-4

❑ Open drawing EX25-2 if it is not already on your screen.
❑ If your drawing does not have a RED layer, make one and be sure it is current.
❑ Draw a 6 × 4 unit rectangle. Insert two CIRCLE blocks into the rectangle, both one unit in diameter. Make a new block of this drawing and name it PLATE-2.
❑ Erase the screen. Set the current layer to 0. Insert both the PLATE-1 and PLATE-2 blocks.
❑ The PLATE-2 block should appear red because it was created on the red layer. PLATE-1 should be black.
❑ Make sure RED is the current layer. Insert the PLATE-1 block into your drawing. It should appear red because it was created on layer 0 and assumes the color of the layer on which it is inserted.
❑ Enter the **BASE** command. Choose an insertion point below and to the left of the objects on the screen.
❑ Save the drawing as A:EX25-4.
❑ Start a new drawing named PLATES.
❑ Insert drawing EX25-4 into your new drawing. The insertion point you pick is the one established using the **BASE** command.
❑ Pick any editing command and select a line of one of the plates. The entire drawing should highlight since the drawing is actually one large block.
❑ Save the drawing as A:EX25-4.

## Presetting block insertion variables

You can dramatically speed the insertion of blocks by presetting the scale or rotation angle. These preset options are available by typing them at the Insertion point: prompt of the **INSERT** command, or when using the **Insert** dialog box, which is discussed in the next section. The preset options not only save time, but also allow you to see the scaled size and rotation angle before you pick the insertion point. This helps you determine if the scale and rotation angle are correct.

Preset options can be used two ways. If the **S** option is entered at the Insertion point: prompt, you are asked for the scale factor, then the insertion point and rotation angle. If you enter PS, a prompt requests the scale factor for insertion display purposes only. After you pick the insertion point, the normal **INSERT** prompts are displayed. This second method is a "temporary" preset. The difference is illustrated in the following examples. The first example inserts the block PLATE at a preset scale factor of 2.

> Command: **INSERT** ↵
> Block name (or ?) ⟨*current*⟩: **PLATE** ↵
>   Insertion point: **S** ↵
>   Scale factor: **2** ↵
>   Insertion point: *(pick an insertion point)*
>   Rotation angle ⟨0⟩: ↵

The next example illustrates a temporary preset of the scale factor.

> Command: **INSERT** ↵
> Block name (or ?) ⟨*current*⟩: **PLATE** ↵
>   Insertion point: **PS** ↵
>   Scale factor: **2** ↵
>   Insertion point: *(pick an insertion point)* X scale factor ⟨1⟩ / Corner / XYZ: ↵
>   Y scale factor (default=X): ↵
>   Rotation angle ⟨0⟩: ↵

The temporary preset allows you to see the preset scale or rotation angle as you drag the block. You can also change the scale and rotation angle by entering a value at the normal prompts. Remember to use temporary preset type P, then the option you wish to preset at the Insertion point: prompt. For example, to temporarily set the rotation angle, enter PR at the Insertion point: prompt. The following list describes the functions of the preset options.

- **S.** Affects the overall scale of X, Y, and Z axes. Rotation angle is also requested.
- **X.** Affects only the X scale. Rotation angle is also requested.
- **Y.** Affects only the Y scale. Rotation angle is also requested.
- **Z.** Affects only the Z scale. Rotation angle is also requested.
- **R.** Sets the rotation angle. The normal **INSERT** scaling options are presented.

In addition, the AutoCAD system variable **INSNAME** (insert name) can be used to store the name of a block you wish to insert. For example, if you will be inserting several copies of the DESK block, you can use **INSNAME** as follows:

> Command: **INSNAME** ↵
> New value of INSNAME, or . for none ⟨""⟩: **DESK** ↵

Now when you use the **INSERT** command, the name DESK appears as the default for the block name.

> Command: **INSERT** ↵
> Block name (or ?) ⟨DESK⟩: *(press [Enter] to accept this block name, or provide another block name and press [Enter])*

As shown here, you may provide another block name at the **INSERT** prompt, such as CHAIR, regardless of the **INSNAME** setting. The name CHAIR is then stored in the **INSNAME** variable. To specify no default block name, enter a period (.) at the **INSNAME** prompt.

## USING THE **INSERT** DIALOG BOX

AUG 7

All of the functions of the **INSERT** command previously discussed can be accessed using the **DDINSERT** command. To access the **DDINSERT** command, you can type DDINSERT at the **Command:** prompt, or pick the **Insert Block** button on the **Draw** toolbar. If the ACADFULL menu file is loaded, it can be accessed by picking **Insert ⟩** and then **Block...** from the **Draw** pull-down menu. All of these methods display the **Insert** dialog box shown in Figure 25-10.

Figure 25-10. Shown is the **Insert** dialog box that is activated by the **DDINSERT** command.

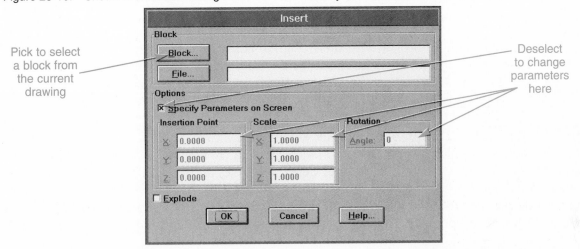

In the **Insert** dialog box, you can choose the block to insert by picking the **Block...** button. When you pick this button, a list of all blocks defined in the current drawing is displayed in the **Defined Blocks** subdialog box. See Figure 25-11. Pick the block name you wish to use and it is displayed in the **Selection:** edit box. If the list of block names is long, and the name you need is not displayed, you can use the scroll bar to view additional blocks or enter the name in the **Selection:** box, and then pick **OK**.

Notice that the presets of **Insertion point**, **Scale**, and **Rotation** in the **Insert** dialog box are initially grayed out. If you wish to preset the insertion point, scale, and rotation angle values, pick the **Specify Parameters on Screen** check box. Now the preset values are no longer grayed out, and can be changed in the dialog box.

If you wish to have the block exploded upon insertion, simply pick the **Explode** check box to turn it on. Exploding and editing blocks is discussed in the next section. When you are finished, pick **OK**. If presets were used, the block is immediately inserted. If presets were not used, the block appears on the crosshairs and the standard **INSERT** command prompts are issued.

Figure 25-11. Picking the **Block...** button in the **Insert** dialog box shows the blocks defined in the current drawing. If the list is long, you can scroll through it or enter the block name in the **Selection:** text box.

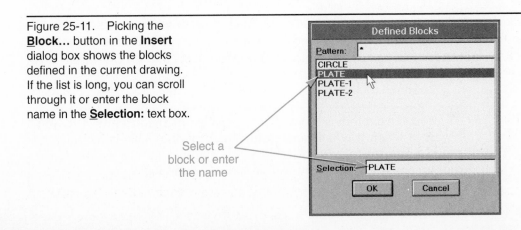

A block's rotation angle can also be based on the current UCS. Should you wish to insert a block at a specific angle based on the current, or an existing UCS, first be sure the proper UCS is restored. Then insert the block and use a zero rotation angle. If you subsequently change the UCS, the inserted blocks retain their original angle.

## EDITING BLOCKS

AUG 7

Blocks must first be broken into their original components before they can be edited. This is especially important when an entire view or drawing has been inserted. Two methods can be used to break blocks apart. The first method, asterisk insertion, is done at the time of insertion. The second, the **EXPLODE** command, can be done at any time.

### Breaking a block apart with asterisk insertions

A block is a single object. Individual objects that make up the block, such as lines, arcs, and circles, cannot be edited. The **MOVE**, **COPY**, **ROTATE**, and **SCALE** commands affect the block as a single item.

If you plan to edit the individual items upon insertion, you can insert a block exploded into its original components. To do this, type an asterisk before the block name:

```
Command: INSERT ↵
Block name (or ?): *PLATE−1 ↵
    Insertion point: (pick a point)
    Scale factor ⟨1⟩: ↵
    Rotation angle ⟨0⟩: ↵
```

The inserted geometry is now not part of a block. It consists of individual objects, which can be edited.

### Exploding the block

The **EXPLODE** command is used to break apart any existing block, polyline, or dimension. To access the **EXPLODE** command, type EXPLODE at the **Command:** prompt, or select the **Explode** button on the **Modify** toolbar. If the ACADFULL menu file is loaded, the command can be accessed by picking **Explode** in the **Modify** pull-down menu.

```
Command: EXPLODE ↵
Select objects: (pick the block)
Select objects: ↵
```

When the block is exploded, the component objects are quickly redrawn. The exploded block is now composed of objects that can be changed individually. To see if **EXPLODE** worked properly, select any object formerly part of the block. Only that entity should highlight. If so, the block was exploded properly.

**NOTE**

You can explode a block that was scaled using different X, Y, and Z values when it was inserted into the drawing. This is technically called a *non-uniformly* scaled block. Previous versions of AutoCAD did not allow exploding non-uniformly scaled blocks.

## Redefining existing blocks

A situation can arise where you discover that a block must be edited. This is an easy process, even if you have placed the block on a drawing many times. To redefine an existing block, follow this procedure:

1. Insert the block to be redefined anywhere on screen.
2. Explode the block you just inserted using the **EXPLODE** command.
3. Edit the block as needed.
4. Recreate the block using the **BLOCK** command.
5. Give the block the same name it had before. Answer Yes to redefine the block.
6. Give the block the same insertion point as the original.
7. All insertions of the block are updated when the **BLOCK** command is complete.

A common mistake is to forget to use the **EXPLODE** command. When you try to create the block again with the same name, the following error message is displayed and the command is aborted:

> Block ⟨name⟩ references itself
> *Invalid*

This means that you are trying to recreate a block that already exists. Enter the **EXPLODE** command and try again.

This concept of a block *referencing itself* may be a little difficult to understand at first, so let's take a closer look at how AutoCAD works with blocks.

A block can be composed of any AutoCAD objects, including *other* blocks. When using the **BLOCK** command to incorporate an existing block into the new block, AutoCAD must make a list of all the objects that compose the new block. This means that AutoCAD must refer to any existing block definitions that are selected to be part of the new block. But if you select an instance (reference) of the block being redefined as a component object for the new definition, a problem occurs. You are trying to redefine a block name using a previous version of the block with the same name. In other words, the new block refers to a block of the same name, or *references itself*.

For example, use a block called BOX, that is composed of four line objects. The block should be changed so that it contains a small circle in the lower left corner. If the original block BOX is exploded, all that is left is the four line objects. After drawing the required circle, the block command is activated and the block named BOX can be redefined by selecting the four lines and the circle as the component objects. Redefining a block destroys the old definition and creates a new one. See Figure 25-12A.

Alternately, if you do not explode the block, but still draw the circle and try to redefine the block, the objects selected to define the revised block BOX would now be a block reference of the block BOX and a circle. The old definition of BOX has not been destroyed, but a new definition has been attempted. Thus AutoCAD is trying to define the block BOX by using an instance of the block BOX. This is referred to as a *circular reference*, and is what is meant by a block referencing itself. See Figure 25-12B.

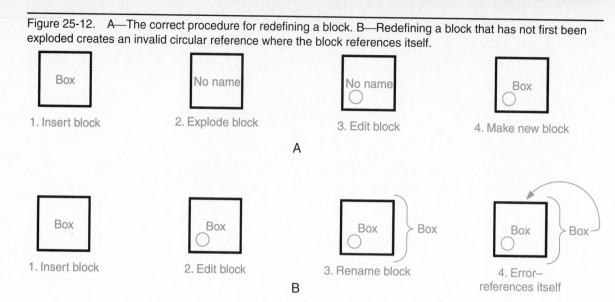

Figure 25-12. A—The correct procedure for redefining a block. B—Redefining a block that has not first been exploded creates an invalid circular reference where the block references itself.

## Creating a block from a drawing file

You can create a block from any existing drawing. This allows you to avoid redrawing the object as a block, thus saving time. Remember, if something has already been drawn, try to use it as a block rather than redrawing it. In this case, use the **INSERT** command in the following manner to define a block named BOLT from an existing drawing file named FASTENER.

Command: **INSERT** ↵
Block name (or ?): **BOLT=FASTENER** ↵
    Insertion point: (press the [Esc] key)

The drawing is not inserted on screen because the command is canceled. However, a block named BOLT is added to the drawing file and can be used like any other block.

---

### EXERCISE 25-5

❑ Open EX25-3.
❑ Insert a block named CHAIR anywhere on the drawing.
❑ Explode the chair you just inserted.
❑ Add a feature to the chair, such as a headrest. Keep it simple.
❑ Make a block named CHAIR of the revised chair.
❑ Answer Yes to redefine the block, and pick the same insertion point as the original chair.
❑ When the **BLOCK** command is completed, all chairs should be updated to reflect the changes.
❑ Save the drawing as A:EX25-5 and quit.

---

## MAKING PERMANENT GLOBAL BLOCKS                    AUG 7

Symbols created with the **BLOCK** command can only be used in the drawing in which they were made. However, you may want to use blocks on many different drawings without having to redraw them. The **WBLOCK** command allows you to create a drawing file (.DWG extension) out of a block. This drawing can then be inserted as a block in any drawing.

There are several ways to use the **WBLOCK** command. To illustrate the first, open drawing EX25-1. Convert your CIRCLE block to a permanent symbol by making it a separate drawing file using the following procedure:

Command: **WBLOCK** ↵

The **Create Drawing File** dialog box appears, displaying a listing of all drawing files in the current directory. Move the pointer to the **File Name:** text box and type the name of the wblock, HOLE, and press [Enter]. Each time you select the **WBLOCK** command, the **Create Drawing File** dialog box appears, unless the **FILEDIA** system variable is set to the value of zero (0).

> Block name: **CIRCLE** ↵

The above sequence wrote a new block, HOLE, to a drawing file on disk. The prompt asked for the name of an existing block. Type CIRCLE to convert it into a separate drawing file named HOLE. In the **File** pull-down menu, select **Management** and then **Utilities...**, or type FILES at the **Command:** prompt. The **File Utilities** dialog box appears; pick **List Files...** to see if HOLE.DWG is now on your disk.

When another drawing is inserted into the current drawing it acts like a block. It is a single object and cannot be edited unless broken into its original components. To assign the new drawing name to the same name as the block, type an equal symbol (=) for the block name as follows:

> Command: **WBLOCK** ↵
> File name: **CIRCLE** ↵
> Block name: **=** ↵

When you enter WBLOCK, the **Create Drawing File** dialog box appears. Pick **Type it...** to obtain the previous prompts.

## Making a new wblock

Suppose you want to create a separate file from a shape you just drew, but have not made a block yet. Enter the **WBLOCK** command, but do not supply a block name. Press [Enter] instead. Then select the insertion point and the objects to be included in the new drawing.

> Command: **WBLOCK** ↵
> File name: **DESK** ↵
> Block Name: ↵
> Insertion base point: *(pick a point)*
> Select objects: *(select objects to be in the new drawing)*
> Select objects: ↵

This sequence is exactly like that of the **BLOCK** command. Remember that this drawing is saved to disk—not to the drawing file. Be sure to specify a path before the file name, if needed. The previous drawing file would be saved in the current hard disk directory because no path was given. If you want to save the drawing file on a floppy disk in the A: drive, enter the filename as A:DESK. A drawing file that is to be saved into the BLOCKS directory on the C: hard drive would be named C:\BLOCKS\DESK.

## Preparing a drawing for use as a symbol

An entire drawing can also be stored as a wblock. Type an asterisk (*) for the block name.

> Command: **WBLOCK** ↵
> File name: *(type a filename and press* [Enter]*)*
> Block name: * ↵

In this case, the whole drawing is saved to disk as if you used the **SAVE** command. The difference is that all unused blocks are deleted from the drawing. If the drawing contains any unused blocks, this method reduces the size of a drawing considerably.

**PROFESSIONAL TIP**

The **WBLOCK**-asterisk method is a good technique to clean your drawing of unused named objects to reduce the file size. Use this routine when you have completed a drawing and know that the unused blocks, layers, styles, and objects are no longer needed.

### Inserting a separate drawing file with the Select Drawing File dialog box

When you use the **DDINSERT** command, you have the option to insert a block or a wblock. Clicking the **File...** button activates the **Select Drawing File** dialog box. See Figure 25-10. You can now scroll through listings in any directory, or on another drive, and pick the file name you need.

If you type INSERT at the **Command:** prompt, you can access the **Select Drawing File** dialog box by entering a tilde (~) at the Block name (or ?): prompt as follows:

```
Command: INSERT ↵
Block name (or ?): ~ ↵
```

You can use the tilde character whenever any AutoCAD command prompt requests a file name. One of several dialog boxes is then displayed, regardless of the **FILEDIA** system variable setting.

---

**EXERCISE 25-6**

❑ Open drawing EX25-2.
❑ Create a drawing file called PLATE-1 using the existing block of the same name.
❑ Select **Management** ⟩ and then **Utilities...** from the **File** pull-down menu. Now, click the **List File...** button to get a listing of your .DWG files. Be sure PLATE-1.DWG is listed.
❑ Start a new drawing called EX25-6.
❑ Insert the PLATE-1 drawing into the current drawing. Any drawing can be inserted into the current drawing.
❑ Save the drawing as A:EX25-6 and quit.

---

### Revising an inserted drawing

One of the basic principles of drawing, design, and engineering is that things will inevitably change. You may find that you have to revise a drawing file that has been used in other drawings. If this happens, you can quickly update any drawing in which the revised drawing is used. For example, if the drawing file named PUMP was used several times in a drawing, simply use the **INSERT** command, and place an equal sign (=) after the block name in the following manner to update all the PUMP symbols:

```
Command: INSERT ↵
Block name (or ?): PUMP= ↵
Block PUMP redefined
Regenerating drawing.
   Insertion point: (press [Esc])
```

All of the PUMP symbols are automatically updated, and by canceling the command, no new symbols are added to the drawing.

Suppose you had inserted a drawing file named FASTENER into your current drawing, but gave it the block name of SCREW. Now you have decided to revise the FASTENER drawing. The SCREW block can be updated using the **INSERT** command as follows:

Command: **INSERT** ↵
Block name (or ?): **SCREW=FASTENER** ↵
Block SCREW redefined
Regenerating drawing.
    Insertion point: *(press* [Esc]*)*

**PROFESSIONAL TIP**

   If you work on projects in which inserted drawings may be revised, it is more productive to use reference drawings instead of inserted drawing files. Reference drawings are used with the **XREF** command, discussed in Chapter 26. All referenced drawings are automatically updated when a drawing file that contains the xrefed material is loaded into AutoCAD.

## CREATING A SYMBOL LIBRARY

   As you become proficient with AutoCAD, begin to construct symbol libraries. A *symbol library* is a collection of related shapes, views, and symbols that are used repeatedly. You may eventually want to incorporate symbols into your screen and tablet menus. This is discussed in detail in *AutoCAD and its Applications—Advanced, Release 13 for Windows*. First, you need to know where symbols (blocks and drawing files) are stored and how they can be inserted into different drawings.

### Blocks vs. separate drawing files

   As discussed earlier, the principal difference between the **BLOCK** command and the **WBLOCK** is that a block is saved with the drawing in which it is created and can only be used in that drawing. The **WBLOCK** command saves a separate individual drawing file that can be used in any drawing. This means that the block. See Figure 25-13. A complete drawing file occupies considerably more disk space than a block.

Figure 25-13.   Blocks can only be used in the drawing where they were created. Drawing files can be inserted into any drawing.

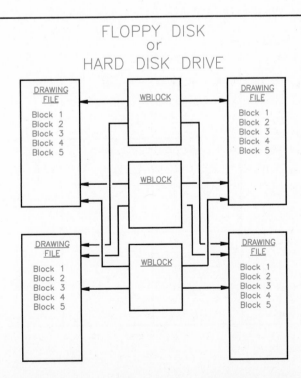

If you decide to use blocks, each person in the office or class must have a copy of the drawing that contains the blocks. This is often done by creating the blocks in a prototype drawing. If drawing files are used, each student or employee must have access to the files.

### Using floppy diskettes

Floppy diskettes are good for temporarily storing backup copies of drawing and data files. They also allow you to transport files from one workstation to another in the absence of a network or modem. However, avoid making floppies the primary means for storage of symbols, especially if you have sufficient room on the hard disk drive, optical drive, or network server drives. Inserting and removing floppy diskettes from a disk drive is tedious and time-consuming because it takes more time for the computer to access the floppy disks. If you must adopt this method, follow these guidelines.

- Create all symbols as separate drawing files.
- Assign one person to initially create the symbols for each specialty.
- Follow class or company symbol standards.
- Create a symbol library listing using a printer or plotter. Include a picture of the symbol, its insertion point, necessary information, and where it is located. A sample is shown in Figure 25-14. Provide all persons who use the symbols with a copy of the listing.
- Save one group of symbols per diskette. For example, individual disks may contain the following types of symbols:
  - ✓ Electronic
  - ✓ Electrical
  - ✓ Piping
  - ✓ Mechanical
  - ✓ Structural
  - ✓ Architectural
  - ✓ Landscaping
  - ✓ Mapping

Figure 25-14. Piping flow diagram blocks used for prototype drawings in the symbol library listing. The colored dot indicates the insertion point, and is not part of the block.

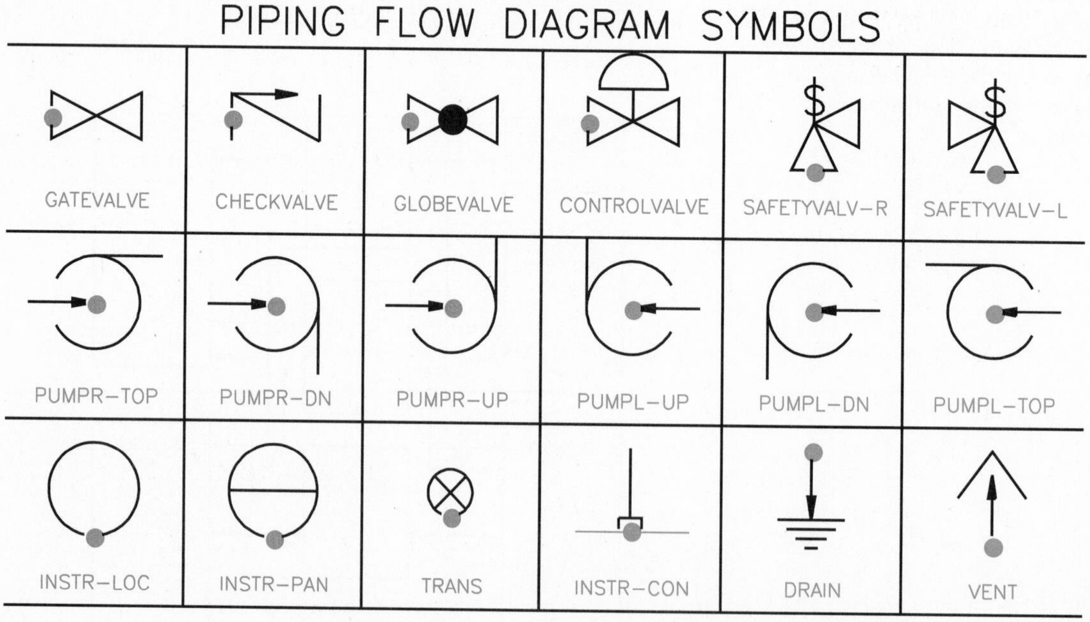

### PIPING FLOW DIAGRAM SYMBOLS

| | | | | | |
|---|---|---|---|---|---|
| GATEVALVE | CHECKVALVE | GLOBEVALVE | CONTROLVALVE | SAFETYVALV−R | SAFETYVALV−L |
| PUMPR−TOP | PUMPR−DN | PUMPR−UP | PUMPL−UP | PUMPL−DN | PUMPL−TOP |
| INSTR−LOC | INSTR−PAN | TRANS | INSTR−CON | DRAIN | VENT |

- Label floppy disks two ways:
  - ✓ Use the DOS LABEL command to assign a name to each floppy disk in the following manner:

        C:\\> **LABEL A:STRUCTURAL** ⏎

    This gives the disk in the A: drive the name of STRUCTURAL. Eleven characters can be used for a label. Use the DOS VOL command to find out the label of a disk.

        C:\\> **VOL A:** ⏎

    DOS responds:

        Volume in drive A is STRUCTURAL
        Volume Serial Number is 2309-OCFA

    A label can also be given to a disk when it is formatted.

        C:\\> **FORMAT A:/V** ⏎

    The /V (volume) switch activates the DOS LABEL command.
  - ✓ Use stick-on floppy disk labels on all disks. Write on the label before attaching it to the disk. Use the same name as the volume label.
- Copy symbol disks and provide a copy for each workstation in the class or office.
- Keep backup copies of all symbol disks in a secure place.
- When symbols are revised, update all copies of diskettes containing the edited symbols.
- Inform all users of any changes to symbols.

Floppy disk formatting and volume labeling may also be easily performed using the Windows File Manager. See Chapter 32 for a description of this capability.

## Using the hard disk drive

The hard disk drive is the best place to store a symbol library. It is easily accessible, quick, and more convenient to use than floppy disks. Symbols should be created with the **WBLOCK** command, as they were with floppy disks. The drawing files can be saved in the current directory (usually \R13) or a subdirectory. If drawing files are stored in the \R13 directory, they are easier to enter the first time. There is less typing at the **INSERT** command. However, storing symbols in separate subdirectories keeps the \R13 directory uncluttered and easy to manage.

A symbol named PUMP is retrieved from the \R13 directory with the **INSERT** command as follows:

        Command: **INSERT** ⏎
        Block name (or ?) ⟨*current*⟩: **PUMP** ⏎

If the same symbol is stored in a subdirectory of \R13 called BLK, it is retrieved the first time as follows:

        Command: **INSERT** ⏎
        Block name (or ?) ⟨*current*⟩: **R13\BLK\PUMP** ⏎

After its initial insertion, the drawing file is saved as a block definition in the current drawing, and can be accessed by just entering its filename.

Drawing files are saved on the hard disk drive using the same systematic approach as with floppy disks. These additional guidelines also apply:

- All workstations in the class or office should have directories and subdirectories with the same names.
- One person should be assigned to update and copy symbol libraries to all workstation hard drives.

- Drawing files should be copied onto each workstation's hard drive from a master disk or network server.
- The master disks and backup disks of the symbol libraries should be kept in separate locations.

## Creating prototype symbol drawings

In addition to obtaining a printed copy, you can display all the symbols on the screen. This technique requires that you create symbols in a prototype drawing. The symbols (blocks) are then inserted into a special area of the drawing outside of the drawing limits, then labeled. They can be copied from this library and placed in the drawing. An example of this arrangement was shown in Figure 25-14. The following steps should be used to create this type of symbol library:

- Draw each symbol on layer 0 and save as a block.
- Increase the limits beyond the needed drawing area to provide space for the symbols. The amount of space required is determined by the number of symbols stored in the library.
- Draw a grid in which to place the symbols (if desired). Insert symbols inside the grid boxes.
- Make a layer named INSERT. Assign a unique color to the layer.
- Use the **DONUT** or **POINT** commands to place a dot or an X at the insertion point of each symbol.
- Label each symbol on the INSERT layer.
- To use a block, copy it from the library to the drawing rather than using the **INSERT** command.

## Using prototype symbol libraries

The symbol library can be used in several different ways. Symbols can be copied directly from the library to the drawing as they are needed. You might also insert one copy of each symbol into the drawing limits when you begin. Then zoom the drawing to display only the limits. This hides the symbol library and also enlarges the view of your work. Use **COPY** to place symbols in your drawing. This method has limitations because you cannot scale or rotate immediately with **COPY**, as you can with **INSERT**.

Turn **Quick Text** mode on so that symbol labels are not recalculated when a regeneration takes place. This saves much time. Descriptive symbol names, like those in Figure 25-13, can be replaced with numbers or letters.

The on-screen library also serves as a reference. You can check the shape, block name, or insertion point of a symbol. When using the on-screen library for this method only, create the library on layers not used in the drawing. The symbol library layers are normally frozen to speed regeneration time. To check a symbol, thaw the library layers.

**PROFESSIONAL TIP**

Create one or more views of your symbol library using the **VIEW** command, especially if you use them for reference purposes. It is faster to display a view than it is to use the **ZOOM** or **PAN** commands.

## Copying a symbol library into a new drawing

A symbol library of blocks that is part of a prototype drawing can be copied into a new drawing file. The incoming blocks are not displayed, only included in the drawing file. It enables you to use blocks created on one drawing without also having to use the drawing. The process is simple. If the drawing PIPEFLOW on the disk in the A: drive contains the needed blocks, enter the following:

> Command: **INSERT** ↵
> Block name (or ?) ⟨*current*⟩: **A:PIPEFLOW** ↵
>   Insertion point: (*press* [Esc] *to cancel*)

The blocks are now included with your drawing. Check this by selecting **BLOCK** and the ? option.

These methods of placing symbol libraries on prototype drawings are just several possibilities. As you learn more about AutoCAD, other avenues will open. After reading the menu customizing chapters in *AutoCAD and its Applications—Advanced, Release 13 for Windows*, you will see additional possibilities. Regardless of the method chosen, it is important that you maintain consistency and adhere to standards.

## Create a symbol library listing

After deciding which method of using symbols is best for you, create a symbol library listing. Distribute it to all persons who will be using the symbols. The list can be a pen or printer plot of the symbol libraries on each prototype drawing. These lists should be updated when revisions are made to symbols. A copy on 8.5″ × 11″ paper should be given to all AutoCAD users. A larger copy should be placed on a wall or bulletin board. Examples of symbol library lists used in engineering offices are shown in Figure 25-15 and Figure 25-16.

Figure 25-15.   Shown are instrumentation loop diagram symbols. (Willamette Industries, Inc.)

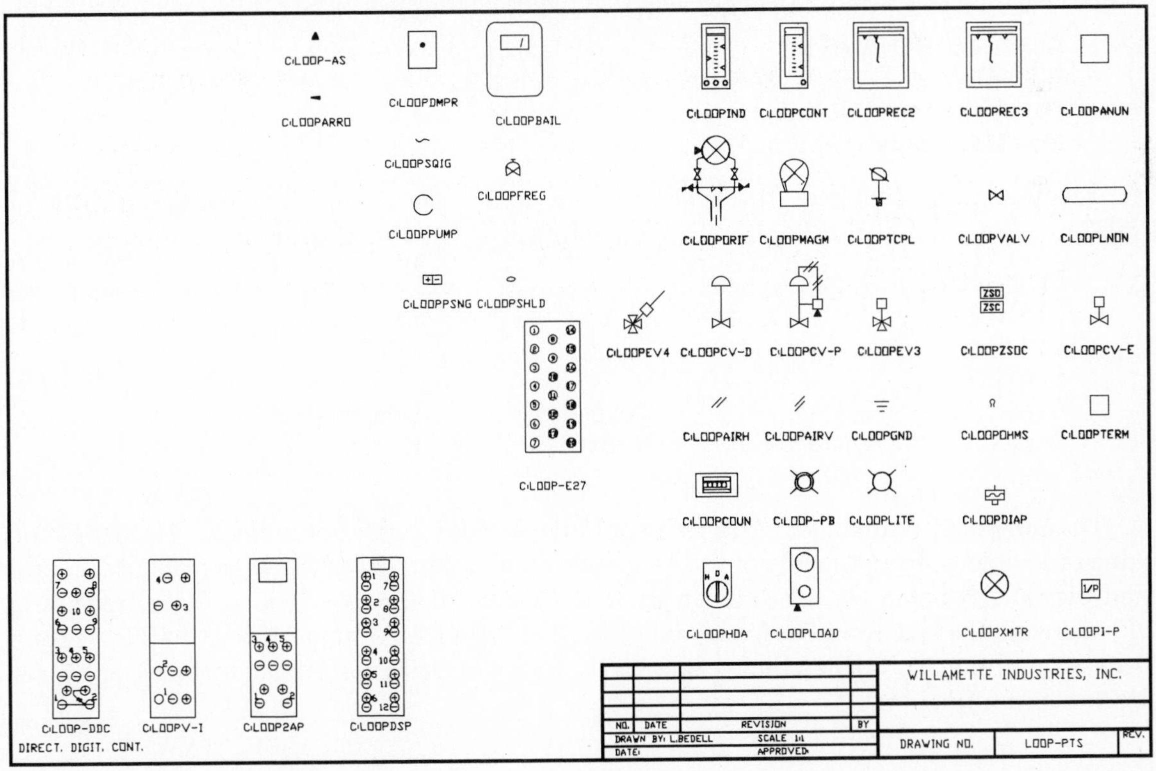

Figure 25-16.   Shown are isometric piping symbols. (Willamette Industries, Inc.)

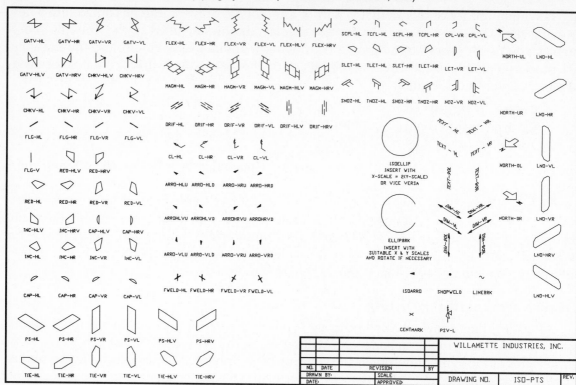

## RENAMING BLOCKS

Block names can be changed with the **RENAME** command. To change the name of the CIRCLE block to HOLE, enter the **RENAME** command as follows:

> Command: **RENAME** ↵
> Block/Dimstyle/LAyer/LType/Style/Ucs/VIew/VPort: **B** ↵
> Old block name: **CIRCLE** ↵
> New block name: **HOLE** ↵

The block name is changed. To check that the name was changed, select the **BLOCK** or **INSERT** command. Use the **?** option to get a listing. The list will appear similar to this:

> Defined blocks.
> PLATE
> HOLE
> PLATE-1

| User Blocks | External Reference | Dependent Blocks | Unnamed Blocks |
|---|---|---|---|
| 3 | 0 | 0 | 0 |

The **RENAME** command in AutoCAD only works for blocks, not wblocks. To change the name of a wblock, from the **File** pull-down menu select **Management ⟩**, select **Utilities...**, and then pick the **Rename file...** button in the **File Utilities** dialog box. You can also rename a wblock using the Windows File Manager or the DOS RENAME command. See Chapter 17 for a discussion of the **File Utilities** dialog box, or Chapter 32, *Using the Windows File Manager*, for additional information.

## Renaming blocks using a dialog box

Blocks may also be renamed from a dialog box. As with the **RENAME** command, you may rename dimension styles, layers, linetypes, text styles, UCS's, named views, and saved viewport configurations. Enter DDRENAME at the **Command:** prompt to activate the **Rename** dialog box shown in Figure 25-17. To rename the CIRCLE block for example, select **Block** from the **Named Objects** list at the left of the dialog box. A list of block names defined in the current drawing appears in the **Items** list at the right. Click CIRCLE and it becomes highlighted in the list. CIRCLE then appears in the **Old Name:** text box. Enter the new block name, HOLE, in the **Rename To:** text box. Click the **Rename To:** button and the new block name HOLE appears in the **Items** list. Click **OK** to exit the **Rename** dialog box.

Figure 25-17.    The **Rename** dialog box allows you to change the name of a block.

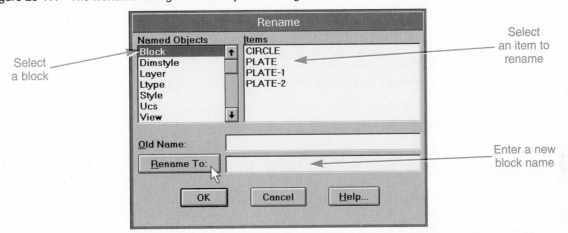

Select a block

Select an item to rename

Enter a new block name

---

**NOTE**     Since AutoCAD does not permit the renaming of layer 0 to a different layer name or the renaming of the CONTINUOUS linetype, these two named entities do not appear in the **Rename** dialog box's **Items** list.

---

## DELETING NAMED ENTITIES

A block is a *named entity*, or *object*. Other such named objects are dimension styles (dimstyles), layers, linetypes, shapes, text styles, applications registered for ADS or AutoLISP, and multiline styles. In many drawing sessions, not all of the named entities in a drawing are used. For example, your prototype drawing may contain several layers, text styles, and blocks that are not used. Since these entities occupy drawing file space, it is good practice to delete, or *purge* the unused objects using the **PURGE** command. You can use **PURGE** in the following manner to delete a block named LINESPEC:

    Command: **PURGE** ↵
    Purge unused Blocks/Dimstyles/LAyers/LTypes/SHapes/STyles/Mlinestyles/All: **B** ↵
    Purge block LINESPEC? ⟨N⟩ **Y** ↵

The **PURGE** command lists all unused blocks individually and gives you the option to answer yes or no. Use the **PURGE** command in the same manner to delete any of the unused entities listed above. The **All** option can be used to delete all unused named objects. This is a good procedure to clean up a drawing after it is completed.

## CHAPTER TEST

*Write your answers in the spaces provided.*

1.  Define "symbol library." _____

    _____

    _____

2.  Which option of the **COLOR** and **LINETYPE** commands should be set, and what dialog box should they be set in, if you want the block to assume the current color and linetype when it is inserted into a drawing? _____

    _____

3.  When should blocks be drawn to fit inside a one unit square? _____

    _____

4.  A block name can be _____ characters long.

5.  To obtain a listing of all blocks in the current drawing, you must _____

    _____

6.  Describe block nesting. _____

    _____

7.  How do you preset block insertion variables using a dialog box? _____

    _____

    _____

8.  Describe the effect of entering negative scale factors when inserting a block.

    _____

9.  Why would the **Corner** option be used when scaling a block during insertion?

    _____

    _____

10. What properties do blocks drawn on a layer other than 0 assume when inserted?

    _____

11. Why would you draw blocks on layer 0? _____

    _____

12. What are the limitations of the **MINSERT** command? _____

    _____

13. What is the purpose of the **BASE** command? _____

    _____

14. What is the purpose of the **INSNAME** system variable? _____

    _____

15. Explain why you would choose to use preset options when inserting a block.

    _____

16. Explain the difference between **PS** and **S** as preset options. _____

    _____

    _____

17. Name the two methods that break a block into its individual entities for editing._____
    _____

18. Suppose you have found that a block was incorrectly drawn. Unfortunately, you have already inserted the block 30 times. How can you edit all of the blocks quickly?
    _____
    _____

19. What is the primary difference between **BLOCK** and **WBLOCK**?_____
    _____
    _____
    _____

20. The **WBLOCK** command asks for block name. What would you enter at the Block name: prompt to make a drawing file out of an existing block? _____

21. What would you enter at the Block name: prompt to remove all unused blocks from a drawing?_____
    _____

22. Suppose you revise a drawing named DESK. However, the DESK drawing had been inserted several times into another drawing as wblocks named DESK2. How would you update the DESK2 insertions? _____
    _____
    _____

23. Why is it best to put symbol libraries on the hard disk drive rather than floppy disks?
    _____
    _____

24. What would you enter at the DOS C:⟩ prompt to name a diskette located in the B: drive CADCLASS? _____

25. How do you request the disk-naming procedure at the DOS prompt when formatting a disk in the A: drive?_____

26. What advantage is offered by having a symbol library of blocks in a prototype drawing, rather than using wblocks? _____
    _____

27. Give the command and entries needed to insert all of the blocks from a drawing named A:STRUCT-1 into the current drawing.
    Command:_____
    Block name (or ?) ⟨*current*⟩: _____
    Insertion point:_____

28. What is the purpose of the **PURGE** command, and what conditions govern its use?
    _____
    _____

## DRAWING PROBLEMS

*Electrical Drafting*

1. Choose one of the diagrams shown and draw it using blocks. Use the following guidelines:
   A. Start a new drawing using an A-size or B-size prototype.
   B. Create a block for each different shape in the drawing.
   C. Arrows should be drawn as a block.
   D. Use a thick polyline for the flow lines.
   E. Label the drawing as shown.
   F. Place a border and title block on the drawing.
   G. Save the drawing as A:P25-1.

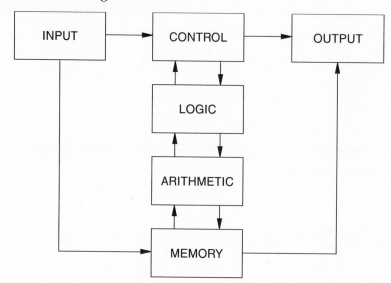

A. COMPUTER FLOW DIAGRAM

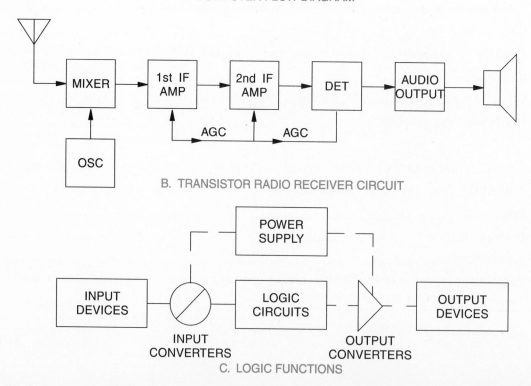

B. TRANSISTOR RADIO RECEIVER CIRCUIT

C. LOGIC FUNCTIONS

2. Create a symbol library for one of the drafting disciplines listed below on a prototype drawing. Then, after checking with your instructor, draw one problem using the library. You can use the prototype drawings in two ways:

*General*

   - Start a new drawing using a standard prototype drawing named PROTO. Name the new drawing NEWDWG.
   - Insert the prototype into the current drawing (perhaps a different size drawing) and cancel at the Insertion point: prompt.

   Specialty areas you might create symbols for include:
   - Mechanical (machine features, fasteners, tolerance symbols).
   - Architectural (doors, windows, fixtures).
   - Structural (steel shapes, bolts, standard footings).
   - Industrial piping (fittings, valves).
   - Piping Flow Diagrams (tanks, valves, pumps).
   - Electrical Schematic (resistors, capacitors, switches).
   - Electrical One-Line (transformers, switches).
   - Electronics (IC chips, test points, components).
   - Logic Diagrams (and gates, nand gates, buffers).
   - Mapping, Civil (survey markers, piping).
   - Geometric Tolerancing (feature control frames).

   Save the drawing as A:P25-2, or choose an appropriate name for the prototype, such as ARCH-PRO or ELEC-PRO.

3. Display the prototype drawing symbol library on the screen and make a print with your printer. If you are not familiar with your printer, read Chapter 12 and consult your printer's reference manuals for specific information on its operation. Put the printed copy of the symbol library in your notebook as a reference.

*General*

4. Open Problem 4 from Chapter 15 (P15-4). The sketch for this drawing is shown below. Erase all copies of the symbols that were made, leaving the original intact. This includes steel column symbols and the bay and column line tags. Then follow these steps:

*Architecture*

   A. Make a block of each of the remaining steel column and tag symbols.

   B. Use the **MINSERT** or **ARRAY** commands to place the symbols in the drawing.

   C. Dimension the drawing as shown in the problem drawing in Chapter 15. Set the proper dimension variables for this type of drawing. Dimensions should be given in feet and inches. Show zero inches as follows: 20'-0".

   D. Save the drawing as A:P25-4.

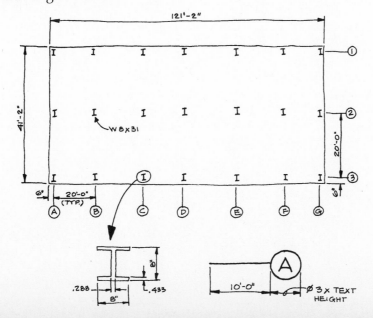

5. Open Problem 5 from Chapter 15 (P15-5). The sketch for this drawing is shown below. Erase all of the desk workstations except one. Then follow these directions:

A. Create a block of the remaining workstation.

B. Insert the block in the drawing using the **MINSERT** command.

C. Dimension one of the workstations as shown in the original problem.

D. Save the drawing as A:P25-5.

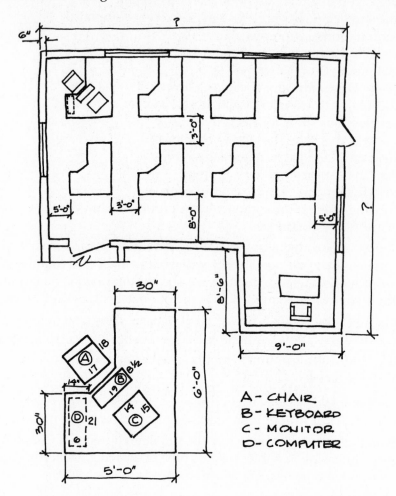

A – CHAIR
B – KEYBOARD
C – MONITOR
D – COMPUTER

*Problems 6 - 10 are presented as engineering sketches. They are not-to-scale, schematic drawings made using symbols. The symbols should first be drawn as blocks and then saved in a symbol library. Use one of the methods discussed in this chapter. Place a border and title block on each of the drawings.*

6.  This is a one-line diagram of an electrical substation. Set limits for an A-size or B-size sheet. Save the drawing as A:P25-6.

*Electrical Drafting*

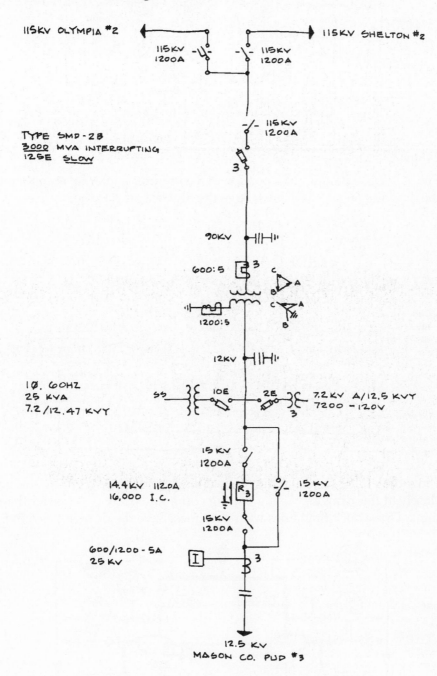

*Electrical Drafting*

7. This is an electrical schematic of a light flasher circuit. Set limits for a B-size sheet. Align components when possible. Eliminate as many bends in the circuit lines as possible. See Appendix H for standard electronic symbols. Save the drawing as A:P25-7.

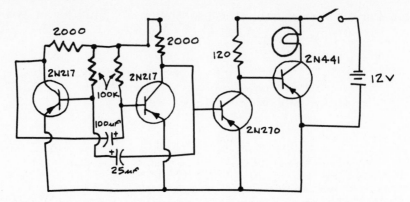

*Electrical Drafting*

8. This is a logic diagram of a portion of a computer's internal components. Create the drawing on a C-size sheet. Save the drawing as A:P25-8.

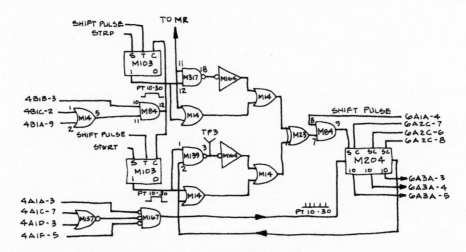

*Piping*

9. Draw the piping flow diagram of a cooling water system on a B-size sheet. Look closely at this drawing. Using editing commands, it may be easier than you think. Draw thick flow lines with polylines. Save the drawing as A:P25-9.

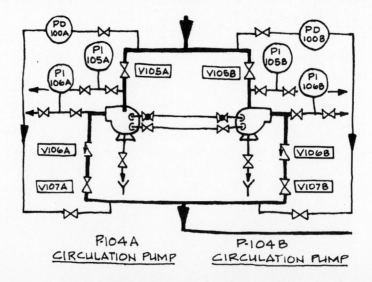

10. This piping flow diagram is part of an industrial effluent treatment system. Draw it on a C-size sheet. Eliminate as many bends in the flow lines as possible. Place arrowheads at all flow line intersections and bends. Flow lines should not run through valves or equipment. Use polylines for thick flow lines. Save the drawing as A:P25-10.

*Piping*

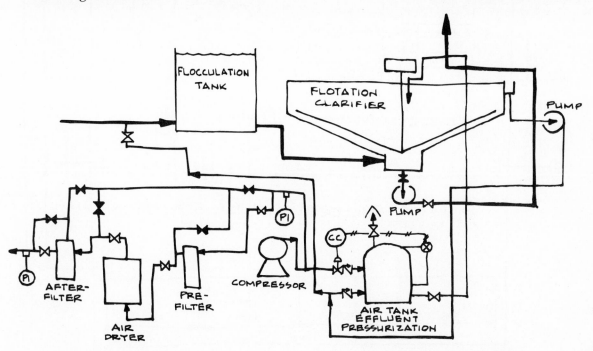

11. The general arrangement of a basement floor plan for a new building is shown at the top of the next page. The engineer has shown one example of each type of equipment. Use the following instructions to complete the drawing:

*Architecture*

A. Drawing should fit on C-size sheet.

B. All text should appear 1/8" high, except bay and column line tags, which are 3/16" high. The text balloons for bay and column lines should be twice the diameter of the text height.

C. The column and bay line steel symbols represent wide-flange structural shapes, and should be 8" wide × 12" high.

D. The PUMP and CHILLER installations (except PUMP #5) should be located per the dimensions given for PUMP #1 and CHILLER #1. Use the dimensions shown on the sketch for other PUMP and CHILLER units.

E. TANK #2 and PUMP #5 (P-5) should be located exactly as TANK #1 and P-4, and should be the same respective sizes.

F. Tanks T-3, T-4, T-5, and T-6 are all the same size, and are aligned 12' from column line A.

G. Plan this drawing carefully and create as many blocks or wblocks as possible to increase your productivity. Dimension the drawing completely as shown, and provide location dimensions for all equipment not shown in the engineer's sketch.

H. Save the drawing as A:P25-11.

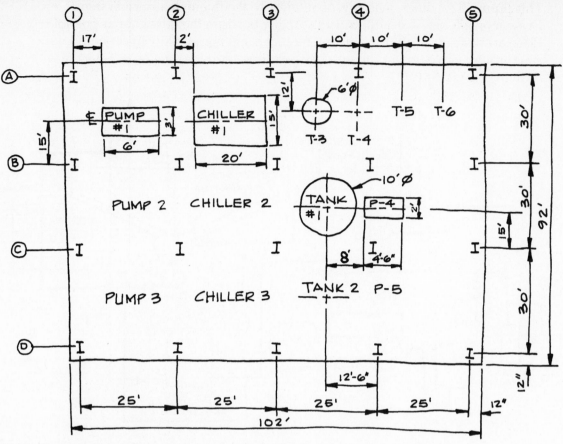

12. The drawing in Problem 25-11 (P25-11) must be revised. The engineer has provided you with a sketch of the necessary revisions. It is up to you to alter the drawing as quickly and efficiently as possible. The dimensions shown on the sketch *do not* need to be added to the drawing; they are provided for construction purposes only. Revise P25-11 so that all CHILLERS, and TANKS #3, #4, #5, and #6 reflect the changes. Save your drawing as A:P25-12.

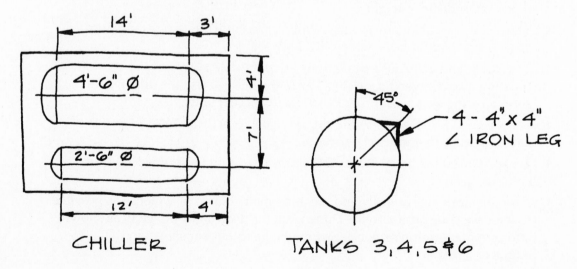

CHILLER                         TANKS 3,4,5 & 6

13. This drawing is an instrumentation loop diagram of software functions for the drying section of a paper machine. Each large box in the drawing represents a specific function or algorithm in the computer program. The smaller blocks on the left and right indicate different signals that are received and sent (input and output) by each function. Lay out the drawing exactly as shown on a B-size or C-size sheet. Use your own title block. Save the drawing as A:P25-13.

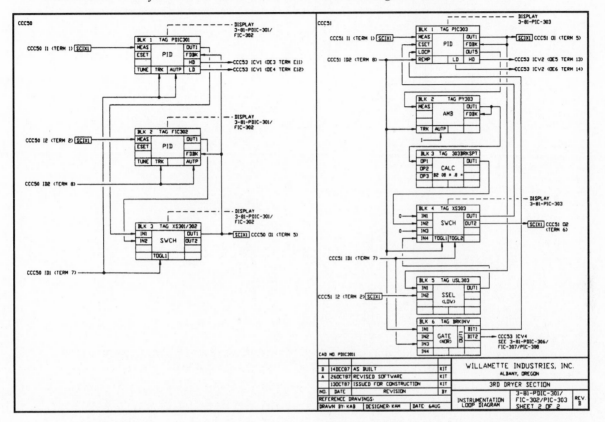

14 - 15. Make multiview drawings from the following drawings. Add any sectioning necessary to completely describe the object. Completely dimension the drawing and apply geometric dimensioning and tolerancing symbols as shown on the sketch. Refer to Appendix H for the proper size and format of geometric dimensioning and tolerancing symbols. Remember that engineering sketches may contain out-of-date symbols and notations. Always check the appropriate standards for correct use of symbols and dimensioning techniques. Be sure to include the following general notes:

INTERPRET DIMENSIONS AND TOLERANCES PER ASME Y14.5M-1994.
REMOVE ALL BURRS AND SHARP EDGES.

Save the drawings as A:P25-14 and A:P25-15, respectively.

Mechanical
Drafting
14.

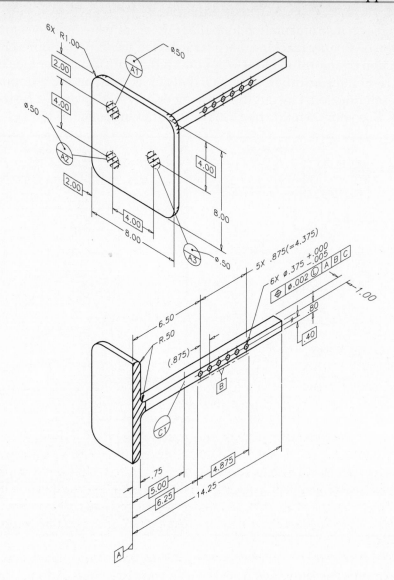

Mechanical
Drafting
15.

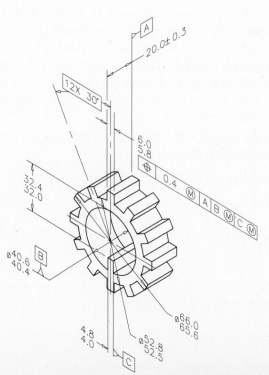

## Chapter 26

AutoCAD R13

# External References and Multiview Layouts

## Learning objectives

After completing this chapter, you will be able to:
- ◯ Define the function of external references.
- ◯ Reference an existing drawing into the current drawing using the **XREF** command.
- ◯ Overlay an existing drawing onto the current drawing.
- ◯ Change the path of external references.
- ◯ Bind dependent symbols to a drawing.
- ◯ Construct multiple viewports in a paper space drawing.
- ◯ Construct a multiview drawing using external references of different scales.
- ◯ Control the display of layers using the **VPLAYER** command.

As you create multiple objects in a drawing by copying, the drawing file grows in size. This is because AutoCAD must maintain a complete description of the geometry of each one of the copied objects. On the other hand, when you use a block to represent repetitive objects, AutoCAD must maintain only one description of the block's geometry. All of the other instances of the block are recorded as X, Y, Z coordinates, and AutoCAD refers to the original *block definition* to obtain the block's data. This decreases the size of a drawing considerably if many blocks are used.

AutoCAD enables you to go even further in your efforts to control the size of drawing files with the use of the **XREF** command. This command allows you to incorporate, or "reference," one or more existing drawings into the current drawing without adding them to the contents of the current file. This procedure is excellent for applications in which existing base drawings, or complex symbols and details must be shared by several users, or used often. This chapter explores the use of the **XREF** command, and illustrates how it can be used to create a paper space multiview architectural layout with a variety of scales.

## USING REFERENCE DRAWINGS                           AUG 7

Any machine or electrical appliance contains a variety of subassemblies and components. These components are assembled to create the final product. The final product occupies a greater amount of space and weighs more than any of the individual parts. In the same way, a drawing composed of a variety of blocks and wblocks grows much larger and occupies more disk space than the individual symbols and components. Imagine creating a design model of an automobile by projecting numerous holograms (laser-generated 3D pictures) onto a viewing area. The design occupies perceived space, yet weighs nothing. When the lasers are turned off, the image of the car vanishes. Yet, the individual components that were projected still exist in computer storage and can be displayed again if needed. That is the principle behind the AutoCAD reference drawing concept.

AutoCAD allows you to *reference* existing drawings to the master drawing you are currently working on. When you externally reference (xref) a drawing, its geometry is not added to the current drawing (as are inserted drawing files), but it is displayed on the screen. This makes for much smaller files. It also allows several people in a class or office to reference the same drawing file, and always be assured that any revisions to the reference drawing (master) will be displayed in any drawing where it is used. To reference drawings, select one of the **Xref** options in the **External Reference** ⟩ cascading submenu in the **File** pull-down menu, pick one of the **Xref** buttons on the **External Reference** toolbar, or type XREF at the **Command:** prompt.

Reference drawings can be used in two basic forms:
- Constructing a drawing using predrawn symbols or details (similar to the use of blocks).
- Laying out a drawing to be plotted that is composed of multiple views or details, using existing drawings. This technique is discussed in detail later in the chapter.

### Benefits of external references

An important benefit of using xrefs is that whenever the master drawing is loaded into AutoCAD, the latest version of the xrefs are displayed. If the xrefs are modified between the time you revise the master and the time you plot it, all of the revisions are automatically reflected. This is because AutoCAD reloads each xref whenever the master drawing is loaded.

Other significant aspects of xrefs is that they can be nested, and you can use as many xrefs as needed for the drawing. This means that a detail referenced to the master drawing can be composed of smaller details that are themselves xrefs. You can also use **OSNAP** options to attach entities or other xrefs to the referenced drawing.

### Attaching an external reference to the current drawing

Using the **XREF** command is similar to the **INSERT** command. Suppose, for example, that you want to add a standard arrangement of a pump and valves to a piping flow diagram. The pump and valve arrangement is named PUMP-VLV, and is located in the \R13\PIPE subdirectory. To use the **Attach** option, pick the **Attach** button on the **External Reference** toolbar, or select the **Attach** option of the **XREF** command as follows:

```
Command: XREF ↵
?/Bind/Detach/Path/Reload/Overlay/⟨Attach⟩: ↵
```

The **Select file to attach** dialog box is now displayed. If the **Attach** button on the **External Reference** toolbar is selected, then this dialog box appears immediately. Now, select the file to attach from the **File Name:** list, and pick the **OK** button.

```
Attach Xref PUMP-VLV: \R13\PIPE\PUMP-VLV.DWG
PUMP-VLV loaded.
Insertion point: (pick an insertion point)
 X scale factor ⟨1⟩ / Corner / XYZ: ↵
 Y scale factor (default=X): ↵
 Rotation angle ⟨0⟩: ↵
```

As you can see, the only outward differences between the **XREF** command and the **INSERT** command are the options of the command. Both of the commands function in a similar manner, yet it is the internal workings of the commands that are different. Remember that xrefs are not added to the drawing file, thereby reducing the size of the master drawing.

### Overlaying the current drawing with an external reference

As you have learned in the previous discussion, you can attach an xref to the current, or master drawing. Then, each time you open the master drawing in AutoCAD, the xref is also loaded, and appears on the screen. This attachment remains permanent until you remove it by picking the **Detach** button on the **External Reference** toolbar, or selecting the **Detach** option of the **XREF** command.

There are many situations in which you may just want to see what your drawing looks like with another drawing overlaid on it. In manual drafting terms, this is called *overlay drafting*, and involves the use of a pin bar, and registered holes punched along the top of all the drawings used in the overlay.

The **Overlay** option of the **XREF** command temporarily lays an existing drawing over the one currently on your screen. Because this is a temporary operation, the overlay xref does not appear on your screen the next time you open the master drawing. This is an important distinction between the **Attach** and **Overlay** options of **XREF**. Use the following to remember the functions of each option.

| Option | Activity |
|---|---|
| **Attach** | xref drawing is loaded each time master drawing is opened. |
| **Overlay** | xref drawing is loaded only when this command option is used. |

## Clipping an external reference

The **XREFCLIP** command combines several functions into one powerful procedure. It enables you to construct a paper space viewport, attach an external reference, and zoom to a specific portion of the drawing. This command is accessed by picking the **Clip** button in the **External Reference** toolbar, or in the **File** pull-down menu by picking **External Reference 〉** and then **Clip**. The following **Command:** prompt entry illustrates the use of the **XREFCLIP** command.

        Command: **XREFCLIP** ⏎
        Initializing…
        Enable paper space? 〈Y〉: ⏎

If you are currently in paper space, this prompt does not appear. If you are in model space and answer Yes to this prompt, the **TILEMODE** variable is set to 0 (off), and all layers and viewports are turned off temporarily.

        Entering Paper space. Use MVIEW to insert Model space viewports.
        Regenerating drawing.
        Xref name: **\R13\ARCH\FOOTING** ⏎
        Clip onto what layer? *(enter a layer name that does not exist)*
        First corner of clip box: *(pick a corner of the clip box)*
        Other corner: *(pick the opposite corner of the clip box)*

The next prompts establish a scale for the drawing inside the new paper space viewport. As you will see in the upcoming tutorial in this chapter, it is important that you plan the drawing and layout early. For example, if the plotted scale of this footing detail is to be 3/4″ = 1′-0″, the scale factor is 16. The plotted drawing is 16 times smaller than the footing. Use that information as follows:

        Enter the ratio of paper space units to model space units…
        Number of paper space units 〈1.0〉 **16** ⏎
        Number of model space units 〈1.0〉 ⏎

The existing layers and viewports are redisplayed and you can accurately position the new viewport containing the clipped reference drawing.

        Insertion point for clip: *(pick an insertion point)*

The screen display shown in Figure 26-1 now shows the original viewport created with **XREFCLIP** and the new one constructed with **XREF Attach**.

Figure 26-1. The **XREFCLIP** command allows you to construct a viewport with a clipped drawing.

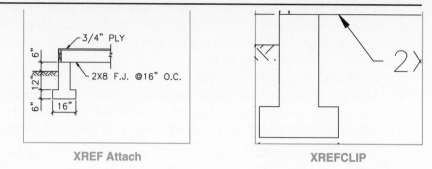

XREF Attach                    XREFCLIP

## XREF command options

A complete discussion of the use of xrefs and the creation of multiview drawings for plotting is discussed in this chapter in the form of an exercise and tutorial. It covers all of the options of the **XREF** command, and the manner in which they can be used to create any type of drawing that is composed of several views, details, or components of varying scales.

A brief description of each of the **XREF** command options is given here to provide a better understanding of their capabilities.

- **?.** Lists the xrefs used in the current drawing. This option is accessed by picking the **List** button on the **External Reference** toolbar, or by selecting **List** in the **External Reference** ⟩ cascading submenu of the **File** pull-down menu. See Figure 26-2.
- **Bind.** Allows you to permanently join an xref to the master drawing. This is similar to using the **INSERT** command. It is useful if you must send a drawing file on disk to a plotting service, or give a copy of the drawing file to a client. However, the **Bind** option does not appear in the **External Reference** ⟩ cascading submenu, or as a toolbar button.

- **Detach.** Removes an xref from the master drawing. It is used if you must delete a detail, view, or portion of a drawing, and wish to remove all its dependent symbols. This option is accessed by picking the **Detach** button on the **External Reference** toolbar, or by selecting **Detach** in the **External Reference** ⟩ cascading submenu of the **File** pull-down menu.

Figure 26-2. The **XREF** options are found in the **External Reference** ⟩ cascading submenu of the **File** pull-down menu.

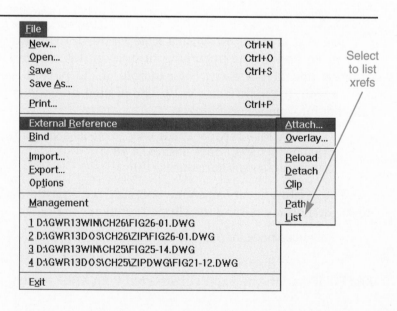

Select to list xrefs

- **Path.** Allows you to change the location (path) of the xref. It is convenient if you must locate the xrefs in a different hard drive directory or disk drive. This option is accessed by picking the **Path** button on the **External Reference** toolbar, or by selecting **Path** in the **External Reference** ⟩ cascading submenu of the **File** pull-down menu.

- **Reload.** Enables you to reload any updated xrefs without reloading the master drawing. It is useful if you know that an xref has been revised by another user while you were working on your drawing. This option is accessed by picking the **Reload** button on the **External Reference** toolbar, or by selecting **Reload** in the **External Reference** ⟩ cascading submenu of the **File** pull-down menu.

- **Overlay.** An xref that has been inserted into the drawing, but does not remain attached when the drawing is saved. Unlike the **Attach** option, AutoCAD does not create a block definition of an overlaid drawing. This option is accessed by picking the **Overlay** button in the **External Reference** toolbar, or by selecting **Overlay...** in the **External Reference** ⟩ cascading submenu of the **File** pull-down menu.

- **Attach.** An xref drawing that has been attached becomes a part of the master drawing in the form of a block definition. Therefore, whenever the master drawing is opened in AutoCAD, the attached xref is automatically loaded. This option is accessed by picking the **Attach** button on the **External Reference** toolbar, or by selecting **Attach...** in the **External Reference** ⟩ cascading submenu of the **File** pull-down menu.

## BINDING DEPENDENT SYMBOLS TO A DRAWING   [ AUG 7 ]

AutoCAD refers to *dependent symbols* as named items such as blocks, dimension styles, layers, linetypes, and text styles. If you reference a drawing, you cannot directly use any of its dependent symbols. For example, a layer that exists only on a referenced drawing cannot be made current in the master drawing in order to draw on it. It is the same for text styles. If one of the dependent symbols, such as a dimension style or linetype, is one that you would like to use on the master drawing, you can permanently *bind*, or affix any of these symbols to the master drawing. After a permanent bind is created, the dependent symbol, such as the text style, can be used on the master drawing.

When a drawing is referenced to the master, the layer names of the xref are given the name of the referenced drawing, followed by the piping (¦) symbol, and then the name of the layer. This naming convention enables you to quickly identify which layers belong to a specific referenced drawing. Figure 26-3A illustrates referenced drawing layer names as they appear in the **Layer Control** dialog box, which is accessed with the **DDLMODES** command. The layer names also appear in the **Current Layer** pop-up list as shown in Figure 26-3B.

Figure 26-3. Layer names on a reference drawing are preceded by the xref drawing name.
A—The **Layer Control** dialog box. B—The **Current Layer** pop-up list.

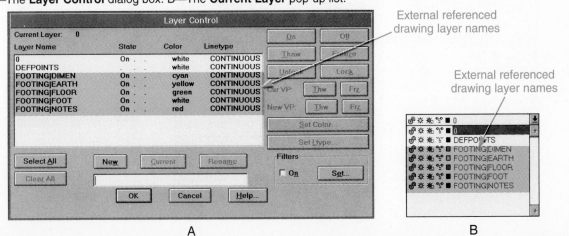

A                                                     B

Remember, you are not allowed to draw on any layer that belongs to an xref. If you wish to use one of these layers, or any other dependent symbol in an xref drawing, use the **XBIND** command. The **XBIND** command is located in the same **File** pull-down menu as **Bind**. The options are shown in Figure 26-4. The command sequence is as follows:

Command: **XBIND** ↵
Block/Dimstyle/LAyer/LType/Style: **LA** ↵
Dependent Layer name(s): **FOOTING|DIMEN,FOOTING|NOTES** ↵
  Scanning...
2 Layer(s) bound.
Command:

When a layer has been bound to the master drawing, it is renamed. The FOOTING|DIMEN layer becomes FOOTING$0$DIMEN. The additional views of the **Layer Control** dialog box and the **Current Layer** pop-up list illustrate this concept. See Figure 26-5.

Keep in mind that when a dependent symbol is bound to the master drawing using **XBIND**, it becomes a permanent part of the drawing, thus increasing the drawing file size.

Figure 26-4.   The **XBIND** command options in the **File** pull-down menu.

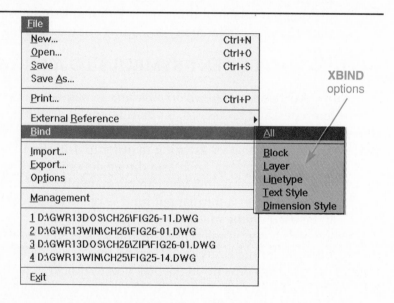

Figure 26-5.   Layers that are bound using the **XBIND** command are renamed. Note the use of the $0$. A—The **Current Layer** pop-up list. B—The **Layer Control** dialog box

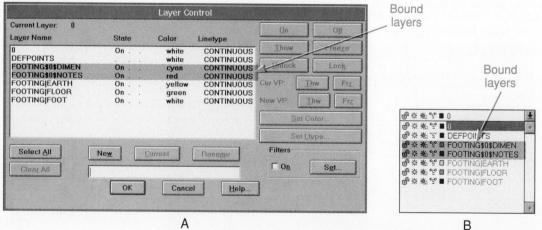

A

B

> **NOTE** You can instruct AutoCAD to create and maintain a log file of the **Attach**, **Detach**, and **Reload** functions used on any drawing containing xrefs. Simply set the **XREFCTL** system variable to 1. AutoCAD creates an .XLG file having the same name as the current drawing, and locates it in the same directory. Each time you load a drawing that contains xrefs, or use the **Attach**, **Detach**, and **Reload** options of the **XREF** command, AutoCAD appends information to the log file. A new heading, or title block, is added to the log file each time the related drawing file is opened. The log file provides the following information:
>
> - Drawing name, date, time, and type of xref operation
> - Nesting level of all xrefs affected by the operation
> - A list of the symbol tables affected by the operation, and the names of the symbols added to the drawing. A few examples of symbol tables are blocks, styles, linetypes, and layers
>
> You can also create a general log file of all activity while in AutoCAD. Select **Preferences...** from the **Options** pull-down menu. This displays the **Preferences** dialog box. Pick **Environment**, then select the **Log File:** check box in the **Files** area at the lower-left of the panel. A log file will be created in the directory that is displayed in the edit box. You can view this ASCII file using Windows Notepad, or any text editor, after exiting AutoCAD.

## CREATING MULTIPLE VIEWPORTS IN PAPER SPACE  AUG 10

Multiview mechanical drawings and architectural construction drawings often contain sections and details drawn at different scales. AutoCAD allows you to lay out a multiview drawing with views of different scales and plot at full scale.

Imagine that you have manually developed three separate drawings of a house floor plan and construction details. Now, assume that you lay a C-size piece of vellum (with preprinted border and title block) on a table. Take the three drawings, each at a different scale, and arrange them on the sheet of vellum. Now, take a full-size photograph of the entire drawing. The photo contains all drawings at the proper scale, including the border and title block. Finally, remove the views from the original sheet of vellum and return them to storage. That's the concept behind creating multiple viewports in paper space.

One of the reasons for creating multiple viewport layouts in paper space using different scales is the ability to plot the layout at the scale of 1:1. This means that scales do not have to be calculated prior to plotting, but they must be considered during the planning stages of your drawing.

### Understanding model space and paper space

Creating a multiple viewport layout requires a basic understanding of two concepts—model space and paper space. Model space is the *space* that you draw and design in. It is the default space you enter when AutoCAD is loaded. All of your drawings and models should be created here. Paper space is the mode that you select when you wish to create a layout of your drawing prior to plotting. The powerful aspect of using paper space is that you can create a layout of several different drawings and views, each with different scales. You can even mix 2D and 3D views in the same paper space layout.

As mentioned in Chapter 10, four commands govern how you work with model space and paper space. The tutorial provided in this chapter will guide you through the use of these commands, but a short preview here will help you understand their functions.

- **TILEMODE = 1.** Represents model space, and the **VPORTS** command is used to establish multiple "tiled" viewports. This is the default setting when you enter AutoCAD.
- **TILEMODE = 0.** Represents paper space, and the **MVIEW** command is used to create multiple floating viewports in paper space.
- **MSPACE.** Command used when **TILEMODE** is set to 0, to move from paper space to one of the floating model space viewports.
- **PSPACE.** Command used when **TILEMODE** is set to 0, to move from one of the floating model space viewports to paper space.
- **MVIEW.** Enables you to *cut* model space viewports into the *paper* of paper space. Can only be used when **TILEMODE** is set to 0. You might even call this command the Xacto™ knife of AutoCAD. Using it, you can cut any number and size of rectangular viewports, at any location on your paper. A viewport created with **MVIEW** is an AutoCAD object, and can be moved, copied, or resized.

---

**NOTE**  The **Create** option of the **MVSETUP** command can also be used to construct an arrangement of viewports in paper space.

---

If this seems a bit confusing to you, try using the following to help you understand the relationship between model and paper space.

| ACTIVITY | SPACE | TILEMODE | COMMAND |
|---|---|---|---|
| Drawing and design | Model | 1 | **VPORTS** (tiled) |
| Plotting and printing layout | Paper | 0 | **MVIEW** (objects) |

After you use these commands and procedures a few times, you will begin to see how easy they are to understand. Everything you draw is constructed in model space. When preparing a drawing or model for plotting, the necessary views are created in paper space.

### Drawing in model space

When you begin a new drawing in AutoCAD for Windows, you are automatically in model space. This is the default setting in the ACAD.DWG file. The standard UCS icon is displayed in the lower-left corner of the screen when you are in model space. In addition, a system variable called **TILEMODE** controls the setting of model space and paper space. The model space default setting of **TILEMODE** is 1, and the paper space setting is 0. Enter the following to change the paper space:

```
Command: TILEMODE ↵
New value for TILEMODE ⟨1⟩: 0 ↵
Entering Paper space. Use MVIEW to insert Model space viewports.
Regenerating drawing.
Command:
```

Note the special paper space UCS icon resembling a triangle is displayed. See Figure 26-6.

---

Figure 26-6.   The paper space
UCS icon resembles a triangle.

The **TILEMODE** variable can also be set using the **View** pull-down menu. Take note of the function of the following three selections in the **View** pull-down menu:

- **Tiled Model Space.** Sets **TILEMODE** to 1 (model space). Use the **VPORTS** command to created tile viewports.
- **Floating Model Space.** Executes the **MSPACE** command and activates the crosshairs in the current viewport. If there are no viewports in paper space, the **MVIEW** command is executed.
- **Paper Space.** Sets **TILEMODE** to 0 (paper space). Use the **MVIEW** command to create viewports in paper space.

PROFESSIONAL
TIP

      All system variable names can be entered at the **Command:** prompt.

## MULTIPLE VIEWPORT CREATION        AUG 10

An overview of creating multiple viewports for plotting will first be discussed to introduce the commands and options, before detailing the creation of a multiview plot. The most important visualization aspect involved in creating a multiview layout is to imagine that the sheet of paper you are creating will contain several cutouts *(viewports)*, through which you can see other drawings *(models)*. See Figure 26-7.

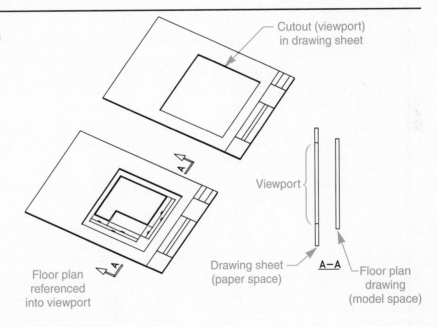

Figure 26-7. Views of other drawings can be seen through viewports "cut into" paper space.

Imagine holding a sheet of paper with a border and title block in front of you. Now, use a knife to cut a rectangle out of the paper. This is a viewport. Place a scaled print (model) of a house floor plan behind the opening. Use your knife to cut another smaller rectangular opening in the paper to the left of the first. Cut a third viewport above the second one. Find scaled prints of a stair detail and a footing detail drawing. Place each of these behind the two new viewports. Now, take a photograph of the completed drawing. That's a simplified version of the process used to create viewports in paper space.

As you know, objects and designs should be created at full size in model space. If you are designing a machine part, you are probably using decimal units. If you are designing a house, you are using architectural units. When constructing each of these, you likely used the full dimensions of the part or house.

Now, imagine the C-size paper is hanging up in front of you, and the first viewport is cut to be 12″ wide and 10″ high. You want to display the floor plan of a house inside the opening. If you then place the full-size model of the floor plan directly behind the C-size paper, the house will extend many feet beyond the edges of the paper. How can you place the drawing within the viewport? You know that the floor plan should be displayed inside the viewport at a scale of 1/4″ = 1′-0″. The scale factor of 1/4″ = 1′-0″ is 48. Therefore, you need to move the floor plan model away from the C-size paper until it is 1/48 (reciprocal of 48) the size it is now. This is accomplished with the **XP** (times paper space) option of the **ZOOM** command discussed later. When you do that, the entire floor plan fits inside the viewport you cut. See Figure 26-8.

Figure 26-8.    The floor plan is placed inside a viewport.

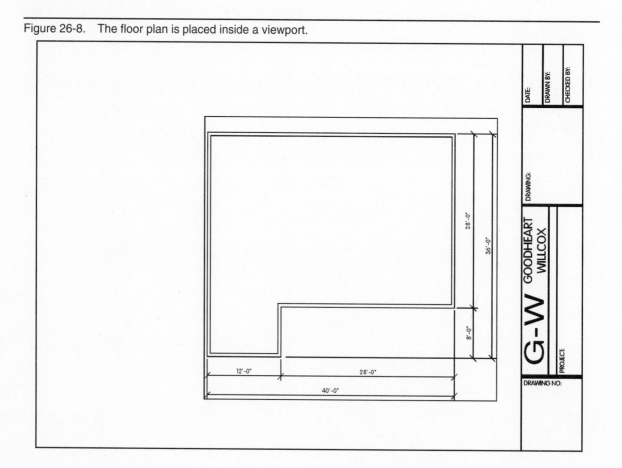

Remember to zoom to the appropriate scale after *referencing (inserting)* a drawing into a viewport so that your multiview plots work properly. Review the brief step-by-step procedure for constructing multiview plots. The first six steps can be omitted if your prototype drawing contains these settings and entities.

1. Set **TILEMODE** to 0 to enter paper space.
2. Set **UNITS** to match the type of drawing you are creating.
3. Set **LIMITS** to match paper size and plotter limits.
4. Make a layer for referenced drawings.
5. Create a border layer or reference a drawing that has a border and title block. You may want to use **MVSETUP** (discussed in Chapter 16).
6. Make a layer for viewport entities, and set this viewport as the current layer.
7. Enter MVIEW and make the size viewport needed.
8. Change to model space.
9. Use the **XREF** command to reference an existing drawing. Insert the drawing at 0,0 and use the remaining defaults.
10. Zoom to the extents of the drawing.
11. Set the scale to the appropriate value using the **XP** option of the **ZOOM** command.
12. Use **VPLAYER** (viewport layer) and either the **Vpvisdflt** (viewport visibility default) or **Freeze** options to freeze layers of this referenced drawing in selected viewports.
13. Return to paper space.
14. Repeat the process using the **MVIEW** command.

## CONSTRUCTING A MULTIVIEW DRAWING FOR PLOTTING  | AUG 7 |

Now that you have a good idea of the multiview plotting process, the following example leads you through the details of the procedure. This example uses a house floor plan, a stair detail, and a footing detail. This drawing is not among the sample drawings furnished with AutoCAD for Windows. Instead, the drawing is based on Exercise 26-1. Complete Exercise 26-1 before working through the example. It is composed of three simple architectural drawings.

## EXERCISE 26-1

❑ If you wish to work along at your computer with the following example of multiview drawing construction, complete this exercise before reading further. It is not necessary to complete this exercise in order to understand the process discussed in the following example, but it may assist you in quickly grasping the concepts of the procedure.

❑ The three drawings shown below—the floor plan, stair detail, and footing detail—should be created for this exercise. They are highly simplified for the purpose of this exercise and explanation, and should not be regarded as complete representations of actual designs. Exact dimensions are not necessary, because the purpose of this exercise is to illustrate the creation of a multiview drawing. You may simplify the drawings further to speed up the exercise.

❑ Each drawing should be created, named, and stored separately with different names. Do not put a border or title block on the drawings. The names are shown in the following table.

| FLOOR.DWG | | | STAIR.DWG | | | FOOTING.DWG | |
|-----------|---|---|-----------|---|---|-------------|---|
| **Layer** | **Color** | | **Layer** | **Color** | | **Layer** | **Color** |
| Wall | White | | Wall | Yellow | | Floor | Green |
| Dimen | Cyan | | Floor | White | | Foot | White |
| Notes | Red | | Stair | Green | | Dimen | Cyan |
| | | | Foot | White | | Notes | Red |
| | | | Dimen | Cyan | | Earth | Yellow |
| | | | Notes | Red | | | |

❑ Use the following scales and scale factors when constructing each of the drawings.

FLOOR.DWG: 1/4″ = 1′-0″ (Scale factor = 48)
STAIR.DWG: 3/8″ = 1′-0″ (Scale factor = 32)
FOOTING.DWG: 3/4″ = 1′-0″ (Scale factor = 16)

The scale factors are important when setting the **DIMSCALE** dimensioning variable, and when establishing text height. Remember to multiply the plotted text height, such as .125, by the scale factor, such as 48, to get the text height to use in AutoCAD (.125 × 48 = 6). The scale factor is also used with the **ZOOM XP** command discussed later in the text.

❑ Save the drawings to a hard disk subdirectory, preferably not in the \R13 directory. Check with your instructor or supervisor before creating or using hard disk space. Save backup copies on a floppy disk.

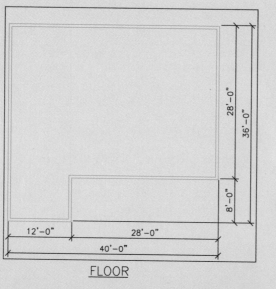

FLOOR

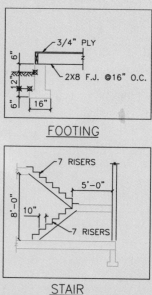

FOOTING

STAIR

## Initial drawing setup

The first aspect of drawing setup is to place a border and title block on the screen. It should be the proper size for the plot you wish to make. This can be accomplished in one of several ways, depending on the depth of your preparation. First, set **TILEMODE** to 0, then do one of the following:

- Draw a border on a separate layer, then draw a title block.
- Draw a border and insert a predrawn title block.
- Insert a predrawn standard border and title block prototype containing all constant text and attributes for variable information.

The method you use is not of primary importance for this example, but it is always best to use existing borders and title blocks for reasons that are discussed later.

**PROFESSIONAL TIP**

This initial setup phase is unnecessary if your school or company uses preprinted border and title block sheets. You might use a *phantom* border and title block sheet on the screen for layout purposes, and to add additional information to the title block. This phantom information can be frozen before plotting.

When setting up a drawing, first enter paper space, then set the units and limits to match the type of drawing you are creating. Be sure that the extents of your border and title block match the maximum active plotting area, or *clip limits* of your plotter. This example uses a standard architectural C-size sheet (18″ × 24″), and assumes that the plotter's active area is .75″ less on all sides, for a total plotting area of 16.5″ × 22.5″.

```
Command: TILEMODE ↵
New value for TILEMODE ⟨1⟩: 0 ↵
Entering Paper space. Use MVIEW to insert Model space viewports.
Regenerating drawing.
Command: UNITS ↵
```

Use the following **UNITS** settings and then reply to the **Command:** prompts.

- Architectural units.
- Units precision = 1/2″.
- Systems of angle measure = Decimal degrees.
- Angles precision = 0.
- Direction for angle 0 = East (0).
- Angles measured counterclockwise.

```
Command: LIMITS ↵
Reset Paper space limits:
ON/OFF/⟨Lower left corner⟩ ⟨0′-0″,0′-0″⟩: ↵
Upper right corner ⟨1′-0″,0′-9″⟩: 26,20 ↵
```

The upper-right corner limit of 26,20 provides additional space on the screen outside the paper limits.

```
Command: ZOOM ↵
All/Center/Dynamic/Extents/Left/Previous/Vmax/Window/⟨Scale(X/XP)⟩: A ↵
Regenerating drawing.
Command:
```

## Creating new layers

The border and title block should be on a separate layer, so you may want to create a new layer, called BORDER or TITLE, and assign it a separate color. Be sure to make this new layer current before you draw the border or use **MVSETUP**.

At this point you can set an appropriate snap grid and visible grid values. If you wish to use an existing border and title block, insert it now, and those values should already be set in the prototype drawing.

One of the principle functions of this example is to use existing drawings of the house floor plan, stairs, and footing. These drawings will not become a part of our new drawing, but they will be "referenced" with the **XREF** command in order to save drawing file space. Therefore, you should also create a new layer for these drawings and name it XREF. Assign the XREF layer the color of 7.

The referenced drawings will fit inside viewports that are made with the **MVIEW** command. These viewports are rectangles and are given the entity name of Viewport. Therefore, they can be edited like any other AutoCAD entity. Create a layer called VIEWPORTS or VPORT for these entities and assign it a color.

The layers of any existing drawings that you reference (xref) into your new drawing remain intact. Therefore, you do not have to create additional layers unless you want to add information to your drawing.

If you do not have an existing C-size architectural border and title block, you can draw a border at this time. Make the BORDER layer current and draw a polyline border using the **RECTANG** command at the dimensions of 16.5″ × 22.5″. Draw a title block if you wish. Your screen should look similar to Figure 26-9.

Figure 26-9.   The border and title block in paper space.

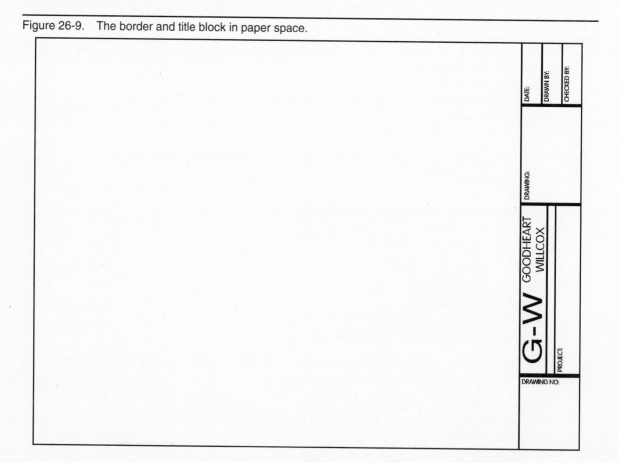

## Creating a viewport in paper space

The process of creating viewports is completed in paper space because viewports are *cut out of the paper*. When creating a drawing in paper space, your screen represents a sheet of paper. You must now create an opening, called a *viewport*, through which you can view a model, design, or drawing. In this case, the model is a floor plan. First, cut an opening in the paper so you can see the floor plan that is behind it. Keep in mind that the sheet of paper measures 18" × 24" and the first viewport to be cut measures 11.5" × 12".

The **MVIEW** command is used to create the viewports. Since viewports are entities, make the VIEWPORTS layer current, so they reside on their own layer. This allows them to be frozen later to avoid being plotted. The first viewport can be located from the lower-left corner of the border by using the **From** object snap mode to locate the corner. Enter the following:

> Command: **MVIEW** ↵
> ON/OFF/Hideplot/Fit/2/3/4/Restore/⟨First Point⟩: **FROM** ↵
> Base point: **INT** ↵
> of (*pick lower-left corner of border*)
> ⟨Offset⟩: **@7,3** ↵
> Other corner: **@12,11.5** ↵
> Regenerating drawing.
> Command:

Your screen should now look like Figure 26-10.

At this point, you can continue creating as many viewports as required. However, this example continues the process, and references a drawing into the new viewport. The other options of the **MVIEW** command are discussed in detail later in this chapter.

Figure 26-10.   A viewport added to the border and title block in paper space.

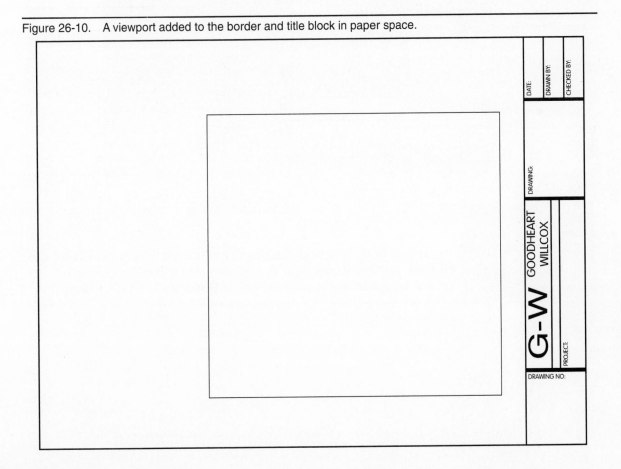

## Placing views in the drawing

A viewport has now been created into which you can insert a view of the 2D or 3D model (drawing) that has been previously created. In this case, we will reference the drawing of the floor plan named FLOOR. Instead of using the **INSERT** command, which combines an existing drawing with the new one, use the **XREF** command so that AutoCAD creates a *reference* to the FLOOR drawing. This allows the size of the new drawing to remain small because the FLOOR drawing has not been combined with it.

The following procedure allows you to enter model space, reference an existing drawing to the new one, and **ZOOM** to see the referenced drawing.

Command: **MSPACE** ↵
Command: **LAYER** ↵
?/Make/Set/New/ON/OFF/Color/Ltype/Freeze/Thaw/LOck/Unlock: **S** ↵
New current layer ⟨VIEWPORTS⟩: **XREF** ↵
?/Make/Set/New/ON/OFF/Color/Ltype/Freeze/Thaw/LOck/Unlock: ↵
Command: **XREF** ↵
?/Bind/Detach/Path/Reload/Overlay/⟨Attach⟩: ↵

The **Select file to attach** dialog box is displayed. See Figure 26-11.

Figure 26-11.   The **Select file to attach** dialog box.

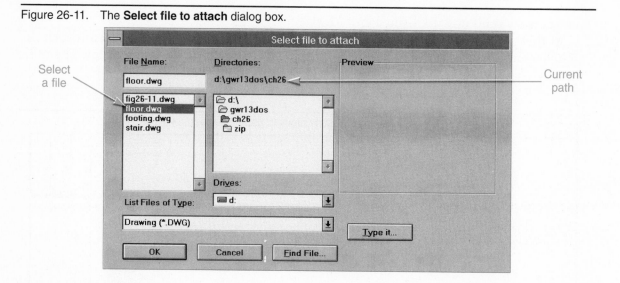

**PROFESSIONAL TIP**

If you have disabled the display of dialog boxes by setting the **FILEDIA** system variable to 0, you can still force the dialog box to appear by entering the tilde (~) at the Select file to attach: prompt.

Select FLOOR.DWG in the dialog box, or enter the drawing name FLOOR at the Xref to Attach: prompt. The following messages and prompts are then displayed:

```
Attach Xref FLOOR: FLOOR.DWG
FLOOR loaded.
Insertion point: 0,0 ↵
    X scale factor ⟨1⟩ / Corner / XYZ: ↵
    Y scale factor (default = X): ↵
    Rotation angle ⟨0⟩: ↵
Command: ZOOM ↵
All/Center/Dynamic/Extents/Left/Previous/Vmax/Window/⟨Scale(X/XP)⟩: E ↵
Command:
```

Your drawing should now resemble the one shown in Figure 26-12.

Figure 26-12.    The floor plan is referenced into the first viewport.

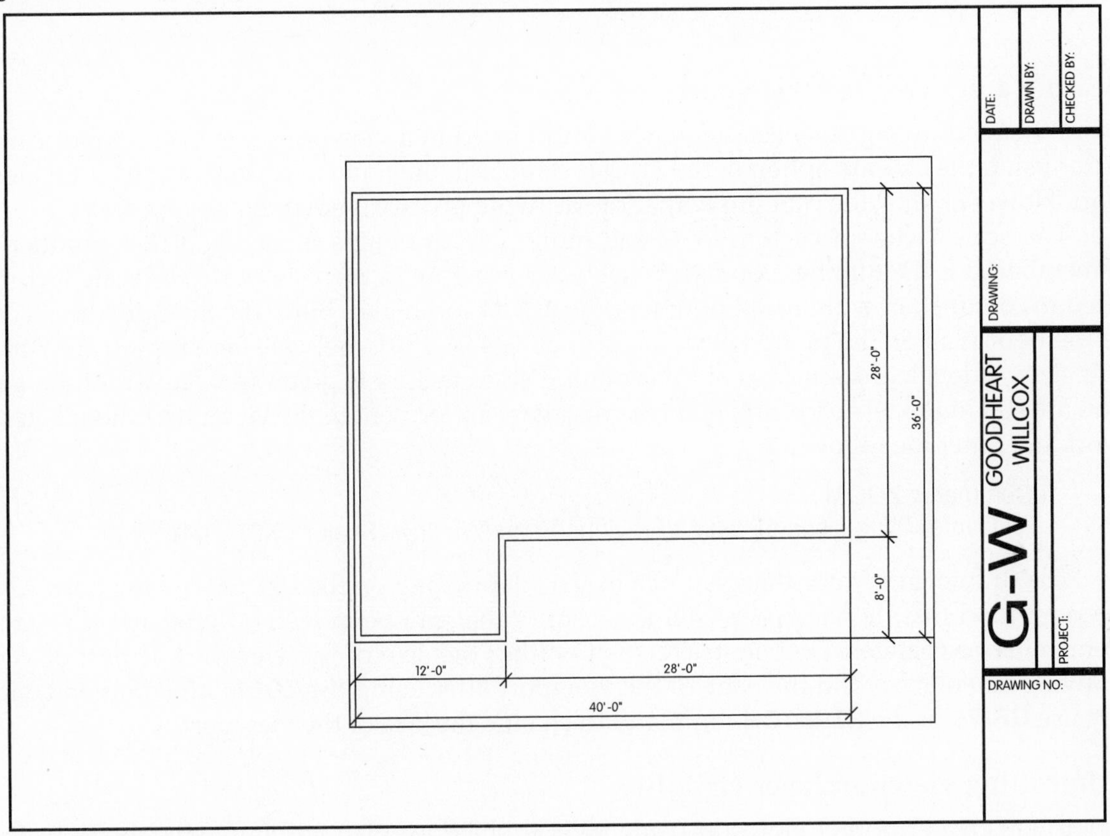

All of the layers on the referenced drawing are added to the new drawing. These layers can be distinguished from existing layers because the drawing name is automatically placed in front of the layer name and separated by a piping symbol (¦). This naming convention is shown in the **Current Layer** name box pop-up list on the toolbar and in the **Layer Control** dialog box, Figure 26-13. To display the **Current Layer** pop-up list, click on the down arrow to the right of the **Current Layer** name box. To access the **Layer Control** dialog box, click the **Layers** button at the far left of the toolbar, select **Layers...** from the **Data** pull-down menu, or enter DDLMODES at the Command: prompt.

Figure 26-13. A—How layers are named on referenced drawings in the **Layer Control** dialog box.
B— How layers are named on referenced drawings in the **Current Layer** pop-up list.

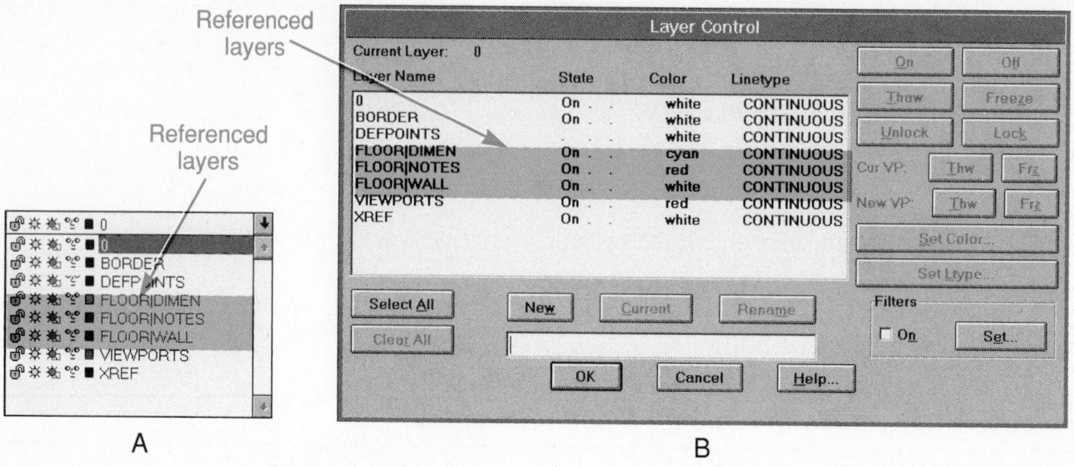

## Scaling a drawing in a viewport

When a drawing has been referenced and placed in a viewport, it is ready to be scaled. After using the **Extents** option of the **ZOOM** command, the referenced drawing fills the viewport. However, this does not imply that the drawing is displayed at the correct scale.

The scale factor of each view of the multiview drawings is an important number to remember; it is the number you use to size your drawing in the viewport. The scale factor is used in conjunction with the **XP** option of the **ZOOM** command. Since the intended final scale of the floor plan on the plotted drawing is to be 1/4" = 1'-0", the scale factor is 48, or 1/48 of full size. A detailed discussion of determining scale factors is given in Chapter 12. Be sure you are still in model space, and that the crosshairs are present in the viewport where you are working. Enter the following:

> Command: **ZOOM** ↵
> All/Center/Dynamic/Extents/Left/Previous/Vmax/Window/⟨Scale(X/XP)⟩: **1/48XP** ↵

The drawing may not change much in size, depending on the size of the viewport. Also, keep in mind that the viewport itself is an entity that can be moved or stretched if needed. Remember to change to paper space when editing the size of the viewport. If part of your drawing extends beyond the edge of the viewport after using the **ZOOM XP** command, simply use **GRIPS** or the **STRETCH** command to change the size of the viewport.

## Controlling viewport layer visibility

If you create another viewport using **MVIEW**, the floor plan will immediately fill it. This is because a viewport is just a window through which you can view a drawing or 3D model that has been referenced to the current drawing. One way to control what is visible in subsequent viewports is to freeze all layers of the FLOOR drawing in any new viewports that are created. The **VPLAYER** (viewport layer) command controls the display of layers in specific viewports, whereas the **LAYER** command controls layers in all viewports.

The following example uses the **VPLAYER** command and the **Vpvisdflt** option to control the display of layers in new viewports.

> Command: **VPLAYER** ↵
> ?/Freeze/Thaw/Reset/Newfrz/Vpvisdflt: **V** ↵
> Layer name(s) to change default viewport visibility: **FLOOR*** ↵
> Change default viewport visibility to Frozen/⟨Thawed⟩: **F** ↵
> ?/Freeze/Thaw/Reset/Newfrz/Vpvisdflt: ↵

The asterisk (*) after the name FLOOR instructs AutoCAD to freeze all of the layers on the FLOOR drawing in subsequent viewports. Look at the **Layer Control** dialog box in Figure 26-14 and note the "N" after the layer name, directly to the left of the color. This indicates the layer is frozen in a new viewport. Any layer's frozen or thawed status in a viewport can also be controlled by using the **Cur VP:** and the **New VP:** buttons on the right side of the **Layer Control** dialog box. Select one of the FLOOR layers, then pick the **Thaw** button of the **New VP:** option. Notice that the "N" is removed. These buttons are the same as using the **VPLAYER** command. The remaining options of the **VPLAYER** command are discussed later in this chapter.

Figure 26-14.   The "N" to the left of the color indicates the layer is frozen in all viewports. Layers can be frozen in selected viewports using the **Cur VP** and **New VP** buttons (shown highlighted here).

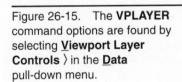
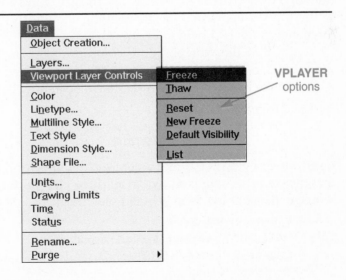

## Using menus to control viewport layer visibility

The **VPLAYER** command options are found in the **Data** pull-down menu by selecting **Viewport Layer Controls** 〉. All of the options of the **VPLAYER** command are displayed in the cascading submenu. See Figure 26-15.

Figure 26-15.   The **VPLAYER** command options are found by selecting **Viewport Layer Controls** 〉 in the **Data** pull-down menu.

### Creating additional viewports

The previous example of creating a viewport and referencing a drawing to it is the same process that is used to create the additional two viewports in our example. In this case, two viewports are created before using the **XREF** command. If you know the number, size, and location of all viewports needed on a multiview drawing, it may save time to create them all at once.

**PROFESSIONAL TIP**

If your class or company uses standard sheet layouts containing several views, create prototype drawings that contain viewports. Viewports can always be added, deleted, or resized on a drawing. Custom prototype drawings with viewports can be added to the list in the **MVSETUP** command.

The following command sequence resets paper space, changes the current layer to VIEWPORT, and uses the **MVIEW** command and grips to create new viewports. It then returns to model space to reference new drawings, and uses the **ZOOM** command to size the drawing in the viewport. The **VPLAYER** command is also used to control layer visibility in new viewports.

> Command: **PSPACE** ↵
> Command: **LAYER** ↵
> ?/Make/Set/New/ON/OFF/Color/Ltype/Freeze/Thaw/LOck/Unlock: **S** ↵
> New current layer ⟨*current*⟩: **VIEWPORTS** ↵
> ?/Make/Set/New/ON/OFF/Color/Ltype/Freeze/Thaw/LOck/Unlock: ↵
> Command: **MVIEW** ↵
> ON/OFF/Hideplot/Fit/2/3/4/Restore/⟨First Point⟩: **.5,3** ↵ (*this is the location relative to the lower-left corner of the border*)
> Other corner: **6.5,9** ↵

Be sure grips are on and pick the viewport you just drew. Copy the viewport to a position directly above the first. Next, use the grips and **STRETCH** command to change the height of the top viewport to 5″ while keeping the width the same. The final arrangement of the three viewports is shown in Figure 26-16.

Now that the viewports are complete, you can begin referencing the remaining two drawings. Change to model space, set the current layer to XREF and pick the lower-left viewport to make it active. The STAIR drawing can now be referenced.

> Command: **XREF** ↵
> ?/Bind/Detach/Path/Reload/Overlay/⟨Attach⟩: ↵
> Xref to Attach ⟨FLOOR⟩: **STAIR** ↵

Insert the drawing at 0,0, and accept the defaults for scale and rotation. Notice in Figure 26-17 that the stair drawing is shown in all three viewports. The **VPLAYER** command must be used to freeze the stair layers in selected viewports.

> Command: **VPLAYER** ↵
> ?/Freeze/Thaw/Reset/Newfrz/Vpvisdflt: **F** ↵
> Layer(s) to Freeze: **STAIR*** ↵
> All/Select/⟨*current*⟩: **S** ↵
> Switching to Paper space.
> Select objects: (*pick the outline of the large and upper-left viewports*)
> Select objects: ↵
> Switching to Model space.
> ?/Freeze/Thaw/Reset/Newfrz/Vpvisdflt: ↵
> Command:

Figure 26-16.   Two additional viewports are placed and sized on the drawing.

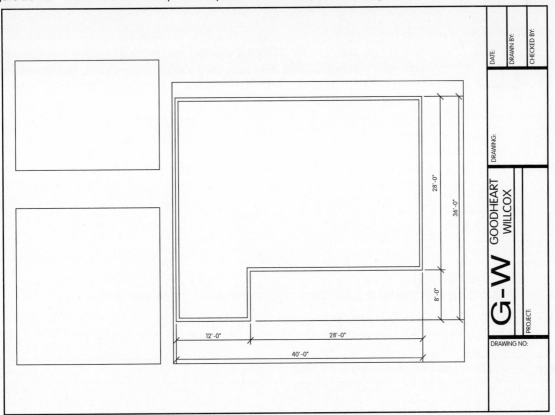

Figure 26-17.   The reference drawing STAIR is displayed in all viewports. **VPLAYER** must be used to restrict its visibility.

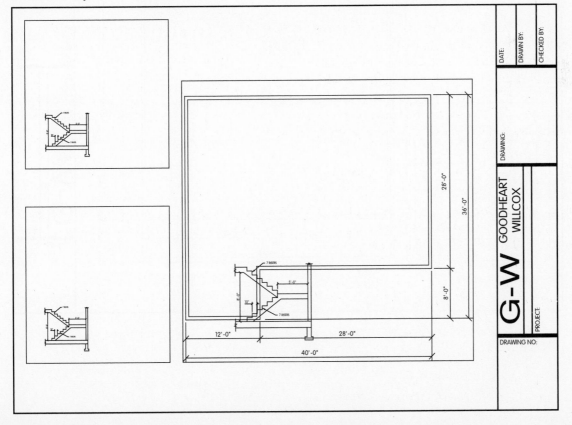

Use the **ZOOM Extents** command to display the drawing completely in the lower-left viewport, then scale the drawing with **ZOOM XP**.

**NOTE**

If you do not use **ZOOM Extents** first, your drawing may disappear after using **ZOOM XP**. This may occur if you pick the insertion point when using the **XREF** command, rather than entering 0,0 for the insertion point.

The plotted scale of the stair detail should be 3/8″ = 1′-0″. The scale factor is calculated as follows:

3/8″ = 1′-0″
.375″ = 12″
12/.375 = 32

The scale factor is 32, but you must use the reciprocal (1/32) for the **ZOOM XP** command.

Command: **ZOOM** ↵
All/Center/Dynamic/Extents/Left/Previous/Vmax/Window/⟨Scale⟩(X/XP)⟩: **1/32XP** ↵

Your drawing should now resemble the one shown in Figure 26-18.

Figure 26-18.   The scaled STAIR drawing in the second viewport.

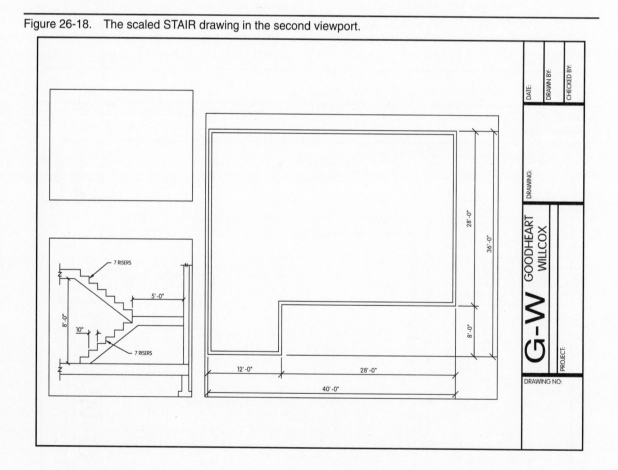

**PROFESSIONAL TIP**

You can use any display command inside a viewport. If a drawing is not centered after using **ZOOM XP**, simply use **PAN** to move it around. If lines of a drawing touch a viewport edge, those lines will not be visible if the viewport layer is frozen or turned off.

The final drawing can now be inserted into the last viewport. Pick the top viewport with your pointing device to make it active. Notice that the current viewport is surrounded by a white line. Crosshairs should now be displayed in the active viewport. Try to prepare the third view by following these steps.

1. Model space should be active.
2. The XREF layer should be current.
3. **XREF Attach** the FOOTING drawing.
4. Freeze the FOOTING layers in the other two viewports with **VPLAYER**.
5. **ZOOM Extents**, then **ZOOM XP** for proper scale. Plotted scale is to be 3/4″ = 1′-0″.
6. Use the **PAN** command if necessary to center the drawing.

When the final drawing has been referenced and scaled, your screen should look like Figure 26-19.

**NOTE**

Be sure to set the current layer to XREF when referencing a drawing so that the inserted drawing is not placed on another layer, such as VIEWPORTS.

**Figure 26-19.**   The new drawing is completed by referencing the footing.

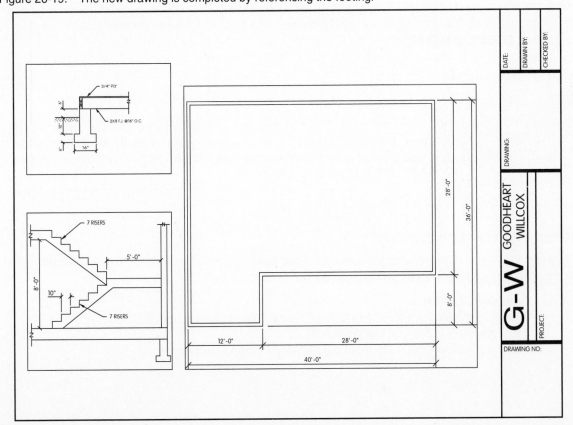

## Adjusting viewport display, size, and location

If you need to adjust a drawing within a viewport, first be sure that you are in model space. Then, pick the desired viewport to make it active, and use an appropriate display command, such as **ZOOM** or **PAN**.

The entire viewport can be moved to another location, but you must first be in paper space. Pick the viewport border and its grips appear. An object inside the viewport is not selected when picked because those objects are in model space. After selection, adjust the location of the viewports. Remember the following when adjusting viewports:

- **Model space.** Adjust the display of a drawing or model inside a specific viewport.
- **Paper space.** Adjust the size or location of a viewport.

> **PROFESSIONAL TIP**
>
> Whenever the **TILEMODE** variable is set to 0 (off) and there are existing model space viewports, you can quickly switch between model space and paper space. Simply click either the **Floating Model Space** button or the **Paper Space** button on the **Standard** toolbar.

## Adding notes and titles

There are two ways in which titles and notes can be added to a multiview drawing. The first method is to add the notations to the original drawing. In this manner, all titles and notes are referenced to the new drawing. This is the best system to use if the titles, scale label, and notes will not change.

However, titles may change. You may want to be sure that all titles of views are the same text style, or you might want to add a special symbol. This is easily completed after the drawings are referenced. The most important thing to remember is that you must be in paper space to add text. You can use new and existing text styles to add titles and notes to a drawing using **DTEXT** or **MTEXT**.

> **PROFESSIONAL TIP**
>
> Paper space viewports can also be placed on the DEFPOINTS layer, which is automatically created when you draw a dimension. Objects on this layer are seen but never plotted. You can also create a DEFPOINTS layer if it does not exist.

## Removing viewport outlines

The viewport outlines can be turned off for plotting purposes, as shown in Figure 26-20. Turn off or freeze the VIEWPORTS layer as follows:

```
Command: LAYER ↵
?/Make/Set/New/ON/OFF/Color/Ltype/Freeze/Thaw/LOck/Unlock: F ↵
Layer name(s) to Freeze: VIEWPORTS ↵
?/Make/Set/New/ON/OFF/Color/Ltype/Freeze/Thaw/LOck/Unlock: ↵
```

Figure 26-20.  The completed drawing with titles added and viewport outlines turned off.

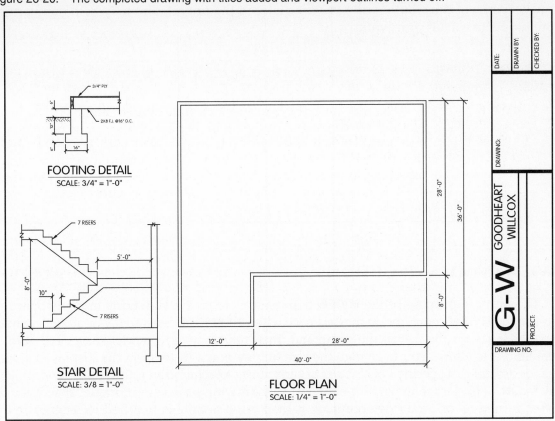

**NOTE**

If you turn off the **VIEWPORTS** layer, and a box still surrounds one of the views, you are probably still in model space. Remember that a box outlines the current viewport in model space. Enter PS at the **Command:** prompt, or click the **Paper Space** button on the **Standard** toolbar to enter paper space and the outline disappears.

## PLOTTING A MULTIVIEW DRAWING

You have already taken care of scaling the views when you referenced them and used the **ZOOM XP** command. The drawing that now appears on your screen in paper space can be plotted at full scale, 1=1, with the **PLOT** command.

Using the **PLOT** command in this manner is a simple procedure, but only if you planned your drawing(s) at the start of the project. The process of creating a properly-scaled multi-view layout will go smoothly if you have planned the project. Review the following items, and keep them in mind when starting any drawing or design project—especially one that involves the creation of a multiview paper space layout.

- Determine the size of paper to be used.
- Determine the type of title block, notes, revision blocks, parts lists, etc. that will appear on the drawing.
- Prepare a quick sketch of the view layouts and their plotted scales.
- Determine the scales to be used for each viewport.
- Establish proper text styles and heights based on the drawing scale factors.
- Set the **DIMSCALE** variable using the proper scale factor when creating drawings in model space.

There is no substitute for planning a project before you begin. It may seem like an unnecessary expense of time, but it will save time later in the project, and may help you become more productive in all your work.

**PROFESSIONAL TIP**

You may never have to specify a scale other than full (1=1) when plotting. Any object or design, whether 2D or 3D, can be referenced into a border and title block drawing, scaled with **ZOOM XP**, and then plotted. Try using the paper space layout procedure for all your drawings, even if they are just a single view. You will find that you need fewer border and title block prototype drawings, and the process will become quicker.

## MVIEW COMMAND OPTIONS

AUG 10

The primary purpose of the **MVIEW** command is to create viewports in paper space. If you use the **MVIEW** command in model space when **TILEMODE** is set to 0, AutoCAD changes to paper space for the rest of the command, then returns you to model space. The **MVIEW** command also allows you to change the size of viewports, fit them in the displayed screen area, or default to a specific value. Brief descriptions of each option follow:

- **ON/OFF.** The contents of a viewport (the drawing or design in model space) can be turned on or off. If viewports are turned off, less time is required to regenerate the drawing.
- **Hideplot.** Allows you to select the viewports you wish to have hidden lines removed from when plotting in paper space. Hidden lines are removed from 3D objects by selecting **ON**, and are shown by selecting **OFF**.
- **Fit.** Creates a viewport to fit the current screen display. You can zoom into an area first, then use the **Fit** option to create a viewport in the windowed area.
- **2/3/4.** AutoCAD automatically creates a configuration of 2, 3, or 4 viewports. The prompt is similar to the same option for the **VPORTS** command. When 2 or 3 is selected, you are prompted for specific locations and arrangements.

      2–Horizontal/⟨Vertical⟩:
      3–Horizontal/Vertical/Above/Below/Left/⟨Right⟩:

  When 4 is selected, four equal size viewports are created within a specified area.
- **Restore.** This option works if you have used the **VPORTS** command to create and save viewport configurations. AutoCAD asks for the configuration name, then allows you to either specify the locations and size of the viewports, or fit it into the current display.

      ?/Name of window configuration to insert ⟨*ACTIVE⟩: (enter the name and
         press [Enter])
      Fit/⟨First Point⟩:

  If you accept the default, you can position and size the new viewports by selecting two points to window an area in paper space. If you select Fit, the restored viewports are scaled to fit the graphics area.
- **⟨First Point⟩.** The default option allows you to select or enter the coordinates of the first corner of the viewport. Then, you are prompted for the other corner and a window is attached to the crosshairs. Pick the opposite corner and the viewport is drawn.

**EXERCISE 26-2**

❑ Use the prototype method to recall the border and title block drawing you used in Exercise 26-1. Name the drawing EX26-2.
❑ Create layers for referenced drawings (XREF) and viewports (VIEWPORT).
❑ Use the **MVIEW 2/3/4** option to create an arrangement of three viewports on the **VIEWPORT** layer. Leave space in the upper-right corner for an additional viewport.
❑ Use the **ZOOM Window** command to display the open area in the upper-right corner of the drawing.
❑ Select the **Fit** option of the **MVIEW** command to create a viewport in the current screen display.
❑ Reference the FLOOR drawing used in Exercise 26-1 into one of the viewports in the group of three viewports. Be sure the XREF layer is current.
❑ Turn off the contents of that viewport with the **OFF** option of the **MVIEW** command.
❑ Save the drawing as A:EX26-2, then quit the drawing session.

## VPLAYER COMMAND OPTIONS                                  | AUG 10 |

The **VPLAYER** (viewport layer) command controls the visibility of layers within selected viewports. This function differs from the **LAYER** command, which controls the visibility of all layers in the drawing. The following list describes the function of each of the **VPLAYER** command options.

- **?.** After entering a question mark, AutoCAD prompts you to select a viewport. If you selected the upper-left viewport in Figure 26-19, the following display appears in the text window:

> Layers currently frozen in viewport 4:
> FLOORIWALL
> FLOORIDIMEN
> FLOORINOTES
> STAIRIDIMEN
> STAIRIFLOOR
> STAIRINOTES
> STAIRISTAIR
> STAIRIWALL
> Switching to Model space:
> ?/Freeze/Thaw/Reset/Newfrz/Vpvisdflt:

- **Freeze.** Enables you to selectively freeze one or more layers in any selected viewport(s).
- **Thaw.** This option allows you to thaw layers that were frozen with the **Freeze** option. As with the **Freeze** option, you can selectively thaw one or more layers in any viewport(s).
- **Reset.** Removes any viewport visibility default settings that were established with the **Vpvisdflt** option, and resets it to the default setting for a layer in a given viewport. This means that if you reset layers in a selected viewport, they become visible.
- **Newfrz.** Enables you to create a new frozen layer in all viewports, then it can be thawed in the viewport in which it is to be displayed. The prompt for this option is:

> ?/Freeze/Thaw/Reset/Newfrz/Vpvisdflt: **N** ↵
> New Viewport frozen layer name(s): **WALLS** ↵
> ?/Freeze/Thaw/Reset/Newfrz/Vpvisdflt: **T** ↵

After entering the **Thaw** option, you can select the viewport(s) in which you want the new layer named WALLS to be visible.

- **Vpvisdflt (viewport visibility default).** This option enables you to control the visibility of layers in new viewports. Use this option if you do not want existing layers to be visible in new viewports.

    > ?/Freeze/Thaw/Reset/Newfrz/Vpvisdflt: **V** ⏎
    > Layer name(s) to change default viewport visibility: *(enter layer name)*

The **VPLAYER** command options are accessed from a cascading submenu by selecting **Viewport Layer Controls** ⟩ from the **Data** pull-down menu. See Figure 26-15. The **MVIEW** command options are found by selecting **Floating Viewports** ⟩ in the **View** pull-down menu. See Figure 26-21.

Figure 26-21. The **MVIEW** command options are found by selecting **Floating Viewports** ⟩ in the **View** pull-down menu.

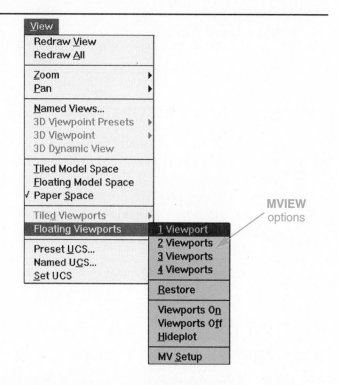

---

## EXERCISE 26-3

❑ Recall the drawing that you constructed in this chapter. It should contain three viewports similar to Figure 26-19, each containing an architectural detail.

❑ Be sure that the VIEWPORTS layer is on so that the viewport outlines are visible.

❑ List the layers currently frozen in the large viewport.

❑ Freeze the DIMEN layers in all viewports. Remember that in each viewport, the DIMEN layer name has been altered. For example, in the STAIR drawing, the layer is STAIR|DIMEN.

❑ Thaw the DIMEN layers in all viewports. Use a wild-card character (*) to thaw them all at once.

❑ Use the **Reset** option of the **VPLAYER** command to remove all **Vpvisdflt** settings. The viewports should become crowded with multiple views. Use **UNDO** to remove the effects of the last command.

❑ Create a new frozen layer with the **Newfrz** option of the **VPLAYER** command, and name it BOM. List the frozen layers in any of the viewports to see if BOM is frozen.

❑ Thaw BOM in the FOOTING viewport, then list the frozen layers in that viewport.

❑ Do not save your drawing.

## XREF COMMAND OPTIONS

Using external references efficiently will allow you to save considerable time and file storage space. Therefore, it is important that you have a good understanding of the functions of **XREF** and its options. The **XREF** command options were discussed earlier in this chapter, but the following section is a brief review of those command options.

The **XREF** command enables you to add existing models or drawings to the current drawing without actually combining the files. AutoCAD creates a reference to an existing drawing. This allows you to keep the size of drawing files to a minimum. The following options are included when the **XREF** command is used.

- **?.** Lists the xrefs used in the current drawing. This option is accessed by entering ? at the ?/Bind/Detach/Path/Reload/Overlay/⟨Attach⟩: prompt, picking the **List** button on the **External Reference** toolbar, or by selecting **List** in the **External Reference** ⟩ cascading submenu of the **File** pull-down menu.

```
Command: XREF ↵
?/Bind/Detach/Path/Reload/Overlay/⟨Attach⟩: ? ↵
Xref(s) to list ⟨*⟩: ↵

Xref Name     Path
FLOOR         \r13\gw\27\floor
FOOTING       \r13\gw\27\footing
STAIR         \r13\gw\27\stair
Total Xref(s): 3
```

- **Bind.** This option permanently attaches an external reference to your drawing. It is a good idea to bind xrefs on drawings that are completed and are to be stored (archived), or drawings that are to be sent to a client, instructor, or service bureau for plotting. However, the **Bind** option does not appear in the **External Reference** ⟩ cascading submenu, or as a toolbar button. This option is accessed by entering B at the ?/Bind/Detach/Path/Reload/Overlay/⟨Attach⟩: prompt.

- **Detach.** Referenced drawings that have been erased from your drawing, or that are no longer needed, can then be detached. AutoCAD deletes the specified xref(s) from the drawing file. This option is accessed by entering D at the ?/Bind/Detach/Path/Reload/Overlay/⟨Attach⟩: prompt, picking the **Detach** button on the **External Reference** toolbar, or by selecting **Detach** in the **External Reference** ⟩ cascading submenu of the **File** pull-down menu.

- **Path.** AutoCAD remembers the location, or "path" of a referenced drawing. If, for any reason, you must move the referenced drawings to another directory or disk drive, use the **Path** option to tell AutoCAD the new location. This option is accessed by entering P at the ?/Bind/Detach/Path/Reload/Overlay/⟨Attach⟩: prompt, picking the **Path** button on the **External Reference** toolbar, or by selecting **Path** in the **External Reference** ⟩ cascading submenu of the **File** pull-down menu. For example, if you were to relocate the FOOTING drawing to the \R13\STRUCT subdirectory, use the following sequence:

```
Command: XREF ↵
?/Bind/Detach/Path/Reload/Overlay/⟨Attach⟩: P ↵
Edit path for which Xref(s): FOOTING ↵
    Scanning...
Xref name: FOOTING
Old path: \r13\gw\27\footing
New path: \R13\STRUCT ↵
```

- **Reload.** You can update any of the referenced drawings at any time by using the **Reload** option. This may be appropriate if someone in the class or office made revisions to a drawing that you referenced. This option is accessed by entering R at the ?/Bind/Detach/Path/Reload/Overlay/⟨Attach⟩: prompt, picking the **Reload** button on the **External Reference** toolbar, or by selecting **R**eload in the **External Reference** ⟩ cascading submenu of the **File** pull-down menu.

  > Xref(s) to reload: **FOOTING** ↵
  > Reload Xref FOOTING: \r13\struct\footing

- **Overlay.** An xref that has been inserted into the drawing, but does not remain attached when the drawing is saved. Unlike the **Attach** option, AutoCAD does not create a block definition of an overlaid drawing. This option is accessed by entering O at the ?/Bind/Detach/Path/Reload/Overlay/⟨Attach⟩: prompt, picking the **Overlay** button on the **External Reference** toolbar, or by selecting **O**verlay... in the **External Reference** ⟩ cascading submenu of the **File** pull-down menu.
- **Attach.** This option enables you to attach an xref to the drawing currently displayed on the screen. This is the default option and can be selected by pressing [Enter] after the initial prompt is displayed. This option is accessed by entering A at the ?/Bind/Detach/Path/Reload/Overlay/⟨Attach⟩: prompt, picking the **Attach** button on the **External Reference** toolbar, or by selecting **A**ttach... in the **External Reference** ⟩ cascading submenu of the **File** pull-down menu.

## CHAPTER TEST

*Write your answers in the spaces provided.*

1. How does the **XREF Overlay** option differ from the **Attach** option? _____

   _____

   _____

2. What command enables you to construct a paper space viewport, attach an external reference, and zoom to a specific portion of the drawing? _____

   _____

3. What effect does the use of referenced drawings have on drawing file size? _____

   _____

4. When are xrefs updated in the master drawing? _____

   _____

5. Why would you want to bind a dependent symbol to a master drawing? _____

   _____

   _____

6. What does the layer name WALL$0$NOTES mean? _____

   _____

   _____

   _____

7. Name the system variable that controls the creation of the xref log file. _____

8. Your drawings should be created in what "space?" _____

   _____

9. Which system variable allows you to switch from model space to paper space? _____

   _____

10. What value should the variable mentioned in Question 9 be set to in order to draw in the space mentioned in Question 8? _____

    _____

11. What value should the variable mentioned in Question 9 be set to in order to use the **MVIEW** command? _____

    _____

12. What is the function of the **MVIEW** command? _____

    _____

13. Why would you want to reference one drawing to another rather than insert it? _____

    _____

    _____

14. Indicate the command, option, and value you would use to specify a scale of 1/2″ = 1′-0″ inside a viewport. _____

15. Name the command and option you would use to freeze all layers of drawings inside any new viewports. _____

16. Do you need to be in paper space or model space in order to resize a viewport? _____

    _____

17. Why would you plot a multiview drawing at full scale (1=1) if it was created with **MVIEW**, and contained several views at different scales? _____

    _____

18. Explain why you should plan your plots. _____

    _____

    _____

## DRAWING PROBLEMS

1. Open one of your dimensioned drawings from Chapter 20. Construct a multiview layout and generate a plot on C-size paper.

   *Mechanical Drafting*

   A. Set **TILEMODE** to 0 and create four viewports of equal size, but separated by 1″ of empty space.

   B. Select each viewport and display a different view of the drawing.

   C. Plot the drawing and be sure to use the scale of 1 = 1.

   D. Save the drawing as A:P26-1.

2. Open one of your dimensioned drawings from Chapter 21. Construct a multiview layout and generate a plot on C-size or B-size paper. Create a single viewport and plot at the scale of 1:1.

   *Mechanical Drafting*

3. Open one of your dimensioned drawings from Chapter 22. Construct a multiview layout and generate a plot on C-size or B-size paper. Create a single viewport and plot at the scale of 1:1.

   *Mechanical Drafting*

*Mechanical Drafting*

4. Open one of your dimensioned drawings from Chapter 23. Construct a multiview layout and generate a plot on C-size or B-size paper. Create a single viewport and plot at the scale of 1:1.

*Mechanical Drafting*

5. Open one of your dimensioned drawings from Chapter 24. Construct a multiview layout and generate a plot on C-size or B-size paper. Create a single viewport and plot at the scale of 1:1.

*Mechanical Drafting*

6. Open one of your dimensioned drawings from Chapter 25. Construct a multiview layout and generate a plot on C-size or B-size paper. Create a single viewport and plot at the scale of 1:1.

AutoCAD R13

# Chapter 27

# Assigning Attributes and Generating a Bill of Materials

## Learning objectives

After completing this chapter, you will be able to:
- ○ Assign visible or hidden values (attributes) to blocks.
- ○ Edit attributes in existing blocks.
- ○ Create a template file for the collection of block attributes.
- ○ Collect attribute values in a bill of materials.

Blocks become more useful when written information is given with them. It is even more helpful to assign information that is visible (displayed) and information that is hidden. From this data, a list, much like a bill of materials, can be requested and printed.

Written or numerical values assigned to blocks are called *attributes* by AutoCAD. Attribute information can be extracted from the drawing, rather than used only as text labels. Examples of blocks with attributes are shown in Figure 27-1. The **ATTDEF** (attribute defined) command allows you to specify attribute text and specify how it is displayed. The **ATTDISP**

Figure 27-1. Examples of blocks with attributes.

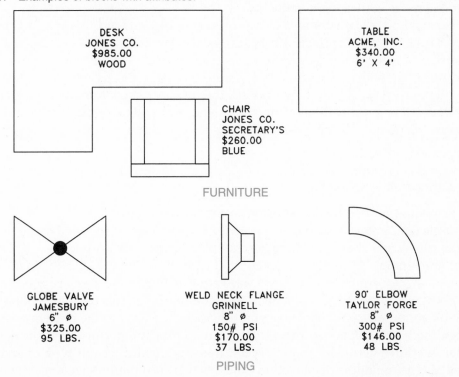

DESK
JONES CO.
$985.00
WOOD

TABLE
ACME, INC.
$340.00
6' X 4'

CHAIR
JONES CO.
SECRETARY'S
$260.00
BLUE

FURNITURE

GLOBE VALVE
JAMESBURY
6" ⌀
$325.00
95 LBS.

WELD NECK FLANGE
GRINNELL
8" ⌀
150# PSI
$170.00
37 LBS.

90° ELBOW
TAYLOR FORGE
8" ⌀
300# PSI
$146.00
48 LBS.

PIPING

(attribute display) command governs which attributes are displayed. You can selectively or collectively edit attributes using the **ATTEDIT** (attribute edit) command. Using the **ATTEXT** (attribute extract) command, you can extract attributes from a drawing in a list or report form.

The creation, editing, and extraction of attributes can also be handled with dialog boxes that are displayed with the **DDATTDEF**, **DDATTE**, **DDMODIFY**, and **DDATTEXT** commands.

## ASSIGNING ATTRIBUTES TO BLOCKS                          | AUG 7 |

The first step in defining block attributes is to decide what information about the block is needed. Then decide how the computer should ask you for the attribute. What is the size? might be such a prompt. The name of the object should be your first attribute. This is followed by items such as manufacturer, type, size, price, and weight.

Suppose you are drawing a valve symbol for a piping flow diagram. You might want to list all product-related data. The number of attributes needed are limited only by the project requirements.

Once the symbol is completed and shown on the screen, select the **ATTDEF** command.

> Command: **ATTDEF** ↵
> Attribute modes — Invisible:N Constant:N Verify:N Preset:N
> Enter (ICVP) to change, RETURN when done:

At this prompt, there are four decisions you must make. All of the options affect the attributes, and all are toggle switches. The default option is **N** for no, or normal.

- **Invisible.** Should the attribute be visible? Type I to make the attribute invisible. It will not be displayed when the block is inserted.
- **Constant.** Should the attribute always be the same? Typing C to turn on the **Constant** option means that all future uses of the block display the same value for the attribute. You will not be prompted for a new value.
- **Verify.** Do you want a prompt to remind you about the value you entered? When creating an attribute, you enter the attribute value at the prompt. To check that the value you entered is correct, turn **Verify** on.
- **Preset.** Should all attributes assume preset values and not display prompts? The **Preset** option creates variable attributes, but disables all attribute prompts during the insertion of a block. Default values are used instead. This works only with normal attributes. The setting does not affect dialog box entry discussed later.

If you do not turn on any of these options, the display shows **Normal**. A normal display means that you will be prompted for all attributes and they will be visible. Request the **Normal** option by pressing [Enter]. The next three prompts let you assign a value to the attribute.

> Attribute tag: **TYPE** ↵
> Attribute prompt: **Enter valve type:** ↵
> Default attribute value: **GATE** ↵

The information needed by the **ATTDEF** prompts is as follows:

- **Attribute tag:.** Enter the name of the attribute here. You must give a name or number. There can be any character in the tag, but blanks are not allowed.
- **Attribute prompt:.** Enter the statement you want the computer to ask when this block is inserted. For example, What is the valve size? or Enter valve size: are good prompts if size is the attribute tag. If **Constant** or **Preset** mode is set, this prompt is not displayed.
- **Default attribute value:.** The entry you type here is placed in the drawing as a default when the block is inserted unless you change it at the prompt. You do not have to enter anything here. You might type a message regarding the type of information needed. The default is displayed in brackets (⟨ ⟩). You might have a message, such as 10 SPACES MAX or NUMBERS ONLY. Only the prompt Attribute value is displayed if the **Constant** mode is set.

The remainder of the **ATTDEF** command is the same series of prompts found with the **DTEXT** command. Since attributes are text, they need to be positioned and sized. The current text style is assigned unless a new one is selected. When you complete the **ATTDEF** command, press [Enter]. A label appears on screen. This is the attribute tag. Do not be dismayed; this is the only time the tag name appears. When the block is inserted, you are asked for information that takes the place of the tag.

When you define a second attribute and reach the text positioning prompt, the previous text is highlighted. This indicates that if [Enter] is pressed, the new text assumes the same justification, and is positioned directly below the highlighted text. If you prefer a different position, enter new values or pick a new point.

When you finish creating attributes, use the **BLOCK** or **WBLOCK** commands as discussed in Chapter 25. When creating the block, be sure to select the objects and all of the attributes that go with that block. When the block is created, it should disappear, as should all of the attributes. If attributes remain on the screen, undo and try again, making sure that all attributes are selected.

## ASSIGNING ATTRIBUTES WITH A DIALOG BOX      AUG 7

All of the aspects of an attribute can be assigned on the screen in a dialog box by using the **DDATTDEF** command. This command activates the **Attribute Definition** dialog box shown in Figure 27-2. To access the **DDATTDEF** command, type DDATTDEF at the **Command:** prompt, or pick the **Define Attribute** button from the **Attribute** toolbar. If the ACADFULL menu file is loaded, select **Attribute...** from the **Construct** pull-down menu.

Figure 27-2.   Attributes can be assigned in the **Attribute Definition** dialog box.

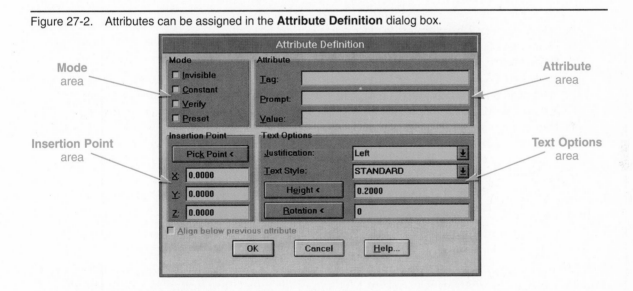

The **Attribute Definition** dialog box is divided into four areas with the following labels: **Mode**, **Attribute**, **Insertion Point**, and **Text Options**. Each of these areas allows you to set the specific aspects of the attribute.

First pick any of the mode buttons you wish to set. Then, pick the **Tag:** edit box and enter the attribute tag. Do the same for **Prompt:** and **Value:**. If you need to change any one of these values, simply double-click on the current entry and type the new value. If you click once in the edit box, you can use any of the cursor keys to edit the text. Each of these edit boxes displays only a limited number of characters. The boxes can contain up to 256 characters. If you type more than the maximum displayable characters, the text scrolls off the left side of the edit box. If you need to view the first part of the text, use the arrow keys to move to that position.

Notice in Figure 27-2 that two pop-up lists (denoted by the arrow along the right of the dialog box) enable you to select the text justification and the text style. If you wish to select centered text, just pick anywhere inside the **Justification:** box, and a list of text alignment options is displayed. When you pick **Center**, the list closes and the word Center appears in the list box. Similarly, if you pick inside the **Text Style:** box, a pop-up list of all text styles in the current drawing is displayed. Pick the style you need, and it is displayed in the list box.

Note the ⟨ symbol on the **Pick Point** ⟨, **Height** ⟨, and **Rotation** ⟨ buttons. Selecting any one of these buttons temporarily returns you to the graphics screen and allows you to indicate to AutoCAD the value on the screen by picking points. Once the point is picked, the dialog box returns. If everything is correct, pick **OK** and the attribute is placed on the screen. Press [Enter] if you want to create another attribute. If you want the next attribute to be placed below the first with the same justification, pick the **Align below previous attribute** check box. When you do this, the **Insertion point** and **Text** options selections are grayed out.

## EDITING ATTRIBUTE DEFINITIONS                                    AUG 7

Occasionally you may need to change certain aspects of attribute text before it is included in a block or wblock. Similar to the options available when editing normal text, the **CHANGE** command may be used to change the attribute text insertion point, text style, height, and rotation angle of selected attribute definitions. The **CHANGE** command also permits you to revise the attribute tag, prompt, and default value (if a default value was initially provided). To access the **CHANGE** command, type CHANGE at the **Command:** prompt. The command sequence and options appear as follows:

```
Command: CHANGE ↵
Select objects: (select the attribute definition[s] to change)
Select objects: (press [Enter] to close the selection set)
Properties/⟨Change point⟩: ↵
Enter text insertion point: (pick a new insertion point or press [Enter])
Text style: STANDARD
New style or RETURN for no change: (enter an existing style name or press [Enter])
New height ⟨0.2000⟩: (enter a new height or press [Enter])
New rotation angle ⟨0⟩: (enter a new angle or press [Enter])
New tag ⟨SIZE⟩: (provide a new tag and press [Enter], or press [Enter] to accept the tag)
New prompt ⟨ENTER THE SIZE⟩: (enter a new prompt and press [Enter], or press
    [Enter] to accept the prompt)
New default value ⟨6"⟩: (provide a new default value and press [Enter], or press
    [Enter] to accept the default value)
```

If you only want to change the tag, prompt, or default value assigned to a text attribute, you may do so quickly using the **DDEDIT** command. To access the **DDEDIT** command, type DDEDIT at the **Command:** prompt, or pick the **Edit Text** button in the **Edit Polyline** flyout on the **Modify** toolbar. If the ACADFULL menu file is loaded, select **Text Edit...** from the **Modify** pulldown menu. However, unlike the **CHANGE** command, **DDEDIT** only allows you to change one attribute definition at a time.

```
Command: DDEDIT ↵
⟨Select an annotation object⟩/Undo: (select one attribute definition to change)
```

The **Edit Attribute Definition** dialog box is now displayed, as shown in Figure 27-3. Revise the **Tag**, **Prompt**, or **Default** values as required in the corresponding edit boxes. If necessary, refer to Chapter 11 to review the editing techniques available in this type of dialog box. When you are done making changes, click the **OK** button and the dialog box is closed. The **DDEDIT** prompt remains on the command line should you want to select another entity or undo the changes you made. When you are finished, press [Enter] to end the command.

Figure 27-3.   The **Edit Attribute Definition** dialog box is used to change the tag, prompt, and default value of an attribute.

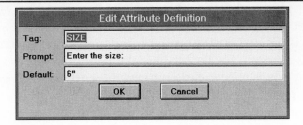

## Editing attribute definitions in a dialog box

The **Modify Attribute Definition** dialog box provides expanded editing capabilities for text attributes. To activate this dialog box, enter DDMODIFY at the **Command:** prompt. It may also be activated by picking the **Properties** button on the **Properties** toolbar, or select **Properties...** from the **Edit** pull-down menu. If either of the last two methods is used, you must select the text attribute to be edited before the dialog box is activated.

As shown in Figure 27-4, you can change the color, linetype, layer, or thickness of the selected attribute in the **Properties** section at the top of the dialog box. Just below the **Properties** section are the **Tag:**, **Prompt**, and **Default:** edit boxes. These edit boxes provide the same capabilities as the **DDEDIT** command described previously.

Figure 27-4.   The **Modify Attribute Definition** dialog box allows all aspects of the attribute's text to be changed.

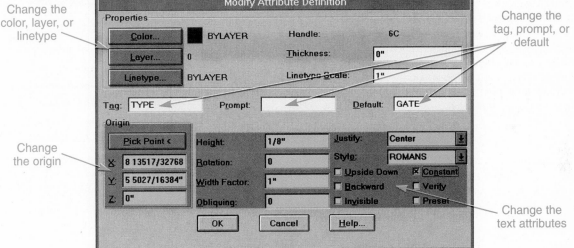

You can change the origin of the text attribute by selecting the **Pick Point** ⟨ button and picking a new point on the screen, or entering new X, Y, or Z coordinates in the appropriate edit boxes. You will also note the options to change the text height, rotation angle, width factor, and obliquing angle.

Clicking the arrow to the right of the **Justify:** box activates a pop-up list from which you may select a new text justification. To change the attribute's text style, click the arrow to the right of the **Style:** box. If another text style is defined in the current drawing, it appears in this pop-up list. Pick the **Upside Down** or **Backward** check boxes if you want these conditions applied to your text attribute.

Perhaps the most powerful feature of the **Modify Attribute Definition** dialog box is the ability to change the attribute modes originally defined for a text attribute. You may recall from the discussion of the **ATTDEF** and **DDATTDEF** commands earlier in this chapter, that an attribute may be defined with **Invisible**, **Constant**, **Verify**, or **Preset** modes. Remember that the **Constant** mode assumes that the values of an attribute will remain unchanged. Therefore, no prompt is defined for the attribute and no prompt is presented when the attribute is inserted.

The example shown in Figure 27-4 illustrates this restriction. Observe that since the **Constant** box is checked, no prompt appears in the **Prompt:** edit box. To revise the attribute definition for normal prompting, pick the **Constant** check box to remove the "X", and enter a prompt in the **Prompt:** edit box. If you want to turn on the **Verify** or **Preset** modes, or change an attribute from visible to invisible, pick the appropriate check box.

## INSERTING BLOCKS WITH ATTRIBUTES

AUG 7

When you use the **INSERT** command to place a block with attributes in your drawing, you are prompted for additional information after the insertion point, scale factors, and rotation angle are specified. The prompt that you entered in the **ATTDEF** command appears, and the default attribute value appears in brackets. Accept the default by pressing [Enter], or provide a new value. Then the attribute is displayed.

Attribute prompts may be answered using a dialog box if the **ATTDIA** system variable is set to a value of 1 (on). After entering the rotation angle at the **INSERT** or **DDINSERT** commands, the **Enter Attributes** dialog box appears. As shown in Figure 27-5, this dialog box can list up to eight attributes. If a block has more than eight attributes, you can display the next page of attributes by clicking the **Next** button.

Figure 27-5.  The **Enter Attributes** dialog box allows you to enter or change attributes when a block is inserted. If the block has more than eight attributes, pick the **Next** button to see the next "page." The button is grayed-out here since there are only three attributes.

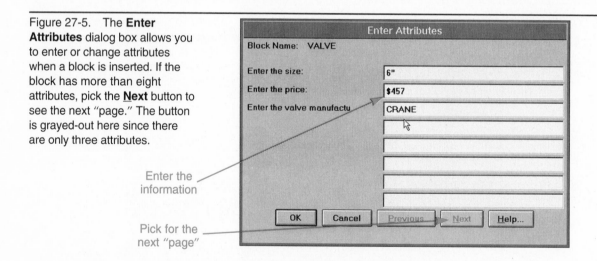

Enter the information

Pick for the next "page"

Responding to attribute prompts in a dialog box has distinct advantages over answering the prompts on the command line. With the dialog box, you can see at a glance whether all the attribute values are correct. To change a value, simply move to the incorrect value and enter a new one. You can quickly move forward through the attributes and buttons in this dialog box by using the [Tab] key. Using the [Shift]+[Tab] key combination cycles through the attributes and buttons in reverse order. When you are finished, click **OK** to close the dialog box. The inserted block with attributes then appears on screen.

**PROFESSIONAL TIP**

Set the value of **ATTDIA** to 1 in your prototype drawing to automatically activate the **Enter Attributes** dialog box whenever you insert a block with attributes.

## Attribute prompt suppression

Some drawings may use blocks with attributes that always retain their default values. In this case, there is no need to be prompted for the attribute values. You can turn off the attribute prompts by entering 0 for the **ATTREQ** system variable.

> Command: **ATTREQ** ↵
> New value for ATTREQ ⟨1⟩: **0** ↵

Try inserting the VALVE block. Notice that none of the attribute prompts appear. The ATTREQ value is saved with the drawing. To display attribute prompts again, change the value of **ATTREQ** back to 1.

PROFESSIONAL
TIP

Part of your project and drawing planning should involve system variable settings such as **ATTREQ**. Setting **ATTREQ** to 0 before using blocks can save time in the drawing process.

## EXERCISE 27-1

☐ Load AutoCAD for Windows and start a new drawing. Name the drawing EX27-1, and use an A-size or B-size architectural prototype drawing.
☐ Draw the valve symbol shown below.

GATE
CRANE
6"
$457

☐ Select the **ATTDEF** command and assign the following attributes:

| TAG | PROMPT | VALUE | MODE |
|-----|--------|-------|------|
| Type | *(None)* | Gate | Constant |
| Mfgr. | Enter the valve manufacturer: | Crane | Invisible |
| Size | Enter the size | 6" | Normal and Preset |
| Price | Enter the price | $457 | Invisible and Verify |

☐ Select the **BLOCK** command. Include the valve and all of the attributes in the block and name it VALVE.
☐ Select the **INSERT** command to place a copy of the VALVE block on your screen. Enter new values for the attributes if you wish. You should be prompted twice for the price if the **Verify** option was set properly.
☐ Save the drawing as A:EX27-1.

## CONTROLLING THE ATTRIBUTE DISPLAY

Attributes are meant to contain valuable information about the blocks in your drawings. This information is normally not displayed on the screen or during plotting. Its principal function is to generate materials lists and to speed accounting. Use the **DTEXT** and **MTEXT** commands for specific labels. You can control the display of attributes on the screen using the **ATTDISP** command.

    Command: **ATTDISP** ↵
    Normal/ON/OFF ⟨Normal⟩:

The **Normal** mode displays attributes exactly as you created them. This is the default mode for **ATTDISP**. The **ON** option displays *all* attributes. The **OFF** position suppresses all attributes.

**PROFESSIONAL TIP**

After attributes have been drawn, added to blocks, and checked for correctness, hide them by turning off **ATTDISP**. If left on, they clutter the screen and lengthen regeneration time.

## CHANGING ATTRIBUTE VALUES

As mentioned earlier, you can freely edit attribute definitions with the **CHANGE**, **DDEDIT**, or **DDMODIFY** commands before they are included in a block. Once the block is created, however, the attributes are part of it and must be changed using the **ATTEDIT** command. To access the **ATTEDIT** command, type ATTEDIT at the **Command:** prompt, or pick the **Edit Attribute Globally** button on the **Attribute** toolbar. If the ACADFULL menu file is loaded, from the **Modify** pull-down menu, select **Attribute** ⟩ and then **Edit Globally**. The **ATTEDIT** command sequence is as follows:

    Command: **ATTEDIT** ↵
    Edit attributes one at a time? ⟨Y⟩

This prompt asks if you want to edit attributes individually. It is possible to change the same attribute on several insertions of the same block. Pressing [Enter] at this prompt allows you to select any number of different attributes. AutoCAD lets you edit them all, one at a time, without leaving the **ATTEDIT** command. If you respond with no, you may change specific letters, words, and values of a single attribute. This can affect all insertions of the same block. For example, suppose a block named RESISTOR was inserted on a drawing in 12 places. However, you misspelled the attribute as RESISTER. Answer N to the Edit attributes one at a time? prompt. This is a *global* attribute editing method.

Each **ATTEDIT** technique allows you to determine the exact block and attribute specifications to edit. These prompts appear:

    Block name specification ⟨*⟩:
    Attribute tag specification ⟨*⟩:
    Attribute value specification ⟨*⟩:

To selectively edit attribute values, respond to the prompt with a name or value. Suppose you enter an attribute and receive the following message:

    0 attributes selected. *Invalid*

You have picked an attribute that was not specified. It is often quicker to press [Enter] for the three specification prompts and then *pick* the attribute you need to edit.

### Editing several insertions of the same attribute

A situation may occur when a block having a wrong or misspelled attribute is inserted several times. For example, in Figure 27-6 the VALVE block was inserted three times with the manufacturer's name as CRANE. Unfortunately, the name was supposed to be POWELL. Enter **ATTEDIT** and respond in the following manner.

> Command: **ATTEDIT** ⏎
> Edit attributes one at a time? ⟨Y⟩ **N** ⏎
> Global edit of attribute values.
> Edit only attributes visible on screen? ⟨Y⟩: ⏎
> Block name specification ⟨*⟩: ⏎
> Attribute tag specification ⟨*⟩: ⏎
> Attribute value specification ⟨*⟩: ⏎
> Select attributes: (*pick* CRANE *on all* VALVE *blocks and press* [Enter] *when completed*)
> (*n*) attributes selected. (*n equals the number of attributes picked*)
> String to change: **CRANE** ⏎ (*words or characters to change*)
> New string: **POWELL** ⏎

After pressing [Enter], CRANE attributes on the blocks selected are changed to read POWELL.

Figure 27-6.   Global editing changes the same attribute on several block insertions.

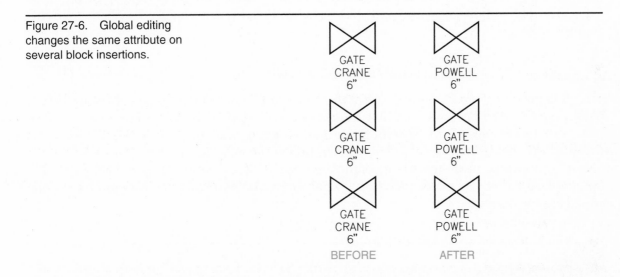

EXERCISE 27-2

❑ If Exercise 27-1 is not on your screen now, open the drawing named EX27-1.
❑ Insert the VALVE block onto your screen in three places, as shown in the diagram below.
❑ In response to the attribute prompts, enter CRANE as the manufacturer, 6″ as the size, and $457 as the price.
❑ Set **ATTDISP** to on.
❑ Use global attribute editing to change the following attributes on all insertions of VALVE.

| FROM | TO |
|---|---|
| Crane | Powell |
| $457.00 | $487.00 |

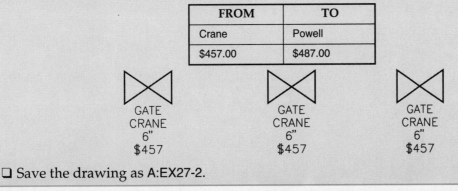

❑ Save the drawing as A:EX27-2.

Use care when assigning the **Constant** mode option to attribute definitions. The **ATTEDIT** command displays the following error message if you attempt to edit an inserted block attribute with a **Constant** setting:

0 attributes selected. *Invalid*

The inserted block must then be exploded and redefined. Assign **Constant** to only those attributes you know will not change.

### Editing different attributes one at a time

Global editing is a more precise method of changing specific attributes and text strings. On the other hand, individual editing allows you to change any value on any attribute. Several attributes and text strings can be changed without leaving the **ATTEDIT** command. After you answer Y to the Edit attributes one at a time prompt, and press [Enter] for the three "specification" options, select the attributes. Press [Enter] when you are finished; then this prompt appears:

(*n*) attributes selected.
Value/Position/Height/Angle/Style/Layer/Color/Next ⟨N⟩:

With this prompt, a small "X" appears at the lower-left corner of the first attribute in the last block selected. The order in which attributes were selected is shown in Figure 27-7A. The order in which AutoCAD picks them for editing is shown in Figure 27-7B. The "X" indicates the attribute that is being edited. The **Next** option is the default. Pressing [Enter] causes the "X" to jump to the next attribute in sequence. The "X" does not jump to the next attribute automatically after you make a change. It remains in case you want to make more than one change to the attribute.

Figure 27-7.   A—The order attributes were selected. B—The order in which AutoCAD edits them.

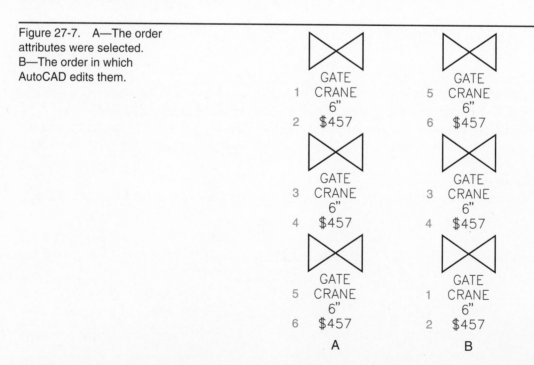

Prompts for all attribute editing options are as follows:

- **Value.** Change or Replace? ⟨R⟩: Pressing [Enter] here indicates you want to replace the attribute. AutoCAD requests a new attribute value. You can change any part of the attribute by typing C for **Change**. AutoCAD responds with String to change and New string prompts. A *string* is any sequence of consecutive characters.
- **Position.** Enter text insertion point:
- **Height.** New height ⟨*current*⟩:
- **Angle.** New rotation angle ⟨0⟩:
- **Style.** Text style: ⟨*current*⟩
    New style or RETURN for no change:
- **Layer.** New layer ⟨*current*⟩:
- **Color.** New color ⟨BYLAYER⟩:

Individual editing of attributes can be used to correct misspelled words, replace words, or change attribute information. Look at the attributes attached to the block in Figure 27-8. The manufacturer was changed from POWELL to CRANE. The price was changed from $565.00 to $556.00. Suppose these are the only two attributes to be edited. The entire command sequence looks like this:

Command: **ATTEDIT** ↵
Edit attributes one at a time? ⟨N⟩ **Y** ↵
Select Attributes: *(select the two attributes)*
2 attributes selected. *(the "X" appears at POWELL, the first attribute selected)*
Value/Position/Height/Angle/Style/Layer/Color/Next ⟨N⟩: **V** ↵
Change or Replace? ⟨R⟩: **R** ↵
New attribute value: **CRANE** ↵
Value/Position/Height/Angle/Style/Layer/Color/Next ⟨N⟩: ↵ *(pressing [Enter] moves
    the "X" to the next attribute, $565.00)*
Value/Position/Height/Angle/Style/Layer/Color/Next ⟨N⟩: **V** ↵
Change or Replace? ⟨R⟩: **C** ↵
String to change: **65** ↵
New string: **56** ↵
Value/Position/Height/Angle/Style/Layer/Color/Next ⟨N⟩: *(press [Enter] at this prompt
    to get out of the* **ATTEDIT** *command and see the final change take place)*

The completed attribute edit is shown in Figure 27-8C.

Figure 27-8.   The attributes
to be changed are indicated
with an "X."

GATE
POWELL
6"
$565

A

GATE
CRANE
6"
$565

B

GATE
CRANE
6"
$556

C

**PROFESSIONAL TIP**

When making blocks that contain attributes, add as many attributes as you think will be needed. If you do not have values for some of them, just enter TO COME as the value, or enter something to remind you that information is needed. Adding an attribute to a block is much more time-consuming than changing an attribute using the **ATTEDIT** command.

## EXERCISE 27-3

❑ Load AutoCAD for Windows and open drawing EX27-2 if it is not already on screen.
❑ Be sure there are three insertions of the VALVE block. Align them as shown in the diagram below.
❑ Set **ATTDISP** to on to display all attributes.
❑ Select the **ATTEDIT** command and choose the individual edit option.
❑ Assuming the blocks are numbered 1 to 3, top to bottom, change the individual attributes to the following values:

| | 1 | 2 | 3 |
|---|---|---|---|
| **Type** | Gate | Gate | Gate |
| **Mfgr.** | Crane | Powell | Jenkins |
| **Size** | 4" | 8" | 10" |
| **Price** | $376.00 | $563.00 | $837.00 |

❑ Connect the valves with straight lines as shown.
❑ Save the drawing as A:EX27-3.

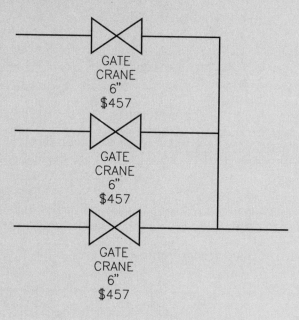

# EDITING ATTRIBUTES USING A DIALOG BOX

AUG 10

The **DDATTE** (dynamic dialog attribute editing) command allows you to edit attributes in a dialog box. You can edit as many block attributes as desired. To access the **DDATTE** command, type DDATTE at the **Command:** prompt, or pick the **Edit Attribute** button on the **Attribute** toolbar. If the ACADFULL menu file is loaded, from the **Modify** pull-down menu select **Attribute** ⟩ and then **Edit...**. After using one of these methods to access **DDATTE**, you are then prompted to select the attribute to be edited. Once selected, the **Edit Attributes** dialog box is activated.

## Editing attributes in a single block

If attributes in one block need editing, enter DDATTE and select the block as follows:

Command: **DDATTE** ↵
Select block: *(select block)*

The **Edit Attributes** dialog box appears on-screen, Figure 27-9. The attributes of the selected block are listed on the left. Their current values are shown in the edit boxes on the right. Move the cursor to the value to be edited and double-click so the box is highlighted, and enter the new value. Remember that if you pick the box, you can move the cursor to the incorrect letter, then use the delete key to remove a letter, type to insert characters, or use [Backspace] to delete. You can then pick **Cancel** or **OK**, or you can press [Enter] to move to the next attribute. If **Cancel** is picked, the attribute value is left unchanged. When finished, pick **OK** at the bottom of the dialog box. The attribute associated with the block is changed. If **Cancel** is picked, no changes are made and the drawing is redisplayed.

Figure 27-9.   The **Edit Attributes** dialog box displays all of the attributes assigned to the selected block. You can change any of these attributes.

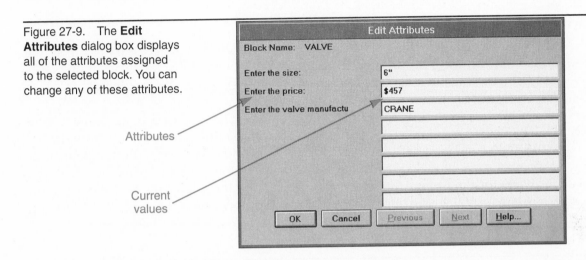

NOTE

When editing attributes using the dialog box, the attribute value can have up to 256 characters. Remember, only a limited number of characters will be displayed in the edit box. The attribute prompt is limited to 23 characters for display purposes only. Longer attribute prompts entered remain intact in the drawing file.

## Redefining a block and its attributes

You may encounter a situation in which an existing block and its associated attributes must be revised. You may need to delete existing attributes, or add new ones, in addition to revising the geometry of the block itself. This could normally be a time-consuming function, but is made easy with the **ATTREDEF** command. To access the **ATTREDEF** command, type ATTREDEF at the **Command:** prompt, or pick the **Redefine Attribute** button on the **Attribute** toolbar. If the ACADFULL menu file is loaded, from a **Modify** pull-down menu select **Attribute** 〉 and then **Redefine**. After using one of these methods to access **ATTREDEF**, you are then prompted to select the attribute to be redefined.

When redefining a block and its attributes, the existing block that is being redefined must be exploded prior to using **ATTREDEF**. If it is not, you will get a Block *nnn* references itself error. The prompts for this command are as follows:

> Command: **ATTREDEF** ↵
> Name of Block you wish to redefine: *(enter block name and press* [Enter]*)*
> Select objects for new Block...
> Select objects: *(select the block geomerty and all new and existing attributes and*
>    *press* [Enter]*)*
> Insertion base point of new block: *(pick insertion base point)*
> Verify attribute values
> Command:

All existing instances of the redefined block and attributes will be immediately updated. If any of the old attributes were omitted from the redefined block, they will not be included in the new version.

## USING ATTRIBUTES TO AUTOMATE DRAFTING DOCUMENTATION

So far you have seen that attributes are extremely powerful tools for assigning textual information to drawing symbols. However, attributes may also be used to automate any detailing or documentation task that requires a great deal of text. Such tasks include title block information, revision block data, and parts list or list of materials generation.

### Attributes and title blocks

After a drawing is completely drawn and dimensioned, it is then necessary to fill out the information in the drawing title block. This is usually one of the more time-consuming tasks associated with drafting documentation. Using the following suggested guidelines, this task can be efficiently automated.

1. The title block format is first drawn using the correct layer(s) and in accordance with industry or company standards. You can use one of the title block formats provided by the **MVSETUP** command discussed in Chapter 19, or create your own. Be sure to include your company or school logo within the title block. If you work in an industry that produces items for the Federal Government, also include the applicable FSCM code in the title block. A typical A-size title block drawn in accordance with the ANSI Y14.1 *Drawing Sheet Size and Format* standard is illustrated in Figure 27-10.

Figure 27-10.    A title block sheet must adhere to applicable standards. This title block is for an A-size sheet and adheres to ANSI Y14.1, *Drawing Sheet Size and Format.*

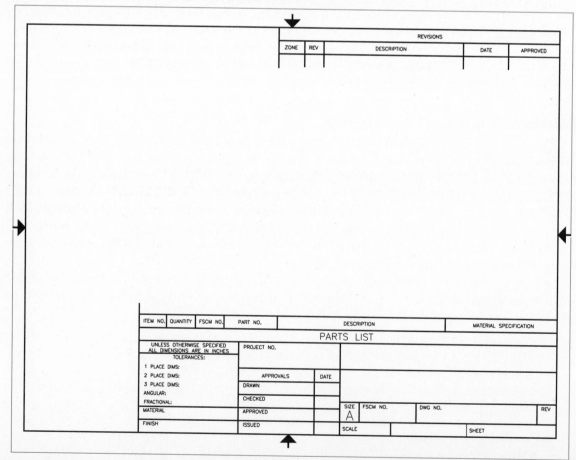

**NOTE** The FSCM (Federal Supply Code for Manufacturers) is a five-digit numeric code identifier applicable to any organization that produces items used by the Federal Government. It also applies to government activities that control design, or are responsible for the development of certain specifications, drawings, or standards that control the design of items.

2. After drawing the title block, create a separate layer for the title block attributes. By placing the attributes on a separate layer, you can easily suppress the title block information by freezing the layer that contains the attributes. This can greatly reduce redraw and regeneration times. When you are ready to plot the finished drawing, simply thaw the frozen layer.

3. Define attributes for each area of the title block. As you create the attributes, determine the appropriate text height and justification modes for each. The attributes should include the drawing title, drawing number, drafter, checker, dates, scale, sheet size, material, finish, revision letter, and tolerance information, as shown in Figure 27-11. Include any other information that may be specific to your organization or application.

4. Assign default values to attributes wherever possible. As an example, if your organization consistently specifies the same overall tolerances on drawing dimensions, the tolerance attributes can be assigned default values.

5. Once you have defined each attribute, **WBLOCK** the entire drawing to disk with a descriptive filename. Some examples of names for an A-size title block are **TITLEA** or **FORMATA**. Be sure to use 0,0 as the insertion point for the title block.

Figure 27-11. This shows attributes that have been defined for each field of a title block.

| ITEM NO. | QUANTITY | FSCM NO. | PART NO. | DESCRIPTION | MATERIAL SPECIFICATION |
|---|---|---|---|---|---|

PARTS LIST

UNLESS OTHERWISE SPECIFIED ALL DIMENSIONS ARE IN INCHES
TOLERANCES:

1 PLACE DIMS: TOL1
2 PLACE DIMS: TOL2
3 PLACE DIMS: TOL3
ANGULAR: ANGL
FRACTIONAL: FRAC

MATERIAL MATERIAL
FINISH FINISH

PROJECT NO. PROJECT

APPROVALS | DATE
DRAWN DRAWN | DATE
CHECKED CHECKED | DATE
APPROVED APPROVED | DATE
ISSUED ISSUED | DATE

TITLE

SIZE A | FSCM NO. | DWG NO. NUMBER | REV REV
SCALE SCALE | SHEET SHEET

Insertion point

**PROFESSIONAL TIP** The size of each title block area imposes limits on the number of characters you can have in a line of text. You can provide a handy cue to yourself by including a reminder in the attribute. When defining an attribute in which you wish to place a reminder, use something like the following when entering text for the attribute prompt:

Attribute prompt: **Enter drawing name ⟨15 characters max⟩:**

Each time the block or prototype drawing is used that contains this attribute, the prompt will display the reminder shown above.

After all of the attributes have been defined, the **WBLOCK** command can be used to create a prototype drawing that can be inserted into a new drawing, or the **BLOCK** command can be used to create a block of defined attributes within the current prototype drawing file. Either method is acceptable, and the uses of both are explained in the following descriptions.

- **WBLOCK method.** The **WBLOCK** command saves a drawing file to disk, so it can be inserted into any other drawing. Prototype drawings used in this manner should be given descriptive names such as TITLE-A, PROTO-A, or TITLBLKA. The name should provide some indication of the drawing size. To utilize the prototype file, begin a new drawing and insert the prototype. After locating and scaling the drawing, the attribute prompts are displayed. As you enter the requested information, it is placed in the title block. This method requires that you begin with a blank drawing, and that you know the information requested by the attribute prompts when you begin. Remember, should you enter information that is incorrect, it can be altered using the **ATTE** (**DDATTE**) command.

- **BLOCK method.** The **BLOCK** command prompts you to select objects. Be sure to select *only* the defined attributes you just created. Do not select the headings of title block areas, or any of the geometry in the title block. When prompted to pick the insertion base point, select a corner of the title block that will be convenient to use each time this block is inserted into a drawing. The bold "X" in Figure 27-11 shows an appropriate location for the insertion base point. The current prototype drawing now contains a block of defined attributes for use in the title block. To begin a new drawing you must open this prototype and give it a new name to protect the integrity of the prototype. The title block data can be entered at any time during the creation of the new drawing. To do so, just use the **INSERT** command, and pick the proper insertion base point. The attribute prompts are then either displayed on the command line or in a dialog box, depending on the value of the **ATTDIA** variable. If **ATTDIA** is set to 1, all of the attributes can be entered in a dialog box like the one shown in Figure 27-12. The **WBLOCK** command can be used to save the defined attributes to disk as a file should you wish to have the ability to use the attributes on any drawing.

Regardless of the method used, title block data can be entered quickly and accurately without the use of text commands. If the attributes are entered in a dialog box, all of the information can be seen at one time, and mistakes can be corrected quickly. Attributes can be easily edited at a later date if necessary. Attribute text height or position can be changed with the **ATTEDIT** command, and the content of the attribute is changed with the **DDATTE** command. The completed title block after insertion of the attribute block is shown in Figure 27-13.

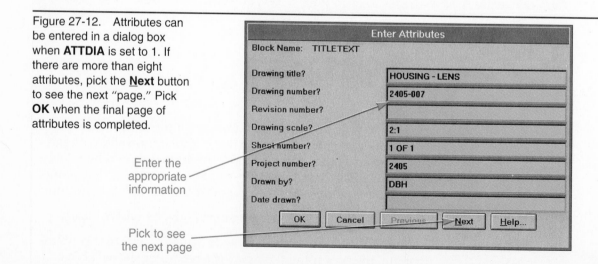

Figure 27-12.    Attributes can be entered in a dialog box when **ATTDIA** is set to 1. If there are more than eight attributes, pick the **Next** button to see the next "page." Pick **OK** when the final page of attributes is completed.

Enter the appropriate information

Pick to see the next page

Figure 27-13.   The title block after insertion of the attributes. When the drawing is complete, dates and approvals can be added with the **DDATTE** command.

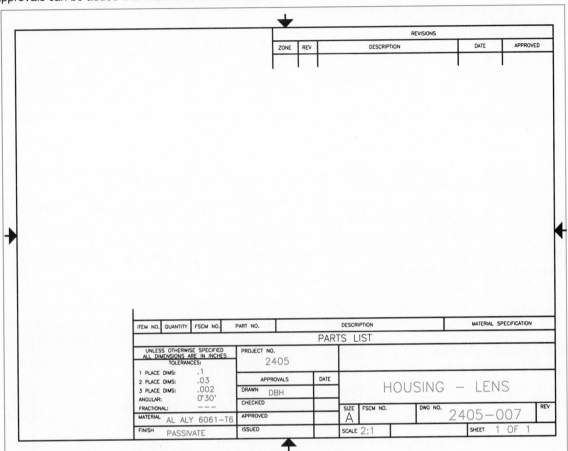

## Attributes and revision blocks

It is almost certain that a detail drawing will require revision at some time in the life cycle of a product. Typical changes that occur include design improvements and the correction of drafting errors. The first time that a drawing is revised, it is usually assigned the revision letter A. If necessary, revision letters continue with B through Z, but the letters I, O, and Q are not used, because they might be confused with numbers.

Title block formats include an area specifically designated to record all drawing changes. This area is normally located at the upper-right of the title block sheet, and is commonly called the *revision block*. The revision block provides space for the revision letter, description of the change, date, and approvals. The zone column is optional, and need only be added if applicable. Zones appear in the margins of a title block sheet and are indicated by alphabetical and numeric entries. They are used for reference purposes the same way as reference letters and numbers are used to identify a street or feature on a road map. Although A-size and B-size title blocks may include zones, they are rarely needed.

Block attributes provide a handy means of completing the necessary information in a revision block. Refer to Figure 27-14 as you follow these guidelines:

- First, create a revision block in the appropriate drawing layer(s).
- Define attributes that describe the zone (optional), revision letter, description of change, and change approval on a separate layer.
- Use left-justified text for the change description attribute, and middle-justified text for the remainder.

Figure 27-14.   The revision block is comprised of lines, attributes, and an insertion point. The border lines must be drawn as part of the block.

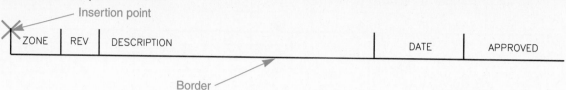

- **WBLOCK** the lines and attributes to disk, or **BLOCK** them into the current prototype drawing. Use a descriptive name such as REVBLK or REV. Keep in mind that each line of the parts list or revision block comes with its own border lines, therefore the borders must be saved with the attributes. Use the upper-left endpoint of the revision block as the insertion point.

Now, after a drawing has been revised, simply insert the revision block at the correct location into the edited drawing. If the **ATTDIA** system variable is set to 1, you can answer the attribute prompts in the **Enter Attributes** dialog box, as illustrated in Figure 27-15. After providing the change information, click the **OK** button and the completed revision block is automatically added to the title block sheet, Figure 27-16.

Figure 27-15.   Drawing revisions are entered in the **Enter Attributes** dialog box when **ATTDIA** is set to 1.

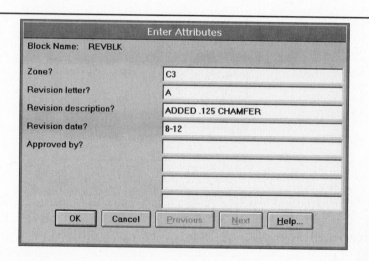

Figure 27-16.   The revision block after it is inserted into the drawing.

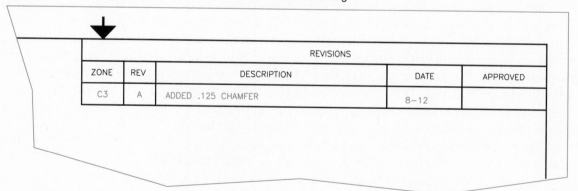

## Attributes and parts lists

Assembly drawings require a parts list, or list of materials, which includes the quantity, FSCM code (optional), part number, description, and item number for each component of the assembly or subassembly. In some organizations, the parts list is generated as a separate document; usually in an 8 1/2″ × 11″ format. In other companies, it is common practice to include the parts list on the face of the assembly drawing. Whether as a separate document or as part of the assembly drawing itself, parts lists provide another example of how attributes may be used to automate the documentation process.

Refer once again to the title block in Figure 27-10. You will observe a section specifically designated for a parts list located just above the title block area. Now, consider the example illustrated in Figure 27-17 as you follow the guidelines:

- First, create a parts list block in the appropriate drawing layer(s).
- Define attributes on a separate layer that describe the quantity, zone (optional), part number, item description, material specification, and item number for the components of an assembly drawing.
- Use left-justified text for the item description attribute and middle-justified text for the remainder.
- **WBLOCK** the parts list block to disk with a descriptive name like PL for parts list, or BOM for bill of materials. Use the lower-left endpoint of the parts list block as the insertion point as shown in Figure 27-17.

Figure 27-17.   Attributes and an insertion point are defined for a parts list block.

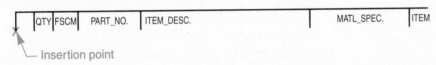

Now, after an assembly drawing has been completed, simply insert the parts list block at the correct location into the drawing. If the **ATTDIA** system variable is set to 1, you can answer the attribute prompts in the **Enter Attributes** dialog box, as illustrated in Figure 27-18.

After providing the parts list information, click the **OK** button and the completed parts list block is automatically added to the title block sheet, Figure 27-19. Repeat the procedure as many times as required for each component of the assembly drawing.

From the preceding examples, you can see that block attributes are powerful entities. Their applications are virtually endless. Can you think of any other drafting procedures that could be similarly automated?

Figure 27-18.   The parts list information is entered in the **Enter Attributes** dialog box when **ATTDIA** is set to 1.

| Enter Attributes | |
| --- | --- |
| Block Name:   BOM | |
| FSCM Number? | |
| Item number? | 1 |
| Material? | AL ALY 6061-T6 |
| Item description? | HOUSING - LENS |
| Part number? | 2405-007 |
| Quantity? | 1 |
| | |
| | |
| OK   Cancel   Previous   Next   Help... | |

Figure 27-19.    The parts list block after it is inserted into a drawing.

| 1 | | 52451 | PLATE, MOUNTING | 6061–T6 ALUM | 1 |
|---|---|---|---|---|---|
| QTY REQD | FSCM NO. | PART OR IDENTIFYING NO. | NOMENCLATURE OR DESCRIPTION | MATERIAL SPECIFICATION | ITEM NO. |

PARTS LIST

---

**PROFESSIONAL TIP**

A truly integrated CAD environment continually seeks out new methods to automate the drafting and design process. In such organizations, the "electronic geometry" embodied in a CAD file is the original, or master, document. If you work in a supervisory capacity, you are probably authorized to "sign-off" completed drawings, or to approve revised drawings. How can you "electronically" add your signature to an AutoCAD drawing? Consider using the following procedure.

- Set the **SKPOLY** system variable to use polylines when you use the **SKETCH** command. Use the **SKETCH** command to reproduce your signature. Sketching your name is a little difficult with a pointing device, but it can be reasonably accomplished with a bit of practice.
- Use the **PEDIT** command to "tweak" the signature into a more acceptable representation of your handwriting.
- **WBLOCK** your signature to a floppy disk. Keep the floppy in your briefcase or locked away in a secure location. Do not store your signature block on the hard drive or on the network drive where anyone can access it.
- When you need to approve a drawing, simply insert and scale your signature block as required in the correct location.

---

## COLLECTING ATTRIBUTE INFORMATION                    AUG 7

AutoCAD provides a method for listing attributes associated with any specified block. It is helpful for tabulating block information. Creating a special *template file* is part of this method. This file is a list of attributes that can be used in a bill of materials by third-party packages, or in databases. It is used with drawings that contain specific blocks and attributes you wish to list. The **ATTEXT** command creates an *extract file* that allows AutoCAD to find and list the attributes specified in the template file. This extract file can display the attributes on the screen or send them to a printer.

### Creating a template file

You often need to be selective in the blocks and attributes that are listed. This requires guidelines for AutoCAD to use when sorting through a drawing. To pick out specific block attributes, these guidelines are in the form of a *template file*. The AutoCAD template file allows you to pick out specific items from blocks and list them. The template file, a simple text file, can be made using database, word processing, or text editor programs.

In addition to listing attributes, the template file can be designed to extract block properties. Those include:

- **Level.** This refers to the nesting level of the block. If the block was nested inside another block, this number would be "2" in the extracted list.
- **Name.** Block name.
- **X.** The X coordinate location of the block insertion point.
- **Y.** The Y coordinate location of the block insertion point.
- **Layer.** Layer name.
- **Orient.** Rotation angle of the block.
- **XScale.** The X coordinate scale factor of the block.
- **YScale.** The Y coordinate scale factor of the block.

**PROFESSIONAL TIP**

Your application determines which properties need to be included in the template file. Template files can be created for different groups or departments of a company. The following chart lists possible attributes for a desk in the left column. Across the top are several different departments in a company. An "X" indicates which item is to be included in that department's template file.

| ATTRIBUTE | SHIPPING | PURCHASING | ACCOUNTING | ENGINEERING |
|-----------|----------|------------|------------|-------------|
| Manufacturer | | X | X | |
| Size | X | X | | X |
| Price | | X | X | |
| Weight | X | | | X |
| Color | | X | | X |
| Material | X | X | | X |

The example template file shown below could be used to extract information from the piping flow diagram in Exercise 27-3.

```
BL:NAME      C010000
BL:LAYER     C005000
BL:X         N008002
BL:Y         N008002
BLANK        C004000
MFGR         C010000
SIZE         C008000
PRICE        C010000
```

You would write this file using database or text editing programs such as the Windows Notepad. Notice that the items that are block characteristics begin with BL:. The items that are block attributes are given the name used at the Attribute tag: prompt of the **ATTDEF** command. The item BLANK is placed in the file to provide spacing between the Y coordinate and MFGR. Had this been omitted there would be no line space between those two items.

The numbers in the right column all begin with either C or N. The C indicates that character information is to be extracted and N represents numeric information. If a character other than a number is included in an attribute, use C instead of N. Notice that the PRICE attribute uses C. That is because the dollar symbol ($) is used in front of the price in the attribute.

The first three numbers after the C or N character indicate the number of spaces allotted for the attribute. There are ten spaces allotted for MFGR. The following three digits specify the number of decimal places in the attribute. The X and Y locations have been assigned two decimal places. This is detailed in Figure 27-20.

Figure 27-20. The template file shows numeric and character entries.

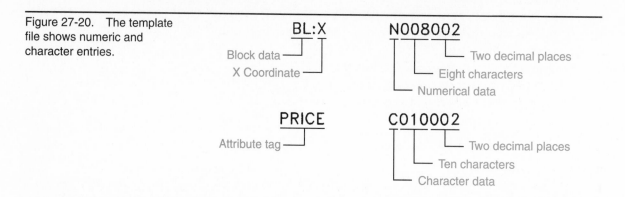

**EXERCISE 27-4**

❑ This exercise guides you through the construction of a template file for the drawing EX27-3. Use the Windows Notepad to create the file.

❑ Open drawing EX27-3 if it is not already on your screen.

❑ Use the [Ctrl]+[Esc] key combination to activate the Windows Task List, select **Program Manager** from the list and click the Switch To button.

❑ When the Accessories group window appears, double-click the Notepad icon to launch Notepad.

❑ Begin entering the following text at the flashing vertical cursor located at the top left of the Notepad window. You may place either a [Tab] or spaces between the columns:

|          |         |
|----------|---------|
| BL:NAME  | C010000 |
| BL:LAYER | C005000 |
| BL:X     | N008002 |
| BL:Y     | N008002 |
| BLANK    | C004000 |
| MFGR     | C010000 |
| SIZE     | C008000 |
| PRICE    | C010000 |

❑ When you are through entering text, your screen should appear as shown below.

❑ Select Save As... from the File pull-down menu, and save the file with the name EX27-3. Notepad automatically adds the .TXT extension to the filename.

❑ Select Exit from the File pull-down menu to exit Notepad and return to AutoCAD.

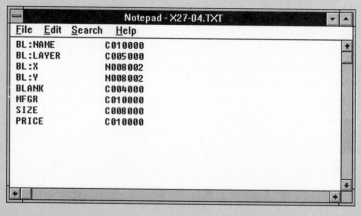

## Listing block attributes

AutoCAD provides three different formats for listing extracted information. The *DXF format* is related to programming and is the most complex. See Chapter 16, *AutoCAD Customization Guide*, for information on the DXF format. The other two—SDF and CDF—are formats that can be used with a variety of other programs. The *SDF (Space Delimited Format)* is the easiest for the average user to interpret. It means that the different *fields*, or groups of data are separated by spaces. The *CDF (Comma Delimited Format)* uses commas instead of spaces to separate fields.

Issue the **ATTEXT** command by entering ATTEXT on the command line. Specify the format you want or type O to list the attributes of specific selected objects. At this point, select the SDF format. The response here needs to be only the first letter.

> Command: **ATTEXT** ↵
> CDF, SDF, or DXF Attribute extract (or Objects)?⟨C⟩: **S** ↵

The **Select Template File** dialog box is then displayed. Select the file you wish to use from the **Files** list box. Note in Figure 27-21 that the file named EX22-3.TXT is selected. Click **OK**, and then the **Create extract file** dialog box appears. If you wish to have the extracted attributes saved in an existing file, select the extract file from the **Files** list box. To save the extracted attributes to a new file, enter a filename in the **File Name:** edit box. The current drawing name is the default. Be sure the extract filename you enter is slightly different than the template filename, for example, EX27-3A.

AutoCAD automatically appends a .TXT to the filename you enter. See Figure 27-22. If you use the same name, your original template file will be deleted. Click **OK** after entering the filename. If all goes well, AutoCAD reports that you have *n* records in extract file. The number of records listed in the file is based on the number of blocks that contain the attributes you were searching for.

Figure 27-21. The **Select Template File** dialog box allows you to choose a file.

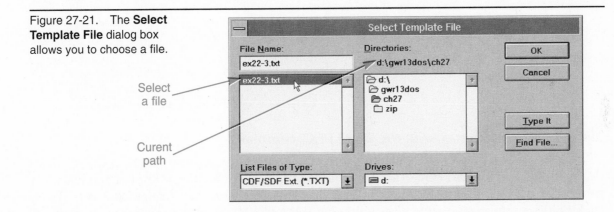

Figure 27-22. The **Create extract file** dialog box allows you to select an existing extract filename, or enter a new extract filename.

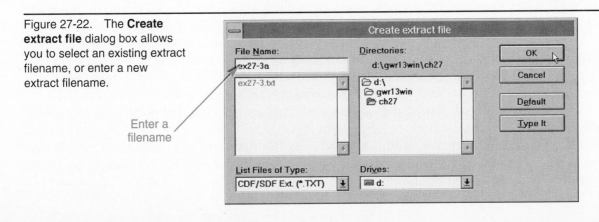

The extract file can be displayed on the screen by opening the file in the Windows Notepad. An example of the extract file in SDF format is shown in Figure 27-23. The same file in CDF format appears in Figure 27-24. Of the three formats discussed, the CDF format appears the most cumbersome. However, it (as well as the SDF format) may be used with specific database programs, such as dBASE. Decide which format is most suitable for your application. Regardless of the extract file format chosen, you may print the file from the Windows Notepad by selecting Print from the File pull-down menu.

Figure 27-23.   An extract file displayed in SDF format in the Windows Notepad.

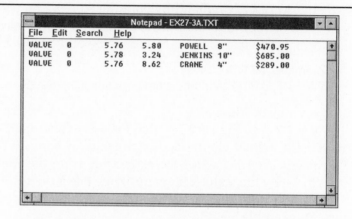

Figure 27-24.   An extract file displayed in CDF format in the Windows Notepad.

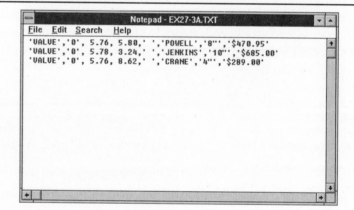

## Listing block attributes with the DDATTEXT command

The **DDATTEXT** command enables you to use dialog boxes for all steps in the attribute extraction process. DDATTEXT can be entered at the **Command:** prompt to activate the **Attribute Extraction** dialog box, Figure 27-25. Select the desired file format, such as SDF, by clicking the appropriate option button. If you want specific blocks in the extract file, click the **Select Objects** ⟩ button, and use any selection method to pick the blocks. If you do not select objects, all blocks in the drawing (specified by the template file) will be used.

Pick the **Template File...** button to select a filename from the **Template File** dialog box. This dialog box is exactly the same as the one shown in Figure 27-21. The output file, or extract file, can be selected by clicking the **Output File...** button. This displays the **Output File** dialog box, which is exactly the same as the **Create extract file** dialog box shown in Figure 27-22.

The bill of materials listing discussed in this chapter is a basic list of each block's selected attributes. As you become familiar with AutoCAD, customize it to meet your needs. Study magazines devoted to AutoCAD and read the *AutoCAD User's Guide.* You will find numerous software packages that generate specialized bills of material containing quantities and totals, rather than just a list of blocks.

Figure 27-25. The **DDATTEXT** command activates the **Attribute Extraction** dialog box.

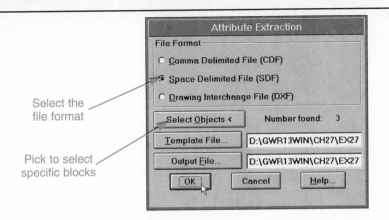

Select the file format

Pick to select specific blocks

**Attribute Extraction**

File Format
- ○ **C**omma Delimited File (CDF)
- ● **S**pace Delimited File (SDF)
- ○ **D**rawing Interchange File (DXF)

Select **O**bjects <    Number found:  3

**T**emplate File...    D:\GWR13WIN\CH27\EX27

Output **F**ile...    D:\GWR13WIN\CH27\EX27

OK    Cancel    Help...

## EXERCISE 27-5

❏ Open EX27-4 if it is not already on your screen.
❏ Select the **ATTEXT** command and enter SDF format.
❏ Enter the template filename as EX27-4. Enter EX27-4A for the extract filename.
❏ Select **ATTEXT** again and display the bill of materials on the screen.

## CHAPTER TEST

*Write your answers in the spaces provided.*

1. Define an "attribute." _____

2. Explain the purpose of the **ATTDEF** command. _____

   _____

3. Define the function of the following four **ATTDEF** modes: _____

   A. **Invisible—** _____

   B. **Constant—** _____

   C. **Verify—** _____

   D. **Preset—** _____

4. What attribute information does the **ATTDEF** command request? _____

   _____

5. Identify the three commands that may be used to edit attributes before they are included within a block. _____

   _____

   _____

6. Which command allows you to change an existing attribute from **Visible** to **Invisible**?___

   _____

7. List the three options for the **ATTDISP** command. _____

   _____

8. What is meant by "global" attribute editing? _____

   _____

9. How does individual attribute editing differ from global editing? _____
_____
_____
_____

10. Identify the purpose of the following two prompts in the global attribute editing routine.
String to change: _____
New string: _____

11. List the different aspects of the attribute that you can change when you edit attributes
one at a time. _____
_____

12. Which command allows you to use a dialog box to create attributes? _____

13. Explain the function of the **DDATTE** command. _____
_____

14. How does editing an attribute with **DDEDIT** differ from using **DDMODIFY**? _____
_____

15. What purpose does the **ATTREQ** system variable serve? _____
_____

16. To enter attributes using the dialog box, you must set the **ATTDIA** system variable to ___
_____.

17. When created, a drawing extract file is given the file extension _____.

18. The command that allows you to create the file type mentioned in Question 17 is
_____.

19. How is character and numerical data specified in a template file? _____
_____

20. How many characters are allowed for an attribute name in the template file? _____
_____

21. How do you create a template file? _____
_____

22. Define all of the aspects of each of the following template file entries.
BL:X _____
N006002 _____
PRICE _____
C010003 _____

23. Describe the difference between CDF and SDF attribute extract formats. _____
_____

24. The first time you create a file using the **ATTEXT** command, it is given a _____
extension.

## DRAWING PROBLEMS

1. Load AutoCAD for Windows and start a new drawing named P27-1. Draw the structural steel wide flange shape shown below using the dimensions given. Do not dimension the drawing. Create attributes for the drawing using the information given. Make a block of the drawing and name it W12X40. Insert the block once to test the attributes.

*Architecture*

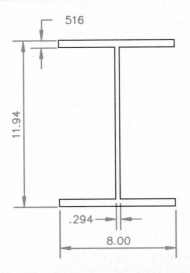

| Attributes | | | |
|---|---|---|---|
| | Steel | W12 x 40 | Visible |
| | Mfgr | Ryerson | Invisible |
| | Price | $.30/lb | Invisible |
| | Weight | 40 lbs/ft | Invisible |
| | Length | 10 ft | Invisible |
| | Code | 03116Wf | Invisible |

2. Load the drawing in Problem 1 (P27-1) and construct the floor plan shown using the dimensions given at a scale of 1/4"=1'-0". Dimension the drawing. Insert the block W12X40 six times as shown. Required attribute data is given in the chart below the drawing. Enter the appropriate information for the attributes as you are prompted for it. Note that the steel columns labeled 3 and 6 require slightly different attribute data. You can speed the drawing process by using **ARRAY** or **COPY**. Save the drawing as A:P27-2.

*Architecture*

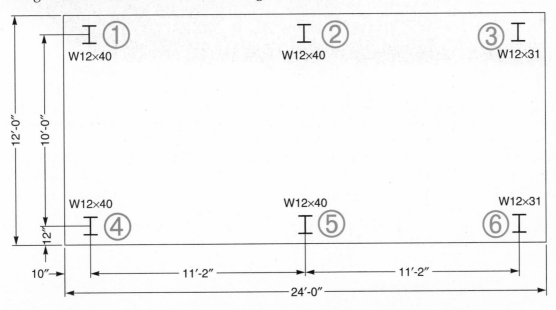

| | Steel | Mfgr | Price | Weight | Length | Code |
|---|---|---|---|---|---|---|
| Blocks ①, ②, ④, & ⑤ | W12×40 | RYERSON | $.30/lb | 40LB/FT | 10' | 03116WF |
| Blocks ③, & ⑥ | W12×31 | RYERSON | $.30/lb | 31LB/FT | 8.5' | 03125WF |

**General**

3. Load Problem 2 (P27-2) into the drawing editor. Create a template file for use in extracting the data from structural steel blocks inserted in Problem 2. Use the following information in your template file:

| ITEM | CHARACTERS | DECIMAL PLACES |
|---|---|---|
| Block name | 8 | 0 |
| Tag | 8 | 0 |
| Mfgr | 20 | 0 |
| Price | 12 | 0 |
| Weight | 8 | 0 |
| Length | 6 | 1 |
| Code | 8 | 0 |

Use the **ATTEXT** command to create a listing of the attribute information. When using **ATTEXT**, give the extract file a slightly different name than the template file. If not, your template file will be converted into the extract file. Using a different name enables you to easily revise the template file to extract different information.

The extract file that is created from Problem 2 should appear as follows:

```
W12X40          RYERSON   $.30/LB    40LB/FT   10FT   03116WF
W12X40          RYERSON   $.30/LB    40LB/FT   10FT   03116WF
W12X40          RYERSON   $.30/LB    40LB/FT   10FT   03116WF
W12X40          RYERSON   $.30/LB    40LB/FT   10FT   03116WF
W12X31          RYERSON   $.29/LB    31LB/FT   8.5FT  03125WF
W12X31          RYERSON   $.29/LB    31LB/FT   8.5FT  03125WF
```

**General**

4. Select one of your drawings from Chapter 25 and create a bill of materials for it using the template file method and the **ATTEXT** command. Follow these guidelines.

   A. The template file should list all of the attributes of each block in the drawing.

   B. Use the SDF format to display the file.

   C. Display the file in the Windows Notepad.

**General**

5. Open the prototype drawing TITLEA from Chapter 11, Problem 1. Define attributes for the title block information, revision block, and parts list as described in this chapter. **WBLOCK** the entire drawing to disk using 0,0 as the insertion base point. Repeat the procedure for drawings TITLEB and TITLEC.

AutoCAD R13

## Chapter 28

# Isometric Drawing

## Learning objectives

After completing this chapter, you will be able to:

- ○ Describe the nature of isometric and oblique views.
- ○ Set an isometric grid.
- ○ Construct isometric objects.
- ○ Create isometric text styles.
- ○ Demonstrate isometric and oblique dimensioning techniques.

Three-dimensional visualization and drawing are skills that every drafter, designer, and engineer should have. This is especially important now that most CAD systems support 3D modeling. However, be aware that there is a distinct difference between drawing a view that *looks* three-dimensional and a *true* 3D model. A 3D model can be rotated on the display screen to view from any angle. The computer calculates the points, lines, and surfaces of the object in space. Three-dimensional models are introduced in Chapter 29. This chapter focuses on creating three-dimensional *looking* views using two-dimensional objects and some special AutoCAD functions.

## PICTORIAL DRAWING OVERVIEW

The word *pictorial* means like a picture. It refers to any realistic form of drawing. Pictorial drawings show height, width, and depth. Several forms of pictorial drawing are used in industry today. The least realistic is *oblique*. However, this is the simplest type. The most realistic is *perspective*, but also the most complex. *Isometric* drawing falls midway between the two as far as realism and complexity are concerned.

## Oblique drawings

An oblique drawing shows objects with one or more parallel faces having true shape and size. A scale is selected for the orthographic, or front faces. Then, an angle for the depth or receding axis is chosen. Three types of oblique drawing are used: *cavalier, cabinet,* and *general*, Figure 28-1. These vary in the angle and scale of the receding axis. Both cavalier and cabinet drawings use an angle of 45°. The receding axis is drawn at half scale for a cabinet view and at full scale for a cavalier. The general oblique is normally drawn at an angle other than 45° and at 3/4 scale for the receding axis.

Figure 28-1.   The three types of oblique drawings differ in the scale, and angle, of the receding axis.

Cavalier          Cabinet          General

## Isometric drawings

Isometric drawings are more realistic than obliques. The entire object appears as if it is tilted toward the viewer. The word *isometric* means equal measure. This equal measure refers to the angle between the three axes (120°) after the object has been tilted. The tilt angle is 35°16′. This is shown in Figure 28-2. The angle of 120° can be hard to locate, so an angle of 30° from horizontal is used when laying out the drawing.

Figure 28-2.   An object is tilted 35°16′ to achieve an isometric view having 120° between the three axes. Notice how the highlighted face corresponds to each view.

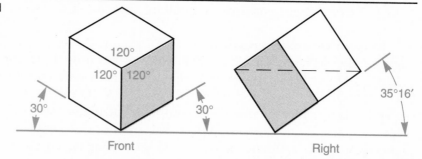

120°
120°  120°
30°           30°
35°16′
Front          Right

**NOTE**

When constructing isometric drawings, remember that lines parallel in the orthogonal views must be parallel in the isometric view.

The most appealing aspect of isometric drawing is that all three axis lines can be measured using the same scale. This saves time, while still producing a pleasing pictorial representation of the object. This type of drawing is produced when you use the **Isometric** option of the **SNAP** command, discussed later.

Closely related to isometric drawing is *dimetric* and *trimetric*. These forms of pictorial drawing differ from isometric in the scales used to measure the three axes. Dimetric drawing uses two different scales, whereas trimetric uses three scales. Using different scales is an attempt to create *foreshortening*. This means the length of the sides appears to recede. The relationship between isometric, dimetric, and trimetric drawings is illustrated in Figure 28-3.

Figure 28-3.   Isometric, dimetric, and trimetric differ in the scales used to draw the three axes. The isometric shown here has the scales represented as one. You can see how the dimetric and trimetric scales vary from that.

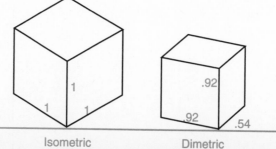

1
1    1
.92
.92    .54
.73
.90    .80
Isometric          Dimetric          Trimetric

## Perspective drawing

The most realistic form of pictorial drawing is perspective. This is done with the aid of *vanishing points*. The eye naturally sees objects in perspective. Look down a long hall and notice that the wall and floor lines seem to converge in the distance at an imaginary point. That point is called the *vanishing point*. The most common types of perspective drawing are *one-point* and *two-point*. These forms of pictorial drawing are often used in architecture. They are also used in the automotive and aircraft industries. Examples of one-point and two-point perspectives are shown in Figure 28-4. A perspective of a 3D model can be produce in AutoCAD using the **DVIEW** command. See *AutoCAD and its Applications—Advanced, Release 13 for Windows* for complete coverage of the **DVIEW** command.

Figure 28-4. An example of a one-point and a two-point perspective.

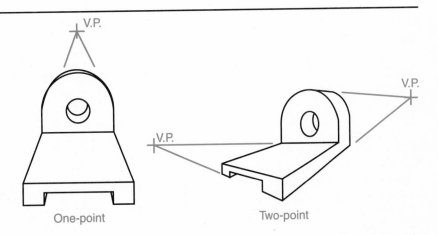

One-point          Two-point

## ISOMETRIC DRAWING

AUG 3

The most common method of pictorial drawing used in industry is isometric. The drawing provides a single view showing three sides that can be measured using the same scale. An isometric view has no perspective and may appear somewhat distorted. Isometric axes are drawn at 30° to horizontal, as shown in Figure 28-5.

The three axes shown in Figure 28-5 represent the width, height, and depth of the object. Lines that appear horizontal in an orthographic view are placed at a 30° angle. Lines that are vertical in an orthographic view are placed vertically. These are parallel to the axes. Any line parallel to the three axes can be measured and is called an *isometric line*. Lines not parallel to the axes cannot be measured and are called *nonisometric lines*. Note the two nonisometric lines in Figure 28-5.

Figure 28-5. Isometric axis layout. Lines not parallel to any of the three axes are called nonisometric.

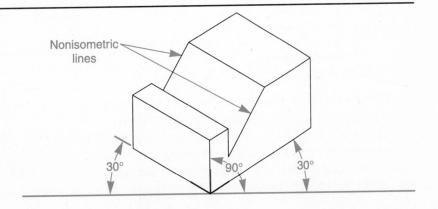

Circular features shown on isometric objects must be oriented properly or they will appear distorted. Figure 28-6 shows the correct orientation of isometric circles on the three principle planes. These circles appear as ellipses on the isometric object. The small diameter of the ellipse must always align on the axis of the hole or circular feature. Notice that the centerline axes of the holes in Figure 28-6 are parallel to one of the isometric planes.

A good basic rule to remember about isometric drawing is that lines parallel in an orthogonal view must be parallel in the isometric view. AutoCAD's **ISOPLANE** feature makes that task, and the positioning of ellipses, easy.

Figure 28-6.   Proper ellipse orientation on isometric planes. The minor axis always aligns with the axis centerline.

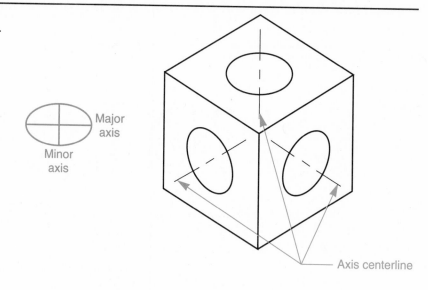

**PROFESSIONAL TIP**

If you are ever in doubt about the proper orientation of an ellipse in an isometric drawing, remember that the minor axis of the ellipse must always be aligned on the centerline axis of the circular feature. This is shown clearly in Figure 28-6.

### Setting the isometric snap

When the grid is turned on, horizontal and vertical lines of dots are displayed. To begin drawing an isometric object it is helpful to have the grid dots at an angle. The angle represents the three axis lines of the isometric layout. This is easy using the **SNAP** command. Enter the **Style** option, then the **Isometric** option. Finally, enter the vertical spacing.

Command: **SNAP** ↵
Snap spacing or ON/OFF/Aspect/Rotate/Style ⟨current⟩: **S** ↵
Standard/Isometric ⟨S⟩: **I** ↵
Vertical spacing ⟨current⟩: **.25** ↵

The grid dots on the screen change to the isometric orientation, as shown in Figure 28-7. If your grid dots are not visible, turn the grid on.

Notice the crosshairs also change and appear angled. This aids you in drawing lines at the proper angles. Try drawing a four-sided surface using the **LINE** command. Draw it so that it appears to be the left side of a box in an isometric layout. See Figure 28-8. To draw nonparallel surfaces, change the angle of the crosshairs to make your task easy.

Figure 28-7. An example of an isometric grid setup in AutoCAD.

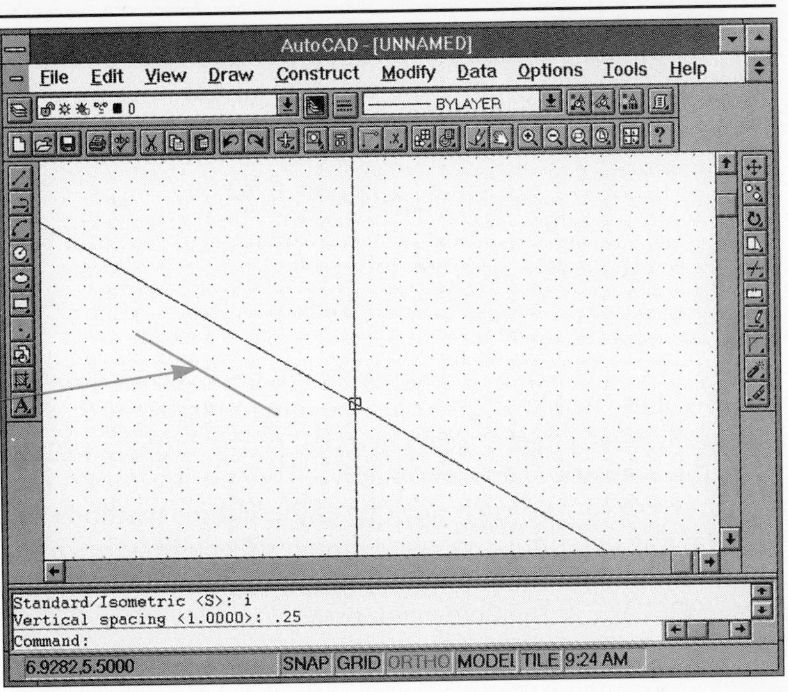

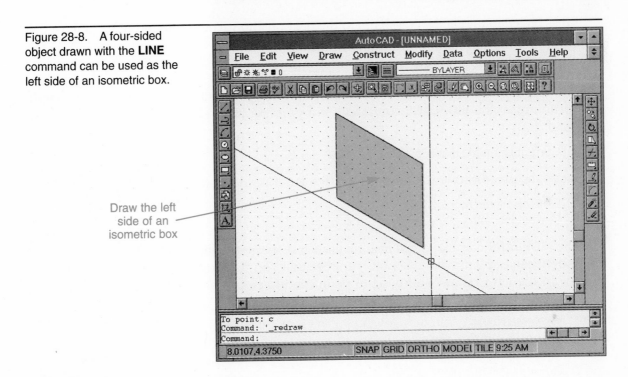

Grid dots align to the isometric orientation

Figure 28-8. A four-sided object drawn with the **LINE** command can be used as the left side of an isometric box.

Draw the left side of an isometric box

## Changing the crosshairs orientation

Drawing an isometric shape is possible without ever changing the angle of the crosshairs. Yet, the drawing process is easier and quicker if the angles of the crosshairs align with the isometric axes. This is a simple task using the [F5] function key. Whenever the isometric snap style is enabled, simply press the [F5] key and the crosshairs immediately change to the next plane. AutoCAD refers to the isometric positions as *isoplanes*. The isoplanes are displayed on the prompt line as a reference.

Command: ⟨Isoplane Left⟩ ⟨Isoplane Top⟩ ⟨Isoplane Right⟩

The three crosshairs positions are shown in Figure 28-9.

Figure 28-9. The three isometric crosshairs positions are set with the **ISOPLANE** command.

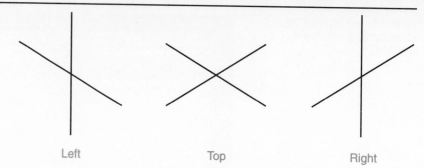

Left                          Top                          Right

Another quick way to toggle through the isoplanes is with the [Ctrl]+[E] key combination. Pressing these two keys performs the same function as the [F5] key. In addition, many multi-button digitizer tablet pucks have one of the buttons programmed to toggle the isoplane when the isometric snap style is active. The specific button varies from manufacturer to manufacturer. For convenience, any one of these three methods can be used during the execution of a drawing or editing function without first exiting the command you are working in.

Another method to toggle the crosshairs' position is with the **ISOPLANE** command. Enter ISOPLANE at the **Command:** prompt as follows:

> Command: **ISOPLANE** ↵
> Left/Top/Right/⟨Toggle⟩: ↵

Press [Enter] to toggle the crosshairs to the next position. The command line displays the new isoplane setting with the following message:

> Current Isometric plane is: Right

You can toggle immediately to the next position by pressing [Enter] at the **Command:** prompt to repeat the **ISOPLANE** command and pressing [Enter] again. The message should now read:

> Current Isometric plane is: Left

To specify the plane of orientation, type the first letter of that position:

> Left/Top/Right/⟨Toggle⟩: **R** ↵
> Current Isometric plane is: Right

The **ISOPLANE** command can also be used transparently while in another command to toggle between isoplanes. For example, suppose that you start to draw a line and then realize you are in the left isoplane and need to be in the top isoplane. The procedure to use is as follows:

> Command: **LINE** ↵
> From point: '**ISOPLANE** ↵
> ⟩⟩Left/Top/Right/⟨Toggle⟩: **T** ↵
> Current Isometric plane is: Top
> Resuming LINE command.
> From point: (pick the start point for the line)

The crosshairs are always in one of the isoplane positions when the isometric snap style is in effect. An exception occurs during a display or editing command when a multiple selection set method (such as a window) is used instead of the single pick selection method. In these cases, the crosshairs then change to the normal vertical and horizontal positions. At the completion of the display or editing command, the crosshairs automatically revert to their former isoplane orientation.

**PROFESSIONAL TIP**

Although the **ISOPLANE** command can be entered transparently, using the function key [F5] or the [Ctrl]+[E] key combination is a more efficient way to toggle the isoplane while inside another command.

## Setting isometric variables with a dialog box

You can quickly pick your isometric variables from the **Drawing Aids** dialog box. To access this dialog box, type DDRMODES at the **Command:** prompt. If the ACADFULL menu file is loaded, you can also select **Drawing Aids...** from the **Options** pull-down menu. The **Drawing Aids** dialog box is displayed. It contains the options for isometric drawing. The **Isometric** buttons are located at the lower right of the dialog box. See Figure 28-10.

To activate the isometric snap grid, pick the **On** check box. Notice that the X spacing for **Grid** and **Snap** are grayed out. You can only set the Y spacing for grid and snap in isometric. Since X spacing relates to horizontal measurements, it is not used in the isometric mode. Horizontal lines on an isometric object are drawn at a 30° angle from horizontal. Three option buttons at the lower right of the dialog box allow you to select the isoplane orientation. Be sure to pick the **On** check boxes for **Snap** and **Grid** if you want to turn them on. Pick **OK** when you have completed all of your settings. To turn off the **Isometric** mode, simply pick the **On** check box in the isometric area so that the "X" disappears. The **Isometric** mode is turned off and you are returned to the drawing editor when you pick **OK**.

Figure 28-10. The **Drawing Aids** dialog box allows you to pick settings needed for isometric drawing. (The **Isometric** options are shown here highlighted.)

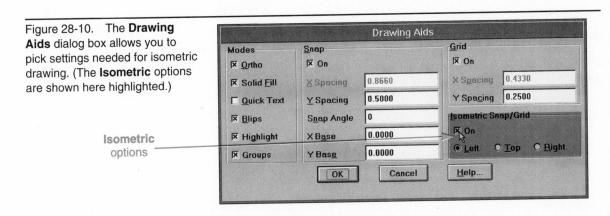

## EXERCISE 28-1

❑ Start a new drawing and name it EX28-1.
❑ Set the grid spacing at .5.
❑ Set the snap style to the **Isometric** option. Specify .25 vertical spacing.
❑ Use the **LINE** command to draw the objects shown. Do not dimension the objects.
❑ Change the **ISOPLANE** orientation as needed.
❑ Save the drawing as A:EX28-1.

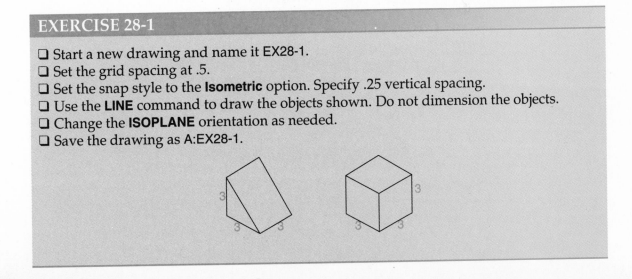

### Isometric ellipses

Placing an isometric ellipse on an object is made easy using AutoCAD. An ellipse is positioned automatically to the current **ISOPLANE** setting. Use the **ELLIPSE** command by picking the **Ellipse Axis End** button on the **Draw** toolbar or typing ELLIPSE at the **Command:** prompt. If the ACADFULL menu file is loaded, you can also select **Ellipse ⟩** and then **Axis, End** from the **Draw** pull-down menu. Do not select the **Center Ellipse** button or **Center** option, because these methods do not allow you to create isocircles. After selecting **Isocircle** from the **ELLIPSE** command options, pick the center point and diameter.

Command: **ELLIPSE** ↵
Arc/Center/Isocircle/⟨Axis endpoint 1⟩: **I** ↵
Center of circle: *(pick a point)*
⟨Circle radius⟩/Diameter:

Three options are available for determining the size of the ellipse at this last prompt.
- When **DRAGMODE** is on, the ellipse changes size as the cursor moves. Set the radius by picking a point.
- Enter a numeric value and press [Enter] to have AutoCAD draw the ellipse a specific radius.
- Type D and you are asked for the circle diameter. Enter a number, press [Enter], and the ellipse appears.

Always check the **ISOPLANE** position before locating an ellipse on your drawing. You can dynamically view the three positions that an ellipse can take. Enter the **ELLIPSE** command, pick the **Isocircle** option, and then toggle the **ISOPLANE** option. See Figure 28-11. The ellipse rotates each time you toggle the crosshairs.

Figure 28-11. The orientation of an isometric ellipse is determined by the **ISOPLANE** position.

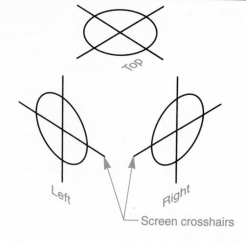

## EXERCISE 28-2

❑ Open EX28-1 if this drawing is not already on your screen.
❑ Select the **ELLIPSE** command to place an ellipse on the three sides of the object.
❑ Draw the ellipses in the following manner:
   1. Pick a radius of .5 using the cursor.
   2. Enter a radius of .75 at the keyboard.
   3. Type D and enter a diameter of .6 at the keyboard.
❑ The finished drawing should look like the example given below.
❑ Save the drawing as A:EX28-2.

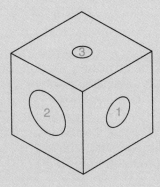

## Constructing isometric arcs

    The **ELLIPSE** command can also be used to draw an isometric arc of any included angle. The **Arc** option of the **ELLIPSE** command saves considerable time when creating elliptical arcs. Use the **ELLIPSE** command by picking the **Ellipse Arc** or **Ellipse Axis End** button on the **Draw** toolbar or by typing ELLIPSE at the **Command:** prompt. If the ACADFULL menu file is loaded, you can also select **Ellipse** ⟩ and then **Arc** in the **Draw** pull-down menu. Use the following steps to construct an isometric arc.

     Command: **ELLIPSE** ↵
     Arc/Center/Isocircle/⟨Axis endpoint 1⟩: **A** ↵
     ⟨Axis endpoint 1⟩/Center/Isocircle: **I** ↵
     Center of circle: *(pick the center of the arc)*
     ⟨Circle radius⟩/Diameter: *(pick the radius or type a value and press* [Enter]*)*
     Parameter/⟨start angle⟩: *(pick a start angle or type a value and press* [Enter]*)*

Remember that angles are drawn counterclockwise from the start point.

     Parameter/Included/⟨end angle⟩: *(pick an end angle or type a value and press* [Enter]*)*
     Command:

    The isometric ellipse in Release 13 is a true ellipse. If selected, grips are displayed at the center and four quadrant points. This simplifies the editing process. See Figure 28-12.

Figure 28-12.   An isometric
ellipse has grips at its four
quadrant points and its center.

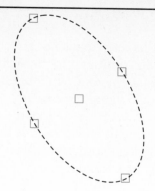

**CAUTION**

It may be tempting to resize or otherwise adjust an isometric
ellipse or arc by selecting one of the grips. Keep in mind that as soon
as you resize an isometric ellipse in this manner its angular value has
changed and it is no longer isometric. If you rotate an isometric ellipse
while **ORTHO** is on, it will not appear in a proper isometric plane. You
*can* rotate an isometric ellipse, but be sure to enter a value of 120° if
you want it to rotate from one of the three isometric planes to another.

Prior to drawing isometric ellipses it is good practice to first place some sort of marker at
the ellipse center point. A good technique is to set **PDMODE** to 3 and use **POINT** to place an X
at the center. This is especially useful if the ellipse does not fall on grid or snap points.

A common application of isometric arcs is drawing fillets or rounds. Once a round is created isometrically, the edge (corner) of the object sits back from its original,  unfilled position. See Figure 28-13A. You can draw the complete object first, then trim away the excess
after locating the fillets. You can also draw the isometric arcs and then the connecting lines.
Either way, the center point of the ellipse is a critical feature, and should be located first. In
Figure 28-13, the arc at the upper left was drawn first, then copied to the upper back position
using grips. Use **ORTHO** to help quickly draw 90° arcs.

The next step is to move the original edge to its new position. This is tangent to the isometric arcs. You can do this by snapping the line to the quadrant point of the arc. See Figure
28-13B. Notice the grips on the line and on the arc. The endpoint of the line is snapped to the
quadrant grip on the arc. The final step is to trim away the excess lines and upper right arc.
The completed feature is shown in Figure 28-13C.

Rounded edges, when viewed straight on, cannot be shown as complete-edge lines that
extend to the ends of the object. Instead, a good technique to use is a broken line in the original location of the edge. This is clearly shown in the figure in Exercise 28-3.

Figure 28-13.   Rounds can be drawn with the **Arc** option of the **ELLIPSE** command.

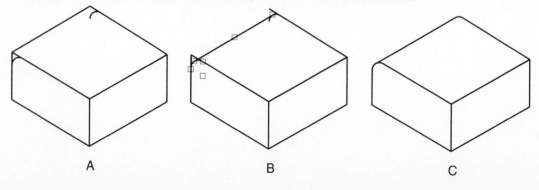

A                                              B                                              C

## EXERCISE 28-3

❏ Load AutoCAD for Windows and begin a new drawing named EX28-3.
❏ Set the grid spacing at .5.
❏ Set the snap style to the **Isometric** option, and specify a .25 vertical spacing.
❏ Use the **LINE** command and draw the object shown below. Do not dimension the object.
❏ Fillets and rounds are all .25 radius.
❏ Change the **ISOPLANE** as needed, and use the **ELLIPSE** command and **Arc** option to complete the object as shown.
❏ Save the drawing as A:EX28-3.

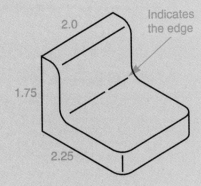

### Creating isometric text styles

Isometric text should appear to lie in one of the isometric planes. Text should not look like it was added at the last minute. Drafters and artists occasionally neglect this aspect of pictorial drawing, and it shows on the final product. Text should align with the plane that it applies to. This involves creating new text styles.

Figure 28-14 illustrates possible orientation of text on an isometric drawing. Text may be located on the object or positioned away from it as a note. These examples were created using only two text styles.

Figure 28-14. Isometric text applications. The text shown here indicates the ISO style used and the angle used.

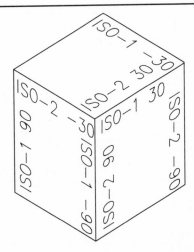

The text styles in Figure 28-14 are based on styles that use either a 30° or –30° obliquing angle. The labels in Figure 28-14 refer to the style numbers given in the chart below. The angle shown in Figure 28-14 indicates the rotation angle entered when using the **DTEXT** command. Find the text sample in Figure 28-14 that says ISO-2 90. This means that the ISO-2 style was used and the text was rotated 90°. This technique can be applied to any font.

| NAME | FONT | OBLIQUING ANGLE |
|------|------|-----------------|
| ISO-1 | Romans | 30° |
| ISO-2 | Romans | –30° |

### EXERCISE 28-4

❑ Load AutoCAD for Windows and open drawing EX28-1.
❑ Create one text style to label the angled (nonisometric) surface of the wedge. See the illustration below.
❑ Create a second style to label the front of the wedge.
❑ Save the drawing as A:EX28-4.

## Drawing solid isometric shapes

Isometric drawing can be used to produce both wireframe constructions and objects that appear to be solid. *Wireframes* are objects that you can see through, as if they are made of wire. The objects you drew in Exercise 28-1 appeared solid even though the surfaces were not colored or filled in.

Using the **SOLID** command, you can construct simple colored shapes that appear to be solid. Keep the following points in mind as you draw an isometric object using the **SOLID** command.

- The sequence of points needed to draw a rectangular shape must be correct.
- A solid fill cannot be drawn with a curved edge.
- An ellipse or circle placed on a solid surface will not open a hole in the solid shading.

The sequence you choose to pick the points is important. Figure 28-15 shows the proper order to construct solid planes.

### PROFESSIONAL TIP

Solids are drawn without the benefit of a rubber band line. Isometric snap and grids are especially helpful when creating solid surfaces.

Figure 28-15. The correct sequence of points to create solid isometric planes.

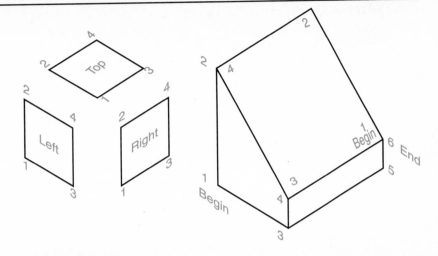

❑ Start a new drawing and name it EX28-5.
❑ Set the grid to .5 and isometric snap to .25.
❑ Set the colors as indicated for each side of the object. Enter the **COLOR** command before drawing each side with the **SOLID** command.
❑ Use the **SOLID** command to construct the object shown. Do not add the labels.
❑ Save the drawing as A:EX28-5.

## ISOMETRIC DIMENSIONING

An important aspect of isometric dimensioning is to place dimension lines, text, and arrowheads in the proper plane. Remember these guidelines:

- The extension lines should always extend the plane being dimensioned.
- The heel of the arrowhead should always be parallel to the extension line.
- The strokes of the text that would normally be vertical should always be parallel with the extension lines or dimension lines.

These techniques, as well as a dimensioned isometric part, are shown in Figure 28-16.

Figure 28-16.   A dimensioned
isometric part. Note the text
and arrowhead orientation in
relation to the extension lines.

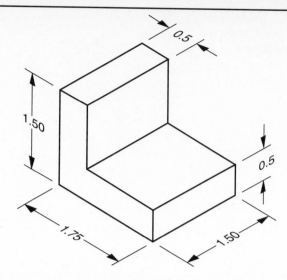

AutoCAD does not automatically dimension isometric objects. You must first create isometric arrowheads and text styles. Then, manually draw the dimension lines and text as they should appear in each of the three isometric planes. This is time-consuming when compared to dimensioning two-dimensional drawings.

You have already learned how to create isometric text styles. These can be set up in an isometric prototype drawing if you draw isometrics often. Examples of arrows for the three isometric planes are shown in Figure 28-17.

Arrowheads can be drawn as open with the **LINE** command or filled-in with the **SOLID** command. Every arrowhead does not have to be drawn individually. First, draw two isometric axes, as shown in Figure 28-18A. Then, draw one arrowhead like the one shown in Figure 28-18B. Use the **MIRROR** command to create additional arrows. As you create new arrows, move them to their proper plane. Save each arrowhead as a block in your isometric prototype drawing. Use names that are easy to remember and type.

Figure 28-17.   Examples of
arrowheads in each of the
three isometric planes.

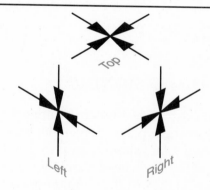

Figure 28-18.   A—Draw the
two isometric axes for arrowhead
placement. B—Draw the first
arrowhead on one of the axis
lines. Then, mirror the arrowhead
to create others.

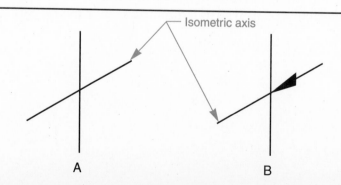

## OBLIQUE DIMENSIONING

AutoCAD has a way to semi-automatically dimension oblique lines. First, the dimensions must be drawn using any of the linear dimensioning commands. Figure 28-19A illustrates an object that has been dimensioned using the **DIMALIGNED** and **DIMVERTICAL** commands. Next, select the **Oblique** option of the **DIMEDIT** command. See Figure 28-19B.

To access the **Oblique** option, type DIMEDIT at the **Command:** prompt and enter O at the Dimension Edit prompt. If the ACADFULL menu file is loaded, you can also select **Dimensioning** ⟩ then select **Oblique** from the **Draw** pull-down menu. See Figure 28-20. Select the dimension and enter the obliquing angle:

> Command: **DIMEDIT** ↵
> Dimension Edit (Home/New/Rotate/Oblique) ⟨Home⟩: **O** ↵
> Select objects: *(pick dimension number 1)*
> Select objects: ↵
> Enter obliquing angle (RETURN for none): **30** ↵
> Dim:

Figure 28-19A shows numbers by each dimension. The following list gives the obliquing angle required for each numbered dimension in order to achieve the finished drawing shown in Figure 28-19B.

| Dimension | Obliquing angle |
|:---:|:---:|
| ① | 30° |
| ② | −30° |
| ③ | 30° |
| ④ | −30° |
| ⑤ | 30° |

This technique creates suitable dimensions for an isometric drawing, and is quicker than the previous method discussed. Keep in mind that the oblique method does not rotate the arrows so that the arrowhead heels are aligned with the extension lines. It also does not draw the dimension text aligned in the plane of the dimension.

---

Figure 28-19.   The **OBLIQUE** dimensioning command requires that you select an existing dimension (shown in A) and enter the desired obliquing angle (shown in B). Refer to the text for the angles represented by the circled numbers.

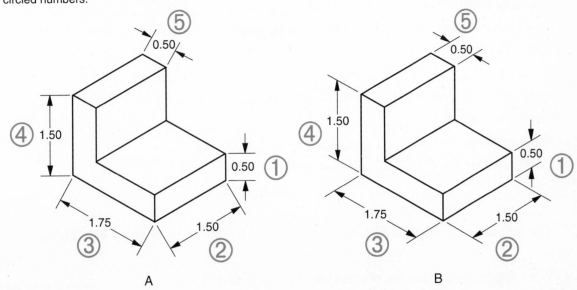

A                              B

Figure 28-20.   The **Oblique** option can be accessed from the **Draw** pull-down menu by selecting **Ob̲lique** from the **Dimensioning** ⟩ cascading submenu.

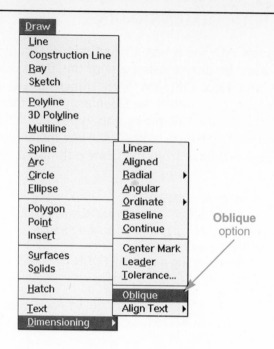

## CHAPTER TEST

*Write your answers in the spaces provided.*

1.  The simplest form of pictorial drawing is _____.

2.  How does isometric drawing differ from oblique drawing? _____
    _____
    _____

3.  How do dimetric and trimetric drawings differ from isometric drawings? _____
    _____
    _____

4.  The most realistic form of pictorial drawing is _____.

5.  Provide the correct entries at the following prompts to set an isometric snap with a spacing of 0.2.

    Command:_____

    Snap spacing or ON/OFF/Aspect/Rotate/Style ⟨*current*⟩:_____

    Standard/Isometric ⟨S⟩: _____

    Vertical spacing ⟨*current*⟩:_____

6.  What function does the **ISOPLANE** command perform?_____
    _____
    _____

7.  The pull-down menu that contains the command to access the **Drawing Aids** dialog box is _____.

8.  What factor determines the orientation of an isometric ellipse? _____
    _____

9. List the three methods to define the size of an isometric ellipse._____
   _____
   _____

10. Which aspect of the **STYLE** command allows you to create text that can be used on an isometric drawing? _____

11. You can create angled surfaces in an isometric drawing using the **SOLID** command. (True/False)._____

12. What command and two options must you select in order to draw isometric arcs? _____
    _____
    _____

13. On what parts of an isometric circle are grips located?_____
    _____
    _____

14. Can grips be used to correctly resize an isometric circle? Explain your answer.
    _____
    _____

15. What technique does AutoCAD provide for dimensioning isometric objects?_____
    _____

16. What value must you enter to achieve the kind of dimensioning referred to in Question 15?
    _____
    _____

## DRAWING PROBLEMS

1 - 13. Before drawing any of the objects, create an isometric prototype drawing. Then, use the prototype to construct each isometric drawing. Items that should be set in the prototype include grid spacing, snap spacing, ortho setting, and text size. Save the prototype as ISOPROTO. Use ISOPROTO as the prototype drawing for the following isometric drawings. Save the drawings as A:P28-*(problem number)*.

*Mechanical Drafting*

1.

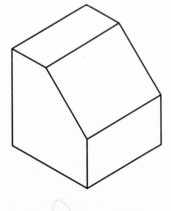

2.

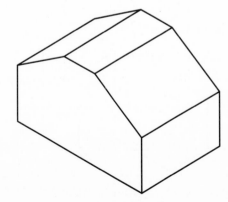

3.

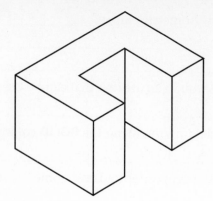

4.

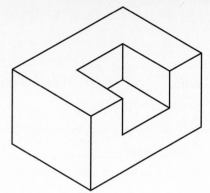

5.

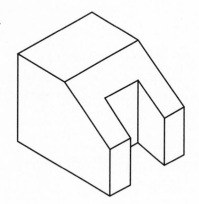

6.

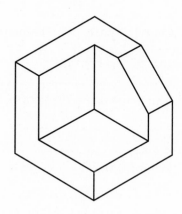

7.

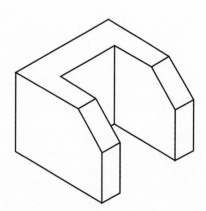

8.

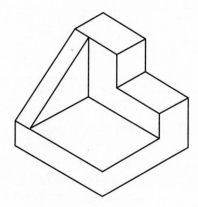

9.

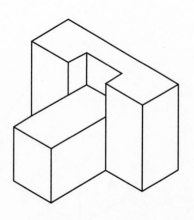

10.

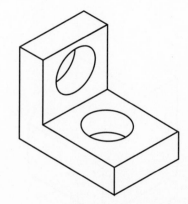

11.

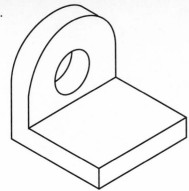

12.

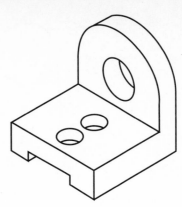

13.

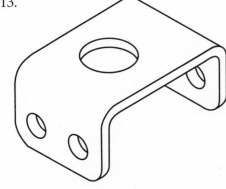

14 - 17. Create isometric drawings using the views shown.

14.

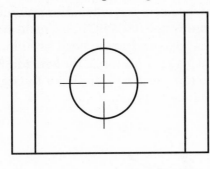

15.

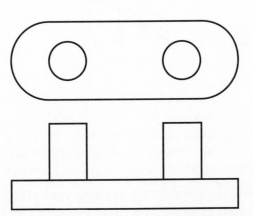

16.

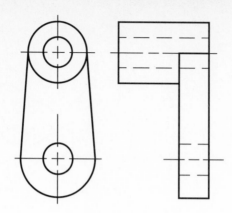

17.

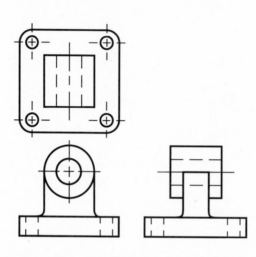

18. Construct a set of isometric arrowheads to use when dimensioning isometric drawings. Load your isometric prototype (ISOPROTO). Create arrowheads for each of the three isometric planes. Save each arrowhead as a block. Name them with the first letter indicating the plane: T for top, L for left, and R for right. Also number them clockwise from the top. See the example for the right isometric plane. Save the prototype again when finished.

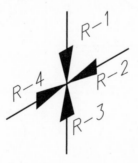

19. Create a set of isometric text styles like those shown in Figure 28-14. Load your prototype drawing and make a complete set in one font. Make additional sets in other fonts if you wish. Enter a text height of 0 so that you can specify the height when placing the text. Save the prototype again when finished.

20. Begin a new drawing named P28-20 using your prototype. Select one of the following problems to dimension fully: problem 2, 6, 10, 11, or 12. When adding dimensions, be sure to use the proper arrowhead and text style for the plane that you are working in. Save the drawing when completed.

**AutoCAD R13**

# Chapter *29*

# Introduction to Three-Dimensional Drawing

## Learning objectives
After completing this chapter, you will be able to:
- ❍ Describe the nature and function of rectangular, spherical, and cylindrical 3D coordinate systems.
- ❍ Use the "right-hand rule" of 3D visualization.
- ❍ Construct extruded and wireframe 3D objects.
- ❍ Display 3D objects at any desired viewpoint.

Computers are especially suited to handle information about points in space. However, in order for computer software to accept and use this information, the drafter or designer must first have good 3D visualization skills. These skills include the ability to see an object in three dimensions, and to visualize it rotating in space. These skills can be obtained by using 3D techniques to construct objects, and by trying to picture two-dimensional sketches and drawings as 3D models.

This chapter provides an introduction to several aspects of 3D drawing and visualization. A thorough discussion of 3D drawing, visualization, and display techniques is provided in *AutoCAD and its Applications—Advanced, Release 13 for Windows.*

## RECTANGULAR 3D COORDINATES

$\boxed{\text{AUG 11}}$

A computer can draw lines because it knows the X and Y values of the endpoints. The line does not really exist in the computer, only the points do. You see one plane and two dimensions in 2D drawing. However, when drawing in 3D, you add another plane and coordinate axis. You define the third dimension with a third coordinate measured along the Z axis. A computer can only draw lines in 3D if it knows the X, Y, and Z coordinate values of each point on the object.

Compare the 2D coordinate system to the 3D system in Figure 29-1. Note that the positive values of Z in the 3D system come up from the X-Y plane of a 2D drawing. Consider the surface of your screen as the new Z plane. Anything behind the screen is negative Z and anything in front of the screen is positive Z.

---

Figure 29-1. A comparison of 2D and 3D coordinate systems.

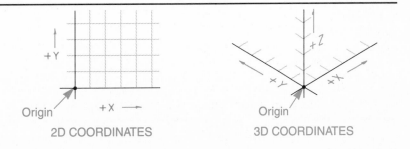

2D COORDINATES        3D COORDINATES

The object in Figure 29-2A is a 2D drawing showing the top view of an object. The XY coordinate values of each point are shown, given the lower-left corner as the origin (0,0). To convert this object to its three-dimensional form, Z values are given to each vertex, or corner. Figure 29-2B shows the object pictorially with the XYZ values of each point listed.

This same object could have been drawn using negative Z coordinates. It would extend behind the screen. Although the sign of the Z value makes no difference to AutoCAD, it may be confusing for you to deal with negative values.

Study the nature of the 3D coordinate system. Be sure you understand Z values before you begin constructing 3D objects. It is especially important that you carefully visualize and plan your design when working with 3D constructions.

Three-dimensional objects can be drawn in AutoCAD using two additional coordinate systems—spherical and cylindrical. These two systems enable you to work with point locations using distances and angles in order to draw a variety of shapes. For a complete discussion of spherical and cylindrical coordinate systems, please refer to *AutoCAD and its Applications—Advanced, Release 13 for Windows.*

Figure 29-2.   Each vertex of a
3D object must have an
X, Y, and Z value.

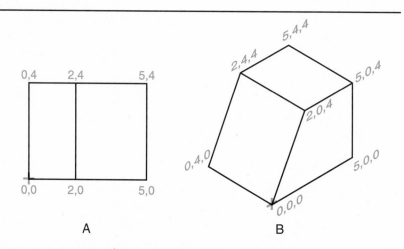

A                    B

## EXERCISE 29-1

❑ Study the multiview sketch below.
❑ Given the 3D coordinate axes, freehand sketch the object pictorially.
❑ Each tick mark is one unit. Use correct dimensions as given in the multiview drawing.
❑ When you complete the freehand sketch, draw the object in AutoCAD with the **LINE** command by entering XYZ coordinates for each point.
❑ Save the drawing as A:EX29-1 and quit.

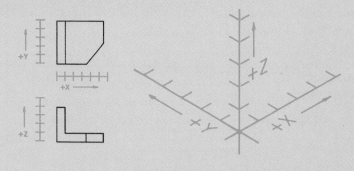

## CREATING EXTRUDED 3D SHAPES

AUG 11

Most shapes drawn with AutoCAD are extruded shapes. *Extruded* means that a 2D shape is given a base elevation and a thickness. The object then rises up, or "extrudes" to its given thickness. The **ELEV** command controls the base elevation and thickness. **ELEV** does not draw, it merely sets the base elevation and thickness for the next objects drawn. **ELEV** can be typed at the **Command:** prompt, or set in the **Object Creation Modes** dialog box by picking **Object Creation...** from the **Data** pull-down menu. The **DDEMODES** command also displays the **Object Creation Modes** dialog box, where the current elevation and thickness can be set. See Figure 29-3.

Figure 29-3.   The **Object Creation Modes** dialog box enables you to set the current elevation.

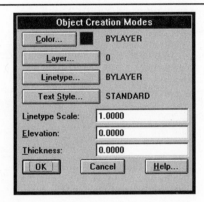

NOTE
Keep in mind that the current elevation is the level on which the next objects will be drawn. Therefore, if you set the elevation at 2.0, then draw the bottom of a machine part, the bottom of that part is now sitting at an elevation of 2.0 units above the zero elevation. On the other hand, the setting of the *thickness* is the value that determines the height of the next object you draw. Therefore, if you want to draw a part 2.0 units high, with the bottom of the part resting on the zero elevation plane, set elevation to 0.0 and thickness to 2.0.

The process of drawing a rectangular box four units long by three units wide by two units high begins with the **ELEV** command:

Command: **ELEV** ↵
New current elevation ⟨0.0000⟩: ↵
New current thickness ⟨0.0000⟩: **2** ↵
Command:

Nothing happens on-screen. Now use the **LINE** command to draw the top view of the rectangular box. Although it appears that you are drawing four lines, you are actually drawing planes. Each plane has a height (the thickness) that you cannot see yet.

Before you display the 3D construction, use the following instructions to add a hexagon and a circle, as shown in Figure 29-4. The hexagon should sit on top of the rectangle and extend three units above. The circle should appear to be a hole through the rectangle. Since the circle and rectangle have the same elevation, there is no need to use the **ELEV** command.

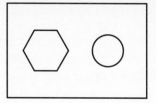

Figure 29-4.   A hexagon and a circle added to the rectangle for the command sequence given in the text.

Before drawing the hexagon, set the base elevation to the top surface of the rectangle and thickness (height) of the hexagon feature using the **ELEV** command as follows:

Command: **ELEV** ↵
New current elevation ⟨0.0000⟩: **2** ↵
New current thickness ⟨2.0000⟩: **3** ↵
Command:

These values can also be set in the **Object Creation Modes** dialog box as shown in Figure 29-5.

Figure 29-5.   The elevation and the thickness values can be set in the **Object Creation Modes** dialog box.

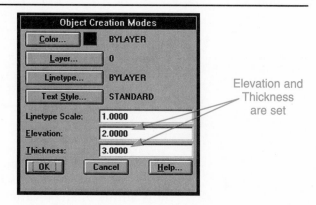

Elevation and Thickness are set

Now, draw the hexagon. The bracketed numbers after each prompt reflect the current values. A "2" was entered for the elevation because the hexagon sits on top of the rectangle, which is two units thick. This is where the hexagon starts. The "3" is the thickness, or height of the hexagon above its starting point.

Next, the elevation and thickness for the circle is set:

Command: **ELEV** ↵
New current elevation ⟨2.0000⟩: **0** ↵
New current thickness ⟨3.0000⟩: **2** ↵
Command:

Now, draw the circle to the right of the hexagon. The object is now ready to be viewed in 3D.

**PROFESSIONAL TIP**

Keep in mind that a "hole" drawn using **ELEV** and **CIRCLE** is not really a hole to AutoCAD. It is a cylinder with solid ends. This becomes clear when you display the objects in a 3D view with hidden lines removed.

## Some 3D drawing hints

- Erasing a line drawn with the **ELEV** thickness value set to a value other than zero erases an entire plane.
- Shapes drawn using the **LINE** and **ELEV** commands are open at the top and bottom.
- Circles drawn with **ELEV** are closed at the ends.
- The **PLINE** and **TRACE** commands give thickness to lines and make them appear as walls in the 3D view.

## THE RIGHT-HAND RULE OF 3D AUG 11

Before we discuss viewing the 3D drawing, it is worthwhile to review a good technique for 3D visualization. Once you understand the following procedure, viewing a 3D object oriented in AutoCAD's rectangular coordinate system should be relatively easy.

The right-hand rule is a graphic representation of positive coordinate values in the three axis directions of a coordinate system. The UCS (User Coordinate System) is based on a concept of visualization called the *right-hand rule*. This requires that you use the thumb, index finger, and middle finger of your right hand and hold them open in front of you, as shown in Figure 29-6.

Figure 29-6. Try positioning your hand like this to understand the relationship of the X, Y, and Z axes.

Although this may seem a bit unusual to do (especially if you are sitting in the middle of a school library or computer lab), it can do wonders for your understanding of the nature of the three axes. It can also help in understanding how the UCS can be rotated about each of the axis lines, or fingers.

Imagine that your thumb represents the X axis, your index finger is the Y axis, and your middle finger is the Z axis. Hold your hand directly in front of you and bend your middle finger so it is pointing directly at you. Now you see the plan view. The positive X axis is pointing to the right and the positive Y axis is pointing up. The positive Z axis comes toward you, and the origin of this system is the palm of your hand.

This concept can be visualized even better if you are sitting at a computer and the AutoCAD graphics screen is displayed. If the UCS icon is not displayed in the lower-left corner of the screen, turn it on as follows:

Command: **UCSICON** ↵
ON/OFF/All/Noorigin/ORigin ⟨ON⟩: **ON** ↵

Now orient your right hand as shown in Figure 29-6 and position it next to the UCS icon on the screen. Your index finger and thumb should point in the same directions as Y and X, respectively, on the UCS icon. Your middle finger will be pointing out of the screen. This technique can also be used to eliminate confusion when the UCS is rotated to odd angles.

When you use the **VPOINT** command (discussed later in this chapter), a tripod appears on the screen. It is composed of three axis lines, which are X, Y, and Z. When you see the tripod, you should be able to make the comparison with the right-hand rule. See Figure 29-7.

Figure 29-7.   Compare the use of three fingers on the right hand and the tripod used by AutoCAD for 3D viewing.

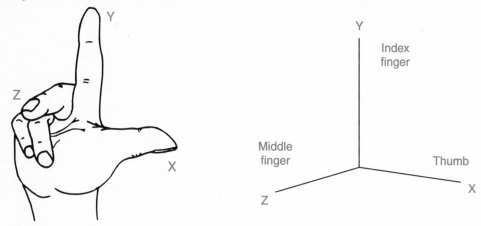

The User Coordinate System (UCS) can be rotated to any position desired. The coordinate system rotates on one of the three axis lines, just like a wheel rotates on an axle. Therefore, if you want to rotate the X plane, keep your thumb stationary, and turn your hand toward or away from you. If you wish to rotate the Y plane, keep your index finger stationary and turn your hand to the left or right. When rotating the Z plane, you must keep your middle finger stationary and rotate your entire arm to the right or left.

If you discover that your 3D visualization skills are weak, or that you are having trouble with the UCS method, don't be afraid to use the right-hand rule. It is a useful technique for improving your 3D visualization skills.

The ability to rotate the UCS around one or more of the three axes can become confusing if proper techniques are not used to visualize the rotation angles. A complete discussion of these techniques is provided in *AutoCAD and its Applications—Advanced, Release 13 for Windows.*

## DISPLAYING 3D DRAWINGS                                 AUG 11

Once you have drawn a 3D object in plan view, you should change your point of view so that the object can be seen in three dimensions. The **VPOINT** command allows you to display the current drawing at any angle. It may be easier to understand the function of this command as establishing your position relative to the object. Imagine that you can position yourself at a coordinate location in 3D space, in relation to the object. The **VPOINT** command basically provides AutoCAD with the XYZ coordinates of your eyes, so the object can be positioned properly. **VPOINT** can be selected from the **View** pull-down menu by picking **3D Viewpoint** ⟩, then **Tripod**. Several preset viewpoints can also be selected by clicking on the appropriate button in the **View** toolbar. See Figure 29-8.

Figure 29-8.   The **View** toolbar contains several preset viewpoints that can be selected by clicking the appropriate button. These are shown here highlighted.

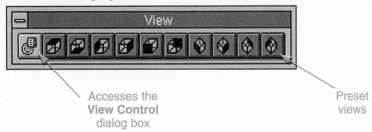

Accesses the
**View Control**
dialog box

Preset
views

Use the **VPOINT** command to establish your position relative to the object by entering VPOINT at the **Command:** prompt as follows:

> Command: **VPOINT** ↵
> Rotate/⟨View point⟩ ⟨0.0000,0.0000,1.0000⟩:

The three numbers reflect the XYZ coordinates of the current viewpoint. You can change these coordinates to select different viewpoints. The **VPOINT** values shown above represent the coordinates for the plan view. This means that your line of sight is along the positive Z axis looking down on the XY plane. Since it is difficult to visualize a numerical viewpoint, you can display a graphic representation of the XYZ axes, and pick the desired viewpoint with your pointing device. To do so, simply press [Enter] at the Rotate/⟨View point⟩: prompt. The screen display changes to one similar to that shown in Figure 29-9.

Figure 29-9.   The **VPOINT** axes display enables you to position yourself in relation to the object.

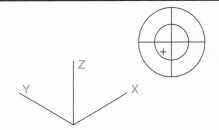

As you move the pointing device, notice what happens on screen. The XYZ coordinate tripod moves and the small crosshairs near the concentric circles also move. The concentric circles represent a compass. When the small crosshairs are inside the small circle, you are viewing the object from above. When the crosshairs are located between the two circles, you are viewing the object from below.

The easiest way to locate the viewpoint is to move the cursor while observing the XYZ axes tripod movement. Pick the location where you are satisfied with the appearance of the axes. It may take some practice. Remember that in the top, or plan view, the X axis is horizontal, Y axis is vertical, and Z axis comes out of the screen. As you move the tripod, keep track of where the crosshairs are located inside the compass. Compare their position to that of the tripod. Move the tripod until it is positioned like the one given in Figure 29-10. Press the pick button. The display should then resemble that figure.

The number of viewpoints you can select is endless. To get an idea of how the axes tripod and compass relate to the viewpoint, see the examples in Figure 29-11. It can be hard to distinguish top from bottom in wireframe views. Therefore, the viewpoints shown in Figure 29-11 are all from above the object and the **HIDE** command has been used to clarify the views. Use the **VPOINT** command to try each of these 3D positions on your computer.

Figure 29-10.   The three axes
and a 3D view display.

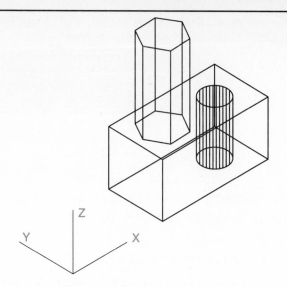

Figure 29-11.   Examples of viewpoint locations and their related axes positions.

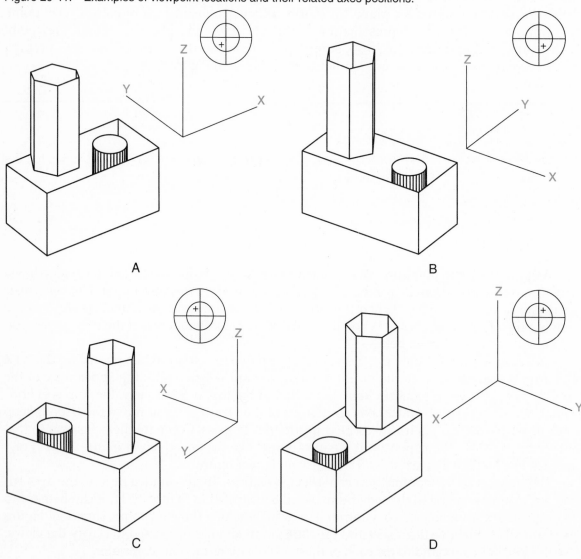

When you are ready to return to the World Coordinate System plan view, use the **PLAN** command. To access the **PLAN** command type PLAN at the **Command:** prompt, or select **3D Viewpoint Presets** from the **View** pull-down menu, select **Plan View**, and then **World** as shown in Figure 29-12. The command sequence is as follows:

> Command: **PLAN** ↵
> ⟨Current UCS⟩/Ucs/World: **W** ↵
> Regenerating drawing.
> Command:

Figure 29-12.   The **PLAN** command can be accessed through the **View** pull-down menu.

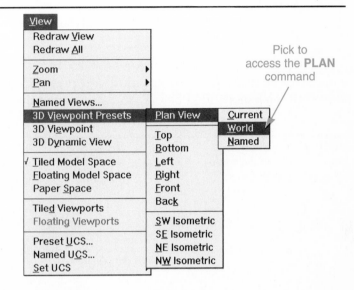

Pick to access the **PLAN** command

As an alternative to the **PLAN** command, you can also type the XYZ coordinates for the plan view using the **VPOINT** command.

> Command: **VPOINT** ↵
> Rotate/⟨View point⟩ ⟨*current*⟩: **0,0,1** ↵
> Regenerating drawing.
> Command:

Either method automatically performs a **ZOOM Extents** operation that fills the graphics window with your original top view. You can use the **ZOOM All** option to redisplay the original drawing limits.

---

## EXERCISE 29-2

❑ Set the grid spacing to .5 and snap spacing to .25.
❑ Set the elevation at 0 and the thickness at 2.
❑ Using the **RECTANG** command, draw a rectangle 2 × 3 units.
❑ Add a 180° arc to each end of the rectangle.
❑ Set the elevation at 2 and the thickness at 3.
❑ Draw a 1 unit diameter circle in the center of the rectangle.
❑ Use the **VPOINT** command to display the 3D view of your drawing. Display it from three viewpoints using the axes tripod.
❑ Save the drawing as A:EX29-2.

## Creating extruded 3D text

Text added on the plan view is displayed in 3D when you use the **VPOINT** command. However, the displayed text does not have thickness, and it always rests on the zero elevation plane. You can give text thickness and change the elevation with the **CHPROP** command. Select the text to change, pick the **Thickness** option, and enter a value.

```
Command: CHPROP ↵
Select objects: (select the text)
Select objects: ↵
Change what property (Color/LAyer/LType/ltScale/Thickness)? T ↵
New thickness ⟨current⟩: 1.5 ↵
Change what property (Color/LAyer/LType/ltScale/Thickness)? ↵
Command:
```

The selected text now has a thickness of 1.5. It is that simple. The **CHPROP** command does not leave the properties prompt until you press [Enter]. Figure 29-13 shows examples of 3D text with thickness added before, and after, using the **HIDE** command.

Figure 29-13.   Thickness applied to 3D text with and without the **HIDE** option.

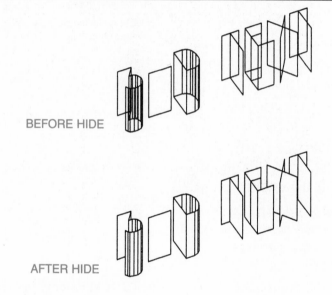

BEFORE HIDE

AFTER HIDE

## Removing hidden lines in 3D displays

The displays shown in Figure 29-10 and Figure 29-13 are wireframe representations, where all edges and vertices can clearly be seen. A wireframe view can be confusing because features that are normally hidden from view are fully displayed. The best way to mask all features that would normally be hidden is to use the **HIDE** command.

Use **HIDE** only after you have selected a 3D viewing angle. To access the **HIDE** command, enter HIDE at the **Command:** prompt or pick the **Hide** button in the **Render** toolbar. If the ACADFULL menu file is loaded, select **Hide** from the **Tools** pull-down menu. The command sequence is as follows:

```
Command: HIDE ↵
Regenerating drawing.
Hiding lines 100% done.
Command:
```

The size and complexity of the drawing and the speed of your computer determines how long you must wait for the lines to be hidden. The final display of the object in Figure 29-10 is shown in Figure 29-14 with hidden lines removed.

Figure 29-14.   Hidden lines removed using the **HIDE** command.

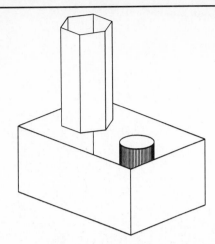

The view in Figure 29-14 may not look exactly as you expected. You probably expected the rectangle to appear solid with a circle in the top representing a hole. Think back to the initial construction of the rectangle. When drawn in the plan view, it consisted of four lines, or planes. It was not drawn with a top or bottom, just four sides. Then you placed a hexagon on top of the box and a cylinder inside. That is what appears in the "hidden line removed" display.

The individual features that compose the object in Figure 29-14 are shown in Figure 29-15. Both wireframe and hidden line views are given.

To redisplay the wireframe view, just select another viewpoint or enter REGEN and press [Enter]. A regeneration displays all lines of the objects.

Figure 29-15.   Individual features of the object in Figure 29-14 in wireframe and with hidden lines removed.

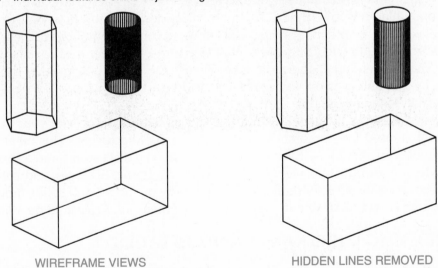

WIREFRAME VIEWS                 HIDDEN LINES REMOVED

## 3D CONSTRUCTION TECHNIQUES

Three-dimensional objects can be drawn in three basic forms—wireframe, surface models, and solid models. The following section discusses the construction of wireframes, and the use of 3D faces to apply a surface to the wireframe. A *wireframe construction* is just that; an object that looks like it was made of wire. You can see through it.

There are not a lot of practical applications for wireframe models unless you are an artist designing a new object using coat hangers. Wireframe models are hard to visualize because it is difficult to determine the angle of view and the nature of the surfaces. For example, compare the two objects in Figure 29-16.

Figure 29-16.   A wireframe
object is harder to visualize
than the surface model.
(Autodesk, Inc.)

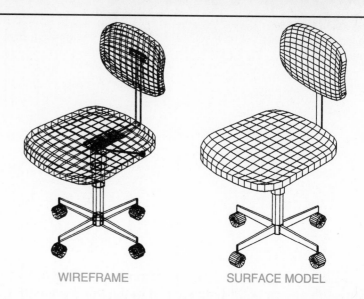

WIREFRAME                          SURFACE MODEL

*Surface modeling*, on the other hand, is much more easily visualized. It looks more like the real object. Surface models can be used to imitate solid models, and most importantly, can be used for shading and rendering models. These shaded and rendered models can then be used in any number of presentation formats, including slide shows, black and white or color prints, walk-through animation, or animation recorded to videotape.

A surface model can also be exported from AutoCAD for use in animation and rendering software, such as Autodesk's 3D Studio. In addition, surface models are the basis for the construction of composite 3D models, often called *virtual worlds*, which are used in the field of virtual reality.

On the other hand, *solid modeling* more closely represents designing an object using the materials from which it is to be made. This type of 3D design involves using primitive solid shapes, such as boxes, cylinders, spheres, and cones, to construct an object. These shapes are added together and subtracted from each other to create a finished product. The solid model can then be shaded, rendered, and more importantly, analyzed to determine mass, volume, moments of inertia, and centroid location. Some third-party programs allow you to perform finite stress analysis on the model.

Before constructing a 3D model, you should determine the purpose of your design. What will the model be used for—presentation, analysis, or manufacturing? This helps you determine which tools you should use to construct the model. The discussions and examples in this chapter provide an introductory view of the uses of wireframe, 3D faces, and basic surfaced objects in order to create 3D constructions. Further study of surface and solids modeling techniques is covered in *AutoCAD and its Applications—Advanced, Release 13 for Windows*.

## CONSTRUCTING WIREFRAMES AND 3D FACES          AUG 11

Wireframes can be constructed using the **LINE**, **PLINE**, **SPLINE**, and **3DPOLY** commands. AutoCAD provides a number of methods to use, but one particularly useful method is called filters. A *filter* is an existing point, or vector, in your drawing file. When using a filter, you instruct AutoCAD to find the coordinate values of a selected point. Then, you supply the missing value, which can be X, Y, Z, or a combination. Filters can be used when working in two-dimensional space or when using a pictorial projection resulting from the **VPOINT** command.

### Using filters to create 3D wireframe objects

When using **LINE**, you must know the XYZ coordinate values of each corner on the object. To draw an object, first decide the easiest and quickest method using the **LINE** command. One technique is to draw the bottom surface. Then, make a copy at the height of the object.

Finally, connect the corners with lines. The filters can be used with the **COPY** command, or by using grips to copy. From the plan view, step through the process in this manner:

> Command: **LINE** ↵
> From point: **3,3** ↵
> To point: **@4,0** ↵
> To point: *(continue picking points to construct the box)*

Next, copy the shape up to the height of 3 units.

> Command: **COPY** ↵
> Select objects: *(select the box using a window or crossing box)*
> Select objects: ↵
> ⟨Base point or displacement⟩/Multiple: *(pick a corner of the box)*
> Second point of displacement: **.XY** ↵
> of *(pick the same corner)* (need Z): **3** ↵
> Command:

Since the shape is copied straight up, the top surface of the cube has the same XY values as the bottom surface. That is why .XY was entered as the second point of displacement. This filter picks up the XY values of the previous point specified and applies them to the location of the new copy. Now, all AutoCAD needs is the Z value, which it requests.

Check your progress by looking at the object using the **VPOINT** command. Enter the coordinates given below. Your display should look like that in Figure 29-17.

> Command: **VPOINT** ↵
> Rotate/⟨View point⟩/⟨*current*⟩: **1,–2,.5** ↵
> Regenerating drawing.
> Command:

Figure 29-17.   A partially constructed box using the **Line** command and XYZ filters.

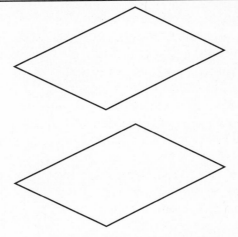

Return the drawing to the plan view and finish the object using **LINE** command and point filters. The four remaining lines are vertical and 3 units long.

> Command: **LINE** ↵
> From point: *(pick the lower-left corner)*
> To point: **.XY** ↵
> of *(pick the lower-left corner again)* (need Z): **3** ↵
> To point: ↵
> Command:

In this example, you instructed the computer to draw a line from the lower-left corner of the object to the same XY position 3 units above. The new line connects the top and bottom planes of the object. The same process can be used to draw the other three vertical lines. If you forget to enter the XY filter at the To point: prompt, AutoCAD will not ask for the Z distance. If this happens, cancel the command and start again. Use the **VPOINT** command again, and your drawing should look like Figure 29-18.

Figure 29-18.   A completed
box using the **LINE** command.

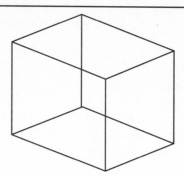

## PROFESSIONAL TIP

If the process of drawing Z axis lines in the plan view is difficult to visualize, there is an easier option; draw them in the pictorial view. After drawing the top and bottom faces of the box, select a viewpoint and zoom in on the object. Now use the **LINE** command to construct the vertical lines using **OSNAP** modes **Endpoint** or **Intersection**. This method allows you to see the lines in 3D as you draw them.

## EXERCISE 29-3

❑ Set the grid spacing at .5, snap spacing at .25, and elevation at 0.
❑ Draw the object below to the dimensions indicated.
❑ Use the **LINE** and **COPY** commands to construct the object.
❑ Construct the top and bottom planes in the plan view. Connect the vertical lines in a 3D view.
❑ Save the drawing as A:EX29-3.

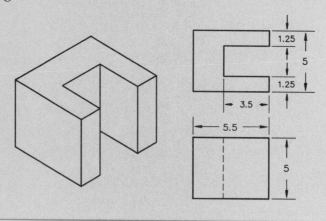

## Constructing 3D faces

Surfaces that appear solid are called *3D faces*. They can be made with the **3DFACE** command. Its prompt structure is similar to that of the **SOLID** command, but you can specify points in either a clockwise or counterclockwise manner. A 3D face must have at least three corners, but cannot have any more than four corners. To access the **3DFACE** command, enter **3DFACE** at the **Command:** prompt or pick the **3D Face** button in the **Render** toolbar. If the ACADFULL menu file is loaded, from the **Draw** pull-down menu select **Surfaces** ⟩ and then **3D Face**.

Draw the familiar box again, beginning with the bottom face, with the elevation set at 0. Then draw the top face. Draw the bottom face using the following command sequence:

> Command: **3DFACE** ⏎
> First point: *(pick a point)*
> Second point: *(pick a point)*
> Third point: *(pick a point)*
> Fourth point: *(pick a point)*
> Third point: ⏎
> Command:

Notice that after you placed the fourth point, a line automatically connected the first point. A prompt then asks for the third point again if you want to continue to draw additional faces. Press [Enter] to end the command.

The 3D face can be copied using the similar steps taken to copy the line surface. Remember to use XY filters for copying, and copy the 3D face using the following command sequence:

> Command: **COPY** ⏎
> Select objects: *(pick the 3D face)*
> Select objects: ⏎
> ⟨Base point or displacement⟩/Multiple: *(pick a corner of the 3D face)*
> Second point of displacement: **.XY** ⏎
> of *(pick the same corner)* (need Z): **3** ⏎
> Command:

Finally, the four sides of the box are drawn. First, set a viewpoint and then connect corners of each 3D face using a running **OSNAP** mode of **Endpoint** or **Intersection**.

> Command: **VPOINT** ⏎
> Rotate/⟨View point⟩/⟨*current*⟩: **–1,–1,.75** ⏎
> Command:

The drawing should look like that shown in Figure 29-19. Zoom in if the view is too small. Complete the box using the **3DFACE** command and pick the points as numbered in Figure 29-19.

---

## PROFESSIONAL TIP

When moving or copying objects in 3D space, it can simplify matters to use the displacement option to specify positioning data. This allows you to specify the X, Y, and Z movement simultaneously. For example, to copy the 3D face to a position 3 units above the original on the Z axis, use the following command sequence:

> Command: **COPY** ⏎
> Select objects: *(pick the 3D face)*
> Select objects: ⏎
> ⟨Base point or displacement⟩/Multiple: **0,0,3** ⏎
> ⟨Second point of displacement⟩: ⏎

Because [Enter] was pressed at the Second point of displacement: prompt, the X,Y,Z values entered are used as a relative displacement instead of a base point. In this example, the object is copied to a position that differs from the original by 0 on the X axis, 0 on the Y axis, and +3 on the Z axis. To move an object +1 on the X, –4 on the Y, and +2 on the Z axis, the displacement value would be 1,–4,2.

Command: **OSNAP** ⏎
Object snap modes: **END** ⏎
Command: **3DFACE** ⏎
First point: *(pick point 1)*
Second point: *(pick point 2)*
Third point: *(pick point 3)*
Fourth point: *(pick point 4)*
Third point: ⏎
Command:

The first face is complete. Now draw the remaining faces in the same manner. The finished box should appear similar to that in Figure 29-20.

How does a 3D face object differ from ones drawn using the **ELEV** and **LINE** commands? For comparison, Figure 29-21 shows boxes drawn using the **ELEV**, **LINE**, and **3DFACE** commands with hidden lines removed by **HIDE**.

---

Figure 29-19.   Top and bottom 3D faces of a box. The numbers indicate the points to pick when using the **3DFACE** command.

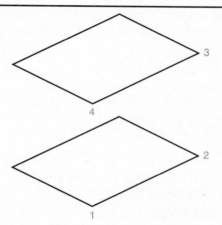

---

Figure 29-20.   A completed **3DFACE** appears to be a wireframe construction before using **HIDE**.

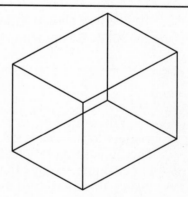

---

Figure 29-21.   Comparison of boxes drawn with **ELEV**, **LINE**, and **3DFACE** after the **HIDE** command is selected.

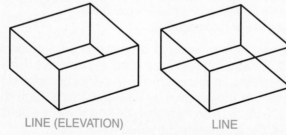

LINE (ELEVATION)                    LINE                         3DFACE

## EXERCISE 29-4

❑ Set the grid spacing at .5, snap spacing at .25, and elevation at 0.

❑ Use the **3DFACE** command to construct the object to the dimensions given.

❑ Draw the bottom, two end faces, and the two top angled surfaces in the plan view. Draw the front and rear V-shaped surfaces in a 3D view. Hint: Each V-shaped end surface must be made of two 3D faces.

❑ Use the **HIDE** command when you complete the object.

❑ Save the drawing as A:EX29-4.

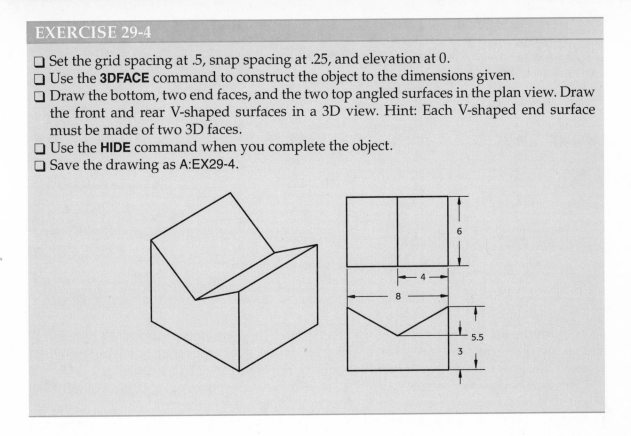

## CONSTRUCTING 3D SURFACE MODELED OBJECTS

Several predrawn 3D objects can be quickly drawn by providing AutoCAD with a location and basic dimensions of the object. The **3D** command can be accessed by typing 3D at the **Command:** prompt, or a number of 3D objects can be selected from the **Surfaces** toolbar. A graphic dialog box display of the objects is also available if ACADFULL menu file is loaded. Pick **Surfaces ⟩** and then **3D Objects...** from the **Draw** pull-down menu. This activates the **3D Objects** dialog box. The buttons displayed on the **Surfaces** toolbar are similar to those in the **3D Objects** dialog box. See Figure 29-22.

Figure 29-22.   A—The **3D Objects** dialog box displays a group of 3D surface modeled objects that can be quickly drawn by supplying a few basic dimensions. B—The same objects can be drawn using the **Surfaces** toolbar.

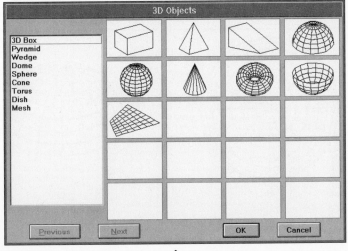

A                                                    B

Figure 29-23. When an image or its name is selected, the image tile and name are both highlighted.

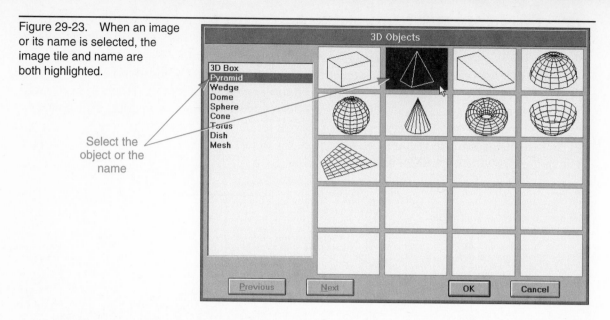

Select the object or the name

Notice the list box to the left of the dialog box. These are the names of all the objects shown. An object can be selected for drawing by picking either the name or the image. When selected, the image and the name are highlighted. See Figure 29-23. Pick **OK**.

Regardless how a 3D object is selected, the first prompt requests a location point for the object. The remaining prompts request sizes in the form of length, width, height, diameter, radius, or number of longitudinal and latitudinal segments. For example, select **Dome** and the command sequence is as follows:

Command: **3D** ↵
Box/Cone/DIsh/DOme/Mesh/Pyramid/Sphere/Torus/Wedge: **DO** ↵
Center of dome: *(pick a point)*
Diameter/⟨radius⟩: *(enter a radius or pick on the screen)*
Number of longitudinal segments ⟨16⟩: ↵
Number of latitudinal segments ⟨16⟩: ↵

The object is drawn in the plan view, as shown in Figure 29-24A. Use the **VPOINT** command to produce a 3D view of the object, and use **HIDE** to remove hidden lines. The illustration in Figure 29-24B provides an explanation of longitudinal and latitudinal segments. Longitudinal refers to an east-west measurement, and latitudinal means north-south. Note that the default of 16 latitudinal segments creates only eight segments in the dome or dish, since these shapes are half of a sphere.

Figure 29-24. A—The plan view of a dome. B—Longitudinal segments are measured east-west, and latitudinal segments are measured north-south.

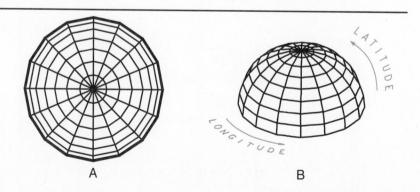

A

B

The group of objects provided in the **3D Objects** dialog box are easy to draw and fun to work with. Remember that if the current display is a plan view and you draw 3D objects, you must use the **VPOINT** command in order to see a 3D view. The illustrations in Figure 29-25 show all of the dimensions required to construct the predrawn 3D objects provided by AutoCAD.

Figure 29-25. These dimensions are required to draw AutoCAD's surfaced 3D surface objects.

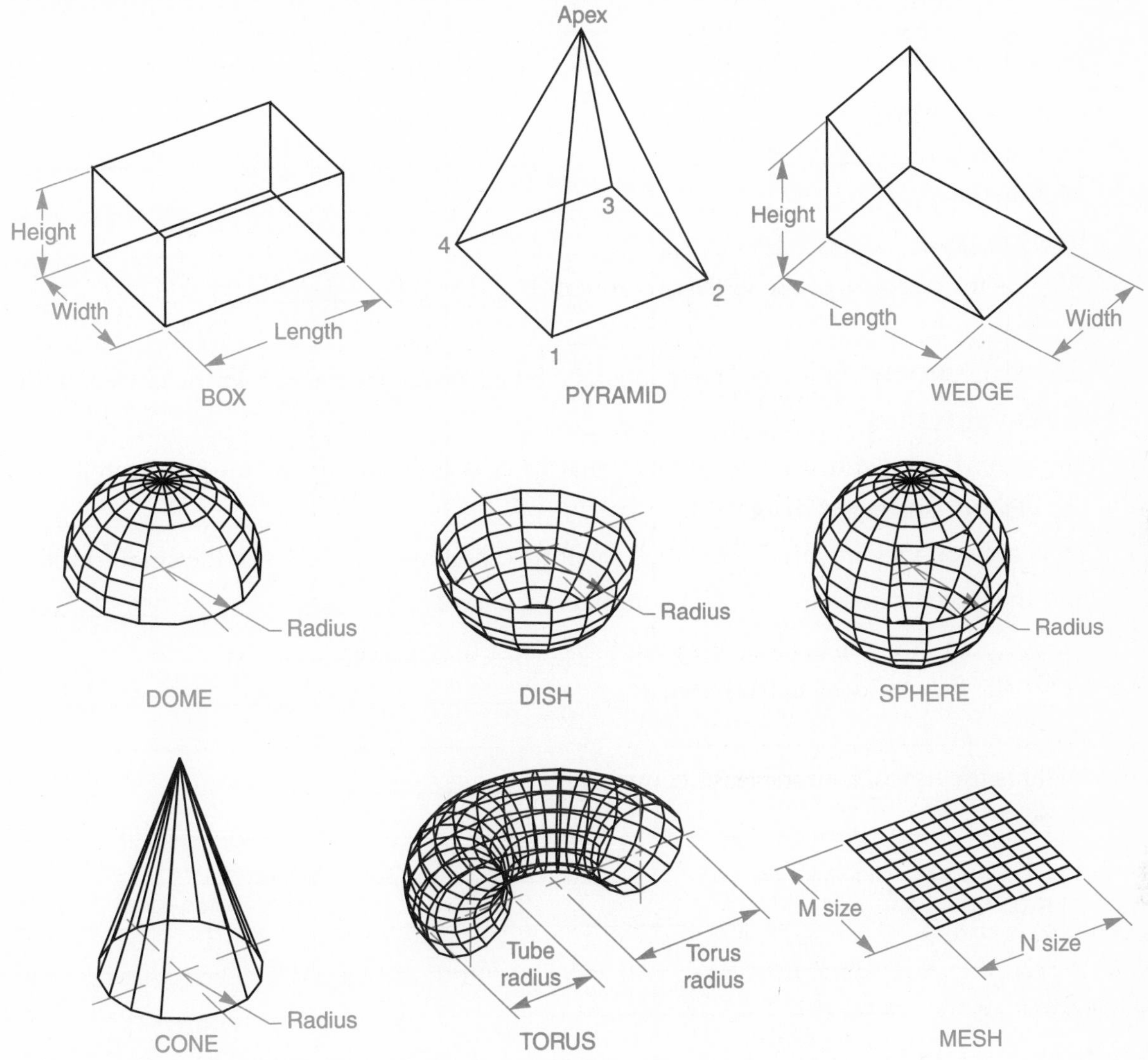

BOX

PYRAMID

WEDGE

DOME

DISH

SPHERE

CONE

TORUS

MESH

## CHAPTER TEST

*Write your answers in the spaces provided.*

1. When looking at the screen, in which direction does the Z coordinate project? _____

   _____

2. Which command displays the **Object Creation Modes** dialog box? _____

3. Which two aspects of 3D can be set in the **Object Creation Modes** dialog box? _____

   _____

   _____

4. Which command allows you to give objects thickness? _____

5. If you draw a line after setting a thickness, what have you actually drawn? _____
   _____

6. What is the purpose of the right-hand rule? _____
   _____
   _____
   _____

7. According to the right-hand rule, name the coordinate axes represented by the
   following fingers:
   Thumb—_____
   Middle finger—_____
   Index finger—_____

8. What is the purpose of the **VPOINT** command? _____
   _____

9. When the **VPOINT** command's tripod is displayed, what are the concentric circles in the
   upper right called? _____

10. How are you viewing an object when the little crosshairs are inside the small circle in
    the **VPOINT** command display? _____

11. How are you viewing an object when the little crosshairs are between the small circle
    and the large circle in the **VPOINT** command display? _____
    _____

12. How do you create 3D extruded text? _____
    _____

13. What is the function of the **HIDE** command?_____
    _____
    _____

14. Define "point filters." _____
    _____
    _____
    _____
    _____

15. Compare the **3DFACE** and **SOLID** commands. _____
    _____
    _____
    _____
    _____

16. How do you select one of AutoCAD's predrawn 3D shapes? _____
    _____
    _____

## DRAWING PROBLEMS

1. Draw Problem 12 from Chapter 28 using the **ELEV** command. Display the object in two different views. Use **HIDE** on one view. Save the drawing as A:P29-1.

*Mechanical Drafting*

2. Draw the object shown below using the **ELEV** command. Display the object in two different views. Use **HIDE** on one view. Save the drawing as A:P29-2.

*Mechanical Drafting*

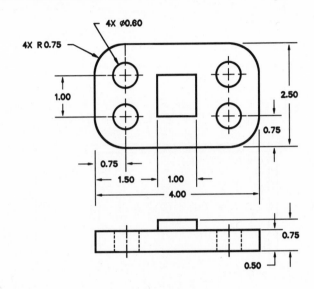

3. Choose Problem 5, 6, 7, 8, or 9 from Chapter 28 and draw it as a wireframe using the **LINE** command. Display the drawing with **VPOINT** in four different views. Save the drawing as A:P29-3.

*Mechanical Drafting*

4. Open drawing P29-3. Use the **3DFACE** command to create faces on the entire part. Display the part in four different views. Save the revised drawing as A:P29-4.

*Mechanical Drafting*

5 - 7. Draw the objects shown below in 3D form. Use the **LINE** and **3DFACE** commands with the dimensions given to create the drawings. Can you create 3D blocks for use in these drawings? Display the drawings from three different viewpoints. Select the **HIDE** command for one of the views. Save the drawings as A:P29-5, A:P29-6, and A:P29-7.

5.

*General*

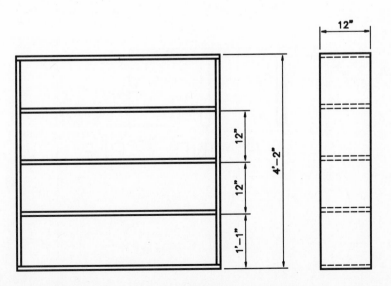

*General*     6.

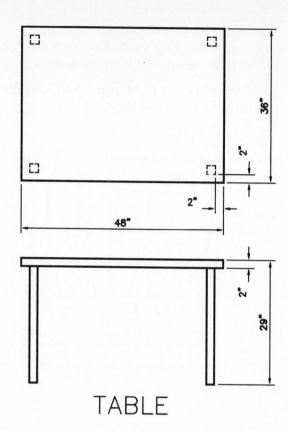

TABLE

*General*     7.

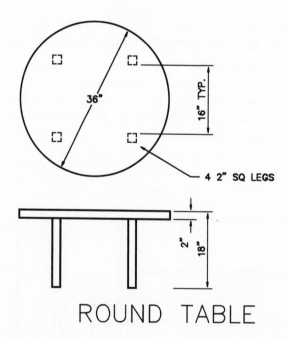

ROUND TABLE

8. Construct a 3D model of the table shown.

   A. Use any 3D construction techniques required.

   B. Use the dimensions given.

   C. Alter the design of the table to include rounded table top corners or rounded feet. Try replacing the rectangular feet shown with spheres.

   D. Use the **DVIEW** command to display the model.

   E. Use the **HIDE** command to remove hidden lines.

   F. Plot the table both in wireframe and with hidden lines removed.

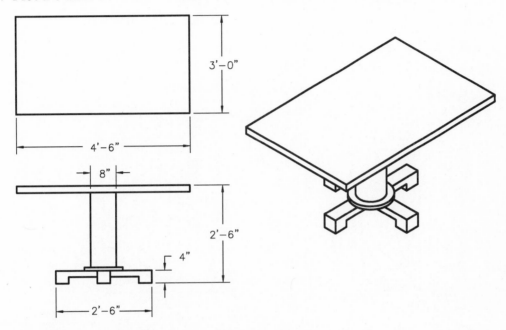

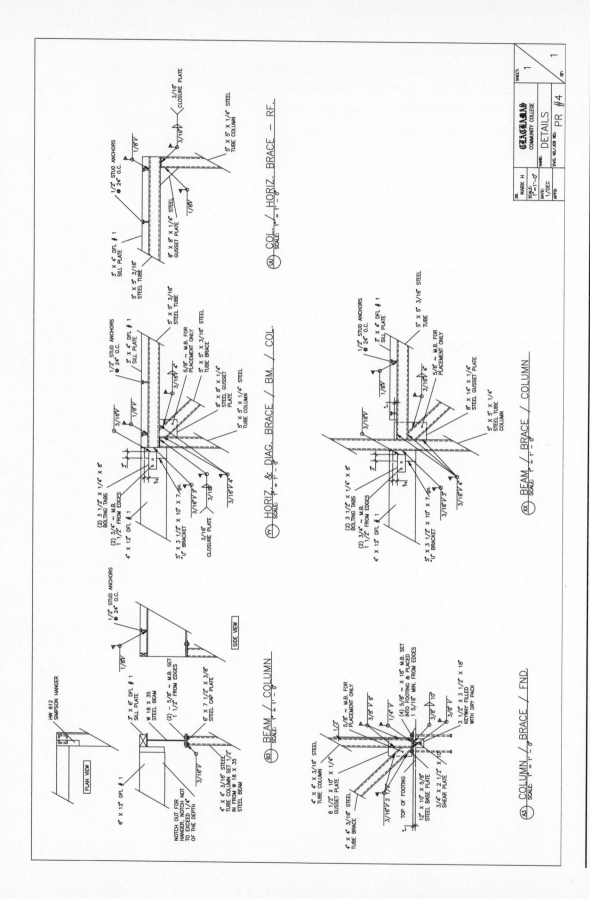

Roof framing details. (Mark Hartman)

# Chapter 30
## AutoCAD R13 External Commands, Script Files, and Slide Shows

### Learning objectives
After completing this chapter, you will be able to:
- ○ Edit the ACAD.PGP file.
- ○ Use a text editor to create script files.
- ○ Create a continuous slide show of existing drawings.
- ○ Use the **SLIDELIB** command to create a slide library.

This chapter introduces you to the use of scripts. A *script* is a series of commands and variables listed in a text file. When the script file is activated by AutoCAD, the entire list of commands is performed without additional input from the user. One useful script is a continuous slide show. It is excellent for client presentations, demonstrations, and for grading drawings.

Word processing or text editor programs can be used to write scripts. There are three tools available under the MS-DOS operating system for writing ASCII (American Standard Code for Information Interchange) text files: the COPY command with the console input source, the EDLIN text editor, and the MS-DOS EDIT text editor. Check for the presence of the last two files on your hard disk drive by typing the following at the DOS prompt:

C:\\> **DIR \DOS\ED*.*** ↵

If EDLIN.COM or EDIT.COM is not listed, consult your instructor or supervisor. In the Microsoft Windows operating environment, the Windows Notepad provides a much faster and more convenient method of creating text files, although both EDLIN and EDIT may still be used.

| | |
|---|---|
| **NOTE**  | The MS-DOS EDIT text editor is available only in DOS versions 5.*x* or later. If you have an earlier version of DOS, this program is not available. Type VER at the DOS prompt to determine your DOS version. The EDLIN line editor is not available if you are using MS-DOS version 6.*x*. |

## USING TEXT EDITORS

The more experienced you become with AutoCAD for Windows, the more you will want to alter the program to suit specific needs. Most of these alterations are done with a text editor program. The EDLIN program that comes with DOS is neither powerful nor flexible enough for production work. While the Windows-supplied Notepad editor is quite capable of performing many of the text editing tasks appropriate for AutoCAD, it cannot accommodate files that exceed 50K (50,000 bytes) in size. However, EDLIN, MS-DOS EDIT, and Notepad are satisfactory for creating simple text files.

## Word processors

Many AutoCAD users rely on full-fledged word processing programs to create their text
files. These word processing files are then saved in ASCII format so that they are readable by
AutoCAD. There are dozens of word processing programs commercially available. The
Windows Write program is a word processor that is included with Microsoft Windows. Like
Notepad, Windows Write may be accessed from the Accessories group window in the Program
Manager, Figure 30-1.

Figure 30-1.   Both the Notepad
text editor and Windows Write
word processor can be accessed
from the Accessories group
window.

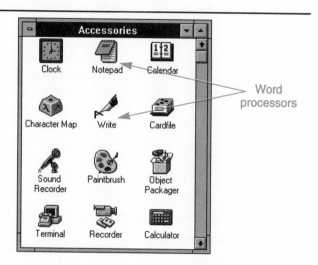

Other Windows-compatible programs with which you might be familiar include Ami
Pro, WordPerfect, and Microsoft Word for Windows. All are excellent tools for producing written
documentation, but exceed what is needed to create text files for AutoCAD. If you choose to
use a word processor, create the text file in "programmer's mode" or "nondocument mode."
This prevents the inclusion of special formatting codes, thus producing an ASCII format file.

## Programmer's text editors

The best type of text editor, however, is a programmer's editor. There are a wide variety
of inexpensive, yet powerful, text editors commercially available that are designed for creating the type of files needed to customize AutoCAD. The Norton Editor is one example of an
excellent programmer's editor.

Programmer's editors are recommended over word processors because of their design,
size, function, ease of use, and price. If you are using versions 5.x or 6.x of MS-DOS, the EDIT
text editor is excellent for many of the custom files you will write for AutoCAD.

# EXTERNAL COMMANDS–THE MS-DOS PROMPT

One of the greatest advantages in using Microsoft Windows is the ability to have an application open in one window, yet be working in another window entirely. This capability allows you to edit a text file with Notepad, or some other Windows-based text editor, without exiting AutoCAD for Windows. Since many of the text files you create will be designed and needed while running AutoCAD, this is a particularly handy feature of Microsoft Windows.

There are times, however, when it would be convenient to run a non-Windows application without exiting AutoCAD for Windows. This capability is provided with the Windows application called **MS-DOS Prompt.** You can access MS-DOS Prompt by returning to the Main group window in the Program Manager and double-clicking the MS-DOS Prompt icon, Figure 30-2. The display screen flashes briefly and you are presented with messages and a prompt similar to the ones shown in Figure 30-3.

Figure 30-2.   The MS-DOS Prompt icon is located in the Main group window.

Pick to access the MS-DOS prompt

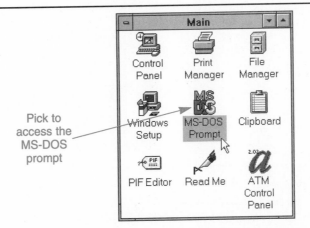

Figure 30-3.   Pressing [Alt]+[Enter] displays the MS-DOS Prompt as a window, instead of a full-screen display.

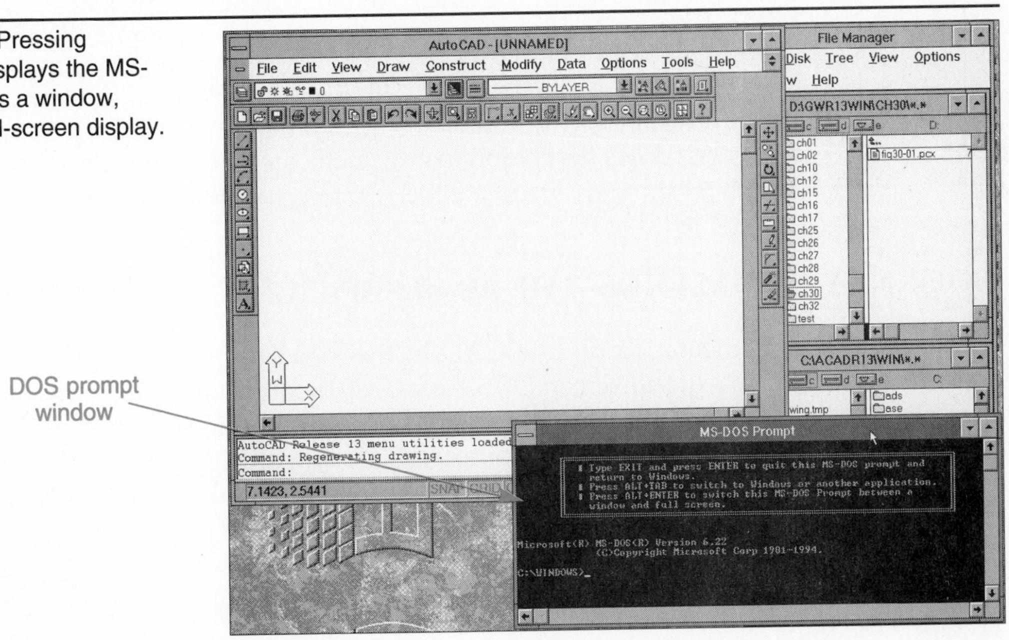

DOS prompt window

Even though MS-DOS Prompt is a Windows application, you may now issue a DOS command or run a non-Windows application at the displayed DOS prompt. You can verify for yourself that MS-DOS Prompt is a Windows application by pressing the [Ctrl]+[Esc] key combination to activate the Windows Task List, Figure 30-4. Also, observe that MS-DOS Prompt exits to the \WINDOWS directory. If necessary, change to the appropriate directory or drive to run your application. From the screen instructions shown above, you have the option to display the DOS prompt in a window by pressing [Alt]+[Enter].

You can leave the DOS prompt as an open window, or minimize it for later use. By pressing the [Alt]+[Tab] key combination, you can switch back to the Windows application you were running before you invoked MS-DOS Prompt. This action does not close MS-DOS Prompt, however. When you are ready to exit MS-DOS Prompt, simply type EXIT and press [Enter].

Figure 30-4.   As with other open Windows applications, the MS-DOS Prompt appears in the Windows Task List box.

Select an application and pick the **Switch To** button

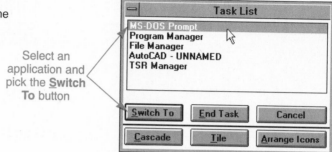

PROFESSIONAL TIP

Be sure to save your AutoCAD drawing before using MS-DOS Prompt. This will ensure that no work is lost in case your computer should "hang" or crash while you are temporarily exited from AutoCAD. Keep in mind that certain DOS commands should not be used when running MS-DOS Prompt. These commands include UNDELETE and CHKDSK with the /F switch. Also, never use disk-compression and optimization programs when running Windows. Exit Windows first before using such commands and program utilities.

# EXTERNAL COMMANDS–THE ACAD.PGP FILE                      ACG 1

Before the implementation of AutoCAD in the Windows environment, it was usually necessary for a user to exit full-screen DOS AutoCAD before using a text editor or issuing an operating system command. Autodesk long ago recognized this limitation and thus provided a means of executing such *external* commands from within AutoCAD. These commands are called external because the functions they invoke are not part of AutoCAD.

Each of these external commands are defined in a file called ACAD.PGP (program parameters). This file is placed in the \R13\COM\SUPPORT subdirectory during the AutoCAD for Windows installation procedure. A portion of the ACAD.PGP file is displayed in the Notepad as shown in Figure 30-5.

Figure 30-5.  An ACAD.PGP
(program parameters) file
opened in Notepad.

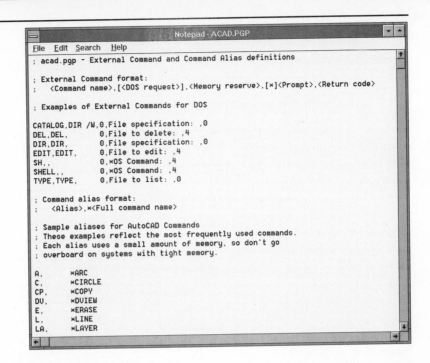

```
Notepad - ACAD.PGP
File  Edit  Search  Help

; acad.pgp - External Command and Command Alias definitions

; External Command format:
;    <Command name>,[<DOS request>],<Memory reserve>,[×]<Prompt>,<Return code>

; Examples of External Commands for DOS

CATALOG,DIR /W,0,File specification: ,0
DEL,DEL,       0,File to delete: ,4
DIR,DIR,       0,File specification: ,0
EDIT,EDIT,     0,File to edit: ,4
SH,,           0,×OS Command: ,4
SHELL,,        0,×OS Command: ,4
TYPE,TYPE,     0,File to list: ,0

; Command alias format:
;    <Alias>,×<Full command name>

; Sample aliases for AutoCAD Commands
; These examples reflect the most frequently used commands.
; Each alias uses a small amount of memory, so don't go
; overboard on systems with tight memory.

A,     ×ARC
C,     ×CIRCLE
CP,    ×COPY
DV,    ×DVIEW
E,     ×ERASE
L,     ×LINE
LA,    ×LAYER
```

To view this file without launching Notepad, enter the DOS TYPE command at the **Command:** prompt as follows:

Command: **TYPE** ↵
File to list: **\R13\COM\SUPPORT\ACAD.PGPIMORE** ↵
CATALOG,DIR /W,    0,File specification:    ,0
DEL,DEL,          0,File to delete:    ,4
DIR,DIR,          0,File specification:    ,0
EDIT,EDIT,        0,File to edit:    ,4
SH,,              0,*OS Command:    ,4
SHELL,,           0,*OS Command:    ,4
TYPE,TYPE,        0,File to list:    ,0

The first word on each line is the command name that should be typed at AutoCAD's **Command:** prompt to execute the external command. The second word represents the DOS command or program to be executed. Although the CATALOG, DEL, and DIR commands are still included in the ACAD.PGP file, they are not valid in AutoCAD for Windows and no longer perform any function. Notice that typing EDIT at the **Command:** prompt runs the MS-DOS EDIT text editor. Each field in the EDIT entry is separated by a comma and is defined as follows:

- **EDIT.** The command to be typed at the AutoCAD **Command:** prompt.
- **EDIT.** The command or program name executed after the external command name is typed. This is the name that would normally be entered at the DOS prompt to run the text editor. If you are using MS-DOS Version 5.*x* or higher, this command runs the EDIT text editor. Instructions on how to edit the ACAD.PGP file for purposes of running your favorite text editor are provided later in this chapter.
- **0.** Previous versions of AutoCAD require a specified memory reserve for the command to function. Release 13 handles this automatically, but a 0 is still required for proper operation.
- **File to edit:.** The prompt that you want to appear after a command is typed.
- **4.** Non-Windows versions of AutoCAD require a code that determines the type of screen mode to display when an external command is completed. To return to the graphics screen, a number 4 is placed in this location. Entering 0 here instructs AutoCAD to remain in text mode. These codes are no longer applicable in AutoCAD for Windows and may be omitted.

## The SH and SHELL commands

The SH and SHELL entries in the ACAD.PGP file perform a function similar to the MS-DOS Prompt Windows application discussed earlier in this chapter. When you enter SH or SHELL on the AutoCAD command line, you are prompted with:

OS Command: *(enter an external command or press* [Enter]*)*

You may enter only one external command at the OS Command: prompt. When the command is completed, you are automatically returned to the AutoCAD graphics window. If you press [Enter] at the OS Command: prompt, the screen flashes briefly and you are presented with the DOS prompt. Thus, pressing [Enter] performs much the same function as MS-DOS Prompt but you are placed in the \R13 directory and not the \WINDOWS directory.

From the Windows Task List box shown in Figure 30-6, you can see two entries titled COMMAND and ***AutoCAD Shell Active***. These entries appear when you "shell out" of AutoCAD for Windows using the SH or SHELL commands. Clicking COMMAND switches you to the DOS prompt, while clicking ***AutoCAD Shell Active*** switches you back to the AutoCAD graphics window. As with MS-DOS Prompt, when you are ready to exit the AutoCAD shell, type EXIT and press [Enter].

---

Figure 30-6. The Windows Task List box reports that the AutoCAD Shell is active.

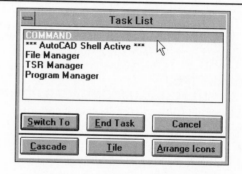

**PROFESSIONAL TIP**

The SH or SHELL command is a handy way to delete a file or do a directory listing from within AutoCAD. If you choose to perform a directory listing, use the command form DIR/P to scroll the directory one page at a time. As with MS-DOS Prompt, take care using certain DOS commands and exit Windows before using any hard disk utility programs.

## Command aliases

AutoCAD allows you to abbreviate command names. This feature was introduced with AutoCAD Release 11 and is called *command aliasing.* A list of predefined aliases furnished with AutoCAD for Windows can be displayed by viewing the contents of the ACAD.PGP file. You can do this by using the **TYPE** command as explained earlier in this chapter, or by loading the file into Notepad or another text editor of your choice. Scroll down past the listing of external commands and you will see the list of command aliases:

```
A,          *ARC
C,          *CIRCLE
CP,         *COPY
DV,         *DVIEW
E,          *ERASE
L,          *LINE
LA,         *LAYER
LT,         *LINETYPE
M,          *MOVE
MS,         *MSPACE
P,          *PAN
PS,         *PSPACE
PL,         *PLINE
R,          *REDRAW
T,          *MTEXT
Z,          *ZOOM
3DLINE,     *LINE
```

If you continue to scroll down into the file, you will find a list of aliases for dimensioning commands. While the MS-DOS Prompt Windows application has virtually eliminated the need to use the ACAD.PGP file for executing external commands, you can easily create your own aliases by editing this file. If you do so, keep the number of aliases to a minimum if your computer does not have a lot of extra memory. Each command alias uses a small amount of memory, which reduces the amount available for drawing purposes.

If you want to add an alias for the **SPLINE** command, for example, enter the following below the **REDRAW** command in the ACAD.PGP file:

```
S,          *SPLINE
```

Be sure to include the asterisk since it indicates to AutoCAD that this is an alias. The revised .PGP file will not work until you exit AutoCAD for Windows and re-enter the program, which reloads the ACAD.PGP file. You can also reload the ACAD.PGP file by entering the **REINIT** command. This displays the **Re-initialization** dialog box shown in Figure 30-7. Clicking the **PGP File** check box in this dialog box, and then clicking **OK** re-initializes the ACAD.PGP file so that your new command alias will work.

---

Figure 30-7.   The **Re-initialization** dialog box.

**NOTE**   The **Re-initialization** dialog box can also be used if you have one of your serial ports, such as COM1, configured for both a plotter and a digitizer. If you physically change the cable from plotter to digitizer, click the **Digitizer** check boxes in both areas of the dialog box; then click **OK**. The digitizer will be re-initialized. If you are using a mouse instead of a digitizer, both **Digitizer** entries in this dialog box are grayed-out.

## Editing the ACAD.PGP file

There are several tools available to edit the ACAD.PGP file. The Windows Notepad, EDLIN, EDIT, or some other text editor may all be used. Probably the easiest editing method is with the Windows Notepad. However, keep in mind that for files that exceed 50K in size, Notepad cannot be used. Fortunately, the ACAD.PGP file is much smaller than that.

You may recall that Notepad was introduced in Chapter 24 as a means to add a customized hatch pattern to the ACAD.PAT file. It was used again in Chapter 27 to create a template file for attribute extraction. If necessary, refer to those chapters to refresh your memory on the use of Notepad.

**PROFESSIONAL TIP**

Always make backup copies of AutoCAD text files before editing them. These files include: ACAD.LIN, ACAD.PAT, and ACAD.PGP. There are other kinds of AutoCAD text files as well, which are discussed in *AutoCAD and its Applications, Advanced—Release 13 for Windows*. Should you "corrupt" one of these files through incorrect editing techniques, simply delete that file and restore the original.

For files that exceed 50K, it is necessary to use EDLIN, EDIT, or another text editor. EDLIN is available in all versions of DOS through 5.x, and the DOS editor is executed by the ACAD.PGP file when EDIT is entered at the AutoCAD **Command:** prompt.

EDLIN is referred to as a line editor. This simply means that editing is done by line number. Unfortunately, this is a very slow and clumsy way to edit a text file. If you are using MS-DOS Version 5.x or 6.x, the EDIT program is far easier to use and much more efficient. This is because EDIT, like Notepad, is a full screen editor that allows you to move the text cursor around the screen easily.

The ACAD.PGP file can be easily altered to specify your personal text editor (TE) instead of EDIT. If you are currently running AutoCAD for Windows, press [Ctrl]+[Esc] to activate the Windows Task List box and return to the Program Manager. Now, open the Main group window and double-click the MS-DOS Prompt icon. When the DOS prompt appears, enter the following:

C:\WINDOWS⟩ **EDIT \R13\COM\SUPPORT\ACAD.PGP** ↵

The display screen will flash briefly and then the ACAD.PGP file is displayed, as shown in Figure 30-8.

Figure 30-8.   The ACAD.PGP file is displayed in the MS-DOS EDIT text editor.

The DOS EDIT is specified

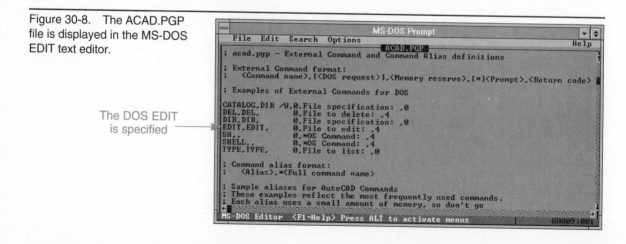

You may freely use any of the text editing keys on your keyboard to move the flashing text cursor around the screen. These keys include the left, right, up, and down arrows, as well as the [Home], [Page Up], [Page Down], [Insert], [Delete], and [End] keys. You can also move the text cursor with your pointing device. Use the down arrow key or your pointing device to move the text cursor to the line labeled:

    EDIT, EDIT,      0,File to edit: ,4

Remove the second word EDIT using the [Backspace] or [Delete] keys, and replace it with the word TE. When you are done, the ACAD.PGP file should appear as shown in Figure 30-9.

To save the edited file, activate the pull-down menus at the top of the screen. You do this by pressing the [Alt] key on the keyboard, and then pressing F to activate the File pull-down menu. Now select Save by pressing S on the keyboard, Figure 30-10. (Your pointing device may also be used to activate the pull-down menus.)

Figure 30-9.   The word EDIT is replaced with TE to specify an external text editor.

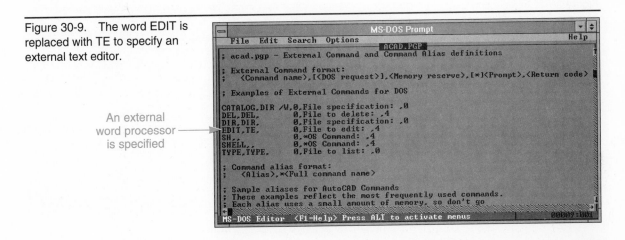

An external word processor is specified

Figure 30-10.   Select Save from the File pull-down menu to save the edited ACAD.PGP file.

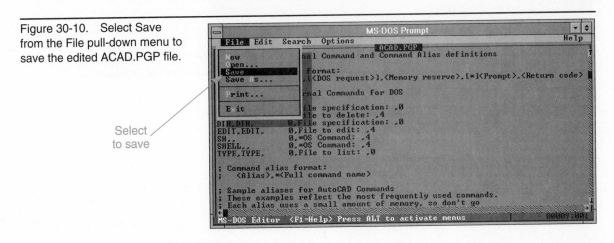

Select to save

Because the ACAD.PGP file is rather small, it will save very quickly and you may not even notice any delay as it is written back to the disk. To exit MS-DOS EDIT, reactivate the menus at the top of the screen by pressing the [Alt] key again. Once more press F to activate the File pull-down menu, and then press X to exit the program, Figure 30-11.

If the file was saved correctly, you are immediately returned to the DOS prompt. If the file was not saved, MS-DOS EDIT displays the dialog box shown in Figure 30-12. This dialog box asks if you want to save the file. Since the default answer to this question is ⟨Yes⟩, simply press [Enter] to save the file and return to the DOS prompt. To return to AutoCAD for Windows, enter EXIT at the DOS prompt.

If you try using the new EDIT command in AutoCAD now, it will not work. This is because AutoCAD is still using the original version of the ACAD.PGP file. You must re-initialize the .PGP file with the **REINIT** command before the EDIT command can function properly.

Figure 30-11.   Selecting Exit from the File pull-down menu exits the EDIT program and returns to the DOS prompt.

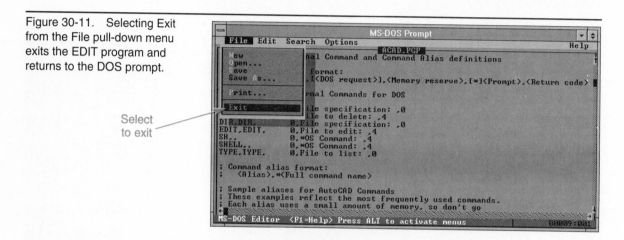

Figure 30-12.   If the file is not saved when you try to exit EDIT, you are given the option of saving before you exit.

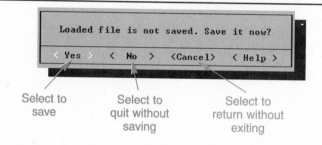

Select to save     Select to quit without saving     Select to return without exiting

---

**EXERCISE 30-1**

❑ Start Windows and load AutoCAD.
❑ Use MS-DOS Prompt and the EDIT program to edit the ACAD.PGP file as described in the previous text. Make sure that you have a backup copy of ACAD.PGP before making your changes.
❑ Save the file, exit MS-DOS Prompt, and use the **REINIT** command.
❑ Test the new EDIT command.

## CREATING SCRIPT FILES TO AUTOMATE AUTOCAD          AUG 6

A *script file* is a list of commands that AutoCAD executes in sequence without input from the user. Scripts enable non-programmers to automate AutoCAD functions. They can be used for specific functions, such as plotting a drawing with the correct **PLOT** command values and settings, or creating a slide show. A good working knowledge of AutoCAD commands and options is needed before you can confidently create a script file.

When writing a script file, put just one command or option per line in the text file. This makes the file easier to fix if the script does not work properly. A RETURN is specified by pressing [Enter] after typing a command. If the next option of a command is a default value to be accepted, press [Enter] again. This leaves a blank line in the script file, which represents pressing [Enter].

The following example shows how a script file can be used to plot a drawing. At your computer, enter these files with Notepad, EDIT, or your favorite text editor. The file extension of the script name must be .SCR. Also, place the file in the \R13\WIN directory of the hard disk. This occurs automatically if you enter EDIT at the **Command:** prompt to run the text editor. If the file is written outside AutoCAD, enter the filename as C:\R13\WIN\FILENAME.SCR.

### A drawing plotting script

In Chapter 12, you learned that you can save plotter settings for a specific drawing in the form of a PCP file. This eliminates setting all of the plot values each time you plot the same drawing. You can automate this process by including all of the plot values in a script file. If you have drawings that will always be plotted with the same settings, use script files to plot them.

The script file on the following page plots a C-size drawing. The contents of the script file are shown in the left column, and a description of each line is given to the right. This script file is named ARCH24-C.SCR. The "ARCH" indicates an architectural drawing, the "24" is the scale factor, and "C" is the paper size.

| | |
|---|---|
| **NOTE**  | When writing a script file, it is important to include every keystroke that is required to accomplish the task at the keyboard. It is also important to know how many plotters and printers are configured in AutoCAD, and how they are listed when using the **PLOT** command at the **Command:** line. |

| | |
|---|---|
| cmddia | *(executes* **CMDDIA** *system variable)* |
| 0 | *(disables the* **Plot Configuration** *dialog box)* |
| plot | *(executes* **PLOT** *command)* |
| E | *(what to plot—extents)* |
| Y | *(Y to change plot settings)* |
| Y | *(Y to change plotters)* |
| 3 | *(description =3 for HP DraftPro)* |
| E | *(what to plot—extents)* |
| Y | *(Y to change plot settings)* |
| N | *(N to not change plotters)* |
| 60 | *(number of seconds to wait for plotter port)* |
| Y | *(Y to request hard clip limits)* |
| Y | *(Y to change plot parameters)* |
| C1 | *(specify color number 1)* |
| 1 | *(pen 1 for color 1)* |
| 0 | *(linetype 0 for color 1)* |
| 15 | *(pen speed for color 1)* |

| 0.010 | (pen width for color 1) |
| C2 | (specify color 2) |
| 2 | (pen 2 for color 2) |
| 0 | (linetype 0 for color 2) |
| 15 | (pen speed for color 2) |
| 0.010 | (pen width for color 2) |
| C3 | (specify color 3) |
| 3 | (pen 3 for color 3) |
| 0 | (linetype 0 for color 3) |
| 15 | (pen speed for color 3) |
| 0.010 | (pen width for color 3) |
| C4 | (specify color 4) |
| 4 | (pen 4 for color 4) |
| 0 | (linetype 0 for color 4) |
| 15 | (pen speed for color 4) |
| 0.010 | (pen width for color 4) |
| X | (exit parameter settings) |
| N | (do not write plot file) |
| I | (size units in inches) |
| 0,0 | (plot origin) |
| C | (paper size) |
| 0 | (plot rotation angle) |
| N | (do not adjust for pen width) |
| N | (do not remove hidden lines) |
| 1=24 | (drawing scale) |

**CAUTION**

A single incorrect entry in a script file can cause it to malfunction. Test the keystrokes at the keyboard before you write the script file, and record them for future reference. When writing a script for plotting purposes, this is an important step. Plotters and printers have different settings, and thus have different prompts in the **PLOT** command. Always step through the **PLOT** command and specify the plotter or printer you wish to use before writing the script file.

**PROFESSIONAL TIP**

Avoid pressing the space bar at the end of a line in the script file. This adds a space, and can cause the script to crash. Plus, finding spaces in a script file can be tedious work.

At the **Command:** prompt, type SCRIPT and then select the filename ARCH24-C.SCR from the **Select Script File** dialog box. See Figure 30-13. Then sit back and watch the script run.

Command: **SCRIPT** ↵

All of the commands, options, and text screens associated with the commands in the script are displayed in rapid succession on the screen. If the script stops before completing, a problem has occurred. Flip the screen to the text window ([F2]) to determine the last command executed. Return to your text editor and correct the problem. Most often, there are too many or too few RETURNs. Another problem is spaces at the end of a line. If you suspect these errors, retype the line.

Figure 30-13.   The **Select Script File** dialog box.

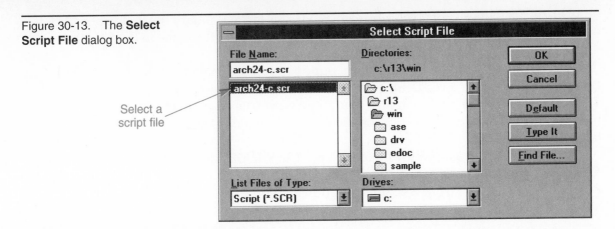

Select a script file

## EXERCISE 30-2

☐ Begin a new drawing named SCRPTEST.

☐ Use the **DTEXT** command to write your name in the lower-right corner.

☐ Save the drawing, but do not exit AutoCAD for Windows.

☐ Use Notepad or MS-DOS EDIT and write a script file named TEST.SCR. The script file should do the following:

  ☐ Draw a circle at coordinates 4,4 with a radius of 1.

  ☐ Change the current color to green.

  ☐ Draw a doughnut centered on the circle with an inside diameter of 2.5 and an outside diameter of 2.8.

☐ Switch back to AutoCAD and use the **SCRIPT** command to run TEST.SCR.

☐ If the script file does not run to completion, use Notepad to correct it. Run the script file again until it works.

## SLIDES AND SLIDE SHOWS

ACG 6

A *slide* in AutoCAD, similar to a slide in photography, is a snapshot of the screen display. Because of its nature, it cannot be edited or plotted. Slides can be viewed one at a time or as a continuous show. This is why slides are excellent for demonstrations, presentations, displays, and grading procedures.

Students and prospective employees can create an impressive portfolio using a slide show. A *slide show* is a group of slides that are displayed at preset intervals. The slide show is controlled by a script file—a list of commands similar to the previous script examples. Each slide is displayed for a specific length of time. The show can be continuous or a single pass.

### Making and viewing slides

Creating slides is easy. First display the drawing for which you need a slide. You might display the entire drawing or zoom to a specific area or feature. AutoCAD creates a slide of the current screen display. Make as many slides of one drawing as you want. For each, select the **MSLIDE** command and provide a filename for the slide. Do not enter a file type, as AutoCAD automatically attaches an .SLD file extension. Pick **Slide**, then **Save...**, from the **Tools** pull-down menu. If **FILEDIA** is set to 1, a dialog box appears. Use **MSLIDE** at the **Command:** prompt as follows:

      Command: **MSLIDE** ↵

The **Create Slide File** dialog box is displayed. This is the standard file dialog box. Pick the drive and directory in which the file is to be stored, then enter the name in the **File Name:** text box, and click the **OK** button.

Slide names should follow a pattern. Suppose you are making slides for a class called CAD1. Filenames such as CAD1SLD1 and CAD1SLD2 are appropriate. If working on project #4305 for the Weyerhauser Company, you might name the slide to reflect the client name or project number, such as WEYERSL1 or 4305SLD1. Slide names can use the full eight characters allowed by DOS.

Viewing a slide is as simple as making one. The **VSLIDE** command asks for the slide filename. Do not enter the .SLD file extension because AutoCAD knows it is looking for a slide. Pick **Slide**, then **View...**, from the **Tools** pull-down menu.

      Command: **VSLIDE** ↵

The **Select Slide File** dialog box appears. Pick the slide you want to display and click **OK**.

Keep the \R13 directory free of drawing, slide, and AutoLISP files. This speeds the computer's access to AutoCAD files. Create a separate hard disk directory for slides or save slides on a floppy disk. If using floppy disks, be sure to give the appropriate filename when creating slides. A filename of A:CAD1SLD1 is entered to place a slide on a floppy disk in the A: disk drive.

      Command: **MSLIDE** ↵
      Slide file: **A:CAD1SLD1** ↵

**PROFESSIONAL TIP**

To create a slide file at the highest resolution, set **VIEWRES** to its maximum value of 20000 before using the **MSLIDE** command. After making the slide, restore **VIEWRES** to its previous value.

**EXERCISE 30-3**

❑ Load any one of your drawings into the drawing editor.
❑ Create a slide of the entire drawing, using an appropriate filename.
❑ Make slides of two more drawings. Use similar naming techniques.
❑ View each of the slides as they are created.
❑ These slides are required to complete the next exercise.

## Writing a slide show script file

A slide show script file contains only two or three commands. This depends on whether it is a single pass or continuous show. The **RSCRIPT** (repeat script) command is used at the end of a continuous script file. Any slide file can be displayed for up to 33 seconds using the **DELAY** command. Delays are given in milliseconds. A delay of four seconds is written as DELAY 4000. The next slide is "preloaded" into computer memory for quick display by placing an asterisk before the slide name. A slide is displayed with the **VSLIDE** command.

A slide show begins with the creation of a script file using a text editor. The following script uses four slides. Each appears for three seconds and the script repeats. Notice that the next slide is preloaded while the previous one is viewed. The file, SHOW.SCR, is created using a text editor as follows:

```
Command: EDIT ↵
File to edit: SHOW.SCR ↵
  *VSLIDE CAD1SLD1 ↵
  *VSLIDE * CAD1SLD2 ↵
  *DELAY 3000 ↵
  *VSLIDE ↵
  *VSLIDE *CAD1SLD3 ↵
  *DELAY 3000 ↵
  *VSLIDE ↵
  *VSLIDE *CAD1SLD4 ↵
  *DELAY 3000 ↵
  *VSLIDE ↵
  *DELAY 3000 ↵
  *RSCRIPT ↵
```

The SHOW.SCR script file is shown as it would be entered in the Windows Notepad, Figure 30-14. Also, do not forget that when using slide files on diskettes, include the disk drive letter and path in front of the filename, such as A:CAD1SLD2. Use this method with each **VSLIDE** command.

Figure 30-14.   The SHOW.SCR script file as it appears in the Windows Notepad.

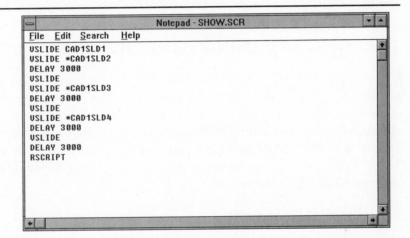

### Viewing the slide show

The slide show is started by entering **SCRIPT** at the **Command:** prompt, or by picking **Run Script...** from the **Tools** pull-down menu. Select the script filename SHOW.SCR from the **Select Script File** dialog box.

The show begins and the commands in the script file are displayed at the **Command:** prompt as the slides appear. To stop the show, press the [Backspace] key. You can then work on a drawing, use DOS commands, or work with a text editor on another script file. When finished, resume the slide show where it left off by typing RESUME. Any script file can be interrupted and restarted in this manner.

Your slide show may run into a bug and not finish the first time through. This is not unusual, so do not panic. Take the following steps to "debug," or correct, problems in your script file.

- Run the script to see where it crashes (quits working).
- Check the command line for the last command that was executed.
- Look for error messages, such as:
    - ✓ Can't open slide file *xxxxx* (Incorrect slide filename).
    - ✓ *xxxxx* Unknown command (Command spelled incorrectly or a space left at the end of the line).

✓ Requires an integer value (Delay value not all numerical characters. Possibly a space at the end of the line).
- Correct the problem in the script file and save the file.
- Test the script.

The most common errors are misspelled commands and spaces at the end of lines. If you suspect there is a space at the end of a line, it is best to retype the line.

If you use Notepad or EDIT, it is easy to see if a space exists. The flashing cursor, when placed at the end of a line, does not rest on the last character. This feature is not possible with EDLIN.

## EXERCISE 30-4

❑ Create a script file named EX30-4. Use Notepad or your own text editor. It is not necessary to be in the AutoCAD drawing editor to create the script file.
❑ Include the three slides created in Exercise 30-3. If these slides have not been created, make slides of any three of your drawings.
❑ Delay each slide for two seconds.
❑ Make the show run continuously.
❑ Run the slide show. Correct any errors and run it again until it recycles without failing.

## CREATING AND USING SLIDE LIBRARIES                            AUG 14

A *slide library* is a list of slide files that can be used not only for slide shows, but also for constructing image tile menus. Image tile menus are groups of slides or vector images displayed in a dialog box. Examples are the Geometric Dimensioning and Tolerancing symbols displayed after selecting **Dimensioning**, then **Tolerance...** in the **Draw** pull-down menu. Image tile menus were known as "icon" menus in previous releases of AutoCAD. Constructing image tile menus is discussed in *AutoCAD and its Applications, Advanced— Release 13 for Windows*.

### Creating the slide library

To create the slide library, you must use a utility program, called SLIDELIB.EXE, that operates from the DOS prompt. By default, the SLIDELIB.EXE utility program is installed in the R13\COM\SUPPORT subdirectory. Be sure to include this path when using the utility. SLIDELIB.EXE can be used to create slide libraries one of two ways. The first method involves listing the slides and their directory location after entering the **SLIDELIB** command. For example, suppose you have four slides of pipe fittings in the \PIPE subdirectory of \R13. List these in a slide library called PIPE in the following manner:

```
Command: SH ⏎
OS Command: \R13\COM\SUPPORT\SLIDELIB PIPE ⏎
SLIDELIB 1.2 (3/8/89)
(C) Copyright 1987-89 Autodesk, Inc.
   All Rights Reserved
\ACAD\PIPE\90ELBOW ⏎
\ACAD\PIPE\45ELBOW ⏎
\ACAD\PIPE\TEE ⏎
\ACAD\PIPE\CAP ⏎
   ⏎
   ⏎
Command:
```

After entering the last slide, press [Enter] three times to end the **SLIDELIB** command. The new slide library file is saved as PIPE.SLB.

The second way to use **SLIDELIB** is to first create a list of the slides you will eventually want in the library. Do this with an ASCII text editor like Notepad or MS-DOS EDIT. This method allows you to accumulate slides over a period of time. Then, when you are ready to create the slide library, the list is prepared. A list of those same pipe fittings would be entered in a file called PIPE.TXT, for example. The list would appear in Notepad or EDIT as follows:

```
90ELBOW
45ELBOW
TEE
CAP
```

After completing the list of slides to include, use the **SLIDELIB** command. The **SLIDELIB** command needs to find the PIPE.TXT file and use it to create a slide library called PIPE.SLB. This can all be handled with one entry at the DOS prompt. But first, you must shell out of AutoCAD for Windows:

```
Command: SH ↵
OS Command: \R13\COM\SUPPORT\SLIDELIB PIPE ⟨PIPE.TXT ↵
SLIDELIB 1.2 (3/8/89)
(C) Copyright 1987-89 Autodesk, Inc.
   All Rights Reserved
Command:
```

The screen flashes briefly and the AutoCAD graphic window is redisplayed. The less-than sign (⟨) instructs the **SLIDELIB** command to take input from the PIPE.TXT file to create a file called PIPE.SLB. To see the results, obtain a directory listing of all .SLB files and look for PIPE.SLB.

## Viewing slide library slides

The **VSLIDE** command also is used to view slides contained in a slide library. Provide the library name plus the slide name in parentheses as follows:

```
Command: VSLIDE ↵
Slide file: (click the Type It button in the dialog box, enter PIPE(90ELBOW) in the
   edit box, and press [Enter])
```

To remove the slide from the screen to display the previous drawing, enter REDRAW.

## Making a slide show using the slide library

The advantage of using a slide library for a slide show is that you do not need to preload slides. A slide show of the four slides in the PIPE.SLB file would appear as follows:

```
VSLIDE PIPE(90ELBOW)
DELAY 1000
VSLIDE PIPE(45ELBOW)
DELAY 1000
VSLIDE PIPE(TEE)
DELAY 1000
VSLIDE PIPE(CAP)
DELAY 1000
REDRAW
```

The **REDRAW** command at the end of the slide show clears the screen and replaces the previous display. An **RSCRIPT** command instead of **REDRAW** repeats the show continuously.

## CHAPTER TEST

*Write your answers in the spaces provided.*

1.  EDLIN is _____.

2.  What precautions should you take when using a word processor to create text files for AutoCAD? _____

    _____

3.  Explain why EDLIN is called a "line editor." _____

    _____

4.  What is the maximum file size (in bytes) that can be handled by the Windows Notepad?

    _____

5.  Which Program Manager group window features MS-DOS Prompt? _____

    _____

6.  What key combination is used to display the Windows Task List? _____

    _____

7.  All DOS commands and program utilities may be executed from MS-DOS Prompt. (True/False) _____

8.  Name the two AutoCAD commands that perform a similar function to MS-DOS Prompt.

    _____

9.  If you edit the ACAD.PGP file from within AutoCAD for Windows, what must you do for the new file definitions to take effect? _____

    _____

10. Describe external commands. _____

    _____

11. Commands located in the ACAD.PGP file are executed by _____.

12. Name the parts of a command listing found in the ACAD.PGP file. _____

    _____

    _____

13. What is a command alias, and how would you write one for the **POLYGON** command?

    _____

14. Define "script file." _____

    _____

15. Why is it a good idea to put one command on each line of a script file? _____

    _____

16. List two common reasons why a script file might not work. _____

    _____

17. The commands that allow you to make and view slides are _____ and

    _____.

18. The file extension that AutoCAD assigns slides is _____.

19. Explain why it is a good idea to keep slide files in a separate directory and not in the \R13 directory. _____

_____

20. List the three commands that are included when writing a slide show. _____

_____

_____

21. To stop a slide show, press the _____ key.

22. To begin a slide show that has been stopped, _____.

23. Briefly explain the two methods used to create a SLIDELIB file. _____

_____

_____

24. Suppose you want to view a slide named VIEW1, which is in a slide library file called VIEWS. How must you enter its name at the Slide file: prompt?

    Slide file: _____

25. What is the principal difference between a slide show script file written for a slide library and one simply written for a group of slides? _____

_____

## PROBLEMS

1. If you use a text editor or word processor other than EDLIN or MS-DOS EDIT, create a new command in the ACAD.PGP file that loads the text editor.

   *General*

2. Create a new command for the ACAD.PGP file that generates a directory listing of all your slide files. Be sure to specify the directory path that contains the slides. For example, if your slides are kept on a floppy disk, the DOS command to execute is: DIR A:*.SLD.

   *General*

3. Write a script file called NOTES.SCR that does the following:

   *General*

   A. Executes the **TEXT** command.
   B. Selects the **Style** option.
   C. Enters a style name.
   D. Selects the last point using the "@" symbol.
   E. Enters a text height of .25.
   F. Enters a rotation angle of 0.
   G. Inserts the text: NOTES:.
   H. Selects the **TEXT** command again.
   I. Enters location coordinates for first note.
   J. Enters a text height of .125.
   K. Enters a rotation angle of 0.
   L. Inserts the text: 1. INTERPRET DIMENSIONS AND TOLERANCES PER ANSI Y14.5.
   M. Enters an [Enter] keystroke.
   N. Inserts the text: 2. REMOVE ALL BURRS AND SHARP EDGES.

O. Enters [Enter] twice to exit the command.

Immediately before this script file is used, select the **ID** command and pick the point where you want the notes to begin. That point will be the "last point" used in the script file for the location of the word NOTES:. The script file, when executed, should draw the following:

NOTES:

1.  INTERPRET DIMENSIONS AND TOLERANCES PER ASME Y14.5.
2.  REMOVE ALL BURRS AND SHARP EDGES.

*General*

4. Create a slide show of your best AutoCAD drawings. This slide show should be considered as part of your portfolio for potential employers. Place all of the slides and the script file on a floppy disk. Make two copies of the portfolio disk on separate floppy disks. Since employers may have different machines, be prepared. Keep the following guidelines in mind:

   A. Do not delay slides longer than 5 seconds. You can always press the [Backspace] key to view a slide longer.

   B. One view of a drawing is sufficient unless the drawing is complex. If so, make additional slides of the drawing's details.

   C. Create a cover slide, or title page slide that gives your name.

   D. Create an ending slide that says THE END.

*General*

5. Create a slide show that illustrates specific types of drawings. For example, you might make a slide show for dimensioned mechanical drawings or for electrical drawings. These specialized slide shows in your portfolio are useful if you apply for a job in a specific discipline. Store all slide shows on the same disk. Identify slide shows by their content as follows:

   MECH.SCR—Mechanical

   ARCH.SCR—Architectural

   PIPE.SCR—Piping

   STRUCT.SCR—Structural

   ELECT.SCR—Electrical or Electronics

   MAP.SCR—Mapping

   CIVIL.SCR—Civil

*General*

6. Create a script file to plot your most frequently used drawing. Use the following guidelines to write the script:

   A. Run a trial plot of the drawing first. Record all of the keystrokes required to plot the drawing correctly.

   B. Check the results of the trial plot to be sure that the use of pens and the location of the drawing on the paper is correct.

   C. Write the script file using the exact keystrokes you recorded.

   D. Test the script and note where problems occur.

   E. Fix the problems in the script file and test the script until it runs properly.

AutoCAD R13

# Chapter *31*
## Digitizing Existing Drawings

### Learning objectives

After completing this chapter, you will be able to:
- Describe the digitizer and the digitizing process.
- Digitize existing drawings into AutoCAD.
- Define scanning and discuss the advantages and disadvantages of scanning over manually digitizing a drawing.

*Digitizing* is the process of transferring information from a digitizing tablet into the computer. You can send commands to the computer by digitizing a command cell on the menu overlay. A *digitizing tablet*, or *digitizer*, is also used to convert existing paper drawings into AutoCAD drawing files. Digitizers range in size from 6″ square to 44″ × 60″. Many schools and industries use 12″ square digitizers to input commands from standard and custom tablet menus.

Most companies do not have the time to convert existing drawings to CAD because they rely on the CAD system for new product drawings. Therefore, an increasing number of businesses digitize existing drawings for other companies. These commercial operations use larger digitizers so that D-size and E-size drawings can be digitized.

Another way to convert existing drawings to CAD files is with a scanner. It sends a light or camera over the drawing to transfer the image to the computer. This technique is called *scanning*.

## THE DIGITIZER

A digitizer consists of a plastic surface, called a *tablet*, and a pointing device for picking locations on the tablet. The digitizer provides extremely accurate location in the form of XY coordinates. Figure 31-1 shows a digitizer and pointing device with a 12″ × 12″ digitizer.

Figure 31-1.   A 12″ × 12″ digitizer with pointing device.

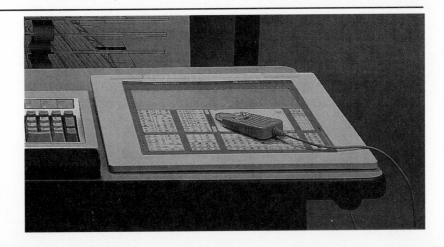

# DIGITIZING AN EXISTING DRAWING

When a company begins converting to CAD, the normal procedure is to have a manual drafting group and a CAD group. Selected new drawings are done on the computer. This situation may continue until the full capabilities of CAD are realized. Manual drafters remain important because older drawings are often revised in the original format.

There comes a time when a company must make a decision to convert existing paper drawings to CAD drawing files. This problem is not confined to paper drawings. Sometimes it is necessary to convert one type of computer-generated drawing to another CAD system. This might be done with a translation program.

In some situations the only solution is to redraw the existing drawings with AutoCAD. Time is usually saved by digitizing the existing drawing, depending on the type of drawing. A digitizer large enough to accommodate the largest drawings is best, but large drawings can also be digitized on small digitizers, if necessary.

The digitizing process consists of a combination of digitized points and AutoCAD drawing and editing commands. Also plan to use **SNAP**, **ORTHO**, and **OSNAP** modes to your best advantage.

## Configuring the tablet

Before digitizing a drawing, you must configure the tablet, even if it was previously configured for another application. This is done to utilize the maximum area on the tablet. To configure the tablet, type TABLET at the **Command:** prompt, followed by typing CFG at the Option: prompt:

    Command: **TABLET** ↵
    Option (ON/OFF/CAL/CFG): **CFG** ↵

Next, AutoCAD asks for the number of tablet menus. Since the entire tablet is used when digitizing an existing drawing, there are no menu areas. Type 0 and press [Enter]. When asked if you want to respecify the screen pointing area, answer Y. Then pick the lower-left corner followed by the upper-right corner. If your digitizer has proximity lights, watch them as you do this. One of the lights is on when the puck is in the screen pointing area, and off when the puck leaves the area. Move the pointing device slowly to the extreme corners until you find the location where the light comes on. This will help you gain use of the entire screen pointing areas when digitizing. See Figure 31-2. The prompt sequence is as follows:

    Enter number of tablet menus desired (0-4) ⟨0⟩: ↵
    Do you want to respecify the screen pointing area? ⟨N⟩: **Y** ↵
    Digitize lower left corner of screen pointing area: (pick the lower-left corner of the
        pointing area)
    Digitize the upper right corner of screen pointing area: (pick the upper-right corner of
        the pointing area)
    Command:

Figure 31-2.  The layout of a common digitizing tablet.

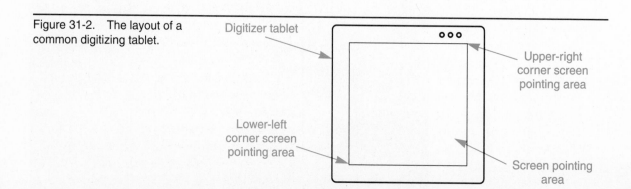

## Preparing the drawing and calibrating the tablet

The next step, calibrating the tablet, aligns the drawing to be digitized with the tablet. Attach the drawing to the tablet using drafting tape. The drawing does not have to be exactly square on the screen pointing area, but it should be flat. Figure 31-3 shows a plot plan attached to the digitizer tablet.

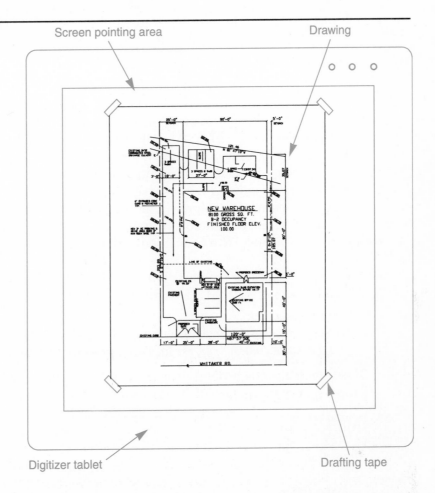

Figure 31-3.   A drawing to be digitized is placed on the tablet.

Screen pointing area

Drawing

Digitizer tablet

Drafting tape

The number of points that you digitize when calibrating the drawing to the tablet determines how accurately the existing drawing coordinates are transferred to the computer. This is called *transformation*. The following are the AutoCAD transformation options:

- *Orthogonal transformation.* AutoCAD allows you to enter two coordinates. Two points work well if the existing drawing is dimensionally accurate. A dimensionally accurate drawing normally has stable length and width measurements, and angles are not distorted.

- *Affine.* This is digitizing three points for calibration. This is necessary when lines are generally parallel, but the horizontal dimensions are stretched in relationship to the vertical dimensions. The calibration of three points provides accuracy by triangulation of three points.

- *Projective calibration.* This is the calibration of four points. When the existing drawing has stretched or has been distorted to the point where parallel lines tend to converge, then the calibration of four points may be necessary.

- *Multiple-point transformation.* This the digitizing of more than four points. AutoCAD mathematically calculates the relationship between the points with accuracy proportional to the number of points digitized. However, nine points are usually the maximum number of points needed, since additional points tend to slow down the transformation process without improving the accuracy.

**PROFESSIONAL TIP**

When selecting points for calibration, choose locations that are as accurate as possible. For example, in mapping applications, pick property corners or bench marks. In mechanical drafting, use datums on the drawing. Select points that are distributed in a wide area around the drawing. In addition, the points should be in a triangular relationship rather than in a straight line.

When attaching a drawing to the digitizer, use the following guidelines:
- Set the limits to correlate with the drawing dimensions. The limits for the drawing in Figure 31-3 should relate to the overall dimensions of the plot, plus space for notes. The plot is approximately 120′ × 200′. Allowing an additional 40′ in the horizontal and vertical directions for dimensions and notes makes the limits 160′ × 240′, or 1920″ × 2880″.
- Set the drawing units to correspond with the type of drawing you are transferring. The drawing in Figure 31-3 is a surveyed plot plan where engineering units are used, angles are measured in degrees/minutes/seconds, the direction of angle 0 is North 90°, and angles are measured clockwise.
- Set the grid and snap to a convenient value. A 20′ (240″) value works well for the plot plan.
- The property lines on the plot plan are based on a survey and are probably accurate. With this in mind, use the UCS command to set the origin to one of the property corners:

    Command: **UCS** ↵
    Origin/ZAxis/3point/Entity/View/X/Y/Z/Prev/Restore/Save/Del/?/⟨World⟩: **O** ↵
    Origin point: ⟨0,0,0⟩: *(pick the lower-left property line corner)*

This establishes the property corner at a 0,0 origin for convenience in locating other property corner points.

**PROFESSIONAL TIP**

Be sure to look straight down on the target point if you are digitizing points using a puck with crosshairs. Looking at an angle through the puck viewing glass results in inaccuracies when picking points.

Now you are ready to calibrate the tablet. The orthogonal, or two-point calibration, is used on the plot plan because the existing drawing is very accurate. To do this, enter the **TABLET** command and respond with CAL (calibrate). At this point, the tablet mode is turned on and the screen cursor no longer appears.

    Command: **TABLET** ↵
    Option (ON/OFF/CAL/CFG): **CAL** ↵

AutoCAD then requests that you digitize two points on the drawing and give the coordinates of each point. These two points may be anywhere, but usually are the endpoints of a vertical line. Drafters often pick two points on the left side of the object, such as the west property line on a plot plan. This begins the orientation of the digitizer in relation to the object as you work from left to right.

AutoCAD next asks for the exact coordinates of the two points. Look at the existing drawing in Figure 31-4 to be digitized as you follow these prompts:

    Digitize point #1: *(pick the lower-left property corner where you set the UCS origin)*
    Enter coordinates for point #1: *(enter 0,0 and press [Enter] to coincide with the UCS origin)*
    Digitize point #2: *(pick the North end of the west property line)*

Figure 31-4. To calibrate the
tablet, carefully select two
points and provide the
coordinates of those points.

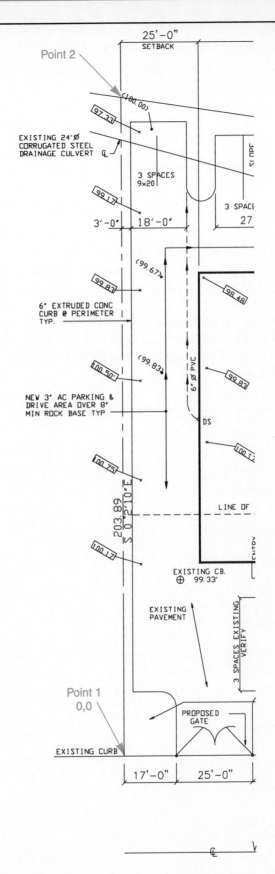

Enter the length of the property line relative to the first point (X = 0, Y = 203.89' or 2446.68") when entering the coordinates for the second point:

> Enter coordinates for point #2: **0,2446.68** ↵

Pressing [Enter] for the third point request automatically makes AutoCAD use the orthogonal transformation format:

> Digitize point #3 (or RETURN to end): ↵

Enter the **TABLET** command and turn the tablet on now that the existing drawing has been calibrated to the digitizer:

> Command: **TABLET** ↵
> Option (ON/OFF/CAL/CFG): **ON** ↵

The screen cursor returns for you to use AutoCAD commands to draw lines and other features. Use the **LINE** command to draw the property boundaries by picking each property corner. Use the **Close** option for the last line. The resulting property boundaries are shown in Figure 31-5.

Proceed by digitizing the buildings, roads, walkways, utilities, and other features using AutoCAD commands such as **LINE**, **PLINE**, **ARC**, and **CIRCLE**. Use the **DIM** command to dimension the plot plan, and use the **DTEXT** command to add notes. The finished drawing is shown in Figure 31-6.

Figure 31-5. Use the **LINE** command to construct the property boundaries.

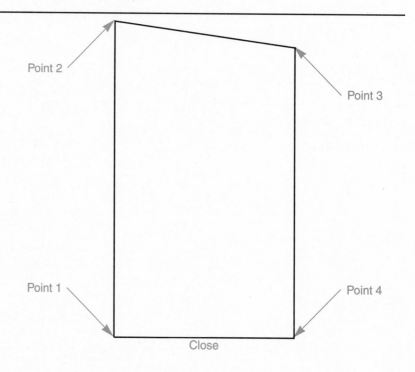

Figure 31-6.  The completed digitized drawing.

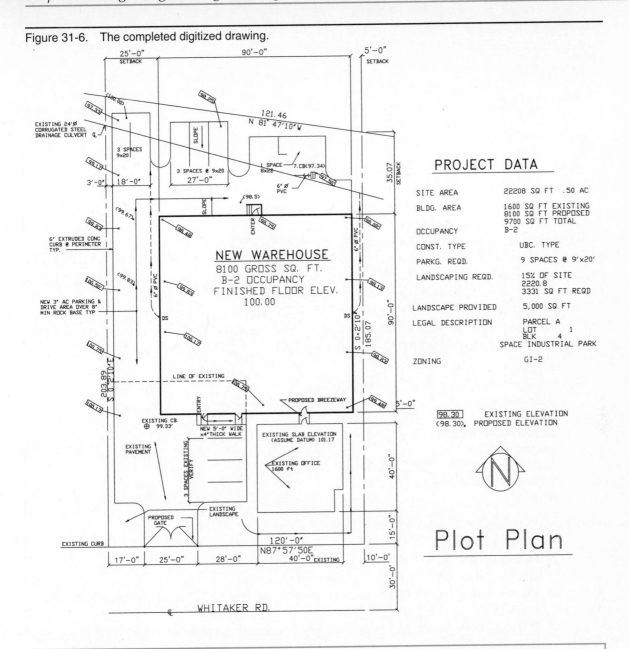

**Plot Plan**

**NOTE**  AutoCAD for Windows can be configured to display screen menus in addition to the toolbar and pull-down menus. This capability is discussed in *AutoCAD and its Applications—Advanced, Release 13 for Windows.* When tablet mode is on, the displayed screen menus are disabled, but commands may still be entered from the keyboard, toolbars, and pull-down menus. To make selections from the screen menus, you must turn tablet mode off by entering OFF at the Option prompt of the **TABLET** command:

Command: **TABLET** ↵
Option (ON/OFF/CAL/CFG): **OFF** ↵

Tablet mode may also be turned on or off with function key [F4], pressing [Ctrl]+[T], or using the **TABMODE** system variable. When using **TABMODE**, 0 is off and 1 is on. Configuring the tablet to menu areas of the AutoCAD menu template overlay is discussed in Appendix I.

**PROFESSIONAL TIP**

Remember, when digitizing an existing drawing, use the **SNAP** and **ORTHO** commands to your advantage. Also be careful when you pick points on the existing drawing. Place the digitizing tablet at a convenient angle. Look directly into the crosshairs of the puck.

The plot plan example in the previous discussion used two calibration points. The existing drawing was very accurate, allowing for two-point calibration to be successfully used. If you successfully enter two points, AutoCAD automatically calculates an orthogonal transformation and ends the command.

Three or more points may be digitized to help provide greater accuracy. The same example could have been used to continue calibrating a third point. The third point would be another property line corner, forming a triangular relationship between the points. Press [Enter] when you have picked three calibration points.

When three points are digitized, AutoCAD calculates the relationship between orthogonal, affine, and projective transformation types. When AutoCAD is finished making the calculations, a table is displayed in the text window, providing you with this information:

| 3 calibration points | | | |
|---|---|---|---|
| Transformation type: | Orthogonal | Affine | Projective |
| Outcome of fit: | success | exact | impossible |
| RMS Error: | 6.324 | | |
| Standard deviation: | 2.941 | | |
| Largest residual: | 9.726 | | |
| At point: | 2 | | |
| Second-largest residual: | 8.975 | | |
| At point: | 1 | | |

These elements can be interpreted as follows:
- **Outcome of fit:.**
  - ✓ **success**—AutoCAD was successful in calibrating the points, and this is the only category that gives the calculation results.
  - ✓ **exact**—There were exactly enough points for AutoCAD to complete the transformation.
  - ✓ **impossible**—AutoCAD was not given enough points to provide a projective transformation.
  - ✓ **failure**—If this message is displayed, there may have been enough points, but AutoCAD was unable to complete a transformation, because of colinear or coincident points.
  - ✓ **canceled**—Can happen in a projective transformation.
- **RMS Error:.** RMS means Root Mean Square, which is a calculation of the accuracy of your calibration points. The smaller this number is, the closer it is to a perfect fit.
- **Standard deviation:.** This indicates how much difference there is between the accuracy of points. If this value is near zero, then the points have nearly the same degree of accuracy.
- **Largest residual:.** Estimates the worst error you might have in the digitized points, and tells you at which point this occurs.
- **Second largest residual:.** Gives the next least accurate calculation.

When you pick more than three points, a successful calibration reports back to you in all three types of transformation with a table similar to this:

| 7 calibration points | | | |
| --- | --- | --- | --- |
| Transformation type: | Orthogonal | Affine | Projective |
| Outcome of fit: | success | success | success |
| RMS Error: | 6.324 | 5.852 | 2.602 |
| Standard deviation: | 2.941 | 2.469 | 0.508 |
| Largest residual: | 9.726 | 8.984 | 4.7634 |
| At point: | 3 | 3 | 3 |
| Second-largest residual: | 8.975 | 8.233 | 4.012 |
| At point: | 5 | 5 | 5 |

Now, AutoCAD allows you to select the desired transformation type or repeat the table by pressing [Enter] at the following prompt:

Select transformation type…
Orthogonal/Affine/Projective?⟨Repeat table⟩: *(press* [Enter] *or type* O, A, *or* P *for the desired transformation type)*
Command:

## Digitizing large drawings

Companies with many large drawings to digitize typically invest in a table-size digitizer. A variety of digitizer sizes and pointing devices were discussed in Chapter 1.

The drawing you plan to digitize may be too large for your tablet. Then you must divide the drawing into sections that fit the tablet area. Establish the coordinates of the boundaries for each section. A large drawing can be divided into four sections, as shown in Figure 31-7. The coordinates of each section are labeled and shown with dots for reference.

Figure 31-7. Dividing a large drawing into sections for digitizing. Label the sections and the coordinates of the points defining the sections.

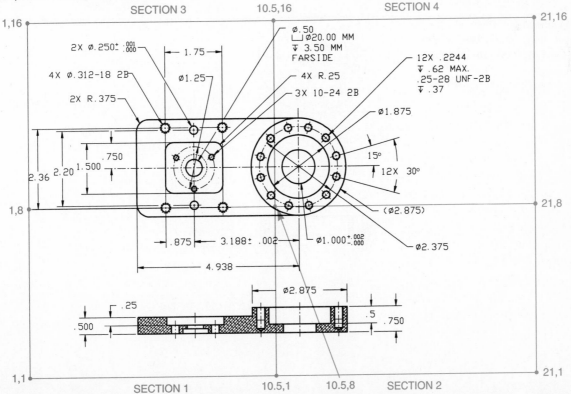

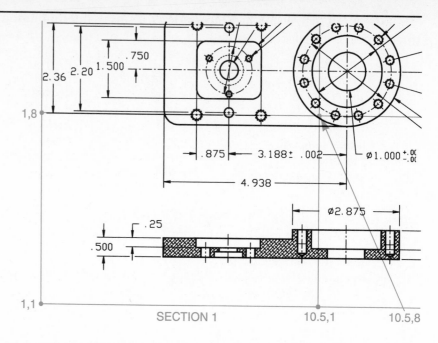

Figure 31-8. Place the first section to be digitized on the tablet and calibrate the tablet.

Next, tape the portion labeled as SECTION 1 to the tablet and calibrate the tablet to the coordinates 1,1 and 1,8. Digitize the portion of the object shown as SECTION 1, Figure 31-8.

Proceed by placing the portion of the drawing labeled as SECTION 2 on the digitizer. Calibrate the tablet to the coordinates 10.5,1 and 10.5,8. Digitize the portion of the object shown as SECTION 2. See Figure 31-9.

Proceed by moving SECTION 3 of the drawing into place on the digitizer. Calibrate the tablet to the coordinates 1,8 and 1,16. Digitize the portion of the object shown as SECTION 3.

Proceed by moving SECTION 4 into place on the digitizer. Calibrate the tablet to the coordinates 10.5,8 and 10.5,16. Digitize the portion of the object shown as SECTION 4. The entire drawing has now been digitized.

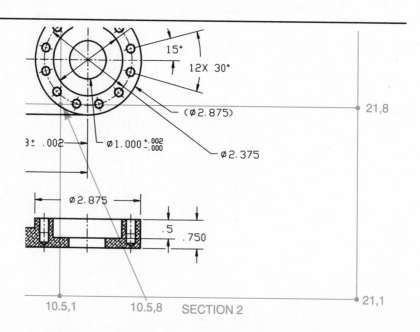

Figure 31-9. Place the second section to be digitized on the tablet and calibrate the tablet.

## OPTICAL SCANNING OF EXISTING DRAWINGS

*Scanning* is a method of automatically digitizing existing drawings to become computer drawings. Scanners work much the same way as taking a photograph of the drawing. One advantage of scanning over manually digitizing drawings is that the entire drawing—including dimensions, symbols, and text—is transferred to the computer. A disadvantage is that some drawings, when scanned, require much editing to make them presentable.

The scanning process picks up images from the drawing. What appears to be a dimension, for example, is only a graphic representation of the dimension, it is not an "entity." If you want the dimensional information to be technically accurate, the dimensions must be edited and redrawn.

After the drawing is scanned, the image is sent to a raster converter that translates information to digital or vector format. A *raster* is an electron beam that generates a matrix of pixels. As you learned previously, pixels make up the drawing image on the display screen. A raster editor is then used to display the images for changes.

Companies using scanners can, in many cases, reproduce existing drawings more efficiently than companies that manually digitize existing drawings. When an existing drawing has been transferred to the computer, it becomes an AutoCAD drawing, which can be edited as necessary.

Scanners transfer drawings from paper, vellum, film, or blueline prints and converts the hardcopy image into a raster data file. An example of a scanner in operation is shown in Figure 31-10.

Figure 31-10.  An optical scanner in operation. (Houston Instrument, A Summagraphics Company)

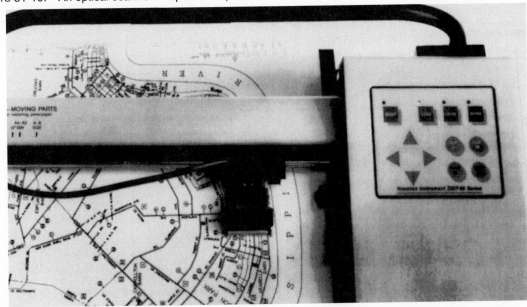

**PROFESSIONAL TIP**

Current technology limits the capability to scan old faded drawings, especially blueprints or faded blueline prints. Raster to vector conversions are not very reliable and text recognition is weak or nonexistent. Text is usually converted to vectors.

A common approach is referred to as overlay, where a raster image is displayed in AutoCAD for on-screen digitizing.

## CHAPTER TEST

*Write your answers on a separate sheet of paper.*

1. Give the command and related entries to configure the tablet so that the entire area is available as the screen pointing area:

   Command:_____

   Option (ON/OFF/CAL/CFG): _____

   Enter number of tablet menus desired (0-4) ⟨0⟩: _____

   Do you want to respecify the screen pointing area? ⟨N⟩: _____

   Digitize lower left corner of screen pointing area: _____

   _____

   Digitize upper right corner of screen pointing area: _____

   _____

2. Give the command and related entries needed to calibrate an existing drawing for digitizing using orthogonal transformation:

   Command:_____

   Option (ON/OFF/CAL/CFG): _____

   Digitize point #1: _____

   Enter coordinates for point #1: _____

   Digitize point #2: _____

   Enter coordinates for point #2: _____

   Digitize point #3 (or RETURN to end): _____

3. List at least three methods to turn the tablet mode on and off. _____

   _____

4. Describe the function of a digitizer. _____

   _____

   _____

5. List the four types of transformation and give the number of points required for each.

   _____

   _____

   _____

   _____

6. Why is it generally unnecessary to digitize more than nine points?_____

   _____

7. List at least three things to consider when digitizing points for drawing transformation.

   _____

   _____

   _____

8. Explain the relationship of the limits, units, grid, and snap to digitizing an existing drawing. _____

_____

_____

9. Why is it important to look straight down into the puck crosshairs when digitizing points? _____

_____

_____

10. Define the following terms related to digitizing three or more points when transferring an existing drawing.

Outcome of fit:

A. success— _____

B. exact— _____

C. impossible— _____

D. largest residual— _____

11. How are sections of a drawing coordinated when a large drawing is digitized? _____

_____

12. Define "scanning." _____

_____

_____

13. List an advantage and a disadvantage of scanning over digitizing drawings. _____

_____

_____

_____

_____

_____

## DRAWING PROBLEMS

1. Make a photocopy of the drawing in Figure 31-6 or 31-7. Use the digitizing process to convert the drawing to AutoCAD.

*Civill Drafting*

2. Make a photocopy of one or more of your previous drawing problem solutions. Use the digitizing process to convert the drawings to AutoCAD.

*Mechanical Drafting*

3. Obtain an existing industrial or class drawing that was created using manual techniques. Use the digitizing process to convert it to AutoCAD.

*General*

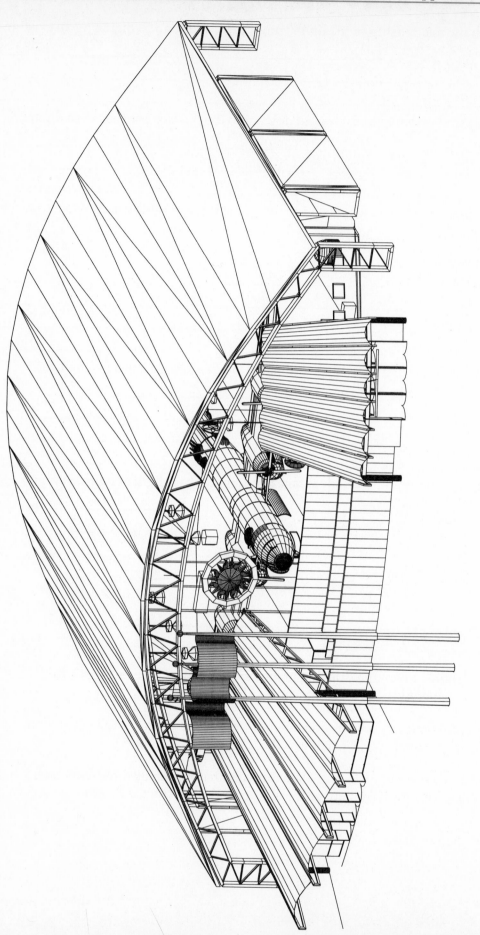

Drawing of an airplane hanger. (David Ward)

**AutoCAD R13**

### Learning objectives

After completing this chapter, you will be able to:

- ○ Identify the various elements of **File Manager**.
- ○ Start applications and print drawing files from **File Manager**.
- ○ Drag and drop AutoCAD-related files into the AutoCAD graphics window.
- ○ Move, copy, delete, and rename files on floppy and hard disks.
- ○ Create and manage directories and subdirectories.
- ○ Format, label, and copy floppy disks.

Prudent file and disk management is of paramount importance to every computer user. This is particularly true in the case of AutoCAD. The loss of a large or complex drawing file through carelessness or negligence is a painful experience. Losing an entire directory of drawing files can be devastating.

A variety of suggestions and procedures for managing AutoCAD-related files have been offered throughout the preceding chapters of this text. For example, Chapter 17 details the use of the **File Utilities** dialog box, in which files can be listed, copied, renamed, and deleted from within AutoCAD for Windows.

In this chapter, you will be introduced to an alternate method of file and disk maintenance using the Microsoft Windows **File Manager**. With **File Manager**, you can perform a wide variety of file manipulation tasks with remarkable ease and assurance. This powerful tool also enables you to create, delete, rename, and move entire directories. You can also use **File Manager** to quickly and easily format and label floppy disks.

**File Manager** can be used to open a drawing file and simultaneously start AutoCAD for Windows in one simple operation. Additionally, the *drag and drop* capability of **File Manager** is explored as a means of inserting drawing files, AutoLISP routines, and text files into the AutoCAD for Windows drawing editor, as well as printing or plotting a drawing with the Windows **Print Manager**. For a complete description of **File Manager**, refer to the *Microsoft Windows User's Guide*.

## INTRODUCTION TO FILE MANAGER

To launch **File Manager**, open the **Main** program group window in the **Program Manager** and double-click the **File Manager** icon. Alternatively, you can click the **File Manager** icon just once and then press [Enter].

### Elements of the File Manager directory window

When you use **File Manager**, all of your work is performed in a *directory window*. This is a graphic representation of the directory structure of your disk and each of the files and directories it contains. When you first start **File Manager**, the directory window displays the contents of the current drive. The directory window is divided in half with a *split bar*. The left half of the directory window displays the *directory tree*, and the right half lists the contents of the current directory. You can drag the split bar to the left or to the right to display more or less of the contents in each side of the directory window.

The directory window for the \R13 directory is shown in Figure 32-1. You can see that R13 is highlighted in the directory tree and is the current directory. This is confirmed by the directory path shown in the title bar of the **File Manager** window and by the R13 *directory icon*, which appears as an open folder in the directory tree. The subdirectories within the R13 directory branch down below and form a tree structure. Each of these subdirectories is connected with a vertical line to the directory one level above them.

Figure 32-1. The **File Manager** directory window lists directories and subdirectories in the left side of the window, and the contents of the current directory to the right.

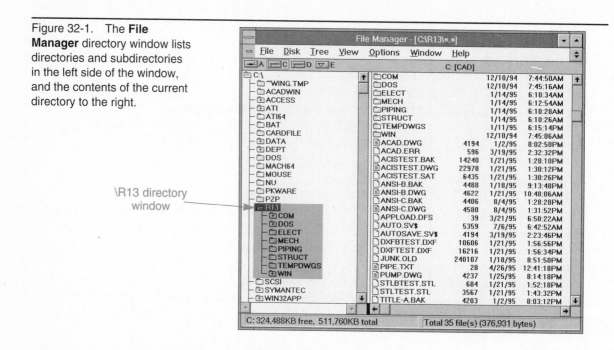

At the right of the directory window is a contents list of the subdirectories and files contained in R13. Each subdirectory in this list is also represented with a directory icon. A *file icon* indicating the file type appears next to each filename. There are icons to represent program files (.EXE and .BAT files), document files (.TXT and .WRI files), and other types of files.

You must first select a file or directory in the **File Manager** directory window before you can work with it. When you want to select a file or directory, place the arrow cursor of your pointing device over the desired file or directory icon and click. More than one file or directory can be selected by pressing and holding the [Shift] key as you click with your pointing device. The item(s) you select is then highlighted and you can proceed with the desired operation. More information about file and directory selection appears later in this chapter.

*Drive icons* represent each of the drives on your computer. These are located at the upper left of the directory window. A drive letter follows each icon. You can see that the floppy disk drive, A:, is represented with a different icon than those used for the hard disks, C: and D:.

You can easily change to one of the available drives with a simple click on the desired drive icon. If you are connected to a network, or are using a RAM drive or CD-ROM device, appropriate icons are displayed for these drives as well. The icon to the left of the drive letter E in Figure 32-1 indicates CD-ROM.

Located just above the file list is the volume label of the current drive. In this example, the volume label C:[CAD] is shown. If no volume label had been assigned, this label would appear as C: only. If you are connected to a network, and the network drive is selected, then the network name is displayed instead of the volume label.

Just below the directory window title bar are the names of the eight **File Manager** pull-down menus. These menu names are: **File**, **Disk**, **Tree**, **View**, **Options**, **Window**, and **Help**. Many of the commands located in these menus are explored later in this chapter.

Finally, as with all Microsoft Windows applications, the **File Manager** window can be moved, resized, closed, and reduced to an icon at any time.

## LAUNCHING APPLICATIONS WITH FILE MANAGER

Many of the files that appear in the **File Manager** directory window are associated with application programs. By double-clicking on the file icon, or on the filename itself, you can load the file and simultaneously start the application with which it is associated. Consider the portion of the directory window shown in Figure 32-2. Double-clicking on the drawing file HVAC.DWG highlights the filename in the directory window. The Windows "hourglass" appears as AutoCAD for Windows loads AutoCAD and opens the HVAC drawing.

Figure 32-2.  Double-clicking a .DWG file icon, or the filename itself, from the **File Manager** directory starts AutoCAD for Windows and loads the selected file into the drawing editor.

| | | | |
|---|---|---|---|
| ⊡DBF | | 12/10/94 | 7:4 |
| ⊡TEMP | | 1/21/95 | 7:0 |
| ⊟ASESMP.DWG | 101758 | 5/22/95 | 1:4 |
| ⊡BMAKE.DCL | 4922 | 6/24/95 | 6:3 |
| ⊡BMAKE.LSP | 19644 | 6/24/95 | 6:3 |
| ⊡CHKLIST.MS | 27 | 5/23/95 | 6:4 |
| ⊟CHROMA.DWG | 31494 | 5/22/95 | 1:4 |
| ⊡CHROMA.LSP | 4291 | 6/24/95 | 6:2 |
| ⊟COLORWH.DWG | 63290 | 5/22/95 | 1:4 |
| ⊡COLORWH.SLD | 16448 | 5/22/95 | 1:4 |
| ⊡DLGTEST.DCL | 5471 | 6/24/95 | 6:2 |
| ⊡DLGTEST.LSP | 7395 | 6/24/95 | 6:2 |
| ⊡ES.SHP | 1377 | 6/24/95 | 6:2 |
| ⊡ES.SHX | 541 | 5/22/95 | 1:4 |
| ⊟FILTER.DWG | 441209 | 5/22/95 | 1:4 |
| ⊟HVAC.DWG | 230082 | 5/22/95 | 1:4 |
| ⊡JULIAN.LSP | 15557 | 6/24/95 | 6:2 |
| ⊟LINKRODS.DWG | 278772 | 5/22/95 | 1:4 |
| ⊟MC.DOC | 4589 | 6/24/95 | 6:2 |
| ⊟MC.EXE | 21389 | 5/22/95 | 1:4 |
| ⊡PC.SHP | 1212 | 6/24/95 | 6:2 |
| ⊡PC.SHX | 464 | 5/22/95 | 1:4 |
| ⊟PNID.DWG | 863494 | 5/22/95 | 1:4 |
| ⊟PSFILPAT.DWG | 16604 | 5/22/95 | 1:4 |
| ⊡SAMPLE.FMP | 776 | 6/24/95 | 6:2 |
| ⊟SASKATCH.DWG | 730480 | 5/22/95 | 1:4 |
| ⊟SEXTANT.DWG | 72399 | 5/22/95 | 1:4 |
| ⊡ST.SHP | 3319 | 6/24/95 | 6:2 |

## DRAG AND DROP OPERATIONS WITH FILE MANAGER

The Windows **File Manager** can also be used to dynamically "drag and drop" file icons into the AutoCAD for Windows graphics window. This powerful capability allows you to insert drawing files as blocks, insert text files as dynamic text, print or plot a drawing, and import IGES, DXF, and PostScript files. Drag and drop can also be used to load menu, font, linetype, shape, script, and slide files, as well as AutoLISP and ADS applications. A file selected for drag and drop with AutoCAD must have one of the following file extensions:

| | | | |
|---|---|---|---|
| .DWG | .DXB | .DXF | .EPS |
| .EXE | .IGS | .LIN | .LSP |
| .MNU | .MNX | .SCR | .SHP |
| .SLD | .TXT | | |

The following table lists the different kinds of drag and drop operations that can be used in AutoCAD for Windows. Also listed are the required filename extensions, the related AutoCAD commands, and the chapters in this text where additional command information can be found.

| Operation | File Extension | Related Command | Related Chapter |
|---|---|---|---|
| Load a linetype file | .LIN | **LINETYPE** | Chapter 6 |
| Insert a text file | .TXT | **DTEXT** | Chapter 11 |
| Load a shape font | .SHX | **STYLE** | Chapter 11 |
| Insert a drawing file | .DWG | **INSERT** | Chapter 25 |
| Print a drawing | .DWG | **PLOT** | Chapter 12 |
| Load a slide file | .SLD | **VSLIDE** | Chapter 30 |
| Run a script file | .SCR | **SCRIPT** | Chapter 30 |
| Import a .DXF file | .DXF | **DXFIN** | Chapter 17 |
| Load a .DXB file | .DXB | **DXBIN** | Chapter 17 |

Additional files that can be used with drag and drop are found in *AutoCAD and its Applications, Advanced—Release 13 for Windows.* The following table lists those files.

| Operation | File Extension | Related Command |
|---|---|---|
| Load an ADS application | .EXE | **XLOAD** |
| Import a PostScript image | .EPS | **PSIN** |
| Load a menu file | .MNU | **MENU** |
| Insert an AutoLISP routine | .LSP | **LOAD** |

## Dragging and dropping a text file

You learned in Chapter 25 that AutoCAD entities, like text, can be saved to disk with the **WBLOCK** command and inserted into other drawing files. A text file created with a text editor outside of AutoCAD for Windows can also be inserted into a drawing file using the **MTEXT** command. This command was covered in Chapter 11.

External text files can also be inserted into a drawing using **File Manager** drag and drop. As an example, look at the NOTES.TXT text file shown in the Windows **Notepad** in Figure 32-3.

Figure 32-3. An external text file with a .TXT extension, like the one shown here in **Notepad**, can be dragged and dropped into the graphics window.

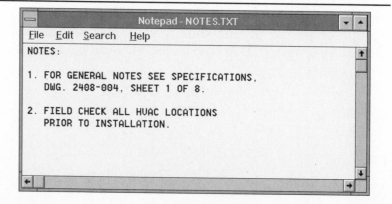

To drag this text file into AutoCAD, do the following:
1. Start both AutoCAD for Windows and **File Manager**. Arrange the display windows so that both are visible.
2. Issue the **DTEXT** command. Select the start point and justification for the text, and respond to the text height and rotation angle prompts. Stop when the Text: prompt appears.
3. Now, open the **File Manager** directory that contains the text file you want.
4. Drag the text file icon next to the desired filename into the AutoCAD graphics window, and then release the mouse (or puck) button, Figure 32-4.
5. After the text appears in the graphics window, the Text: prompt remains displayed. At this point, you can enter additional text or press [Enter] to end the **DTEXT** command. The text is inserted in the current text style and on the current layer. See Figure 32-5.

Figure 32-4.   After beginning the DTEXT command and answering the prompts for text height and rotation, drag the text file icon into the AutoCAD graphics window.

Drag the icon for the text file and drop it in the drawing editor

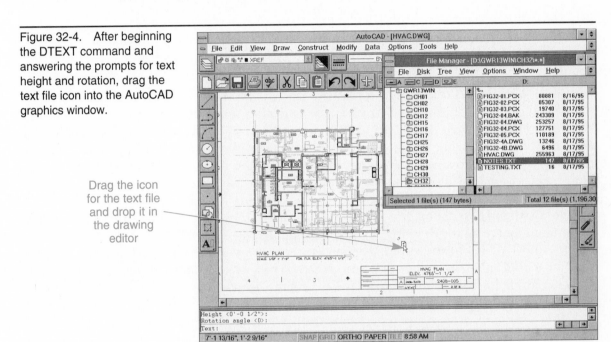

Figure 32-5.   The external text is inserted in the current text style, layer, and color.

The text is inserted

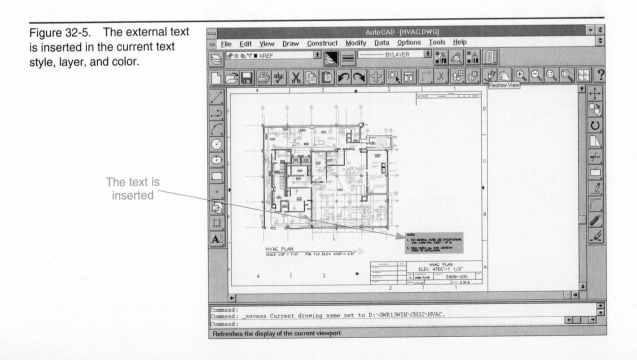

External text files can be created with **Notepad**, MS-DOS **EDIT**, or your own ASCII text editor. Remember that the text file must have a .TXT extension. Without this extension, a text file has no association with an application. If you attempt to drag and drop a text file without a .TXT extension, AutoCAD displays the alert box shown in Figure 32-6.

Also, remember that dragging and dropping text files works only with the **DTEXT** command, and not the **TEXT** command. If you attempt to drag and drop a text file when using the **TEXT** command, AutoCAD will not perform the operation.

Figure 32-6. A—The **Drag and Drop** alert box tells you that no association exists for a text file without a .TXT extension.

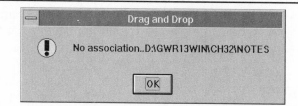

### Using drag and drop to print a drawing

If you are using the system printer, you can drag a drawing file icon directly to the Windows **Print Manager**. AutoCAD for Windows need not be loaded beforehand. Dragging and dropping a drawing file icon into **Print Manager** automatically starts AutoCAD. The drawing file icon you select is inserted into the drawing editor using the **FILEOPEN** command. This command allows you to open a file without using a dialog box, regardless of the setting of the **FILEDIA** system variable. Once the drawing appears in the graphics window, the **Plot Configuration** dialog box is displayed. You can then modify the printing parameters as required and print the drawing.

If AutoCAD is already running when you use drag and drop to print a drawing, the **Drawing Modification** dialog box appears on the display screen. You can then save or discard any changes made to the current drawing before the drawing to be printed is opened in the drawing editor.

This drag and drop operation can be used when the Windows system printer is the desired output device, but is not valid if you want to plot a drawing on a pen or electrostatic plotter. To print a drawing on the system printer using drag and drop, do the following:

1. Open the **Main** group window and double-click the **Print Manager** icon to launch **Print Manager**, Figure 32-7.

Figure 32-7. The **Print Manager** icon is located in the **Main program** group.

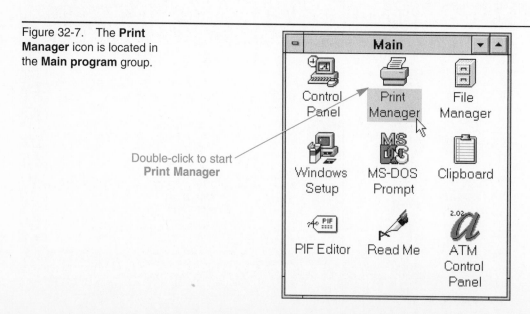

2. Once the **Print Manager** window is displayed, click the **Minimize** button (the down arrow at the upper right of the window). This makes **Print Manager** an icon. See Figure 32-8.
3. Launch **File Manager** and arrange the window so that the **Print Manager** icon is visible on your display screen.
4. Open the **File Manager** directory that contains the drawing you wish to print.
5. Drag the drawing file icon onto the **Print Manager** icon and release the mouse (or puck) button. In Figure 32-9, the SEXTANT.DWG file icon is dragged into **Print Manager**.
6. AutoCAD for Windows is then automatically started (unless it is already running), and the **Plot Configuration** dialog box is opened, Figure 32-10.
7. Make any desired changes to the printing configuration and click **OK**.

Figure 32-8. Click the **Minimize** button at the upper right of the **Print Manager** window to reduce **Print Manager** to an icon.

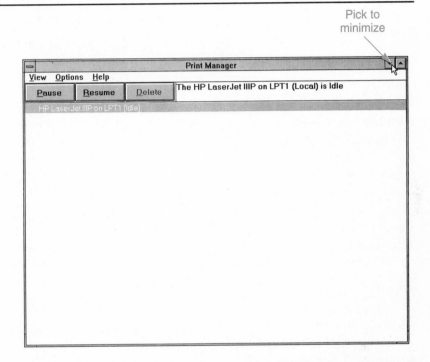

Figure 32-9. You can drag a drawing file icon to the **Print Manager** icon to print the drawing.

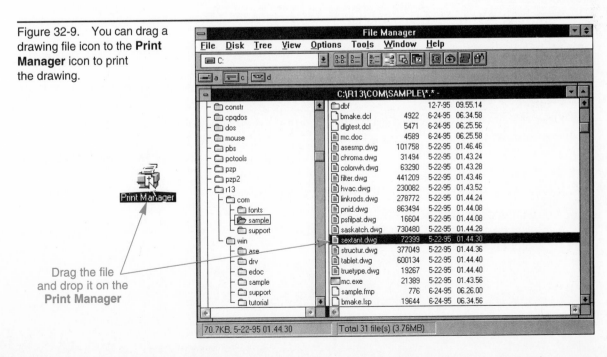

Figure 32-10. When you drop a drawing file icon into **Print Manager**, AutoCAD is loaded and the **Plot Configuration** dialog box is displayed.

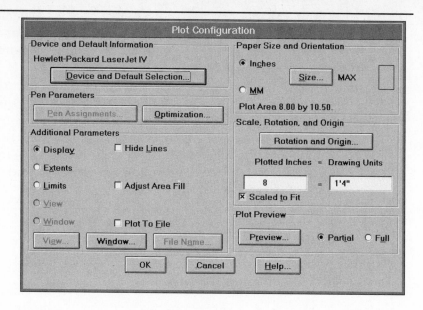

## PROFESSIONAL TIP

You can also drag a drawing file icon directly into **Print Manager** without first reducing **Print Manager** to an icon. See Chapter 12 for detailed information about printing or plotting a drawing. For more information about **Print Manager**, refer to the *Microsoft Windows User's Guide*.

## Using drag and drop to insert a drawing file

Drag and drop can also be used to insert any drawing into the current drawing session. This method is very similar to the **INSERT** command discussed in Chapter 25. Like **INSERT**, the drawing that you drag and drop becomes a block. Therefore, be sure to explode it after insertion, if necessary.

1. Start both AutoCAD for Windows and **File Manager**. Once again, arrange the display windows so that both are visible.
2. Make sure that the **Command:** prompt is displayed at the bottom of the AutoCAD graphics window.
3. Now, open the **File Manager** directory that contains the drawing file that you want to insert.
4. Drag the drawing file icon next to the filename into the AutoCAD graphics window and then release the mouse (or puck) button.
5. The **INSERT** command is echoed in the AutoCAD prompt area. Answer the prompts for the drawing insertion point, scale, and rotation angle.
6. If necessary, explode the inserted drawing as follows:

   Command: **EXPLODE** ⏎
   Select objects: (*type* L *or* LAST *and press* [Enter])
   Select objects: ⏎

**EXERCISE 32-1**

❏ Start Windows and launch both **File Manager** and AutoCAD. Arrange the open display windows to resemble those shown in Figure 32-4.

❏ Open a directory containing one or more .DWG files. Using the method described on the previous page, drag a drawing file icon into the AutoCAD graphics window. Answer the prompts for insertion point, scale, and rotation angle and then explode the inserted drawing.

❏ Use **Notepad** to create a simple text file like that shown in Figure 32-3. Make the notes specific to your particular application.

❏ Activate the AutoCAD graphics window and issue the **DTEXT** command. Pick a start point for the text, and accept the default text height and rotation angle values.

❏ Drag the text file you created with **Notepad** into the graphics window.

❏ If you are connected to a printer, try using drag and drop to print a drawing file with **Print Manager** as described earlier in this chapter.

## Automatic startup of **File Manager**

The drag and drop capabilities of **File Manager** make it an excellent companion application for AutoCAD for Windows. As such, you may want to have **File Manager** open and readily accessible whenever you are working with AutoCAD. Having both programs start together automatically is quite convenient, and is simple to accomplish. This is because when Microsoft Windows is installed on a computer, a group window named **StartUp** is created, Figure 32-11A. As you can see from the illustration, the Windows installation program initially creates an empty group window. However, if you move or copy a program item icon into the **StartUp** window, the application represented by the program item icon is started automatically whenever Windows is loaded. As an example, consider the **StartUp** group window shown in Figure 32-11B. This window contains the program item icons for four applications—**AutoCAD for Windows**, **File Manager**, **Notepad**, and **Clock**.

Figure 32-11.  A—The **StartUp** group is created when Microsoft Windows is installed. B—Place the program icons for any programs you want started every time Windows starts in the **StartUp** program group. Here, the **AutoCAD for Windows**, **File Manager**, and **Notepad** program icons are copied to the **StartUp** group window.

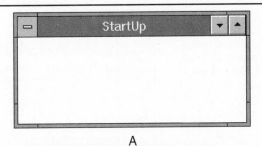

A

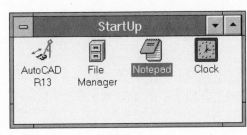

B

Figure 32-12. Each of the applications in the **StartUp** window are loaded when Windows is started.

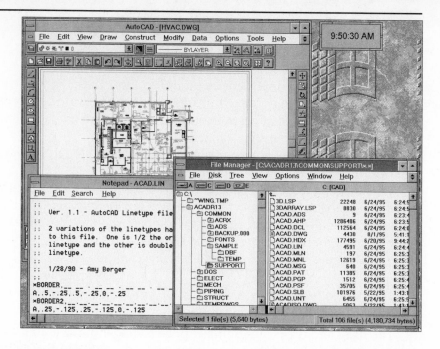

This is a reasonable selection of applications because these four programs work so well together. Now, whenever Microsoft Windows is started, the four items in the **StartUp** group window are automatically loaded and displayed simultaneously on the Windows desktop, Figure 32-12.

You can set up a **StartUp** group window like this one using the following procedure:

1. Return to **Program Manager** and open the **StartUp**, **AutoCAD**, **Main**, and **Accessories** group windows so that the program item icons are clearly visible, Figure 32-13.
2. Drag and drop the AutoCAD program item icon from the **AutoCAD** group window into the **StartUp** group window. However, you may want to make a copy of the program item icon before dragging it. To do so, click the program item icon and hold down the [Ctrl] key as you drag the icon into the **StartUp** group window.

Figure 32-13. Drag any icon to the StartUp program group that you want to start when Windows starts.

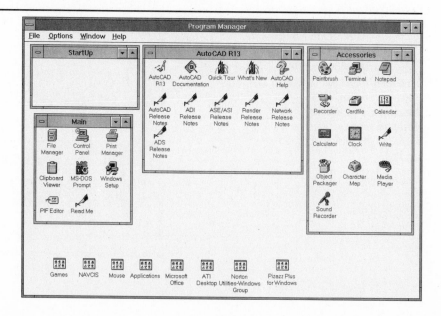

3. Repeat the procedure for the **File Manager**, **Notepad**, and **Clock** program item icons.
4. Resize the **StartUp** group window to your personal liking.
5. Now, exit Windows and then restart it.
6. Each of the programs in the **StartUp** window is automatically loaded after Windows starts up.

Once each application is opened, you may want to move and resize each of the display windows. After the AutoCAD graphics and text windows are sized and positioned to your satisfaction, the new window settings are automatically saved in the ACAD.INI file. See *AutoCAD and its Applications, Advanced—Release 13 for Windows* for detailed information about the ACAD.INI file.

When you have the **File Manager** directory window sized and positioned satisfactorily, select **Save Settings on Exit** from the **File Manager Options** pull-down menu, Figure 32-14. The new size and position of **File Manager** is now stored for future sessions.

Figure 32-14.   The **Options** pull-down menu of **File Manager**.

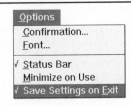

## Some additional start up considerations

If you like, you can choose to have an application load automatically at Windows start up but be reduced to an icon to conserve desktop workspace. When you want to use the application, simply double-click the icon on the desktop to open the minimized application.

As an example, suppose you use **Notepad** on a frequent basis, but do not want the **Notepad** display window opened on screen after Windows is started. Return to **Program Manager**, open the **StartUp** group window, and click the **Notepad** program item icon to highlight it. Now, select **Properties...** from the **File** pull-down menu in **Program Manager** (or press [Alt]+[Enter]) to display the **Program Item Properties** dialog box. Click the **Run Minimized** check box, and then click **OK** to exit the dialog box, Figure 32-15. The next time Windows is started, the minimized **Notepad** icon will appear at the bottom of the screen. Simply double-click on the icon when you want to work with **Notepad**.

Figure 32-15.   Clicking the **Run Minimized** check box in the **Program Item Properties** dialog box starts an application as a minimized icon.

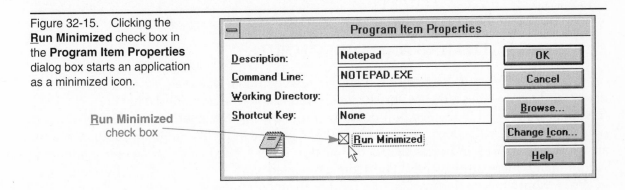

Also, keep in mind that every open application in Windows takes memory and free system resources (FSR's) away from AutoCAD. For this reason, use some discretion when adding program item icons to the **StartUp** window. If you notice some degradation in AutoCAD performance, you can monitor your available system resources by returning to **Program Manager** and selecting **About Program Manager...** from the **Help** pull-down menu. This displays the **About Program Manager** dialog box shown in Figure 32-16. Free memory and system resources are displayed at the bottom of this dialog box. If 30% or less is reported free for system resources, you should close some of your applications or add additional memory to your computer.

Figure 32-16. Free memory and system resources can be monitored in the **About Program Manager** dialog box.

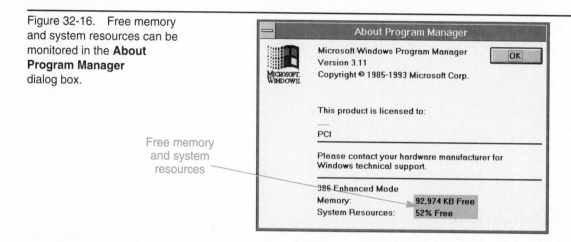

Free memory and system resources

### EXERCISE 32-2

❏ Check with your system administrator or instructor before performing this exercise.
❏ Create a **StartUp** window using the techniques described in the preceding text. Be sure to include AutoCAD for Windows and **File Manager** in the **StartUp** window.
❏ Use some discretion when adding program item icons to the window. Remember that each open application requires additional memory.
❏ After you are satisfied with your **StartUp** configuration, resize and position the windows to your personal taste. Save the new settings.
❏ Return to **Program Manager** and check the amount of free resources displayed in the **About Program Manager** dialog box.

## WORKING WITH FILES AND DIRECTORIES

Managing files and directories is a simple task with **File Manager**. You can move, copy, delete, and rename files and directories quickly and easily. The commands that perform these functions are located in the **File** pull-down menu of the **File Manager**, Figure 32-17. You will note that, like the pull-down menus in AutoCAD, several of the menu items are followed by an ellipsis (...). This indicates that a dialog box is associated with the menu command. Additionally, there are keyboard shortcuts associated with several of the commands. The keyboard shortcuts are displayed to the right of the menu items.

Figure 32-17.   The **File** pull-down
menu of **File Manager**.

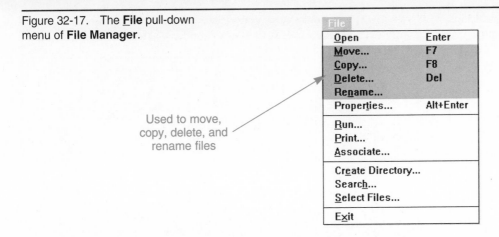

Used to move,
copy, delete, and
rename files

## Directory window display options

When working with **File Manager**, it is often useful to display more than one directory listing in the directory window. This simplifies moving files between drives and directories, and allows you to see the results of your operations. In Figure 32-18, the contents of the A: drive are displayed at the top of the directory window, and the C:\R13 directory listing appears at the bottom. This type of window arrangement is called a *tiled display*. Two or more listings can be displayed in this fashion. You can drag the *split bar* left or right to display more, or less, of the contents of the directory window.

Alternatively, you can choose to arrange your directory windows in a *cascading display*, Figure 32-19. In this example, the contents of C:\R13 are displayed in the active window, while the inactive windows report the directory listings for the A: and D: drives.

Figure 32-18.   A tiled display shows all directory windows on the screen.

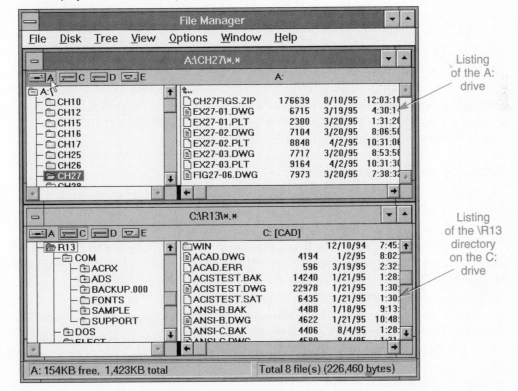

Listing
of the A:
drive

Listing
of the \R13
directory
on the C:
drive

Figure 32-19. A cascading display shows the active directory window on the top, and the inactive directory windows behind it.

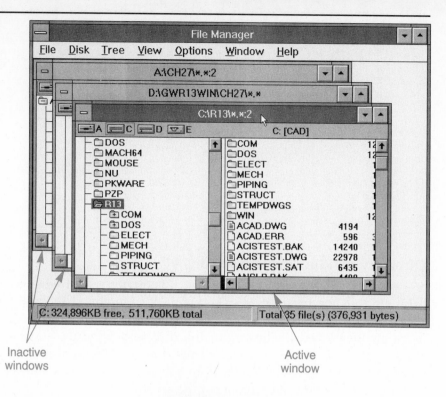

Inactive windows

Active window

Figure 32-20. The **Window** pull-down menu of **File Manager**.

Select to open a new window

| Window |  |
|---|---|
| New Window |  |
| Cascade | Shift+F5 |
| Tile | Shift+F4 |
| Arrange Icons |  |
| Refresh | F5 |
| √ 1 C:\R13\*.*:2 |  |

Use the **New Window** menu option when you want to open a new directory window. This option is located in the **Window** pull-down menu in the **File Manager**, Figure 32-20. You can also open a new window by double-clicking one of the drive icons at the upper-left of the **File Manager** display window. Once a new directory window is opened, arrange the windows in a tiled or cascading display for easier viewing. The **Cascade** and **Tile** options are also located in the **Window** pull-down menu of the **File Manager**.

## Selecting files and directories

Before you can work with a file or directory, it must first be selected. As mentioned at the beginning of this chapter, simply place the arrow cursor of your pointing device over the desired file or directory icon (or name) and click.

If you want to select more than one file or directory, press and hold the [Ctrl] key as you click with your pointing device. The [Shift] key can be used to select several items in sequence. In Windows terminology, selecting more than one item is called *extending a selection*. The items you select are then highlighted and you can proceed with the desired operation.

For example, look at the three drawing files shown highlighted in Figure 32-21. These three drawing files are selected in consecutive sequence by first picking the STRUCTUR.DWG file. Then, the [Shift] key is pressed and held as the TRUETYPE.DWG file is picked. Any file (or files) located between the two is included in the selection. In the example shown, the file TABLET.DWG is located between STRUCTUR.DWG and TRUETYPE.DWG, and is therefore selected.

There will be occasions when you want to extend a selection, but you do not want the files selected in a consecutive fashion. You can easily select files out of sequence by pressing and holding the [Ctrl] key as you make your selection. This method is shown in Figure 32-22.

Figure 32-21. To select a group of sequential files, select the first file, hold the [Shift] key, and then select the last file.

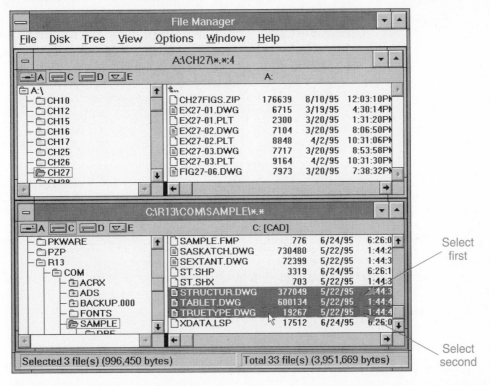

Figure 32-22. To select individual files, hold down the [Ctrl] key as you select them.

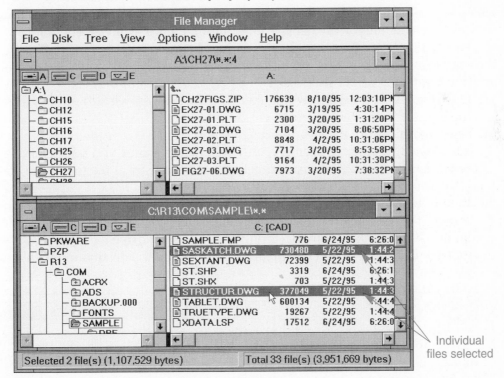

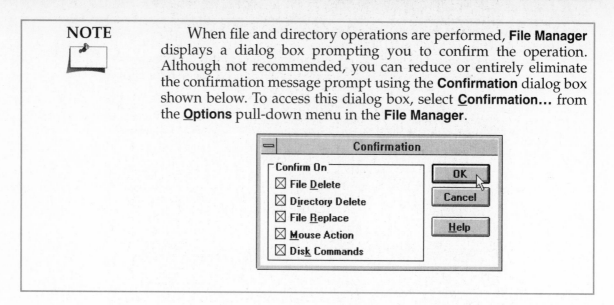

**NOTE**      When file and directory operations are performed, **File Manager** displays a dialog box prompting you to confirm the operation. Although not recommended, you can reduce or entirely eliminate the confirmation message prompt using the **Confirmation** dialog box shown below. To access this dialog box, select **Confirmation...** from the **Options** pull-down menu in the **File Manager**.

If you should inadvertently select a file or directory, and would like to cancel your selection, press and hold the [Ctrl] key as you pick the highlighted item. The item is removed from the selection.

## Moving and copying files

You can easily move and copy files between directories and drives by dragging the file icons with your pointing device. If you like, you can move or copy an entire directory. However, before moving or copying files or directories, it is a good idea to display both the source and destination directories or drives in separate display windows. The *source* is where you are moving or copying from. The *destination* is where you are moving or copying to. This is essential if you are using your pointing device for these operations.

As an alternative to using your pointing device, you can use the **Move...** and **Copy...** commands in the **File** pull-down menu of the **File Manager**. To move a file from one directory or drive to another, do the following:

1. Open the directory window that contains the file you wish to move. Click the file to be moved.
2. Select **Move...** from the **File** pull-down menu.
3. The **Move** dialog box appears, Figure 32-23. The filename you selected is displayed in the **From:** text box and the current directory name appears at the top of the dialog box. This is the source.
4. Enter the drive and directory for the file destination in the **To:** text box. In the example shown, the file STRUCTUR.DWG is being moved from the \R13\COM\SAMPLE directory on the C: drive to the PROJECTS directory on the D: drive.
5. Pick the **OK** button when you are finished entering the destination path name.

Figure 32-23.   The **Move** dialog box.

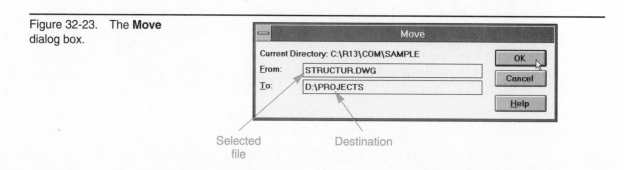

Remember that *moving* a file removes it from its source location and relocates it to a different destination. To *copy* a file from one directory or drive to another, do the following:

1. Open the directory window that contains the file you wish to copy. Click the file to be copied.
2. Select **Copy...** from the **File** pull-down menu.
3. The **Copy** dialog box then appears, Figure 32-24. The filename you selected is displayed in the **From:** text box and the current directory name appears at the top of the dialog box. This is the source.
4. Enter the drive and directory for the file destination in the **To:** text box. In the example shown, the file FILTER.DWG is being copied from the \R13\COM\SAMPLE directory on the C: drive to the A: drive.
5. Click the **OK** button when you are finished entering the destination directory name or drive letter.

Keep in mind that several files can be selected for moving or copying. When you extend your file selection, each selected filename appears in the **From:** text box in the **Move** and **Copy** dialog boxes.

---

Figure 32-24.   The **Copy** dialog box.

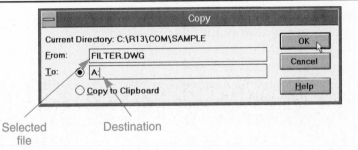

Keep a formatted floppy disk in your machine while working with AutoCAD for Windows. Whenever you save one of your drawing files to the hard disk, activate the **File Manager** window and use the **Copy** command to copy the saved drawing to your floppy as a backup file.

PROFESSIONAL TIP

## Deleting and renaming files

You can use **File Manager** to delete individual files or entire directories. When you delete a directory, all files and subdirectories within it are also deleted. To delete a file, do the following:

1. Open the directory window that contains the file or directory you wish to delete. Select the file or directory to be deleted.
2. Now, press the [Delete] key on your keyboard or select **Delete...** from the **File** pull-down menu. The **Delete** dialog box appears and the file or directory you selected is displayed in the **Delete:** text box. Click **OK** to complete the operation.
3. If you like, you can enter a different file or directory name in the **Delete:** text box. You can also use an asterisk (*) as a wild card character. In the example shown in Figure 32-25, this wild card is used to delete all of the .BAK drawing backup files in the \R13\TEMPDWGS directory.

Figure 32-25. The **Delete** dialog box. Enter a filename or use wild card characters.

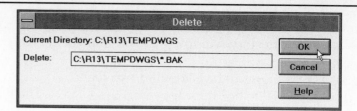

CAUTION

As with all delete operations, slow down and think carefully before deleting any files or directories. File recovery and undelete utilities cannot always recover a deleted file.

Renaming files or directories is also easily accomplished with **File Manager**. To rename a file or directory, do the following:

1. Open the directory window that contains the file or directory you wish to rename. Select the file or directory to be renamed.
2. Select **Rename...** from the **File** pull-down menu.
3. The **Rename** dialog box appears, Figure 32-26. The file or directory name you selected is displayed in the **From:** text box.
4. Enter the desired new file or directory name in the **To:** text box. In the example shown, the file HVAC.DWG is renamed to HVAC-2.DWG.
5. Click the **OK** button when you are finished entering the new file or directory name.

Figure 32-26. The **Rename** dialog box.

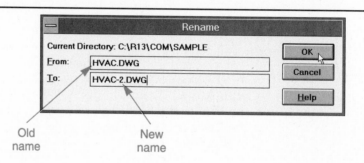

Old name                    New name

PROFESSIONAL TIP

If you rename a drawing file that has been externally referenced (xref) into another drawing, AutoCAD will not be able to find that file the next time the drawing containing that xref is opened in the drawing editor. To fix the problem, use the **XREF** command **Reload** option and reload the renamed drawing. Additionally, if you rename a directory that contains an xref, AutoCAD also will not be able to resolve the xref the next time the drawing containing the external reference is opened. This is because the directory path name to the xref is now different. This is easily remedied using the **XREF** command **Path** option. See Chapter 26 for detailed information about the **XREF** command and its options.

## Creating a new directory

Organizing the files on your hard disk is a very important component of computer system maintenance. It is often desirable to keep block symbols, hatch patterns, and script files in separate subdirectories. Once you have created a new directory, you can move and copy files and subdirectories there from other locations on your hard disk. Creating directories is a simple task with **File Manager**. However, remember that the same naming conventions used for filenames apply to directory names. To create a directory, do the following:

1. Arrange the **File Manager** directory window so that the directory tree is clearly visible at the left of the directory window.
2. Click the directory icon or name where you want the new subdirectory to appear.
3. Select **Create Directory...** from the **File** pull-down menu.
4. The **Create Directory** dialog box then appears, Figure 32-27. The current directory name is displayed at the top of the dialog box.
5. Enter the desired new directory name in the **Name:** text box. In the example shown, a new subdirectory named BLOCKS is created under the \R13 directory.
6. If you want to create the directory somewhere other than in the current directory, you must type in the full path to the new directory in the **Name:** text box.
7. Click the **OK** button when you are finished entering the new directory name.

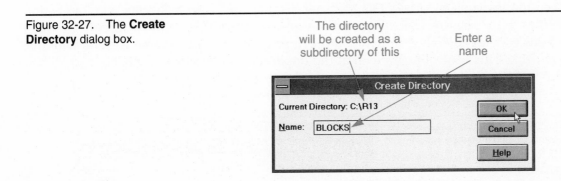

Figure 32-27.   The **Create Directory** dialog box.

The directory will be created as a subdirectory of this

Enter a name

> NOTE          Creating a directory using **File Manager** is the same as using the MKDIR (make directory) command in MS-DOS.

## Searching for files

There will be times when you cannot remember the location of a file or directory on your hard disk. AutoCAD for Windows provides a means of locating files and directories using the **Find File** function. This capability is discussed in Chapter 5, *Saving Drawings*.

A similar function can be performed with the **Search** command in **File Manager**. This command searches for files and directories on all, or part, of the current drive. You can search for a single file, or you can use wild cards to search for a group of files. Once the files are found, they are listed in the **Search Results** window. For example, if you want to search for all the drawing files in all the subdirectories located under the \R13 directory, then do the following:

1. Arrange the **File Manager** directory window so that the directory tree is clearly visible at the left of the directory window.
2. Select the \R13 directory from which to start the search.
3. Select **Search...** from the **File** pull-down menu.
4. The **Search** dialog box then appears, Figure 32-28. To search for all drawing files, enter *.DWG in the **Search For:** text box.

Figure 32-28.  The **Search** dialog box.

Enter search criteria

Enter where to start the search from

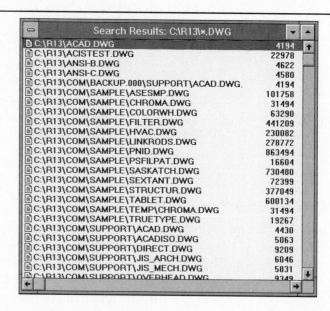

5. The current directory name appears in the **Start From:** text box. If you want to start the search from a different directory, type the desired directory name in this text box.

6. If the **Search All Subdirectories** check box is on (checked), **File Manager** automatically searches all of the subdirectories located under the directory name specified in the **Start From:** text box. If you want to limit the search to the current directory only, turn off this check box.

7. Click the **OK** button when you are ready to begin the search. To cancel the search, press the [Esc] key or pick the **Cancel** button.

8. When the search is complete, **File Manager** displays the **Search Results** window listing the files found, Figure 32-29. Files can be selected from this window to perform such tasks as copying, deleting, moving, and printing. To close the **Search Results** window, double-click the control menu icon at the upper-left of the window. This is a small box containing a single dash located in the upper-left corner.

Figure 32-29.  The **Search Results** window displays each of the files found that match the search criteria.

| Search Results: C:\R13\*.DWG | |
| --- | --- |
| C:\R13\ACAD.DWG | 4194 |
| C:\R13\ACISTEST.DWG | 22978 |
| C:\R13\ANSI-B.DWG | 4622 |
| C:\R13\ANSI-C.DWG | 4580 |
| C:\R13\COM\BACKUP.000\SUPPORT\ACAD.DWG. | 4194 |
| C:\R13\COM\SAMPLE\ASESMP.DWG | 101758 |
| C:\R13\COM\SAMPLE\CHROMA.DWG | 31494 |
| C:\R13\COM\SAMPLE\COLORWH.DWG | 63290 |
| C:\R13\COM\SAMPLE\FILTER.DWG | 441209 |
| C:\R13\COM\SAMPLE\HVAC.DWG | 230082 |
| C:\R13\COM\SAMPLE\LINKRODS.DWG | 278772 |
| C:\R13\COM\SAMPLE\PNID.DWG | 863494 |
| C:\R13\COM\SAMPLE\PSFILPAT.DWG | 16604 |
| C:\R13\COM\SAMPLE\SASKATCH.DWG | 730480 |
| C:\R13\COM\SAMPLE\SEXTANT.DWG | 72399 |
| C:\R13\COM\SAMPLE\STRUCTUR.DWG | 377049 |
| C:\R13\COM\SAMPLE\TABLET.DWG | 600134 |
| C:\R13\COM\SAMPLE\TEMP\CHROMA.DWG | 31494 |
| C:\R13\COM\SAMPLE\TRUETYPE.DWG | 19267 |
| C:\R13\COM\SUPPORT\ACAD.DWG | 4430 |
| C:\R13\COM\SUPPORT\ACADISO.DWG | 5063 |
| C:\R13\COM\SUPPORT\DIRECT.DWG | 9209 |
| C:\R13\COM\SUPPORT\JIS_ARCH.DWG | 6046 |
| C:\R13\COM\SUPPORT\JIS_MECH.DWG | 5831 |
| C:\R13\COM\SUPPORT\OVERHEAD.DWG | 9349 |

❑ Insert one of your disks in the A: drive and open a new directory window for the drive.

❑ Arrange the directory windows in a tiled display with the contents of the A: drive displayed in the top window and the contents of the C:\R13 directory displayed in the bottom window.

❑ Activate the A: drive window so that it is current.

❑ Make a directory on the A: drive called CLASSES and another called PROJECTS.

❑ Make two subdirectories in the CLASSES directory called CAD-I and CAD-II.

❑ Rename the two subdirectories to CAD-1 and CAD-2.

❑ Make two subdirectories in the PROJECTS directory called P-100 and P-200.

❑ Copy a group of drawing files from the hard disk to one of the subdirectories under either CLASSES or PROJECTS. Be sure to open a directory window for the subdirectory before copying the files. Extend your selection of drawing files as described in this chapter.

❑ Check the directory window to verify that the files were copied correctly. Now, delete the subdirectory and all the files it contains.

❑ Delete all the directories created in this exercise.

## DISK OPERATIONS USING **FILE MANAGER**

A variety of disk operations can also be performed with **File Manager**. These operations include formatting, labeling, and copying disks. Each of these functions is located in the **File Manager Disk** pull-down menu, Figure 32-30.

Figure 32-30. The **Disk** pull-down menu of **File Manager**.

Used to copy, label, or format a disk

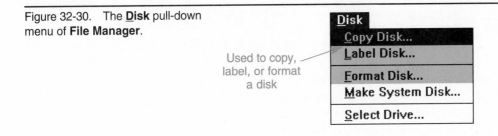

### Formatting a floppy disk

Whenever you purchase new floppy disks, you must first format them before they can be used. The formatting process prepares a floppy disk so that information can then be copied to it. Formatting and labeling a disk is another of the procedures made simple by **File Manager**. If the disk you intend to format has previously been used, **File Manager** detects this and informs you accordingly before it removes any existing data from the disk. To format a floppy disk, do the following:

1. Insert a floppy disk in the appropriate disk drive.
2. Select **Format Disk...** from the **Disk** pull-down menu.
3. The **Format Disk** dialog box then appears, Figure 32-31. Specify the drive letter in the **Disk In:** text box or use the pop-up list to the right of the text box to select the desired drive.
4. Specify the capacity of the disk to be formatted in the **Capacity:** text box, or use the pop-up list to the right of the text box to select the correct capacity.
5. If you want to provide a label for the disk, enter the desired label name in the **Label:** text box. A label is an identifying name for the disk. The name is shown in the title bar of the directory window. A label name cannot exceed eleven characters and spaces are not permitted.

6. In the example shown in Figure 32-31, a 1.44 MB floppy is to be formatted in the B: drive. This disk will be used to store custom hatch patterns and the label HATCHPATS is entered in the **Label:** text box.

7. Once you have specified the appropriate drive, disk capacity, and entered a label (if desired), click the **OK** button to begin formatting the disk.

8. When the formatting is complete, another dialog box appears and asks you if you want to format another disk. Pick **Yes** or **No** as appropriate.

Figure 32-31.   The **Format Disk** dialog box.

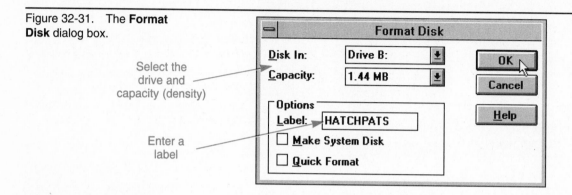

Select the drive and capacity (density)

Enter a label

PROFESSIONAL TIP

      Get in the habit of providing a volume label for each disk you format. Write the volume label name on the adhesive label that comes with the floppy disk before attaching it to the disk. Attempting to write on the label after attaching it to the disk can damage the floppy.

    Notice that the **Options** section of the **Format Disk** dialog box contains two check boxes. These check boxes perform the following functions:

- **Make System Disk.** This option allows you to include MS-DOS operating system files on the disk you are formatting. These files include two hidden files and the COMMAND.COM file. Such a disk is called a *system disk* and can be used to boot up your computer. This option would not be used if you are formatting a floppy disk for backup purposes.

- **Quick Format.** When **File Manager** formats a floppy disk, it checks for any bad sectors. These bad sectors are unusable portions of the floppy disk. If you are reformatting a used floppy and are reasonably certain that it contains no bad sectors, you can speed up the formatting process by checking the **Quick Format** check box. The disk will then not be scanned for bad sectors.

PROFESSIONAL TIP

      A system disk should always be created on a *bootable* drive—usually A:—and should normally contain no files other than those installed by Windows. The system disk that you create should always be kept with you when you work at a computer. If you work at more than one computer, keep a system disk at each location. Should you ever encounter a problem that prevents the computer from booting, turn the power off, insert the system disk in the A: drive, and turn the power back on again. The computer will boot from the A: drive and you will then have access to the hard drive in order to solve the problem.

**CAUTION**

Always use caution when formatting a disk. Remember that in addition to preparing a new disk, formatting will erase any existing data on a previously formatted disk. Unless you are running MS-DOS Version 5 or higher, or have a disk recovery utility program, you *cannot* recover information on a disk that is accidentally formatted.

## Labeling a disk

You can assign or change a label for both floppy and hard disks using **File Manager**, even after the disk has been formatted. The procedure is as follows:

1. If you are labeling a floppy disk, insert it in the appropriate floppy disk drive.
2. Select the drive icon at the upper-left of the directory window for the disk you want to label. Alternatively, you can pick **Select Drive...** from the **Disk** pull-down menu and specify the desired drive from a dialog box.
3. Now, select **Label Disk** from the **Disk** pull-down menu.
4. The **Label Disk** dialog box then appears, Figure 32-32. Enter the new label in the **Label:** text box. In the example shown, the label BACKUP is entered in the text box.
5. Click the **OK** button when you are finished.

Figure 32-32. The **Label Disk** dialog box.

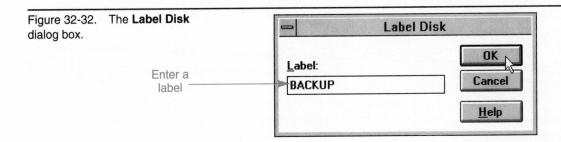

Enter a label

## Copying a disk

Throughout this text you have been advised to always make a backup copy of your AutoCAD drawings on floppy disks. It is also a good idea to have a second backup of your original backup. You can easily copy the contents of one floppy disk to another using **File Manager**. To copy a floppy disk, do the following:

1. Insert the source floppy disk in the drive you want to copy from. If your computer has two of the same drives, insert the destination floppy disk in the second drive. The destination disk is called the *target* disk.
2. Select the drive icon for the source disk at the upper left of the **File Manager** directory window.
3. Select **Copy Disk...** from the **Disk** pull-down menu. If your computer has two floppy disk drives, the **Copy Disk** dialog box appears, Figure 32-33. If your computer has only one floppy disk drive, the dialog box does not appear and you are asked to insert the source disk.
4. If you have not already selected the source disk drive icon, you can specify the drive letter using the pop-up list to the right of the **Source In:** text box. In the example shown, drive A: is the source disk.
5. Select the letter of the destination drive from the pop-up list to the right of the **Destination In:** text box. In this example, the destination disk is in the B: drive. Click the **OK** button when you are finished.
6. The contents of drive A: are then copied to drive B:.

Figure 32-33. The **Copy Disk** dialog box.

Select the source and destination

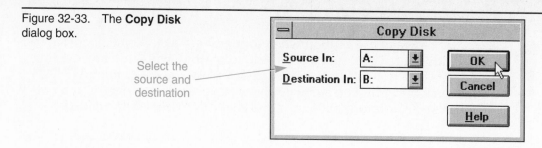

**CAUTION**

The **Copy Disk** command not only copies, it formats! Therefore, there is no need to spend time formatting a floppy disk before making a copy. Be certain your destination disk is blank or only has unneeded files on it.

## Protecting your disks

Dust, heat, cold, magnets, cigarette smoke, and coffee do great damage to your disks. Placing your disk on or near any other electrical or magnetic device can quickly ruin your files. This includes your digitizer tablet! A ringing telephone can even be a dangerous enemy of the disk because of its magnetic field. Beyond physical damage, you or someone else could write over the files on a disk, or put files on the wrong disk, making them difficult or impossible to find.

The easiest way to protect the data on your floppy disk from accidental erasure is to use the write-protect tab. A 3.5″ disk uses a small, sliding tab located on the bottom side of the disk. Notice that the write-protect tab is in effect when it is moved toward the edge of the disk. Use the point of a pen or your fingernail to slide the tab. For 5.25″ disks, the write-protect tab is a small, rectangular adhesive-backed piece that is placed over the write-protect notch. See Figure 32-34.

When the tab is covering the notch, or moved to the write-protect position, you cannot format, save, or copy files to that disk. However, the files can be read from the disk. **File Manager** displays a dialog box with a write-protect/access error message if you attempt to format or save to a write-protected disk. If you must use the disk for writing or formatting purposes, simply remove the tab or move it to the appropriate position.

Figure 32-34. A—Protect your 5.25″ disks by placing a write-protect tab over the notch on the disk. B—On a 3.5″ disk, move the write-protect tab to the "Read Only" position.

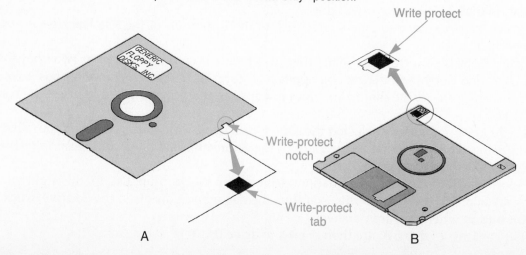

---

**EXERCISE 32-4**

❏ Insert one of your floppy disks containing drawing problems in the A: drive.
❏ Use the **Label Disk** command to name the floppy disk PROBLEMS.
❏ Copy a drawing file from the floppy to the \R13 directory on the hard disk.
❏ Use the **Search** command to list only .DWG files in the \R13 directory to verify that the file was copied.
❏ Change the name of the file you previously copied to \R13 to TEST.BAK.
❏ Use the **Search** command to list only .BAK files in the \R13 directory to verify that the file was renamed.
❏ Delete TEST.BAK from the hard disk.
❏ Use the **Copy Disk** command to make a backup copy of one of your floppy disks.

---

**NOTE**    This chapter has introduced you to only some of the features within **File Manager**. Become familiar with *all* of the functions offered by this useful tool. By making **File Manager** an integral part of your daily work, you can greatly increase your productivity.

---

## CHAPTER TEST

*Write your answers in the spaces provided.*

1. What is a directory window?_____

_____

_____

2. How do you select more than one file or directory in consecutive order from the directory window?_____

_____

_____

3. How do you select more than one file or directory out of sequence from the directory window? _____

_____

_____

_____

4. Once a file or directory is selected, how do you cancel your selection? _____

_____

_____

5. Which AutoCAD command must be used when dragging and dropping an external text file?_____

6. What three-letter file extension is valid when using drag and drop to place text in an AutoCAD drawing? _____

7. You can use drag and drop to plot a drawing on a pen plotter. (True/False) _____

8. What is the purpose of the directory window split bar? _____
_____
_____
_____

9. What action should be performed after dragging and dropping a drawing file into the
AutoCAD graphics window? _____
_____

10. Why should you not place too many program items in the **StartUp** program group?
_____
_____
_____

11. How do you monitor available system resources in Microsoft Windows? _____
_____
_____
_____
_____

12. Suppose you want to place a drawing file from the \R13 directory on one of your floppies, and then remove the drawing from the hard disk. Which **File Manager** command
accomplishes this in one operation? _____
_____
_____

13. When you delete a directory, all the files and subdirectories within it are also deleted.
(True/False) _____

14. You must first format a disk before using the **Copy Disk** command. (True/False) _____

15. Which **File Manager** command is used to assign a name to a previously formatted disk?
_____
_____

16. The **Copy Disk** command can be used on a computer with only one disk drive.
(True/False) _____

17. Why should you exercise caution when using the **Copy Disk** command? _____
_____
_____
_____

18. Describe how you can protect your floppy disks from having data written to them
accidentally. _____
_____
_____
_____

## PROBLEMS

*Obtain the permission of your instructor or system administrator before creating or deleting directories, formatting or labeling disks, deleting files, or using any* **File Manager** *command that can alter the structure of the hard disk files and directories.*

1. This problem involves making new subdirectories and copying drawing files to them.

   *General*

   A. Make your own subdirectory under the \R13 directory. Name it using your initials.

   B. Make the new subdirectory current.

   C. Copy all of your drawing files from one floppy disk to the subdirectory.

   D. Make a subdirectory within your new directory and name it BAK.

   E. Make the BAK subdirectory current.

   F. Copy all of your .BAK files into the BAK subdirectory.

   G. Open a separate directory window for each of your subdirectories. Display the directory windows in a tiled fashion.

2. Make a new subdirectory of the directory you created in Problem 1. Name the new subdirectory TEST.

   *General*

   A. Copy the contents of the BAK subdirectory into TEST.

   B. Open a new directory window for the TEST subdirectory.

   C. Rename one of the files in the TEST subdirectory to HEY.YOU.

   D. Use the **Search** command and list all files with a .YOU file extension.

   E. Copy the HEY.YOU file to the BAK subdirectory and rename it WHO.ME.

   F. Use the **Search** command and list all files with a .ME file extension.

   G. Copy WHO.ME to one of your floppy disks and name it YES.YOU.

   H. Delete the three files you just created.

   I. Activate the BAK subdirectory and delete it and all the files it contains.

3. Format four disks in a row without exiting the **Format Disk** command. Provide volume labels for the disks as they are formatted. When all formatting is complete, use the **Label Disk** command and change the names of each disk label.

   *General*

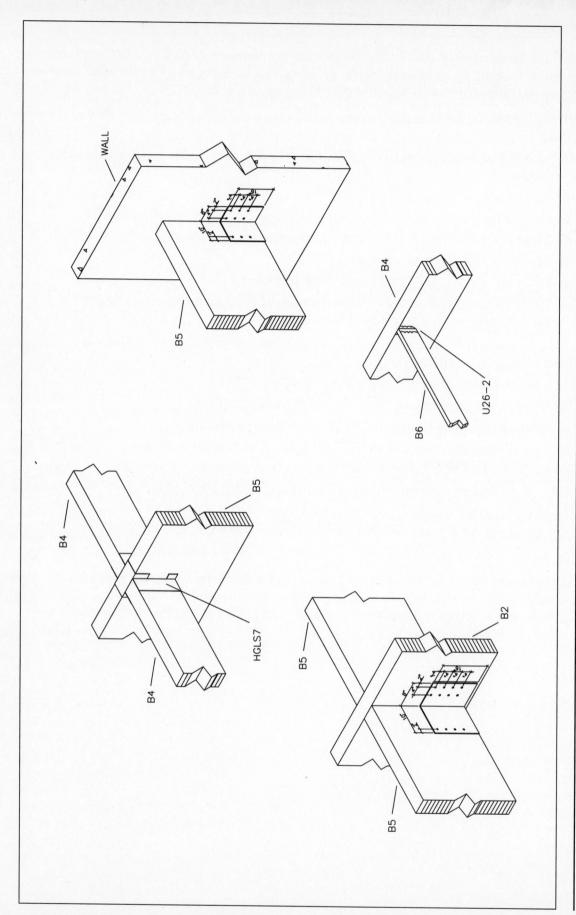

## Chapter 33

# AutoCAD R13  AutoCAD Release 13 and Windows 95

## Learning objectives

After completing this chapter, you will be able to:
- ○ Identify the differences between Windows 95 and Windows 3.1.
- ○ Install AutoCAD Release 13 for Windows in the Windows 95 environment.
- ○ Use AutoCAD for Windows in Windows 95.
- ○ Explain how to manage files using Windows 95.

Windows 95 is an operating system designed to take advantage of the 32-bit architecture of 386, 486, and Pentium (Intel or compatible) computers. Windows 95 is very different from Windows 3.1 and Windows for Workgroups 3.11. This chapter will look at three aspects that will directly affect you when installing and using AutoCAD in the Windows 95 environment.

First, this chapter looks at how Windows 95 is different. Secondly, how to install AutoCAD and how it functions in the Windows 95 operating system are examined. Finally, managing files with Windows 95 is explained.

Note: Windows 3.1 and Windows for Workgroups 3.11 operate very similar to each other. Therefore, this chapter will explain how Windows 95 and Windows 3.1 relate to each other. However, in certain instances where Windows 3.1 and Windows for Workgroups 3.11 have different features or operate differently, how Windows 95 relates to Windows for Workgroups 3.11 will be explained as well.

## HOW IS WINDOWS 95 DIFFERENT?

There are many features in Windows 95 that are new or operate differently than in Windows 3.1. While this text does not look at every new feature, the next sections give you an overview of the important changes you need to know to install and use AutoCAD, and to manage files.

### Operating system

One of the biggest changes in Windows 95 is that it is an operating system, like DOS. What this means is that Windows 95 provides the basic instructions to the computer. With a DOS system, even though Windows 3.1 may start automatically when you turn on your computer, all of the basic instructions to the computer are provided by DOS. Windows 3.1 is simply a graphic interface running on top of DOS.

Windows 95 has a DOS compatibility box that allows you to run DOS programs. In fact, most DOS programs run faster in Windows 95. You also have the option of shutting down your computer and restarting in DOS mode.

## A different look

The first change that you may actually *notice* is that Windows 95 *looks* different, Figure 33-1. There is no longer the **Program Manager** found in Windows 3.1. Instead, there is the **Task Bar** located along the bottom edge of the screen. Also, located in the top-left corner of the screen are two icons. These are called **My Computer** and **Recycle Bin**. **My Computer** has taken over some of the functions of **Program Manager** found in Windows 3.1. **Recycle Bin** is the undelete function of Windows 95. The **Task Bar**, **My Computer**, and **Recycle Bin** are covered later in this chapter.

Figure 33-1.   Windows 95 looks and operates much different from Windows 3.1. Located along the bottom of the screen is the **Task Bar**. This is used to start or switch between programs. The **My Computer** icon performs other functions of **Program Manager** in Windows 3.1.

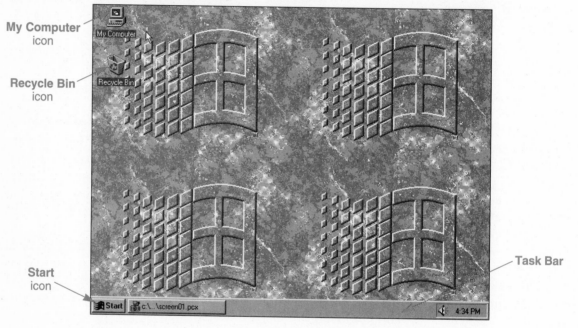

**NOTE**          The names of the icons given in this chapter are the default names after installing Windows 95. If you have changed the names on your system, the icons will have the new names.

## Managing files and installing programs

Another change is that **File Manager** from Windows 3.1 has been replaced by **Windows Explorer**. This is explained in more detail later in the section called *Managing Files Using Windows 95*. Another change, as mentioned earlier, is how programs are installed in Windows 95. This is examined in more detail in the section called *Installing AutoCAD in Windows 95*.

## Starting programs

A very big change in Windows 95 is how programs are launched (started). In Windows 3.1, you open the program group that contains the program icon and double-click on the icon. However, in Windows 95 you will notice that there are no program groups. To start a program, click on **Start** located on the **Task Bar** and select the appropriate item. This feature is discussed in more detail in the section called *Using AutoCAD in Windows 95*.

## Multitasking

Another important change is in how you perform multitasking. *Multitasking* means running two or more programs at the same time. For example, you have AutoCAD and a desktop publishing program running. You create a simple illustration in AutoCAD and want to place it in a desktop layout. You "cut" the object from AutoCAD, then switch to the desktop publishing program and "paste" the object. This is an example of multitasking.

In Windows 3.1, to switch between programs, hold down the [Alt] key and press the [Tab] key until the name of the program you want is displayed. Then, release the [Alt] key and that program is shown in the foreground.

However, switching between programs in Windows 95 is different. As mentioned earlier, there is the **Task Bar** located along the bottom edge of the screen. The **Task Bar** is always shown no matter what program is active, Figure 33-2. When a program is started, a button appears on the **Task Bar**. The button for the currently active program appears "pushed in," Figure 33-3. Other programs that are running also have a button on the **Task Bar**. These programs are referred to as *minimized*. This means that they are running, but are not the currently active program. To switch between programs in Windows 95, simply click on the appropriate button on the **Task Bar**. That program then becomes the currently active program.

The "[Alt][Tab]" function still exists in Windows 95. However, it operates differently from Windows 3.1. When you press and hold the [Alt] key, a box appears in the middle of the screen with an icon for each open program. The icon for the current program has a small box, or frame, around it. As you press the [Tab] key, the small box moves between the icons. When the box is around the icon for the program that you want, release the [Alt] key.

Figure 33-2. The **Task Bar** located along the bottom of the screen (shown here highlighted) is always shown.

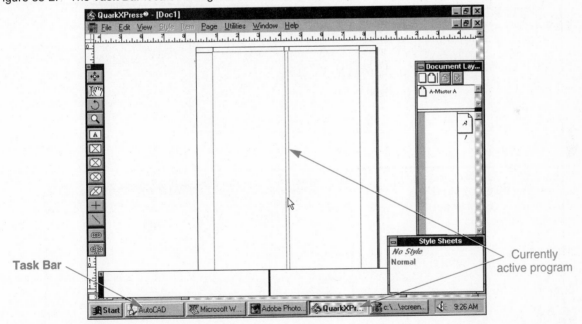

Figure 33-3. The button on the **Task Bar** for the currently active program is "pushed in." To switch to another program that is minimized, simply click on its button. The **Start** icon is used to start other programs.

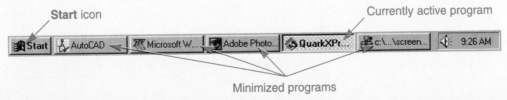

# INSTALLING AUTOCAD IN WINDOWS 95

Installing new programs in Windows 95 is very different from Windows 3.1. Though the basics of "telling" the computer to install a new program from a floppy disk (or CD-ROM) remains, *how* you tell the computer to do this has changed. The following installation procedure is used for any program.

## Installing a program

To install a new program, first double-click on the **My Computer** icon found in the upper-left corner of the screen. This opens the **My Computer** window, Figure 33-4. In this window, you will notice several icons. (Icons are sometimes called *objects* in Windows 95.) There is **Control Panel**, **Printers**, **3 1/2 Floppy [A:]**, **Hard drive [C:]**, and **[D:]**. Note: Your system may have different icons, depending on the setup.

Next, double-click on the **Control Panel**. This opens the **Control Panel** window, Figure 33-5. This window is similar to the **Control Panel** in Windows 3.1. The **Control Panel** is where you can change various system settings, such as the display, system sounds, and adding/removing printers.

Double-click on the **Add/Remove Programs** icon. This opens the **Add/Remove Programs Properties** window, Figure 33-6. In this window, you will see three tabs along the top labeled **Install/Uninstall**, **Windows Setup**, and **Startup Disk**.

Figure 33-4.   The **My Computer** window.

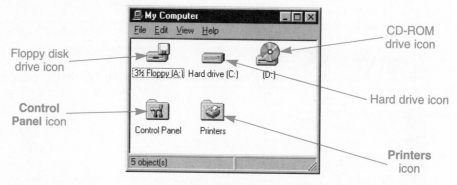

Figure 33-5.   Double-click on the **Add/Remove Programs** icon found in **Control Panel** to install a new program.

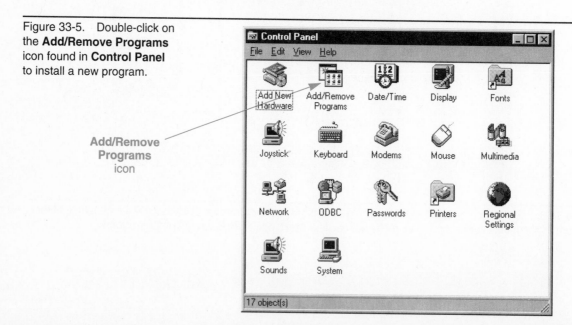

Figure 33-6. To install a new program, make sure the **Install/Uninstall** tab is on top. Then, select the **Install...** button.

Install/Uninstall tab

Pick to install a new program

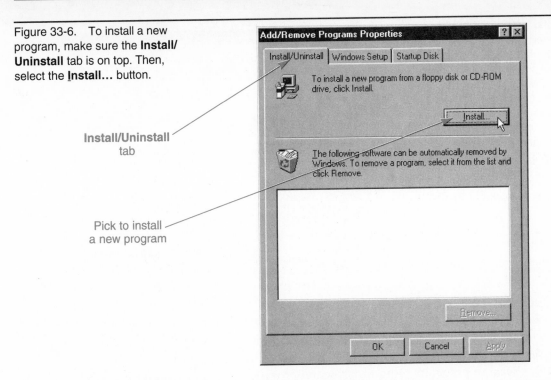

Click on the **Install/Uninstall** tab, if it is not already on top. Then, click on the **Install...** button. This opens the **Install Program From Floppy Disk or CD-ROM** window, Figure 33-7. Insert Disk 1, the personalization disk, of AutoCAD for Windows into the floppy drive and insert the CD into the CD-ROM drive. Click on the **Next ⟩** button.

Windows automatically searches for the installation program. When it finds the program, the path and program name are displayed in the **Run Installation Program** window, Figure 33-8. If this information is incorrect, click on the **Browse...** button and locate the correct program. Once the information is correct, click on the **Finish** button and follow the on-screen prompts.

Figure 33-7. The **Install Program From Floppy Disk or CD-ROM** window prompts you to insert the first installation disk. Then, pick the **Next...** button.

Pick to continue

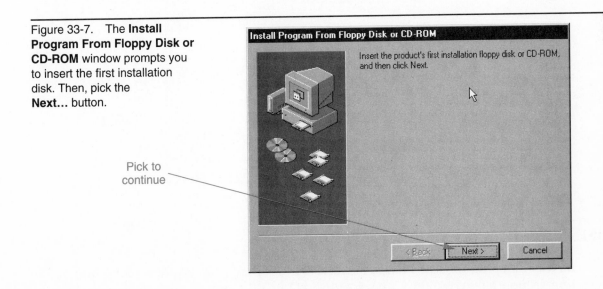

Figure 33-8.   Windows 95 automatically searches the floppy and CD-ROM drive for an installation program. If the program it finds, shown in the **Command line for installation program:** box, is incorrect, pick the **B**r**owse...** button and locate the correct program. Otherwise, pick the **Finish** button.

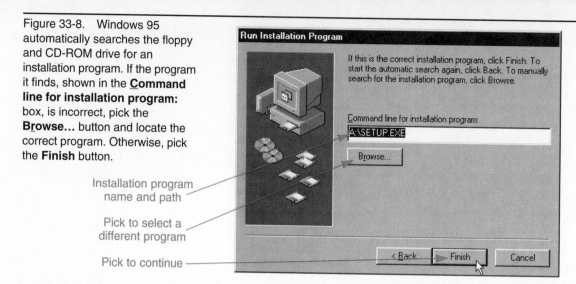

Installation program name and path

Pick to select a different program

Pick to continue

**Differences**. To install a program in Windows 3.1, you first have to select the **File** menu, then the **R**un... command. Then, in the **Run** dialog box, you must manually enter the correct path and filename, or pick the **B**r**owse...** button and manually search for the program.

Windows 95 automatically searches for the installation program. If Windows 95 has located the wrong program, you must search for the program manually. However, the "browsing" feature has changed for Windows 95, Figure 33-9. Select the proper drive and file type. Once the file is located, highlight it and pick the **Open** button.

Figure 33-9.   This window appears when you pick the **Browse** button in the **Run Installation Program** window. Use the **Browse** window to locate the correct installation program. When you have located the correct program, highlight it and pick the **Open** button.

Select the proper drive

Files found

Select the type of file

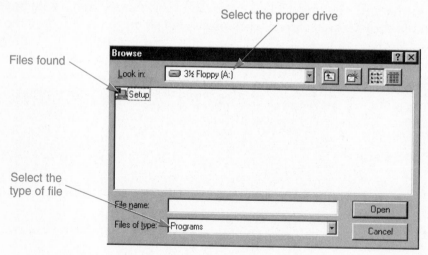

## USING AUTOCAD IN WINDOWS 95

The way that programs are *launched* (started) is different from Windows 3.1. Though the following section tells you how to start AutoCAD in Windows 95, the same procedure is used to start any program. In addition, Windows 95 slightly changes how AutoCAD works. This is covered in the section *How AutoCAD Operates in Windows 95*.

**NOTE**        The AutoCAD Release 13 c4 maintenance release is the first Windows 95 compliant version of Release 13. Prior versions of Release 13 may function within Windows 95, but may also have some problems. These problems may include improper dialog box colors and functions, and an inability for AutoCAD to run some of its internal applications. You can avoid these and other problems by using AutoCAD Release 13 c4 with Windows 95.

## Starting AutoCAD in Windows 95

To start AutoCAD once it is installed, click on **Start** located on the **Task Bar**, Figure 33-10. This opens a pop-up menu with several selections, Figure 33-11. Some of the menu items include **Programs**, **Sh<u>u</u>t Down...**, and **<u>H</u>elp**.

Move your cursor to the **<u>P</u>rograms** selection. You can click on the selection, or wait a second for Windows to automatically highlight it. Another pop-up menu appears, Figure 33-12. The items in this list are similar to the program groups in Windows 3.1. In fact, if you installed Windows 95 over an existing copy of Windows 3.1, the names of the program groups are carried over to Windows 95 and appear in this list.

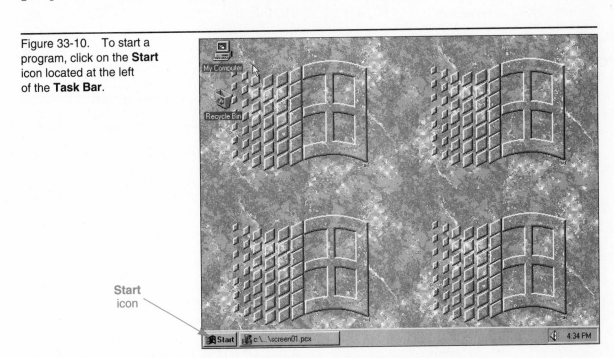

Figure 33-10.   To start a program, click on the **Start** icon located at the left of the **Task Bar**.

Start icon

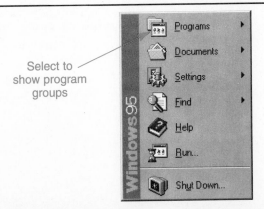

Figure 33-11.   After you click on the **Start** icon, this pop-up menu appears. To start a program, choose the **Programs** selection.

Select to show program groups

Figure 33-12. This pop-up
menu appears when you select
**Programs** from the pop-up
menu shown in Figure 33-11.
The selections in this pop-up
menu are similar to the program
groups in Windows 3.1.

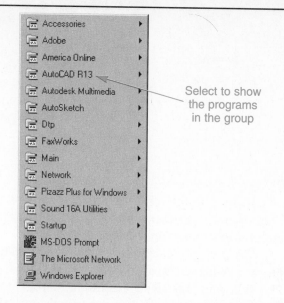

Select to show
the programs
in the group

Figure 33-13. When you
choose a "group" in the pop-up
menu shown in Figure 33-12,
the programs in that group are
shown. Single-click on the
program that you want to start.

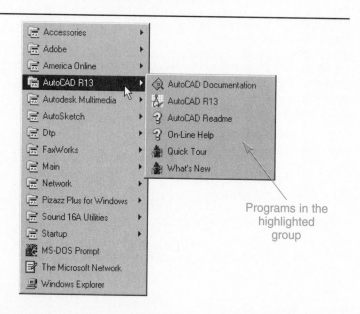

Programs in the
highlighted
group

Move your cursor to the **AutoCAD R13** selection, and another list appears, Figure 33-13. This list contains the names of the programs "under" the selection highlighted in the previous menu. Notice that the **AutoCAD R13** group has six programs.

To start AutoCAD, move your cursor to the **AutoCAD R13** icon (selection) and click. You only have to click once. In Windows 3.1, you have to double-click on an icon to start the program.

**Differences.** To start a program in Windows 3.1, you have to first open the program group that contains the program's icon. Then, you must double-click on the program's icon to launch it.

To start a program in Windows 95, click on **Start** located on the **Task Bar** and select **Programs**. Then, select the appropriate menu item and single-click on the appropriate program selection.

## How AutoCAD operates in Windows 95

AutoCAD operates nearly the same in Windows 95 as it does in Windows 3.1. In fact, the only real differences are in the visual appearance and a few extra tools that Windows 95 provides.

One of the first things you will notice when AutoCAD is started in Windows 95 is that the titles are aligned to the left, not centered, Figure 33-14. The next thing you will likely notice right away is the **Task Bar** at the bottom of the screen.

You will also notice that the file control menu appears as the AutoCAD icon, Figure 33-15. When you activate the menu, notice that the options are the same as those found in Windows 3.1, except that the **Switch To...** command has been removed. This is due to the addition of the **Task Bar** in Windows 95. The commands in the file control menu all operate the same. However, the menu looks slightly different. The file control menu for the drawing window also appears as the AutoCAD icon, Figure 33-16.

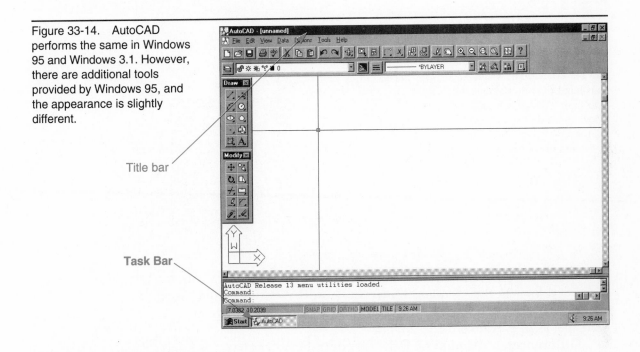

Figure 33-14.  AutoCAD performs the same in Windows 95 and Windows 3.1. However, there are additional tools provided by Windows 95, and the appearance is slightly different.

Title bar

Task Bar

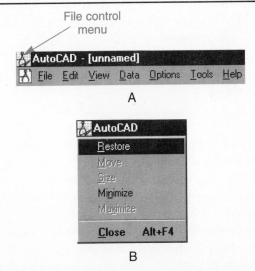

Figure 33-15.  The file control menu in Windows 95 appears as the program's icon. A—Here, the file control menu is for AutoCAD, therefore the AutoCAD icon is shown. B—The commands in the file control pull-down menu operate the same as in Windows 3.1. However, the menu looks a bit different.

File control menu

AutoCAD - [unnamed]
File  Edit  View  Data  Options  Tools  Help

A

AutoCAD
Restore
Move
Size
Minimize
Maximize

Close    Alt+F4

B

Figure 33-16.   The file control menu for the AutoCAD drawing window also appears as the AutoCAD icon.

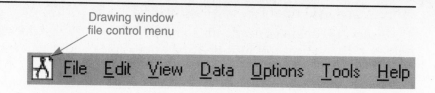

Drawing window file control menu

**WIN 95**

**WIN 95**

The final thing to point out is the three buttons on the right side of the AutoCAD title bar. These are the minimize, maximize/window, and close application buttons, Figure 33-17. The minimize button has a short horizontal line on it. The maximize/window button has two overlapping windows on it. The close application button has an X on it.

By picking the maximize/window button, you can switch between a full screen and a window of AutoCAD. When AutoCAD is minimized, the AutoCAD button on the **Task Bar** no longer appears "pushed in." By single-clicking on the close application button, the program is closed.

Figure 33-17.   The three buttons on the right side of the title bar are used to minimize, maximize/window, or close the application. The three buttons shown here on the bottom perform the same functions to the drawing window.

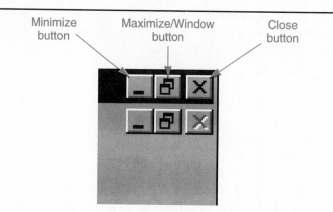

Minimize button        Maximize/Window button        Close button

Another aspect of Windows 95 is the ability to use long filenames. (Long filenames are discussed later in this chapter.) However, AutoCAD does not allow you to enter long filenames. When naming your drawing, you are limited to eight characters and the .DWG extension, just as in Windows 3.1.

**Differences.** In Windows 3.1, the file control menu appears as a square with a horizontal line in it. On the right side of the AutoCAD title bar, there are two buttons. One is to minimize AutoCAD and the other is to maximize/window AutoCAD. In addition, the titles for Windows 3.1 are centered.

In Windows 95, the file control menus appear as the AutoCAD icon. Also, there are three buttons on the right side of the AutoCAD title bar for minimizing/maximizing/closing AutoCAD. Finally, titles are aligned to the left of the title bar in Windows 95.

## Placing AutoCAD on your desktop

The *desktop* is what appears when Windows 95 starts. The **Task Bar**, **My Computer** icon, and **Recycle Bin** icon are all on the desktop. You can also add shortcuts to your desktop. A *shortcut* simply tells the computer to open a file. A shortcut can appear in **Windows Explorer** as a file, or it can be placed on the desktop as an icon. The following procedure can be used to create a shortcut for any program. Placing a shortcut on your desktop is also explained.

**Creating a shortcut.** First, start **Windows Explorer** using the **Start** button located on the **Task Bar**. To create a shortcut for AutoCAD, highlight ACAD.EXE in the \R13\WIN directory. Then, select **Create Shortcut** from the **File** menu. A file appears in the \R13\WIN directory with the name Shortcut to ACAD.EXE. If you double-click on this file, AutoCAD is launched.

**Placing a shortcut on the Desktop.** To place a shortcut on your desktop, first highlight the file in **Windows Explorer**. Then, drag the shortcut to the **Desktop** in **Windows Explorer** (**Desktop** is the top of the tree in **Windows Explorer**). When you close **Windows Explorer**, an icon with the name Shortcut to ACAD.EXE is on the desktop. When you double-click on this icon, AutoCAD is launched.

**Renaming a shortcut.** If you wish to rename the shortcut, you can select it in **Windows Explorer** and rename it using the **Rename** command in the **File** menu. This can be done either before or after you have "dragged" the shortcut to the Desktop.

## MANAGING FILES USING WINDOWS 95

The **File Manager** in Windows 3.1 has been replaced in Windows 95 with **Windows Explorer**. **Windows Explorer** operates much differently than **File Manager**. The next sections cover how to manage your files using **Windows Explorer**.

### Overview of Windows Explorer

To start **Windows Explorer**, click on **Start** on the **Task Bar**. Then select **Programs** and **Windows Explorer** (located at the bottom of the list), Figure 33-18. The **Windows Explorer** window opens with the title **Exploring** and the name of the current drive or directory, Figure 33-19. Also, an **Exploring** button appears on the **Task Bar**. Note: Directories are often called *folders* in Windows 95.

You will notice that there is a tree similar to the one found in **File Manager**. However, where the top of the tree in **File Manager** is the root directory of a drive (such as the hard drive), in **Windows Explorer** the top of the directory is called **Desktop**. Also, the first branches are **My Computer** and **Recycle Bin**.

**WIN 95**

Under **My Computer**, the next branches are the disk drives installed on your computer. The floppy drive, hard drive, and CD-ROM drive (if installed) are listed. You can double-click on the drive you want to view to expand the directories on that drive.

You will also notice a toolbar along the top of the window, much like the one found in Windows for Workgroups 3.11. On the toolbar, you will find a button with a file folder having an up arrow on it. This can be used to move up one level in the tree.

**Differences.** In Windows 3.1, **File Manager** shows a directory tree for the current drive. At the top of the tree is the root directory. Different drives can be viewed at the same time by opening multiple windows.

Figure 33-18.   To launch
**Windows Explorer**, select
**Start**, **Programs**, then
**Windows Explorer**.

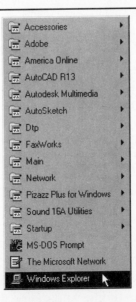

Accessories
Adobe
America Online
AutoCAD R13
Autodesk Multimedia
AutoSketch
Dtp
FaxWorks
Main
Network
Pizazz Plus for Windows
Sound 16A Utilities
Startup
MS-DOS Prompt
The Microsoft Network
Windows Explorer

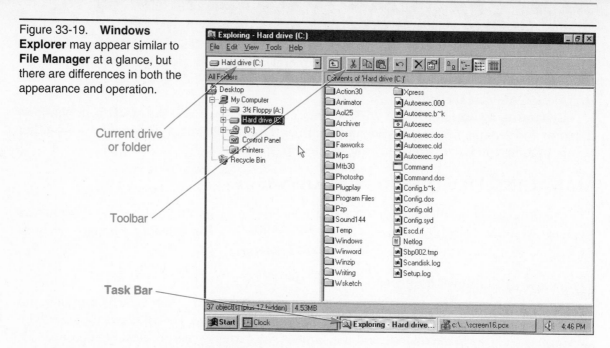

Figure 33-19. **Windows Explorer** may appear similar to **File Manager** at a glance, but there are differences in both the appearance and operation.

In Windows 95, **Windows Explorer** also shows a tree, but the top of the tree is **Desktop**. The tree contains all of the disk drives installed on your computer. You can expand the tree on a drive by double-clicking on its icon.

## Selecting files

To select a single file, simply highlight that file with your cursor. To select several files in a series, highlight the first file, hold down the [Shift] key, and then select the last file in the series. The entire series is highlighted. To select several individual files, hold down the [Ctrl] as you select the files.

**Differences.** Files are selected in the same way in both Windows 3.1 and Windows 95. There have been no changes to this function. The [Ctrl] and [Shift] keys are still used to select groups of files.

## Copying and moving files

To copy a file to a different location on the same drive, highlight the file and hold down the [Shift] key as you drag it to the location where you want the copy. To copy a file to a different drive, simply highlight the file and drag it to the location on the other drive where you want it. In either case, you will notice a small square with a plus in it next to the cursor as you drag the file.

To move a file to a different location on the same drive, simply highlight it and drag it with the cursor to the new location. To move a file to a different drive, hold down the [Shift] key as you drag it. In either case, you will notice that as you drag the file, only the filename and icon are dragged with the cursor. There is no box with a plus in it that follows the cursor.

**Differences.** The major differences between copying/moving files in **File Manager** and **Windows Explorer** is in the visual appearance and menu options. In addition, formatting a disk is not done in **Windows Explorer**, but in **Control Panel**. For complete information on the menu options, see the documentation that comes with Windows 95. Formatting a disk is covered later in the section called *Formatting a Disk*.

## Deleting and undeleting files

WIN 95

To delete a file, highlight the file and click on the **Delete** button on the toolbar. You are then asked Are you sure you want to send *filename* to the RecycleBin?. Pick the **Yes** button. You can also select a group of files and delete them all at the same time.

**PROFESSIONAL TIP**

To quickly delete a file or group of files, simply highlight them and press the [Delete] key.

**WIN 95**

To undelete a file, minimize **Windows Explorer** by selecting the button in the upper-right corner with a horizontal bar on it. Then, double-click on the **Recycle Bin** icon on the desktop (the main Windows 95 screen). This opens the **Recycle Bin** window, Figure 33-20. Highlight the file or files you want to undelete and select **R̲estore** from the **F̲ile** menu. The file is restored to its original location and removed from the **Recycle Bin**.

Deleted files are not kept in the **Recycle Bin** forever. If you "empty" the **Recycle Bin**, the files are permanently erased. Also, if your hard drive has most of the space used, new files that are saved may overwrite files in the **Recycle Bin**. In addition, if you defragment your hard drive, the files in the **Recycle Bin** will be lost.

**Differences.** The undelete function in Windows 3.1 is located in the **F̲ile** menu of **File Manager**. In Windows for Workgroups 3.11, the undelete function can also be placed as a tool on the toolbar. To use this command, simply select the file(s) and select the command. You will then be asked to provide the first letter of the filename, as DOS substitutes a ? for the first letter. In addition, you can only delete files that were in the current directory.

**WFW**

The undelete function in Windows 95 is separate from **Windows Explorer** and called **Recycle Bin**. To undelete a file, open **Recycle Bin**. Then select the file(s) and pick **R̲estore** from the **F̲ile** menu. You do not need to enter the first letter of the filename, as Windows 95 retains the entire filename and location.

Figure 33-20.   The undelete function in Windows 95 is **Recycle Bin**. All deleted files are moved here, no matter the original location. **Recycle Bin** keeps the entire filename and location.

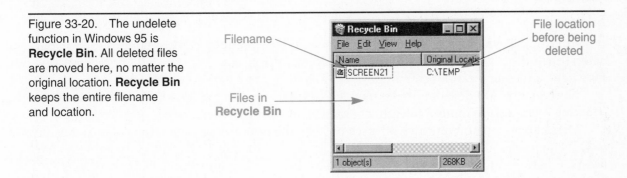

## Formatting a disk

To format a disk in Windows 95, single-click on **3 1/2 Floppy Drive [A:]** found in **My Computer** (if the disk is in the A: drive). The icon is highlighted. Then, select **Format…** from the **F̲ile** menu. This opens the **Format - 3 1/2 Floppy [A:]** window (if you are using the A: drive), Figure 33-21.

Select the density (**Ca̲pacity:**) and format type. You can also add a label to the disk or make it a system disk (**Copy s̲ystem files**). When you have made the appropriate selections, click on the **S̲tart** button. A meter appears at the bottom of the window showing the progress of the format.

**Differences.** To format a disk in Windows 3.1, select **Format Disk…** from the **D̲isk** menu in **File Manager**. Then, specify the drive and density of the disk. You also have the option of labeling the disk or making it a system disk.

To format a disk in Windows 95, first open **Control Panel**. Then, single-click on the drive icon where your disk is. Select **Format…** from the **F̲ile** menu. Finally, select the appropriate options and start the formatting.

Figure 33-21.  When formatting
a disk, select appropriate options
and click on the **Start** button.

Select the
disk size

Select the
type of format

Select to make
a system disk

Progress
meter

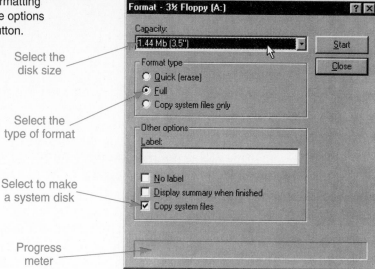

**PROFESSIONAL TIP**

If you don't know what is on the disk, double-click on the drive icon. This will show any files that may be on the disk. If there are no files on the disk, this window will be blank. Then, close the window and proceed with the format.

## Filenames

In Windows 95, you can use long filenames. *Long filenames* can contain up to 255 characters, including spaces. In addition, the file extension can also be 255 characters long. However, a filename cannot contain \ ? : " < > | as these are reserved characters.

Note: AutoCAD does *not* make use of long filenames in Windows 95. When naming a drawing, you still are limited to eight characters and the .DWG extension.

**Differences.** Since Windows 3.1 uses DOS as the operating system, the rules that apply to DOS filenames also apply to Windows 3.1. In DOS, a filename can only contain eight characters, a period, and a three character extension. In addition, a filename cannot contain \ ? : " < > | as these are reserved characters.

## CHAPTER TEST

*Write your answers in the space provided.*

1. What is multitasking? _____

_____

_____

2. True or false. When using Windows 95, DOS provides the basic commands to the computer. _____

3. Where is the **Install/Remove Programs** icon located? _____

_____

4. True or false. When installing a program, Windows 95 will automatically look for an installation program on your floppy or CD-ROM drive. _____

5. How do you launch a program in Windows 95? _____

_____

_____

6. What program is used in Windows 95 to manage files? _____

7. Explain the two ways that can be used to multitask in the Windows 95 environment.

A. _____

_____

B. _____

_____

8. How do you format a disk in Windows 95? _____

_____

_____

9. How many characters can a filename have in Windows 95? _____

10. How do you undelete a file in Windows 95? _____

_____

_____

_____

## PROBLEMS

*Here is a mixture of activities to develop your skills using Windows 95. Do not save files on disk drives where you are not authorized to do so. This section assumes that you have Windows 95 installed on your computer.*

1. Find a program that you can install on your computer (such as the Goodheart-Willcox Student Work Disks). Install that program in Windows 95. Note how the Windows 95 installation process is different from Windows 3.1.

2. Using Windows 95, format an unformatted disk, or a disk with files you no longer need.

3. Using **Windows Explorer**, create a directory on the hard drive using your name. Copy the entire directory tree from your work diskette into that directory.

4. Using **Windows Explorer**, create directories on the diskette from Problem 3 for each chapter in this book. Move your drawings for each chapter into the appropriate directory.

5. Delete the directory tree from the hard drive that you created in Problem 4.

AutoCAD R13

# Appendix *A*

# Installing and Configuring AutoCAD for Windows

Before you can use AutoCAD for Windows, it must be installed onto the hard disk and then configured to work with your specific hardware. When AutoCAD is installed on the hard disk, you begin the ongoing process of disk and system management. This involves creating storage space for files and maintaining them.

The configuration procedure should have to be used only once, unless equipment is upgraded or new peripherals are added. To use two or more different menu systems, you can duplicate and alter AutoCAD's standard configuration file, ACAD.CFG.

## INSTALLING AUTOCAD FOR WINDOWS

Before installing AutoCAD for Windows, follow these preparation and setup steps:
- Have Microsoft Windows installed and running.
- Determine the hard disk drive to install AutoCAD on.
- If installing from disks, make backup copies of the AutoCAD diskettes.
- Label the backup disks.

These steps require only a few minutes and can prevent problems later.

### Making backup copies of the AutoCAD disks

Always make backup copies of original disks before installing the software. Be sure you have the correct number of blank disks before starting to copy the AutoCAD disks. Attach labels to the blank disks that contain the disk name, number, and AutoCAD serial number.

Disks can be easily copied and formatted at the same time using File Manager. A complete discussion of File Manager is contained in Chapter 32. To copy the contents of one floppy disk to another, activate the Program Manager and double-click the File Manager icon. Select Copy Disk... from the Disk pull-down menu. The Copy Disk dialog box is displayed. See Figure A-1.

The procedure allows you to copy the entire contents of the *source* disk to the *destination* disk. The disks must be compatible in order to be copied. For example, if your computer has a 5.25" drive and a 3.5" drive, you cannot use Copy Disk to copy between those two drives. Instead, use only one of the drives as both the source and destination. Notice in Figure A-1 that the B drive is used for the disk copy procedure.

Figure A-1.   Use Copy Disk
in the File Manager to back up
copies of your AutoCAD disks.

| Copy Disk | | |
|---|---|---|
| Source In: | B: | OK |
| Destination In: | B: | Cancel |
| | | Help |

> **CAUTION**
>
> Windows warns you that all data on the destination drive will be erased. This is because the destination disk is formatted as files are copied to it. Always check the contents of a disk before using the Copy Disk or Format Disk selections in the Disk pull-down menu.

Insert a disk into the drive and click the OK button, or press [Enter]. If you are copying on a single drive, you will be prompted to insert the destination disk. Follow the instructions until the File Manager window becomes active again. Follow the same procedure to copy all of the program disks.

## Using the CD-ROM

Release 13 is the first version of AutoCAD that is available on CD-ROM. This format is less expensive, and requires the use of only one flexible disk. In addition, the CD-ROM has greater integrity than disks, and many of the extra precautions required when handling and storing floppy disks are not concerns with a CD. Advantages of a CD are the speed of the installation, and the need to handle only a single installation disk. Once the installation of files begins from the CD, the computer can be left unattended, since there are no disks to remove or insert.

The installation process discussed here is based on the use of a CD-ROM, but is similar if installing from disks. The main difference when using disks is that you are prompted to insert the next disk.

## Installing Win32s

Windows 3.1 is a 16 bit platform, and AutoCAD Release 13 for Windows runs in 32 bit mode. Therefore, if you are using Windows 3.1 on a computer that is incapable of running Win32s applications, it is necessary to install the Win32s files before you run AutoCAD. If you begin installing AutoCAD, you may be prompted to install Win32s. It is not necessary to terminate the installation of AutoCAD, because Win32s can be installed after AutoCAD. These files can be installed quickly using the following steps:

1. Start Windows and be sure to terminate any other applications that are running.
2. Insert the Win32s disk 1 into the disk drive or insert the CD-ROM into the CD-ROM drive. This procedure describes the steps required to use a CD-ROM.
3. Activate Windows Program Manager, pick Run... from the File pull-down menu, then pick the Browse... button. In the Drives: pop-up list select the drive letter that represents your CD-ROM drive, E: in this example. Scroll through the Directories: list and double-click the WIN32S folder icon. Next double-click the DISK1 folder icon. Pick SETUP.EXE in the files list and pick the OK button, Figure A-2A. The file E:\WIN32S\DISK1\SETUP.EXE should be displayed in the Command Line: edit box. See Figure A-2B. Pick the OK button.

Figure A-2.    A—Pick SETUP.EXE in the files list to install the Win32s files. B—Pick OK to run SETUP.EXE.

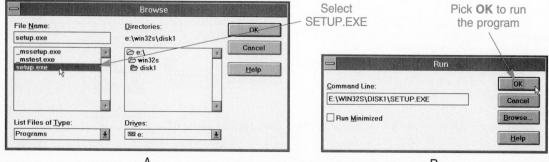

A                                                                                                              B

4. Win32s will be installed on your hard drive. After it is installed, you will be asked if you want to install a game called Freecell that can be used to test the Win32s installation. It is suggested that you install Freecell and test the game to be sure the installation went smoothly. If you agree to the installation you are asked to verify the installation path for Freecell. See Figure A-3.

5. Windows will be restarted after the Win32s installation. At this time you can install AutoCAD if you have not done so.

Figure A-3. You can test the Win32s setup by installing the game Freecell.

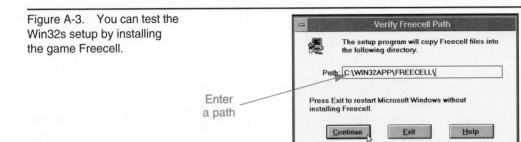

## Installing the Windows WHIP driver

Autodesk has developed a special accelerated display list driver for Windows called WHIP. It is reported to perform certain display operations faster that the other two drivers that are shipped with AutoCAD. The WHIP driver must first be installed before it can be configured for use. This procedure is similar to that used to install Win32s. Follow steps 1 and 2 given for the Win32s installation. Follow step 3 as indicated previously, but open the \WING directory folder on the CD-ROM drive, then open the \WING\DISK subdirectory folder. See Figure A-4A. Select the SETUP.EXE file then pick OK. The Run dialog box should appear, as shown in Figure A-4B. Pick OK and the WHIP driver files are installed. This driver will now be listed under video displays during the configuration of AutoCAD.

Figure A-4. To install the WHIP driver, select the setup program from the \WING\DISK directory.

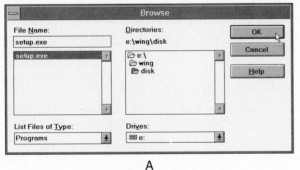
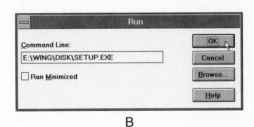

A                B

## Installing AutoCAD

Installing AutoCAD for Windows is a simple process, but it does require that you are somewhat prepared before beginning. First, be sure that you have enough hard disk space for the program files.

A typical installation of AutoCAD for Windows requires approximately 46MB of hard disk space and a complete installation requires approximately 49MB. The setup process warns you if there is not enough disk space to install the files you have selected. Approximate hard disk storage areas required for some of the components are as follows.

| Files | Disk Space |
|---|---|
| • Complete installation | 49MB |
| • Custom installation | varies |
| • Typical installation | 46MB |
| • Executables and Support | 23MB |
| • AutoCAD Learning tools | 5MB |
| • Application Development Tools | 2MB |
| • External Database Access | 9MB |
| • Example & Sample files | 4MB |
| • AutoCAD Fonts (all fonts and .SHX source files) | 2MB |
|   • TrueType = 1MB | |
|   • PostScript = 575K | |
| • Speller Dictionaries | 227K |
| • Electronic Documentation Viewer | 1MB |

In an effort to run smoothly through the setup process, know the following information before starting.

Disk drive on which to install AutoCAD. _____

Portion of the AutoCAD files to install. _____

Dealer's name. _____

Dealer's telephone number. _____

---

**NOTE**      If you are installing AutoCAD from disks, use only your backup disks for installation, not the original disks. If you have not yet created backup disks as explained at the beginning of this chapter, do so before you continue. If you are installing from a CD, you should also make a backup copy of the installation disk before continuing.

---

After you have created backup disks of all of the AutoCAD program disks, you are ready to install the software. Insert the Installation Disk into the disk drive and activate the Program Manager window. Pick Run... from the File pull-down menu and the Run dialog box is displayed. A blinking cursor appears in the Command Line: text box. Enter the name of the drive in which you inserted the Installation Disk followed by SETUP as follows:

**A:SETUP**

Substitute the appropriate letter for the disk drive you are using. See Figure A-5.

Click the OK button, or press [Enter]. The AutoCAD for Windows setup program begins and you are then asked for specific information that becomes a permanent part of the Executable disk. This is both a security measure, and also enables AutoCAD to display the name and phone number of your dealer.

---

Figure A-5.   If the correct program name appears in the text box, pick OK to run the program.

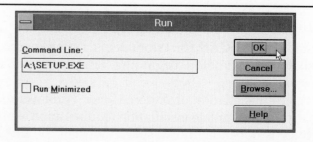

Enter the information requested, and use the [Tab] key to move between the text box fields. Click the <u>O</u>K button when you are finished. The same information is redisplayed, and you are given a chance to change your mind or correct anything you enter. This information becomes a permanent part of your disk, so make any necessary changes at this point. See Figure A-6.

Release 13 is the first time that users can install both DOS and Windows versions of AutoCAD at the same time. The next screen allows you to choose the version(s) you wish to install. See Figure A-7. Pick **OK** after making your selection.

The next screen provides three choices for the amount of files that are installed onto your hard disk. See Figure A-8. If hard disk space is a concern to you, choose the <u>M</u>inimum button. This installation requires 23MB of hard disk space. If you are unsure about which components to install, but have plenty of hard disk space, choose the <u>T</u>ypical button. Since this button is the default, pressing [Enter] selects the Typical Installation.

Figure A-6.   If your personal information is incorrect, pick Cancel and re-enter the information.

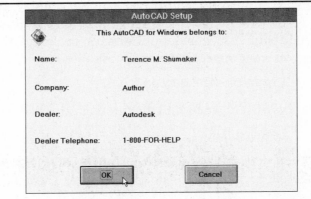

Figure A-7.   This display allows you to select either the DOS or Windows version, or both.

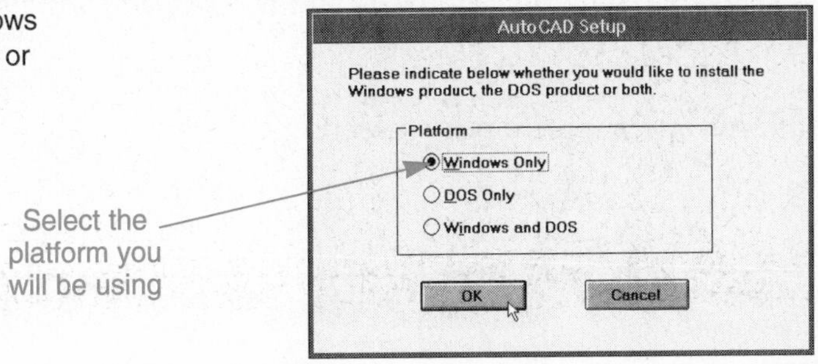

Select the platform you will be using

Figure A-8.   Choose either a typical, custom, or minimum installation.

Select the type of installation

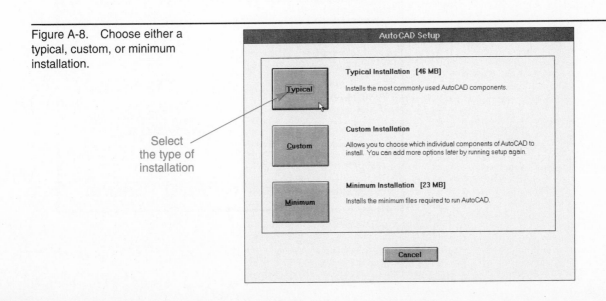

This discussion describes the custom installation, which allows you to pick only those components of AutoCAD that you wish to install. This selection should only be used if you are familiar with AutoCAD, and the files required for its operation.

**NOTE**    Regardless of the type of installation you select, you can always run the setup program again later and choose additional components to install. Just run the setup program as described at the beginning of this appendix. Then, use the <u>C</u>ustom button as described below to select the items you wish to install.

After selecting the <u>C</u>ustom button you are required to select the components of AutoCAD that you wish to install. See Figure A-9. If you planned your installation as mentioned previously, refer to those notes now. If you are unsure about the applications that will be needed, install all files. Refer to the checklist below to help you decide what to install. Just remember, you'll need about 49 megabytes of storage space for all files.

✓ If you want to install the minimum files required to run AutoCAD, select:

> Executables and Support

✓ If you wish to work with the tutorials supplied with AutoCAD, select:

> Learning Tools

✓ If you wish to have access to AutoCAD Development System (ADS) files (additional sample programs with an .EXP, .EXE, or .C extension), select:

> Application Development Tools

✓ If you will be working with databases and SQL, select:

> External Database Access

✓ Install all fonts and shape files by selecting:

> Fonts

Figure A-9.   If you choose to do a custom install, you can select the components to install.

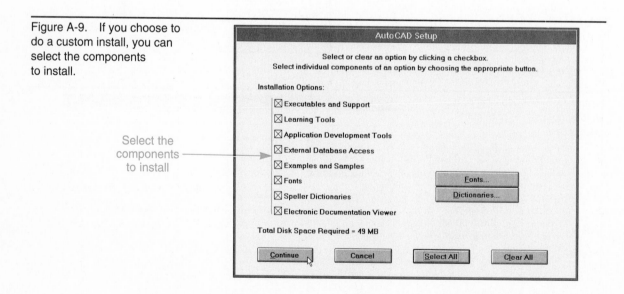

Select the components to install

Figure A-10.   Select the type of fonts to install.

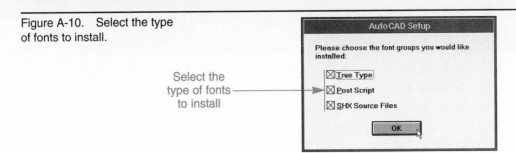

Select the type of fonts to install

Should you wish to select specific categories of fonts, pick the Fonts... button and the dialog box shown in Figure A-10 is displayed. TrueType fonts are scaleable and maintain their appearance regardless of their size. PostScript fonts can only be used with a PostScript hardcopy device. The SHX source files are the ASCII format files for all standard AutoCAD fonts. Pick OK when you have selected the items you need.

✓ If you wish to install more than one language dictionary, select:

> Speller Dictionaries

Pick the Dictionaries... button to obtain a list of the spelling dictionaries available to you. Select all those you will need and pick OK.

✓ To gain access to the electronic documentation, select:

> Electronic Documentation Viewer

You next need to indicate the hard disk drive and directory that AutoCAD Windows-specific files are to be installed on, and also the directory in which to place shared files. The default drive and directory names are displayed. See Figure A-11. Edit the drive letter and directory name if desired, otherwise pick OK to use the default. Shared files are those used by both the DOS and Windows versions of Release 13.

Figure A-11.   Select the hard drive and directories where you want to install AutoCAD and shared files.

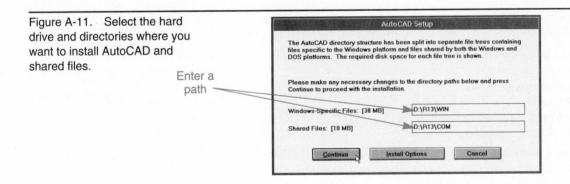

Enter a path

The next two screens will indicate that the directories you selected either exist or do not exist. If the directories do not exist you are asked if you want them created. See Figure A-12. Pick Yes to create them. If the directories already exist, you are asked if you wish to continue. Press [Enter] to accept the default, unless you wish to change the names. If you pick the No button you are returned to the dialog box displayed in Figure A-11. You can change the drive and directory at this point.

After you accept the drive and directory names, the installation begins. The next screen prompts you for the name of your CD-ROM drive. Enter the proper name of your CD-ROM and pick OK. See Figure A-13.

When the installation is complete, a new Windows program group is created, and all of the required program item icons are placed inside. See Figure A-14.

Figure A-12.   If the directories that you specified do not exist, you will get these alert boxes.

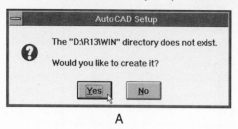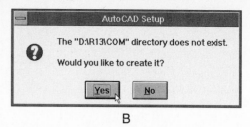

A                                                    B

Figure A-13.   Insert the CD in
your CD-ROM drive and pick OK.

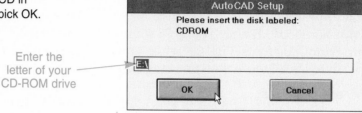

Enter the
letter of your
CD-ROM drive

Figure A-14.   The AutoCAD
R13 program group is created
when installation is complete.

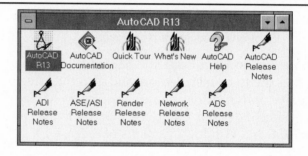

At this time you can resize the window as needed. To launch AutoCAD, click the
AutoCAD R13 icon to highlight it, then click Open in the File pull-down menu, or, just double-
click on the AutoCAD R13 icon. If you are opening AutoCAD for the first time after running
the setup program, you must configure it for all display, input, and output devices attached
to your computer.

## CONFIGURING AUTOCAD FOR WINDOWS

The configuration process allows you to tell AutoCAD the specific brands and styles of
equipment you are using. Before you begin, make a list of the following pieces of equipment
that comprise your workstation:

Video Display_____

Input Device (Digitizer or Mouse) _____

   Size _____

   Number of buttons _____

Plotter _____

Printer _____

Once you have a list of your equipment, the configuring process should go quickly.

Because this is the first time starting AutoCAD, it will proceed past the copyright notice
and display the following message in the text window:

AutoCAD is not yet configured.
You may specify the devices to which AutoCAD will interface.

The following prompt is given in the text window:

Available video displays:
    1.   'WHIP' - HEIDI (TM) Accelerated Display driver - Autodesk, Inc
    2.   Accelerated Disp. drvr. by Rasterex (Int'l) a.s for Autodesk, Inc
    3.   Windows Display driver - by Autodesk, Inc
Select device number or ? to repeat list ⟨1⟩:

There are a wide variety of video graphics adapters on the market. If drivers for one of these devices have been installed in your computer, the list that is displayed on your screen may contain additional selections. Also, if you did not install the WHIP driver as discussed previously, it will not be shown in the list. Unless you will be using a display driver that was supplied with your video graphics board, select the default number 1 and press [Enter].

If the default driver is WHIP you are asked:

Would you like to configure the WHIP driver? ⟨N⟩ *(Press* [Enter] *to accept the default of* NO*)*

---

**NOTE**      Video display boards (graphics cards), usually come with special drivers that are supplied on a diskette. These drivers may enable you to utilize special features, colors, and resolutions not available with the standard Windows and Autodesk drivers. Always consult the documentation provided with your video card for instructions to install special drivers.

---

You are next asked if you want to correct the aspect ratio of your screen. Select the default of No unless you know that the aspect ratio is incorrect.

After configuring your video display, you are asked to choose a digitizer. This is actually referring to the pointing device since you can select pointing devices other than digitizers. You are given the following list:

Available digitizers:
    1.   Current System Pointing Device
    2.   Calcomp 2500 (obsolete) and 3300 Series ADI 4.2 - by Autodesk, Inc
    3.   Hitachi HICOMSCAN HDG Series ADI 4.2 - by Autodesk, Inc
    4.   Kurta IS/ONE ⟨obsolete⟩ ADI 4.2 - by Autodesk, Inc
    5.   Kurta XLC, IS/THREE ⟨obsolete⟩, ADI 4.2 - by Autodesk, Inc
    6.   Kurta XLP, ADI 4.2 - by Autodesk, Inc
    7.   Summagraphics MicroGrid v1.1 (Series II or later) ADI 4.2 - by Autodesk, Inc
    8.   Summagraphics MM Series v2.0, ADI 4.2 - by Autodesk, Inc
    9.   Wintab Compatible Digitizer ADI 4.2 - by Autodesk, Inc
Select device number or ? to repeat list ⟨1⟩: *(enter your selection and press* [Enter]*)*

You are next asked a variety of questions regarding digitizer size, number of buttons, and mouse scaling parameters. This depends on which pointing device you selected.

The configuration process continues, presenting available plotters and printers. Choose the appropriate hardware and answer the ensuing questions. After the printer or plotter is configured, you are required to provide the following information:

- Authorization number.
- Default login name—The default name is the one entered when AutoCAD was installed.
- Enable file locking? (Y/N)
- Available spelling dialects:
    1.   American English
    2.   British English (ise)
    3.   British English (ize)

- Select dialect number or ? to repeat list ⟨1⟩:
- Run the executable from a read-only directory? (Y/N)

After answering the previous questions, the current AutoCAD configuration is displayed in the text window. This is only a display; you cannot change anything here. If you wish to change something, you may do so at the Configuration menu after pressing [Enter] at the following prompt:

>Press RETURN to continue: ↵

Pressing [Enter] displays the Configuration menu in the text window. Correct any configuration errors or add a piece of equipment that you may have forgotten. Press [Enter] if you do not wish to configure any additional equipment or change the hardware you chose.

>Configuration menu
>
>    0.   Exit to drawing editor
>    1.   Show current configuration
>    2.   Allow detailed configuration
>    3.   Configure video display
>    4.   Configure digitizer
>    5.   Configure plotter
>    6.   Configure system console
>    7.   Configure operating parameters
>
>Enter selection ⟨0⟩: ↵

**NOTE**     After this initial configuration, you can at anytime configure additional equipment or change the hardware by selecting **Configure** from the **Options** pull-down menu while in AutoCAD.

You are now given the choice to save the configuration. Be sure to press [Enter] at the following prompt, or enter Y, to save the configuration file:

>If you answer N to the following question, all configuration
>changes you have just made will be discarded.
>Keep configuration changes? ⟨Y⟩ ↵

The AutoCAD graphics window then appears, and you can begin a drawing session. Test the equipment you configured and reconfigure those which do not operate properly.

When you enter the AutoCAD graphics window for a drawing session, if you have a digitizer, notice that the entire surface of the digitizer tablet represents the screen. The tablet menu will not work until you use the **TABLET** command to configure it. This is explained in detail in Chapter 31 *Digitizing Existing Drawings*. After the tablet is configured, this information is added to the ACAD.CFG file, which is saved in the \R13\WIN subdirectory.

## ALTERNATE CONFIGURATIONS

The ACAD.CFG file contains all of the information needed to allow AutoCAD to work with the equipment you specified during configuration. It also includes information about the screen and tablet menus, and additional system variable settings.

As you gain experience with AutoCAD, you will use additional configurations of tablet and menus, and possibly different input devices. Creating and maintaining multiple configuration files is discussed in Appendix C *Hard Disk Management*.

If you plan to work with projects that require different menus, become familiar with multiple configuration techniques. These eliminate the need to reconfigure the tablet and load new menus each time you begin a new project or work on a different drawing.

# Appendix

# System Requirements for AutoCAD for Windows

This appendix lists the system requirements for AutoCAD Release 13 for Windows and outlines the hardware, software, and data exchange options available for this latest AutoCAD release. It is intended to be used as a guide for configuring the AutoCAD system that best meets your needs. Your local authorized AutoCAD dealer will provide you with detailed information about system configuration options and assist you in selecting the platform, peripherals, and companion programs that are right for you. See the AutoCAD Release 13 *Installation Guide for Windows* for detailed information on peripheral configurations and settings.

## SOFTWARE AND HARDWARE

The following software and hardware is required to run AutoCAD Release 13 for Windows. Optional software and hardware is noted as such.

- DOS 5.0 or later
- Microsoft Windows, Version 3.1 running in enhanced mode or Windows for Workgroups, Version 3.11 or later (AutoCAD for Windows does not run in real or standard mode)
- Microsoft's Win32s Version 1.20 or later (Autodesk supplies this with the installation)
- 16MB RAM (minimum)
- Intel 386, Intel 486, Pentium processor or compatible
- 80387 math coprocessor (or 80486 internal)
- 37MB of hard disk space
- 40MB of disk swap space (minimum)
- CD-ROM drive and 1.44MB 3.5" floppy drive
- Windows-supported display adapter
- Mouse
- IBM-compatible parallel port (Serial port optional for digitizers and some plotters)
- Hardware lock (for networks and single-user international)
- AutoCAD for Windows supports Windows-compatible video displays with the resolution of 640 × 480 or greater. Autodesk supplies two ADI display drivers with AutoCAD for Windows—DSACAD.DLL and DSDLWIN.DLL. The drivers are dynamic-link library (.DLL) files. Because both drivers are compatible with your installed Windows 3.1 display driver, the AutoCAD window can show graphics at the same resolution and with the same color as your Windows driver.
- AutoCAD for Windows supports the following digitizers:
  - CalComp 2500 Series Tablets
  - CalComp 3300 Series Tablets
  - Hitachi HDG Series Tablet
  - Kurta Tablet IS/ONE*
  - Kurta Tablet IS/THREE*, Kurta XLC
  - Summagraphics MM Series Tablet, Kurta XLP

- • Summagraphics MicroGrid Series II & III Tablets
- • Wintab Compatible Tablets
- • AutoCAD for Windows offers the following plotters:
  - • Raster File Format
  - • Canon Laser Beam Printer
  - • CalComp ColorMaster Plotter
  - • CalComp DrawingMaster Plotter
  - • CalComp Electrostatic Plotter
  - • CalComp Pen Plotter
  - • AutoCAD File Format
  - • Houston Instruments DMP Series
  - • Hewlett-Packard HP-GL/2 Plotter
  - • Hewlett-Packard Laserjet Printer (PCL)
  - • Hewlett-Packard Plotter (HP-GL)
  - • Hewlett-Packard Color Printer
  - • Windows System Printer
  - • Null Plotter

# Hard Disk and System Management

Any business—be it a bakery or engineering firm—relies on structure, organization, and standard procedures. A business lacking in one of these areas does not operate efficiently.

The widespread use of computers in business and industry has introduced another facet to business operations. Computer systems can be used within the company structure for organization and procedure; or computers can contain the structure and organize procedures. In either case, the method in which computer systems are managed greatly affects the operation of the entire company.

Effective management of an AutoCAD system in a school or business means paying careful attention to the following items:
- The structure and makeup of the hard disk.
- The location of all files and drawings.
- Storage procedures for student/employee drawing files.
- Drawing file backup procedures.
- The kind of prototype drawings used for specific projects.
- The location and use of symbol libraries and reference drawings.
- The location and use of special screen and tablet menus.
- Drawing naming procedures.
- Drawing file creation procedures.
- Creation and distribution of new symbols and menus.
- Timely updating of software and hardware.
- Hardware maintenance.

Effective procedures and management techniques must be practiced by all students or employees. In addition, look for ways that standards can be improved and revised for greater efficiency. Read the section in Chapter 1 on system management and the section in Chapter 25 on creating and using symbol libraries.

## DOS HARD DISK STRUCTURE

The hard disk drive is the heart of the AutoCAD computer system. It is the storage center for AutoCAD and other programs you use. In addition, it may hold hundreds of additional files, including drawings, menus, AutoLISP programs, slides, scripts, and text files. The manner in which you work with the hard disk and arrange its contents can affect your productivity and efficiency at the computer. Take some time to learn the nature of the hard disk drive.

### The root directory and its contents

The root directory is the trunk of the hard disk tree from which every other directory, subdirectory, and file branches. After your computer is set up, the root directory contains only a \DOS directory. See Figure C-1. No other programs are on the hard disk. In addition to the DOS directory, two files occupy the root directory. These files are COMMAND.COM and

Figure C-1.    The root directory
contains only the DOS directory
when the computer is set up
and DOS is installed.

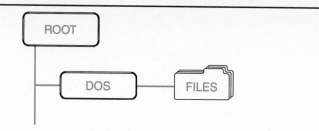

AUTOEXEC.BAT. A third file, CONFIG.SYS, should be placed in the root directory when Windows is installed.

Before a program is installed on the hard disk, a directory should first be created. The program files are copied into that directory. Program files should not be placed in the root directory. The default name for the AutoCAD directory is \R13, and all AutoCAD files reside in it and its subdirectories. After AutoCAD and Windows are installed, the structure of the hard disk resembles Figure C-2.

The AutoCAD installation program creates a directory tree that contains a location for files required by the Windows version. The AutoCAD directory is named \R13 by default, and the subdirectory for Windows-specific files is named \R13\WIN. In addition, a shared subdirectory, named \R13\COM, is created in which files used by both the DOS and Windows versions are stored. Thus, after installation, the R13 directory is completely free of files, and contains only the two subdirectories mentioned above. See Figure C-2.

The files that reside in the \R13 subdirectories are the only ones required by AutoCAD. Any files that you create should be stored in either the appropriate subdirectory, or in new subdirectories. See Chapter 32 *Using the Windows File Manager* for information on creating directories and subdirectories. Additional information is provided in this appendix for creating and maintaining an efficient directory tree.

Figure C-2.    AutoCAD files are
stored in the \R13 directory.

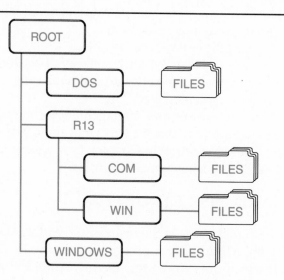

## Designing and building a hard disk tree

When you install AutoCAD using the SETUP program provided on the disks, several subdirectories are automatically created, depending on which files you instruct AutoCAD to install. These subdirectories are created so that the \R13 directory is not filled with files it does not need. Take some time to look at the contents of these subdirectories and notice the files that are stored there.

**PROFESSIONAL TIP**

If you are responsible for hard disk organization and management in your school or company, it is a good idea to keep a printed copy of the contents of each subdirectory. Get a print of each directory and subdirectory immediately after installing the software. Periodically check the contents of each directory and look for unnecessary files. Compare the contents with your printed list. Then, delete all unnecessary files. You can automate this process with a batch file. This file can delete all file types, such as .DWG, that are not supposed to be in the directory.

After installing the software, you will be faced with other decisions about where to store new files that must go on the hard disk. Only you can decide which files should be saved on the hard disk and where they are to be saved. Regardless of the decisions you make, they should be based on careful consideration of the following:

### Questions to ask

✓ Are the computers used for training or production?
✓ Will the computers be used for demonstrations?
✓ Will the system hardware be upgraded often?
✓ How often will drawings be saved to the hard disk?
✓ How many drawings, from how many users, are to be saved on the hard disk?
✓ Will custom menus, AutoLISP, and ADS programs be used?
✓ Will users have their own subdirectories?

### Points to consider

✓ Load new software in its own directory.
✓ Store nonessential files in subdirectories of the parent software directory.
✓ Use short names or abbreviations for directory names.
✓ If you have multiple hard drives, leave an empty buffer of at least five megabytes per hard drive for work space over and above the working space required by software such as AutoCAD.
✓ If users have their own subdirectory, encourage them to work in it, not in the program directory.

When you answer these questions, and keep these points in mind, you can better estimate what to store on the hard disk and how it should be structured.

Regardless of what you store on the hard disk, have a plan for it. Drawings should not be saved in the \R13 directory. Users should not be allowed to save files in the root directory. Decide on the nature of the hard disk structure and then stick to it. Make sure that all users are informed by documenting and distributing standard procedures to all who use the system. Place copies of procedures at each workstation.

Files to be used in conjunction with AutoCAD should be located in subdirectories of the \R13 directory. Possible subdirectories include drawings, AutoLISP files, drivers, slides, and user directories. Within each of these subdirectories reside the individual files. This is clearly illustrated in Figure C-3. The subdirectories of \R13 in Figure C-3 are some of those that are automatically created when AutoCAD is installed. If you plan to store files within the AutoCAD directory tree, plan on creating new subdirectories with names such as DRAW-INGS, LISP, and SCRIPTS. When specific types of files are kept in their own subdirectories, file maintenance is easier.

Figure C-3. Specific subdirectories in the \R13 directory are for files that are used with AutoCAD. These subdirectories are automatically created when AutoCAD is installed.

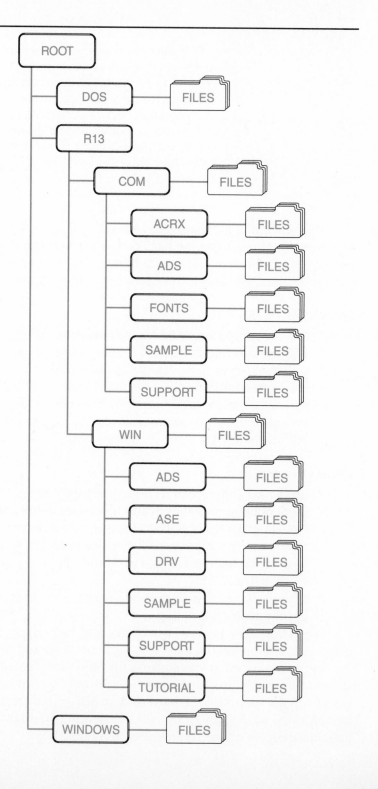

Your hard disk planning should take into account future software. New programs should be stored in their own directories on the hard disk, and managed in the same fashion as the AutoCAD files. The structure of a well-planned and closely managed hard disk should appear like that shown in Figure C-4.

Figure C-4.   The directory structure of a well-managed hard disk appears clean and organized.

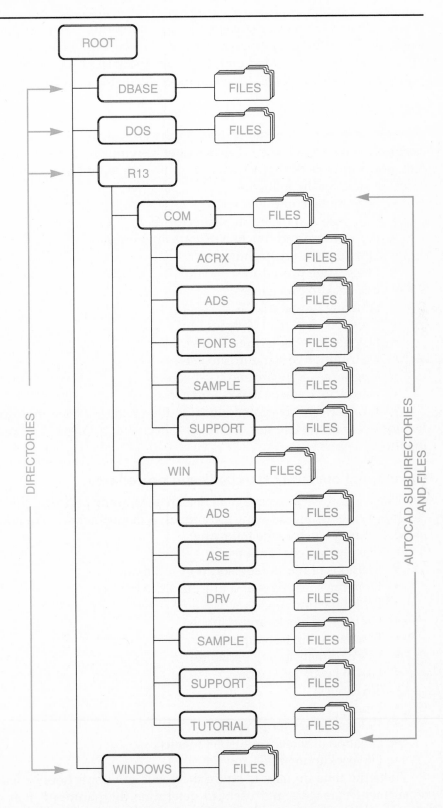

# MANAGING THE AUTOCAD SYSTEM

One of your goals as an AutoCAD user should be to keep the computer system as efficient as possible. This means being organized and knowledgeable of school or company standards. Also know who has the authority to manage the system, and follow the system manager's guidelines.

If you are the system manager, develop standards and procedures, relay these to system users, and distribute up-to-date documentation, symbol libraries, menus, and standards. Revise standards as needed and distribute these to all users. In addition, handle software updates in a consistent and timely manner. Make the maintenance of hardware a priority.

## The system manager

One or two people, depending on the size of the department or company, should be assigned as system manager. The manager has control over all functions of the computer system, preventing inconsistencies in procedure, drawing format, and file storage. The manager is responsible for the following:

- Scheduling computer use.
- Structure of the hard disk directories.
- Appearance and function of start-up menus.
- Drawing naming techniques.
- File storage procedures.
- File backup procedures.
- Drawing file access.
- Creation of symbol libraries.
- Development of written standards.
- Distribution of standards to users.
- Upgrading software and hardware.
- Hardware hygiene and maintenance.

When tasks are delegated, such as the creation of symbol library shapes, be sure to include accurate sketches or drawings. Check and approve final drawings before distributing them to users.

## Developing operating standards and procedures

The basis of system management is that everyone performs their job using the same procedures, symbols, and drawing techniques. A department that operates smoothly is probably using standards such as the following:

- File naming conventions.
- Methods of file storage: location and name.
- Drawing sheet sizes and title blocks to be used.
- Prototype drawings.
- Creation of blocks and symbols.
- Dimensioning techniques.
- Use of dimensioning variables.
- Use of layers and colors.
- Text styles.
- Line types.
- Color schemes for plotting.
- Creation of screen and tablet menus.
- File backup methods and times.

Take the time initially to study the needs of your school or company. Meet with other department managers and users to determine the nature of their drawings. Always gain input from people who use the system and avoid making blanket decisions on your own.

Once needs have been established, develop a plan for implementing the required standards and procedures. Assign specific tasks to students or employees. Assemble the materials as they are completed and distribute the documentation and procedures to all users.

When developing procedures, begin with start-up procedures and work through the drawing process. Develop prototype drawings for specific types of projects first. The final aspects of system development should be screen and tablet menus and AutoLISP programs.

## File maintenance

The integrity of files must be protected by all who work with the system. Procedures for file maintenance must be documented. Files of every type, including .DWG, .SLD, .BAT, .LSP, .MNU, and .BAK must have a secure storage area. This can be hard disk directories, floppy disks, or magnetic tape storage areas, kept clean of nonessential files. File maintenance procedures should include the following:

- Location of essential AutoCAD files.
- Location of backup AutoCAD files.
- Print the contents of all hard disk directories for each workstation.
- Location and contents of all prototype drawings, supplemented with printed listings.
- Location and contents of all batch files and associated menus.
- Location of all user files, including drawings, slides, and text files.
- Proper creation of drawings using prototypes, layers, dimensioning techniques, linetypes, text styles, and symbols.
- Storage and backup methods for drawing files.
- Storage of printed or plotted copies of all drawing files.

## Symbol libraries and menus

The development of symbol libraries and menus is a primary concern of managing an AutoCAD system. Symbols must be consistent and up-to-date. Menus must also be consistent throughout the department or company. A vital aspect of maintaining standards and consistency is a facility for updating symbol libraries and menus. This task should be given to certain students or employees and the results distributed to all users. Maintaining symbol libraries and menus includes the following:

- Standards for drawing symbols.
- System for naming symbols (blocks).
- System for block storage.
- Post a printed or plotted copy of all symbol libraries, their names, and locations.
- Creation and maintenance of custom screen and tablet menus.
- Use of custom menus by specific departments.
- Revisions to custom menus.
- Upgrading of menus on all hard disks.

## Maintaining the software

Software upgrades and releases are issued regularly. If you purchase upgrades, converting to the new version should be smooth and have little, if any, effect on production. Establish a procedure for upgrading all computers in the classroom or office. Inform all users of changes by providing a printed listing of new features. Offer training sessions on the new release if necessary. Make backup copies of the new software and store the originals in a safe place.

## Maintain the management system

All systems require continuous maintenance to function efficiently. Enable users to contribute to the function of the system. Foster creativity by inviting suggestions from users. Meet with users and managers on a regular basis to learn what is functioning well and what is not. Remember, the system will function efficiently if a majority of those using it enjoy working with the system, and are encouraged to contribute to its growth and development.

# Pull-down and Cascading Menus—AutoCAD Release 13 for Windows

**File**
New... Ctrl+N
Open... Ctrl+O
Save Ctrl+S
Save As...
Save R12 DWG...

Print... Ctrl+P

External Reference ▶
Bind ▶

Import...
Export...
Options ▶

Management ▶

1 C:\R13\WIN\FILE1.DWG
2 C:\R13\WIN\FILE2.DWG
3 C:\R13\WIN\FILE3.DWG
4 C:\R13\WIN\FILE4.DWG

Exit

Utilities...
Audit
Recover...

WMF Options...
PostScript Quality
PostScript Display

PostScript Prolog

All

Block
Layer
Linetype
Text Style
Dimension Style

Attach...
Overlay...

Reload
Detach
Clip

Path
List

**Edit**
Undo Ctrl+Z
Redo

Cut Ctrl+X
Copy Ctrl+C
Copy View
Paste Ctrl+V
Paste Special...

Properties...

Object Snap ▶
Point Filters ▶

Snap Ctrl+B
Grid Ctrl+G
Ortho Ctrl+L

Select Objects ▶
Group Objects...

Inquiry ▶

Links...
Insert Object...

List

Locate Point
Distance
Area
Mass Properties

Window
Crossing
Group
Previous
Last
All
Window Polygon
Crossing Polygon
Fence

Add
Remove

Selection Filters...
Group Selection
Hatch Selection

.X
.Y
.Z
.XY
.XZ
.YZ

From

Endpoint
Midpoint
Intersection
Apparent Intersection
Center
Quadrant
Perpendicular
Tangent
Node
Insertion
Nearest
Quick,

None

**View**
Redraw View
Redraw All

Zoom ▶
Pan ▶

Named Views...
3D Viewpoint Presets ▶
3D Viewpoint ▶
3D Dynamic View

Tiled Model Space
Floating Model Space
Paper Space

Tiled Viewports ▶
Floating Viewports ▶

Preset UCS...
Named UCS...
Set UCS ▶

World
Origin
Z Axis Vector
3 Point
Object
View
X Axis Rotate
Y Axis Rotate
Z Axis Rotate
Previous

Restore
Save
Delete

List

1 Viewport
2 Viewports
3 Viewports
4 Viewports

Restore

Viewports On
Viewports Off
Hideplot

MV Setup

Layout...

1 Viewport
2 Viewports
3 Viewports
4 Viewports

Restore
Delete
Join

Save

Rotate...
Tripod
Vector

Plan View ▶

Top
Bottom
Left
Right
Front
Back

SW Isometric
SE Isometric
NE Isometric
NW Isometric

Current
World
Named

Point

Left
Right
Up
Down

Up-Left
Up-Right
Down-Left
Down-Right

In
Out

Window
All
Previous
Scale
Dynamic
Center
Left
Limits
Extents
Vmax

**Draw**
Line
Construction Line
Ray
Sketch

Polyline
3D Polyline
Multiline

Spline
Arc ▶
Circle ▶
Ellipse ▶

Polygon
Point
Insert

Surfaces ▶
Solids ▶

Hatch ▶

Text ▶
Dimensioning ▶

Linear
Aligned
Radial ▶
Angular
Ordinate ▶
Baseline
Continue

Center Mark
Leader
Tolerance...

Oblique
Align Text ▶

Home
Rotate

Left
Center
Right

Automatic
X-Datum
Y-Datum

Radius
Diameter

Text
Dynamic Text
Single-Line Text

Hatch...
PostScript Fill

Box
Sphere
Cylinder ▶
Cone ▶
Wedge ▶
Torus

Extrude
Revolve

Slice
Section
Interference

AME Convert

Center
Corner

Elliptical
Center

Elliptical
Center

Center
Corner

3D Objects...
3D Face

Edge
3D Mesh

Revolved Surface
Tabulated Surface
Ruled Surface
Edge Surface

Block...
Multiple Blocks

Shape

Point
Divide
Measure

Rectangle
Polygon
2D Solid

Center
Axis, End

Arc

Center, Radius
Center, Diameter

2 Points
3 Points

Tan, Tan, Radius
Tan, Tan, Tan

Donut

3 Points
Start, Center, End
Start, Center, Angle
Start, Center, Length
Start, End, Angle
Start, End, Direction
Start, End, Radius
Center, Start, End
Center, Start, Angle
Center, Start, Length
Continue

**Construct**
Copy
Offset
Mirror
Array ▶

Chamfer
Fillet

Region
Bounding Polyline

Union
Subtract
Intersection

Block
Attribute...

3D Array ▶
3D Mirror
3D Rotate

Rectangular
Polar

Rectangular
Polar

# AutoCAD Menu Tree

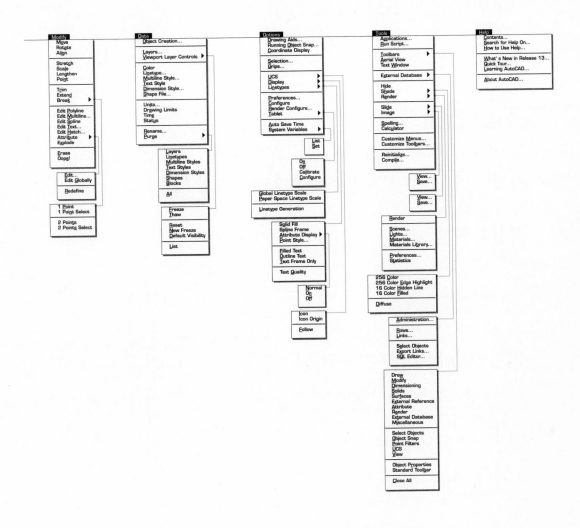

**Modify**
- Move
- Rotate
- Align
- Stretch
- Scale
- Lengthen
- Point
- Trim
- Extend
- Break ▶
- Edit Polyline
- Edit Multiline...
- Edit Spline
- Edit Text...
- Edit Hatch...
- Attribute ▶
- Explode
- Erase
- Oops!
- Edit...
- Edit Globally
- Redefine
- 1 Point
- 1 Point Select
- 2 Points
- 2 Points Select

**Data**
- Object Creation...
- Layers...
- Viewport Layer Controls ▶
- Color
- Linetype...
- Multiline Style...
- Text Style
- Dimension Style...
- Shape File...
- Units...
- Drawing Limits
- Time
- Status
- Rename...
- Purge ▶
- Layers
- Linetypes
- Multiline Styles
- Text Styles
- Dimension Styles
- Shapes
- Blocks
- All
- Freeze
- Thaw
- Reset
- New Freeze
- Default Visibility
- List

**Options**
- Drawing Aids...
- Running Object Snap...
- Coordinate Display
- Selection...
- Grips...
- UCS ▶
- Display ▶
- Linetypes ▶
- Preferences...
- Configure
- Render Configure...
- Tablet ▶
- Auto Save Time
- System Variables ▶
- List
- Set
- On
- Off
- Calibrate
- Configure
- Global Linetype Scale
- Paper Space Linetype Scale
- Linetype Generation
- Solid Fill
- Spline Frame
- Attribute Display ▶
- Point Style...
- Filled Text
- Outline Text
- Text Frame Only
- Text Quality
- Normal
- On
- Off
- Icon
- Icon Origin
- Follow

**Tools**
- Applications...
- Run Script...
- Toolbars ▶
- Aerial View
- Text Window
- External Database ▶
- Hide
- Shade ▶
- Render ▶
- Slide ▶
- Image ▶
- Spelling...
- Calculator
- Customize Menus...
- Customize Toolbars...
- Reinitialize...
- Compile...
- View...
- Save...
- View...
- Save...
- Render
- Scenes...
- Lights...
- Materials...
- Materials Library...
- Preferences...
- Statistics
- 256 Color
- 256 Color Edge Highlight
- 16 Color Hidden Line
- 16 Color Filled
- Diffuse
- Administration...
- Rows...
- Links...
- Select Objects
- Export Links...
- SQL Editor...
- Draw
- Modify
- Dimensioning
- Solids
- Surfaces
- External Reference
- Attribute
- Render
- External Database
- Miscellaneous
- Select Objects
- Object Snap
- Point Filters
- UCS
- View
- Object Properties
- Standard Toolbar
- Close All

**Help**
- Contents...
- Search for Help On...
- How to Use Help...
- What's New in Release 13...
- Quick Tour...
- Learning AutoCAD...
- About AutoCAD...

# Screen Menus—AutoCAD Release 13 for Windows

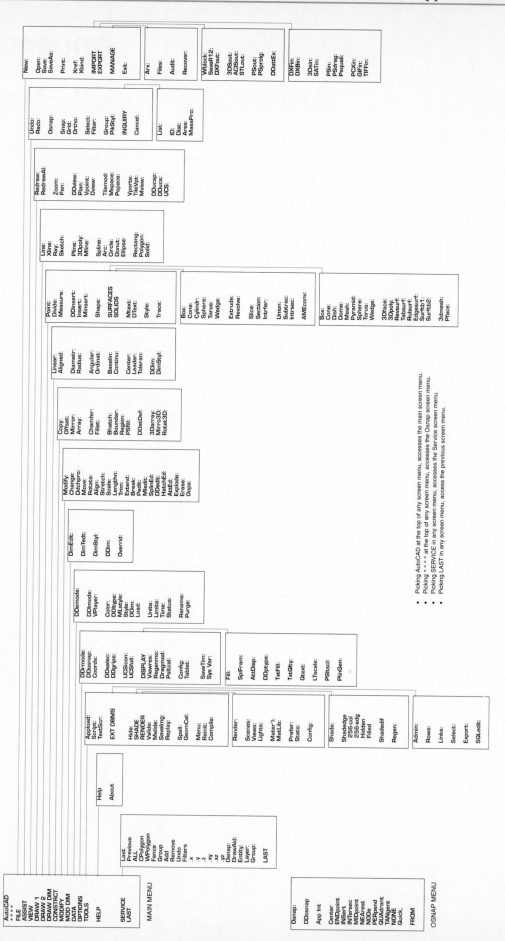

# AutoCAD Prototype Drawing and System Variable Defaults with Descriptions; Drawing Sheet Sizes and Scale Parameters

The following listing shows the AutoCAD system variables that can be stored within a prototype drawing file. The value of each of these variables is written into the drawing file when the drawing is saved, so that the next time the drawing is opened the values remain the same. Setting the values for most of these variables can be done by entering the associated command or by using the **SETVAR** command. Some variable values are derived by AutoCAD from the current condition of the drawing or the drawing environment, and cannot be directly set. These are referred to as "read-only".

Each listing provides a brief description of the variable and the default setting when no prototype drawing is referenced. The symbol ⌐ (eyeglasses) indicates that the variable is read-only.

| Variable Name | Default Value | Description |
|---|---|---|
| ANGBASE | 0.0000 | Direction for base angle 0 relative to current UCS. |
| ANGDIR | 0 | Counter-clockwise (0) or clockwise (1) angle measurement. |
| ATTDIA | 0 | Prompt on **Command:** line or use dialog box. |
| ATTMODE | 1 | Display mode for block attributes. |
| ATTREQ | 1 | Use attribute defaults or request values from user. |
| AUNITS | 0 | Format for angular units. |
| AUPREC | 0 | Precision of angular units. |
| BACKZ | ⌐ | Back clipping plane offset from the target plane. |
| BLIPMODE | 1 | Controls display of marker blips. |
| CECOLOR | BYLAYER | Color of newly-created objects. |
| CELTSCALE | 1.0000 | Individual object linetype scaling for new objects. |
| CELTYPE | BYLAYER | Linetype for newly-created objects. |
| CHAMFERA | 0.0000 | First chamfer distance. |
| CHAMFERB | 0.0000 | Second chamfer distance. |
| CHAMFERC | 0.0000 | Chamfer length. |
| CHAMFERD | 0.0000 | Chamfer angle. |
| CLAYER | "0" | Currently active layer. |
| COORDS | 1 | Controls dynamic coordinate updating. |
| CVPORT | 2 | Identification number of current viewport. |
| DELOBJ | 1 | Controls deletion of objects used to create other objects. |
| DIMALT | off | Enables or disables alternate units dimensioning. |
| DIMALTD | 2 | Decimal places for alternate units dimensions. |
| DIMALTF | 25.4 | Alternate units dimension scale factor. |
| DIMALTTD | 2 | Decimal places for alternate units tolerance values. |

| Variable Name | Default Value | Description |
|---|---|---|
| DIMALTTZ | 0 | Zero suppression for alternate units tolerance values. |
| DIMALTU | 2 | Units format for alternate units dimensions. |
| DIMALTZ | 0 | Zero suppression for alternate units dimension values. |
| DIMAPOST | "" | Prefix/suffix for alternate units dimensions. |
| DIMASO | on | Toggles associative dimensioning. |
| DIMASZ | 0.1800 | Dimension line and arrowhead size. |
| DIMAUNIT | 0 | Unit format for angular dimension values. |
| DIMBLK | "" | Block name to use for both arrowheads. |
| DIMBLK1 | "" | Block name to use for first arrowhead. |
| DIMBLK2 | "" | Block name to use for second arrowhead. |
| DIMCEN | 0.0900 | Center mark size. |
| DIMCLRD | 0 | Dimension line, arrowhead and leader line color. |
| DIMCLRE | 0 | Dimension extension line color. |
| DIMCLRT | 0 | Dimension text color. |
| DIMDEC | 4 | Decimal places for dimension values. |
| DIMDLE | 0.0000 | Dimension line extension beyond extension lines. |
| DIMDLI | 0.3800 | Incremental spacing between baseline dimensions. |
| DIMEXE | 0.1800 | Extension line distance beyond dimension line. |
| DIMEXO | 0.0625 | Distance from origin to begin extension line. |
| DIMFIT | 3 | Controls placement of text and arrowheads. |
| DIMGAP | 0.0900 | Gap size between dimension line and dimension text. |
| DIMJUST | 0 | Horizontal justification of dimension text. |
| DIMLFAC | 1.0000 | Linear units scale factor for dimension values. |
| DIMLIM | off | Toggles creation of limits style dimensions. |
| DIMPOST | "" | Prefix/suffix for primary units dimension values. |
| DIMRND | 0.0000 | Rounding value for dimensions. |
| DIMSAH | off | Toggles use of separate arrowhead blocks. |
| DIMSCALE | 1.0000 | Global dimension feature scale factor. |
| DIMSD1 | off | Toggles suppression of first dimension line. |
| DIMSD2 | off | Toggles suppression of second dimension line. |
| DIMSE1 | off | Toggles suppression of first extension line. |
| DIMSE2 | off | Toggles suppression of second extension line. |
| DIMSHO | on | Controls dynamic update of dimensions while dragging. |
| DIMSOXD | off | Suppress dimension lines outside of extension lines. |
| DIMSTYLE | ⌒ | Name of current dimension style. |
| DIMTAD | 0 | Toggles placement of text above dimension line. |
| DIMTDEC | 4 | Decimal places for primary units tolerance values. |
| DIMTFAC | 1.0000 | Scale factor for tolerance text size relative to dimensions. |
| DIMTIH | on | Orientation of text inside extension lines. |
| DIMTIX | off | Toggles forced placement of text between extension lines. |
| DIMTM | 0.0000 | Lower tolerance value for limits or toleranced dimensions. |
| DIMTOFL | off | Toggles forced dimension line creation. |
| DIMTOH | on | Orientation of text outside extension lines. |
| DIMTOL | off | Toggles creation of tolerance style dimensions. |
| DIMTOLJ | 1 | Vertical justification for dimension tolerance text. |
| DIMTP | 0.0000 | Upper tolerance value for limits or toleranced dimensions. |
| DIMTSZ | 0.0000 | Size for dimension line tick marks instead of arrowheads. |
| DIMTVP | 0.0000 | Vertical position of text above/below dimension line. |

| Variable Name | Default Value | Description |
|---|---|---|
| DIMTXSTY | STANDARD | Text style used for dimension text. |
| DIMTXT | 0.1800 | Size of dimension text. |
| DIMTZIN | 0 | Zero suppression for primary units tolerance values. |
| DIMUNIT | 2 | Units format for primary dimension values. |
| DIMUPT | off | Controls user placement of dimension line/text. |
| DIMZIN | 0 | Zero suppression for primary units dimensions. |
| DISPSILH | 0 | Toggles display of wire frame curve silhouettes. |
| DRAGMODE | 2 | Controls object "dragging" feature. |
| DWGCODEPAGE | ∽ | **SYSCODEPAGE** value when drawing was created. |
| ELEVATION | 0.0000 | Current 3D elevation relative to current UCS. |
| EXPLMODE | 1 | **EXPLODE** support for nonuniformly scaled blocks. |
| EXTMAX | ∽ | Upper-right extents of drawing. |
| EXTMIN | ∽ | Lower-left extents of drawing. |
| FACETRES | 0.5 | Smoothness of shaded and hidden line removed objects. |
| FILLETRAD | 0.0000 | Current fillet radius setting. |
| FILLMODE | 1 | Toggles fill for solid objects. |
| FRONTZ | ∽ | Front clipping plane offset from the target plane. |
| GRIDMODE | 0 | Toggles display of grid. |
| GRIDUNIT | 0.0000, 0.0000 | Current grid spacing in drawing units. |
| HANDLES | ∽ | Provides support for applications requiring handle access. |
| HPBOUND | 1 | Object type created by **BHATCH** and **BOUNDARY**. |
| INSBASE | 0.0000, 0.0000 | Insertion point set by **BASE** command. |
| ISOLINES | 4 | Number of isolines per surface on 3D objects. |
| LASTPOINT | 0.0000, 0.0000, 0.0000 | Last entered UCS coordinates for current space. |
| LENSLENGTH | ∽ | Length of lens in millimeters for perspective view. |
| LIMCHECK | 0 | Toggles active limit checking for object creation. |
| LIMMAX | 12.0000, 9.0000 | Upper-right limits. |
| LIMMIN | 0.0000, 0.0000 | Lower-left limits. |
| LTSCALE | 1.0000 | Current global linetype scale. |
| LUNITS | 2 | Current display format for linear units. |
| LUPREC | 4 | Current linear units precision value. |
| MIRRTEXT | 1 | Toggles mirroring technique for text objects. |
| ORTHOMODE | 0 | Toggles orthogonal drawing control. |
| OSMODE | 0 | Current **Object Snap** mode bit value. |
| PDMODE | 0 | Current **POINT** object display mode. |
| PDSIZE | 0.0000 | Current **POINT** object display size. |
| PELLIPSE | 0 | Controls the object type created with **ELLIPSE**. |
| PICKSTYLE | 3 | Controls group and associative hatch selection. |
| PLINEGEN | 0 | Toggles linetype generation along a polyline. |
| PLINEWID | 0.0000 | Current polyline width value. |
| PLOTROTMODE | 1 | Controls the orientation of plots. |
| PSLTSCALE | 1 | Paper space linetype scale factor. |
| PSQUALITY | 75 | Controls rendering quality and fill on postscript images. |
| QTEXTMODE | 0 | Toggles quick text display mode. |
| RASTERPREVIEW | 0 | Toggles drawing preview saving and sets format. |
| REGENMODE | 1 | Toggles automatic drawing regeneration. |
| SHADEDGE | 3 | Controls edge shading during rendering. |
| SHADEDIF | 70 | Sets ratio of diffuse reflective light to ambient light. |

| Variable Name | Default Value | Description |
|---|---|---|
| SKETCHINC | 0.1000 | Current **SKETCH** record increment value. |
| SKPOLY | 0 | Toggles creation of polyline objects by **SKETCH**. |
| SNAPANG | 0 | Snap/grid rotation angle in current viewport. |
| SNAPBASE | 0.0000, 0.0000 | Snap/grid origin point in current viewport. |
| SNAPISOPAIR | 0 | Isometric plane for current viewport. |
| SNAPMODE | 0 | Toggles snap mode. |
| SNAPSTYL | 0 | Current snap style. |
| SNAPUNIT | 1.0000, 1.0000 | Snap spacing for current viewport. |
| SPLFRAME | 0 | Toggles display of frames for spline-fit polylines. |
| SPLINESEGS | 8 | Current number of segments generated for each spline. |
| SPLINETYPE | 6 | Current type of spline generation by **PEDIT**. |
| SURFTAB1 | 6 | Tabulations generated for **RULESURF/TABSURF**, and M direction mesh density for **REVSURF/EDGESURF**. |
| SURFTAB2 | 6 | N direction mesh density for **REVSURF** and **EDGESURF**. |
| SURFTYPE | 6 | Surface fitting type performed by **PEDIT** Smooth. |
| SURFU | 6 | M direction surface density. |
| SURFV | 6 | N direction surface density. |
| SYSCODEPAGE | ∿ | System code page specified in ACAD.XMF. |
| TARGET | ∿ | Location of target point in current viewport. |
| TDCREATE | ∿ | Time and date when the current drawing was created. |
| TDINDWG | ∿ | Total editing time for the current drawing. |
| TDUPDATE | ∿ | Time and date of last update and save. |
| TDUSRTIMER | ∿ | User timer time elapsed. |
| TEXTFILL | 1 | Controls fill for Bitstream/TrueType/Adobe Type 1 fonts. |
| TEXTQLTY | 50 | Resolution for Bitstream/TrueType/Adobe Type 1 fonts. |
| TEXTSIZE | 0.2000 | Default height of text drawn in current style. |
| TEXTSTYLE | STANDARD | Current text style name. |
| THICKNESS | 0.0000 | Current 3D thickness. |
| TILEMODE | 1 | Controls access to paper space. |
| TRACEWID | 0.0500 | Current width for **TRACE** objects. |
| TREEDEPTH | 3020 | Maximum number of branches for tree-structured spatial index. |
| UCSFOLLOW | 0 | Toggles automatic change to plan view of current UCS. |
| UCSICON | 1 | Controls the display of the UCS icon. |
| UCSNAME | ∿ | Name of the current UCS for the current space. |
| UCSORG | ∿ | Origin point for the current UCS for the current space. |
| UCSXDIR | ∿ | X direction for the current UCS for the current space. |
| UCSYDIR | ∿ | Y direction for the current UCS for the current space. |
| UNITMODE | 0 | Current units display format. |
| VIEWCTR | ∿ | Center point location for current view in current viewport. |
| VIEWDIR | ∿ | Viewing direction of the current view in current viewport. |
| VIEWMODE | ∿ | Current viewing mode for the current viewport. |
| VIEWSIZE | ∿ | Height of the current view in the current viewport. |
| VIEWTWIST | ∿ | View twist angle for current viewport. |
| VISRETAIN | 0 | Controls visibility of layers in xref files. |
| VSMAX | ∿ | Upper-right corner of the current viewport virtual screen. |
| VSMIN | ∿ | Lower-left corner of the current viewport virtual screen. |
| WORLDVIEW | 1 | Controls automatic change of UCS for **DVIEW/VPOINT**. |

The following listing shows the AutoCAD system variables that are saved with the AutoCAD configuration. These variables are not associated with, or saved, in the drawing file. The values will be the same in the next drawing session as they are when you leave the current drawing. The default values shown here represent the values existing prior to AutoCAD's initial configuration. The symbol ↭ indicates that the variable is read-only.

| Variable Name | Default Value | Description |
| --- | --- | --- |
| APERTURE | 10 | Object snap target aperture height. |
| AUDITCTL | 0 | Toggles AutoCAD's creation of an audit file (.ADT). |
| CMDDIA | 1 | Enables/disables dialog boxes for a variety of commands. |
| CMLJUST | 0 | Current multiline justification. |
| CMLSCALE | 1.0000 | Scale factor for multiline features. |
| CMLSTYLE | "" | Current multiline style name. |
| DCTCUST | "" | Current custom dictionary filename and path. |
| DCTMAIN | "" | Main dictionary filename. |
| DRAGP1 | 10 | Sets regen-drag input sampling rate. |
| DRAGP2 | 25 | Sets fast-drag input sampling rate. |
| FFLIMIT | 0 | Maximum number of Post Script/TrueType fonts that can be stored in memory. |
| FILEDIA | 1 | Enables/disables file dialog boxes. |
| FONTALT | "" | Font file to be used when specified file is not found. |
| FONTMAP | "" | Font mapping file to be used when specified file is not found. |
| GRIPBLOCK | 0 | Controls assignment of grips within block objects. |
| GRIPCOLOR | 5 | Color of nonselected grips. |
| GRIPHOT | 1 | Color of selected grips. |
| GRIPS | 1 | Toggles availability of grip editing modes. |
| GRIPSIZE | 3 | Size of grip box in pixels. |
| MAXSORT | 200 | Maximum number of symbols or filenames sorted by listing commands. |
| MENUCTL | 1 | Toggles screen menu switching in response to commands. |
| MTEXTED | "" | Name of text editor for editing **MTEXT** objects. |
| PICKADD | 1 | Toggles additive selection of objects. |
| PICKAUTO | 1 | Toggles automatic windowing during selection process. |
| PICKBOX | 3 | Object selection pickbox height in pixels. |
| PICKDRAG | 0 | Controls selection window drawing method. |
| PICKFIRST | 1 | Controls selection and editing sequence. |
| PLOTID | "" | Current default plotter description. |
| PLOTTER | 0 | Current default plotter identification. |
| PROJMODE | 1 | Controls projection mode for **TRIM/EXTEND**. |
| PSPROLOG | "" | Name for prologue section read from ACAD.PSF for **PSOUT**. |
| SAVEFILE | ↭ | Current autosave destination filename. |
| SAVETIME | 120 | Autosave interval, in minutes. |
| SCREENBOXES | ↭ | Number of available boxes in screen menu area. |
| SCREENMODE | ↭ | Current graphics/text state of the AutoCAD display. |
| SORTENTS | 96 | Controls object sort order operations. |
| TEMPPREFIX | ↭ | Directory name for placement of temporary files. |
| TOOLTIPS | 1 | Toggles display of toolbar **ToolTips**. |
| TREEMAX | 10000000 | Limits maximum number of nodes in spatial index tree. |
| XREFCTL | 0 | Controls creation of .XLG files (xref log). |

The following listing shows the AutoCAD system variables that are not saved at all. These variables revert to default values when opening an existing drawing or starting a new one. Many of these variables are read-only, and reference drawing or operating system specific information. Other variables in this section are used to change standard features of AutoCAD, and are restored to default values in subsequent editing sessions to avoid unexpected results in common drafting procedures. Many of the variables shown here are commonly referenced or set when customizing. The symbol ↶ indicates that the variable is read-only.

| Variable Name | Default Value | Description |
|---|---|---|
| **ACADPREFIX** | ↶ | Current support directory search path. |
| **ACADVER** | ↶ | Current AutoCAD version number, including patch level. |
| **AFLAGS** | 0 | Current attribute flags settings. |
| **AREA** | ↶ | Stores the last area calculated by **AREA/LIST/DBLIST**. |
| **CDATE** | ↶ | Current date and time presented as a real number. |
| **CHAMMODE** | 0 | Current chamfer method. |
| **CIRCLERAD** | 0.0000 | Radius of last circle drawn. |
| **CMDACTIVE** | ↶ | Indicates what type of command is active. |
| **CMDECHO** | 1 | Controls echo of prompts and commands during the AutoLISP (command) function. |
| **CMDNAMES** | ↶ | Name of the currently active command(s). |
| **DATE** | ↶ | Current Julian date. |
| **DBMOD** | ↶ | Drawing modification status. |
| **DIASTAT** | ↶ | Exit method of last dialog session. |
| **DISTANCE** | ↶ | Last distance calculated by **DIST**. |
| **DONUTID** | 0.5000 | Default ID for doughnuts. |
| **DONUTOD** | 1.0000 | Default OD for doughnuts. |
| **DWGNAME** | ↶ | Name of current drawing. |
| **DWGPREFIX** | ↶ | Directory path for current drawing. |
| **DWGTITLED** | ↶ | Indicates if current drawing has been named. |
| **DWGWRITE** | 1 | Toggles initial state of "read-only" switch for **OPEN**. |
| **EDGEMODE** | 0 | Cutting and boundary edge determination method for **TRIM/EXTEND**. |
| **EXPERT** | 0 | Suppression level of warnings and double-checks. |
| **HIGHLIGHT** | 1 | Toggles highlighting of selected objects. |
| **HPANG** | 0.0000 | Current default hatch pattern angle. |
| **HPDOUBLE** | 0 | Toggles double hatching for **U** user-defined patterns. |
| **HPNAME** | "" | Current default hatch pattern name. |
| **HPSCALE** | 1.0000 | Current default hatch pattern scale. |
| **HPSPACE** | 1.0000 | Current spacing for **U** user-defined patterns. |
| **INSNAME** | "" | Name of last block inserted. |
| **LASTANGLE** | ↶ | Last angle entered or drawn. |
| **LOCALE** | ↶ | ISO language code for running AutoCAD version. |
| **LOGINNAME** | ↶ | Currently configured user login name. |
| **MAXACTVP** | 16 | Maximum number of active model space viewports. |
| **MENUECHO** | 0 | Controls level of menu echo. |
| **MENUNAME** | ↶ | Currently loaded menu file and path names. |
| **MODEMACRO** | "" | Displays text on status line—used in DIESEL. |
| **OFFSETDIST** | -1.0000 | Last entered offset distance. |

*Appendix E*  AutoCAD Prototype Drawing and System Variable Defaults with Descriptions; Drawing Sheet Sizes and Scale Parameters

1081

| Variable Name | Default Value | Description |
|---|---|---|
| **PERIMETER** | ∿ | Last perimeter value calculated by **AREA/LIST/DBLIST**. |
| **PFACEVMAX** | ∿ | Maximum number of vertices per face. |
| **PLATFORM** | ∿ | Current operating system. |
| **POLYSIDES** | 4 | Default number of polygon sides. |
| **POPUPS** | ∿ | Support level of display driver for pull-down menus. |
| **RE-INIT** | 0 | Controls action of **REINIT** command. |
| **RIASPECT** | 0.0000 | Aspect ratio for imported raster images. |
| **RIBACKG** | 0 | Background color for imported raster images. |
| **RIEDGE** | 0 | Edge detection feature for imported raster images. |
| **RIGAMUT** | 256 | Number of colors used for imported raster images. |
| **RIGREY** | 0 | Gray-scale conversion for imported raster images. |
| **RITHRESH** | 0 | Controls importing an image based on luminance. |
| **SAVENAME** | ∿ | Default drawing save name. |
| **SCREENSIZE** | ∿ | Current viewport size in pixels. |
| **SHPNAME** | "" | Default shape file name. |
| **TABMODE** | 0 | Enables/disables tablet mode. |
| **TEXTEVAL** | 0 | Controls evaluation method for text strings. |
| **TRIMMODE** | 1 | Controls object trimming for **FILLET** and **CHAMFER**. |
| **UNDOCTL** | ∿ | Current status of **UNDO** feature. |
| **UNDOMARKS** | ∿ | The number of **UNDO** marks that have been placed. |
| **WORLDUCS** | ∿ | Comparison of current UCS to World UCS. |

### Prototype Drawing Sheet Size Parameters

| Drawing Scale | D-size (34″ × 22″) Drawing Limits | C-size (22″ × 17″) Drawing Limits | B-size (17″ × 11″) Drawing Limits |
|---|---|---|---|
| 1″ = 1″ | 34,22 | 22,17 | 17,11 |
| 1/2″ = 1″ | 68,44 | 44,34 | 34,22 |
| 1/4″ = 1″ | 136,88 | 88,68 | 68,44 |
| 1/8″ = 1″ | 272,176 | 176,136 | 136,88 |
| 1″ = 1′-0″ | 408,264 | 264,204 | 204,132 |
| 3/4″ = 1′-0″ | 544,352 | 352,272 | 272,176 |
| 1/2″ = 1′-0″ | 816,528 | 528,408 | 408,264 |
| 3/8″ = 1′-0″ | 1088,704 | 704,544 | 544,352 |
| 1/4″ = 1′-0″ | 1632,1056 | 1056,816 | 816,528 |
| 3/16″ = 1′-0″ | 2176,1408 | 1408,1088 | 1088,704 |
| 1/8″ = 1′-0″ | 3264,2112 | 2112,1632 | 1632,1056 |
| 3/32″ = 1′-0″ | 4352,2816 | 2816,2176 | 2176,1408 |
| 1/16″ = 1′-0″ | 6528,4224 | 4224,3264 | 3264,2112 |

### Prototype Drawing Scale Parameters

| Drawing Scale | Dimension Scale (DIMSCALE) | Linetype Scale (LTSCALE) | Inversion Scale of Border & Parts List Blocks |
|---|---|---|---|
| 1″ = 1″ | 1 | .5 | 1 = 1 |
| 1/2″ = 1″ | 2 | 1 | 1 = 2 |
| 1/4″ = 1″ | 4 | 2 | 1 = 4 |
| 1/8″ = 1″ | 8 | 4 | 1 = 8 |
| 1″ = 1′-0″ | 12 | 6 | 1 = 12 |
| 3/4″ = 1′-0″ | 16 | 8 | 1 = 16 |
| 1/2″ = 1′-0″ | 24 | 12 | 1 = 24 |
| 3/8″ = 1′-0″ | 32 | 16 | 1 = 32 |
| 1/4″ = 1′-0″ | 48 | 24 | 1 = 48 |
| 3/16″ = 1′-0″ | 64 | 32 | 1 = 64 |
| 1/8″ = 1′-0″ | 96 | 48 | 1 = 96 |
| 3/32″ = 1′-0″ | 128 | 64 | 1 = 128 |
| 1/16″ = 1′-0″ | 192 | 96 | 1 = 192 |

# Appendix F

## Sample Tablet Menus

The tablet menu templates illustrated here show how the AutoCAD menu template can be altered to suit the needs of a company or individual. The menu shown in Figure F-1 is used creating electrical loop and wiring diagrams. Look closely at some of the special commands. Also note that different menus can be called from this template.

Figure F-1. Tablet menu for electrical loop and wiring diagrams. (Fitzgerald, Hagan & Hackathorn, Inc., Norwest Engineering)

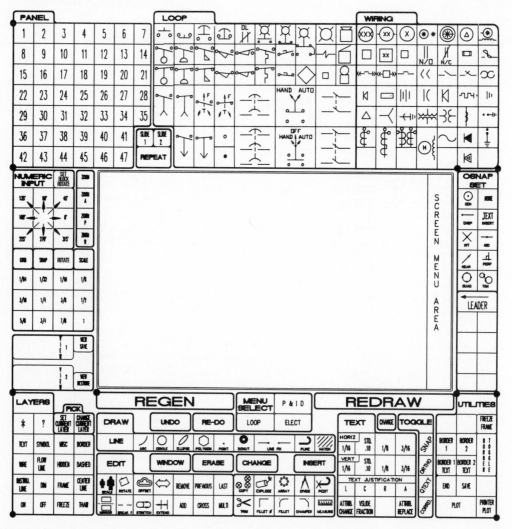

The tablet menu template shown in Figure F-2 was developed specifically for isometric piping drawings. All symbols are displayed in an orderly manner at the top of the menu. Note the section at the left of the screen area for isometric text.

Figure F-2. Tablet menu template for isometric piping symbols. (Fitzgerald, Hagan & Hackathorn, Inc., Norwest Engineering)

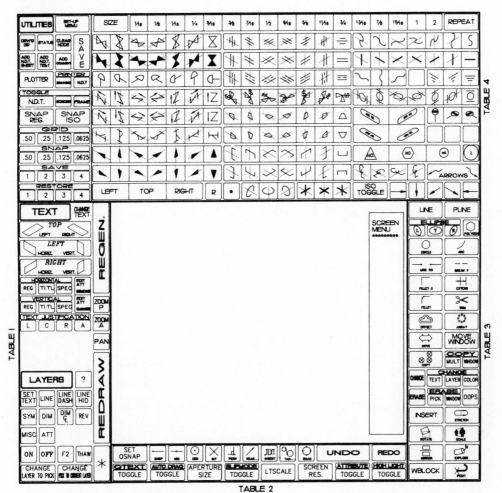

The tablet menu template shown in Figure F-3 was created for instrumentation loop diagrams. This menu does not have the detail as those shown earlier, but still reflects the needs of the individual using it. Notice the conversion chart on the right side of the template. Also note the cursor button references inside the screen area.

Figure F-3. Tablet menu template for instrumentation loop diagrams. (Courtesy R.L. Dunn, Harris Group, Inc.)

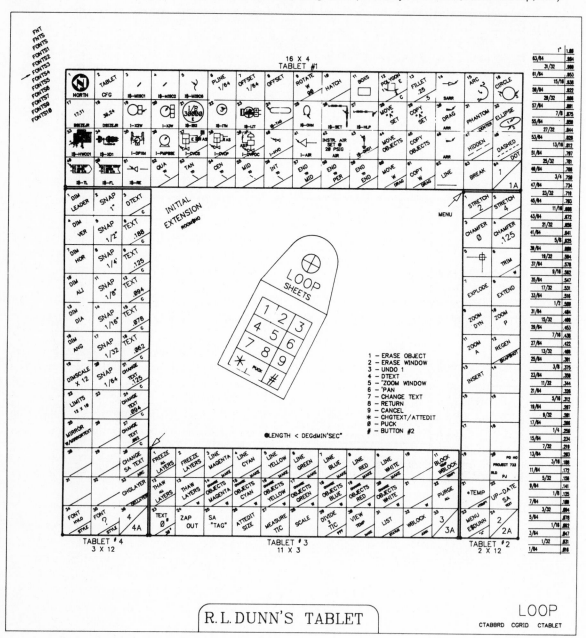

The following is a list of ANSI/ASME drafting standards or related documents. They are ANSI/ASME adopted, unless another standard developing organization, such as ANSI/NFPA, is indicated.

## ABBREVIATIONS

Y1.1-1989, *Abbreviations for Use on Drawings and in Text*

## CHARTS AND GRAPHS (Y15)

Y15.1M-1979 (R1993), *Illustrations for Publication and Projection*

Y15.2M-1979 (R1986), *Time-Series Charts*

Y15.3M-1979 (R1986), *Process Charts*

## DIMENSIONS

B4.1-1967 (R1987), *Preferred Limits and Fits for Cylindrical Parts*

B4.2-1978 (R1994), *Preferred Metric Limits and Fits*

B4.3-1978 (R1994), *General Tolerances for Metric Dimensioned Products*

B4.4M-1981 (R1987), *Inspection of Workpieces*

B32.1-1952 (R1994), *Preferred Thickness for Uncoated, Thin, Flat Metals (Under 0.250/in.)*

B32.2-1969 (R1994), *Preferred Diameters for Round Wire-0.500 Inches and Under*

B32.3M-1984 (R1994), *Preferred Metric Sizes for Flat Metal Products*

B32.4M-1980 (R1994), *Preferred Metric Sizes for Round, Square, Rectangle, and Hexagon Metal Products*

B32.5-1977 (R1994), *Preferred Metric Sizes for Tubular Metal Products Other Than Pipe*

B32.6M-1984 (R1994), *Preferred Metric Equivalents of Inch Sizes for Tubular Metal Products Other Than Pipe*

B36.10M-1985, *Welded and Seamless Wrought Steel Pipe*

B36.19M-1985, *Stainless Steel Pipe*

## DRAFTING STANDARDS

Y14.1-1980 (R1987), *Drawing Sheet Size and Format*

Y14.1M-1992, *Metric Drawing Sheet Size and Format*

Y14.2M-1992, *Line Conventions and Lettering*

Y14.3M-1992, *Multi- and Sectional-View Drawings*

Y14.4M-1989 (R1994), *Pictorial Drawings*

Y14.5M-1994, *Dimensioning and Tolerancing*

Y14.5.1-1994, *Mathematical Definition of Y14.5*

Y14.5.2, *Certification of GD&T Professionals*

Y14.6M-1978 (R1993), *Screw Thread Representation*

14.6aM-1981 (R1993), *Engineering Drawing and Related Documentation Practices (Screw Thread Representation) (Metric Supplement)*

Y14.7.1-1971 (R1993), *Gear Drawing Standards-Part 1-Spur, Helical, Double Helical, and Rack*

Y14.7.2-1978 (R1994), *Gear and Spline Drawing Standards-Part 2-Bevel and Hypoid Gears*

Y14.8M-1989 (R1993), *Castings and Forgings*

Y14.13M-1981 (R1992), *Engineering Drawing and Related Documentation Practices-Mechanical Spring Representation*

Y14.18M-1986 (R1993), *Engineering Drawings and Related Documentation Practices-Optical Parts*

Y14.24M-1989, *Types and Applications of Engineering Drawings*

14.34M-1989 (R1993), *Parts Lists, Data Lists, and Index Lists*

Y14.35M-1992, *Revision of Engineering Drawings and Associated Documents*

Y14.36-1978 (R1993), *Surface Texture Symbols*

Y14 Report 1, *Digital Representation of Physical Object Shapes*

Y14 Report 2, *Guidelines for Documenting of Computer Systems Used in Computer-Aided Preparation of Product Definition Data-User Instructions*

Y14 Report 3, *Guidelines for Documenting of Computer Systems Used in Computer-Aided Preparation of Product Definition Data-Design Requirements*

Y14 Report 4-1989, *A Structural Language Format for Basic Shape Description*

ANSI/US PRO/IPO-100-1993, *Digital Representation for Communication of Product Definition Data (Replaced ANSI Y14.26M-1981)*

## GRAPHIC SYMBOLS

Y32.2-1975, *Electrical and Electronic Diagrams*

Y32.2.3-1949 (R1988), *Pipe Fittings, Valves, and Piping*

Y32.2.4-1949 (R1993), *Heating, Ventilating, and Air Conditioning*

Y32.2.6-1950 (R1993), *Heat/Power Apparatus*

Y32.4-1977 (R1987), *Plumbing Fixture Diagrams Used in Architectural and Building Construction*

Y32.7-1972 (R1987), *Railroad Maps and Profiles*

Y32.9-1972 (R1989), *Electrical Wiring and Layout Diagrams Used in Architecture and Building*

Y32.10-1967 (R1987), *Fluid Power Diagrams*

Y32.11-1961 (R1993), *Process Flow Diagrams in the Petroleum and Chemical Industries*

Y32.18-1972 (R1993), *Mechanical and Acoustical Elements as Used in Schematic Diagrams*

ANSI/AWS A2.4-91, *Symbols for Welding, Brazing, and Nondestructive Examination*

ANSI/IEEE 200-1975 (R1989), *Reference Designations for Electrical and Electronics Parts and Equipment*

ANSI/IEEE 315-1975 (R1989), *Electrical and Electronics Diagrams (Including Reference Designation Class Designation Letters)*

ANSI/IEEE 623-1976 (R1989), *Grid and Mapping Used in Cable Television Systems*

ANSI/ISA S5.1-1984 (R1992), *Instrumentation Symbols and Identification*

ANSI/NFPA 170-1991, *Public Fire Safety Symbols*

## LETTER SYMBOLS

Y10.1-1972 (R1988), *Glossary of Terms Concerning Letter Symbols*

Y10.3M-1984, *Mechanics and Time-Related Phenomena*

Y10.4-1982 (R1988), *Heat and Thermodynamics*

Y10.11-1984, *Acoustics*

Y10.12-1955 (R1988), *Chemical Engineering*

Y10.17-1961 (R1988), *Greek Letters Used as Letter Symbols for Engineering Math*

Y10.18 1967 (R1977), *Illuminating Engineering*

ANSI/IEEE 260-1978 (R1992), *SI Units and Certain Other Units of Measurement*

## METRIC SYSTEM

SI-1, *Orientation and Guide for use of SI (Metric) Units*

SI-2, *SI Units in Strength of Materials*

SI-3, *SI Units in Dynamics*

SI-4, *SI Units in Thermodynamics*

SI-5, *SI Units in Fluid Mechanics*

SI-6, *SI Units in Kinematics*

SI-7, *SI Units in Heat Transfer*

SI-8, *SI Units in Vibration*

SI-9, *Metrification of Codes and Standards SI (Metric) Units*

SI-10, *Steam Charts, SI (Metric) and U.S. Customary Units*

# Appendix *H*

# Drafting Symbols

## STANDARD DIMENSIONING SYMBOLS

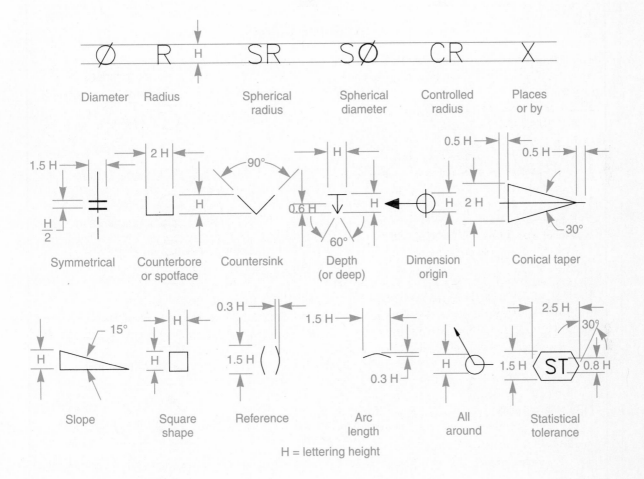

H = lettering height

# GEOMETRIC DIMENSIONING AND TOLERANCING SYMBOLS

Additional GD&T information is found in *Geometric Dimensioning and Tolerancing* by David A. Madsen, and is available through Goodheart-Willcox.

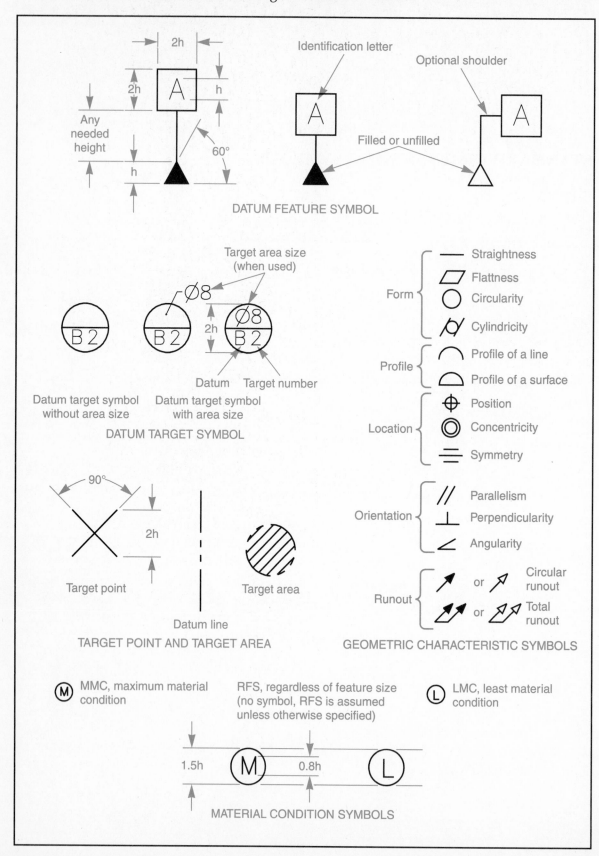

# GEOMETRIC DIMENSIONING AND TOLERANCING SYMBOLS, Cont.

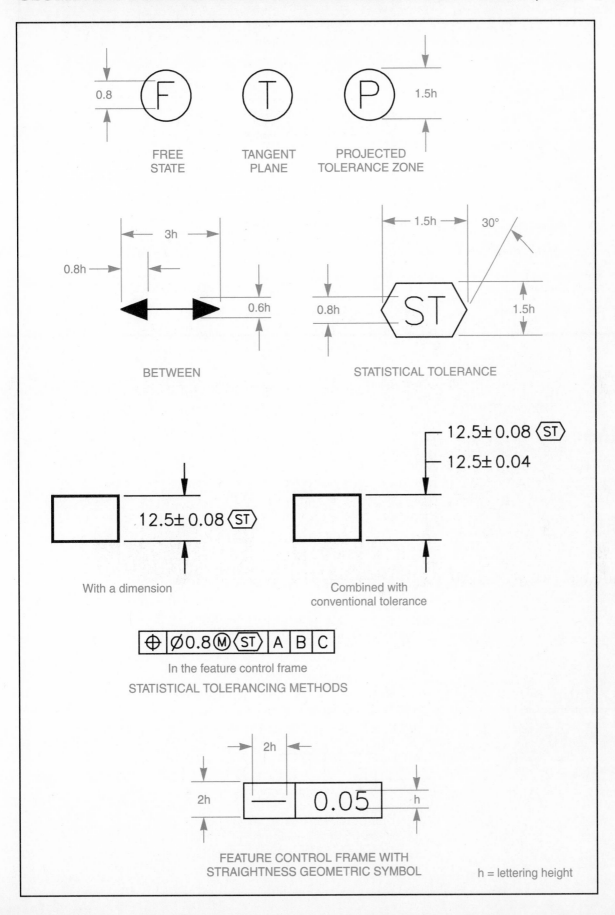

FREE
STATE

TANGENT
PLANE

PROJECTED
TOLERANCE ZONE

BETWEEN

STATISTICAL TOLERANCE

With a dimension

Combined with
conventional tolerance

In the feature control frame

STATISTICAL TOLERANCING METHODS

FEATURE CONTROL FRAME WITH
STRAIGHTNESS GEOMETRIC SYMBOL

h = lettering height

# GEOMETRIC DIMENSIONING AND TOLERANCING SYMBOLS, Cont.

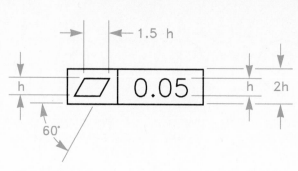

FEATURE CONTROL FRAME WITH THE FLATNESS
GEOMETRIC CHARACTERISTIC SYMBOL

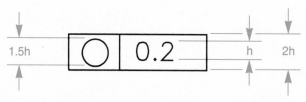

FEATURE CONTROL FRAME WITH CIRCULARITY
GEOMETRIC CHARACTERISTIC SYMBOL

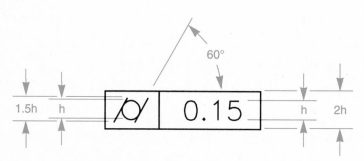

FEATURE CONTROL FRAME WITH CYLINDRICITY
GEOMETRIC CHARACTERISTIC SYMBOL

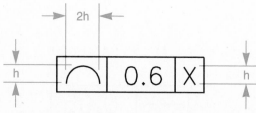

FEATURE CONTROL FRAME WITH PROFILE
OF A LINE GEOMETRIC CHARACTERISTIC
SYMBOL AND A DATUM REFERENCE

h = lettering height

# GEOMETRIC DIMENSIONING AND TOLERANCING SYMBOLS, Cont.

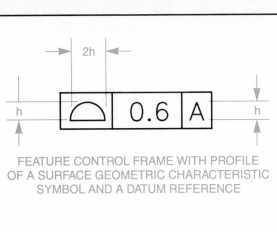

FEATURE CONTROL FRAME WITH PROFILE
OF A SURFACE GEOMETRIC CHARACTERISTIC
SYMBOL AND A DATUM REFERENCE

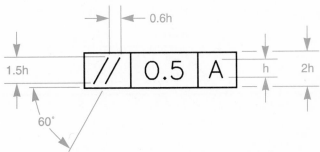

FEATURE CONTROL FRAME WITH
PARALLELISM GEOMETRIC CHARACTERISTIC
SYMBOL AND A DATUM REFERENCE

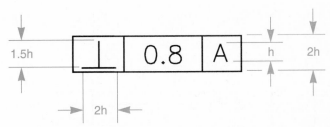

FEATURE CONTROL FRAME WITH
PERPENDICULARITY GEOMETRIC CHARACTERISTIC
SYMBOL AND A DATUM REFERENCE

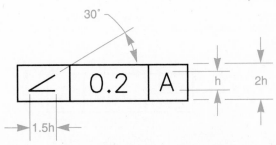

FEATURE CONTROL FRAME WITH
ANGULARITY GEOMETRIC CHARACTERISTIC
SYMBOL AND A DATUM REFERENCE

h = lettering height

# GEOMETRIC DIMENSIONING AND TOLERANCING SYMBOLS, Cont.

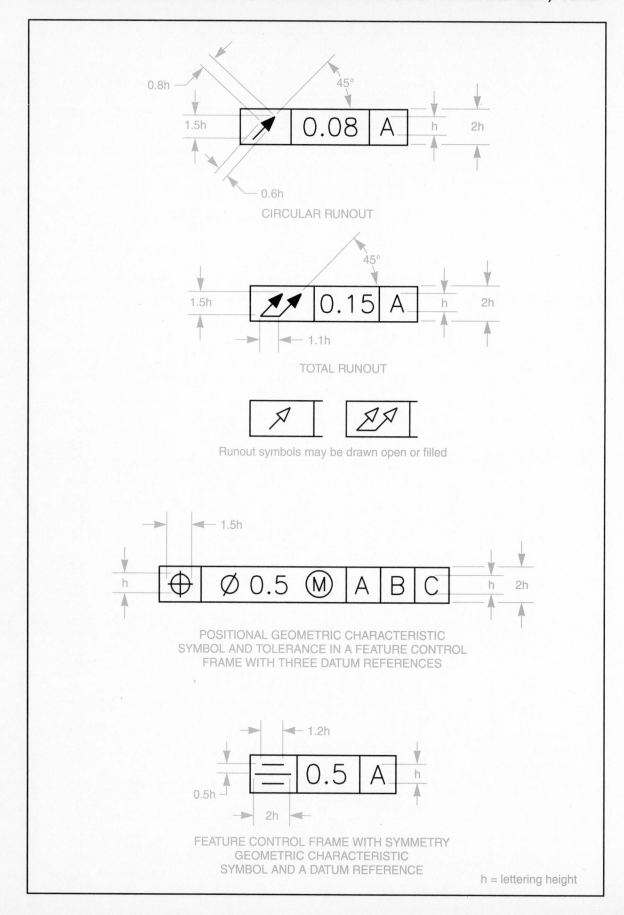

CIRCULAR RUNOUT

TOTAL RUNOUT

Runout symbols may be drawn open or filled

POSITIONAL GEOMETRIC CHARACTERISTIC
SYMBOL AND TOLERANCE IN A FEATURE CONTROL
FRAME WITH THREE DATUM REFERENCES

FEATURE CONTROL FRAME WITH SYMMETRY
GEOMETRIC CHARACTERISTIC
SYMBOL AND A DATUM REFERENCE

h = lettering height

# COMMON SINGLE LINE PIPE FITTING SYMBOLS

Additional pipe drafting information is found in *Process Pipe Drafting* by Terence M. Shumaker, and is available through Goodheart-Willcox.

| Name | Screwed | | | Buttwelded | | |
|---|---|---|---|---|---|---|
| | Left side | Front | Right side | Left side | Front | Right side |
| 90° Elbow | | | | | | |
| 45° Elbow | | | | | | |
| Tee | | | | | | |
| 45° Lateral | | | | | | |
| Cross | | | | | | |
| Cap | | | | | | |
| Concentric Reducer | | | | | | |
| Eccentric Reducer | | | | | | |
| Union | | | | | | |
| Coupling | | | | | | |

# COMMON SYMBOLS FOR ELECTRICAL DIAGRAMS

Amplifier

Antenna, general

Antenna, dipole

Antenna, dipole

Antenna, counterpoise

Battery, long line positive

Multicell battery

Capacitor, general

Capacitor, variable

Capacitor, polarized

Circuit breaker

Ground

Chassis ground

Connectors, jack and plug

Engaged connectors

Triode with directly heated cathode and envelope connection to base terminal

Pentode using elongated envelope

Twin triode using elongated envelope

Voltage regulator, also, glow lamp

Phototube

Inductor, winding, reactor, general

Magnetic core inductor

Adjustable inductor

Balast lamp

Fluorescent, 2-terminal lamp

Incandescent lamp

Microphone

Receiver, earphone

Resistor, general

Resistor, adjustable

Resistor, variable

Transformer, general

Transformer, magnetic core

Shielded transformer, magnetic core

Auto–transformer, adjustable

# COMMON ARCHITECTURAL SYMBOLS

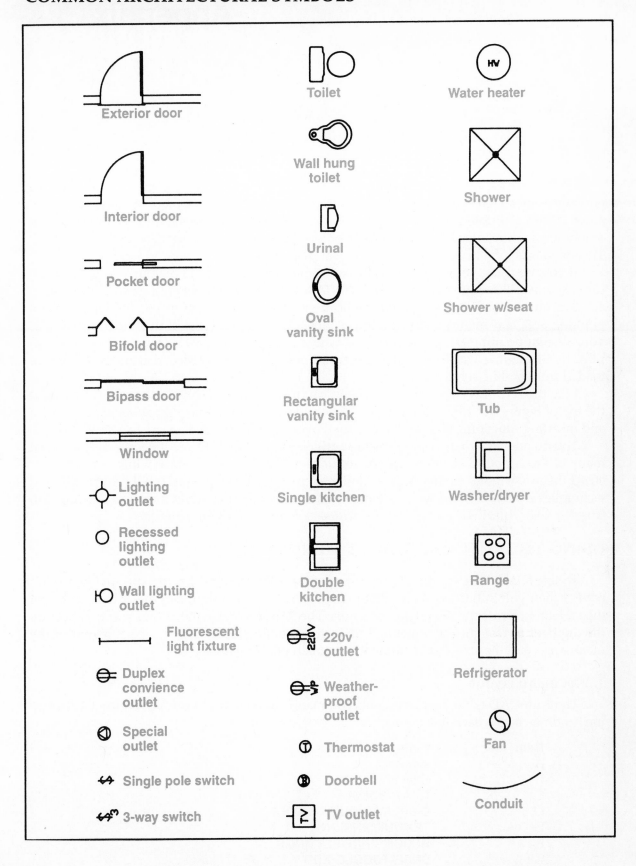

| | | |
|---|---|---|
| Exterior door | Toilet | Water heater |
| Interior door | Wall hung toilet | Shower |
| Pocket door | Urinal | Shower w/seat |
| Bifold door | Oval vanity sink | Tub |
| Bipass door | Rectangular vanity sink | Washer/dryer |
| Window | Single kitchen | Range |
| Lighting outlet | Double kitchen | Refrigerator |
| Recessed lighting outlet | 220v outlet | Fan |
| Wall lighting outlet | Weatherproof outlet | Conduit |
| Fluorescent light fixture | Thermostat | |
| Duplex convience outlet | Doorbell | |
| Special outlet | TV outlet | |
| Single pole switch | | |
| 3-way switch | | |

# Configuring
# the Digitizer

If you have a digitizer, the AutoCAD standard tablet menu is an alternative to keyboard entry or using screen commands. The tablet menu template is a thick piece of plastic that measures 11″ × 12″. Printed on it are most of the commands available in AutoCAD. Some commands are accompanied by small symbols, or icons, that indicate the function of the command. The menu is helpful because it provides a clear display of various AutoCAD commands.

If you are using your digitizer as the sole pointing device for all of your Windows applications, you will require a driver called WINTAB. The WINTAB driver configures a digitizer to act as a mouse for Windows-based applications, but permits you to use the tablet screen pointing area and menus when running AutoCAD. You must install the WINTAB driver as your system pointing device in Windows before starting AutoCAD. These drivers are supplied by the digitizer tablet manufacturers, and not by Autodesk. Most drivers can be downloaded from on-line services.

Like the screen menus, the tablet menu can be customized. Notice the empty spaces at the top of Figure I-1. This space is available for adding commands or symbols to aid picking and inserting functions. You can have several overlays for this area.

You do not have to use the template supplied with AutoCAD. Most people discover that many of the AutoCAD commands are not used for specific types of drawings, so they construct their own tablet menus. This is similar to creating screen menus, but there are different techniques involved when making tablet menus. Customizing tablet menus is discussed in Chapter 20 of *AutoCAD and its Applications–Advanced, R13 for Windows.*

## USING THE AUTOCAD TABLET MENU

To use a tablet menu, the digitizer must first be configured for the specific menu you have. When you initially configure AutoCAD to recognize a digitizer, the entire surface of the tablet represents the screen pointing area. The **TABLET** command allows you to configure the digitizer to recognize the menu. This includes telling AutoCAD the exact layout of the menu areas and the size and position of the screen pointing area.

### Tablet menu layout

The AutoCAD tablet menu presents commands in related groups. See Figure I-1. Notice the headings below each menu area.

| Item | Group |
|------|-------|
| A | **Monitor** |
| B | **User area** |
| C | **DRAW/ZOOM** |
| D | **DISPLAY/INQUIRY/LAYER** |
| E | **TEXT/DIMENSION** |
| F | **BLOCK/XREF/SETTINGS** |
| G | **SNAP/TOGGLE/EDIT** |
| H | **UTILITY** |
| I | **NUMERIC** |

Figure I-1.   The AutoCAD tablet menu template.  (Autodesk, Inc.)

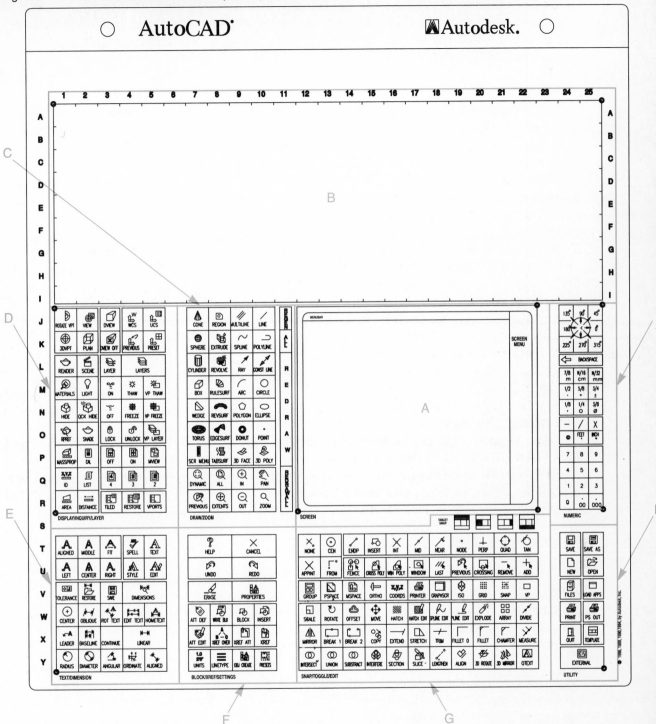

Find the **TEMPLATE** command in the **UTILITY** section in the lower-right corner of the template. This command allows the digitizer to recognize additional third-party software packages or your own custom menu. Each third-party package must work with AutoCAD, and must be installed on your hard disk drive for this command to work.

In order for the **TEMPLATE** command to work, you must set the **Alt Menu File:** value on the **Environment** page in the **Preference** dialog box. To set this value, first select **Preferences...** from the **Options** pull-down menu. Then, select the **Environment** tab in the **Preferences** dialog box. Locate the **Alt Menu File:** edit box and enter the name of your custom menu. For example, to use the CADPIPE menu located in the D:\CADPIPE directory, enter D:\CADPIPE\PIPING.MNU in the edit box. Finally, pick the **OK** button.

Now, when you pick **TEMPLATE** it looks for the **Alt Menu File:** value and loads the menu. Keep in mind that the alternate menu can be an entirely new menu composed of button, screen, pull-down, and tablet menus.

### Configuring the tablet menu

The **TABLET** command allows you to tell AutoCAD the layout of the tablet menu. It prompts for three corners of each menu area and the number of columns and rows in each area. The screen pointing area is defined by picking two opposite corners. Three corners of each menu area are marked with small doughnuts. As you read the following example, look at Figure I-2. It illustrates how the standard AutoCAD tablet menu is configured and shows the doughnuts marking menu area corners.

Figure I-2.   Small doughnuts mark the corners of the menu areas on the AutoCAD template. (Autodesk, Inc.)

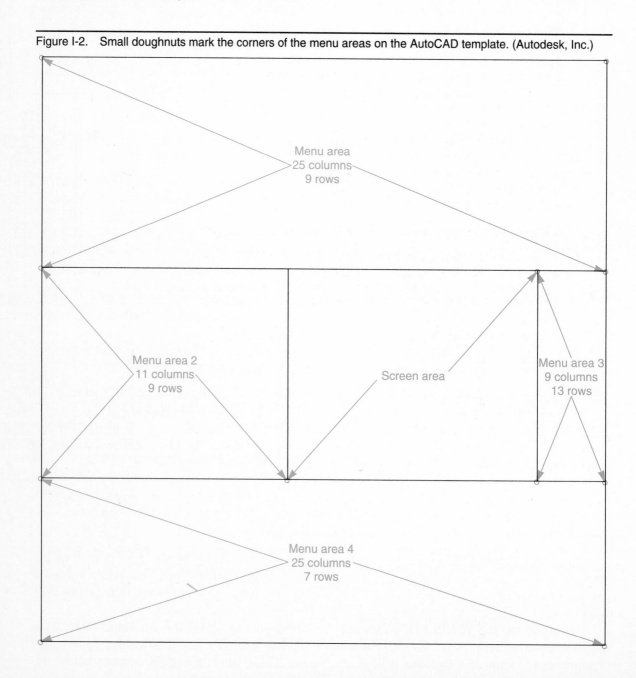

```
Command: TABLET ↵
Option (ON/OFF/CAL/CFG): CFG ↵
Enter number of tablet menus desired (0-4) ⟨0⟩: 4↵
Do you want to realign tablet menu areas? ⟨N⟩ Y ↵
Digitize upper left corner of menu area 1: (pick the doughnut at the upper-left corner)
Digitize lower left corner of menu area 1: (pick the point)
Digitize lower right corner of menu area 1: (pick the point)
Enter the number of columns for menu area 1(n - nnnn)⟨25⟩: ↵
Enter the number of rows for menu area 1(n - nnnn)⟨9⟩: ↵
```

You have now given AutoCAD the location of menu area 1 and specified the number of boxes that are available. The command continues with menu area 2:

```
Digitize upper left corner of menu area 2: (pick the point)
Digitize lower left corner of menu area 2: (pick the point)
Digitize lower right corner of menu area 2: (pick the point)
Enter the number of columns for menu area 2(n - nnnn)⟨11⟩: ↵
Enter the number of rows for menu area 2(n - nnnn)⟨9⟩: ↵
Digitize upper left corner of menu area 3: (pick the point)
Digitize lower left corner of menu area 3: (pick the point)
Digitize lower right corner of menu area 3: (pick the point)
Enter the number of columns for menu area 3(n - nnn)⟨9⟩: ↵
Enter the number of rows for menu area 3(n - nnnn)⟨13⟩: ↵
Digitize upper left corner of menu area 4: (pick the point)
Digitize lower left corner of menu area 4: (pick the point)
Digitize lower right corner of menu area 4: (pick the point)
Enter the number of columns for menu area 4(n - nnnn)⟨25⟩: ↵
Enter the number of rows for menu area 4(n - nnnn)⟨7⟩: ↵
```

Next, you must locate opposite corners of the screen pointing area:

```
Do you want to specify the Floating Screen Pointing Area? ⟨N⟩: Y ↵
Do you want the Floating Screen Pointing Area to be the same size as the Fixed Screen
  Pointing Area? ⟨Y⟩: (enter Y or N; If you enter Y, digitize the lower-left and upper-
  right corners of the floating screen pointing area when prompted.)
The F12 key will toggle the Floating Screen Pointing Area ON and OFF.
Would you like to specify a button to toggle the Floating Screen
Area? ⟨N⟩: (enter Y or N)
Command:
```

If you choose to use a digitizer puck button as the toggle, press the button of your choice. Do not press the pick button.

The tablet configuration is saved in the ACAD.CFG file, which is in your R13\WIN directory. The system reads this file when loading AutoCAD to determine what kind of equipment you are using. It also determines which menu is current. Use this same process when configuring the tablet for your custom menus.

If screen menus are enabled, configuring the AutoCAD template is made quicker by selecting the **TABLET** command from the screen menu. Pick **OPTIONS** in the **Root Menu**, then pick **Tablet:**, or pick **Tablet** in the **Options** pull-down menu.

Select the **Re-Cfg** option from the **Tablet:** screen menu. The configuration prompts appear as shown earlier, but you do not have to enter the number of columns and rows. The **Re-Cfg** option assumes you are reconfiguring the AutoCAD template. Therefore, it only requires the locations of the menu areas and the screen pointing area. Use this option when you wish to return to the standard AutoCAD template after using a custom menu.

## Swapping template areas

Look at the digitizer template below the monitor area and you can see the "Tablet swap" icons. These four picks allow you to swap each of the four tablet areas. The black area of each icon indicates the area that is swapped when the icon is picked. In addition, a prompt on the monitor indicates the type of swap. For example, if you pick area 1, the current custom menu picks are removed and the entire area is available for an alternate custom menu. Customizing this area is discussed in Chapter 20 of *AutoCAD and its Applications–Advanced, R13 for Windows*. The following list indicates the area swapped and the prompt.

- Area 1 prompt:
  Alternate tablet area 1 loaded.
  This area is for your personal applications and menu items.
- Area 2 prompt:
  Alternate tablet area 2 loaded.
  Zoom and other commands issue [Esc]'s: **VPOINT** and **DVIEW** in current UCS mode.
- Area 3 prompt:
  Alternate tablet area 3 loaded.
  Select Metric units from the Numeric menu.
- Area 4 prompt:
  Alternate tablet area 4 loaded.
  Object snap modes issue running modes: commands repeat.

Any of the areas can be swapped back to the default menu by just picking the icon again. You can have more than one swapped menu at a time. If you are unsure if any of the tablet areas have been swapped, it is easy to check. Just pick a tablet area and the prompt will indicate if the swap area is loaded or unloaded. The following prompt is displayed when a pick on a tabelt swap icon unloads the swapped area and returns to the default configuration:

Alternate tablet area 1 unloaded.

The configuration of alternate tablet areas is saved in the configuration file. Therefore, when AutoCAD is loaded, or a new drawing is opened, AutoCAD displays the Alternate tablet area *n* loaded message for each of the swapped areas that are loaded. This provides you with an additional reminder.

The prompt that is issued after picking a swap icon can be shortened or eliminated if you decide that you do not need to see it. Use the **EXPERT** system variable to change the prompt. A value of 0 for **EXPERT** displays the entire prompt. A value of 1 to 3 displays only the first part of the prompt:

Alternate tablet area 3 loaded.

A value of 4 for the **EXPERT** variable displays no prompt when a swap icon is picked. A value of 3 displays an abbreviated prompt. Set the variable as follows:

Command: **EXPERT** ↵
New value for EXPERT ⟨0⟩: **3** ↵

# INDEX